Pro C# 5.0 and the .NET 4.5 Framework

Sixth Edition

Andrew Troelsen

Pro C# 5.0 and the .NET 4.5 Framework, Sixth Edition

ISBN-13 (pbk): 978-1-4302-4233-8

ISBN-13 (electronic): 978-1-4302-4234-5

Printed and bound in the United States of America 9 8 7 6 5 4 3

President and Publisher: Paul Manning
Lead Editor: Ewan Buckingham
Technical Reviewer: Andy Olsen
Editorial Board: Steve Anglin, Ewan Buckingham, Gary Cornell, Louise Corrigan, Morgan Ertel, Jonathan Gennick, Jonathan Hassell, Robert Hutchinson, Michelle Lowman, James Markham, Matthew Moodie, Jeff Olson, Jeffrey Pepper, Douglas Pundick, Ben Renow-Clarke, Dominic Shakeshaft, Gwenan Spearing, Matt Wade, Tom Welsh, Steve Weiss
Coordinating Editor: Christine Ricketts
Copy Editors: Ralph and Vanessa Moore
Compositor: SPi Global
Indexer: SPi Global
Artist: SPi Global
Cover Designer: Anna Ishchenko

Distributed to the book trade worldwide by Springer Science+Business Media New York, 233 Spring Street, 6th Floor, New York, NY 10013. Phone 1-800-SPRINGER, fax (201) 348-4505, e-mail orders-ny@springer-sbm.com, or visit www.springeronline.com.

For information on translations, please e-mail rights@apress.com, or visit www.apress.com.

Apress and friends of ED books may be purchased in bulk for academic, corporate, or promotional use. eBook versions and licenses are also available for most titles. For more information, reference our Special Bulk Sales–eBook Licensing web page at www.apress.com/bulk-sales.

Any source code or other supplementary materials referenced by the author in this text is available to readers at www.apress.com. For detailed information about how to locate your book's source code, go to www.apress.com/source-code.

This edition of the text is dedicated to the two most important people in my life. First to my wife Mandy, who was crazy enough to bring up the idea of adoption.

Second, to my son Soren Wade Troelsen. Words can't express how much I love you. However, I will say one thing:

Grrrrrrawwwwhhhh!

You can ask me about this when you get older.

Contents at a Glance

Contents

About the Author

■ **Andrew Troelsen** fondly recalls his very first computer, an Atari 400 complete with a tape deck storage device and a black-and-white TV serving as a monitor (which his parents permitted him to have in his bedroom—thanks guys!).

Andrew is employed with Intertech (`www.intertech.com`), a .NET/Java training and consulting center located in Minneapolis, Minnesota.

He has authored a number of books, including *Developer's Workshop to COM and ATL 3.0* (Wordware Publishing, 2000), *COM and .NET Interoperability* (Apress, 2002), and *Visual Basic 2008 and the .NET 3.5 Platform: An Advanced Guide* (Apress, 2008).

About the Technical Reviewer

■ **Andy Olsen** runs a software training company based in the UK, delivering training in .NET, Java, web, and mobile technologies in Europe, the U.S., and Asia. Andy has been working with .NET since the days of the first beta and is actively involved with the latest features in the .NET 4.5 platform. Andy lives by the sea in Swansea with his wife Jayne and their children, Emily and Tom. Andy enjoys running along the sea front (with copious coffee stops along the way), skiing, and following the Swans! Andy can be reached at andyo@olsensoft.com

Acknowledgments

One might think that it would be easier to update a book, rather than create a new book from the ground up. In my experience, I feel it is the exact opposite. While I am the individual responsible for the overall content, this book would never have been published if a number of people had not worked tirelessly beside me.

Huge thanks are in order to my technical editor, Andy Olsen. As always, Andy made many excellent suggestions (I only wish I had the time to incorporate everything—maybe in the next edition!).

To the folks at Apress, you have continued to show me why I am grateful to be working with you. Thanks to all for taking my raw manuscript and transforming it into a professional, high-quality, published text.

Introduction

Many moons ago (circa 2001), I was given the opportunity to write a book on a forthcoming Microsoft technology that was, at the time, dubbed NGWS (Next Generation Windows Software). As I began to examine the source code provided by Microsoft, I noticed numerous code comments referring to the "COOL" (Common Object Oriented Language) programming language.

While I worked on my first initial manuscript of *C# and the .NET Platform* using a pre-alpha build (and no documentation to speak of), NGWS was eventually rebranded as the Microsoft .NET platform. COOL, as you might guess, is what we now know today as C#.

The first edition of this book was released in step with .NET 1.0, beta 2. Since then, I have updated the text to account for the numerous updates to the C# programming language, as well as the explosion of new APIs introduced with each new release of the .NET platform.

Over the years, this book has (thankfully and gratefully) been very well received, by the press (a JOLT award finalist and ReferenceWare programming book of the year), readers, and various university programs in computer science and software engineering.

It has been just wonderful to communicate with readers and educators around the globe. Thank you for all of your suggestions, comments, and (yes) criticism. I might not be able to respond to every e-mail, but everything is taken under consideration, to be sure.

We're a Team, You and I

Technology authors write for a demanding group of people (I should know—I'm one of them). You know that building software solutions using any platform or language is extremely complicated and is very specific to your department, company, client base, and subject matter. Perhaps you work in the electronic publishing industry, develop systems for the state or local government, or work at NASA or a branch of the military. Speaking for myself, I have developed children's educational software (Oregon Trail/Amazon Trail), various n-tier systems, and projects within the medical and financial industries. The chances are almost 100 percent that the code you write at your place of employment has little to do with the code I write at mine (unless we happened to work together previously!).

Therefore, in this book, I have deliberately chosen to avoid creating demonstrations that tie the example code to a specific industry or vein of programming. Given this, I explain C#, OOP, the CLR, and the .NET base class libraries using industry-agnostic examples. Rather than having every blessed example fill a grid with data, calculate payroll, or whatnot, I'll stick to subject matter we can all relate to: automobiles (with some geometric structures and employee payroll systems thrown in for good measure). And that's where you come in.

My job is to explain the C# programming language and the core aspects of the .NET platform the best I possibly can. As well, I will do everything I can to equip you with the tools and strategies you need to continue your studies at this book's conclusion.

Your job is to take this information and apply it to your specific programming assignments. I obviously understand that your projects most likely don't revolve around automobiles with friendly pet names (Zippy the BMW, or a Yugo named Clunker, among others), but that's what applied knowledge is all about!

Rest assured, once you understand the topics and concepts presented within this text, you will be in a perfect position to build .NET solutions that map to your own unique programming environment.

An Overview of This Book

Pro C# 5.0 and the .NET 4.5 Framework, Sixth Edition, is logically divided into eight distinct parts, each of which contains a number of related chapters. Here is a part-by-part and chapter-by-chapter breakdown of the text.

Part I: Introducing C# and the .NET Platform

The purpose of Part 1 is to acclimate you to the nature of the .NET platform and various development tools (many of which are open source) used during the construction of .NET applications.

Chapter 1: The Philosophy of .NET

This first chapter functions as the backbone for the remainder of the text. The primary goal of this chapter is to acquaint you with a number of .NET-centric building blocks, such as the Common Language Runtime (CLR), Common Type System (CTS), Common Language Specification (CLS), and base class libraries. Here, you will take an initial look at the C# programming language and the .NET assembly format. As well, you will learn the role of the .NET platform within the Windows 8 operating system, and understand the distinction between a Windows 8 app and a .NET application.

Chapter 2: Building C# Applications

The goal of this chapter is to introduce you to the process of compiling C# source code files using various tools and techniques. You will begin by learning how to use the command-line compiler (`csc.exe`) and C# response files. Over the remainder of the chapter, you will examine numerous code editors and integrated development environments (IDEs), including Notepad++, SharpDevelop, Visual C# Express, and Visual Studio. You will also learn how to configure your development machine with a local installation of the all-important .NET Framework 4.5 SDK documentation.

Part II: Core C# Programming

The topics presented in this part of the book are quite important because you will use them regardless of which type of .NET software you intend to develop (e.g., web applications, desktop GUI applications, code libraries, or Windows services). Here, you will learn about the fundamental data types of .NET, work with text manipulation, and learn the role of various C# parameter modifiers (including optional and named arguments).

Chapter 3: Core C# Programming Constructs, Part I

This chapter begins your formal investigation of the C# programming language. Here, you will learn about the role of the Main() method and numerous details regarding the intrinsic data types of the .NET platform, including the manipulation of textual data using System.String and System.Text.StringBuilder. You will also examine iteration and decision constructs, narrowing and widening operations, and the unchecked keyword.

Chapter 4: Core C# Programming Constructs, Part II

This chapter completes your examination of the core aspects of C#, beginning with the construction of overloaded type methods and defining parameters using the out, ref, and params keywords. This chapter will examine two C# features called *arguments* and *optional parameters*. You will also learn how to create and manipulate arrays of data, define nullable data types (with the ? and ?? operators), and understand the distinction between value types (including enumerations and custom structures) and reference types.

Part III: Object-Oriented Programming with C#

In this section you will come to understand the core constructs of the C# language, including the details of *object-oriented programming* (OOP). This part will also examine how to process runtime exceptions, and dive into the details of working with strongly typed interfaces.

Chapter 5: Understanding Encapsulation

This chapter begins your examination of object-oriented programming (OOP) using the C# programming language. After you are introduced to the pillars of OOP (encapsulation, inheritance, and polymorphism), the remainder of this chapter will show you how to build robust class types using constructors, properties, static members, constants, and read-only fields. You will wrap up with an examination of partial type definitions, object initialization syntax, and automatic properties.

Chapter 6: Understanding Inheritance and Polymorphism

Here, you will examine the remaining pillars of OOP (inheritance and polymorphism), which allow you to build families of related class types. As you do this, you will examine the role of virtual methods, abstract methods (and abstract base classes), and the nature of the polymorphic interface. Last but not least, this chapter will explain the role of the supreme base class of the .NET platform, System.Object.

Chapter 7: Understanding Structured Exception Handling

The point of this chapter is to discuss how to handle runtime anomalies in your code base through the use of *structured exception handling*. Not only will you learn about the C# keywords that allow you to handle such problems (try, catch, throw, and finally), but you will also come to understand the distinction between application-level and system-level exceptions. In addition, this chapter will examine various tools within Visual Studio that allow you to debug the exceptions that escape your notice.

Chapter 8: Working with Interfaces

The material in this chapter builds upon your understanding of object-based development by covering the topic of *interface-based programming*. Here, you will learn how to define classes and structures that support multiple behaviors, how to discover these behaviors at runtime, and how to selectively hide particular behaviors using explicit interface implementation. In addition to creating a number of custom interfaces, you will also learn how to implement standard interfaces found within the .NET platform. You will use these to build objects that can be sorted, copied, enumerated, and compared.

Part IV: Advanced C# Programming

This section of the book will deepen your understanding of the C# language by walking you through a number of more advanced (but very important) concepts. Here, you will complete your examination of the .NET type system by examining interfaces and delegates. You will also learn about the role of generics, take a first look at Language Integrated Query (LINQ), and examine a number of more advanced features of C# (e.g., extension methods, partial methods, and pointer manipulation).

Chapter 9: Collections and Generics

This chapter explores the topic of *generics*. As you will see, generic programming gives you a way to create types and type members, which contain various *placeholders* that can be specified by the caller. In a nutshell, generics greatly enhance application performance and type safety. Not only will you explore various generic types within the System.Collections.Generic namespace, but you will also learn how to build your own generic methods and types (with and without constraints).

Chapter 10: Delegates, Events, and Lambda Expressions

The purpose of Chapter 10 is to demystify the *delegate* type. Simply put, a .NET delegate is an object that *points* to other methods in your application. Using this type, you can build systems that allow multiple objects to engage in a two-way conversation. After you have examined the use of .NET delegates, you will then be introduced to the C# event keyword, which you can use to simplify the manipulation of raw delegate programming. You will wrap up this chapter by investigating the role of the C# lambda operator (=>) and exploring the connection between delegates, anonymous methods, and lambda expressions.

Chapter 11: Advanced C# Language Features

This chapter deepens your understanding of the C# programming language by introducing you to a number of advanced programming techniques. Here, you will learn how to overload operators and create custom conversion routines (both implicit and explicit) for your types. You will also learn how to build and interact with *type indexers*, as well as work with *extension methods, anonymous types, partial methods*, and C# pointers using an *unsafe* code context.

Chapter 12: LINQ to Objects

This chapter will begin your examination of Language Integrated Query (LINQ). LINQ allows you to build strongly typed *query expressions* that can be applied to a number of LINQ targets to manipulate *data* in the broadest sense of the word. Here, you will learn about LINQ to Objects, which allows you to apply LINQ expressions to containers of data (e.g., arrays, collections, and custom types). This information will serve you well as you encounter a number of additional LINQ APIs throughout the remainder of this book (e.g., LINQ to XML, LINQ to DataSet, PLINQ, and LINQ to Entities).

Chapter 13: Understanding Object Lifetime

The final chapter of this section examines how the CLR manages memory using the .NET garbage collector. Here you will come to understand the role of application roots, object generations, and the System.GC type. Once you understand the basics, you will examine the topics of *disposable objects* (using the IDisposable interface) and the finalization process (using the System.Object.Finalize() method). This chapter will also investigate the Lazy<T> class, which allows you to define data that will not be allocated until requested by a caller. As you will see, this feature can be very helpful when you want to ensure you do not clutter the heap with objects that are not actually required by your programs.

Part V: Programming with .NET Assemblies

Part 5 dives into the details of the .NET assembly format. Not only will you learn how to deploy and configure .NET code libraries, but you will also come to understand the internal composition of a .NET binary image. This part also explains the role of .NET attributes and the role of resolving type information at runtime. This section will also explain the role of the Dynamic Language Runtime (DLR) and the C# dynamic keyword. Later chapters will examine some fairly advanced topics regarding assemblies, such as application domains, the syntax of CIL, and the construction of in-memory assemblies.

Chapter 14: Building and Configuring Class Libraries

At a very high level, *assembly* is the term used to describe a *.dll or *.exe binary file created with a .NET compiler. However, the true story of .NET assemblies is far richer than that. Here, you will learn the distinction between single-file and multifile assemblies, as well as how to build and deploy each entity. You'll also examine how you can configure private and shared assemblies using XML-based *.config files and publisher policy assemblies. Along the way, you will investigate the internal structure of the global assembly cache (GAC).

Chapter 15: Type Reflection, Late Binding, and Attribute-Based Programming

Chapter 15 continues your examination of .NET assemblies by checking out the process of runtime type discovery using the System.Reflection namespace. Using the types of this namespace, you can build applications that can read an assembly's metadata on the fly. You will also learn how to load and create types at runtime dynamically using *late binding*. The final topic of this chapter will explore the role of

.NET attributes (both standard and custom). To illustrate the usefulness of each of these topics, the chapter shows you how to construct an extendable Windows Forms application.

Chapter 16: Dynamic Types and the Dynamic Language Runtime

.NET 4.0 introduces a new aspect of the .NET runtime environment called the *dynamic language runtime*. Using the DLR and the C# 2010 dynamic keyword, you can define data that is not truly resolved until runtime. Using these features simplifies some very complex .NET programming tasks dramatically. In this chapter, you will learn some practical uses of dynamic data, including how to leverage the .NET reflection APIs in a streamlined manner, as well as how to communicate with legacy COM libraries with a minimum of fuss and bother.

Chapter 17: Processes, AppDomains, and Object Contexts

Now that you have a solid understanding of assemblies, this chapter dives deeper into the composition of a loaded .NET executable. The goal of this chapter is to illustrate the relationship between processes, application domains, and contextual boundaries. These topics provide the proper foundation for Chapter 19, where you will examine the construction of multithreaded applications.

Chapter 18: Understanding CIL and the Role of Dynamic Assemblies

The goal of the final chapter in this section is twofold. In the first half (more or less), you will examine the syntax and semantics of CIL in much greater detail than in previous chapters. The remainder of this chapter will cover the role of the System.Reflection.Emit namespace. You can use these types to build software that can generate .NET assemblies in memory at runtime. Formally speaking, assemblies defined and executed in memory are termed *dynamic assemblies*.

Part VI: Introducing the .NET Base Class Libraries

By this point in the text, you have a solid handle on the C# language and the details of the .NET assembly format. Part 6 leverages your newfound knowledge by exploring a number of commonly used services found within the base class libraries, including the creation of multithreaded applications, file I/O, and database access using ADO.NET. This part also covers the construction of distributed applications using Windows Communication Foundation (WCF), workflow-enabled applications that use the Windows Workflow Foundation (WF) API, and the LINQ to XML API.

Chapter 19: Multithreaded, Parallel, and Async Programming

This chapter examines how to build multithreaded applications and illustrates a number of techniques you can use to author thread-safe code. The chapter opens by revisiting the .NET delegate type to ensure, explaining a delegate's intrinsic support for asynchronous method invocations. Next, you will investigate the types within the System.Threading namespace. The remainder of this chapter covers the *Task Parallel Library* (TPL). Using the TPL, .NET developers can build applications that distribute their workload across all available CPUs in a wickedly simple manner. At this point, you will also learn about the role of *Parallel LINQ* (PINQ), which provides a way to create LINQ queries that scale across multiple machine cores. We wrap up by examining some new C# keywords introduced in .NET 4.5, which integrate asynchronous method calls directly into the language.

Chapter 20: File I/O and Object Serialization

The System.IO namespace allows you to interact with a machine's file and directory structure. Over the course of this chapter, you will learn how to create (and destroy) a directory system programmatically. You will also learn how to move data into and out of various streams (e.g., file based, string based, and memory based). The latter part of this chapter will examine the object serialization services of the .NET platform. Simply put, *serialization* allows you to persist the state of an object (or a set of related objects) into a stream for later use. *Deserialization* (as you might expect) is the process of plucking an object from the stream into memory for consumption by your application. After you understand the basics, you will learn how to customize the serialization process using the ISerializable interface and a set of .NET attributes.

Chapter 21: ADO.NET Part I: The Connected Layer

In this first of three database-centric chapters, you will take your first look at the database access API of the .NET platform, ADO.NET. Specifically, this chapter will introduce you to the role of .NET data providers and how to communicate with a relational database using the *connected layer* of ADO.NET, which is represented by connection objects, command objects, transaction objects, and data reader objects. Be aware that this chapter will also walk you through the creation of a custom database and the first iteration of a custom data access library (AutoLotDAL.dll); you will use this library throughout the remainder of this book.

Chapter 22: ADO.NET Part II: The Disconnected Layer

This chapter continues your study of database manipulation by examining the *disconnected layer* of ADO.NET. Here, you will learn the role of the DataSet type and data adapter objects. You will also learn about the many tools of Visual Studio 2010 that can greatly simplify the creation of data-driven applications. Along the way, you will learn how to bind DataTable objects to user interface elements, as well as how to apply LINQ queries to in-memory DataSet objects using LINQ to DataSet.

Chapter 23: ADO.NET Part III: The Entity Framework

This chapter wraps up your investigation of ADO.NET by examining the role of the *Entity Framework* (EF). Essentially, EF is a way for you to author data-access code using strongly typed classes that directly map to your business model. Here, you will come to understand the role of EF Object Services, the Entity Client and Object Context, and the composition of an *.edmx file. While doing so, you will learn to interact with relational databases using LINQ to Entities. You will also build the final version of your custom data-access library (AutoLotDAL.dll), which you will use in several of the remaining chapters of the book.

Chapter 24: Introducing LINQ to XML

Chapter 14 introduced you to the core LINQ programming model—specifically LINQ to Objects. Here, you will deepen your understanding of Language Integrated Query by examining how to apply LINQ queries to XML documents. You will begin by learning about the "warts" that were present in .NET's initial foray into XML manipulation as you use the types of the System.Xml.dll assembly. With this brief history lesson behind you, you will explore how to create XML documents in memory, how to persist them to the hard drive, and how to navigate their contents using the LINQ programming model (LINQ to XML).

Chapter 25: Introducing Windows Communication Foundation

Until this point in the book, all of the sample applications have executed on a single computer. In this chapter, you will learn about the *Windows Communication Foundation* (WCF) API that allows you to build distributed applications in a symmetrical manner, regardless of their underlying plumbing. This chapter will expose you to the construction of WCF services, hosts, and clients. As you will see, WCF services are extremely flexible because they allow clients and hosts to leverage XML-based configuration files to specify addresses, bindings, and contracts declaratively.

Chapter 26: Introducing Windows Workflow Foundation

In this chapter, you will begin by learning about the role of a workflow-enabled application, and you will come to understand the various ways to model business processes using the .NET 4.0 WF API. Next, you will examine the scope of the WF activity library, as well as learn how to build custom activities that will use the custom database access library you created earlier in the book.

Part VII: Windows Presentation Foundation

.NET 3.0 introduced programmers to an amazing API called *Windows Presentation Foundation* (WFP). This API has quickly become the heir apparent to the Windows Forms desktop programming model. In essence, WPF allows you to build desktop applications that incorporate vector graphics, interactive animations, and data-binding operations using a declarative markup grammar called *XAML*. Furthermore, the WPF control architecture provides a trivial way to restyle the look-and-feel of a typical control radically using little more than some well-formed XAML.

Chapter 27: Introducing Windows Presentation Foundation and XAML

Essentially, WPF allows you to build extremely interactive and media-rich front ends for desktop applications (and indirectly, web applications). Unlike Windows Forms, this supercharged UI framework integrates a number of key services (e.g., 2D and 3D graphics, animations, and rich documents) into a single, unified object model. In this chapter, you will begin your examination of WPF and the Extendable Application Markup Language (XAML). Here, you will learn how to build WPF programs without XAML, as well as using nothing but XAML, and by using a combination of both approaches. You will wrap up the chapter by building a custom XAML editor that you will use for the remainder of the WPF-centric chapters.

Chapter 28: Programming with WPF Controls

This chapter will expose you to the process of using intrinsic WPF controls and layout managers. For example, you will learn to build menu systems, splitter windows, toolbars, and status bars. This chapter will also introduce you to a number of WPF APIs (and their related controls), including the WPF Documents API, the WPF Ink API, and the data-binding model. Just as importantly, this chapter will begin your investigation of Expression Blend IDE, which simplifies the task of creating rich UIs for a WPF application.

Chapter 29: WPF Graphics Rendering Services

WPF is a graphically intensive API; given this fact, WPF provides three ways to render graphics: *shapes*, *drawings and geometries*, and *visuals*. In this chapter, you will evaluate each option and learn about a number of important graphics primitives (e.g., brushes, pens, and transformations) along the way. This chapter will also examine a number of ways in which Expression Blend can help you simplify the process of creating WPF graphics, as well as how to perform hit-testing operations against graphical data.

Chapter 30: WPF Resources, Animations, and Styles

This chapter will introduce you to three important (and interrelated) topics that will deepen your understanding of the Windows Presentation Foundation API. The first order of business is to learn the role of *logical resources*. As you will see, the logical resource (also termed an *object resource*) system provides a way for you to name and refer to commonly used objects within a WPF application. Next, you will learn how to define, execute, and control an *animation* sequence. Despite what you might be thinking, however, WPF animations are not limited to the confines of video game or multimedia applications. You will wrap up the chapter by learning about the role of WPF *styles*. Similar to a web page that uses CSS or the ASP.NET theme engine, a WPF application can define a common look-and-feel for a set of controls.

Chapter 31: Dependency Properties, Routed Events, and Templates

This chapter begins by examining two topics that are important when creating a custom control: *dependency properties* and *routed events*. After you understand these topics, you will learn about the role of a *default template*, as well as how to view them programmatically at runtime. After this foundation has been laid, the remainder of this chapter will examine how to build custom templates.

Part VIII: ASP.NET Web Forms

Part 8 is devoted to an examination of constructing web applications using the ASP.NET programming API. Microsoft designed ASP.NET to model the creation of desktop user interfaces by layering an event-driven, object-oriented framework on top of a standard HTTP request/response.

Chapter 32: Introducing ASP.NET Web Forms

This chapter begins your study of web application development using ASP.NET. As you will see, server-side scripting code has now been replaced with real object-oriented languages (e.g., C# and VB .NET). This chapter will examine the construction of an ASP.NET web page, the underlying programming model, and other key aspects of ASP.NET, such as your choice of web server and the use of web.config files.

Chapter 33: ASP.NET Web Controls, Master Pages, and Themes

Whereas the previous chapter showed you how to construct ASP.NET Page objects, this chapter will examine the controls that populate the internal control tree. Here, you will examine the core ASP.NET *web controls*, including validation controls, the intrinsic site navigation controls, and various data-binding operations. This chapter will also illustrate the role of *master pages* and the *ASP.NET theme engine*, which is a server-side alternative to traditional style sheets.

Chapter 34: ASP.NET State Management Techniques

This chapter extends your understanding of ASP.NET by examining various ways to handle state management under .NET. Like classic ASP, ASP.NET allows you to create cookies and application-level and session-level variables quite easily. However, ASP.NET also introduces a new state management technique: the *application cache*. After you look at the numerous ways to handle state with ASP.NET, you will examine the role of the HttpApplication base class and learn how to alter the runtime behavior of your web application dynamically using the web.config file.

Downloadable Appendixes

As if 34 chapters were not enough, I have made two additional chapters available for download from the home page of this book at the Apress web site (www.apress.com). The first appendix covers the basics of the Windows Forms API, which is used for a few of the UI examples in this text. The second appendix examines the platform-independent nature of .NET via the Mono platform.

Downloadable Appendix A: Programming with Windows Forms

The original desktop GUI toolkit that shipped with the .NET platform is called *Windows Forms*. This appendix will walk you through the role of this UI framework and illustrate how to build main windows, dialog boxes, and menu systems. You will also learn about the role of form inheritance and see how to render 2D graphical data using the System.Drawing namespace. You will wrap things up by building a (semicapable) painting application that illustrates the various topics discussed throughout this appendix.

Downloadable Appendix B: Platform-Independent .NET Development with Mono

Last but not least, Appendix B covers how to use an open source implementation of the .NET platform named *Mono*. You can use Mono to build feature-rich .NET applications that can be created, deployed, and executed upon a variety of operating systems, including Mac OS X, Solaris, and numerous Linux distributions. Given that Mono is largely comparable with Microsoft's .NET platform, you already know most of what Mono has to offer. Therefore, this appendix will focus on the Mono installation process, Mono development tools, and Mono runtime engine.

Obtaining This Book's Source Code

You can find all of the code examples contained in this book available as a free download from the Source Code/Download area of the Apress website. Simply navigate to www.apress.com, select the Source Code/Download link, and look up this title by name. Once you are on the home page for Pro C# 5

With this book, you can download a self-extracting *.zip file. After you unzip the contents, you will find that the code has been partitioned on a chapter-by-chapter basis.

On a related note, be aware that you will find "Source Code" notes, such as the following, in many of the book's chapters. These notes serve as your visual cue that you can load the example under discussion into Visual Studio for further examination and modification.

■ **Source Code** This is a source code note that refers you to a specific directory in the ZIP archive.

To open a solution into Visual Studio, use the File ➤ Open ➤ Project/Solution menu option, and then navigate to the correct *.sln file within the correct subdirectory of the unzipped archive.

Obtaining Updates for This Book

As you read through this text, you might find an occasional grammatical or code error (although I sure hope not). If this is the case, please accept my apologies. Being human, I am sure that a glitch or two might be present, despite my best efforts. If this is the case, you can obtain the current errata list from the Apress web site at www.apress.com (again, this is located on the home page for this book), as well as information on how to notify me of any errors you might find.

Contacting Me

If you have any questions regarding this book's source code, are in need of clarification for a given example, or simply would like to offer your thoughts regarding the .NET platform, feel free to drop me a line at the following e-mail address (to ensure your messages don't end up in my junk mail folder, please include "C# SixthEd" in the Subject line somewhere):

atroelsen@intertech.com

Please understand that I will do my best to get back to you in a timely fashion; however, like yourself, I get busy from time to time. If I don't respond within a week or two, please be aware that I am not trying to be a jerk, nor am I trying to avoid talking to you. I'm just busy (or, if I'm lucky, on vacation somewhere). So, then! Thanks for buying this text (or at least looking at it in the bookstore while you try to decide whether you will buy it). I hope you enjoy reading this book and putting your newfound knowledge to good use.

— Andrew Troelsen

## PART I

Introducing C# and .NET Platform

CHAPTER 1

The Philosophy of .NET

Microsoft's .NET platform (and the related C# programming language) were formally introduced circa 2002, and have quickly become a mainstay of modern day software development. As mentioned in the book's introductory section, the goal of this text is twofold. The first order of business is to provide you with deep and detailed examination of the syntax and semantics of C#. The second (equally important) order of business is to illustrate the use of numerous .NET APIs, including database access with ADO.NET and the Entity Framework (EF), the LINQ technology set, WPF, WCF, WF, and web site development using ASP.NET. As they say, the journey of a thousand miles begins with a single step; and with this I welcome you to Chapter 1.

The point of this first chapter is to lay the conceptual groundwork for the remainder of the book. Here you will find a high-level discussion of a number of .NET-related topics such as assemblies, the Common Intermediate Language (CIL), and just-in-time (JIT) compilation. In addition to previewing some keywords of the C# programming language, you will also come to understand the relationship between various aspects of the .NET Framework, such as the Common Language Runtime (CLR), the Common Type System (CTS), and the Common Language Specification (CLS).

This chapter also provides you with a survey of the functionality supplied by the .NET 4.5 base class libraries, sometimes abbreviated as BCLs. Here, you will also overview the language-agnostic and platform-independent nature of the .NET platform (yes, it's true; .NET is not confined to the Windows operating system) and be provided with a brief overview regarding .NET's role in constructing applications under the Windows 8 operating system. As you would hope, many of these topics are explored in further detail throughout the remainder of this text.

An Initial Look at the .NET Platform

Before Microsoft released the C# language and .NET platform, software developers who created applications for the Windows family of operating system frequently made use of the COM programming model. COM (which stands for the *Component Object Model*) allowed individuals to build libraries of code that could be shared across diverse programming languages. For example, a C++ programmer could build a COM library that could be used by a Visual Basic developer. The language-independent nature of COM was certainly useful; however, COM was plagued by complicated infrastructure, a fragile deployment model, and was only possible on the Windows operating system.

Despite the complexity and limitations of COM, countless applications have been successful created with this architecture. However, nowadays, a majority of applications created for the Windows family of operating systems are not created with the COM model. Rather, desktop applications, web sites, OS services, and libraries of reusable data access/business logic are created using the .NET platform.

Some Key Benefits of the .NET Platform

As mentioned, C# and the .NET platform were first introduced to the world in 2002 and were intended to offer a much more powerful, more flexible, and simpler programming model than COM. As you will see during the remainder of this book, the .NET Framework is a software platform for building systems on the Windows family of operating systems, as well as on numerous non-Microsoft operating systems such as Mac OS X and various Unix/Linux distributions. To set the stage, here is a quick rundown of some core features provided courtesy of .NET:

> *Interoperability with existing code:* This is (of course) a good thing. Existing COM binaries can commingle (i.e., interop) with newer .NET software and vice versa. As of .NET 4.0 onward, interoperability has been further simplified with the addition of the dynamic keyword (covered in Chapter 16).

> *Support for numerous programming languages:* .NET applications can be created using any number of programming languages (C#, Visual Basic, F#, and so on).

> *A common runtime engine shared by all .NET-aware languages:* One aspect of this engine is a well-defined set of types that each .NET-aware language understands.

> *Language integration:* .NET supports cross-language inheritance, cross-language exception handling, and cross-language debugging of code. For example, you can define a base class in C#, and extend this type in Visual Basic.

> *A comprehensive base class library:* This library provides shelter from the complexities of low-level API calls and offers a consistent object model used by all .NET-aware languages.

> *A simplified deployment model:* Unlike COM, .NET libraries are not registered into the system registry. Furthermore, the .NET platform allows multiple versions of the same *.dll to exist in harmony on a single machine.

You will see each of these topics (and many more) examined in the chapters to come.

Introducing the Building Blocks of the .NET Platform (the CLR, CTS, and CLS)

Now that you know some of the major benefits provided by .NET, let's preview three key (and interrelated) topics that make it all possible: the CLR, CTS, and CLS. From a programmer's point of view, .NET can be understood as a runtime environment and a comprehensive base class library. The runtime layer is properly referred to as the *Common Language Runtime*, or *CLR*. The primary role of the CLR is to locate, load, and manage .NET objects on your behalf. The CLR also takes care of a number of low-level details such as memory management, application hosting, coordinating threads, and performing security checks (among other low-level details).

Another building block of the .NET platform is the *Common Type System*, or *CTS*. The CTS specification fully describes all possible data types and all programming constructs supported by the runtime, specifies how these entities can interact with each other, and details how they are represented in the .NET metadata format (more information on metadata later in this chapter; see Chapter 15 for complete details).

Understand that a given .NET-aware language might not support each and every feature defined by the CTS. The *Common Language Specification, or CLS,* is a related specification that defines a subset of common types and programming constructs that all .NET programming languages can agree on. Thus, if you build .NET types that expose only CLS-compliant features, you can rest assured that all .NET-aware languages can consume them. Conversely, if you make use of a data type or programming construct that is outside of the bounds of the CLS, you cannot guarantee that every .NET programming language can interact with your .NET code library. Thankfully, as you will see later in this chapter, it is very simple to tell your C# compiler to check all of your code for CLS compliance.

The Role of the Base Class Libraries

In addition to the CLR and CTS/CLS specifications, the .NET platform provides a base class library that is available to all .NET programming languages. Not only does this base class library encapsulate various primitives such as threads, file input/output (I/O), graphical rendering systems, and interaction with various external hardware devices, but it also provides support for a number of services required by most real-world applications.

The base class libraries define types that can be used to build any type of software application. For example, you can use ASP.NET to build web sites, WCF to build networked services, WPF to build desktop GUI applications, and so forth. As well, the base class libraries provide types to interact with XML documents, the local directory and file system on a given computer, communicate with a relational databases (via ADO.NET), and so forth. From a high level, you can visualize the relationship between the CLR, CTS, CLS, and the base class library, as shown in Figure 1-1.

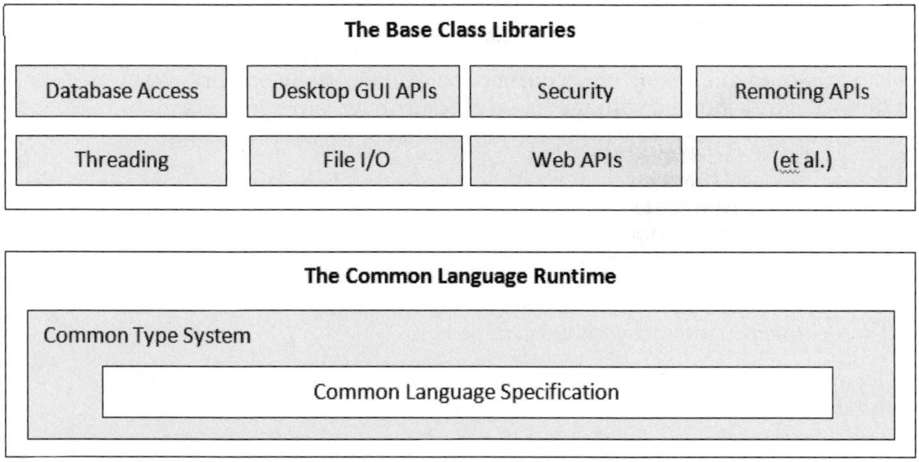

Figure 1-1. *The CLR, CTS, CLS, and base class library relationship*

What C# Brings to the Table

C# is a programming language whose core syntax looks *very* similar to the syntax of Java. However, to call C# a Java clone is inaccurate. In reality, both C# and Java are members of the C family of programming languages (e.g., C, Objective C, C++) and, therefore, share a similar syntax.

The truth of the matter is that many of C#'s syntactic constructs are modeled after various aspects of Visual Basic (VB) and C++. For example, like VB, C# supports the notion of class properties (as opposed to traditional getter and setter methods) and optional parameters. Like C++, C# allows you to overload operators, as well as create structures, enumerations, and callback functions (via delegates).

Moreover, as you work through this text, you will quickly see that C# supports a number of features traditionally found in various functional languages (e.g., LISP or Haskell) such as lambda expressions and anonymous types. Furthermore, with the advent of LINQ (*Language Integrated Query*), C# supports a number of constructs that make it quite unique in the programming landscape. Nevertheless, the bulk of C# is indeed influenced by C-based languages.

Due to the fact that C# is a hybrid of numerous languages, the result is a product that is as syntactically clean—if not cleaner—as Java, is about as simple as VB, and provides just about as much power and flexibility as C++. Here is a partial list of core C# features that are found in all versions of the language.

> No pointers required! C# programs typically have no need for direct pointer manipulation (although you are free to drop down to that level if absolutely necessary, as shown in Chapter 11).

> Automatic memory management through garbage collection. Given this, C# does not support a delete keyword.

> Formal syntactic constructs for classes, interfaces, structures, enumerations, and delegates.

> The C++-like ability to overload operators for a custom type, without the complexity (e.g., making sure to "return *this to allow chaining" is not your problem).

> Support for attribute-based programming. This brand of development allows you to annotate types and their members to further qualify their behavior. For example, if you mark a method with the [Obsolete] attribute, programmers will see your custom warning message print out if they attempt to make use of the decorated member.

With the release of .NET 2.0 (circa 2005), the C# programming language was updated to support numerous new bells and whistles, most notability the following:

> The ability to build generic types and generic members. Using generics, you are able to build very efficient and type-safe code that defines numerous *placeholders* specified at the time you interact with the generic item.

> Support for anonymous methods, which allow you to supply an inline function anywhere a delegate type is required.

> The ability to define a single type across multiple code files (or if necessary, as an in-memory representation) using the partial keyword.

.NET 3.5 (released circa 2008) added even more functionality to the C# programming language, including the following features:

> Support for strongly typed queries (e.g., LINQ) used to interact with various forms of data. You will first encounter LINQ in Chapter 12.

> Support for anonymous types that allow you to model the *shape* of a type rather than its behavior.

> The ability to extend the functionality of an existing type (without subclassing) using extension methods.

Inclusion of a lambda operator (=>), which even further simplifies working with .NET delegate types.

A new object initialization syntax, which allows you to set property values at the time of object creation.

.NET 4.0 (released in 2010) updated C# yet again with a handful of features. For example:

Support for optional method parameters, as well as named method arguments.

Support for dynamic lookup of members at runtime via the dynamic keyword. As you will see in Chapter 18 this provides a unified approach to invoking members on the fly, regardless of which framework the member implemented (COM, IronRuby, IronPython, or via .NET reflection services).

Working with generic types is much more intuitive, given that you can easily map generic data to and from general System.Object collections via covariance and contravariance.

And that brings us to the current version of C# found with .NET 4.5. The current version of C# provides a pair of new keywords (async and await), which massively simplify multithreaded and asynchronous programming. If you have worked with previous versions of C#, you might recall that calling methods via secondary threads required a fair amount of cryptic code and the use of various .NET namespaces. Given that C# now supports language keywords that handle this complexity for you, the process of calling methods asynchronously is almost as easy as calling a method in a synchronous manner. Chapter 19 will cover these topics in detail.

Managed vs. Unmanaged Code

Perhaps the most important point to understand about the C# language is that it can produce code that can execute only within the .NET runtime (you could never use C# to build a native COM server or an unmanaged C/C++ application). Officially speaking, the term used to describe the code targeting the .NET runtime is *managed code*. The binary unit that contains the managed code is termed an *assembly* (more details on assemblies in just a bit). Conversely, code that cannot be directly hosted by the .NET runtime is termed *unmanaged code*.

Additional .NET-Aware Programming Languages

Understand that C# is not the only language that can be used to build .NET applications. Out of the box, Visual Studio provides you with five managed languages, specifically, C#, Visual Basic, C++/CLI, JavaScript, and F#.

■ **Note** F# is a .NET language based on the syntax of functional languages. While F# can be used as a purely functional language, it also has support for OOP constructs and the .NET base class libraries. If you are interested in learning more about this managed language, navigate online to the official F# homepage, http://msdn.microsoft.com/fsharp.

In addition to the managed languages provided by Microsoft, there are .NET compilers for Smalltalk, Ruby, Python, COBOL, and Pascal (to name a few). Although this book focuses almost exclusively on C#, you might be interested in the following web site:

www.dotnetlanguages.net

If you click the Resources link at the top of the homepage, you will find a list of .NET programming languages and related links where you are able to download various compilers (see Figure 1-2).

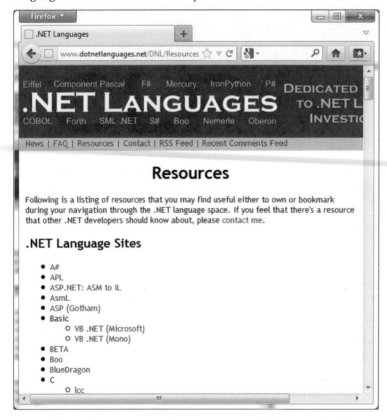

Figure 1-2. DotNetLanguages.net is one of many sites documenting known .NET programming languages

While I assume you are primarily interested in building .NET programs using the syntax of C#, I encourage you to visit this site, as you are sure to find many .NET languages worth investigating at your leisure (LISP.NET, anyone?).

Life in a Multilanguage World

As developers first come to understand the language-agnostic nature of .NET, numerous questions arise. The most prevalent of these questions would have to be, "If all .NET languages compile down to managed code, why do we need more than one language/compiler?"

There are a number of ways to answer this question. First, we programmers are a *very* particular lot when it comes to our choice of programming language. Some of us prefer languages full of semicolons and curly brackets with as few language keywords as possible. Others enjoy a language that offers more *human-readable* syntactic tokens (such as Visual Basic). Still others might want to leverage their mainframe skills while moving to the .NET platform (via the COBOL .NET compiler).

Now, be honest. If Microsoft were to build a single "official" .NET language derived from the BASIC family of languages, can you really say all programmers would be happy with this choice? Or, if the only "official" .NET language was based on Fortran syntax, imagine all the folks out there who would ignore .NET altogether. Because the .NET runtime couldn't care less which language was used to build a block of managed code, .NET programmers can stay true to their syntactic preferences and share the compiled code among teammates, departments, and external organizations (regardless of which .NET language others choose to use).

Another excellent byproduct of integrating various .NET languages into a single, unified software solution is the simple fact that all programming languages have their own sets of strengths and weaknesses. For example, some programming languages offer excellent intrinsic support for advanced mathematical processing. Others offer superior support for financial calculations, logical calculations, interaction with mainframe computers, and so forth. When you take the strengths of a particular programming language and then incorporate the benefits provided by the .NET platform, everybody wins.

Of course, in reality the chances are quite good that you will spend much of your time building software using your .NET language of choice. However, once you master the syntax of one .NET language, it is very easy to learn another. This is also quite beneficial, especially to the software consultants of the world. If your language of choice happens to be C# but you are placed at a client site that has committed to Visual Basic, you are still able to leverage the functionality of the .NET Framework, and you should be able to understand the overall structure of the code base with minimal fuss and bother.

An Overview of .NET Assemblies

Regardless of which .NET language you choose to program with, understand that despite the fact that .NET binaries take the same file extension as unmanaged Windows binaries (*.dll or *.exe), they have absolutely no internal similarities. Specifically, .NET binaries do not contain platform-specific instructions, but rather platform-agnostic *Intermediate Language* (*IL*) and type metadata. Figure 1-3 shows the big picture of the story thus far.

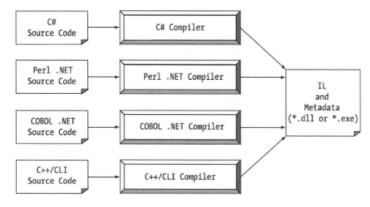

Figure 1-3. All .NET-aware compilers emit IL instructions and metadata

> ■ **Note** There is one point to be made regarding the abbreviation "IL." IL is also known as Microsoft Intermediate Language (MSIL) or alternatively as the Common Intermediate Language (CIL). Thus, as you read the .NET literature, understand that IL, MSIL, and CIL are all describing the same concept. In this text, I will use the abbreviation CIL to refer to this low-level instruction set.

When a *.dll or *.exe has been created using a .NET-aware compiler, the binary blob is termed an *assembly*. You will examine numerous details of .NET assemblies in Chapter 14. However, to facilitate the current discussion, you do need to understand some basic properties of this new file format.

As mentioned, an assembly contains CIL code, which is conceptually similar to Java bytecode in that it is not compiled to platform-specific instructions until absolutely necessary. Typically, "absolutely necessary" is the point at which a block of CIL instructions (such as a method implementation) is referenced for use by the .NET runtime.

In addition to CIL instructions, assemblies also contain *metadata* that describes in vivid detail the characteristics of every "type" within the binary. For example, if you have a class named SportsCar, the type metadata describes details such as SportsCar's base class, which interfaces are implemented by SportsCar (if any), as well as a full description of each member supported by the SportsCar type. .NET metadata is always present within an assembly, and is automatically generated by a .NET-aware language compiler.

Finally, in addition to CIL and type metadata, assemblies themselves are also described using metadata, which is officially termed a *manifest*. The manifest contains information about the current version of the assembly, culture information (used for localizing string and image resources), and a list of all externally referenced assemblies that are required for proper execution. You'll examine various tools that can be used to examine an assembly's types, metadata, and manifest information over the course of the next few chapters.

The Role of the Common Intermediate Language

Let's examine CIL code, type metadata, and the assembly manifest in a bit more detail. CIL is a language that sits above any particular platform-specific instruction set. For example, the following C# code models a trivial calculator. Don't concern yourself with the exact syntax for now, but do notice the format of the Add() method in the Calc class.

```
// Calc.cs
using System;

namespace CalculatorExample
{
  // This class contains the app's entry point.
  class Program
  {
    static void Main()
    {
      Calc c = new Calc();
      int ans = c.Add(10, 84);
      Console.WriteLine("10 + 84 is {0}.", ans);
```

```
      // Wait for user to press the Enter key before shutting down.
      Console.ReadLine();
    }
  }

  // The C# calculator.
  class Calc
  {
    public int Add(int x, int y)
    { return x + y; }
  }
}
```

After you compile this code file using the C# compiler (csc.exe), you end up with a single-file *.exe assembly that contains a manifest, CIL instructions, and metadata describing each aspect of the Calc and Program classes.

■ **Note** Chapter 2 examines the details of compiling code using the C# compiler, as well as the use of graphical IDEs such as Microsoft Visual Studio (among others).

For example, if you were to open this assembly using ildasm.exe (examined a little later in this chapter), you would find that the Add() method is represented using CIL such as the following:

```
.method public hidebysig instance int32 Add(int32 x,
    int32 y) cil managed
{
  // Code size 9 (0x9)
  .maxstack  2
  .locals init (int32 V_0)
  IL_0000:  nop
  IL_0001:  ldarg.1
  IL_0002:  ldarg.2
  IL_0003:  add
  IL_0004:  stloc.0
  IL_0005:  br.s IL_0007
  IL_0007:  ldloc.0
  IL_0008:  ret
} // end of method Calc::Add
```

Don't worry if you are unable to make heads or tails of the resulting CIL for this method—Chapter 17 will describe the basics of the CIL programming language. The point to concentrate on is that the C# compiler emits CIL, not platform-specific instructions.

Now, recall that this is true of all .NET-aware compilers. To illustrate, assume you created this same application using Visual Basic, rather than C#.

```
' Calc.vb
Imports System

Namespace CalculatorExample
```

```
' A VB "Module" is a class that contains only
' static members.
Module Program
  Sub Main()
    Dim c As New Calc
    Dim ans As Integer = c.Add(10, 84)
    Console.WriteLine("10 + 84 is {0}.", ans)
    Console.ReadLine()
  End Sub
End Module

Class Calc
  Public Function Add(ByVal x As Integer, ByVal y As Integer) As Integer
    Return x + y
  End Function
End Class

End Namespace
```

If you examine the CIL for the Add() method, you find similar instructions (slightly tweaked by the Visual Basic compiler, vbc.exe).

```
.method public instance int32 Add(int32 x,
  int32 y) cil managed
{
  // Code size 8 (0x8)
  .maxstack  2
  .locals init (int32 V_0)
  IL_0000:  ldarg.1
  IL_0001:  ldarg.2
  IL_0002:  add.ovf
  IL_0003:  stloc.0
  IL_0004:  br.s IL_0006
  IL_0006:  ldloc.0
  IL_0007:  ret
} // end of method Calc::Add
```

■ **Source Code** The Calc.cs and Calc.vb code files are included under the Chapter 1 subdirectory.

Benefits of CIL

At this point, you might be wondering exactly what is gained by compiling source code into CIL rather than directly to a specific instruction set. One benefit is language integration. As you have already seen, each .NET-aware compiler produces nearly identical CIL instructions. Therefore, all languages are able to interact within a well-defined binary arena.

Furthermore, given that CIL is platform-agnostic, the .NET Framework itself is platform-agnostic, providing the same benefits Java developers have grown accustomed to (e.g., a single code base running on numerous operating systems). In fact, there is an international standard for the C# language and a large subset of the .NET platform and implementations already exist for many non-Windows operating systems (more details at the conclusion of this chapter).

Compiling CIL to Platform-Specific Instructions

Due to the fact that assemblies contain CIL instructions rather than platform-specific instructions, CIL code must be compiled on the fly before use. The entity that compiles CIL code into meaningful CPU instructions is a JIT compiler, which sometimes goes by the friendly name of *Jitter*. The .NET runtime environment leverages a JIT compiler for each CPU targeting the runtime, each optimized for the underlying platform.

For example, if you are building a .NET application to be deployed to a handheld device (such as a Windows mobile device), the corresponding Jitter is well equipped to run within a low-memory environment. On the other hand, if you are deploying your assembly to a back-end company server (where memory is seldom an issue), the Jitter will be optimized to function in a high-memory environment. In this way, developers can write a single body of code that can be efficiently JIT compiled and executed on machines with different architectures.

Furthermore, as a given Jitter compiles CIL instructions into corresponding machine code, it will cache the results in memory in a manner suited to the target operating system. In this way, if a call is made to a method named `PrintDocument()`, the CIL instructions are compiled into platform-specific instructions on the first invocation and retained in memory for later use. Therefore, the next time `PrintDocument()` is called, there is no need to recompile the CIL.

■ **Note** It is also possible to perform a "pre-JIT" of an assembly when installing your application using the `ngen.exe` command-line tool that ships with the .NET 4.5 Framework SDK. Doing so can improve startup time for graphically intensive applications.

The Role of .NET Type Metadata

In addition to CIL instructions, a .NET assembly contains full, complete, and accurate metadata, which describes each and every type (e.g., class, structure, enumeration) defined in the binary, as well as the members of each type (e.g., properties, methods, events). Thankfully, it is always the job of the compiler (not the programmer) to emit the latest and greatest type metadata. Because .NET metadata is so wickedly meticulous, assemblies are completely self-describing entities.

To illustrate the format of .NET type metadata, let's take a look at the metadata that has been generated for the `Add()` method of the C# `Calc` class you examined previously (the metadata generated for the Visual Basic version of the `Add()` method is similar).

```
TypeDef #2 (02000003)
-------------------------------------------------
  TypDefName: CalculatorExample.Calc  (02000003)
  Flags    : [NotPublic] [AutoLayout] [Class]
  [AnsiClass] [BeforeFieldInit]  (00100001)
  Extends  : 01000001 [TypeRef] System.Object
  Method #1 (06000003)
```

```
-----------------------------------------------------------
MethodName: Add (06000003)
Flags     : [Public] [HideBySig] [ReuseSlot]   (00000086)
RVA       : 0x00002090
ImplFlags : [IL] [Managed]   (00000000)
CallCnvntn: [DEFAULT]
hasThis
ReturnType: I4
   2 Arguments
   Argument #1:   I4
   Argument #2:   I4
   2 Parameters
   (1) ParamToken : (08000001) Name : x flags: [none] (00000000)
   (2) ParamToken : (08000002) Name : y flags: [none] (00000000)
```

Metadata is used by numerous aspects of the .NET runtime environment, as well as by various development tools. For example, the IntelliSense feature provided by tools such as Visual Studio is made possible by reading an assembly's metadata at design time. Metadata is also used by various object-browsing utilities, debugging tools, and the C# compiler itself. To be sure, metadata is the backbone of numerous .NET technologies including Windows Communication Foundation (WCF), reflection, late binding, and object serialization. Chapter 15 will formalize the role of .NET metadata.

The Role of the Assembly Manifest

Last but not least, remember that a .NET assembly also contains metadata that describes the assembly itself (technically termed a *manifest*). Among other details, the manifest documents all external assemblies required by the current assembly to function correctly, the assembly's version number, copyright information, and so forth. Like type metadata, it is always the job of the compiler to generate the assembly's manifest. Here are some relevant details of the manifest generated when compiling the Calc.cs code file shown earlier in this chapter (assume we instructed the compiler to name our assembly Calc.exe).

```
.assembly extern mscorlib
{
  .publickeytoken = (B7 7A 5C 56 19 34 E0 89 )
  .ver 4:0:0:0
}
.assembly Calc
{
  .hash algorithm 0x00008004
  .ver 0:0:0:0
}
.module Calc.exe
.imagebase 0x00400000
.subsystem 0x00000003
.file alignment 0x00000200
.corflags 0x00000001
```

In a nutshell, this manifest documents the set of external assemblies required by Calc.exe (via the .assembly extern directive) as well as various characteristics of the assembly itself (e.g., version number, module name). Chapter 14 will examine the usefulness of manifest data in much more detail.

Understanding the Common Type System

A given assembly may contain any number of distinct types. In the world of .NET, *type* is simply a general term used to refer to a member from the set {class, interface, structure, enumeration, delegate}. When you build solutions using a .NET-aware language, you will most likely interact with many of these types. For example, your assembly might define a single class that implements some number of interfaces. Perhaps one of the interface methods takes an enumeration type as an input parameter and returns a structure to the caller.

Recall that the CTS is a formal specification that documents how types must be defined in order to be hosted by the CLR. Typically, the only individuals who are deeply concerned with the inner workings of the CTS are those building tools and/or compilers that target the .NET platform. It is important, however, for all .NET programmers to learn about how to work with the five types defined by the CTS in their language of choice. Following is a brief overview.

CTS Class Types

Every .NET-aware language supports, at the very least, the notion of a *class type*, which is the cornerstone of OOP (Object Oriented Programming). A class may be composed of any number of members (such as constructors, properties, methods, and events) and data points (fields). In C#, classes are declared using the class keyword, like so:

```
// A C# class type with 1 method.
class Calc
{
  public int Add(int x, int y)
  {
    return x + y;
  }
}
```

Chapter 5 will begin your formal examination of building class types with C#; however, Table 1-1 documents a number of characteristics pertaining to class types.

Table 1-1. CTS Class Characteristics

Class Characteristic	Meaning in Life
Is the class sealed or not?	Sealed classes cannot function as a base class to other classes.
Does the class implement any interfaces?	An interface is a collection of abstract members that provide a contract between the object and object user. The CTS allows a class to implement any number of interfaces.
Is the class abstract or concrete?	Abstract classes cannot be directly instantiated, but are intended to define common behaviors for derived types. Concrete classes can be instantiated directly.

Class Characteristic	Meaning in Life
What is the visibility of this class?	Each class must be configured with a visibility keyword such as public or internal. Basically, this controls if the class may be used by external assemblies or only from within the defining assembly.

CTS Interface Types

Interfaces are nothing more than a named collection of abstract member definitions, which may be supported (i.e., implemented) by a given class or structure. In C#, interface types are defined using the interface keyword. By convention, all .NET interfaces begin with a capital letter I, as in the following example:

```
// A C# interface type is usually
// declared as public, to allow types in other
// assemblies to implement their behavior.
public interface IDraw
{
  void Draw();
}
```

On their own, interfaces are of little use. However, when a class or structure implements a given interface in its unique way, you are able to request access to the supplied functionality using an interface reference in a polymorphic manner. Interface-based programming will be fully explored in Chapter 8.

CTS Structure Types

The concept of a structure is also formalized under the CTS. If you have a C background, you should be pleased to know that these user-defined types (UDTs) have survived in the world of .NET (although they behave a bit differently under the hood). Simply put, a *structure* can be thought of as a lightweight class type having value-based semantics. For more details on the subtleties of structures, see Chapter 4. Typically, structures are best suited for modeling geometric and mathematical data and are created in C# using the struct keyword, as follows:

```
// A C# structure type.
struct Point
{
  // Structures can contain fields.
  public int xPos, yPos;

  // Structures can contain parameterized constructors.
  public Point(int x, int y)
  { xPos = x; yPos = y;}

  // Structures may define methods.
  public void PrintPosition()
  {
    Console.WriteLine("({0}, {1})", xPos, yPos);
  }
}
```

CTS Enumeration Types

Enumerations are a handy programming construct that allow you to group name/value pairs. For example, assume you are creating a video game application that allows the player to select one of three character categories (Wizard, Fighter, or Thief). Rather than keeping track of simple numerical values to represent each possibility, you could build a strongly typed enumeration using the enum keyword.

```
// A C# enumeration type.
enum CharacterType
{
  Wizard = 100,
  Fighter = 200,
  Thief = 300
}
```

By default, the storage used to hold each item is a 32-bit integer; however, it is possible to alter this storage slot if need be (e.g., when programming for a low-memory device such as a mobile device). Also, the CTS demands that enumerated types derive from a common base class, System.Enum. As you will see in Chapter 4, this base class defines a number of interesting members that allow you to extract, manipulate, and transform the underlying name/value pairs programmatically.

CTS Delegate Types

Delegates are the .NET equivalent of a type-safe, C-style function pointer. The key difference is that a .NET delegate is a *class* that derives from System.MulticastDelegate, rather than a simple pointer to a raw memory address. In C#, delegates are declared using the delegate keyword.

```
// This C# delegate type can "point to" any method
// returning an int and taking two ints as input.
delegate int BinaryOp(int x, int y);
```

Delegates are critical when you want to provide a way for one object to forward a call to another object and provide the foundation for the .NET event architecture. As you will see in Chapters 11 and 19, delegates have intrinsic support for multicasting (i.e., forwarding a request to multiple recipients) and asynchronous method invocations (i.e., invoking the method on a secondary thread).

CTS Type Members

Now that you have previewed each of the types formalized by the CTS, realize that most types take any number of *members*. Formally speaking, a type member is constrained by the set {constructor, finalizer, static constructor, nested type, operator, method, property, indexer, field, read-only field, constant, event}.

The CTS defines various *adornments* that may be associated with a given member. For example, each member has a given visibility trait (e.g., public, private, protected). Some members may be declared as abstract (to enforce a polymorphic behavior on derived types) as well as virtual (to define a canned, but overridable, implementation). Also, most members may be configured as static (bound at the class level) or instance (bound at the object level). The creation of type members is examined over the course of the next several chapters.

■ **Note** As described in Chapter 9, the C# language also supports the creation of generic types and generic members.

Intrinsic CTS Data Types

The final aspect of the CTS to be aware of for the time being is that it establishes a well-defined set of fundamental data types. Although a given language typically has a unique keyword used to declare a fundamental data type, all .NET language keywords ultimately resolve to the same CTS type defined in an assembly named mscorlib.dll. Consider Table 1-2, which documents how key CTS data types are expressed in various .NET languages.

Table 1-2. The Intrinsic CTS Data Types

CTS Data Type	VB Keyword	C# Keyword	C++/CLI Keyword
System.Byte	Byte	byte	unsigned char
System.SByte	SByte	sbyte	signed char
System.Int16	Short	short	short
System.Int32	Integer	int	int or long
System.Int64	Long	long	__int64
System.UInt16	UShort	ushort	unsigned short
System.UInt32	UInteger	uint	unsigned int or unsigned long
System.UInt64	ULong	ulong	unsigned __int64
System.Single	Single	float	float
System.Double	Double	double	double
System.Object	Object	object	object^
System.Char	Char	char	wchar_t
System.String	String	string	String^
System.Decimal	Decimal	decimal	Decimal
System.Boolean	Boolean	bool	bool

Given the fact that the unique keywords of a managed language are simply shorthand notations for a real type in the System namespace, we no longer have to worry about overflow/underflow conditions for numerical data, or how strings and Booleans are internally represented across different languages. Consider the following code snippets, which define 32-bit numerical variables in C# and Visual Basic, using language keywords as well as the formal CTS data type:

```
// Define some "ints" in C#.
int i = 0;
System.Int32 j = 0;

' Define some "ints" in VB.
Dim i As Integer = 0
Dim j As System.Int32 = 0
```

Understanding the Common Language Specification

As you are aware, different languages express the same programming constructs in unique, language-specific terms. For example, in C# you denote string concatenation using the plus operator (+), while in VB you typically make use of the ampersand (&). Even when two distinct languages express the same programmatic idiom (e.g., a function with no return value), the chances are very good that the syntax will appear quite different on the surface.

```
// C# method returning nothing.
public void MyMethod()
{
  // Some interesting code...
}

' VB method returning nothing.
Public Sub MyMethod()
  ' Some interesting code...
End Sub
```

As you have already seen, these minor syntactic variations are inconsequential in the eyes of the .NET runtime, given that the respective compilers (csc.exe or vbc.exe, in this case) emit a similar set of CIL instructions. However, languages can also differ with regard to their overall level of functionality. For example, a .NET language might or might not have a keyword to represent unsigned data, and might or might not support pointer types. Given these possible variations, it would be ideal to have a baseline to which all .NET-aware languages are expected to conform.

The CLS is a set of rules that describe in vivid detail the minimal and complete set of features a given .NET-aware compiler must support to produce code that can be hosted by the CLR, while at the same time be accessed in a uniform manner by all languages that target the .NET platform. In many ways, the CLS can be viewed as a *subset* of the full functionality defined by the CTS.

The CLS is ultimately a set of rules that compiler builders must conform to if they intend their products to function seamlessly within the .NET universe. Each rule is assigned a simple name (e.g., CLS Rule 6) and describes how this rule affects those who build the compilers as well as those who (in some way) interact with them. The crème de la crème of the CLS is Rule 1.

> *Rule 1:* CLS rules apply only to those parts of a type that are exposed outside the defining assembly.

Given this rule, you can (correctly) infer that the remaining rules of the CLS do not apply to the logic used to build the inner workings of a .NET type. The only aspects of a type that must conform to the CLS are the member definitions themselves (i.e., naming conventions, parameters, and return types). The implementation logic for a member may use any number of non-CLS techniques, as the outside world won't know the difference.

To illustrate, the following C# Add() method is not CLS compliant, as the parameters and return values make use of unsigned data (which is not a requirement of the CLS):

```
class Calc
{
  // Exposed unsigned data is not CLS compliant!
  public ulong Add(ulong x, ulong y)
  {
    return x + y;
  }
}
```

However, if you were to only make use of unsigned data internally in a method, as follows:

```
class Calc
{
  public int Add(int x, int y)
  {
    // As this ulong variable is only used internally,
    // we are still CLS compliant.
    ulong temp = 0;
    ...
    return x + y;
  }
}
```

you have still conformed to the rules of the CLS and can rest assured that all .NET languages are able to invoke the Add() method.

Of course, in addition to Rule 1, the CLS defines numerous other rules. For example, the CLS describes how a given language must represent text strings, how enumerations should be represented internally (the base type used for storage), how to define static members, and so forth. Luckily, you don't have to commit these rules to memory to be a proficient .NET developer. Again, by and large, an intimate understanding of the CTS and CLS specifications is typically only of interest to tool/compiler builders.

Ensuring CLS Compliance

As you will see over the course of this book, C# does define a number of programming constructs that are not CLS compliant. The good news, however, is that you can instruct the C# compiler to check your code for CLS compliance using a single .NET attribute.

```
// Tell the C# compiler to check for CLS compliance.
[assembly: CLSCompliant(true)]
```

Chapter 15 dives into the details of attribute-based programming. Until then, simply understand that the [CLSCompliant] attribute will instruct the C# compiler to check each and every line of code against the rules of the CLS. If any CLS violations are discovered, you receive a compiler error and a description of the offending code.

Understanding the Common Language Runtime

In addition to the CTS and CLS specifications, the final TLA (three-letter abbreviation) to contend with at the moment is the CLR. Programmatically speaking, the term *runtime* can be understood as a collection of services that are required to execute a given compiled unit of code. For example, when Java developers deploy software to a new computer, they need to ensure the machine has been installed with the Java Virtual Machine (JVM) in order to run their software.

The .NET platform offers yet another runtime system. The key difference between the .NET runtime and the various other runtimes I just mentioned is the fact that the .NET runtime provides a single, well-defined runtime layer that is shared by *all* languages and platforms that are .NET-aware.

The crux of the CLR is physically represented by a library named `mscoree.dll` (a.k.a. the Common Object Runtime Execution Engine). When an assembly is referenced for use, `mscoree.dll` is loaded automatically, which in turn loads the required assembly into memory. The runtime engine is responsible for a number of tasks. First and foremost, it is the agent in charge of resolving the location of an assembly and finding the requested type within the binary by reading the contained metadata. The CLR then lays out the type in memory, compiles the associated CIL into platform-specific instructions, performs any necessary security checks, and then executes the code in question.

In addition to loading your custom assemblies and creating your custom types, the CLR will also interact with the types contained within the .NET base class libraries when required. Although the entire base class library has been broken into a number of discrete assemblies, the key assembly is `mscorlib.dll`, which contains a large number of core types that encapsulate a wide variety of common programming tasks, as well as the core data types used by all .NET languages. When you build .NET solutions, you automatically have access to this particular assembly.

Figure 1-4 illustrates the workflow that takes place between your source code (which is making use of base class library types), a given .NET compiler, and the .NET execution engine.

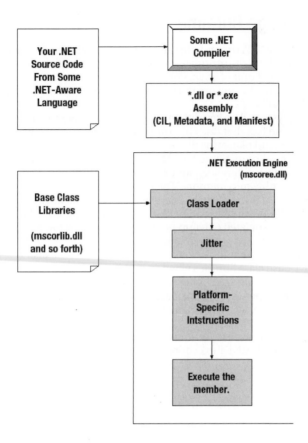

Figure 1-4. *mscoree.dll in action*

The Assembly/Namespace/Type Distinction

Each of us understands the importance of code libraries. The point of framework libraries is to give developers a well-defined set of existing code to leverage in their applications. However, the C# language does not come with a language-specific code library. Rather, C# developers leverage the language-neutral .NET libraries. To keep all the types within the base class libraries well organized, the .NET platform makes extensive use of the *namespace* concept.

A namespace is a grouping of semantically related types contained in an assembly or possibly spread across multiple related assemblies. For example, the System.IO namespace contains file I/O-related types, the System.Data namespace defines basic database types, and so on. It is very important to point out that a single assembly (such as mscorlib.dll) can contain any number of namespaces, each of which can contain any number of types.

To clarify, Figure 1-5 shows a screenshot of the Visual Studio Object Browser utility. This tool allows you to examine the assemblies referenced by your current project, the namespaces within a particular assembly, the types within a given namespace, and the members of a specific type. Note that the mscorlib.dll assembly contains many different namespaces (such as System.IO), each with its own semantically related types (e.g., BinaryReader).

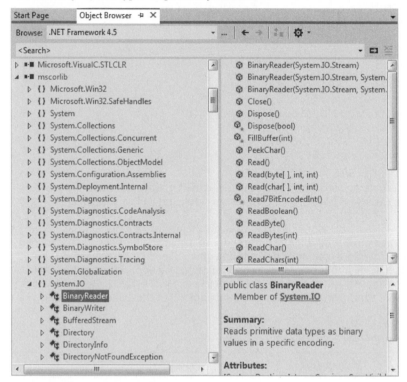

Figure 1-5. *A single assembly can have any number of namespaces*

The key difference between this approach and a language-specific library is that any language targeting the .NET runtime makes use of the *same* namespaces and *same* types. For example, the following three programs all illustrate the ubiquitous "Hello World" application, written in C#, VB, and C++/CLI:

```
// Hello world in C#.
using System;

public class MyApp
{
  static void Main()
  {
    Console.WriteLine("Hi from C#");
  }
}
```

```
' Hello world in VB.
Imports System
```

```
Public Module MyApp
  Sub Main()
    Console.WriteLine("Hi from VB")
  End Sub
End Module

// Hello world in C++/CLI.
#include "stdafx.h"
using namespace System;

int main(array<System::String ^> ^args)
{
  Console::WriteLine(L"Hi from C++/CLI");
  return 0;
}
```

Notice that each language is making use of the Console class defined in the System namespace. Beyond some obvious syntactic variations, these three applications look and feel very much alike, both physically and logically.

Clearly, your primary goal as a .NET developer is to get to know the wealth of types defined in the (numerous) .NET namespaces. The most fundamental namespace to get your hands around initially is named System. This namespace provides a core body of types that you will need to leverage time and again as a .NET developer. In fact, you cannot build any sort of functional C# application without at least making a reference to the System namespace, as the core data types (e.g., System.Int32, System.String) are defined here. Table 1-3 offers a rundown of some (but certainly not all) of the .NET namespaces grouped by related functionality.

Table 1-3. A Sampling of .NET Namespaces

.NET Namespace	Meaning in Life
System	Within System, you find numerous useful types dealing with intrinsic data, mathematical computations, random number generation, environment variables, and garbage collection, as well as a number of commonly used exceptions and attributes.
System.Collections System.Collections.Generic	These namespaces define a number of stock container types, as well as base types and interfaces that allow you to build customized collections.
System.Data System.Data.Common System.Data.EntityClient System.Data.SqlClient	These namespaces are used for interacting with relational databases using ADO.NET.
System.IO System.IO.Compression System.IO.Ports	These namespaces define numerous types used to work with file I/O, compression of data, and port manipulation.

.NET Namespace	Meaning in Life
System.Reflection System.Reflection.Emit	These namespaces define types that support runtime type discovery as well as dynamic creation of types.
System.Runtime.InteropServices	This namespace provides facilities to allow .NET types to interact with unmanaged code (e.g., C-based DLLs and COM servers) and vice versa.
System.Drawing System.Windows.Forms	These namespaces define types used to build desktop applications using .NET's original UI toolkit (Windows Forms).
System.Windows System.Windows.Controls System.Windows.Shapes	The System.Windows namespace is the root for several namespaces that represent the Windows Presentation Foundation (WPF) UI toolkit.
System.Linq System.Xml.Linq System.Data.DataSetExtensions	These namespaces define types used when programming against the LINQ API.
System.Web	This is one of many namespaces that allow you to build ASP.NET web applications.
System.ServiceModel	This is one of many namespaces used to build distributed applications using the Windows Communication Foundation API.
System.Workflow.Runtime System.Workflow.Activities	These are two of many namespaces that define types used to build "workflow-enabled" applications using the Windows Workflow Foundation API.
System.Threading System.Threading.Tasks	This namespace defines numerous types to build multithreaded applications that can distribute workloads across multiple CPUs.
System.Security	Security is an integrated aspect of the .NET universe. In the security-centric namespaces, you find numerous types dealing with permissions, cryptography, and so on.
System.Xml	The XML-centric namespaces contain numerous types used to interact with XML data.

The Role of the Microsoft Root Namespace

I'm sure you noticed while reading over the listings in Table 1-3, that System is the root namespace for a majority of nested namespaces (e.g., System.IO, System.Data). As it turns out, however, the .NET base class library defines a number of topmost root namespaces beyond System, the most useful of which is named Microsoft.

Any namespace nested within Microsoft (e.g., Microsoft.CSharp, Microsoft.ManagementConsole, Microsoft.Win32) contains types that are used to interact with services unique to the Windows operating system. Given this point, you should not assume that these types could be used successfully on other .NET-enabled operating systems such as Mac OS X. For the most part, this text will not dig into the details of the Microsoft rooted namespaces, so be sure to consult the .NET Framework 4.5 SDK documentation if you are interested.

■ **Note** Chapter 2 will illustrate the use of the .NET Framework 4.5 SDK documentation, which provides details regarding every namespace, type, and member found within the base class libraries.

Accessing a Namespace Programmatically

It is worth reiterating that a namespace is nothing more than a convenient way for us mere humans to logically understand and organize related types. Consider again the System namespace. From your perspective, you can assume that System.Console represents a class named Console that is contained within a namespace called System. However, in the eyes of the .NET runtime, this is not so. The runtime engine only sees a single class named System.Console.

In C#, the using keyword simplifies the process of referencing types defined in a particular namespace. Here is how it works. Let's say you are interested in building a graphical desktop application using the WPF API. While learning the types each namespace contains takes study and experimentation, here are some possible candidates to reference in your program.

```
// Here are some possible namespaces used to build a WPF application.
using System;                      // General base class library types.
using System.Windows.Shapes;       // Graphical rendering types.
using System.Windows.Controls;     // Windows Forms GUI widget types.
using System.Data;                 // General data-centric types.
using System.Data.SqlClient;       // MS SQL Server data-access types.
```

Once you have specified some number of namespaces (and set a reference to the assemblies that define them), you are free to create instances of the types they contain. For example, if you are interested in creating an instance of the Button class (defined in the System.Windows.Controls namespace), you can write the following:

```
// Explicitly list the namespaces used by this file.
using System;
using System.Windwos.Controls;

class MyGUIBuilder
{
  public void BuildUI()
  {
    // Create a button control.
    Button btnOK = new Button();
    ...
  }
}
```

Because your code file is importing the `System.Windows.Controls` namespace, the compiler is able to resolve the `Bitmap` class as a member of this namespace. If you did not import the `System.Windows.Controls` namespace, you would be issued a compiler error. However, you are free to declare variables using a *fully qualified name* as well.

```
// Not listing System.Drawing namespace!
using System;

class MyGUIBuilder
{
  public void BuildUI()
  {
    // Using fully qualified name.
    System.Windows.Controls.Button btnOK =
      new System.Windows.Controls.Button();
    ...
  }
}
```

While defining a type using the fully qualified name provides greater readability, I think you'd agree that the C# using keyword reduces keystrokes. In this text, I will avoid the use of fully qualified names (unless there is a definite ambiguity to be resolved) and opt for the simplified approach of the C# using keyword.

However, always remember that the using keyword is simply a shorthand notation for specifying a type's fully qualified name, and either approach results in the *exact* same underlying CIL (given the fact that CIL code always makes use of fully qualified names) and has no effect on performance or the size of the assembly.

Referencing External Assemblies

In addition to specifying a namespace via the C# using keyword, you also need to tell the C# compiler the name of the assembly containing the actual CIL definition for the referenced type. As mentioned, many core .NET namespaces are defined within mscorlib.dll. However, the System.Drawing.Bitmap class is contained within a separate assembly named System.Drawing.dll. A vast majority of the .NET Framework assemblies are located under a specific directory termed the *global assembly cache* (GAC). On a Windows machine, this can be located by default under C:\Windows\Assembly, as shown in Figure 1-6.

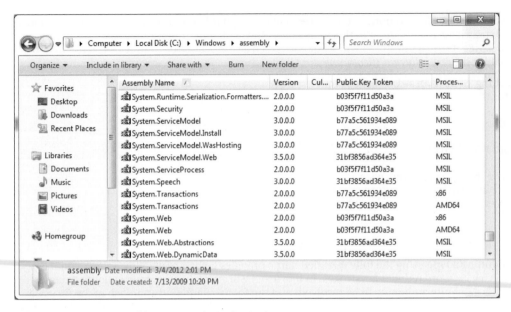

Figure 1-6. Many .NET libraries reside in the GAC

Depending on the development tool you are using to build your .NET applications, you will have various ways to inform the compiler which assemblies you want to include during the compilation cycle. You'll examine how to do so in Chapter 2, so I'll hold off on the details for now.

■ **Note** Beginning with .NET 4.0, Microsoft has opted to isolate .NET 4.0 and .NET 4.5 assemblies in a unique location, which is independent from C:\Windows\Assembly. Chapter 14 will address this point in detail.

Exploring an Assembly Using ildasm.exe

If you are beginning to feel a tad overwhelmed at the thought of gaining mastery over every namespace in the .NET platform, just remember that what makes a namespace unique is that it contains types that are somehow *semantically related*. Therefore, if you have no need for a user interface beyond a simple Console Application, you can forget all about the desktop and web namespaces (among others). If you are building a painting application, the database namespaces are most likely of little concern. Like any new set of prefabricated code, you learn as you go.

The Intermediate Language Disassembler utility (ildasm.exe), which ships with the .NET Framework 4.5 SDK, allows you to load up any .NET assembly and investigate its contents, including the associated manifest, CIL code, and type metadata. This tool allows a programmer to dive deeply into how their C# code maps to CIL, and ultimately helps one understand the inner workings of the .NET platform. While you never *need* to use ildasm.exe to become a proficient .NET programmer, I highly recommend you fire up this tool from time to time to better understand how your C# code maps to runtime concepts.

■ **Note** You can easily run ildasm.exe by opening a Developer Command Prompt, and type "ildasm" (without the quotes) followed by the Enter key. Chapter 2 will explain how to open this "special" command window, as well as other tools loaded from the command line.

After you launch ildasm.exe, proceed to the File   Open menu command and navigate to an assembly you would like to explore. By way of illustration, Figure 1-7 shows the Calc.exe assembly generated based on the Calc.cs file shown earlier in this chapter. ildasm.exe presents the structure of an assembly using a familiar tree-view format.

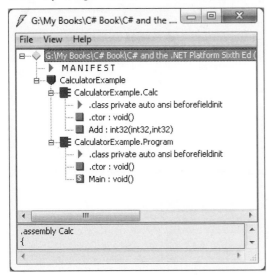

Figure 1-7. *ildasm.exe allows you to see the CIL code, manifest, and metadata within a .NET assembly*

Viewing CIL Code

In addition to showing the namespaces, types, and members contained in a given assembly, ildasm.exe also allows you to view the CIL instructions for a given member. For example, if you were to double-click the Main() method of the Program class, a separate window would display the underlying CIL (see Figure 1-8).

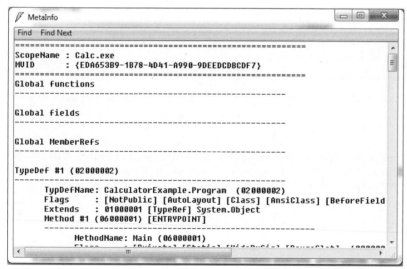

```
.method private hidebysig static void  Main() cil managed
{
  .entrypoint
  // Code size       42 (0x2a)
  .maxstack  3
  .locals init (class CalculatorExample.Calc V_0,
           int32 V_1)
  IL_0000:  nop
  IL_0001:  newobj      instance void CalculatorExample.Calc::.ctor()
  IL_0006:  stloc.0
  IL_0007:  ldloc.0
  IL_0008:  ldc.i4.s    10
  IL_000a:  ldc.i4.s    84
  IL_000c:  callvirt    instance int32 CalculatorExample.Calc::Add(int32,
                                                                  int32)
  IL_0011:  stloc.1
  IL_0012:  ldstr       "10 + 84 is {0}."
  IL_0017:  ldloc.1
  IL_0018:  box         [mscorlib]System.Int32
  IL_001d:  call        void [mscorlib]System.Console::WriteLine(string,
                                                                 object)
  IL_0022:  nop
```

Figure 1-8. Viewing the underlying CIL

Viewing Type Metadata

If you want to view the type metadata for the currently loaded assembly, press Ctrl+M. Figure 1-9 shows the metadata for the Calc.Add() method.

```
ScopeName : Calc.exe
MVID      : {EDA653B9-1B78-4D41-A990-9DEEDCDBCDF7}
===========================================================
Global functions
-----------------------------------------------------------

Global fields
-----------------------------------------------------------

Global MemberRefs
-----------------------------------------------------------

TypeDef #1 (02000002)
-----------------------------------------------------------
     TypDefName: CalculatorExample.Program  (02000002)
     Flags     : [NotPublic] [AutoLayout] [Class] [AnsiClass] [BeforeField
     Extends   : 01000001 [TypeRef] System.Object
     Method #1 (06000001) [ENTRYPOINT]
     -----------------------------------------------------
         MethodName: Main (06000001)
```

Figure 1-9. Viewing type metadata via ildasm.exe

Viewing Assembly Metadata (a.k.a. the Manifest)

Finally, if you are interested in viewing the contents of the assembly's manifest, simply double-click the MANIFEST icon (see Figure 1-10).

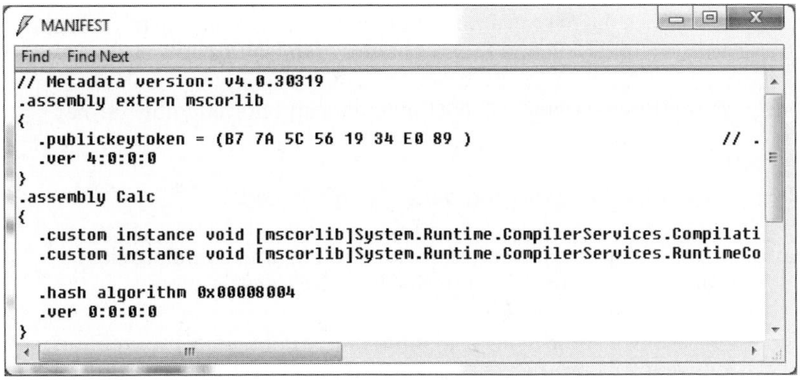

```
// Metadata version: v4.0.30319
.assembly extern mscorlib
{
  .publickeytoken = (B7 7A 5C 56 19 34 E0 89 )                           // .
  .ver 4:0:0:0
}
.assembly Calc
{
  .custom instance void [mscorlib]System.Runtime.CompilerServices.Compilati
  .custom instance void [mscorlib]System.Runtime.CompilerServices.RuntimeCo

  .hash algorithm 0x00008004
  .ver 0:0:0:0
}
```

Figure 1-10. Viewing manifest data via `ildasm.exe`

To be sure, `ildasm.exe` has more options than shown here, and I will illustrate additional features of the tool where appropriate in the text.

The Platform-Independent Nature of .NET

Allow me to briefly comment on the platform-independent nature of the .NET platform. To the surprise of most developers, .NET assemblies can be developed and executed on non-Microsoft operating systems, including Mac OS X, various Linux distributions, Solaris, as well as iOS and Android mobile devices (via the MonoTouch API). To understand how this is possible, you need to come to terms with yet another abbreviation in the .NET universe: CLI (Common Language Infrastructure).

When Microsoft released the C# programming language and the .NET platform, they also crafted a set of formal documents that described the syntax and semantics of the C# and CIL languages, the .NET assembly format, core .NET namespaces, and the mechanics of a hypothetical .NET runtime engine (known as the Virtual Execution System, or VES).

These documents have been submitted to (and ratified by) Ecma International (www.ecma-international.org) as official international standards. The specifications of interest are as follows:

> *ECMA-334:* The C# Language Specification

> *ECMA-335:* The Common Language Infrastructure (CLI)

The importance of these documents becomes clear when you understand that they enable third parties to build distributions of the .NET platform for any number of operating systems and/or processors. ECMA-335 is the more "meaty" of the two specifications, so much so that is has been broken into various partitions, including those seen in Table 1-4.

Table 1-4. Partitions of the CLI

Partitions of ECMA-335	Meaning in Life
Partition I: Concepts and Architecture	Describes the overall architecture of the CLI, including the rules of the CTS and CLS, and the mechanics of the .NET runtime engine.
Partition II: Metadata Definition and Semantics	Describes the details of .NET metadata and the assembly format.
Partition III: CIL Instruction Set	Describes the syntax and semantics of CIL code.
Partition IV: Profiles and Libraries	Gives a high-level overview of the minimal and complete class libraries that must be supported by a .NET distribution.
Partition V: Debug Interchange Format	Describes a standard way to interchange debugging information between CLI producers and consumers.
Partition VI: Annexes	Provides a collection of odds-and-ends details such as class library design guidelines and the implementation details of a CIL compiler.

Be aware that Partition IV (Profiles and Libraries) defines only a *minimal* set of namespaces that represent the core services expected by a CLI distribution (e.g., collections, console I/O, file I/O, threading, reflection, network access, core security needs, XML data manipulation). The CLI does *not* define namespaces that facilitate web development (ASP.NET), database access (ADO.NET), or desktop graphical user interface (GUI) application development (Windows Presentation Foundation or Windows Forms).

The good news, however, is that the mainstream .NET distributions extend the CLI libraries with Microsoft-compatible equivalents of ASP.NET implementations and ADO.NET implementations (and so on) in order to provide full-featured, production-level development platforms. To date, there are two major implementations of the CLI (beyond Microsoft's Windows-specific offering). Although this text focuses on the creation of .NET applications using Microsoft's .NET distribution, Table 1-5 provides information regarding the Mono and Portable .NET projects.

Table 1-5. Open Source .NET Distributions

Distribution	Meaning in Life
www.mono-project.com	The Mono project is an open source distribution of the CLI that targets various Linux distributions (e.g., SuSe, Fedora), Mac OS X, iOS devices (iPad, iPhone), Android devices, and (surprise!) Windows.
www.dotgnu.org	Portable.NET is another open source distribution of the CLI that runs on numerous operating systems. Portable.NET aims to target as many operating systems as possible (e.g., Windows, AIX, Mac OS X, Solaris, all major Linux distributions).

Both Mono and Portable.NET provide an ECMA-compliant C# compiler, .NET runtime engine, code samples, documentation, as well as numerous development tools that are functionally equivalent to the tools that ship with Microsoft's .NET Framework 4.5 SDK.

■ **Note** An introduction to creating cross-platform .NET applications using Mono can be found in Appendix A.

A Brief Word Regarding Windows 8 Applications

To close this chapter, allow me to briefly comment on how the Microsoft .NET platform relates to a *brand-new* set of technologies introduced with the Windows 8 operating system. If you have not yet had time to explore Windows 8, let me just say that the new user interface is radically different than any previous version of Microsoft Windows (in fact, I'd say it is as radical as the shift from Windows 3.11 to Windows 95—for those of you old enough to remember). Figure 1-11 illustrates the new start screen of Windows 8 OS.

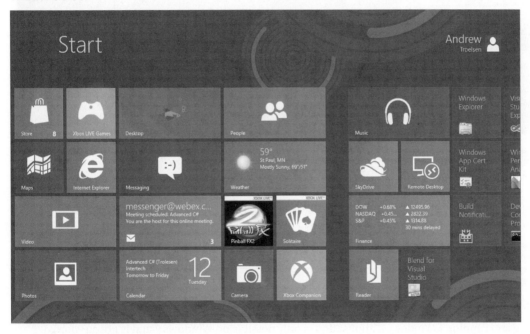

Figure 1-11. The Windows 8 start screen

As seen in Figure 1-11, the Windows 8 start screen supports a tiled layout, where each tile represents an application installed on the machine. Unlike a typical Windows desktop application, Windows 8 applications are built for touch-screen interactions. They are also run in full-screen renderings and lack the usual "chrome" (e.g., menu systems, status bars, and toolbar buttons) we see in many desktop applications. Figure 1-12 shows a partial view of a Windows 8 weather application.

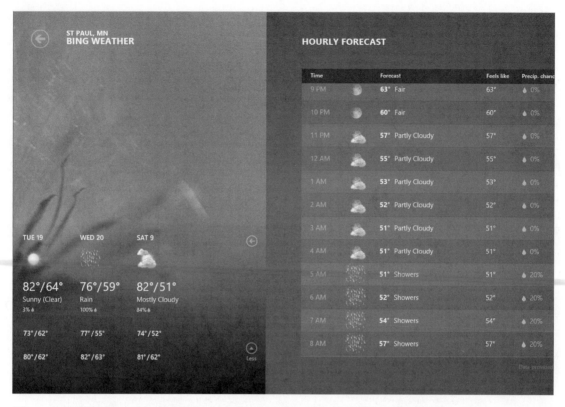

Figure 1-12. Windows 8 applications are full-screeen, graphically rich desktop applications

---

■ **Note** Building a Windows 8 application requires developers to adhere to an entirely new set of UI design guidelines, data storage methodologies, and user input options. To be sure, a "Win8" app is much more than a tile installed on the Windows 8 start screen.

Building Windows 8 Applications

Creating and running a Windows 8 application is only possible on Windows 8 and is not supported under Windows 7. In fact, if you install Visual Studio on Windows 7 (or earlier), you will not even see Windows 8 project templates appear in the New Project dialog box.

Programming a Windows 8 application requires developers to tap into an entirely new runtime layer termed (appropriately enough) *Windows Runtime* (WinRT). Be very aware that WinRT is *not* the .NET CLR, however it does offer some similar services such as garbage collection, support for multiple programming languages (including C#), and so forth.

In addition, these applications are created using a completely new set of namespaces, all of which begin with the root name `Windows`. Figure 1-13 shows various WinRT namespaces displayed in the Visual Studio object browser.

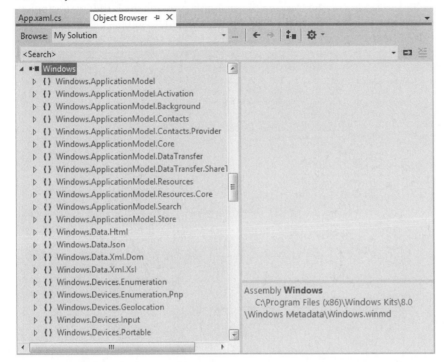

Figure 1-13. The `Windows.*` *namespaces are only used to build Windows 8 applications*

As luck would have it, the `Windows.*` namespaces offer functionality that mirrors many APIs of the .NET base class libraries. In fact, from a programming point of view, building an application for WinRT feels very similar to building a .NET application for the CLR. For example, Windows 8 applications can be constructed using C# (as well as with Visual Basic, JavaScript, or C++).

As well, many of the `Windows.*` namespaces offer similar (though not identical) functionality as is found in the .NET base class libraries. By way of one example, later in this text (see Chapters 27–31), you will examine a .NET technology termed *Windows Presentation Foundation* (WPF). Here, you will learn about an XML-based grammar named *XAML*. Should you begin to explore how to Windows 8 applications, you will be happy to see that they are created using XAML as well (or possibly using HTML5, if your language of choice is JavaScript), and have a very similar programming model to a WPF program constructed with the .NET platform.

The Role of .NET Under Windows 8

In addition to the `Windows.*` namespaces, Windows 8 applications can also make use of a large subset of the .NET platform. Collectively, the .NET APIs for Windows 8 applications, provide support for generic collections, LINQ, XML document processing, I/O services, security services, and other topics explored in this book. This is certainly a good thing, as many topics explored in this book will map directly to the construction of a Windows 8 application.

Also be aware that even though the classic Windows desktop is not the default display under Windows 8, it is still accessible by clicking on the Desktop tile or simply pressing the Windows button on your computer keyboard. Once opened, the OS will display a desktop that looks almost identical to the Windows 7 desktop (see Figure 1-14).

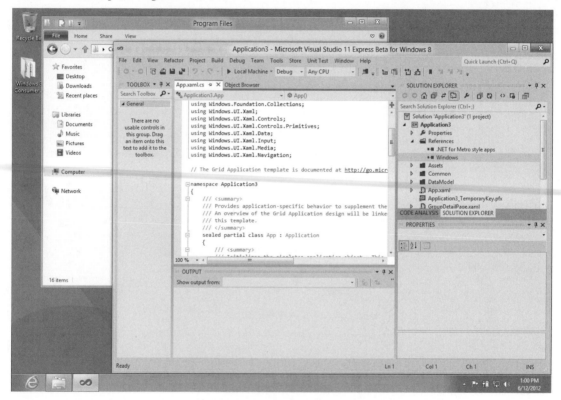

Figure 1-14. *The desktop of Windows 8 allows you to run non-Windows 8 applications*

Here you are able to run all of your expected desktop applications including Visual Studio, Word, Excel, Photoshop and whatnot. As well, if you are building .NET applications under Windows 8, the applications will run within the Windows 8 desktop environment.

So, the short answer is that the Microsoft .NET platform is alive and well under Windows 8, and will be a key part of your development efforts. Just keep in mind that .NET proper is not used to build Windows 8 applications. Rather, you will make use of new libraries (Windows.*), a new runtime (WinRT), and a subset of .NET proper (the .NET APIs) to create such a program.

This text will not examine the process of building Windows 8 applications using WinRT, but will focus exclusively on the .NET platform. However, do keep in mind that a majority of topics examined in this text will most certainly prepare you to explore Windows 8 application development in the future, should you have the need.

Summary

The point of this chapter was to lay out the conceptual framework necessary for the remainder of this book. I began by examining a number of limitations and complexities found within the technologies prior to .NET, and followed up with an overview of how .NET and C# attempt to simplify the current state of affairs.

.NET basically boils down to a runtime execution engine (`mscoree.dll`) and base class library (`mscorlib.dll` and associates). The Common Language Runtime (CLR) is able to host any .NET binary (a.k.a. assembly) that abides by the rules of managed code. As you have seen, assemblies contain CIL instructions (in addition to type metadata and the assembly manifest) that are compiled to platform-specific instructions using a just-in-time (JIT) compiler. In addition, you explored the role of the Common Language Specification (CLS) and Common Type System (CTS).

This was followed by an examination of the `ildasm.exe` and `reflector.exe` object browsing utilities, as well as coverage of how to configure a machine to host .NET applications using the full and client profiles. I wrapped up by briefly addressing the platform-independent nature of C# and the .NET platform (a topic further examined in Appendix A) and how the .NET platform is positioned within the Windows 8 operating system.

CHAPTER 2

Building C# Applications

As a C# programmer, you may choose among numerous tools to build .NET applications. The point of this chapter is to provide a tour of various .NET development options, including, of course, Visual Studio proper. The chapter opens, however, with an examination of working with the C# command-line compiler, `csc.exe`, and the simplest of all text editors, the Notepad application that ships with the Microsoft Windows OS, as well as the freely downloadable Notepad++.

While you could work through this entire text using nothing other than `csc.exe` and a basic text editor, I'd bet you are also interested in working with feature-rich integrated development environments (IDEs). To address this need, you will be introduced to a free, open source .NET IDE named SharpDevelop. Then, after briefly examining the Visual C# Express IDE (which is also free), you will be given a guided tour of the key features of Visual Studio Professional.

■ **Note** Over the course of this chapter, you will encounter some C# syntax we have not formally examined. If you are unfamiliar with the syntax, don't fret. Chapter 3 will formally begin your examination of the C# language.

The Role of the .NET Framework 4.5 SDK

One common misconception regarding .NET development is the belief that programmers must purchase a copy of Visual Studio in order to build their C# applications. The truth of the matter is that you are able to build any sort of .NET program using the freely downloadable .NET Framework 4.5 Software Development Kit (SDK).

This SDK provides you with numerous managed compilers, command-line utilities, sample code, the .NET class libraries, and a complete documentation system. Now, be aware that if you are going to be using Visual Studio proper or Visual C# Express, you have no need to manually download or install the .NET Framework 4.5 SDK. When you install either of these products, the SDK is installed automatically, thereby giving you everything you need out of the box. However, if you are *not* going to be using a Microsoft IDE as you work through this text, be sure to install the SDK before proceeding.

■ **Note** The .NET Framework 4.5 SDK setup program (`dotNetFx45_Full_x86_x64.exe`) can be obtained from the .NET download web site (`http://msdn.microsoft.com/netframework`).

The Developer Command Prompt

When you install the .NET Framework 4.5 SDK, Visual Studio, or Visual C# Express, you will end up with a number of new directories on your local hard drive, each of which contains various .NET development tools. Many of these tools are driven from the command prompt, so if you wish to use these utilities from any Windows command window, you will need to register these paths with the operating system.

   While you could update your machine's PATH variable manually to do so, you can save yourself some time by simply making use of the Developer Command Prompt (see Figure 2-1) that is accessible from the Start ➤ All Programs ➤ Microsoft Visual Studio 11 ➤ Visual Studio Tools folder.

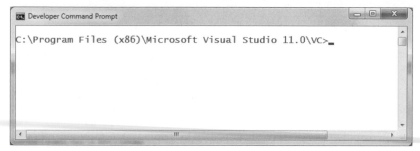

Figure 2-1. *The Developer Command Prompt*

   The benefit of using this particular command prompt is that it has been preconfigured to provide access to each of the .NET development tools. Assuming you have a .NET development environment installed, type the following command and press the Enter key:

```
csc -?
```

   If all is well, you should see a list of command-line arguments of the C# command-line compiler (where csc stands for the *C-sharp compiler*). As you can see, this command-line compiler has a bevy of options; however, in practice you will only need to make use of a handful of settings to build C# programs at the command prompt.

Building C# Applications Using csc.exe

While it is true that you might never decide to build a large-scale application using nothing but the C# command-line compiler, it is important to understand the basics of how to compile your code files by hand. I can think of a few reasons you should get a grip on the process.

- The most obvious reason is the simple fact that you might not have a copy of Visual Studio or another graphical IDE.

- You might be in a college or university setting where you are prohibited from using code-generation tools/IDEs in the classroom.

- You plan to make use of automated build tools, such as msbuild.exe, which require you to know the command-line options of the tools you are utilizing.

- You want to deepen your understanding of C#. When you use graphical IDEs to build applications, you are ultimately instructing csc.exe how to manipulate your C# input files. In this light, it's edifying to see what takes place behind the scenes.

Another nice by-product of working with csc.exe in the raw is that you become that much more comfortable manipulating other command-line tools included with the .NET Framework 4.5 SDK. As you will see throughout this book, a number of important utilities are accessible only from the command line (such as gacutil.exe, ngen.exe, ilasm.exe, and aspnet_regiis.exe).

To illustrate how to build a .NET application IDE-free, we will build a simple executable assembly named TestApp.exe using the C# command-line compiler and Notepad. First, you need some source code. Open Notepad (using the Start ➤ All Programs ➤ Accessories menu option) and enter the following trivial C# class definition:

```csharp
// A simple C# application.
using System;

class TestApp
{
  static void Main()
  {
    Console.WriteLine("Testing! 1, 2, 3");
  }
}
```

After you have finished, save the file in a convenient location (e.g., C:\CscExample) as TestApp.cs. Now let's get to know the core options of the C# compiler.

■ **Note** C# code files take a *.cs file extension. Unlike Java, the name of the file need not have any mapping to the name of the type (or types) it is defining.

Specifying Input and Output Targets

The first point of interest is to understand how to specify the name and type of assembly to create (e.g., a console application named MyShell.exe, a code library named MathLib.dll, a Windows Presentation Foundation application named Halo8.exe, and so forth). Each possibility is represented by a specific flag passed into csc.exe as a command-line parameter (see Table 2-1).

Table 2-1. Common Output Options of the C# Compiler

Option	Meaning in Life
/out	This option is used to specify the name of the assembly to be created. By default, the assembly name is the same as the name of the initial input *.cs file.
/target:exe	This option builds an executable console application. This is the default assembly output type, and thus may be omitted when building this type of application.
/target:library	This option builds a single-file *.dll assembly.

Option	Meaning in Life
/target:winexe	Although you are free to build graphical user interface–based applications using the /target:exe option, /target:winexe prevents a console window from appearing in the background.

■ **Note** The options sent to the command-line compiler (as well as most other command-line tools) can be prefixed with either a dash (-) or a slash (/).

To compile TestApp.cs into a console application named TestApp.exe, change to the directory containing your source code file using the cd ("change directory") command:

```
cd C:\CscExample
```

Then, enter the following command set (note that command-line flags must come before the name of the input files, not after):

```
csc /target:exe TestApp.cs
```

Here I did not explicitly specify an /out flag; therefore, the executable will be named TestApp.exe given that TestApp is the name of the input file. Also be aware that most of the C# compiler flags support an abbreviated version, such as /t rather than /target (you can view all abbreviations by entering csc -? at the command prompt).

```
csc /t:exe TestApp.cs
```

Furthermore, given that the /t:exe flag is the default output used by the C# compiler, you could also compile TestApp.cs simply by typing the following:

```
csc TestApp.cs
```

TestApp.exe can now be run from the command line by typing the name of the executable, as shown in Figure 2-2.

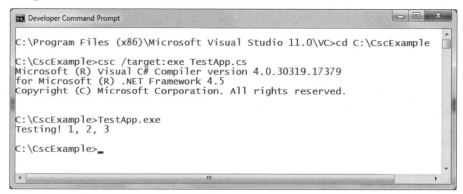

Figure 2-2. Compiling and running TestApp.exe

Referencing External Assemblies

Next, let's examine how to compile an application that makes use of types defined in a separate .NET assembly. And just in case you are wondering how the C# compiler understood your reference to the System.Console type, recall from Chapter 1 that mscorlib.dll is *automatically referenced* during the compilation process (if for some strange reason you wish to disable this feature, you may specify the /nostdlib option of csc.exe).

Let's update the TestApp application to display a Windows Forms message box. Open your TestApp.cs file and modify it as follows:

```
using System;

// Add this!
using System.Windows.Forms;

class TestApp
{
  static void Main()
  {
    Console.WriteLine("Testing! 1, 2, 3");

    // Add this!
    MessageBox.Show("Hello...");
  }
}
```

Notice you are importing the System.Windows.Forms namespace via the C# using keyword (introduced in Chapter 1). Recall that when you explicitly list the namespaces used within a given *.cs file, you avoid the need to make use of fully qualified names of a type (which can lead to hand cramps).

At the command line, you must inform csc.exe which assembly contains the namespaces you are using. Given that you have made use of the System.Windows.Forms.MessageBox class, you must specify the System.Windows.Forms.dll assembly using the /reference flag (which can be abbreviated to /r).

```
csc /r:System.Windows.Forms.dll TestApp.cs
```

If you now rerun your application, you should see a message box appear (see Figure 2-3) in addition to the console output.

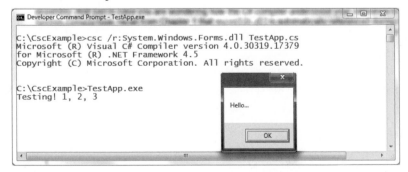

Figure 2-3. Your first graphical user interface application

Referencing Multiple External Assemblies

On a related note, what if you need to reference numerous external assemblies using csc.exe? Simply list each assembly using a semicolon-delimited list. You don't need to specify multiple external assemblies for the current example, but some sample usage follows:

```
csc /r:System.Windows.Forms.dll;System.Drawing.dll *.cs
```

■ **Note** As explained a bit later in this chapter, the C# compiler will automatically reference a set of core .NET assemblies (such as System.Windows.Forms.dll), even if they are not specified using the /r flag.

Compiling Multiple Source Files

The current incarnation of the TestApp.exe application was created using a single *.cs source code file. While it is perfectly permissible to have all of your .NET types defined in a single *.cs file, most projects are composed of multiple *.cs files to keep your code base a bit more flexible. Assume you have authored a new class contained in a new file named HelloMsg.cs.

```
// The HelloMessage class
using System;
using System.Windows.Forms;

class HelloMessage
{
  public void Speak()
  {
    MessageBox.Show("Hello...");
  }
}
```

Now, update your initial TestApp class to make use of this new class type and comment out the previous Windows Forms logic.

```
using System;

// Don't need this anymore.
// using System.Windows.Forms;

class TestApp
{
  static void Main()
  {
    Console.WriteLine("Testing! 1, 2, 3");

    // Don't need this anymore either.
    // MessageBox.Show("Hello...");
```

```
    // Use the HelloMessage class!
    HelloMessage h = new HelloMessage();
    h.Speak();
  }
}
```

You can compile your C# files by listing each input file explicitly.

```
csc /r:System.Windows.Forms.dll TestApp.cs HelloMsg.cs
```

As an alternative, the C# compiler allows you to make use of the wildcard character (*) to inform csc.exe to include all *.cs files contained in the project directory as part of the current build.

```
csc /r:System.Windows.Forms.dll *.cs
```

When you run the program again, the output is identical to the previous compiled code. The only difference between the two applications is the fact that the current logic has been split among multiple files.

Working with C# Response Files

As you might guess, if you were to build a complex C# application at the command prompt, you would have to specify a tedious number of input options to inform the compiler how to process your source code. To help lessen your typing burden, the C# compiler honors the use of *response files.*

C# response files contain all the instructions to be used during the compilation of your current build. By convention, these files end in a *.rsp (response) extension. Assume that you have created a response file named TestApp.rsp that contains the following options (as you can see, comments are denoted with the # character):

```
# This is the response file
# for the TestApp.exe example
# of Chapter 2.

# External assembly references.
/r:System.Windows.Forms.dll

# output and files to compile (using wildcard syntax).
/target:exe /out:TestApp.exe *.cs
```

Now, assuming this file is saved in the same directory as the C# source code files to be compiled, you are able to build your entire application as follows (note the use of the @ symbol):

```
csc @TestApp.rsp
```

If the need should arise, you can also specify multiple *.rsp files as input (e.g., csc @FirstFile.rsp @SecondFile.rsp @ThirdFile.rsp). If you take this approach, be aware that the compiler processes the command options as they are encountered. Therefore, command-line arguments in a later *.rsp file can override options in a previous response file.

Also note that flags listed explicitly on the command line before a response file will be overridden by the specified *.rsp file. Thus, if you were to enter the following:

```
csc /out:MyCoolApp.exe @TestApp.rsp
```

the name of the assembly would still be TestApp.exe (rather than MyCoolApp.exe), given the /out:TestApp.exe flag listed in the TestApp.rsp response file. However, if you list flags after a response file, the flag will override settings in the response file.

■ **Note** The effect of the /reference flag is cumulative. Regardless of where you specify external assemblies (before, after, or within a response file), the end result is a summation of each reference assembly.

The Default Response File (csc.rsp)

The final point to be made regarding response files is that the C# compiler has an associated default response file (csc.rsp), which is located in the same directory as csc.exe itself (which is by default installed under C:\Windows\Microsoft.NET\Framework\<version>, where <version> is a given version of the platform). If you were to open this file using Notepad, you will find that numerous .NET assemblies have already been specified using the /r: flag, including various libraries for web development, LINQ programming, data access, and other core libraries (beyond mscorlib.dll).

When you are building your C# programs using csc.exe, this response file will be automatically referenced, even when you supply a custom *.rsp file. Given the presence of the default response file, the current TestApp.exe application could be successfully compiled using the following command set (as System.Windows.Forms.dll is referenced within csc.rsp):

```
csc /out:TestApp.exe *.cs
```

In the event that you wish to disable the automatic reading of csc.rsp, you can specify the /noconfig option.

```
csc @TestApp.rsp /noconfig
```

■ **Note** If you reference assemblies (via the /r option) that you do not actually make use of, they are ignored by the compiler. Therefore, you have no need to worry about "code bloat." If you reference a library you do not actually make use of, it is ignored by the compiler.

Obviously, the C# command-line compiler has many other options that can be used to control how the resulting .NET assembly is to be generated. You'll see other important features where necessary over the course of this text; however, full details of these options can be found within the .NET Framework 4.5 SDK documentation.

■ **Source Code** The CscExample application can be found under the Chapter 2 subdirectory.

Building .NET Applications Using Notepad++

Another simple text editor I'd like to quickly point out is the freely downloadable Notepad++ application. This tool can be obtained from `http://notepad-plus.sourceforge.net`. Unlike the primitive Windows Notepad application, Notepad++ allows you to author code in a variety of languages and supports various plug-in utilities. In addition, Notepad++ provides a few other niceties, including the following:

- Out-of-the-box support for C# keywords (including keyword color coding)

- Support for *syntax folding*, which allows you to collapse and expand groups of code statements within the editor (similar to Visual Studio /C# Express)

- The ability to zoom in/zoom out text via Ctrl-mouse wheel

- Configurable autocompletion for a variety of C# keywords and .NET namespaces

Regarding this last point, the Ctrl+space keyboard combination will activate C# autocompletion support (see Figure 2-4).

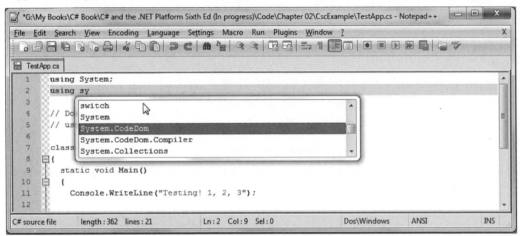

Figure 2-4. Autocompletion using Notepad++

■ **Note** The options displayed by the autocomplete window can be modified and extended. Simply open up the `C:\Program Files (x86)\Notepad++\plugins\APIs\cs.xml` file for editing, and add any additional entries.

I won't go into too many details of Notepad++ beyond what we have examined here. If you require more assistance, select the Help content menu option.

Building .NET Applications Using SharpDevelop

As you might agree, authoring C# code with Notepad++ is a step in the right direction, compared to Notepad. However, these tools do not provide rich IntelliSense capabilities for C# code, designers for building graphical user interfaces, project templates, or database manipulation utilities. To address such needs, allow me to introduce the next .NET development option: SharpDevelop (also known as *#Develop*).

SharpDevelop is an open source and feature-rich IDE that you can utilize to build .NET assemblies using C#, VB, Iron Ruby, Iron Python, C++ F#, or a Python-inspired .NET language named Boo. Beyond the fact that this IDE is completely free, it is interesting to note that it was written entirely in C#. In fact, you have the choice to download and compile the *.cs files manually or run a setup.exe program to install SharpDevelop on your development machine. Both distributions can be obtained from http://www.sharpdevelop.com.

SharpDevelop provides numerous productivity enhancements. Here is a hit list of some of the major benefits.

- Support for multiple .NET languages, .NET versions and project types

- IntelliSense, code completion, and code snippet capabilities

- An Add Reference dialog box to reference external assemblies, including assemblies deployed to the global assembly cache (GAC)

- Integrated GUI designers for desktop and web applications

- Integrated object browsing and code definition utilities

- Visual database designer utilities

- A C#-to-VB (and vice versa) code-conversion utility

Impressive for a free IDE, is it not? Although this chapter doesn't cover each of these points in detail, let's walk through a few items of interest.

■ **Note** The current version of SharpDevelop (4.2) does support all C# or .NET 4.5 features. Be sure to check the SharpDevelop web site for future releases.

Building a Simple Test Project

After you have installed SharpDevelop, the File ➤ New ➤ Solution menu option allows you to pick which type of project you wish to generate (and in which .NET language). For example, assume you have created a C# Windows Application solution named MySDWinApp (see Figure 2-5).

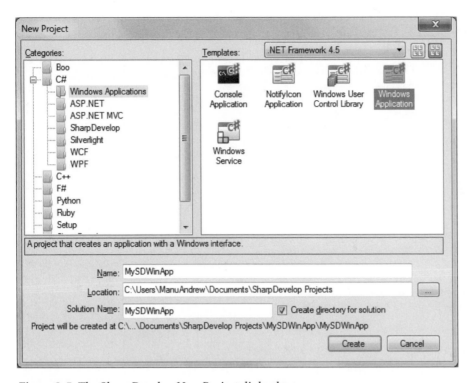

Figure 2-5. The SharpDevelop New Project dialog box

Like Visual Studio, you have a Windows Forms GUI designer toolbox (to drag and drop controls onto the designer), and a Properties window to set up the look and feel of each UI item. Figure 2-6 illustrates configuring a button control using the IDE (note that I clicked on the Design tab mounted on the bottom of the opened code file).

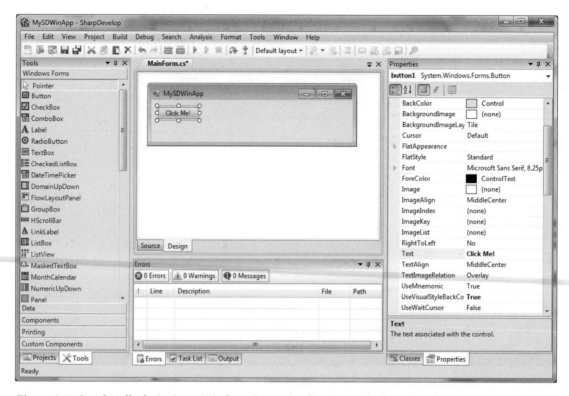

Figure 2-6. *Graphically designing a Windows Forms Application with SharpDevelop*

If you were to click the Source button mounted to the bottom of the form's designer, you would find the expected IntelliSense, code completion, and integrated help features (see Figure 2-7).

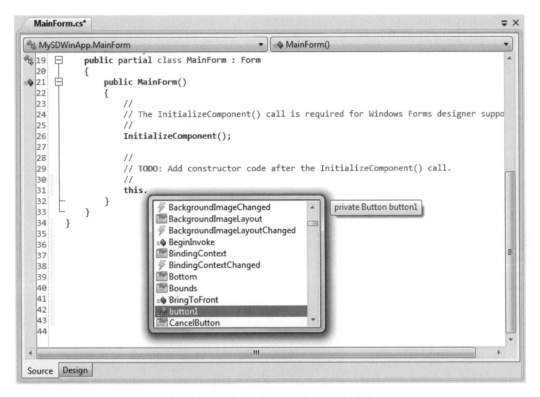

Figure 2-7. SharpDevelop supports numerous code-generation utilities

SharpDevelop was designed to mimic much of the same functionality found within Microsoft's .NET IDEs (which we will examine next). Given this point, I won't dive into all of the features of this open source .NET IDE. If you require more information, simply use the provided Help menu.

■ **Note** MonoDevelop is an open source IDE based on the SharpDevelop code base. MonoDevelop is the preferred IDE for .NET programmers building applications for Mac OS X or Linux operating systems using the Mono platform. Consult http://monodevelop.com/ for more details on this IDE.

Building .NET Applications Using Visual C# Express

Microsoft provides a line of IDEs that fall under the designation of *Express* products (http://msdn.microsoft.com/express). To date, there are various members of the Express family (all of which are *completely free* and supported and maintained by Microsoft Corporation), including the following:

- *Visual Web Developer Express*: A lightweight tool for building dynamic ASP.NET web sites and WCF services

- *Visual Basic Express*: A streamlined programming tool ideal for novice programmers who want to learn how to build applications using the user-friendly syntax of Visual Basic

- *Visual C# Express and Visual C++ Express*: Targeted IDEs for students and enthusiasts who wish to learn the fundamentals of computer science in their syntax of choice

- *SQL Server Express*: An entry-level, database management system geared toward hobbyists, enthusiasts, and student developers

Some Unique Features of Visual C# Express

By and large, the Express products are slimmed-down versions of their Visual Studio proper counterparts and are primarily targeted at .NET hobbyists and students. Like SharpDevelop, Visual C# Express provides various object browsing tools, GUI designers for desktop applications, the Add References dialog box, IntelliSense capabilities, and code expansion templates.

However, Visual C# Express offers a few (important) features currently not available in SharpDevelop, including the following:

- Rich support for Windows Presentation Foundation (WPF) XAML applications

- The ability to download additional free templates that support Xbox 360 development, WPF applications with Twitter integration, and much more

Because the look and feel of Visual C# Express is so similar to that of Visual Studio proper (and, to some degree, SharpDevelop), I do not provide a walk-through of this particular IDE here. You are free to use this IDE as you work through the book, but do be aware that Visual C# Express does not support project templates for building ASP.NET web sites. If you wish to also build web applications, be sure to also download Visual Web Developer, also available from http://msdn.microsoft.com/express.

Building .NET Applications Using Visual Studio

If you are a professional .NET software engineer, the chances are extremely good that your employer has purchased Microsoft's premier IDE, Visual Studio, for your development endeavors (http://msdn.microsoft.com/vstudio). This tool is far and away the most feature-rich, enterprise-ready IDE examined in this chapter. Of course, this power comes at a price, which will vary based on the version of Visual Studio you purchase. As you might suspect, each version supplies a unique set of features.

■ **Note** There are a staggering number of members within the Visual Studio family. My assumption during the remainder of this text is that you have chosen to make use of Visual Studio Professional as your IDE of choice.

Although I will assume you have a copy of Visual Studio Professional, understand that owning a copy of this IDE is *not required* to use this edition of the text. In the worst case, I might examine an option that is not provided by your IDE (such as Microsoft C# Express or SharpDevelop). However, rest assured that all of this book's sample code will compile just fine when processed by your tool of choice.

■ **Note** After you download the source code for this book from the Source Code/Downloads area of the Apress web site (http://www.apress.com), you may load the current example into Visual Studio (or C# Express) by double-clicking the example's *.sln file. If you are not using Visual Studio / C# Express, you will need to manually insert the provided *.cs files into your IDE's project work space.

Some Unique Features of Visual Studio

Visual Studio ships with the expected GUI designers, code snippet support, database manipulation tools, object and project browsing utilities, and an integrated help system. Unlike many of the IDEs we have already examined, Visual Studio provides numerous additions. Here is a partial list.

- Visual XML editors/designers

- Support for Windows mobile device development

- Support for Microsoft Office development

- Designer support for Windows Workflow Foundation projects

- Integrated support for code refactoring

- Visual class designer tools

To be completely honest, Visual Studio provides so many features that it would take an entire book (a rather large book at that) to fully describe every aspect of the IDE. *This is not that book.* However, I do want to point out some of the major features in the pages that follow. As you progress through the text, you'll learn more about the Visual Studio IDE where appropriate.

■ **Note** If you have used a previous version of Microsoft Visual Studio, you will quickly notice that the entire look and feel has changed quite a bit. If you find the default "Dark" theme is a tad too dark for your liking, you can change to the "Light" theme by selecting the Tools ➤ Options menu and picking from the Color Theme drop-down list box in the Environment ➤ General section. All screen shots in this text are shown in the "Light" theme.

Targeting the .NET Framework Using the New Project Dialog Box

If you are following along, create a new C# Console Application (named VsExample) using the File ➤ New ➤ Project menu item. As you can see in Figure 2-8, Visual Studio supports the ability to select which version of the .NET Framework you wish to build against (2.0, 3.0, 3.5, 4.0, or 4.5) using the drop-down list box on the top-center of the New Project dialog box. For each project in this text, you can simply leave the default selection of .NET Framework 4.5.

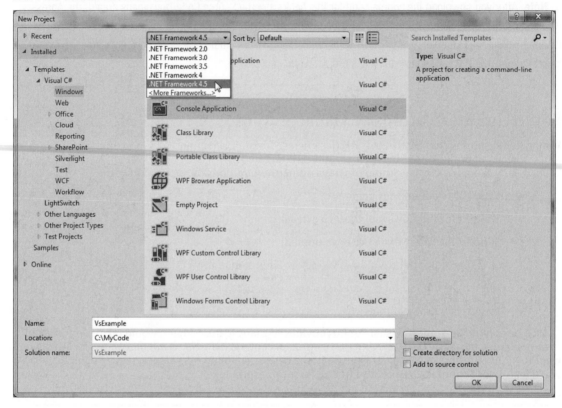

Figure 2-8. Visual Studio allows you to target a particular version of the .NET Framework

Using the Solution Explorer Utility

The Solution Explorer utility (accessible from the View menu) allows you to view the set of all content files and referenced assemblies that comprise the current project (see Figure 2-9). Also notice, that you can expand a given file (such as Program.cs) to see the code types defined within the file in question. As you move through this text, I'll point out other useful features of the Solution Explorer where necessary; however, feel free to take some time to tinker with each option, if you so choose.

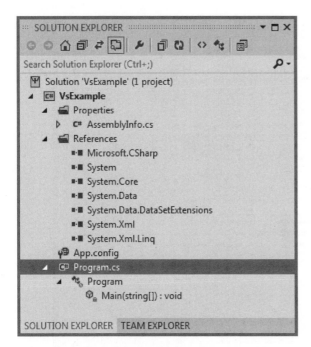

Figure 2-9. *The Solution Explorer utility*

Notice that the References folder of Solution Explorer displays a list of each assembly you have currently referenced, which will differ based on the type of project you select and the version of the Framework you are compiling against. Because you have created a Console Application, you will find a minimal set of libraries is automatically included (such as System.dll, System.Core.dll, System.Data.dll, and so forth).

■ **Note** Recall from Chapter 1 that the primary .NET library is named mscorlib.dll. This library will not be shown in the Solution Explorer; however, you have access to all the contained types regardless.

Referencing External Assemblies

When you need to reference additional assemblies, right-click the References folder and select Add Reference. At this point, you can select your assembly from the resulting dialog box (this is essentially the way Visual Studio allows you to specify the /reference option of the command-line compiler). The Framework tab (see Figure 2-10) displays a number of commonly used .NET assemblies; however, the Browse tab allows you to navigate to any .NET assembly on your hard drive. Also, the very useful Recent tab keeps a running tally of frequently referenced assemblies you have used in other projects.

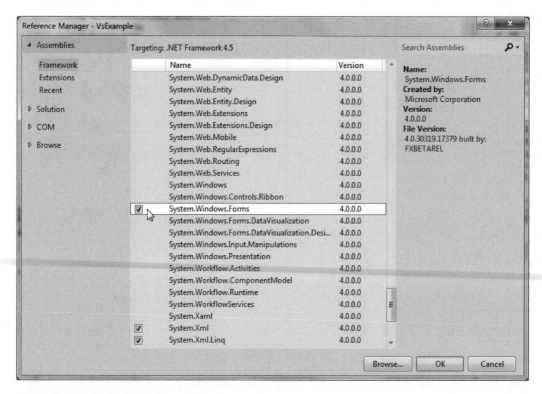

Figure 2-10. *The Add Reference dialog box*

By way of a simple test, locate the `System.Windows.Forms.dll` assembly from the Framework area, and check the related check box. After you do so (and close the dialog), you will see this library appear under the References folder of your Solution Explorer. You can delete this reference by selecting it in the Solution Explorer and pressing the Delete key on your keyboard (or via the Delete menu option of a right mouse click).

Viewing Project Properties

Finally, notice an icon named Properties within Solution Explorer. When you double-click this item, you are presented with a sophisticated project configuration editor (see Figure 2-11).

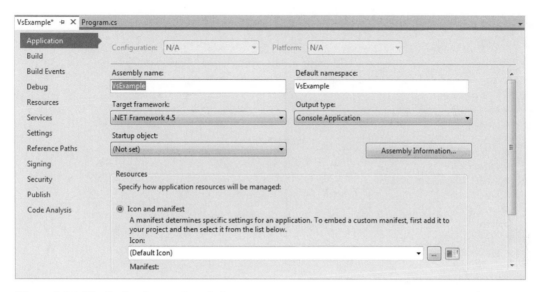

Figure 2-11. *The Project Properties window*

You will see various aspects of the Project Properties window as you progress through this book. However, if you take some time to poke around, you will see that you can establish various security settings, strongly name your assembly (see Chapter 14), deploy your application, insert application resources, and configure pre- and post-build events.

The Class View Utility

The next tool to examine is the Class View utility, which you can load from the View menu. The purpose of this utility is to show all of the types in your current project from an object-oriented perspective (rather than the default file-based view of Solution Explorer). The top pane displays the set of namespaces and their types, while the bottom pane displays the currently selected type's members (see Figure 2-12).

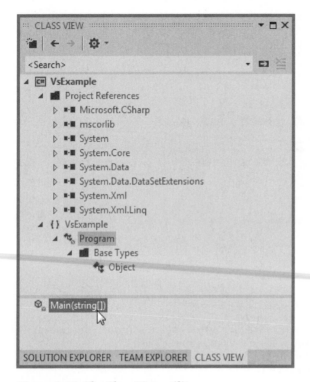

Figure 2-12. The Class View utility

When you double-click on a type or type member using the Class View tool, Visual Studio will automatically open the correct C# code file, and place your mouse cursor at the correct location. Another nice feature of the Visual Studio Class View tool is that you are able to open up any referenced assembly and drill into the contained namespaces, types, and members.

The Object Browser Utility

Visual Studio also provides a second utility to investigate the set of referenced assemblies within your current project. Activate the Object Browser using the View menu, and then select the assembly you wish to investigate (see Figure 2-13).

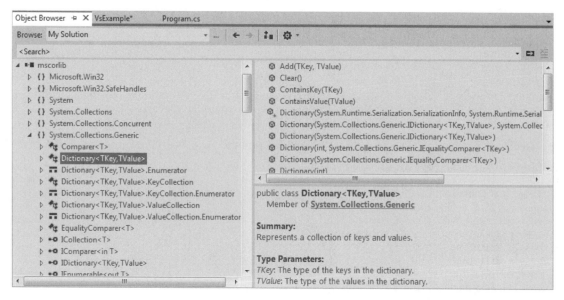

Figure 2-13. *The Object Browser utility*

Integrated Support for Code Refactoring

One major feature that ships with Visual Studio is support to *refactor* existing code. Simply put, refactoring is a formal and mechanical process whereby you improve an existing code base. In the bad old days, refactoring typically involved a ton of manual labor. Luckily, Visual Studio does a great deal to automate the refactoring process by supporting a number of commonly used techniques.

Using the Refactor menu (which will only be available when a code file is open in the IDE for editing), related keyboard shortcuts, smart tags, and/or context-sensitive mouse clicks, you can dramatically reshape your code with minimal fuss and bother. Table 2-2 defines some common refactorings recognized by Visual Studio.

Table 2-2. *Visual Studio Refactorings*

Refactoring Technique	Meaning in Life
Extract Method	Allows you to define a new method based on a selection of code statements
Encapsulate Field	Turns a public field into a private field encapsulated by a C# property
Extract Interface	Defines a new interface type based on a set of existing type members
Reorder Parameters	Provide a way to reorder member arguments

Refactoring Technique	Meaning in Life
Remove Parameters	Remove a given argument from the current list of parameters (as you would expect)
Rename	Allows you to rename a code token (method name, field, local variable, and so on) throughout a project

To illustrate refactoring in action, update your Main() method with the following simple code:

```
static void Main(string[] args)
{
  // Set up Console UI (CUI)
  Console.Title = "My Rocking App";
  Console.ForegroundColor = ConsoleColor.Yellow;
  Console.BackgroundColor = ConsoleColor.Blue;
  Console.WriteLine("***********************************");
  Console.WriteLine("***** Welcome to My Rocking App *****");
  Console.WriteLine("***********************************");
  Console.BackgroundColor = ConsoleColor.Black;

  // Wait for Enter key to be pressed.
  Console.ReadLine();
}
```

While there is nothing wrong with the preceding code as it now stands, imagine that you want to display this welcome message at various places throughout your program. Rather than retyping the same exact console user interface logic, it would be ideal to have a helper function that could be called to do so. Given this, you will apply the Extract Method refactoring to your existing code.

First, select each code statement within Main() (except the final call to Console.ReadLine()) using the editor. Then right-click the selected text and select the Extract Method option within the Refactor context menu (see Figure 2-14).

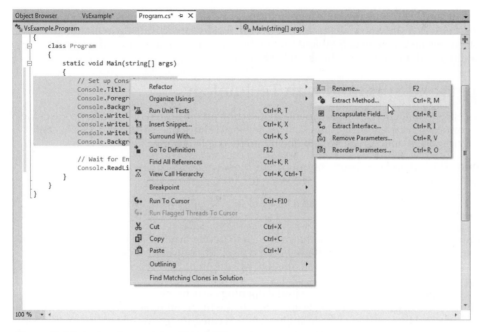

Figure 2-14. *Activating a code refactoring*

Name your new method ConfigureCUI using the resulting dialog box. When you have finished, you will find that your Main() method calls the newly generated ConfigureCUI() method, which now contains the previously selected code.

```csharp
class Program
{
  static void Main(string[] args)
  {
    ConfigureCUI();

    // Wait for key press to close.
    Console.ReadLine();
  }

  private static void ConfigureCUI()
  {
    // Set up Console UI (CUI)
    Console.Title = "My Rocking App";
    Console.ForegroundColor = ConsoleColor.Yellow;
    Console.BackgroundColor = ConsoleColor.Blue;
    Console.WriteLine("**********************************");
    Console.WriteLine("***** Welcome to My Rocking App *****");
    Console.WriteLine("**********************************");
    Console.BackgroundColor = ConsoleColor.Black;
  }
}
```

This is a simple example of using the built-in refactorings of Visual Studio, and you'll see additional examples here and there over the course of this text. However, feel free to activate the remaining refactoring options to see their net effect firsthand (remember, we are not going to use the current VsExample project for anything later in the book, so hack away).

Code Snippets and Surround with Technology

Visual Studio (as well as Visual C# Express) is capable of inserting prefabricated blocks of C# code using menu selections, context-sensitive mouse clicks, and/or keyboard shortcuts. The number of available code expansions is impressive and can be broken down into two main groups.

- *Snippets*: These templates insert common code blocks at the location of the mouse cursor.

- *Surround With*: These templates wrap a block of selected statements within a relevant scope.

To see this functionality firsthand, assume that you wish to iterate over the incoming parameters of the Main() method using a foreach construct. Rather than typing the code in by hand, you can activate the foreach code snippet. When you have done so, the IDE will dump out a foreach code template at the current location of the mouse cursor.

To illustrate, place the mouse cursor after the initial opening curly bracket of Main(). One way to activate a code snippet is to right-click the mouse and activate the Insert Snippet (or Surround With) menu option. Here, you will find a list of all code snippets of this category (press the Esc key to dismiss the pop-up menu). As a shortcut, however, you can simply type in the name of the code snippet, foreach in this case. In Figure 2-15, notice how the icon for a code snippet looks a bit like a torn piece of paper.

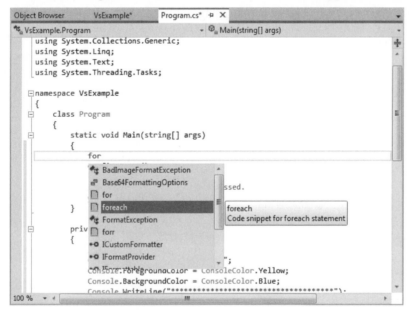

Figure 2-15. *Activating a code snippet*

After you find the snippet you want to activate, press the Tab key twice. This will autocomplete the entire snippet and leave you with a set of placeholders that you can fill in to complete the snippet. If you press the Tab key, you can cycle between each placeholder and fill in the gaps (press the Esc key to exit the code snippet edit mode). For our example, we can change the first placeholder (the var keyword) with the string data type; the second placeholder (the item variable name) with arg; and the final placeholder with the name of the incoming string array parameter, leaving us with the following:

```
static void Main(string[] args)
{
  foreach (string arg in args)
  {

  }
...
}
```

If you were to right-click in an open C# code file and select the Surround With menu, you would likewise be presented with a list of options. When using Surround With snippets, typically you first select a block of code statements to represent what should be used to wrap them (e.g., try/catch block). Be sure to take time to explore these predefined code expansion templates, as they can radically speed up the development process.

■ **Note** All code expansion templates are XML-based descriptions of the code to generate within the IDE. Using Visual Studio (as well as Visual C# Express), you can create your own custom code templates. Details of how to do so can be found in my article "Investigating Code Snippet Technology" at http://msdn.microsoft.com /en-US/library/ms379562.

The Visual Class Designer

Visual Studio gives you the ability to design classes and other types (such as interfaces or delegates) in a visual manner (this functionality is not included in Visual C# Express). The Class Designer utility allows you to view and modify the relationships of the types (classes, interfaces, structures, enumerations, and delegates) in your project. Using this tool, you are able to visually add (or remove) members to (or from) a type and have your modifications reflected in the corresponding C# file. Also, as you modify a given C# file, changes are reflected in the class diagram.

To work with this aspect of Visual Studio, the first step is to insert a new class diagram file. There are many ways to do so, one of which is to click the View Class Diagram button located on Solution Explorer's right side (see Figure 2-16; be sure your project—not the containing solution—is the selected item in the window).

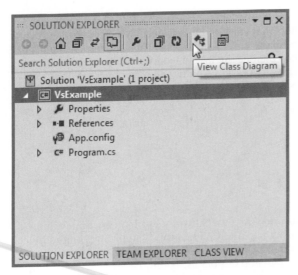

Figure 2-16. *Inserting a class diagram file into the current project*

After you do so, you will find class icons that represent the types found in your current project. If you click the arrow icon for a given type, you can show or hide the type's members (see Figure 2-17).

■ **Note** Using the Class Designer toolbar, you can fine-tune the display options of the designer surface.

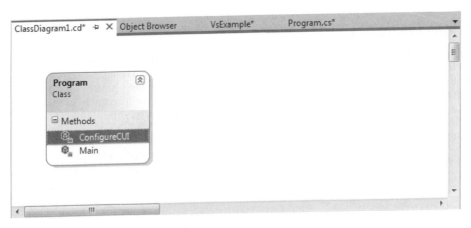

Figure 2-17. *The Class Diagram viewer*

The Class Designer utility works in conjunction with two other aspects of Visual Studio: the Class Details window (activated using the View ➤ Other Windows menu) and the Class Designer Toolbox (activated using the View ➤ Toolbox menu item). The Class Details window not only shows you the details of the currently selected item in the diagram, but also allows you to modify existing members and insert new members on the fly (see Figure 2-18).

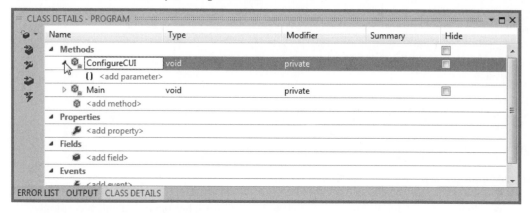

Figure 2-18. *The Class Details window*

The Class Designer Toolbox, which can also be activated using the View menu, allows you to insert new types (and create relationships between these types) into your project visually (see Figure 2-19). (Be aware you must have a class diagram as the active window to view this toolbox.) As you do so, the IDE automatically creates new C# type definitions in the background.

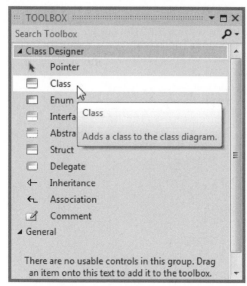

Figure 2-19. *The Class Designer Toolbox*

By way of example, drag a new Class from the Class Designer Toolbox onto your Class Designer. Name this class Car in the resulting dialog box. Now, using the Class Details window, add a public string field named petName (see Figure 2-20).

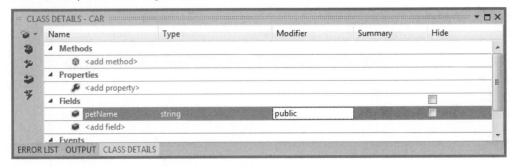

Figure 2-20. *Adding a field with the Class Details window*

If you now look at the C# definition of the Car class, you will see it has been updated accordingly (minus the additional code comments seen below).

```
public class Car
{
  // Public data is typically a bad idea; however,
  // it keeps this example simple.
  public string petName;
}
```

Now, activate the designer file once again and drag another new Class onto the designer and name it SportsCar. Now, select the Inheritance icon from the Class Designer Toolbox and click the top of the SportsCar icon. Next, click the mouse on top of the Car class icon. If you performed these steps correctly, you have just derived the SportsCar class from Car (see Figure 2-21).

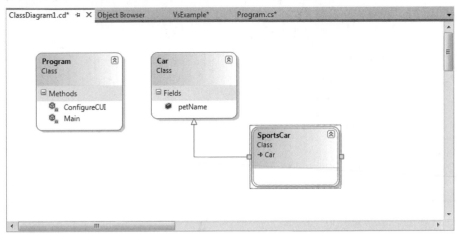

Figure 2-21. *Visually deriving from an existing class*

To complete this example, update the generated SportsCar class with a public method named GetPetName(), authored as follows:

```
public class SportsCar : Car
{
  public string GetPetName()
  {
    petName = "Fred";
    return petName;
  }
}
```

You will make use of these (and other) visual tools of Visual Studio over the course of this book. However, you should now feel a bit more comfortable regarding the basics of the IDE.

■ **Note** The concept of inheritance will be fully examined in Chapter 6.

The Integrated .NET Framework 4.5 SDK Documentation System

The final aspect of Visual Studio you *must* be comfortable with from the outset is the fully integrated help system. The .NET Framework 4.5 SDK documentation is extremely good, very readable, and full of useful information. Given the huge number of predefined .NET types (which number well into the thousands), you must be willing to roll up your sleeves and dig into the provided documentation. If you resist, you are doomed to a long, frustrating, and painful existence as a .NET developer.

If you have an Internet connection, you can view the .NET Framework 4.5 SDK documentation online at the following web address:

```
http://msdn.microsoft.com/library
```

From here, use the tree view navigation on the main page to navigate to the .NET Development area, and select .NET Framework 4.5. After you have done so, you will find the all-important .NET Framework Class Library link, which documents every single type in every single .NET namespace (Figure 2-22).

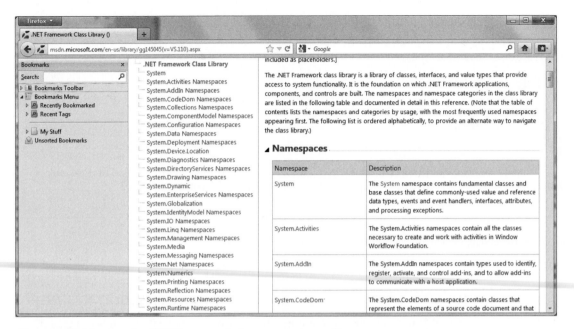

Figure 2-22. *Viewing the .NET Framework documentation online*

During the installation of Visual Studio, you will be given the option to install the same help system locally to your computer (which can be very helpful when you don't have an active Internet connection). If you wish to perform a local installation of the help system after the fact, navigate to the All Programs ➤ Microsoft Visual Studio 11 ➤ Microsoft Help Viewer tool using your Windows Start button. After you have done so, you can then elect to add the help documentation you are interested in using the Manage Content tab, as seen in Figure 2-23 (if hard drive space allows, I'd recommend adding all possible documentation).

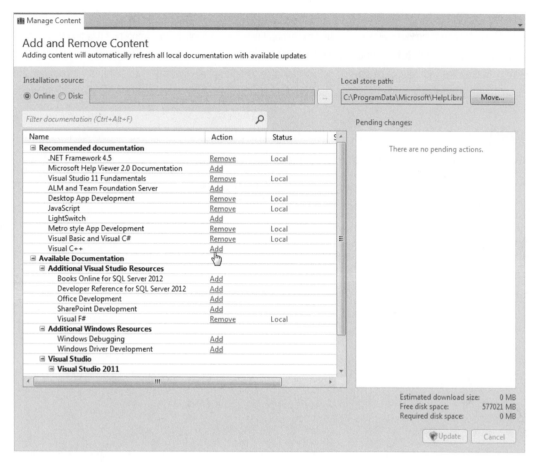

Figure 2-23. The Help Library Manager allows you to download a local copy of the .NET Framework 4.5 SDK Documentation

Regardless if you have installed the help system locally or are going online, the simplest way to interact with the documentation is to highlight a C# keyword, type name or member name within the Visual Studio code window, and press the F1 key. This will automatically open a documentation window for the selected item. For example, select the `string` keyword within your `Car` class definition. After you press F1, you will see the Help page for the `string` type appear.

Another useful aspect of the documentation is the Search tab of the display. Here you can enter in the name of any namespace, type, or member and navigate to the correct location. If you were to try to search for the `System.Reflection` namespace, you would be able to learn about the details of this namespace, examine the contained types, view code examples, and so forth.

■ **Note** At the risk of sounding like a broken record, I really can't emphasize enough how important it is that you learn to use the .NET Framework 4.5 SDK documentation. No book, no matter how lengthy, can cover every aspect of the .NET platform. Make sure you take some time to get comfortable using the help system—you'll thank yourself later.

Summary

So as you can see, you have many new toys at your disposal! The point of this chapter was to provide you with a tour of the major programming tools a C# programmer may leverage during the development process. You began the journey by learning how to generate .NET assemblies using nothing other than the free C# compiler (csc.exe) and Notepad/Notepad++ applications, and were walked through the process of using these tools to edit and compile *.cs code files.

You were also introduced three feature-rich IDEs, starting with the open source SharpDevelop, followed by Microsoft's Visual C# Express and Visual Studio Professional. While this chapter only scratched the surface of each tool's functionality, you should be in a good position to explore your chosen IDE at your leisure (and remember that you'll see additional features of Visual Studio as you progress through the book).

## PART II

Core C# Programming

CHAPTER 3

Core C# Programming Constructs, Part I

This chapter begins your formal investigation of the C# programming language by presenting a number of bite-sized, stand-alone topics you must be comfortable with as you explore the .NET Framework. The first order of business is to understand how to build your program's *application object* and to examine the composition of an executable program's entry point: the Main() method. Next, you will investigate the fundamental C# data types (and their equivalent types in the System namespace) including an examination of the System.String and System.Text.StringBuilder classes.

After you know the details of the fundamental .NET data types, you will then examine a number of data type conversion techniques, including narrowing operations, widening operations, and the use of the checked and unchecked keywords.

This chapter will also examine the role of the C# var keyword, which allows you to *implicitly* define a local variable. As you will see later in this book, implicit typing is extremely helpful, if not occasionally mandatory, when working with the LINQ technology set. We wrap up this chapter by quickly examining the C# keywords and operators which allow you to control the flow of an application using various looping and decision constructs.

The Anatomy of a Simple C# Program

C# demands that all program logic be contained within a type definition (recall from Chapter 1 that *type* is a general term referring to a member of the set {class, interface, structure, enumeration, delegate}). Unlike many other languages, in C# it is not possible to create global functions or global points of data. Rather, all data members and all methods must be contained within a type definition. To get the ball rolling, create a new Console Application project named SimpleCSharpApp. You might agree that the code within the initial Program.cs file is rather uneventful.

```
using System;
using System.Collections.Generic;
using System.Linq;
using System.Text;
using System.Threading.Tasks;

namespace SimpleCSharpApp
{
  class Program
  {
    static void Main(string[] args)
```

```
        {
        }
    }
}
```

Given this, update the `Main()` method of your `Program` class with the following code statements:

```
class Program
{
  static void Main(string[] args)
  {
    // Display a simple message to the user.
    Console.WriteLine("***** My First C# App *****");
    Console.WriteLine("Hello World!");
    Console.WriteLine();

    // Wait for Enter key to be pressed before shutting down.
    Console.ReadLine();
  }
}
```

■ **Note** C# is a case-sensitive programming language. Therefore, *Main* is not the same as *main*, and *Readline* is not the same as *ReadLine*. Be aware that all C# keywords are lowercase (e.g., `public`, `lock`, `class`, `dynamic`), while namespaces, types, and member names begin (by convention) with an initial capital letter and have capitalized the first letter of any embedded words (e.g., `Console.WriteLine`, `System.Windows.MessageBox`, `System.Data.SqlClient`). As a rule of thumb, whenever you receive a compiler error regarding "undefined symbols," be sure to check your spelling and casing first!

Here we have a definition for a class type that supports a single method named `Main()`. By default, Visual Studio names the class defining `Main()` *Program*; however, you are free to change this if you so choose. Every executable C# application (console program, Windows desktop program, or Windows service) must contain a class defining a `Main()` method, which is used to signify the entry point of the application.

Formally speaking, the class that defines the `Main()` method is termed the *application object*. While it is possible for a single executable application to have more than one application object (which can be useful when performing unit tests), you must inform the compiler which `Main()` method should be used as the entry point via the /main option of the command-line compiler, or via the Startup Object drop-down list box, located under the Application tab of the Visual Studio project properties editor (see Chapter 2).

Note that the signature of `Main()` is adorned with the `static` keyword, which will be examined in detail in Chapter 5. For the time being, simply understand that static members are scoped to the class level (rather than the object level) and can thus be invoked without the need to first create a new class instance.

In addition to the `static` keyword, this `Main()` method has a single parameter, which happens to be an array of strings (`string[] args`). Although you are not currently bothering to process this array, this parameter may contain any number of incoming command-line arguments (you'll see how to access them momentarily). Finally, this Main() method has been set up with a void return value, meaning we do not explicitly define a return value using the return keyword before exiting the method scope.

The logic of Program is within Main() itself. Here, you make use of the Console class, which is defined within the System namespace. Among its set of members is the static WriteLine() which, as you might assume, sends a text string and carriage return to the standard output. You also make a call to Console.ReadLine() to ensure the command prompt launched by the Visual Studio IDE remains visible during a debugging session until you press the Enter key. You will learn more about the System.Console class shortly.

Variations on the Main() Method

By default, Visual Studio will generate a Main() method that has a void return value and an array of string types as the single input parameter. This is not the only possible form of Main(), however. It is permissible to construct your application's entry point using any of the following signatures (assuming it is contained within a C# class or structure definition):

```
// int return type, array of strings as the parameter.
static int Main(string[] args)
{
  // Must return a value before exiting!
  return 0;
}

// No return type, no parameters.
static void Main()
{
}

// int return type, no parameters.
static int Main()
{
  // Must return a value before exiting!
  return 0;
}
```

■ **Note** The Main() method may also be defined as public as opposed to private, which is assumed if you do not supply a specific access modifier. Visual Studio automatically defines a program's Main() method as implicitly private.

Obviously, your choice of how to construct Main() will be based on two questions. First, do you want to return a value to the system when Main() has completed and your program terminates? If so, you need to return an int data type rather than void. Second, do you need to process any user-supplied, command-line parameters? If so, they will be stored in the array of strings. Let's examine all of our options in more detail.

Specifying an Application Error Code

While a vast majority of your Main() methods will return void as the return value, the ability to return an int from Main() keeps C# consistent with other C-based languages. By convention, returning the value 0 indicates the program has terminated successfully, while another value (such as -1) represents an error condition (be aware that the value 0 is automatically returned, even if you construct a Main() method prototyped to return void).

On the Windows operating system, an application's return value is stored within a system environment variable named %ERRORLEVEL%. If you were to create an application that programmatically launches another executable (a topic examined in Chapter 17), you can obtain the value of %ERRORLEVEL% using the static System.Diagnostics.Process.ExitCode property.

Given that an application's return value is passed to the system at the time the application terminates, it is obviously not possible for an application to obtain and display its final error code while running. However, to illustrate how to view this error level upon program termination, begin by updating the Main() method, as follows:

```
// Note we are now returning an int, rather than void.
static int Main(string[] args)
{
    // Display a message and wait for Enter key to be pressed.
    Console.WriteLine("***** My First C# App *****");
    Console.WriteLine("Hello World!");
    Console.WriteLine();
    Console.ReadLine();

    // Return an arbitrary error code.
    return -1;
}
```

Now let's capture the return value of Main() with the help of a batch file. Using Windows Explorer, navigate to the folder containing your compiled application (for example, C:\SimpleCSharpApp\bin\Debug). Add a new text file (named SimpleCSharpApp.bat) to the Debug folder that contains the following instructions (if you have not authored *.bat files before, don't concern yourself with the details; this is a test . . . this is only a test):

```
@echo off

rem A batch file for SimpleCSharpApp.exe
rem which captures the app's return value.

SimpleCSharpApp
@if "%ERRORLEVEL%" == "0" goto success

:fail
  echo This application has failed!
  echo return value = %ERRORLEVEL%
  goto end
:success
  echo This application has succeeded!
  echo return value = %ERRORLEVEL%
  goto end
:end
```

```
echo All Done.
```

At this point, open a Developer Command Prompt (see Chapter 2) and navigate to the folder containing your executable and new *.bat file. Execute the batch logic by typing its name and pressing the Enter key. You should find the output shown below, given that your Main() method is returning -1. Had the Main() method returned 0, you would see the message "This application has succeeded!" print to the console.

```
***** My First C# App *****
Hello World!

This application has failed!
return value = -1
All Done.
```

Again, a vast majority (if not all) of your C# applications will use void as the return value from Main(), which, as you recall, implicitly returns the error code of zero. To this end, the Main() methods used in this text (beyond the current example) will indeed return void (and the remaining projects will certainly not need to make use of batch files to capture return codes).

Processing Command-Line Arguments

Now that you better understand the return value of the Main() method, let's examine the incoming array of string data. Assume that you now wish to update your application to process any possible command-line parameters. One way to do so is using a C# for loop. (Note that C#'s iteration constructs will be examined in some detail near the end of this chapter.)

```
static int Main(string[] args)
{
...
  // Process any incoming args.
  for(int i = 0; i < args.Length; i++)
    Console.WriteLine("Arg: {0}", args[i]);

  Console.ReadLine();
  return -1;
}
```

Here, you are checking to see whether the array of strings contains some number of items using the Length property of System.Array. As you'll see in Chapter 4, all C# arrays actually alias the System.Array class, and therefore, share a common set of members. As you loop over each item in the array, its value is printed to the console window. Supplying the arguments at the command line is equally simple, as shown here:

```
C:\SimpleCSharpApp\bin\Debug>SimpleCSharpApp.exe /arg1 -arg2

***** My First C# App *****
Hello World!
```

```
Arg: /arg1
Arg: -arg2
```

As an alternative to the standard for loop, you may iterate over an incoming string array using the C# foreach keyword. Here is some sample usage (but again, you will see specifics of looping constructs later in this chapter).

```
// Notice you have no need to check the size of the array when using "foreach".
static int Main(string[] args)
{
...
  // Process any incoming args using foreach.
  foreach(string arg in args)
    Console.WriteLine("Arg: {0}", arg);

  Console.ReadLine();
  return -1;
}
```

Finally, you are also able to access command-line arguments using the static GetCommandLineArgs() method of the System.Environment type. The return value of this method is an array of strings. The first index identifies the name of the application itself, while the remaining elements in the array contain the individual command-line arguments. Note that when using this approach, it is no longer necessary to define Main() as taking a string array as the input parameter, although there is no harm in doing so.

```
static int Main(string[] args)
{
...
  // Get arguments using System.Environment.
  string[] theArgs = Environment.GetCommandLineArgs();
  foreach(string arg in theArgs)
    Console.WriteLine("Arg: {0}", arg);

  Console.ReadLine();
  return -1;
}
```

Of course, it is up to you to determine which command-line arguments your program will respond to (if any) and how they must be formatted (such as with a - or / prefix). Here, we simply passed in a series of options that were printed directly to the command prompt. Assume, however, you were creating a new video game and programmed your application to process an option named -godmode. If the user starts your application with the flag, you know he is, in fact, *a cheater* and you can take an appropriate course of action.

Specifying Command-Line Arguments with Visual Studio

In the real world, an end user has the option of supplying command-line arguments when starting a program. However, during the development cycle, you might wish to specify possible command-line flags for testing purposes. To do so with Visual Studio, double-click the Properties icon from Solution Explorer and select the Debug tab on the left side. From there, specify values using the command-line arguments text box (see Figure 3-1).

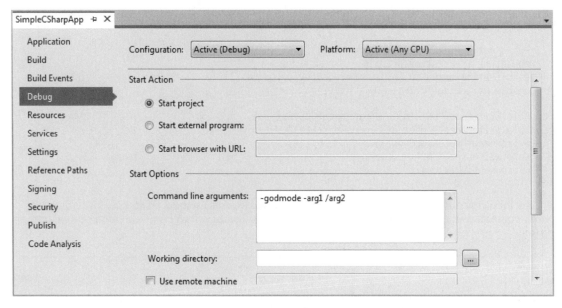

Figure 3-1. Setting command arguments via Visual Studio

After you have established such command-line arguments, they will automatically be passed to the Main() method when debugging or running your application within the Visual Studio IDE.

An Interesting Aside: Some Additional Members of the System.Environment Class

The Environment class exposes a number of extremely helpful methods beyond GetCommandLineArgs(). Specifically, this class allows you to obtain a number of details regarding the operating system currently hosting your .NET application using various static members. To illustrate the usefulness of System.Environment, update your Main() method to call a helper method named ShowEnvironmentDetails().

```
static int Main(string[] args)
{
...
  // Helper method within the Program class.
  ShowEnvironmentDetails();

  Console.ReadLine();
  return -1;
}
```

Implement this method within your Program class to call various members of the Environment type.

```
static void ShowEnvironmentDetails()
{
  // Print out the drives on this machine,
  // and other interesting details.
  foreach (string drive in Environment.GetLogicalDrives())
    Console.WriteLine("Drive: {0}", drive);

  Console.WriteLine("OS: {0}", Environment.OSVersion);
  Console.WriteLine("Number of processors: {0}",
    Environment.ProcessorCount);
  Console.WriteLine(".NET Version: {0}",
    Environment.Version);
}
```

The following output shows a possible test run of invoking this method. Of course, if you did not specify command-line arguments via the Visual Studio Debug tab, you will not find them printed to the console.

```
***** My First C# App *****

Hello World!

Arg: -godmode
Arg: -arg1
Arg: /arg2

Drive: C:\
Drive: D:\
Drive: E:\
Drive: F:\
Drive: G:\
Drive: H:\
Drive: I:\
OS: Microsoft Windows NT 6.1.7601 Service Pack 1
Number of processors: 4
.NET Version: 4.0.30319.17020
```

The Environment type defines members other than those shown in the previous example. Table 3-1 documents some additional properties of interest; however, be sure to check out the .NET Framework 4.5 SDK documentation for full details.

Table 3-1. Select Properties of System.Environment

Property	Meaning in Life
ExitCode	Gets or sets the exit code for the application
Is64BitOperatingSystem	Returns a bool to represent if the host machine is running a 64-bit OS
MachineName	Gets the name of the current machine
NewLine	Gets the newline symbol for the current environment
SystemDirectory	Returns the full path to the system directory
UserName	Returns the name of the user that started this application
Version	Returns a Version object that represents the version of the .NET platform

■ **Source Code** The SimpleCSharpApp project is located under the Chapter 3 subdirectory.

The System.Console Class

Almost all of the example applications created over the course of the initial chapters of this book make extensive use of the System.Console class. While it is true that a console user interface (CUI) is not as enticing as a graphical user interface (GUI) or web-application, restricting the early examples to console programs will allow us to keep focused on the syntax of C# and the core aspects of the .NET platform, rather than dealing with the complexities of building desktop GUIs or web sites.

As its name implies, the Console class encapsulates input, output, and error-stream manipulations for console-based applications. Table 3-2 lists some (but definitely not all) members of interest. As you can see, the Console class does provide some members that can spice up a simple command-line application, such as the ability to change background and foreground colors and issue beep noises (in a variety of frequencies!).

Table 3-2. Select Members of System.Console

Member	Meaning in Life
Beep()	This method forces the console to emit a beep of a specified frequency and duration.
BackgroundColor ForegroundColor	These properties set the background/foreground colors for the current output. They may be assigned any member of the ConsoleColor enumeration.

Member	Meaning in Life
BufferHeight BufferWidth	These properties control the height/width of the console's buffer area.
Title	This property sets the title of the current console.
WindowHeight WindowWidth WindowTop WindowLeft	These properties control the dimensions of the console in relation to the established buffer.
Clear()	This method clears the established buffer and console display area.

Basic Input and Output with the Console Class

In addition to the members in Table 3-2, the Console type defines a set of methods to capture input and output, all of which are static and are, therefore, called by prefixing the name of the class (Console) to the method name. As you have seen, WriteLine() pumps a text string (including a carriage return) to the output stream. The Write() method pumps text to the output stream without a carriage return. ReadLine() allows you to receive information from the input stream up until the Enter key is pressed, while Read() is used to capture a single character from the input stream.

To illustrate basic I/O using the Console class, create a new Console Application project named BasicConsoleIO and update your Main() method to call a helper method named GetUserData():

```
class Program
{
  static void Main(string[] args)
  {
    Console.WriteLine("***** Basic Console I/O *****");
    GetUserData();
    Console.ReadLine();
  }
}
```

■ **Note** In Chapter 2, you briefly examined Visual Studio code snippets. The cw code snippet is quite useful during the early chapters of this text, in that it will automatically expand to Console.WriteLine()! To test this for yourself, type in cw somewhere within your Main() method and hit the Tab key twice. Sadly, there is no code snippet for Console.ReadLine().

Implement this method within the Program class with logic that prompts the user for some bits of information and echoes each item to the standard output stream. For example, we could ask the user for his or her name and age (which we will treat as a text value for simplicity, rather than the expected numerical value), as follows:

```
static void GetUserData()
{
  // Get name and age.
  Console.Write("Please enter your name: ");
  string userName = Console.ReadLine();
  Console.Write("Please enter your age: ");
  string userAge = Console.ReadLine();

  // Change echo color, just for fun.
  ConsoleColor prevColor = Console.ForegroundColor;
  Console.ForegroundColor = ConsoleColor.Yellow;

  // Echo to the console.
  Console.WriteLine("Hello {0}!  You are {1} years old.",
    userName, userAge);

  // Restore previous color.
  Console.ForegroundColor = prevColor;
}
```

Not surprisingly, when you run this application, the input data is printed to the console (using a custom color to boot!).

Formatting Console Output

During these first few chapters, you might have noticed numerous occurrences of tokens such as {0} and {1} embedded within various string literals. The .NET platform supports a style of string formatting slightly akin to the printf() statement of C. Simply put, when you are defining a string literal that contains segments of data whose value is not known until runtime, you are able to specify a placeholder within the literal using this curly-bracket syntax. At runtime, the value(s) passed into Console.WriteLine() are substituted for each placeholder.

The first parameter to WriteLine() represents a string literal that contains optional placeholders designated by {0}, {1}, {2}, and so forth. Be very aware that the first ordinal number of a curly-bracket placeholder always begins with 0. The remaining parameters to WriteLine() are simply the values to be inserted into the respective placeholders.

■ **Note** If you have more uniquely numbered curly-bracket placeholders than fill arguments, you will receive a format exception at runtime. However, if you have more fill arguments than placeholders, the unused fill arguments are ignored.

It is permissible for a given placeholder to repeat within a given string. For example, if you are a Beatles fan and want to build the string "9, Number 9, Number 9", you would write:

```
// John says...
Console.WriteLine("{0}, Number {0}, Number {0}", 9);
```

Also know that it is possible to position each placeholder in any location within a string literal, and it need not follow an increasing sequence. For example, consider the following code snippet:

```
// Prints: 20, 10, 30
Console.WriteLine("{1}, {0}, {2}", 10, 20, 30);
```

Formatting Numerical Data

If you require more elaborate formatting for numerical data, each placeholder can optionally contain various format characters. Table 3-3 shows the most common formatting options.

Table 3-3. .NET Numerical Format Characters

String Format Character	Meaning in Life
C or c	Used to format currency. By default, the flag will prefix the local cultural symbol (a dollar sign [$] for U.S. English).
D or d	Used to format decimal numbers. This flag may also specify the minimum number of digits used to pad the value.
E or e	Used for exponential notation. Casing controls whether the exponential constant is uppercase (E) or lowercase (e).
F or f	Used for fixed-point formatting. This flag may also specify the minimum number of digits used to pad the value.
G or g	Stands for *general*. This character can be used to format a number to fixed or exponential format.
N or n	Used for basic numerical formatting (with commas).
X or x	Used for hexadecimal formatting. If you use an uppercase X, your hex format will also contain uppercase characters.

These format characters are suffixed to a given placeholder value using the colon token (e.g., {0:C}, {1:d}, {2:X}). To illustrate, update the Main() method to call a new helper function named FormatNumericalData(). Implement this method in your Program class to format a fixed numerical value in a variety of ways.

```
// Now make use of some format tags.
static void FormatNumericalData()
{
  Console.WriteLine("The value 99999 in various formats:");
  Console.WriteLine("c format: {0:c}", 99999);
  Console.WriteLine("d9 format: {0:d9}", 99999);
  Console.WriteLine("f3 format: {0:f3}", 99999);
  Console.WriteLine("n format: {0:n}", 99999);
```

```
    // Notice that upper- or lowercasing for hex
    // determines if letters are upper- or lowercase.
    Console.WriteLine("E format: {0:E}", 99999);
    Console.WriteLine("e format: {0:e}", 99999);
    Console.WriteLine("X format: {0:X}", 99999);
    Console.WriteLine("x format: {0:x}", 99999);
}
```

The following output shows the result of calling the FormatNumericalData() method.

```
The value 99999 in various formats:

c format: $99,999.00
d9 format: 000099999
f3 format: 99999.000
n format: 99,999.00
E format: 9.999900E+004
e format: 9.999900e+004
X format: 1869F
x format: 1869f
```

You'll see additional formatting examples where required throughout this text; however, if you are interested in digging into .NET string formatting further, look up the topic *"Formatting types"* within the .NET Framework 4.5 SDK documentation.

■ **Source Code** The BasicConsoleIO project is located under the Chapter 3 subdirectory.

Formatting Numerical Data Beyond Console Applications

On a final note, be aware that the use of the .NET string formatting characters is not limited to console programs. This same formatting syntax can be used when calling the static string.Format() method. This can be helpful when you need to compose textual data at runtime for use in any application type (e.g., desktop GUI app, ASP.NET web app, and so forth).

The string.Format() method returns a new string object, which is formatted according to the provided flags. After this point, you are free to use the textual data as you see fit. For example, assume you are building a graphical WPF desktop application and need to format a string for display in a message box. The following code illustrates how to do so, but be aware that this code will not compile until you reference the PresentationFramework.dll assembly for use by your project (see Chapter 2 for information on referencing libraries using Visual Studio).

```
static void DisplayMessage()
{
    // Using string.Format() to format a string literal.
    string userMessage = string.Format("100000 in hex is {0:x}",
        100000);
```

```
    // You need to reference PresentationFramework.dll
    // in order to compile this line of code!
    System.Windows.MessageBox.Show(userMessage);
}
```

System Data Types and Corresponding C# Keywords

Like any programming language, C# defines keywords for fundamental data types, which are used to represent local variables, class data member variables, method return values, and parameters. Unlike other programming languages, however, these keywords are much more than simple compiler-recognized tokens. Rather, the C# data type keywords are actually shorthand notations for full-blown types in the System namespace. Table 3-4 lists each system data type, its range, the corresponding C# keyword, and the type's compliance with the common language specification (CLS).

■ **Note** Recall from Chapter 1 that CLS-compliant .NET code can be used by any managed programming language. If you expose non–CLS-compliant data from your programs, other languages might not be able to make use of it.

Table 3-4. *The Intrinsic Data Types of C#*

C# Shorthand	CLS Compliant?	System Type	Range	Meaning in Life
bool	Yes	System.Boolean	true or false	Represents truth or falsity
sbyte	No	System.SByte	−128 to 127	Signed 8-bit number
byte	Yes	System.Byte	0 to 255	Unsigned 8-bit number
short	Yes	System.Int16	−32,768 to 32,767	Signed 16-bit number
ushort	No	System.UInt16	0 to 65,535	Unsigned 16-bit number
int	Yes	System.Int32	−2,147,483,648 to 2,147,483,647	Signed 32-bit number
uint	No	System.UInt32	0 to 4,294,967,295	Unsigned 32-bit number
long	Yes	System.Int64	−9,223,372,036,854,775,808 to 9,223,372,036,854,775,807	Signed 64-bit number
ulong	No	System.UInt64	0 to 18,446,744,073,709,551,615	Unsigned 64-bit number

char	Yes	System.Char	U+0000 to U+ffff	Single 16-bit Unicode character
float	Yes	System.Single	$-3.4 \ 10^{38}$ to $+3.4 \ 10^{38}$	32-bit floating-point number
double	Yes	System.Double	$\pm 5.0 \ 10^{-324}$ to $\pm 1.7 \ 10^{308}$	64-bit floating-point number
decimal	Yes	System.Decimal	$(-7.9 \times 10^{28}$ to $7.9 \times 10^{28}) / (10^{0 \text{ to } 28})$	128-bit signed number
string	Yes	System.String	Limited by system memory	Represents a set of Unicode characters
Object	Yes	System.Object	Can store any data type in an object variable	The base class of all types in the .NET universe

■ **Note** By default, a floating-point number is treated as a `double`. To declare a `float` variable, use the suffix `f` or `F` to the raw numerical value (`5.3F`); suffix `m` or `M` to a floating-point number to declare a decimal (`300.5M`). Finally, raw whole numbers default to an `int` data type. To set the underlying data type to a `long`, suffix `l` or `L` (`4L`).

Variable Declaration and Initialization

When you are declaring a local variable (e.g., a variable within a member scope), you do so by specifying the data type followed by the variable's name. To begin, create a new Console Application project named BasicDataTypes. Update the `Program` class with the following helper method that is called from within `Main()`:

```
static void LocalVarDeclarations()
{
  Console.WriteLine("=> Data Declarations:");
  // Local variables are declared as so:
  // dataType varName;
  int myInt;
  string myString;

  Console.WriteLine();
}
```

Be aware that it is a *compiler error* to make use of a local variable before assigning an initial value. Given this, it is good practice to assign an initial value to your local data points at the time of declaration. You may do so on a single line, or by separating the declaration and assignment into two code statements.

```
static void LocalVarDeclarations()
{
  Console.WriteLine("=> Data Declarations:");
  // Local variables are declared and initialized as follows:
  // dataType varName = initialValue;
  int myInt = 0;

  // You can also declare and assign on two lines.
  string myString;
  myString = "This is my character data";

  Console.WriteLine();
}
```

It is also permissible to declare multiple variables of the same underlying type on a single line of code, as in the following three bool variables:

```
static void LocalVarDeclarations()
{
  Console.WriteLine("=> Data Declarations:");
  int myInt = 0;
  string myString;
  myString = "This is my character data";

  // Declare 3 bools on a single line.
  bool b1 = true, b2 = false, b3 = b1;
  Console.WriteLine();
}
```

Since the C# bool keyword is simply a shorthand notation for the System.Boolean structure, it is also possible to allocate any data type using its full name (of course, the same point holds true for any C# data type keyword). Here is the final implementation of LocalVarDeclarations(), which illustrates various ways to declare a local variable.

```
static void LocalVarDeclarations()
{
  Console.WriteLine("=> Data Declarations:");
  // Local variables are declared and initialized as follows:
  // dataType varName = initialValue;
  int myInt = 0;

  string myString;
  myString = "This is my character data";

  // Declare 3 bools on a single line.
  bool b1 = true, b2 = false, b3 = b1;

  // Use System.Boolean data type to declare a bool.
  System.Boolean b4 = false;

  Console.WriteLine("Your data: {0}, {1}, {2}, {3}, {4}, {5}",
      myInt, myString, b1, b2, b3, b4);
```

```
  Console.WriteLine();
}
```

Intrinsic Data Types and the new Operator

All intrinsic data types support what is known as a *default constructor* (see Chapter 5). This feature allows you to create a variable using the new keyword, which automatically sets the variable to its default value.

- bool variables are set to false.

- Numeric data is set to 0 (or 0.0 in the case of floating-point data types).

- char variables are set to a single empty character.

- BigInteger variables are set to 0.

- DateTime variables are set to 1/1/0001 12:00:00 AM.

- Object references (including strings) are set to null.

■ **Note** The BigInteger data type seen in the previous list will be explained in just a bit.

Although it is more cumbersome to use the new keyword when creating a basic data type variable, the following is syntactically well-formed C# code:

```
static void NewingDataTypes()
{
  Console.WriteLine("=> Using new to create variables:");
  bool b = new bool();              // Set to false.
  int i = new int();                // Set to 0.
  double d = new double();          // Set to 0.
  DateTime dt = new DateTime();     // Set to 1/1/0001 12:00:00 AM
  Console.WriteLine("{0}, {1}, {2}, {3}", b, i, d, dt);
  Console.WriteLine();
}
```

The Data Type Class Hierarchy

It is very interesting to note that even the primitive .NET data types are arranged in a *class hierarchy*. If you are new to the world of inheritance, you will discover the full details in Chapter 6. Until then, just understand that types at the top of a class hierarchy provide some default behaviors that are granted to the derived types. The relationship between these core system types can be understood as shown in Figure 3-2.

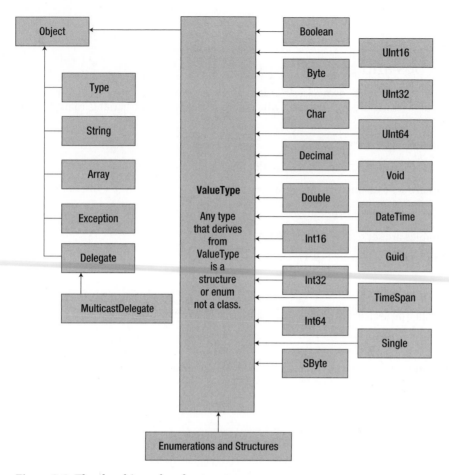

Figure 3-2. The class hierarchy of system types

Notice that each of these types ultimately derive from System.Object, which defines a set of methods (e.g., ToString(), Equals(), GetHashCode()) common to all types in the .NET base class libraries (these methods are fully detailed in Chapter 6).

Also note that many numerical data types derive from a class named System.ValueType. Descendents of ValueType are automatically allocated on the stack and, therefore, have a very predictable lifetime and are quite efficient. On the other hand, types that do not have System.ValueType in their inheritance chain (such as System.Type, System.String, System.Array, System.Exception, and System.Delegate) are not allocated on the stack, but on the garbage-collected heap. (More information on this distinction can be found in Chapter 4.)

Without getting too hung up on the details of System.Object and System.ValueType, just understand that because a C# keyword (such as int) is simply shorthand notation for the corresponding system type (in this case, System.Int32), the following is perfectly legal syntax, given that System.Int32 (the C# int) eventually derives from System.Object and, therefore, can invoke any of its public members, as illustrated by this additional helper function:

```
static void ObjectFunctionality()
{
  Console.WriteLine("=> System.Object Functionality:");

  // A C# int is really a shorthand for System.Int32,
  // which inherits the following members from System.Object.
  Console.WriteLine("12.GetHashCode() = {0}", 12.GetHashCode());
  Console.WriteLine("12.Equals(23) = {0}", 12.Equals(23));
  Console.WriteLine("12.ToString() = {0}", 12.ToString());
  Console.WriteLine("12.GetType() = {0}", 12.GetType());
  Console.WriteLine();
}
```

If you were to call this method from within Main(), you would find the output shown in here:

```
=> System.Object Functionality:

12.GetHashCode() = 12
12.Equals(23) = False
12.ToString() = 12
12.GetType() = System.Int32
```

Members of Numerical Data Types

To continue experimenting with the intrinsic C# data types, understand that the numerical types of .NET support MaxValue and MinValue properties that provide information regarding the range a given type can store. In addition to the MinValue/MaxValue properties, a given numerical system type may define further useful members. For example, the System.Double type allows you to obtain the values for epsilon and infinity (which might be of interest to those of you with a mathematical flare). To illustrate, consider the following helper function:

```
static void DataTypeFunctionality()
{
  Console.WriteLine("=> Data type Functionality:");

  Console.WriteLine("Max of int: {0}", int.MaxValue);
  Console.WriteLine("Min of int: {0}", int.MinValue);
  Console.WriteLine("Max of double: {0}", double.MaxValue);
  Console.WriteLine("Min of double: {0}", double.MinValue);
  Console.WriteLine("double.Epsilon: {0}", double.Epsilon);
  Console.WriteLine("double.PositiveInfinity: {0}",
    double.PositiveInfinity);
  Console.WriteLine("double.NegativeInfinity: {0}",
    double.NegativeInfinity);
  Console.WriteLine();
}
```

Members of System.Boolean

Next, consider the System.Boolean data type. The only valid assignment a C# bool can take is from the set {true | false}. Given this point, it should be clear that System.Boolean does not support a MinValue/MaxValue property set, but rather TrueString/FalseString (which yields the string "True" or "False", respectively). For example:

```
Console.WriteLine("bool.FalseString: {0}", bool.FalseString);
Console.WriteLine("bool.TrueString: {0}", bool.TrueString);
```

Members of System.Char

C# textual data is represented by the string and char keywords, which are simple shorthand notations for System.String and System.Char, both of which are Unicode under the hood. As you might already know, a string represents a contiguous set of characters (e.g., "Hello"), while the char can represent a single slot in a string (e.g., 'H').

The System.Char type provides you with a great deal of functionality beyond the ability to hold a single point of character data. Using the static methods of System.Char, you are able to determine whether a given character is numerical, alphabetical, a point of punctuation, or whatnot. Consider the following method:

```
static void CharFunctionality()
{
  Console.WriteLine("=> char type Functionality:");

  char myChar = 'a';
  Console.WriteLine("char.IsDigit('a'): {0}", char.IsDigit(myChar));
  Console.WriteLine("char.IsLetter('a'): {0}", char.IsLetter(myChar));
  Console.WriteLine("char.IsWhiteSpace('Hello There', 5): {0}",
    char.IsWhiteSpace("Hello There", 5));
  Console.WriteLine("char.IsWhiteSpace('Hello There', 6): {0}",
    char.IsWhiteSpace("Hello There", 6));
  Console.WriteLine("char.IsPunctuation('?'): {0}",
    char.IsPunctuation('?'));
  Console.WriteLine();
}
```

As illustrated in the previous method, many members of System.Char have two calling conventions: a single character, or a string with a numerical index that specifies the position of the character to test.

Parsing Values from String Data

The .NET data types provide the ability to generate a variable of their underlying type given a textual equivalent (e.g., parsing). This technique can be extremely helpful when you wish to convert a bit of user input data (such as a selection from a GUI-based, drop-down list box) into a numerical value. Consider the following parsing logic within a method named ParseFromStrings():

```
static void ParseFromStrings()
{
  Console.WriteLine("=> Data type parsing:");
```

```
  bool b = bool.Parse("True");
  Console.WriteLine("Value of b: {0}", b);
  double d = double.Parse("99.884");
  Console.WriteLine("Value of d: {0}", d);
  int i = int.Parse("8");
  Console.WriteLine("Value of i: {0}", i);
  char c = Char.Parse("w");
  Console.WriteLine("Value of c: {0}", c);
  Console.WriteLine();
}
```

System.DateTime and System.TimeSpan

The System namespace defines a few useful data types for which there are no C# keywords, such as the DateTime and TimeSpan structures (I'll leave the investigation of System.Guid and System.Void, as shown in Figure 3-2, to interested readers; but do be aware that these two data types in the System namespace are seldom useful in most applications).

The DateTime type contains data that represents a specific date (month, day, year) and time value, both of which may be formatted in a variety of ways using the supplied members. The TimeSpan structure allows you to easily define and transform units of time using various members.

```
static void UseDatesAndTimes()
{
  Console.WriteLine("=> Dates and Times:");

  // This constructor takes (year, month, day).
  DateTime dt = new DateTime(2011, 10, 17);

  // What day of the month is this?
  Console.WriteLine("The day of {0} is {1}", dt.Date, dt.DayOfWeek);

  // Month is now December.
  dt = dt.AddMonths(2);
  Console.WriteLine("Daylight savings: {0}", dt.IsDaylightSavingTime());

  // This constructor takes (hours, minutes, seconds).
  TimeSpan ts = new TimeSpan(4, 30, 0);
  Console.WriteLine(ts);

  // Subtract 15 minutes from the current TimeSpan and
  // print the result.
  Console.WriteLine(ts.Subtract(new TimeSpan(0, 15, 0)));
}
```

The System.Numerics.dll Assembly

The System.Numerics namespace defines a structure named BigInteger. As its name implies, the BigInteger data type can be used when you need to represent *humongous* numerical values, which are not constrained by a fixed upper or lower limit.

■ **Note** The System.Numerics namespace defines a second structure named Complex, which allows you to model mathematically complex numerical data (e.g., imaginary units, real data, hyperbolic tangents). Consult the .NET Framework 4.5 SDK documentation if you are interested.

While many of your .NET applications might never need to make use of the BigInteger structure, if you do find the need to define a massive numerical value, your first step is to reference the System.Numerics.dll assembly into your project. If you wish to follow along with the current example, perform the following tasks:

1. Select the Project ➤ Add Reference... menu option of Visual Studio.

2. Locate and select the System.Numerics.dll assembly within the list of presented libraries.

3. Press the Add button, then the Close button.

After you have done so, add the following using directive to the file, which will be using the BigInteger data type:

```
// BigInteger lives here!
using System.Numerics;
```

At this point, you can create a BigInteger variable using the new operator. Within the constructor, you can specify a numerical value, including floating-point data. However, recall that when you define a literal whole number (such as 500), the runtime will default the data type to an int. Likewise, literal floating-point data (such as 55.333) will default to a double. How, then, can you set BigInteger to a massive value while not overflowing the default data types used for raw numerical values?

The simplest approach is to establish the massive numerical value as a text literal, which can be converted into a BigInteger variable via the static Parse() method. If required, you can also pass in a byte array directly to the constructor of the BigInteger class.

■ **Note** After you assign a value to a BigInteger variable, you cannot change it, as the data is immutable. However, the BigInteger class defines a number of members that will return new BigInteger objects based on your data modifications (such as the static Multiply() method used in the proceeding code sample).

In any case, after you have defined a BigInteger variable, you will find this class defines very similar members as other intrinsic C# data types (e.g., float, int). In addition, the BigInteger class defines several static members that allow you to apply basic mathematical expressions (such as adding and multiplying) to BigInteger variables. Here is an example of working with the BigInteger class.

```
static void UseBigInteger()
{
  Console.WriteLine("=> Use BigInteger:");
  BigInteger biggy =
    BigInteger.Parse("9999999999999999999999999999999999999999999999");
```

```
  Console.WriteLine("Value of biggy is {0}", biggy);
  Console.WriteLine("Is biggy an even value?: {0}", biggy.IsEven);
  Console.WriteLine("Is biggy a power of two?: {0}", biggy.IsPowerOfTwo);
  BigInteger reallyBig = BigInteger.Multiply(biggy,
    BigInteger.Parse("88888888888888888888888888888888888888888888"));
  Console.WriteLine("Value of reallyBig is {0}", reallyBig);
}
```

It is also important to note that the BigInteger data type responds to C#'s intrinsic mathematical operators, such as +, -, and *. Therefore, rather than calling BigInteger.Multiply() to multiply two huge numbers, you could author the following code:

```
BigInteger reallyBig2 = biggy * reallyBig;
```

At this point, I hope you understand that the C# keywords representing basic data types have a corresponding type in the .NET base class libraries, each of which exposes a fixed functionality. While I have not detailed each member of these data types, you are in a great position to dig into the details as you see fit. Be sure to consult the .NET Framework 4.5 SDK documentation for full details regarding the various .NET data types—you will likely be surprised at the amount of built in functionality.

■ **Source Code** The BasicDataTypes project is located under the Chapter 3 subdirectory.

Working with String Data

System.String provides a number of methods you would expect from such a utility class, including methods that return the length of the character data, find substrings within the current string, and convert to and from uppercase/lowercase. Table 3-5 lists some (but by no means all) of the interesting members.

Table 3-5. Select Members of System.String

String Member	Meaning in Life
Length	This property returns the length of the current string.
Compare()	This static method compares two strings.
Contains()	This method determines whether a string contains a specific substring.
Equals()	This method tests whether two string objects contain identical character data.
Format()	This static method formats a string using other primitives (e.g., numerical data, other strings) and the {0} notation examined earlier in this chapter.
Insert()	This method inserts a string within a given string.

String Member	Meaning in Life
PadLeft() PadRight()	These methods are used to pad a string with some characters.
Remove() Replace()	Use these methods to receive a copy of a string with modifications (characters removed or replaced).
Split()	This method returns a String array containing the substrings in this instance that are delimited by elements of a specified char array or string array.
Trim()	This method removes all occurrences of a set of specified characters from the beginning and end of the current string.
ToUpper() ToLower()	These methods create a copy of the current string in uppercase or lowercase format, respectively.

Basic String Manipulation

Working with the members of System.String is as you would expect. Simply declare a string variable and make use of the provided functionality via the dot operator. Be aware that a few of the members of System.String are static members and are, therefore, called at the class (rather than the object) level. Assume you have created a new Console Application project named FunWithStrings. Author the following method, which should be called from within Main():

```
static void BasicStringFunctionality()
{
  Console.WriteLine("=> Basic String functionality:");
  string firstName = "Freddy";
  Console.WriteLine("Value of firstName: {0}", firstName);
  Console.WriteLine("firstName has {0} characters.", firstName.Length);
  Console.WriteLine("firstName in uppercase: {0}", firstName.ToUpper());
  Console.WriteLine("firstName in lowercase: {0}", firstName.ToLower());
  Console.WriteLine("firstName contains the letter y?: {0}",
    firstName.Contains("y"));
  Console.WriteLine("firstName after replace: {0}", firstName.Replace("dy", ""));
  Console.WriteLine();
}
```

Not too much to say here, as this method simply invokes various members, such as ToUpper() and Contains(), on a local string variable to yield various formats and transformations. Here is the initial output:

```
***** Fun with Strings *****

=> Basic String functionality:
Value of firstName: Freddy
```

```
firstName has 6 characters.
firstName in uppercase: FREDDY
firstName in lowercase: freddy
firstName contains the letter y?: True
firstName after replace: Fred
```

While this output might not seem too surprising, the output seen via calling the Replace() method is a bit misleading. In reality, the firstName variable has not changed at all; rather, we receive back a new string in a modified format. We will revisit the immutable nature of strings in just a few moments.

String Concatenation

string variables can be connected together to build larger strings via the C# + operator. As you might know, this technique is formally termed *string concatenation*. Consider the following new helper function:

```
static void StringConcatenation()
{
  Console.WriteLine("=> String concatenation:");
  string s1 = "Programming the ";
  string s2 = "PsychoDrill (PTP)";
  string s3 = s1 + s2;
  Console.WriteLine(s3);
  Console.WriteLine();
}
```

You might be interested to know that the C# + symbol is processed by the compiler to emit a call to the static String.Concat() method. Given this, it is possible to perform string concatenation by calling String.Concat() directly (although you really have not gained anything by doing so—in fact, you have incurred additional keystrokes!).

```
static void StringConcatenation()
{
  Console.WriteLine("=> String concatenation:");
  string s1 = "Programming the ";
  string s2 = "PsychoDrill (PTP)";
  string s3 = String.Concat(s1, s2);
  Console.WriteLine(s3);
  Console.WriteLine();
}
```

Escape Characters

As in other C-based languages, C# string literals may contain various *escape characters*, which qualify how the character data should be printed to the output stream. Each escape character begins with a backslash, followed by a specific token. In case you are a bit rusty on the meanings behind these escape characters, Table 3-6 lists the more common options.

Table 3-6. *String Literal Escape Characters*

Character	Meaning in Life
\'	Inserts a single quote into a string literal.
\"	Inserts a double quote into a string literal.
\\	Inserts a backslash into a string literal. This can be quite helpful when defining file or network paths.
\a	Triggers a system alert (beep). For console programs, this can be an audio clue to the user.
\n	Inserts a new line (on Windows platforms).
\r	Inserts a carriage return.
\t	Inserts a horizontal tab into the string literal.

For example, to print a string that contains a tab between each word, you can make use of the \t escape character. Or assume you wish to create a string literal that contains quotation marks, another that defines a directory path, and a final string literal that inserts three blank lines after printing the character data. To do so without compiler errors, you would need to make use of the \", \\, and \n escape characters. Also, to annoy any person within a 10-foot radius from you, notice that I have embedded an alarm within each string literal (to trigger a beep). Consider the following:

```
static void EscapeChars()
{
  Console.WriteLine("=> Escape characters:\a");
  string strWithTabs = "Model\tColor\tSpeed\tPet Name\a ";
  Console.WriteLine(strWithTabs);

  Console.WriteLine("Everyone loves \"Hello World\"\a ");
  Console.WriteLine("C:\\MyApp\\bin\\Debug\a ");

  // Adds a total of 4 blank lines (then beep again!).
  Console.WriteLine("All finished.\n\n\n\a ");
  Console.WriteLine();
}
```

Defining Verbatim Strings

When you prefix a string literal with the @ symbol, you have created what is termed a *verbatim string*. Using verbatim strings, you disable the processing of a literal's escape characters and print out a string as is. This can be most useful when working with strings representing directory and network paths. Therefore, rather than making use of \\ escape characters, you can simply write the following:

```
// The following string is printed verbatim,
// thus all escape characters are displayed.
Console.WriteLine(@"C:\MyApp\bin\Debug");
```

Also note that verbatim strings can be used to preserve white space for strings that flow over multiple lines.

```
// White space is preserved with verbatim strings.
string myLongString = @"This is a very
    very
        very
            long string";
Console.WriteLine(myLongString);
```

Using verbatim strings, you can also directly insert a double quote into a literal string by doubling the " token.

```
Console.WriteLine(@"Cerebus said ""Darrr! Pret-ty sun-sets""");
```

Strings and Equality

As fully explained in Chapter 4, a *reference type* is an object allocated on the garbage-collected managed heap. By default, when you perform a test for equality on reference types (via the C# == and != operators), you will be returned true if the references are pointing to the same object in memory. However, even though the string data type is indeed a reference type, the equality operators have been redefined to compare the *values* of string objects, not the object in memory to which they refer.

```
static void StringEquality()
{
  Console.WriteLine("=> String equality:");
  string s1 = "Hello!";
  string s2 = "Yo!";
  Console.WriteLine("s1 = {0}", s1);
  Console.WriteLine("s2 = {0}", s2);
  Console.WriteLine();

  // Test these strings for equality.
  Console.WriteLine("s1 == s2: {0}", s1 == s2);
  Console.WriteLine("s1 == Hello!: {0}", s1 == "Hello!");
  Console.WriteLine("s1 == HELLO!: {0}", s1 == "HELLO!");
  Console.WriteLine("s1 == hello!: {0}", s1 == "hello!");
  Console.WriteLine("s1.Equals(s2): {0}", s1.Equals(s2));
  Console.WriteLine("Yo.Equals(s2): {0}", "Yo!".Equals(s2));
  Console.WriteLine();
}
```

The C# equality operators perform a case-sensitive, character-by-character equality test on string objects. Therefore, "Hello!" is not equal to "HELLO!", which is also different from "hello!". Also, keeping the connection between string and System.String in mind, notice that we are able to test for equality using the Equals() method of String as well as the baked-in equality operators. Finally, given that every string literal (such as "Yo") is a valid System.String instance, we are able to access string-centric functionality from a fixed sequence of characters.

Strings Are Immutable

One of the interesting aspects of System.String is that after you assign a string object with its initial value, the character data *cannot be changed*. At first glance, this might seem like a flat-out lie, given that we are always reassigning strings to new values and because the System.String type defines a number of methods that appear to modify the character data in one way or another (such as uppercasing and lowercasing). However, if you look more closely at what is happening behind the scenes, you will notice the methods of the string type are, in fact, returning you a brand-new string object in a modified format.

```
static void StringsAreImmutable()
{
  // Set initial string value.
  string s1 = "This is my string.";
  Console.WriteLine("s1 = {0}", s1);

  // Uppercase s1?
  string upperString = s1.ToUpper();
  Console.WriteLine("upperString = {0}", upperString);

  // Nope! s1 is in the same format!
  Console.WriteLine("s1 = {0}", s1);
}
```

If you examine the relevant output that follows, you can verify that the original string object (s1) is not uppercased when calling ToUpper(). Rather, you are returned a *copy* of the string in a modified format.

```
s1 = This is my string.
upperString = THIS IS MY STRING.
s1 = This is my string.
```

The same law of immutability holds true when you use the C# assignment operator. To illustrate, implement the following StringsAreImmutable2() method:

```
static void StringsAreImmutable2()
{
  string s2 = "My other string";
  s2 = "New string value";
}
```

Now, compile your application and load the assembly into ildasm.exe (see Chapter 1). The following output shows what you would find if you were to generate CIL code for the StringsAreImmutable2() method:

```
.method private hidebysig static void  StringsAreImmutable2() cil managed
{
  // Code size       14 (0xe)
  .maxstack  1
```

```
.locals init ([0] string s2)
IL_0000:  nop
IL_0001:  ldstr        "My other string"
IL_0006:  stloc.0
IL_0007:  ldstr        "New string value"
IL_000c:  stloc.0
IL_000d:  ret
} // end of method Program::StringAreImmutable2
```

Although we have yet to examine the low-level details of the CIL, note the numerous calls to the ldstr (load string) opcode. Simply put, the ldstr opcode of the CIL loads a new string object on the managed heap. The previous string object that contained the value "My other string" will eventually be garbage collected.

So, what exactly are we to gather from this insight? In a nutshell, the string class can be inefficient and result in bloated code if misused, especially when performing string concatenation. If you need to represent basic character data such as a U.S. Social Security number, first or last names, or simple bits of text used within your application, the string class is the perfect choice.

However, if you are building an application that makes heavy use of frequently changing textual data (such as a word processing program), it would be a very bad idea to represent the word processing data using string objects, as you will most certainly (and often indirectly) end up making unnecessary copies of string data. So what is a programmer to do? Glad you asked.

The System.Text.StringBuilder Type

Given that the string type can be inefficient when used with reckless abandon, the .NET base class libraries provide the System.Text namespace. Within this (relatively small) namespace lives a class named StringBuilder. Like the System.String class, the StringBuilder defines methods that allow you to replace or format segments, for example. When you wish to use this type in your C# code files, your first step is to make sure the following namespace is imported into your code file (this should already be the case for a new Visual Studio project):

```
// StringBuilder lives here!
using System.Text;
```

What is unique about the StringBuilder is that when you call members of this type, you are directly modifying the object's internal character data (making it more efficient), not obtaining a copy of the data in a modified format. When you create an instance of the StringBuilder, you can supply the object's initial startup values via one of many *constructors*. If you are new to the topic of constructors, simply understand that constructors allow you to create an object with an initial state when you apply the new keyword. Consider the following usage of StringBuilder:

```
static void FunWithStringBuilder()
{
  Console.WriteLine("=> Using the StringBuilder:");
  StringBuilder sb = new StringBuilder("**** Fantastic Games ****");
  sb.Append("\n");
  sb.AppendLine("Half Life");
  sb.AppendLine("Morrowind");
  sb.AppendLine("Deus Ex" + "2");
  sb.AppendLine("System Shock");
  Console.WriteLine(sb.ToString());
```

101

```
    sb.Replace("2", " Invisible War");
    Console.WriteLine(sb.ToString());
    Console.WriteLine("sb has {0} chars.", sb.Length);
    Console.WriteLine();
}
```

Here, we have constructed a StringBuilder set to the initial value "**** Fantastic Games ****". As you can see, we are appending to the internal buffer and are able to replace or remove characters at will. By default, a StringBuilder is only able to initially hold a string of 16 characters or fewer (but will expand automatically if necessary); however, this default starting value can be changed via an additional constructor argument.

```
// Make a StringBuilder with an initial size of 256.
StringBuilder sb = new StringBuilder("**** Fantastic Games ****", 256);
```

If you append more characters than the specified limit, the StringBuilder object will copy its data into a new instance and grow the buffer by the specified limit.

■ **Source Code** The FunWithStrings project is located under the Chapter 3 subdirectory.

Narrowing and Widening Data Type Conversions

Now that you understand how to work with intrinsic C# data types, let's examine the related topic of *data type conversion*. Assume you have a new Console Application project named TypeConversions that defines the following class:

```
class Program
{
    static void Main(string[] args)
    {
        Console.WriteLine("***** Fun with type conversions *****");

        // Add two shorts and print the result.
        short numb1 = 9, numb2 = 10;
        Console.WriteLine("{0} + {1} = {2}",
            numb1, numb2, Add(numb1, numb2));
        Console.ReadLine();
    }

    static int Add(int x, int y)
    {
        return x + y;
    }
}
```

Notice that the Add() method expects to be sent two int parameters. However, the Main() method is, in fact, sending in two short variables. While this might seem like a complete and total mismatch of data types, the program compiles and executes without error, returning the expected result of 19.

The reason the compiler treats this code as syntactically sound is due to the fact that there is no possibility for loss of data. Given that the maximum value of a short (32,767) is well within the maximum range of an int (2,147,483,647), the compiler implicitly *widens* each short to an int. Formally speaking, *widening* is the term used to define an implicit *upward cast* that does not result in a loss of data.

■ **Note** Look up "Type Conversion Tables" in the .NET Framework 4.5 SDK documentation if you wish to see permissible widening (and narrowing, also see the following) conversions for each C# data type.

Although this implicit widening worked in our favor for the previous example, other times this "feature" can be the source of compile-time errors. For example, assume that you have set values to numb1 and numb2 that (when added together) overflow the maximum value of a short. Also, assume you are storing the return value of the Add() method within a new local short variable, rather than directly printing the result to the console.

```
static void Main(string[] args)
{
  Console.WriteLine("***** Fun with type conversions *****");

  // Compiler error below!
  short numb1 = 30000, numb2 = 30000;
  short answer = Add(numb1, numb2);

  Console.WriteLine("{0} + {1} = {2}",
    numb1, numb2, answer);
  Console.ReadLine();
}
```

In this case, the compiler reports the following error:

```
Cannot implicitly convert type 'int' to 'short'. An explicit conversion exists (are you
missing a cast?)
```

The problem is that although the Add() method is capable of returning an int with the value 60,000 (as this fits within the range of a System.Int32), the value cannot be stored in a short, as it overflows the bounds of this data type. Formally speaking, the CLR was unable to apply a *narrowing operation*. As you can guess, narrowing is the logical opposite of widening, in that a larger value is stored within a smaller data type variable.

It is important to point out that all narrowing conversions result in a compiler error, even when you can reason that the narrowing conversion should indeed succeed. For example, the following code also results in a compiler error:

```
// Another compiler error!
static void NarrowingAttempt()
{
  byte myByte = 0;
  int myInt = 200;
```

```
    myByte = myInt;

    Console.WriteLine("Value of myByte: {0}", myByte);
}
```

Here, the value contained within the int variable (myInt) is safely within the range of a byte; therefore, you would expect the narrowing operation to not result in a runtime error. However, given that C# is a language built with type safety in mind, we do indeed receive a compiler error.

When you wish to inform the compiler that you are willing to deal with a possible loss of data due to a narrowing operation, you must apply an *explicit cast* using the C# casting operator (). Consider the following update to the Program type.

```
class Program
{
  static void Main(string[] args)
  {
    Console.WriteLine("***** Fun with type conversions *****");
    short numb1 = 30000, numb2 = 30000;

    // Explicitly cast the int into a short (and allow loss of data).
    short answer = (short)Add(numb1, numb2);

    Console.WriteLine("{0} + {1} = {2}",
      numb1, numb2, answer);
    NarrowingAttempt();
    Console.ReadLine();
  }

  static int Add(int x, int y)
  {
    return x + y;
  }

  static void NarrowingAttempt()
  {
    byte myByte = 0;
    int myInt = 200;

    // Explicitly cast the int into a byte (no loss of data).
    myByte = (byte)myInt;
    Console.WriteLine("Value of myByte: {0}", myByte);
  }
}
```

At this point, our code compiles; however, the result of our addition is completely incorrect:

```
***** Fun with type conversions *****
30000 + 30000 = -5536
Value of myByte: 200
```

As you have just witnessed, an explicit cast allows you to force the compiler to apply a narrowing conversion, even when doing so may result in a loss of data. In the case of the NarrowingAttempt() method, this was not a problem, as the value 200 can fit snuggly within the range of a byte. However, in the case of adding the two shorts within Main(), the end result is completely unacceptable (30,000 + 30,000 = -5536?).

If you are building an application where loss of data is always unacceptable, C# provides the checked and unchecked keywords to ensure data loss does not escape undetected.

The checked Keyword

Let's begin by learning the role of the checked keyword. Assume you have a new method within Program that attempts to add two bytes, each of which has been assigned a value that is safely below the maximum (255). If you were to add the values of these types (casting the returned int to a byte), you would assume that the result would be the exact sum of each member.

```
static void ProcessBytes()
{
  byte b1 = 100;
  byte b2 = 250;
  byte sum = (byte)Add(b1, b2);

  // sum should hold the value 350. However, we find the value 94!
  Console.WriteLine("sum = {0}", sum);
}
```

If you were to view the output of this application, you might be surprised to find that sum contains the value 94 (rather than the expected 350). The reason is simple. Given that a System.Byte can hold a value only between 0 and 255 (inclusive, for a grand total of 256 slots), sum now contains the overflow value (350 – 256 = 94). By default, if you take no corrective course of action, overflow/underflow conditions occur without error.

To handle overflow or underflow conditions in your application, you have two options. Your first choice is to leverage your wits and programming skills to handle all overflow/underflow conditions manually. Of course, the problem with this technique is the simple fact that you are human, and even your best attempts might result in errors that have escaped your eyes.

Thankfully, C# provides the checked keyword. When you wrap a statement (or a block of statements) within the scope of the checked keyword, the C# compiler emits additional CIL instructions that test for overflow conditions that may result when adding, multiplying, subtracting, or dividing two numerical data types.

If an overflow has occurred, you will receive a runtime exception: System.OverflowException. Chapter 7 will examine all the details of structured exception handling and the use of the try and catch keywords. Without getting too hung up on the specifics at this point, observe the following update:

```
static void ProcessBytes()
{
  byte b1 = 100;
  byte b2 = 250;

  // This time, tell the compiler to add CIL code
  // to throw an exception if overflow/underflow
  // takes place.
  try
  {
```

```
    byte sum = checked((byte)Add(b1, b2));
    Console.WriteLine("sum = {0}", sum);
  }
  catch (OverflowException ex)
  {
    Console.WriteLine(ex.Message);
  }
}
```

Notice that the return value of Add() has been wrapped within the scope of the checked keyword. Because the sum is greater than a byte, we trigger a runtime exception. Notice the error message printed out via the Message property:

```
Arithmetic operation resulted in an overflow.
```

If you wish to force overflow checking to occur over a block of code statements, you can do so by defining a "checked scope" as follows:

```
try
{
  checked
  {
    byte sum = (byte)Add(b1, b2);
    Console.WriteLine("sum = {0}", sum);
  }
}
catch (OverflowException ex)
{
  Console.WriteLine(ex.Message);
}
```

In either case, the code in question will be evaluated for possible overflow conditions automatically, which will trigger an overflow exception if encountered.

Setting Project-Wide Overflow Checking

If you are creating an application that should never allow silent overflow to occur, you might find yourself in the annoying position of wrapping numerous lines of code within the scope of the checked keyword. As an alternative, the C# compiler supports the /checked flag. When enabled, all of your arithmetic will be evaluated for overflow without the need to make use of the C# checked keyword. If overflow has been discovered, you will still receive a runtime exception.

To enable this flag using Visual Studio, open your project's property page and click the Advanced button on the Build tab. From the resulting dialog box, select the Check for arithmetic overflow/underflow check box (see Figure 3-3).

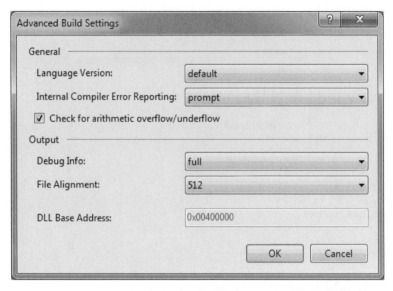

Figure 3-3. Enabling project-wide overflow/underflow data checking

Enabling this setting can be very helpful when you're creating a debug build. After all of the overflow exceptions have been squashed out of the code base, you're free to disable the /checked flag for subsequent builds (which will increase the runtime performance of your application).

The unchecked Keyword

Now, assuming you have enabled this project-wide setting, what are you to do if you have a block of code where data loss *is* acceptable? Given that the /checked flag will evaluate all arithmetic logic, C# provides the unchecked keyword to disable the throwing of an overflow exception on a case-by-case basis. This keyword's use is identical to that of the checked keyword in that you can specify a single statement or a block of statements.

```
// Assuming /checked is enabled,
// this block will not trigger
// a runtime exception.
unchecked
{
  byte sum = (byte)(b1 + b2);
  Console.WriteLine("sum = {0} ", sum);
}
```

So, to summarize the C# checked and unchecked keywords, remember that the default behavior of the .NET runtime is to ignore arithmetic overflow/underflow. When you want to selectively handle discrete statements, make use of the checked keyword. If you wish to trap overflow errors throughout your application, enable the /checked flag. Finally, the unchecked keyword may be used if you have a block of code where overflow is acceptable (and thus should not trigger a runtime exception).

■ **Source Code** The TypeConversions project is located under the Chapter 3 subdirectory.

Understanding Implicitly Typed Local Variables

Up until this point in the chapter, when we have been defining local variables, we've *explicitly* specified the underlying data type of each variable being declared.

```
static void DeclareExplicitVars()
{
  // Explicitly typed local variables
  // are declared as follows:
  // dataType variableName = initialValue;
  int myInt = 0;
  bool myBool = true;
  string myString = "Time, marches on...";
}
```

While many (including yours truly) would argue that is it is always good practice to explicitly specify the data type of each variable, the C# language does provide for *implicitly typing* of local variables using the var keyword. The var keyword can be used in place of specifying a specific data type (such as int, bool, or string). When you do so, the compiler will automatically infer the underlying data type based on the initial value used to initialize the local data point.

To illustrate the role of implicit typing, create a new Console Application project named ImplicitlyTypedLocalVars. Notice how the local variables within the previous method can now be declared as follows:

```
static void DeclareImplicitVars()
{
  // Implicitly typed local variables
  // are declared as follows:
  // var variableName = initialValue;
  var myInt = 0;
  var myBool = true;
  var myString = "Time, marches on...";
}
```

■ **Note** Strictly speaking, var is not a C# keyword. It is permissible to declare variables, parameters, and fields named "var" without compile-time errors. However, when the var token is used as a data type, it is contextually treated as a keyword by the compiler.

In this case, the compiler is able to infer, given the initially assigned value, that myInt is, in fact, a System.Int32, myBool is a System.Boolean, and myString is indeed of type System.String. You can verify this by printing out the type name via *reflection*. As you will see in much more detail in Chapter 15, *reflection* is the act of determining the composition of a type at runtime. For example, using reflection, you can determine the data type of an implicitly typed local variable. Update your method with the following code statements:

```
static void DeclareImplicitVars()
{
  // Implicitly typed local variables.
  var myInt = 0;
  var myBool = true;
  var myString = "Time, marches on...";

  // Print out the underlying type.
  Console.WriteLine("myInt is a: {0}", myInt.GetType().Name);
  Console.WriteLine("myBool is a: {0}", myBool.GetType().Name);
  Console.WriteLine("myString is a: {0}", myString.GetType().Name);
}
```

■ **Note** Be aware that you can use this implicit typing for any type including arrays, generic types (see Chapter 9), and your own custom types. You'll see other examples of implicit typing over the course of this book.

If you were to call the DeclareImplicitVars() method from within Main(), you'd find the output shown here.

```
***** Fun with Implicit Typing *****

myInt is a: Int32
myBool is a: Boolean
myString is a: String
```

Restrictions on Implicitly Typed Variables

There are various restrictions regarding the use of the var keyword. First and foremost, implicit typing applies *only* to local variables in a method or property scope. It is illegal to use the var keyword to define return values, parameters, or field data of a custom type. For example, the following class definition will result in various compile-time errors:

```
class ThisWillNeverCompile
{
  // Error! var cannot be used as field data!
  private var myInt = 10;

  // Error! var cannot be used as a return value
  // or parameter type!
  public var MyMethod(var x, var y){}
}
```

Also, local variables declared with the var keyword *must* be assigned an initial value at the exact time of declaration and *cannot* be assigned the initial value of null. This last restriction should make sense, given that the compiler cannot infer what sort of type in memory the variable would be pointing to based only on null.

```
// Error! Must assign a value!
var myData;

// Error! Must assign value at exact time of declaration!
var myInt;
myInt = 0;

// Error! Can't assign null as initial value!
var myObj = null;
```

It is permissible, however, to assign an inferred local variable to null after its initial assignment (provided it is a reference type).

```
// OK, if SportsCar is a reference type!
var myCar = new SportsCar();
myCar = null;
```

Furthermore, it is permissible to assign the value of an implicitly typed local variable to the value of other variables, implicitly typed or not.

```
// Also OK!
var myInt = 0;
var anotherInt = myInt;

string myString = "Wake up!";
var myData = myString;
```

Also, it is permissible to return an implicitly typed local variable to the caller, provided the method return type is the same underlying type as the var-defined data point.

```
static int GetAnInt()
{
  var retVal = 9;
  return retVal;
}
```

Implicit Typed Data Is Strongly Typed Data

Be very aware that implicit typing of local variables results in strongly typed data. Therefore, use of the var keyword is not the same technique used with scripting languages (such as JavaScript or Perl) or the COM Variant data type, where a variable can hold values of different types over its lifetime in a program (often termed *dynamic typing*).

■ **Note** C# does allow for dynamic typing in C# using a keyword called—surprise, surprise—dynamic. You will learn about this aspect of the language in Chapter 16.

Rather, type inference keeps the strongly typed aspect of the C# language and affects only the declaration of variables at compile time. After that, the data point is treated as if it were declared with that type; assigning a value of a different type into that variable will result in a compile-time error.

```csharp
static void ImplicitTypingIsStrongTyping()
{
  // The compiler knows "s" is a System.String.
  var s = "This variable can only hold string data!";
  s = "This is fine...";

  // Can invoke any member of the underlying type.
  string upper = s.ToUpper();

  // Error! Can't assign numerical data to a string!
  s = 44;
}
```

Usefulness of Implicitly Typed Local Variables

Now that you have seen the syntax used to declare implicitly typed local variables, I am sure you are wondering when to make use of this construct. First and foremost, using var to declare local variables simply for the sake of doing so really brings little to the table. Doing so can be confusing to others reading your code, as it becomes harder to quickly determine the underlying data type and, therefore, more difficult to understand the overall functionality of the variable. So, if you know you need an int, declare an int!

However, as you will see beginning in Chapter 12, the LINQ technology set makes use of *query expressions* that can yield dynamically created result sets based on the format of the query itself. In these cases, implicit typing is extremely helpful, as we do not need to explicitly define the type that a query may return, which in some cases would be literally impossible to do. Without getting hung up on the following LINQ example code, see if you can figure out the underlying data type of subset:

```csharp
static void LinqQueryOverInts()
{
  int[] numbers = { 10, 20, 30, 40, 1, 2, 3, 8 };

  // LINQ query!
  var subset = from i in numbers where i < 10 select i;

  Console.Write("Values in subset: ");
  foreach (var i in subset)
  {
    Console.Write("{0} ", i);
  }
  Console.WriteLine();

  // Hmm...what type is subset?
  Console.WriteLine("subset is a: {0}", subset.GetType().Name);
  Console.WriteLine("subset is defined in: {0}", subset.GetType().Namespace);
}
```

You might be assuming that the subset data type is an array of integers. That seems to be the case, but in fact, it is a low level LINQ data type that you would never know about unless you have been doing

LINQ for a very long time, or open the compiled image in `ildasm.exe`. The good news is that when you are using LINQ, you seldom (if ever) care about the underlying type of the query's return value; you will simply assign the value to an implicitly typed local variable.

In fact, it could be argued that the *only time* one would make use of the `var` keyword is when defining data returned from a LINQ query. Remember, if you know you need an `int`, just declare an `int`! Overuse of implicit typing (via the var keyword) is considered by most developers to be poor style in production code.

■ **Source Code** The ImplicitlyTypedLocalVars project can be found under the Chapter 3 subdirectory.

C# Iteration Constructs

All programming languages provide ways to repeat blocks of code until a terminating condition has been met. Regardless of which language you have used in the past, I would guess the C# iteration statements should not raise too many eyebrows and should require little explanation. C# provides the following four iteration constructs:

- `for` loop
- `foreach`/`in` loop
- `while` loop
- `do`/`while` loop

Let's quickly examine each looping construct in turn, using a new Console Application project named IterationsAndDecisions.

■ **Note** I will keep this final section of the chapter short and to the point, as I am assuming you have experience using similar keywords (`if`, `for`, `switch`, etc.) in your current programming language. If you require more information, look up the topics "Iteration Statements (C# Reference)," "Jump Statements (C# Reference)," and "Selection Statements (C# Reference)" within the .NET Framework 4.5 SDK documentation.

The for Loop

When you need to iterate over a block of code a fixed number of times, the `for` statement provides a good deal of flexibility. In essence, you are able to specify how many times a block of code repeats itself, as well as the terminating condition. Without belaboring the point, here is a sample of the syntax.

```
// A basic for loop.
static void ForLoopExample()
{
  // Note! "i" is only visible within the scope of the for loop.
```

```
  for(int i = 0; i < 4; i++)
  {
    Console.WriteLine("Number is: {0} ", i);
  }
  // "i" is not visible here.
}
```

All of your old C, C++, and Java tricks still hold when building a C# for statement. You can create complex terminating conditions, build endless loops, loop in reverse (via the -- operator) and make use of the goto, continue, and break jump keywords.

The foreach Loop

The C# foreach keyword allows you to iterate over all items in a container without the need to test for an upper limit. Unlike a for loop however, the foreach loop will only walk the container in a linear (n+1) fashion (thus, you cannot go backward through the container, skip every third element, or whatnot).

However, when you simply need to walk a collection item-by-item, the foreach loop is the perfect choice. Here are two examples using foreach—one to traverse an array of strings and the other to traverse an array of integers. Notice that the data type before the in keyword represents the type of data in the container:

```
// Iterate array items using foreach.
static void ForEachLoopExample()
{
  string[] carTypes = {"Ford", "BMW", "Yugo", "Honda" };
  foreach (string c in carTypes)
    Console.WriteLine(c);

  int[] myInts = { 10, 20, 30, 40 };
  foreach (int i in myInts)
    Console.WriteLine(i);
}
```

The item after the in keyword can be a simple array (seen here) or more specifically, any class implementing the IEnumerable interface. As you will see in Chapter 9, the .NET base class libraries ship with a number of collections that contain implementations of common abstract data types (ADTs). Any of these items (such as the generic List<T>) can be used within a foreach loop.

Use of Implicit Typing Within foreach Constructs

It is also possible to make use of implicit typing within a foreach looping construct. As you would expect, the compiler will correctly infer the correct "type of type." Recall the LINQ example method seen earlier in this chapter. Given that we don't know the exact underlying data type of the subset variable, we can iterate over the result set using implicit typing:

```
static void LinqQueryOverInts()
{
  int[] numbers = { 10, 20, 30, 40, 1, 2, 3, 8 };

  // LINQ query!
  var subset = from i in numbers where i < 10 select i;
```

```
    Console.Write("Values in subset: ");
    foreach (var i in subset)
    {
      Console.Write("{0} ", i);
    }
  }
```

The while and do/while Looping Constructs

The while looping construct is useful should you wish to execute a block of statements until some terminating condition has been reached. Within the scope of a while loop, you will need to ensure this terminating event is indeed established; otherwise, you will be stuck in an endless loop. In the following example, the message "In while loop" will be continuously printed until the user terminates the loop by entering *yes* at the command prompt:

```
static void WhileLoopExample()
{
  string userIsDone = "";

  // Test on a lower-class copy of the string.
  while(userIsDone.ToLower() != "yes")
  {
    Console.WriteLine("In while loop");
    Console.Write("Are you done? [yes] [no]: ");
    userIsDone = Console.ReadLine();
  }
}
```

Closely related to the while loop is the do/while statement. Like a simple while loop, do/while is used when you need to perform some action an undetermined number of times. The difference is that do/while loops are guaranteed to execute the corresponding block of code at least once. In contrast, it is possible that a simple while loop may never execute if the terminating condition is false from the onset.

```
static void DoWhileLoopExample()
{
  string userIsDone = "";

  do
  {
    Console.WriteLine("In do/while loop");
    Console.Write("Are you done? [yes] [no]: ");
    userIsDone = Console.ReadLine();
  }while(userIsDone.ToLower() != "yes"); // Note the semicolon!
}
```

Decision Constructs and the Relational/Equality Operators

Now that you can iterate over a block of statements, the next related concept is how to control the flow of program execution. C# defines two simple constructs to alter the flow of your program, based on various contingencies:

- The if/else statement
- The switch statement

The if/else Statement

First up is the if/else statement. Unlike in C and C++, the if/else statement in C# operates only on Boolean expressions, not ad hoc values such as –1 or 0.

Equality and Relational Operators

C# if/else statements typically involve the use of the C# operators shown in Table 3-7 in order to obtain a literal Boolean value.

Table 3-7. C# Relational and Equality Operators

C# Equality/Relational Operator	Example Usage	Meaning in Life
==	if(age == 30)	Returns true only if each expression is the same.
!=	if("Foo" != myStr)	Returns true only if each expression is different.

>
<=
>=
	if(bonus < 2000)
	if(bonus > 2000)
	if(bonus <= 2000)
	if(bonus >= 2000)
		Returns true if expression A (bonus) is less than, greater than, less than or equal to, or greater than or equal to expression B (2000).

Again, C and C++ programmers need to be aware that the old tricks of testing a condition for a value not equal to zero will not work in C#. Let's say you want to see whether the string you are working with is longer than zero characters. You might be tempted to write:

```
static void IfElseExample()
{
  // This is illegal, given that Length returns an int, not a bool.
  string stringData = "My textual data";
  if(stringData.Length)
  {
    Console.WriteLine("string is greater than 0 characters");
  }
}
```

If you wish to make use of the String.Length property to determine truth or falsity, you need to modify your conditional expression to resolve to a Boolean.

```
// Legal, as this resolves to either true or false.
if(stringData.Length > 0)
{
  Console.WriteLine("string is greater than 0 characters");
}
```

Conditional Operators

An if statement may be composed of complex expressions as well and can contain else statements to perform more complex testing. The syntax is identical to C(++) and Java. To build complex expressions, C# offers an expected set of conditional logical operators, as shown in Table 3-8.

Table 3-8. C# Conditional Operators

Operator	Example	Meaning in Life
&&	if(age == 30 && name == "Fred")	AND operator. Returns true if all expressions are true.
||	if(age == 30 || name == "Fred")	OR operator. Returns true if at least one expression is true.
!	if(!myBool)	NOT operator. Returns true if false, or false if true.

■ **Note** The && and || operators both "short circuit" when necessary. This means that after a complex expression has been determined to be false, the remaining subexpressions will not be checked. If you require all expressions to be tested regardless, you can use the related & and | operators.

The switch Statement

The other simple selection construct offered by C# is the switch statement. As in other C-based languages, the switch statement allows you to handle program flow based on a predefined set of choices. For example, the following Main() logic prints a specific string message based on one of two possible selections (the default case handles an invalid selection).

```
// Switch on a numerical value.
static void SwitchExample()
{
  Console.WriteLine("1 [C#], 2 [VB]");
  Console.Write("Please pick your language preference: ");

  string langChoice = Console.ReadLine();
  int n = int.Parse(langChoice);

  switch (n)
  {
    case 1:
      Console.WriteLine("Good choice, C# is a fine language.");
    break;
    case 2:
```

```
      Console.WriteLine("VB: OOP, multithreading, and more!");
    break;
    default:
      Console.WriteLine("Well...good luck with that!");
    break;
  }
}
```

■ **Note** C# demands that each case (including `default`) that contains executable statements have a terminating `break` or `goto` to avoid fall-through.

One nice feature of the C# switch statement is that you can evaluate string data in addition to numeric data. Here is an updated switch statement that does this very thing (notice we have no need to parse the user data into a numeric value with this approach).

```
static void SwitchOnStringExample()
{
  Console.WriteLine("C# or VB");
  Console.Write("Please pick your language preference: ");

  string langChoice = Console.ReadLine();
  switch (langChoice)
  {
    case "C#":
      Console.WriteLine("Good choice, C# is a fine language.");
    break;
    case "VB":
      Console.WriteLine("VB: OOP, multithreading and more!");
    break;
    default:
      Console.WriteLine("Well...good luck with that!");
    break;
  }
}
```

It is also possible to switch on an enumeration data type. As you will see in Chapter 4, the C# enum keyword allows you to define a custom set of name/value pairs. To whet your appetite, consider the following final helper function, which performs a switch test on the System.DayOfWeek enum. You'll notice some syntax we have not yet examined, but focus on the issue of switching over the enum itself; the missing pieces will be filled in over the chapters to come:

```
static void SwitchOnEnumExample()
{
  Console.Write("Enter your favorite day of the week: ");
  DayOfWeek favDay;

  try
  {
```

```
      favDay = (DayOfWeek)Enum.Parse(typeof(DayOfWeek), Console.ReadLine());
  }
  catch (Exception)
  {
    Console.WriteLine("Bad input!");
    return;
  }

  switch (favDay)
  {
    case DayOfWeek.Friday:
      Console.WriteLine("Yes, Friday rules!");
    break;
    case DayOfWeek.Monday:
      Console.WriteLine("Another day, another dollar");
    break;
    case DayOfWeek.Saturday:
      Console.WriteLine("Great day indeed.");
    break;
    case DayOfWeek.Sunday:
      Console.WriteLine("Football!!");
    break;
    case DayOfWeek.Thursday:
      Console.WriteLine("Almost Friday...");
    break;
    case DayOfWeek.Tuesday:
      Console.WriteLine("At least it is not Monday");
    break;
    case DayOfWeek.Wednesday:
      Console.WriteLine("A fine day.");
    break;
  }
}
```

■ **Source Code** The IterationsAndDecisions project is located under the Chapter 3 subdirectory.

Summary

The goal of this chapter was to expose you to numerous core aspects of the C# programming language. Here, we examined the commonplace constructs in any application you may be interested in building. After examining the role of an application object, you learned that every C# executable program must have a type defining a Main() method, which serves as the program's entry point. Within the scope of Main(), you typically create any number of objects that work together to breathe life into your application.

Next, we dove into the details of the built-in data types of C# and came to understand that each data type keyword (e.g., int) is really a shorthand notation for a full-blown type in the System namespace (System.Int32, in this case). Given this, each C# data type has a number of built-in members. Along the same vein, you also learned about the role of *widening* and *narrowing,* as well as the role of the checked and unchecked keywords.

We wrapped up by checking out the role of implicit typing using the var keyword. As we discussed, the most useful place for implicit typing is when working with the LINQ programming model. Finally, we quickly examined the various iteration and decision constructs supported by C#.

Now that you have an understanding of some of the basic nuts and bolts, the next chapter (Chapter 4) will complete our examination of core language features. After that, you will be well prepared to examine the object-oriented features of C# beginning in Chapter 5.

Core C# Programming Constructs, Part II

This chapter picks up where the Chapter 3 left off, and completes your investigation of the core aspects of the C# programming language. We begin by examining various details regarding the construction of C# methods, exploring the out, ref, and params keywords. Along the way, you will also examine the role of optional and named parameters.

After you examine the topic of *method overloading,* the next task is to investigate the details behind manipulating arrays using the syntax of C# and get to know the functionality contained within the related System.Array class type.

In addition, this chapter provides a discussion regarding the construction of enumeration and structure types, including a fairly detailed examination of the distinction between a *value type* and a *reference type.* We wrap this up by examining the role of nullable data types and the ? and ?? operators. After you have completed this chapter, you will be in a perfect position to learn the object-oriented capabilities of C#, beginning in Chapter 5.

Methods and Parameter Modifiers

To begin this chapter, let's examine the details of defining methods. Just like the Main() method (see Chapter 3), your custom methods may or may not take parameters and may or may not return values to the caller. As you will see over the next several chapters, methods can be implemented within the scope of classes or structures (as well as prototyped within interface types) and may be decorated with various keywords (e.g., static, virtual, public, new) to qualify their behavior. At this point in the text, each of our methods has followed the following basic format:

```
// Recall that static methods can be called directly
// without creating a class instance.
class Program
{
  // static returnType MethodName(paramater list) { /* Implementation */ }
  static int Add(int x, int y){ return x + y; }
}
```

While the definition of a method in C# is quite straightforward, there are a handful of keywords that you can use to control how arguments are passed to the method in question. These are listed in Table 4-1.

Table 4-1. *C# Parameter Modifiers*

Parameter Modifier	Meaning in Life
(None)	If a parameter is not marked with a parameter modifier, it is assumed to be passed by value, meaning the called method receives a copy of the original data.
out	Output parameters must be assigned by the method being called, and therefore, are passed by reference. If the called method fails to assign output parameters, you are issued a compiler error.
ref	The value is initially assigned by the caller and may be optionally reassigned by the called method (as the data is also passed by reference). No compiler error is generated if the called method fails to assign a ref parameter.
params	This parameter modifier allows you to send in a variable number of arguments as a single logical parameter. A method can have only a single params modifier, and it must be the final parameter of the method. In reality, you might not need to use the params modifier all too often; however, be aware that numerous methods within the base class libraries do make use of this C# language feature.

To illustrate the use of these keywords, create a new Console Application project named FunWithMethods. Now, let's walk through the role of each keyword.

The Default by Value Parameter-Passing Behavior

The default manner in which a parameter is sent into a function is *by value*. Simply put, if you do not mark an argument with a parameter modifier, a copy of the data is passed into the function. As explained at the end of this chapter, exactly *what* is copied will depend on whether the parameter is a value type or a reference type. For the time being, assume the following method within the Program class that operates on two numerical data types passed by value:

```
// Arguments are passed by value by default.
static int Add(int x, int y)
{
  int ans = x + y;

  // Caller will not see these changes
  // as you are modifying a copy of the
  // original data.
  x = 10000;
  y = 88888;
  return ans;
}
```

Numerical data falls under the category of *value types*. Therefore, if you change the values of the parameters within the scope of the member, the caller is blissfully unaware, given that you are changing the values on a *copy* of the caller's original data:

```
static void Main(string[] args)
{
  Console.WriteLine("***** Fun with Methods *****\n");

  // Pass two variables in by value.
  int x = 9, y = 10;
  Console.WriteLine("Before call: X: {0}, Y: {1}", x, y);
  Console.WriteLine("Answer is: {0}", Add(x, y));
  Console.WriteLine("After call: X: {0}, Y: {1}", x, y);
  Console.ReadLine();
}
```

As you would hope, the values of x and y remain identical before and after the call to Add(), as shown in the following output, as the data points were sent in by value. Thus, any changes on these parameters within the Add() method are not seen by the caller, as the Add() method is operating on a copy of the data.

```
***** Fun with Methods *****

Before call: X: 9, Y: 10
Answer is: 19
After call: X: 9, Y: 10
```

The out Modifier

Next, you have the use of *output parameters*. Methods that have been defined to take output parameters (via the out keyword) are under obligation to assign them to an appropriate value before exiting the method scope (if you fail to do so, you will receive compiler errors).

To illustrate, here is an alternative version of the Add() method that returns the sum of two integers using the C# out modifier (note the physical return value of this method is now void):

```
// Output parameters must be assigned by the called method.
static void Add(int x, int y, out int ans)
{
  ans = x + y;
}
```

Calling a method with output parameters also requires the use of the out modifier. However, the local variables that are passed as output variables are not required to be assigned before passing them in as output arguments (if you do so, the original value is lost after the call). The reason the compiler allows you to send in seemingly unassigned data is due to the fact that the method being called *must* make an assignment. The following code is an example:

```
static void Main(string[] args)
{
  Console.WriteLine("***** Fun with Methods *****");
...
  // No need to assign initial value to local variables
  // used as output parameters, provided the first time
  // you use them is as output arguments.
  int ans;
  Add(90, 90, out ans);
  Console.WriteLine("90 + 90 = {0}", ans);
  Console.ReadLine();
}
```

The previous example is intended to be illustrative in nature; you really have no reason to return the value of your summation using an output parameter. However, the C# out modifier does serve a very useful purpose: it allows the caller to obtain multiple outputs from a single method invocation.

```
// Returning multiple output parameters.
static void FillTheseValues(out int a, out string b, out bool c)
{
  a = 9;
  b = "Enjoy your string.";
  c = true;
}
```

The caller would be able to invoke the FillTheseValues() method. Remember that you must use the out modifier when you invoke the method, as well as when you implement the method:

```
static void Main(string[] args)
{
  Console.WriteLine("***** Fun with Methods *****");
...
  int i; string str; bool b;
  FillTheseValues(out i, out str, out b);

  Console.WriteLine("Int is: {0}", i);
  Console.WriteLine("String is: {0}", str);
  Console.WriteLine("Boolean is: {0}", b);
  Console.ReadLine();
}
```

Finally, always remember that a method that defines output parameters *must* assign the parameter to a valid value before exiting the method scope. Therefore, the following code will result in a compiler error, as the output parameter has not been assigned within the method scope:

```
static void ThisWontCompile(out int a)
{
  Console.WriteLine("Error! Forgot to assign output arg!");
}
```

The ref Modifier

Now consider the use of the C# ref parameter modifier. Reference parameters are necessary when you wish to allow a method to operate on (and usually change the values of) various data points declared in the caller's scope (such as a sorting or swapping routine). Note the distinction between output and reference parameters:

- Output parameters do not need to be initialized before they passed to the method. The reason for this is that the method must assign output parameters before exiting.

- Reference parameters must be initialized before they are passed to the method. The reason for this is that you are passing a reference to an existing variable. If you don't assign it to an initial value, that would be the equivalent of operating on an unassigned local variable.

Let's check out the use of the ref keyword by way of a method that swaps two string variables (of course, any two data types could be used here, including int, bool, float, and so on):

```
// Reference parameters.
public static void SwapStrings(ref string s1, ref string s2)
{
  string tempStr = s1;
  s1 = s2;
  s2 = tempStr;
}
```

This method can be called as follows:

```
static void Main(string[] args)
{
  Console.WriteLine("***** Fun with Methods *****");
...
  string str1 = "Flip";
  string str2 = "Flop";
  Console.WriteLine("Before: {0}, {1} ", str1, str2);
  SwapStrings(ref str1, ref str2);
  Console.WriteLine("After: {0}, {1} ", str1, str2);
  Console.ReadLine();
}
```

Here, the caller has assigned an initial value to local string data (str1 and str2). After the call to SwapStrings() returns, str1 now contains the value "Flop", while str2 reports the value "Flip":

```
Before: Flip, Flop
After: Flop, Flip
```

■ **Note** The C# `ref` keyword will be revisited later in this chapter in the section "Understanding Value Types and Reference Types." As you will see, the behavior of this keyword changes just a bit depending on whether the argument is a value type or reference type.

The params Modifier

C# supports the use of *parameter arrays* using the `params` keyword. To understand this language feature, you must (as the name implies) understand how to manipulate C# arrays. If this is not the case, you might wish to return to this section after you read the section "Array Manipulation in C#," later in this chapter.

The `params` keyword allows you to pass into a method a variable number of identically typed parameters (or classes related by inheritance) as a *single logical parameter*. As well, arguments marked with the `params` keyword can be processed if the caller sends in a strongly typed array or a comma-delimited list of items. Yes, this can be confusing! To clear things up, assume you wish to create a function that allows the caller to pass in any number of arguments and return the calculated average.

If you were to prototype this method to take an array of doubles, this would force the caller to first define the array, then fill the array, and finally pass it into the method. However, if you define `CalculateAverage()` to take a params of `double[]` data types, the caller can simply pass a comma-delimited list of doubles. The .NET runtime will automatically package the set of doubles into an array of type double behind the scenes:

```
// Return average of "some number" of doubles.
static double CalculateAverage(params double[] values)
{
  Console.WriteLine("You sent me {0} doubles.", values.Length);

  double sum = 0;
  if(values.Length == 0)
    return sum;

  for (int i = 0; i < values.Length; i++)
    sum += values[i];
  return (sum / values.Length);
}
```

This method has been defined to take a parameter array of doubles. What this method is in fact saying is, "Send me any number of doubles (including zero) and I'll compute the average." Given this, you can call `CalculateAverage()` in any of the following ways:

```
static void Main(string[] args)
{
  Console.WriteLine("***** Fun with Methods *****");
...
  // Pass in a comma-delimited list of doubles...
  double average;
  average = CalculateAverage(4.0, 3.2, 5.7, 64.22, 87.2);
  Console.WriteLine("Average of data is: {0}", average);
```

```
    // ...or pass an array of doubles.
    double[] data = { 4.0, 3.2, 5.7 };
    average = CalculateAverage(data);
    Console.WriteLine("Average of data is: {0}", average);

    // Average of 0 is 0!
    Console.WriteLine("Average of data is: {0}", CalculateAverage());
    Console.ReadLine();
}
```

If you did not make use of the params modifier in the definition of CalculateAverage(), the first invocation of this method would result in a compiler error, as the compiler would be looking for a version of CalculateAverage() that took five double arguments.

■ **Note** To avoid any ambiguity, C# demands a method only support single `params` argument, which must be the final argument in the parameter list.

As you might guess, this technique is nothing more than a convenience for the caller, given that the array is created by the CLR as necessary. By the time the array is within the scope of the method being called, you are able to treat it as a full-blown .NET array that contains all the functionality of the System.Array base class library type. Consider the following output:

```
You sent me 5 doubles.
Average of data is: 32.864
You sent me 3 doubles.
Average of data is: 4.3
You sent me 0 doubles.
Average of data is: 0
```

Defining Optional Parameters

C# allows you to create methods that can take *optional arguments*. This technique allows the caller to invoke a single method while omitting arguments deemed unnecessary, provided the caller is happy with the specified defaults.

■ **Note** As you will see in Chapter 16, a key motivation for adding optional arguments to C# is to simplify interacting with COM objects. Several Microsoft object models (e.g., Microsoft Office) expose their functionality via COM objects, many of which were written long ago to make use of optional parameters, which earlier versions of C# did not support.

To illustrate working with optional arguments, assume you have a method named EnterLogData(), which defines a single optional parameter:

```
static void EnterLogData(string message, string owner = "Programmer")
{
  Console.Beep();
  Console.WriteLine("Error: {0}", message);
  Console.WriteLine("Owner of Error: {0}", owner);
}
```

Here, the final string argument has been assigned the default value of "Programmer", via an assignment within the parameter definition. Given this, we can call EnterLogData() from within Main() in two manners:

```
static void Main(string[] args)
{
  Console.WriteLine("***** Fun with Methods *****");
...
  EnterLogData("Oh no! Grid can't find data");
  EnterLogData("Oh no! I can't find the payroll data", "CFO");

  Console.ReadLine();
}
```

Because the first invocation of EnterLogData() did not specify a second string argument, we would find that the programmer is the one responsible for losing data for the grid, while the CFO misplaced the payroll data (as specified by the second argument in the second method call).

One very important thing to be aware of, is that the value assigned to an optional parameter must be known at compile time, and cannot be resolved at runtime (if you attempt to do so, you'll receive compile-time errors!). To illustrate, assume you wish to update EnterLogData() with the following extra optional parameter:

```
// Error! The default value for an optional arg must be known
// at compile time!
static void EnterLogData(string message,
            string owner = "Programmer", DateTime timeStamp = DateTime.Now)
{
  Console.Beep();
  Console.WriteLine("Error: {0}", message);
  Console.WriteLine("Owner of Error: {0}", owner);
  Console.WriteLine("Time of Error: {0}", timeStamp);
}
```

This will not compile, as the value of the Now property of the DateTime class is resolved at runtime, not compile time.

■ **Note** To avoid ambiguity, optional parameters must always be packed onto the *end* of a method signature. It is a compiler error to have optional parameters listed before nonoptional parameters.

Invoking Methods Using Named Parameters

Another language feature found in C# is support for *named arguments*. To be honest, at first glance, this language construct might appear to do little more than result in confusing code. And to continue being completely honest, this could be the case! Similar to optional arguments, including support for named parameters is largely motivated by the desire to simplify the process of working with the COM interoperability layer (again, see Chapter 16).

Named arguments allow you to invoke a method by specifying parameter values in any order you choose. Thus, rather than passing parameters solely by position (as you will do in most cases), you can choose to specify each argument by name using a colon operator. To illustrate the use of named arguments, assume we have added the following method to the Program class:

```
static void DisplayFancyMessage(ConsoleColor textColor,
  ConsoleColor backgroundColor, string message)
{
  // Store old colors to restore after message is printed.
  ConsoleColor oldTextColor = Console.ForegroundColor;
  ConsoleColor oldbackgroundColor = Console.BackgroundColor;

  // Set new colors and print message.
  Console.ForegroundColor = textColor;
  Console.BackgroundColor = backgroundColor;

  Console.WriteLine(message);

  // Restore previous colors.
  Console.ForegroundColor = oldTextColor;
  Console.BackgroundColor = oldbackgroundColor;
}
```

Now, the way DisplayFancyMessage() was written, you would expect the caller to invoke this method by passing two ConsoleColor variables followed by a string type. However, using named arguments, the following calls are completely fine:

```
static void Main(string[] args)
{
  Console.WriteLine("***** Fun with Methods *****");
...
  DisplayFancyMessage(message: "Wow!  Very Fancy indeed!",
    textColor: ConsoleColor.DarkRed,
    backgroundColor: ConsoleColor.White);

  DisplayFancyMessage(backgroundColor: ConsoleColor.Green,
    message: "Testing...",
    textColor: ConsoleColor.DarkBlue);
  Console.ReadLine();
}
```

One minor gotcha regarding named arguments is that if you begin to invoke a method using positional parameters, they must be listed before any named parameters. In other words, named arguments must always be packed onto the end of a method call. The following code is an example:

```
// This is OK, as positional args are listed before named args.
DisplayFancyMessage(ConsoleColor.Blue,
  message: "Testing...",
  backgroundColor: ConsoleColor.White);
// This is an ERROR, as positional args are listed after named args.
DisplayFancyMessage(message: "Testing...",
  backgroundColor: ConsoleColor.White,
  ConsoleColor.Blue);
```

This restriction aside, you might still be wondering when you would ever want to use this language feature. After all, if you need to specify three arguments to a method, why bother flipping around their position?

Well, as it turns out, if you have a method that defines optional arguments, this feature can actually be really helpful. Assume `DisplayFancyMessage()` has been rewritten to now support optional arguments, as you have assigned fitting defaults:

```
static void DisplayFancyMessage(ConsoleColor textColor = ConsoleColor.Blue,
  ConsoleColor backgroundColor = ConsoleColor.White,
  string message = "Test Message")
{
  ...
}
```

Given that each argument has a default value, named arguments allow the caller to specify only the parameter(s) for which they do not wish to receive the defaults. Therefore, if the caller wants the value "Hello!" to appear in blue text surrounded by a white background, they can simply specify:

```
DisplayFancyMessage(message: "Hello!");
```

Or, if the caller wants to see "Test Message" print out with a green background containing blue text, they can invoke `DisplayFancyMessage()`:

```
DisplayFancyMessage(backgroundColor: ConsoleColor.Green);
```

As you can see, optional arguments and named parameters do tend to work hand in hand. To wrap up our examination of building C# methods, I need to address the topic of *method overloading*.

■ **Source Code** The FunWithMethods application is located under the Chapter 4 subdirectory.

Understanding Method Overloading

Like other modern object-oriented languages, C# allows a method to be *overloaded*. Simply put, when you define a set of identically named methods that differ by the number (or type) of parameters, the method in question is said to be overloaded.

To understand why overloading is so useful, consider life as an old-school Visual Basic 6.0 (VB6) developer. Assume you are using VB6 to build a set of methods that return the sum of various incoming data types (Integers, Doubles, and so on). Given that VB6 does not support method overloading, you would be required to define a unique set of methods that essentially do the same thing (return the sum of the arguments):

```
' VB6 code examples.
Public Function AddInts(ByVal x As Integer, ByVal y As Integer) As Integer
  AddInts = x + y
End Function

Public Function AddDoubles(ByVal x As Double, ByVal y As Double) As Double
  AddDoubles = x + y
End Function

Public Function AddLongs(ByVal x As Long, ByVal y As Long) As Long
  AddLongs = x + y
End Function
```

Not only can code such as this become tough to maintain, but the caller must now be painfully aware of the name of each method. Using overloading, you are able to allow the caller to call a single method named Add(). Again, the key is to ensure that each version of the method has a distinct set of arguments (methods differing only by return type are not unique enough).

■ **Note** As explained in Chapter 9, it is possible to build generic methods that take the concept of overloading to the next level. Using generics, you can define *type placeholders* for a method implementation that are specified at the time you invoke the member in question.

To check this out firsthand, create a new Console Application project named MethodOverloading. Now, consider the following class definition:

```
// C# code.
class Program
{
  static void Main(string[] args)
  {
  }

  // Overloaded Add() method.
  static int Add(int x, int y)
  { return x + y; }

  static double Add(double x, double y)
  { return x + y; }

  static long Add(long x, long y)
  { return x + y; }
}
```

The caller can now simply invoke Add() with the required arguments and the compiler is happy to comply, given the fact that the compiler is able to resolve the correct implementation to invoke given the provided arguments:

```
static void Main(string[] args)
{
  Console.WriteLine("***** Fun with Method Overloading *****\n");

  // Calls int version of Add()
  Console.WriteLine(Add(10, 10));

  // Calls long version of Add()
  Console.WriteLine(Add(900000000000, 900000000000));

  // Calls double version of Add()
  Console.WriteLine(Add(4.3, 4.4));

  Console.ReadLine();
}
```

The Visual Studio IDE provides assistance when calling overloaded methods to boot. When you type in the name of an overloaded method (such as our good friend Console.WriteLine()), IntelliSense will list each version of the method in question. Note that you are able to cycle through each version of an overloaded method using the up and down arrow keys shown in Figure 4-1.

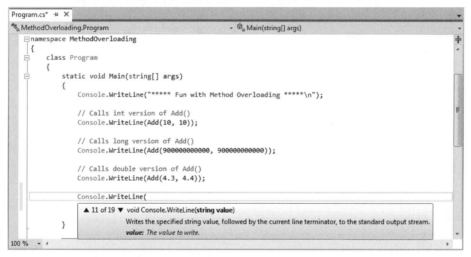

Figure 4-1. *Visual Studio IntelliSense for overloaded methods*

■ **Source Code** The MethodOverloading application is located under the Chapter 4 subdirectory.

That wraps up our initial examination of building methods using the syntax of C#. Next, let's check out how to build and manipulate arrays, enumerations, and structures.

Understanding C# Arrays

As I would guess you are already aware, an *array* is a set of data items, accessed using a numerical index.
More specifically, an array is a set of contiguous data points of the same type (an array of ints, an array
of strings, an array of SportsCars, and so on). Declaring, filling, and accessing an array with C# is quite
straightforward. To illustrate, create a new Console Application project (named FunWithArrays) that
contains a helper method named SimpleArrays(), invoked from within Main():

```
class Program
{
  static void Main(string[] args)
  {
    Console.WriteLine("***** Fun with Arrays *****");
    SimpleArrays();
    Console.ReadLine();
  }

  static void SimpleArrays()
  {
    Console.WriteLine("=> Simple Array Creation.");
    // Create an array of ints containing 3 elements indexed 0, 1, 2
    int[] myInts = new int[3];

    // Create a 100 item string array, indexed 0 - 99
    string[] booksOnDotNet = new string[100];
    Console.WriteLine();
  }
}
```

Look closely at the previous code comments. When declaring a C# array using this syntax, the
number used in the array declaration represents the total number of items, not the upper bound. Also
note that the lower bound of an array always begins at 0. Thus, when you write int[] myInts = new
int[3], you end up with an array holding three elements, indexed at positions 0, 1, 2.

After you have defined an array variable, you are then able to fill the elements index by index as
shown in the updated SimpleArrays() method:

```
static void SimpleArrays()
{
  Console.WriteLine("=> Simple Array Creation.");
  // Create and fill an array of 3 Integers
  int[] myInts = new int[3];
  myInts[0] = 100;
  myInts[1] = 200;
  myInts[2] = 300;

  // Now print each value.
  foreach(int i in myInts)
    Console.WriteLine(i);
  Console.WriteLine();
}
```

■ **Note** Do be aware that if you declare an array, but do not explicitly fill each index, each item will be set to the default value of the data type (e.g., an array of `bools` will be set to `false` or an array of `ints` will be set to 0).

C# Array Initialization Syntax

In addition to filling an array element by element, you are also able to fill the items of an array using C# *array initialization syntax*. To do so, specify each array item within the scope of curly brackets ({}). This syntax can be helpful when you are creating an array of a known size and wish to quickly specify the initial values. For example, consider the following alternative array declarations:

```
static void ArrayInitialization()
{
  Console.WriteLine("=> Array Initialization.");

  // Array initialization syntax using the new keyword.
  string[] stringArray = new string[]
    { "one", "two", "three" };
  Console.WriteLine("stringArray has {0} elements", stringArray.Length);

  // Array initialization syntax without using the new keyword.
  bool[] boolArray = { false, false, true };
  Console.WriteLine("boolArray has {0} elements", boolArray.Length);

  // Array initialization with new keyword and size.
  int[] intArray = new int[4] { 20, 22, 23, 0 };
  Console.WriteLine("intArray has {0} elements", intArray.Length);
  Console.WriteLine();
}
```

Notice that when you make use of this "curly bracket" syntax, you do not need to specify the size of the array (seen when constructing the `stringArray` variable), given that this will be inferred by the number of items within the scope of the curly brackets. Also notice that use of the new keyword is optional (shown when constructing the `boolArray` type).

In the case of the `intArray` declaration, again recall the numeric value specified represents the number of elements in the array, not the value of the upper bound. If there is a mismatch between the declared size and the number of initializers (whether you have too many or too few initializers), you are issued a compile-time error. The following is an example:

```
// OOPS! Mismatch of size and elements!
int[] intArray = new int[2] { 20, 22, 23, 0 };
```

Implicitly Typed Local Arrays

In Chapter 3, you learned about the topic of implicitly typed local variables. Recall that the var keyword allows you to define a variable, whose underlying type is determined by the compiler. In a similar vein, the var keyword can be used to define *implicitly typed local arrays*. Using this technique, you can allocate a new array variable without specifying the type contained within the array itself:

```
static void DeclareImplicitArrays()
{
  Console.WriteLine("=> Implicit Array Initialization.");

  // a is really int[].
  var a = new[] { 1, 10, 100, 1000 };
  Console.WriteLine("a is a: {0}", a.ToString());

  // b is really double[].
  var b = new[] { 1, 1.5, 2, 2.5 };
  Console.WriteLine("b is a: {0}", b.ToString());

  // c is really string[].
  var c = new[] { "hello", null, "world" };
  Console.WriteLine("c is a: {0}", c.ToString());
  Console.WriteLine();
}
```

Of course, just as when you allocate an array using explicit C# syntax, the items in the array's initialization list must be of the same underlying type (e.g., all ints, all strings, or all SportsCars). Unlike what you might be expecting, an implicitly typed local array does not default to System.Object; thus, the following generates a compile-time error:

```
// Error! Mixed types!
var d = new[] { 1, "one", 2, "two", false };
```

Defining an Array of Objects

In most cases, when you define an array, you do so by specifying the explicit type of item that can be within the array variable. While this seems quite straightforward, there is one notable twist. As you will come to understand in Chapter 6, System.Object is the ultimate base class to each and every type (including fundamental data types) in the .NET type system. Given this fact, if you were to define an array of System.Object data types, the subitems could be anything at all. Consider the following ArrayOfObjects() method (which again can be invoked from Main() for testing):

```
static void ArrayOfObjects()
{
  Console.WriteLine("=> Array of Objects.");

  // An array of objects can be anything at all.
  object[] myObjects = new object[4];
  myObjects[0] = 10;
  myObjects[1] = false;
  myObjects[2] = new DateTime(1969, 3, 24);
  myObjects[3] = "Form & Void";
  foreach (object obj in myObjects)
  {
    // Print the type and value for each item in array.
    Console.WriteLine("Type: {0}, Value: {1}", obj.GetType(), obj);
  }
  Console.WriteLine();
}
```

Here, as you are iterating over the contents of myObjects, you print out the underlying type of each item using the GetType() method of System.Object, as well as the value of the current item. Without going into too much detail regarding System.Object.GetType() at this point in the text, simply understand that this method can be used to obtain the fully qualified name of the item (Chapter 15 examines the topic of type information and reflection services in detail). The following output shows the result of calling ArrayOfObjects().

```
=> Array of Objects.
Type: System.Int32, Value: 10
Type: System.Boolean, Value: False
Type: System.DateTime, Value: 3/24/1969 12:00:00 AM
Type: System.String, Value: Form & Void
```

Working with Multidimensional Arrays

In addition to the single-dimension arrays you have seen thus far, C# also supports two varieties of multidimensional arrays. The first of these is termed a *rectangular array*, which is simply an array of multiple dimensions, where each row is of the same length. To declare and fill a multidimensional rectangular array, proceed as follows:

```
static void RectMultidimensionalArray()
{
  Console.WriteLine("=> Rectangular multidimensional array.");
  // A rectangular MD array.
  int[,] myMatrix;
  myMatrix = new int[6,6];

  // Populate (6 * 6) array.
  for(int i = 0; i < 6; i++)
    for(int j = 0; j < 6; j++)
      myMatrix[i, j] = i * j;

  // Print (6 * 6) array.
  for(int i = 0; i < 6; i++)
  {
    for(int j = 0; j < 6; j++)
      Console.Write(myMatrix[i, j] + "\t");
    Console.WriteLine();
  }
  Console.WriteLine();
}
```

The second type of multidimensional array is termed a *jagged array*. As the name implies, jagged arrays contain some number of inner arrays, each of which may have a different upper limit. For example:

```
static void JaggedMultidimensionalArray()
{
  Console.WriteLine("=> Jagged multidimensional array.");
  // A jagged MD array (i.e., an array of arrays).
  // Here we have an array of 5 different arrays.
```

```csharp
int[][] myJagArray = new int[5][];

// Create the jagged array.
for (int i = 0; i < myJagArray.Length; i++)
  myJagArray[i] = new int[i + 7];

// Print each row (remember, each element is defaulted to zero!).
for(int i = 0; i < 5; i++)
{
  for(int j = 0; j < myJagArray[i].Length; j++)
    Console.Write(myJagArray[i][j] + " ");
  Console.WriteLine();
}
Console.WriteLine();
}
```

Figure 4-2 shows the output of calling each of the RectMultidimensionalArray() and JaggedMultidimensionalArray() methods within Main().

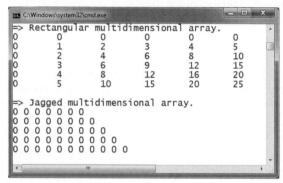

Figure 4-2. *Rectangular and jagged multidimensional arrays*

Arrays As Arguments or Return Values

After you have created an array, you are free to pass it as an argument or receive it as a member return value. For example, the following PrintArray() method takes an incoming array of ints and prints each member to the console, while the GetStringArray() method populates an array of strings and returns it to the caller:

```csharp
static void PrintArray(int[] myInts)
{
  for(int i = 0; i < myInts.Length; i++)
    Console.WriteLine("Item {0} is {1}", i, myInts[i]);
}

static string[] GetStringArray()
{
  string[] theStrings = {"Hello", "from", "GetStringArray"};
  return theStrings;
}
```

These methods may be invoked as you would expect:

```
static void PassAndReceiveArrays()
{
  Console.WriteLine("=> Arrays as params and return values.");
  // Pass array as parameter.
  int[] ages = {20, 22, 23, 0} ;
  PrintArray(ages);

  // Get array as return value.
  string[] strs = GetStringArray();
  foreach(string s in strs)
    Console.WriteLine(s);

  Console.WriteLine();
}
```

At this point, hopefully you feel comfortable with the process of defining, filling, and examining the contents of a C# array variable. To complete the picture, let's now examine the role of the System.Array class.

The System.Array Base Class

Every array you create gathers much of its functionality from the System.Array class. Using these common members, you are able to operate on an array using a consistent object model. Table 4-2 gives a rundown of some of the more interesting members (be sure to check the .NET Framework 4.5 SDK documentation for full details).

Table 4-2. Select Members of System.Array

Member of Array Class	Meaning in Life
Clear()	This static method sets a range of elements in the array to empty values (0 for numbers, null for object references, false for booleans).
CopyTo()	This method is used to copy elements from the source array into the destination array.
Length	This property returns the number of items within the array.
Rank	This property returns the number of dimensions of the current array.
Reverse()	This static method reverses the contents of a one-dimensional array.
Sort()	This static method sorts a one-dimensional array of intrinsic types. If the elements in the array implement the IComparer interface, you can also sort your custom types (see Chapter 9).

Let's see some of these members in action. The following helper method makes use of the static Reverse() and Clear() methods to pump out information about an array of string types to the console:

```
static void SystemArrayFunctionality()
{
  Console.WriteLine("=> Working with System.Array.");
  // Initialize items at startup.
  string[] gothicBands = {"Tones on Tail", "Bauhaus", "Sisters of Mercy"};

  // Print out names in declared order.
  Console.WriteLine("-> Here is the array:");
  for (int i = 0; i < gothicBands.Length; i++)
  {
    // Print a name.
    Console.Write(gothicBands[i] + ", ");
  }
  Console.WriteLine("\n");

  // Reverse them...
  Array.Reverse(gothicBands);
  Console.WriteLine("-> The reversed array");
  // ... and print them.
  for (int i = 0; i < gothicBands.Length; i++)
  {
    // Print a name.
    Console.Write(gothicBands[i] + ", ");
  }
  Console.WriteLine("\n");

  // Clear out all but the final member.
  Console.WriteLine("-> Cleared out all but one...");
  Array.Clear(gothicBands, 1, 2);
  for (int i = 0; i < gothicBands.Length; i++)
  {
    // Print a name.
    Console.Write(gothicBands[i] + ", ");
  }
  Console.WriteLine();
}
```

If you invoke this method from within Main(), you will get the output shown here:

```
=> Working with System.Array.
-> Here is the array:
Tones on Tail, Bauhaus, Sisters of Mercy,

-> The reversed array
Sisters of Mercy, Bauhaus, Tones on Tail,

-> Cleared out all but one...
Sisters of Mercy, , ,
```

Notice that many members of System.Array are defined as static members and are, therefore, called at the class level (for example, the Array.Sort() or Array.Reverse() methods). Methods such as these are passed in the array you wish to process. Other methods of System.Array (such as the Length property) are bound at the object level, thus you are able to invoke the member directly on the array.

■ **Source Code** The FunWithArrays application is located under the Chapter 4 subdirectory.

Understanding the enum Type

Recall from Chapter 1 that the .NET type system is composed of classes, structures, enumerations, interfaces, and delegates. To begin exploration of these types, let's check out the role of the *enumeration* (or simply, enum) using a new Console Application project named FunWithEnums.

■ **Note** Do not confuse the term "enum" with "enumerator"; they are completely different concepts. An enum is a custom data type of name/value pairs. An enumerator is a class or structure that implements a .NET interface named IEnumerable. Typically, this interface is implemented on collection classes, as well as the System.Array class. As you will see later in Chapter 8, objects that support IEnumerable can work within the foreach loop.

When building a system, it is often convenient to create a set of symbolic names that map to known numerical values. For example, if you are creating a payroll system, you might want to refer to the type of employees using constants such as vice president, manager, contractor, and grunt. C# supports the notion of custom enumerations for this very reason. For example, here is an enumeration named EmpType:

```
// A custom enumeration.
enum EmpType
{
  Manager,       // = 0
  Grunt,         // = 1
  Contractor,    // = 2
  VicePresident  // = 3
}
```

The EmpType enumeration defines four named constants, corresponding to discrete numerical values. By default, the first element is set to the value zero (0), followed by an n + 1 progression. You are free to change the initial value as you see fit. For example, if it made sense to number the members of EmpType as 102 through 105, you could do so as follows:

```
// Begin with 102.
enum EmpType
{
  Manager = 102,
  Grunt,         // = 103
```

```
  Contractor,   // = 104
  VicePresident // = 105
}
```

Enumerations do not necessarily need to follow a sequential ordering, and need not have unique values. If (for some reason or another) it makes sense to establish your EmpType as shown here, the compiler continues to be happy:

```
// Elements of an enumeration need not be sequential!
enum EmpType
{
  Manager = 10,
  Grunt = 1,
  Contractor = 100,
  VicePresident = 9
}
```

Controlling the Underlying Storage for an enum

By default, the storage type used to hold the values of an enumeration is a System.Int32 (the C# int); however, you are free to change this to your liking. C# enumerations can be defined in a similar manner for any of the core system types (byte, short, int, or long). For example, if you want to set the underlying storage value of EmpType to be a byte rather than an int, you can write the following:

```
// This time, EmpType maps to an underlying byte.
enum EmpType : byte
{
  Manager = 10,
  Grunt = 1,
  Contractor = 100,
  VicePresident = 9
}
```

Changing the underlying type of an enumeration can be helpful if you are building a .NET application that will be deployed to a low-memory device (such as a Windows Phone 7 device) and need to conserve memory wherever possible. Of course, if you do establish your enumeration to use a byte as storage, each value must be within its range! For example, the following version of EmpType will result in a compiler error, as the value 999 cannot fit within the range of a byte:

```
// Compile-time error!  999 is too big for a byte!
enum EmpType : byte
{
  Manager = 10,
  Grunt = 1,
  Contractor = 100,
  VicePresident = 999
}
```

Declaring enum Variables

Once you have established the range and storage type of your enumeration, you can use it in place of so-called "magic numbers." Because enumerations are nothing more than a user-defined data type, you are able to use them as function return values, method parameters, local variables, and so forth. Assume you have a method named AskForBonus(), taking an EmpType variable as the sole parameter. Based on the value of the incoming parameter, you will print out a fitting response to the pay bonus request:

```
class Program
{
  static void Main(string[] args)
  {
    Console.WriteLine("**** Fun with Enums *****");
    // Make a contractor type.
    EmpType emp = EmpType.Contractor;
    AskForBonus(emp);
    Console.ReadLine();
  }

  // Enums as parameters.
  static void AskForBonus(EmpType e)
  {
    switch (e)
    {
      case EmpType.Manager:
        Console.WriteLine("How about stock options instead?");
      break;
      case EmpType.Grunt:
        Console.WriteLine("You have got to be kidding...");
      break;
      case EmpType.Contractor:
        Console.WriteLine("You already get enough cash...");
      break;
      case EmpType.VicePresident:
        Console.WriteLine("VERY GOOD, Sir!");
      break;
    }
  }
}
```

Notice that when you are assigning a value to an enum variable, you must scope the enum name (EmpType) to the value (Grunt). Because enumerations are a fixed set of name/value pairs, it is illegal to set an enum variable to a value that is not defined directly by the enumerated type:

```
static void ThisMethodWillNotCompile()
{
  // Error! SalesManager is not in the EmpType enum!
  EmpType emp = EmpType.SalesManager;

  // Error! Forgot to scope Grunt value to EmpType enum!
  emp = Grunt;
}
```

The System.Enum Type

The interesting thing about .NET enumerations is that they gain functionality from the System.Enum class type. This class defines a number of methods that allow you to interrogate and transform a given enumeration. One helpful method is the static Enum.GetUnderlyingType(), which as the name implies, returns the data type used to store the values of the enumerated type (System.Byte in the case of the current EmpType declaration).

```
static void Main(string[] args)
{
  Console.WriteLine("**** Fun with Enums *****");
  // Make a contractor type.
  EmpType emp = EmpType.Contractor;
  AskForBonus(emp);

  // Print storage for the enum.
  Console.WriteLine("EmpType uses a {0} for storage",
    Enum.GetUnderlyingType(emp.GetType()));
  Console.ReadLine();
}
```

If you were to consult the Visual Studio object browser, you would be able to verify that the Enum.GetUnderlyingType() method requires you to pass in a System.Type as the first parameter. As fully examined in Chapter 15, Type represents the metadata description of a given .NET entity.

One possible way to obtain metadata (as shown previously) is to use the GetType() method, which is common to all types in the .NET base class libraries. Another approach is to make use of the C# typeof operator. One benefit of doing so is that you do not need to have a variable of the entity you wish to obtain a metadata description of:

```
// This time use typeof to extract a Type.
Console.WriteLine("EmpType uses a {0} for storage",
    Enum.GetUnderlyingType(typeof(EmpType)));
```

Dynamically Discovering an enum's Name/Value Pairs

Beyond the Enum.GetUnderlyingType() method, all C# enumerations support a method named ToString(), which returns the string name of the current enumeration's value. The following code is an example:

```
static void Main(string[] args)
{
  Console.WriteLine("**** Fun with Enums *****");
  EmpType emp = EmpType.Contractor;
  AskForBonus(emp);

  // Prints out "emp is a Contractor".
  Console.WriteLine("emp is a {0}.", emp.ToString());
  Console.ReadLine();
}
```

If you are interested in discovering the value of a given enumeration variable, rather than its name, you can simply cast the enum variable against the underlying storage type. The following is an example:

```
static void Main(string[] args)
{
  Console.WriteLine("**** Fun with Enums *****");
  EmpType emp = EmpType.Contractor;
  ...

  // Prints out "Contractor = 100".
  Console.WriteLine("{0} = {1}", emp.ToString(), (byte)emp);
  Console.ReadLine();
}
```

■ **Note** The static `Enum.Format()` method provides a finer level of formatting options by specifying a desired format flag. Consult the .NET Framework 4.5 SDK documentation for full details of the `System.Enum.Format()` method.

`System.Enum` also defines another static method named `GetValues()`. This method returns an instance of `System.Array`. Each item in the array corresponds to a member of the specified enumeration. Consider the following method, which will print out each name/value pair within any enumeration you pass in as a parameter:

```
// This method will print out the details of any enum.
static void EvaluateEnum(System.Enum e)
{
  Console.WriteLine("=> Information about {0}", e.GetType().Name);

  Console.WriteLine("Underlying storage type: {0}",
    Enum.GetUnderlyingType(e.GetType()));
  // Get all name/value pairs for incoming parameter.
  Array enumData = Enum.GetValues(e.GetType());
  Console.WriteLine("This enum has {0} members.", enumData.Length);
  // Now show the string name and associated value, using the D format
  // flag (see Chapter 3).
  for(int i = 0; i < enumData.Length; i++)
  {
    Console.WriteLine("Name: {0}, Value: {0:D}",
      enumData.GetValue(i));
  }
  Console.WriteLine();
}
```

To test this new method, update your `Main()` method to create variables of several enumeration types declared in the `System` namespace (as well as an `EmpType` enumeration for good measure). The following code is an example:

```
static void Main(string[] args)
{
  Console.WriteLine("**** Fun with Enums *****");
  ...
```

```
  EmpType e2 = EmpType.Contractor;

  // These types are enums in the System namespace.
  DayOfWeek day = DayOfWeek.Monday;
  ConsoleColor cc = ConsoleColor.Gray;

  EvaluateEnum(e2);
  EvaluateEnum(day);
  EvaluateEnum(cc);
  Console.ReadLine();
}
```

The output is shown in Figure 4-3.

Figure 4-3. *Dynamically discovering name/value pairs of enumeration types*

As you will see over the course of this text, enumerations are used extensively throughout the .NET base class libraries. For example, ADO.NET makes use of numerous enumerations to represent the state of a database connection (e.g., opened or closed) or the state of a row in a DataTable (e.g., changed, new, or detached). Therefore, when you make use of any enumeration, always remember that you are able to interact with the name/value pairs using the members of System.Enum.

■ **Source Code** The FunWithEnums project is located under the Chapter 4 subdirectory.

Understanding the Structure Type

Now that you understand the role of enumeration types, let's examine the use of .NET *structures* (or simply *structs*). Structure types are well suited for modeling mathematical, geometrical, and other "atomic" entities in your application. A structure (like an enumeration) is a user-defined type; however, structures are not simply a collection of name/value pairs. Rather, structures are types that can contain any number of data fields and members that operate on these fields.

■ **Note** If you have a background in OOP, you can think of a structure as a "lightweight class type," given that structures provide a way to define a type that supports encapsulation, but cannot be used to build a family of related types. When you need to build a family of related types through inheritance, you will need to make use of class types.

On the surface, the process of defining and using structures is very simple, but as they say, the devil is in the details. To begin understanding the basics of structure types, create a new project named FunWithStructures. In C#, structures are defined using the struct keyword. Define a new structure named Point, which defines two member variables of type int and a set of methods to interact with said data:

```
struct Point
{
  // Fields of the structure.
  public int X;
  public int Y;

  // Add 1 to the (X, Y) position.
  public void Increment()
  {
    X++; Y++;
  }

  // Subtract 1 from the (X, Y) position.
  public void Decrement()
  {
    X--; Y--;
  }

  // Display the current position.
  public void Display()
  {
    Console.WriteLine("X = {0}, Y = {1}", X, Y);
```

```
  }
}
```

Here, you have defined your two integer fields (X and Y) using the public keyword, which is an access control modifier (Chapter 5 furthers this discussion). Declaring data with the public keyword ensures the caller has direct access to the data from a given Point variable (via the dot operator).

■ **Note** It is typically considered bad style to define public data within a class or structure. Rather, you will want to define *private* data, which can be accessed and changed using *public* properties. These details will be examined in Chapter 5.

Here is a Main() method that takes our Point type out for a test drive:

```
static void Main(string[] args)
{
  Console.WriteLine("***** A First Look at Structures *****\n");

  // Create an initial Point.
  Point myPoint;
  myPoint.X = 349;
  myPoint.Y = 76;
  myPoint.Display();

  // Adjust the X and Y values.
  myPoint.Increment();
  myPoint.Display();
  Console.ReadLine();
}
```

The output is as you would expect:

```
***** A First Look at Structures *****

X = 349, Y = 76
X = 350, Y = 77
```

Creating Structure Variables

When you want to create a structure variable, you have a variety of options. Here, you simply create a Point variable and assign each piece of public field data before invoking its members. If you do *not* assign each piece of public field data (X and Y in our case) before making use of the structure, you will receive a compiler error:

```
// Error! Did not assign Y value.
Point p1;
p1.X = 10;
```

```
p1.Display();

// OK! Both fields assigned before use.
Point p2;
p2.X = 10;
p2.Y = 10;
p2.Display();
```

As an alternative, we can create structure variables using the C# new keyword, which will invoke the structure's *default constructor*. By definition, a default constructor does not take any arguments. The benefit of invoking the default constructor of a structure is that each piece of field data is automatically set to its default value:

```
// Set all fields to default values
// using the default constructor.
Point p1 = new Point();

// Prints X=0,Y=0.
p1.Display();
```

It is also possible to design a structure with a *custom constructor*. This allows you to specify the values of field data upon variable creation, rather than having to set each data member field by field. Chapter 5 will provide a detailed examination of constructors; however, to illustrate, update the Point structure with the following code:

```
struct Point
{
  // Fields of the structure.
  public int X;
  public int Y;

  // A custom constructor.
  public Point(int XPos, int YPos)
  {
    X = XPos;
    Y = YPos;
  }
...
}
```

With this, we could now create Point variables, as follows:

```
// Call custom constructor.
Point p2 = new Point(50, 60);

// Prints X=50,Y=60.
p2.Display();
```

As mentioned, working with structures on the surface is quite simple. However, to deepen your understanding of this type, you need to explore the distinction between a .NET value type and a .NET reference type.

■ **Source Code** The FunWithStructures project is located under the Chapter 4 subdirectory.

Understanding Value Types and Reference Types

■ **Note** The following discussion of value types and reference types assumes that you have a background in object-oriented programming. If this is not the case, you might want to skip to the final section in this chapter, "Understanding C# Nullable Types," and return to this section after you have read Chapters 5 and 6.

Unlike arrays, strings, or enumerations, C# structures do not have an identically named representation in the .NET library (that is, there is no System.Structure class), but are implicitly derived from System.ValueType. Simply put, the role of System.ValueType is to ensure that the derived type (e.g., any structure) is allocated on the *stack,* rather than the garbage-collected *heap.* Simply put, data allocated on the stack can be created and destroyed very quickly, as its lifetime is determined by the defining scope. Heap allocated data, on the other hand, is monitored by the .NET garbage collector, and has a lifetime that is determined by a large number of factors, which will be examined in Chapter 13.

Functionally, the only purpose of System.ValueType is to override the virtual methods defined by System.Object to use value-based, versus reference-based, semantics. As you might know, overriding is the process of changing the implementation of a virtual (or possibly abstract) method defined within a base class. The base class of ValueType is System.Object. In fact, the instance methods defined by System.ValueType are identical to those of System.Object:

```
// Structures and enumerations implicitly extend System.ValueType.
public abstract class ValueType : object
{
  public virtual bool Equals(object obj);
  public virtual int GetHashCode();
  public Type GetType();
  public virtual string ToString();
}
```

Given the fact that value types are using value-based semantics, the lifetime of a structure (which includes all numerical data types [int, float], as well as any enum or structure) is very predictable. When a structure variable falls out of the defining scope, it is removed from memory immediately:

```
// Local structures are popped off
// the stack when a method returns.
static void LocalValueTypes()
{
  // Recall! "int" is really a System.Int32 structure.
  int i = 0;

  // Recall! Point is a structure type.
  Point p = new Point();
} // "i" and "p" popped off the stack here!
```

Value Types, References Types, and the Assignment Operator

When you assign one value type to another, a member-by-member copy of the field data is achieved. In the case of a simple data type such as System.Int32, the only member to copy is the numerical value. However, in the case of your Point, the X and Y values are copied into the new structure variable. To illustrate, create a new Console Application project named ValueAndReferenceTypes, then copy your previous Point definition into your new namespace. Next, add the following method to your Program type:

```
// Assigning two intrinsic value types results in
// two independent variables on the stack.
static void ValueTypeAssignment()
{
  Console.WriteLine("Assigning value types\n");

  Point p1 = new Point(10, 10);
  Point p2 = p1;

  // Print both points.
  p1.Display();
  p2.Display();

  // Change p1.X and print again. p2.X is not changed.
  p1.X = 100;
  Console.WriteLine("\n=> Changed p1.X\n");
  p1.Display();
  p2.Display();
}
```

Here, you have created a variable of type Point (named p1) that is then assigned to another Point (p2). Because Point is a value type, you have two copies of the MyPoint type on the stack, each of which can be independently manipulated. Therefore, when you change the value of p1.X, the value of p2.X is unaffected:

```
Assigning value types

X = 10, Y = 10
X = 10, Y = 10
=> Changed p1.X
X = 100, Y = 10
X = 10, Y = 10
```

In stark contrast to value types, when you apply the assignment operator to reference types (meaning all class instances), you are redirecting what the reference variable points to in memory. To illustrate, create a new class type named PointRef that has the exact same members as the Point structures, beyond renaming the constructor to match the class name:

```
// Classes are always reference types.
class PointRef
{
  // Same members as the Point structure...
```

```
// Be sure to change your constructor name to PointRef!
public PointRef(int XPos, int YPos)
{
  X = XPos;
  Y = YPos;
}
}
```

Now, make use of your PointRef type within the following new method. Note that beyond using the PointRef class, rather than the Point structure, the code is identical to the ValueTypeAssignment() method.

```
static void ReferenceTypeAssignment()
{
  Console.WriteLine("Assigning reference types\n");
  PointRef p1 = new PointRef(10, 10);
  PointRef p2 = p1;

  // Print both point refs.
  p1.Display();
  p2.Display();

  // Change p1.X and print again.
  p1.X = 100;
  Console.WriteLine("\n=> Changed p1.X\n");
  p1.Display();
  p2.Display();
}
```

In this case, you have two references pointing to the same object on the managed heap. Therefore, when you change the value of X using the p1 reference, p2.X reports the same value. Assuming you have called this new method within Main(), your output should look like the following:

```
Assigning reference types

X = 10, Y = 10
X = 10, Y = 10
=> Changed p1.X
X = 100, Y = 10
X = 100, Y = 10
```

Value Types Containing Reference Types

Now that you have a better feeling for the basic differences between value types and reference types, let's examine a more complex example. Assume you have the following reference (class) type that maintains an informational string that can be set using a custom constructor:

```
class ShapeInfo
{
  public string infoString;
```

```
  public ShapeInfo(string info)
  {
    infoString = info;
  }
}
```

Now assume that you want to contain a variable of this class type within a value type named Rectangle. To allow the caller to set the value of the inner ShapeInfo member variable, you also provide a custom constructor. Here is the complete definition of the Rectangle type:

```
struct Rectangle
{
  // The Rectangle structure contains a reference type member.
  public ShapeInfo rectInfo;

  public int rectTop, rectLeft, rectBottom, rectRight;

  public Rectangle(string info, int top, int left, int bottom, int right)
  {
    rectInfo = new ShapeInfo(info);
    rectTop = top;   rectBottom = bottom;
    rectLeft = left; rectRight = right;
  }

  public void Display()
  {
    Console.WriteLine("String = {0}, Top = {1}, Bottom = {2}, " +
      "Left = {3}, Right = {4}",
      rectInfo.infoString, rectTop, rectBottom, rectLeft, rectRight);
  }
}
```

At this point, you have contained a reference type within a value type. The million dollar question now becomes, what happens if you assign one Rectangle variable to another? Given what you already know about value types, you would be correct in assuming that the integer data (which is indeed a structure- System.Int32) should be an independent entity for each Rectangle variable. But what about the internal reference type? Will the object's *state* be fully copied, or will the reference to that object be copied? To answer this question, define the following method and invoke it from Main():

```
static void ValueTypeContainingRefType()
{
  // Create the first Rectangle.
  Console.WriteLine("-> Creating r1");
  Rectangle r1 = new Rectangle("First Rect", 10, 10, 50, 50);

  // Now assign a new Rectangle to r1.
  Console.WriteLine("-> Assigning r2 to r1");
  Rectangle r2 = r1;

  // Change some values of r2.
  Console.WriteLine("-> Changing values of r2");
  r2.rectInfo.infoString = "This is new info!";
  r2.rectBottom = 4444;
```

```
// Print values of both rectangles.
  r1.Display();
  r2.Display();
}
```

The output can be seen in the following:

```
-> Creating r1
-> Assigning r2 to r1
-> Changing values of r2
String = This is new info!, Top = 10, Bottom = 50, Left = 10, Right = 50
String = This is new info!, Top = 10, Bottom = 4444, Left = 10, Right = 50
```

As you can see, when you change the value of the informational string using the r2 reference, the r1 reference displays the same value. By default, when a value type contains other reference types, assignment results in a copy of the references. In this way, you have two independent structures, each of which contains a reference pointing to the same object in memory (i.e., a shallow copy). When you want to perform a deep copy, where the state of internal references is fully copied into a new object, one approach is to implement the ICloneable interface (as you will do in Chapter 8).

■ **Source Code** The ValueAndReferenceTypes project is located under the Chapter 4 subdirectory.

Passing Reference Types by Value

Reference types or value types can, obviously, be passed as parameters to methods. However, passing a reference type (e.g., a class) by reference is quite different from passing it by value. To understand the distinction, assume you have a simple Person class defined in a new Console Application project named RefTypeValTypeParams, defined as follows:

```
class Person
{
  public string personName;
  public int personAge;

  // Constructors.
  public Person(string name, int age)
  {
    personName = name;
    personAge = age;
  }
  public Person(){}

  public void Display()
  {
    Console.WriteLine("Name: {0}, Age: {1}", personName, personAge);
  }
```

```
}
```

Now, what if you create a method that allows the caller to send in the Person object by value (note the lack of parameter modifiers, such as out or ref):

```
static void SendAPersonByValue(Person p)
{
  // Change the age of "p"?
  p.personAge = 99;

  // Will the caller see this reassignment?
  p = new Person("Nikki", 99);
}
```

Notice how the SendAPersonByValue() method attempts to reassign the incoming Person reference to a new Person object, as well as change some state data. Now let's test this method using the following Main() method:

```
static void Main(string[] args)
{
  // Passing ref-types by value.
  Console.WriteLine("***** Passing Person object by value *****");
  Person fred = new Person("Fred", 12);
  Console.WriteLine("\nBefore by value call, Person is:");
  fred.Display();

  SendAPersonByValue(fred);
  Console.WriteLine("\nAfter by value call, Person is:");
  fred.Display();
  Console.ReadLine();
}
```

The following is the output of this call:

```
***** Passing Person object by value *****

Before by value call, Person is:
Name: Fred, Age: 12

After by value call, Person is:
Name: Fred, Age: 99
```

As you can see, the value of personAge has been modified. This behavior seems to fly in the face of what it means to pass a parameter "by value." Given that you were able to change the state of the incoming Person, what was copied? The answer: a copy of the reference to the caller's object. Therefore, as the SendAPersonByValue() method is pointing to the same object as the caller, it is possible to alter the object's state data. What is not possible is to reassign what the reference *is pointing to*.

Passing Reference Types by Reference

Now assume you have a SendAPersonByReference() method, which passes a reference type by reference (note the ref parameter modifier):

```
static void SendAPersonByReference(ref Person p)
{
  // Change some data of "p".
  p.personAge = 555;

  // "p" is now pointing to a new object on the heap!
  p = new Person("Nikki", 999);
}
```

As you might expect, this allows complete flexibility of how the callee is able to manipulate the incoming parameter. Not only can the callee change the state of the object, but if it so chooses, it may also reassign the reference to a new Person object. Now ponder the following updated Main() method:

```
static void Main(string[] args)
{
  // Passing ref-types by ref.
  Console.WriteLine("***** Passing Person object by reference *****");
  ...

  Person mel = new Person("Mel", 23);
  Console.WriteLine("Before by ref call, Person is:");
  mel.Display();

  SendAPersonByReference(ref mel);
  Console.WriteLine("After by ref call, Person is:");
  mel.Display();
  Console.ReadLine();
}
```

Notice the following output:

```
***** Passing Person object by reference *****
Before by ref call, Person is:
Name: Mel, Age: 23
After by ref call, Person is:
Name: Nikki, Age: 999
```

As you can see, an object named Mel returns after the call as an object named Nikki, as the method was able to change what the incoming reference pointed to in memory. The golden rule to keep in mind when passing reference types is the following:

- If a reference type is passed by reference, the callee may change the values of the object's state data, as well as the object it is referencing.

- If a reference type is passed by value, the callee may change the values of the object's state data, but *not* the object it is referencing.

■ **Source Code** The RefTypeValTypeParams project is located under the Chapter 4 subdirectory.

Final Details Regarding Value Types and Reference Types

To wrap up this topic, consider the information in Table 4-3, which summarizes the core distinctions between value types and reference types.

Table 4-3. *Value Types and Reference Types Comparison*

Intriguing Question	Value Type	Reference Type
Where are objects allocated?	Allocated on the stack.	Allocated on the managed heap.
How is a variable represented?	Value type variables are local copies.	Reference type variables are pointing to the memory occupied by the allocated instance.
What is the base type?	Implicitly extends `System.ValueType`.	Can derive from any other type (except `System.ValueType`), as long as that type is not "sealed" (more details on this in Chapter 6).
Can this type function as a base to other types?	No. Value types are always sealed and cannot be inherited from.	Yes. If the type is not sealed, it may function as a base to other types.
What is the default parameter passing behavior?	Variables are passed by value (i.e., a copy of the variable is passed into the called function).	For value types, the object is copied-by-value. For reference types, the reference is copied-by-value.
Can this type override `System.Object.Finalize()`?	No. Value types are never placed onto the heap and, therefore, do not need to be finalized.	Yes, indirectly (more details on this in Chapter 13).
Can I define constructors for this type?	Yes, but the default constructor is reserved (i.e., your custom constructors must all have arguments).	But, of course!
When do variables of this type die?	When they fall out of the defining scope.	When the object is garbage collected.

Despite their differences, value types and reference types both have the ability to implement interfaces and may support any number of fields, methods, overloaded operators, constants, properties, and events.

Understanding C# Nullable Types

To wrap up this chapter, let's examine the role of *nullable data type* using a final Console Application named NullableTypes. As you know, C# data types have a fixed range and are represented as a type in the System namespace. For example, the System.Boolean data type can be assigned a value from the set {true, false}. Now, recall that all of the numerical data types (as well as the Boolean data type) are *value types*. Value types can never be assigned the value of null, as that is used to establish an empty object reference:

```
static void Main(string[] args)
{
  // Compiler errors!
  // Value types cannot be set to null!
  bool myBool = null;
  int myInt = null;

  // OK! Strings are reference types.
  string myString = null;
}
```

C# supports the concept of *nullable data types*. Simply put, a nullable type can represent all the values of its underlying type, plus the value null. Thus, if we declare a nullable bool, it could be assigned a value from the set {true, false, null}. This can be extremely helpful when working with relational databases, given that it is quite common to encounter undefined columns in database tables. Without the concept of a nullable data type, there is no convenient manner in C# to represent a numerical data point with no value.

To define a nullable variable type, the question mark symbol (?) is suffixed to the underlying data type. Do note that this syntax is only legal when applied to value types. If you attempt to create a nullable reference type (including strings), you are issued a compile-time error. Like a nonnullable variable, local nullable variables must be assigned an initial value before you can use them:

```
static void LocalNullableVariables()
{
  // Define some local nullable variables.
  int? nullableInt = 10;
  double? nullableDouble = 3.14;
  bool? nullableBool = null;
  char? nullableChar = 'a';
  int?[] arrayOfNullableInts = new int?[10];

  // Error! Strings are reference types!
  // string? s = "oops";
}
```

In C#, the ? suffix notation is a shorthand for creating an instance of the generic System.Nullable<T> structure type. Although we will not examine generics until Chapter 9, it is important to understand that the System.Nullable<T> type provides a set of members that all nullable types can make use of.

For example, you are able to programmatically discover whether the nullable variable indeed has been assigned a null value using the HasValue property or the != operator. The assigned value of a nullable type may be obtained directly or via the Value property. In fact, given that the ? suffix is just a shorthand for using Nullable<T>, you could implement your LocalNullableVariables() method as follows:

```
static void LocalNullableVariablesUsingNullable()
{
  // Define some local nullable types using Nullable<T>.
  Nullable<int> nullableInt = 10;
  Nullable<double> nullableDouble = 3.14;
  Nullable<bool> nullableBool = null;
  Nullable<char> nullableChar = 'a';
  Nullable<int>[] arrayOfNullableInts = new int?[10];
}
```

Working with Nullable Types

As stated, nullable data types can be particularly useful when you are interacting with databases, given that columns in a data table may be intentionally empty (e.g., undefined). To illustrate, assume the following class, which simulates the process of accessing a database that has a table containing two columns that may be null. Note that the GetIntFromDatabase() method is not assigning a value to the nullable integer member variable, while GetBoolFromDatabase() is assigning a valid value to the bool? member:

```
class DatabaseReader
{
  // Nullable data field.
  public int? numericValue = null;
  public bool? boolValue = true;

  // Note the nullable return type.
  public int? GetIntFromDatabase()
  { return numericValue; }

  // Note the nullable return type.
  public bool? GetBoolFromDatabase()
  { return boolValue; }
}
```

Now, assume the following Main() method, which invokes each member of the DatabaseReader class, and discovers the assigned values using the HasValue and Value members, as well as using the C# equality operator (not equal, to be exact):

```
static void Main(string[] args)
{
  Console.WriteLine("***** Fun with Nullable Data *****\n");
  DatabaseReader dr = new DatabaseReader();

  // Get int from "database".
  int? i = dr.GetIntFromDatabase();
  if (i.HasValue)
    Console.WriteLine("Value of 'i' is: {0}", i.Value);
```

```
  else
    Console.WriteLine("Value of 'i' is undefined.");

  // Get bool from "database".
  bool? b = dr.GetBoolFromDatabase();
  if (b != null)
    Console.WriteLine("Value of 'b' is: {0}", b.Value);
  else
    Console.WriteLine("Value of 'b' is undefined.");
  Console.ReadLine();
}
```

The ?? Operator

The final aspect to be aware of with nullable types is that they can make use of the C# ?? operator. This operator allows you to assign a value to a nullable type if the retrieved value is in fact null. For this example, assume you want to assign a local nullable integer to 100 if the value returned from GetIntFromDatabase() is null (of course, this method is programmed to *always* return null, but I am sure you get the general idea):

```
static void Main(string[] args)
{
  Console.WriteLine("***** Fun with Nullable Data *****\n");
  DatabaseReader dr = new DatabaseReader();
...
  // If the value from GetIntFromDatabase() is null,
  // assign local variable to 100.
  int myData = dr.GetIntFromDatabase() ?? 100;
  Console.WriteLine("Value of myData: {0}", myData);
  Console.ReadLine();
}
```

The benefit of using the ?? operator is that it provides a more compact version of a traditional if/else condition. However, if you want, you could have authored the following functionally equivalent code to ensure that if a value comes back as null, it will indeed be set to the value 100:

```
// Long-hand notation not using ?? syntax.
int? moreData = dr.GetIntFromDatabase();
if (!moreData.HasValue)
    moreData = 100;
Console.WriteLine("Value of moreData: {0}", moreData);
```

With this, our initial investigation of the C# programming language is complete! In Chapter 5, you will begin to dig into the details of object-oriented development.

■ **Source Code** The NullableTypes application is located under the Chapter 4 subdirectory.

Summary

This chapter began with an examination of several C# keywords that allow you to build custom methods. Recall that by default, parameters are passed by value; however, you may pass a parameter by reference if you mark it with ref or out. You also learned about the role of optional or named parameters and how to define and invoke methods taking parameter arrays.

After we investigated the topic of method overloading, the bulk of this chapter examined several details regarding how arrays, enumerations, and structures are defined in C# and represented within the .NET base class libraries. Along the way, you examined several details regarding value types and reference types, including how they respond when passing them as parameters to methods, and how to interact with nullable data types using the ? and ?? operators.

■ ■ ■

## PART III

Object-Oriented Programming with C#

CHAPTER 5

Understanding Encapsulation

In the Chapters 3 and 4, you investigated a number of core syntactical constructs that are commonplace to any .NET application you might be developing. Here, you will begin your examination of the object-oriented capabilities of C#. The first order of business is to examine the process of building well-defined class types that support any number of *constructors*. After you understand the basics of defining classes and allocating objects, the remainder of this chapter will examine the role of *encapsulation*. Along the way, you will learn how to define class properties, and come to understand the role of static members, object initialization syntax, read-only fields, constant data, and partial classes.

Introducing the C# Class Type

As far as the .NET platform is concerned, the most fundamental programming construct is the *class type*. Formally, a class is a user-defined type that is composed of field data (often called *member variables*) and members that operate on this data (such as constructors, properties, methods, events, and so forth). Collectively, the set of field data represents the "state" of a class instance (otherwise known as an *object*). The power of object-oriented languages, such as C#, is that by grouping data and related functionality in a unified class definition, you are able to model your software after entities in the real world.

To get the ball rolling, create a new C# Console Application named SimpleClassExample. Next, insert a new class file (named Car.cs) into your project using the Project ➤ Add Class... menu selection. Choose the Class icon from the resulting dialog box, as shown in Figure 5-1, and click the Add button.

A class is defined in C# using the class keyword. Here is the simplest possible declaration:

```
class Car
{
}
```

After you have defined a class type, you will need to consider the set of member variables that will be used to represent its state. For example, you might decide that cars maintain an int data type to represent the current speed and a string data type to represent the car's friendly pet name. Given these initial design notes, update your Car class as follows:

```
class Car
{
  // The 'state' of the Car.
  public string petName;
  public int currSpeed;
}
```

Figure 5-1. *Inserting a new C# class type*

Notice that these member variables are declared using the public access modifier. Public members of a class are directly accessible once an object of this type has been created. Recall the term "object" is used to describe an instance of a given class type created using the new keyword.

■ **Note** Field data of a class should seldom (if ever) be defined as public. To preserve the integrity of your state data, it is a far better design to define data as private (or possibly protected) and allow controlled access to the data via properties (as shown later in this chapter). However, to keep this first example as simple as possible, public data fits the bill.

After you have defined the set of member variables that represent the state of the class, the next design step is to establish the members that model its behavior. For this example, the Car class will define one method named SpeedUp() and another named PrintState(). Update your class as so:

```
class Car
{
  // The 'state' of the Car.
  public string petName;
  public int currSpeed;

  // The functionality of the Car.
  public void PrintState()
  {
    Console.WriteLine("{0} is going {1} MPH.", petName, currSpeed);
  }
```

```
  public void SpeedUp(int delta)
  {
    currSpeed += delta;
  }
}
```

PrintState() is more or less a diagnostic function that will simply dump the current state of a given Car object to the command window. SpeedUp() will increase the speed of the Car by the amount specified by the incoming int parameter. Now, update your Main() method in the Program class with the following code:

```
static void Main(string[] args)
{
  Console.WriteLine("***** Fun with Class Types *****\n");

  // Allocate and configure a Car object.
  Car myCar = new Car();
  myCar.petName = "Henry";
  myCar.currSpeed = 10;

  // Speed up the car a few times and print out the
  // new state.
  for (int i = 0; i <= 10; i++)
  {
    myCar.SpeedUp(5);
    myCar.PrintState();
  }
  Console.ReadLine();
}
```

After you run your program, you will see that the Car variable (myCar) maintains its current state throughout the life of the application, as shown in the following code:

```
***** Fun with Class Types *****

Henry is going 15 MPH.
Henry is going 20 MPH.
Henry is going 25 MPH.
Henry is going 30 MPH.
Henry is going 35 MPH.
Henry is going 40 MPH.
Henry is going 45 MPH.
Henry is going 50 MPH.
Henry is going 55 MPH.
Henry is going 60 MPH.
Henry is going 65 MPH.
```

Allocating Objects with the new Keyword

As shown in the previous code example, objects must be allocated into memory using the new keyword. If you do not make use of the new keyword and attempt to make use of your class variable in a subsequent code statement, you will receive a compiler error. For example, the following Main() method will not compile:

```
static void Main(string[] args)
{
  Console.WriteLine("***** Fun with Class Types *****\n");

  // Error! Forgot to use 'new' to create object!
  Car myCar;
  myCar.petName = "Fred";
}
```

To correctly create an object using the new keyword, you may define and allocate a Car object on a single line of code:

```
static void Main(string[] args)
{
  Console.WriteLine("***** Fun with Class Types *****\n");
  Car myCar = new Car();
  myCar.petName = "Fred";
}
```

As an alternative, if you wish to define and allocate a class instance on separate lines of code, you may do so as follows:

```
static void Main(string[] args)
{
  Console.WriteLine("***** Fun with Class Types *****\n");
  Car.myCar;
  myCar = new Car();
  myCar.petName = "Fred";
}
```

Here, the first code statement simply declares a reference to a yet-to-be-determined Car object. It is not until you assign a reference to an object that this reference points to a valid object in memory.

In any case, at this point we have a trivial class that defines a few points of data and some basic operations. To enhance the functionality of the current Car class, we need to understand the role of *constructors*.

Understanding Constructors

Given that objects have state (represented by the values of an object's member variables), a programmer will typically want to assign relevant values to the object's field data before use. Currently, the Car class demands that the petName and currSpeed fields be assigned on a field-by-field basis. For the current example, this is not too problematic, given that we have only two public data points. However, it is not uncommon for a class to have dozens of fields to contend with. Clearly, it would be undesirable to author 20 initialization statements to set 20 points of data!

Thankfully, C# supports the use of *constructors*, which allow the state of an object to be established at the time of creation. A constructor is a special method of a class that is called indirectly when creating an object using the new keyword. However, unlike a "normal" method, constructors never have a return value (not even void) and are always named identically to the class they are constructing.

The Role of the Default Constructor

Every C# class is provided with a freebee *default constructor* that you may redefine if need be. By definition, a default constructor never takes arguments. After allocating the new object into memory, the default constructor ensures that all field data of the class is set to an appropriate default value (see Chapter 3 for information regarding the default values of C# data types).

If you are not satisfied with these default assignments, you may redefine the default constructor to suit your needs. To illustrate, update your C# Car class as follows:

```
class Car
{
  // The 'state' of the Car.
  public string petName;
  public int currSpeed;

  // A custom default constructor.
  public Car()
  {
    petName = "Chuck";
    currSpeed = 10;
  }
...
}
```

In this case, we are forcing all Car objects to begin life named Chuck at a rate of 10 mph. With this, you are able to create a Car object set to these default values as follows:

```
static void Main(string[] args)
{
  Console.WriteLine("***** Fun with Class Types *****\n");

  // Invoking the default constructor.
  Car chuck = new Car();

  // Prints "Chuck is going 10 MPH."
  chuck.PrintState();
...
}
```

Defining Custom Constructors

Typically, classes define additional constructors beyond the default. In doing so, you provide the object user with a simple and consistent way to initialize the state of an object directly at the time of creation. Ponder the following update to the Car class, which now supports a total of three constructors:

```
class Car
{
  // The 'state' of the Car.
  public string petName;
```

```
  public int currSpeed;

  // A custom default constructor.
  public Car()
  {
    petName = "Chuck";
    currSpeed = 10;
  }

  // Here, currSpeed will receive the
  // default value of an int (zero).
  public Car(string pn)
  {
    petName = pn;
  }

  // Let caller set the full state of the Car.
  public Car(string pn, int cs)
  {
    petName = pn;
    currSpeed = cs;
  }
...
}
```

Keep in mind that what makes one constructor different from another (in the eyes of the C# compiler) is the number of and type of constructor arguments. Recall from Chapter 4, when you define a method of the same name that differs by the number or type of arguments, you have *overloaded* the method. Thus, the Car class has overloaded the constructor to provide a number of ways to create an object at the time of declaration. In any case, you are now able to create Car objects using any of the public constructors. For example:

```
static void Main(string[] args)
{
  Console.WriteLine("***** Fun with Class Types *****\n");

  // Make a Car called Chuck going 10 MPH.
  Car chuck = new Car();
  chuck.PrintState();

  // Make a Car called Mary going 0 MPH.
  Car mary = new Car("Mary");
  mary.PrintState();

  // Make a Car called Daisy going 75 MPH.
  Car daisy = new Car("Daisy", 75);
  daisy.PrintState();
...
}
```

The Default Constructor Revisited

As you have just learned, all classes are provided with a free default constructor. Thus, if you insert a new class into your current project named Motorcycle, defined like so:

```
class Motorcycle
{
  public void PopAWheely()
  {
    Console.WriteLine("Yeeeeeee Haaaaaeewww!");
  }
}
```

you are able to create an instance of the Motorcycle type via the default constructor out of the box:

```
static void Main(string[] args)
{
  Console.WriteLine("***** Fun with Class Types *****\n");
  Motorcycle mc = new Motorcycle();
  mc.PopAWheely();
...
}
```

However, as soon as you define a custom constructor with any number of parameters, the default constructor is silently removed from the class and is no longer available! Think of it this way: if you do not define a custom constructor, the C# compiler grants you a default in order to allow the object user to allocate an instance of your type with field data set to the correct default values. However, when you define a unique constructor, the compiler assumes you have taken matters into your own hands.

Therefore, if you wish to allow the object user to create an instance of your type with the default constructor, as well as your custom constructor, you must *explicitly* redefine the default. To this end, understand that in a vast majority of cases, the implementation of the default constructor of a class is intentionally empty, as all you require is the ability to create an object with default values. Consider the following update to the Motorcycle class:

```
class Motorcycle
{
  public int driverIntensity;

  public void PopAWheely()
  {
    for (int i = 0; i <= driverIntensity; i++)
    {
      Console.WriteLine("Yeeeeeee Haaaaaeewww!");
    }
  }

  // Put back the default constructor, which will
  // set all data members to default vaules.
  public Motorcycle() {}

  // Our custom constructor.
  public Motorcycle(int intensity)
  {
```

```
    driverIntensity = intensity;
  }
}
```

■ **Note** Now that you better understand the role of class constructors, here is a nice short cut. The Visual Studio IDE provides the `ctor` code snippet. When you type "ctor" and press the Tab key twice, the IDE will automatically define a custom default constructor! You can then add custom parameters and implementation logic. Give it a try.

The Role of the this Keyword

C# supplies a this keyword that provides access to the current class instance. One possible use of the this keyword is to resolve scope ambiguity, which can arise when an incoming parameter is named identically to a data field of the class. Of course, ideally you would simply adopt a naming convention that does not result in such ambiguity; however, to illustrate this use of the this keyword, update your Motorcycle class with a new string field (named name) to represent the driver's name. Next, add a method named SetDriverName() implemented as follows:

```
class Motorcycle
{
  public int driverIntensity;

  // New members to represent the name of the driver.
  public string name;
  public void SetDriverName(string name)
  {
    name = name;
  }
...
}
```

Although this code will compile just fine, Visual Studio will display a warning message informing you that you have assigned a variable back to itself! To illustrate, update Main() to call SetDriverName() and then print out the value of the name field. You might be surprised to find that the value of the name field is an empty string!

```
// Make a Motorcycle with a rider named Tiny?
Motorcycle c = new Motorcycle(5);
c.SetDriverName("Tiny");
c.PopAWheely();
Console.WriteLine("Rider name is {0}", c.name); // Prints an empty name value!
```

The problem is that the implementation of SetDriverName() is assigning the incoming parameter *back to itself* given that the compiler assumes name is referring to the variable currently in the method scope rather than the name field at the class scope. To inform the compiler that you wish to set the current object's name data field to the incoming name parameter, simply use this to resolve the ambiguity:

```
public void SetDriverName(string name)
{
  this.name = name;
}
```

Do understand that if there is no ambiguity, you are not required to make use of the this keyword when a class wishes to access its own data fields or members, as this is implied. For example, if we rename the string data member from name to driverName (which will also require you to update your Main() method) the use of this is optional as there is no longer a scope ambiguity:

```
class Motorcycle
{
  public int driverIntensity;
  public string driverName;

  public void SetDriverName(string name)
  {
    // These two statements are functionally the same.
    driverName = name;
    this.driverName = name;
  }
...
}
```

Even though there is little to be gained when using this in unambiguous situations, you might still find this keyword useful when implementing class members, as IDEs such as SharpDevelop and Visual Studio will enable IntelliSense when this is specified. This can be very helpful when you have forgotten the name of a class member and want to quickly recall the definition. Consider Figure 5-2.

Figure 5-2. The IntelliSense of this

Chaining Constructor Calls Using this

Another use of the this keyword is to design a class using a technique termed *constructor chaining*. This design pattern is helpful when you have a class that defines multiple constructors. Given the fact that constructors often validate the incoming arguments to enforce various business rules, it can be quite common to find redundant validation logic within a class's constructor set. Consider the following updated Motorcycle:

```
class Motorcycle
{
  public int driverIntensity;
  public string driverName;

  public Motorcycle() { }

  // Redundent constructor logic!
  public Motorcycle(int intensity)
  {
    if (intensity > 10)
    {
      intensity = 10;
    }
    driverIntensity = intensity;
  }

  public Motorcycle(int intensity, string name)
  {
    if (intensity > 10)
    {
      intensity = 10;
    }
    driverIntensity = intensity;
    driverName = name;
  }
...
}
```

Here (perhaps in an attempt to ensure the safety of the rider) each constructor is ensuring that the intensity level is never greater than 10. While this is all well and good, you do have redundant code statements in two constructors. This is less than ideal, as you are now required to update code in multiple locations if your rules change (for example, if the intensity should not be greater than 5).

One way to improve the current situation is to define a method in the Motorcycle class that will validate the incoming argument(s). If you were to do so, each constructor could make a call to this method before making the field assignment(s). While this approach does allow you to isolate the code you need to update when the business rules change, you are now dealing with the following redundancy:

```
class Motorcycle
{
  public int driverIntensity;
  public string driverName;
```

```
// Constructors.
public Motorcycle() { }

public Motorcycle(int intensity)
{
  SetIntensity(intensity);
}

public Motorcycle(int intensity, string name)
{
  SetIntensity(intensity);
  driverName = name;
}

public void SetIntensity(int intensity)
{
  if (intensity > 10)
  {
    intensity = 10;
  }
  driverIntensity = intensity;
}
...
}
```

A cleaner approach is to designate the constructor that takes the *greatest number·of arguments* as the "master constructor" and have its implementation perform the required validation logic. The remaining constructors can make use of the this keyword to forward the incoming arguments to the master constructor and provide any additional parameters as necessary. In this way, you only need to worry about maintaining a single constructor for the entire class, while the remaining constructors are basically empty.

Here is the final iteration of the Motorcycle class (with one additional constructor for the sake of illustration). When chaining constructors, note how the this keyword is "dangling" off the constructor's declaration (via a colon operator) outside the scope of the constructor itself:

```
class Motorcycle
{
  public int driverIntensity;
  public string driverName;

  // Constructor chaining.
  public Motorcycle() {}
  public Motorcycle(int intensity)
    : this(intensity, "") {}
  public Motorcycle(string name)
    : this(0, name) {}

  // This is the 'master' constructor that does all the real work.
  public Motorcycle(int intensity, string name)
  {
    if (intensity > 10)
    {
```

```
      intensity = 10;
    }
    driverIntensity = intensity;
    driverName = name;
  }
...
}
```

Understand that using the this keyword to chain constructor calls is never mandatory. However, when you make use of this technique, you do tend to end up with a more maintainable and concise class definition. Again, using this technique you can simplify your programming tasks, as the real work is delegated to a single constructor (typically the constructor that has the most parameters), while the other constructors simply "pass the buck."

■ **Note** Recall from Chapter 4 that C# supports optional parameters. If you make use of optional parameters in your class constructors, you can achieve the same benefits as constructor chaining, with considerably less code. You will see how to do so in just a moment.

Observing Constructor Flow

On a final note, do know that once a constructor passes arguments to the designated master constructor (and that constructor has processed the data), the constructor invoked originally by the caller will finish executing any remaining code statements. To clarify, update each of the constructors of the Motorcycle class with a fitting call to Console.WriteLine():

```
class Motorcycle
{
  public int driverIntensity;
  public string driverName;

  // Constructor chaining.
  public Motorcycle()
  {
    Console.WriteLine("In default ctor");
  }

  public Motorcycle(int intensity)
    : this(intensity, "")
  {
    Console.WriteLine("In ctor taking an int");
  }

  public Motorcycle(string name)
    : this(0, name)
  {
    Console.WriteLine("In ctor taking a string");
  }
```

```
  // This is the 'master' constructor that does all the real work.
  public Motorcycle(int intensity, string name)
  {
    Console.WriteLine("In master ctor ");
    if (intensity > 10)
    {
      intensity = 10;
    }
    driverIntensity = intensity;
    driverName = name;
  }
...
}
```

Now, ensure your Main() method exercises a Motorcycle object as follows:

```
static void Main(string[] args)
{
  Console.WriteLine("***** Fun with class Types *****\n");

  // Make a Motorcycle.
  Motorcycle c = new Motorcycle(5);
  c.SetDriverName("Tiny");
  c.PopAWheely();
  Console.WriteLine("Rider name is {0}", c.driverName);
  Console.ReadLine();
}
```

With this, ponder the output from the previous Main() method:

```
***** Fun with class Types *****

In master ctor
In ctor taking an int
Yeeeeeee Haaaaaeewww!
Yeeeeeee Haaaaaeewww!
Yeeeeeee Haaaaaeewww!
Yeeeeeee Haaaaaeewww!
Yeeeeeee Haaaaaeewww!
Yeeeeeee Haaaaaeewww!
Rider name is Tiny
```

As you can see, the flow of constructor logic is as follows:

- You create your object by invoking the constructor requiring a single int.
- This constructor forwards the supplied data to the master constructor and provides any additional start-up arguments not specified by the caller.
- The master constructor assigns the incoming data to the object's field data.

- Control is returned to the constructor originally called, and executes any remaining code statements.

The nice thing about using constructor chaining, is that this programming pattern will work with any version of the C# language and .NET platform. However, if you are targeting .NET 4.0 and higher, you can further simplify your programming tasks by making use of optional arguments as an alternative to traditional constructor chaining.

Revisiting Optional Arguments

In Chapter 4, you learned about optional and named arguments. Recall that optional arguments allow you to define supplied default values to incoming arguments. If the caller is happy with these defaults, they are not required to specify a unique value, however they may do so to provide the object with custom data. Consider the following version of Motorcycle, which now provides a number of ways to construct objects using a *single* constructor definition:

```
class Motorcycle
{
  // Single constructor using optional args.
  public Motorcycle(int intensity = 0, string name = "")
  {
    if (intensity > 10)
    {
      intensity = 10;
    }
    driverIntensity = intensity;
    driverName = name;
  }
...
}
```

With this one constructor, you are now able to create a new Motorcycle object using zero, one, or two arguments. Recall that named argument syntax allows you to essentially skip over acceptable default settings (see Chapter 3).

```
static void MakeSomeBikes()
{
  // driverName = "", driverIntensity = 0
  Motorcycle m1 = new Motorcycle();
  Console.WriteLine("Name= {0}, Intensity= {1}",
    m1.driverName, m1.driverIntensity);

  // driverName = "Tiny", driverIntensity = 0
  Motorcycle m2 = new Motorcycle(name:"Tiny");
  Console.WriteLine("Name= {0}, Intensity= {1}",
    m2.driverName, m2.driverIntensity);

  // driverName = "", driverIntensity = 7
  Motorcycle m3 = new Motorcycle(7);
  Console.WriteLine("Name= {0}, Intensity= {1}",
    m3.driverName, m3.driverIntensity);
}
```

While the use of optional/named arguments is a very slick way to streamline how you define the set of constructors used by a given class, do always remember that this syntax is only valid under .NET 4.0 or higher. If you need to build classes that can run under any version of the .NET platform, it is best to stick to classical constructor chaining techniques.

In any case, at this point you are able to define a class with field data (a.k.a., member variables) and various operations such as methods and constructors. Next up, let's formalize the role of the static keyword.

■ **Source Code** The SimpleClassExample project is included under the Chapter 5 subdirectory.

Understanding the static Keyword

A C# class may define any number of *static members*, which are declared using the static keyword. When you do so, the member in question must be invoked directly from the class level, rather than from an object reference variable. To illustrate the distinction, consider your good friend System.Console. As you have seen, you do not invoke the WriteLine() method from the object level:

```
// Error! WriteLine() is not an object level method!
Console c = new Console();
c.WriteLine("I can't be printed...");
```

but instead simply prefix the class name to the static WriteLine() member:

```
// Correct! WriteLine() is a static method.
Console.WriteLine("Much better! Thanks...");
```

Simply put, static members are items that are deemed (by the class designer) to be so commonplace that there is no need to create an instance of the class before invoking the member. While any class can define static members, they are quite commonly found within "utility classes." By definition, a utility class is a class that does not maintain any object-level state and is not created with the new keyword. Rather, a utility class exposes all functionality as class-level (a.k.a., static) members.

For example, if you were to use the Visual Studio object browser (via the View ➤ Object Browser menu item) to view the System namespace of mscorlib.dll, you would see that all of the members of the Console, Math, Environment, and GC classes (among others) expose all of their functionality via static members. These are but a few utility classes found within the .NET base class libraries.

Again, be aware that static members are not only found in utility classes; they can be part of any class definition at all. Just remember that static members promote a given item to the class level rather than the object level. As you will see over the next few sections, the static keyword can be applied to the following:

- Data of a class

- Methods of a class

- Properties of a class

- A constructor

- The entire class definition

Let's see each of our options, beginning with the concept of static data.

■ **Note** You will examine the role of static properties later in this chapter, during our examination of properties themselves.

Defining Static Field Data

Most of the time when designing a class, you define data as instance-level data; said another way, as nonstatic data. When you define instance-level data, you know that every time you create a new object, the object maintains its own independent copy of the data. In contrast, when you define *static* data of a class, the memory is shared by all objects of that category.

To see the distinction, create a new Console Application project named StaticDataAndMembers. Now, insert a new class into your project named SavingsAccount. Begin by defining a point of instance-level data (to model the current balance) and a custom constructor to set the initial balance:

```
// A simple savings account class.
class SavingsAccount
{
  // Instance-level data.
  public double currBalance;

  public SavingsAccount(double balance)
  {
    currBalance = balance;
  }
}
```

When you create SavingsAccount objects, memory for the currBalance field is allocated for each object. Thus, you could create five different SavingsAccount objects, each with their own unique balance. Furthermore, if you change the balance on one account, the other objects are not affected.

Static data, on the other hand, is allocated once and shared among all objects of the same class category. Add a static point of data named currInterestRate to the SavingsAccount class, which is set to a default value of 0.04:

```
// A simple savings account class.
class SavingsAccount
{
  // Instance-level data.
  public double currBalance;

  // A static point of data.
  public static double currInterestRate = 0.04;

  public SavingsAccount(double balance)
  {
    currBalance = balance;
  }
}
```

If you were to create three instances of SavingsAccount in Main() as follows:

```
static void Main(string[] args)
{
  Console.WriteLine("***** Fun with Static Data *****\n");
  SavingsAccount s1 = new SavingsAccount(50);
  SavingsAccount s2 = new SavingsAccount(100);
  SavingsAccount s3 = new SavingsAccount(10000.75);
  Console.ReadLine();
}
```

the in-memory data allocation would look something like Figure 5-3.

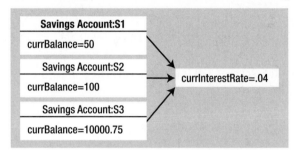

Figure 5-3. *Static data is allocated once and shared among all instances of the class*

Here, our assumption is that all saving accounts should have the same interest rate. Because static data is shared by all objects of the same category, if you were to change it in any way, all objects will "see" the new value the next time they access the static data, as they are all essentially looking at the same memory location. To understand how to change (or obtain) static data, we need to consider the role of static methods.

Defining Static Methods

Let's update the SavingsAccount class to define two static methods. The first static method (GetInterestRate()) will return the current interest rate, while the second static method (SetInterestRate()) will allow you to change the interest rate:

```
// A simple savings account class.
class SavingsAccount
{
  // Instance-level data.
  public double currBalance;

  // A static point of data.
  public static double currInterestRate = 0.04;

  public SavingsAccount(double balance)
  {
    currBalance = balance;
  }
```

```
    // Static members to get/set interest rate.
    public static void SetInterestRate(double newRate)
    { currInterestRate = newRate; }

    public static double GetInterestRate()
    { return currInterestRate; }
}
```

Now, observe the following usage:

```
static void Main(string[] args)
{
    Console.WriteLine("***** Fun with Static Data *****\n");
    SavingsAccount s1 = new SavingsAccount(50);
    SavingsAccount s2 = new SavingsAccount(100);

    // Print the current interest rate.
    Console.WriteLine("Interest Rate is: {0}", SavingsAccount.GetInterestRate());

    // Make new object, this does NOT 'reset' the interest rate.
    SavingsAccount s3 = new SavingsAccount(10000.75);
    Console.WriteLine("Interest Rate is: {0}", SavingsAccount.GetInterestRate());

    Console.ReadLine();
}
```

The output of the previous Main() is seen here:

```
***** Fun with Static Data *****

Interest Rate is: 0.04
Interest Rate is: 0.04
```

As you can see, when you create new instances of the SavingsAccount class, the value of the static data is not reset, as the CLR will allocate the static data into memory exactly one time. After that point, all objects of type SavingsAccount operate on the same value for the static currInterestRate field.

When designing any C# class, one of your design challenges is to determine which pieces of data should be defined as static members, and which should not. While there are no hard and fast rules, remember that a static data field is shared by all objects of that type. Therefore, if you are defining a point of data that *all* objects should share between them, static is the way to go.

Consider what would happen if the interest rate variable were *not* defined using the static keyword. This would mean every SavingsAccount object would have its own copy of the currInterestRate field. Now, assume you created 100 SavingsAccount objects, and need to change the interest rate. That would require you to call the SetInterestRate() method 100 times! Clearly, this would not be a very useful way to model "shared data." Again, static data is perfect when you have a value that should be common to all objects of that category.

■ **Note** It is a compiler error for a static member to reference nonstatic members in its implementation. On a related note, it is an error to use the `this` operator in a static member as "this" implies an object!

Defining Static Constructors

A typical constructor is used to set the value of an object's instance-level data at the time of creation. However, what would happen if you attempted to assign the value of a static point of data in a typical constructor? You might be surprised to find that the value is reset each time you create a new object!

To illustrate, assume you have updated the SavingsAccount class constructor as follows (also note we are no longer assigning the currInterestRate field inline):

```
class SavingsAccount
{
  public double currBalance;
  public static double currInterestRate;

  // Notice that our constructor is setting
  // the static currInterestRate value.
  public SavingsAccount(double balance)
  {
    currInterestRate = 0.04;  // This is static data!
    currBalance = balance;
  }
...
}
```

Now, assume you have authored the following code in Main():

```
static void Main( string[] args )
{
  Console.WriteLine("***** Fun with Static Data *****\n");

  // Make an account.
  SavingsAccount s1 = new SavingsAccount(50);

  // Print the current interest rate.
  Console.WriteLine("Interest Rate is: {0}", SavingsAccount.GetInterestRate());

  // Try to change the interest rate via property.
  SavingsAccount.SetInterestRate(0.08);

  // Make a second account.
  SavingsAccount s2 = new SavingsAccount(100);

  // Should print 0.08...right??
  Console.WriteLine("Interest Rate is: {0}", SavingsAccount.GetInterestRate());
  Console.ReadLine();
}
```

If you execute the previous `Main()` method, you would see that that the `currInterestRate` variable is reset each time you create a new `SavingsAccount` object, and it is always set to `0.04`. Clearly, setting the value of static data in a normal instance-level constructor sort of defeats the whole purpose. Every time you make a new object, the class-level data is reset! One approach to setting a static field is to use member initialization syntax, as you did originally:

```
class SavingsAccount
{
  public double currBalance;

  // A static point of data.
  public static double currInterestRate = 0.04;
...
}
```

This approach will ensure the static field is assigned only once, regardless of how many objects you create. However, what if the value for your static data needed to be obtained at runtime? For example, in a typical banking application, the value of an interest rate variable would be read from a database or external file. To perform such tasks requires a method scope such as a constructor to execute the code statements.

For this very reason, C# allows you to define a static constructor, which allows you to safely set the values of your static data. Consider the following update to our class:

```
class SavingsAccount
{
  public double currBalance;
  public static double currInterestRate;

  public SavingsAccount(double balance)
  {
    currBalance = balance;
  }

  // A static constructor!
  static SavingsAccount()
  {
    Console.WriteLine("In static ctor!");
    currInterestRate = 0.04;
  }
...
}
```

Simply put, a static constructor is a special constructor that is an ideal place to initialize the values of static data when the value is not known at compile time (e.g., you need to read in the value from an external file, a database, generate a random number, or whatnot). If you were to rerun the previous `Main()` method, you would find the output you expect. Note that the message "In static ctor!" only prints out one time, as the CLR calls all static constructors before first use (and never calls them again for that instance of the application):

```
***** Fun with Static Data *****

In static ctor!
Interest Rate is: 0.04
Interest Rate is: 0.08
```

Here are a few points of interest regarding static constructors:

- A given class may define only a single static constructor. In other words, the static constructor cannot be overloaded.

- A static constructor does not take an access modifier and cannot take any parameters.

- A static constructor executes exactly one time, regardless of how many objects of the type are created.

- The runtime invokes the static constructor when it creates an instance of the class or before accessing the first static member invoked by the caller.

- The static constructor executes before any instance-level constructors.

Given this modification, when you create new SavingsAccount objects, the value of the static data is preserved, as the static member is set only one time within the static constructor, regardless of the number of objects created.

■ **Source Code** The StaticDataAndMembers project is included under the Chapter 5 subdirectory.

Defining Static Classes

It is also possible to apply the static keyword directly on the class level. When a class has been defined as static, it is not creatable using the new keyword, and it can contain only members or data fields marked with the static keyword. If this is not the case, you receive compiler errors.

■ **Note** Recall that a class (or structure) that only exposes static functionality is often termed a utility class. When designing a utility class, it is good practice to apply the static keyword to the class definition.

At first glance, this might seem like a fairly odd feature, given that a class that cannot be created does not appear all that helpful. However, if you create a class that contains nothing but static members and/or constant data, the class has no need to be allocated in the first place! To illustrate, create a new Console Application named SimpleUtilityClass. Next, define the following class:

```
// Static classes can only
// contain static members!
static class TimeUtilClass
{
  public static void PrintTime()
  { Console.WriteLine(DateTime.Now.ToShortTimeString()); }

  public static void PrintDate()
  { Console.WriteLine(DateTime.Today.ToShortDateString()); }
}
```

Given that this class has been defined with the static keyword, you cannot create an instance of TimeUtilClass using the new keyword. Rather, all functionality is exposed from the class level:

```
static void Main(string[] args)
{
  Console.WriteLine("***** Fun with Static Classes *****\n");

  // This is just fine.
  TimeUtilClass.PrintDate();
  TimeUtilClass.PrintTime();
  // Compiler error! Can't create static classes!
  TimeUtilClass u = new TimeUtilClass ();

  Console.ReadLine();
}
```

At this point in the chapter, you hopefully feel comfortable defining simple class types containing constructors, fields, and various static (and nonstatic) members. Now that you have the basics of class construction under your belt, you can formally investigate the three pillars of object-oriented programming.

■ **Source Code** The SimpleUtilityClass project is located under the Chapter 5 subdirectory.

Defining the Pillars of OOP

All object-oriented languages (C#, Java, C++, Visual Basic, etc.) must contend with three core principals, often called the pillars of object-oriented programming (OOP):

- *Encapsulation:* How does this language hide an object's internal implementation details and preserve data integrity?

- *Inheritance:* How does this language promote code reuse?

- *Polymorphism:* How does this language let you treat related objects in a similar way?

Before digging into the syntactic details of each pillar, it is important that you understand the basic role of each. Here is an overview of each pillar, which will be examined in full detail over the remainder of this chapter and the next.

The Role of Encapsulation

The first pillar of OOP is called *encapsulation*. This trait boils down to the language's ability to hide unnecessary implementation details from the object user. For example, assume you are using a class named DatabaseReader, which has two primary methods named Open() and Close():

```
// Assume this class encapsulates the details of opening and closing a database.
DatabaseReader dbReader = new DatabaseReader();
dbReader.Open(@"C:\AutoLot.mdf");

// Do something with data file and close the file.
dbReader.Close();
```

The fictitious DatabaseReader class encapsulates the inner details of locating, loading, manipulating, and closing a data file. Programmers love encapsulation, as this pillar of OOP keeps coding tasks simpler. There is no need to worry about the numerous lines of code that are working behind the scenes to carry out the work of the DatabaseReader class. All you do is create an instance and send the appropriate messages (e.g., "Open the file named AutoLot.mdf located on my C drive").

Closely related to the notion of encapsulating programming logic is the idea of data protection. Ideally, an object's state data should be specified using the private (or possibly protected) keyword. In this way, the outside world must ask politely in order to change or obtain the underlying value. This is a good thing, as publicly declared data points can easily become corrupted (hopefully by accident rather than intent!). You will formally examine this aspect of encapsulation in just a bit.

The Role of Inheritance

The next pillar of OOP, *inheritance,* boils down to the language's ability to allow you to build new class definitions based on existing class definitions. In essence, inheritance allows you to extend the behavior of a base (or *parent*) class by inheriting core functionality into the derived subclass (also called a *child class*). Figure 5-4 shows a simple example.

You can read the diagram in Figure 5-4 as "A Hexagon is-a Shape that is-an Object." When you have classes related by this form of inheritance, you establish *"is-a" relationships* between types. The "is-a" relationship is termed *inheritance.*

Here, you can assume that Shape defines some number of members that are common to all descendents (maybe a value to represent the color to draw the shape, and other values to represent the height and width). Given that the Hexagon class extends Shape, it inherits the core functionality defined by Shape and Object, as well as defines additional hexagon-related details of its own (whatever those may be).

■ **Note** Under the .NET platform, System.Object is always the topmost parent in any class hierarchy, which defines some general functionality for all types (fully described in Chapter 6).

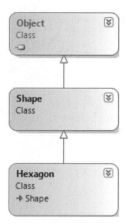

Figure 5-4. The "is-a" relationship

There is another form of code reuse in the world of OOP: the containment/delegation model also known as the *"has-a" relationship* or aggregation. This form of reuse is not used to establish parent/child relationships. Rather, the "has-a" relationship allows one class to define a member variable of another class and expose its functionality (if required) to the object user indirectly.

For example, assume you are again modeling an automobile. You might want to express the idea that a car "has-a" radio. It would be illogical to attempt to derive the Car class from a Radio, or vice versa (a Car "is-a" Radio? I think not!). Rather, you have two independent classes working together, where the Car class creates and exposes the Radio's functionality:

```
class Radio
{
  public void Power(bool turnOn)
  {
    Console.WriteLine("Radio on: {0}", turnOn);
  }
}

class Car
{
  // Car 'has-a' Radio.
  private Radio myRadio = new Radio();

  public void TurnOnRadio(bool onOff)
  {
    // Delegate call to inner object.
    myRadio.Power(onOff);
  }
}
```

Notice that the object user has no clue that the Car class is making use of an inner Radio object.

```
static void Main(string[] args)
{
  // Call is forwarded to Radio internally.
```

```
    Car viper = new Car();
    viper.TurnOnRadio(false);
}
```

The Role of Polymorphism

The final pillar of OOP is *polymorphism*. This trait captures a language's ability to treat related objects in a similar manner. Specifically, this tenant of an object-oriented language allows a base class to define a set of members (formally termed the *polymorphic interface*) that are available to all descendents. A class's polymorphic interface is constructed using any number of *virtual* or *abstract* members (see Chapter 6 for full details).

In a nutshell, a *virtual member* is a member in a base class that defines a default implementation that may be changed (or more formally speaking, *overridden*) by a derived class. In contrast, an *abstract method* is a member in a base class that does not provide a default implementation, but does provide a signature. When a class derives from a base class defining an abstract method, it *must* be overridden by a derived type. In either case, when derived types override the members defined by a base class, they are essentially redefining how they respond to the same request.

To preview polymorphism, let's provide some details behind the shapes hierarchy shown in Figure 5-5. Assume that the Shape class has defined a virtual method named Draw() that takes no parameters. Given the fact that every shape needs to render itself in a unique manner, subclasses such as Hexagon and Circle are free to override this method to their own liking (see Figure 5-5).

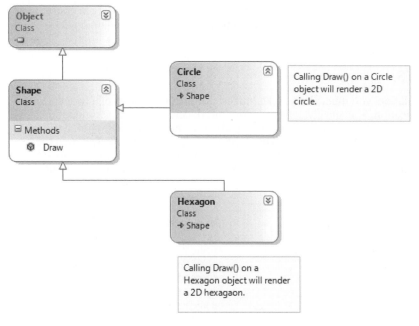

Figure 5-5. Classical polymorphism

After a polymorphic interface has been designed, you can begin to make various assumptions in your code. For example, given that Hexagon and Circle derive from a common parent (Shape), an array of Shape types could contain anything deriving from this base class. Furthermore, given that Shape defines a polymorphic interface to all derived types (the Draw() method in this example), you can assume each member in the array has this functionality.

Consider the following Main() method, which instructs an array of Shape-derived types to render themselves using the Draw() method:

```
class Program
{
  static void Main(string[] args)
  {
    Shape[] myShapes = new Shape[3];
    myShapes[0] = new Hexagon();
    myShapes[1] = new Circle();
    myShapes[2] = new Hexagon();

    foreach (Shape s in myShapes)
    {
      // Use the polymorphic interface!
      s.Draw();
    }
    Console.ReadLine();
  }
}
```

This wraps up our brisk overview of the pillars of OOP. Now that you have the theory in your mind, the remainder of this chapter explores further details of how encapsulation is handled under C#. Chapter 6 will tackle the details of inheritance and polymorphism.

C# Access Modifiers

When working with encapsulation, you must always take into account which aspects of a type are visible to various parts of your application. Specifically, types (classes, interfaces, structures, enumerations, and delegates) as well as their members (properties, methods, constructors, and fields) are defined using a specific keyword to control how "visible" the item is to other parts of your application. Although C# defines numerous keywords to control access, they differ on where they can be successfully applied (type or member). Table 5-1 documents the role of each access modifier and where it may be applied.

Table 5-1. *C# Access Modifiers*

C# Access Modifier	May Be Applied To	Meaning in Life
public	Types or type members	Public items have no access restrictions. A public member can be accessed from an object, as well as any derived class. A public type can be accessed from other external assemblies.
private	Type members or nested types	Private items can only be accessed by the class (or structure) that defines the item.

protected	Type members or nested types	Protected items can be used by the class which defines it, and any child class. However, protected items cannot be accessed from the outside world using the C# dot operator.
internal	Types or type members	Internal items are accessible only within the current assembly. Therefore, if you define a set of internal types within a .NET class library, other assemblies are not able to make use of them.
protected internal	Type members or nested types	When the protected and internal keywords are combined on an item, the item is accessible within the defining assembly, the defining class, and by derived classes.

In this chapter, you are only concerned with the public and private keywords. Later chapters will examine the role of the internal and protected internal modifiers (useful when you build .NET code libraries) and the protected modifier (useful when you are creating class hierarchies).

The Default Access Modifiers

By default, type members are *implicitly private* while types are *implicitly internal.* Thus, the following class definition is automatically set to internal, while the type's default constructor is automatically set to private:

```
// An internal class with a private default constructor.
class Radio
{
  Radio(){}
}
```

To allow other parts of a program to invoke members of an object, you must mark them as publicly accessible. As well, if you wish to expose the Radio to external assemblies (again, useful when building .NET code libraries; see Chapter 14), you will need to add the public modifier.

```
// A public class with a public default constructor.
public class Radio
{
  public Radio(){}
}
```

Access Modifiers and Nested Types

As mentioned in Table 5-1, the private, protected, and protected internal access modifiers can be applied to a *nested type*. Chapter 6 will examine nesting in detail. What you need to know at this point, however, is that a nested type is a type declared directly within the scope of class or structure. By way of example, here is a private enumeration (named `CarColor`) nested within a public class (named `SportsCar`):

```csharp
public class SportsCar
{
  // OK! Nested types can be marked private.
  private enum CarColor
  {
    Red, Green, Blue
  }
}
```

Here, it is permissible to apply the `private` access modifier on the nested type. However, nonnested types (such as the `SportsCar`) can only be defined with the `public` or `internal` modifiers. Therefore, the following class definition is illegal:

```csharp
// Error! Nonnested types cannot be marked private!
private class SportsCar
{}
```

The First Pillar: C#'s Encapsulation Services

The concept of encapsulation revolves around the notion that an object's internal data should not be directly accessible from an object instance. Rather, class data is defined as private. If the caller wants to alter the state of an object, the user does so indirectly using public members. To illustrate the need for encapsulation services, assume you have created the following class definition:

```csharp
// A class with a single public field.
class Book
{
  public int numberOfPages;
}
```

The problem with public data is that the data itself has no ability to "understand" whether the current value to which they are assigned is valid with regard to the current business rules of the system. As you know, the upper range of a C# int is quite large (2,147,483,647). Therefore, the compiler allows the following assignment:

```csharp
// Humm. That is one heck of a mini-novel!
static void Main(string[] args)
{
  Book miniNovel = new Book();
  miniNovel.numberOfPages = 30000000;
}
```

Although you have not overflowed the boundaries of an `int` data type, it should be clear that a mini-novel with a page count of 30,000,000 pages is a bit unreasonable. As you can see, public fields do not provide a way to trap logical upper (or lower) limits. If your current system has a business rule that states a book must be between 1 and 1,000 pages, you are at a loss to enforce this programmatically. Because of this, public fields typically have no place in a production-level class definition.

■ **Note** To be more specific, members of a class that represent an object's state should not be marked as public. As you will see later in this chapter, public constants and public read-only fields are a-okay.

Encapsulation provides a way to preserve the integrity of an object's state data. Rather than defining public fields (which can easily foster data corruption), you should get in the habit of defining *private data*, which is indirectly manipulated using one of two main techniques:

- Define a pair of public accessor (get) and mutator (set) methods.

- Define a public .NET property.

Whichever technique you choose, the point is that a well-encapsulated class should protect its data and hide the details of how it operates from the prying eyes of the outside world. This is often termed *black box programming*. The beauty of this approach is that an object is free to change how a given method is implemented under the hood. It does this without breaking any existing code making use of it, provided that the parameters and return values of the method remain constant.

Encapsulation Using Traditional Accessors and Mutators

Over the remaining pages in this chapter, you will be building a fairly complete class that models a general employee. To get the ball rolling, create a new Console Application named EmployeeApp and insert a new class file (named Employee.cs) using the Project Add class menu item. Update the Employee class with the following fields, methods, and constructors:

```
class Employee
{
  // Field data.
  private string empName;
  private int empID;
  private float currPay;

  // Constructors.
  public Employee() {}
  public Employee(string name, int id, float pay)
  {
    empName = name;
    empID = id;
    currPay = pay;
  }

  // Methods.
  public void GiveBonus(float amount)
  {
    currPay += amount;
  }

  public void DisplayStats()
  {
    Console.WriteLine("Name: {0}", empName);
```

```
    Console.WriteLine("ID: {0}", empID);
    Console.WriteLine("Pay: {0}", currPay);
  }
}
```

Notice that the fields of the Employee class are currently defined using the private keyword. Given this, the empName, empID, and currPay fields are not directly accessible from an object variable. Therefore, the following logic in Main() would result in compiler errors:

```
static void Main(string[] args)
{
  // Error! Cannot directly access private members
  // from an object!
  Employee emp = new Employee();
  emp.empName = "Marv";
}
```

If you want the outside world to interact with a worker's full name, a traditional approach (which is very common in Java) is to define an accessor (get method) and a mutator (set method). The role of a "get" method is to return to the caller the current value of the underlying state data. A "set" method allows the caller to change the current value of the underlying state data, as long as the defined business rules are met.

To illustrate, let's encapsulate the empName field. To do so, add the following public methods to the Employee class. Notice that the SetName() method performs a test on the incoming data, to ensure the string is 15 characters or less. If it is not, an error prints to the console and returns without making a change to the empName field:

■ **Note** If this were a production level class, you would also make to check the character length for an employee's name within your constructor logic. Ignore this detail for the time being, as you will clean up this code in just a bit when you examine .NET property syntax.

```
class Employee
{
  // Field data.
  private string empName;
  ...

  // Accessor (get method).
  public string GetName()
  {
    return empName;
  }

  // Mutator (set method).
  public void SetName(string name)
  {
    // Do a check on incoming value
    // before making assignment.
```

```
    if (name.Length > 15)
      Console.WriteLine("Error!  Name must be less than 16 characters!");
    else
      empName = name;
  }
}
```

This technique requires two uniquely named methods to operate on a single data point. To test your new methods, update your Main() method as follows:

```
static void Main(string[] args)
{
  Console.WriteLine("***** Fun with Encapsulation *****\n");
  Employee emp = new Employee("Marvin", 456, 30000);
  emp.GiveBonus(1000);
  emp.DisplayStats();

  // Use the get/set methods to interact with the object's name.
  emp.SetName("Marv");
  Console.WriteLine("Employee is named: {0}", emp.GetName());
  Console.ReadLine();
}
```

Because of the code in your SetName() method, if you attempted to specify more than 16 characters (see the following), you would find the hard-coded error message printed to the console:

```
static void Main(string[] args)
{
  Console.WriteLine("***** Fun with Encapsulation *****\n");
...
  // Longer than 16 characters! Error will print to console.
  Employee emp2 = new Employee();
  emp2.SetName("Xena the warrior princess");

  Console.ReadLine();
}
```

So far, so good. You have encapsulated the private empName field using two public methods named GetName() and SetName(). If you were to further encapsulate the data in the Employee class, you would need to add various additional methods (such as GetID(), SetID(), GetCurrentPay(), SetCurrentPay()). Each of the mutator methods could have within it various lines of code to check for additional business rules. While this could certainly be done, the C# language has a useful alternative notation to encapsulate class data.

Encapsulation Using .NET Properties

Although you can encapsulate a piece of field data using traditional get and set methods, .NET languages prefer to enforce data encapsulation state data using *properties*. First of all, understand that properties are just a simplification for "real" accessor and mutator methods. Therefore, as a class designer, you are still able to perform any internal logic necessary before making the value assignment (e.g., uppercase the value, scrub the value for illegal characters, check the bounds of a numerical value, and so on).

Here is the updated `Employee` class, now enforcing encapsulation of each field using property syntax rather than traditional get and set methods:

```
class Employee
{
  // Field data.
  private string empName;
  private int empID;
  private float currPay;

  // Properties!
  public string Name
  {
    get { return empName; }
    set
    {
      if (value.Length > 15)
        Console.WriteLine("Error!  Name must be less than 16 characters!");
      else
        empName = value;
    }
  }

  // We could add additional business rules to the sets of these properties;
  // however, there is no need to do so for this example.
  public int ID
  {
    get { return empID; }
    set { empID = value; }
  }
  public float Pay
  {
    get { return currPay; }
    set { currPay = value; }
  }
...
}
```

A C# property is composed by defining a get scope (accessor) and set scope (mutator) directly within the property itself. Notice that the property specifies the type of data it is encapsulating by what appears to be a return value. Also take note that, unlike a method, properties do not make use of parentheses (not even empty parentheses) when being defined. Consider the commentary on your current ID property:

```
// The 'int' represents the type of data this property encapsulates.
// The data type must be identical to the related field (empID).
public int ID  // Note lack of parentheses.
{
  get { return empID; }
  set { empID = value; }
}
```

Within a "set" scope of a property, you use a token named value, which is used to represent the incoming value used to assign the property by the caller. This token is *not* a true C# keyword, but is what is known as a *contextual keyword*. When the token value is within the set scope of the property, it always represents the value being assigned by the caller, and it will always be the same underlying data type as the property itself. Thus, notice how the Name property can still test the range of the string as so:

```
public string Name
{
  get { return empName; }
  set
  {
    // Here, value is really a string.
    if (value.Length > 15)
      Console.WriteLine("Error! Name must be less than 16 characters!");
    else
      empName = value;
  }
}
```

After you have these properties in place, it appears to the caller that it is getting and setting a *public point* of data; however, the correct get and set block is called behind the scenes to preserve encapsulation:

```
static void Main(string[] args)
{
  Console.WriteLine("***** Fun with Encapsulation *****\n");
  Employee emp = new Employee("Marvin", 456, 30000);
  emp.GiveBonus(1000);
  emp.DisplayStats();

  // Set and get the Name property.
  emp.Name = "Marv";
  Console.WriteLine("Employee is named: {0}", emp.Name);
  Console.ReadLine();
}
```

Properties (as opposed to accessors and mutators) also make your types easier to manipulate, in that properties are able to respond to the intrinsic operators of C#. To illustrate, assume that the Employee class type has an internal private member variable representing the age of the employee. Here is the relevant update (notice the use of constructor chaining):

```
class Employee
{
...
  // New field and property.
  private int empAge;
  public int Age
  {
    get { return empAge; }
    set { empAge = value; }
  }

  // Updated constructors.
  public Employee() {}
```

```
public Employee(string name, int id, float pay)
  :this(name, 0, id, pay){}

public Employee(string name, int age, int id, float pay)
{
  empName = name;
  empID = id;
  empAge = age;
  currPay = pay;
}

// Updated DisplayStats() method now accounts for age.
public void DisplayStats()
{
  Console.WriteLine("Name: {0}", empName);
  Console.WriteLine("ID: {0}", empID);
  Console.WriteLine("Age: {0}", empAge);
  Console.WriteLine("Pay: {0}", currPay);
}
}
```

Now assume you have created an Employee object named joe. On his birthday, you want to increment the age by one. Using traditional accessor and mutator methods, you would need to write code such as the following:

```
Employee joe = new Employee();
joe.SetAge(joe.GetAge() + 1);
```

However, if you encapsulate empAge using a property named Age, you are able to simply write

```
Employee joe = new Employee();
joe.Age++;
```

Using Properties Within a Class Definition

Properties, specifically the "set" portion of a property, are common places to package up the business rules of your class. Currently, the Employee class has a Name property that ensures the name is no more than 15 characters. The remaining properties (ID, Pay, and Age) could also be updated with any relevant logic.

While this is well and good, also consider what a class constructor typically does internally. It will take the incoming parameters, check for valid data, and then make assignments to the internal private fields. Currently, your master constructor does *not* test the incoming string data for a valid range, so you could update this member as so:

```
public Employee(string name, int age, int id, float pay)
{
  // Humm, this seems like a problem...
  if (name.Length > 15)
    Console.WriteLine("Error! Name must be less than 16 characters!");
  else
    empName = name;

  empID = id;
  empAge = age;
```

```
  currPay = pay;
}
```

I am sure you can see the problem with this approach. The Name property and your master constructor are performing the same error checking! If you were also making checks on the other data points, you would have a good deal of duplicate code. To streamline your code, and isolate all of your error checking to a central location, you will do well if you *always* use properties within your class whenever you need to get or set the values. Consider the following updated constructor:

```
public Employee(string name, int age, int id, float pay)
{
  // Better! Use properties when setting class data.
  // This reduces the amount of duplicate error checks.
  Name = name;
  Age = age;
  ID = id;
  Pay = pay;
}
```

Beyond updating constructors to use properties when assigning values, it is good practice to use properties throughout a class implementation, to ensure your business rules are always enforced. In many cases, the only time when you directly make reference to the underlying private piece of data is within the property itself. With this in mind, here is your updated Employee class:

```
class Employee
{
  // Field data.
  private string empName;
  private int empID;
  private float currPay;
  private int empAge;

  // Constructors.
  public Employee() { }
  public Employee(string name, int id, float pay)
    :this(name, 0, id, pay){}
  public Employee(string name, int age, int id, float pay)
  {
    Name = name;
    Age = age;
    ID = id;
    Pay = pay;
  }

  // Methods.
  public void GiveBonus(float amount)
  { Pay += amount; }

  public void DisplayStats()
  {
    Console.WriteLine("Name: {0}", Name);
    Console.WriteLine("ID: {0}", ID);
    Console.WriteLine("Age: {0}", Age);
```

```
    Console.WriteLine("Pay: {0}", Pay);
  }

  // Properties as before...
  ...
}
```

Read-Only and Write-Only Properties

When encapsulating data, you might want to configure a *read-only property*. To do so, simply omit the set block. Likewise, if you want to have a *write-only property*, omit the get block. For example, assume you wanted a new property named SocialSecurityNumber, which encapsulates a private string variable named empSSN. If you want to make this a read-only property, you could write:

```
public string SocialSecurityNumber
{
  get { return empSS; }
}
```

Now assume our class constructor has a new parameter to let the caller set the SSN of the object. Since the SocialSecurityNumber property is read only, we cannot set the value as so:

```
public Employee(string name, int age, int id, float pay, string ssn)
{
  Name = name;
  Age = age;
  ID = id;
  Pay = pay;
  // OOPS! This is no longer possible if the property is read
  // only.
  SocialSecurityNumber = ssn;
}
```

Unless we are willing to redesign the property as read/write, your only choice would be to use the underlying empSSN member variable within your constructor logic as so:

```
public Employee(string name, int age, int id, float pay, string ssn)
{
  ...
  empSSN = ssn;
}
```

To wrap up the story thus far, recall that C# prefers properties to encapsulate data. These syntactic entities are used for the same purpose as traditional accessor (get)/mutator (set) methods. The benefit of properties is that the users of your objects are able to manipulate the internal data point using a single named item.

■ **Source Code** The EmployeeApp project can be found under the Chapter 5 subdirectory.

Revisiting the static Keyword: Defining Static Properties

Earlier in this chapter, you examined the role of the static keyword. Now that you understand the use of C# property syntax, we can formalize static properties. In the StaticDataAndMembers project, our SavingsAccount class had two public static properties to get and set the interest rate. However, it would be more standard to wrap this data point in a property. Thus, if you would rather not have two methods to get and set the interest rate, you could instead define this following class property (note the use of the static keyword):

```
// A simple savings account class.
class SavingsAccount
{
  // Instance-level data.
  public double currBalance;

  // A static point of data.
  private static double currInterestRate = 0.04;

  // A static property.
  public static double InterestRate
  {
    get { return currInterestRate; }
    set { currInterestRate = value; }
  }
...
}
```

If you want to use this property in place of the previous static methods, you could update your Main() method as so:

```
// Print the current interest rate via property.
Console.WriteLine("Interest Rate is: {0}", SavingsAccount.InterestRate);
```

Understanding Automatic Properties

When you are building properties to encapsulate your data, it is common to find that the set scopes have code to enforce business rules of your program. However, in some cases you may not need any implementation logic beyond simply getting and setting the value. This means you can end up with a lot of code looking like the following:

```
// A Car type using standard property
// syntax.
class Car
{
  private string carName = "";
  public string PetName
  {
    get { return carName; }
    set { carName = value; }
  }
}
```

In these cases, it can become rather verbose to define private backing fields and simple property definitions multiple times. By way of an example, if you are modeling a class that requires 15 private points of field data, you end up authoring 15 related properties that are little more than thin wrappers for encapsulation services.

To streamline the process of providing simple encapsulation of field data, you may use *automatic property syntax*. As the name implies, this feature will offload the work of defining a private backing field and the related C# property member to the compiler using a new bit of syntax. To illustrate, create a new Console Application named AutoProps. Now, consider the reworking of the Car class, which uses this syntax to quickly create three properties:

```
class Car
{
  // Automatic properties!
  public string PetName { get; set; }
  public int Speed { get; set; }
  public string Color { get; set; }
}
```

■ **Note** Visual Studio provides the prop code snippet. If you type "prop" and press the Tab key twice, the IDE will generate starter code for a new automatic property! You can then use the Tab key to cycle through each part of the definition to fill in the details. Give it a try!

When defining automatic properties, you simply specify the access modifier, underlying data type, property name, and empty get/set scopes. At compile time, your type will be provided with an autogenerated private backing field and a fitting implementation of the get/set logic.

■ **Note** The name of the autogenerated private backing field is not visible within your C# code base. The only way to see it is to make use of a tool such as ildasm.exe.

Unlike traditional C# properties, however, it is *not* possible to build read-only or write-only automatic properties. While you might think you can just omit the get; or set; within your property declaration as follows:

```
// Read-only property? Error!
public int MyReadOnlyProp { get; }

// Write only property? Error!
public int MyWriteOnlyProp { set; }
```

this will result in a compiler error. When you are defining an automatic property, it must support both read and write functionality. Recall the following:

```
// Automatic properties must be read and write.
public string PetName { get; set; }
```

Interacting with Automatic Properties

Because the compiler will define the private backing field at compile time, the class defining automatic properties will always need to use property syntax to get and set the underlying value. This is important to note because many programmers make direct use of the private fields *within* a class definition, which is not possible in this case. For example, if the Car class were to provide a DisplayStats() method, it would need to implement this method using the property name:

```
class Car
{
  // Automatic properties!
  public string PetName { get; set; }
  public int Speed { get; set; }
  public string Color { get; set; }

  public void DisplayStats()
  {
    Console.WriteLine("Car Name: {0}", PetName);
    Console.WriteLine("Speed: {0}", Speed);
    Console.WriteLine("Color: {0}", Color);
  }
}
```

When you are using an object defined with automatic properties, you will be able to assign and obtain the values using the expected property syntax:

```
static void Main(string[] args)
{
  Console.WriteLine("***** Fun with Automatic Properties *****\n");

  Car c = new Car();
  c.PetName = "Frank";
  c.Speed = 55;
  c.Color = "Red";

  Console.WriteLine("Your car is named {0}? That's odd...",
    c.PetName);
  c.DisplayStats();

  Console.ReadLine();
}
```

Regarding Automatic Properties and Default Values

When you use automatic properties to encapsulate numerical or Boolean data, you are able to use the autogenerated type properties straightaway within your code base, as the hidden backing fields will be assigned a safe default value that can be used directly. However, be very aware that if you use automatic property syntax to wrap another class variable, the hidden private reference type will also be set to a default value of null.

Consider the following new class named Garage, which makes use of two automatic properties (of course, a real garage class would maintain a collection of Car objects; however, we will ignore that detail for the time being):

```
class Garage
{
  // The hidden int backing field is set to zero!
  public int NumberOfCars { get; set; }

  // The hidden Car backing field is set to null!
  public Car MyAuto { get; set; }
}
```

Given C#'s default values for field data, you would be able to print out the value of NumberOfCars as is (as it is automatically assigned the value of zero), but if you directly invoke MyAuto, you will receive a "null reference exception" at runtime, as the Car member variable used in the background has not been assigned to a new object:

```
static void Main(string[] args)
{
  ...
  Garage g = new Garage();

  // OK, prints default value of zero.
  Console.WriteLine("Number of Cars: {0}", g.NumberOfCars);

  // Runtime error! Backing field is currently null!
  Console.WriteLine(g.MyAuto.PetName);
  Console.ReadLine();
}
```

Given that the private backing fields are created at compile time, you will be unable to make use of C# field initialization syntax to allocate the reference type directly with the new keyword. Therefore, this work will need to be done with class constructors to ensure the object comes to life in a safe manner. For example:

```
class Garage
{
  // The hidden backing field is set to zero!
  public int NumberOfCars { get; set; }

  // The hidden backing field is set to null!
  public Car MyAuto { get; set; }

  // Must use constructors to override default
  // values assigned to hidden backing fields.
  public Garage()
  {
    MyAuto = new Car();
    NumberOfCars = 1;
  }
  public Garage(Car car, int number)
  {
    MyAuto = car;
    NumberOfCars = number;
  }
}
```

With this update, you could now place a Car object into the Garage object as so:

```
static void Main(string[] args)
{
  Console.WriteLine("***** Fun with Automatic Properties *****\n");

  // Make a car.
  Car c = new Car();
  c.PetName = "Frank";
  c.Speed = 55;
  c.Color = "Red";
  c.DisplayStats();

  // Put car in the garage.
  Garage g = new Garage();
  g.MyAuto = c;
  Console.WriteLine("Number of Cars in garage: {0}", g.NumberOfCars);
  Console.WriteLine("Your car is named: {0}", g.MyAuto.PetName);

  Console.ReadLine();
}
```

As you most likely agree, this is a very nice feature of the C# programming language, as you can define a number of properties for a class using a streamlined syntax. Be aware, of course, that if you are building a property that requires additional code beyond getting and setting the underlying private field (such as data validation logic, writing to an event log, communicating with a database, etc.), you will be required to define a "normal" .NET property type by hand. C# automatic properties never do more than provide simple encapsulation for an underlying piece of (compiler-generated) private data.

■ **Source Code** The AutoProps project can be found under the Chapter 5 subdirectory.

Understanding Object Initialization Syntax

As seen throughout this chapter, a constructor allows you specify start-up values when creating a new object. On a related note, properties allow you to get and set underlying data in a safe manner. When you are working with other people's classes, including the classes found within the .NET base class library, it is not too uncommon to discover that there is not a single constructor that allows you to set every piece of underlying state data. Given this point, a programmer is typically forced to pick the best constructor possible, after which he or she makes assignments using a handful of provided properties.

To help streamline the process of getting an object up and running, C# offers *object initializer syntax*. Using this technique, it is possible to create a new object variable and assign a slew of properties and/or public fields in a few lines of code. Syntactically, an object initializer consists of a comma-delimited list of specified values, enclosed by the { and } tokens. Each member in the initialization list maps to the name of a public field or public property of the object being initialized.

To see this syntax in action, create a new Console Application named ObjectInitializers. Now, consider a simple class named Point, created using automatic properties (which is not mandatory for this example, but helps us write some very concise code):

```
class Point
{
  public int X { get; set; }
  public int Y { get; set; }

  public Point(int xVal, int yVal)
  {
    X = xVal;
    Y = yVal;
  }
  public Point() { }

  public void DisplayStats()
  {
    Console.WriteLine("[{0}, {1}]", X, Y);
  }
}
```

Now consider how we can make Point objects using any of the following approaches:

```
static void Main(string[] args)
{
  Console.WriteLine("***** Fun with Object Init Syntax *****\n");

  // Make a Point by setting each property manually.
  Point firstPoint = new Point();
  firstPoint.X = 10;
  firstPoint.Y = 10;
  firstPoint.DisplayStats();

  // Or make a Point via a custom constructor.
  Point anotherPoint = new Point(20, 20);
  anotherPoint.DisplayStats();

  // Or make a Point using object init syntax.
  Point finalPoint = new Point { X = 30, Y = 30 };
  finalPoint.DisplayStats();
  Console.ReadLine();
}
```

The final Point variable is not making use of a custom constructor (as one might do traditionally), but is rather setting values to the public X and Y properties. Behind the scenes, the type's default constructor is invoked, followed by setting the values to the specified properties. To this end, object initialization syntax is just shorthand notations for the syntax used to create a class variable using a default constructor, and setting the state data property by property.

Calling Custom Constructors with Initialization Syntax

The previous examples initialized Point types by implicitly calling the default constructor on the type:

```
// Here, the default constructor is called implicitly.
Point finalPoint = new Point { X = 30, Y = 30 };
```

If you want to be very clear about this, it is permissible to explicitly call the default constructor as follows:

```
// Here, the default constructor is called explicitly.
Point finalPoint = new Point() { X = 30, Y = 30 };
```

Do be aware that when you are constructing a type using the new initialization syntax, you are able to invoke *any* constructor defined by the class. Our Point type currently defines a two-argument constructor to set the (*x*, *y*) position. Therefore, the following Point declaration results in an X value of 100 and a Y value of 100, regardless of the fact that our constructor arguments specified the values 10 and 16:

```
// Calling a custom constructor.
Point pt = new Point(10, 16) { X = 100, Y = 100 };
```

Given the current definition of your Point type, calling the custom constructor while using initialization syntax is not terribly useful (and more than a bit verbose). However, if your Point type provides a new constructor that allows the caller to establish a color (via a custom enum named PointColor), the combination of custom constructors and object initialization syntax becomes clear. Assume you have updated Point as follows:

```
public enum PointColor
{ LightBlue, BloodRed, Gold }

class Point
{
  public int X { get; set; }
  public int Y { get; set; }
  public PointColor Color{ get; set; }

  public Point(int xVal, int yVal)
  {
    X = xVal;
    Y = yVal;
    Color = PointColor.Gold;
  }

  public Point(PointColor ptColor)
  {
    Color = ptColor;
  }

  public Point()
    : this(PointColor.BloodRed){ }

  public void DisplayStats()
  {
    Console.WriteLine("[{0}, {1}]", X, Y);
    Console.WriteLine("Point is {0}", Color);
  }
}
```

With this new constructor, you can now create a gold point (positioned at 90, 20) as follows:

```
// Calling a more interesting custom constructor with init syntax.
Point goldPoint = new Point(PointColor.Gold){ X = 90, Y = 20 };
goldPoint.DisplayStats();
```

Initializing Inner Types

As briefly mentioned earlier in this chapter (and fully examined in Chapter 6), the "has-a" relationship allows us to compose new classes by defining member variables of existing classes. For example, assume you now have a Rectangle class, which makes use of the Point type to represent its upper-left/bottom-right coordinates. Since automatic properties set all internal class variables to null, you will implement this new class using "traditional" property syntax:

```
class Rectangle
{
  private Point topLeft = new Point();
  private Point bottomRight = new Point();

  public Point TopLeft
  {
    get { return topLeft; }
    set { topLeft = value; }
  }
  public Point BottomRight
  {
    get { return bottomRight; }
    set { bottomRight = value; }
  }

  public void DisplayStats()
  {
    Console.WriteLine("[TopLeft: {0}, {1}, {2} BottomRight: {3}, {4}, {5}]",
      topLeft.X, topLeft.Y, topLeft.Color,
      bottomRight.X, bottomRight.Y, bottomRight.Color);
  }
}
```

Using object initialization syntax, you could create a new Rectangle variable and set the inner Points as follows:

```
// Create and initialize a Rectangle.
Rectangle myRect = new Rectangle
{
  TopLeft = new Point { X = 10, Y = 10 },
  BottomRight = new Point { X = 200, Y = 200}
};
```

Again, the benefit of object initialization syntax is that it basically decreases the number of keystrokes (assuming there is not a suitable constructor). Here is the traditional approach to establishing a similar Rectangle:

```
// Old-school approach.
Rectangle r = new Rectangle();
Point p1 = new Point();
```

```
p1.X = 10;
p1.Y = 10;
r.TopLeft = p1;
Point p2 = new Point();
p2.X = 200;
p2.Y = 200;
r.BottomRight = p2;
```

While you might feel object initialization syntax can take a bit of getting used to, once you get comfortable with the code, you'll be quite pleased at how quickly you can establish the state of a new object with minimal fuss and bother.

To wrap up this chapter, allow me to close with three bite-sized topics that will round out your understanding of building well-encapsulated classes: constant data, read-only fields, and partial class definitions.

■ **Source Code** The ObjectInitilizers project can be found under the Chapter 5 subdirectory.

Working with Constant Field Data

C# offers the const keyword to define constant data, which can never change after the initial assignment. As you might guess, this can be helpful when you are defining a set of known values for use in your applications that are logically connected to a given class or structure.

Assume you are building a utility class named MyMathClass that needs to define a value for the value PI (which you will assume to be 3.14). Begin by creating a new Console Application project named ConstData. Given that you would not want to allow other developers to change this value in code, PI could be modeled with the following constant:

```
namespace ConstData
{
  class MyMathClass
  {
    public const double PI = 3.14;
  }

  class Program
  {
    static void Main(string[] args)
    {
      Console.WriteLine("***** Fun with Const *****\n");
      Console.WriteLine("The value of PI is: {0}", MyMathClass.PI);
      // Error! Can't change a constant!
      // MyMathClass.PI = 3.1444;

      Console.ReadLine();
    }
  }
}
```

Notice that you are referencing the constant data defined by MyMathClass using a class name prefix (i.e., MyMathClass.PI). This is due to the fact that constant fields of a class are implicitly *static*. However, it is permissible to define and access a local constant variable within a type member. By way of example:

```
static void LocalConstStringVariable()
{
  // A local constant data point can be directly accessed.
  const string fixedStr = "Fixed string Data";
  Console.WriteLine(fixedStr);

  // Error!
  fixedStr = "This will not work!";
}
```

Regardless of where you define a constant piece of data, the one point to always remember is that the initial value assigned to the constant must be specified at the time you define the constant. Thus, if you were to modify your MyMathClass in such a way that the value of PI is assigned in a class constructor as follows:

```
class MyMathClass
{
  // Try to set PI in ctor?
  public const double PI;

  public MyMathClass()
  {
    // Error!
    PI = 3.14;
  }
}
```

you would receive a compile-time error. The reason for this restriction has to do with the fact the value of constant data must be known at compile time. Constructors, as you know, are invoked at runtime.

Understanding Read-Only Fields

Closely related to constant data is the notion of *read-only field data* (which should not be confused with a read-only property). Like a constant, a read-only field cannot be changed after the initial assignment. However, unlike a constant, the value assigned to a read-only field can be determined at runtime and, therefore, can legally be assigned within the scope of a constructor, but nowhere else.

This can be very helpful when you don't know the value of a field until runtime, perhaps because you need to read an external file to obtain the value, but wish to ensure that the value will not change after that point. For the sake of illustration, assume the following update to MyMathClass:

```
class MyMathClass
{
  // Read-only fields can be assigned in ctors,
  // but nowhere else.
  public readonly double PI;

  public MyMathClass ()
  {
    PI = 3.14;
```

```
    }
}
```

Again, any attempt to make assignments to a field marked readonly outside the scope of a constructor results in a compiler error:

```
class MyMathClass
{
  public readonly double PI;
  public MyMathClass ()
  {
    PI = 3.14;
  }

  // Error!
  public void ChangePI()
  { PI = 3.14444;}
}
```

Static Read-Only Fields

Unlike a constant field, read-only fields are not implicitly static. Thus, if you want to expose PI from the class level, you must explicitly make use of the static keyword. If you know the value of a static read-only field at compile time, the initial assignment looks very similar to that of a constant (however in this case, it would be easier to simply use the const keyword in the first place, as we are assigning the data field at the time of declaration):

```
class MyMathClass
{
  public static readonly double PI = 3.14;
}

class Program
{
  static void Main(string[] args)
  {
    Console.WriteLine("***** Fun with Const *****");
    Console.WriteLine("The value of PI is: {0}", MyMathClass.PI);
    Console.ReadLine();
  }
}
```

However, if the value of a static read-only field is not known until runtime, you must make use of a static constructor as described earlier in this chapter:

```
class MyMathClass
{
  public static readonly double PI;

  static MyMathClass()
  { PI = 3.14; }
}
```

■ **Source Code** The ConstData project is included under the Chapter 5 subdirectory.

Understanding Partial Types

Last but not least, it is important to understand the role of the C# partial keyword. A production-level class could very easily consist of hundreds and hundreds of lines of code. As well, given that a typical class is defined within a single *.cs file, you could end up with a very long file indeed. When you are creating your classes, it is often the case that much of the code can be basically ignored after it is accounted for. For example, field data, properties, and constructors tend to remain as-is during production, while methods tend to be modified quite often.

If you want, you can partition a single class across multiple C# files, to isolate the boilerplate code from more readily useful members. To illustrate, open up the EmployeeApp project you created previously in this chapter into Visual Studio, and after you have done so, open the Employee.cs file for editing. Currently, this single file contains code of all aspects of the class:

```
class Employee
{
  // Field Data

  // Constructors

  // Methods

  // Properties
}
```

Using partial classes, you could choose to move the constructors and field data into a brand new file named Employee.Internal.cs (please note, the name of the file is irrelevant; here I just tacked on the work internal to represent the guts of the class). The first step is to add the partial keyword to the current class definition and cut the code to be placed into the new file:

```
// Employee.cs
partial class Employee
{
  // Methods

  // Properties
}
```

Next, assuming you have inserted a new class file into your project, you can move the data fields and constructors to the new file using a simple cut/paste operation. In addition, you *must* add the partial keyword to this aspect of the class definition. For example:

```
// Employee.Internal.cs
partial class Employee
{
  // Field data

  // Constructors
}
```

■ **Note** Remember that every aspect of a partial class definition must be marked with the `partial` keyword!

After you compile the modified project, you should see no difference whatsoever. The whole idea of a partial class is only realized during design time. After the application has been compiled, there is just a single, unified class within the assembly. The only requirement when defining partial types is that the type's name (`Employee` in this case) is identical and defined within the same .NET namespace.

To be honest, you will most likely not need to make use of partial class definitions too often. However, Visual Studio uses them in the background all the time. Later in this book, when you start to look into GUI application development using Windows Presentation Foundation or ASP.NET, you'll see that Visual Studio isolates designer-generated code into a partial class, leaving you to focus on your application-specific programming logic.

■ **Source Code** The EmployeeAppPartial project can be found under the Chapter 5 subdirectory.

Summary

The point of this chapter was to introduce you to the role of the C# class type. As you have seen, classes can take any number of *constructors* that enable the object user to establish the state of the object upon creation. This chapter also illustrated several class design techniques (and related keywords). Recall that the `this` keyword can be used to obtain access to the current object, the `static` keyword allows you to define fields and members that are bound at the class (not object) level, and the `const` keyword (and `readonly` modifier) allows you to define a point of data that can never change after the initial assignment.

The bulk of this chapter dug into the details of the first pillar of OOP: encapsulation. Here you learned about the access modifiers of C# and the role of type properties, object initialization syntax, and partial classes. With this behind you, you are now able to turn to the next chapter where you will learn to build a family of related classes using inheritance and polymorphism.

CHAPTER 6

Understanding Inheritance and Polymorphism

Chapter 5 examined the first pillar of OOP: encapsulation. At that time, you learned how to build a single well-defined class type with constructors and various members (constructors, fields, properties, methods, constants, and read-only fields). This chapter will focus on the remaining two pillars of OOP: inheritance and polymorphism.

First, you will learn how to build families of related classes using *inheritance*. As you will see, this form of code reuse allows you to define common functionality in a parent class that can be leveraged, and possibly altered, by child classes. Along the way, you will learn how to establish a *polymorphic interface* into class hierarchies using virtual and abstract members, as well as the role of explicit casting. We'll wrap up by examining the role of the ultimate parent class in the .NET base class libraries: System.Object.

The Basic Mechanics of Inheritance

Recall from Chapter 5 that inheritance is the aspect of OOP that facilitates code reuse. Specifically speaking, code reuse comes in two flavors: inheritance (the "is-a" relationship) and the containment/delegation model (the "has-a" relationship). Let's begin this chapter by examining the classical inheritance model of the "is-a" relationship.

When you establish "is-a" relationships between classes, you are building a dependency between two or more class types. The basic idea behind classical inheritance is that new classes can be created using existing classes as a starting point. To begin with a very simple example, create a new Console Application project named BasicInheritance. Now assume you have designed a class named Car that models some basic details of an automobile:

```
// A simple base class.
class Car
{
  public readonly int maxSpeed;
  private int currSpeed;

  public Car(int max)
  {
    maxSpeed = max;
  }
  public Car()
  {
    maxSpeed = 55;
  }
```

```
  public int Speed
  {
    get { return currSpeed; }
    set
    {
      currSpeed = value;
      if (currSpeed > maxSpeed)
      {
        currSpeed = maxSpeed;
      }
    }
  }
}
```

Notice that the Car class is making use of encapsulation services to control access to the private currSpeed field using a public property named Speed. At this point, you can exercise your Car type as follows:

```
static void Main(string[] args)
{
  Console.WriteLine("***** Basic Inheritance *****\n");
  // Make a Car object and set max speed.
  Car myCar = new Car(80);

  // Set the current speed, and print it.
  myCar.Speed = 50;
  Console.WriteLine("My car is going {0} MPH", myCar.Speed);
  Console.ReadLine();
}
```

Specifying the Parent Class of an Existing Class

Now assume you want to build a new class named MiniVan. Like a basic Car, you want to define the MiniVan class to support data for a maximum speed, current speed, and a property named Speed to allow the object user to modify the object's state. Clearly, the Car and MiniVan classes are related; in fact, it can be said that a MiniVan "*is-a*" type of Car. The "is-a" relationship (formally termed *classical inheritance*) allows you to build new class definitions that extend the functionality of an existing class.

The existing class that will serve as the basis for the new class is termed a base or parent class. The role of a base class is to define all the common data and members for the classes that extend it. The extending classes are formally termed derived or child classes. In C#, you make use of the colon operator on the class definition to establish an "is-a" relationship between classes. Assume you have authored the following new MiniVan class:

```
// MiniVan "is-a" Car.
class MiniVan : Car
{
}
```

Currently, this new class has not defined any members whatsoever. So, what have you gained by extending your MiniVan from the Car base class? Simply put, MiniVan objects now have access to each public member defined within the parent class.

■ **Note** Although constructors are typically defined as public, a derived class never inherits the constructors of a parent class. Constructors are only used to construct the class that they are defined within.

Given the relation between these two class types, you could now make use of the MiniVan class like so:

```
static void Main(string[] args)
{
  Console.WriteLine("***** Basic Inheritance *****\n");
...
  // Now make a MiniVan object.
  MiniVan myVan = new MiniVan();
  myVan.Speed = 10;
  Console.WriteLine("My van is going {0} MPH",
    myVan.Speed);
  Console.ReadLine();
}
```

Again, notice that although you have not added any members to the MiniVan class, you have direct access to the public Speed property of your parent class, and have thus reused code. This is a far better approach than creating a MiniVan class that has the exact same members as Car, such as a Speed property. If you did duplicate code between these two classes, you would need to now maintain two bodies of code, which is certainly a poor use of your time.

Always remember, that inheritance preserves encapsulation; therefore, the following code results in a compiler error, as private members can never be accessed from an object reference.

```
static void Main(string[] args)
{
  Console.WriteLine("***** Basic Inheritance *****\n");
...
  // Make a MiniVan object.
  MiniVan myVan = new MiniVan();
  myVan.Speed = 10;
  Console.WriteLine("My van is going {0} MPH",
    myVan.Speed);

  // Error! Can't access private members!
  myVan.currSpeed = 55;
  Console.ReadLine();
}
```

On a related note, if the MiniVan defined its own set of members, it would still not be able to access any private member of the Car base class. Remember, private members can *only* be accessed by the class that defines it. For example, the following method in MiniVan would result in a compiler error:

```
// MiniVan derives from Car.
class MiniVan : Car
{
  public void TestMethod()
  {
```

215

```
    // OK! Can access public members
    // of a parent within a derived type.
    Speed = 10;

    // Error! Cannot access private
    // members of parent within a derived type.
    currSpeed = 10;
  }
}
```

Regarding Multiple Base Classes

Speaking of base classes, it is important to keep in mind that C# demands that a given class have exactly *one* direct base class. It is not possible to create a class type that directly derives from two or more base classes (this technique [which is supported in unmanaged C++] is known as *multiple inheritance*, or simply *MI*). If you attempted to create a class that specifies two direct parent classes, as shown in the following code, you will receive compiler errors.

```
// Illegal! C# does not allow
// multiple inheritance for classes!
class WontWork
  : BaseClassOne, BaseClassTwo
{}
```

As you will see in Chapter 8, the .NET platform does allow a given class, or structure, to implement any number of discrete interfaces. In this way, a C# type can exhibit a number of behaviors while avoiding the complexities associated with MI. On a related note, while a class can have only one direct base class, it is permissible for an interface to directly derive from multiple interfaces. Using this technique, you can build sophisticated interface hierarchies that model complex behaviors (again, see Chapter 8).

The sealed Keyword

C# supplies another keyword, sealed, that prevents inheritance from occurring. When you mark a class as sealed, the compiler will not allow you to derive from this type. For example, assume you have decided that it makes no sense to further extend the MiniVan class:

```
// The MiniVan class cannot be extended!
sealed class MiniVan : Car
{
}
```

If you (or a teammate) were to attempt to derive from this class, you would receive a compile-time error:

```
// Error! Cannot extend
// a class marked with the sealed keyword!
class DeluxeMiniVan
  : MiniVan
{}
```

Most often, sealing a class makes the best sense when you are designing a utility class. For example, the System namespace defines numerous sealed classes. You can verify this for yourself by opening up the Visual Studio Object Browser (via the View menu) and selecting the String class within the System namespace of the mscorlib.dll assembly. Notice in Figure 6-1 the use of the sealed keyword seen within the Summary window.

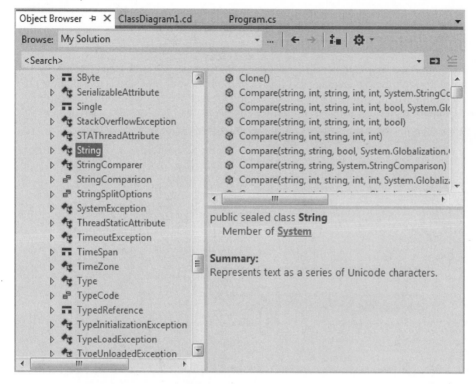

Figure 6-1. The base class libraries define numerous sealed types, such as System.String

Thus, just like the MiniVan, if you attempted to build a new class that extends System.String, you will receive a compile-time error:

```
// Another error! Cannot extend
// a class marked as sealed!
class MyString
  : String
{}
```

■ **Note** In Chapter 4, you learned that C# structures are always implicitly sealed (see Table 4-3). Therefore, you can never derive one structure from another structure, a class from a structure, or a structure from a class. Structures can only be used to model stand-alone, atomic, user-defined data types. If you want to leverage the is-a relationship, you must use classes.

As you would guess, there are many more details to inheritance that you will come to know during the remainder of this chapter. For now, simply keep in mind that the colon operator allows you to establish base/derived class relationships, while the sealed keyword prevents subsequent inheritance from occurring.

Revising Visual Studio Class Diagrams

In Chapter 2, I briefly mentioned that Visual Studio allows you to establish base/derived class relationships visually at design time. To leverage this aspect of the IDE, your first step is to include a new class diagram file into your current project. To do so, access the Project Add New Item menu option and select the Class Diagram icon (in Figure 6-2, I renamed the file from ClassDiagram1.cd to Cars.cd).

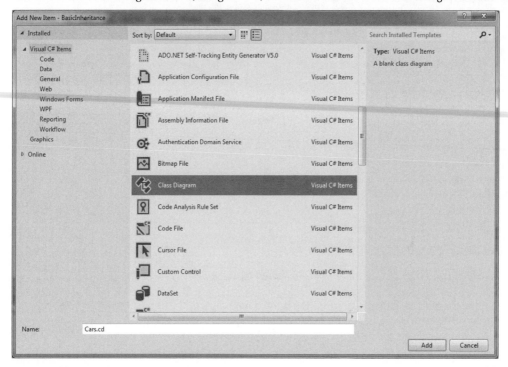

Figure 6-2. Inserting a new class diagram

After you click the Add button, you will be presented with a blank designer surface. To add types to a class designer, simply drag each file from the Solution Explorer window onto the surface. Also recall that if you delete an item from the visual designer (simply by selecting it and pressing the Delete key), this will not destroy the associated source code, but simply removes the item off the designer surface. The current class hierarchy is shown in Figure 6-3.

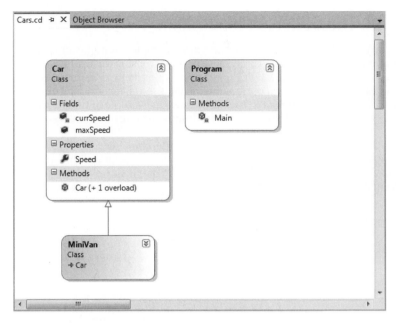

Figure 6-3. *The visual designer of Visual Studio*

■ **Note** As a shortcut, if you wish to automatically add all of your project's current types to a designer surface, select the Project node within the Solution Explorer and then click the View Class Diagram button in the upper right of the Solution Explorer window.

Beyond simply displaying the relationships of the types within your current application, recall from Chapter 2 that you can also create brand new types and populate their members using the Class Designer toolbox and Class Details window.

If you want to make use of these visual tools during the remainder of the book, feel free. However, always make sure you analyze the generated code so you have a solid understanding of what these tools have done on your behalf.

■ **Source Code** The BasicInheritance project is located under the Chapter 6 subdirectory.

The Second Pillar of OOP: The Details of Inheritance

Now that you have seen the basic syntax of inheritance, let's create a more complex example and get to know the numerous details of building class hierarchies. To do so, you will be reusing the Employee class you designed in Chapter 5. To begin, create a brand new C# Console Application named Employees.

Next, activate the Project ➤ Add Existing Item menu option and navigate to the location of your Employee.cs and Employee.Internals.cs files you created in the EmployeeApp example of Chapter 5. Select each of them (via a Ctrl+click) and click the Add button. Visual Studio responds by copying each file into the current project.

Before you start to build some derived classes, you have one detail to attend to. Because the original Employee class was created in a project named EmployeeApp, the class has been wrapped within an identically named .NET namespace. Chapter 14 will examine namespaces in detail; however, for simplicity, rename the current namespace (in both file locations) to Employees in order to match your new project name:

```
// Be sure to change the namespace name in both C# files!
namespace Employees
{
  partial class Employee
  {...}
}
```

■ **Note** As a sanity check, compile and run your new project by pressing Ctrl+F5. The program will not do anything at this point; however, this will ensure you do not have any compiler errors.

Your goal is to create a family of classes that model various types of employees in a company. Assume that you want to leverage the functionality of the Employee class to create two new classes (SalesPerson and Manager). The new SalesPerson class "is-an" Employee (as is a Manager). Remember that under the classical inheritance model, base classes (such as Employee) are used to define general characteristics that are common to all descendents. Subclasses (such as SalesPerson and Manager) extend this general functionality while adding more specific functionality.

For your example, you will assume that the Manager class extends Employee by recording the number of stock options, while the SalesPerson class maintains the number of sales made. Insert a new class file (Manager.cs) that defines the Manager class with the following automatic property:

```
// Managers need to know their number of stock options.
class Manager : Employee
{
  public int StockOptions { get; set; }
}
```

Next, add another new class file (SalesPerson.cs) that defines the SalesPerson class with a fitting automatic property:

```
// Salespeople need to know their number of sales.
class SalesPerson : Employee
{
  public int SalesNumber { get; set; }
```

```
}
```

Now that you have established an "is-a" relationship, SalesPerson and Manager have automatically inherited all public members of the Employee base class. To illustrate, update your Main() method as follows:

```
// Create a subclass object and access base class functionality.
static void Main(string[] args)
{
  Console.WriteLine("***** The Employee Class Hierarchy *****\n");
  SalesPerson fred = new SalesPerson();
  fred.Age = 31;
  fred.Name = "Fred";
  fred.SalesNumber = 50;
  Console.ReadLine();
}
```

Controlling Base Class Creation with the base Keyword

Currently, SalesPerson and Manager can only be created using the freebee default constructor (see Chapter 5). With this in mind, assume you have added a new six-argument constructor to the Manager type, which is invoked as follows:

```
static void Main(string[] args)
{
...
  // Assume Manager has a constructor matching this signature:
  // (string fullName, int age, int empID,
  //  float currPay, string ssn, int numbOfOpts)
  Manager chucky = new Manager("Chucky", 50, 92, 100000, "333-23-2322", 9000);
  Console.ReadLine();
}
```

If you look at the parameter list, you can clearly see that most of these arguments should be stored in the member variables defined by the Employee base class. To do so, you might implement this custom constructor on the Manager class as follows:

```
public Manager(string fullName, int age, int empID,
               float currPay, string ssn, int numbOfOpts)
{
  // This property is defined by the Manager class.
  StockOptions = numbOfOpts;

  // Assign incoming parameters using the
  // inherited properties of the parent class.
  ID = empID;
  Age = age;
  Name = fullName;
  Pay = currPay;

  // OOPS! This would be a compiler error,
  // if the SSN property were read-only!
  SocialSecurityNumber = ssn;
```

```
}
```

The first issue with this approach is that if you defined any property as read-only (for example, the `SocialSecurityNumber` property), you are unable to assign the incoming `string` parameter to this field, as seen in the final code statement of this custom constructor.

The second issue is that you have indirectly created a rather inefficient constructor, given the fact that under C#, unless you say otherwise, the default constructor of a base class is called automatically before the logic of the derived constructor is executed. After this point, the current implementation accesses numerous public properties of the `Employee` base class to establish its state. Thus, you have really made seven hits (five inherited properties and two constructor calls) during the creation of a `Manager` object!

To help optimize the creation of a derived class, you will do well to implement your subclass constructors to explicitly call an appropriate custom base class constructor, rather than the default. In this way, you are able to reduce the number of calls to inherited initialization members (which saves processing time). Let's retrofit the custom constructor of the `Manager` type to do this very thing using the base keyword:

```
public Manager(string fullName, int age, int empID,
               float currPay, string ssn, int numbOfOpts)
  : base(fullName, age, empID, currPay, ssn)
{
  // This property is defined by the Manager class.
  StockOptions = numbOfOpts;
}
```

Here, the base keyword is hanging off the constructor signature (much like the syntax used to chain constructors on a single class using the this keyword, as was discussed in Chapter 5), which always indicates a derived constructor is passing data to the immediate parent constructor. In this situation, you are explicitly calling the five-parameter constructor defined by `Employee` and saving yourself unnecessary calls during the creation of the child class. The custom `SalesPerson` constructor looks almost identical:

```
// As a general rule, all subclasses should explicitly call an appropriate
// base class constructor.
public SalesPerson(string fullName, int age, int empID,
    float currPay, string ssn, int numbOfSales)
  : base(fullName, age, empID, currPay, ssn)
{
  // This belongs with us!
  SalesNumber = numbOfSales;
}
```

■ **Note** You may use the base keyword whenever a subclass wishes to access a public or protected member defined by a parent class. Use of this keyword is not limited to constructor logic. You will see examples using base in this manner during the examination of polymorphism, later in this chapter.

Finally, recall that once you add a custom constructor to a class definition, the default constructor is silently removed. Therefore, be sure to redefine the default constructor for the SalesPerson and Manager types. For example:

```
// Add back the default ctor
// in the Manager class as well.
public SalesPerson() {}
```

Keeping Family Secrets: The protected Keyword

As you already know, public items are directly accessible from anywhere, while private items can only be accessed by the class that has defined them. Recall from Chapter 5 that C# takes the lead of many other modern object languages and provides an additional keyword to define member accessibility: protected.

When a base class defines protected data or protected members, it establishes a set of items that can be accessed directly by any descendent. If you want to allow the SalesPerson and Manager child classes to directly access the data sector defined by Employee, you can update the original Employee class definition as follows:

```
// Protected state data.
partial class Employee
{
  // Derived classes can now directly access this information.
  protected string empName;
  protected int empID;
  protected float currPay;
  protected int empAge;
  protected string empSSN;
...
}
```

The benefit of defining protected members in a base class is that derived types no longer have to access the data indirectly using public methods or properties. The possible downfall, of course, is that when a derived type has direct access to its parent's internal data, it is very possible to accidentally bypass existing business rules found within public properties. When you define protected members, you are creating a level of trust between the parent and child class, as the compiler will not catch any violation of your type's business rules.

Finally, understand that as far as the object user is concerned, protected data is regarded as private (as the user is "outside" of the family). Therefore, the following is illegal:

```
static void Main(string[] args)
{
  // Error! Can't access protected data from object instance.
  Employee emp = new Employee();
  emp.empName = "Fred";
}
```

■ **Note** Although `protected` field data can break encapsulation, it is quite safe (and useful) to define `protected` methods. When building class hierarchies, it is very common to define a set of methods that are only for use by derived types and are not intended for use by the outside world.

Adding a Sealed Class

Recall that a *sealed* class cannot be extended by other classes. As mentioned, this technique is most often used when you are designing a utility class. However, when building class hierarchies, you might find that a certain branch in the inheritance chain should be "capped off," as it makes no sense to further extend the linage. For example, assume you have added yet another class to your program (PTSalesPerson) that extends the existing SalesPerson type. Figure 6-4 shows the current update.

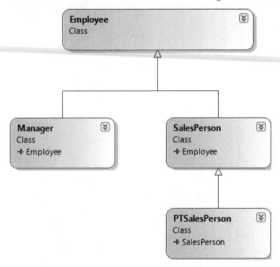

Figure 6-4. The PTSalesPerson *class*

PTSalesPerson is a class representing, of course, a part-time salesperson. For the sake of argument, let's say that you want to ensure that no other developer is able to subclass from PTSalesPerson. (After all, how much more part-time can you get than "part-time"?) Again, to prevent others from extending a class, make use of the sealed keyword:

```
sealed class PTSalesPerson : SalesPerson
{
  public PTSalesPerson(string fullName, int age, int empID,
                       float currPay, string ssn, int numbOfSales)
    :base (fullName, age, empID, currPay, ssn, numbOfSales)
  {
  }
    // Assume other members here...
}
```

Programming for Containment/Delegation

Recall that code reuse comes in two flavors. You have just explored the classical "is-a" relationship. Before you examine the third pillar of OOP (polymorphism), let's examine the "has-a" relationship (also known as the *containment/delegation model* or *aggregation*). Assume you have created a new class that models an employee benefits package, as follows:

```
// This new type will function as a contained class.
class BenefitPackage
{
  // Assume we have other members that represent
  // dental/health benefits, and so on.
  public double ComputePayDeduction()
  {
    return 125.0;
  }
}
```

Obviously, it would be rather odd to establish an "is-a" relationship between the BenefitPackage class and the employee types. (Employee "is-a" BenefitPackage? I don't think so.) However, it should be clear that some sort of relationship between the two could be established. In short, you would like to express the idea that each employee "has-a" BenefitPackage. To do so, you can update the Employee class definition as follows:

```
// Employees now have benefits.
partial class Employee
{
  // Contain a BenefitPackage object.
  protected BenefitPackage empBenefits = new BenefitPackage();
...
}
```

At this point, you have successfully contained another object. However, to expose the functionality of the contained object to the outside world requires delegation. *Delegation* is simply the act of adding public members to the containing class that make use of the contained object's functionality.

For example, you could update the Employee class to expose the contained empBenefits object using a custom property, as well as make use of its functionality internally using a new method named GetBenefitCost():

```
public partial class Employee
{
  // Contain a BenefitPackage object.
  protected BenefitPackage empBenefits = new BenefitPackage();

  // Expose certain benefit behaviors of object.
  public double GetBenefitCost()
  { return empBenefits.ComputePayDeduction(); }

  // Expose object through a custom property.
  public BenefitPackage Benefits
  {
    get { return empBenefits; }
    set { empBenefits = value; }
```

```
    }
  ...
}
```

In the following updated `Main()` method, notice how you can interact with the internal `BenefitsPackage` type defined by the `Employee` type:

```
static void Main(string[] args)
{
  Console.WriteLine("***** The Employee Class Hierarchy *****\n");
  ...
  Manager chucky = new Manager("Chucky", 50, 92, 100000, "333-23-2322", 9000);
  double cost = chucky.GetBenefitCost();
  Console.ReadLine();
}
```

Understanding Nested Type Definitions

Chapter 5 briefly mentioned the concept of nested types, which is a spin on the "has-a" relationship you have just examined. In C# (as well as other .NET languages), it is possible to define a type (enum, class, interface, struct, or delegate) directly within the scope of a class or structure. When you have done so, the nested (or "inner") type is considered a member of the nesting (or "outer") class, and in the eyes of the runtime can be manipulated like any other member (fields, properties, methods, and events). The syntax used to nest a type is quite straightforward:

```
public class OuterClass
{
  // A public nested type can be used by anybody.
  public class PublicInnerClass {}

  // A private nested type can only be used by members
  // of the containing class.
  private class PrivateInnerClass {}
}
```

Although the syntax is fairly clear, understanding why you would want to do this might not be readily apparent. To understand this technique, ponder the following traits of nesting a type:

- Nested types allow you to gain complete control over the access level of the inner type, as they may be declared privately (recall that non-nested classes cannot be declared using the `private` keyword).

- Because a nested type is a member of the containing class, it can access private members of the containing class.

- Often, a nested type is only useful as a helper for the outer class, and is not intended for use by the outside world.

When a type nests another class type, it can create member variables of the type, just as it would for any point of data. However, if you want to make use of a nested type from outside of the containing type, you must qualify it by the scope of the nesting type. Consider the following code:

```
static void Main(string[] args)
{
  // Create and use the public inner class. OK!
  OuterClass.PublicInnerClass inner;
  inner = new OuterClass.PublicInnerClass();

  // Compiler Error! Cannot access the private class.
  OuterClass.PrivateInnerClass inner2;
  inner2 = new OuterClass.PrivateInnerClass();
}
```

To make use of this concept within the employees example, assume you have now nested the
BenefitPackage directly within the Employee class type:

```
partial class Employee
{
  public class BenefitPackage
  {
    // Assume we have other members that represent
    // dental/health benefits, and so on.
    public double ComputePayDeduction()
    {
      return 125.0;
    }
  }
...
}
```

The nesting process can be as "deep" as you require. For example, assume you want to create an
enumeration named BenefitPackageLevel, which documents the various benefit levels an employee
may choose. To programmatically enforce the tight connection between Employee, BenefitPackage, and
BenefitPackageLevel, you could nest the enumeration as follows:

```
// Employee nests BenefitPackage.
public partial class Employee
{
  // BenefitPackage nests BenefitPackageLevel.
  public class BenefitPackage
  {
    public enum BenefitPackageLevel
    {
      Standard, Gold, Platinum
    }

    public double ComputePayDeduction()
    {
      return 125.0;
    }
  }
...
}
```

Because of the nesting relationships, note how you are required to make use of this enumeration:

```
static void Main(string[] args)
{
...
  // Define my benefit level.
  Employee.BenefitPackage.BenefitPackageLevel myBenefitLevel =
    Employee.BenefitPackage.BenefitPackageLevel.Platinum;
  Console.ReadLine();
}
```

Excellent! At this point, you have been exposed to a number of keywords (and concepts) that allow you to build hierarchies of related types via classical inheritance, containment, and nested types. If the details aren't crystal clear right now, don't sweat it. You will be building a number of additional hierarchies over the remainder of this book. Next up, let's examine the final pillar of OOP: polymorphism.

The Third Pillar of OOP: C#'s Polymorphic Support

Recall that the Employee base class defined a method named GiveBonus(), which was originally implemented as follows:

```
public partial class Employee
{
  public void GiveBonus(float amount)
  {
    Pay += amount;
  }
...
}
```

Because this method has been defined with the public keyword, you can now give bonuses to salespeople and managers (as well as part-time salespeople):

```
static void Main(string[] args)
{
  Console.WriteLine("***** The Employee Class Hierarchy *****\n");

  // Give each employee a bonus?
  Manager chucky = new Manager("Chucky", 50, 92, 100000, "333-23-2322", 9000);
  chucky.GiveBonus(300);
  chucky.DisplayStats();
  Console.WriteLine();

  SalesPerson fran = new SalesPerson("Fran", 43, 93, 3000, "932-32-3232", 31);
  fran.GiveBonus(200);
  fran.DisplayStats();
  Console.ReadLine();
}
```

The problem with the current design is that the publicly inherited GiveBonus() method operates identically for all subclasses. Ideally, the bonus of a salesperson or part-time salesperson should take into account the number of sales. Perhaps managers should gain additional stock options in conjunction with a monetary bump in salary. Given this, you are suddenly faced with an interesting question: "How can related types respond differently to the same request?" Again, glad you asked!

The virtual and override Keywords

Polymorphism provides a way for a subclass to define its own version of a method defined by its base class, using the process termed *method overriding*. To retrofit your current design, you need to understand the meaning of the virtual and override keywords. If a base class wants to define a method that *may be* (but does not have to be) overridden by a subclass, it must mark the method with the virtual keyword:

```
partial class Employee
{
  // This method can now be "overridden" by a derived class.
  public virtual void GiveBonus(float amount)
  {
    Pay += amount;
  }
...
}
```

■ **Note** Methods that have been marked with the virtual keyword are (not surprisingly) termed *virtual methods*.

When a subclass wants to change the implementation details of a virtual method, it does so using the override keyword. For example, the SalesPerson and Manager could override GiveBonus() as follows (assume that PTSalesPerson will not override GiveBonus() and, therefore, simply inherits the version defined by SalesPerson):

```
class SalesPerson : Employee
{
...
  // A salesperson's bonus is influenced by the number of sales.
  public override void GiveBonus(float amount)
  {
    int salesBonus = 0;
    if (SalesNumber >= 0 && SalesNumber <= 100)
      salesBonus = 10;
    else
    {
      if (SalesNumber >= 101 && SalesNumber <= 200)
        salesBonus = 15;
      else
        salesBonus = 20;
    }
    base.GiveBonus(amount * salesBonus);
  }
}

class Manager : Employee
{
...
```

```
    public override void GiveBonus(float amount)
    {
      base.GiveBonus(amount);
      Random r = new Random();
      StockOptions += r.Next(500);
    }
}
```

Notice how each overridden method is free to leverage the default behavior using the base keyword. In this way, you have no need to completely reimplement the logic behind GiveBonus(), but can reuse (and possibly extend) the default behavior of the parent class.

Also assume that the current DisplayStats() method of the Employee class has been declared virtually. By doing so, each subclass can override this method to account for displaying the number of sales (for salespeople) and current stock options (for managers). For example, consider the Manager's version of the DisplayStats() method (the SalesPerson class would implement DisplayStats() in a similar manner to show the number of sales):

```
public override void DisplayStats()
{
  base.DisplayStats();
  Console.WriteLine("Number of Stock Options: {0}", StockOptions);
}
```

Now that each subclass can interpret what these virtual methods means to itself, each object instance behaves as a more independent entity:

```
static void Main(string[] args)
{
  Console.WriteLine("***** The Employee Class Hierarchy *****\n");

  // A better bonus system!
  Manager chucky = new Manager("Chucky", 50, 92, 100000, "333-23-2322", 9000);
  chucky.GiveBonus(300);
  chucky.DisplayStats();
  Console.WriteLine();

  SalesPerson fran = new SalesPerson("Fran", 43, 93, 3000, "932-32-3232", 31);
  fran.GiveBonus(200);
  fran.DisplayStats();
  Console.ReadLine();
}
```

The following output shows a possible test run of your application thus far:

```
***** The Employee Class Hierarchy *****

Name: Chucky
ID: 92
Age: 50
Pay: 100300
SSN: 333-23-2322
Number of Stock Options: 9337

Name: Fran
ID: 93
Age: 43
Pay: 5000
SSN: 932-32-3232
Number of Sales: 31
```

Overriding Virtual Members Using the Visual Studio IDE

As you might have already noticed, when you are overriding a member, you must recall the type of each and every parameter—not to mention the method name and parameter passing conventions (ref, out, and params). Visual Studio has a very helpful feature that you can make use of when overriding a virtual member. If you type the word "override" within the scope of a class type (then hit the spacebar), IntelliSense will automatically display a list of all the overridable members defined in your parent classes, as you see in Figure 6-5.

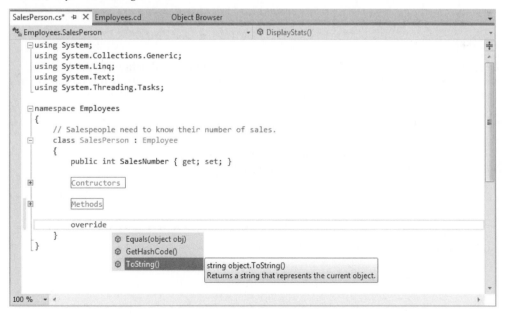

Figure 6-5. Quickly viewing overridable methods à la Visual Studio

When you select a member and hit the Enter key, the IDE responds by automatically filling in the method stub on your behalf. Note that you also receive a code statement that calls your parent's version of the virtual member (you are free to delete this line if it is not required). For example, if you used this technique when overriding the DisplayStats() method, you might find the following autogenerated code:

```
public override void DisplayStats()
{
  base.DisplayStats();
}
```

Sealing Virtual Members

Recall that the sealed keyword can be applied to a class type to prevent other types from extending its behavior via inheritance. As you might remember, you sealed PTSalesPerson as you assumed it made no sense for other developers to extend this line of inheritance any further.

On a related note, sometimes you might not wish to seal an entire class, but simply want to prevent derived types from overriding particular virtual methods. For example, assume you do not want part-time salespeople to obtain customized bonuses. To prevent the PTSalesPerson class from overriding the virtual GiveBonus() method, you could effectively seal this method in the SalesPerson class as follows:

```
// SalesPerson has sealed the GiveBonus() method!
class SalesPerson : Employee
{
...
  public override sealed void GiveBonus(float amount)
  {
    ...
  }
}
```

Here, SalesPerson has indeed overridden the virtual GiveBonus() method defined in the Employee class; however, it has explicitly marked it as sealed. Thus, if you attempted to override this method in the PTSalesPerson class, you receive compile-time errors, as shown in the following code:

```
sealed class PTSalesPerson : SalesPerson
{
  public PTSalesPerson(string fullName, int age, int empID,
                       float currPay, string ssn, int numbOfSales)
    :base (fullName, age, empID, currPay, ssn, numbOfSales)
  {
  }

  // Compiler error! Can't override this method
  // in the PTSalesPerson class, as it was sealed.
  public override void GiveBonus(float amount)
  {
  }
}
```

Understanding Abstract Classes

Currently, the Employee base class has been designed to supply various data members for its descendents, as well as supply two virtual methods (GiveBonus() and DisplayStats()) that may be overridden by a given descendent. While this is all well and good, there is a rather odd byproduct of the current design; you can directly create instances of the Employee base class:

```
// What exactly does this mean?
Employee X = new Employee();
```

In this example, the only real purpose of the Employee base class is to define common members for all subclasses. In all likelihood, you did not intend anyone to create a direct instance of this class, reason being that the Employee type itself is too general of a concept. For example, if I were to walk up to you and say, "I'm an employee!" I would bet your very first question to me would be, "What *kind* of employee are you?" Are you a consultant, trainer, admin assistant, copyeditor, or White House aide?

Given that many base classes tend to be rather nebulous entities, a far better design for this example is to prevent the ability to directly create a new Employee object in code. In C#, you can enforce this programmatically by using the abstract keyword in the class definition, thus creating an *abstract base class*:

```
// Update the Employee class as abstract
// to prevent direct instantiation.
abstract partial class Employee
{
  ...
}
```

With this, if you now attempt to create an instance of the Employee class, you are issued a compile-time error:

```
// Error! Cannot create an instance of an abstract class!
Employee X = new Employee();
```

At first glance, it might seem very strange to define a class that you cannot directly create. Recall however that base classes (abstract or not) are very useful, in that they contain all of the common data and functionality of derived types. Using this form of abstraction, we are able to model that the "idea" of an employee is completely valid; it is just not a concrete entity. Also understand that although we cannot *directly* create an abstract class, it is still assembled in memory when derived classes are created. Thus, it is perfectly fine (and common) for abstract classes to define any number of constructors that are called *indirectly* when derived classes are allocated.

At this point, you have constructed a fairly interesting employee hierarchy. You will add a bit more functionality to this application later in this chapter when examining C# casting rules. Until then, Figure 6-6 illustrates the crux of your current design.

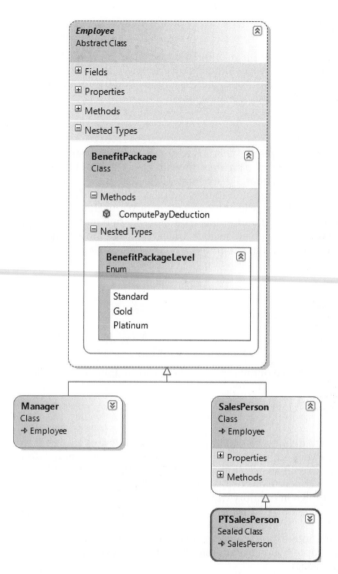

Figure 6-6. The Employee hierarchy

■ **Source Code** The Employees project is included under the Chapter 6 subdirectory.

Understanding the Polymorphic Interface

When a class has been defined as an abstract base class (via the abstract keyword), it may define any number of *abstract members*. Abstract members can be used whenever you wish to define a member that does *not* supply a default implementation, but *must* be accounted for by each derived class. By doing so, you enforce a *polymorphic interface* on each descendent, leaving them to contend with the task of providing the details behind your abstract methods.

Simply put, an abstract base class's polymorphic interface simply refers to its set of virtual and abstract methods. This is much more interesting than first meets the eye, as this trait of OOP allows you to build easily extendable and flexible software applications. To illustrate, you will be implementing (and slightly modifying) the hierarchy of shapes briefly examined in Chapter 5 during the overview of the pillars of OOP. To begin, create a new C# Console Application project named Shapes.

In Figure 6-7, notice that the Hexagon and Circle types each extend the Shape base class. Like any base class, Shape defines a number of members (a PetName property and Draw() method, in this case) that are common to all descendents.

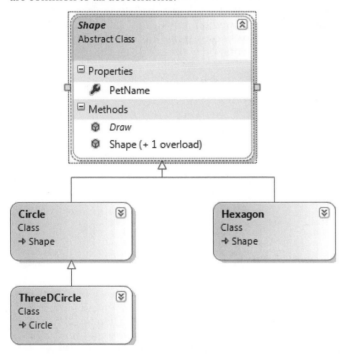

Figure 6-7. The shapes hierarchy

Much like the employee hierarchy, you should be able to tell that you don't want to allow the object user to create an instance of Shape directly, as it is too abstract of a concept. Again, to prevent the direct creation of the Shape type, you could define it as an abstract class. As well, given that you wish the derived types to respond uniquely to the Draw() method, let's mark it as virtual and define a default implementation:

```
// The abstract base class of the hierarchy.
abstract class Shape
{
  public Shape(string name = "NoName")
  { PetName = name; }

  public string PetName { get; set; }

  // A single virtual method.
  public virtual void Draw()
  {
    Console.WriteLine("Inside Shape.Draw()");
  }
}
```

Notice that the virtual Draw() method provides a default implementation that simply prints out a message that informs you that you are calling the Draw() method within the Shape base class. Now recall that when a method is marked with the virtual keyword, the method provides a default implementation that all derived types automatically inherit. If a child class so chooses, it *may* override the method but does not *have* to. Given this, consider the following implementation of the Circle and Hexagon types:

```
// Circle DOES NOT override Draw().
class Circle : Shape
{
  public Circle() {}
  public Circle(string name) : base(name){}
}

// Hexagon DOES override Draw().
class Hexagon : Shape
{
  public Hexagon() {}
  public Hexagon(string name) : base(name){}
  public override void Draw()
  {
    Console.WriteLine("Drawing {0} the Hexagon", PetName);
  }
}
```

The usefulness of abstract methods becomes crystal clear when you once again remember that subclasses are *never required* to override virtual methods (as in the case of Circle). Therefore, if you create an instance of the Hexagon and Circle types, you'd find that the Hexagon understands how to "draw" itself correctly or at least print out an appropriate message to the console. The Circle, however, is more than a bit confused:

```
static void Main(string[] args)
{
  Console.WriteLine("***** Fun with Polymorphism *****\n");

  Hexagon hex = new Hexagon("Beth");
  hex.Draw();
```

```
  Circle cir = new Circle("Cindy");
  // Calls base class implementation!
  cir.Draw();
  Console.ReadLine();
}
```

Now consider the following output of the previous Main() method:

```
***** Fun with Polymorphism *****

Drawing Beth the Hexagon
Inside Shape.Draw()
```

Clearly, this is not a very intelligent design for the current hierarchy. To force each child class to override the Draw() method, you can define Draw() as an abstract method of the Shape class, which by definition means you provide no default implementation whatsoever. To mark a method as abstract in C#, you use the abstract keyword. Notice that abstract members do not provide any implementation whatsoever:

```
abstract class Shape
{
  // Force all child classes to define how to be rendered.
  public abstract void Draw();
  ...
}
```

■ **Note** Abstract methods can only be defined in abstract classes. If you attempt to do otherwise, you will be issued a compiler error.

Methods marked with abstract are pure protocol. They simply define the name, return type (if any), and parameter set (if required). Here, the abstract Shape class informs the derived types "I have a method named Draw() that takes no arguments and returns nothing. If you derive from me, you figure out the details."

Given this, you are now obligated to override the Draw() method in the Circle class. If you do not, Circle is also assumed to be a noncreatable abstract type that must be adorned with the abstract keyword (which is obviously not very useful in this example). Here is the code update:

```
// If we did not implement the abstract Draw() method, Circle would also be
// considered abstract, and would have to be marked abstract!
class Circle : Shape
{
  public Circle() {}
  public Circle(string name) : base(name) {}
  public override void Draw()
  {
    Console.WriteLine("Drawing {0} the Circle", PetName);
```

```
    }
}
```

The short answer is that you can now make the assumption that anything deriving from Shape does indeed have a unique version of the Draw() method. To illustrate the full story of polymorphism, consider the following code:

```
static void Main(string[] args)
{
  Console.WriteLine("***** Fun with Polymorphism *****\n");

  // Make an array of Shape-compatible objects.
  Shape[] myShapes = {new Hexagon(), new Circle(), new Hexagon("Mick"),
    new Circle("Beth"), new Hexagon("Linda")};

  // Loop over each item and interact with the
  // polymorphic interface.
  foreach (Shape s in myShapes)
  {
    s.Draw();
  }
  Console.ReadLine();
}
```

Here is the output from the modified Main() method:

```
***** Fun with Polymorphism *****

Drawing NoName the Hexagon
Drawing NoName the Circle
Drawing Mick the Hexagon
Drawing Beth the Circle
Drawing Linda the Hexagon
```

This Main() method illustrates polymorphism at its finest. Although it is not possible to *directly* create an instance of an abstract base class (the Shape), you are able to freely store references to any subclass with an abstract base variable. Therefore, when you are creating an array of Shapes, the array can hold any object deriving from the Shape base class (if you attempt to place Shape-incompatible objects into the array, you receive a compiler error).

Given that all items in the myShapes array do indeed derive from Shape, you know they all support the same "polymorphic interface" (or said more plainly, they all have a Draw() method). As you iterate over the array of Shape references, it is at runtime that the underlying type is determined. At this point, the correct version of the Draw() method is invoked in memory.

This technique also makes it very simple to safely extend the current hierarchy. For example, assume you derived more classes from the abstract Shape base class (Triangle, Square, etc.). Due to the polymorphic interface, the code within your foreach loop would not have to change in the slightest, as the compiler enforces that only Shape-compatible types are placed within the myShapes array.

Understanding Member Shadowing

C# provides a facility that is the logical opposite of method overriding, termed *shadowing*. Formally speaking, if a derived class defines a member that is identical to a member defined in a base class, the derived class has shadowed the parent's version. In the real world, the possibility of this occurring is the greatest when you are subclassing from a class you (or your team) did not create yourselves (for example, if you purchase a third-party .NET software package).

For the sake of illustration, assume you receive a class named ThreeDCircle from a coworker (or classmate) that defines a subroutine named Draw() taking no arguments:

```
class ThreeDCircle
{
  public void Draw()
  {
    Console.WriteLine("Drawing a 3D Circle");
  }
}
```

You figure that a ThreeDCircle "is-a" Circle, so you derive from your existing Circle type:

```
class ThreeDCircle : Circle
{
  public void Draw()
  {
    Console.WriteLine("Drawing a 3D Circle");
  }
}
```

After you recompile, you find the following warning:

```
'Shapes.ThreeDCircle.Draw()' hides inherited member 'Shapes.Circle.Draw()'. To make the
current member override that implementation, add the override keyword. Otherwise add the new
keyword.
```

The problem is that you have a derived class (ThreeDCircle) that contains a method that is identical to an inherited method. To address this issue, you have two options. You could simply update the parent's version of Draw() using the override keyword (as suggested by the compiler). With this approach, the ThreeDCircle type is able to extend the parent's default behavior as required. However, if you don't have access to the code defining the base class (again, as would be the case in many third-party libraries), you would be unable to modify the Draw() method as a virtual member, as you don't have access to the code file!

As an alternative, you can include the new keyword to the offending Draw() member of the derived type (ThreeDCircle, in this example). Doing so explicitly states that the derived type's implementation is intentionally designed to effectively ignore the parent's version (again, in the real world, this can be helpful if external .NET software somehow conflicts with your current software).

```
// This class extends Circle and hides the inherited Draw() method.
class ThreeDCircle : Circle
{
  // Hide any Draw() implementation above me.
  public new void Draw()
```

```
    {
        Console.WriteLine("Drawing a 3D Circle");
    }
}
```

You can also apply the new keyword to any member type inherited from a base class (field, constant, static member, or property). As a further example, assume that ThreeDCircle wants to hide the inherited PetName property:

```
class ThreeDCircle : Circle
{
    // Hide the PetName property above me.
    public new string PetName { get; set; }

    // Hide any Draw() implementation above me.
    public new void Draw()
    {
        Console.WriteLine("Drawing a 3D Circle");
    }
}
```

Finally, be aware that it is still possible to trigger the base class implementation of a shadowed member using an explicit cast, as described in the next section. For example, the following code shows:

```
static void Main(string[] args)
{
...
    // This calls the Draw() method of the ThreeDCircle.
    ThreeDCircle o = new ThreeDCircle();
    o.Draw();

    // This calls the Draw() method of the parent!
    ((Circle)o).Draw();
    Console.ReadLine();
}
```

■ **Source Code** The Shapes project can be found under the Chapter 6 subdirectory.

Understanding Base Class/Derived Class Casting Rules

Now that you can build a family of related class types, you need to learn the rules of class *casting operations*. To do so, let's return to the Employees hierarchy created earlier in this chapter. Under the .NET platform, the ultimate base class in the system is System.Object. Therefore, everything "is-an" Object and can be treated as such. Given this fact, it is legal to store an instance of any type within an object variable:

```
static void CastingExamples()
{
    // A Manager "is-a" System.Object, so we can
```

```
  // store a Manager reference in an object variable just fine.
  object frank = new Manager("Frank Zappa", 9, 3000, 40000, "111-11-1111", 5);
}
```

In the `Employees` example, `Managers`, `SalesPerson`, and `PTSalesPerson` types all extend `Employee`, so you can store any of these objects in a valid base class reference. Therefore, the following statements are also legal:

```
static void CastingExamples()
{
  // A Manager "is-a" System.Object, so we can
  // store a Manager reference in an object variable just fine.
  object frank = new Manager("Frank Zappa", 9, 3000, 40000, "111-11-1111", 5);

  // A Manager "is-an" Employee too.
  Employee moonUnit = new Manager("MoonUnit Zappa", 2, 3001, 20000, "101-11-1321", 1);

  // A PTSalesPerson "is-a" SalesPerson.
  SalesPerson jill = new PTSalesPerson("Jill", 834, 3002, 100000, "111-12-1119", 90);
}
```

The first law of casting between class types is that when two classes are related by an "is-a" relationship, it is always safe to store a derived object within a base class reference. Formally, this is called an *implicit cast*, as "it just works" given the laws of inheritance. This leads to some powerful programming constructs. For example, assume you have defined a new method within your current Program class:

```
static void GivePromotion(Employee emp)
{
  // Increase pay...
  // Give new parking space in company garage...

  Console.WriteLine("{0} was promoted!", emp.Name);
}
```

Because this method takes a single parameter of type `Employee`, you can effectively pass any descendent from the `Employee` class into this method directly, given the "is-a" relationship:

```
static void CastingExamples()
{
  // A Manager "is-a" System.Object, so we can
  // store a Manager reference in an object variable just fine.
  object frank = new Manager("Frank Zappa", 9, 3000, 40000, "111-11-1111", 5);

  // A Manager "is-an" Employee too.
  Employee moonUnit = new Manager("MoonUnit Zappa", 2, 3001, 20000, "101-11-1321", 1);
  GivePromotion(moonUnit);

  // A PTSalesPerson "is-a" SalesPerson.
  SalesPerson jill = new PTSalesPerson("Jill", 834, 3002, 100000, "111-12-1119", 90);
  GivePromotion(jill);
}
```

The previous code compiles given the implicit cast from the base class type (Employee) to the derived type. However, what if you also wanted to fire Frank Zappa (currently stored in a general System.Object reference)? If you pass the frank object directly into this method, you will find a compiler error as follows:

```
// Error!
object frank = new Manager("Frank Zappa", 9, 3000, 40000, "111-11-1111", 5);
GivePromotion(frank);
```

The problem is that you are attempting to pass in a variable which IS-NOT-A Employee, but a more general System.Object. Given the fact that object is higher up the inheritance chain than Employee, the compiler will not allow for an implicit cast, in an effort to keep your code as type-safe as possible.

Even though you can figure out that the object reference is pointing to an Employee-compatible class in memory, the compiler cannot, as that will not be known until runtime. You can satisfy the compiler by performing an *explicit cast*. This is the second law of casting: you can, in such cases, explicitly downcast using the C# casting operator. The basic template to follow when performing an explicit cast looks something like the following:

```
(ClassIWantToCastTo)referenceIHave
```

Thus, to pass the object variable into the GivePromotion() method, you must author the following code:

```
// OK!
GivePromotion((Manager)frank);
```

The C# as Keyword

Be very aware that explicit casting is evaluated at *runtime*, not compile time. Therefore, if you were to author the following C# code:

```
// Ack! You can't cast frank to a Hexagon, but this compiles fine!
Hexagon hex = (Hexagon)frank;
```

you would compile without error, but would receive a runtime error, or more formally a *runtime exception*. Chapter 7 will examine the full details of structured exception handling; however, it is worth pointing out, for the time being, that when you are performing an explicit cast, you can trap the possibility of an invalid cast using the try and catch keywords (again, see Chapter 7 for full details):

```
// Catch a possible invalid cast.
try
{
  Hexagon hex = (Hexagon)frank;
}
catch (InvalidCastException ex)
{
  Console.WriteLine(ex.Message);
}
```

While this is a fine example of defensive programming, C# provides the as keyword to quickly determine at runtime whether a given type is compatible with another. When you use the as keyword, you are able to determine compatibility by checking against a null return value. Consider the following:

```
// Use "as" to test compatability.
Hexagon hex2 = frank as Hexagon;
if (hex2 == null)
  Console.WriteLine("Sorry, frank is not a Hexagon...");
```

The C# is Keyword

Given that the GivePromotion() method has been designed to take any possible type derived from Employee, one question on your mind may be how this method can determine which derived type was sent into the method. On a related note, given that the incoming parameter is of type Employee, how can you gain access to the specialized members of the SalesPerson and Manager types?

In addition to the as keyword, the C# language provides the is keyword to determine whether two items are compatible. Unlike the as keyword, however, the is keyword returns false, rather than a null reference, if the types are incompatible. Consider the following implementation of the GivePromotion() method:

```
static void GivePromotion(Employee emp)
{
  Console.WriteLine("{0} was promoted!", emp.Name);

  if (emp is SalesPerson)
  {
    Console.WriteLine("{0} made {1} sale(s)!", emp.Name,
      ((SalesPerson)emp).SalesNumber);
    Console.WriteLine();
  }
  if (emp is Manager)
  {
    Console.WriteLine("{0} had {1} stock options...", emp.Name,
      ((Manager)emp).StockOptions);
    Console.WriteLine();
  }
}
```

Here, you are performing a runtime check to determine what the incoming base class reference is actually pointing to in memory. After you determine whether you received a SalesPerson or Manager type, you are able to perform an explicit cast to gain access to the specialized members of the class. Also notice that you are not required to wrap your casting operations within a try/catch construct, as you know that the cast is safe if you enter either if scope, given your conditional check.

The Master Parent Class: System.Object

To wrap up this chapter, I'd like to examine the details of the master parent class in the .NET platform: Object. As you were reading the previous section, you might have noticed that the base classes in your hierarchies (Car, Shape, Employee) never explicitly specify their parent classes:

```
// Who is the parent of Car?
class Car
{...}
```

In the .NET universe, every type ultimately derives from a base class named System.Object (which can be represented by the C# object keyword [lowercase "o"]). The Object class defines a set of common members for every type in the framework. In fact, when you do build a class that does not explicitly define its parent, the compiler automatically derives your type from Object. If you want to be very clear in your intentions, you are free to define classes that derive from Object as follows:

```
// Here we are explicitly deriving from System.Object.
class Car : object
{...}
```

Like any class, System.Object defines a set of members. In the following formal C# definition, note that some of these items are declared virtual, which specifies that a given member may be overridden by a subclass, while others are marked with static (and are therefore called at the class level):

```
public class Object
{
  // Virtual members.
  public virtual bool Equals(object obj);
  protected virtual void Finalize();
  public virtual int GetHashCode();
  public virtual string ToString();

  // Instance-level, nonvirtual members.
  public Type GetType();
  protected object MemberwiseClone();

  // Static members.
  public static bool Equals(object objA, object objB);
  public static bool ReferenceEquals(object objA, object objB);
}
```

Table 6-1 offers a rundown of the functionality provided by some of the methods you're most likely to make use of.

Table 6-1. *Core Members of System.Object*

Instance Method of Object Class	Meaning in Life
Equals()	By default, this method returns true only if the items being compared refer to the exact same item in memory. Thus, Equals() is used to compare object references, not the state of the object. Typically, this method is overridden to return true only if the objects being compared have the same internal state values (that is, value-based semantics).
	Be aware that if you override Equals(), you should also override GetHashCode(), as these methods are used internally by Hashtable types to retrieve subobjects from the container.
	Also recall from Chapter 4, that the ValueType class overrides this method for all structures, so they work with value-based comparisons.

`Finalize()`	For the time being, you can understand this method (when overridden) is called to free any allocated resources before the object is destroyed. I talk more about the CLR garbage collection services in Chapter 9.
`GetHashCode()`	This method returns an `int` that identifies a specific object instance.
`ToString()`	This method returns a string representation of this object, using the `<namespace>.<type name>` format (termed the *fully qualified name*). This method will often be overridden by a subclass to return a tokenized string of name/value pairs that represent the object's internal state, rather than its fully qualified name.
`GetType()`	This method returns a Type object that fully describes the object you are currently referencing. In short, this is a Runtime Type Identification (RTTI) method available to all objects (discussed in greater detail in Chapter 15).
`MemberwiseClone()`	This method exists to return a member-by-member copy of the current object, which is often used when cloning an object (see Chapter 8).

To illustrate some of the default behavior provided by the `Object` base class, create a final C# Console Application named ObjectOverrides. Insert a new C# class type that contains the following empty class definition for a type named `Person`:

```
// Remember! Person extends Object.
class Person {}
```

Now, update your `Main()` method to interact with the inherited members of `System.Object` as follows:

```
class Program
{
  static void Main(string[] args)
  {
    Console.WriteLine("***** Fun with System.Object *****\n");
    Person p1 = new Person();

    // Use inherited members of System.Object.
    Console.WriteLine("ToString: {0}", p1.ToString());
    Console.WriteLine("Hash code: {0}", p1.GetHashCode());
    Console.WriteLine("Type: {0}", p1.GetType());

    // Make some other references to p1.
    Person p2 = p1;
    object o = p2;
```

245

```
      // Are the references pointing to the same object in memory?
      if (o.Equals(p1) && p2.Equals(o))
      {
        Console.WriteLine("Same instance!");
      }
      Console.ReadLine();
    }
}
```

Here is the output of the current Main() method:

```
***** Fun with System.Object *****

ToString: ObjectOverrides.Person
Hash code: 46104728
Type: ObjectOverrides.Person
Same instance!
```

First, notice how the default implementation of ToString() returns the fully qualified name of the current type (ObjectOverrides.Person). As you will see later during the examination of building custom namespaces in Chapter 14, every C# project defines a "root namespace," which has the same name of the project itself. Here, you created a project named ObjectOverrides; thus, the Person type (as well as the Program class) have both been placed within the ObjectOverrides namespace.

The default behavior of Equals() is to test whether two variables are pointing to the same object in memory. Here, you create a new Person variable named p1. At this point, a new Person object is placed on the managed heap. p2 is also of type Person. However, you are not creating a *new* instance, but rather assigning this variable to reference p1. Therefore, p1 and p2 are both pointing to the same object in memory, as is the variable o (of type object, which was thrown in for good measure). Given that p1, p2, and o all point to the same memory location, the equality test succeeds.

Although the canned behavior of System.Object can fit the bill in a number of cases, it is quite common for your custom types to override some of these inherited methods. To illustrate, update the Person class to support some properties representing an individual's first name, last name, and age, each of which can be set by a custom constructor:

```
// Remember! Person extends Object.
class Person
{
  public string FirstName { get; set; }
  public string LastName { get; set; }
  public int Age { get; set; }

  public Person(string fName, string lName, int personAge)
  {
    FirstName = fName;
    LastName = lName;
    Age = personAge;
  }
  public Person(){}
}
```

Overriding System.Object.ToString()

Many classes (and structures) that you create can benefit from overriding ToString() in order to return a string textual representation of the type's current state. This can be quite helpful for purposes of debugging (among other reasons). How you choose to construct this string is a matter of personal choice; however, a recommended approach is to separate each name/value pair with semicolons and wrap the entire string within square brackets (many types in the .NET base class libraries follow this approach). Consider the following overridden ToString() for your Person class:

```
public override string ToString()
{
  string myState;
  myState = string.Format("[First Name: {0}; Last Name: {1}; Age: {2}]",
    FirstName, LastName, Age);
  return myState;
}
```

This implementation of ToString() is quite straightforward, given that the Person class only has three pieces of state data. However, always remember that a proper ToString() override should also account for any data defined *up the chain of inheritance*.

When you override ToString() for a class extending a custom base class, the first order of business is to obtain the ToString() value from your parent using the base keyword. After you have obtained your parent's string data, you can append the derived class's custom information.

Overriding System.Object.Equals()

Let's also override the behavior of Object.Equals() to work with value-based semantics. Recall that by default, Equals() returns true only if the two objects being compared reference the same object instance in memory. For the Person class, it may be helpful to implement Equals() to return true if the two variables being compared contain the same state values (e.g., first name, last name, and age).

First of all, notice that the incoming argument of the Equals() method is a general System. Object. Given this, your first order of business is to ensure the caller has indeed passed in a Person object, and as an extra safeguard, to make sure the incoming parameter is not a null reference.

After you have established the caller has passed you an allocated Person, one approach to implement Equals() is to perform a field-by-field comparison against the data of the incoming object to the data of the current object:

```
public override bool Equals(object obj)
{
  if (obj is Person && obj != null)
  {
    Person temp;
    temp = (Person)obj;
    if (temp.FirstName == this.FirstName
        && temp.LastName == this.LastName
        && temp.Age == this.Age)
    {
      return true;
    }
    else
    {
      return false;
```

```
    }
  }
  return false;
}
```

Here, you are examining the values of the incoming object against the values of your internal values (note the use of the this keyword). If the name and age of each are identical, you have two objects with the exact same state data and, therefore, return true. Any other possibility results in returning false.

While this approach does indeed work, you can certainly imagine how labor intensive it would be to implement a custom Equals() method for nontrivial types that may contain dozens of data fields. One common shortcut is to leverage your own implementation of ToString(). If a class has a prim-and-proper implementation of ToString() that accounts for all field data up the chain of inheritance, you can simply perform a comparison of the object's string data:

```
public override bool Equals(object obj)
{
  // No need to cast "obj" to a Person anymore,
  // as everything has a ToString() method.
  return obj.ToString() == this.ToString();
}
```

Notice in this case that we no longer need to check whether the incoming argument is of the correct type (a Person, in our example), as everything in .NET supports a ToString() method. Even better, we no longer need to perform a property-by-property equality check, as we are not simply testing the value returned from ToString().

Overriding System.Object.GetHashCode()

When a class overrides the Equals() method, you should also override the default implementation of GetHashCode(). Simply put, a *hash code* is a numerical value that represents an object as a particular state. For example, if you create two string variables that hold the value Hello, you would obtain the same hash code. However, if one of the string objects were in all lowercase (hello), you would obtain different hash codes.

By default, System.Object.GetHashCode() uses your object's current location in memory to yield the hash value. However, if you are building a custom type that you intend to store in a Hashtable type (within the System.Collections namespace), you should always override this member, as the Hashtable will be internally invoking Equals() and GetHashCode() to retrieve the correct object.

■ **Note** To be more specific, the System.Collections.Hashtable class calls GetHashCode() internally to gain a general idea where the object is located, but a subsequent (internal) call to Equals() determines the exact match.

Although you are not going to place your Person into a System.Collections.Hashtable, for completion, let's override GetHashCode(). There are many algorithms that can be used to create a hash code, some fancy, others not so fancy. Most of the time, you are able to generate a hash code value by leveraging the System.String's GetHashCode() implementation.

Given that the String class already has a solid hash code algorithm that is using the character data of the String to compute a hash value, if you can identify a piece of field data on your class that should be unique for all instances (such as a Social Security number), simply call GetHashCode() on that point of field data. Thus, if the Person class defined a SSN property, we could author the following code:

```
// Assume we have an SSN property as so.
class Person
{
  public string SSN {get; set;}

  // Return a hash code based on a point of unique string data.
  public override int GetHashCode()
  {
    return SSN.GetHashCode();
  }
}
```

If you cannot find a single point of unique string data, but you have overridden ToString(), call GetHashCode() on your own string representation:

```
// Return a hash code based on the person's ToString() value.
public override int GetHashCode()
{
  return this.ToString().GetHashCode();
}
```

Testing Your Modified Person Class

Now that you have overridden the virtual members of Object, update Main() to test your updates.

```
static void Main(string[] args)
{
  Console.WriteLine("***** Fun with System.Object *****\n");

  // NOTE: We want these to be identical to test
  // the Equals() and GetHashCode() methods.
  Person p1 = new Person("Homer", "Simpson", 50);
  Person p2 = new Person("Homer", "Simpson", 50);

  // Get stringified version of objects.
  Console.WriteLine("p1.ToString() = {0}", p1.ToString());
  Console.WriteLine("p2.ToString() = {0}", p2.ToString());

  // Test overridden Equals().
  Console.WriteLine("p1 = p2?: {0}", p1.Equals(p2));

  // Test hash codes.
  Console.WriteLine("Same hash codes?: {0}", p1.GetHashCode() == p2.GetHashCode());
  Console.WriteLine();

  // Change age of p2 and test again.
  p2.Age = 45;
  Console.WriteLine("p1.ToString() = {0}", p1.ToString());
  Console.WriteLine("p2.ToString() = {0}", p2.ToString());
  Console.WriteLine("p1 = p2?: {0}", p1.Equals(p2));
```

```
    Console.WriteLine("Same hash codes?: {0}", p1.GetHashCode() == p2.GetHashCode());
    Console.ReadLine();
}
```

The output can be seen here:

```
***** Fun with System.Object *****

p1.ToString() = [First Name: Homer; Last Name: Simpson; Age: 50]
p2.ToString() = [First Name: Homer; Last Name: Simpson; Age: 50]
p1 = p2?: True
Same hash codes?: True

p1.ToString() = [First Name: Homer; Last Name: Simpson; Age: 50]
p2.ToString() = [First Name: Homer; Last Name: Simpson; Age: 45]
p1 = p2?: False
Same hash codes?: False
```

The Static Members of System.Object

In addition to the instance-level members you have just examined, System.Object does define two (very helpful) static members that also test for value-based or reference-based equality. Consider the following code:

```
static void StaticMembersOfObject()
{
    // Static members of System.Object.
    Person p3 = new Person("Sally", "Jones", 4);
    Person p4 = new Person("Sally", "Jones", 4);
    Console.WriteLine("P3 and P4 have same state: {0}", object.Equals(p3, p4));
    Console.WriteLine("P3 and P4 are pointing to same object: {0}",
        object.ReferenceEquals(p3, p4));
}
```

Here, you are able to simply send in two objects (of any type) and allow the System.Object class to determine the details automatically.

■ **Source Code** The ObjectOverrides project is located under the Chapter 6 subdirectory.

Summary

This chapter explored the role and details of inheritance and polymorphism. Over these pages you were introduced to numerous new keywords and tokens to support each of these techniques. For example, recall that the colon token is used to establish the parent class of a given type. Parent types are able to define any number of virtual and/or abstract members to establish a polymorphic interface. Derived types override such members using the override keyword.

In addition to building numerous class hierarchies, this chapter also examined how to explicitly cast between base and derived types, and wrapped up by diving into the details of the cosmic parent class in the .NET base class libraries: `System.Object`.

CHAPTER 7

Understanding Structured Exception Handling

In this chapter, you will learn how to handle runtime anomalies in your C# code through the use of *structured exception handling* (often cryptically abbreviated as SEH). Not only will you examine the C# keywords that allow you to handle such matters (`try`, `catch`, `throw`, `finally`), you will also come to understand the distinction between application-level and system-level exceptions, as well as the role of the `System.Exception` base class. This discussion will lead into the topic of building custom exceptions and, finally, to a quick look at the exception-centric debugging tools of Visual Studio.

Ode to Errors, Bugs, and Exceptions

Despite what our (sometimes inflated) egos may tell us, no programmer is perfect. Writing software is a complex undertaking, and given this complexity, it is quite common for even the best software to ship with various "problems." Sometimes the problem is caused by "bad code" (such as overflowing the bounds of an array). Other times, a problem is caused by bogus user input that has not been accounted for in the application's code base (e.g., a phone number input field assigned to the value "Chucky"). Now, regardless of the cause of the problem, the end result is that the application does not work as expected. To help frame the upcoming discussion of structured exception handling, allow me to provide definitions for three commonly used anomaly-centric terms:

- *Bugs:* These are, simply put, errors made by the programmer. For example, suppose you are programming with unmanaged C++. If you fail to delete dynamically allocated memory, resulting in a memory leak, you have a bug.

- *User errors:* User errors, on the other hand, are typically caused by the individual running your application, rather than by those who created it. For example, an end user who enters a malformed string into a text box could very well generate an error *if* you fail to handle this faulty input in your code base.

- *Exceptions:* Exceptions are typically regarded as runtime anomalies that are difficult, if not impossible, to account for while programming your application. Possible exceptions include attempting to connect to a database that no longer exists, opening a corrupted XML file, or trying to contact a machine that is currently offline. In each of these cases, the programmer (or end user) has little control over these "exceptional" circumstances.

Given these definitions, it should be clear that .NET structured *exception* handling is a technique for dealing with runtime *exceptions*. However, even for the bugs and user errors that have escaped your view, the CLR will often generate a corresponding exception that identifies the problem at hand. The .NET base class libraries define numerous exceptions, such as FormatException, IndexOutOfRangeException, FileNotFoundException, ArgumentOutOfRangeException, and so forth.

Within the .NET nomenclature, an "exception" accounts for bugs, bogus user input, and runtime errors, even though we programmers may view each of these as a distinct issue. However, before we get too far ahead of ourselves, let's formalize the role of structured exception handling and check out how it differs from traditional error-handling techniques.

■ **Note** To make the code examples used in this book as clean as possible, I will not catch every possible exception that may be thrown by a given method in the base class libraries. In your production-level projects, you should, of course, make liberal use of the techniques presented in this chapter.

The Role of .NET Exception Handling

Prior to .NET, error handling under the Windows operating system was a confused mishmash of techniques. Many programmers rolled their own error-handling logic within the context of a given application. For example, a development team could define a set of numerical constants that represented known error conditions, and make use of them as method return values. By way of an example, consider the following partial C code:

```
/* A very C-style error trapping mechanism. */
#define E_FILENOTFOUND 1000

int UseFileSystem()
{
  // Assume something happens in this function
  // that causes the following return value.
  return E_FILENOTFOUND;
}

void main()
{
  int retVal = UseFileSystem();
  if(retVal == E_FILENOTFOUND)
    printf("Cannot find file...");
}
```

This approach is less than ideal, given the fact that the constant E_FILENOTFOUND is little more than a numerical value, and is far from being a helpful agent regarding how to deal with the problem. Ideally, you would like to wrap the error's name, a descriptive message, and other helpful information about this error condition into a single, well-defined package (which is exactly what happens under structured exception handling).

In addition to a developer's ad hoc techniques, the Windows API defines hundreds of error codes that come by way of #defines, HRESULTs, and far too many variations on the simple Boolean (bool, BOOL, VARIANT_BOOL, and so on). Furthermore, many C++ COM developers made use of a small set of standard

COM interfaces (e.g., `ISupportErrorInfo`, `IErrorInfo`, `ICreateErrorInfo`) to return meaningful error information to a COM client.

The obvious problem with these older techniques is the tremendous lack of symmetry. Each approach is more or less tailored to a given technology, a given language, and perhaps even a given project. To put an end to this madness, the .NET platform provides a standard technique to send and trap runtime errors: structured exception handling (SEH).

The beauty of this approach is that developers now have a unified approach to error handling, which is common to all languages targeting the .NET platform. Therefore, the way in which a C# programmer handles errors is syntactically similar to that of a VB programmer, or a C++ programmer using C++/CLI.

As an added bonus, the syntax used to throw and catch exceptions across assemblies and machine boundaries is identical. For example, if you use C# to build a Windows Communication Foundation (WCF) service, you can throw a SOAP fault to a remote caller, using the same keywords that allow you to throw an exception between methods in the same application.

Another bonus of .NET exceptions is that rather than receiving a cryptic numerical value that simply identifies the problem at hand, exceptions are objects that contain a human-readable description of the problem, as well as a detailed snapshot of the call stack that triggered the exception in the first place. Furthermore, you are able to give the end user help-link information that points the user to a URL that provides details about the error, as well as custom programmer-defined data.

The Building Blocks of .NET Exception Handling

Programming with structured exception handling involves the use of four interrelated entities:

- A class type that represents the details of the exception

- A member that *throws* an instance of the exception class to the caller under the correct circumstances

- A block of code on the caller's side that invokes the exception-prone member

- A block of code on the caller's side that will process (or *catch*) the exception, should it occur

The C# programming language offers four keywords (`try`, `catch`, `throw`, and `finally`) that allow you to throw and handle exceptions. The object that represents the problem at hand is a class extending `System.Exception` (or a descendent thereof). Given this fact, let's check out the role of this exception-centric base class.

The System.Exception Base Class

All exceptions ultimately derive from the `System.Exception` base class, which in turn derives from `System.Object`. Here is the crux of this class (note that some of these members are virtual and may thus be overridden by derived classes):

```
public class Exception : ISerializable, _Exception
{
  // Public constructors
  public Exception(string message, Exception innerException);
  public Exception(string message);
  public Exception();
...
```

```
// Methods
public virtual Exception GetBaseException();
public virtual void GetObjectData(SerializationInfo info,
  StreamingContext context);

// Properties
public virtual IDictionary Data { get; }
public virtual string HelpLink { get; set; }
public Exception InnerException { get; }
public virtual string Message { get; }
public virtual string Source { get; set; }
public virtual string StackTrace { get; }
public MethodBase TargetSite { get; }
...
}
```

As you can see, many of the properties defined by System.Exception are read-only in nature. This is due to the fact that derived types will typically supply default values for each property. For example, the default message of the IndexOutOfRangeException type is "Index was outside the bounds of the array."

■ **Note** The Exception class implements two .NET interfaces. Although we have yet to examine interfaces (see Chapter 8), just understand that the _Exception interface allows a .NET exception to be processed by an unmanaged code base (such as a COM application), while the ISerializable interface allows an exception object to be persisted across boundaries (such as a machine boundary).

Table 7-1 describes the most important members of System.Exception.

Table 7-1. Core Members of the System.Exception Type

System.Exception Property	Meaning in Life
Data	This read-only property retrieves a collection of key/value pairs (represented by an object implementing IDictionary) that provide additional, programmer-defined information about the exception. By default, this collection is empty.
HelpLink	This property gets or sets a URL to a help file or web site describing the error in full detail.
InnerException	This read-only property can be used to obtain information about the previous exception(s) that caused the current exception to occur. The previous exception(s) are recorded by passing them into the constructor of the most current exception.

Message	This read-only property returns the textual description of a given error. The error message itself is set as a constructor parameter.
Source	This property gets or sets the name of the assembly, or the object, that threw the current exception.
StackTrace	This read-only property contains a string that identifies the sequence of calls that triggered the exception. As you might guess, this property is very useful during debugging or if you wish to dump the error to an external error log.
TargetSite	This read-only property returns a MethodBase object, which describes numerous details about the method that threw the exception (invoking ToString() will identify the method by name).

The Simplest Possible Example

To illustrate the usefulness of structured exception handling, we need to create a class that will throw an exception under the correct (or one might say *exceptional*) circumstances. Assume we have created a new C# Console Application project (named SimpleException) that defines two class types (Car and Radio) associated by the "has-a" relationship. The Radio type defines a single method that turns the radio's power on or off:

```
class Radio
{
  public void TurnOn(bool on)
  {
    if(on)
      Console.WriteLine("Jamming...");
    else
      Console.WriteLine("Quiet time...");
  }
}
```

In addition to leveraging the Radio class via containment/delegation, the Car class (shown next) is defined in such a way that if the user accelerates a Car object beyond a predefined maximum speed (specified using a constant member variable named MaxSpeed), its engine explodes, rendering the Car unusable (captured by a private bool member variable named carIsDead).

Beyond these points, the Car type has a few properties to represent the current speed and a user supplied "pet name," as well as various constructors to set the state of a new Car object. Here is the complete definition (with code annotations):

```
class Car
{
  // Constant for maximum speed.
  public const int MaxSpeed = 100;

  // Car properties.
  public int CurrentSpeed {get; set;}
  public string PetName {get; set;}
```

```csharp
// Is the car still operational?
private bool carIsDead;

// A car has-a radio.
private Radio theMusicBox = new Radio();

// Constructors.
public Car() {}
public Car(string name, int speed)
{
  CurrentSpeed = speed;
  PetName = name;
}

public void CrankTunes(bool state)
{
  // Delegate request to inner object.
  theMusicBox.TurnOn(state);
}

// See if Car has overheated.
public void Accelerate(int delta)
{
  if (carIsDead)
    Console.WriteLine("{0} is out of order...", PetName);
  else
  {
    CurrentSpeed += delta;
    if (CurrentSpeed > MaxSpeed)
    {
      Console.WriteLine("{0} has overheated!", PetName);
      CurrentSpeed = 0;
      carIsDead = true;
    }
    else
      Console.WriteLine("=> CurrentSpeed = {0}", CurrentSpeed);
  }
}
}
```

Now, if we implement a Main() method that forces a Car object to exceed the predefined maximum speed (set to 100, in the Car class) as shown here:

```csharp
static void Main(string[] args)
{
  Console.WriteLine("***** Simple Exception Example *****");
  Console.WriteLine("=> Creating a car and stepping on it!");
  Car myCar = new Car("Zippy", 20);
  myCar.CrankTunes(true);

  for (int i = 0; i < 10; i++)
    myCar.Accelerate(10);
```

```
  Console.ReadLine();
}
```

we would see the following output:

```
***** Simple Exception Example *****
=> Creating a car and stepping on it!
Jamming...
=> CurrentSpeed = 30
=> CurrentSpeed = 40
=> CurrentSpeed = 50
=> CurrentSpeed = 60
=> CurrentSpeed = 70
=> CurrentSpeed = 80
=> CurrentSpeed = 90
=> CurrentSpeed = 100
Zippy has overheated!
Zippy is out of order...
```

Throwing a General Exception

Now that we have a functional Car class, I'll demonstrate the simplest way to throw an exception. The current implementation of Accelerate() simply displays an error message if the caller attempts to speed up the Car beyond its upper limit.

To retrofit this method to throw an exception if the user attempts to speed up the automobile after it has met its maker, you want to create and configure a new instance of the System.Exception class, setting the value of the read-only Message property via the class constructor. When you want to send the exception object back to the caller, use the C# throw keyword. Here is the relevant code update to the Accelerate() method:

```csharp
// This time, throw an exception if the user speeds up beyond MaxSpeed.
public void Accelerate(int delta)
{
  if (carIsDead)
    Console.WriteLine("{0} is out of order...", PetName);
  else
  {
    CurrentSpeed += delta;
    if (CurrentSpeed >= MaxSpeed)
    {
      carIsDead = true;
      CurrentSpeed = 0;

      // Use the "throw" keyword to raise an exception.
      throw new Exception(string.Format("{0} has overheated!", PetName));
    }
    else
      Console.WriteLine("=> CurrentSpeed = {0}", CurrentSpeed);
  }
}
```

Before examining how a caller would catch this exception, let's look at a few points of interest. First of all, when you are throwing an exception, it is always up to you to decide exactly what constitutes the error in question, and when an exception should be thrown. Here, you are making the assumption that if the program attempts to increase the speed of a Car object that has expired, a System.Exception object should be thrown to indicate the Accelerate() method cannot continue (which may or may not be a valid assumption; this will be a judgment call on your part based on the application you are creating).

Alternatively, you could implement Accelerate() to recover automatically without needing to throw an exception in the first place. By and large, exceptions should be thrown only when a more terminal condition has been met (for example, not finding a necessary file, failing to connect to a database, and the like). Deciding exactly what justifies throwing an exception is a design issue you must always contend with. For our current purposes, assume that asking a doomed automobile to increase its speed is cause to throw an exception.

Catching Exceptions

Because the Accelerate() method now throws an exception, the caller needs to be ready to handle the exception, should it occur. When you are invoking a method that may throw an exception, you make use of a try/catch block. After you have caught the exception object, you are able to invoke the members of the exception object to extract the details of the problem.

What you do with this data is largely up to you. You might wish to log this information to a report file, write the data to the Windows event log, e-mail a system administrator, or display the problem to the end user. Here, you will simply dump the contents to the console window:

```
// Handle the thrown exception.
static void Main(string[] args)
{
  Console.WriteLine("***** Simple Exception Example *****");
  Console.WriteLine("=> Creating a car and stepping on it!");
  Car myCar = new Car("Zippy", 20);
  myCar.CrankTunes(true);

  // Speed up past the car's max speed to
  // trigger the exception.
  try
  {
    for(int i = 0; i < 10; i++)
      myCar. Accelerate(10);
  }
  catch(Exception e)
  {
    Console.WriteLine("\n*** Error! ***");
    Console.WriteLine("Method: {0}", e.TargetSite);
    Console.WriteLine("Message: {0}", e.Message);
    Console.WriteLine("Source: {0}", e.Source);
  }

  // The error has been handled, processing continues with the next statement.
  Console.WriteLine("\n***** Out of exception logic *****");
  Console.ReadLine();
}
```

In essence, a try block is a section of statements that may throw an exception during execution. If an exception is detected, the flow of program execution is sent to the appropriate catch block. On the other hand, if the code within a try block does not trigger an exception, the catch block is skipped entirely, and all is right with the world. The following output shows a test run of this program.

```
***** Simple Exception Example *****
=> Creating a car and stepping on it!
Jamming...
=> CurrentSpeed = 30
=> CurrentSpeed = 40
=> CurrentSpeed = 50
=> CurrentSpeed = 60
=> CurrentSpeed = 70
=> CurrentSpeed = 80
=> CurrentSpeed = 90

*** Error! ***
Method: Void Accelerate(Int32)
Message: Zippy has overheated!
Source: SimpleException

***** Out of exception logic *****
```

As you can see, after an exception has been handled, the application is free to continue on from the point after the catch block. In some circumstances, a given exception could be critical enough to warrant the termination of the application. However, in a good number of cases, the logic within the exception handler will ensure the application can continue on its merry way (although it could be slightly less functional, such as not being able to connect to a remote data source).

Configuring the State of an Exception

Currently, the System.Exception object configured within the Accelerate() method simply establishes a value exposed to the Message property (via a constructor parameter). As shown previously in Table 7-1, however, the Exception class also supplies a number of additional members (TargetSite, StackTrace, HelpLink, and Data) that can be useful in further qualifying the nature of the problem. To spruce up our current example, let's examine further details of these members on a case-by-case basis.

The TargetSite Property

The System.Exception.TargetSite property allows you to determine various details about the method that threw a given exception. As shown in the previous Main() method, printing the value of TargetSite will display the return type, name, and parameter types of the method that threw the exception. However, TargetSite does not return just a vanilla-flavored string, but rather a strongly typed System.Reflection.MethodBase object. This type can be used to gather numerous details regarding the offending method, as well as the class that defines the offending method. To illustrate, assume the previous catch logic has been updated as follows:

```
static void Main(string[] args)
{
...
  // TargetSite actually returns a MethodBase object.
  catch(Exception e)
  {
    Console.WriteLine("\n*** Error! ***");
    Console.WriteLine("Member name: {0}", e.TargetSite);
    Console.WriteLine("Class defining member: {0}",
      e.TargetSite.DeclaringType);
    Console.WriteLine("Member type: {0}", e.TargetSite.MemberType);
    Console.WriteLine("Message: {0}", e.Message);
    Console.WriteLine("Source: {0}", e.Source);
  }
  Console.WriteLine("\n***** Out of exception logic *****");
  Console.ReadLine();
}
```

This time, you make use of the MethodBase.DeclaringType property to determine the fully qualified name of the class that threw the error (SimpleException.Car, in this case) as well as the MemberType property of the MethodBase object to identify the type of member (such as a property vs. a method) where this exception originated. In this case, the catch logic would display the following:

```
*** Error! ***
Member name: Void Accelerate(Int32)
Class defining member: SimpleException.Car
Member type: Method
Message: Zippy has overheated!
Source: SimpleException
```

The StackTrace Property

The System.Exception.StackTrace property allows you to identify the series of calls that resulted in the exception. Be aware that you never set the value of StackTrace, as it is established automatically at the time the exception is created. To illustrate, assume you have once again updated your catch logic:

```
catch(Exception e)
{
  ...
  Console.WriteLine("Stack: {0}", e.StackTrace);
}
```

If you were to run the program, you would find the following stack trace is printed to the console (your line numbers and file paths may differ, of course):

```
Stack: at SimpleException.Car.Accelerate(Int32 delta)
in c:\MyApps\SimpleException\car.cs:line 65 at SimpleException.Program.Main()
in c:\MyApps\SimpleException\Program.cs:line 21
```

The string returned from StackTrace documents the sequence of calls that resulted in the throwing of this exception. Notice how the bottommost line number of this string identifies the first call in the sequence, while the topmost line number identifies the exact location of the offending member. Clearly, this information can be quite helpful during the debugging or logging of a given application, as you are able to "follow the flow" of the error's origin.

The HelpLink Property

While the TargetSite and StackTrace properties allow programmers to gain an understanding of a given exception, this information is of little use to the end user. As you have already seen, the System.Exception.Message property can be used to obtain human-readable information that can be displayed to the current user. In addition, the HelpLink property can be set to point the user to a specific URL or standard Windows help file that contains more detailed information.

By default, the value managed by the HelpLink property is an empty string. If you want to fill this property with a more interesting value, you need to do so before throwing the System.Exception object. Here are the relevant updates to the Car.Accelerate() method:

```
public void Accelerate(int delta)
{
  if (carIsDead)
    Console.WriteLine("{0} is out of order...", PetName);
  else
  {
    CurrentSpeed += delta;
    if (CurrentSpeed >= MaxSpeed)
    {
      carIsDead = true;
      CurrentSpeed = 0;

      // We need to call the HelpLink property, thus we need to
      // create a local variable before throwing the Exception object.
      Exception ex =
        new Exception(string.Format("{0} has overheated!", PetName));
      ex.HelpLink = "http://www.CarsRUs.com";
      throw ex;
    }
    else
      Console.WriteLine("=> CurrentSpeed = {0}", CurrentSpeed);
  }
}
```

The catch logic could now be updated to print out this help link information as follows:

```
catch(Exception e)
{
  ...
  Console.WriteLine("Help Link: {0}", e.HelpLink);
}
```

The Data Property

The Data property of System.Exception allows you to fill an exception object with relevant auxiliary information (such as a time stamp). The Data property returns an object implementing an interface named IDictionary, defined in the System.Collections namespace. Chapter 8 examines the role of interface-based programming, as well as the System.Collections namespace. For the time being, just understand that dictionary collections allow you to create a set of values that are retrieved using a specific key. Observe the next update to the Car.Accelerate() method:

```
public void Accelerate(int delta)
{
  if (carIsDead)
    Console.WriteLine("{0} is out of order...", PetName);
  else
  {
    CurrentSpeed += delta;
    if (CurrentSpeed >= MaxSpeed)
    {
      carIsDead = true;
      CurrentSpeed = 0;

      // We need to call the HelpLink property, thus we need
      // to create a local variable before throwing the Exception object.
      Exception ex =
        new Exception(string.Format("{0} has overheated!", PetName));
      ex.HelpLink = "http://www.CarsRUs.com";

      // Stuff in custom data regarding the error.
      ex.Data.Add("TimeStamp",
        string.Format("The car exploded at {0}", DateTime.Now));
      ex.Data.Add("Cause", "You have a lead foot.");
      throw ex;
    }
    else
      Console.WriteLine("=> CurrentSpeed = {0}", CurrentSpeed);
  }
}
```

To successfully enumerate over the key/value pairs, you must first make sure to specify a using directive for the System.Collections namespace, since you will use a DictionaryEntry type in the file containing the class implementing your Main() method:

```
using System.Collections;
```

Next, you need to update the catch logic to test that the value returned from the Data property is not null (the default value). After that, you make use of the Key and Value properties of the DictionaryEntry type to print the custom data to the console:

```
catch (Exception e)
{
...
  // By default, the data field is empty, so check for null.
  Console.WriteLine("\n-> Custom Data:");
```

```
  if (e.Data != null)
  {
    foreach (DictionaryEntry de in e.Data)
      Console.WriteLine("-> {0}: {1}", de.Key, de.Value);
  }
}
```

With this, here's the final output you'd see:

```
***** Simple Exception Example *****
=> Creating a car and stepping on it!
Jamming...
=> CurrentSpeed = 30
=> CurrentSpeed = 40
=> CurrentSpeed = 50
=> CurrentSpeed = 60
=> CurrentSpeed = 70
=> CurrentSpeed = 80
=> CurrentSpeed = 90

*** Error! ***
Member name: Void Accelerate(Int32)
Class defining member: SimpleException.Car
Member type: Method
Message: Zippy has overheated!
Source: SimpleException
Stack: at SimpleException.Car.Accelerate(Int32 delta)
       at SimpleException.Program.Main(String[] args)
Help Link: http://www.CarsRUs.com

-> Custom Data:
-> TimeStamp: The car exploded at 5/12/2012 9:02:12 PM
-> Cause: You have a lead foot.

***** Out of exception logic *****
```

The Data property is very useful in that it allows us to pack in custom information regarding the error at hand, without requiring the building of a brand-new class type to extend the Exception base class. As helpful as the Data property may be, however, it is still common for .NET developers to build strongly typed exception classes, which handle custom data using strongly typed properties.

This approach allows the caller to catch a specific exception-derived type, rather than having to dig into a data collection to obtain additional details. To understand how to do this, we need to examine the distinction between system-level and application-level exceptions.

■ **Source Code** The SimpleException project is included under the Chapter 7 subdirectory.

System-Level Exceptions (System.SystemException)

The .NET base class libraries define many classes that ultimately derive from System.Exception. For example, the System namespace defines core exception objects such as ArgumentOutOfRangeException, IndexOutOfRangeException, StackOverflowException, and so forth. Other namespaces define exceptions that reflect the behavior of that namespace. For example, System.Drawing.Printing defines printing exceptions, System.IO defines input/output-based exceptions, System.Data defines database-centric exceptions, and so forth.

Exceptions that are thrown by the .NET platform are (appropriately) called *system exceptions*. These exceptions are generally regarded as nonrecoverable, fatal errors. System exceptions derive directly from a base class named System.SystemException, which in turn derives from System.Exception (which derives from System.Object):

```
public class SystemException : Exception
{
  // Various constructors.
}
```

Given that the System.SystemException type does not add any additional functionality beyond a set of custom constructors, you might wonder why SystemException exists in the first place. Simply put, when an exception type derives from System.SystemException, you are able to determine that the .NET runtime is the entity that has thrown the exception, rather than the code base of the executing application. You can verify this quite simply using the is keyword:

```
// True! NullReferenceException is-a SystemException.
NullReferenceException nullRefEx = new NullReferenceException();
Console.WriteLine("NullReferenceException is-a SystemException? : {0}",
                  nullRefEx is SystemException);
```

Application-Level Exceptions (System.ApplicationException)

Given that all .NET exceptions are class types, you are free to create your own application-specific exceptions. However, due to the fact that the System.SystemException base class represents exceptions thrown from the CLR, you might naturally assume that you should derive your custom exceptions from the System.Exception type. You could do this, but you could instead derive from the System.ApplicationException class:

```
public class ApplicationException : Exception
{
  // Various constructors.
}
```

Like SystemException, ApplicationException does not define any additional members beyond a set of constructors. Functionally, the only purpose of System.ApplicationException is to identify the source of the error. When you handle an exception deriving from System.ApplicationException, you can assume the exception was raised by the code base of the executing application, rather than by the .NET base class libraries or .NET runtime engine.

■ **Note** In practice, few .NET developers build custom exceptions that extend `ApplicationException`. Rather, it is more common to simply subclass `System.Exception`; however, either approach is technically valid.

Building Custom Exceptions, Take One

While you can always throw instances of `System.Exception` to signal a runtime error (as shown in the first example), it is sometimes advantageous to build a *strongly typed exception* that represents the unique details of your current problem. For example, assume you want to build a custom exception (named `CarIsDeadException`) to represent the error of speeding up a doomed automobile. The first step is to derive a new class from `System.Exception`/`System.ApplicationException` (by convention, all exception classes end with the "Exception" suffix; in fact, this is a .NET best practice).

■ **Note** As a rule, all custom exception classes should be defined as public classes (recall, the default access modifier of a non-nested type is internal). The reason is that exceptions are often passed outside of assembly boundaries, and should therefore be accessible to the calling code base.

Create a new Console Application project named CustomException, and copy the previous `Car.cs` and `Radio.cs` files into your new project using the Project Add Existing Item menu option (for clarity, be sure to change the namespace that defines the `Car` and `Radio` types from `SimpleException` to `CustomException`). Next, add the following class definition:

```
// This custom exception describes the details of the car-is-dead condition.
// (Remember, you can also simply extend Exception.)
public class CarIsDeadException : ApplicationException
{}
```

As with any class, you are free to include any number of custom members that can be called within the catch block of the calling logic. You are also free to override any virtual members defined by your parent classes. For example, we could implement the `CarIsDeadException` by overriding the virtual `Message` property.

As well, rather than populating a data dictionary (via the `Data` property) when throwing our exception, our constructor allows the sender to pass in a time stamp and reason for the error. Finally, the time stamp data and cause of the error can be obtained using strongly typed properties:

```
public class CarIsDeadException : ApplicationException
{
  private string messageDetails = String.Empty;
  public DateTime ErrorTimeStamp {get; set;}
  public string CauseOfError {get; set;}

  public CarIsDeadException(){}
  public CarIsDeadException(string message,
    string cause, DateTime time)
  {
```

```
    messageDetails = message;
    CauseOfError = cause;
    ErrorTimeStamp = time;
  }

  // Override the Exception.Message property.
  public override string Message
  {
    get
    {
      return string.Format("Car Error Message: {0}", messageDetails);
    }
  }
}
```

Here, the CarIsDeadException class maintains a private field (messageDetails) that represents data regarding the current exception, which can be set using a custom constructor. Throwing this exception from the Accelerate() method is straightforward. Simply allocate, configure, and throw a CarIsDeadException type rather than a System.Exception (notice that in this case, we no longer need to fill the data collection manually):

```
// Throw the custom CarIsDeadException.
public void Accelerate(int delta)
{
...
  CarIsDeadException  ex =
   new CarIsDeadException (string.Format("{0} has overheated!", PetName),
                            "You have a lead foot", DateTime.Now);
  ex.HelpLink = "http://www.CarsRUs.com";
  throw ex;
...
}
```

To catch this incoming exception, your catch scope can now be updated to catch a specific CarIsDeadException type (however, given that CarIsDeadException "is-a" System.Exception, it is still permissible to catch a System.Exception as well):

```
static void Main(string[] args)
{
  Console.WriteLine("***** Fun with Custom Exceptions *****\n");
  Car myCar = new Car("Rusty", 90);

  try
  {
    // Trip exception.
    myCar.Accelerate(50);
  }
  catch (CarIsDeadException e)
  {
    Console.WriteLine(e.Message);
    Console.WriteLine(e.ErrorTimeStamp);
    Console.WriteLine(e.CauseOfError);
  }
```

```
    Console.ReadLine();
}
```

So, now that you understand the basic process of building a custom exception, you might wonder when you are required to do so. Typically, you only need to create custom exceptions when the error is tightly bound to the class issuing the error (for example, a custom file-centric class that throws a number of file-related errors, a `Car` class that throws a number of car-related errors, a data access object that throws errors regarding a particular database table, and so forth). In doing so, you provide the caller with the ability to handle numerous exceptions on a descriptive error-by-error basis.

Building Custom Exceptions, Take Two

The current `CarIsDeadException` type has overridden the virtual `System.Exception.Message` property in order to configure a custom error message, and has supplied two custom properties to account for additional bits of data. In reality, however, you are not required to override the virtual `Message` property, as you could simply pass the incoming message to the parent's constructor as follows:

```
public class CarIsDeadException : ApplicationException
{
  public DateTime ErrorTimeStamp { get; set; }
  public string CauseOfError { get; set; }

  public CarIsDeadException() { }

  // Feed message to parent constructor.
  public CarIsDeadException(string message, string cause, DateTime time)
    :base(message)
  {
    CauseOfError = cause;
    ErrorTimeStamp = time;
  }
}
```

Notice that this time you have *not* defined a string variable to represent the message, and have *not* overridden the `Message` property. Rather, you are simply passing the parameter to your base class constructor. With this design, a custom exception class is little more than a uniquely named class deriving from `System.ApplicationException` (with additional properties if appropriate), devoid of any base class overrides.

Don't be surprised if most (if not all) of your custom exception classes follow this simple pattern. Many times, the role of a custom exception is not necessarily to provide additional functionality beyond what is inherited from the base classes, but to supply a *strongly named type* that clearly identifies the nature of the error, so the client can provide different handler-logic for different types of exceptions.

Building Custom Exceptions, Take Three

If you want to build a truly prim-and-proper custom exception class, you would want to make sure your type adheres to .NET best practices. Specifically, this requires that your custom exception does the following:

- Derives from `Exception`/`ApplicationException`

- Is marked with the `[System.Serializable]` attribute

- Defines a default constructor

- Defines a constructor that sets the inherited Message property

- Defines a constructor to handle "inner exceptions"

- Defines a constructor to handle the serialization of your type

Now, based on your current background with .NET, you might have no experience regarding the role of attributes or object serialization, which is just fine. I'll address these topics later in the text (see Chapter 15 for information on attributes and Chapter 20 for details on serialization services). However, to complete our examination of building custom exceptions, here is the final iteration of CarIsDeadException, which accounts for each of these special constructors (the other custom properties and constructors would be as seen in the example found in "Building Custom Exceptions, Take Two"):

```
[Serializable]
public class CarIsDeadException : ApplicationException
{
  public CarIsDeadException() { }
  public CarIsDeadException(string message) : base( message ) { }
  public CarIsDeadException(string message,
                            System.Exception inner)
    : base( message, inner ) { }
  protected CarIsDeadException(
    System.Runtime.Serialization.SerializationInfo info,
    System.Runtime.Serialization.StreamingContext context)
    : base( info, context ) { }

  // Any additional custom properties, constructors and data members...
}
```

Given that building custom exceptions that adhere to .NET best practices really differ by only their name, you will be happy to know that Visual Studio provides a code snippet template named "Exception" (see Figure 7-1) that will autogenerate a new exception class that adheres to .NET best practices. (Recall from Chapter 2, a code snippet can be activated by typing its name [exception, in this case] and pressing the Tab key twice.)

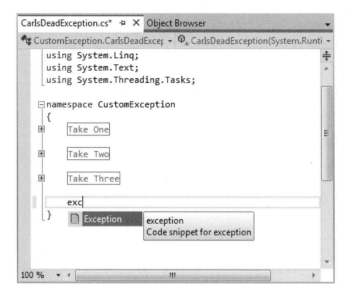

Figure 7-1. The Exception code snippet template

■ **Source Code** The CustomException project is included under the Chapter 7 subdirectory.

Processing Multiple Exceptions

In its simplest form, a try block has a single catch block. In reality, though, you often run into situations where the statements within a try block could trigger *numerous* possible exceptions. Create a new C# Console Application project named ProcessMultipleExceptions, add the Car.cs, Radio.cs, and CarIsDeadException.cs files from the previous CustomException example into the new project (via Project ➤ Add Existing Item), and update your namespace names accordingly.

Now, update the Car's Accelerate() method to also throw a predefined base class library ArgumentOutOfRangeException if you pass an invalid parameter (which we will assume is any value less than zero). Note the constructor of this exception class takes the name of the offending argument as the first string, followed by a message describing the error.

```
// Test for invalid argument before proceeding.
public void Accelerate(int delta)
{
  if(delta < 0)
    throw new
      ArgumentOutOfRangeException("delta", "Speed must be greater than zero!");
  ...
}
```

The catch logic could now specifically respond to each type of exception:

271

```
static void Main(string[] args)
{
  Console.WriteLine("***** Handling Multiple Exceptions *****\n");
  Car myCar = new Car("Rusty", 90);
  try
  {
    // Trip Arg out of range exception.
    myCar.Accelerate(-10);
  }
  catch (CarIsDeadException e)
  {
    Console.WriteLine(e.Message);
  }
  catch (ArgumentOutOfRangeException e)
  {
    Console.WriteLine(e.Message);
  }
  Console.ReadLine();
}
```

When you are authoring multiple catch blocks, you must be aware that when an exception is thrown, it will be processed by the "first available" catch. To illustrate exactly what the "first available" catch means, assume you retrofitted the previous logic with an additional catch scope that attempts to handle all exceptions beyond CarIsDeadException and ArgumentOutOfRangeException by catching a general System.Exception as follows:

```
// This code will not compile!
static void Main(string[] args)
{
  Console.WriteLine("***** Handling Multiple Exceptions *****\n");
  Car myCar = new Car("Rusty", 90);

  try
  {
    // Trigger an argument out of range exception.
    myCar.Accelerate(-10);
  }
  catch(Exception e)
  {
    // Process all other exceptions?
    Console.WriteLine(e.Message);
  }
  catch (CarIsDeadException e)
  {
    Console.WriteLine(e.Message);
  }
  catch (ArgumentOutOfRangeException e)
  {
    Console.WriteLine(e.Message);
  }
  Console.ReadLine();
}
```

This exception-handling logic generates compile-time errors. The problem is due to the fact that the first catch block can handle *anything* derived from System.Exception (given the "is-a" relationship), including the CarIsDeadException and ArgumentOutOfRangeException types. Therefore, the final two catch blocks are unreachable!

The rule of thumb to keep in mind is to make sure your catch blocks are structured such that the very first catch is the most specific exception (i.e., the most derived type in an exception-type inheritance chain), leaving the final catch for the most general (i.e., the base class of a given exception inheritance chain, in this case System.Exception).

Thus, if you want to define a catch block that will handle any errors beyond CarIsDeadException and ArgumentOutOfRangeException, you could write the following:

```
// This code compiles just fine.
static void Main(string[] args)
{
  Console.WriteLine("***** Handling Multiple Exceptions *****\n");
  Car myCar = new Car("Rusty", 90);
  try
  {
    // Trigger an argument out of range exception.
    myCar.Accelerate(-10);
  }
  catch (CarIsDeadException e)
  {
    Console.WriteLine(e.Message);
  }
  catch (ArgumentOutOfRangeException e)
  {
    Console.WriteLine(e.Message);
  }
  // This will catch any other exception
  // beyond CarIsDeadException or
  // ArgumentOutOfRangeException.
  catch (Exception e)
  {
    Console.WriteLine(e.Message);
  }
  Console.ReadLine();
}
```

■ **Note** Where at all possible, always favor catching specific exception classes, rather than a general System.Exception. Though it might appear to make life simple in the short term (you may think, "Ah! This catches all the other things I don't care about."), in the long term you could end up with strange runtime crashes, as a more serious error was not directly dealt with in your code. Remember, a final catch block that deals with System.Exception tends to be very general indeed.

General catch Statements

C# also supports a "general" catch scope that does not explicitly receive the exception object thrown by a given member:

```
// A generic catch.
static void Main(string[] args)
{
  Console.WriteLine("***** Handling Multiple Exceptions *****\n");
  Car myCar = new Car("Rusty", 90);
  try
  {
    myCar.Accelerate(90);
  }
  catch
  {
    Console.WriteLine("Something bad happened...");
  }
  Console.ReadLine();
}
```

Obviously, this is not the most informative way to handle exceptions, since you have no way to obtain meaningful data about the error that occurred (such as the method name, call stack, or custom message). Nevertheless, C# does allow for such a construct, which can be helpful when you want to handle all errors in a very, very general fashion.

Rethrowing Exceptions

When you catch an exception, it is permissible for the logic in a try block to *rethrow* the exception up the call stack to the previous caller. To do so, simply use the throw keyword within a catch block. This passes the exception up the chain of calling logic, which can be helpful if your catch block is only able to partially handle the error at hand:

```
// Passing the buck.
static void Main(string[] args)
{
...
  try
  {
    // Speed up car logic...
  }
  catch(CarIsDeadException e)
  {
    // Do any partial processing of this error and pass the buck.
    throw;
  }
...
}
```

Be aware that in this example code, the ultimate receiver of CarIsDeadException is the CLR, because it is the Main() method rethrowing the exception. Because of this, your end user is presented with a system-supplied error dialog box. Typically, you would only rethrow a partial handled exception to a caller that has the ability to handle the incoming exception more gracefully.

Notice as well that we are not explicitly rethrowing the CarIsDeadException object, but rather making use of the throw keyword with no argument. We're not creating a new exception object; we're just rethrowing the original exception object (with all its original information). Doing so preserves the context of the original target.

Inner Exceptions

As you might suspect, it is entirely possible to trigger an exception at the time you are handling another exception. For example, assume you are handling a CarIsDeadException within a particular catch scope, and during the process you attempt to record the stack trace to a file on your C: drive named carErrors.txt (you must specify you are using the System.IO namespace to gain access to these I/O-centric types):

```
catch(CarIsDeadException e)
{
  // Attempt to open a file named carErrors.txt on the C drive.
  FileStream fs = File.Open(@"C:\carErrors.txt", FileMode.Open);
  ...
}
```

Now, if the specified file is not located on your C: drive, the call to File.Open() results in a FileNotFoundException! Later in this text, you will learn all about the System.IO namespace where you'll discover how to programmatically determine whether a file exists on the hard drive before attempting to open the file in the first place (thereby avoiding the exception altogether). However, to stay focused on the topic of exceptions, assume the exception has been raised.

When you encounter an exception while processing another exception, best practice states that you should record the new exception object as an "inner exception" within a new object of the same type as the initial exception. (That was a mouthful!) The reason you need to allocate a new object of the exception being handled is that the only way to document an inner exception is via a constructor parameter. Consider the following code:

```
catch (CarIsDeadException e)
{
  try
  {
    FileStream fs = File.Open(@"C:\carErrors.txt", FileMode.Open);
    ...
  }
  catch (Exception e2)
  {
    // Throw an exception that records the new exception,
    // as well as the message of the first exception.
    throw new CarIsDeadException(e.Message, e2);
  }
}
```

Notice in this case, we have passed in the FileNotFoundException object as the second parameter to the CarIsDeadException constructor. After we have configured this new object, we throw it up the call stack to the next caller, which in this case would be the Main() method.

Given that there is no "next caller" after Main() to catch the exception, we would be again presented with an error dialog box. Much like the act of rethrowing an exception, recording inner exceptions is usually only useful when the caller has the ability to gracefully catch the exception in the first place. If this is the case, the caller's catch logic can make use of the InnerException property to extract the details of the inner exception object.

The finally Block

A try/catch scope may also define an optional finally block. The purpose of a finally block is to ensure that a set of code statements will *always* execute, exception (of any type) or not. To illustrate, assume you want to always power down the car's radio before exiting Main(), regardless of any handled exception:

```
static void Main(string[] args)
{
  Console.WriteLine("***** Handling Multiple Exceptions *****\n");
  Car myCar = new Car("Rusty", 90);
  myCar.CrankTunes(true);

  try
  {
    // Speed up car logic.
  }
  catch(CarIsDeadException e)
  {
    // Process CarIsDeadException.
  }
  catch(ArgumentOutOfRangeException e)
  {
    // Process ArgumentOutOfRangeException.
  }
  catch(Exception e)
  {
    // Process any other Exception.
  }
  finally
  {
    // This will always occur. Exception or not.
    myCar.CrankTunes(false);
  }
  Console.ReadLine();
}
```

If you did not include a finally block, the radio would not be turned off if an exception is encountered (which might or might not be problematic). In a more real-world scenario, when you need to dispose of objects, close a file, or detach from a database (or whatever), a finally block ensures a location for proper cleanup.

Who Is Throwing What?

Given that a method in the .NET Framework could throw any number of exceptions under various circumstances, a logical question is, "How do I know which exceptions may be thrown by a given base class library method?" The ultimate answer is simple: consult the .NET Framework 4.5 SDK documentation. Each method in the help system documents the exceptions a given member may throw. As a quick alternative, Visual Studio allows you to view the list of all exceptions thrown by a base class library member (if any) simply by hovering your mouse cursor over the member name in the code window (see Figure 7-2).

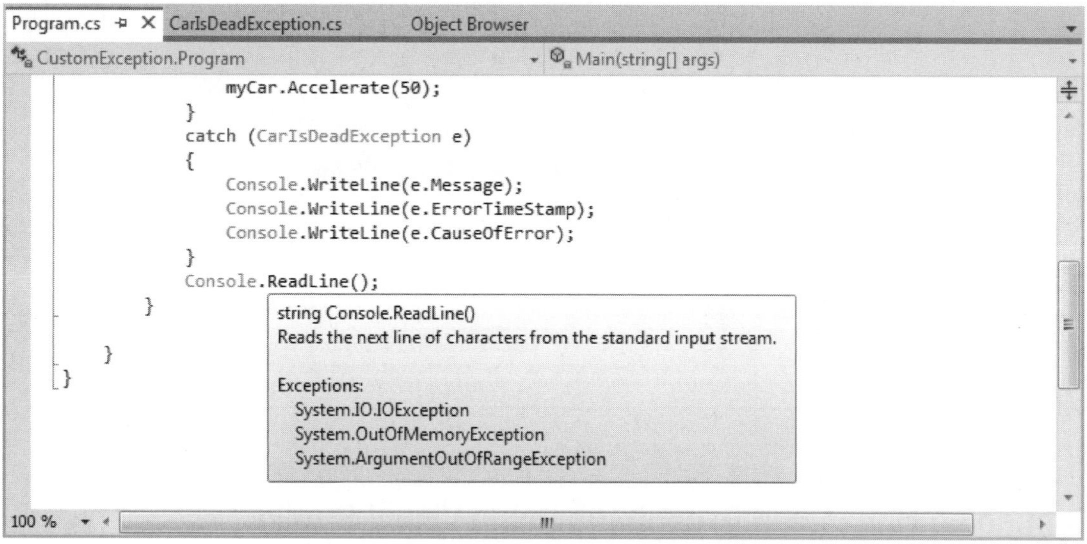

```
Program.cs  ⇄ X   CarIsDeadException.cs      Object Browser                                          ▼
CustomException.Program                              ▼  Main(string[] args)                          ▼

                    myCar.Accelerate(50);                                                            ÷
            }
            catch (CarIsDeadException e)
            {
                Console.WriteLine(e.Message);
                Console.WriteLine(e.ErrorTimeStamp);
                Console.WriteLine(e.CauseOfError);
            }
            Console.ReadLine();
        }
                         ┌──────────────────────────────────────────────────────────┐
                         │ string Console.ReadLine()                                  │
    }                    │ Reads the next line of characters from the standard input stream. │
                         │                                                            │
 }                       │ Exceptions:                                                │
                         │     System.IO.IOException                                  │
                         │     System.OutOfMemoryException                            │
                         │     System.ArgumentOutOfRangeException                     │
                         └──────────────────────────────────────────────────────────┘

100 %   ▼  ◄                                         Ⅲ                                          ►
```

Figure 7-2. Identifying the exceptions thrown from a given method

---

■ **Note** For those coming to .NET from a Java background, understand that type members are not prototyped with the set of exceptions they may throw (in other words, .NET does not support checked exceptions). For better or for worse, you are not required to handle each and every exception thrown from a given member.

The Result of Unhandled Exceptions

At this point, you might be wondering what would happen if you do not handle an exception thrown in your direction. Assume that the logic in Main() increases the speed of the Car object beyond the maximum speed, without the benefit of try/catch logic:

```
static void Main(string[] args)
{
  Console.WriteLine("***** Handling Multiple Exceptions *****\n");
  Car myCar = new Car("Rusty", 90);
  myCar.Accelerate(500);
  Console.ReadLine();
}
```

The result of ignoring an exception would be rather obstructive to the end user of your application, as an "unhandled exception" dialog box is displayed (see Figure 7-3).

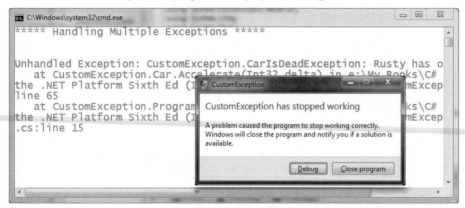

Figure 7-3. The result of not dealing with exceptions

Debugging Unhandled Exceptions Using Visual Studio

Do be aware that Visual Studio supplies a number of tools that help you debug unhandled custom exceptions. Again, assume you have increased the speed of a Car object beyond the maximum. If you start a debugging session within Visual Studio (using the Debug ➤ Start Debugging menu selection), Visual Studio automatically breaks at the time the uncaught exception is thrown. Better yet, you are presented with a window (see Figure 7-4) displaying the value of the Message property.

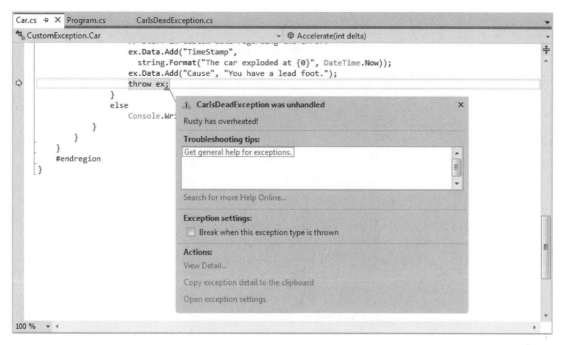

Figure 7-4. Debugging unhandled custom exceptions with Visual Studio

---

■ **Note** If you fail to handle an exception thrown by a method in the .NET base class libraries, the Visual Studio debugger breaks at the statement that called the offending method.

If you click the View Detail link, you will find the details regarding the state of the object (see Figure 7-5).

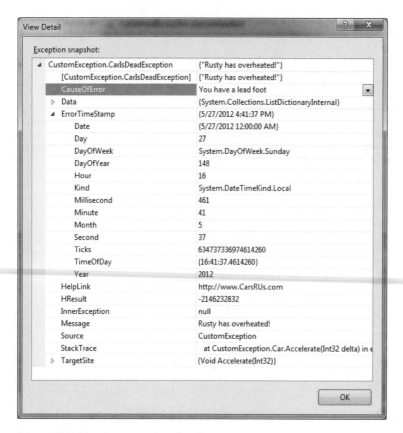

Figure 7-5. Viewing exception details

■ **Source Code** The ProcessMultipleExceptions project is included under the Chapter 7 subdirectory.

Summary

In this chapter, you examined the role of structured exception handling. When a method needs to send an error object to the caller, it will allocate, configure, and throw a specific System.Exception derived type via the C# throw keyword. The caller is able to handle any possible incoming exceptions using the C# catch keyword and an optional finally scope.

When you are creating your own custom exceptions, you ultimately create a class type deriving from System.ApplicationException, which denotes an exception thrown from the currently executing application. In contrast, error objects deriving from System.SystemException represent critical (and fatal) errors thrown by the CLR. Last but not least, this chapter illustrated various tools within Visual Studio that can be used to create custom exceptions (according to .NET best practices) as well as debug exceptions.

CHAPTER 8

Working with Interfaces

This chapter builds upon your current understanding of object-oriented development by examining the topic of interface-based programming. Here you'll learn how to define and implement interfaces, and come to understand the benefits of building types that support multiple behaviors. Along the way, I'll also discuss a number of related topics, such as obtaining interface references, explicit interface implementation, and the construction of interface hierarchies. We'll also examine a number of standard interfaces defined within the .NET base class libraries. As you will see, your custom classes and structures are free to implement these predefined interfaces to support a number of useful behaviors, such as object cloning, object enumeration, and object sorting.

Understanding Interface Types

To begin this chapter, allow me to provide a formal definition of the *interface type*. An *interface* is nothing more than a named set of *abstract members*. Recall from Chapter 6 that abstract methods are pure protocol in that they do not provide a default implementation. The specific members defined by an interface depend on the exact behavior it is modeling. Said another way, an interface expresses a *behavior* that a given class or structure may choose to support. Furthermore, as you will see in this chapter, a class or structure can support as many interfaces as necessary, thereby supporting (in essence) multiple behaviors.

As you might guess, the .NET base class libraries ship with hundreds of predefined interface types that are implemented by various classes and structures. For example, as you will see in Chapter 21, ADO.NET ships with multiple data providers that allow you to communicate with a particular database management system. Thus, under ADO.NET we have numerous connection objects to choose from (SqlConnection, OleDbConnection, OdbcConnection, etc.).

Regardless of the fact that each connection object has a unique name, is defined within a different namespace, and (in some cases) is bundled within a different assembly, all connection objects implement a common interface named IDbConnection:

```
// The IDbConnection interface defines a common
// set of members supported by all connection objects.
public interface IDbConnection : IDisposable
{
  // Methods
  IDbTransaction BeginTransaction();
  IDbTransaction BeginTransaction(IsolationLevel il);
  void ChangeDatabase(string databaseName);
  void Close();
  IDbCommand CreateCommand();
  void Open();
```

```
    // Properties
    string ConnectionString { get; set;}
    int ConnectionTimeout { get; }
    string Database { get; }
    ConnectionState State { get; }
}
```

■ **Note** By convention, .NET interfaces are prefixed with a capital letter "I." When you are creating your own custom interfaces, it is considered a best practice to do the same.

Don't concern yourself with the details of what these members actually do at this point. Simply understand that the IDbConnection interface defines a set of members that are common to all ADO.NET connection objects. Given this, you are guaranteed that every connection object supports members such as Open(), Close(), CreateCommand(), and so forth. Furthermore, given that interface members are always abstract, each connection object is free to implement these methods in its own unique manner.

As you work through the remainder of this book, you'll be exposed to dozens of interfaces that ship with the .NET base class libraries. As you will see, these interfaces can be implemented on your own custom classes and structures to define types that integrate tightly within the framework.

Interface Types vs. Abstract Base Classes

Given your work in Chapter 6, the interface type might seem very similar to an abstract base class. Recall that when a class is marked as abstract, it *may* define any number of abstract members to provide a polymorphic interface to all derived types. However, even when a class does define a set of abstract members, it is also free to define any number of constructors, field data, nonabstract members (with implementation), and so on. Interfaces, on the other hand, contain *only* abstract member definitions.

The polymorphic interface established by an abstract parent class suffers from one major limitation in that *only derived types* support the members defined by the abstract parent. However, in larger software systems, it is very common to develop multiple class hierarchies that have no common parent beyond System.Object. Given that abstract members in an abstract base class apply only to derived types, we have no way to configure types in different hierarchies to support the same polymorphic interface. By way of example, assume you have defined the following abstract class:

```
public abstract class CloneableType
{
    // Only derived types can support this
    // "polymorphic interface." Classes in other
    // hierarchies have no access to this abstract
    // member.
    public abstract object Clone();
}
```

Given this definition, only members that extend CloneableType are able to support the Clone() method. If you create a new set of classes that do not extend this base class, you can't gain this polymorphic interface. Also, you might recall that C# does not support multiple inheritance for classes. Therefore, if you wanted to create a MiniVan that is-a Car and is-a CloneableType, you are unable to do so:

```
// Nope! Multiple inheritance is not possible in C#
// for classes.
public class MiniVan : Car, CloneableType
{
}
```

As you would guess, interface types come to the rescue. After an interface has been defined, it can be implemented by any class or structure, in any hierarchy, within any namespace or any assembly (written in any .NET programming language). As you can see, interfaces are *highly* polymorphic. Consider the standard .NET interface named ICloneable, defined in the System namespace. This interface defines a single method named Clone():

```
public interface ICloneable
{
  object Clone();
}
```

If you examine the .NET Framework 4.5 SDK documentation, you'll find that a large number of seemingly unrelated types (System.Array, System.Data.SqlClient.SqlConnection, System.OperatingSystem, System.String, etc.) all implement this interface. Although these types have no common parent (other than System.Object), we can treat them polymorphically via the ICloneable interface type.

For example, if you had a method named CloneMe() that took an ICloneable interface parameter, you could pass this method any object that implements said interface. Consider the following simple Program class defined within a Console Application named ICloneableExample:

```
class Program
{
  static void Main(string[] args)
  {
    Console.WriteLine("***** A First Look at Interfaces *****\n");

    // All of these classes support the ICloneable interface.
    string myStr = "Hello";
    OperatingSystem unixOS = new OperatingSystem(PlatformID.Unix, new Version());
    System.Data.SqlClient.SqlConnection sqlCnn =
      new System.Data.SqlClient.SqlConnection();

    // Therefore, they can all be passed into a method taking ICloneable.
    CloneMe(myStr);
    CloneMe(unixOS);
    CloneMe(sqlCnn);
    Console.ReadLine();
  }

  private static void CloneMe(ICloneable c)
  {
    // Clone whatever we get and print out the name.
    object theClone = c.Clone();
    Console.WriteLine("Your clone is a: {0}",
      theClone.GetType().Name);
  }
}
```

When you run this application, the class name of each class prints out to the console, via the GetType() method you inherit from System.Object. As explained in Chapter 15, this method (and .NET reflection services) allow you to understand the composition of any type at runtime. In any case, the output of the previous program is shown next:

```
***** A First Look at Interfaces *****

Your clone is a: String
Your clone is a: OperatingSystem
Your clone is a: SqlConnection
```

Another limitation of abstract base classes is that *each derived type* must contend with the set of abstract members and provide an implementation. To see this problem, recall the shapes hierarchy we defined in Chapter 6. Assume we defined a new abstract method in the Shape base class named GetNumberOfPoints(), which allows derived types to return the number of points required to render the shape:

```
abstract class Shape
{
...
  // Every derived class must now support this method!
  public abstract byte GetNumberOfPoints();
}
```

Clearly, the only class that has any points in the first place is Hexagon. However, with this update, *every* derived class (Circle, Hexagon, and ThreeDCircle) must now provide a concrete implementation of this function, even if it makes no sense to do so. Again, the interface type provides a solution. If you define an interface that represents the behavior of "having points," you can simply plug it into the Hexagon type, leaving Circle and ThreeDCircle untouched.

■ **Source Code** The ICloneableExample project is located under the Chapter 8 subdirectory.

Defining Custom Interfaces

Now that you better understand the overall role of interface types, let's see an example of defining and implementing custom interfaces. To begin, create a brand-new Console Application named CustomInterface. Using the Project ➤ Add Existing Item menu option, insert the file(s) containing your shape type definitions (Shape.cs and DerivedShapes.cs in the book's solution code) created back in Chapter 6 during the Shapes example. After you have done so, rename the namespace that defines your shape-centric types to CustomInterface (simply to avoid having to import namespace definitions in your new project):

```
namespace CustomInterface
{
  // Your shape types defined here...
}
```

Now, insert a new interface into your project named IPointy using the Project ➤ Add New Item menu option, as shown in Figure 8-1.

Figure 8-1. *Interfaces, like classes, can be defined in any *.cs file*

At a syntactic level, an interface is defined using the C# interface keyword. Unlike a class, interfaces never specify a base class (not even System.Object; however, as you will see later in this chapter, an interface can specify base interfaces). Moreover, the members of an interface never specify an access modifier (as all interface members are implicitly public and abstract). To get the ball rolling, here is a custom interface defined in C#:

```
// This interface defines the behavior of "having points."
public interface IPointy
{
  // Implicitly public and abstract.
  byte GetNumberOfPoints();
}
```

Remember that when you define interface members, you do not define an implementation scope for the members in question. Interfaces are pure protocol and, therefore, never define an implementation (that is up to the supporting class or structure). Hence, the following version of IPointy would result in various compiler errors:

```
// Ack! Errors abound!
public interface IPointy
{
  // Error! Interfaces cannot have data fields!
  public int numbOfPoints;
```

```
  // Error! Interfaces do not have constructors!
  public IPointy() { numbOfPoints = 0;};

  // Error! Interfaces don't provide an implementation of members!
  byte GetNumberOfPoints() { return numbOfPoints; }
}
```

In any case, this initial IPointy interface defines a single method. However, .NET interface types are also able to define any number of property prototypes. For example, let's update the IPointy interface to use a read-only property rather than a traditional accessor method:

```
// The pointy behavior as a read-only property.
public interface IPointy
{
  // A read-write property in an interface would look like:
  // retType PropName { get; set; }
  //
  // while a write-only property in an interface would be:
  // retType PropName { set; }

  byte Points { get; }
}
```

■ **Note** Interface types can also contain event (see Chapter 10) and indexer (see Chapter 11) definitions.

Interface types are quite useless on their own, as they are nothing more than a named collection of abstract members. For example, you can't allocate interface types as you would a class or structure:

```
// Ack! Illegal to allocate interface types.
static void Main(string[] args)
{
  IPointy p = new IPointy();  // Compiler error!
}
```

Interfaces do not bring much to the table until they are implemented by a class or structure. Here, IPointy is an interface that expresses the behavior of "having points." The idea is simple: some classes in the shapes hierarchy have points (such as the Hexagon), while others (such as the Circle) do not.

Implementing an Interface

When a class (or structure) chooses to extend its functionality by supporting interfaces, it does so using a comma-delimited list in the type definition. Be aware that the direct base class must be the first item listed after the colon operator. When your class type derives directly from System.Object, you are free to simply list the interface(s) supported by the class, as the C# compiler will extend your types from System.Object if you do not say otherwise. On a related note, given that structures always derive from System.ValueType (see Chapter 4), simply list each interface directly after the structure definition. Ponder the following examples:

```
// This class derives from System.Object and
// implements a single interface.
public class Pencil : IPointy
{...}

// This class also derives from System.Object
// and implements a single interface.
public class SwitchBlade : object, IPointy
{...}

// This class derives from a custom base class
// and implements a single interface.
public class Fork : Utensil, IPointy
{...}

// This struct implicitly derives from System.ValueType and
// implements two interfaces.
public struct PitchFork : ICloneable, IPointy
{...}
```

Understand that implementing an interface is an all-or-nothing proposition. The supporting type is not able to selectively choose which members it will implement. Given that the IPointy interface defines a single read-only property, this is not too much of a burden. However, if you are implementing an interface that defines ten members (such as the IDbConnection interface shown earlier), the type is now responsible for fleshing out the details of all ten abstract members.

For this example, insert a new class type named Triangle that is-a Shape and supports IPointy. Note that the implementation of the read-only Points property simply returns the correct number of points (3).

```
// New Shape derived class named Triangle.
class Triangle : Shape, IPointy
{
  public Triangle() { }
  public Triangle(string name) : base(name) { }
  public override void Draw()
  { Console.WriteLine("Drawing {0} the Triangle", PetName); }

  // IPointy implementation.
  public byte Points
  {
    get { return 3; }
  }
}
```

Now, update your existing Hexagon type to also support the IPointy interface type:

```
// Hexagon now implements IPointy.
class Hexagon : Shape, IPointy
{
  public Hexagon(){ }
  public Hexagon(string name) : base(name){ }
  public override void Draw()
  { Console.WriteLine("Drawing {0}  the Hexagon", PetName); }
```

```
// IPointy implementation.
public byte Points
{
  get { return 6; }
}
}
```

To sum up the story so far, the Visual Studio class diagram shown in Figure 8-2 illustrates IPointy-compatible classes using the popular "lollipop" notation. Notice again that Circle and ThreeDCircle do not implement IPointy, as this behavior makes no sense for these particular classes.

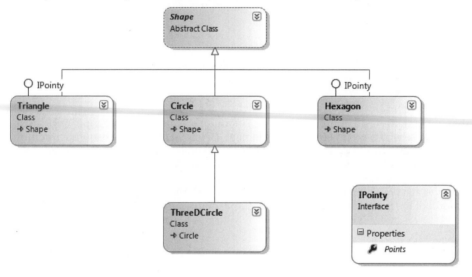

Figure 8-2. *The shapes hierarchy, now with interfaces*

■ **Note** To display or hide interface names on the class designer, right-click on the interface icon and select the Collapse or Expand option.

Invoking Interface Members at the Object Level

Now that you have some classes that support the IPointy interface, the next question is how you interact with the new functionality. The most straightforward way to interact with functionality supplied by a given interface is to invoke the members directly from the object level (provided the interface members are not implemented explicitly; more details later in the section "Explicit Interface Implementation"). For example, consider the following Main() method:

```
static void Main(string[] args)
{
  Console.WriteLine("***** Fun with Interfaces *****\n");
```

```
  // Call Points property defined by IPointy.
  Hexagon hex = new Hexagon();
  Console.WriteLine("Points: {0}", hex.Points);
  Console.ReadLine();
}
```

This approach works fine in this particular case, given that you are well aware that the Hexagon type has implemented the interface in question and, therefore, has a Points property. Other times, however, you might not be able to determine which interfaces are supported by a given type. For example, suppose you have an array containing 50 Shape-compatible types, only some of which support IPointy. Obviously, if you attempt to invoke the Points property on a type that has not implemented IPointy, you would receive an error. So how can you dynamically determine if a class or structure supports the correct interface?

One way to determine at runtime whether a type supports a specific interface is to make use of an explicit cast. If the type does not support the requested interface, you receive an InvalidCastException. To handle this possibility gracefully, use structured exception handling as in the following example:

```
static void Main(string[] args)
{
...
  // Catch a possible InvalidCastException.
  Circle c = new Circle("Lisa");
  IPointy itfPt = null;
  try
  {
    itfPt = (IPointy)c;
    Console.WriteLine(itfPt.Points);
  }
  catch (InvalidCastException e)
  {
    Console.WriteLine(e.Message);
  }

  Console.ReadLine();
}
```

While you could use try/catch logic and hope for the best, it would be ideal to determine which interfaces are supported before invoking the interface members in the first place. Let's see two ways of doing so.

Obtaining Interface References: The as Keyword

You can determine whether a given type supports an interface by using the as keyword, introduced in Chapter 6. If the object can be treated as the specified interface, you are returned a reference to the interface in question. If not, you receive a null reference. Therefore, be sure to check against a null value before proceeding:

```
static void Main(string[] args)
{
...
  // Can we treat hex2 as IPointy?
  Hexagon hex2 = new Hexagon("Peter");
```

```
    IPointy itfPt2 = hex2 as IPointy;

    if(itfPt2 != null)
      Console.WriteLine("Points: {0}", itfPt2.Points);
    else
      Console.WriteLine("OOPS! Not pointy...");
    Console.ReadLine();
}
```

Notice that when you use the as keyword, you have no need to use try/catch logic, given that if the reference is not null, you know you are calling on a valid interface reference.

Obtaining Interface References: The is Keyword

You may also check for an implemented interface using the is keyword (also first discussed in Chapter 6). If the object in question is not compatible with the specified interface, you are returned the value false. On the other hand, if the type is compatible with the interface in question, you can safely call the members without needing to use try/catch logic.

To illustrate, assume we have an array of Shape types containing some members that implement IPointy. Notice how we are able to determine which items in the array support this interface using the is keyword, as shown in this retrofitted Main() method:

```
static void Main(string[] args)
{
  Console.WriteLine("***** Fun with Interfaces *****\n");

  // Make an array of Shapes.
  Shape[] myShapes = { new Hexagon(), new Circle(),
                    new Triangle("Joe"), new Circle("JoJo")} ;

  for(int i = 0; i < myShapes.Length; i++)
  {
    // Recall the Shape base class defines an abstract Draw()
    // member, so all shapes know how to draw themselves.
    myShapes[i].Draw();

    // Who's pointy?
    if(myShapes[i] is IPointy)
      Console.WriteLine("-> Points: {0}", ((IPointy) myShapes[i]).Points);
    else
      Console.WriteLine("-> {0}\'s not pointy!", myShapes[i].PetName);
    Console.WriteLine();
  }
  Console.ReadLine();
}
```

The output is as follows:

```
***** Fun with Interfaces *****

Drawing NoName the Hexagon
-> Points: 6

Drawing NoName the Circle
-> NoName's not pointy!

Drawing Joe the Triangle
-> Points: 3

Drawing JoJo the Circle
-> JoJo's not pointy!
```

Interfaces As Parameters

Given that interfaces are valid .NET types, you may construct methods that take interfaces as parameters, as illustrated by the CloneMe() method earlier in this chapter. For the current example, assume you have defined another interface named IDraw3D:

```
// Models the ability to render a type in stunning 3D.
public interface IDraw3D
{
  void Draw3D();
}
```

Next, assume that two of your three shapes (ThreeDCircle and Hexagon) have been configured to support this new behavior:

```
// Circle supports IDraw3D.
class ThreeDCircle : Circle, IDraw3D
{
...
  public void Draw3D()
  { Console.WriteLine("Drawing Circle in 3D!"); }
}

// Hexagon supports IPointy and IDraw3D.
class Hexagon : Shape, IPointy, IDraw3D
{
...
  public void Draw3D()
  { Console.WriteLine("Drawing Hexagon in 3D!"); }
}
```

Figure 8-3 presents the updated Visual Studio class diagram.

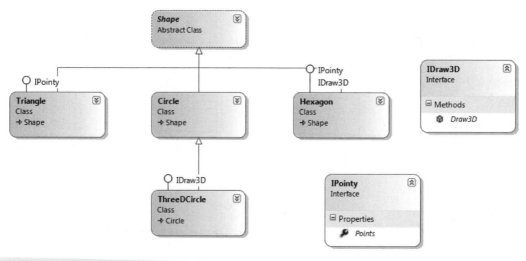

Figure 8-3. *The updated shapes hierarchy*

If you now define a method taking an IDraw3D interface as a parameter, you can effectively send in any object implementing IDraw3D. (If you attempt to pass in a type not supporting the necessary interface, you receive a compile-time error.) Consider the following method defined within your Program class:

```
// I'll draw anyone supporting IDraw3D.
static void DrawIn3D(IDraw3D itf3d)
{
  Console.WriteLine("-> Drawing IDraw3D compatible type");
  itf3d.Draw3D();
}
```

We could now test whether an item in the Shape array supports this new interface, and if so, pass it into the DrawIn3D() method for processing:

```
static void Main(string[] args)
{
  Console.WriteLine("***** Fun with Interfaces *****\n");
  Shape[] myShapes = { new Hexagon(), new Circle(),
                       new Triangle(), new Circle("JoJo") } ;
  for(int i = 0; i < myShapes.Length; i++)
  {
    ...
    // Can I draw you in 3D?
    if(myShapes[i] is IDraw3D)
      DrawIn3D((IDraw3D)myShapes[i]);
  }
}
```

Here is the output of the updated application. Notice that only the Hexagon object prints out in 3D, as the other members of the Shape array do not implement the IDraw3D interface.

```
***** Fun with Interfaces *****

Drawing NoName the Hexagon
-> Points: 6
-> Drawing IDraw3D compatible type
Drawing Hexagon in 3D!

Drawing NoName the Circle
-> NoName's not pointy!

Drawing Joe the Triangle
-> Points: 3

Drawing JoJo the Circle
-> JoJo's not pointy!
```

Interfaces As Return Values

Interfaces can also be used as method return values. For example, you could write a method that takes an array of Shape objects and returns a reference to the first item that supports IPointy:

```
// This method returns the first object in the
// array that implements IPointy.
static IPointy FindFirstPointyShape(Shape[] shapes)
{
  foreach (Shape s in shapes)
  {
    if (s is IPointy)
      return s as IPointy;
  }
  return null;
}
```

You could interact with this method as follows:

```
static void Main(string[] args)
{
  Console.WriteLine("***** Fun with Interfaces *****\n");
  // Make an array of Shapes.
  Shape[] myShapes = { new Hexagon(), new Circle(),
                    new Triangle("Joe"), new Circle("JoJo")};

  // Get first pointy item.
  // To be safe, you'd want to check firstPointyItem for null before proceeding.
  IPointy firstPointyItem = FindFirstPointyShape(myShapes);
  Console.WriteLine("The item has {0} points", firstPointyItem.Points);
...
}
```

Arrays of Interface Types

Recall that the same interface can be implemented by numerous types, even if they are not within the same class hierarchy and do not have a common parent class beyond System.Object. This can yield some very powerful programming constructs. For example, assume you have developed three new class types within your current project that model kitchen utensils (via Knife and Fork classes) and another modeling gardening equipment (à la PitchFork). Consider Figure 8-4.

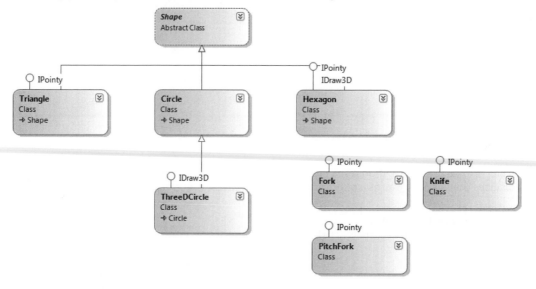

Figure 8-4. *Recall that interfaces can be "plugged into" any type in any part of a class hierarchy*

If you defined the PitchFork, Fork, and Knife types, you could now define an array of IPointy-compatible objects. Given that these members all support the same interface; you can iterate through the array and treat each item as an IPointy-compatible object, regardless of the overall diversity of the class hierarchies:

```
static void Main(string[] args)
{
...
  // This array can only contain types that
  // implement the IPointy interface.
  IPointy[] myPointyObjects = {new Hexagon(), new Knife(),
    new Triangle(), new Fork(), new PitchFork()};

  foreach(IPointy i in myPointyObjects)
    Console.WriteLine("Object has {0} points.", i.Points);
  Console.ReadLine();
}
```

Just to highlight the importance of this example, remember this: when you have an array of a given interface, the array can contain any class or structure which implements that interface.

Implementing Interfaces Using Visual Studio

Although interface-based programming is a very powerful technique, implementing interfaces may entail a healthy amount of typing. Given that interfaces are a named set of abstract members, you are required to type in the definition and implementation for *each* interface method on *each* type that supports the behavior. Therefore, if you want to support an interface that defines a total of five methods and three properties, you need to account for all eight members (or else you will receive compiler errors).

As you would hope, Visual Studio supports various tools that make the task of implementing interfaces less burdensome. By way of a simple test, insert a final class into your current project named PointyTestClass. When you implement IPointy (or any interface for that matter), you might have noticed that when you complete typing the interface's name (or when you position the mouse cursor on the interface name in the code window), the first letter is underlined (formally termed a *smart tag*). When you click the smart tag, you will be presented with a drop-down list that allows you to implement the interface (see Figure 8-5).

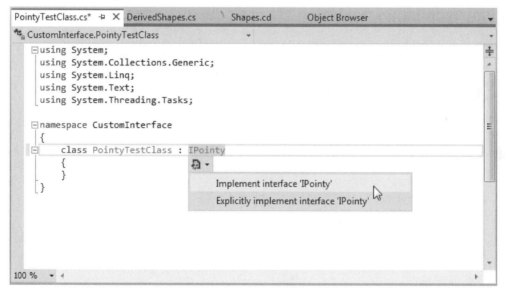

Figure 8-5. Implementing interfaces using Visual Studio

Notice you are presented with two options, the second of which (explicit interface implementation) will be examined in the next section. For the time being, select the first option and you'll see that Visual Studio has generated stub code for you to update (note that the default implementation throws a System.NotImplementedException, which can obviously be deleted).

```
namespace CustomInterface
{
  class PointyTestClass : IPointy
  {
    public byte Points
    {
      get { throw new NotImplementedException(); }
    }
  }
}
```

■ **Note** Visual Studio also supports extract interface refactoring, available from the Refactor menu. This allows you to pull out a new interface definition from an existing class definition. For example, you might be halfway through writing a class when it dawns on you that you can generalize the behavior into an interface (and thereby open up the possibility of alternative implementations).

Explicit Interface Implementation

As shown earlier in this chapter, a single class or structure can implement any number of interfaces. Given this, there is always the possibility you might implement interfaces that contain identical members and, therefore, have a name clash to contend with. To illustrate various manners in which you can resolve this issue, create a new Console Application named InterfaceNameClash. Now design three interfaces that represent various locations to which an implementing type could render its output:

```
// Draw image to a form.
public interface IDrawToForm
{
  void Draw();
}

// Draw to buffer in memory.
public interface IDrawToMemory
{
  void Draw();
}

// Render to the printer.
public interface IDrawToPrinter
{
  void Draw();
}
```

Notice that each interface defines a method named Draw(), with the identical signature (which happen to be no arguments). If you now want to support each of these interfaces on a single class type named Octagon, the compiler would allow the following definition:

```
class Octagon : IDrawToForm, IDrawToMemory, IDrawToPrinter
{
  public void Draw()
  {
    // Shared drawing logic.
    Console.WriteLine("Drawing the Octagon...");
  }
}
```

Although the code compiles cleanly, we do have a possible problem. Simply put, providing a single implementation of the Draw() method does not allow us to take unique courses of action based on which interface is obtained from an Octagon object. For example, the following code will invoke the same Draw() method, regardless of which interface you obtain:

```
static void Main(string[] args)
{
  Console.WriteLine("***** Fun with Interface Name Clashes *****\n");
  // All of these invocations call the
  // same Draw() method!
  Octagon oct = new Octagon();

  IDrawToForm itfForm = (IDrawToForm)oct;
  itfForm.Draw();

  IDrawToPrinter itfPriner = (IDrawToPrinter)oct;
  itfPriner.Draw();

  IDrawToMemory itfMemory = (IDrawToMemory)oct;
  itfMemory.Draw();

  Console.ReadLine();
}
```

Clearly, the sort of code required to render the image to a window is quite different from the code needed to render the image to a networked printer or a region of memory. When you implement several interfaces that have identical members, you can resolve this sort of name clash using *explicit interface implementation* syntax. Consider the following update to the Octagon type:

```
class Octagon : IDrawToForm, IDrawToMemory, IDrawToPrinter
{
  // Explicitly bind Draw() implementations
  // to a given interface.
  void IDrawToForm.Draw()
  {
    Console.WriteLine("Drawing to form...");
  }
  void IDrawToMemory.Draw()
  {
    Console.WriteLine("Drawing to memory...");
  }
  void IDrawToPrinter.Draw()
  {
    Console.WriteLine("Drawing to a printer...");
```

```
    }
}
```

As you can see, when explicitly implementing an interface member, the general pattern breaks down to:

```
returnType InterfaceName.MethodName(params){}
```

Note that when using this syntax, you do not supply an access modifier; explicitly implemented members are automatically private. For example, the following is illegal syntax:

```
// Error! No access modifer!
public void IDrawToForm.Draw()
{
  Console.WriteLine("Drawing to form...");
}
```

Because explicitly implemented members are always implicitly private, these members are no longer available from the object level. In fact, if you were to apply the dot operator to an Octagon type, you would find that IntelliSense does not show you any of the Draw() members. As expected, you must make use of explicit casting to access the required functionality. For example:

```
static void Main(string[] args)
{
  Console.WriteLine("***** Fun with Interface Name Clashes *****\n");
  Octagon oct = new Octagon();

  // We now must use casting to access the Draw()
  // members.
  IDrawToForm itfForm = (IDrawToForm)oct;
  itfForm.Draw();

  // Shorthand notation if you don't need
  // the interface variable for later use.
  ((IDrawToPrinter)oct).Draw();

  // Could also use the "as" keyword.
  if(oct is IDrawToMemory)
    ((IDrawToMemory)oct).Draw();

  Console.ReadLine();
}
```

While this syntax is quite helpful when you need to resolve name clashes, you can use explicit interface implementation simply to hide more "advanced" members from the object level. In this way, when the object user applies the dot operator, he or she will see only a subset of the type's overall functionality. However, those who require the more advanced behaviors can extract out the desired interface via an explicit cast.

■ **Source Code** The InterfaceNameClash project is located under the Chapter 8 subdirectory.

Designing Interface Hierarchies

Interfaces can be arranged in an interface hierarchy. Like a class hierarchy, when an interface extends an existing interface, it inherits the abstract members defined by the parent(s). Of course, unlike class-based inheritance, derived interfaces never inherit true implementation. Rather, a derived interface simply extends its own definition with additional abstract members.

Interface hierarchies can be useful when you want to extend the functionality of an existing interface without breaking existing code bases. To illustrate, create a new Console Application named InterfaceHierarchy. Now, let's design a new set of rendering-centric interfaces such that IDrawable is the root of the family tree:

```
public interface IDrawable
{
  void Draw();
}
```

Given that IDrawable defines a basic drawing behavior, we could now create a derived interface that extends this interface with the ability to render in modified formats. For example:

```
public interface IAdvancedDraw : IDrawable
{
  void DrawInBoundingBox(int top, int left, int bottom, int right);
  void DrawUpsideDown();
}
```

Given this design, if a class were to implement IAdvancedDraw, it would now be required to implement each and every member defined up the chain of inheritance (specifically, the Draw(), DrawInBoundingBox(), and DrawUpsideDown() methods):

```
public class BitmapImage : IAdvancedDraw
{
  public void Draw()
  {
    Console.WriteLine("Drawing...");
  }

  public void DrawInBoundingBox(int top, int left, int bottom, int right)
  {
    Console.WriteLine("Drawing in a box...");
  }

  public void DrawUpsideDown()
  {
    Console.WriteLine("Drawing upside down!");
  }
}
```

Now, when we make use of the `BitmapImage`, we are able to invoke each method at the object level (as they are all `public`), as well as extract out a reference to each supported interface explicitly via casting:

```
static void Main(string[] args)
{
  Console.WriteLine("***** Simple Interface Hierarchy *****");

  // Call from object level.
  BitmapImage myBitmap = new BitmapImage();
  myBitmap.Draw();
  myBitmap.DrawInBoundingBox(10, 10, 100, 150);
  myBitmap.DrawUpsideDown();

  // Get IAdvancedDraw explicitly.
  IAdvancedDraw iAdvDraw = myBitmap as IAdvancedDraw;
  if(iAdvDraw != null)
    iAdvDraw.DrawUpsideDown();

  Console.ReadLine();
}
```

■ **Source Code** The InterfaceHierarchy project is located under the Chapter 8 subdirectory.

Multiple Inheritance with Interface Types

Unlike class types, a single interface can extend multiple base interfaces, allowing us to design some very powerful and flexible abstractions. Create a new Console Application project named MIInterfaceHierarchy. Here is another collection of interfaces that model various rendering and shape abstractions. Notice that the IShape interface is extending both IDrawable and IPrintable:

```
// Multiple inheritance for interface types is a-okay.
interface IDrawable
{
   void Draw();
}

interface IPrintable
{
   void Print();
   void Draw(); // <-- Note possible name clash here!
}

// Multiple interface inheritance. OK!
interface IShape : IDrawable, IPrintable
{
   int GetNumberOfSides();
}
```

Figure 8-6 illustrates the current interface hierarchy.

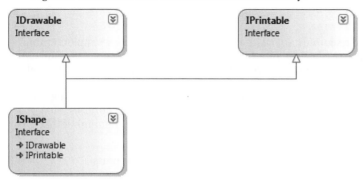

Figure 8-6. *Unlike classes, interfaces can extend multiple interface types*

Now, the million dollar question is, if you have a class supporting IShape, how many methods will it be required to implement? The answer: it depends. If you want to provide a simple implementation of the Draw() method, you need only provide three members, as shown in the following Rectangle type:

```
class Rectangle : IShape
{
  public int GetNumberOfSides()
  { return 4; }

  public void Draw()
  { Console.WriteLine("Drawing..."); }

  public void Print()
  { Console.WriteLine("Prining..."); }
}
```

If you'd rather have specific implementations for each Draw() method (which in this case would make the most sense), you can resolve the name clash using explicit interface implementation, as shown in the following Square type:

```
class Square : IShape
{
  // Using explicit implementation to handle member name clash.
  void IPrintable.Draw()
  {
    // Draw to printer ...
  }
  void IDrawable.Draw()
  {
    // Draw to screen ...
  }
  public void Print()
  {
    // Print ...
  }
```

```
    public int GetNumberOfSides()
    { return 4; }
}
```

Hopefully, at this point you feel more comfortable with the process of defining and implementing custom interfaces using the C# syntax. To be honest, interface-based programming can take a while to get comfortable with, so if you are in fact still scratching your head just a bit, this is a perfectly normal reaction.

Do be aware, however, that interfaces are a fundamental aspect of the .NET Framework. Regardless of the type of application you are developing (web-based, desktop GUIs, data-access libraries, etc.), working with interfaces will be part of the process. To summarize the story thus far, remember that interfaces can be extremely useful when

- You have a single hierarchy where only a subset of the derived types supports a common behavior.

- You need to model a common behavior that is found across multiple hierarchies with no common parent class beyond System.Object.

Now that you have drilled into the specifics of building and implementing custom interfaces, the remainder of this chapter examines a number of predefined interfaces contained within the .NET base class libraries.

■ **Source Code** The MIInterfaceHierarchy project is located under the Chapter 8 subdirectory.

The IEnumerable and IEnumerator Interfaces

To begin examining the process of implementing existing .NET interfaces, let's first look at the role of IEnumerable and IEnumerator. Recall that C# supports a keyword named foreach that allows you to iterate over the contents of any array type:

```
// Iterate over an array of items.
int[] myArrayOfInts = {10, 20, 30, 40};

foreach(int i in myArrayOfInts)
{
  Console.WriteLine(i);
}
```

While it might seem that only array types can make use of this construct, the truth of the matter is any type supporting a method named GetEnumerator() can be evaluated by the foreach construct. To illustrate, begin by creating a new Console Application project named CustomEnumerator. Next, add the Car.cs and Radio.cs files defined in the SimpleException example of Chapter 7 (via the Project ➤ Add Existing Item menu option).

■ **Note** You might want to rename the namespace containing the Car and Radio types to CustomEnumerator, to avoid having to import the CustomException namespace within this new project.

Now, insert a new class named Garage that stores a set of Car objects within a System.Array:

```
// Garage contains a set of Car objects.
public class Garage
{
  private Car[] carArray = new Car[4];

  // Fill with some Car objects upon startup.
  public Garage()
  {
    carArray[0] = new Car("Rusty", 30);
    carArray[1] = new Car("Clunker", 55);
    carArray[2] = new Car("Zippy", 30);
    carArray[3] = new Car("Fred", 30);
  }
}
```

Ideally, it would be convenient to iterate over the Garage object's subitems using the foreach construct, just like an array of data values:

```
// This seems reasonable ...
public class Program
{
  static void Main(string[] args)
  {
    Console.WriteLine("***** Fun with IEnumerable / IEnumerator *****\n");
    Garage carLot = new Garage();

    // Hand over each car in the collection?
    foreach (Car c in carLot)
    {
      Console.WriteLine("{0} is going {1} MPH",
        c.PetName, c.CurrentSpeed);
    }
    Console.ReadLine();
  }
}
```

Sadly, the compiler informs you that the Garage class does not implement a method named GetEnumerator(). This method is formalized by the IEnumerable interface, which is found lurking within the System.Collections namespace.

■ **Note** In Chapter 9, you will learn about the role of generics and the `System.Collections.Generic` namespace. As you will see, this namespace contains generic versions of `IEnumerable`/`IEnumerator` that provide a more type-safe way to iterate over subobjects.

Classes or structures that support this behavior advertise that they are able to expose contained subitems to the caller (in this example, the `foreach` keyword itself). Here is the definition of this standard .NET interface:

```
// This interface informs the caller
// that the object's subitems can be enumerated.
public interface IEnumerable
{
    IEnumerator GetEnumerator();
}
```

As you can see, the `GetEnumerator()` method returns a reference to yet another interface named `System.Collections.IEnumerator`. This interface provides the infrastructure to allow the caller to traverse the internal objects contained by the `IEnumerable`-compatible container:

```
// This interface allows the caller to
// obtain a container's subitems.
public interface IEnumerator
{
    bool MoveNext ();         // Advance the internal position of the cursor.
    object Current { get;}    // Get the current item (read-only property).
    void Reset ();            // Reset the cursor before the first member.
}
```

If you want to update the Garage type to support these interfaces, you could take the long road and implement each method manually. While you are certainly free to provide customized versions of `GetEnumerator()`, `MoveNext()`, `Current`, and `Reset()`, there is a simpler way. As the `System.Array` type (as well as many other collection classes) already implements `IEnumerable` and `IEnumerator`, you can simply delegate the request to the `System.Array` as follows:

```
using System.Collections;
...
public class Garage : IEnumerable
{
    // System.Array already implements IEnumerator!
    private Car[] carArray = new Car[4];

    public Garage()
    {
        carArray[0] = new Car("FeeFee", 200);
        carArray[1] = new Car("Clunker", 90);
        carArray[2] = new Car("Zippy", 30);
        carArray[3] = new Car("Fred", 30);
    }
```

```
public IEnumerator GetEnumerator()
{
    // Return the array object's IEnumerator.
    return carArray.GetEnumerator();
}
}
```

After you have updated your Garage type, you can safely use the type within the C# foreach construct. Furthermore, given that the GetEnumerator() method has been defined publicly, the object user could also interact with the IEnumerator type:

```
// Manually work with IEnumerator.
IEnumerator i = carLot.GetEnumerator();
i.MoveNext();
Car myCar = (Car)i.Current;
Console.WriteLine("{0} is going {1} MPH", myCar.PetName, myCar.CurrentSpeed);
```

However, if you prefer to hide the functionality of IEnumerable from the object level, simply make use of explicit interface implementation:

```
IEnumerator IEnumerable.GetEnumerator()
{
    // Return the array object's IEnumerator.
    return carArray.GetEnumerator();
}
```

By doing so, the casual object user will not find the Garage's GetEnumerator() method, while the foreach construct will obtain the interface in the background when necessary.

■ **Source Code** The CustomEnumerator project is located under the Chapter 8 subdirectory.

Building Iterator Methods with the yield Keyword

In earlier versions of the .NET platform, when you wanted to build a custom collection (such as Garage) that supported foreach enumeration, implementing the IEnumerable interface (and possibly the IEnumerator interface) was your only option. However, there's an alternative way to build types that work with the foreach loop via *iterators*.

Simply put, an *iterator* is a member that specifies how a container's internal items should be returned when processed by foreach. While the iterator method must still be named GetEnumerator(), and the return value must still be of type IEnumerator, your custom class does not need to implement any of the expected interfaces.

To illustrate, create a new Console Application project named CustomEnumeratorWithYield and insert the Car, Radio, and Garage types from the previous example (again, renaming your namespace definitions to the current project if you like). Now, retrofit the current Garage type as follows:

```
public class Garage : IEnumerator
{
    private Car[] carArray = new Car[4];
    ...
    // Iterator method.
```

```
    public IEnumerator GetEnumerator()
    {
      foreach (Car c in carArray)
      {
        yield return c;
      }
    }
}
```

Notice that this implementation of GetEnumerator() iterates over the subitems using internal foreach logic and returns each Car to the caller using the yield return syntax. The yield keyword is used to specify the value (or values) to be returned to the caller's foreach construct. When the yield return statement is reached, the current location in the container is stored, and execution is restarted from this location the next time the iterator is called.

Iterator methods are not required to make use of the foreach keyword to return its contents. It is also permissible to define this iterator method as follows:

```
public IEnumerator GetEnumerator()
{
  yield return carArray[0];
  yield return carArray[1];
  yield return carArray[2];
  yield return carArray[3];
}
```

In this implementation, notice that the GetEnumerator() method is explicitly returning a new value to the caller with each pass through. Doing so for this example makes little sense, given that if we were to add more objects to the carArray member variable, our GetEnumerator() method would now be out of sync. Nevertheless, this syntax can be useful when you want to return local data from a method for processing by the foreach syntax.

Building a Named Iterator

It is also interesting to note that the yield keyword can technically be used within any method, regardless of its name. These methods (which are technically called *named iterators*) are also unique in that they can take any number of arguments. When building a named iterator, be very aware that the method will return the IEnumerable interface, rather than the expected IEnumerator-compatible type. To illustrate, you could add the following method to the Garage type:

```
public IEnumerable GetTheCars(bool ReturnRevesed)
{
  // Return the items in reverse.
  if (ReturnRevesed)
  {
    for (int i = carArray.Length; i != 0; i--)
    {
      yield return carArray[i-1];
    }
  }
  else
  {
    // Return the items as placed in the array.
```

```
    foreach (Car c in carArray)
    {
      yield return c;
    }
  }
}
```

Notice that the new method allows the caller to obtain the subitems in sequential order, as well as in reverse order, if the incoming parameter has the value true. You could now interact with our new method as follows:

```
static void Main(string[] args)
{
  Console.WriteLine("***** Fun with the Yield Keyword *****\n");
  Garage carLot = new Garage();

  // Get items using GetEnumerator().
  foreach (Car c in carLot)
  {
    Console.WriteLine("{0} is going {1} MPH",
      c.PetName, c.CurrentSpeed);
  }

  Console.WriteLine();

  // Get items (in reverse!) using named iterator.
  foreach (Car c in carLot.GetTheCars(true))
  {
    Console.WriteLine("{0} is going {1} MPH",
      c.PetName, c.CurrentSpeed);
  }
  Console.ReadLine();
}
```

As you might agree, named iterators are helpful constructs, in that a single custom container can define multiple ways to request the returned set.

So, to wrap up our look at building enumerable objects, remember that for your custom types to work with the C# foreach keyword, the container must define a method named GetEnumerator(), which has been formalized by the IEnumerable interface type. The implementation of this method is typically achieved by simply delegating it to the internal member that is holding onto the subobjects; however, it is also possible to make use of the yield return syntax to provide multiple "named iterator" methods.

■ **Source Code** The CustomEnumeratorWithYield project is located under the Chapter 8 subdirectory.

307

The ICloneable Interface

As you might recall from Chapter 6, System.Object defines a method named MemberwiseClone(). This method is used to obtain a *shallow copy* of the current object. Object users do not call this method directly, as it is protected. However, a given object may call this method itself during the *cloning* process. To illustrate, create a new Console Application named CloneablePoint that defines a class named Point:

```
// A class named Point.
public class Point
{
  public int X {get; set;}
  public int Y {get; set;}

  public Point(int xPos, int yPos) { X = xPos; Y = yPos;}
  public Point(){}

  // Override Object.ToString().
  public override string ToString()
  {  return string.Format("X = {0}; Y = {1}", X, Y ); }
}
```

Given what you already know about reference types and value types (see Chapter 4), you are aware that if you assign one reference variable to another, you have two references pointing to the same object in memory. Thus, the following assignment operation results in two references to the same Point object on the heap; modifications using either reference affect the same object on the heap:

```
static void Main(string[] args)
{
  Console.WriteLine("***** Fun with Object Cloning *****\n");
  // Two references to same object!
  Point p1 = new Point(50, 50);
  Point p2 = p1;
  p2.X = 0;
  Console.WriteLine(p1);
  Console.WriteLine(p2);
  Console.ReadLine();
}
```

When you want to give your custom type the ability to return an identical copy of itself to the caller, you may implement the standard ICloneable interface. As shown at the start of this chapter, this type defines a single method named Clone():

```
public interface ICloneable
{
  object Clone();
}
```

Obviously, the implementation of the Clone() method varies among your classes. However, the basic functionality tends to be the same: copy the values of your member variables into a new object instance of the same type, and return it to the user. To illustrate, ponder the following update to the Point class:

```
// The Point now supports "clone-ability."
public class Point : ICloneable
{
  public int X { get; set; }
  public int Y { get; set; }

  public Point(int xPos, int yPos) { X = xPos; Y = yPos; }
  public Point() { }

  // Override Object.ToString().
  public override string ToString()
  { return string.Format("X = {0}; Y = {1}", X, Y); }

  // Return a copy of the current object.
  public object Clone()
  { return new Point(this.X, this.Y); }
}
```

In this way, you can create exact stand-alone copies of the Point type, as illustrated by the following code:

```
static void Main(string[] args)
{
  Console.WriteLine("***** Fun with Object Cloning *****\n");
  // Notice Clone() returns a plain object type.
  // You must perform an explicit cast to obtain the derived type.
  Point p3 = new Point(100, 100);
  Point p4 = (Point)p3.Clone();

  // Change p4.X (which will not change p3.X).
  p4.X = 0;

  // Print each object.
  Console.WriteLine(p3);
  Console.WriteLine(p4);
  Console.ReadLine();
}
```

While the current implementation of Point fits the bill, you can streamline things just a bit. Because the Point type does not contain any internal reference type variables, you could simplify the implementation of the Clone() method as follows:

```
public object Clone()
{
  // Copy each field of the Point member by member.
  return this.MemberwiseClone();
}
```

Be aware, however, that if the Point did contain any reference type member variables, MemberwiseClone() will copy the references to those objects (i.e., a *shallow copy*). If you want to support a true *deep copy*, you will need to create a new instance of any reference type variables during the cloning process. Let's see an example next.

A More Elaborate Cloning Example

Now assume the Point class contains a reference type member variable of type PointDescription. This class maintains a point's friendly name as well as an identification number expressed as a System.Guid (a globally unique identifier [GUID] is a statistically unique 128-bit number). Here is the implementation:

```
// This class describes a point.
public class PointDescription
{
  public string PetName {get; set;}
  public Guid PointID {get; set;}

  public PointDescription()
  {
    PetName = "No-name";
    PointID = Guid.NewGuid();
  }
}
```

The initial updates to the Point class itself included modifying ToString() to account for these new bits of state data, as well as defining and creating the PointDescription reference type. To allow the outside world to establish a pet name for the Point, you also update the arguments passed into the overloaded constructor:

```
public class Point : ICloneable
{
  public int X { get; set; }
  public int Y { get; set; }
  public PointDescription desc = new PointDescription();

  public Point(int xPos, int yPos, string petName)
  {
    X = xPos; Y = yPos;
    desc.PetName = petName;
  }
  public Point(int xPos, int yPos)
  {
    X = xPos; Y = yPos;
  }
  public Point() { }

  // Override Object.ToString().
  public override string ToString()
  {
    return string.Format("X = {0}; Y = {1}; Name = {2};\nID = {3}\n",
    X, Y, desc.PetName, desc.PointID);
  }

  // Return a copy of the current object.
  public object Clone()
  { return this.MemberwiseClone(); }
}
```

Notice that you did not yet update your Clone() method. Therefore, when the object user asks for a clone using the current implementation, a shallow (member-by-member) copy is achieved. To illustrate, assume you have updated Main() as follows:

```
static void Main(string[] args)
{
  Console.WriteLine("***** Fun with Object Cloning *****\n");
  Console.WriteLine("Cloned p3 and stored new Point in p4");
  Point p3 = new Point(100, 100, "Jane");
  Point p4 = (Point)p3.Clone();

  Console.WriteLine("Before modification:");
  Console.WriteLine("p3: {0}", p3);
  Console.WriteLine("p4: {0}", p4);
  p4.desc.PetName = "My new Point";
  p4.X = 9;

  Console.WriteLine("\nChanged p4.desc.petName and p4.X");
  Console.WriteLine("After modification:");
  Console.WriteLine("p3: {0}", p3);
  Console.WriteLine("p4: {0}", p4);
  Console.ReadLine();
}
```

Notice in the following output that while the value types have indeed been changed, the internal reference types maintain the same values, as they are "pointing" to the same objects in memory (specifically, note that the pet name for both objects is now "My new Point").

```
***** Fun with Object Cloning *****

Cloned p3 and stored new Point in p4
Before modification:
p3: X = 100; Y = 100; Name = Jane;
ID = 133d66a7-0837-4bd7-95c6-b22ab0434509

p4: X = 100; Y = 100; Name = Jane;
ID = 133d66a7-0837-4bd7-95c6-b22ab0434509


Changed p4.desc.petName and p4.X
After modification:
p3: X = 100; Y = 100; Name = My new Point;
ID = 133d66a7-0837-4bd7-95c6-b22ab0434509

p4: X = 9; Y = 100; Name = My new Point;
ID = 133d66a7-0837-4bd7-95c6-b22ab0434509
```

To have your Clone() method make a complete deep copy of the internal reference types, you need to configure the object returned by MemberwiseClone() to account for the current point's name (the

System.Guid type is in fact a structure, so the numerical data is indeed copied). Here is one possible implementation:

```
// Now we need to adjust for the PointDescription member.
public object Clone()
{
  // First get a shallow copy.
  Point newPoint = (Point)this.MemberwiseClone();

  // Then fill in the gaps.
  PointDescription currentDesc = new PointDescription();
  currentDesc.PetName = this.desc.PetName;
  newPoint.desc = currentDesc;
  return newPoint;
}
```

If you rerun the application once again and view the output (see below), you see that the Point returned from Clone() does copy its internal reference type member variables (note the pet name is now unique for both p3 and p4).

```
***** Fun with Object Cloning *****

Cloned p3 and stored new Point in p4
Before modification:
p3: X = 100; Y = 100; Name = Jane;
ID = 51f64f25-4b0e-47ac-ba35-37d263496406

p4: X = 100; Y = 100; Name = Jane;
ID = 0d3776b3-b159-490d-b022-7f3f60788e8a


Changed p4.desc.petName and p4.X
After modification:
p3: X = 100; Y = 100; Name = Jane;
ID = 51f64f25-4b0e-47ac-ba35-37d263496406

p4: X = 9; Y = 100; Name = My new Point;
ID = 0d3776b3-b159-490d-b022-7f3f60788e8a
```

To summarize the cloning process, if you have a class or structure that contains nothing but value types, implement your Clone() method using MemberwiseClone(). However, if you have a custom type that maintains other reference types, you might want to create a new object that takes into account each reference type member variable, in order to get a "deep copy."

■ **Source Code** The CloneablePoint project is located under the Chapter 8 subdirectory.

The IComparable Interface

The System.IComparable interface specifies a behavior that allows an object to be sorted based on some specified key. Here is the formal definition:

```
// This interface allows an object to specify its
// relationship between other like objects.
public interface IComparable
{
  int CompareTo(object o);
}
```

■ **Note** The generic version of this interface (IComparable<T>) provides a more type-safe manner to handle comparisons between objects. You'll examine generics in Chapter 9.

Let's assume you have a new Console Application named ComparableCar that defines the following updated Car class (notice that we have basically just added a new property to represent a unique ID for each car and a modified constructor):

```
public class Car
{
...
  public int CarID {get; set;}
  public Car(string name, int currSp, int id)
  {
    CurrentSpeed = currSp;
    PetName = name;
    CarID = id;
  }
...
}
```

Now assume you have an array of Car objects as follows:

```
static void Main(string[] args)
{
  Console.WriteLine("***** Fun with Object Sorting *****\n");

  // Make an array of Car objects.
  Car[] myAutos = new Car[5];
  myAutos[0] = new Car("Rusty", 80, 1);
  myAutos[1] = new Car("Mary", 40, 234);
  myAutos[2] = new Car("Viper", 40, 34);
  myAutos[3] = new Car("Mel", 40, 4);
  myAutos[4] = new Car("Chucky", 40, 5);

  Console.ReadLine();
}
```

The System.Array class defines a static method named Sort(). When you invoke this method on an array of intrinsic types (int, short, string, etc.), you are able to sort the items in the array in numeric/alphabetic order, as these intrinsic data types implement IComparable. However, what if you were to send an array of Car types into the Sort() method as follows?

```
// Sort my cars? Not yet!
Array.Sort(myAutos);
```

If you run this test, you would get a runtime exception, as the Car class does not support the necessary interface. When you build custom types, you can implement IComparable to allow arrays of your types to be sorted. When you flesh out the details of CompareTo(), it will be up to you to decide what the baseline of the ordering operation will be. For the Car type, the internal CarID seems to be the logical candidate:

```
// The iteration of the Car can be ordered
// based on the CarID.
public class Car : IComparable
{
...
  // IComparable implementation.
  int IComparable.CompareTo(object obj)
  {
    Car temp = obj as Car;
    if (temp != null)
    {
      if (this.CarID > temp.CarID)
        return 1;
      if (this.CarID < temp.CarID)
        return -1;
      else
        return 0;
    }
    else
      throw new ArgumentException("Parameter is not a Car!");
  }
}
```

As you can see, the logic behind CompareTo() is to test the incoming object against the current instance based on a specific point of data. The return value of CompareTo() is used to discover whether this type is less than, greater than, or equal to the object it is being compared with (see Table 8-1).

Table 8-1. CompareTo() Return Values

CompareTo() Return Value	Description
Any number less than zero	This instance comes before the specified object in the sort order.
Zero	This instance is equal to the specified object.
Any number greater than zero	This instance comes after the specified object in the sort order.

We can streamline the previous implementation of CompareTo() given the fact that the C# int data type (which is just a shorthand notation for the CLR System.Int32) implements IComparable. You could implement the Car's CompareTo() as follows:

```
int IComparable.CompareTo(object obj)
{
  Car temp = obj as Car;
  if (temp != null)
    return this.CarID.CompareTo(temp.CarID);
  else
    throw new ArgumentException("Parameter is not a Car!");
}
```

In either case, so that your Car type understands how to compare itself to like objects, you can write the following user code:

```
// Exercise the IComparable interface.
static void Main(string[] args)
{
  // Make an array of Car objects.
  ...
  // Display current array.
  Console.WriteLine("Here is the unordered set of cars:");
  foreach(Car c in myAutos)
    Console.WriteLine("{0} {1}", c.CarID, c.PetName);

  // Now, sort them using IComparable!
  Array.Sort(myAutos);
  Console.WriteLine();

  // Display sorted array.
  Console.WriteLine("Here is the ordered set of cars:");
  foreach(Car c in myAutos)
    Console.WriteLine("{0} {1}", c.CarID, c.PetName);
  Console.ReadLine();
}
```

Here is the output from the previous Main() method:

```
***** Fun with Object Sorting *****

Here is the unordered set of cars:
1 Rusty
234 Mary
34 Viper
4 Mel
5 Chucky

Here is the ordered set of cars:
1 Rusty
4 Mel
5 Chucky
```

```
34 Viper
234 Mary
```

Specifying Multiple Sort Orders with IComparer

In this version of the Car type, you used the car's ID as the base for the sort order. Another design might have used the pet name of the car as the basis for the sorting algorithm (to list cars alphabetically). Now, what if you wanted to build a Car that could be sorted by ID *as well as* by pet name? If this is the type of behavior you are interested in, you need to make friends with another standard interface named IComparer, defined within the System.Collections namespace as follows:

```
// A general way to compare two objects.
interface IComparer
{
  int Compare(object o1, object o2);
}
```

■ **Note** The generic version of this interface (IComparer<T>) provides a more type-safe manner to handle comparisons between objects. You'll examine generics in Chapter 9.

Unlike the IComparable interface, IComparer is typically *not* implemented on the type you are trying to sort (i.e., the Car). Rather, you implement this interface on any number of helper classes, one for each sort order (pet name, car ID, etc.). Currently, the Car type already knows how to compare itself against other cars based on the internal car ID. Therefore, allowing the object user to sort an array of Car objects by pet name will require an additional helper class that implements IComparer. Here's the code (be sure to import the System.Collections namespace in the code file):

```
// This helper class is used to sort an array of Cars by pet name.
public class PetNameComparer : IComparer
{
  // Test the pet name of each object.
  int IComparer.Compare(object o1, object o2)
  {
    Car t1 = o1 as Car;
    Car t2 = o2 as Car;
    if(t1 != null && t2 != null)
      return String.Compare(t1.PetName, t2.PetName);
    else
      throw new ArgumentException("Parameter is not a Car!");
  }
}
```

The object user code is able to make use of this helper class. System.Array has a number of overloaded Sort() methods, one that just happens to take an object implementing IComparer.

```
static void Main(string[] args)
{
...
  // Now sort by pet name.
  Array.Sort(myAutos, new PetNameComparer());

  // Dump sorted array.
  Console.WriteLine("Ordering by pet name:");
  foreach(Car c in myAutos)
    Console.WriteLine("{0} {1}", c.CarID, c.PetName);
...
}
```

Custom Properties and Custom Sort Types

It is worth pointing out that you can make use of a custom static property in order to help the object user along when sorting your Car types by a specific data point. Assume the Car class has added a static read-only property named SortByPetName that returns an instance of an object implementing the IComparer interface (PetNameComparer, in this case):

```
// We now support a custom property to return
// the correct IComparer interface.
public class Car : IComparable
{
  ...
  // Property to return the PetNameComparer.
  public static IComparer SortByPetName
  { get { return (IComparer)new PetNameComparer(); } }
}
```

The object user code can now sort by pet name using a strongly associated property, rather than just "having to know" to use the stand-alone PetNameComparer class type:

```
// Sorting by pet name made a bit cleaner.
Array.Sort(myAutos, Car.SortByPetName);
```

■ **Source Code** The ComparableCar project is located under the Chapter 8 subdirectory.

Hopefully, at this point you not only understand how to define and implement your own interfaces, but also understand their usefulness. To be sure, interfaces are found within every major .NET namespace, and you will continue working with various standard interfaces over the remainder of this text.

Summary

An interface can be defined as a named collection of *abstract members*. Because an interface does not provide any implementation details, it is common to regard an interface as a behavior that may be supported by a given type. When two or more classes implement the same interface, you can treat each type the same way (interface-based polymorphism) even if the types are defined within unique class hierarchies.

C# provides the interface keyword to allow you to define a new interface. As you have seen, a type can support as many interfaces as necessary using a comma-delimited list. Furthermore, it is permissible to build interfaces that derive from multiple base interfaces.

In addition to building your custom interfaces, the .NET libraries define a number of standard (i.e., framework-supplied) interfaces. As you have seen, you are free to build custom types that implement these predefined interfaces to gain a number of desirable traits such as cloning, sorting, and enumerating.

Advanced C# Programming

CHAPTER 9

Collections and Generics

Any application you create with the .NET platform will need to contend with the issue of maintaining and manipulating a set of data points in memory. These data points can come from any variety of locations including a relational database, a local text file, an XML document, a web service call, or perhaps via user provided input.

When the .NET platform was first released, programmers frequently used the classes of the System.Collections namespace to store and interact with bits of data used within an application. In .NET 2.0, the C# programming language was enhanced to support a feature termed *generics*; and with this change, a brand new namespace was introduced in the base class libraries: System.Collections.Generic.

This chapter will provide you will an overview of the various collection (generic and nongeneric) namespaces and types found within the .NET base class libraries. As you will see, generic containers are often favored over their nongeneric counterparts because they typically provide greater type safety and performance benefits. After you've seen learned how to create and manipulate the generic items found in the framework, the remainder of this chapter will examine how to build your own generic methods and generic types. As you do this, you will learn about the role of *constraints (and the corresponding C# where keyword)*, which allow you to build extremely type-safe classes.

The Motivation for Collection Classes

The most primitive container one could use to hold application data is undoubtedly the array. As you saw in Chapter 4, C# arrays allow you to define a set of identically typed items (including an array of System.Objects, which essentially represents an array of any type of data) of a fixed upper limit. Also recall from Chapter 4 that all C# array variables gather a good deal of functionality from the System.Array class. By way of a quick review, consider the following Main() method, which creates an array of textual data and manipulates its contents in various ways:

```
static void Main(string[] args)
{
  // Make an array of string data.
  string[] strArray = {"First", "Second", "Third" };

  // Show number of items in array using Length property.
  Console.WriteLine("This array has {0} items.", strArray.Length);
  Console.WriteLine();

  // Display contents using enumerator.
  foreach (string s in strArray)
  {
```

```
      Console.WriteLine("Array Entry: {0}", s);
    }
    Console.WriteLine();

    // Reverse the array and print again.
    Array.Reverse(strArray);
    foreach (string s in strArray)
    {
      Console.WriteLine("Array Entry: {0}", s);
    }

    Console.ReadLine();
}
```

While basic arrays can be useful to manage small amounts of fixed-size data, there are many other times where you require a more flexible data structure, such as a dynamically growing and shrinking container, or a container that can hold objects that meet only a specific criteria (e.g., only objects deriving from a specific base class or only objects implementing a particular interface). When you make use of a simple array, always remember they are "fixed size." If you make an array of three items, you only get three items; therefore, the following code would result in a runtime exception (an IndexOutOfRangeException, to be exact):

```
static void Main(string[] args)
{
    // Make an array of string data.
    string[] strArray = { "First", "Second", "Third" };

    // Try to add a new item at the end?? Runtime error!
    strArray[3] = "new item?";
    ...
}
```

To help overcome the limitations of a simple array, the .NET base class libraries ship with a number of namespaces containing *collection classes*. Unlike a simple C# array, collection classes are built to dynamically resize themselves on the fly as you insert or remove items. Moreover, many of the collection classes offer increased type safety and are highly optimized to process the contained data in a memory-efficient manner. As you read over this chapter, you will quickly notice that a collection class can belong to one of two broad categories:

- Nongeneric collections (primarily found in the System.Collections namespace)

- Generic collections (primarily found in the System.Collections.Generic namespace)

Nongeneric collections are typically designed to operate on System.Object types and are, therefore, very loosely typed containers (however, some nongeneric collections do operate only on a specific type of data, such as string objects). In contrast, generic collections are much more type safe, given that you must specify the "type of type" they contain upon creation. As you will see, the telltail sign of any generic item is the "type parameter" marked with angled brackets (for example, List<T>). We will examine the details of generics (including the many benefits they provide) a bit later in this chapter. For now, let's examine some of the key nongeneric collection types in the System.Collections and System.Collections.Specialized namespaces.

The System.Collections Namespace

When the .NET platform was first released, programmers frequently used the nongeneric collection classes found within the System.Collections namespace, which contains a set of classes used to manage and organize large amounts of in-memory data. Table 9-1 documents some of the more commonly used collection classes of this namespace, and the core interfaces they implement.

■ **Note** Any .NET application built with .NET 2.0 or higher should ignore the classes in System.Collections in favor of the corresponding classes in System.Collections.Generic. However, it is important to know the basics of the nongeneric collection classes, as you might have some legacy software to maintain.

Table 9-1. Useful Types of System.Collections

System.Collections Class	Meaning in Life	Key Implemented Interfaces
ArrayList	Represents a dynamically sized collection of objects listed in sequential order.	IList, ICollection, IEnumerable, and ICloneable
BitArray	Manages a compact array of bit values, which are represented as Booleans, where true indicates that the bit is on (1) and false indicates the bit is off (0).	ICollection, IEnumerable, and ICloneable
Hashtable	Represents a collection of key/value pairs that are organized based on the hash code of the key.	IDictionary, ICollection, IEnumerable, and ICloneable
Queue	Represents a standard first-in, first-out (FIFO) collection of objects.	ICollection, IEnumerable, and ICloneable
SortedList	Represents a collection of key/value pairs that are sorted by the keys and are accessible by key and by index.	IDictionary, ICollection, IEnumerable, and ICloneable
Stack	A last-in, first-out (LIFO) stack providing push and pop (and peek) functionality.	ICollection, IEnumerable, and ICloneable

The interfaces implemented by these collection classes provide huge insights into their overall functionality. Table 9-2 documents the overall nature of these key interfaces, some of which you worked with firsthand in Chapter 8.

Table 9-2. Key Interfaces Supported by Classes of System.Collections

System.Collections Interface	Meaning in Life
ICollection	Defines general characteristics (e.g., size, enumeration, and thread safety) for all nongeneric collection types.
ICloneable	Allows the implementing object to return a copy of itself to the caller.
IDictionary	Allows a nongeneric collection object to represent its contents using key/value pairs.
IEnumerable	Returns an object implementing the IEnumerator interface (see next table entry).
IEnumerator	Enables foreach style iteration of collection items.
IList	Provides behavior to add, remove, and index items in a sequential list of objects.

An Illustrative Example: Working with the ArrayList

Based on your experience, you might have some firsthand experience using (or implementing) some of these classic data structures such as stacks, queues, and lists. If this is not the case, I'll provide some further details on their differences when we examine their generic counterparts a bit later in this chapter. Until then, here is a Main() method making use of an ArrayList object. Notice that we can add (or remove) items on the fly and the container automatically resizes itself accordingly:

```
// You must import System.Collections to access the ArrayList.
static void Main(string[] args)
{
  ArrayList strArray = new ArrayList();
  strArray.AddRange(new string[] { "First", "Second", "Third" });

  // Show number of items in ArrayList.
  Console.WriteLine("This collection has {0} items.", strArray.Count);
  Console.WriteLine();

  // Add a new item and display current count.
  strArray.Add("Fourth!");
  Console.WriteLine("This collection has {0} items.", strArray.Count);

  // Display contents.
  foreach (string s in strArray)
  {
    Console.WriteLine("Entry: {0}", s);
  }
  Console.WriteLine();
}
```

As you would guess, the `ArrayList` class has many useful members beyond the `Count` property and `AddRange()` and `Add()` methods, so be sure you consult the .NET Framework documentation for full details. On a related note, the other classes of `System.Collections` (`Stack`, `Queue`, and so on) are also fully documented in the .NET help system.

However, it is very important to point out that a majority of your .NET projects will most likely *not* make use of the collection classes in the `System.Collections` namespace! To be sure, these days it is far more common to make use of the generic counterpart classes found in the `System.Collections.Generic` namespace. Given this point, I won't comment on (or provide code examples for) the remaining nongeneric classes found in `System.Collections`.

A Survey of System.Collections.Specialized Namespace

`System.Collections` is not the only .NET namespace that contains nongeneric collection classes. For example, the `System.Collections.Specialized` namespace defines a number of (pardon the redundancy) specialized collection types. Table 9-3 documents some of the more useful types in this particular collection-centric namespace, all of which are nongeneric.

Table 9-3. *Useful Classes of System.Collections.Specialized*

System.Collections.Specialized Type	Meaning in Life
HybridDictionary	This class implements `IDictionary` by using a `ListDictionary` while the collection is small, and then switching to a `Hashtable` when the collection gets large.
ListDictionary	This class is useful when you need to manage a small number of items (10 or so) that can change over time. This class makes use of a singly linked list to maintain its data.
StringCollection	This class provides an optimal way to manage large collections of string data.
BitVector32	This class provides a simple structure that stores Boolean values and small integers in 32 bits of memory.

Beyond these concrete types, this namespace also contains many additional interfaces and abstract base classes that you can use as a starting point for creating custom collection classes. While these "specialized" types might be just what your projects require in some situations, I won't comment on their usage here. Again, in many cases, you will likely find that the `System.Collections.Generic` namespace provides classes with similar functionality and additional benefits.

> ■ **Note** There are two additional collection-centric namespaces (System.Collections.ObjectModel and System.Collections.Concurrent) in the .NET base class libraries. You will examine the former namespace later in this chapter, after you are comfortable with the topic of generics. System.Collections.Concurrent provides thread-safe collection classes (see Chapter 19 for information on multithreading).

The Problems of Nongeneric Collections

While it is true that many successful .NET applications have been built over the years using these nongeneric collection classes (and interfaces), history has shown that use of these types can result in a number of issues.

The first issue is that using the System.Collections and System.Collections.Specialized classes can result in some poorly performing code, especially when you are manipulating numerical data (e.g., value types). As you'll see momentarily, the CLR must perform a number of memory transfer operations when you store structures in any nongeneric collection class prototyped to operate on System.Objects, which can hurt runtime execution speed.

The second issue is that most of the nongeneric collection classes are not type safe because (again) they were developed to operate on System.Objects, and they could therefore contain anything at all. If a .NET developer needed to create a highly type-safe collection (e.g., a container that can hold objects implementing only a certain interface), the only real choice was to create a brand new collection class by hand. Doing so was not too labor intensive, but it was a tad bit on the tedious side.

Before you look at how to use generics in your programs, you'll find it helpful to examine the issues of nongeneric collection classes a bit closer; this will help you better understand the problems generics intend to solve in the first place. If you want to follow along, create a new Console Application named IssuesWithNonGenericCollections. Next, make sure you import the System.Collections namespace to the top of your C# code file:

```
using System.Collections;
```

The Issue of Performance

As you might recall from Chapter 4, the .NET platform supports two broad categories of data: value types and reference types. Given that .NET defines two major categories of types, you might occasionally need to represent a variable of one category as a variable of the other category. To do so, C# provides a simple mechanism, termed *boxing*, to store the data in a value type within a reference variable. Assume that you have created a local variable of type int in a method called SimpleBoxUnboxOperation(). If, during the course of your application, you were to represent this value type as a reference type, you would *box* the value, as follows:

```
static void SimpleBoxUnboxOperation()
{
  // Make a ValueType (int) variable.
  int myInt = 25;

  // Box the int into an object reference.
  object boxedInt = myInt;
```

```
}
```

Boxing can be formally defined as the process of explicitly assigning a value type to a System.Object variable. When you box a value, the CLR allocates a new object on the heap and copies the value type's value (25, in this case) into that instance. What is returned to you is a reference to the newly allocated heap-based object.

The opposite operation is also permitted through *unboxing*. Unboxing is the process of converting the value held in the object reference back into a corresponding value type on the stack. Syntactically speaking, an unboxing operation looks like a normal casting operation. However, the semantics are quite different. The CLR begins by verifying that the receiving data type is equivalent to the boxed type; and if so, it copies the value back into a local stack-based variable. For example, the following unboxing operations work successfully, given that the underlying type of the boxedInt is indeed an int:

```
static void SimpleBoxUnboxOperation()
{
  // Make a ValueType (int) variable.
  int myInt = 25;

  // Box the int into an object reference.
  object boxedInt = myInt;

  // Unbox the reference back into a corresponding int.
  int unboxedInt = (int)boxedInt;
}
```

When the C# compiler encounters boxing/unboxing syntax, it emits CIL code that contains the box/unbox op codes. If you were to examine your compiled assembly using ildasm.exe, you would find the following:

```
.method private hidebysig static void SimpleBoxUnboxOperation() cil managed
{
  // Code size 19 (0x13)
  .maxstack  1
  .locals init ([0] int32 myInt, [1] object boxedInt, [2] int32 unboxedInt)
  IL_0000:  nop
  IL_0001:  ldc.i4.s 25
  IL_0003:  stloc.0
  IL_0004:  ldloc.0
  IL_0005:  box   [mscorlib]System.Int32
  IL_000a:  stloc.1
  IL_000b:  ldloc.1
  IL_000c:  unbox.any [mscorlib]System.Int32
  IL_0011:  stloc.2
  IL_0012:  ret
} // end of method Program::SimpleBoxUnboxOperation
```

Remember that unlike when performing a typical cast, you *must* unbox into an appropriate data type. If you attempt to unbox a piece of data into the incorrect data type, an InvalidCastException exception will be thrown. To be perfectly safe, you should wrap each unboxing operation in try/catch logic; however, this would be quite labor intensive to do for every unboxing operation. Consider the following code update, which will throw an error because you're attempting to unbox the boxed int into a long:

```
static void SimpleBoxUnboxOperation()
{
  // Make a ValueType (int) variable.
  int myInt = 25;

  // Box the int into an object reference.
  object boxedInt = myInt;

  // Unbox in the wrong data type to trigger
  // runtime exception.
  try
  {
    long unboxedInt = (long)boxedInt;
  }
  catch (InvalidCastException ex)
  {
    Console.WriteLine(ex.Message);
  }
}
```

At first glance, boxing/unboxing might seem like a rather uneventful language feature that is more academic than practical. After all, you will seldom need to store a local value type in a local object variable, as seen here. However, it turns out that the boxing/unboxing process is quite helpful because it allows you to assume everything can be treated as a System.Object, while the CLR takes care of the memory-related details on your behalf.

Let's look at a practical use of these techniques. Assume you have created a nongeneric System.Collections.ArrayList to hold onto a batch of numeric (stack-allocated) data. If you were to examine the members of ArrayList, you would find they are prototyped to operate on System.Object data. Now consider the Add(), Insert(), and Remove() methods, as well as the class indexer:

```
public class ArrayList : object,
  IList, ICollection, IEnumerable, ICloneable
{
...
  public virtual int Add(object value);
  public virtual void Insert(int index, object value);
  public virtual void Remove(object obj);
  public virtual object this[int index] {get; set; }
}
```

ArrayList has been built to operate on objects, which represent data allocated on the heap, so it might seem strange that the following code compiles and executes without throwing an error:

```
static void WorkWithArrayList()
{
  // Value types are automatically boxed when
  // passed to a method requesting an object.
  ArrayList myInts = new ArrayList();
  myInts.Add(10);
  myInts.Add(20);
  myInts.Add(35);
}
```

Although you pass in numerical data directly into methods requiring an object, the runtime automatically boxes the stack-based data on your behalf. Later, if you want to retrieve an item from the ArrayList using the type indexer, you must unbox the heap-allocated object into a stack-allocated integer using a casting operation. Remember that the indexer of the ArrayList is returning System.Objects, not System.Int32s:

```
static void WorkWithArrayList()
{
  // Value types are automatically boxed when
  // passed to a member requesting an object.
  ArrayList myInts = new ArrayList();
  myInts.Add(10);
  myInts.Add(20);
  myInts.Add(35);

  // Unboxing occurs when a object is converted back to
  // stack-based data.
  int i = (int)myInts[0];

  // Now it is reboxed, as WriteLine() requires object types!
  Console.WriteLine("Value of your int: {0}", i);
}
```

Again, note that the stack-allocated System.Int32 is boxed prior to the call to ArrayList.Add(), so it can be passed in the required System.Object. Also note that the System.Object is unboxed back into a System.Int32 once it is retrieved from the ArrayList via the casting operation, only to be boxed *again* when it is passed to the Console.WriteLine() method, as this method is operating on System.Object variables.

Boxing and unboxing are convenient from a programmer's viewpoint, but this simplified approach to stack/heap memory transfer comes with the baggage of performance issues (in both speed of execution and code size) and a lack of type safety. To understand the performance issues, ponder the steps that must occur to box and unbox a simple integer.

1. A new object must be allocated on the managed heap.

2. The value of the stack-based data must be transferred into that memory location.

3. When unboxed, the value stored on the heap-based object must be transferred back to the stack.

4. The now unused object on the heap will (eventually) be garbage collected.

Although this particular WorkWithArrayList() method won't cause a major bottleneck in terms of performance, you could certainly feel the impact if an ArrayList contained thousands of integers that your program manipulates on a somewhat regular basis. In an ideal world, you could manipulate stack-based data in a container without any performance issues. Ideally, it would be nice if you did not have to have to bother plucking data from this container using try/catch scopes (this is exactly what generics let you achieve).

The Issue of Type Safety

We touched on the issue of type safety when we looked at unboxing operations. Recall that you must unbox your data into the same data type it was declared as before boxing. However, there is another aspect of type safety you must keep in mind in a generic-free world: the fact that a majority of the classes of System.Collections can typically hold anything whatsoever because their members are prototyped to operate on System.Objects. For example, this method builds an ArrayList of random bits of unrelated data:

```
static void ArrayListOfRandomObjects()
{
  // The ArrayList can hold anything at all.
  ArrayList allMyObjects = new ArrayList();
  allMyObjects.Add(true);
  allMyObjects.Add(new OperatingSystem(PlatformID.MacOSX, new Version(10, 0)));
  allMyObjects.Add(66);
  allMyObjects.Add(3.14);
}
```

In some cases, you will require an extremely flexible container that can hold literally anything (as seen here). However, most of the time you desire a *type-safe* container that can operate only on a particular type of data point. For example, you might need a container that can hold only database connections, bitmaps, or IPointy-compatible objects.

Prior to generics, the only way you could address this issue of type safety was to create a custom (strongly typed) collection class manually. Assume you wish to create a custom collection that can contain only objects of type Person:

```
public class Person
{
  public int Age {get; set;}
  public string FirstName {get; set;}
  public string LastName {get; set;}

  public Person(){}
  public Person(string firstName, string lastName, int age)
  {
    Age = age;
    FirstName = firstName;
    LastName = lastName;
  }

  public override string ToString()
  {
    return string.Format("Name: {0} {1}, Age: {2}",
      FirstName, LastName, Age);
  }
}
```

To build a *collection which can hold only* Person *objects*, you could define a System.Collections.ArrayList member variable within a class named PersonCollection and configure all members to operate on strongly typed Person objects, rather than on System.Object types. Here is a simple example (a production-level custom collection could support many additional members and might extend an abstract base class from the System.Collections or System.Collections.Specialized namespace):

```
public class PersonCollection : IEnumerable
{
  private ArrayList arPeople = new ArrayList();

  // Cast for caller.
  public Person GetPerson(int pos)
  { return (Person)arPeople[pos]; }

  // Insert only Person objects.
  public void AddPerson(Person p)
  { arPeople.Add(p); }

  public void ClearPeople()
  { arPeople.Clear(); }

  public int Count
  { get { return arPeople.Count; } }

  // Foreach enumeration support.
  IEnumerator IEnumerable.GetEnumerator()
  { return arPeople.GetEnumerator(); }
}
```

Notice that the PersonCollection class implements the IEnumerable interface, which allows a foreach-like iteration over each contained item. Also notice that your GetPerson() and AddPerson() methods have been prototyped to operate only on Person objects, not bitmaps, strings, database connections, or other items. With these types defined, you are now assured of type safety, given that the C# compiler will be able to determine any attempt to insert an incompatible data type:

```
static void UsePersonCollection()
{
  Console.WriteLine("***** Custom Person Collection *****\n");
  PersonCollection myPeople = new PersonCollection();
  myPeople.AddPerson(new Person("Homer", "Simpson", 40));
  myPeople.AddPerson(new Person("Marge", "Simpson", 38));
  myPeople.AddPerson(new Person("Lisa", "Simpson", 9));
  myPeople.AddPerson(new Person("Bart", "Simpson", 7));
  myPeople.AddPerson(new Person("Maggie", "Simpson", 2));

  // This would be a compile-time error!
  // myPeople.AddPerson(new Car());

  foreach (Person p in myPeople)
    Console.WriteLine(p);
}
```

While custom collections do ensure type safety, this approach leaves you in a position where you must create an (almost identical) custom collection for each unique data type you want to contain. Thus, if you need a custom collection that can operate only on classes deriving from the Car base class, you need to build a highly similar collection class:

```
public class CarCollection : IEnumerable
{
  private ArrayList arCars = new ArrayList();

  // Cast for caller.
  public Car GetCar(int pos)
  { return (Car) arCars[pos]; }

  // Insert only Car objects.
  public void AddCar(Car c)
  { arCars.Add(c); }

  public void ClearCars()
  { arCars.Clear(); }

  public int Count
  { get { return arCars.Count; } }

  // Foreach enumeration support.
  IEnumerator IEnumerable.GetEnumerator()
  { return arCars.GetEnumerator(); }
}
```

However, a custom collection class does nothing to solve the issue of boxing/unboxing penalties. Even if you were to create a custom collection named IntCollection that you designed to operate only on System.Int32 items, you would have to allocate some type of object to hold the data (e.g., System.Array and ArrayList):

```
public class IntCollection : IEnumerable
{
  private ArrayList arInts = new ArrayList();

  // Get an int (performs unboxing!).
  public int GetInt(int pos)
  { return (int)arInts[pos]; }

  // Insert an int (performs boxing)!
  public void AddInt(int i)
  { arInts.Add(i); }

  public void ClearInts()
  { arInts.Clear(); }

  public int Count
  { get { return arInts.Count; } }

  IEnumerator IEnumerable.GetEnumerator()
  { return arInts.GetEnumerator(); }
}
```

Regardless of which type you might choose to hold the integers, you cannot escape the boxing dilemma using nongeneric containers.

A First Look at Generic Collections

When you use generic collection classes, you rectify all of the previous issues, including boxing/unboxing penalties and a lack of type safety. Also, the need to build a custom (generic) collection class becomes quite rare. Rather than having to build unique classes that can contain people, cars, and integers, you can use a generic collection class and specify the type of type.

Consider the following method, which uses the generic List<T> class (in the System.Collections.Generic namespace) to contain various types of data in a strongly typed manner (don't fret the details of generic syntax at this time):

```
static void UseGenericList()
{
  Console.WriteLine("***** Fun with Generics *****\n");

  // This List<> can hold only Person objects.
  List<Person> morePeople = new List<Person>();
  morePeople.Add(new Person ("Frank", "Black", 50));
  Console.WriteLine(morePeople[0]);

  // This List<> can hold only integers.
  List<int> moreInts = new List<int>();
  moreInts.Add(10);
  moreInts.Add(2);
  int sum = moreInts[0] + moreInts[1];

  // Compile-time error! Can't add Person object
  // to a list of ints!
  // moreInts.Add(new Person());
}
```

The first List<T> object can contain only Person objects. Therefore, you do not need to perform a cast when plucking the items from the container, which makes this approach more type safe. The second List<T> can contain only integers, all of which are allocated on the stack; in other words, there is no hidden boxing or unboxing as you found with the nongeneric ArrayList. Here is a short list of the benefits generic containers provide over their nongeneric counterparts.

- Generics provide better performance because they do not result in boxing or unboxing penalties when storing value types.

- Generics are type safe because they can contain only the type of type you specify.

- Generics greatly reduce the need to build custom collection types because you specify the "type of type" when creating the generic container.

■ **Source Code** You can find the IssuesWithNonGenericCollections project under the Chapter 9 subdirectory.

The Role of Generic Type Parameters

You can find generic classes, interfaces, structures, and delegates throughout the .NET base class libraries, and these might be part of any .NET namespace. Also be very aware that generics have far more uses then simply defining a collection class. To be sure, you will see many different generics used in the remainder of this book for various reasons.

■ **Note** Only classes, structures, interfaces, and delegates can be written generically; enum types cannot.

When you see a generic item listed in the .NET Framework documentation or the Visual Studio object browser, you will notice a pair of angled brackets with a letter or other token sandwiched within. Figure 9-1 shows the Visual Studio object browser displaying a number of generic items located within the System.Collections.Generic namespace, including the highlighted List<T> class.

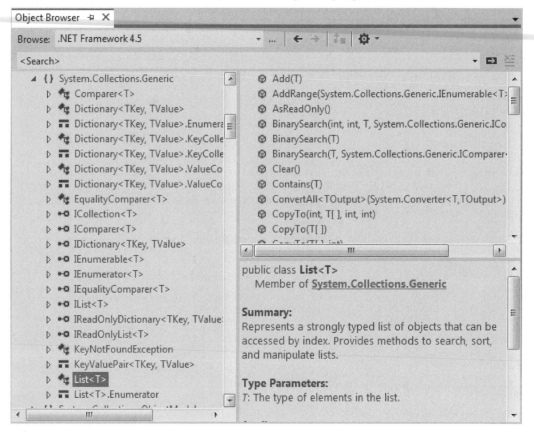

Figure 9-1. Generic items supporting type parameters

Formally speaking, you call these tokens *type parameters*; however, in more user-friendly terms, you can simply call them *placeholders*. You can read the symbol <T> as "*of T*." Thus, you can read IEnumerable<T> as IEnumerable *of T*; or, to say it another way, IEnumerable *of type T*.

■ **Note** The name of a type parameter (placeholder) is irrelevant, and it is up to the developer who created the generic item. However, typically *T* is used to represent types, *TKey* or *K* is used for keys, and *TValue* or *V* is used for values.

When you create a generic object, implement a generic interface, or invoke a generic member, it is up to you to supply a value to the type parameter. You'll see many examples in this chapter, and throughout the remainder of the text. However, to set the stage, let's see the basics of interacting with generic types and members.

Specifying Type Parameters for Generic Classes/Structures

When you create an instance of a generic class or structure, you specify the type parameter when you declare the variable and when you invoke the constructor. As you saw in the preceding code example, UseGenericList() defined two List<T> objects:

```
// This List<> can hold only Person objects.
List<Person> morePeople = new List<Person>();
```

You can read the preceding snippet as *a List<> of T, where T is of type Person*. Or, more simply, you can read it as *a list of person objects.* After you specify the type parameter of a generic item, it cannot be changed (remember: generics are all about type safety). When you specify a type parameter for a generic class or structure, all occurrences of the placeholder(s) are now replaced with your supplied value.

If you were to view the full declaration of the generic List<T> class using the Visual Studio object browser, you would see that the placeholder T is used throughout the definition of the List<T> type. Here is a partial listing (note the items in **bold**):

```
// A partial listing of the List<T> class.
namespace System.Collections.Generic
{
  public class List<T> :
    IList<T>, ICollection<T>, IEnumerable<T>, IReadOnlyList<T>
    IList, ICollection, IEnumerable
  {
...
    public void Add(T item);
    public ReadOnlyCollection<T> AsReadOnly();
    public int BinarySearch(T item);
    public bool Contains(T item);
    public void CopyTo(T[] array);
    public int FindIndex(System.Predicate<T> match);
    public T FindLast(System.Predicate<T> match);
    public bool Remove(T item);
    public int RemoveAll(System.Predicate<T> match);
    public T[] ToArray();
    public bool TrueForAll(System.Predicate<T> match);
```

```
    public T this[int index] { get; set; }
  }
}
```

When you create a List<T> specifying Person objects, it is as if the List<T> type were defined as follows:

```
namespace System.Collections.Generic
{
  public class List<Person> :
    IList<Person>, ICollection<Person>, IEnumerable<Person>, IReadOnlyList<Person>
    IList, ICollection, IEnumerable
  {
...
    public void Add(Person item);
    public ReadOnlyCollection<Person> AsReadOnly();
    public int BinarySearch(Person item);
    public bool Contains(Person item);
    public void CopyTo(Person[] array);
    public int FindIndex(System.Predicate<Person> match);
    public Person FindLast(System.Predicate<Person> match);
    public bool Remove(Person item);
    public int RemoveAll(System.Predicate<Person> match);
    public Person[] ToArray();
    public bool TrueForAll(System.Predicate<Person> match);
    public Person this[int index] { get; set; }
  }
}
```

Of course, when you create a generic List<T> variable, the compiler does not literally create a brand new implementation of the List<T> class. Rather, it will address only the members of the generic type you actually invoke.

Specifying Type Parameters for Generic Members

It is fine for a nongeneric class or structure to support a handful of generic members (e.g., methods and properties). In these cases, you would also need to specify the placeholder value at the time you invoke the method. For example, System.Array supports a several generic methods. Specifically, the nongeneric static Sort() method now has a generic counterpart named Sort<T>(). Consider the following code snippet, where T is of type int:

```
int[] myInts = { 10, 4, 2, 33, 93 };

// Specify the placeholder to the generic
// Sort<>() method.
Array.Sort<int>(myInts);

foreach (int i  in myInts)
{
  Console.WriteLine(i);
}
```

Specifying Type Parameters for Generic Interfaces

It is common to implement generic interfaces when you build classes or structures that need to support various framework behaviors (e.g., cloning, sorting, and enumeration). In Chapter 8, you learned about a number of nongeneric interfaces, such as IComparable, IEnumerable, IEnumerator, and IComparer. Recall that the nongeneric IComparable interface was defined like this:

```
public interface IComparable
{
  int CompareTo(object obj);
}
```

In Chapter 8, you also implemented this interface on your Car class to enable sorting in a standard array. However, the code required several runtime checks and casting operations because the parameter was a general System.Object:

```
public class Car : IComparable
{
...
  // IComparable implementation.
  int IComparable.CompareTo(object obj)
  {
    Car temp = obj as Car;
    if (temp != null)
    {
      if (this.CarID > temp.CarID)
        return 1;
      if (this.CarID < temp.CarID)
        return -1;
      else
        return 0;
    }
    else
      throw new ArgumentException("Parameter is not a Car!");
  }
}
```

Now assume you use the generic counterpart of this interface:

```
public interface IComparable<T>
{
  int CompareTo(T obj);
}
```

In this case, your implementation code will be cleaned up considerably:

```
public class Car : IComparable<Car>
{
...
  // IComparable<T> implementation.
  int IComparable<Car>.CompareTo(Car obj)
  {
    if (this.CarID > obj.CarID)
      return 1;
```

```
      if (this.CarID < obj.CarID)
        return -1;
      else
        return 0;
  }
}
```

Here, you do not need to check whether the incoming parameter is a Car because it can *only* be a Car! If someone were to pass in an incompatible data type, you would get a compile-time error. Now that you have a better handle on how to interact with generic items, as well as the role of type parameters (a.k.a. placeholders), you're ready to examine the classes and interfaces of the System.Collections.Generic namespace.

The System.Collections.Generic Namespace

When you are building a .NET application and need a way to manage in-memory data, the classes of System.Collections.Generic will most likely fit the bill. At the opening of this chapter, I briefly mentioned some of the core nongeneric interfaces implemented by the nongeneric collection classes. Not too surprisingly, the System.Collections.Generic namespace defines generic replacements for many of them.

In fact, you can find a number of the generic interfaces that extend their nongeneric counterparts. This might seem odd; however, by doing so, implementing classes will also support the legacy functionally found in their nongeneric siblings. For example, IEnumerable<T> extends IEnumerable. Table 9-4 documents the core generic interfaces you'll encounter when working with the generic collection classes.

Table 9-4. Key Interfaces Supported by Classes of System.Collections.Generic

System.Collections.Generic Interface	Meaning in Life
ICollection<T>	Defines general characteristics (e.g., size, enumeration, and thread safety) for all generic collection types.
IComparer<T>	Defines a way to compare to objects.
IDictionary<TKey, TValue>	Allows a generic collection object to represent its contents using key/value pairs.
IEnumerable<T>	Returns the IEnumerator<T> interface for a given object.
IEnumerator<T>	Enables foreach-style iteration over a generic collection.
IList<T>	Provides behavior to add, remove, and index items in a sequential list of objects.
ISet<T>	Provides the base interface for the abstraction of sets.

The `System.Collections.Generic` namespace also defines several classes that implement many of these key interfaces. Table 9-5 describes some commonly used classes of this namespace, the interfaces they implement, and their basic functionality.

Table 9-5. Classes of System.Collections.Generic

Generic Class	Supported Key Interfaces	Meaning in Life
`Dictionary<TKey, TValue>`	`ICollection<T>`, `IDictionary<TKey, TValue>`, `IEnumerable<T>`	This represents a generic collection of keys and values.
`LinkedList<T>`	`ICollection<T>`, `IEnumerable<T>`	This represents a doubly linked list.
`List<T>`	`ICollection<T>`, `IEnumerable<T>`, `IList<T>`	This is a dynamically resizable sequential list of items.
`Queue<T>`	`ICollection` (Not a typo! This is the nongeneric collection interface) , `IEnumerable<T>`	This is a generic implementation of a first-in, first-out (FIFO) list.
`SortedDictionary<TKey, TValue>`	`ICollection<T>`, `IDictionary<TKey, TValue>`, `IEnumerable<T>`	This is a generic implementation of a sorted set of key/value pairs.
`SortedSet<T>`	`ICollection<T>`, `IEnumerable<T>`, `ISet<T>`	This represents a collection of objects that is maintained in sorted order with no duplication.
`Stack<T>`	`ICollection` (Not a typo! This is the nongeneric collection interface) , `IEnumerable<T>`	This is a generic implementation of a last-in, first-out (LIFO) list.

The `System.Collections.Generic` namespace also defines many auxiliary classes and structures that work in conjunction with a specific container. For example, the `LinkedListNode<T>` type represents a node within a generic `LinkedList<T>`, the `KeyNotFoundException` exception is raised when attempting to grab an item from a container using a nonexistent key, and so forth.

It is also worth pointing out that `mscorlib.dll` and `System.dll` are not the only assemblies that add new types to the `System.Collections.Generic` namespace. For example, `System.Core.dll` adds the `HashSet<T>` class to the mix. Be sure to consult the .NET Framework documentation for full details of the `System.Collections.Generic` namespace.

In any case, your next task is to learn how to use some of these generic collection classes. Before you do however, allow me to illustrate a C# language feature (first introduced in .NET 3.5) that simplifies the way you populate generic (and nongeneric) collection containers with data.

Understanding Collection Initialization Syntax

In Chapter 4, you learned about *object initialization syntax,* which allows you to set properties on a new variable at the time of construction. Closely related to this is *collection initialization syntax.* This C# language feature makes it possible to populate many containers (such as ArrayList or List<T>) with items by using syntax similar to what you use to populate a basic array.

■ **Note** You can apply collection initialization syntax only to classes that support an Add() method, which is formalized by the ICollection<T>/ICollection interfaces.

Consider the following examples:

```
// Init a standard array.
int[] myArrayOfInts = { 0, 1, 2, 3, 4, 5, 6, 7, 8, 9 };
```

```
// Init a generic List<> of ints.
List<int> myGenericList = new List<int> { 0, 1, 2, 3, 4, 5, 6, 7, 8, 9 };
```

```
// Init an ArrayList with numerical data.
ArrayList myList = new ArrayList { 0, 1, 2, 3, 4, 5, 6, 7, 8, 9 };
```

If your container is managing a collection of classes or a structure, you can blend object initialization syntax with collection initialization syntax to yield some functional code. You might recall the Point class from Chapter 5, which defined two properties named X and Y. If you wanted to build a generic List<T> of Point objects, you could write the following:

```
List<Point> myListOfPoints = new List<Point>
{
  new Point { X = 2, Y = 2 },
  new Point { X = 3, Y = 3 },
  new Point(PointColor.BloodRed){ X = 4, Y = 4 }
};
```

```
foreach (var pt in myListOfPoints)
{
  Console.WriteLine(pt);
}
```

Again, the benefit of this syntax is that you save yourself numerous keystrokes. While the nested curly brackets can become difficult to read if you don't mind your formatting, imagine the amount of code that would be required to fill the following List<T> of Rectangles if you did not have collection initialization syntax (you might recall from Chapter 4 that you created a Rectangle class that contained two properties encapsulating Point objects):

```
List<Rectangle> myListOfRects = new List<Rectangle>
{
  new Rectangle {TopLeft = new Point { X = 10, Y = 10 },
              BottomRight = new Point { X = 200, Y = 200}},
  new Rectangle {TopLeft = new Point { X = 2, Y = 2 },
```

```
                    BottomRight = new Point { X = 100, Y = 100}},
    new Rectangle {TopLeft = new Point { X = 5, Y = 5 },
                    BottomRight = new Point { X = 90, Y = 75}}
};

foreach (var r in myListOfRects)
{
  Console.WriteLine(r);
}
```

Working with the List<T> Class

Create a brand new Console Application project named FunWithGenericCollections. Note that your initial C# code file already imports the System.Collections.Generic namespace.

The first generic class you will examine is List<T>, which you've already seen once or twice in this chapter. The List<T> class is bound to be your most frequently used type in the System.Collections.Generic namespace because it allows you to resize the contents of the container dynamically. To illustrate the basics of this type, ponder the following method in your Program class, which leverages List<T> to manipulate the set of Person objects seen earlier in this chapter; you might recall that these Person objects defined three properties (Age, FirstName, and LastName) and a custom ToString() implementation:

```
static void UseGenericList()
{
  // Make a List of Person objects, filled with
  // collection/object init syntax.
  List<Person> people = new List<Person>()
  {
    new Person {FirstName= "Homer", LastName="Simpson", Age=47},
    new Person {FirstName= "Marge", LastName="Simpson", Age=45},
    new Person {FirstName= "Lisa", LastName="Simpson", Age=9},
    new Person {FirstName= "Bart", LastName="Simpson", Age=8}
  };

  // Print out # of items in List.
  Console.WriteLine("Items in list: {0}", people.Count);

  // Enumerate over list.
  foreach (Person p in people)
    Console.WriteLine(p);

  // Insert a new person.
  Console.WriteLine("\n->Inserting new person.");
  people.Insert(2, new Person { FirstName = "Maggie", LastName = "Simpson", Age = 2 });
  Console.WriteLine("Items in list: {0}", people.Count);

  // Copy data into a new array.
  Person[] arrayOfPeople = people.ToArray();
  for (int i = 0; i < arrayOfPeople.Length; i++)
  {
    Console.WriteLine("First Names: {0}", arrayOfPeople[i].FirstName);
  }
```

```
}
```

Here, you use initialization syntax to populate your List<T> with objects, as a shorthand notation for calling Add() *multiple* times. After you print out the number of items in the collection (as well as enumerate over each item), you invoke Insert(). As you can see, Insert() allows you to plug a new item into the List<T> at a specified index.

Finally, notice the call to the ToArray() method, which returns an array of Person objects based on the contents of the original List<T>. From this array, you loop over the items again using the array's indexer syntax. If you call this method from within Main(), you get the following output:

```
***** Fun with Generic Collections *****

Items in list: 4
Name: Homer Simpson, Age: 47
Name: Marge Simpson, Age: 45
Name: Lisa Simpson, Age: 9
Name: Bart Simpson, Age: 8

->Inserting new person.
Items in list: 5
First Names: Homer
First Names: Marge
First Names: Maggie
First Names: Lisa
First Names: Bart
```

The List<T> class defines many additional members of interest, so be sure to consult the .NET Framework documentation for more information. Next, let's look at a few more generic collections, specifically Stack<T>, Queue<T>, and SortedSet<T>. This should get you in a great position to understand your basic choices regarding how to hold your custom application data.

Working with the Stack<T> Class

The Stack<T> class represents a collection that maintains items using a last-in, first-out manner. As you might expect, Stack<T> defines members named Push() and Pop() to place items onto or remove items from the stack. The following method creates a stack of Person objects:

```
static void UseGenericStack()
{
  Stack<Person> stackOfPeople = new Stack<Person>();
  stackOfPeople.Push(new Person
    { FirstName = "Homer", LastName = "Simpson", Age = 47 });
  stackOfPeople.Push(new Person
    { FirstName = "Marge", LastName = "Simpson", Age = 45 });
  stackOfPeople.Push(new Person
    { FirstName = "Lisa", LastName = "Simpson", Age = 9 });
```

```
    // Now look at the top item, pop it, and look again.
    Console.WriteLine("First person is: {0}", stackOfPeople.Peek());
    Console.WriteLine("Popped off {0}", stackOfPeople.Pop());

    Console.WriteLine("\nFirst person is: {0}", stackOfPeople.Peek());
    Console.WriteLine("Popped off {0}", stackOfPeople.Pop());

    Console.WriteLine("\nFirst person item is: {0}", stackOfPeople.Peek());
    Console.WriteLine("Popped off {0}", stackOfPeople.Pop());

    try
    {
      Console.WriteLine("\nnFirst person is: {0}", stackOfPeople.Peek());
      Console.WriteLine("Popped off {0}", stackOfPeople.Pop());
    }
    catch (InvalidOperationException ex)
    {
      Console.WriteLine("\nError! {0}", ex.Message);
    }
}
```

Here, you build a stack that contains three people, added in the order of their first names: Homer, Marge, and Lisa. As you peek into the stack, you will always see the object at the top first; therefore, the first call to Peek() reveals the third Person object. After a series of Pop() and Peek() calls, the stack eventually empties, at which time additional Peek() and Pop() calls raise a system exception. You can see the output for this here:

```
***** Fun with Generic Collections *****

First person is: Name: Lisa Simpson, Age: 9
Popped off Name: Lisa Simpson, Age: 9

First person is: Name: Marge Simpson, Age: 45
Popped off Name: Marge Simpson, Age: 45

First person item is: Name: Homer Simpson, Age: 47
Popped off Name: Homer Simpson, Age: 47

Error! Stack empty.
```

Working with the Queue<T> Class

Queues are containers that ensure items are accessed in a first-in, first-out manner. Sadly, we humans are subject to queues all day long: lines at the bank, lines at the movie theater, and lines at the morning coffeehouse. When you need to model a scenario in which items are handled on a first-come, first-served basis, you will find the Queue<T> class fits the bill. In addition to the functionality provided by the supported interfaces, Queue defines the key members shown in Table 9-6.

Table 9-6. Members of the Queue<T> Type

Select Member of Queue<T>	Meaning in Life
Dequeue()	Removes and returns the object at the beginning of the Queue<T>.
Enqueue()	Adds an object to the end of the Queue<T>.
Peek()	Returns the object at the beginning of the Queue<T> without removing it.

Now let's put these methods to work. You can begin by leveraging your Person class again and building a Queue<T> object that simulates a line of people waiting to order coffee. First, assume you have the following static helper method:

```
static void GetCoffee(Person p)
{
  Console.WriteLine("{0} got coffee!", p.FirstName);
}
```

Now assume you have this additional helper method, which calls GetCoffee() internally:

```
static void UseGenericQueue()
{
  // Make a Q with three people.
  Queue<Person> peopleQ = new Queue<Person>();
  peopleQ.Enqueue(new Person {FirstName= "Homer",
    LastName="Simpson", Age=47});
  peopleQ.Enqueue(new Person {FirstName= "Marge",
    LastName="Simpson", Age=45});
  peopleQ.Enqueue(new Person {FirstName= "Lisa",
    LastName="Simpson", Age=9});

  // Peek at first person in Q.
  Console.WriteLine("{0} is first in line!", peopleQ.Peek().FirstName);

  // Remove each person from Q.
  GetCoffee(peopleQ.Dequeue());
  GetCoffee(peopleQ.Dequeue());
  GetCoffee(peopleQ.Dequeue());
  // Try to de-Q again?
  try
  {
    GetCoffee(peopleQ.Dequeue());
  }
  catch(InvalidOperationException e)
  {
    Console.WriteLine("Error! {0}", e.Message);
  }
}
```

Here, you insert three items into the Queue<T> class using its Enqueue() method. The call to Peek() allows you to view (but not remove) the first item currently in the Queue. Finally, the call to Dequeue() removes the item from the line and sends it into the GetCoffee() helper function for processing. Note that if you attempt to remove items from an empty queue, a runtime exception is thrown. Here is the output you receive when calling this method:

```
***** Fun with Generic Collections *****

Homer is first in line!
Homer got coffee!
Marge got coffee!
Lisa got coffee!
Error! Queue empty.
```

Working with the SortedSet<T> Class

The SortedSet<T> class is useful because it automatically ensures that the items in the set are sorted when you insert or remove items. However, you do need to inform the SortedSet<T> class exactly *how* you want it to sort the objects, by passing in as a constructor argument an object that implements the generic IComparer<T> interface.

Begin by creating a brand new class named SortPeopleByAge, which implements IComparer<T>, where T is of type Person. Recall that this interface defines a single method named Compare(), where you can author whatever logic you require for the comparison. Here is a simple implementation of this class:

```
class SortPeopleByAge : IComparer<Person>
{
  public int Compare(Person firstPerson, Person secondPerson)
  {
    if (firstPerson.Age > secondPerson.Age)
      return 1;
    if (firstPerson.Age < secondPerson.Age)
      return -1;
    else
      return 0;
  }
}
```

Now update your Program class with the following new method, which I assume you will call from Main():

```
static void UseSortedSet()
{
  // Make some people with different ages.
  SortedSet<Person> setOfPeople = new SortedSet<Person>(new SortPeopleByAge())
  {
    new Person {FirstName= "Homer", LastName="Simpson", Age=47},
    new Person {FirstName= "Marge", LastName="Simpson", Age=45},
    new Person {FirstName= "Lisa", LastName="Simpson", Age=9},
    new Person {FirstName= "Bart", LastName="Simpson", Age=8}
  };
```

345

```
  // Note the items are sorted by age!
  foreach (Person p in setOfPeople)
  {
    Console.WriteLine(p);
  }
  Console.WriteLine();

  // Add a few new people, with various ages.
  setOfPeople.Add(new Person { FirstName = "Saku", LastName = "Jones", Age = 1 });
  setOfPeople.Add(new Person { FirstName = "Mikko", LastName = "Jones", Age = 32 });

  // Still sorted by age!
  foreach (Person p in setOfPeople)
  {
    Console.WriteLine(p);
  }
}
```

When you run your application, the listing of objects is now always ordered based on the value of the Age property, regardless of the order you inserted or removed objects:

```
***** Fun with Generic Collections *****

Name: Bart Simpson, Age: 8
Name: Lisa Simpson, Age: 9
Name: Marge Simpson, Age: 45
Name: Homer Simpson, Age: 47

Name: Saku Jones, Age: 1
Name: Bart Simpson, Age: 8
Name: Lisa Simpson, Age: 9
Name: Mikko Jones, Age: 32
Name: Marge Simpson, Age: 45
Name: Homer Simpson, Age: 47
```

■ **Note** You can find the FunWithGenericCollections project under the Chapter 9 subdirectory.

The System.Collections.ObjectModel Namespace

Now that you understand the basics of how to work with generic classes, we can briefly examine an additional collection-centric namespace, System.Collections.ObjectModel. This is a relatively small namespace, which contains a handful of classes. Table 9-7 documents the two classes that you should most certainly be aware of.

Table 9-7. Useful Members of System.Collections.ObjectModel

System.Collections.ObjectModel Type	Meaning in Life
ObservableCollection<T>	Represents a dynamic data collection that provides notifications when items get added, removed, or when the whole list is refreshed.
ReadOnlyObservableCollection<T>	Represents a read-only version of ObservableCollection<T>.

The ObservableCollection<T> class is very useful in that it has the ability to inform external objects when its contents have changed in some way (as you might guess, working with ReadOnlyObservableCollection<T> is very similar, but read-only in nature).

Working with ObservableCollection<T>

Create a new Console Application named FunWithObservableCollection, and import the System.Collections.ObjectModel namespace into your initial C# code file. In many ways, working with the ObservableCollection<T> is identical to working with List<T>, given that both of these classes implement the same core interfaces. What makes the ObservableCollection<T> class unique is that this class supports an event named CollectionChanged. This event will fire whenever a new item is inserted, a current item is removed (or relocated), or if the entire collection is modified.

Like any event, CollectionChanged is defined in terms of a delegate, which in this case is NotifyCollectionChangedEventHandler. This delegate can call any method that takes an object as the first parameter, and a NotifyCollectionChangedEventArgs as the second. Consider the following Main() method, which populates an observable collection containing Person objects and wires up the CollectionChanged event:

```
class Program
{
  static void Main(string[] args)
  {
    // Make a collection to observe and add a few Person objects.
    ObservableCollection<Person> people = new ObservableCollection<Person>()
    {
      new Person{ FirstName = "Peter", LastName = "Murphy", Age = 52 },
      new Person{ FirstName = "Kevin", LastName = "Key", Age = 48 },
    };

    // Wire up the CollectionChanged event.
    people.CollectionChanged += people_CollectionChanged;
  }

  static void people_CollectionChanged(object sender,
    System.Collections.Specialized.NotifyCollectionChangedEventArgs e)
  {
    throw new NotImplementedException();
  }
}
```

```
}
```

The incoming NotifyCollectionChangedEventArgs parameter defines two important properties, OldItems and NewItems, which will give you a list of items that were currently in the collection before the event fired, and the new items that were involved in the change. However, you will want to examine these lists only under the correct circumstances. Recall that the CollectionChanged event can fire when items are added, removed, relocated, or reset. To discover which of these actions triggered the event, you can use the Action property of NotifyCollectionChangedEventArgs. The Action property can be tested against any of the following members of the NotifyCollectionChangedAction enumeration:

```
public enum NotifyCollectionChangedAction
{
  Add = 0,
  Remove = 1,
  Replace = 2,
  Move = 3,
  Reset = 4,
}
```

Here is an implementation of the CollectionChanged event handler that will traverse the old and new set when an item has been inserted or removed to the collection at hand:

```
static void people_CollectionChanged(object sender,
  System.Collections.Specialized.NotifyCollectionChangedEventArgs e)
{
  // What was the action that caused the event?
  Console.WriteLine("Action for this event: {0}", e.Action);

  // They removed something.
  if (e.Action == System.Collections.Specialized.NotifyCollectionChangedAction.Remove)
  {
    Console.WriteLine("Here are the OLD items:");
    foreach (Person p in e.OldItems)
    {
      Console.WriteLine(p.ToString());
    }
    Console.WriteLine();
  }

  // They added something.
  if (e.Action == System.Collections.Specialized.NotifyCollectionChangedAction.Add)
  {
    // Now show the NEW items that were inserted.
    Console.WriteLine("Here are the NEW items:");
    foreach (Person p in e.NewItems)
    {
      Console.WriteLine(p.ToString());
    }
  }
}
```

Now, assuming you have updated your Main() method to add and remove an item, you will see output similar to the following:

```
Action for this event: Add
Here are the NEW items:
Name:  Fred Smith, Age: 32

Action for this event: Remove
Here are the OLD items:
Name: Peter Murphy, Age: 52
```

That wraps up our examination of the various collection-centric namespaces in the .NET base class libraries. To conclude our chapter, we will now examine how we can build our own custom generic methods and custom generic types.

■ **Source Code** You can find the FunWithObservableCollection project under the Chapter 9 subdirectory.

Creating Custom Generic Methods

While most developers typically use the existing generic types within the base class libraries, it is also possible to build your own generic members and custom generic types. Let's look at how to incorporate custom generics into your own projects. The first step is to build a generic swap method. Begin by creating a new console application named CustomGenericMethods.

When you build custom generic methods, you achieve a supercharged version of traditional method overloading. In Chapter 2, you learned that overloading is the act of defining multiple versions of a single method, which differ by the number of, or type of, parameters.

While overloading is a useful feature in an object-oriented language, one problem is that you can easily end up with a ton of methods that essentially do the same thing. For example, assume you need to build some methods that can switch two pieces of data using a simple swap routine. You might begin by authoring a new method that can operate on integers, like this:

```
// Swap two integers.
static void Swap(ref int a, ref int b)
{
  int temp;
  temp = a;
  a = b;
  b = temp;
}
```

So far, so good. But now assume you also need to swap two Person objects; this would require authoring a new version of Swap():

```
// Swap two Person objects.
static void Swap(ref Person a, ref Person b)
{
  Person temp;
  temp = a;
  a = b;
```

```
    b = temp;
}
```

No doubt, you can see where this is going. If you also needed to swap floating-point numbers, bitmaps, cars, buttons, and whatnot, you would have to build even more methods, which would become a maintenance nightmare. You could build a single (nongeneric) method that operated on object parameters, but then you face all the issues you examined earlier in this chapter, including boxing, unboxing, a lack of type safety, explicit casting, and so on.

Whenever you have a group of overloaded methods that differ only by incoming arguments, this is your clue that generics could make your life easier. Consider the following generic Swap<T> method that can swap any two Ts:

```
// This method will swap any two items.
// as specified by the type parameter <T>.
static void Swap<T>(ref T a, ref T b)
{
  Console.WriteLine("You sent the Swap() method a {0}",
    typeof(T));
  T temp;
  temp = a;
  a = b;
  b = temp;
}
```

Notice how a generic method is defined by specifying the type parameters after the method name, but before the parameter list. Here, you state that the Swap<T>() method can operate on any two parameters of type <T>. To spice things up a bit, you also print out the type name of the supplied placeholder to the console using C#'s typeof() operator. Now consider the following Main() method, which swaps integers and strings:

```
static void Main(string[] args)
{
  Console.WriteLine("***** Fun with Custom Generic Methods *****\n");

  // Swap 2 ints.
  int a = 10, b = 90;
  Console.WriteLine("Before swap: {0}, {1}", a, b);
  Swap<int>(ref a, ref b);
  Console.WriteLine("After swap: {0}, {1}", a, b);
  Console.WriteLine();

  // Swap 2 strings.
  string s1 = "Hello", s2 = "There";
  Console.WriteLine("Before swap: {0} {1}!", s1, s2);
  Swap<string>(ref s1, ref s2);
  Console.WriteLine("After swap: {0} {1}!", s1, s2);

  Console.ReadLine();
}
```

The output looks like this:

```
***** Fun with Custom Generic Methods *****

Before swap: 10, 90
You sent the Swap() method a System.Int32
After swap: 90, 10

Before swap: Hello There!
You sent the Swap() method a System.String
After swap: There Hello!
```

The major benefit of this approach is that you have only one version of Swap<T>() to maintain, yet it can operate on any two items of a given type in a type-safe manner. Better yet, stack-based items stay on the stack, while heap-based items stay on the heap!

Inference of Type Parameters

When you invoke generic methods such as Swap<T>, you can optionally omit the type parameter if (and only if) the generic method requires arguments because the compiler can infer the type parameter based on the member parameters. For example, you could swap two System.Boolean values by adding the following code to Main():

```
// Compiler will infer System.Boolean.
bool b1 = true, b2 = false;
Console.WriteLine("Before swap: {0}, {1}", b1, b2);
Swap(ref b1, ref b2);
Console.WriteLine("After swap: {0}, {1}", b1, b2);
```

Even though the compiler is able to discover the correct type parameter based on the data type used to declare b1 and b2, you should get in the habit of always specifying the type parameter explicitly:

```
Swap<string>(ref b1, ref b2);
```

This makes it clear to your fellow programmers that this method is indeed generic. Moreover, inference of type parameters works only if the generic method has at least one parameter. For example, assume you have the following generic method in your Program class:

```
static void DisplayBaseClass<T>()
{
  // BaseType is a method used in reflection,
  // which will be examined in Chapter 15
  Console.WriteLine("Base class of {0} is: {1}.",
    typeof(T), typeof(T).BaseType);
}
```

In this case, you must supply the type parameter upon invocation:

```
static void Main(string[] args)
{
...
  // Must supply type parameter if
```

```
  // the method does not take params.
  DisplayBaseClass<int>();
  DisplayBaseClass<string>();

  // Compiler error! No params? Must supply placeholder!
  // DisplayBaseClass();
  Console.ReadLine();
}
```

Currently, the generic Swap<T> and DisplayBaseClass<T> methods are defined within the application's Program class. Of course, as with any method, you are free to define these members in a separate class type (MyGenericMethods) if you would prefer to do it that way:

```
public static class MyGenericMethods
{
  public static void Swap<T>(ref T a, ref T b)
  {
    Console.WriteLine("You sent the Swap() method a {0}",
      typeof(T));
    T temp;
    temp = a;
    a = b;
    b = temp;
  }

  public static void DisplayBaseClass<T>()
  {
    Console.WriteLine("Base class of {0} is: {1}.",
      typeof(T), typeof(T).BaseType);
  }
}
```

The static Swap<T> and DisplayBaseClass<T> methods have been scoped within a new static class type, so you need to specify the type's name when invoking either member, as in this example:

```
MyGenericMethods.Swap<int>(ref a, ref b);
```

Of course, generic methods do not need to be static. If Swap<T> and DisplayBaseClass<T> were instance level (and defined in a nonstatic class), you would simply make an instance of MyGenericMethods and invoke them using the object variable:

```
MyGenericMethods c = new MyGenericMethods();
c.Swap<int>(ref a, ref b);
```

■ **Source Code** You can find the CustomGenericMethods project under the Chapter 9 subdirectory.

Creating Custom Generic Structures and Classes

Now that you understand how to define and invoke generic methods, it's time to turn your attention to the construction of a generic structure (the process of building a generic class is identical) within a new Console Application project named GenericPoint. Assume you have built a generic Point structure that supports a single type parameter that represents the underlying storage for the (*x*, *y*) coordinates. The caller can then create Point<T> types as follows:

```
// Point using ints.
Point<int> p = new Point<int>(10, 10);

// Point using double.
Point<double> p2 = new Point<double>(5.4, 3.3);
```

Here is the complete definition of Point<T>, with some analysis to follow:

```
// A generic Point structure.
public struct Point<T>
{
  // Generic state date.
  private T xPos;
  private T yPos;

  // Generic constructor.
  public Point(T xVal, T yVal)
  {
    xPos = xVal;
    yPos = yVal;
  }

  // Generic properties.
  public T X
  {
    get { return xPos; }
    set { xPos = value; }
  }

  public T Y
  {
    get { return yPos; }
    set { yPos = value; }
  }

  public override string ToString()
  {
    return string.Format("[{0}, {1}]", xPos, yPos);
  }

  // Reset fields to the default value of the
  // type parameter.
  public void ResetPoint()
  {
```

```
    xPos = default(T);
    yPos = default(T);
  }
}
```

The default Keyword in Generic Code

As you can see, Point<T> leverages its type parameter in the definition of the field data, constructor arguments, and property definitions. Notice that, in addition to overriding ToString(), Point<T> defines a method named ResetPoint() that uses some new syntax you have not yet seen:

```
// The "default" keyword is overloaded in C#.
// When used with generics, it represents the default
// value of a type parameter.
public void ResetPoint()
{
  X = default(T);
  Y = default(T);
}
```

With the introduction of generics, the C# default keyword has been given a dual identity. In addition to its use within a switch construct, it can also be used to set a type parameter to its default value. This is helpful because a generic type does not know the actual placeholders up front, which means it cannot safely assume what the default value will be. The defaults for a type parameter are as follows:

- Numeric values have a default value of 0.

- Reference types have a default value of null.

- Fields of a structure are set to 0 (for value types) or null (for reference types).

For Point<T>, you can set the X and Y values to 0 directly because it is safe to assume the caller will supply only numerical data. However, you can also increase the overall flexibility of the generic type by using the default(T) syntax. In any case, you can now exercise the methods of Point<T>:

```
static void Main(string[] args)
{
  Console.WriteLine("***** Fun with Generic Structures *****\n");

  // Point using ints.
  Point<int> p = new Point<int>(10, 10);
  Console.WriteLine("p.ToString()={0}", p.ToString());
  p.ResetPoint();
  Console.WriteLine("p.ToString()={0}", p.ToString());
  Console.WriteLine();

  // Point using double.
  Point<double> p2 = new Point<double>(5.4, 3.3);
  Console.WriteLine("p2.ToString()={0}", p2.ToString());
  p2.ResetPoint();
  Console.WriteLine("p2.ToString()={0}", p2.ToString());
```

```
  Console.ReadLine();
```

```
***** Fun with Generic Structures *****

p.ToString()=[10, 10]
p.ToString()=[0, 0]

p2.ToString()=[5.4, 3.3]
p2.ToString()=[0, 0]
```

■ **Source Code** You can find the GenericPoint project under the Chapter 9 subdirectory.

Constraining Type Parameters

As this chapter illustrates, any generic item has at least one type parameter that you need to specify at the time you interact with the generic type or member. This alone allows you to build some type-safe code; however, the .NET platform allows you to use the where keyword to get extremely specific about what a given type parameter must look like.

Using this keyword, you can add a set of constraints to a given type parameter, which the C# compiler will check at compile time. Specifically, you can constrain a type parameter as described in Table 9-8.

Table 9-8. Possible Constraints for Generic Type Parameters

Generic Constraint	Meaning in Life
where T : struct	The type parameter <T> must have System.ValueType in its chain of inheritance (i.e., <T> must be a structure).
where T : class	The type parameter <T> must not have System.ValueType in its chain of inheritance (i.e., <T> must be a reference type).
where T : new()	The type parameter <T> must have a default constructor. This is helpful if your generic type must create an instance of the type parameter because you cannot assume you know the format of custom constructors. Note that this constraint must be listed last on a multiconstrained type.
where T : NameOfBaseClass	The type parameter <T> must be derived from the class specified by NameOfBaseClass.

Generic Constraint	Meaning in Life
where T : NameOfInterface	The type parameter <T> must implement the interface specified by NameOfInterface. You can separate multiple interfaces as a comma-delimited list.

Unless you need to build some extremely type-safe custom collections, you might never need to use the where keyword in your C# projects. Regardless, the following handful of (partial) code examples illustrate how to work with the where keyword.

Examples Using the where Keyword

Begin by assuming that you have created a custom generic class, and you want to ensure that the type parameter has a default constructor. This could be useful when the custom generic class needs to create instances of the T because the default constructor is the only constructor that is potentially common to all types. Also, constraining T in this way lets you get compile-time checking; if T is a reference type, the programmer remembered to redefine the default in the class definition (you might recall that the default constructor is removed in classes when you define your own):

```
// MyGenericClass derives from object, while
// contained items must have a default ctor.
public class MyGenericClass<T> where T : new()
{
  ...
}
```

Notice that the where clause specifies which type parameter is being constrained, followed by a colon operator. After the colon operator, you list each possible constraint (in this case, a default constructor). Here is another example:

```
// MyGenericClass derives from object, while
// contained items must be a class implementing IDrawable
// and must support a default ctor.
public class MyGenericClass<T> where T : class, IDrawable, new()
{
  ...
}
```

In this case, T has three requirements. It must be a reference type (not a structure), as marked with the class token. Second, T must implement the IDrawable interface. Third, it must also have a default constructor. Multiple constraints are listed in a comma-delimited list; however, you should be aware that the new() constraint must always be listed last! Thus, the following code will not compile:

```
// Error! new() constraint must be listed last!
public class MyGenericClass<T> where T : new(), class, IDrawable
{
  ...
}
```

If you ever create a custom generic collection class that specifies multiple type parameters, you can specify a unique set of constraints for each, using separate where clauses:

```
// <K> must extend SomeBaseClass and have a default ctor,
// while <T> must be a structure and implement the
// generic IComparable interface.
public class MyGenericClass<K, T> where K : SomeBaseClass, new()
    where T : struct, IComparable<T>
{
  ...
}
```

You will rarely encounter cases where you need to build a complete custom generic collection class; however, you can use the where keyword on generic methods, as well. For example, if you want to specify that your generic Swap<T>() method can operate only on structures, you would update the method like this:

```
// This method will swap any structure, but not classes.
static void Swap<T>(ref T a, ref T b) where T : struct
{
  ...
}
```

Note that if you were to constrain the Swap() method in this manner, you would no longer be able to swap string objects (as is shown in the sample code) because string is a reference type.

The Lack of Operator Constraints

I want to make one more comment on generic methods and constraints as this chapter draws to a close. It might come as a surprise to you to find out that, when creating generic methods, you will get a compiler error if you apply any C# operators (+, -, *, ==, etc.) on the type parameters. For example, imagine the usefulness of a class that can Add(), Subtract(), Multiply(), and Divide() generic types:

```
// Compiler error! Cannot apply
// operators to type parameters!
public class BasicMath<T>
{
  public T Add(T arg1, T arg2)
  { return arg1 + arg2; }
  public T Subtract(T arg1, T arg2)
  { return arg1 - arg2; }
  public T Multiply(T arg1, T arg2)
  { return arg1 * arg2; }
  public T Divide(T arg1, T arg2)
  { return arg1 / arg2; }
}
```

Unfortunately, the preceding BasicMath class will not compile. While this might seem like a major restriction, you need to remember that generics are generic. Of course, the numerical data can work just fine with the binary operators of C#. However, for the sake of argument, if <T> were a custom class or structure type, the compiler could assume the class supports the +, -, *, and / operators. Ideally, C# would allow a generic type to be constrained by supported operators, as in this example:

```
// Illustrative code only!
public class BasicMath<T> where T : operator +, operator -,
  operator *, operator /
{
```

```
  public T Add(T arg1, T arg2)
  { return arg1 + arg2; }
  public T Subtract(T arg1, T arg2)
  { return arg1 - arg2; }
  public T Multiply(T arg1, T arg2)
  { return arg1 * arg2; }
  public T Divide(T arg1, T arg2)
  { return arg1 / arg2; }
}
```

Alas, operator constraints are not supported under the current version of C#. However, it is possible (albeit it requires a bit more work) to achieve the desired effect by defining an interface that supports these operators (C# interfaces can define operators!) and then specifying an interface constraint of the generic class. In any case, this wraps up this book's initial look at building custom generic types. In Chapter 10, you will pick up the topic of generics once again in the course of examining the .NET delegate type.

Summary

This chapter began by examining the nongeneric collection types of System.Collections and System.Collections.Specialized, including the various issues associated with many nongeneric containers, including a lack of type safety and the runtime overhead of boxing and unboxing operations. As mentioned, for these very reasons, modern-day .NET programs will typically make use of the generic collection classes found in System.Collections.Generic and System.Collections.ObjectModel.

As you have seen, a generic item allows you to specify placeholders (type parameters) that you specify at the time of object creation (or invocation, in the case of generic methods). While you will most often simply use the generic types provided in the .NET base class libraries, you will also be able to create your own generic types (and generic methods). When you do so, you have the option of specifying any number of constraints (using the where keyword) to increase the level of type safety and ensure that you perform operations on types of a *known quantity* that are guaranteed to exhibit certain basic capabilities.

As a final note, remember that generics are found in numerous locations within the .NET base class libraries. Here, we focused specifically on generic collections. However, as you work through the remainder of this book (and when you dive into the platform on your own terms), you will certainly find generic classes, structures, and delegates located in a given namespace. As well, be on the lookout for generic members of a nongeneric class!

Delegates, Events, and Lambda Expressions

Up to this point in the text, most of the applications you developed added various bits of code to Main(), which, in some way or another, sent requests *to* a given object. However, many applications require that an object be able to communicate *back to* the entity that created it using a callback mechanism. While callback mechanisms can be used in any application, they are especially critical for graphical user interfaces in that controls (such as a button) need to invoke external methods under the correct circumstances (when the button is clicked, when the mouse enters the button surface, and so forth).

Under the .NET platform, the *delegate* type is the preferred means of defining and responding to callbacks within applications. Essentially, the .NET delegate type is a type-safe object that "points to" a method or a list of methods that can be invoked at a later time. Unlike a traditional C++ function pointer, however, .NET delegates are classes that have built-in support for multicasting and asynchronous method invocation.

In this chapter, you will learn how to create and manipulate delegate types, then you'll investigate the C# event keyword, which streamlines the process of working with delegate types. Along the way, you will also examine several delegate- and event-centric language features of C#, including anonymous methods and method group conversions.

I wrap up this chapter by examining *lambda expressions*. Using the C# lambda operator (=>), you can specify a block of code statements (and the parameters to pass to those code statements) wherever a strongly typed delegate is required. As you will see, a lambda expression is little more than an anonymous method in disguise, and provides a simplified approach to working with delegates.

Understanding the .NET Delegate Type

Before formally defining .NET delegates, let's gain a bit of perspective. Historically, the Windows API made frequent use of C-style function pointers to create entities termed *callback functions,* or simply *callbacks*. Using callbacks, programmers were able to configure one function to report back to (call back) another function in the application. With this approach, Windows developers were able to handle button-clicking, mouse-moving, menu-selecting, and general bidirectional communications between two entities in memory.

The problem with standard C-style callback functions is that they represent little more than a raw address in memory. Ideally, you should be able to configure callbacks to include additional type-safe information such as the number of (and types of) parameters and the return type (if any) of the method pointed to. Sadly, this is not the case in traditional callback functions and, as you might suspect, they can therefore be a frequent source of bugs, hard crashes, and other runtime disasters. Nevertheless, callbacks are useful entities.

In the .NET Framework, callbacks are still possible, and this functionality is accomplished in a much safer and more object-oriented manner using *delegates*. In essence, a delegate is a type-safe object that points to another method (or possibly a list of methods) in the application, which can be invoked at a later time. Specifically, a delegate maintains three important pieces of information:

- The *address* of the method on which it makes calls
- The *parameters* (if any) of this method
- The *return type* (if any) of this method

■ **Note** .NET delegates can point to either static or instance methods.

After a delegate object has been created and given the necessary information, it may dynamically invoke the method(s) it points to at runtime. Every delegate in the .NET Framework (including your custom delegates) is automatically endowed with the ability to call its methods *synchronously* or *asynchronously*. This fact greatly simplifies programming tasks, given that you can call a method on a secondary thread of execution without manually creating and managing a Thread object.

■ **Note** We will examine the asynchronous behavior of delegate types during our investigation of threading and asynchronous calls in Chapter 19. In this chapter, we are concerned only with the synchronous aspects of the delegate type.

Defining a Delegate Type in C#

When you want to create a delegate type in C#, you use the delegate keyword. The name of your delegate type can be whatever you desire. However, you must define the delegate to match the signature of the method(s) it will point to. For example, the following delegate type (named BinaryOp) can point to any method that returns an integer and takes two integers as input parameters (you will build and use this delegate yourself a bit later in this chapter, so hang tight for now):

```
// This delegate can point to any method,
// taking two integers and returning an integer.
public delegate int BinaryOp(int x, int y);
```

When the C# compiler processes delegate types, it automatically generates a sealed class deriving from System.MulticastDelegate. This class (in conjunction with its base class, System.Delegate) provides the necessary infrastructure for the delegate to hold onto a list of methods to be invoked at a later time. For example, if you were to examine the BinaryOp delegate using ildasm.exe, you would find the class shown in Figure 10-1.

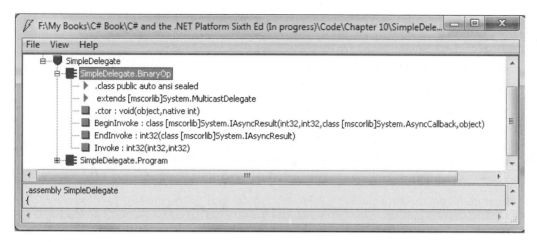

Figure 10-1. *The C# delegate keyword represents a sealed class deriving from* System.MulticastDelegate

As you can see, the compiler-generated BinaryOp class defines three public methods. Invoke() is perhaps the key method, as it is used to invoke each method maintained by the delegate object in a *synchronous* manner, meaning the caller must wait for the call to complete before continuing on its way. Strangely enough, the synchronous Invoke() method may not need to be called explicitly from your C# code. As you will see in just a bit, Invoke()is called behind the scenes when you make use of the appropriate C# syntax.

BeginInvoke() and EndInvoke() provide the ability to call the current method *asynchronously* on a separate thread of execution. If you have a background in multithreading, you know that one of the most common reasons developers create secondary threads of execution is to invoke methods that require time to complete. Although the .NET base class libraries supply several namespaces devoted to multithreaded and parallel programming, delegates provide this functionality out of the box.

Now, how exactly does the compiler know how to define the Invoke(), BeginInvoke(), and EndInvoke() methods? To understand the process, here is the crux of the compiler-generated BinaryOp class type (bold italic marks the items specified by the defined delegate type):

```
sealed class BinaryOp : System.MulticastDelegate
{
  public int Invoke(int x, int y);
  public IAsyncResult BeginInvoke(int x, int y,
    AsyncCallback cb, object state);
  public int EndInvoke(IAsyncResult result);
}
```

First, notice that the parameters and return type defined for the Invoke() method exactly match the definition of the BinaryOp delegate. The initial parameters to BeginInvoke() members (two integers, in our case) are also based on the BinaryOp delegate; however, BeginInvoke() will always provide two final parameters (of type AsyncCallback and object) that are used to facilitate asynchronous method invocations. Finally, the return type of EndInvoke() is identical to the original delegate declaration and will always take as a sole parameter an object implementing the IAsyncResult interface.

Let's see another example. Assume you have defined a delegate type that can point to any method returning a string and receiving three System.Boolean input parameters:

```
public delegate string MyDelegate(bool a, bool b, bool c);
```

This time, the compiler-generated class breaks down as follows:

```
sealed class MyDelegate : System.MulticastDelegate
{
  public string Invoke(bool a, bool b, bool c);
  public IAsyncResult BeginInvoke(bool a, bool b, bool c,
    AsyncCallback cb, object state);
  public string EndInvoke(IAsyncResult result);
}
```

Delegates can also "point to" methods that contain any number of out or ref parameters (as well as array parameters marked with the params keyword). For example, assume the following delegate type:

```
public delegate string MyOtherDelegate(out bool a, ref bool b, int c);
```

The signatures of the Invoke() and BeginInvoke() methods look as you would expect; however, check out the EndInvoke() method, which now includes the set of all out/ref arguments defined by the delegate type:

```
public sealed class MyOtherDelegate : System.MulticastDelegate
{
  public string Invoke(out bool a, ref bool b, int c);
  public IAsyncResult BeginInvoke(out bool a, ref bool b, int c,
    AsyncCallback cb, object state);
  public string EndInvoke(out bool a, ref bool b, IAsyncResult result);
}
```

To summarize, a C# delegate type definition results in a sealed class with three compiler-generated methods whose parameter and return types are based on the delegate's declaration. The following pseudo-code approximates the basic pattern:

```
// This is only pseudo-code!
public sealed class DelegateName : System.MulticastDelegate
{
  public delegateReturnValue Invoke(allDelegateInputRefAndOutParams);

  public IAsyncResult BeginInvoke(allDelegateInputRefAndOutParams,
    AsyncCallback cb, object state);

  public delegateReturnValue EndInvoke(allDelegateRefAndOutParams,
    IAsyncResult result);
}
```

The System.MulticastDelegate and System.Delegate Base Classes

So, when you build a type using the C# delegate keyword, you are indirectly declaring a class type that derives from System.MulticastDelegate. This class provides descendants with access to a list that contains the addresses of the methods maintained by the delegate object, as well as several additional methods (and a few overloaded operators) to interact with the invocation list. Here are some select members of System.MulticastDelegate:

```
public abstract class MulticastDelegate : Delegate
{
  // Returns the list of methods "pointed to."
```

```
public sealed override Delegate[] GetInvocationList();

// Overloaded operators.
public static bool operator ==(MulticastDelegate d1, MulticastDelegate d2);
public static bool operator !=(MulticastDelegate d1, MulticastDelegate d2);

// Used internally to manage the list of methods maintained by the delegate.
private IntPtr _invocationCount;
private object _invocationList;
}
```

System.MulticastDelegate obtains additional functionality from its parent class, System.Delegate. Here is a partial snapshot of the class definition:

```
public abstract class Delegate : ICloneable, ISerializable
{
    // Methods to interact with the list of functions.
    public static Delegate Combine(params Delegate[] delegates);
    public static Delegate Combine(Delegate a, Delegate b);
    public static Delegate Remove(Delegate source, Delegate value);
    public static Delegate RemoveAll(Delegate source, Delegate value);

    // Overloaded operators.
    public static bool operator ==(Delegate d1, Delegate d2);
    public static bool operator !=(Delegate d1, Delegate d2);

    // Properties that expose the delegate target.
    public MethodInfo Method { get; }
    public object Target { get; }
}
```

Now, understand that you can never directly derive from these base classes in your code (it is a compiler error to do so). Nevertheless, when you use the delegate keyword, you have indirectly created a class that "is-a" MulticastDelegate. Table 10-1 documents the core members common to all delegate types.

Table 10-1. Select Members of System.MultcastDelegate/System.Delegate

Member	Meaning in Life
Method	This property returns a System.Reflection.MethodInfo object that represents details of a static method maintained by the delegate.
Target	If the method to be called is defined at the object level (rather than a static method), Target returns an object that represents the method maintained by the delegate. If the value returned from Target equals null, the method to be called is a static member.
Combine()	This static method adds a method to the list maintained by the delegate. In C#, you trigger this method using the overloaded += operator as a shorthand notation.

Member	Meaning in Life
GetInvocationList()	This method returns an array of System.Delegate objects, each representing a particular method that may be invoked.
Remove() RemoveAll()	These static methods remove a method (or all methods) from the delegate's invocation list. In C#, the Remove() method can be called indirectly using the overloaded -= operator.

The Simplest Possible Delegate Example

To be sure, delegates can cause some confusion when encountered for the first time. Thus, to get the ball rolling, let's take a look at a very simple Console Application program (named SimpleDelegate) that makes use of the BinaryOp delegate type you've seen previously. Here is the complete code, with analysis to follow:

```
namespace SimpleDelegate
{
  // This delegate can point to any method,
  // taking two integers and returning an integer.
  public delegate int BinaryOp(int x, int y);

  // This class contains methods BinaryOp will
  // point to.
  public class SimpleMath
  {
    public static int Add(int x, int y)
    { return x + y; }
    public static int Subtract(int x, int y)
    { return x - y; }
  }

  class Program
  {
    static void Main(string[] args)
    {
      Console.WriteLine("***** Simple Delegate Example *****\n");

      // Create a BinaryOp delegate object that
      // "points to" SimpleMath.Add().
      BinaryOp b = new BinaryOp(SimpleMath.Add);

      // Invoke Add() method indirectly using delegate object.
      Console.WriteLine("10 + 10 is {0}", b(10, 10));
      Console.ReadLine();
    }
  }
}
```

Again, notice the format of the BinaryOp delegate type declaration; it specifies that BinaryOp delegate objects can point to any method taking two integers and returning an integer (the actual name of the method pointed to is irrelevant). Here, we have created a class named SimpleMath, which defines two static methods that match the pattern defined by the BinaryOp delegate.

When you want to insert the target method to a given delegate object, simply pass in the name of the method to the delegate's constructor:

```
// Create a BinaryOp delegate object that
// "points to" SimpleMath.Add().
BinaryOp b = new BinaryOp(SimpleMath.Add);
```

At this point, you are able to invoke the member pointed to using a syntax that looks like a direct function invocation:

```
// Invoke() is really called here!
Console.WriteLine("10 + 10 is {0}", b(10, 10));
```

Under the hood, the runtime actually calls the compiler-generated Invoke() method on your MulticastDelegate derived class. You can verify this for yourself if you open your assembly in ildasm.exe and examine the CIL code within the Main() method:

```
.method private hidebysig static void Main(string[] args) cil managed
{
...
  callvirt instance int32 SimpleDelegate.BinaryOp::Invoke(int32, int32)
}
```

C# does not require you to explicitly call Invoke() within your code base. Because BinaryOp can point to methods that take two arguments, the following code statement is also permissible:

```
Console.WriteLine("10 + 10 is {0}", b.Invoke(10, 10));
```

Recall that .NET delegates are *type safe*. Therefore, if you attempt to pass a delegate a method that does not match the pattern, you receive a compile-time error. To illustrate, assume the SimpleMath class now defines an additional method named SquareNumber(), which takes a single integer as input:

```
public class SimpleMath
{
...
  public static int SquareNumber(int a)
  { return a * a; }
}
```

Given that the BinaryOp delegate can point *only* to methods that take two integers and return an integer, the following code is illegal and will not compile:

```
// Compiler error! Method does not match delegate pattern!
BinaryOp b2 = new BinaryOp(SimpleMath.SquareNumber);
```

Investigating a Delegate Object

Let's spice up the current example by creating a static method (named DisplayDelegateInfo()) within the Program class. This method will print out the names of the method(s) maintained by a delegate object, as well as the name of the class defining the method. To do this, we will iterate over the System.Delegate array returned by GetInvocationList(), invoking each object's Target and Method properties:

```
static void DisplayDelegateInfo(Delegate delObj)
{
  // Print the names of each member in the
  // delegate's invocation list.
  foreach (Delegate d in delObj.GetInvocationList())
  {
    Console.WriteLine("Method Name: {0}", d.Method);
    Console.WriteLine("Type Name: {0}", d.Target);
  }
}
```

Assuming you have updated your Main() method to actually call this new helper method:

```
BinaryOp b = new BinaryOp(SimpleMath.Add);
DisplayDelegateInfo(b);
```

you would find the output shown next:

```
***** Simple Delegate Example *****

Method Name: Int32 Add(Int32, Int32)
Type Name:
10 + 10 is 20
```

Notice that the name of the target class (SimpleMath) is currently *not* displayed when calling the Target property. The reason has to do with the fact that our BinaryOp delegate is pointing to a *static method* and, therefore, there is no object to reference! However, if we update the Add() and Subtract() methods to be nonstatic (simply by deleting the static keywords), we could create an instance of the SimpleMath class and specify the methods to invoke using the object reference:

```
static void Main(string[] args)
{
  Console.WriteLine("***** Simple Delegate Example *****\n");

  // .NET delegates can also point to instance methods as well.
  SimpleMath m = new SimpleMath();
  BinaryOp b = new BinaryOp(m.Add);

  // Show information about this object.
  DisplayDelegateInfo(b);

  Console.WriteLine("10 + 10 is {0}", b(10, 10));
  Console.ReadLine();
}
```

In this case, we would find the output shown here:

```
***** Simple Delegate Example *****

Method Name: Int32 Add(Int32, Int32)
Type Name: SimpleDelegate.SimpleMath
```

```
10 + 10 is 20
```

■ **Note** The SimpleDelegate project is located under the Chapter 10 subdirectory.

Sending Object State Notifications Using Delegates

Clearly, the previous SimpleDelegate example was intended to be purely illustrative in nature, given that there would be no compelling reason to define a delegate simply to add two numbers. To provide a more realistic use of delegate types, let's use delegates to define a Car class that has the ability to inform external entities about its current engine state. To do so, we will take the following steps:

1. Define a new delegate type that will be used to send notifications to the caller.

2. Declare a member variable of this delegate in the Car class.

3. Create a helper function on the Car that allows the caller to specify the method to call back on.

4. Implement the Accelerate() method to invoke the delegate's invocation list under the correct circumstances.

To begin, create a new Console Application project named CarDelegate. Now, define a new Car class that looks initially like this:

```
public class Car
{
  // Internal state data.
  public int CurrentSpeed { get; set; }
  public int MaxSpeed { get; set; }
  public string PetName { get; set; }

  // Is the car alive or dead?
  private bool carIsDead;

  // Class constructors.
  public Car() { MaxSpeed = 100; }
  public Car(string name, int maxSp, int currSp)
  {
    CurrentSpeed = currSp;
    MaxSpeed = maxSp;
    PetName = name;
  }
}
```

Now, consider the following updates, which address the first three points:

```
public class Car
{
  ...
  // 1) Define a delegate type.
```

```
public delegate void CarEngineHandler(string msgForCaller);

// 2) Define a member variable of this delegate.
private CarEngineHandler listOfHandlers;

// 3) Add registration function for the caller.
public void RegisterWithCarEngine(CarEngineHandler methodToCall)
{
  listOfHandlers = methodToCall;
}
}
```

Notice in this example that we define the delegate types directly within the scope of the Car class, which is certainly not necessary, but does help enforce the idea that the delegate works naturally with this particular class. Our delegate type, CarEngineHandler, can point to any method taking a single string as input and void as a return value.

Next, note that we declare a private member variable of our delegate (named listOfHandlers), and a helper function (named RegisterWithCarEngine()) that allows the caller to assign a method to the delegate's invocation list.

■ **Note** Strictly speaking, we could have defined our delegate member variable as public, therefore avoiding the need to create additional registration methods. However, by defining the delegate member variable as private, we are enforcing encapsulation services and providing a more type-safe solution. You'll revisit the risk of public delegate member variables later in this chapter when you look at the C# event keyword.

At this point, we need to create the Accelerate() method. Recall, the point here is to allow a Car object to send engine-related messages to any subscribed listener. Here is the update:

```
// 4) Implement the Accelerate() method to invoke the delegate's
//    invocation list under the correct circumstances.
public void Accelerate(int delta)
{
  // If this car is "dead," send dead message.
  if (carIsDead)
  {
    if (listOfHandlers != null)
      listOfHandlers("Sorry, this car is dead...");
  }
  else
  {
    CurrentSpeed += delta;

    // Is this car "almost dead"?
    if (10 == (MaxSpeed - CurrentSpeed)
        && listOfHandlers != null)
    {
      listOfHandlers("Careful buddy! Gonna blow!");
```

```
  }

    if (CurrentSpeed >= MaxSpeed)
      carIsDead = true;
    else
      Console.WriteLine("CurrentSpeed = {0}", CurrentSpeed);
  }
}
```

Notice that before we invoke the methods maintained by the listOfHandlers member variable, we are checking it against a null value. The reason is that it will be the job of the caller to allocate these objects by calling the RegisterWithCarEngine() helper method. If the caller does not call this method and we attempt to invoke the delegate's invocation list, we will trigger a NullReferenceException at runtime. Now that we have the delegate infrastructure in place, observe the updates to the Program class:

```
class Program
{
  static void Main(string[] args)
  {
    Console.WriteLine("***** Delegates as event enablers *****\n");

    // First, make a Car object.
    Car c1 = new Car("SlugBug", 100, 10);

    // Now, tell the car which method to call
    // when it wants to send us messages.
    c1.RegisterWithCarEngine(new Car.CarEngineHandler(OnCarEngineEvent));

    // Speed up (this will trigger the events).
    Console.WriteLine("***** Speeding up *****");
    for (int i = 0; i < 6; i++)
      c1.Accelerate(20);
    Console.ReadLine();
  }

  // This is the target for incoming events.
  public static void OnCarEngineEvent(string msg)
  {
    Console.WriteLine("\n***** Message From Car Object *****");
    Console.WriteLine("=> {0}", msg);
    Console.WriteLine("*********************************\n");
  }
}
```

The Main() method begins by simply making a new Car object. Since we are interested in hearing about the engine events, our next step is to call our custom registration function, RegisterWithCarEngine(). Recall that this method expects to be passed an instance of the nested CarEngineHandler delegate, and as with any delegate, we specify a "method to point to" as a constructor parameter. The trick in this example is that the method in question is located back in the Program class! Again, notice that the OnCarEngineEvent() method is a dead-on match to the related delegate in that it takes a string as input and returns void. Consider the output of the current example:

```
***** Delegates as event enablers *****

***** Speeding up *****
CurrentSpeed = 30
CurrentSpeed = 50
CurrentSpeed = 70

***** Message From Car Object *****
=> Careful buddy! Gonna blow!
********************************

CurrentSpeed = 90

***** Message From Car Object *****
=> Sorry, this car is dead...
********************************
```

Enabling Multicasting

Recall that .NET delegates have the built-in ability to *multicast*. In other words, a delegate object can maintain a list of methods to call, rather than just a single method. When you want to add multiple methods to a delegate object, you simply make use of the overloaded += operator, rather than a direct assignment. To enable multicasting on the Car class, we could update the RegisterWithCarEngine()method, like so:

```
public class Car
{
  // Now with multicasting support!
  // Note we are now using the += operator, not
  // the assignment operator (=).
  public void RegisterWithCarEngine(CarEngineHandler methodToCall)
  {
    listOfHandlers += methodToCall;
  }
...
}
```

When you use the += operator on a delegate object, the compiler resolves this to a call on the static Delegate.Combine() method. In fact, you could call Delegate.Combine() directly; however, the += operator offers a simpler alternative. There is no need to modify your current RegisterWithCarEngine() method, but here is an example if using Delegate.Combine() rather than the += operator:

```
public void RegisterWithCarEngine( CarEngineHandler methodToCall )
{
  if (listOfHandlers == null)
    listOfHandlers = methodToCall;
  else
    Delegate.Combine(listOfHandlers, methodToCall);
}
```

In any case, the caller can now register multiple targets for the same callback notification. Here, our second handler prints the incoming message in uppercase, just for display purposes:

```
class Program
{
  static void Main(string[] args)
  {
    Console.WriteLine("***** Delegates as event enablers *****\n");

    // First, make a Car object.
    Car c1 = new Car("SlugBug", 100, 10);

    // Register multiple targets for the notifications.
    c1.RegisterWithCarEngine(new Car.CarEngineHandler(OnCarEngineEvent));
    c1.RegisterWithCarEngine(new Car.CarEngineHandler(OnCarEngineEvent2));

    // Speed up (this will trigger the events).
    Console.WriteLine("***** Speeding up *****");
    for (int i = 0; i < 6; i++)
      c1.Accelerate(20);
    Console.ReadLine();
  }

  // We now have TWO methods that will be called by the Car
  // when sending notifications.
  public static void OnCarEngineEvent(string msg)
  {
    Console.WriteLine("\n***** Message From Car Object *****");
    Console.WriteLine("=> {0}", msg);
    Console.WriteLine("********************************\n");
  }

  public static void OnCarEngineEvent2(string msg)
  {
    Console.WriteLine("=> {0}", msg.ToUpper());
  }
}
```

Removing Targets from a Delegate's Invocation List

The Delegate class also defines a static Remove() method that allows a caller to dynamically remove a method from a delegate object's invocation list. This makes it simple to allow the caller to "unsubscribe" from a given notification at runtime. While you could call Delegate.Remove() directly in code, C# developers can use the -= operator as a convenient shorthand notation. Let's add a new method to the Car class that allows a caller to remove a method from the invocation list:

```
public class Car
{
...
  public void UnRegisterWithCarEngine(CarEngineHandler methodToCall)
  {
    listOfHandlers -= methodToCall;
```

```
    }
}
```

With the current updates to the Car class, we could stop receiving the engine notification on the second handler by updating Main() as follows:

```
static void Main(string[] args)
{
  Console.WriteLine("***** Delegates as event enablers *****\n");

  // First, make a Car object.
  Car c1 = new Car("SlugBug", 100, 10);
  c1.RegisterWithCarEngine(new Car.CarEngineHandler(OnCarEngineEvent));

  // This time, hold onto the delegate object,
  // so we can unregister later.
  Car.CarEngineHandler handler2 = new Car.CarEngineHandler(OnCarEngineEvent2);
  c1.RegisterWithCarEngine(handler2);

  // Speed up (this will trigger the events).
  Console.WriteLine("***** Speeding up *****");
  for (int i = 0; i < 6; i++)
    c1.Accelerate(20);

  // Unregister from the second handler.
  c1.UnRegisterWithCarEngine(handler2);

  // We won't see the "uppercase" message anymore!
  Console.WriteLine("***** Speeding up *****");
  for (int i = 0; i < 6; i++)
    c1.Accelerate(20);

  Console.ReadLine();
}
```

One difference in Main() is that this time we are creating a Car.CarEngineHandler object and storing it in a local variable so we can use this object to unregister with the notification later on. Thus, the second time we speed up the Car object, we no longer see the uppercase version of the incoming message data, as we have removed this target from the delegate's invocation list.

■ **Source Code** The CarDelegate project is located under the Chapter 10 subdirectory.

Method Group Conversion Syntax

In the previous CarDelegate example, we explicitly created instances of the Car.CarEngineHandler delegate object in order to register and unregister with the engine notifications:

```
static void Main(string[] args)
{
  Console.WriteLine("***** Delegates as event enablers *****\n");

  Car c1 = new Car("SlugBug", 100, 10);
  c1.RegisterWithCarEngine(new Car.CarEngineHandler(OnCarEngineEvent));

  Car.CarEngineHandler handler2 =
    new Car.CarEngineHandler(OnCarEngineEvent2);
  c1.RegisterWithCarEngine(handler2);
...
}
```

To be sure, if you need to call any of the inherited members of MulticastDelegate or Delegate, manually creating a delegate variable is the most straightforward way of doing so. However, in most cases, you don't really need to hang onto the delegate object. Rather, you typically only need to use the delegate object in order to pass in the method name as a constructor parameter.

As a simplification, C# provides a shortcut termed *method group conversion*. This feature allows you to supply a direct method name, rather than a delegate object, when calling methods that take delegates as arguments.

■ **Note** As you will see later in this chapter, you can also use method group conversion syntax to simplify how you register with a C# event.

To illustrate, create a new Console Application named CarDelegateMethodGroupConversion and insert the file containing the Car class you defined in the CarDelegate project (and update the namespace name in the Car.cs file to match your new namespace name). Now, consider the following Program class, which uses method group conversion to register and unregister from the engine notifications:

```
class Program
{
  static void Main(string[] args)
  {
    Console.WriteLine("***** Method Group Conversion *****\n");
    Car c1 = new Car();

    // Register the simple method name.
    c1.RegisterWithCarEngine(CallMeHere);

    Console.WriteLine("***** Speeding up *****");
    for (int i = 0; i < 6; i++)
      c1.Accelerate(20);

    // Unregister the simple method name.
    c1.UnRegisterWithCarEngine(CallMeHere);
```

```
      // No more notifications!
      for (int i = 0; i < 6; i++)
        c1.Accelerate(20);

      Console.ReadLine();
    }

    static void CallMeHere(string msg)
    {
      Console.WriteLine("=> Message from Car: {0}", msg);
    }
  }
}
```

Notice that we are not directly allocating the associated delegate object, but rather simply specifying a method that matches the delegate's expected signature (a method returning void and taking a single string, in this case). Understand that the C# compiler is still ensuring type safety. Thus, if the CallMeHere() method did not take a string and return void, we would be issued a compiler error.

■ **Source Code** The CarDelegateMethodGroupConversion project is located under the Chapter 10 subdirectory.

Understanding Generic Delegates

In the previous chapter, I mentioned that C# allows you to define generic delegate types. For example, assume you want to define a delegate type that can call any method returning void and receiving a single parameter. If the argument in question may differ, you could model this using a type parameter. To illustrate, consider the following code within a new Console Application named GenericDelegate:

```
namespace GenericDelegate
{
  // This generic delegate can call any method
  // returning void and taking a single type parameter.
  public delegate void MyGenericDelegate<T>(T arg);

  class Program
  {
    static void Main(string[] args)
    {
      Console.WriteLine("***** Generic Delegates *****\n");

      // Register targets.
      MyGenericDelegate<string> strTarget =
        new MyGenericDelegate<string>(StringTarget);
      strTarget("Some string data");

      MyGenericDelegate<int> intTarget =
        new MyGenericDelegate<int>(IntTarget);
      intTarget(9);
      Console.ReadLine();
```

```
  }

  static void StringTarget(string arg)
  {
    Console.WriteLine("arg in uppercase is: {0}", arg.ToUpper());
  }

  static void IntTarget(int arg)
  {
    Console.WriteLine("++arg is: {0}", ++arg);
  }
 }
}
```

Notice that MyGenericDelegate<T> defines a single type parameter that represents the argument to pass to the delegate target. When creating an instance of this type, you are required to specify the value of the type parameter, as well as the name of the method the delegate will invoke. Thus, if you specified a string type, you send a string value to the target method:

```
// Create an instance of MyGenericDelegate<T>
// with string as the type parameter.
MyGenericDelegate<string> strTarget =
  new MyGenericDelegate<string>(StringTarget);
strTarget("Some string data");
```

Given the format of the strTarget object, the StringTarget() method must now take a single string as a parameter:

```
static void StringTarget(string arg)
{
  Console.WriteLine("arg in uppercase is: {0}", arg.ToUpper());
}
```

■ **Source Code** The GenericDelegate project is located under the Chapter 10 subdirectory.

The Generic Action<> and Func<> Delegates

Over the course of this chapter, you have seen that when you want to use delegates to enable callbacks in your applications, you typically follow the steps shown here:

- Define a custom delegate that matches the format of the method being pointed to.

- Create an instance of your custom delegate, passing in a method name as a constructor argument.

- Invoke the method indirectly, via a call to Invoke() on the delegate object.

When you take this approach, you typically end up with a number of custom delegates that might never be used beyond the current task at hand (e.g., MyGenericDelegate<T>, CarEngineHandler, and so forth). While it may certainly be the case that you do indeed need to have a custom, uniquely named delegate for your project, other times the exact *name* of the delegate is irrelevant. In many cases, you simply want "some delegate" that takes a set of arguments and possibly has a return value other than void. In these cases, you can make use of the framework's built-in Action<> and Func<> delegates. To illustrate their usefulness, create a new Console Application project type named ActionAndFuncDelegates.

The generic Action<> delegate is defined in the System namespaces of mscorlib.dll and System.Core.dll assemblies. You can use this generic delegate to "point to" a method that takes up to *16 arguments* (that ought to be enough!) and returns void. Now recall, because Action<> is a generic delegate, you will need to specify the underlying types of each parameter as well.

Update your Program class to define a new static method that takes three (or so) unique parameters, for example:

```
// This is a target for the Action<> delegate.
static void DisplayMessage(string msg, ConsoleColor txtColor, int printCount)
{
  // Set color of console text.
  ConsoleColor previous = Console.ForegroundColor;
  Console.ForegroundColor = txtColor;

  for (int i = 0; i < printCount; i++)
  {
    Console.WriteLine(msg);
  }

  // Restore color.
  Console.ForegroundColor = previous;
}
```

Now, rather than building a custom delegate manually to pass the program's flow to the DisplayMessage() method, we can use the out-of-the-box Action<> delegate, as so:

```
static void Main(string[] args)
{
  Console.WriteLine("***** Fun with Action and Func *****");

  // Use the Action<> delegate to point to DisplayMessage.
  Action<string, ConsoleColor, int> actionTarget =
    new Action<string, ConsoleColor, int>(DisplayMessage);
  actionTarget("Action Message!", ConsoleColor.Yellow, 5);

  Console.ReadLine();
}
```

As you can see, using the Action<> delegate saves you the bother of defining a custom delegate. However, recall that the Action<> delegate can point only to methods that take a void return value. If you want to point to a method that does have a return value (and don't want to bother writing the custom delegate yourself), you can use Func<>.

The generic Func<> delegate can point to methods that (like Action<>) take up to 16 parameters and a custom return value. To illustrate, add the following new method to the Program class:

```
// Target for the Func<> delegate.
static int Add(int x, int y)
{
```

```
        return x + y;
}
```

Earlier in the chapter, I had you build a custom `BinaryOp` delegate to "point to" addition and subtraction methods. However, we can simplify our efforts using a version of `Func<>` that takes a total of three type parameters. Be aware that the *final* type parameter of `Func<>` is *always* the return value of the method. Just to solidify that point, assume the `Program` class also defines the following method:

```
static string SumToString(int x, int y)
{
  return (x + y).ToString();
}
```

Now, our `Main()` method can call each of these methods, as so:

```
Func<int, int, int> funcTarget = new Func<int, int, int>(Add);
int result = funcTarget.Invoke(40, 40);
Console.WriteLine("40 + 40 = {0}", result);

Func<int, int, string> funcTarget2 = new Func<int, int, string>(SumToString);
string sum = funcTarget2(90, 300);
Console.WriteLine(sum);
```

So, given that `Action<>` and `Func<>` can save you the step of manually defining a custom delegate, you might be wondering if you should use them all the time. The answer, like so many aspects of programming is "it depends." In many cases, `Action<>` and `Func<>` will be the preferred course of action (no pun intended). However, if you need a delegate that has a custom name that you feel helps better capture your problem domain, building a custom delegate is as simple as a single code statement. You'll see both approaches as you work over the remainder of this text.

■ **Note** Many important .NET APIs make considerable use of `Action<>` and `Func<>` delegates, including the parallel programming framework and LINQ (among others).

That wraps up our initial look at the .NET delegate type. We will look at some additional details of working with delegates at the conclusion of this chapter and again in Chapter 19 during our examination of multithreading and asynchronous calls. Next, let's move on to the related topic of the C# event keyword.

■ **Source Code** The ActionAndFuncDelegates project is located under the Chapter 10 subdirectory.

Understanding C# Events

Delegates are fairly interesting constructs in that they enable objects in memory to engage in a two-way conversation. However, working with delegates in the raw can entail the creation of some boilerplate code (defining the delegate, declaring necessary member variables, and creating custom registration and unregistration methods to preserve encapsulation, etc.).

Moreover, when you use delegates in the raw as your application's callback mechanism, if you do not define a class's delegate member variables as private, the caller will have direct access to the delegate objects. In this case, the caller could reassign the variable to a new delegate object (effectively deleting the current list of functions to call) and, worse yet, the caller would be able to directly invoke the delegate's invocation list. To illustrate this problem, consider the following reworking (and simplification) of the Car class from the previous CarDelegate example:

```
public class Car
{
  public delegate void CarEngineHandler(string msgForCaller);

  // Now a public member!
  public CarEngineHandler listOfHandlers;

  // Just fire out the Exploded notification.
  public void Accelerate(int delta)
  {
    if (listOfHandlers != null)
      listOfHandlers("Sorry, this car is dead...");
  }
}
```

Notice that we no longer have private delegate member variables encapsulated with custom registration methods. Because these members are indeed public, the caller can directly access the listOfHandlers member variable and reassign this type to new CarEngineHandler objects and invoke the delegate whenever it so chooses:

```
class Program
{
  static void Main(string[] args)
  {
    Console.WriteLine("***** Agh! No Encapsulation! *****\n");
    // Make a Car.
    Car myCar = new Car();
    // We have direct access to the delegate!
    myCar.listOfHandlers = new Car.CarEngineHandler(CallWhenExploded);
    myCar.Accelerate(10);

    // We can now assign to a whole new object...
    // confusing at best.
    myCar.listOfHandlers = new Car.CarEngineHandler(CallHereToo);
    myCar.Accelerate(10);

    // The caller can also directly invoke the delegate!
    myCar.listOfHandlers.Invoke("hee, hee, hee...");
    Console.ReadLine();
```

```
    }

    static void CallWhenExploded(string msg)
    { Console.WriteLine(msg); }

    static void CallHereToo(string msg)
    { Console.WriteLine(msg); }
}
```

Exposing public delegate members breaks encapsulation, which not only can lead to code that is hard to maintain (and debug), but could also open your application to possible security risks! Here is the output of the current example:

```
***** Agh! No Encapsulation! *****

Sorry, this car is dead...
Sorry, this car is dead...
hee, hee, hee...
```

Obviously, you would not want to give other applications the power to change what a delegate is pointing to or to invoke the members without your permission. Given this, it is common practice to declare private delegate member variables.

■ **Source Code** The PublicDelegateProblem project is located under the Chapter 10 subdirectory.

The C# event Keyword

As a shortcut, so you don't have to build custom methods to add or remove methods to a delegate's invocation list, C# provides the event keyword. When the compiler processes the event keyword, you are automatically provided with registration and unregistration methods, as well as any necessary member variables for your delegate types. These delegate member variables are *always* declared private and, therefore, they are not directly exposed from the object firing the event. To be sure, the event keyword can be used to simplify how a custom class sends out notifications to external objects.

Defining an event is a two-step process. First, you need to define a delegate type that will hold the list of methods to be called when the event is fired. Next, you declare an event (using the C# event keyword) in terms of the related delegate type.

To illustrate the event keyword, create a new Console Application named CarEvents. In this iteration of the Car class, we will define two events named AboutToBlow and Exploded. These events are associated to a single delegate type named CarEngineHandler. Here are the initial updates to the Car class:

```
public class Car
{
    // This delegate works in conjunction with the
    // Car's events.
    public delegate void CarEngineHandler(string msg);
```

379

```
// This car can send these events.
public event CarEngineHandler Exploded;
public event CarEngineHandler AboutToBlow;
...
}
```

Sending an event to the caller is as simple as specifying the event by name, along with any required parameters as defined by the associated delegate. To ensure that the caller has indeed registered with the event, you will want to check the event against a null value before invoking the delegate's method set. With these points in mind, here is the new iteration of the Car's Accelerate() method:

```
public void Accelerate(int delta)
{
  // If the car is dead, fire Exploded event.
  if (carIsDead)
  {
    if (Exploded != null)
      Exploded("Sorry, this car is dead...");
  }
  else
  {
    CurrentSpeed += delta;

    // Almost dead?
    if (10 == MaxSpeed - CurrentSpeed
      && AboutToBlow != null)
    {
      AboutToBlow("Careful buddy!  Gonna blow!");
    }

    // Still OK!
    if (CurrentSpeed >= MaxSpeed)
      carIsDead = true;
    else
      Console.WriteLine("CurrentSpeed = {0}", CurrentSpeed);
  }
}
```

With this, you have configured the car to send two custom events without having to define custom registration functions or declare delegate member variables. You will see the usage of this new automobile in just a moment, but first, let's check the event architecture in a bit more detail.

Events Under the Hood

When the compiler processes the C# event keyword, it generates two hidden methods, one having an add_ prefix, the other having a remove_ prefix. Each prefix is followed by the name of the C# event. For example, the Exploded event results in two hidden methods named add_Exploded() and remove_Exploded(). If you were to check out the CIL instructions behind add_AboutToBlow(), you would find a call to the Delegate.Combine() method. Consider the partial CIL code:

```
.method public hidebysig specialname instance void
add_AboutToBlow(class CarEvents.Car/CarEngineHandler 'value') cil managed
{
...
  call class [mscorlib]System.Delegate
  [mscorlib]System.Delegate::Combine(
    class [mscorlib]System.Delegate, class [mscorlib]System.Delegate)
...
}
```

As you would expect, remove_AboutToBlow() will call Delegate.Remove() on your behalf:

```
.method public hidebysig specialname instance void
  remove_AboutToBlow(class CarEvents.Car/CarEngineHandler 'value')
  cil managed
{
...
  call class [mscorlib]System.Delegate
    [mscorlib]System.Delegate::Remove(
      class [mscorlib]System.Delegate, class [mscorlib]System.Delegate)
...
}
```

Finally, the CIL code representing the event itself makes use of the .addon and .removeon directives to map the names of the correct add_XXX() and remove_XXX() methods to invoke:

```
.event CarEvents.Car/EngineHandler AboutToBlow
{
  .addon instance void CarEvents.Car::add_AboutToBlow
    (class CarEvents.Car/CarEngineHandler)

  .removeon instance void CarEvents.Car::remove_AboutToBlow
    (class CarEvents.Car/CarEngineHandler)
}
```

Now that you understand how to build a class that can send C# events (and are aware that events are little more than a typing time saver), the next big question is how to listen to the incoming events on the caller's side.

Listening to Incoming Events

C# events also simplify the act of registering the caller-side event handlers. Rather than having to specify custom helper methods, the caller simply makes use of the += and -= operators directly (which triggers the correct add_XXX() or remove_XXX() method in the background). When you want to register with an event, follow the pattern shown here:

```
// NameOfObject.NameOfEvent += new RelatedDelegate(functionToCall);
//
Car.CarEngineHandler d = new Car.CarEngineHandler(CarExplodedEventHandler);
myCar.Exploded += d;
```

When you want to detach from a source of events, use the -= operator, using the following pattern:

```
// NameOfObject.NameOfEvent -= new RelatedDelegate(functionToCall);
//
myCar.Exploded -= d;
```

Given these very predictable patterns, here is the refactored Main() method, now using the C# event registration syntax:

```
class Program
{
  static void Main(string[] args)
  {
    Console.WriteLine("***** Fun with Events *****\n");
    Car c1 = new Car("SlugBug", 100, 10);

    // Register event handlers.
    c1.AboutToBlow += new Car.CarEngineHandler(CarIsAlmostDoomed);
    c1.AboutToBlow += new Car.CarEngineHandler(CarAboutToBlow);

    Car.CarEngineHandler d = new Car.CarEngineHandler(CarExploded);
    c1.Exploded += d;

    Console.WriteLine("***** Speeding up *****");
    for (int i = 0; i < 6; i++)
      c1.Accelerate(20);

    // Remove CarExploded method
    // from invocation list.
    c1.Exploded -= d;

    Console.WriteLine("\n***** Speeding up *****");
    for (int i = 0; i < 6; i++)
      c1.Accelerate(20);
    Console.ReadLine();
  }

  public static void CarAboutToBlow(string msg)
  { Console.WriteLine(msg); }

  public static void CarIsAlmostDoomed(string msg)
  { Console.WriteLine("=> Critical Message from Car: {0}", msg); }

  public static void CarExploded(string msg)
  { Console.WriteLine(msg); }
}
```

To even further simplify event registration, you can use method group conversion. Consider the following iteration of Main():

```
static void Main(string[] args)
{
  Console.WriteLine("***** Fun with Events *****\n");
  Car c1 = new Car("SlugBug", 100, 10);
```

```
// Register event handlers.
c1.AboutToBlow += CarIsAlmostDoomed;
c1.AboutToBlow += CarAboutToBlow;
c1.Exploded += CarExploded;

Console.WriteLine("***** Speeding up *****");
for (int i = 0; i < 6; i++)
  c1.Accelerate(20);

c1.Exploded -= CarExploded;

Console.WriteLine("\n***** Speeding up *****");
for (int i = 0; i < 6; i++)
  c1.Accelerate(20);

Console.ReadLine();
}
```

Simplifying Event Registration Using Visual Studio

Visual Studio offers assistance with the process of registering event handlers. When you apply the +=
syntax during event registration, you will find an IntelliSense window displayed, inviting you to hit the
Tab key to autocomplete the associated delegate instance (see Figure 10-2), which is captured using
method group conversion syntax.

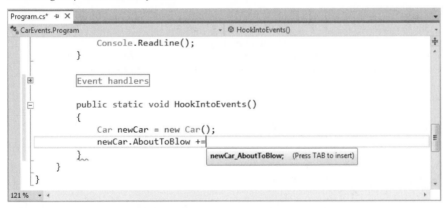

Figure 10-2. Delegate selection IntelliSense

After you hit the Tab key, you are invited to enter the name of the event handler to be generated (or
simply accept the default name), as shown in Figure 10-3.

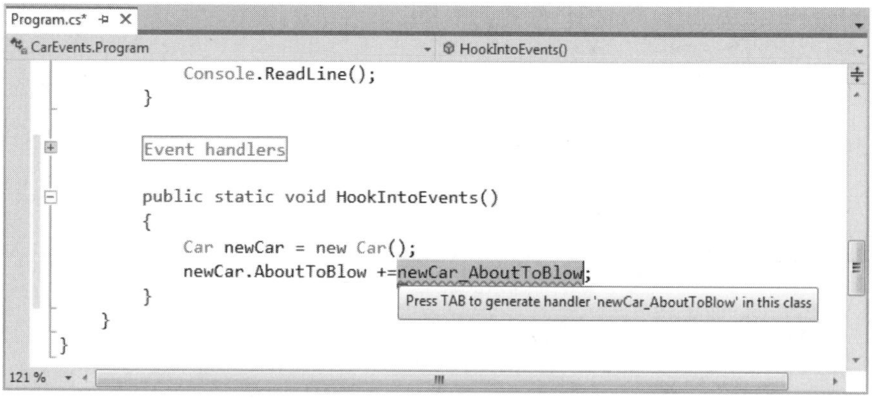

Figure 10-3. Delegate target format IntelliSense

When you hit the Tab key again, you will be provided with stub code in the correct format of the delegate target (note that this method has been declared static due to the fact that the event was registered within a static method):

```
static void newCar_AboutToBlow(string msg)
{
  // Delete the following line and add your code!
  throw new NotImplementedException();
}
```

IntelliSense is available to all .NET events in the base class libraries. This IDE feature is a massive time saver, given that it saves you from having to search the .NET help system to figure out both the correct delegate to use with a particular event and the format of the delegate target method.

■ **Source Code** The CarEvents project is located under the Chapter 10 subdirectory.

Creating Custom Event Arguments

Truth be told, there is one final enhancement we could make to the current iteration of the Car class that mirrors Microsoft's recommended event pattern. As you begin to explore the events sent by a given type in the base class libraries, you will find that the first parameter of the underlying delegate is a System.Object, while the second parameter is a descendant of System.EventArgs.

The System.Object argument represents a reference to the object that sent the event (such as the Car), while the second parameter represents information regarding the event at hand. The System.EventArgs base class represents an event that is not sending any custom information:

```
public class EventArgs
{
  public static readonly EventArgs Empty;
  public EventArgs();
}
```

For simple events, you can pass an instance of EventArgs directly. However, when you want to pass along custom data, you should build a suitable class deriving from EventArgs. For our example, assume you have a class named CarEventArgs, which maintains a string representing the message sent to the receiver:

```
public class CarEventArgs : EventArgs
{
  public readonly string msg;
  public CarEventArgs(string message)
  {
    msg = message;
  }
}
```

With this, you would now update the CarEngineHandler delegate type definition as follows (the events would be unchanged):

```
public class Car
{
  public delegate void CarEngineHandler(object sender, CarEventArgs e);
...
}
```

Here, when firing the events from within the Accelerate() method, you would now need to supply a reference to the current Car (via the this keyword) and an instance of the CarEventArgs type. For example, consider the following partial update:

```
public void Accelerate(int delta)
{
  // If the car is dead, fire Exploded event.
  if (carIsDead)
  {
    if (Exploded != null)
      Exploded(this, new CarEventArgs("Sorry, this car is dead..."));
  }
...
}
```

On the caller's side, all you would need to do is update your event handlers to receive the incoming parameters and obtain the message via the read-only field. For example:

```
public static void CarAboutToBlow(object sender, CarEventArgs e)
{
  Console.WriteLine("{0} says: {1}", sender, e.msg);
}
```

If the receiver wants to interact with the object that sent the event, you can explicitly cast the System.Object. From this reference, you can make use of any public member of the object that sent the event notification:

```
public static void CarAboutToBlow(object sender, CarEventArgs e)
{
  // Just to be safe, perform a
  // runtime check before casting.
  if (sender is Car)
```

```
  {
    Car c = (Car)sender;
    Console.WriteLine("Critical Message from {0}: {1}", c.PetName, e.msg);
  }
}
```

■ **Source Code** The PrimAndProperCarEvents project is located under the Chapter 10 subdirectory.

The Generic EventHandler<T> Delegate

Given that so many custom delegates take an object as the first parameter and an EventArgs descendant as the second, you could further streamline the previous example by using the generic EventHandler<T> type, where T is your custom EventArgs type. Consider the following update to the Car type (notice how we no longer need to define a custom delegate type at all):

```
public class Car
{
  public event EventHandler<CarEventArgs> Exploded;
  public event EventHandler<CarEventArgs> AboutToBlow;
...
}
```

The Main() method could then use EventHandler<CarEventArgs> anywhere we previously specified CarEventHandler (or, once again, use method group conversion):

```
static void Main(string[] args)
{
  Console.WriteLine("***** Prim and Proper Events *****\n");

  // Make a car as usual.
  Car c1 = new Car("SlugBug", 100, 10);

  // Register event handlers.
  c1.AboutToBlow += CarIsAlmostDoomed;
  c1.AboutToBlow += CarAboutToBlow;

  EventHandler<CarEventArgs> d = new EventHandler<CarEventArgs>(CarExploded);
  c1.Exploded += d;
...
}
```

Great! At this point, you have seen the core aspects of working with delegates and events in the C# language. While you could use this information for just about all of your callback needs, we will wrap up this chapter with a look at some final simplifications, specifically anonymous methods and lambda expressions.

Understanding C# Anonymous Methods

As you have seen, when a caller wants to listen to incoming events, it must define a custom method in a class (or structure) that matches the signature of the associated delegate. For example:

```
class Program
{
  static void Main(string[] args)
  {
    SomeType t = new SomeType();

    // Assume "SomeDelegate" can point to methods taking no
    // args and returning void.
    t.SomeEvent += new SomeDelegate(MyEventHandler);
  }

  // Typically only called by the SomeDelegate object.
  public static void MyEventHandler()
  {
    // Do something when event is fired.
  }
}
```

When you think about it, however, methods such as MyEventHandler() are seldom intended to be called by any part of the program other than the invoking delegate. As far as productivity is concerned, it is a bit of a bother (though in no way a show-stopper) to manually define a separate method to be called by the delegate object.

To address this point, it is possible to associate an event directly to a block of code statements at the time of event registration. Formally, such code is termed an *anonymous method*. To illustrate the syntax, check out the following Main() method, which handles the events sent from the Car class using anonymous methods, rather than specifically named event handlers:

```
class Program
{
  static void Main(string[] args)
  {
    Console.WriteLine("***** Anonymous Methods *****\n");
    Car c1 = new Car("SlugBug", 100, 10);

    // Register event handlers as anonymous methods.
    c1.AboutToBlow += delegate
    {
      Console.WriteLine("Eek! Going too fast!");
    };

    c1.AboutToBlow += delegate(object sender, CarEventArgs e)
    {
```

```
      Console.WriteLine("Message from Car: {0}", e.msg);
    };

    c1.Exploded += delegate(object sender, CarEventArgs e)
    {
      Console.WriteLine("Fatal Message from Car: {0}", e.msg);
    };

    // This will eventually trigger the events.
    for (int i = 0; i < 6; i++)
      c1.Accelerate(20);

    Console.ReadLine();
  }
}
```

■ **Note** The final curly bracket of an anonymous method must be terminated by a semicolon. If you fail to do so, you are issued a compilation error.

Again, notice that the Program type no longer defines specific static event handlers such as CarAboutToBlow() or CarExploded(). Rather, the unnamed (a.k.a. anonymous) methods are defined inline at the time the caller is handling the event using the += syntax. The basic syntax of an anonymous method matches the following pseudo-code:

```
class Program
{
  static void Main(string[] args)
  {
    SomeType t = new SomeType();
    t.SomeEvent += delegate (optionallySpecifiedDelegateArgs)
    { /* statements */ };
  }
}
```

When handling the first AboutToBlow event within the previous Main() method, notice that you are not specifying the arguments passed from the delegate:

```
c1.AboutToBlow += delegate
{
  Console.WriteLine("Eek! Going too fast!");
};
```

Strictly speaking, you are not required to receive the incoming arguments sent by a specific event. However, if you want to make use of the possible incoming arguments, you will need to specify the parameters prototyped by the delegate type (as shown in the second handling of the AboutToBlow and Exploded events). For example:

```
c1.AboutToBlow += delegate(object sender, CarEventArgs e)
{
  Console.WriteLine("Critical Message from Car: {0}", e.msg);
};
```

Accessing Local Variables

Anonymous methods are interesting in that they are able to access the local variables of the method that defines them. Formally speaking, such variables are termed *outer variables* of the anonymous method. A few important points about the interaction between an anonymous method scope and the scope of the defining method should be mentioned:

- An anonymous method cannot access ref or out parameters of the defining method.

- An anonymous method cannot have a local variable with the same name as a local variable in the outer method.

- An anonymous method can access instance variables (or static variables, as appropriate) in the outer class scope.

- An anonymous method can declare local variables with the same name as outer class member variables (the local variables have a distinct scope and hide the outer class member variables).

Assume our Main() method defined a local integer named aboutToBlowCounter. Within the anonymous methods that handle the AboutToBlow event, we will increment this counter by one and print out the tally before Main() completes:

```
static void Main(string[] args)
{
  Console.WriteLine("***** Anonymous Methods *****\n");
  int aboutToBlowCounter = 0;

  // Make a car as usual.
  Car c1 = new Car("SlugBug", 100, 10);

  // Register event handlers as anonymous methods.
  c1.AboutToBlow += delegate
  {
    aboutToBlowCounter++;
    Console.WriteLine("Eek!  Going too fast!");
  };

  c1.AboutToBlow += delegate(object sender, CarEventArgs e)
  {
    aboutToBlowCounter++;
    Console.WriteLine("Critical Message from Car: {0}", e.msg);
  };

...
```

```
    Console.WriteLine("AboutToBlow event was fired {0} times.",
      aboutToBlowCounter);
    Console.ReadLine();
}
```

After you run this updated `Main()` method, you will find the final `Console.WriteLine()` reports the `AboutToBlow` event was fired twice.

■ **Source Code** The AnonymousMethods project is located under the Chapter 10 subdirectory.

Understanding Lambda Expressions

To conclude our look at the .NET event architecture, we will examine C# *lambda expressions*. As just explained, C# supports the ability to handle events "inline" by assigning a block of code statements directly to an event using anonymous methods, rather than building a stand-alone method to be called by the underlying delegate. Lambda expressions are nothing more than a very concise way to author anonymous methods and ultimately simplify how we work with the .NET delegate type.

To set the stage for our examination of lambda expressions, create a new Console Application named SimpleLambdaExpressions. To begin, consider the `FindAll()` method of the generic `List<T>` class. This method can be called when you need to extract out a subset of items from the collection, and is prototyped like so:

```
// Method of the System.Collections.Generic.List<T> class.
public List<T> FindAll(Predicate<T> match)
```

As you can see, this method returns a new `List<T>` that represents the subset of data. Also notice that the sole parameter to `FindAll()` is a generic delegate of type `System.Predicate<T>`. This delegate can point to any method returning a `bool`, and takes a single type parameter as the only input parameter:

```
// This delegate is used by FindAll() method
// to extract out the subset.
public delegate bool Predicate<T>(T obj);
```

When you call `FindAll()`, each item in the `List<T>` is passed to the method pointed to by the `Predicate<T>` object. The implementation of said method will perform some calculations to see whether the incoming data matches the necessary criteria, and return `true` or `false`. If this method returns `true`, the item will be added to the new `List<T>` that represents the subset (got all that?).

Before we see how lambda expressions can simplify working with `FindAll()`, let's work the problem out in longhand notation, using the delegate objects directly. Add a method (named `TraditionalDelegateSyntax()`) within your `Program` type that interacts with the `System.Predicate<T>` type to discover the even numbers in a `List<T>` of integers:

```
class Program
{
  static void Main(string[] args)
  {
    Console.WriteLine("***** Fun with Lambdas *****\n");
    TraditionalDelegateSyntax();
```

```
    Console.ReadLine();
}

static void TraditionalDelegateSyntax()
{
    // Make a list of integers.
    List<int> list = new List<int>();
    list.AddRange(new int[] { 20, 1, 4, 8, 9, 44 });

    // Call FindAll() using traditional delegate syntax.
    Predicate<int> callback = new Predicate<int>(IsEvenNumber);
    List<int> evenNumbers = list.FindAll(callback);

    Console.WriteLine("Here are your even numbers:");
    foreach (int evenNumber in evenNumbers)
    {
        Console.Write("{0}\t", evenNumber);
    }
    Console.WriteLine();
}

// Target for the Predicate<> delegate.
static bool IsEvenNumber(int i)
{
    // Is it an even number?
    return (i % 2) == 0;
}
}
```

Here, we have a method (IsEvenNumber()) that is in charge of testing the incoming integer parameter to see whether it is even or odd via the C# modulo operator, %. If you execute your application, you will find the numbers 20, 4, 8, and 44 print out to the console.

While this traditional approach to working with delegates behaves as expected, the IsEvenNumber() method is invoked only in very limited circumstances—specifically when we call FindAll(), which leaves us with the baggage of a full method definition. If we were to instead use an anonymous method, our code would clean up considerably. Consider the following new method of the Program class:

```
static void AnonymousMethodSyntax()
{
    // Make a list of integers.
    List<int> list = new List<int>();
    list.AddRange(new int[] { 20, 1, 4, 8, 9, 44 });

    // Now, use an anonymous method.
    List<int> evenNumbers = list.FindAll(delegate(int i)
        { return (i % 2) == 0; } );

    Console.WriteLine("Here are your even numbers:");
    foreach (int evenNumber in evenNumbers)
    {
        Console.Write("{0}\t", evenNumber);
    }
```

```
  Console.WriteLine();
}
```

In this case, rather than directly creating a `Predicate<T>` delegate type and then authoring a stand-alone method, we are able to inline a method anonymously. While this is a step in the right direction, we are still required to use the `delegate` keyword (or a strongly typed `Predicate<T>`), and we must ensure that the parameter list is a dead-on match:

```
List<int> evenNumbers = list.FindAll(
  delegate(int i)
  {
    return (i % 2) == 0;
  }
);
```

Lambda expressions can be used to simplify the call to `FindAll()` even more. When you make use of lambda syntax, there is no trace of the underlying delegate object whatsoever. Consider the following new method to the `Program` class:

```
static void LambdaExpressionSyntax()
{
  // Make a list of integers.
  List<int> list = new List<int>();
  list.AddRange(new int[] { 20, 1, 4, 8, 9, 44 });

  // Now, use a C# lambda expression.
  List<int> evenNumbers = list.FindAll(i => (i % 2) == 0);

  Console.WriteLine("Here are your even numbers:");
  foreach (int evenNumber in evenNumbers)
  {
    Console.Write("{0}\t", evenNumber);
  }
  Console.WriteLine();
}
```

In this case, notice the rather strange statement of code passed into the `FindAll()` method, which is in fact a lambda expression. In this iteration of the example, there is no trace whatsoever of the `Predicate<T>` delegate (or the delegate keyword, for that matter). All we have specified is the lambda expression:

```
i => (i % 2) == 0
```

Before I break this syntax down, first understand that lambda expressions can be used anywhere you would have used an anonymous method or a strongly typed delegate (typically with far fewer keystrokes). Under the hood, the C# compiler translates the expression into a standard anonymous method making use of the `Predicate<T>` delegate type (which can be verified using `ildasm.exe` or `reflector.exe`). Specifically, the following code statement:

```
// This lambda expression...
List<int> evenNumbers = list.FindAll(i => (i % 2) == 0);
```

is compiled into the following approximate C# code:

```
// ...becomes this anonymous method.
List<int> evenNumbers = list.FindAll(delegate (int i)
{
  return (i % 2) == 0;
});
```

Dissecting a Lambda Expression

A lambda expression is written by first defining a parameter list, followed by the => token (C#'s token for the lambda operator found in the *lambda calculus*), followed by a set of statements (or a single statement) that will process these arguments. From a very high level, a lambda expression can be understood as follows:

```
ArgumentsToProcess => StatementsToProcessThem
```

Within our LambdaExpressionSyntax() method, things break down like so:

```
// "i" is our parameter list.
// "(i % 2) == 0" is our statement set to process "i".
List<int> evenNumbers = list.FindAll(i => (i % 2) == 0);
```

The parameters of a lambda expression can be explicitly or implicitly typed. Currently, the underlying data type representing the i parameter (an integer) is determined implicitly. The compiler is able to figure out that i is an integer based on the context of the overall lambda expression and the underlying delegate. However, it is also possible to explicitly define the type of each parameter in the expression, by wrapping the data type and variable name in a pair of parentheses, as follows:

```
// Now, explicitly state the parameter type.
List<int> evenNumbers = list.FindAll((int i) => (i % 2) == 0);
```

As you have seen, if a lambda expression has a single, implicitly typed parameter, the parentheses may be omitted from the parameter list. If you want to be consistent regarding your use of lambda parameters, you can *always* wrap the parameter list within parentheses, leaving us with this expression:

```
List<int> evenNumbers = list.FindAll((i) => (i % 2) == 0);
```

Finally, notice that currently our expression has not been wrapped in parentheses (we have of course wrapped the modulo statement to ensure it is executed first before the test for equality). Lambda expressions do allow for the statement to be wrapped as follows:

```
// Now, wrap the expression as well.
List<int> evenNumbers = list.FindAll((i) => ((i % 2) == 0));
```

Now that you have seen the various ways to build a lambda expression, how can we read this lambda statement in human-friendly terms? Leaving the raw mathematics behind, the following explanation fits the bill:

```
// My list of parameters (in this case, a single integer named i)
// will be processed by the expression (i % 2) == 0.
List<int> evenNumbers = list.FindAll((i) => ((i % 2) == 0));
```

Processing Arguments Within Multiple Statements

Our first lambda expression was a single statement that ultimately evaluated to a Boolean. However, as you know, many delegate targets must perform a number of code statements. For this reason, C# allows you to build lambda expressions using multiple statement blocks. When your expression must process the parameters using multiple lines of code, you can do so by denoting a scope for these statements using the expected curly brackets. Consider the following example update to our LambdaExpressionSyntax() method:

```
static void LambdaExpressionSyntax()
{
  // Make a list of integers.
  List<int> list = new List<int>();
  list.AddRange(new int[] { 20, 1, 4, 8, 9, 44 });

  // Now process each argument within a group of
  // code statements.
  List<int> evenNumbers = list.FindAll((i) =>
  {
    Console.WriteLine("value of i is currently: {0}", i);
    bool isEven = ((i % 2) == 0);
    return isEven;
  });

  Console.WriteLine("Here are your even numbers:");
  foreach (int evenNumber in evenNumbers)
  {
    Console.Write("{0}\t", evenNumber);
  }
  Console.WriteLine();
}
```

In this case, our parameter list (again, a single integer named i) is being processed by a set of code statements. Beyond the calls to Console.WriteLine(), our modulo statement has been broken into two code statements for increased readability. Assuming each of the methods we've looked at in this section are called from within Main():

```
static void Main(string[] args)
{
  Console.WriteLine("***** Fun with Lambdas *****\n");
  TraditionalDelegateSyntax();
  AnonymousMethodSyntax();
  Console.WriteLine();
  LambdaExpressionSyntax();
  Console.ReadLine();
}
```

we will find the following output:

```
***** Fun with Lambdas *****

Here are your even numbers:
20      4       8       44
Here are your even numbers:
20      4       8       44

value of i is currently: 20
value of i is currently: 1
value of i is currently: 4
value of i is currently: 8
value of i is currently: 9
value of i is currently: 44
Here are your even numbers:
20      4       8       44
```

■ **Source Code** The SimpleLambdaExpressions project can be found under the Chapter 10 subdirectory.

Lambda Expressions with Multiple (or Zero) Parameters

The lambda expressions you have seen here processed a single parameter. This is not a requirement, however, as a lambda expression may process multiple arguments (or none). To illustrate the first scenario, create a Console Application named LambdaExpressionsMultipleParams. Next, assume the following incarnation of the SimpleMath type:

```
public class SimpleMath
{
  public delegate void MathMessage(string msg, int result);
  private MathMessage mmDelegate;

  public void SetMathHandler(MathMessage target)
  {mmDelegate = target; }

  public void Add(int x, int y)
  {
    if (mmDelegate != null)
      mmDelegate.Invoke("Adding has completed!", x + y);
  }
}
```

Notice that the MathMessage delegate is expecting two parameters. To represent them as a lambda expression, our Main() method might be written as follows:

```
static void Main(string[] args)
{
  // Register with delegate as a lambda expression.
```

```
SimpleMath m = new SimpleMath();
m.SetMathHandler((msg, result) =>
  {Console.WriteLine("Message: {0}, Result: {1}", msg, result);});

// This will execute the lambda expression.
m.Add(10, 10);
Console.ReadLine();
}
```

Here, we are leveraging type inference, as our two parameters have not been strongly typed for simplicity. However, we could call SetMathHandler(), as follows:

```
m.SetMathHandler((string msg, int result) =>
  {Console.WriteLine("Message: {0}, Result: {1}", msg, result);});
```

Finally, if you are using a lambda expression to interact with a delegate taking no parameters at all, you may do so by supplying a pair of empty parentheses as the parameter. Thus, assuming you have defined the following delegate type:

```
public delegate string VerySimpleDelegate();
```

you could handle the result of the invocation as follows:

```
// Prints "Enjoy your string!" to the console.
VerySimpleDelegate d = new VerySimpleDelegate( () => {return "Enjoy your string!";} );
Console.WriteLine(d());
```

■ **Source Code** The LambdaExpressionsMultipleParams project can be found under the Chapter 10 subdirectory.

Retrofitting the CarEvents Example Using Lambda Expressions

Given that the whole reason for lambda expressions is to provide a clean, concise manner to define an anonymous method (and therefore indirectly a manner to simplify working with delegates), let's retrofit the PrimAndProperCarEvents project we created earlier in this chapter. Here is a simplified version of that project's Program class, which makes use of lambda expression syntax (rather than the raw delegates) to hook into each event sent from the Car object:

```
static void Main(string[] args)
{
  Console.WriteLine("***** More Fun with Lambdas *****\n");

  // Make a car as usual.
  Car c1 = new Car("SlugBug", 100, 10);

  // Hook into events with lambdas!
  c1.AboutToBlow += (sender, e) => { Console.WriteLine(e.msg);};
  c1.Exploded += (sender, e) => { Console.WriteLine(e.msg); };
```

```
  // Speed up (this will generate the events).
  Console.WriteLine("\n***** Speeding up *****");
  for (int i = 0; i < 6; i++)
    c1.Accelerate(20);

  Console.ReadLine();
}
```

Hopefully, at this point you can see the overall role of lambda expressions and understand how they provide a "functional manner" to work with anonymous methods and delegate types. Although the lambda operator (=>) might take a bit to get used to, always remember a lambda expression can be broken down to the following simple equation:

```
ArgumentsToProcess => StatementsToProcessThem
```

It is worth pointing out that the LINQ programming model also makes substantial use of lambda expressions to help simplify your coding efforts. You will examine LINQ beginning in Chapter 12.

■ **Source Code** The CarEventsWithLambdas project can be found under the Chapter 10 subdirectory.

Summary

In this chapter, you have examined a number of ways in which multiple objects can partake in a bidirectional conversation. First, you looked at the C# delegate keyword, which is used to indirectly construct a class derived from System.MulticastDelegate. As you saw, a delegate object maintains a list of methods to call when told to do so. These invocations may be made synchronously (using the Invoke() method) or asynchronously (via the BeginInvoke() and EndInvoke() methods). Again, the asynchronous nature of .NET delegate types will be examined in Chapter 19.

You then examined the C# event keyword, which, when used in conjunction with a delegate type, can simplify the process of sending your event notifications to waiting callers. As shown via the resulting CIL, the .NET event model maps to hidden calls on the System.Delegate/System.MulticastDelegate types. In this light, the C# event keyword is purely optional in that it simply saves you some typing time.

This chapter also explored a C# language feature termed *anonymous methods*. Using this syntactic construct, you are able to directly associate a block of code statements to a given event. As you have seen, anonymous methods are free to ignore the parameters sent by the event and have access to the "outer variables" of the defining method. You also examined a simplified way to register events using *method group conversion*.

Finally, we wrapped things up by looking at the C# *lambda operator,* =>. As shown, this syntax is a great shorthand notation for authoring anonymous methods, where a stack of arguments can be passed into a group of statements for processing. Any method in the .NET platform that takes a delegate object as an argument can be substituted with a related lambda expression, which will typically simplify your code base quite a bit.

CHAPTER 11

Advanced C# Language Features

In this chapter, you'll deepen your understanding of the C# programming language by examining a number of more advanced syntactic constructs. To begin, you'll learn how to implement and use an *indexer method*. This C# mechanism enables you to build custom types that provide access to internal subitems using an array-like syntax. After you learn how to build an indexer method, you'll see how to overload various operators (+, -, <, >, and so forth), and how to create custom explicit and implicit conversion routines for your types (and you'll learn why you might want to do this).

Next, you'll examine topics that are particularly useful when working with LINQ-centric APIs (though you can use them outside of the context of LINQ)—specifically extension methods and anonymous types.

To wrap things up, you'll learn how to create an "unsafe" code context in order to directly manipulate unmanaged pointers. While it is certainly true that using pointers in C# applications is a fairly infrequent activity, understanding how to do so can be helpful in some circumstances that involve complex interoperability scenarios.

Understanding Indexer Methods

As a programmer, you are certainly familiar with the process of accessing individual items contained within a simple array using the index operator ([ ]). For example:

```
static void Main(string[] args)
{
  // Loop over incoming command-line arguments
  // using index operator.
  for(int i = 0; i < args.Length; i++)
    Console.WriteLine("Args: {0}", args[i]);

  // Declare an array of local integers.
  int[] myInts = { 10, 9, 100, 432, 9874};

  // Use the index operator to access each element.
  for(int j = 0; j < myInts.Length; j++)
    Console.WriteLine("Index {0} = {1} ", j,  myInts[j]);
  Console.ReadLine();
}
```

This code is by no means a major newsflash. However, the C# language provides the capability to design custom classes and structures that may be indexed just like a standard array, by defining an *indexer method.* This particular feature is most useful when you are creating custom collection classes (generic or nongeneric).

Before examining how to implement a custom indexer, let's begin by seeing one in action. Assume you have added support for an indexer method to the custom PersonCollection type developed in Chapter 9 (specifically, the IssuesWithNonGenericCollections project). While you have not yet added the indexer, observe the following usage within a new Console Application named SimpleIndexer:

```csharp
// Indexers allow you to access items in an array-like fashion.
class Program
{
  static void Main(string[] args)
  {
    Console.WriteLine("***** Fun with Indexers *****\n");

    PersonCollection myPeople = new PersonCollection();

    // Add objects with indexer syntax.
    myPeople[0] = new Person("Homer", "Simpson", 40);
    myPeople[1] = new Person("Marge", "Simpson", 38);
    myPeople[2] = new Person("Lisa", "Simpson", 9);
    myPeople[3] = new Person("Bart", "Simpson", 7);
    myPeople[4] = new Person("Maggie", "Simpson", 2);

    // Now obtain and display each item using indexer.
    for (int i = 0; i < myPeople.Count; i++)
    {
      Console.WriteLine("Person number: {0}", i);
      Console.WriteLine("Name: {0} {1}",
        myPeople[i].FirstName, myPeople[i].LastName);
      Console.WriteLine("Age: {0}", myPeople[i].Age);
      Console.WriteLine();
    }
  }
}
```

As you can see, indexers allow you to manipulate the internal collection of subobjects just like a standard array. Now for the big question: how do you configure the PersonCollection class (or any custom class or structure) to support this functionality? An indexer is represented as a slightly modified C# property definition. In its simplest form, an indexer is created using the this[] syntax. Here is the required update for the PersonCollection class:

```csharp
// Add the indexer to the existing class definition.
public class PersonCollection : IEnumerable
{
  private ArrayList arPeople = new ArrayList();

  // Custom indexer for this class.
  public Person this[int index]
  {
    get { return (Person)arPeople[index]; }
    set { arPeople.Insert(index, value); }
  }
...
```

```
}
```

Apart from using the this keyword, the indexer looks just like any other C# property declaration. For example, the role of the get scope is to return the correct object to the caller. Here, we are doing so by delegating the request to the indexer of the ArrayList object, as this class also supports an indexer. The set scope is in charge of adding new Person objects, this is achieved by calling the Insert() method of the ArrayList.

Indexers are yet another form of syntactic sugar, given that this functionality can also be achieved using "normal" public methods such as AddPerson() or GetPerson(). Nevertheless, when you support indexer methods on your custom collection types, they integrate well into the fabric of the .NET base class libraries.

While creating indexer methods is quite commonplace when you are building custom collections, do remember that generic types give you this very functionality out of the box. Consider the following method, which makes use of a generic List<T> of Person objects. Note that you can simply use the indexer of List<T> directly. For example:

```
static void UseGenericListOfPeople()
{
  List<Person> myPeople = new List<Person>();
  myPeople.Add(new Person("Lisa", "Simpson", 9));
  myPeople.Add(new Person("Bart", "Simpson", 7));

  // Change first person with indexer.
  myPeople[0] = new Person("Maggie", "Simpson", 2);

  // Now obtain and display each item using indexer.
  for (int i = 0; i < myPeople.Count; i++)
  {
    Console.WriteLine("Person number: {0}", i);
    Console.WriteLine("Name: {0} {1}", myPeople[i].FirstName,
      myPeople[i].LastName);
    Console.WriteLine("Age: {0}", myPeople[i].Age);
    Console.WriteLine();
  }
}
```

■ **Source Code** The SimpleIndexer project is located under the Chapter 11 subdirectory.

Indexing Data Using String Values

The current PersonCollection class defined an indexer that allowed the caller to identify subitems using a numerical value. Understand, however, that this is not a requirement of an indexer method. Suppose you'd prefer to contain the Person objects using a System.Collections.Generic.Dictionary<TKey, TValue> rather than an ArrayList. Given that Dictionary types allow access to the contained types using a string token (such as a person's first name), you could define an indexer as follows:

```
public class PersonCollection : IEnumerable
{
  private Dictionary<string, Person> listPeople =
    new Dictionary<string, Person>();

  // This indexer returns a person based on a string index.
  public Person this[string name]
  {
    get { return (Person)listPeople[name]; }
    set { listPeople[name] = value; }
  }

  public void ClearPeople()
  { listPeople.Clear(); }

  public int Count
  { get { return listPeople.Count; } }

  IEnumerator IEnumerable.GetEnumerator()
  { return listPeople.GetEnumerator(); }
}
```

The caller would now be able to interact with the contained Person objects as shown here:

```
static void Main(string[] args)
{
  Console.WriteLine("***** Fun with Indexers *****\n");

  PersonCollection myPeople = new PersonCollection();

  myPeople["Homer"] = new Person("Homer", "Simpson", 40);
  myPeople["Marge"] = new Person("Marge", "Simpson", 38);

  // Get "Homer" and print data.
  Person homer = myPeople["Homer"];
  Console.WriteLine(homer.ToString());

  Console.ReadLine();
}
```

Again, if you were to use the generic Dictionary<TKey, TValue> type directly, you'd gain the indexer method functionality out of the box, without building a custom, nongeneric class supporting a string indexer. Nevertheless, do understand that the data type of any indexer will be based on how the supporting collection type allows the caller to retrieve subitems.

■ **Source Code** The StringIndexer project is located under the Chapter 11 subdirectory.

Overloading Indexer Methods

Understand that indexer methods may be overloaded on a single class or structure. Thus, if it makes sense to allow the caller to access subitems using a numerical index *or* a string value, you might define multiple indexers for a single type. By way of example, in ADO.NET (.NET's native database-access API), the DataSet class supports a property named Tables, which returns to you a strongly typed DataTableCollection type. As it turns out, DataTableCollection defines *three* indexers to get and set DataTable objects—one by ordinal position, and the others by a friendly string moniker and optional containing namespace, as shown here:

```
public sealed class DataTableCollection : InternalDataCollectionBase
{
...
  // Overloaded indexers!
  public DataTable this[string name] { get; }
  public DataTable this[string name, string tableNamespace] { get; }
  public DataTable this[int index] { get; }
}
```

It is very common for types in the base class libraries to support indexer methods. So be aware, even if your current project does not require you to build custom indexers for your classes and structures, that many types already support this syntax.

Indexers with Multiple Dimensions

You can also create an indexer method that takes multiple parameters. Assume you have a custom collection that stores subitems in a 2D array. If this is the case, you may define an indexer method as follows:

```
public class SomeContainer
{
  private int[,] my2DintArray = new int[10, 10];

  public int this[int row, int column]
  {  /* get or set value from 2D array */  }
}
```

Again, unless you are building a highly stylized custom collection class, you won't have much need to build a multidimensional indexer. Still, once again ADO.NET showcases how useful this construct can be. The ADO.NET DataTable is essentially a collection of rows and columns, much like a piece of graph paper or the general structure of a Microsoft Excel spreadsheet.

While DataTable objects are typically populated on your behalf using a related "data adapter," the following code illustrates how to manually create an in-memory DataTable containing three columns (for the first name, last name, and age of each record). Notice how once we have added a single row to the DataTable, we use a multidimensional indexer to drill into each column of the first (and only) row. (If you are following along, you'll need to import the System.Data namespace into your code file.)

```
static void MultiIndexerWithDataTable()
{
  // Make a simple DataTable with 3 columns.
  DataTable myTable = new DataTable();
  myTable.Columns.Add(new DataColumn("FirstName"));
  myTable.Columns.Add(new DataColumn("LastName"));
```

```
myTable.Columns.Add(new DataColumn("Age"));

// Now add a row to the table.
myTable.Rows.Add("Mel", "Appleby", 60);

// Use multidimension indexer to get details of first row.
Console.WriteLine("First Name: {0}", myTable.Rows[0][0]);
Console.WriteLine("Last Name: {0}", myTable.Rows[0][1]);
Console.WriteLine("Age : {0}", myTable.Rows[0][2]);
}
```

Do be aware that we'll take a rather deep dive into ADO.NET beginning with Chapter 21, so if some of the previous code seems unfamiliar, fear not. The main point of this example is that indexer methods can support multiple dimensions, and if used correctly, can simplify the way you interact with contained subobjects in custom collections.

Indexer Definitions on Interface Types

Indexers can be defined on a given .NET interface type to allow supporting types to provide a custom implementation. Here is a simple example of an interface that defines a protocol for obtaining string objects using a numerical indexer:

```
public interface IStringContainer
{
  string this[int index] { get; set; }
}
```

With this interface definition, any class or structure that implements this interface must now support a read/write indexer that manipulates subitems using a numerical value. Here is a partial implementation of such as class:

```
class SomeClass : IStringContainer
{
  private List<string> myStrings = new List<string>();

  public string this[int index]
  {
    get { return myStrings[index]; }
    set { myStrings.Insert(index, value); }
  }
}
```

That wraps up the first major topic of this chapter. Now let's examine a language feature that lets you build custom classes or structures that respond uniquely to the intrinsic operators of C#. Next, allow me to introduce the concept of *operator overloading*.

Understanding Operator Overloading

C#, like any programming language, has a canned set of tokens that are used to perform basic operations on intrinsic types. For example, you know that the + operator can be applied to two integers in order to yield a larger integer:

```
// The + operator with ints.
int a = 100;
int b = 240;
int c = a + b;   // c is now 340
```

Once again, this is no major newsflash, but have you ever stopped and noticed how the same + operator can be applied to most intrinsic C# data types? For example, consider this code:

```
// + operator with strings.
string s1 = "Hello";
string s2 = " world!";
string s3 = s1 + s2;   // s3 is now "Hello world!"
```

In essence, the + operator functions in specific ways based on the supplied data types (strings or integers, in this case). When the + operator is applied to numerical types, the result is the summation of the operands. However, when the + operator is applied to string types, the result is string concatenation.

The C# language gives you the capability to build custom classes and structures that also respond uniquely to the same set of basic tokens (such as the + operator). While not every possible C# operator can be overloaded, many can, as shown in Table 11-1.

Table 11-1. Overloadability of C# Operators

C# Operator	Overloadability
+, -,! , ~, ++, --, true, false	These unary operators can be overloaded.
+, -, *, /, %, &, |, ^, <<, >>	These binary operators can be overloaded.
==,!=, <, >, <=, >=	These comparison operators can be overloaded. C# demands that "like" operators (i.e., < and >, <= and >=, == and !=) are overloaded together.
[]	The [ ] operator cannot be overloaded. As you saw earlier in this chapter, however, the indexer construct provides the same functionality.
()	The () operator cannot be overloaded. As you will see later in this chapter, however, custom conversion methods provide the same functionality.
+=, -=, *=, /=, %=, &=, |=, ^=, <<=, >>=	Shorthand assignment operators cannot be overloaded; however, you receive them as a freebie when you overload the related binary operator.

Overloading Binary Operators

To illustrate the process of overloading binary operators, assume the following simple Point class is defined in a new Console Application named OverloadedOps:

```
// Just a simple, everyday C# class.
public class Point
{
  public int X {get; set;}
  public int Y {get; set;}

  public Point(int xPos, int yPos)
  {
    X = xPos;
    Y = yPos;
  }

  public override string ToString()
  {
    return string.Format("[{0}, {1}]", this.X, this.Y);
  }
}
```

Now, logically speaking, it makes sense to "add" Points together. For example, if you added together two Point variables, you should receive a new Point that is the summation of the X and Y values. Of course, it might also be helpful to subtract one Point from another. Ideally, you would like to be able to author the following code:

```
// Adding and subtracting two points?
static void Main(string[] args)
{
  Console.WriteLine("***** Fun with Overloaded Operators *****\n");

  // Make two points.
  Point ptOne = new Point(100, 100);
  Point ptTwo = new Point(40, 40);
  Console.WriteLine("ptOne = {0}", ptOne);
  Console.WriteLine("ptTwo = {0}", ptTwo);

  // Add the points to make a bigger point?
  Console.WriteLine("ptOne + ptTwo: {0} ", ptOne + ptTwo);

  // Subtract the points to make a smaller point?
  Console.WriteLine("ptOne - ptTwo: {0} ", ptOne - ptTwo);
  Console.ReadLine();
}
```

However, as our Point now stands, we will receive compile-time errors, as the Point type does not know how to respond to the + or - operators. To equip a custom type to respond uniquely to intrinsic operators, C# provides the operator keyword, which you can use only in conjunction with the static keyword. When you overload a binary operator (such as + and -), you will most often pass in two arguments that are the same type as the defining class (a Point in this example), as illustrated in the following code update:

```
// A more intelligent Point type.
public class Point
{
...
```

```
// Overloaded operator +.
public static Point operator + (Point p1, Point p2)
{
  return new Point(p1.X + p2.X, p1.Y + p2.Y);
}

// Overloaded operator -.
public static Point operator - (Point p1, Point p2)
{
  return new Point(p1.X - p2.X, p1.Y - p2.Y);
}
}
```

The logic behind operator + is simply to return a brand-new Point object based on the summation of the fields of the incoming Point parameters. Thus, when you write pt1 + pt2, under the hood you can envision the following hidden call to the static operator + method:

```
// Pseudo-code: Point p3 = Point.operator+ (p1, p2)
Point p3 = p1 + p2;
```

Likewise, p1 – p2 maps to the following:

```
// Pseudo-code: Point p4 = Point.operator- (p1, p2)
Point p4 = p1 - p2;
```

With this update, our program now compiles, and we find we are able to add and subtract Point objects, as seen in the following output:

```
ptOne = [100, 100]
ptTwo = [40, 40]
ptOne + ptTwo: [140, 140]
ptOne - ptTwo: [60, 60]
```

When you are overloading a binary operator, you are not required to pass in two parameters of the same type. If it makes sense to do so, one of the arguments can differ. For example, here is an overloaded operator + that allows the caller to obtain a new Point that is based on a numerical adjustment:

```
public class Point
{
...
  public static Point operator + (Point p1, int change)
  {
    return new Point(p1.X + change, p1.Y + change);
  }

  public static Point operator + (int change, Point p1)
  {
    return new Point(p1.X + change, p1.Y + change);
  }
}
```

Notice that you need *both* versions of the method if you want the arguments to be passed in either order (i.e., you can't just define one of the methods and expect the compiler to automatically support the other one). We are now able to use these new versions of operator + as follows:

```
// Prints [110, 110].
Point biggerPoint = ptOne + 10;
Console.WriteLine("ptOne + 10 = {0}", biggerPoint);

// Prints [120, 120].
Console.WriteLine("10 + biggerPoint = {0}", 10 + biggerPoint);
Console.WriteLine();
```

And What of the += and −+ Operators?

If you are coming to C# from a C++ background, you might lament the loss of overloading the shorthand assignment operators (+=, -=, and so forth). Don't despair. In terms of C#, the shorthand assignment operators are automatically simulated if a type overloads the related binary operator. Thus, given that the Point structure has already overloaded the + and - operators, you can write the following:

```
// Overloading binary operators results in a freebie shorthand operator.
static void Main(string[] args)
{
...
  // Freebie +=
  Point ptThree = new Point(90, 5);
  Console.WriteLine("ptThree = {0}", ptThree);
  Console.WriteLine("ptThree += ptTwo: {0}", ptThree += ptTwo);

  // Freebie -=
  Point ptFour = new Point(0, 500);
  Console.WriteLine("ptFour = {0}", ptFour);
  Console.WriteLine("ptFour -= ptThree: {0}", ptFour -= ptThree);
  Console.ReadLine();
}
```

Overloading Unary Operators

C# also allows you to overload various unary operators, such as ++ and --. When you overload a unary operator, you also must use the static keyword with the operator keyword; however, in this case you simply pass in a single parameter that is the same type as the defining class/structure. For example, if you were to update the Point with the following overloaded operators:

```
public class Point
{
...
  // Add 1 to the X/Y values for the incoming Point.
  public static Point operator ++(Point p1)
  {
    return new Point(p1.X+1, p1.Y+1);
  }
```

```
  // Subtract 1 from the X/Y values for the incoming Point.
  public static Point operator --(Point p1)
  {
    return new Point(p1.X-1, p1.Y-1);
  }
}
```

you could increment and decrement Point's x and y values like this:

```
static void Main(string[] args)
{
...
  // Applying the ++ and -- unary operators to a Point.
  Point ptFive = new Point(1, 1);
  Console.WriteLine("++ptFive = {0}", ++ptFive);  // [2, 2]
  Console.WriteLine("--ptFive = {0}", --ptFive);  // [1, 1]

  // Apply same operators as postincrement/decrement.
  Point ptSix = new Point(20, 20);
  Console.WriteLine("ptSix++ = {0}", ptSix++);  // [20, 20]
  Console.WriteLine("ptSix-- = {0}", ptSix--);  // [21, 21]
  Console.ReadLine();
}
```

Notice in the preceding code example we are applying our custom ++ and -- operators in two different manners. In C++, it is possible to overload pre- and postincrement/decrement operators separately. This is not possible in C#. However, the return value of the increment/decrement is automatically handled "correctly" free of charge (i.e., for an overloaded ++ operator, pt++ has the value of the unmodified object as its value within an expression, while ++pt has the new value applied before use in the expression).

Overloading Equality Operators

As you might recall from Chapter 6, System.Object.Equals() can be overridden to perform value-based (rather than referenced-based) comparisons between reference types. If you choose to override Equals() (and the often related System.Object.GetHashCode() method), it is trivial to overload the equality operators (== and !=). To illustrate, here is the updated Point type:

```
// This incarnation of Point also overloads the == and != operators.
public class Point
{
...
  public override bool Equals(object o)
  {
    return o.ToString() == this.ToString();
  }

  public override int GetHashCode()
  {
    return this.ToString().GetHashCode();
  }
```

```
// Now let's overload the == and != operators.
public static bool operator ==(Point p1, Point p2)
{
  return p1.Equals(p2);
}

public static bool operator !=(Point p1, Point p2)
{
  return !p1.Equals(p2);
}
}
```

Notice how the implementation of operator == and operator != simply makes a call to the overridden Equals() method to get the bulk of the work done. Given this, you can now exercise your Point class as follows:

```
// Make use of the overloaded equality operators.
static void Main(string[] args)
{
...
  Console.WriteLine("ptOne == ptTwo : {0}", ptOne == ptTwo);
  Console.WriteLine("ptOne != ptTwo : {0}", ptOne != ptTwo);
  Console.ReadLine();
}
```

As you can see, it is quite intuitive to compare two objects using the well-known == and != operators, rather than making a call to Object. Equals(). If you do overload the equality operators for a given class, keep in mind that C# demands that if you override the == operator, you *must* also override the != operator (if you forget, the compiler will let you know).

Overloading Comparison Operators

In Chapter 8, you learned how to implement the IComparable interface in order to compare the relationship between two like objects. You can, in fact, also overload the comparison operators (<, >, <=, and >=) for the same class. As with the equality operators, C# demands that if you overload <, you must also overload >. The same holds true for the <= and >= operators. If the Point type overloaded these comparison operators, the object user could now compare Points, as follows:

```
// Using the overloaded < and > operators.
static void Main(string[] args)
{
...
  Console.WriteLine("ptOne < ptTwo : {0}", ptOne < ptTwo);
  Console.WriteLine("ptOne > ptTwo : {0}", ptOne > ptTwo);
  Console.ReadLine();
}
```

Assuming you have implemented the IComparable interface (or better yet, the generic equivalent), overloading the comparison operators is trivial. Here is the updated class definition:

```
// Point is also comparable using the comparison operators.
public class Point : IComparable<Point>
{
```

```
...
  public int CompareTo(Point other)
  {
    if (this.X > other.X && this.Y > other.Y)
      return 1;
    if (this.X < other.X && this.Y < other.Y)
      return -1;
    else
      return 0;
  }

  public static bool operator <(Point p1, Point p2)
  { return (p1.CompareTo(p2) < 0); }

  public static bool operator >(Point p1, Point p2)
  { return (p1.CompareTo(p2) > 0); }

  public static bool operator <=(Point p1, Point p2)
  { return (p1.CompareTo(p2) <= 0); }

  public static bool operator >=(Point p1, Point p2)
  { return (p1.CompareTo(p2) >= 0); }
}
```

Final Thoughts Regarding Operator Overloading

As you have seen, C# provides the capability to build types that can respond uniquely to various intrinsic, well-known operators. Now, before you go and retrofit all your classes to support such behavior, you must be sure that the operator(s) you are about to overload make some sort of logical sense in the world at large.

For example, let's say you overloaded the multiplication operator for the MiniVan class. What exactly would it mean to multiply two MiniVan objects? Not much. In fact, it would be very confusing for teammates to see the following use of MiniVan objects:

```
// Huh?! This is far from intuitive...
MiniVan newVan = myVan * yourVan;
```

Overloading operators is generally useful only when you're building atomic data types. Text, points, rectangles, fractions, and hexagons make good candidates for operator overloading. People, managers, cars, database connections, and web pages do not. As a rule of thumb, if an overloaded operator makes it *harder* for the user to understand a type's functionality, don't do it. Use this feature wisely.

■ **Source Code** The OverloadedOps project is located under the Chapter 11 subdirectory.

Understanding Custom Type Conversions

Let's now examine a topic closely related to operator overloading: custom type conversions. To set the stage for the discussion, let's quickly review the notion of explicit and implicit conversions between numerical data and related class types.

Recall: Numerical Conversions

In terms of the intrinsic numerical types (sbyte, int, float, etc.), an *explicit conversion* is required when you attempt to store a larger value in a smaller container, as this could result in a loss of data. Basically, this is your way to tell the compiler, "Leave me alone, I know what I am trying to do." Conversely, an *implicit conversion* happens automatically when you attempt to place a smaller type in a destination type that will not result in a loss of data:

```
static void Main()
{
  int a = 123;
  long b = a;        // Implicit conversion from int to long.
  int c = (int) b;   // Explicit conversion from long to int.
}
```

Recall: Conversions Among Related Class Types

As shown in Chapter 6, class types may be related by classical inheritance (the "is-a" relationship). In this case, the C# conversion process allows you to cast up and down the class hierarchy. For example, a derived class can always be implicitly cast to a base type. However, if you want to store a base class type in a derived variable, you must perform an explicit cast, like so:

```
// Two related class types.
class Base{}
class Derived : Base{}

class Program
{
  static void Main(string[] args)
  {
    // Implicit cast between derived to base.
    Base myBaseType;
    myBaseType = new Derived();

    // Must explicitly cast to store base reference
    // in derived type.
    Derived myDerivedType = (Derived)myBaseType;
  }
}
```

This explicit cast works due to the fact that the Base and Derived classes are related by classical inheritance. However, what if you have two class types in *different hierarchies* with no common parent (other than System.Object) that require conversions? Given that they are not related by classical inheritance, typical casting operations offer no help.

On a related note, consider value types (structures). Assume you have two .NET structures named Square and Rectangle. Given that structures cannot leverage classic inheritance (as they are always sealed), you have no natural way to cast between these seemingly related types.

While you could create helper methods in the structures (such as Rectangle.ToSquare()), C# lets you build custom conversion routines that allow your types to respond to the () casting operator. Therefore, if you configured the structures correctly, you would be able to use the following syntax to explicitly convert between them as follows:

```
// Convert a Rectangle to a Square!
Rectangle rect;
rect.Width = 3;
rect.Height = 10;
Square sq = (Square)rect;
```

Creating Custom Conversion Routines

Begin by creating a new Console Application named CustomConversions. C# provides two keywords, explicit and implicit, that you can use to control how your types respond during an attempted conversion. Assume you have the following structure definitions:

```
public struct Rectangle
{
  public int Width {get; set;}
  public int Height {get; set;}

  public Rectangle(int w, int h) : this()
  {
    Width = w; Height = h;
  }

  public void Draw()
  {
    for (int i = 0; i < Height; i++)
    {
      for (int j = 0; j < Width; j++)
      {
        Console.Write("*");
      }
      Console.WriteLine();
    }
  }

  public override string ToString()
  {
    return string.Format("[Width = {0}; Height = {1}]",
      Width, Height);
  }
}

public struct Square
{
  public int Length {get; set;}
```

```csharp
public Square(int l) : this()
{
  Length = l;
}

public void Draw()
{
  for (int i = 0; i < Length; i++)
  {
    for (int j = 0; j < Length; j++)
    {
      Console.Write("*");
    }
    Console.WriteLine();
  }
}

public override string ToString()
{ return string.Format("[Length = {0}]", Length); }

// Rectangles can be explicitly converted
// into Squares.
public static explicit operator Square(Rectangle r)
{
  Square s = new Square();
  s.Length = r.Height;
  return s;
}
}
```

■ **Note** You'll notice in the Square and Rectangle constructors, I am explicitly chaining to the default constructor. The reason is that if you have a structure, which makes use of automatic property syntax (as we do here), the default constructor must be explicitly called (from all custom constructors) to initialize the private backing fields. Yes, this is a very quirky rule of C#, but after all, this is an advanced topics chapter.

Notice that this iteration of the Square type defines an explicit conversion operator. Like the process of overloading an operator, conversion routines make use of the C# operator keyword, in conjunction with the explicit or implicit keyword, and must be defined as static. The incoming parameter is the entity you are converting *from*, while the operator type is the entity you are converting *to*.

In this case, the assumption is that a square (being a geometric pattern in which all sides are of equal length) can be obtained from the height of a rectangle. Thus, you are free to convert a Rectangle into a Square, as follows:

```csharp
static void Main(string[] args)
{
  Console.WriteLine("***** Fun with Conversions *****\n");
```

```
// Make a Rectangle.
Rectangle r = new Rectangle(15, 4);
Console.WriteLine(r.ToString());
r.Draw();

Console.WriteLine();

// Convert r into a Square,
// based on the height of the Rectangle.
Square s = (Square)r;
Console.WriteLine(s.ToString());
s.Draw();
Console.ReadLine();
}
```

The output can be seen here:

```
***** Fun with Conversions *****

[Width = 15; Height = 4]

**************
**************
**************
**************

[Length = 4]
****
****
****
****
```

While it may not be all that helpful to convert a Rectangle into a Square within the same scope, assume you have a function that has been designed to take Square parameters.

```
// This method requires a Square type.
static void DrawSquare(Square sq)
{
  Console.WriteLine(sq.ToString());
  sq.Draw();
}
```

Using your explicit conversion operation on the Square type, you can now pass in Rectangle types for processing using an explicit cast, like so:

```
static void Main(string[] args)
{
...
  // Convert Rectangle to Square to invoke method.
  Rectangle rect = new Rectangle(10, 5);
```

```
    DrawSquare((Square)rect);
    Console.ReadLine();
}
```

Additional Explicit Conversions for the Square Type

Now that you can explicitly convert Rectangles into Squares, let's examine a few additional explicit conversions. Given that a square is symmetrical on all sides, it might be helpful to provide an explicit conversion routine that allows the caller to cast from an integer type into a Square (which, of course, will have a side length equal to the incoming integer). Likewise, what if you were to update Square such that the caller can cast *from* a Square into an int? Here is the calling logic:

```
static void Main(string[] args)
{
...
    // Converting an int to a Square.
    Square sq2 = (Square)90;
    Console.WriteLine("sq2 = {0}", sq2);

    // Converting a Square to an int.
    int side = (int)sq2;
    Console.WriteLine("Side length of sq2 = {0}", side);
    Console.ReadLine();
}
```

and here is the update to the Square class:

```
public struct Square
{
...
    public static explicit operator Square(int sideLength)
    {
        Square newSq = new Square();
        newSq.Length = sideLength;
        return newSq;
    }

    public static explicit operator int (Square s)
    {return s.Length;}
}
```

To be honest, converting from a Square into an integer may not be the most intuitive (or useful) operation. However, it does point out a very important fact regarding custom conversion routines: the compiler does not care what you convert to or from, as long as you have written syntactically correct code.

Thus, as with overloading operators, just because you can create an explicit cast operation for a given type does not mean you should. Typically, this technique will be most helpful when you're creating .NET structure types, given that they are unable to participate in classical inheritance (where casting comes for free).

Defining Implicit Conversion Routines

So far, you have created various custom *explicit* conversion operations. However, what about the following *implicit* conversion?

```
static void Main(string[] args)
{
...
  Square s3 = new Square();
  s3.Length = 83;

  // Attempt to make an implicit cast?
  Rectangle rect2 = s3;

  Console.ReadLine();
}
```

This code will not compile, given that you have not provided an implicit conversion routine for the Rectangle type. Now here is the catch: it is illegal to define explicit and implicit conversion functions on the same type if they do not differ by their return type or parameter set. This might seem like a limitation; however, the second catch is that when a type defines an *implicit* conversion routine, it is legal for the caller to make use of the *explicit* cast syntax!

Confused? To clear things up, let's add an implicit conversion routine to the Rectangle structure using the C# implicit keyword (note that the following code assumes the width of the resulting Rectangle is computed by multiplying the side of the Square by 2):

```
public struct Rectangle
{
...
  public static implicit operator Rectangle(Square s)
  {
    Rectangle r = new Rectangle();
    r.Height = s.Length;

    // Assume the length of the new Rectangle with
    // (Length x 2).
    r.Width = s.Length * 2;
    return r;
  }
}
```

With this update, you are now able to convert between types, as follows:

```
static void Main(string[] args)
{
...
  // Implicit cast OK!
  Square s3 = new Square();
  s3.Length= 7;
  Rectangle rect2 = s3;
  Console.WriteLine("rect2 = {0}", rect2);
```

```
    // Explicit cast syntax still OK!
    Square s4 = new Square();
    s4.Length = 3;
    Rectangle rect3 = (Rectangle)s4;
    Console.WriteLine("rect3 = {0}", rect3);
    Console.ReadLine();
}
```

That wraps up our look at defining custom conversion routines. As with overloaded operators, remember that this bit of syntax is simply a shorthand notation for "normal" member functions, and in this light it is always optional. When used correctly, however, custom structures can be used more naturally, as they can be treated as true class types related by inheritance.

■ **Source Code** The CustomConversions project is located under the Chapter 11 subdirectory.

Understanding Extension Methods

.NET 3.5 introduced the concept of *extension methods*, which allow you to add new methods or properties to a class or structure, without modifying the original type in any direct manner. So where might this be helpful? Consider the following possibilities.

First off, say you have a given class that is in production. It becomes clear over time that this class should support a handful of new members. If you were to modify the current class definition directly, you risk the possibility of breaking backward compatibility with older code bases making use of it, as they might not have been compiled with the latest and greatest class definition. One way to ensure backward compatibility would be to create a new derived class from the existing parent; however, now you have two classes to maintain. As we all know, code maintenance is least glamorous part of a software engineer's job description.

Now consider this situation. Let's say you have a structure (or maybe a sealed class) and would like to add new members so that it behaves polymorphically in your system. Since structures and sealed classes cannot be extended, your only choice is to add the members to the type, once again risking backward compatibility!

Using extension methods, you are able to modify types without subclassing and without modifying the type directly. To be sure, this technique is essentially a smoke and mirror show. The new functionality is only offered to a type if the extension methods have been referenced for use in your current project.

Defining Extension Methods

When you define extension methods, the first restriction is that they must be defined within a static class (see Chapter 5) and, therefore, each extension method must be declared with the static keyword. The second point is that all extension methods are marked as such by using the this keyword as a modifier on the first (and only the first) parameter of the method in question. The "this qualified" parameter represents the item being extended.

To illustrate, create a new Console Application named ExtensionMethods. Now, assume you are authoring a class named MyExtensions that defines two extension methods. The first method allows any object to use a brand-new method named DisplayDefiningAssembly() that makes use of types in the System.Reflection namespace to display the name of the assembly containing the type in question.

■ **Note** You will formally examine the reflection API in Chapter 15. If you are new to the topic, simply understand that reflection allows you to discover the structure of assemblies, types, and type members at runtime.

The second extension method, named ReverseDigits(), allows any int to obtain a new version of itself where the value is reversed digit by digit. For example, if an integer with the value 1234 called ReverseDigits(), the integer returned is set to the value 4321. Consider the following class implementation (be sure to import the System.Reflection namespace if you are following along):

```
static class MyExtensions
{
  // This method allows any object to display the assembly
  // it is defined in.
  public static void DisplayDefiningAssembly(this object obj)
  {
    Console.WriteLine("{0} lives here: => {1}\n", obj.GetType().Name,
      Assembly.GetAssembly(obj.GetType()).GetName().Name);
  }

  // This method allows any integer to reverse its digits.
  // For example, 56 would return 65.
  public static int ReverseDigits(this int i)
  {
    // Translate int into a string, and then
    // get all the characters.
    char[] digits = i.ToString().ToCharArray();

    // Now reverse items in the array.
    Array.Reverse(digits);

    // Put back into string.
    string newDigits = new string(digits);

    // Finally, return the modified string back as an int.
    return int.Parse(newDigits);
  }
}
```

Again, note how the first parameter of each extension method has been qualified with the this keyword, before defining the parameter type. It is always the case that the first parameter of an extension method represents the type being extended. Given that DisplayDefiningAssembly() has been prototyped to extend System.Object, every type now has this new member, as Object is the parent to all types in the .NET platform. However, ReverseDigits() has been prototyped to only extend integer types and, therefore, if anything other than an integer attempts to invoke this method, you will receive a compile-time error.

> ■ **Note** Understand that a given extension method can have multiple parameters, but *only* the first parameter can be qualified with this. The additional parameters would be treated as normal incoming parameters for use by the method.

Invoking Extension Methods

Now that we have these extension methods in place, consider the following Main() method:

```
static void Main(string[] args)
{
  Console.WriteLine("***** Fun with Extension Methods *****\n");

  // The int has assumed a new identity!
  int myInt = 12345678;
  myInt.DisplayDefiningAssembly();

  // So has the DataSet!
  System.Data.DataSet d = new System.Data.DataSet();
  d.DisplayDefiningAssembly();

  // And the SoundPlayer!
  System.Media.SoundPlayer sp = new System.Media.SoundPlayer();
  sp.DisplayDefiningAssembly();

  // Use new integer functionality.
  Console.WriteLine("Value of myInt: {0}", myInt);
  Console.WriteLine("Reversed digits of myInt: {0}", myInt.ReverseDigits());

  Console.ReadLine();
}
```

Here is the output (minus the beeping):

```
***** Fun with Extension Methods *****

Int32 lives here: => mscorlib

DataSet lives here: => System.Data

SoundPlayer lives here: => System

Value of myInt: 12345678
Reversed digits of myInt: 87654321
```

Importing Extension Methods

When you define a class containing extension methods, it will no doubt be defined within a .NET namespace. If this namespace is different from the namespace using the extension methods, you will need to make use of the expected C# using keyword. When you do, your code file has access to all extension methods for the type being extended. This is important to remember, because if you do not explicitly import the correct namespace, the extension methods are not available for that C# code file.

In effect, although it can appear on the surface that extension methods are global in nature, they are in fact limited to the namespaces that define them or the namespaces that import them. Thus, if we wrap the MyExtensions class into a namespace named MyExtensionMethods, as follows:

```
namespace MyExtensionMethods
{
  static class MyExtensions
  {
    ...
  }
}
```

other namespaces in the project would need to explicitly import the MyExtensionMethods namespace to gain the extension methods defined by our class.

■ **Note** It is common practice to not only isolate extension methods into a dedicated .NET namespace, but into a dedicated class library. In this way, new applications can "opt-in" to extensions by explicitly referencing the correct library. Chapter 14 will examine the details of building and using custom .NET class libraries.

The IntelliSense of Extension Methods

Given the fact that extension methods are not literally defined on the type being extended, it is certainly possible to become confused when examining an existing code base. For example, assume you have imported a namespace that defined some number of extension methods authored by a teammate. As you are authoring your code, you might create a variable of the extended type, apply the dot operator, and find dozens of new methods that are not members of the original class definition!

Thankfully, Visual Studio's IntelliSense mechanism marks all extension methods with a unique, down-arrow icon (see Figure 11-1).

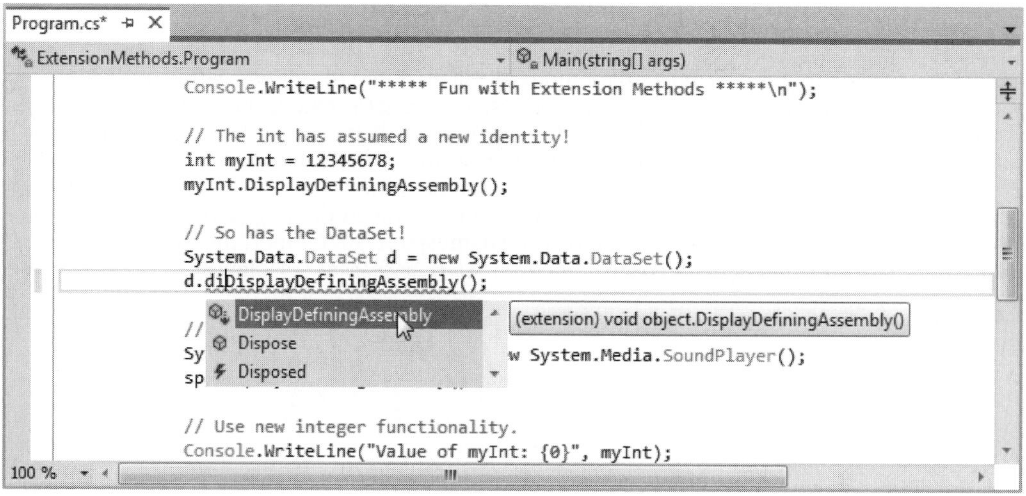

```
Program.cs*  ⊣  ✕
ExtensionMethods.Program                          ▾  Main(string[] args)                      ▾
        Console.WriteLine("***** Fun with Extension Methods *****\n");

        // The int has assumed a new identity!
        int myInt = 12345678;
        myInt.DisplayDefiningAssembly();

        // So has the DataSet!
        System.Data.DataSet d = new System.Data.DataSet();
        d.diDisplayDefiningAssembly();

         ⊘  DisplayDefiningAssembly   ▲   (extension) void object.DisplayDefiningAssembly()
        Sy  ⊘  Dispose                    w System.Media.SoundPlayer();
        sp  ⚡ Disposed                ▾

        // Use new integer functionality.
        Console.WriteLine("Value of myInt: {0}", myInt);
100 %   ▾  ◂                     III                              ▸
```

Figure 11-1. The IntelliSense of extension methods

Any method marked with this visual icon is a friendly reminder that the method is defined outside of the original class definition via an extension method.

■ **Source Code** The ExtensionMethods project can be found under the Chapter 11 subdirectory.

Extending Types Implementing Specific Interfaces

At this point, you have seen how to extend classes (and, indirectly, structures that follow the same syntax) with new functionality via extension methods. It is also possible to define an extension method that can only extend a class or structure that implements the correct interface. For example, you could say something to the effect of "if a class or structure implements IEnumerable<T>, then that type gets the following new members." Of course, it is possible to demand that a type support any interface at all, including your own custom interfaces.

To illustrate, create a new Console Application named InterfaceExtensions. The goal here is to add a new method to any type that implements IEnumerable, which would include any array and many nongeneric collection classes (recall from Chapter 8 that the generic IEnumerable<T> interface extends the nongeneric IEnumerable interface). Add the following extension class to your new project:

```
static class AnnoyingExtensions
{
  public static void PrintDataAndBeep(this System.Collections.IEnumerable iterator)
  {
    foreach (var item in iterator)
    {
      Console.WriteLine(item);
      Console.Beep();
```

```
      }
   }
}
```

Given that the `PrintDataAndBeep()` method can be used by any class or structure that implements `IEnumerable`, we could test via the following `Main()` method:

```
static void Main( string[] args )
{
  Console.WriteLine("***** Extending Interface Compatible Types *****\n");

  // System.Array implements IEnumerable!
  string[] data = { "Wow", "this", "is", "sort", "of", "annoying",
                    "but", "in", "a", "weird", "way", "fun!"};
  data.PrintDataAndBeep();

  Console.WriteLine();

  // List<T> implements IEnumerable!
  List<int> myInts = new List<int>() {10, 15, 20};
  myInts.PrintDataAndBeep();

  Console.ReadLine();
}
```

That wraps up our examination of C# extension methods. Remember that this particular language feature can be very useful whenever you want to extend the functionality of a type, but do not want to subclass (or can not subclass if the type is sealed), for the purposes of polymorphism. As you will see later in the text, extension methods play a key role for LINQ APIs. In fact, you will see that under the LINQ APIs, one of the most common items being extended is a class or structure implementing (surprise!) the generic version of `IEnumerable`.

■ **Source Code** The InterfaceExtension project can be found under the Chapter 11 subdirectory.

Understanding Anonymous Types

As an OO programmer, you know the benefits of defining classes to represent the state and functionality of a given item you are attempting to model. To be sure, whenever you need to define a class that is intended to be reused across projects and provides numerous bits of functionality through a set of methods, events, properties, and custom constructors, creating a new C# class is common practice.

However, there are other times when you would like to define a class simply to model a set of encapsulated (and somehow related) data points without any associated methods, events, or other specialized functionality. Furthermore, what if this type is to be used only by a handful of methods in your program? It would be rather a bother to define a full class definition as shown below; when you know full well this class will be used only in a handful of places. To accentuate this point, here is the rough outline of what you might need to do when you need to create a "simple" data type that follows typical value-based semantics:

```
class SomeClass
{
  // Define a set of private member variables...

  // Make a property for each member variable...

  // Override ToString() to account for key member variables...

  // Override GetHashCode() and Equals() to work with value-based equality...
}
```

As you can see, it is not necessarily so simple. Not only do you need to author a fair amount of code, but you have another class to maintain in your system. For temporary data such as this, it would be useful to whip up a custom data type on the fly. For example, let's say that you need to build a custom method that receives a set of incoming parameters. You would like to take these parameters and use them to create a new data type for use in this method scope. Further, you would like to quickly print out this data using the typical ToString() method and perhaps use other members of System.Object. You can do this very thing using anonymous type syntax.

Defining an Anonymous Type

When you define an anonymous type, you do so by making use of the var keyword (see Chapter 3) in conjunction with object initialization syntax (see Chapter 5). We must use the var keyword because the compiler will automatically generate a new class definition at compile time (and we never see the name of this class in our C# code). The initialization syntax is used to tell the compiler to create private backing fields and (read-only) properties for the newly created type.

To illustrate, create a new Console Application named AnonymousTypes. Now, add the following method to your Program class, which composes a new type, on the fly, using the incoming parameter data:

```
static void BuildAnonType( string make, string color, int currSp )
{
  // Build anon type using incoming args.
  var car = new { Make = make, Color = color, Speed = currSp };

  // Note you can now use this type to get the property data!
  Console.WriteLine("You have a {0} {1} going {2} MPH",
    car.Color, car.Make, car.Speed);

  // Anon types have custom implementations of each virtual
  // method of System.Object. For example:
  Console.WriteLine("ToString() == {0}", car.ToString());
}
```

You can call this method from Main(), as expected. However, do note that an anonymous type can also be created using hard-coded values, as seen here:

```
static void Main(string[] args)
{
  Console.WriteLine("***** Fun with Anonymous Types *****\n");

  // Make an anonymous type representing a car.
  var myCar = new { Color = "Bright Pink", Make = "Saab", CurrentSpeed = 55 };
```

```
    // Now show the color and make.
    Console.WriteLine("My car is a {0} {1}.", myCar.Color, myCar.Make);

    // Now call our helper method to build anonymous type via args.
    BuildAnonType("BMW", "Black", 90);

    Console.ReadLine();
}
```

So, at this point, simply understand that anonymous types allow you to quickly model the "shape" of data with very little overhead. This technique is little more than a way to whip up a new data type on the fly, which supports barebones encapsulation via properties and acts according to value-based semantics. To understand that last point, let's see how the C# compiler builds out anonymous types at compile time, and specifically, how it overrides the members of System.Object.

The Internal Representation of Anonymous Types

All anonymous types are automatically derived from System.Object and, therefore, support each of the members provided by this base class. Given this, we could invoke ToString(), GetHashCode(), Equals(), or GetType() on the implicitly typed myCar object. Assume our Program class defines the following static helper function:

```
static void ReflectOverAnonymousType(object obj)
{
  Console.WriteLine("obj is an instance of: {0}", obj.GetType().Name);
  Console.WriteLine("Base class of {0} is {1}",
    obj.GetType().Name,
    obj.GetType().BaseType);
  Console.WriteLine("obj.ToString() == {0}", obj.ToString());
  Console.WriteLine("obj.GetHashCode() == {0}", obj.GetHashCode());
  Console.WriteLine();
}
```

Now assume we invoke this method from Main(), passing in the myCar object as the parameter, like so:

```
static void Main(string[] args)
{
  Console.WriteLine("***** Fun with Anonymous Types *****\n");

  // Make an anonymous type representing a car.
  var myCar = new {Color = "Bright Pink", Make = "Saab", CurrentSpeed = 55};

  // Reflect over what the compiler generated.
  ReflectOverAnonymousType(myCar);
...

  Console.ReadLine();
}
```

The output will look similar to the following:

```
***** Fun with Anonymous Types *****

obj is an instance of: <>f__AnonymousType0`3
Base class of <>f__AnonymousType0`3 is System.Object
obj.ToString() = { Color = Bright Pink, Make = Saab, CurrentSpeed = 55 }
obj.GetHashCode() = -439083487
```

First, notice that in this example, the myCar object is of type <>f__AnonymousType0`3 (your name may differ). Remember that the assigned type name is completely determined by the compiler and is not directly accessible in your C# code base.

Perhaps most important, notice that each name/value pair defined using the object initialization syntax is mapped to an identically named read-only property and a corresponding private read-only backing field. The following C# code approximates the compiler-generated class used to represent the myCar object (which again can be verified using ildasm.exe):

```
internal sealed class <>f__AnonymousType0<<Color>j__TPar,
  <Make>j__TPar, <CurrentSpeed>j__TPar>
{
  // Read-only fields.
  private readonly <Color>j__TPar <Color>i__Field;
  private readonly <CurrentSpeed>j__TPar <CurrentSpeed>i__Field;
  private readonly <Make>j__TPar <Make>i__Field;

  // Default constructor.
  public <>f__AnonymousType0(<Color>j__TPar Color,
    <Make>j__TPar Make, <CurrentSpeed>j__TPar CurrentSpeed);
  // Overridden methods.
  public override bool Equals(object value);
  public override int GetHashCode();
  public override string ToString();

  // Read-only properties.
  public <Color>j__TPar Color { get; }
  public <CurrentSpeed>j__TPar CurrentSpeed { get; }
  public <Make>j__TPar Make { get; }
}
```

The Implementation of ToString() and GetHashCode()

All anonymous types automatically derive from System.Object and are provided with an overridden version of Equals(), GetHashCode(), and ToString(). The ToString() implementation simply builds a string from each name/value pair. For example:

```
public override string ToString()
{
  StringBuilder builder = new StringBuilder();
  builder.Append("{ Color = ");
  builder.Append(this.<Color>i__Field);
  builder.Append(", Make = ");
  builder.Append(this.<Make>i__Field);
  builder.Append(", CurrentSpeed = ");
  builder.Append(this.<CurrentSpeed>i__Field);
  builder.Append(" }");
  return builder.ToString();
}
```

The GetHashCode() implementation computes a hash value using each anonymous type's member variables as input to the System.Collections.Generic.EqualityComparer<T> type. Using this implementation of GetHashCode(), two anonymous types will yield the same hash value if (and only if) they have the same set of properties that have been assigned the same values. Given this implementation, anonymous types are well-suited to be contained within a Hashtable container.

The Semantics of Equality for Anonymous Types

While the implementation of the overridden ToString() and GetHashCode() methods is fairly straightforward, you might be wondering how the Equals() method has been implemented. For example, if we were to define two "anonymous cars" variables that specify the same name/value pairs, would these two variables be considered equal or not? To see the results firsthand, update your Program type with the following new method:

```
static void EqualityTest()
{
  // Make 2 anonymous classes with identical name/value pairs.
  var firstCar = new { Color = "Bright Pink", Make = "Saab", CurrentSpeed = 55 };
  var secondCar = new { Color = "Bright Pink", Make = "Saab", CurrentSpeed = 55 };

  // Are they considered equal when using Equals()?
  if (firstCar.Equals(secondCar))
    Console.WriteLine("Same anonymous object!");
  else
    Console.WriteLine("Not the same anonymous object!");

  // Are they considered equal when using ==?
  if (firstCar == secondCar)
    Console.WriteLine("Same anonymous object!");
  else
    Console.WriteLine("Not the same anonymous object!");

  // Are these objects the same underlying type?
  if (firstCar.GetType().Name == secondCar.GetType().Name)
    Console.WriteLine("We are both the same type!");
  else
    Console.WriteLine("We are different types!");
```

```
    // Show all the details.
    Console.WriteLine();
    ReflectOverAnonymousType(firstCar);
    ReflectOverAnonymousType(secondCar);
}
```

Assuming you have called this method from within `Main()`. Here is the (somewhat surprising) output:

```
My car is a Bright Pink Saab.
You have a Black BMW going 90 MPH
ToString() == { Make = BMW, Color = Black, Speed = 90 }

Same anonymous object!
Not the same anonymous object!
We are both the same type!

obj is an instance of: <>f__AnonymousType0`3
Base class of <>f__AnonymousType0`3 is System.Object
obj.ToString() == { Color = Bright Pink, Make = Saab, CurrentSpeed = 55 }
obj.GetHashCode() == -439083487

obj is an instance of: <>f__AnonymousType0`3
Base class of <>f__AnonymousType0`3 is System.Object
obj.ToString() == { Color = Bright Pink, Make = Saab, CurrentSpeed = 55 }
obj.GetHashCode() == -439083487
```

When you run this test code, you will see that the first conditional test where you call `Equals()` returns true and, therefore, the message "Same anonymous object!" prints out to the screen. This is because the compiler-generated `Equals()` method makes use of value-based semantics when testing for equality (e.g., checking the value of each field of the objects being compared).

However, the second conditional test, which makes use of the C# equality operator (`==`), prints out "Not the same anonymous object!", which might seem at first glance to be a bit counterintuitive. This result is due to the fact that anonymous types do *not* receive overloaded versions of the C# equality operators (`==` and `!=`). Given this, when you test for equality of anonymous types using the C# equality operators (rather than the `Equals()` method), the *references*, not the values maintained by the objects, are being tested for equality.

Last but not least, in our final conditional test (where we examine the underlying type name), we find that the anonymous types are instances of the same compiler-generated class type (in this example, `<>f__AnonymousType0`3`), due to the fact that `firstCar` and `secondCar` have the same properties (`Color`, `Make`, and `CurrentSpeed`).

This illustrates an important but subtle point: the compiler will only generate a new class definition when an anonymous type contains *unique* names of the anonymous type. Thus, if you declare identical anonymous types (again, meaning the same names) within the same assembly, the compiler generates only a single anonymous type definition.

Anonymous Types Containing Anonymous Types

It is possible to create an anonymous type that is composed of other anonymous types. For example, assume you want to model a purchase order that consists of a timestamp, a price point, and the automobile purchased. Here is a new (slightly more sophisticated) anonymous type representing such an entity:

```
// Make an anonymous type that is composed of another.
var purchaseItem = new {
  TimeBought = DateTime.Now,
  ItemBought = new {Color = "Red", Make = "Saab", CurrentSpeed = 55},
  Price = 34.000};

ReflectOverAnonymousType(purchaseItem);
```

At this point, you should understand the syntax used to define anonymous types, but you might still be wondering exactly where (and when) to use this new language feature. To be blunt, anonymous type declarations should be used sparingly, typically only when making use of the LINQ technology set (see Chapter 12). You would never want to abandon the use of strongly typed classes/structures simply for the sake of doing so, given anonymous types' numerous limitations, which include the following:

- You don't control the name of the anonymous type.

- Anonymous types always extend System.Object.

- The fields and properties of an anonymous type are always read-only.

- Anonymous types cannot support events, custom methods, custom operators, or custom overrides.

- Anonymous types are always implicitly sealed.

- Anonymous types are always created using the default constructor.

However, when programming with the LINQ technology set, you will find that in many cases this syntax can be very helpful when you want to quickly model the overall *shape* of an entity rather than its functionality.

■ **Source Code** The AnonymousTypes project can be found under the Chapter 11 subdirectory.

Working with Pointer Types

And now, the final topic of the chapter, which most likely will be the least-used of all C# features for the vast majority of your .NET projects.

■ **Note** In the examples that follow, I'm assuming you have some background in C(++) pointer manipulation. If this is not true, feel free to skip this topic entirely. Using pointers will not be a common task for the vast majority of C# applications.

In Chapter 4, you learned that the .NET platform defines two major categories of data: value types and reference types. Truth be told, however, there is a third category: *pointer types*. To work with pointer types, we get specific operators and keywords that allow us to bypass the CLR's memory-management scheme and take matters into our own hands (see Table 11-2).

Table 11-2. Pointer-Centric C# Operators and Keywords

Operator/Keyword	Meaning in Life
*	This operator is used to create a pointer variable (i.e., a variable that represents a direct location in memory). As in C(++), this same operator is used for pointer indirection.
&	This operator is used to obtain the address of a variable in memory.
->	This operator is used to access fields of a type that is represented by a pointer (the unsafe version of the C# dot operator).
[]	This operator (in an unsafe context) allows you to index the slot pointed to by a pointer variable (if you're a C++ programmer, you will recall the interplay between a pointer variable and the [ ] operator).
++, --	In an unsafe context, the increment and decrement operators can be applied to pointer types.
+, -	In an unsafe context, the addition and subtraction operators can be applied to pointer types.
==,!=, <, >, <=, =>	In an unsafe context, the comparison and equality operators can be applied to pointer types.
stackalloc	In an unsafe context, the stackalloc keyword can be used to allocate C# arrays directly on the stack.
fixed	In an unsafe context, the fixed keyword can be used to temporarily fix a variable so that its address can be found.

Now, before we dig into the details, let me again point out that you will *seldom if ever* need to make use of pointer types. Although C# does allow you to drop down to the level of pointer manipulations, understand that the .NET runtime has absolutely no clue of your intentions. Thus, if you mismanage a pointer, you are the one in charge of dealing with the consequences. Given these warnings, when exactly would you need to work with pointer types? There are two common situations:

- You are looking to optimize select parts of your application by directly manipulating memory outside the management of the CLR.

- You are calling methods of a C-based .dll or COM server that demand pointer types as parameters. Even in this case, you can often bypass pointer types in favor of the System.IntPtr type and members of the System.Runtime.InteropServices.Marshal type.

In the event that you do decide to make use of this C# language feature, you are required to inform the C# compiler (csc.exe) of your intentions by enabling your project to support "unsafe code." To do so at the command line, simply supply the following /unsafe flag as an argument:

```
csc /unsafe *.cs
```

From Visual Studio, you will need to access your project's Properties page and check the Allow Unsafe Code box from the Build tab (see Figure 11-2). To experiment with pointer types, create a new Console Application project named UnsafeCode and enable unsafe code, and make sure you enable this setting.

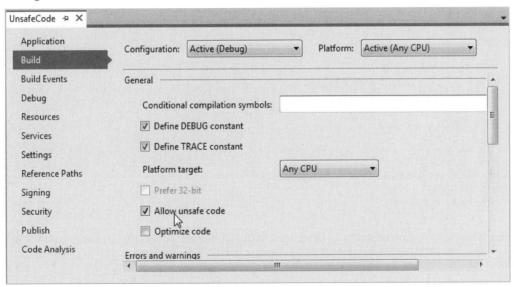

Figure 11-2. Enabling unsafe code using Visual Studio

The unsafe Keyword

When you wish to work with pointers in C#, you must specifically declare a block of "unsafe code" using the unsafe keyword (any code that is not marked with the unsafe keyword is considered "safe" automatically). For example, the following Program class declares a scope of unsafe code within the safe Main() method:

```
class Program
{
  static void Main(string[] args)
  {
    unsafe
    {
      // Work with pointer types here!
    }

    // Can't work with pointers here!
  }
}
```

In addition to declaring a scope of unsafe code within a method, you can build structures, classes, type members, and parameters that are "unsafe." Here are a few examples to gnaw on (no need to define the Node or Node2 types in your current project):

```
// This entire structure is "unsafe" and can
// be used only in an unsafe context.
unsafe struct Node
{
  public int Value;
  public Node* Left;
  public Node* Right;
}

// This struct is safe, but the Node2* members
// are not. Technically, you may access "Value" from
// outside an unsafe context, but not "Left" and "Right".
public struct Node2
{
  public int Value;

  // These can be accessed only in an unsafe context!
  public unsafe Node2* Left;
  public unsafe Node2* Right;
}
```

Methods (static or instance level) may be marked as unsafe as well. For example, assume you know that a particular static method will make use of pointer logic. To ensure that this method can be called only from an unsafe context, you could define the method as follows:

```
unsafe static void SquareIntPointer(int* myIntPointer)
{
  // Square the value just for a test.
  *myIntPointer *= *myIntPointer;
}
```

The configuration of our method demands that the caller invoke SquareIntPointer() as follows:

```
static void Main(string[] args)
{
  unsafe
  {
```

```
  int myInt = 10;

  // OK, because we are in an unsafe context.
  SquareIntPointer(&myInt);
  Console.WriteLine("myInt: {0}", myInt);
}

int myInt2 = 5;

// Compiler error! Must be in unsafe context!
SquareIntPointer(&myInt2);
Console.WriteLine("myInt: {0}", myInt2);
}
```

If you would rather not force the caller to wrap the invocation within an unsafe context, you could update Main() with the unsafe keyword. In this case, the following code would compile:

```
unsafe static void Main(string[] args)
{
  int myInt2 = 5;
  SquareIntPointer(&myInt2);
  Console.WriteLine("myInt: {0}", myInt2);
}
```

If you run this Main() method, you will see the following output:

```
myInt: 25
```

Working with the * and & Operators

After you have established an unsafe context, you are then free to build pointers to data types using the * operator and obtain the address of what is being pointed to using the & operator. Unlike in C or C++, in C# the * operator is applied to the underlying type only, not as a prefix to each pointer variable name. For example, consider the following code, which illustrates both the correct and incorrect ways to declare pointers to integer variables:

```
// No! This is incorrect under C#!
int *pi, *pj;

// Yes! This is the way of C#.
int* pi, pj;
```

Consider the following unsafe method:

```
unsafe static void PrintValueAndAddress()
{
  int myInt;

  // Define an int pointer, and
  // assign it the address of myInt.
  int* ptrToMyInt = &myInt;
```

```
  // Assign value of myInt using pointer indirection.
  *ptrToMyInt = 123;

  // Print some stats.
  Console.WriteLine("Value of myInt {0}", myInt);
  Console.WriteLine("Address of myInt {0:X}", (int)&ptrToMyInt);
}
```

An Unsafe (and Safe) Swap Function

Of course, declaring pointers to local variables simply to assign their value (as in the previous example) is never required and not altogether useful. To illustrate a more practical example of unsafe code, assume you want to build a swap function using pointer arithmetic:

```
unsafe public static void UnsafeSwap(int* i, int* j)
{
  int temp = *i;
  *i = *j;
  *j = temp;
}
```

Very C-like, don't you think? However, given your work in previously, you should be aware that you could write the following safe version of your swap algorithm using the C# ref keyword:

```
public static void SafeSwap(ref int i, ref int j)
{
  int temp = i;
  i = j;
  j = temp;
}
```

The functionality of each method is identical, thus reinforcing the point that direct pointer manipulation is not a mandatory task under C#. Here is the calling logic using a safe Main(), with an unsafe context:

```
static void Main(string[] args)
{
  Console.WriteLine("***** Calling method with unsafe code *****");

  // Values for swap.
  int i = 10, j = 20;

  // Swap values "safely."
  Console.WriteLine("\n***** Safe swap *****");
  Console.WriteLine("Values before safe swap: i = {0}, j = {1}", i, j);
  SafeSwap(ref i, ref j);
  Console.WriteLine("Values after safe swap: i = {0}, j = {1}", i, j);

  // Swap values "unsafely."
  Console.WriteLine("\n***** Unsafe swap *****");
  Console.WriteLine("Values before unsafe swap: i = {0}, j = {1}", i, j);
```

```
  unsafe { UnsafeSwap(&i, &j); }

  Console.WriteLine("Values after unsafe swap: i = {0}, j = {1}", i, j);
  Console.ReadLine();
}
```

Field Access via Pointers (the -> Operator)

Now assume you have defined a simple, safe Point structure, as follows:

```
struct Point
{
  public int x;
  public int y;

  public override string ToString()
  {
    return string.Format("({0}, {1})", x, y);
  }
}
```

If you declare a pointer to a Point type, you will need to make use of the pointer field-access operator (represented by ->) to access its public members. As shown in Table 11-2, this is the unsafe version of the standard (safe) dot operator (.). In fact, using the pointer indirection operator (*), it is possible to dereference a pointer to (once again) apply the dot operator notation. Check out the unsafe method:

```
unsafe static void UsePointerToPoint()
{
  // Access members via pointer.
  Point point;
  Point* p = &point;
  p->x = 100;
  p->y = 200;
  Console.WriteLine(p->ToString());

  // Access members via pointer indirection.
  Point point2;
  Point* p2 = &point2;
  (*p2).x = 100;
  (*p2).y = 200;
  Console.WriteLine((*p2).ToString());
}
```

The stackalloc Keyword

In an unsafe context, you may need to declare a local variable that allocates memory directly from the call stack (and is, therefore, not subject to .NET garbage collection). To do so, C# provides the stackalloc keyword, which is the C# equivalent to the _alloca function of the C runtime library. Here is a simple example:

```
unsafe static void UnsafeStackAlloc()
{
  char* p = stackalloc char[256];
  for (int k = 0; k < 256; k++)
    p[k] = (char)k;
}
```

Pinning a Type via the fixed Keyword

As you saw in the previous example, allocating a chunk of memory within an unsafe context may be facilitated via the stackalloc keyword. By the very nature of this operation, the allocated memory is cleaned up as soon as the allocating method has returned (as the memory is acquired from the stack). However, assume a more complex example. During our examination of the -> operator, you created a value type named Point. Like all value types, the allocated memory is popped off the stack once the executing scope has terminated. For the sake of argument, assume Point was instead defined as a *reference* type, like so:

```
class PointRef  // <= Renamed and retyped.
{
  public int x;
  public int y;
  public override string ToString()
  {
    return string.Format("({0}, {1})", x, y);
  }
}
```

As you are aware, if the caller declares a variable of type Point, the memory is allocated on the garbage-collected heap. The burning question then becomes, "What if an unsafe context wants to interact with this object (or any object on the heap)?" Given that garbage collection can occur at any moment, imagine the problems encountered when accessing the members of Point at the very point in time such a sweep of the heap is under way. Theoretically, it is possible that the unsafe context is attempting to interact with a member that is no longer accessible or has been repositioned on the heap after surviving a generational sweep (which is an obvious problem).

To lock a reference type variable in memory from an unsafe context, C# provides the fixed keyword. The fixed statement sets a pointer to a managed type and "pins" that variable during the execution of the code. Without fixed, pointers to managed variables would be of little use, since garbage collection could relocate the variables unpredictably. (In fact, the C# compiler will not allow you to set a pointer to a managed variable except in a fixed statement.)

Thus, if you create a PointRef type and want to interact with its members, you must write the following code (or receive a compiler error):

```
unsafe public static void UseAndPinPoint()
{
  PointRef pt = new PointRef ();
  pt.x = 5;
  pt.y = 6;

  // Pin pt in place so it will not
  // be moved or GC-ed.
  fixed (int* p = &pt.x)
  {
```

```
  // Use int* variable here!
}

// pt is now unpinned, and ready to be GC-ed once
// the method completes.
  Console.WriteLine ("Point is: {0}", pt);
}
```

In a nutshell, the fixed keyword allows you to build a statement that locks a reference variable in memory, such that its address remains constant for the duration of the statement (or scope block). Any time you interact with a reference type from within the context of unsafe code, pinning the reference is a must.

The sizeof Keyword

The final unsafe-centric C# keyword to consider is sizeof. As in C(++), the C# sizeof keyword is used to obtain the size in bytes of a value type (never a reference type), and it may only be used within an unsafe context. As you might imagine, this ability can prove helpful when you're interacting with unmanaged C-based APIs. Its usage is straightforward.

```
unsafe static void UseSizeOfOperator()
{
  Console.WriteLine("The size of short is {0}.", sizeof(short));
  Console.WriteLine("The size of int is {0}.", sizeof(int));
  Console.WriteLine("The size of long is {0}.", sizeof(long));
}
```

As sizeof will evaluate the number of bytes for any System.ValueType-derived entity, you can obtain the size of custom structures as well. For example, we could pass the Point structure into sizeof, as follows:

```
unsafe static void UseSizeOfOperator()
{
...
  Console.WriteLine("The size of Point is {0}.", sizeof(Point));
}
```

■ **Source Code** The UnsafeCode project can be found under the Chapter 11 subdirectory.

That wraps up our look at some of the more advanced features of the C# programming language. To make sure we are all on the same page here, I again must say that a majority of your .NET projects might never need to directly use these features (especially pointers). Nevertheless, as you will see in later chapters, some topics are quite useful, if not required, when working with the LINQ APIs, most notably extension methods and anonymous types.

Summary

The purpose of this chapter was to deepen your understanding of the C# programming language. First, you investigated various advanced type construction techniques (indexer methods, overloaded operators, and custom conversion routines).

Next, you examined the role of extension methods and anonymous types. As you'll see in some detail in the next chapter, these features are very useful when working with LINQ-centric APIs (though you can use them anywhere in your code, should they be useful). Recall that anonymous methods allow you to quickly model the "shape" of a type, while extension methods allow you to tack on new functionality to types, without the need to subclass.

You spent the remainder of this chapter examining a small set of lesser-known keywords (sizeof, unsafe, and so forth), and during the process learned how to work with raw pointer types. As stated throughout our examination of pointer types, the vast majority of your C# applications will never need to make use of them.

CHAPTER 12

LINQ to Objects

Regardless of the type of application you are creating using the .NET platform, your program will certainly need to access some form of data as it executes. To be sure, data can be found in numerous locations, including XML files, relational databases, in-memory collections, and primitive arrays. Historically speaking, based on the location of said data, programmers needed to make use of very different and unrelated APIs. The Language Integrated Query (LINQ) technology set, introduced initially in .NET 3.5, provides a concise, symmetrical, and strongly typed manner to access a wide variety of data stores. In this chapter, you will begin your investigation of LINQ, by focusing on LINQ to Objects.

Before you dive into LINQ to Objects proper, the first part of this chapter quickly reviews the key C# programming constructs that enable LINQ. As you work through this chapter, you will find that implicitly typed local variables, object initialization syntax, lambda expressions, extension methods, and anonymous types will be quite useful (if not occasionally mandatory).

After this supporting infrastructure is reviewed, the remainder of the chapter will introduce you to the LINQ programming model and its role in the .NET platform. Here, you will come to learn the role of query operators and query expressions, which allow you to define statements that will interrogate a data source to yield the requested result set. Along the way, you will build numerous LINQ examples that interact with data contained within arrays as well as various collection types (both generic and nongeneric) and understand the assemblies, namespaces, and types that represent the LINQ to Objects API.

■ **Note** The information in this chapter is the foundation for future chapters of the book that examine additional LINQ technologies, including LINQ to XML (Chapter 24), Parallel LINQ (Chapter 19), and LINQ to Entities (Chapter 23).

LINQ-Specific Programming Constructs

From a very high level, LINQ can be understood as a strongly typed query language, embedded directly into the grammar of C# itself. Using LINQ, you can build any number of expressions that have a look-and-feel similar to that of a database SQL query. However, a LINQ query can be applied to any number of data stores, including stores that have nothing to do with a literal relational database.

■ **Note** Although LINQ queries look similar to SQL queries, the syntax is *not* identical. In fact, many LINQ queries seem to be the exact opposite format of a similar database query! If you attempt to map LINQ directly to SQL, you will surely become frustrated. To keep your sanity, I'd recommend that you try your best to regard LINQ queries as unique statements, which just "happen to look" similar to SQL.

When LINQ was first introduced to the .NET platform in version 3.5, the C# and VB languages were each expanded with a large number of new programming constructs used to support the LINQ technology set. Specifically, the C# language uses the following core LINQ-centric features:

- Implicitly typed local variables

- Object/collection initialization syntax

- Lambda expressions

- Extension methods

- Anonymous types

These features have already been explored in detail within various chapters of the text. However, to get the ball rolling, let's quickly review each feature in turn, just to make sure we are all in the proper mindset.

Implicit Typing of Local Variables

In Chapter 3, you learned about the var keyword of C#. This keyword allows you to define a local variable without explicitly specifying the underlying data type. The variable, however, is strongly typed, as the compiler will determine the correct data type based on the initial assignment. Recall the following code example from Chapter 3:

```
static void DeclareImplicitVars()
{
  // Implicitly typed local variables.
  var myInt = 0;
  var myBool = true;
  var myString = "Time, marches on...";

  // Print out the underlying type.
  Console.WriteLine("myInt is a: {0}", myInt.GetType().Name);
  Console.WriteLine("myBool is a: {0}", myBool.GetType().Name);
  Console.WriteLine("myString is a: {0}", myString.GetType().Name);
}
```

This language feature is very helpful, and often mandatory, when using LINQ. As you will see during this chapter, many LINQ queries will return a sequence of data types, which are not known until compile time. Given that the underlying data type is not known until the application is compiled, you obviously can't declare a variable explicitly!

Object and Collection Initialization Syntax

Chapter 5 explored the role of object initialization syntax, which allows you to create a class or structure variable, and set any number of its public properties, in one fell swoop. The end result is a very compact (yet still easy on the eyes) syntax that can be used to get your objects ready for use. Also recall from Chapter 9, the C# language allows you to use a very similar syntax to initialize collections of objects. Consider the following code snippet, which uses collection initialization syntax to fill a List<T> of Rectangle objects, each of which maintains two Point objects to represent an (x,y) position:

```
List<Rectangle> myListOfRects = new List<Rectangle>
{
  new Rectangle {TopLeft = new Point { X = 10, Y = 10 },
                 BottomRight = new Point { X = 200, Y = 200}},
  new Rectangle {TopLeft = new Point { X = 2, Y = 2 },
                 BottomRight = new Point { X = 100, Y = 100}},
  new Rectangle {TopLeft = new Point { X = 5, Y = 5 },
                 BottomRight = new Point { X = 90, Y = 75}}
};
```

While you are never required to use collection/object initialization syntax, doing so results in a more compact code base. Furthermore, this syntax, when combined with implicit typing of local variables, allows you to declare an anonymous type, which is very useful when creating a LINQ projection. You'll learn about LINQ projections later in this chapter.

Lambda Expressions

The C# lambda operator (=>) was fully explored in Chapter 10. Recall that this operator allows you to build a lambda expression, which can be used any time you invoke a method that requires a strongly typed delegate as an argument. Lambdas greatly simplify how you work with .NET delegates, in that they reduce the amount of code you have to author by hand. Recall that a lambda expression can be broken down into the following usage:

```
( ArgumentsToProcess ) => { StatementsToProcessThem }
```

In Chapter 10, I walked you through how to interact with the FindAll() method of the generic List<T> class using three different approaches. After working with the raw Predicate<T> delegate and a C# anonymous method, you eventually arrived with the following (extremely concise) iteration that used the following lambda expression:

```
static void LambdaExpressionSyntax()
{
  // Make a list of integers.
  List<int> list = new List<int>();
  list.AddRange(new int[] { 20, 1, 4, 8, 9, 44 });

  // C# lambda expression.
  List<int> evenNumbers = list.FindAll(i => (i % 2) == 0);

  Console.WriteLine("Here are your even numbers:");
  foreach (int evenNumber in evenNumbers)
  {
    Console.Write("{0}\t", evenNumber);
  }
```

```
    Console.WriteLine();
}
```

Lambdas will be very useful when working with the underlying object model of LINQ. As you will soon find out, the C# LINQ query operators are simply a shorthand notation for calling true-blue methods on a class named System.Linq.Enumerable. These methods typically always require delegates (the Func<> delegate in particular) as parameters, which are used to process your data to yield the correct result set. Using lambdas, you can streamline your code, and allow the compiler to infer the underlying delegate.

Extension Methods

C# extension methods allow you to tack on new functionality to existing classes without the need to subclass. As well, extension methods allow you to add new functionality to sealed classes and structures, which could never be subclassed in the first place. Recall from Chapter 11, when you author an extension method, the first parameter is qualified with the this keyword, and marks the type being extended. Also recall that extension methods must always be defined within a static class and must, therefore, also be declared using the static keyword. For example:

```
namespace MyExtensions
{
  static class ObjectExtensions
  {
    // Define an extension method to System.Object.
    public static void DisplayDefiningAssembly(this object obj)
    {
      Console.WriteLine("{0} lives here:\n\t->{1}\n", obj.GetType().Name,
        Assembly.GetAssembly(obj.GetType()));
    }
  }
}
```

To use this extension, an application must import the namespace defining the extension (and possibly set a reference to the external assembly). At this point, simply import the defining namespace, and code away:

```
static void Main(string[] args)
{
  // Since everything extends System.Object, all classes and structures
  // can use this extension.
  int myInt = 12345678;
  myInt.DisplayDefiningAssembly();

  System.Data.DataSet d = new System.Data.DataSet();
  d.DisplayDefiningAssembly();
  Console.ReadLine();
}
```

When you are working with LINQ, you will seldom, if ever, be required to manually build your own extension methods. However, as you create LINQ query expressions, you will actually be making use of numerous extension methods already defined by Microsoft. In fact, each C# LINQ query operator is a shorthand notation for making a manual call on an underlying extension method, typically defined by the System.Linq.Enumerable utility class.

Anonymous Types

The final C# language feature I'd like to quickly review is that of anonymous types, which was explored in Chapter 11. This feature can be used to quickly model the "shape" of data, by allowing the compiler to generate a new class definition at compile time, based on a supplied set of name/value pairs. Recall that this type will be composed using value-based semantics, and each virtual method of System.Object will be overridden accordingly. To define an anonymous type, declare an implicitly typed variable and specify the data's shape using object initialization syntax:

```
// Make an anonymous type that is composed of another.
var purchaseItem = new {
  TimeBought = DateTime.Now,
  ItemBought = new {Color = "Red", Make = "Saab", CurrentSpeed = 55},
  Price = 34.000};
```

LINQ makes frequent use of anonymous types when you want to project new forms of data on the fly. For example, assume you have a collection of Person objects, and want to use LINQ to obtain information on the age and Social Security number of each. Using a LINQ projection, you can allow the compiler to generate a new anonymous type that contains your information.

Understanding the Role of LINQ

That wraps up our quick review of the C# language features that allow LINQ to work its magic. However, why have LINQ in the first place? Well, as software developers, it is hard to deny that the vast majority of our programming time is spent obtaining and manipulating data. When speaking of "data," it is very easy to immediately envision information contained within relational databases. However, another popular location for data is within XML documents (*.config files, locally persisted DataSets, or in-memory data returned from WCF services).

Data can be found in numerous places beyond these two common homes for information. For instance, say you have an array or generic List<T> type containing 300 integers, and you want to obtain a subset that meets a given criterion (e.g., only the odd or even members in the container, only prime numbers, only nonrepeating numbers greater than 50). Or perhaps you are making use of the reflection APIs and need to obtain only metadata descriptions for each class deriving from a particular parent class within an array of Types. Indeed, data is *everywhere*.

Prior to .NET 3.5, interacting with a particular flavor of data required programmers to make use of very diverse APIs. Consider, for example, Table 12-1, which illustrates several common APIs used to access various types of data (I'm sure you can think of many other examples).

Table 12-1. *Ways to Manipulate Various Types of Data*

The Data You Want	How to Obtain It
Relational data	System.Data.dll, System.Data.SqlClient.dll, etc.
XML document data	System.Xml.dll
Metadata tables	The System.Reflection namespace
Collections of objects	System.Array and the System.Collections/System.Collections.Generic namespaces

Of course, nothing is wrong with these approaches to data manipulation. In fact, you can (and will) certainly make direct use of ADO.NET, the XML namespaces, reflection services, and the various collection types. However, the basic problem is that each of these APIs is an island unto itself, which offers very little in the way of integration. True, it is possible (for example) to save an ADO.NET DataSet as XML, and then manipulate it via the System.Xml namespaces, but nonetheless, data manipulation remains rather asymmetrical.

The LINQ API is an attempt to provide a consistent, symmetrical manner in which programmers can obtain and manipulate "data" in the broad sense of the term. Using LINQ, you are able to create directly within the C# programming language constructs called *query expressions*. These query expressions are based on numerous query operators that have been intentionally designed to look and feel very similar (but not quite identical) to a SQL expression.

The twist, however, is that a query expression can be used to interact with numerous types of data—even data that has nothing to do with a relational database. Strictly speaking, "LINQ" is the term used to describe this overall approach to data access. However, based on where you are applying your LINQ queries, you will encounter various terms, such as the following:

- *LINQ to Objects:* This term refers to the act of applying LINQ queries to arrays and collections.

- *LINQ to XML:* This term refers to the act of using LINQ to manipulate and query XML documents.

- *LINQ to DataSet:* This term refers to the act of applying LINQ queries to ADO.NET DataSet objects.

- *LINQ to Entities:* This aspect of LINQ allows you to make use of LINQ queries within the ADO.NET Entity Framework (EF) API.

- *Parallel LINQ* (a.k.a. *PLINQ*): This allows for parallel processing of data returned from a LINQ query.

To be sure, Microsoft seems quite dedicated to integrating LINQ support deeply within the .NET programming environment. Today, LINQ is an integral part of the .NET base class libraries, managed languages, and Visual Studio itself.

LINQ Expressions Are Strongly Typed

It is also very important to point out that a LINQ query expression (unlike a traditional SQL statement) is *strongly typed*. Therefore, the C# compiler will keep us honest and make sure that these expressions are syntactically well formed. On a related note, query expressions have metadata representation within the assembly that makes use of them, as the C# LINQ query operators always make a rich underlying object model. Tools such as Visual Studio can use this metadata for useful features such as IntelliSense, autocompletion, and so forth.

The Core LINQ Assemblies

As mentioned in Chapter 2, the New Project dialog of Visual Studio has the option of selecting which version of the .NET platform you wish to compile against. When you opt to compile against .NET 3.5 or higher, each of the project templates will automatically reference the key LINQ assemblies, which can be viewed using the Solution Explorer. Table 12-2 documents the role of the key LINQ assemblies. However, you will encounter additional LINQ libraries over the remainder of this book.

Table 12-2. *Core LINQ-Centric Assemblies*

Assembly	Meaning in Life
System.Core.dll	Defines the types that represent the core LINQ API. This is the one assembly you must have access to if you want to use any LINQ API, including LINQ to Objects.
System.Data.DataSetExtensions.dll	Defines a handful of types to integrate ADO.NET types into the LINQ programming paradigm (LINQ to DataSet).
System.Xml.Linq.dll	Provides functionality for using LINQ with XML document data (LINQ to XML).

In order to work with LINQ to Objects, you must make sure that every C# code file that contains LINQ queries imports the System.Linq namespace (primarily defined within System.Core.dll). If you do not do so, you will run into a number of problems. As a very good rule of thumb, if you see a compiler error looking similar to this:

```
Error 1 Could not find an implementation of the query pattern for source type 'int[]'.
'Where' not found.  Are you missing a reference to 'System.Core.dll' or a using directive
for 'System.Linq'?
```

the chances are extremely good that your C# file does not have the following using directive (and believe me, I speak from experience!):

```
using System.Linq;
```

Applying LINQ Queries to Primitive Arrays

To begin examining LINQ to Objects, let's build an application that will apply LINQ queries to various array objects. Create a Console Application named LinqOverArray, and define a static helper method within the Program class named QueryOverStrings(). In this method, create a string array containing six or so items of your liking (here I listed out a batch of video games I am currently attempting to finish). Make sure to have at least two entries that contain numerical values, and a few that have embedded spaces.

```
static void QueryOverStrings()
{
  // Assume we have an array of strings.
  string[] currentVideoGames = {"Morrowind", "Uncharted 2",
                                "Fallout 3", "Daxter", "System Shock 2"};
}
```

Now, update Main() to invoke QueryOverStrings():

```
static void Main(string[] args)
{
  Console.WriteLine("***** Fun with LINQ to Objects *****\n");
  QueryOverStrings();
  Console.ReadLine();
}
```

When you have any array of data, it is very common to extract a subset of items based on a given requirement. Maybe you want to obtain only the subitems that contain a number (e.g., System Shock 2, Uncharted 2, and Fallout 3), have more or less than some number of characters, or don't contain embedded spaces (e.g., Morrowind or Daxter). While you could certainly perform such tasks using members of the System.Array type and a bit of elbow grease, LINQ query expressions can greatly simplify the process.

Going on the assumption that you wish to obtain from the array only items that contain an embedded blank space, and you want these items listed in alphabetical order, you could build the following LINQ query expression:

```
static void QueryOverStrings()
{
  // Assume we have an array of strings.
  string[] currentVideoGames = {"Morrowind", "Uncharted 2",
    "Fallout 3", "Daxter", "System Shock 2"};

  // Build a query expression to find the items in the array
  // that have an embedded space.
  IEnumerable<string> subset = from g in currentVideoGames
                    where g.Contains(" ") orderby g select g;

  // Print out the results.
  foreach (string s in subset)
    Console.WriteLine("Item: {0}", s);
}
```

Notice that the query expression created here makes use of the from, in, where, orderby, and select LINQ query operators. You will dig into the formalities of query expression syntax later in this chapter. However, even now you should be able to read this statement roughly as "Give me the items inside of currentVideoGames that contain a space, ordered alphabetically."

Here, each item that matches the search criteria has been given the name "g" (as in "game"); however, any valid C# variable name would do:

```
IEnumerable<string> subset = from game in currentVideoGames
                    where game.Contains(" ") orderby
                    game select game;
```

Notice that the returned sequence is held in a variable named subset, typed as a type that implements the generic version of IEnumerable<T>, where T is of type System.String (after all, you are querying an array of strings). After you obtain the result set, you then simply print out each item using a standard foreach construct. If you run your application, you will find the following output:

```
***** Fun with LINQ to Objects *****
Item: Fallout 3
Item: System Shock 2
```

Item: Uncharted 2

Once Again, Without LINQ

To be sure, LINQ is never mandatory. If you so choose, you could have found the same result set by forgoing LINQ altogether and making use of programming primitives such as if statements and for loops. Here is a method that yields the same result as the QueryOverStrings() method, but in a much more verbose manner:

```
static void QueryOverStringsLongHand()
{
  // Assume we have an array of strings.
  string[] currentVideoGames = {"Morrowind", "Uncharted 2",
    "Fallout 3", "Daxter", "System Shock 2"};

  string[] gamesWithSpaces = new string[5];

  for (int i = 0; i < currentVideoGames.Length; i++)
  {
    if (currentVideoGames[i].Contains(" "))
      gamesWithSpaces[i] = currentVideoGames[i];
  }

  // Now sort them.
  Array.Sort(gamesWithSpaces);

  // Print out the results.
  foreach (string s in gamesWithSpaces)
  {
    if( s != null)
      Console.WriteLine("Item: {0}", s);
  }
  Console.WriteLine();
}
```

While I am sure you can think of ways to tweak the previous method, the fact remains that LINQ queries can be used to radically simplify the process of extracting new subsets of data from a source. Rather than building nested loops, complex if/else logic, temporary data types, and so on, the C# compiler will perform the dirty work on your behalf, once you create a fitting LINQ query.

Reflecting over a LINQ Result Set

Now, assume the Program class defines an additional helper function named ReflectOverQueryResults() that will print out various details of the LINQ result set (note the parameter is a System.Object, to account for multiple types of result sets):

```
static void ReflectOverQueryResults(object resultSet)
{
  Console.WriteLine("***** Info about your query *****");
  Console.WriteLine("resultSet is of type: {0}", resultSet.GetType().Name);
```

```
    Console.WriteLine("resultSet location: {0}",
        resultSet.GetType().Assembly.GetName().Name);
}
```

Assuming you have called this method within QueryOverStrings() directly after printing out the obtained subset, if you run the application, you will see the subset is really an instance of the generic OrderedEnumerable<TElement, TKey> type (represented in terms of CIL code as OrderedEnumerable`2), which is an internal abstract type residing in the System.Core.dll assembly:

```
***** Info about your query *****

resultSet is of type: OrderedEnumerable`2
resultSet location: System.Core
```

■ **Note** Many of the types that represent a LINQ result are hidden by the Visual Studio object browser. These are low-level types not intended for direct use in your applications.

LINQ and Implicitly Typed Local Variables

While the current sample program makes it relatively easy to determine that the result set can be captured as an enumeration of string object (e.g., IEnumerable<string>), I would guess that it is *not* clear that subset is really of type OrderedEnumerable<TElement, TKey>.

Given the fact that LINQ result sets can be represented using a good number of types in various LINQ-centric namespaces, it would be tedious to define the proper type to hold a result set, because in many cases the underlying type may not be obvious or even directly accessible from your code base (and as you will see, in some cases the type is generated at compile time).

To further accentuate this point, consider the following additional helper method defined within the Program class (which I assume you will invoke from within the Main() method):

```
static void QueryOverInts()
{
    int[] numbers = {10, 20, 30, 40, 1, 2, 3, 8};

    // Print only items less than 10.
    IEnumerable<int> subset = from i in numbers where i < 10 select i;

    foreach (int i in subset)
        Console.WriteLine("Item: {0}", i);
    ReflectOverQueryResults(subset);
}
```

In this case, the subset variable is a completely different underlying type. This time, the type implementing the IEnumerable<int> interface is a low-level class named WhereArrayIterator<T>:

```
Item: 1
Item: 2
Item: 3
Item: 8

***** Info about your query *****
resultSet is of type: WhereArrayIterator`1
resultSet location: System.Core
```

Given the fact that the exact underlying type of a LINQ query is certainly not obvious, these first examples have represented the query results as an IEnumerable<T> variable, where T is the type of data in the returned sequence (string, int, etc). However, this is still rather cumbersome. To add insult to injury, given that IEnumerable<T> extends the nongeneric IEnumerable interface, it would also be permissible to capture the result of a LINQ query as follows:

```
System.Collections.IEnumerable subset =
  from i in numbers where i < 10 select i;
```

Thankfully, implicit typing cleans things up considerably when working with LINQ queries:

```
static void QueryOverInts()
{
  int[] numbers = {10, 20, 30, 40, 1, 2, 3, 8};

  // Use implicit typing here...
  var subset = from i in numbers where i < 10 select i;

  // ...and here.
  foreach (var i in subset)
    Console.WriteLine("Item: {0} ", i);
  ReflectOverQueryResults(subset);
}
```

As a rule of thumb, you will always want to make use of implicit typing when capturing the results of a LINQ query. Just remember, however, that (in a vast majority of cases), the *real* return value is a type implementing the generic IEnumerable<T> interface.

Exactly what this type is under the covers (OrderedEnumerable<TElement, TKey>, WhereArrayIterator<T>, etc) is irrelevant, and not necessary to discover. As seen in the previous code example, you can simply use the var keyword within a foreach construct to iterate over the fetched data.

LINQ and Extension Methods

Although the current example does not have you author any extension methods directly, you are in fact using them seamlessly in the background. LINQ query expressions can be used to iterate over data containers that implement the generic IEnumerable<T> interface. However, the .NET System.Array class type (used to represent our array of strings and array of integers) does *not* implement this contract:

```
// The System.Array type does not seem to implement the correct
// infrastructure for query expressions!
public abstract class Array : ICloneable, IList, ICollection,
  IEnumerable, IStructuralComparable, IStructuralEquatable
```

```
{
  ...
}
```

While `System.Array` does not directly implement the `IEnumerable<T>` interface, it indirectly gains the required functionality of this type (as well as many other LINQ-centric members) via the static `System.Linq.Enumerable` class type.

This utility class defines a good number of generic extension methods (such as `Aggregate<T>()`, `First<T>()`, `Max<T>()`, etc.), which `System.Array` (and other types) acquire in the background. Thus, if you apply the dot operator on the `currentVideoGames` local variable, you will find a good number of members *not* found within the formal definition of `System.Array` (see Figure 12-1).

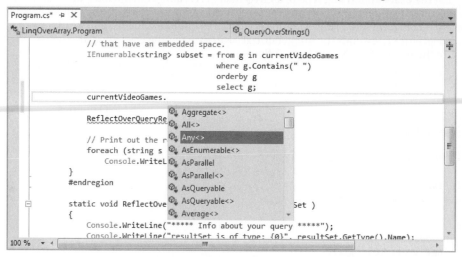

Figure 12-1. The System.Array type has been extended with members of System.Linq.Enumerable

The Role of Deferred Execution

Another important point regarding LINQ query expressions is that they are not actually evaluated until you iterate over the sequence. Formally speaking, this is termed *deferred execution*. The benefit of this approach is that you are able to apply the same LINQ query multiple times to the same container, and rest assured you are obtaining the latest and greatest results. Consider the following update to the `QueryOverInts()` method:

```
static void QueryOverInts()
{
  int[] numbers = { 10, 20, 30, 40, 1, 2, 3, 8 };

  // Get numbers less than ten.
  var subset = from i in numbers where i < 10 select i;

  // LINQ statement evaluated here!
  foreach (var i in subset)
    Console.WriteLine("{0} < 10", i);
```

```
  Console.WriteLine();

  // Change some data in the array.
  numbers[0] = 4;

  // Evaluated again!
  foreach (var j in subset)
    Console.WriteLine("{0} < 10", j);

  Console.WriteLine();
  ReflectOverQueryResults(subset);
}
```

If you were to execute the program yet again, you would find the following output. Notice that the second time you iterate over the requested sequence, you find an additional member, as you set the first item in the array to be a value less than ten:

```
1 < 10
2 < 10
3 < 10
8 < 10

4 < 10
1 < 10
2 < 10
3 < 10
8 < 10
```

One very useful aspect of Visual Studio is that if you set a breakpoint before the evaluation of a LINQ query, you are able to view the contents during a debugging session. Simply locate your mouse cursor above the LINQ result set variable (subset in Figure 12-2). When you do, you will be given the option of evaluating the query at that time by expanding the Results View option.

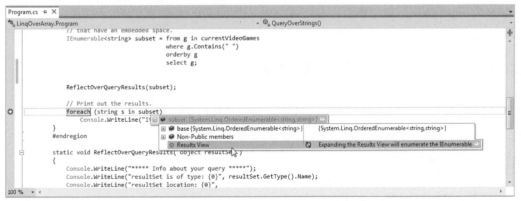

Figure 12-2. Debugging LINQ expressions

The Role of Immediate Execution

When you need to evaluate a LINQ expression from outside the confines of foreach logic, you are able to call any number of extension methods defined by the Enumerable type as ToArray<T>(), ToDictionary<TSource,TKey>(), and ToList<T>(). These methods will cause a LINQ query to execute at the exact moment you call them, to obtain a snapshot of the data. After you have done so, the snapshot of data may be independently manipulated:

```
static void ImmediateExecution()
{
  int[] numbers = { 10, 20, 30, 40, 1, 2, 3, 8 };

  // Get data RIGHT NOW as int[].
  int[] subsetAsIntArray =
    (from i in numbers where i < 10 select i).ToArray<int>();

  // Get data RIGHT NOW as List<int>.
  List<int> subsetAsListOfInts =
    (from i in numbers where i < 10 select i).ToList<int>();
}
```

Notice that the entire LINQ expression is wrapped within parentheses to cast it into the correct underlying type (whatever that might be) in order to call the extension methods of Enumerable.

Also recall from Chapter 9 that when the C# compiler can unambiguously determine the type parameter of a generic, you are not required to specify the type parameter. Thus, you could also call ToArray<T>() (or ToList<T>() for that matter) as follows:

```
int[] subsetAsIntArray =
  (from i in numbers where i < 10 select i).ToArray();
```

The usefulness of immediate execution is very obvious when you need to return the results of a LINQ query to an external caller. And, as luck would have it, this happens to be the next topic of this chapter.

■ **Source Code** The LinqOverArray project can be found under the Chapter 12 subdirectory.

Returning the Result of a LINQ Query

It is possible to define a field within a class (or structure) whose value is the result of a LINQ query. To do so, however, you cannot make use of implicit typing (as the var keyword cannot be used for fields) and the target of the LINQ query cannot be instance-level data; therefore, it must be static. Given these limitations, you will seldom need to author code like the following:

```
class LINQBasedFieldsAreClunky
{
  private static string[] currentVideoGames = {"Morrowind", "Uncharted 2",
    "Fallout 3", "Daxter", "System Shock 2"};

  // Can't use implicit typing here! Must know type of subset!
  private IEnumerable<string> subset = from g in currentVideoGames
```

```
    where g.Contains(" ") orderby g select g;

  public void PrintGames()
  {
   foreach (var item in subset)
   {
    Console.WriteLine(item);
   }
  }
}
```

More often than not, LINQ queries are defined within the scope of a method or property. Moreover, to simplify your programming, the variable used to hold the result set will be stored in an implicitly typed local variable using the var keyword. Now, recall from Chapter 3 that implicitly typed variables cannot be used to define parameters, return values, or fields of a class or structure.

Given this point, you might wonder exactly how you could return a query result to an external caller. The answer is, it depends. If you have a result set consisting of strongly typed data, such as an array of strings or a List<T> of Cars, you could abandon the use of the var keyword and use a proper IEnumerable<T> or IEnumerable type (again, as IEnumerable<T> extends IEnumerable). Consider the following example for a new Console Application named LinqRetValues:

```
class Program
{
  static void Main(string[] args)
  {
    Console.WriteLine("***** LINQ Transformations *****\n");
    IEnumerable<string> subset = GetStringSubset();

    foreach (string item in subset)
    {
      Console.WriteLine(item);
    }

    Console.ReadLine();
  }

  static IEnumerable<string> GetStringSubset()
  {
    string[] colors = {"Light Red", "Green",
      "Yellow", "Dark Red", "Red", "Purple"};

    // Note subset is an IEnumerable<string>-compatible object.
    IEnumerable<string> theRedColors = from c in colors
      where c.Contains("Red") select c;

    return theRedColors;
  }
}
```

The results are as expected:

```
Light Red
Dark Red
Red
```

Returning LINQ Results via Immediate Execution

This example works as expected, only because the return value of the GetStringSubset() and the LINQ query within this method has been strongly typed. If you used the var keyword to define the subset variable, it would be permissible to return the value *only* if the method is still prototyped to return IEnumerable<string> (and if the implicitly typed local variable is in fact compatible with the specified return type).

Because it is a bit inconvenient to operate on IEnumerable<T>, you could make use of immediate execution. For example, rather than returning IEnumerable<string>, you could simply return a string[], provided that you transform the sequence to a strongly typed array. Consider this new method of the Program class, which does this very thing:

```
static string[] GetStringSubsetAsArray()
{
  string[] colors = {"Light Red", "Green",
    "Yellow", "Dark Red", "Red", "Purple"};

  var theRedColors = from c in colors
    where c.Contains("Red") select c;

  // Map results into an array.
  return theRedColors.ToArray();
}
```

With this, the caller can be blissfully unaware that their result came from a LINQ query, and simply work with the array of strings as expected. For example:

```
foreach (string item in GetStringSubsetAsArray())
{
    Console.WriteLine(item);
}
```

Immediate execution is also critical when attempting to return to the caller the results of a LINQ projection. You'll examine this topic a bit later in the chapter. Next up, let's look at how to apply LINQ queries to generic and nongeneric collection objects.

■ **Source Code** The LinqRetValues project can be found under the Chapter 12 subdirectory.

Applying LINQ Queries to Collection Objects

Beyond pulling results from a simple array of data, LINQ query expressions can also manipulate data within members of the System.Collections.Generic namespace, such as the List<T> type. Create a new Console Application project named LinqOverCollections, and define a basic Car class that maintains a current speed, color, make, and pet name as shown in the following code:

```
class Car
{
  public string PetName {get; set;}
  public string Color {get; set;}
  public int Speed {get; set;}
  public string Make {get; set;}
}
```

Now, within your Main() method define a local List<T> variable of type Car, and make use of object initialization syntax to fill the list with a handful of new Car objects:

```
static void Main(string[] args)
{
  Console.WriteLine("***** LINQ over Generic Collections *****\n");

  // Make a List<> of Car objects.
  List<Car> myCars = new List<Car>() {
    new Car{ PetName = "Henry", Color = "Silver", Speed = 100, Make = "BMW"},
    new Car{ PetName = "Daisy", Color = "Tan", Speed = 90, Make = "BMW"},
    new Car{ PetName = "Mary", Color = "Black", Speed = 55, Make = "VW"},
    new Car{ PetName = "Clunker", Color = "Rust", Speed = 5, Make = "Yugo"},
    new Car{ PetName = "Melvin", Color = "White", Speed = 43, Make = "Ford"}
  };

  Console.ReadLine();
}
```

Accessing Contained Subobjects

Applying a LINQ query to a generic container is no different than doing so with a simple array, as LINQ to Objects can be used on any type implementing IEnumerable<T>. This time, your goal is to build a query expression to select only the Car objects within the myCars list, where the speed is greater than 55.

After you get the subset, you will print out the name of each Car object by calling the PetName property. Assume you have the following helper method (taking a List<Car> parameter), which is called from within Main():

```
static void GetFastCars(List<Car> myCars)
{
  // Find all Car objects in the List<>, where the Speed is
  // greater than 55.
  var fastCars = from c in myCars where c.Speed > 55 select c;

  foreach (var car in fastCars)
  {
    Console.WriteLine("{0} is going too fast!", car.PetName);
```

```
    }
}
```

Notice that your query expression is grabbing only those items from the List<T> where the Speed property is greater than 55. If you run the application, you will find that "Henry" and "Daisy" are the only two items that match the search criteria.

If you want to build a more complex query, you might wish to find only the BMWs that have a Speed value above 90. To do so, simply build a compound Boolean statement using the C# && operator:

```
static void GetFastBMWs(List<Car> myCars)
{
    // Find the fast BMWs!
    var fastCars = from c in myCars where c.Speed > 90 && c.Make == "BMW" select c;
    foreach (var car in fastCars)
    {
        Console.WriteLine("{0} is going too fast!", car.PetName);
    }
}
```

In this case, the only pet name printed out is "Henry".

Applying LINQ Queries to Nongeneric Collections

Recall that the query operators of LINQ are designed to work with any type implementing IEnumerable<T> (either directly or via extension methods). Given that System.Array has been provided with such necessary infrastructure, it might surprise you that the legacy (nongeneric) containers within System.Collections have not. Thankfully, it is still possible to iterate over data contained within nongeneric collections using the generic Enumerable.OfType<T>() extension method.

The OfType<T>() method is one of the few members of Enumerable that does not extend generic types. When calling this member off a nongeneric container implementing the IEnumerable interface (such as the ArrayList), simply specify the type of item within the container to extract a compatible IEnumerable<T> object. In code, you can store this data point using an implicitly typed variable.

Consider the following new method, which fills an ArrayList with a set of Car objects (be sure to import the System.Collections namespace into your Program.cs file).

```
static void LINQOverArrayList()
{
    Console.WriteLine("***** LINQ over ArrayList *****");

    // Here is a nongeneric collection of cars.
    ArrayList myCars = new ArrayList() {
        new Car{ PetName = "Henry", Color = "Silver", Speed = 100, Make = "BMW"},
        new Car{ PetName = "Daisy", Color = "Tan", Speed = 90, Make = "BMW"},
        new Car{ PetName = "Mary", Color = "Black", Speed = 55, Make = "VW"},
        new Car{ PetName = "Clunker", Color = "Rust", Speed = 5, Make = "Yugo"},
        new Car{ PetName = "Melvin", Color = "White", Speed = 43, Make = "Ford"}
    };

    // Transform ArrayList into an IEnumerable<T>-compatible type.
    var myCarsEnum = myCars.OfType<Car>();
```

```
// Create a query expression targeting the compatible type.
var fastCars = from c in myCarsEnum where c.Speed > 55 select c;

foreach (var car in fastCars)
{
  Console.WriteLine("{0} is going too fast!", car.PetName);
}
}
```

Similar to the previous examples, this method, when called from Main() will display only the names "Henry" and "Daisy", based on the format of our LINQ query.

Filtering Data Using OfType<T>()

As you know, nongeneric types are capable of containing any combination of items, as the members of these containers (again, such as the ArrayList) are prototyped to receive System.Objects. For example, assume an ArrayList contains a variety of items, only a subset of which are numerical. If you want to obtain a subset that contains only numerical data, you can do so using OfType<T>(), since it filters out each element whose type is different from the given type during the iterations:

```
static void OfTypeAsFilter()
{
  // Extract the ints from the ArrayList.
  ArrayList myStuff = new ArrayList();
  myStuff.AddRange(new object[] { 10, 400, 8, false, new Car(), "string data" });
  var myInts = myStuff.OfType<int>();

  // Prints out 10, 400, and 8.
  foreach (int i in myInts)
  {
    Console.WriteLine("Int value: {0}", i);
  }
}
```

At this point, you have had a chance to apply LINQ queries to arrays, generic collections, and nongeneric collections. These containers held both C# primitive types (integers, string data) as well as custom classes. The next task is to learn about many additional LINQ operators that can be used to build more complex and useful queries.

■ **Source Code** The LinqOverCollections project can be found under the Chapter 12 subdirectory.

Investigating the C# LINQ Query Operators

C# defines a good number of query operators out of the box. Table 12-3 documents some of the more commonly used query operators.

■ **Note** The .NET Framework 4.5 SDK documentation provides full details regarding each of the C# LINQ operators. Look up the topic "LINQ General Programming Guide" for more information.

Table 12-3. Common LINQ Query Operators

Query Operators	Meaning in Life
from, in	Used to define the backbone for any LINQ expression, which allows you to extract a subset of data from a fitting container.
where	Used to define a restriction for which items to extract from a container.
select	Used to select a sequence from the container.
join, on, equals, into	Performs joins based on specified key. Remember, these "joins" do not need to have anything to do with data in a relational database.
orderby, ascending, descending	Allows the resulting subset to be ordered in ascending or descending order.
group, by	Yields a subset with data grouped by a specified value.

In addition to the partial list of operators shown in Table 12-3, the System.Linq.Enumerable class provides a set of methods that do not have a direct C# query operator shorthand notation, but are instead exposed as extension methods. These generic methods can be called to transform a result set in various manners (Reverse<>(), ToArray<>(), ToList<>(), etc.). Some are used to extract singletons from a result set, others perform various set operations (Distinct<>(), Union<>(), Intersect<>(), etc.), and still others aggregate results (Count<>(), Sum<>(), Min<>(), Max<>(), etc.).

To begin digging into more intricate LINQ queries, create a new Console Application named FunWithLinqExpressions. Next, you need to define an array or collection of some sample data. For this project, you will make an array of ProductInfo objects, defined in the following code:

```
class ProductInfo
{
  public string Name {get; set;}
  public string Description {get; set;}
  public int NumberInStock {get; set;}

  public override string ToString()
  {
    return string.Format("Name={0}, Description={1}, Number in Stock={2}",
      Name, Description, NumberInStock);
  }
}
```

Now populate an array with a batch of ProductInfo objects within your Main() method:

```
static void Main(string[] args)
{
  Console.WriteLine("***** Fun with Query Expressions *****\n");

  // This array will be the basis of our testing...
  ProductInfo[] itemsInStock = new[] {
    new ProductInfo{ Name = "Mac's Coffee",
                     Description = "Coffee with TEETH",
                     NumberInStock = 24},
    new ProductInfo{ Name = "Milk Maid Milk",
                     Description = "Milk cow's love",
                     NumberInStock = 100},
    new ProductInfo{ Name = "Pure Silk Tofu",
                     Description = "Bland as Possible",
                     NumberInStock = 120},
    new ProductInfo{ Name = "Cruchy Pops",
                     Description = "Cheezy, peppery goodness",
                     NumberInStock = 2},
    new ProductInfo{ Name = "RipOff Water",
                     Description = "From the tap to your wallet",
                     NumberInStock = 100},
    new ProductInfo{ Name = "Classic Valpo Pizza",
                     Description = "Everyone loves pizza!",
                     NumberInStock = 73}
  };

  // We will call various methods here!
  Console.ReadLine();
}
```

Basic Selection Syntax

Because the syntactical correctness of a LINQ query expression is validated at compile time, you need to remember that the ordering of these operators is critical. In the simplest terms, every LINQ query expression is built using the from, in, and select operators. Here is the general template to follow:

```
var result = from matchingItem in container select matchingItem;
```

The item after the from operator represents an item that matches the LINQ query criteria, which can be named anything you choose. The item after the in operator represents the data container to search (an array, collection, XML document, etc.).

Here is a very simple query, doing nothing more than selecting every item in the container (similar in behavior to a database Select * SQL statement). Consider the following:

```
static void SelectEverything(ProductInfo[] products)
{
  // Get everything!
  Console.WriteLine("All product details:");
  var allProducts = from p in products select p;

  foreach (var prod in allProducts)
  {
```

```
      Console.WriteLine(prod.ToString());
    }
}
```

To be honest, this query expression is not entirely useful, given that your subset is identical to that of the data in the incoming parameter. If you want, you could use this incoming parameter to extract only the Name values of each car using the following selection syntax:

```
static void ListProductNames(ProductInfo[] products)
{
  // Now get only the names of the products.
  Console.WriteLine("Only product names:");
  var names = from p in products select p.Name;

  foreach (var n in names)
  {
    Console.WriteLine("Name: {0}", n);
  }
}
```

Obtaining Subsets of Data

To obtain a specific subset from a container, you can make use of the where operator. When doing so, the general template now becomes the following code:

```
var result = from item in container where BooleanExpression select item;
```

Notice that the where operator expects an expression that resolves to a Boolean. For example, to extract from the ProductInfo[] argument only the items that have more than 25 items on hand, you could author the following code:

```
static void GetOverstock(ProductInfo[] products)
{
  Console.WriteLine("The overstock items!");

  // Get only the items where we have more than
  // 25 in stock.
  var overstock = from p in products where p.NumberInStock > 25 select p;

  foreach (ProductInfo c in overstock)
  {
    Console.WriteLine(c.ToString());
  }
}
```

As seen earlier in this chapter, when you are building a where clause, it is permissible to make use of any valid C# operators to build complex expressions. For example, recall the query that only extracts out the BMWs going at least 100 mph:

```
// Get BMWs going at least 100 mph.
var onlyFastBMWs = from c in myCars
                   where c.Make == "BMW" && c.Speed >= 100 select c;
```

```
foreach (Car c in onlyFastBMWs)
{
  Console.WriteLine("{0} is going {1} MPH", c.PetName, c.Speed);
}
```

Projecting New Data Types

It is also possible to project new forms of data from an existing data source. Let's assume that you want to take the incoming ProductInfo[] parameter and obtain a result set that accounts only for the name and description of each item. To do so, you can define a select statement that dynamically yields a new anonymous type:

```
static void GetNamesAndDescriptions(ProductInfo[] products)
{
  Console.WriteLine("Names and Descriptions:");
  var nameDesc = from p in products select new { p.Name, p.Description };

  foreach (var item in nameDesc)
  {
    // Could also use Name and Description properties directly.
    Console.WriteLine(item.ToString());
  }
}
```

Always remember that when you have a LINQ query that makes use of a projection, you have no way of knowing the underlying data type, as this is determined at compile time. In these cases, the var keyword is mandatory. As well, recall that you cannot create methods with implicitly typed return values. Therefore, the following method would not compile:

```
static var GetProjectedSubset(ProductInfo[] products)
{
    var nameDesc = from p in products select new { p.Name, p.Description };
    return nameDesc;   // Nope!
}
```

When you need to return projected data to a caller, one approach is to transform the query result into a .NET System.Array object using the ToArray() extension method. Thus, if you were to update your query expression as follows:

```
// Return value is now an Array.
static Array GetProjectedSubset(ProductInfo[] products)
{
  var nameDesc = from p in products select new { p.Name, p.Description };

  // Map set of anonymous objects to an Array object.
  return nameDesc.ToArray();
}
```

you could invoke and process the data from Main() as follows:

```
Array objs = GetProjectedSubset(itemsInStock);
foreach (object o in objs)
{
  Console.WriteLine(o);   // Calls ToString() on each anonymous object.
```

```
}
```

Note that you must use a literal System.Array object and cannot make use of the C# array declaration syntax, given that you don't know the underlying type of type, as you are operating on a compiler-generated anonymous class! Also note that you are not specifying the type parameter to the generic ToArray<T>() method, as you once again don't know the underlying data type until compile time, which is too late for your purposes.

The obvious problem is that you lose any strong typing, as each item in the Array object is assumed to be of type Object. Nevertheless, when you need to return a LINQ result set that is the result of a projection operation, transforming the data into an Array type (or another suitable container via other members of the Enumerable type) is mandatory.

Obtaining Counts Using Enumerable

When you are projecting new batches of data, you may need to discover exactly how many items have been returned into the sequence. Any time you need to determine the number of items returned from a LINQ query expression, simply make use of the Count() extension method of the Enumerable class. For example, the following method will find all string objects in a local array that have a length greater than six characters:

```
static void GetCountFromQuery()
{
  string[] currentVideoGames = {"Morrowind", "Uncharted 2",
                       "Fallout 3", "Daxter", "System Shock 2"};

  // Get count from the query.
  int numb =
  (from g in currentVideoGames where g.Length > 6 select g).Count();

  // Print out the number of items.
  Console.WriteLine("{0} items honor the LINQ query.", numb);
}
```

Reversing Result Sets

You can reverse the items within a result set quite simply using the Reverse<T>() extension method of the Enumerable class. For example, the following method selects all items from the incoming ProductInfo[] parameter, in reverse:

```
static void ReverseEverything(ProductInfo[] products)
{
  Console.WriteLine("Product in reverse:");
  var allProducts = from p in products select p;
  foreach (var prod in allProducts.Reverse())
  {
    Console.WriteLine(prod.ToString());
  }
}
```

Sorting Expressions

As you have seen over this chapter's initial examples, a query expression can take an orderby operator to sort items in the subset by a specific value. By default, the order will be ascending; thus, ordering by a string would be alphabetical, ordering by numerical data would be lowest to highest, and so forth. If you need to view the results in a descending order, simply include the descending operator. Ponder the following method:

```
static void AlphabetizeProductNames(ProductInfo[] products)
{
  // Get names of products, alphabetized.
  var subset = from p in products orderby p.Name select p;

  Console.WriteLine("Ordered by Name:");
  foreach (var p in subset)
  {
    Console.WriteLine(p.ToString());
  }
}
```

Although ascending order is the default, you are able to make your intentions very clear by making use of the ascending operator:

```
var subset = from p in products orderby p.Name ascending select p;
```

If you want to get the items in descending order, you can do so via the descending operator:

```
var subset = from p in products orderby p.Name descending select p;
```

LINQ As a Better Venn Diagramming Tool

The Enumerable class supports a set of extension methods that allows you to use two (or more) LINQ queries as the basis to find unions, differences, concatenations, and intersections of data. First, consider the Except() extension method, which will return a LINQ result set that contains the differences between two containers, which in this case, is the value "Yugo":

```
static void DisplayDiff()
{
  List<string> myCars = new List<String> {"Yugo", "Aztec", "BMW"};
  List<string> yourCars = new List<String>{"BMW", "Saab", "Aztec" };

  var carDiff =(from c in myCars select c)
    .Except(from c2 in yourCars select c2);

  Console.WriteLine("Here is what you don't have, but I do:");
  foreach (string s in carDiff)
    Console.WriteLine(s);  // Prints Yugo.
}
```

The Intersect() method will return a result set that contains the common data items in a set of containers. For example, the following method returns the sequence, "Aztec" and "BMW".

```
static void DisplayIntersection()
{
```

```
    List<string> myCars = new List<String> { "Yugo", "Aztec", "BMW" };
    List<string> yourCars = new List<String> { "BMW", "Saab", "Aztec" };

    // Get the common members.
    var carIntersect = (from c in myCars select c)
      .Intersect(from c2 in yourCars select c2);

    Console.WriteLine("Here is what we have in common:");
    foreach (string s in carIntersect)
      Console.WriteLine(s);   // Prints Aztec and BMW.
}
```

The Union() method, as you would guess, returns a result set that includes all members of a batch of LINQ queries. Like any proper union, you will not find repeating values if a common member appears more than once. Therefore, the following method will print out the values "Yugo", "Aztec", "BMW", and "Saab":

```
static void DisplayUnion()
{
    List<string> myCars = new List<String> { "Yugo", "Aztec", "BMW" };
    List<string> yourCars = new List<String> { "BMW", "Saab", "Aztec" };

    // Get the union of these containers.
    var carUnion = (from c in myCars select c)
      .Union(from c2 in yourCars select c2);

    Console.WriteLine("Here is everything:");
    foreach (string s in carUnion)
      Console.WriteLine(s);   // Prints all common members.
}
```

Finally, the Concat() extension method returns a result set that is a direct concatenation of LINQ result sets. For example, the following method prints out the results "Yugo", "Aztec", "BMW", "BMW", "Saab", and "Aztec":

```
static void DisplayConcat()
{
    List<string> myCars = new List<String> { "Yugo", "Aztec", "BMW" };
    List<string> yourCars = new List<String> { "BMW", "Saab", "Aztec" };

    var carConcat = (from c in myCars select c)
      .Concat(from c2 in yourCars select c2);

    // Prints:
    // Yugo Aztec BMW BMW Saab Aztec.
    foreach (string s in carConcat)
      Console.WriteLine(s);
}
```

Removing Duplicates

When you call the Concat()extension method, you could very well end up with redundant entries in the fetched result, which could be exactly what you want in some cases. However, in other cases, you might want to remove duplicate entries in your data. To do so, simply call the Distinct() extension method, as seen here:

```
static void DisplayConcatNoDups()
{
  List<string> myCars = new List<String> { "Yugo", "Aztec", "BMW" };
  List<string> yourCars = new List<String> { "BMW", "Saab", "Aztec" };

  var carConcat = (from c in myCars select c)
    .Concat(from c2 in yourCars select c2);

  // Prints:
  // Yugo Aztec BMW Saab Aztec.
  foreach (string s in carConcat.Distinct())
    Console.WriteLine(s);
}
```

LINQ Aggregation Operations

LINQ queries can also be designed to perform various aggregation operations on the result set. The Count() extension method is one such aggregation example. Other possibilities include obtaining an average, max, min, or sum of values using the Max(), Min(), Average(), or Sum() members of the Enumerable class. Here is a simple example:

```
static void AggregateOps()
{
  double[] winterTemps = { 2.0, -21.3, 8, -4, 0, 8.2 };

  // Various aggregation examples.
  Console.WriteLine("Max temp: {0}",
    (from t in winterTemps select t).Max());

  Console.WriteLine("Min temp: {0}",
    (from t in winterTemps select t).Min());

  Console.WriteLine("Avarage temp: {0}",
    (from t in winterTemps select t).Average());

  Console.WriteLine("Sum of all temps: {0}",
    (from t in winterTemps select t).Sum());
}
```

These examples should give you enough knowledge to feel comfortable with the process of building LINQ query expressions. While there are additional operators you have not yet examined, you will see further examples later in this text when you learn about related LINQ technologies. To wrap up your first look at LINQ, the remainder of this chapter will dive into the details between the C# LINQ query operators and the underlying object model.

■ **Source Code** The FunWithLinqExpressions project can be found under the Chapter 12 subdirectory.

The Internal Representation of LINQ Query Statements

At this point, you have been introduced to the process of building query expressions using various C# query operators (such as from, in, where, orderby, and select). Also, you discovered that some functionality of the LINQ to Objects API can only be accessed when calling extension methods of the Enumerable class. The truth of the matter, however, is that when compiled, the C# compiler actually translates all C# LINQ operators into calls on methods of the Enumerable class. In fact, if you were really a glutton for punishment, you could build all of your LINQ statements using nothing but the underlying object model.

A great many of the methods of Enumerable have been prototyped to take delegates as arguments. In particular, many methods require a generic delegate named Func<>, which was introduced to you during our examination of generic delegates in Chapter 9. Consider the Where() method of Enumerable, which is called on your behalf when you use the C# where LINQ query operator:

```
// Overloaded versions of the Enumerable.Where<T>() method.
// Note the second parameter is of type System.Func<>.
public static IEnumerable<TSource> Where<TSource>(this IEnumerable<TSource> source,
    System.Func<TSource,int,bool> predicate)

public static IEnumerable<TSource> Where<TSource>(this IEnumerable<TSource> source,
    System.Func<TSource,bool> predicate)
```

The Func<> delegate (as the name implies) represents a pattern for a given function with a set of up to 16 arguments and a return value. If you were to examine this type using the Visual Studio object browser, you would notice various forms of the Func<> delegate. For example:

```
// The various formats of the Func<> delegate.
public delegate TResult Func<T1,T2,T3,T4,TResult>(T1 arg1, T2 arg2, T3 arg3, T4 arg4)

public delegate TResult Func<T1,T2,T3,TResult>(T1 arg1, T2 arg2, T3 arg3)

public delegate TResult Func<T1,T2,TResult>(T1 arg1, T2 arg2)

public delegate TResult Func<T1,TResult>(T1 arg1)

public delegate TResult Func<TResult>()
```

Given that many members of System.Linq.Enumerable demand a delegate as input, when invoking them, you can either manually create a new delegate type and author the necessary target methods, make use of a C# anonymous method, or define a proper lambda expression. Regardless of which approach you take, the end result is identical.

While it is true that making use of C# LINQ query operators is far and away the simplest way to build a LINQ query expression, let's walk through each of these possible approaches, just so you can see the connection between the C# query operators and the underlying Enumerable type.

Building Query Expressions with Query Operators (Revisited)

To begin, create a new Console Application named LinqUsingEnumerable. The Program class will define a series of static helper methods (each of which is called within the Main() method) to illustrate the various manners in which you can build LINQ query expressions.

The first method, QueryStringsWithOperators(), offers the most straightforward way to build a query expression and is identical to the code seen in the LinqOverArray example found earlier in this chapter:

```
static void QueryStringWithOperators()
{
  Console.WriteLine("***** Using Query Operators *****");

  string[] currentVideoGames = {"Morrowind", "Uncharted 2",
    "Fallout 3", "Daxter", "System Shock 2"};

  var subset = from game in currentVideoGames
               where game.Contains(" ") orderby game select game;

  foreach (string s in subset)
    Console.WriteLine("Item: {0}", s);
}
```

The obvious benefit of using C# query operators to build query expressions is the fact that the Func<> delegates and calls on the Enumerable type are out of sight and out of mind, as it is the job of the C# compiler to perform this translation. To be sure, building LINQ expressions using various query operators (from, in, where, or orderby) is the most common and straightforward approach.

Building Query Expressions Using the Enumerable Type and Lambda Expressions

Keep in mind that the LINQ query operators used here are simply shorthand versions for calling various extension methods defined by the Enumerable type. Consider the following QueryStringsWithEnumerableAndLambdas() method, which is processing the local string array now making direct use of the Enumerable extension methods:

```
static void QueryStringsWithEnumerableAndLambdas()
{
  Console.WriteLine("***** Using Enumerable / Lambda Expressions *****");

  string[] currentVideoGames = {"Morrowind", "Uncharted 2",
    "Fallout 3", "Daxter", "System Shock 2"};

  // Build a query expression using extension methods
  // granted to the Array via the Enumerable type.
  var subset = currentVideoGames.Where(game => game.Contains(" "))
    .OrderBy(game => game).Select(game => game);

  // Print out the results.
  foreach (var game in subset)
    Console.WriteLine("Item: {0}", game);
  Console.WriteLine();
}
```

Here, you begin by calling the Where() extension method on the currentVideoGames string array. Recall that the Array class receives this via an extension method granted by Enumerable. The Enumerable.Where() method requires a System.Func<T1, TResult> delegate parameter. The first type parameter of this delegate represents the IEnumerable<T> compatible data to process (an array of strings in this case), while the second type parameter represents the method result data, which is obtained from a single statement fed into the lambda expression.

The return value of the Where() method is hidden from view in this code example, but under the covers you are operating on an OrderedEnumerable type. From this object, you call the generic OrderBy() method, which also requires a Func<> delegate parameter. This time, you are simply passing each item in turn via a fitting lambda expression. The end result of calling OrderBy() is a new ordered sequence of the initial data.

Last but not least, you call the Select() method off the sequence returned from OrderBy(), which results in the final set of data that is stored in an implicitly typed variable named subset.

To be sure, this "longhand" LINQ query is a bit more complex to tease apart than the previous C# LINQ query operator example. Part of the complexity is, no doubt, due to the chaining together of calls using the dot operator. Here is the exact same query, with each step broken into discrete chunks:

```
static void QueryStringsWithEnumerableAndLambdas2()
{
  Console.WriteLine("***** Using Enumerable / Lambda Expressions *****");

  string[] currentVideoGames = {"Morrowind", "Uncharted 2",
    "Fallout 3", "Daxter", "System Shock 2"};

  // Break it down!
  var gamesWithSpaces = currentVideoGames.Where(game => game.Contains(" "));
  var orderedGames = gamesWithSpaces.OrderBy(game => game);
  var subset = orderedGames.Select(game => game);

  foreach (var game in subset)
    Console.WriteLine("Item: {0}", game);
  Console.WriteLine();
}
```

As you might agree, building a LINQ query expression using the methods of the Enumerable class directly is much more verbose than making use of the C# query operators. As well, given that the methods of Enumerable require delegates as parameters, you will typically need to author lambda expressions to allow the input data to be processed by the underlying delegate target.

Building Query Expressions Using the Enumerable Type and Anonymous Methods

Given that C# lambda expressions are simply shorthand notations for working with anonymous methods, consider the third query expression created within the QueryStringsWithAnonymousMethods() helper function:

```
static void QueryStringsWithAnonymousMethods()
{
  Console.WriteLine("***** Using Anonymous Methods *****");

  string[] currentVideoGames = {"Morrowind", "Uncharted 2",
    "Fallout 3", "Daxter", "System Shock 2"};
```

```
  // Build the necessary Func<> delegates using anonymous methods.
  Func<string, bool> searchFilter =
    delegate(string game) { return game.Contains(" "); };
  Func<string, string> itemToProcess = delegate(string s) { return s; };

  // Pass the delegates into the methods of Enumerable.
  var subset = currentVideoGames.Where(searchFilter)
    .OrderBy(itemToProcess).Select(itemToProcess);

  // Print out the results.
  foreach (var game in subset)
    Console.WriteLine("Item: {0}", game);
  Console.WriteLine();
}
```

This iteration of the query expression is even more verbose, because you are manually creating the Func<> delegates used by the Where(), OrderBy(), and Select() methods of the Enumerable class. On the plus side, the anonymous method syntax does keep all the delegate processing contained within a single method definition. Nevertheless, this method is functionally equivalent to the QueryStringsWithEnumerableAndLambdas() and QueryStringsWithOperators() methods created in the previous sections.

Building Query Expressions Using the Enumerable Type and Raw Delegates

Finally, if you want to build a query expression using the *really verbose approach*, you could avoid the use of lambdas/anonymous method syntax and directly create delegate targets for each Func<> type. Here is the final iteration of your query expression, modeled within a new class type named VeryComplexQueryExpression:

```
class VeryComplexQueryExpression
{
  public static void QueryStringsWithRawDelegates()
  {
    Console.WriteLine("***** Using Raw Delegates *****");

    string[] currentVideoGames = {"Morrowind", "Uncharted 2",
      "Fallout 3", "Daxter", "System Shock 2"};

    // Build the necessary Func<> delegates.
    Func<string, bool> searchFilter = new Func<string, bool>(Filter);
    Func<string, string> itemToProcess = new Func<string,string>(ProcessItem);

    // Pass the delegates into the methods of Enumerable.
    var subset = currentVideoGames
      .Where(searchFilter).OrderBy(itemToProcess).Select(itemToProcess);

    // Print out the results.
    foreach (var game in subset)
      Console.WriteLine("Item: {0}", game);
    Console.WriteLine();
```

```
    }

    // Delegate targets.
    public static bool Filter(string game) {return game.Contains(" ");}
    public static string ProcessItem(string game) { return game; }
}
```

You can test this iteration of your string processing logic by calling this method within the Main() method of the Program class, as follows:

```
VeryComplexQueryExpression.QueryStringsWithRawDelegates();
```

If you were to now run the application to test each possible approach, it should not be too surprising that the output is identical, regardless of the path taken. Keep the following points in mind regarding how LINQ query expressions are represented under the covers:

- Query expressions are created using various C# query operators.

- Query operators are simply shorthand notations for invoking extension methods defined by the System.Linq.Enumerable type.

- Many methods of Enumerable require delegates (Func<> in particular) as parameters.

- Any method requiring a delegate parameter can instead be passed a lambda expression.

- Lambda expressions are simply anonymous methods in disguise (which greatly improve readability).

- Anonymous methods are shorthand notations for allocating a raw delegate and manually building a delegate target method.

Whew! That might have been a bit deeper under the hood than you wanted to have gone, but I hope this discussion has helped you understand what the user-friendly C# query operators are actually doing behind the scenes.

■ **Note** The LinqUsingEnumerable project can be found under the Chapter 12 subdirectory.

Summary

LINQ is a set of related technologies that attempts to provide a single, symmetrical manner to interact with diverse forms of data. As explained over the course of this chapter, LINQ can interact with any type implementing the IEnumerable<T> interface, including simple arrays as well as generic and nongeneric collections of data.

As you have seen, working with LINQ technologies is accomplished using several C# language features. For example, given the fact that LINQ query expressions can return any number of result sets, it is common to make use of the var keyword to represent the underlying data type. As well, lambda expressions, object initialization syntax, and anonymous types can all be used to build very functional and compact LINQ queries.

More importantly, you have seen how the C# LINQ query operators are simply shorthand notations for making calls on static members of the System.Linq.Enumerable type. As shown, most members of Enumerable operate on Func<T> delegate types, which can take literal method addresses, anonymous methods, or lambda expressions as input to evaluate the query.

CHAPTER 13

Understanding Object Lifetime

At this point in the text, you have learned a great deal about how to build custom class types using C#. Now you will see how the CLR manages allocated class instances (a.k.a. objects) via *garbage collection*. C# programmers never directly deallocate a managed object from memory (recall there is no delete keyword in the C# language). Rather, .NET objects are allocated to a region of memory termed the *managed heap*, where they will be automatically destroyed by the garbage collector "sometime in the future."

After you have looked at the core details of the collection process, you'll learn how to programmatically interact with the garbage collector using the System.GC class type (which is something you will typically not be required to do for a majority of your .NET projects). Next, you'll examine how the virtual System.Object.Finalize() method and IDisposable interface can be used to build classes that release internal *unmanaged resources* in a predictable and timely manner.

You will also delve into some new functionality of the garbage collector introduced with .NET 4.0, including background garbage collections and lazy instantiation using the generic System.Lazy<> class. By the time you have completed this chapter, you will have a solid understanding of how .NET objects are managed by the CLR.

Classes, Objects, and References

To frame the topics covered in this chapter, it is important to further clarify the distinction between classes, objects, and reference variables. Recall that a class is nothing more than a blueprint that describes how an instance of this type will look and feel in memory. Classes, of course, are defined within a code file (which in C# takes a *.cs extension by convention). Consider the following simple Car class defined within a new C# Console Application project named SimpleGC:

```
// Car.cs
public class Car
{
  public int CurrentSpeed {get; set;}
  public string PetName {get; set;}

  public Car(){}
  public Car(string name, int speed)
  {
    PetName = name;
    CurrentSpeed = speed;
  }
  public override string ToString()
  {
```

```
        return string.Format("{0} is going {1} MPH",
            PetName, CurrentSpeed);
    }
}
```

After a class has been defined, you may allocate any number of objects using the C# new keyword. Understand, however, that the new keyword returns a *reference* to the object on the heap, not the actual object itself. If you declare the reference variable as a local variable in a method scope, it is stored on the stack for further use in your application. When you want to invoke members on the object, apply the C# dot operator to the stored reference, like so:

```
class Program
{
  static void Main(string[] args)
  {
    Console.WriteLine("***** GC Basics *****");

    // Create a new Car object on
    // the managed heap. We are
    // returned a reference to this
    // object ("refToMyCar").
    Car refToMyCar = new Car("Zippy", 50);

    // The C# dot operator (.) is used
    // to invoke members on the object
    // using our reference variable.
    Console.WriteLine(refToMyCar.ToString());
    Console.ReadLine();
  }
}
```

Figure 13-1 illustrates the class, object, and reference relationship.

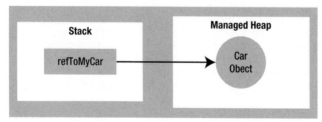

Figure 13-1. References to objects on the managed heap

■ **Note** Recall from Chapter 4 that structures are *value types* that are always allocated directly on the stack and are never placed on the .NET managed heap. Heap allocation occurs only when you are creating instances of classes.

The Basics of Object Lifetime

When you are building your C# applications, you are correct to assume that the .NET runtime environment (a.k.a. the CLR) will take care of the managed heap without your direct intervention. In fact, the golden rule of .NET memory management is simple:

■ **Rule** Allocate a class instance onto the managed heap using the new keyword and forget about it.

Once instantiated, the garbage collector will destroy an object when it is no longer needed. The next obvious question, of course, is, "How does the garbage collector determine when an object is no longer needed?" The short (i.e., incomplete) answer is that the garbage collector removes an object from the heap only if it is *unreachable* by any part of your code base. Assume you have a method in your Program class that allocates a local Car object as follows:

```
static void MakeACar()
{
  // If myCar is the only reference to the Car object,
  // it *may* be destroyed when this method returns.
  Car myCar = new Car();
}
```

Notice that this Car reference (myCar) has been created directly within the MakeACar() method and has not been passed outside of the defining scope (via a return value or ref/out parameters). Thus, once this method call completes, the myCar reference is no longer reachable, and the associated Car object is now a candidate for garbage collection. Understand, however, that you can't guarantee that this object will be reclaimed from memory immediately after MakeACar() has completed. All you can assume at this point is that when the CLR performs the next garbage collection, the myCar object could be safely destroyed.

As you will most certainly discover, programming in a garbage-collected environment greatly simplifies your application development. In stark contrast, C++ programmers are painfully aware that if they fail to manually delete heap-allocated objects, memory leaks are never far behind. In fact, tracking down memory leaks is one of the most time-consuming (and tedious) aspects of programming in unmanaged environments. By allowing the garbage collector to take charge of destroying objects, the burden of memory management has been lifted from your shoulders and placed onto those of the CLR.

The CIL of new

When the C# compiler encounters the new keyword, it emits a CIL newobj instruction into the method implementation. If you compile the current example code and investigate the resulting assembly using ildasm.exe, you'd find the following CIL statements within the MakeACar() method:

```
.method private hidebysig static void MakeACar() cil managed
{
  // Code size 8 (0x8)
  .maxstack  1
  .locals init ([0] class SimpleGC.Car myCar)
  IL_0000:  nop
  IL_0001:  newobj instance void SimpleGC.Car::.ctor()
```

```
  IL_0006:  stloc.0
  IL_0007:  ret
} // end of method Program::MakeACar
```

Before we examine the exact rules that determine when an object is removed from the managed heap, let's check out the role of the CIL newobj instruction in a bit more detail. First, understand that the managed heap is more than just a random chunk of memory accessed by the CLR. The .NET garbage collector is quite a tidy housekeeper of the heap, given that it will compact empty blocks of memory (when necessary) for purposes of optimization.

To aid in this endeavor, the managed heap maintains a pointer (commonly referred to as the *next object pointer* or *new object pointer*) that identifies exactly where the next object will be located. That said, the newobj instruction tells the CLR to perform the following core operations:

- Calculate the total amount of memory required for the object to be allocated (including the memory required by the data members and the base classes).

- Examine the managed heap to ensure that there is indeed enough room to host the object to be allocated. If there is, the specified constructor is called and the caller is ultimately returned a reference to the new object in memory, whose address just happens to be identical to the last position of the next object pointer.

- Finally, before returning the reference to the caller, advance the next object pointer to point to the next available slot on the managed heap.

The basic process is illustrated in Figure 13-2.

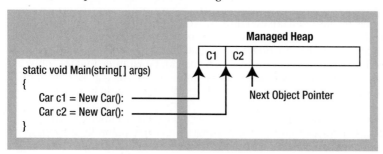

Figure 13-2. *The details of allocating objects onto the managed heap*

As your application is busy allocating objects, the space on the managed heap may eventually become full. When processing the newobj instruction, if the CLR determines that the managed heap does not have sufficient memory to allocate the requested type, it will perform a garbage collection in an attempt to free up memory. Thus, the next rule of garbage collection is also quite simple:

■ **Rule** If the managed heap does not have sufficient memory to allocate a requested object, a garbage collection will occur.

Exactly *how* this garbage collection occurs, however, depends on which version of the .NET platform your application is running under. You'll look at the differences a bit later in this chapter.

Setting Object References to null

C/C++ programmers often set pointer variables to null to ensure they are no longer referencing unmanaged memory. Given this, you might wonder what the end result is of assigning object references to null under C#. For example, assume the MakeACar() subroutine has now been updated as follows:

```
static void MakeACar()
{
  Car myCar = new Car();
  myCar = null;
}
```

When you assign object references to null, the compiler generates CIL code that ensures the reference (myCar, in this example) no longer points to any object. If you once again made use of ildasm.exe to view the CIL code of the modified MakeACar(), you would find the ldnull opcode (which pushes a null value on the virtual execution stack) followed by a stloc.0 opcode (which sets the null reference on the variable):

```
.method private hidebysig static void  MakeACar() cil managed
{
  // Code size 10 (0xa)
  .maxstack  1
  .locals init ([0] class SimpleGC.Car myCar)
  IL_0000:  nop
  IL_0001:  newobj instance void SimpleGC.Car::.ctor()
  IL_0006:  stloc.0
  IL_0007:  ldnull
  IL_0008:  stloc.0
  IL_0009:  ret
} // end of method Program::MakeACar
```

What you must understand, however, is that assigning a reference to null does not in any way force the garbage collector to fire up at that exact moment and remove the object from the heap. The only thing you have accomplished is explicitly clipping the connection between the reference and the object it previously pointed to. Given this point, setting references to null under C# is far less consequential than doing so in other C-based languages; however, doing so will certainly not cause any harm.

The Role of Application Roots

Now, back to the topic of how the garbage collector determines when an object is no longer needed. To understand the details, you need to be aware of the notion of *application roots*. Simply put, a *root* is a storage location containing a reference to an object on the managed heap. Strictly speaking, a root can fall into any of the following categories:

- References to global objects (though these are not allowed in C#, CIL code does permit allocation of global objects)

- References to any static objects/static fields

- References to local objects within an application's code base

- References to object parameters passed into a method

- References to objects waiting to be *finalized* (described later in this chapter)

- Any CPU register that references an object

During a garbage collection process, the runtime will investigate objects on the managed heap to determine whether they are still reachable (i.e., rooted) by the application. To do so, the CLR will build an *object graph*, which represents each reachable object on the heap. Object graphs are explained in some detail during the discussion of object serialization in Chapter 20. For now, just understand that object graphs are used to document all reachable objects. As well, be aware that the garbage collector will never graph the same object twice, thus avoiding the nasty circular reference count found in COM programming.

Assume the managed heap contains a set of objects named A, B, C, D, E, F, and G. During a garbage collection, these objects (as well as any internal object references they may contain) are examined for active roots. After the graph has been constructed, unreachable objects (which we will assume are objects C and F) are marked as garbage. Figure 13-3 diagrams a possible object graph for the scenario just described (you can read the directional arrows using the phrase *depends on* or *requires*, for example, E depends on G and B, A depends on nothing, and so on).

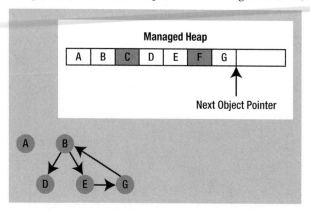

Figure 13-3. *Object graphs are constructed to determine which objects are reachable by application roots*

After objects have been marked for termination (C and F in this case—as they are not accounted for in the object graph), they are swept from memory. At this point, the remaining space on the heap is compacted, which in turn causes the CLR to modify the set of active application roots (and the underlying pointers) to refer to the correct memory location (this is done automatically and transparently). Last but not least, the next object pointer is readjusted to point to the next available slot. Figure 13-4 illustrates the resulting readjustment.

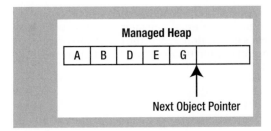

Figure 13-4. *A clean and compacted heap*

■ **Note** Strictly speaking, the garbage collector makes use of two distinct heaps, one of which is specifically used to store very large objects. This heap is less frequently consulted during the collection cycle, given possible performance penalties involved with relocating large objects. Regardless, it is safe to consider the managed heap as a single region of memory.

Understanding Object Generations

When the CLR is attempting to locate unreachable objects, is does not literally examine each and every object placed on the managed heap. Doing so, obviously, would involve considerable time, especially in larger (i.e., real-world) applications.

To help optimize the process, each object on the heap is assigned to a specific "generation." The idea behind generations is simple: the longer an object has existed on the heap, the more likely it is to stay there. For example, the class that defined the main window of a desktop application will be in memory until the program terminates. Conversely, objects that have only recently been placed on the heap (such as an object allocated within a method scope) are likely to be unreachable rather quickly. Given these assumptions, each object on the heap belongs to one of the following generations:

- *Generation 0*: Identifies a newly allocated object that has never been marked for collection.

- *Generation 1*: Identifies an object that has survived a garbage collection (i.e., it was marked for collection but was not removed due to the fact that the sufficient heap space was acquired).

- *Generation 2*: Identifies an object that has survived more than one sweep of the garbage collector.

■ **Note** Generations 0 and 1 are termed *ephemeral generations*. As explained in the next section, you will see that the garbage collection process does treat ephemeral generations differently.

The garbage collector will investigate all generation 0 objects first. If marking and sweeping (or said more plainly, getting rid of) these objects results in the required amount of free memory, any surviving objects are promoted to generation 1. To see how an object's generation affects the collection process, ponder Figure 13-5, which diagrams how a set of surviving generation 0 objects (A, B, and E) are promoted once the required memory has been reclaimed.

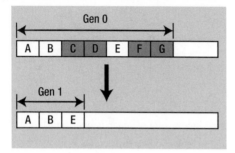

Figure 13-5. *Generation 0 objects that survive a garbage collection are promoted to generation 1*

If all generation 0 objects have been evaluated, but additional memory is still required, generation 1 objects are then investigated for reachability and collected accordingly. Surviving generation 1 objects are then promoted to generation 2. If the garbage collector *still* requires additional memory, generation 2 objects are evaluated. At this point, if a generation 2 object survives a garbage collection, it remains a generation 2 object, given the predefined upper limit of object generations.

The bottom line is that by assigning a generational value to objects on the heap, newer objects (such as local variables) will be removed quickly, while older objects (such as a program's main Window) are not "bothered" as often.

Concurrent Garbage Collection Under .NET 1.0–3.5

Prior to .NET 4.0, the runtime would clean up unused objects using a technique termed *concurrent garbage collection.* Under this model, when a collection takes place for any generation 0 or generation 1 objects (recall these are *ephemeral generations*), the garbage collector temporarily suspends all active *threads* within the current process to ensure that the application does not access the managed heap during the collection process.

We will examine the topic of threads in Chapter 19; for the time being, simply regard a thread as a path of execution within a running executable. After the garbage collection cycle has completed, the suspended threads are permitted to carry on their work. Thankfully, the .NET 3.5 (and earlier) garbage collector was highly optimized; you seldom (if ever) noticed this brief interruption in your application.

As an optimization, concurrent garbage collection allowed objects that were not located in one of the ephemeral generations to be cleaned up on a dedicated thread. This decreased (but didn't eliminate) the need for the .NET runtime to suspend active threads. Moreover, concurrent garbage collection allowed your program to continue allocating objects on the heap during the collection of nonephemeral generations.

Background Garbage Collection Under .NET 4.0 and Greater

Beginning with .NET 4.0, the garbage collector is able to deal with thread suspension when it cleans up objects on the managed heap, using *background garbage collection*. Despite its name, this does not mean that all garbage collection now takes place on additional background threads of execution. Rather, if a background garbage collection is taking place for objects living in a nonephemeral generation, the .NET runtime is now able to collect objects on the ephemeral generations using a dedicated background thread.

On a related note, the .NET 4.0 and higher garbage collection has been improved to further reduce the amount of time a given thread involved with garbage collection details must be suspended. The end result of these changes is that the process of cleaning up unused objects living in generation 0 or generation 1 has been optimized and can result in better runtime performance of your programs (which is really important for real-time systems that require small, and predictable, GC stop time).

Do understand, however, that the introduction of this new garbage collection model has no effect on how you build your .NET applications. For all practical purposes, you can simply allow the .NET garbage collector to perform its work without your direct intervention (and be happy that the folks at Microsoft are improving the collection process in a transparent manner).

The System.GC Type

The mscorlib.dll assembly provides a class type named System.GC that allows you to programmatically interact with the garbage collector using a set of static members. Now, do be very aware that you will seldom (if ever) need to make use of this class directly in your code. Typically, the only time you will use the members of System.GC is when you are creating classes that make internal use of *unmanaged resources*. This could be the case if you are building a class that makes calls into the Windows C-based API using the .NET platform invocation protocol, or perhaps due to some very low-level and complicated COM interop logic. Table 13-1 provides a rundown of some of the more interesting members (consult the .NET Framework 4.5 SDK documentation for complete details).

Table 13-1. Select Members of the System.GC Type

System.GC Member	Description
AddMemoryPressure() RemoveMemoryPressure()	Allows you to specify a numerical value that represents the calling object's "urgency level" regarding the garbage collection process. Be aware that these methods should alter pressure in tandem and, thus, never remove more pressure than the total amount you have added.
Collect()	Forces the GC to perform a garbage collection. This method has been overloaded to specify a generation to collect, as well as the mode of collection (via the GCCollectionMode enumeration).
CollectionCount()	Returns a numerical value representing how many times a given generation has been swept.
GetGeneration()	Returns the generation to which an object currently belongs.

System.GC Member	Description
GetTotalMemory()	Returns the estimated amount of memory (in bytes) currently allocated on the managed heap. A Boolean parameter specifies whether the call should wait for garbage collection to occur before returning.
MaxGeneration	Returns the maximum number of generations supported on the target system. Under Microsoft's .NET 4.0, there are three possible generations: 0, 1, and 2.
SuppressFinalize()	Sets a flag indicating that the specified object should not have its Finalize() method called.
WaitForPendingFinalizers()	Suspends the current thread until all finalizable objects have been finalized. This method is typically called directly after invoking GC.Collect().

To illustrate how the System.GC type can be used to obtain various garbage collection–centric details, consider the following Main() method, which makes use of several members of GC:

```
static void Main(string[] args)
{
  Console.WriteLine("***** Fun with System.GC *****");

  // Print out estimated number of bytes on heap.
  Console.WriteLine("Estimated bytes on heap: {0}",
    GC.GetTotalMemory(false));

  // MaxGeneration is zero based, so add 1 for display purposes.
  Console.WriteLine("This OS has {0} object generations.\n",
    (GC.MaxGeneration + 1));

  Car refToMyCar = new Car("Zippy", 100);
  Console.WriteLine(refToMyCar.ToString());

  // Print out generation of refToMyCar object.
  Console.WriteLine("Generation of refToMyCar is: {0}",
    GC.GetGeneration(refToMyCar));

  Console.ReadLine();
}
```

Forcing a Garbage Collection

Again, the whole purpose of the .NET garbage collector is to manage memory on our behalf. However, in some very rare circumstances, it may be beneficial to programmatically force a garbage collection using GC.Collect(). Here are two common situations where you might consider interacting with the collection process:

- Your application is about to enter into a block of code that you don't want interrupted by a possible garbage collection.

- Your application has just finished allocating an extremely large number of objects and you want to remove as much of the acquired memory as soon as possible.

If you determine it could be beneficial to have the garbage collector check for unreachable objects, you could explicitly trigger a garbage collection, as follows:

```
static void Main(string[] args)
{
...
  // Force a garbage collection and wait for
  // each object to be finalized.
  GC.Collect();
  GC.WaitForPendingFinalizers();
...
}
```

When you manually force a garbage collection, you should always make a call to GC.WaitForPendingFinalizers(). With this approach, you can rest assured that all *finalizable objects* (described in the next section) have had a chance to perform any necessary cleanup before your program continues. Under the hood, GC.WaitForPendingFinalizers() will suspend the calling thread during the collection process. This is a good thing, as it ensures your code does not invoke methods on an object currently being destroyed!

The GC.Collect() method can also be supplied a numerical value that identifies the oldest generation on which a garbage collection will be performed. For example, to instruct the CLR to investigate only generation 0 objects, you would write the following:

```
static void Main(string[] args)
{
...
  // Only investigate generation 0 objects.
  GC.Collect(0);
  GC.WaitForPendingFinalizers();
...
}
```

As well, the Collect() method can also be passed in a value of the GCCollectionMode enumeration as a second parameter, to fine-tune exactly how the runtime should force the garbage collection. This enum defines the following values:

```
public enum GCCollectionMode
{
  Default,    // Forced is the current default.
  Forced,     // Tells the runtime to collect immediately!
  Optimized   // Allows the runtime to determine
              // whether the current time is optimal to reclaim objects.
}
```

As with any garbage collection, calling GC.Collect()promotes surviving generations. To illustrate, assume that our Main() method has been updated as follows:

```
static void Main(string[] args)
{
  Console.WriteLine("***** Fun with System.GC *****");

  // Print out estimated number of bytes on heap.
  Console.WriteLine("Estimated bytes on heap: {0}",
    GC.GetTotalMemory(false));

  // MaxGeneration is zero based.
  Console.WriteLine("This OS has {0} object generations.\n",
    (GC.MaxGeneration + 1));
  Car refToMyCar = new Car("Zippy", 100);
  Console.WriteLine(refToMyCar.ToString());

  // Print out generation of refToMyCar.
  Console.WriteLine("\nGeneration of refToMyCar is: {0}",
    GC.GetGeneration(refToMyCar));

  // Make a ton of objects for testing purposes.
  object[] tonsOfObjects = new object[50000];
  for (int i = 0; i < 50000; i++)
    tonsOfObjects[i] = new object();

  // Collect only gen 0 objects.
  GC.Collect(0, GCCollectionMode.Forced);
  GC.WaitForPendingFinalizers();

  // Print out generation of refToMyCar.
  Console.WriteLine("Generation of refToMyCar is: {0}",
    GC.GetGeneration(refToMyCar));

  // See if tonsOfObjects[9000] is still alive.
  if (tonsOfObjects[9000] != null)
  {
    Console.WriteLine("Generation of tonsOfObjects[9000] is: {0}",
      GC.GetGeneration(tonsOfObjects[9000]));
  }
  else
    Console.WriteLine("tonsOfObjects[9000] is no longer alive.");

  // Print out how many times a generation has been swept.
  Console.WriteLine("\nGen 0 has been swept {0} times",
    GC.CollectionCount(0));
  Console.WriteLine("Gen 1 has been swept {0} times",
    GC.CollectionCount(1));
  Console.WriteLine("Gen 2 has been swept {0} times",
    GC.CollectionCount(2));
  Console.ReadLine();
}
```

Here, we have purposely created a very large array of object types (50,000 to be exact) for testing purposes. As you can see from the output that follows, even though this Main() method made only one explicit request for a garbage collection (via the GC.Collect() method), the CLR performed a number of them in the background.

```
***** Fun with System.GC *****
Estimated bytes on heap: 70240
This OS has 3 object generations.

Zippy is going 100 MPH

Generation of refToMyCar is: 0
Generation of refToMyCar is: 1
Generation of tonsOfObjects[9000] is: 1

Gen 0 has been swept 1 times
Gen 1 has been swept 0 times
Gen 2 has been swept 0 times
```

At this point, I hope you feel more comfortable regarding the details of object lifetime. In the next section, we'll examine the garbage collection process a bit further by addressing how you can build *finalizable objects,* as well as *disposable objects.* Be very aware that the following techniques are typically necessary only if you are building C# classes that maintain internal unmanaged resources.

■ **Source Code** The SimpleGC project is included under the Chapter 13 subdirectory.

Building Finalizable Objects

In Chapter 6, you learned that the supreme base class of .NET, System.Object, defines a virtual method named Finalize(). The default implementation of this method does nothing whatsoever:

```
// System.Object
public class Object
{
  ...
  protected virtual void Finalize() {}
}
```

When you override Finalize() for your custom classes, you establish a specific location to perform any necessary cleanup logic for your type. Given that this member is defined as protected, it is not possible to directly call an object's Finalize() method from a class instance via the dot operator. Rather, the *garbage collector* will call an object's Finalize() method (if supported) before removing the object from memory.

■ **Note** It is illegal to override `Finalize()` on structure types. This makes perfect sense given that structures are value types, which are never allocated on the heap to begin with and, therefore, are not garbage collected! However, if you create a structure that contains unmanaged resources that need to be cleaned up, you can implement the `IDisposable` interface (described shortly).

Of course, a call to `Finalize()` will (eventually) occur during a "natural" garbage collection or possibly when you programmatically force a collection via `GC.Collect()`. In addition, a type's finalizer method will automatically be called when the application domain hosting your application is unloaded from memory. Depending on your background in .NET, you may know that application domains (or simply AppDomains) are used to host an executable assembly and any necessary external code libraries. If you are not familiar with this .NET concept, you will be by the time you've finished Chapter 17. For now, note that when your AppDomain is unloaded from memory, the CLR automatically invokes finalizers for every finalizable object created during its lifetime.

Now, despite what your developer instincts may tell you, the vast majority of your C# classes will not require any explicit cleanup logic or a custom finalizer. The reason is simple: if your classes are just making use of other managed objects, everything will eventually be garbage-collected. The only time you would need to design a class that can clean up after itself is when you are using *unmanaged* resources (such as raw OS file handles, raw unmanaged database connections, chunks of unmanaged memory, or other unmanaged resources). Under the .NET platform, unmanaged resources are obtained by directly calling into the API of the operating system using Platform Invocation Services (PInvoke) or as a result of some very elaborate COM interoperability scenarios. Given this, consider the next rule of garbage collection:

■ **Rule** The only compelling reason to override `Finalize()` is if your C# class is making use of unmanaged resources via PInvoke or complex COM interoperability tasks (typically via various members defined by the `System.Runtime.InteropServices.Marshal` type). The reason is that under these scenarios, you are manipulating memory that the CLR cannot manage.

Overriding System.Object.Finalize()

In the rare case that you do build a C# class that uses unmanaged resources, you will obviously want to ensure that the underlying memory is released in a predictable manner. Suppose you have created a new C# Console Application named SimpleFinalize and inserted a class named `MyResourceWrapper` that uses an unmanaged resource (whatever that might be) and you want to override `Finalize()`. The odd thing about doing so in C# is that you can't do it using the expected override keyword.

```
class MyResourceWrapper
{
  // Compile-time error!
  protected override void Finalize(){ }
}
```

Rather, when you want to configure your custom C# class types to override the Finalize() method, you make use of a (C++-like) destructor syntax to achieve the same effect. The reason for this alternative form of overriding a virtual method is that when the C# compiler processes the finalizer syntax, it automatically adds a good deal of required infrastructure within the implicitly overridden Finalize() method (shown in just a moment).

C# finalizers look very similar to constructors in that they are named identically to the class they are defined within. In addition, finalizers are prefixed with a tilde symbol (~). Unlike a constructor, however, a finalizer never takes an access modifier (they are implicitly protected), never takes parameters, and can't be overloaded (only one finalizer per class).

Following is a custom finalizer for MyResourceWrapper that will issue a system beep when invoked. Obviously, this example is only for instructional purposes. A real-world finalizer would do nothing more than free any unmanaged resources and would *not* interact with other managed objects, even those referenced by the current object, as you can't assume they are still alive at the point the garbage collector invokes your Finalize() method.

```
// Override System.Object.Finalize() via finalizer syntax.
class MyResourceWrapper
{
  ~MyResourceWrapper()
  {
    // Clean up unmanaged resources here.

    // Beep when destroyed (testing purposes only!)
    Console.Beep();
  }
}
```

If you were to examine this C# destructor using ildasm.exe, you would see that the compiler inserts some necessary error-checking code. First, the code statements within the scope of your Finalize() method are placed within a try block (see Chapter 7). The related finally block ensures that your base classes' Finalize() method will always execute, regardless of any exceptions encountered within the try scope.

```
.method family hidebysig virtual instance void
  Finalize() cil managed
{
  // Code size       13 (0xd)
  .maxstack  1
  .try
  {
    IL_0000:  ldc.i4      0x4e20
    IL_0005:  ldc.i4      0x3e8
    IL_000a:  call
    void [mscorlib]System.Console::Beep(int32, int32)
    IL_000f:  nop
    IL_0010:  nop
    IL_0011:  leave.s     IL_001b
  }  // end .try
  finally
  {
    IL_0013:  ldarg.0
    IL_0014:
```

```
        call instance void [mscorlib]System.Object::Finalize()
    IL_0019:  nop
    IL_001a:  endfinally
} // end handler
IL_001b:  nop
IL_001c:  ret
} // end of method MyResourceWrapper::Finalize
```

If you then tested the MyResourceWrapper type, you would find that a system beep occurs when the application terminates, given that the CLR will automatically invoke finalizers upon AppDomain shutdown.

```
static void Main(string[] args)
{
  Console.WriteLine("***** Fun with Finalizers *****\n");
  Console.WriteLine("Hit the return key to shut down this app");
  Console.WriteLine("and force the GC to invoke Finalize()");
  Console.WriteLine("for finalizable objects created in this AppDomain.");
  Console.ReadLine();
  MyResourceWrapper rw = new MyResourceWrapper();
}
```

■ **Source Code** The SimpleFinalize project is included under the Chapter 13 subdirectory.

Detailing the Finalization Process

Not to beat a dead horse, but always remember that the role of the Finalize() method is to ensure that a .NET object can clean up unmanaged resources when it is garbage-collected. Thus, if you are building a class that does not make use of unmanaged memory (by far the most common case), finalization is of little use. In fact, if at all possible, you should design your types to avoid supporting a Finalize() method for the very simple reason that finalization takes time.

When you allocate an object onto the managed heap, the runtime automatically determines whether your object supports a custom Finalize() method. If so, the object is marked as *finalizable*, and a pointer to this object is stored on an internal queue named the *finalization queue*. The finalization queue is a table maintained by the garbage collector that points to each and every object that must be finalized before it is removed from the heap.

When the garbage collector determines it is time to free an object from memory, it examines each entry on the finalization queue and copies the object off the heap to yet another managed structure termed the *finalization reachable table* (often abbreviated as *freachable*, and pronounced "eff-reachable"). At this point, a separate thread is spawned to invoke the Finalize() method for each object on the freachable table *at the next garbage collection*. Given this, it will take, at the very least, two garbage collections to truly finalize an object.

The bottom line is that while finalization of an object does ensure an object can clean up unmanaged resources, it is still nondeterministic in nature, and due to the extra behind-the-curtains processing, considerably slower.

Building Disposable Objects

As you have seen, finalizers can be used to release unmanaged resources when the garbage collector kicks in. However, given that many unmanaged objects are "precious items" (such as raw database or file handles), it could be valuable to release them as soon as possible instead of relying on a garbage collection to occur. As an alternative to overriding Finalize(), your class could implement the IDisposable interface, which defines a single method named Dispose() as follows:

```
public interface IDisposable
{
  void Dispose();
}
```

When you do implement the IDisposable interface, the assumption is that when the *object user* is finished using the object, the object user manually calls Dispose() before allowing the object reference to drop out of scope. In this way, an object can perform any necessary cleanup of unmanaged resources without incurring the hit of being placed on the finalization queue and without waiting for the garbage collector to trigger the class's finalization logic.

■ **Note** Structures and class types can both implement IDisposable (unlike overriding Finalize(), which is reserved for class types), as the object user (not the garbage collector) invokes the Dispose() method.

To illustrate the use of this interface, create a new C# Console Application named SimpleDispose. Here is an updated MyResourceWrapper class that now implements IDisposable, rather than overriding System.Object.Finalize():

```
// Implementing IDisposable.
class MyResourceWrapper : IDisposable
{
  // The object user should call this method
  // when they finish with the object.
  public void Dispose()
  {
    // Clean up unmanaged resources...

    // Dispose other contained disposable objects...

    // Just for a test.
    Console.WriteLine("***** In Dispose! *****");
  }
}
```

Notice that a Dispose() method is not only responsible for releasing the type's unmanaged resources, but can also call Dispose() on any other contained disposable methods. Unlike with Finalize(), it is perfectly safe to communicate with other managed objects within a Dispose() method. The reason is simple: the garbage collector has no clue about the IDisposable interface and will never call Dispose(). Therefore, when the object user calls this method, the object is still living a productive life on the managed heap and has access to all other heap-allocated objects. The calling logic, shown here, is straightforward:

```
class Program
{
  static void Main(string[] args)
  {
    Console.WriteLine("***** Fun with Dispose *****\n");
    // Create a disposable object and call Dispose()
    // to free any internal resources.
    MyResourceWrapper rw = new MyResourceWrapper();
    rw.Dispose();
    Console.ReadLine();
  }
}
```

Of course, before you attempt to call Dispose() on an object, you will want to ensure the type supports the IDisposable interface. While you will typically know which base class library types implement IDisposable by consulting the .NET Framework 4.5 SDK documentation, a programmatic check can be accomplished using the is or as keywords discussed in Chapter 6.

```
class Program
{
  static void Main(string[] args)
  {
    Console.WriteLine("***** Fun with Dispose *****\n");
    MyResourceWrapper rw = new MyResourceWrapper();
    if (rw is IDisposable)
      rw.Dispose();
    Console.ReadLine();
  }
}
```

This example exposes yet another rule regarding memory management:

■ **Rule** It is a good idea to call Dispose() on any object you directly create if the object supports IDisposable. The assumption you should make is that if the class designer chose to support the Dispose() method, the type has some cleanup to perform. If you forget, memory will eventually be cleaned up (so don't panic), but it could take longer than necessary.

There is one caveat to the previous rule. A number of types in the base class libraries that do implement the IDisposable interface provide a (somewhat confusing) alias to the Dispose() method, in an attempt to make the disposal-centric method sound more natural for the defining type. By way of an example, while the System.IO.FileStream class implements IDisposable (and therefore supports a Dispose() method), it also defines the following Close() method that is used for the same purpose:

```
// Assume you have imported
// the System.IO namespace...
static void DisposeFileStream()
{
  FileStream fs = new FileStream("myFile.txt", FileMode.OpenOrCreate);

  // Confusing, to say the least!
  // These method calls do the same thing!
  fs.Close();
  fs.Dispose();
}
```

While it does feel more natural to "close" a file rather than "dispose" of one, this doubling up of cleanup methods can be confusing. For the few types that do provide an alias, just remember that if a type implements IDisposable, calling Dispose() is always a safe course of action.

Reusing the C# using Keyword

When you are handling a managed object that implements IDisposable, it is quite common to make use of structured exception-handling to ensure the type's Dispose() method is called in the event of a runtime exception, like so:

```
static void Main(string[] args)
{
  Console.WriteLine("***** Fun with Dispose *****\n");
  MyResourceWrapper rw = new MyResourceWrapper ();
  try
  {
    // Use the members of rw.
  }
  finally
  {
    // Always call Dispose(), error or not.
    rw.Dispose();
  }
}
```

While this is a fine example of defensive programming, the truth of the matter is that few developers are thrilled by the prospects of wrapping each and every disposable type within a try/finally block just to ensure the Dispose() method is called. To achieve the same result in a much less obtrusive manner, C# supports a special bit of syntax that looks like this:

```
static void Main(string[] args)
{
  Console.WriteLine("***** Fun with Dispose *****\n");
  // Dispose() is called automatically when the
  // using scope exits.
  using(MyResourceWrapper rw = new MyResourceWrapper())
  {
    // Use rw object.
  }
}
```

If you looked at the following CIL code of the Main() method using ildasm.exe, you would find the using syntax does indeed expand to try/finally logic, with the expected call to Dispose():

```
.method private hidebysig static void Main(string[] args) cil managed
{
...
  .try
  {
    ...
  }  // end .try
  finally
  {
...
  IL_0012:  callvirt instance void
    SimpleFinalize.MyResourceWrapper::Dispose()
  }  // end handler
...
} // end of method Program::Main
```

■ **Note** If you attempt to "use" an object that does not implement IDisposable, you will receive a compiler error.

While this syntax does remove the need to manually wrap disposable objects within try/finally logic, the C# using keyword unfortunately now has a double meaning (importing namespaces and invoking a Dispose() method). Nevertheless, when you are working with .NET types that support the IDisposable interface, this syntactical construct will ensure that the object "being used" will automatically have its Dispose() method called once the using block has exited.

Also, be aware that it is possible to declare multiple objects *of the same type* within a using scope. As you would expect, the compiler will inject code to call Dispose() on each declared object.

```
static void Main(string[] args)
{
  Console.WriteLine("***** Fun with Dispose *****\n");

  // Use a comma-delimited list to declare multiple objects to dispose.
  using(MyResourceWrapper rw = new MyResourceWrapper(),
                        rw2 = new MyResourceWrapper())
  {
    // Use rw and rw2 objects.
  }
}
```

■ **Source Code** The SimpleDispose project is included under the Chapter 13 subdirectory.

Building Finalizable and Disposable Types

At this point, we have seen two different approaches to constructing a class that cleans up internal unmanaged resources. On the one hand, you can use a finalizer. Using this technique, you have the peace of mind that comes with knowing the object cleans itself up when garbage-collected (whenever that may be) without the need for user interaction. On the other hand, you can implement IDisposable to provide a way for the object user to clean up the object as soon as it is finished. However, if the caller forgets to call Dispose(), the unmanaged resources may be held in memory indefinitely.

As you might suspect, it is possible to blend both techniques into a single class definition. By doing so, you gain the best of both models. If the object user does remember to call Dispose(), you can inform the garbage collector to bypass the finalization process by calling GC.SuppressFinalize(). If the object user forgets to call Dispose(), the object will eventually be finalized and have a chance to free up the internal resources. The good news is that the object's internal unmanaged resources will be freed one way or another.

Here is the next iteration of MyResourceWrapper, which is now finalizable and disposable, defined in a C# Console Application named FinalizableDisposableClass:

```
// A sophisticated resource wrapper.
public class MyResourceWrapper : IDisposable
{
  // The garbage collector will call this method if the
  // object user forgets to call Dispose().
  ~MyResourceWrapper()
  {
    // Clean up any internal unmanaged resources.
    // Do **not** call Dispose() on any managed objects.
  }

  // The object user will call this method to clean up
  // resources ASAP.
  public void Dispose()
  {
    // Clean up unmanaged resources here.
    // Call Dispose() on other contained disposable objects.

    // No need to finalize if user called Dispose(),
    // so suppress finalization.
    GC.SuppressFinalize(this);
  }
}
```

Notice that this Dispose() method has been updated to call GC.SuppressFinalize(), which informs the CLR that it is no longer necessary to call the destructor when this object is garbage-collected, given that the unmanaged resources have already been freed via the Dispose() logic.

A Formalized Disposal Pattern

The current implementation of MyResourceWrapper does work fairly well; however, we are left with a few minor drawbacks. First, the Finalize() and Dispose() methods each have to clean up the same unmanaged resources. This could result in duplicate code, which can easily become a nightmare to maintain. Ideally, you would define a private helper function that is called by either method.

Next, you'd like to make sure that the Finalize() method does not attempt to dispose of any managed objects, while the Dispose() method should do so. Finally, you'd also like to be certain the object user can safely call Dispose() multiple times without error. Currently, our Dispose() method has no such safeguards.

To address these design issues, Microsoft defined a formal, prim-and-proper disposal pattern that strikes a balance between robustness, maintainability, and performance. Here is the final (and annotated) version of MyResourceWrapper, which makes use of this official pattern:

```csharp
class MyResourceWrapper : IDisposable
{
  // Used to determine if Dispose()
  // has already been called.
  private bool disposed = false;

  public void Dispose()
  {
    // Call our helper method.
    // Specifying "true" signifies that
    // the object user triggered the cleanup.
    CleanUp(true);

    // Now suppress finalization.
    GC.SuppressFinalize(this);
  }

  private void CleanUp(bool disposing)
  {
    // Be sure we have not already been disposed!
    if (!this.disposed)
    {
      // If disposing equals true, dispose all
      // managed resources.
      if (disposing)
      {
        // Dispose managed resources.
      }
      // Clean up unmanaged resources here.
    }
    disposed = true;
  }

  ~MyResourceWrapper()
  {
    // Call our helper method.
    // Specifying "false" signifies that
    // the GC triggered the cleanup.
    CleanUp(false);
  }
}
```

Notice that MyResourceWrapper now defines a private helper method named CleanUp(). By specifying true as an argument, we indicate that the object user has initiated the cleanup, so we should clean up all managed *and* unmanaged resources. However, when the garbage collector initiates the cleanup, we specify false when calling CleanUp() to ensure that internal disposable objects are *not* disposed (as we can't assume they are still in memory!). Last but not least, our bool member variable (disposed) is set to true before exiting CleanUp() to ensure that Dispose() can be called numerous times without error.

■ **Note** After an object has been "disposed," it's still possible for the client to invoke members on it, as it is still in memory. Therefore, a robust resource wrapper class would also need to update each member of the class with additional coding logic that says, in effect, "If I am disposed, do nothing and return from the member."

To test our final iteration of MyResourceWrapper, add a call to Console.Beep() within the scope of your finalizer, like so:

```
~MyResourceWrapper()
{
  Console.Beep();
  // Call our helper method.
  // Specifying "false" signifies that
  // the GC triggered the cleanup.
  CleanUp(false);
}
```

Next, update Main() as follows:

```
static void Main(string[] args)
{
  Console.WriteLine("***** Dispose() / Destructor Combo Platter *****");

  // Call Dispose() manually. This will not call the finalizer.
  MyResourceWrapper rw = new MyResourceWrapper();
  rw.Dispose();

  // Don't call Dispose(). This will trigger the finalizer
  // and cause a beep.
  MyResourceWrapper rw2 = new MyResourceWrapper();
}
```

Notice that we are explicitly calling Dispose() on the rw object, so the destructor call is suppressed. However, we have "forgotten" to call Dispose() on the rw2 object and, therefore, when the application terminates, we hear a single beep. If you were to comment out the call to Dispose() on the rw object, you would hear two beeps.

■ **Source Code** The FinalizableDisposableClass project is included under the Chapter 13 subdirectory.

That concludes our investigation of how the CLR manages your objects via garbage collection. While there are additional (somewhat esoteric) details regarding the collection process I haven't covered here (such as weak references and object resurrection), you are now in a perfect position for further exploration on your own. To wrap this chapter up, we will examine a programming feature called "lazy instantiation" of objects.

Understanding Lazy Object Instantiation

When you are creating classes, you might occasionally need to account for a particular member variable in code, which might never actually be needed, in that the object user might not call the method (or property) that makes use of it. Fair enough. However, this can be very problematic if the member variable in question requires a large amount of memory to be instantiated.

For example, assume you are writing a class that encapsulates the operations of a digital music player. In addition to the expected methods, such as Play(), Pause(), and Stop(), you also want to provide the ability to return a collection of Song objects (via a class named AllTracks), which represents every single digital music file on the device.

If you'd like to follow along, create a new Console Application named LazyObjectInstantiation, and define the following class types:

```
// Represents a single song.
class Song
{
  public string Artist { get; set; }
  public string TrackName { get; set; }
  public double TrackLength { get; set; }
}

// Represents all songs on a player.
class AllTracks
{
  // Our media player can have a maximum
  // of 10,000 songs.
  private Song[] allSongs = new Song[10000];

  public AllTracks()
  {
    // Assume we fill up the array
    // of Song objects here.
    Console.WriteLine("Filling up the songs!");
  }
}

// The MediaPlayer has-an AllTracks object.
class MediaPlayer
{
  // Assume these methods do something useful.
  public void Play() { /* Play a song */ }
  public void Pause() { /* Pause the song */ }
  public void Stop() { /* Stop playback */ }
```

```
private AllTracks allSongs = new AllTracks();

public AllTracks GetAllTracks()
{
  // Return all of the songs.
  return allSongs;
}
}
```

The current implementation of MediaPlayer makes the assumption that the object user will want to obtain a list of songs via the GetAllTracks() method. Well, what if the object user does *not* need to obtain this list? In our current implementation, the AllTracks member variable will still be allocated, thereby creating 10,000 Song objects in memory, as follows:

```
static void Main(string[] args)
{
  Console.WriteLine("***** Fun with Lazy Instantiation *****\n");

  // This caller does not care about getting all songs,
  // but indirectly created 10,000 objects!
  MediaPlayer myPlayer = new MediaPlayer();
  myPlayer.Play();

  Console.ReadLine();
}
```

Clearly, you would rather not create 10,000 objects that nobody will use, as that will add a good deal of stress to the .NET garbage collector. While you could manually add some code to ensure the allSongs object is created only if used (perhaps using the factory method design pattern), there is an easier way.

The base class libraries provide a very useful generic class named Lazy<>, defined in the System namespace of mscorlib.dll. This class allows you to define data that will *not* be created unless your code base actually makes use of it. As this is a generic class, you must specify the type of item to be created on first use, which can be any type with the .NET base class libraries or a custom type you have authored yourself. To enable lazy instantiation of the AllTracks member variable, you can simply replace this:

```
// The MediaPlayer has-an AllTracks object.
class MediaPlayer
{
...
  private AllTracks allSongs = new AllTracks();

  public AllTracks GetAllTracks()
  {
    // Return all of the songs.
    return allSongs;
  }
}
```

with this:

```
// The MediaPlayer has-an Lazy<AllTracks> object.
class MediaPlayer
{
...
```

```
  private Lazy<AllTracks> allSongs = new Lazy<AllTracks>();

  public AllTracks GetAllTracks()
  {
    // Return all of the songs.
    return allSongs.Value;
  }
}
```

Beyond the fact that we are now representing the AllTracks member variable as a Lazy<> type, notice that the implementation of the previous GetAllTracks() method has also been updated. Specifically, we must make use of the read-only Value property of the Lazy<> class to obtain the actual stored data (in this case, the AllTracks object that is maintaining the 10,000 Song objects).

With this simple update, notice how the following updated Main() method will indirectly allocate the Song objects only if GetAllTracks() is indeed called:

```
static void Main(string[] args)
{
  Console.WriteLine("***** Fun with Lazy Instantiation *****\n");

  // No allocation of AllTracks object here!
  MediaPlayer myPlayer = new MediaPlayer();
  myPlayer.Play();

  // Allocation of AllTracks happens when you call GetAllTracks().
  MediaPlayer yourPlayer = new MediaPlayer();
  AllTracks yourMusic = yourPlayer.GetAllTracks();

  Console.ReadLine();
}
```

■ **Note** Lazy object instantiation is not only useful to decrease allocation of unnecessary objects. You can also use this technique if a given member has expensive creation code, such as invoking a remote method, communication with a relational database, or whatnot.

Customizing the Creation of the Lazy Data

When you declare a Lazy<> variable, the actual internal data type is created using the default constructor, like so:

```
// Default constructor of AllTracks is called when the Lazy<>
// variable is used.
private Lazy<AllTracks> allSongs = new Lazy<AllTracks>();
```

While this might be fine in some cases, what if the AllTracks class had some additional constructors, and you want to ensure the correct one is called? Furthermore, what if you have some extra work do to (beyond simply creating the AllTracks object) when the Lazy<> variable is made? As luck would have it, the Lazy<> class allows you to specify a generic delegate as an optional parameter, which will specify a method to call during the creation of the wrapped type.

The generic delegate in question is of type System.Func<>, which can point to a method that returns the same data type being created by the related Lazy<> variable and can take up to 16 arguments (which are typed using generic type parameters). In most cases, you will not need to specify any parameters to pass to the method pointed to by Func<>. Furthermore, to greatly simplify the use of the required Func<>, I'd recommend using a lambda expression (see Chapter 10 to review the delegate/lambda relationship).

With this in mind, the following is a final version of MediaPlayer that adds a bit of custom code when the wrapped AllTracks object is created. Remember, this method must return a new instance of the type wrapped by Lazy<> before exiting, and you can use any constructor you choose (here, we are still invoking the default constructor of AllTracks).

```
class MediaPlayer
{
...

  // Use a lambda expression to add additional code
  // when the AllTracks object is made.
  private Lazy<AllTracks> allSongs = new Lazy<AllTracks>( () =>
    {
      Console.WriteLine("Creating AllTracks object!");
      return new AllTracks();
    }
  );

  public AllTracks GetAllTracks()
  {
    // Return all of the songs.
    return allSongs.Value;
  }
}
```

Sweet! Hopefully you can see the usefulness of the Lazy<> class. Essentially, this generic class allows you to ensure expensive objects are allocated only when the object user requires them. If you find this topic useful for your projects, you might also want to look up the System.Lazy<> class in the .NET Framework 4.5 SDK documentation for further examples of how to program for "lazy instantiation."

■ **Source Code** The LazyObjectInstantiation project is included under the Chapter 13 subdirectory.

Summary

The point of this chapter was to demystify the garbage collection process. As you have seen, the garbage collector will only run when it is unable to acquire the necessary memory from the managed heap (or when a given AppDomain unloads from memory). When a collection does occur, you can rest assured that Microsoft's collection algorithm has been optimized by the use of object generations, secondary threads for the purpose of object finalization, and a managed heap dedicated to hosting large objects.

This chapter also illustrated how to programmatically interact with the garbage collector using the System.GC class type. As mentioned, the only time you will really need to do so is when you are building finalizable or disposable class types that operate on unmanaged resources.

Recall that finalizable types are classes that have provided a destructor (effectively overriding the Finalize() method) to clean up unmanaged resources at the time of garbage collection. Disposable objects, on the other hand, are classes (or structures) that implement the IDisposable interface, which should be called by the object user when it is finished using said objects. Finally, you learned about an official "disposal" pattern that blends both approaches.

We wrapped up this chapter with a look at a generic class named Lazy<>. As you have seen, you can use this class to delay the creation of an expensive (in terms of memory consumption) object until the caller actually requires it. By doing so, you can help reduce the number of objects stored on the managed heap and also ensure expensive objects are created only when actually required by the caller.

■ ■ ■

## PART V

Programming with .NET Assemblies

CHAPTER 14

Building and Configuring Class Libraries

During the first four sections of this text, you have created a number of "stand-alone" executable applications, in which all of the programming logic was packaged within a single executable file (*.exe). These executable assemblies were making use of little more than the primary .NET class library, mscorlib.dll. While some simple .NET programs may be constructed using nothing more than the .NET base class libraries, chances are it will be commonplace for you (or your teammates) to isolate reusable programming logic into *custom* class libraries (*.dll files) that can be shared among applications.

In this chapter, you will learn about various ways to package your types into custom libraries of code. To begin, you'll learn the details of partitioning types into .NET namespaces. After this, you will examine the class library project templates of Visual Studio and learn the distinction between private and shared assemblies.

Next, you'll explore exactly how the .NET runtime resolves the location of an assembly, and you'll come to understand the global assembly cache (GAC), XML application configuration files (*.config files), publisher policy assemblies, and the System.Configuration namespace.

Defining Custom Namespaces

Before diving into the aspects of library deployment and configuration, the first task it to learn the details of packaging your custom types into .NET namespaces. Up to this point in the text, you've been building small test programs that leverage existing namespaces in the .NET universe (System, in particular). However, when you build larger applications with many types, it can be very helpful to group your related types into custom namespaces. In C#, this is accomplished using the namespace keyword. Explicitly defining custom namespaces is even more important when creating .NET *.dll assemblies, as other developers will need to reference the library and import your custom namespaces in order to use your types.

To investigate the issues firsthand, begin by creating a new Console Application named CustomNamespaces. Now, assume you are developing a collection of geometric classes named Square, Circle, and Hexagon. Given their similarities, you would like to group them all together into a unique namespace called MyShapes within the CustomNamespaces.exe assembly. You have two basic approaches. First, you can choose to define all classes in a single C# file (ShapesLib.cs) as follows:

```
// ShapesLib.cs
using System;

namespace MyShapes
{
  // Circle class
  public class Circle { /* Interesting members... */ }
```

```
    // Hexagon class
    public class Hexagon { /* More interesting members... */ }

    // Square class
    public class Square { /* Even more interesting members... */ }
}
```

While the C# compiler has no problems with a single C# code file containing multiple types, this can be cumbersome when you want to reuse class definitions in new projects. For example, say you are building a new project and only need to use the Circle class. If all types are defined in a single code file, you are more or less stuck with the entire set. Therefore, as an alternative, you can split a single namespace across multiple C# files. To ensure each type is packaged into the same logical group, simply wrap the given class definitions in the same namespace scope, like so:

```
// Circle.cs
using System;

namespace MyShapes
{
    // Circle class
    public class Circle { /* Interesting methods... */ }
}

// Hexagon.cs
using System;

namespace MyShapes
{
    // Hexagon class
    public class Hexagon { /* More interesting methods... */ }
}

// Square.cs
using System;

namespace MyShapes
{
    // Square class
    public class Square { /* Even more interesting methods... */ }
}
```

In both cases, notice how the MyShapes namespace acts as the conceptual "container" of these classes. When another namespace (such as CustomNamespaces) wishes to use types in a separate namespace, you make use of the using keyword, just as you would when using namespaces of the .NET base class libraries, as follows:

```
// Bring in a namespace from the base class libraries.
using System;

// Make use of types defined the MyShapes namespace.
using MyShapes;
```

```
namespace CustomNamespaces
{
  public class Program
  {
    static void Main(string[] args)
    {
      Hexagon h = new Hexagon();
      Circle c = new Circle();
      Square s = new Square();
    }
  }
}
```

For this particular example, the assumption is that the C# file(s) that define the MyShapes namespace are part of the same Console Application project that contains the file defining the CustomNamespaces namespace; in other words, all of the files are used to compile a single .NET executable assembly. If you defined the MyShapes namespace within an external assembly, you would also need to set a reference to that library before you could compile successfully. You'll learn all the details of building applications that make use of external libraries during the course of this chapter.

Resolving Name Clashes with Fully Qualified Names

Technically speaking, you are not required to use the C# using keyword when referring to types defined in external namespaces. You could use the *fully qualified name* of the type, which, as you may recall from Chapter 1, is the type's name prefixed with the defining namespace. For example:

```
// Note we are not importing MyShapes anymore!
using System;

namespace CustomNamespaces
{
  public class Program
  {
    static void Main(string[] args)
    {
      MyShapes.Hexagon h = new MyShapes.Hexagon();
      MyShapes.Circle c = new MyShapes.Circle();
      MyShapes.Square s = new MyShapes.Square();
    }
  }
}
```

Typically, there is no need to use a fully qualified name. Not only does it require a greater number of keystrokes, it also makes no difference whatsoever in terms of code size or execution speed. In fact, in CIL code, types are *always* defined with the fully qualified name. In this light, the C# using keyword is simply a typing time saver.

However, fully qualified names can be very helpful (and sometimes necessary) to avoid potential name clashes when using multiple namespaces that contain identically named types. Assume you have a new namespace termed My3DShapes, which defines the following three classes, capable of rendering a shape in stunning 3D:

```
// Another shape-centric namespace.
using System;
```

```
namespace My3DShapes
{
  // 3D Circle class.
  public class Circle { }

  // 3D Hexagon class.
  public class Hexagon { }

  // 3D Square class.
  public class Square { }
}
```

If you update the Program class as seen next, you are issued a number of compile-time errors, because both namespaces define identically named classes:

```
// Ambiguities abound!
using System;
using MyShapes;
using My3DShapes;

namespace CustomNamespaces
{
  public class Program
  {
    static void Main(string[] args)
    {
      // Which namespace do I reference?
      Hexagon h = new Hexagon(); // Compiler error!
      Circle c = new Circle();   // Compiler error!
      Square s = new Square();   // Compiler error!
    }
  }
}
```

The ambiguity can be resolved using the type's fully qualified name, like so:

```
// We have now resolved the ambiguity.
static void Main(string[] args)
{
  My3DShapes.Hexagon h = new My3DShapes.Hexagon();
  My3DShapes.Circle c = new My3DShapes.Circle();
  MyShapes.Square s = new MyShapes.Square();
}
```

Resolving Name Clashes with Aliases

The C# using keyword also lets you create an alias for a type's fully qualified name. When you do so, you define a token that is substituted for the type's full name at compile time. Defining aliases provides a second way to resolve name clashes. For example:

```
using System;
using MyShapes;
```

```
using My3DShapes;

// Resolve the ambiguity using a custom alias.
using The3DHexagon = My3DShapes.Hexagon;

namespace CustomNamespaces
{
  class Program
  {
    static void Main(string[] args)
    {
      // This is really creating a My3DShapes.Hexagon class.
      The3DHexagon h2 = new The3DHexagon();
...
    }
  }
}
```

This alternative using syntax also lets you create an alias for a lengthy namespace. One of the longer namespaces in the base class library is System.Runtime.Serialization.Formatters.Binary, which contains a member named BinaryFormatter. If you wish, you can create an instance of the BinaryFormatter as follows:

```
using bfHome = System.Runtime.Serialization.Formatters.Binary;

namespace MyApp
{
  class ShapeTester
  {
    static void Main(string[] args)
    {
      bfHome.BinaryFormatter b = new bfHome.BinaryFormatter();
      ...
    }
  }
}
```

as well as with a traditional using directive:

```
using System.Runtime.Serialization.Formatters.Binary;

namespace MyApp
{
  class ShapeTester
  {
    static void Main(string[] args)
    {
      BinaryFormatter b = new BinaryFormatter();
      ...
    }
  }
}
```

At this point in the game, there is no need to concern yourself with what the `BinaryFormatter` class is used for (you'll examine this class in Chapter 20). For now, simply remember that the C# using keyword can be used to define aliases for lengthy fully qualified names or, more commonly, to resolve name clashes that can arise when importing multiple namespaces that define identically named types.

■ **Note** Be aware that overuse of C# aliases can result in a confusing code base. If other programmers on your team are unaware of your custom aliases, they could assume the aliases refer to types in the .NET base class libraries and become quite confused when they can't find these tokens in the .NET 4.5 Framework SDK documentation!

Creating Nested Namespaces

When organizing your types, you are free to define namespaces within other namespaces. The .NET base class libraries do so in numerous places to provide deeper levels of type organization. For example, the IO namespace is nested within System, to yield System.IO. If you want to create a root namespace containing the existing My3DShapes namespace, you can update your code as follows:

```
// Nesting a namespace.
namespace Chapter14
{
  namespace My3DShapes
  {
    // 3D Circle class.
    public class Circle{ }

    // 3D Hexagon class.
    public class Hexagon{ }

    // 3D Square class.
    public class Square{ }
  }
}
```

In many cases, the role of a root namespace is simply to provide a further level of scope and, therefore, it may not define any types directly within its scope (as in the case of the Chapter14 namespace). If this is the case, a nested namespace can be defined using the following compact form:

```
// Nesting a namespace (take two).
namespace Chapter14.My3DShapes
{
  // 3D Circle class.
  public class Circle{ }

  // 3D Hexagon class.
  public class Hexagon{ }
```

```
  // 3D Square class.
  public class Square{ }
}
```

Given that you have now nested the My3DShapes namespace within the Chapter14 root namespace, you need to update any existing using directives and type aliases, like so:

```
using Chapter14.My3DShapes;
using The3DHexagon = Chapter14.My3DShapes.Hexagon;
```

The Default Namespace of Visual Studio

On a final namespace-related note, it is worth pointing out that, by default, when you create a new C# project using Visual Studio, the name of your application's default namespace will be identical to the project name. From this point on, when you insert new code files using the Project ➤ Add New Item menu selection, types will automatically be wrapped within the default namespace. If you want to change the name of the default namespace, simply access the Default namespace option using the Application tab of the project's Properties window (see Figure 14-1).

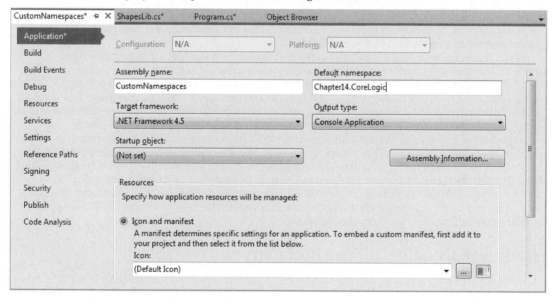

Figure 14-1. Configuring the default namespace

With this update, any new item inserted into the project will be wrapped within the Chapter14.CoreLogic namespace (and, obviously, if another namespace wishes to use these types, the correct using directive must be applied).

So far, so good. Now that you have seen some details regarding how to package your custom types into well-organized namespaces, let's quickly review the benefits and format of the .NET assembly. After this, we will delve into the details of creating, deploying, and configuring your custom class libraries.

■ **Source Code** The CustomNamespaces project is located under the Chapter 14 subdirectory.

The Role of .NET Assemblies

.NET applications are constructed by piecing together any number of *assemblies*. Simply put, an assembly is a versioned, self-describing binary file hosted by the CLR. Now, despite the fact that .NET assemblies have exactly the same file extensions (*.exe or *.dll) as previous Windows binaries, they have very little in common with those files under the hood. Thus, to set the stage for the information to come, let's consider some of the benefits provided by the assembly format.

Assemblies Promote Code Reuse

As you have built your Console Applications over the previous chapters, it might have seemed that *all* of the applications' functionality was contained within the executable assembly you were constructing. In reality, your applications were leveraging numerous types contained within the always accessible .NET code library, mscorlib.dll (recall that the C# compiler references mscorlib.dll automatically), and in the case of some examples, System.Core.dll.

As you might know, a *code library* (also termed a *class library*) is a *.dll that contains types intended to be used by external applications. When you are creating executable assemblies, you will no doubt be leveraging numerous system-supplied and custom code libraries as you create your application. Do be aware, however, that a code library need not take a *.dll file extension. It is perfectly possible (although not very common) for an executable assembly to make use of types defined within an external executable file. In this light, a referenced *.exe can also be considered a code library.

Regardless of how a code library is packaged, the .NET platform allows you to reuse types in a language-independent manner. For example, you could create a code library in C# and reuse that library in any other .NET programming language. It is possible not only to allocate types across languages, but also to derive from them. A base class defined in C# could be extended by a class authored in Visual Basic. Interfaces defined in F# can be implemented by structures defined in C#, and so forth. The point is that when you begin to break apart a single monolithic executable into numerous .NET assemblies, you achieve a *language-neutral* form of code reuse.

Assemblies Establish a Type Boundary

Recall that a type's *fully qualified name* is composed by prefixing the type's namespace (e.g., System) to its name (e.g., Console). Strictly speaking, however, the assembly in which a type resides further establishes a type's identity. For example, if you have two uniquely named assemblies (say, MyCars.dll and YourCars.dll) that both define a namespace (CarLibrary) containing a class named SportsCar, they are considered unique types in the .NET universe.

Assemblies Are Versionable Units

.NET assemblies are assigned a four-part numerical version number of the form *<major>.<minor>.<build>.<revision>*. (If you do not explicitly provide a version number, the assembly is automatically assigned a version of 1.0.0.0, given the default Visual Studio project settings.) This number, in conjunction with an optional *public key value*, allows multiple versions of the same assembly to coexist in harmony on a single machine. Formally speaking, assemblies that provide public key information are termed *strongly named.* As you will see in this chapter, by using a strong name, the CLR is able to ensure that the correct version of an assembly is loaded on behalf of the calling client.

Assemblies Are Self-Describing

Assemblies are regarded as *self-describing,* in part because they record every external assembly they must have access to in order to function correctly. Thus, if your assembly requires System.Windows.Forms.dll and System.Core.dll, this will be documented in the assembly's *manifest.* Recall from Chapter 1 that a manifest is a blob of metadata that describes the assembly itself (name, version, required external assemblies, etc.).

In addition to manifest data, an assembly contains metadata that describes the composition (member names, implemented interfaces, base classes, constructors, and so forth) of every contained type. Because an assembly is documented in such detail, the CLR does *not* consult the Windows system registry to resolve its location (quite the radical departure from Microsoft's legacy COM programming model). As you will discover during this chapter, the CLR makes use of an entirely new scheme to resolve the location of external code libraries.

Assemblies Are Configurable

Assemblies can be deployed as "private" or "shared." Private assemblies reside in the same directory (or possibly a subdirectory) as the client application that uses them. Shared assemblies, on the other hand, are libraries intended to be consumed by numerous applications on a single machine and are deployed to a specific directory termed the *global assembly cache,* or *GAC.*

Regardless of how you deploy your assemblies, you are free to author XML-based configuration files. Using these configuration files, you can instruct the CLR to "probe" for assemblies at a specific location, load a specific version of a referenced assembly for a particular client, or consult an arbitrary directory on your local machine, your network location, or a web-based URL. You'll learn a good deal more about XML configuration files throughout this chapter.

Understanding the Format of a .NET Assembly

Now that you've learned about several benefits provided by the .NET assembly, let's shift gears and get a better idea of how an assembly is composed under the hood. Structurally speaking, a .NET assembly (*.dll or *.exe) consists of the following elements:

- A Windows file header

- A CLR file header

- CIL code

- Type metadata

- An assembly manifest

- Optional embedded resources

While the first two elements (the Windows and CLR headers) are blocks of data you can typically always ignore, they do deserve some brief consideration. Here's an overview of each element.

The Windows File Header

The Windows file header establishes the fact that the assembly can be loaded and manipulated by the Windows family of operating systems. This header data also identifies the kind of application (console-based, GUI-based, or *.dll code library) to be hosted by Windows. If you open a .NET assembly using the dumpbin.exe utility (via a Developer Command Prompt) and specify the /headers flag as so:

```
dumpbin /headers CarLibrary.dll
```

you can view an assembly's Windows header information. Here is the (partial) Windows header information for the CarLibrary.dll assembly you will build a bit later in this chapter (if you would like to run dumpbin.exe yourself right now, you can specify the name of any *.dll or *.exe you wrote during this book in place of CarLibrary.dll):

```
Dump of file CarLibrary.dll

PE signature found
File Type: DLL

FILE HEADER VALUES
             14C machine (x86)
               3 number of sections
        4B37DCD8 time date stamp Sun Dec 27 16:16:56 2011
               0 file pointer to symbol table
               0 number of symbols
              E0 size of optional header
            2102 characteristics
                   Executable
                   32 bit word machine
                   DLL

OPTIONAL HEADER VALUES
             10B magic # (PE32)
            8.00 linker version
             E00 size of code
             600 size of initialized data
               0 size of uninitialized data
            2CDE entry point (00402CDE)
            2000 base of code
            4000 base of data
          400000 image base (00400000 to 00407FFF)
            2000 section alignment
             200 file alignment
            4.00 operating system version
            0.00 image version
            4.00 subsystem version
               0 Win32 version
            8000 size of image
             200 size of headers
               0 checksum
               3 subsystem (Windows CUI)
```

...

Now, remember that the vast majority of .NET programmers will never need to concern themselves with the format of the header data embedded in a .NET assembly. Unless you happen to be building a new .NET language compiler (where you *would* care about such information), you are free to remain blissfully unaware of the grimy details of the header data. Do be aware, however, that this information is used under the covers when Windows loads the binary image into memory.

The CLR File Header

The CLR header is a block of data that all .NET assemblies must support (and do support, courtesy of the C# compiler) in order to be hosted by the CLR. In a nutshell, this header defines numerous flags that enable the runtime to understand the layout of the managed file. For example, flags exist that identify the location of the metadata and resources within the file, the version of the runtime the assembly was built against, the value of the (optional) public key, and so forth. If you supply the /clrheader flag to dumpbin.exe like so:

dumpbin /clrheader CarLibrary.dll

you are presented with the internal CLR header information for a given .NET assembly, as shown here:

```
Dump of file CarLibrary.dll

File Type: DLL

  clr Header:
            48 cb
          2.05 runtime version
          2164 [     A74] RVA [size] of MetaData Directory
             1 flags
                 IL Only
             0 entry point token
             0 [       0] RVA [size] of Resources Directory
             0 [       0] RVA [size] of StrongNameSignature Directory
             0 [       0] RVA [size] of CodeManagerTable Directory
             0 [       0] RVA [size] of VTableFixups Directory
             0 [       0] RVA [size] of ExportAddressTableJumps Directory
             0 [       0] RVA [size] of ManagedNativeHeader Directory

  Summary
        2000 .reloc
        2000 .rsrc
        2000 .text
```

Again, as a .NET developer, you will not need to concern yourself with the gory details of an assembly's CLR header information. Just understand that every .NET assembly contains this data, which is used behind the scenes by the .NET runtime as the image data loads into memory. Now let's turn our attention to some information that is much more useful in our day-to-day programming tasks.

CIL Code, Type Metadata, and the Assembly Manifest

At its core, an assembly contains CIL code, which, as you recall, is a platform- and CPU-agnostic intermediate language. At runtime, the internal CIL is compiled on the fly using a just-in-time (JIT) compiler, according to platform- and CPU-specific instructions. Given this design, .NET assemblies can indeed execute on a variety of architectures, devices, and operating systems. (Although you can live a happy and productive life without understanding the details of the CIL programming language, Chapter 18 offers an introduction to the syntax and semantics of CIL.)

An assembly also contains metadata that completely describes the format of the contained types, as well as the format of external types referenced by this assembly. The .NET runtime uses this metadata to resolve the location of types (and their members) within the binary, lay out types in memory, and facilitate remote method invocations. You'll check out the details of the .NET metadata format in Chapter 15 during our examination of reflection services.

An assembly must also contain an associated *manifest* (also referred to as *assembly metadata*). The manifest documents each *module* within the assembly, establishes the version of the assembly, and also documents any *external* assemblies referenced by the current assembly. As you will see over the course of this chapter, the CLR makes extensive use of an assembly's manifest during the process of locating external assembly references.

Optional Assembly Resources

Finally, a .NET assembly may contain any number of embedded resources, such as application icons, image files, sound clips, or string tables. In fact, the .NET platform supports *satellite assemblies* that contain nothing but localized resources. This can be useful if you want to partition your resources based on a specific culture (English, German, etc.) for the purposes of building international software. The topic of building satellite assemblies is outside the scope of this text; consult the .NET 4.5 Framework documentation for information on satellite assemblies if you are interested.

Building and Consuming Custom Class Library

To begin exploring the world of .NET class libraries, you'll first create a *.dll assembly (named CarLibrary) that contains a small set of public types. To build a code library using Visual Studio, select the Class Library project workspace via the File ➤ New Project... menu option (see Figure 14-2).

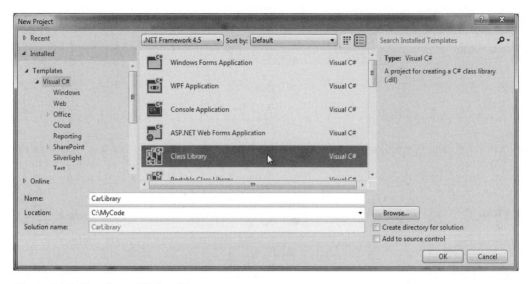

Figure 14-2. *Creating a C# class library*

The design of your automobile library begins with an abstract base class named Car that defines various state data via automatic property syntax. This class also has a single abstract method named TurboBoost(), which makes use of a custom enumeration (EngineState) representing the current condition of the car's engine, as seen here:

```
using System;
using System.Collections.Generic;
using System.Linq;
using System.Text;
using System.Threading.Tasks;

namespace CarLibrary
{
  // Represents the state of the engine.
  public enum EngineState
  { engineAlive, engineDead }

  // The abstract base class in the hierarchy.
  public abstract class Car
  {
    public string PetName {get; set;}
    public int CurrentSpeed {get; set;}
    public int MaxSpeed {get; set;}

    protected EngineState egnState = EngineState.engineAlive;
    public EngineState EngineState
    {
      get { return egnState; }
    }
```

```
      public abstract void TurboBoost();

      public Car(){}
      public Car(string name, int maxSp, int currSp)
      {
        PetName = name; MaxSpeed = maxSp; CurrentSpeed = currSp;
      }
    }
}
```

Now assume you have two direct descendants of the Car type named MiniVan and SportsCar. Each overrides the abstract TurboBoost() method by displaying an appropriate message via a Windows Forms message box. Insert a new C# class file into your project, named DerivedCars.cs, which contains the following code:

```
using System;
using System.Collections.Generic;
using System.Linq;
using System.Text;
using System.Threading.Tasks;

// Keep reading! This won't compile until you reference a .NET library.
using System.Windows.Forms;

namespace CarLibrary
{
  public class SportsCar : Car
  {
    public SportsCar(){ }
    public SportsCar(string name, int maxSp, int currSp)
      : base (name, maxSp, currSp){ }

    public override void TurboBoost()
    {
      MessageBox.Show("Ramming speed!", "Faster is better...");
    }
  }

  public class MiniVan : Car
  {
    public MiniVan(){ }
    public MiniVan(string name, int maxSp, int currSp)
      : base (name, maxSp, currSp){ }

    public override void TurboBoost()
    {
      // Minivans have poor turbo capabilities!
      egnState = EngineState.engineDead;
      MessageBox.Show("Eek!", "Your engine block exploded!");
    }
  }
}
```

Notice how each subclass implements TurboBoost() using the Windows Form's MessageBox class, which is defined in the System.Windows.Forms.dll assembly. For your assembly to make use of the types defined within this external assembly, the CarLibrary project must set a reference to this binary via the Add Reference dialog box (see Figure 14-3), which you can access through the Visual Studio Project ➤ Add Reference menu selection.

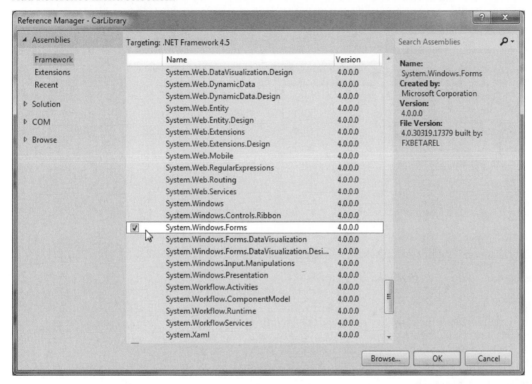

Figure 14-3. *Referencing external .NET assemblies using the Add Reference dialog box*

It is *really* important to understand that the assemblies displayed in the Framework area of the Add Reference dialog box do not represent each and every assembly on your machine. The Add Reference dialog box will *not* display your custom libraries, and it does *not* display all libraries located in the Global Assembly Cache (GAC; more details later in the chapter). Rather, this dialog box simply presents a list of common assemblies that Visual Studio is preprogrammed to display. When you are building applications that require the use of an assembly not listed within the Add Reference dialog box, you need to click the Browse node to manually navigate to the *.dll or *.exe in question.

■ **Note** Be aware that the Recent section of the Add Reference dialog box keeps a running list of previously referenced assemblies. This can be handy, as many .NET projects tend to use the same core set of external libraries.

Exploring the Manifest

Before using CarLibrary.dll from a client application, let's check out how the code library is composed under the hood. Assuming you have compiled this project, load CarLibrary.dll into ildasm.exe via the File ➤ Open menu, and navigate to the \bin\Debug subdirectory of your CarLibrary project. When you are done, you should see your library displayed in the IL disassembler tool (see Figure 14-4).

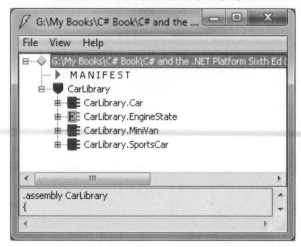

Figure 14-4. CarLibrary.dll loaded into ildasm.exe

Now, open the manifest of CarLibrary.dll by double-clicking the MANIFEST icon. The first code block in a manifest specifies all external assemblies required by the current assembly to function correctly. As you recall, CarLibrary.dll made use of types within mscorlib.dll and System.Windows.Forms.dll, both of which are listed in the manifest using the .assembly extern token, as seen here:

```
.assembly extern mscorlib
{
  .publickeytoken = (B7 7A 5C 56 19 34 E0 89 )
  .ver 4:0:0:0
}
.assembly extern System.Windows.Forms
{
  .publickeytoken = (B7 7A 5C 56 19 34 E0 89 )
  .ver 4:0:0:0
}
```

Here, each .assembly extern block is qualified by the .publickeytoken and .ver directives. The .publickeytoken instruction is present only if the assembly has been configured with a *strong name* (more details on strong names in the section "Understanding Strong Names," later in this chapter). The .ver token defines (of course) the numerical version identifier of the referenced assembly.

After the external references, you will find a number of .custom tokens that identify assembly-level attributes (copyright information, company name, assembly version, etc.). Here is a (very) partial listing of this particular chunk of manifest data:

```
.assembly CarLibrary
{
  .custom instance void ...AssemblyDescriptionAttribute...
  .custom instance void ...AssemblyConfigurationAttribute...
  .custom instance void ...RuntimeCompatibilityAttribute...
  .custom instance void ...TargetFrameworkAttribute...
  .custom instance void ...AssemblyTitleAttribute...
  .custom instance void ...AssemblyTrademarkAttribute...
  .custom instance void ...AssemblyCompanyAttribute...
  .custom instance void ...AssemblyProductAttribute...
  .custom instance void ...AssemblyCopyrightAttribute...
...
  .ver 1:0:0:0
}
.module CarLibrary.dll
```

Typically, these settings are established visually using the Properties editor of your current project. Now, switching back to Visual Studio, if you click the Properties icon within the Solution Explorer, you can click the "Assembly Information..." button located on the (automatically selected) Application tab. This will bring up the GUI editor shown in Figure 14-5.

Figure 14-5. Editing assembly information using Visual Studio's Properties editor

When you save your changes, the GUI editor updates your project's AssemblyInfo.cs file, which is maintained by Visual Studio and can be viewed by expanding the Properties node of the Solution Explorer (see Figure 14-6).

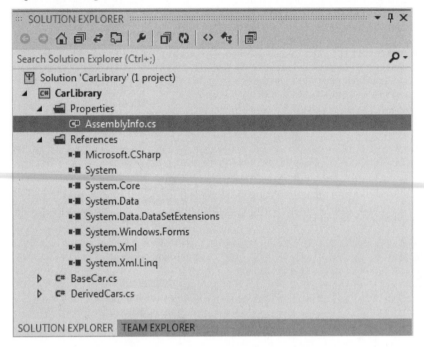

Figure 14-6. *The AssemblyInfo.cs file is updated as you use the GUI Properties editor*

If you view the contents of this C# file, you'll see a number of .NET *attributes* sandwiched between square brackets. For example:

```
[assembly: AssemblyTitle("CarLibrary")]
[assembly: AssemblyDescription("")]
[assembly: AssemblyConfiguration("")]
[assembly: AssemblyCompany("")]
[assembly: AssemblyProduct("CarLibrary")]
[assembly: AssemblyCopyright("Copyright © 2012")]
[assembly: AssemblyTrademark("")]
[assembly: AssemblyCulture("")]
```

Chapter 15 examines the role of attributes in depth, so don't sweat the details at this point. For now, just be aware that a majority of the attributes in AssemblyInfo.cs will be used to update the .custom token values within an assembly manifest.

Exploring the CIL

Recall that an assembly does not contain platform-specific instructions; rather, it contains platform-agnostic common intermediate language (CIL) instructions. When the .NET runtime loads an assembly into memory, the underlying CIL is compiled (using the JIT compiler) into instructions that can be understood by the target platform. For example, back in ildasm.exe, if you double-click the TurboBoost() method of the SportsCar class, ildasm.exe will open a new window showing the CIL tokens that implement this method.

```
.method public hidebysig virtual instance void
  TurboBoost() cil managed
{
  // Code size       18 (0x12)
  .maxstack  8
  IL_0000:  nop
  IL_0001:  ldstr  "Ramming speed!"
  IL_0006:  ldstr  "Faster is better..."
  IL_000b:  call   valuetype [System.Windows.Forms]System.Windows.Forms.DialogResult
    [System.Windows.Forms]System.Windows.Forms.MessageBox::Show(string, string)
  IL_0010:  pop
  IL_0011:  ret
} // end of method SportsCar::TurboBoost
```

Again, while most .NET developers don't need to be deeply concerned with the details of CIL on a daily basis, Chapter 18 provides more details on its syntax and semantics. Believe it or not, understanding the grammar of CIL can be helpful when you are building more complex applications that require advanced services, such as runtime construction of assemblies (again, see Chapter 18).

Exploring the Type Metadata

Before we build some applications that make use of our custom .NET library, if you press the Ctrl+M keystroke combination in ildasm.exe, you can see the metadata for each type within the CarLibrary.dll assembly (see Figure 14-7).

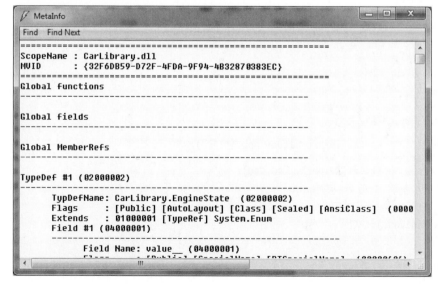

Figure 14-7. Type metadata for the types within CarLibrary.dll

As explained in the next chapter, an assembly's metadata is a very important element of the .NET platform, and serves as the backbone for numerous technologies (object serialization, late binding, extendable applications, etc.). In any case, now that you have looked inside the CarLibrary.dll assembly, you can build some client applications that make use of your types.

■ **Source Code** The CarLibrary project is located under the Chapter 14 subdirectory.

Building a C# Client Application

Because each of the CarLibrary types has been declared using the public keyword, other .NET applications are able to use them as well. Recall that you may also define types using the C# internal keyword (in fact, this is the default C# access mode). Internal types can be used only by the assembly in which they are defined. External clients can neither see nor create types marked with the internal keyword.

To use your library's functionality, create a new C# Console Application project named CSharpCarClient. After you have done so, set a reference to CarLibrary.dll using the Browse node of the Add Reference dialog box (if you compiled CarLibrary.dll using Visual Studio, your assembly is located under the \bin\Debug subdirectory of the CarLibrary project folder). At this point, you can build your client application to make use of the external types. Update your initial C# file as follows:

```
using System;
using System.Collections.Generic;
using System.Linq;
using System.Text;
using System.Threading.Tasks;

// Don't forget to import the CarLibrary namespace!
using CarLibrary;

namespace CSharpCarClient
{
  public class Program
  {
    static void Main(string[] args)
    {
      Console.WriteLine("***** C# CarLibrary Client App *****");
      // Make a sports car.
      SportsCar viper = new SportsCar("Viper", 240, 40);
      viper.TurboBoost();

      // Make a minivan.
      MiniVan mv = new MiniVan();
      mv.TurboBoost();

      Console.WriteLine("Done. Press any key to terminate");
      Console.ReadLine();
    }
```

```
    }
}
```

This code looks just like the code of the other applications developed thus far in the book. The only point of interest is that the C# client application is now making use of types defined within a separate custom library. Go ahead and run your program and verify that you see the display of various message boxes.

You might be wondering exactly what happened when you referenced CarLibrary.dll using the Add Reference dialog box. If you click the Show All Files button of the Solution Explorer, you will notice that Visual Studio added a copy of the original CarLibrary.dll into the \bin\Debug folder of the CSharpCarClient project folder (see Figure 14-8).

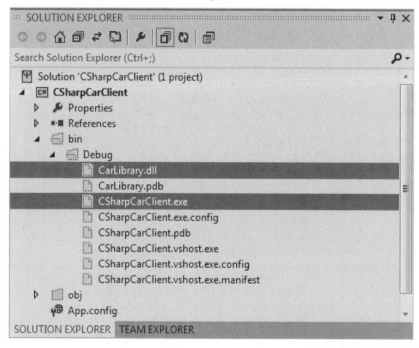

Figure 14-8. Visual Studio copies private assemblies to the client's directory

As explained shortly, CarLibrary.dll has been configured as a "private" assembly (which is the automatic behavior for all Visual Studio Class Library projects). When you reference private assemblies in new applications (such as CSharpCarClient.exe), the IDE responds by placing a copy of the library in the client application's output directory.

■ **Source Code** The CSharpCarClient project is located under the Chapter 14 subdirectory.

Building a Visual Basic Client Application

Recall that the .NET platform allows developers to share compiled code across programming languages. To illustrate the language-agnostic attitude of the .NET platform, let's create another Console Application (VisualBasicCarClient), this time using Visual Basic (see Figure 14-9). Once you have created the project, set a reference to CarLibrary.dll using the Add Reference dialog box, which can be activated by the Project ➤ Add Reference menu option.

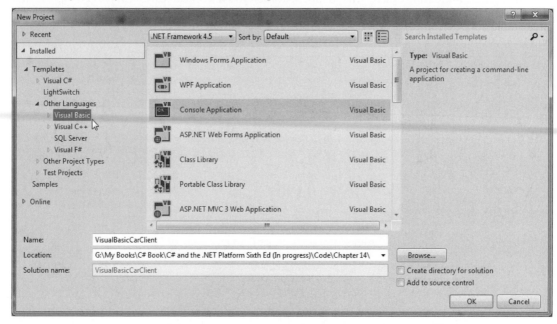

Figure 14-9. *Creating a Visual Basic Console Application*

Like C#, Visual Basic allows you to list each namespace used within the current file. However, Visual Basic offers the Imports keyword rather than the C# using keyword, so add the following Imports statement within the Module1.vb code file:

```
Imports CarLibrary

Module Module1
  Sub Main()
  End Sub
End Module
```

Notice that the Main() method is defined within a Visual Basic module type. In a nutshell, modules are a Visual Basic notation for defining a class that can contain only static methods (much like a C# static class). In any case, to exercise the MiniVan and SportsCar types using the syntax of Visual Basic, update your Main() method as follows:

```
Sub Main()
  Console.WriteLine("***** VB CarLibrary Client App *****")
```

```
' Local variables are declared using the Dim keyword.
Dim myMiniVan As New MiniVan()
myMiniVan.TurboBoost()

Dim mySportsCar As New SportsCar()
mySportsCar.TurboBoost()
Console.ReadLine()
End Sub
```

When you compile and run your application, you will once again find a series of message boxes displayed. Furthermore, this new client application has its own local copy of `CarLibrary.dll` located under the bin\Debug folder.

Cross-Language Inheritance in Action

A very enticing aspect of .NET development is the notion of *cross-language inheritance*. To illustrate, let's create a new Visual Basic class that derives from SportsCar (which was authored using C#). First, add a new class file to your current Visual Basic application (by selecting the Project ➤ Add Class menu option) named PerformanceCar.vb. Update the initial class definition by deriving from the SportsCar type using the Inherits keyword. Then, override the abstract TurboBoost() method using the Overrides keyword, like so:

```
Imports CarLibrary

' This VB class is deriving from the C# SportsCar.
Public Class PerformanceCar
  Inherits SportsCar

  Public Overrides Sub TurboBoost()
    Console.WriteLine("Zero to 60 in a cool 4.8 seconds...")
  End Sub

End Class
```

To test this new class type, update the module's Main() method as follows:

```
Sub Main()
...
  Dim dreamCar As New PerformanceCar()

  ' Use Inherited property.
  dreamCar.PetName = "Hank"
  dreamCar.TurboBoost()
  Console.ReadLine()
End Sub
```

Notice that the dreamCar object is able to invoke any public member (such as the PetName property) found up the chain of inheritance, regardless of the fact that the base class was defined in a completely different language and in a completely different assembly! The ability to extend classes across assembly boundaries in a language-independent manner is a very natural aspect of the .NET development cycle. This makes it very easy to use compiled code written by individuals who would rather not build their shared code with C#.

■ **Source Code** The VisualBasicCarClient project is located under the Chapter 14 subdirectory.

Understanding Private Assemblies

Technically speaking, the class libraries you've created thus far in this chapter have been deployed as *private assemblies*. Private assemblies must be located within the same directory as the client application that's using them (the *application directory*) or a subdirectory thereof. Recall that when you set a reference to CarLibrary.dll while building the CSharpCarClient.exe and VisualBasicCarClient.exe applications, Visual Studio responded by placing a copy of CarLibrary.dll within the client's application directory (at least, after the first compilation).

When a client program uses the types defined within this external assembly, the CLR simply loads the local copy of CarLibrary.dll. Because the .NET runtime does not consult the system registry when searching for referenced assemblies, you can relocate the CSharpCarClient.exe (or VisualBasicCarClient.exe) and CarLibrary.dll assemblies to a new location on your machine and run the application (this is often termed *Xcopy deployment*).

Uninstalling (or replicating) an application that makes exclusive use of private assemblies is a no-brainer: simply delete (or copy) the application folder. More important, you do not need to worry that the removal of private assemblies will break any other applications on the machine.

The Identity of a Private Assembly

The full identity of a private assembly consists of the friendly name and numerical version, both of which are recorded in the assembly manifest. The *friendly name* is simply the name of the module that contains the assembly's manifest minus the file extension. For example, if you examine the manifest of the CarLibrary.dll assembly, you find the following:

```
.assembly CarLibrary
{
...
   .ver 1:0:0:0
}
```

Given the isolated nature of a private assembly, it should make sense that the CLR does not bother to use the version number when resolving its location. The assumption is that private assemblies do not need to have any elaborate version checking, as the client application is the only entity that "knows" of its existence. Because of this, it is (very) possible for a single machine to have multiple copies of the same private assembly in various application directories.

Understanding the Probing Process

The .NET runtime resolves the location of a private assembly using a technique called *probing*, which is much less invasive than it sounds. Probing is the process of mapping an external assembly request to the location of the requested binary file. Strictly speaking, a request to load an assembly may be either *implicit* or *explicit*. An implicit load request occurs when the CLR consults the manifest in order to resolve the location of an assembly defined using the .assembly extern tokens. For example:

```
// An implicit load request.
.assembly extern CarLibrary
```

```
{ ... }
```

An explicit load request occurs programmatically using the Load() or LoadFrom() method of the System.Reflection.Assembly class type, typically for the purposes of late binding and dynamic invocation of type members. You'll examine these topics further in Chapter 15, but for now you can see an example of an explicit load request in the following code:

```
// An explicit load request based on a friendly name.
Assembly asm = Assembly.Load("CarLibrary");
```

In either case, the CLR extracts the friendly name of the assembly and begins probing the client's application directory for a file named CarLibrary.dll. If this file cannot be located, an attempt is made to locate an executable assembly based on the same friendly name (for example, CarLibrary.exe). If neither file can be located in the application directory, the runtime gives up and throws a FileNotFoundException exception at runtime.

■ **Note** Technically speaking, if a copy of the requested assembly cannot be found within the client's application directory, the CLR will also attempt to locate a client subdirectory with the exact same name as the assembly's friendly name (e.g., C:\MyClient\CarLibrary). If the requested assembly resides within this subdirectory, the CLR will load the assembly into memory.

Configuring Private Assemblies

While it is possible to deploy a .NET application by simply copying all required assemblies to a single folder on the user's hard drive, you will most likely want to define a number of subdirectories to group related content. For example, assume you have an application directory named C:\MyApp that contains CSharpCarClient.exe. Under this folder might be a subfolder named MyLibraries that contains CarLibrary.dll.

Regardless of the intended relationship between these two directories, the CLR will *not* probe the MyLibraries subdirectory unless you supply a configuration file. Configuration files contain various XML elements that allow you to influence the probing process. Configuration files must have the same name as the launching application and take a *.config file extension, and they must be deployed in the client's application directory. Thus, if you wish to create a configuration file for CSharpCarClient.exe, it must be named CSharpCarClient.exe.config, and be located (for this example) under the C:\MyApp directory.

To illustrate the process, create a new directory on your C: drive named MyApp using Windows Explorer. Next, copy CSharpCarClient.exe and CarLibrary.dll to this new folder, and run the program by double-clicking the executable. Your program should run successfully at this point.

Now, create a new subdirectory under C:\MyApp named MyLibraries (see Figure 14-10), and move CarLibrary.dll to this location.

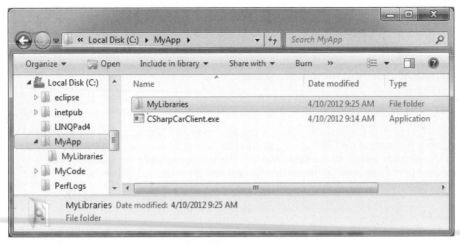

Figure 14-10. CarLibrary.dll now resides under the MyLibraries subdirectory

Try to run your client program again by double-clicking the executable. Because the CLR could not locate an assembly named CarLibrary directly within the application directory, you are presented with a rather nasty unhandled FileNotFoundException exception.

To instruct the CLR to probe under the MyLibraries subdirectory, create a new configuration file named CSharpCarClient.exe.config using any text editor, and save the file in the folder containing the CSharpCarClient.exe application, which in this example is C:\MyApp. Open this file and enter the following content exactly as shown (be aware that XML is case sensitive!):

```
<configuration>
  <runtime>
    <assemblyBinding xmlns="urn:schemas-microsoft-com:asm.v1">
      <probing privatePath="MyLibraries"/>
    </assemblyBinding>
  </runtime>
</configuration>
```

.NET *.config files always open with a root element named <configuration>. The nested <runtime> element may specify an <assemblyBinding> element, which nests a further element named <probing>. The privatePath attribute is the key point in this example, as it is used to specify the subdirectories relative to the application directory where the CLR should probe.

Once you've finished creating CSharpCarClient.exe.config, run the client by double-clicking the executable in Windows Explorer. You should find that CSharpCarClient.exe executes without a hitch (if this is not the case, double-check your *.config file for typos).

Do note that the <probing> element does not specify *which* assembly is located under a given subdirectory. In other words, you cannot say, "CarLibrary is located under the MyLibraries subdirectory, but MathLibrary is located under the OtherStuff subdirectory." The <probing> element simply instructs the CLR to investigate all specified subdirectories for the requested assembly until the first match is encountered.

■ **Note** Be very aware that the privatePath attribute cannot be used to specify an absolute (C:\SomeFolder\SomeSubFolder) or relative (..\SomeFolder\AnotherFolder) path! If you need to specify a directory outside the client's application directory, you will need to use a completely different XML element named <codeBase> (more details on this element later in the chapter).

Multiple subdirectories can be assigned to the privatePath attribute using a semicolon-delimited list. You have no need to do so at this time, but here is an example that informs the CLR to consult the MyLibraries and MyLibraries\Tests client subdirectories:

```
<probing privatePath="MyLibraries;MyLibraries\Tests"/>
```

Next, for testing purposes, change the name of your configuration file (in one way or another) and attempt to run the program once again. The client application should now fail. Remember that *.config files must be prefixed with the same name as the related client application. By way of a final test, open your configuration file for editing and capitalize any of the XML elements. Once the file is saved, your client should fail to run once again (as XML is case sensitive).

■ **Note** Understand that the CLR will load the very first assembly it finds during the probing process. For example, if the C:\MyApp folder did contain a copy of CarLibrary.dll, it will be loaded into memory, while the copy under MyLibraries is effectively ignored.

The Role of the App.Config File

While you are always able to create XML configuration files by hand using your text editor of choice, Visual Studio allows you create a configuration file during the development of the client program. The first step is to elect to insert a new Application Configuration file item into your project via the Project ➤ Add New Item menu option. Notice in Figure 14-11, you have left the name of this file as the suggested App.config.

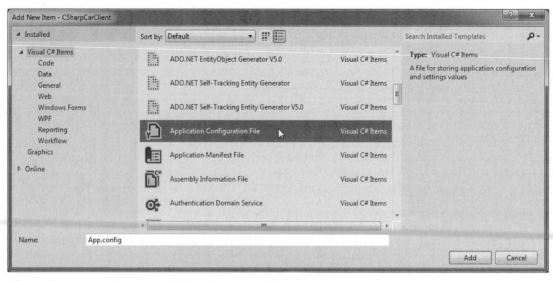

Figure 14-11. *Inserting a new XML configuration file*

If you open this file for viewing, you'll see a minimal set of instructions, to which you will add additional elements:

```
<?xml version="1.0" encoding="utf-8" ?>
<configuration>
</configuration>
```

Now, here is the cool thing. Each time you compile your project, Visual Studio will automatically copy the data in App.config to a new file in the \bin\Debug directory using the proper naming convention (such as CSharpCarClient.exe.config). However, this behavior will happen only if your configuration file is indeed named App.config; see Figure 14-12.

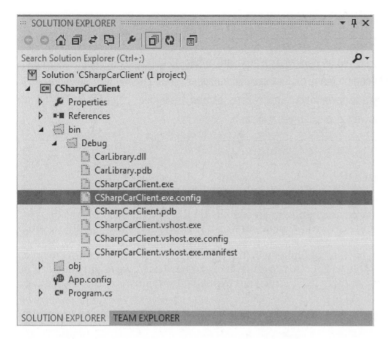

Figure 14-12. *The contents of App.config will be copied to a correctly named *.config in your output directory*

Using this approach, all you need to do is maintain `App.config`, and Visual Studio will ensure your application directory contains the latest and greatest configuration data (even if you happen to rename your project).

Understanding Shared Assemblies

Now that you understand how to deploy and configure a private assembly, you can begin to examine the role of a *shared assembly*. Like a private assembly, a shared assembly is a collection of types intended for reuse among projects. The most obvious difference between shared and private assemblies is the fact that a single copy of a shared assembly can be used by several applications on the same machine.

Consider the fact that all the applications created in this text that required access to `mscorlib.dll`. If you were to look in the application directory of each of these clients, you would *not* find a private copy of this .NET assembly. The reason is that `mscorlib.dll` has been deployed as a shared assembly. Clearly, if you need to create a machine-wide class library, this is the way to go.

■ **Note** Deciding whether a code library should be deployed as a private or shared library is yet another design issue to contend with, and this will be based on many project-specific details. As a rule of thumb, when you are building libraries that need to be used by a wide variety of applications, shared assemblies can be quite helpful in that they can be updated to new versions very easily (as you will see).

The Global Assembly Cache

As suggested in the previous paragraph, a shared assembly is not deployed within the same directory as the application that uses it. Rather, shared assemblies are installed into the Global Assembly Cache (GAC). However, the exact location of the GAC will depend on which versions of the .NET platform you installed on the target computer.

Machines that have not installed .NET 4.0 or higher will find the GAC is located in a subdirectory of your Windows directory named Assembly (e.g., C:\Windows\assembly). These days, we might consider this the "historical GAC," as it can only contain .NET libraries compiled on versions 1.0, 2.0, 3.0, or 3.5. See Figure 14-13.

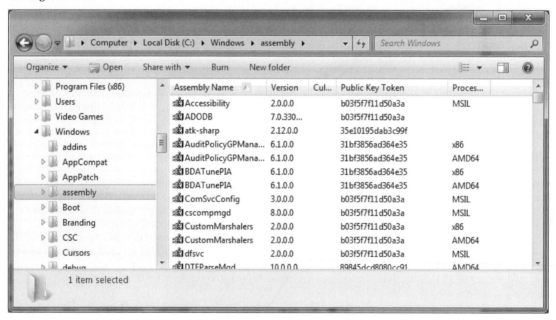

Figure 14-13. The "historical" global assembly cache (GAC)

■ **Note** You cannot install executable assemblies (*.exe) into the GAC. Only assemblies that take the *.dll file extension can be deployed as a shared assembly.

With the release of .NET 4.0, Microsoft decided to isolate .NET 4.0 and higher libraries to a separate location, specifically C:\Windows\Microsoft.NET\assembly\GAC_MSIL (Figure 14-14).

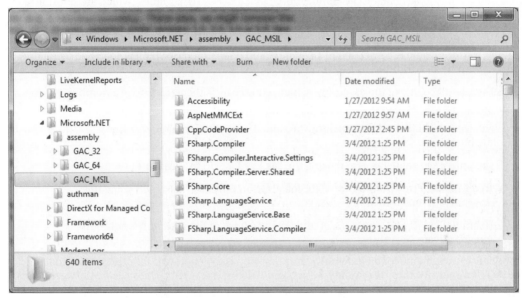

Figure 14-14. The .NET 4.0 and higher global assembly cache (GAC)

Under this new folder, you will find a set of subdirectories, each of which is named identically to the friendly name of a particular code library (for example, \System.Windows.Forms, \System.Core, and so on). Beneath a given friendly name folder, you'll find yet another subdirectory that always takes the following naming convention:

v4.0_major.minor.build.revision_publicKeyTokenValue

The "v4.0" prefix denotes that the library compiled under .NET version 4.0 or higher. That prefix is followed by a single underscore, then the version of the library in question (for example, 1.0.0.0). After a pair of underscores, you'll see another number termed the *publickeytoken value*. As you will see in the next section, the public key value is part of the assembly's "strong name." Finally, under this folder, you will find a copy of the *.dll in question.

In this book, I am assuming you are building applications using .NET 4.5; therefore, if you install a library to the GAC, it will be installed under C:\Windows\Microsoft.NET\assembly\GAC_MSIL. However, be very aware that if you were to configure a Class Library project to be compiled using version 3.5 or earlier, you would find shared libraries installed under C:\Windows\assembly.

Understanding Strong Names

Before you can deploy an assembly to the GAC, you must assign it a *strong name*, which is used to uniquely identify the publisher of a given .NET binary. Understand that a "publisher" can be an individual programmer (such as yourself), a department within a given company, or an entire company itself.

In some ways, a strong name is the modern-day .NET equivalent of the COM globally unique identifier (GUID) identification scheme. If you have a COM background, you might recall that AppIDs are GUIDs that identify a particular COM application. Unlike COM GUID values (which are nothing more than 128-bit numbers), strong names are based (in part) on two cryptographically related keys (*public keys* and *private keys*), which are much more unique and resistant to tampering than a simple GUID.

Formally, a strong name is composed of a set of related data, much of which is specified using the following assembly-level attributes:

- The friendly name of the assembly (which, you recall, is the name of the assembly minus the file extension)

- The version number of the assembly (assigned using the [AssemblyVersion] attribute)

- The public key value (assigned using the [AssemblyKeyFile] attribute)

- An optional culture identity value for localization purposes (assigned using the [AssemblyCulture] attribute)

- An embedded *digital signature*, created using a hash of the assembly's contents and the private key value

To provide a strong name for an assembly, your first step is to generate public/private key data using the .NET Framework 4.5 sn.exe utility (which you'll do in a moment). The sn.exe utility generates a file (typically ending with the *.snk [Strong Name Key] file extension) that contains data for two distinct but mathematically related keys, the public key and the private key. Once the C# compiler is made aware of the location of your *.snk file, it will record the full public key value in the assembly manifest using the .publickey token at the time of compilation.

The C# compiler will also generate a hash code based on the contents of the entire assembly (CIL code, metadata, and so forth). As you recall from Chapter 6, a *hash code* is a numerical value that is statistically unique for a fixed input. Thus, if you modify any aspect of a .NET assembly (even a single character in a string literal) the compiler yields a different hash code. This hash code is combined with the private key data within the *.snk file to yield a digital signature embedded within the assembly's CLR header data. The process of strongly naming an assembly is illustrated in Figure 14-15.

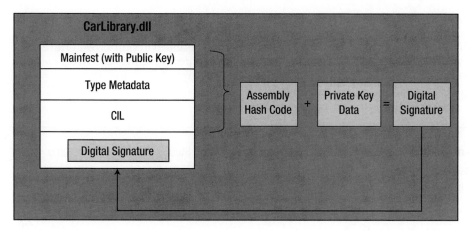

Figure 14-15. At compile time, a digital signature is generated and embedded into the assembly based, in part, on public and private key data

Understand that the actual private key data is not listed anywhere within the manifest, but is used only to digitally sign the contents of the assembly (in conjunction with the generated hash code). Again, the whole idea of using public/private key data is to ensure that no two companies, departments, or individuals have the same identity in the .NET universe. In any case, once the process of assigning a strong name is complete, the assembly may be installed into the GAC.

■ **Note** Strong names also provide a level of protection against potential evildoers tampering with your assembly's contents. Given this point, it is considered a .NET best practice to strongly name every assembly (including *.exe assemblies), regardless of whether it is deployed to the GAC.

Generating Strong Names at the Command Line

Let's walk through the process of assigning a strong name to the CarLibrary assembly created earlier in this chapter. These days, you will most likely generate the required *.snk file using Visual Studio. However, in the bad old days (circa 2003), the only option for strongly signing an assembly was to do so at the command line. Let's see how to do this.

The first order of business is to generate the required key data using the sn.exe utility. Although this tool has numerous command-line options, all you need to concern yourself with for the moment is the -k flag, which instructs the tool to generate a new file containing the public/private key information. Create a new folder on your C drive named MyTestKeyPair and change to that directory using the Developer Command Prompt. Next, issue the following command to generate a file named MyTestKeyPair.snk:

```
sn –k MyTestKeyPair.snk
```

Now that you have your key data, you need to inform the C# compiler exactly where MyTestKeyPair.snk is located. Recall from earlier in this chapter, when you create any new C# project workspace using Visual Studio, one of the initial project files (located under the Properties node of Solution Explorer) is named AssemblyInfo.cs. This file contains a number of attributes that describe the assembly itself. The [AssemblyKeyFile] assembly-level attribute can be added to your AssemblyInfo.cs file to inform the compiler of the location of a valid *.snk file. Simply specify the path as a string parameter. For example:

```
[assembly: AssemblyKeyFile(@"C:\MyTestKeyPair\MyTestKeyPair.snk")]
```

■ **Note** When you manually specify the [AssemblyKeyFile] attribute, Visual Studio will generate a warning informing you to use the /keyfile option of csc.exe or to establish the key file via the Visual Studio Properties window. You'll use the IDE to do so in just a moment (so feel free to ignore the generated warning).

Because the version of a shared assembly is one aspect of a strong name, selecting a version number for CarLibrary.dll is a necessary detail. In the AssemblyInfo.cs file, you will find another attribute named [AssemblyVersion]. Initially, the value is set to 1.0.0.0.

```
[assembly: AssemblyVersion("1.0.0.0")]
```

A .NET version number is composed of the four parts (*<major>.<minor>.<build>.<revision>*). While specifying a version number is entirely up to you, you can instruct Visual Studio to automatically increment the build and revision numbers as part of each compilation using the wildcard token, rather than with a specific build and revision value. We have no need to do so for this example; however, consider the following:

```
// Format: <Major number>.<Minor number>.<Build number>.<Revision number>
// Valid values for each part of the version number are between 0 and 65535.
[assembly: AssemblyVersion("1.0.*")]
```

At this point, the C# compiler has all the information needed to generate strong name data (as you are not specifying a unique culture value via the [AssemblyCulture] attribute, you "inherit" the culture of your current machine, which in my case would be US English).

Compile your CarLibrary code library, open your assembly into ildasm.exe, and check the manifest. You will now see that a new .publickey tag is used to document the full public key information, while the .ver token records the version specified via the [AssemblyVersion] attribute (see Figure 14-16).

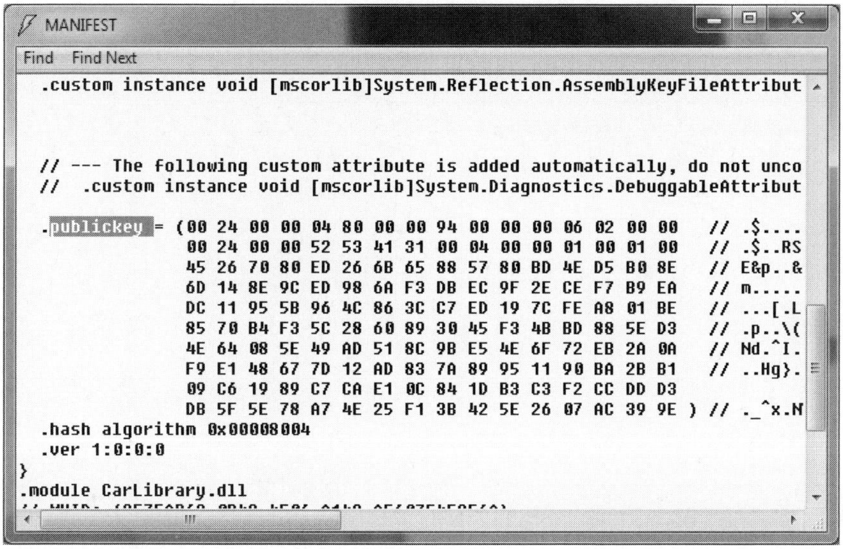

Figure 14-16. *A strongly named assembly records the public key in the manifest*

Great! At this point, we could deploy our shared CarLibrary.dll assembly to the GAC. However, remember that these days, .NET developers can use Visual Studio to create strongly named assemblies using a friendly user interface rather than the cryptic sn.exe command-line tool. Before seeing how to do so, be sure you delete (or comment out) the following line of code from your AssemblyInfo.cs file (assuming you manually added this line during this section of the text):

```
// [assembly: AssemblyKeyFile(@"C:\MyTestKeyPair\MyTestKeyPair.snk")]
```

Generating Strong Names Using Visual Studio

Visual Studio allows you to specify the location of an existing *.snk file using the project's Properties page, as well as generate a new *.snk file. To do so for the CarLibrary project, first double-click the Properties icon of the Solution Explorer, and select the Signing tab. Next, select the "Sign the assembly" check box, and choose the <New...> option from the drop-down list (see Figure 14-17).

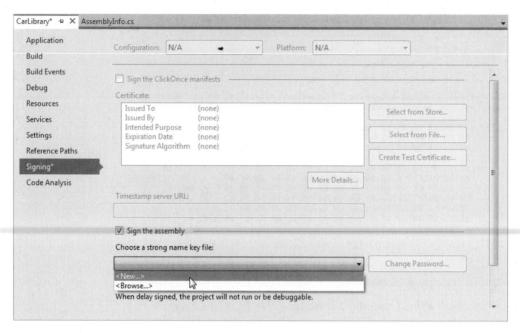

Figure 14-17. *Creating a new *.snk file using Visual Studio*

After you have done so, you will be asked to provide a name for your new *.snk file (such as myKeyPair.snk) and you'll have the option to password-protect your file (which is not required for this example); see Figure 14-18.

Figure 14-18. *Naming the new *.snk file using Visual Studio*

At this point, you will see your *.snk file within the Solution Explorer (Figure 14-19). Every time you build your application, this data will be used to assign a proper strong name to the assembly.

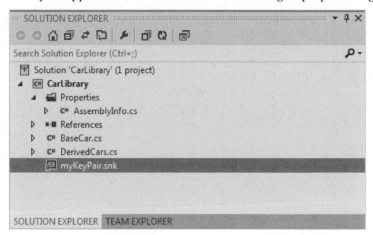

Figure 14-19. Visual Studio will now strongly sign your assembly with each compilation

■ **Note** Recall that the Application tab of the Properties editor provides a button named Assembly Information. When clicked, the button displays a dialog box that allows you to establish numerous assembly-level attributes, including the version number, copyright information, and so forth.

Installing Strongly Named Assemblies to the GAC

The final step is to install the (now strongly named) CarLibrary.dll into the GAC. While the preferred way to deploy assemblies to the GAC in a production setting is to create a Windows MSI installer package (or use a commercial installer program such as InstallShield), the .NET Framework 4.5 SDK ships with a command-line tool named gacutil.exe, which can be useful for quick tests.

■ **Note** You must have administrator rights to interact with the GAC on your machine, which may including adjusting the User Access Control (UAC) settings.

Table 14-1 documents some relevant options of gacutil.exe (specify the /? flag when you run the program to see each option).

Table 14-1. *Various Options of gacutil.exe*

Option	Meaning in Life
-i	Installs a strongly named assembly into the GAC
-u	Uninstalls an assembly from the GAC
-l	Displays the assemblies (or a specific assembly) in the GAC

To install a strongly named assembly using gacutil.exe, first open a Developer Command Prompt, and then change to the directory containing CarLibrary.dll. For example (your path may differ):

```
cd C:\MyCode\CarLibrary\bin\Debug
```

Next, install the library using the -i command, like so:

```
gacutil –i CarLibrary.dll
```

After you have done so, you can verify that the library has been deployed by specifying the -l command as follows (note that you omit the file extension when using the -l command):

```
gacutil –l CarLibrary
```

If all is well, you should see the following output to the Console window (you will find a unique PublicKeyToken value, as expected):

```
The Global Assembly Cache contains the following assemblies:

CarLibrary, Version=1.0.0.0, Culture=neutral, PublicKeyToken=33a2bc294331e8b9,

processorArchitecture=MSIL
```

Furthermore, if you were to navigate to C:\Windows\Microsoft.NET\assembly\GAC_MSIL, you would find a new CarLibrary folder with the correct subdirectory structure (see Figure 14-20).

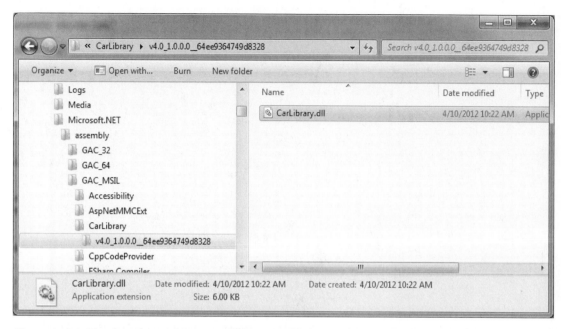

Figure 14-20. The shared CarLibrary assembly in the GAC

Consuming a Shared Assembly

When you are building applications that use a shared assembly, the only difference from consuming a private assembly is in how you reference the library using Visual Studio. In reality, there is no difference as far as the tool is concerned—you still use the Add Reference dialog box.

When you need to reference a private assembly, you could use the Browse button to navigate to the correct subdirectory of the GAC. However, you can also simply navigate to the location of the strongly named assembly (such as the /bin/debug folder of a class library project) and reference the copy. When Visual Studio finds a strongly named library, it will not copy the library to the output folder of the client application. In any case, Figure 14-21 shows the referenced library.

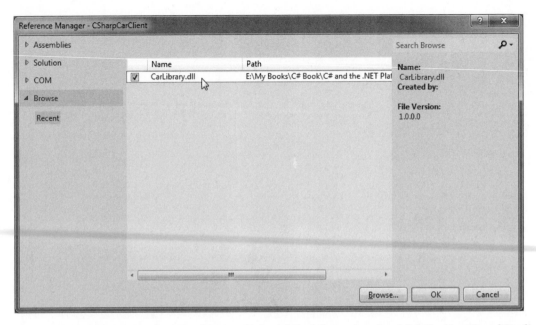

Figure 14-21. Referencing the strongly named, shared CarLibrary (version 1.0.0.0) using Visual Studio

To illustrate, create a new C# Console Application named SharedCarLibClient and reference your
CarLibrary.dll assembly as just described. As you would hope, you can now see an icon in your
Solution Explorer's Reference folder. If you select this icon and then view the Properties window
(accessible from the Visual Studio View menu), you'll notice that the Copy Local property of the selected
CarLibrary is now set to False. In any case, author the following test code in your new client application:

```
using System;
using System.Collections.Generic;
using System.Linq;
using System.Text;
using System.Threading.Tasks;

using CarLibrary;

namespace SharedCarLibClient
{
  class Program
  {
    static void Main(string[] args)
    {
      Console.WriteLine("***** Shared Assembly Client *****");
      SportsCar c = new SportsCar();
      c.TurboBoost();
      Console.ReadLine();
    }
  }
}
```

After you have compiled your client application, navigate to the directory that contains SharedCarLibClient.exe using Windows Explorer and notice that Visual Studio has *not* copied CarLibrary.dll to the client's application directory. When you reference an assembly whose manifest contains a .publickey value, Visual Studio assumes the strongly named assembly will most likely be deployed to the GAC and, therefore, does not bother to copy the binary.

Exploring the Manifest of SharedCarLibClient

Recall that when you generate a strong name for an assembly, the entire public key is recorded in the assembly manifest. On a related note, when a client references a strongly named assembly, its manifest records a condensed hash value of the full public key, denoted by the .publickeytoken tag. If you open the manifest of SharedCarLibClient.exe using ildasm.exe, you would find the following (your public key token value will of course differ, as it is computed based on the public key value):

```
.assembly extern CarLibrary
{
  .publickeytoken = (33 A2 BC 29 43 31 E8 B9 )
  .ver 1:0:0:0
}
```

If you compare the value of the public key token recorded in the client manifest with the public key token value shown in the GAC, you will find a dead-on match. Recall that a public key represents one aspect of the strongly named assembly's identity. Given this, the CLR will only load version 1.0.0.0 of an assembly named CarLibrary that has a public key that can be hashed down to the value 33A2BC294331E8B9. If the CLR does not find an assembly meeting this description in the GAC (and did not find a private assembly named CarLibrary in the client's directory), a FileNotFoundException exception is thrown.

■ **Source Code** The SharedCarLibClient application can be found under the Chapter 14 subdirectory.

Configuring Shared Assemblies

Like private assemblies, shared assemblies can be configured using a client *.config file. Of course, because shared assemblies are deployed to a well-known location (the GAC), you don't use the <privatePath> element as you did for private assemblies (although if the client is using both shared and private assemblies, the <privatePath> element may still exist in the *.config file).

You can use application configuration files in conjunction with shared assemblies whenever you wish to instruct the CLR to bind to a *different* version of a specific assembly, effectively bypassing the value recorded in the client's manifest. This can be useful for a number of reasons. For example, imagine that you have shipped version 1.0.0.0 of an assembly and later discover a major bug. One corrective action would be to rebuild the client application to reference the correct version of the bug-free assembly (say, 1.1.0.0) and redistribute the updated client and new library to every target machine.

Another option is to ship the new code library and a *.config file that automatically instructs the runtime to bind to the new (bug-free) version. As long as the new version has been installed into the GAC, the original client runs without recompilation, redistribution, or fear of having to update your resume.

Here's another example: you have shipped the first version of a bug-free assembly (1.0.0.0), and after a month or two, you add new functionality to the assembly to yield version 2.0.0.0. Obviously, existing client applications that were compiled against version 1.0.0.0 have no clue about these new types, given that their code base makes no reference to them.

New client applications, however, wish to make reference to the new functionality in version 2.0.0.0. Under .NET, you are free to ship version 2.0.0.0 to the target machines, and have version 2.0.0.0 run alongside the older version 1.0.0.0. If necessary, existing clients can be dynamically redirected to load version 2.0.0.0 (to gain access to the implementation refinements), using an application configuration file without needing to recompile and redeploy the client application.

Freezing the Current Shared Assembly

To illustrate how to dynamically bind to a specific version of a shared assembly, open Windows Explorer and copy the current version of the compiled CarLibrary.dll assembly (1.0.0.0) into a distinct subdirectory (I called mine CarLibrary Version 1.0.0.0) to symbolize the freezing of this version (see Figure 14-22).

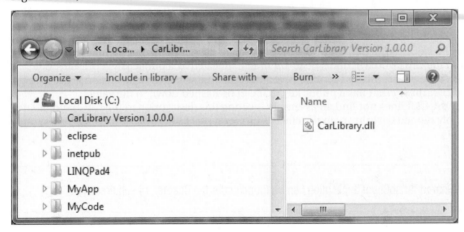

Figure 14-22. *Freezing the current version of CarLibrary.dll*

Building a Shared Assembly Version 2.0.0.0

Now, open your existing CarLibrary project and update your code base with a new enum type named MusicMedia that defines the following four possible musical devices:

```
// Which type of music player does this car have?
public enum MusicMedia
{
  musicCd,
  musicTape,
  musicRadio,
  musicMp3
}
```

As well, add a new public method to the Car type that allows the caller to turn on one of the given media players (be sure to import the System.Windows.Forms namespace if necessary), like so:

```
public abstract class Car
{
...
  public void TurnOnRadio(bool musicOn, MusicMedia mm)
  {
    if(musicOn)
      MessageBox.Show(string.Format("Jamming {0}", mm));
    else
      MessageBox.Show("Quiet time...");
  }
}
```

Update the constructors of the Car class to display a MessageBox that verifies you are indeed using CarLibrary 2.0.0.0 as follows:

```
public abstract class Car
{
...
  public Car()
  {
    MessageBox.Show("CarLibrary Version 2.0!");
  }
  public Car(string name, int maxSp, int currSp)
  {
    MessageBox.Show("CarLibrary Version 2.0!");
    PetName = name; MaxSpeed = maxSp; CurrentSpeed = currSp;
  }
...
}
```

Last but not least, before you recompile your new library, update the version to be 2.0.0.0. Recall you can do so in a visual manner by double-clicking the Properties icon of the Solution Explorer and clicking the "Assembly Information..." button on the Application tab. After you do, simply update the Assembly Version number (see Figure 14-23).

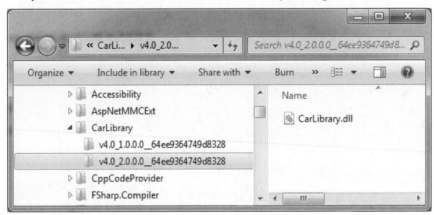

Figure 14-23. Setting the version number of CarLibrary.dll to 2.0.0.0

If you look in your project's \bin\Debug folder, you'll see that you have a new version of this assembly (2.0.0.0), while version 1.0.0.0 is safe in storage in the CarLibrary Version 1.0.0.0 directory. Install this new assembly into the 4.0 GAC using gacutil.exe, as described earlier in this chapter. Notice that you now have two versions of the same assembly (see Figure 14-24).

Figure 14-24. Side-by-side execution of a shared assembly

If you run the current SharedCarLibClient.exe program by double-clicking the icon in Windows Explorer, you should *not* see the "CarLibrary Version 2.0!" message box appear, as the manifest is specifically requesting version 1.0.0.0. How then can you instruct the CLR to bind to version 2.0.0.0? Glad you asked!

■ **Note** Visual Studio will automatically reset references when you compile your applications! Therefore, if you run your SharedCarLibClient.exe application within Visual Studio, it will grab CarLibrary.dll version 2.0.0.0! If you accidentally ran your application in this way, simply delete the current CarLibrary.dll reference and select version 1.0.0.0 (which I suggested you place in a folder named CarLibrary Version 1.0.0.0).

Dynamically Redirecting to Specific Versions of a Shared Assembly

When you want to tell the CLR to load a version of a shared assembly other than the version listed in the manifest, you can build a *.config file that contains a <dependentAssembly> element. When doing so, you will need to create an <assemblyIdentity> subelement that specifies the friendly name of the assembly listed in the client manifest (CarLibrary, for this example) and an optional culture attribute (which can be assigned an empty string or omitted altogether if you wish to use the default culture for the machine). Moreover, the <dependentAssembly> element will define a <bindingRedirect> subelement to define the version *currently* in the manifest (via the oldVersion attribute) and the version in the GAC to load instead (via the newVersion attribute).

Update the current configuration file in the application directory of SharedCarLibClient named SharedCarLibClient.exe.config that contains the following XML data.

■ **Note** The value of your public key token will be different from what you see in the following markup. To find your public key token value, recall you can open the client into ildasm.exe, double click the MANIFEST icon, and copy the value to your clipboard (just be sure to remove the blank spaces!).

```xml
<?xml version="1.0" encoding="utf-8" ?>
<configuration>
  <!--Runtime binding info -->
  <runtime>
    <assemblyBinding xmlns="urn:schemas-microsoft-com:asm.v1">
      <dependentAssembly>
        <assemblyIdentity name="CarLibrary"
                          publicKeyToken="64ee9364749d8328"
                          culture="neutral"/>
        <bindingRedirect oldVersion= "1.0.0.0"
                         newVersion= "2.0.0.0"/>
      </dependentAssembly>
    </assemblyBinding>
  </runtime>
</configuration>
```

Now run the SharedCarLibClient.exe program by double-clicking the executable from Windows Explorer. You should see the message that version 2.0.0.0 has loaded.

Multiple <dependentAssembly> elements can appear within a client's configuration file. Although there's no need for this example, assume that the manifest of SharedCarLibClient.exe also references version 2.5.0.0 of an assembly named MathLibrary. If you wanted to redirect to version 3.0.0.0 of MathLibrary (in addition to version 2.0.0.0 of CarLibrary), the SharedCarLibClient.exe.config file would look like the following:

```
<configuration>
  <runtime>
    <assemblyBinding xmlns="urn:schemas-microsoft-com:asm.v1">
      <!-- Controls Binding to CarLibrary -->
      <dependentAssembly>
        <assemblyIdentity name="CarLibrary"
                          publicKeyToken="64ee9364749d8328"
                          culture=""/>
        <bindingRedirect oldVersion= "1.0.0.0" newVersion= "2.0.0.0"/>
      </dependentAssembly>

      <!-- Controls Binding to MathLibrary -->
      <dependentAssembly>
        <assemblyIdentity name="MathLibrary"
                          publicKeyToken="64ee9364749d8328"
                          culture=""/>
        <bindingRedirect oldVersion= "2.5.0.0" newVersion= "3.0.0.0"/>
      </dependentAssembly>
    </assemblyBinding>
  </runtime>
</configuration>
```

■ **Note** It is possible to specify a range of old version numbers via the oldVersion attribute; for example, <bindingRedirect oldVersion="1.0.0.0-1.2.0.0" newVersion="2.0.0.0"/> informs the CLR to use version 2.0.0.0 for any older version within the range of 1.0.0.0 to 1.2.0.0.

Understanding Publisher Policy Assemblies

The next configuration issue we'll examine is the role of *publisher policy assemblies*. As you've just seen, *.config files can be constructed to bind to a specific version of a shared assembly, thereby bypassing the version recorded in the client manifest. While this is all well and good, imagine you're an administrator who now needs to reconfigure *all* client applications on a given machine to rebind to version 2.0.0.0 of the CarLibrary.dll assembly. Given the strict naming convention of a configuration file, you would need to duplicate the same XML content in numerous locations (assuming you are, in fact, aware of the locations of the executables using CarLibrary!). Clearly this would be a maintenance nightmare.

Publisher policy allows the publisher of a given assembly (you, your department, your company, or what have you) to ship a binary version of a *.config file that is installed into the GAC along with the newest version of the associated assembly. The benefit of this approach is that client application directories do *not* need to contain specific *.config files. Rather, the CLR will read the current manifest and attempt to find the requested version in the GAC. However, if the CLR finds a publisher policy assembly, it will read the embedded XML data and perform the requested redirection *at the level of the GAC.*

Publisher policy assemblies are created at the command line using a .NET utility named al.exe (the assembly linker). Though this tool provides many options, building a publisher policy assembly requires passing in only the following input parameters:

- The location of the *.config or *.xml file containing the redirecting instructions

- The name of the resulting publisher policy assembly

- The location of the *.snk file used to sign the publisher policy assembly

- The version numbers to assign the publisher policy assembly being constructed

If you wanted to build a publisher policy assembly that controls CarLibrary.dll, the command set would be as follows (which must be entered on a single line within the command window):

```
al /link: CarLibraryPolicy.xml /out:policy.1.0.CarLibrary.dll
/keyf:C:\MyKey\myKey.snk /v:1.0.0.0
```

Here, the XML content is contained within a file named CarLibraryPolicy.xml. The name of the output file (which must be in the format policy.<major>.<minor>.assemblyToConfigure) is specified using the obvious /out flag. In addition, note that the name of the file containing the public/private key pair will also need to be supplied via the /keyf option. Remember, publisher policy files are shared and, therefore, must have strong names!

Once the al.exe tool has executed, the result is a new assembly that can be placed into the GAC to force all clients to bind to version 2.0.0.0 of CarLibrary.dll, without the use of a specific client application configuration file. Using this technique, you can design a machine-wide redirection for all applications using a specific version (or range of versions) of an existing assembly.

Disabling Publisher Policy

Now, assume you (as a system administrator) have deployed a publisher policy assembly (and the latest version of the related assembly) to the GAC of a client machine. As luck would have it, nine of the ten affected applications rebind to version 2.0.0.0 without error. However, the remaining client application (for whatever reason) blows up when accessing CarLibrary.dll 2.0.0.0. (As we all know, it is next to impossible to build backward-compatible software that works 100 percent of the time.)

In such a case, it is possible to build a configuration file for a specific troubled client that instructs the CLR to *ignore* the presence of any publisher policy files installed in the GAC. The remaining client applications that are happy to consume the newest .NET assembly will simply be redirected via the installed publisher policy assembly. To disable publisher policy on a client-by-client basis, author a (properly named) *.config file that makes use of the <publisherPolicy> element and set the apply attribute to no. When you do so, the CLR will load the version of the assembly originally listed in the client's manifest.

```
<configuration>
  <runtime>
    <assemblyBinding xmlns="urn:schemas-microsoft-com:asm.v1">
      <publisherPolicy apply="no" />
    </assemblyBinding>
  </runtime>
```

```
</configuration>
```

Understanding the <codeBase> Element

Application configuration files can also specify *code bases*. The <codeBase> element can be used to instruct the CLR to probe for dependent assemblies located at arbitrary locations (such as network end points, or an arbitrary machine path outside a client's application directory).

If the value assigned to a <codeBase> element is located on a remote machine, the assembly will be downloaded on demand to a specific directory in the GAC termed the *download cache*. Given what you have learned about deploying assemblies to the GAC, it should make sense that assemblies loaded from a <codeBase> element will need to be assigned a strong name (after all, how else could the CLR install remote assemblies to the GAC?). If you are interested, you can view the content of your machine's download cache by supplying the /ldl option to gacutil.exe, like so:

```
gacutil /ldl
```

■ **Note** Technically speaking, the <codeBase> element can be used to probe for assemblies that do not have a strong name. However, the assembly's location must be relative to the client's application directory (and, thus, is little more than an alternative to the <privatePath> element).

To see the <codeBase> element in action, create a Console Application named CodeBaseClient, set a reference to CarLibrary.dll version 2.0.0.0, and update the initial file as follows:

```csharp
using System;
using System.Collections.Generic;
using System.Linq;
using System.Text;
using System.Threading.Tasks;

using CarLibrary;

namespace CodeBaseClient
{
  class Program
  {
    static void Main(string[] args)
    {
      Console.WriteLine("***** Fun with CodeBases *****");
      SportsCar c = new SportsCar();
      Console.WriteLine("Sports car has been allocated.");
      Console.ReadLine();
    }
  }
}
```

Given that CarLibrary.dll has been deployed to the GAC, you are able to run the program as is. However, to illustrate the use of the <codeBase> element, create a new folder under your C: drive (perhaps C:\MyAsms) and place a copy of CarLibrary.dll version 2.0.0.0 into this directory.

Now, add an App.config file (or edit an existing App.config) to the CodeBaseClient project (as explained earlier in this chapter) and author the following XML content (remember that your .publickeytoken value will differ; consult your GAC as required):

```
<configuration>
...
  <runtime>
    <assemblyBinding xmlns="urn:schemas-microsoft-com:asm.v1">
      <dependentAssembly>
        <assemblyIdentity name="CarLibrary" publicKeyToken="33A2BC294331E8B9" />
        <codeBase version="2.0.0.0" href="file:///C:/MyAsms/CarLibrary.dll" />
      </dependentAssembly>
    </assemblyBinding>
  </runtime>
</configuration>
```

As you can see, the <codeBase> element is nested within the <assemblyIdentity> element, which makes use of the name and publicKeyToken attributes to specify the friendly name and associated publicKeyToken values. The <codeBase> element itself specifies the version and location (via the href property) of the assembly to load. If you were to delete version 2.0.0.0 of CarLibrary.dll from the GAC, this client would still run successfully, as the CLR is able to locate the external assembly under C:\MyAsms.

▪ **Note** If you place assemblies at random locations on your development machine, you are in effect re-creating the system registry (and the related DLL hell), given that if you move or rename the folder containing your binaries, the current bind will fail. With that in mind, use <codeBase> with caution.

The <codeBase> element can also be helpful when referencing assemblies located on a remote networked machine. Assume you have permission to access a folder located at http://www.MySite.com. To download the remote *.dll to the GAC's download cache on your local machine, you could update the <codeBase> element as follows:

```
<codeBase version="2.0.0.0"
  href="http://www.MySite.com/Assemblies/CarLibrary.dll" />
```

▪ **Source Code** The CodeBaseClient application can be found under the Chapter 14 subdirectory.

The System.Configuration Namespace

Currently, all of the *.config files shown in this chapter have made use of well-known XML elements that are read by the CLR to resolve the location of external assemblies. In addition to these recognized elements, it is perfectly permissible for a client configuration file to contain application-specific data that has nothing to do with binding heuristics. Given this, it should come as no surprise that the .NET Framework provides a namespace that allows you to programmatically read the data within a client configuration file.

The System.Configuration namespace provides a small set of types you can use to read custom data from a client's *.config file. These custom settings must be contained within the scope of an <appSettings> element. The <appSettings> element contains any number of <add> elements that define key/value pairs to be obtained programmatically.

For example, assume you have an App.config file for a Console Application named AppConfigReaderApp that defines two application specific values, listed like so:

```xml
<?xml version="1.0" encoding="utf-8" ?>
<configuration>
  <startup>
    <supportedRuntime version="v4.0" sku=".NETFramework,Version=v4.5" />
  </startup>

  <!-- Custom App settings -->
  <appSettings>
    <add key="TextColor" value="Green" />
    <add key="RepeatCount" value="8" />
  </appSettings>
</configuration>
```

Reading these values for use by the client application is as simple as calling the instance-level GetValue() method of the System.Configuration.AppSettingsReader type. As shown in the following code, the first parameter to GetValue() is the name of the key in the *.config file, whereas the second parameter is the underlying type of the key (obtained via the C# typeof operator):

```csharp
using System;
using System.Collections.Generic;
using System.Linq;
using System.Text;
using System.Threading.Tasks;

using System.Configuration;

namespace AppConfigReaderApp
{
  class Program
  {
    static void Main(string[] args)
    {
      Console.WriteLine("***** Reading <appSettings> Data *****\n");

      // Get our custom data from the *.config file.
      AppSettingsReader ar = new AppSettingsReader();
      int numbOfTimes = (int)ar.GetValue("RepeatCount", typeof(int));
```

```
    string textColor = (string)ar.GetValue("TextColor", typeof(string));

    Console.ForegroundColor =
      (ConsoleColor)Enum.Parse(typeof(ConsoleColor), textColor);

    // Now print a message correctly.
    for (int i = 0; i < numbOfTimes; i++)
      Console.WriteLine("Howdy!");
    Console.ReadLine();
    }
  }
}
```

■ **Source Code** The AppConfigReaderApp application can be found under the Chapter 14 subdirectory.

The Configuration File Schema Documentation

In this chapter, you were introduced to the role of XML configuration files. Here, we focused on a few settings we can add to the <runtime> element that control how the CLR will attempt to locate externally required libraries. As you work on upcoming chapters of this book (and as you move beyond this book and begin to build larger scale software), you will quickly notice that use of XML configuration files is commonplace.

To be sure, the .NET platform uses *.config files in numerous APIs. For example, in Chapter 25, you will see that Windows Communication Foundation (WCF) uses configuration files to establish complex network settings. Later in this text when you examine web development via ASP.NET, you'll quickly note that the web.config file contains the same type of instructions as a desktop App.config file.

Because a given .NET configuration file can contain a large number of instructions, you should be aware that the entire schema of this XML file is documented in the .NET help system. Specifically, if you do a search for the topic "Configuration File Schema for the .NET Framework" in the help system, you will be given a detailed explanation of each element (see Figure 14-25).

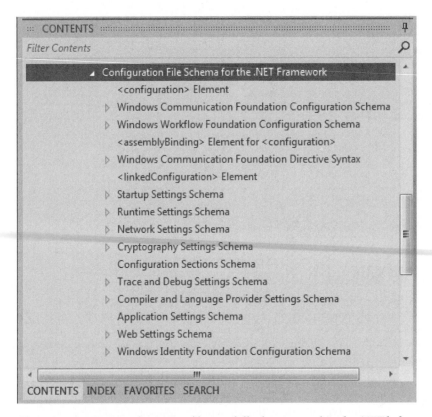

Figure 14-25. XML configuration files are fully documented in the .NET help system

Summary

This chapter examined the role of .NET class libraries (a.k.a. .NET *.dlls). As you have seen, class libraries are .NET binaries that contain logic intended to be reused across a variety of projects. Recall that libraries can be deployed in two primary ways, specifically privately or shared. Private assemblies are deployed to the client folder or a subdirectory thereof, provided you have a proper XML configuration file. Shared assemblies are libraries that can be used by any application on the machine, and can also be influenced by the settings in a client-side configuration file.

You learned how shared assemblies are marked with a "strong name," which essentially establishes a unique identify for a library in the eyes of the CLR. As well, you learned about various command-line tools (sn.exe and gacutil.exe) that are used during the development and deployment of shared libraries.

The chapter wrapped up by examining the role of publisher policies and the process of storing and retrieving custom settings using the System.Configuration namespace.

CHAPTER 15

Type Reflection, Late Binding, and Attribute-Based Programming

As shown in Chapter 14, assemblies are the basic unit of deployment in the .NET universe. Using the integrated object browsers of Visual Studio (and numerous other IDEs), you are able to examine the types within a project's referenced set of assemblies. Furthermore, external tools such as ildasm.exe allow you to peek into the underlying CIL code, type metadata, and assembly manifest for a given .NET binary. In addition to this design-time investigation of .NET assemblies, you are also able to *programmatically* obtain this same information using the System.Reflection namespace. To this end, the first task of this chapter is to define the role of reflection and the necessity of .NET metadata.

The remainder of the chapter examines a number of closely related topics, all of which hinge upon reflection services. For example, you'll learn how a .NET client may employ dynamic loading and late binding to activate types it has no compile-time knowledge of. You'll also learn how to insert custom metadata into your .NET assemblies through the use of system-supplied and custom attributes. To put all of these (seemingly esoteric) topics into perspective, the chapter closes by demonstrating how to build several "snap-in objects" that you can plug into an extendable desktop GUI application.

The Necessity of Type Metadata

The ability to fully describe types (classes, interfaces, structures, enumerations, and delegates) using metadata is a key element of the .NET platform. Numerous .NET technologies, such as Windows Communication Foundation (WCF), and object serialization require the ability to discover the format of types at runtime. Furthermore, cross-language interoperability, numerous compiler services, and an IDE's IntelliSense capabilities all rely on a concrete description of *type*.

Recall that the ildasm.exe utility allows you to view an assembly's type metadata using the Ctrl+M keyboard option (see Chapter 1). Thus, if you were to open any of the *.dll or *.exe assemblies created over the course of this book (such as the CarLibrary.dll created in the Chapter 14) using ildasm.exe and press Ctrl+M, you would find the relevant type metadata (see Figure 15-1).

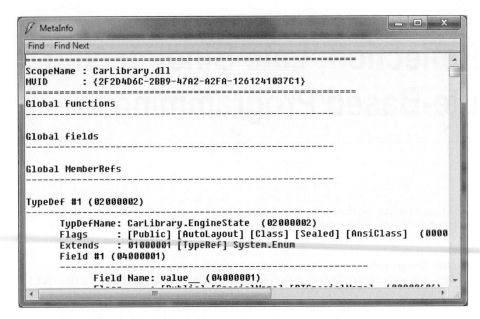

Figure 15-1. Viewing an assembly's metadata using ildasm.exe

As you can see, ildasm.exe's display of .NET type metadata is very verbose (the actual binary format is much more compact). In fact, if I were to list the entire metadata description representing the CarLibrary.dll assembly, it would span several pages. Given that this act would be a woeful waste of paper, let's just glimpse into some key metadata descriptions of the CarLibrary.dll assembly.

■ **Note** Don't be too concerned with the exact syntax of each and every piece of .NET metadata in the next few sections. The bigger point to absorb is that .NET metadata is very descriptive and lists each internally defined (and externally referenced) type found within a given code base.

Viewing (Partial) Metadata for the EngineState Enumeration

Each type defined within the current assembly is documented using a TypeDef #n token (where TypeDef is short for *type definition*). If the type being described uses a type defined within a separate .NET assembly, the referenced type is documented using a TypeRef #n token (where TypeRef is short for *type reference*). A TypeRef token is a pointer (if you will) to the referenced type's full metadata definition in an external assembly. In a nutshell, .NET metadata is a set of tables that clearly mark all type definitions (TypeDefs) and referenced types (TypeRefs), all of which can be viewed using ildasm.exe's metadata window.

As far as CarLibrary.dll goes, one TypeDef is the metadata description of the CarLibrary.EngineState enumeration (your number may differ; TypeDef numbering is based on the order in which the C# compiler processes the file).

```
TypeDef #2 (02000003)
-------------------------------------------------------
  TypDefName: CarLibrary.EngineState  (02000003)
  Flags     : [Public] [AutoLayout] [Class] [Sealed] [AnsiClass]  (00000101)
  Extends   : 01000001 [TypeRef] System.Enum
  Field #1 (04000006)
-------------------------------------------------------
    Field Name: value__ (04000006)
    Flags      : [Public] [SpecialName] [RTSpecialName]  (00000606)
    CallCnvntn: [FIELD]
    Field type:  I4

  Field #2 (04000007)
-------------------------------------------------------
    Field Name: engineAlive (04000007)
    Flags      : [Public] [Static] [Literal] [HasDefault]  (00008056)
    DefltValue: (I4) 0
    CallCnvntn: [FIELD]
    Field type:  ValueClass CarLibrary.EngineState
...
```

Here, the TypDefName token is used to establish the name of the given type, which in this case is the custom CarLibrary.EngineState enum. The Extends metadata token is used to document the base type of a given .NET type (in this case, the referenced type, System.Enum). Each field of an enumeration is marked using the Field #n token. For brevity, I have simply listed the metadata for CarLibrary.EngineState.engineAlive.

Viewing (Partial) Metadata for the Car Type

Here is a partial dump of the Car class that illustrates the following:

- How fields are defined in terms of .NET metadata

- How methods are documented via .NET metadata

- How an automatic property is represented in .NET metadata

```
TypeDef #3 (02000004)
-------------------------------------------------------
  TypDefName: CarLibrary.Car  (02000004)
  Flags : [Public] [AutoLayout] [Class] [Abstract]
          [AnsiClass] [BeforeFieldInit]  (00100081)
  Extends : 01000002 [TypeRef] System.Object
...

  Field #2 (0400000a)
-------------------------------------------------------
  Field Name: <PetName>k__BackingField (0400000A)
  Flags     : [Private]  (00000001)
  CallCnvntn: [FIELD]
  Field type:  String

...
```

```
Method #1 (06000001)
-------------------------------------------------------
  MethodName: get_PetName (06000001)
  Flags     : [Public] [HideBySig] [ReuseSlot] [SpecialName]  (00000886)
  RVA       : 0x000020d0
  ImplFlags : [IL] [Managed]  (00000000)
  CallCnvntn: [DEFAULT]
  hasThis
  ReturnType: String
  No arguments.

...

  Method #2 (06000002)
-------------------------------------------------------
  MethodName: set_PetName (06000002)
  Flags     : [Public] [HideBySig] [ReuseSlot] [SpecialName]  (00000886)
  RVA       : 0x000020e7
  ImplFlags : [IL] [Managed]  (00000000)
  CallCnvntn: [DEFAULT]
  hasThis
  ReturnType: Void
  1 Arguments
    Argument #1:  String
  1 Parameters
    (1) ParamToken : (08000001) Name : value flags: [none] (00000000)
...

Property #1 (17000001)
-------------------------------------------------------
  Prop.Name : PetName (17000001)
  Flags     : [none] (00000000)
  CallCnvntn: [PROPERTY]
  hasThis
  ReturnType: String
  No arguments.
  DefltValue:
  Setter    : (06000002) set_PetName
  Getter    : (06000001) get_PetName
  0 Others
  ...
```

First, note that the Car class metadata marks the type's base class (System.Object) and includes various flags that describe how this type was constructed (e.g., [Public], [Abstract], and whatnot). Methods (such as our Car's constructor) are described in regard to their parameters, return value, and name.

Note how an automatic property results in a compiler-generated private backing field (which was named <PetName>k__BackingField) and two compiler-generated methods (in the case of a read/write property) named, in this example, get_PetName() and set_PetName(). Finally, the actual property itself is mapped to the internal get/set methods using the .NET metadata Getter/Setter tokens.

Examining a TypeRef

Recall that an assembly's metadata will describe not only the set of internal types (Car, EngineState, etc.), but also any external types the internal types reference. For example, given that CarLibrary.dll has defined two enumerations, you find a TypeRef block for the System.Enum type, as follows:

```
TypeRef #1 (01000001)
-------------------------------------------------------
Token:            0x01000001
ResolutionScope:  0x23000001
TypeRefName:      System.Enum
```

Documenting the Defining Assembly

The ildasm.exe metadata window also allows you to view the .NET metadata that describes the assembly itself using the Assembly token. As you can see from the following (partial) listing, information documented within the Assembly table is (surprise, surprise!) the same information that can be viewable via the MANIFEST icon. The following is a partial dump of the manifest of CarLibrary.dll (version 2.0.0.0):

```
Assembly
-------------------------------------------------------
  Token: 0x20000001
  Name : CarLibrary
  Public Key    : 00 24 00 00 04 80 00 00  // Etc...

  Hash Algorithm : 0x00008004
  Major Version: 0x00000002
  Minor Version: 0x00000000
  Build Number: 0x00000000
  Revision Number: 0x00000000
  Locale: <null>
  Flags : [PublicKey] ...
```

Documenting Referenced Assemblies

In addition to the Assembly token and the set of TypeDef and TypeRef blocks, .NET metadata also makes use of AssemblyRef #n tokens to document each external assembly. Given that the CarLibrary.dll makes use of the System.Windows.Forms.MessageBox class, you find an AssemblyRef for the System.Windows.Forms assembly, as shown in the following code:

```
AssemblyRef #2 (23000002)
-------------------------------------------------------
  Token: 0x23000002
  Public Key or Token: b7 7a 5c 56 19 34 e0 89
  Name: System.Windows.Forms
  Version: 4.0.0.0
  Major Version: 0x00000004
  Minor Version: 0x00000000
  Build Number: 0x00000000
  Revision Number: 0x00000000
  Locale: <null>
```

```
HashValue Blob:
Flags: [none] (00000000)
```

Documenting String Literals

The final point of interest regarding .NET metadata is the fact that each and every string literal in your code base is documented under the User Strings token.

```
User Strings
-------------------------------------------------------
70000001 : (11) L"Jamming {0}"
70000019 : (13) L"Quiet time..."
70000035 : (23) L"CarLibrary Version 2.0!"
70000065 : (14) L"Ramming speed!"
70000083 : (19) L"Faster is better..."
700000ab : (16) L"Time to call AAA"
700000cd : (16) L"Your car is dead"
```

■ **Note** As illustrated in this last metadata listing, always be aware that all strings are clearly documented in the assembly metadata. This could have huge security consequences if you were to use string literals to capture passwords, credit card numbers, or other sensitive information.

The next question on your mind may be (in the best-case scenario) "How can I leverage this information in my applications?" or (in the worst-case scenario) "Why should I care about metadata?" To address both points of view, allow me to introduce .NET reflection services. Be aware that the usefulness of the topics presented over the pages that follow may be a bit of a head-scratcher until this chapter's endgame. So hang tight.

■ **Note** You will also find a number of CustomAttribute tokens displayed by the MetaInfo window, which documents the attributes applied within the code base. You'll learn about the role of .NET attributes later in this chapter.

Understanding Reflection

In the .NET universe, *reflection* is the process of runtime type discovery. Using reflection services, you are able to programmatically obtain the same metadata information displayed by ildasm.exe using a friendly object model. For example, through reflection, you can obtain a list of all types contained within a given *.dll or *.exe assembly, including the methods, fields, properties, and events defined by a given type. You can also dynamically discover the set of interfaces supported by a given type, the parameters of a method, and other related details (base classes, namespace information, manifest data, and so forth).

Like any namespace, System.Reflection (which is defined in mscorlib.dll) contains a number of related types. Table 15-1 lists some of the core items you should be familiar with.

Table 15-1. *A Sampling of Members of the System.Reflection Namespace*

Type	Meaning in Life
Assembly	This abstract class contains a number of static methods that allow you to load, investigate, and manipulate an assembly.
AssemblyName	This class allows you to discover numerous details behind an assembly's identity (version information, culture information, and so forth).
EventInfo	This abstract class holds information for a given event.
FieldInfo	This abstract class holds information for a given field.
MemberInfo	This is the abstract base class that defines common behaviors for the EventInfo, FieldInfo, MethodInfo, and PropertyInfo types.
MethodInfo	This abstract class contains information for a given method.
Module	This abstract class allows you to access a given module within a multifile assembly.
ParameterInfo	This class holds information for a given parameter.
PropertyInfo	This abstract class holds information for a given property.

To understand how to leverage the System.Reflection namespace to programmatically read .NET metadata, you need to first come to terms with the System.Type class.

The System.Type Class

The System.Type class defines a number of members that can be used to examine a type's metadata, a great number of which return types from the System.Reflection namespace. For example, Type.GetMethods() returns an array of MethodInfo objects, Type.GetFields() returns an array of FieldInfo objects, and so on. The complete set of members exposed by System.Type is quite expansive; however, Table 15-2 offers a partial snapshot of the members supported by System.Type (see the .NET Framework 4.5 SDK documentation for full details).

Table 15-2. Select Members of System.Type

Type	Meaning in Life
IsAbstract IsArray IsClass IsCOMObject IsEnum IsGenericTypeDefinition IsGenericParameter IsInterface IsPrimitive IsNestedPrivate IsNestedPublic IsSealed IsValueType	These properties (among others) allow you to discover a number of basic traits about the Type you are referring to (e.g., if it is an abstract entity, an array, a nested class, and so forth).
GetConstructors() GetEvents() GetFields() GetInterfaces() GetMembers() GetMethods() GetNestedTypes() GetProperties()	These methods (among others) allow you to obtain an array representing the items (interface, method, property, etc.) you are interested in. Each method returns a related array (e.g., GetFields() returns a FieldInfo array, GetMethods() returns a MethodInfo array, etc.). Be aware that each of these methods has a singular form (e.g., GetMethod(), GetProperty(), etc.) that allows you to retrieve a specific item by name, rather than an array of all related items.
FindMembers()	This method returns a MemberInfo array based on search criteria.
GetType()	This static method returns a Type instance given a string name.
InvokeMember()	This method allows "late binding" for a given item. You'll learn about late binding later in this chapter.

Obtaining a Type Reference Using System.Object.GetType()

You can obtain an instance of the Type class in a variety of ways. However, the one thing you cannot do is directly create a Type object using the new keyword, as Type is an abstract class. Regarding your first choice, recall that System.Object defines a method named GetType(), which returns an instance of the Type class that represents the metadata for the current object.

```
// Obtain type information using a SportsCar instance.
SportsCar sc = new SportsCar();
Type t = sc.GetType();
```

Obviously, this approach will only work if you have compile-time knowledge of the type you wish to reflect over (SportsCar in this case) and currently have an instance of the type in memory. Given this restriction, it should make sense that tools such as ildasm.exe do not obtain type information by directly calling System.Object.GetType() for each type, given the ildasm.exe was not compiled against your custom assemblies.

Obtaining a Type Reference Using typeof()

The next way to obtain type information is using the C# typeof operator, like so:

```
// Get the type using typeof.
Type t = typeof(SportsCar);
```

Unlike System.Object.GetType(), the typeof operator is helpful in that you do not need to first create an object instance to extract type information. However, your code base must still have compile-time knowledge of the type you are interested in examining, as typeof expects the strongly typed name of the type.

Obtaining a Type Reference Using System.Type.GetType()

To obtain type information in a more flexible manner, you may call the static GetType() member of the System.Type class and specify the fully qualified string name of the type you are interested in examining. Using this approach, you do *not* need to have compile-time knowledge of the type you are extracting metadata from, given that Type.GetType() takes an instance of the omnipresent System.String.

■ **Note** When I say you do not need compile-time knowledge when calling Type.GetType(), I am referring to the fact that this method can take any string value whatsoever (rather than a strongly typed variable). Of course, you would still need to know the name of the type in a "stringified" format!

The Type.GetType() method has been overloaded to allow you to specify two Boolean parameters, one of which controls whether an exception should be thrown if the type cannot be found, and the other of which establishes the case sensitivity of the string. To illustrate, ponder the following:

```
// Obtain type information using the static Type.GetType() method
// (don't throw an exception if SportsCar cannot be found and ignore case).
Type t = Type.GetType("CarLibrary.SportsCar", false, true);
```

In the previous example, notice that the string you are passing into GetType() makes no mention of the assembly containing the type. In this case, the assumption is that the type is defined within the currently executing assembly. However, when you wish to obtain metadata for a type within an external private assembly, the string parameter is formatted using the type's fully qualified name, followed by a comma, followed by the friendly name of the assembly containing the type, like so:

```
// Obtain type information for a type within an external assembly.
Type t = Type.GetType("CarLibrary.SportsCar, CarLibrary");
```

As well, do know that the string passed into Type.GetType() may specify a plus token (+) to denote a *nested type*. Assume you wish to obtain type information for an enumeration (SpyOptions) nested within a class named JamesBondCar. To do so, you would write the following:

```
// Obtain type information for a nested enumeration
// within the current assembly.
Type t =  Type.GetType("CarLibrary.JamesBondCar+SpyOptions");
```

Building a Custom Metadata Viewer

To illustrate the basic process of reflection (and the usefulness of System.Type), let's create a Console Application named MyTypeViewer. This program will display details of the methods, properties, fields, and supported interfaces (in addition to some other points of interest) for any type within mscorlib.dll (recall all .NET applications have automatic access to this core framework class library) or a type within MyTypeViewer itself. Once the application has been created, be sure to import the System.Reflection namespace.

```
// Need to import this namespace to do any reflection!
using System.Reflection;
```

Reflecting on Methods

The Program class will be updated to define a number of static methods, each of which takes a single System.Type parameter and returns void. First you have ListMethods(), which (as you might guess) prints the name of each method defined by the incoming type. Notice how Type.GetMethods() returns an array of System.Reflection.MethodInfo objects, which can be enumerated over using a standard foreach loop, as follows:

```
// Display method names of type.
static void ListMethods(Type t)
{
  Console.WriteLine("***** Methods *****");
  MethodInfo[] mi = t.GetMethods();
  foreach(MethodInfo m in mi)
    Console.WriteLine("->{0}", m.Name);
  Console.WriteLine();
}
```

Here, you are simply printing the name of the method using the MethodInfo.Name property. As you might guess, MethodInfo has many additional members that allow you to determine whether the method is static, virtual, generic, or abstract. As well, the MethodInfo type allows you to obtain the method's return value and parameter set. You'll spruce up the implementation of ListMethods() in just a bit.

If you wish, you could also build a fitting LINQ query to enumerate the names of each method. Recall from Chapter 12, LINQ to Objects allows you to build strongly typed queries that can be applied to in-memory object collections. As a good rule of thumb, whenever you find blocks of looping or decision programming logic, you could make use of a related LINQ query. For example, you could rewrite the previous method as so:

```
static void ListMethods(Type t)
{
  Console.WriteLine("***** Methods *****");
  var methodNames = from n in t.GetMethods() select n.Name;
  foreach (var name in methodNames)
    Console.WriteLine("->{0}", name);
  Console.WriteLine();
}
```

Reflecting on Fields and Properties

The implementation of ListFields() is similar. The only notable difference is the call to Type.GetFields() and the resulting FieldInfo array. Again, to keep things simple, you are printing out only the name of each field using a LINQ query.

```
// Display field names of type.
static void ListFields(Type t)
{
  Console.WriteLine("***** Fields *****");
  var fieldNames = from f in t.GetFields() select f.Name;
  foreach (var name in fieldNames)
    Console.WriteLine("->{0}", name);
  Console.WriteLine();
}
```

The logic to display a type's properties is similar as well.

```
// Display property names of type.
static void ListProps(Type t)
{
  Console.WriteLine("***** Properties *****");
  var propNames = from p in t.GetProperties() select p.Name;
  foreach (var name in propNames)
    Console.WriteLine("->{0}", name);
  Console.WriteLine();
}
```

Reflecting on Implemented Interfaces

Next, you will author a method named ListInterfaces() that will print out the names of any interfaces supported on the incoming type. The only point of interest here is that the call to GetInterfaces() returns an array of System.Types! This should make sense given that interfaces are, indeed, types.

```
// Display implemented interfaces.
static void ListInterfaces(Type t)
{
  Console.WriteLine("***** Interfaces *****");
  var ifaces = from i in t.GetInterfaces() select i;
  foreach(Type i in ifaces)
    Console.WriteLine("->{0}", i.Name);
}
```

■ **Note** Be aware that a majority of the "get" methods of System.Type (GetMethods(), GetInterfaces(), etc.) have been overloaded to allow you to specify values from the BindingFlags enumeration. This provides a greater level of control on exactly what should be searched for (e.g., only static members, only public members, include private members, etc.). Consult the .NET Framework 4.5 SDK documentation for details.

Displaying Various Odds and Ends

Last but not least, you have one final helper method that will simply display various statistics (indicating whether the type is generic, what the base class is, whether the type is sealed, and so forth) regarding the incoming type.

```
// Just for good measure.
static void ListVariousStats(Type t)
{
  Console.WriteLine("***** Various Statistics *****");
  Console.WriteLine("Base class is: {0}", t.BaseType);
  Console.WriteLine("Is type abstract? {0}", t.IsAbstract);
  Console.WriteLine("Is type sealed? {0}", t.IsSealed);
  Console.WriteLine("Is type generic? {0}", t.IsGenericTypeDefinition);
  Console.WriteLine("Is type a class type? {0}", t.IsClass);
  Console.WriteLine();
}
```

Implementing Main()

The Main() method of the Program class prompts the user for the fully qualified name of a type. Once you obtain this string data, you pass it into the Type.GetType() method and send the extracted System.Type into each of your helper methods. This process repeats until the user enters **Q** to terminate the application.

```
static void Main(string[] args)
{
  Console.WriteLine("***** Welcome to MyTypeViewer *****");
  string typeName = "";

  do
  {
    Console.WriteLine("\nEnter a type name to evaluate");
    Console.Write("or enter Q to quit: ");

    // Get name of type.
    typeName = Console.ReadLine();

    // Does user want to quit?
    if (typeName.ToUpper() == "Q")
    {
      break;
    }

    // Try to display type.
    try
    {
      Type t = Type.GetType(typeName);
      Console.WriteLine("");
      ListVariousStats(t);
      ListFields(t);
      ListProps(t);
```

```
        ListMethods(t);
        ListInterfaces(t);
    }
    catch
    {
      Console.WriteLine("Sorry, can't find type");
    }
  } while (true);
}
```

At this point, MyTypeViewer.exe is ready to take out for a test drive. For example, run your application and enter the following fully qualified names (be aware that the manner in which you invoked Type.GetType() requires case-sensitive string names):

- System.Int32

- System.Collections.ArrayList

- System.Threading.Thread

- System.Void

- System.IO.BinaryWriter

- System.Math

- System.Console

- MyTypeViewer.Program

For example, here is some partial output when specifying System.Math:

```
***** Welcome to MyTypeViewer *****

Enter a type name to evaluate
or enter Q to quit: System.Math

***** Various Statistics *****
Base class is: System.Object
Is type abstract? True
Is type sealed? True
Is type generic? False
Is type a class type? True

***** Fields *****
->PI
->E

***** Properties *****

***** Methods *****
->Acos
->Asin
->Atan
```

```
->Atan2
->Ceiling
->Ceiling
->Cos
...
```

Reflecting on Generic Types

When you call Type.GetType() in order to obtain metadata descriptions of generic types, you must make use of a special syntax involving a "back tick" character (`) followed by a numerical value that represents the number of type parameters the type supports. For example, if you wish to print out the metadata description of System.Collections.Generic.List<T>, you would need to pass the following string into your application:

```
System.Collections.Generic.List`1
```

Here, you are using the numerical value of 1, given that List<T> has only one type parameter. However, if you wish to reflect over Dictionary<TKey, TValue>, you would supply the value 2, like so:

```
System.Collections.Generic.Dictionary`2
```

Reflecting on Method Parameters and Return Values

So far, so good! Let's make a minor enhancement to the current application. Specifically, you will update the ListMethods() helper function to list not only the name of a given method, but also the return type and incoming parameter types. The MethodInfo type provides the ReturnType property and GetParameters() method for these very tasks. In the following modified code, notice that you are building a string that contains the type and name of each parameter using a nested foreach loop (without the use of LINQ):

```
static void ListMethods(Type t)
{
  Console.WriteLine("***** Methods *****");
  MethodInfo[] mi = t.GetMethods();
  foreach (MethodInfo m in mi)
  {
    // Get return type.
    string retVal = m.ReturnType.FullName;
    string paramInfo = "( ";
    // Get params.
    foreach (ParameterInfo pi in m.GetParameters())
    {
      paramInfo += string.Format("{0} {1} ", pi.ParameterType, pi.Name);
    }
    paramInfo += " )";

    // Now display the basic method sig.
    Console.WriteLine("->{0} {1} {2}", retVal, m.Name, paramInfo);
  }
  Console.WriteLine();
}
```

If you now run this updated application, you will find that the methods of a given type are much more detailed. If you enter your good friend, `System.Object`, as input to the program, the following methods will display:

```
***** Methods *****
->System.String ToString (  )
->System.Boolean Equals ( System.Object obj  )
->System.Boolean Equals ( System.Object objA System.Object objB  )
->System.Boolean ReferenceEquals ( System.Object objA System.Object objB  )
->System.Int32 GetHashCode (  )
->System.Type GetType (  )
```

The current implementation of `ListMethods()` is helpful, in that you can directly investigate each parameter and method return type using the `System.Reflection` object model. As an extreme shortcut, be aware that each of the XXXInfo types (`MethodInfo`, `PropertyInfo`, `EventInfo`, etc.) have overridden `ToString()` to display the signature of the item requested. Thus, you could also implement `ListMethods()` as follows (once again using LINQ, where you simply select all `MethodInfo` objects, rather than only the `Name` values):

```
static void ListMethods(Type t)
{
  Console.WriteLine("***** Methods *****");
  var methodNames = from n in t.GetMethods() select n;
  foreach (var name in methodNames)
    Console.WriteLine("->{0}", name);
  Console.WriteLine();
}
```

Interesting stuff, huh? Clearly the `System.Reflection` namespace and `System.Type` class allow you to reflect over many other aspects of a type beyond what `MyTypeViewer` is currently displaying. As you would hope, you can obtain a type's events, get the list of any generic parameters for a given member, and glean dozens of other details.

Nevertheless, at this point you have created a (somewhat capable) object browser. The major limitation, of course, is that you have no way to reflect beyond the current assembly (`MyTypeViewer`) or the always accessible `mscorlib.dll`. This begs the question, "How can I build applications that can load (and reflect over) assemblies not referenced at compile time?" Glad you asked.

■ **Source Code** The MyTypeViewer project can be found under the Chapter 15 subdirectory.

Dynamically Loading Assemblies

In Chapter 14, you learned all about how the CLR consults the assembly manifest when probing for an externally referenced assembly. However, there will be many times when you need to load assemblies on the fly programmatically, even if there is no record of said assembly in the manifest. Formally speaking, the act of loading external assemblies on demand is known as a *dynamic load*.

System.Reflection defines a class named Assembly. Using this class, you are able to dynamically load an assembly, as well as discover properties about the assembly itself. Using the Assembly type, you are able to dynamically load private or shared assemblies, as well as load an assembly located at an arbitrary location. In essence, the Assembly class provides methods (Load() and LoadFrom(), in particular) that allow you to programmatically supply the same sort of information found in a client-side *.config file.

To illustrate dynamic loading, create a brand-new Console Application named ExternalAssemblyReflector. Your task is to construct a Main() method that prompts for the friendly name of an assembly to load dynamically. You will pass the Assembly reference into a helper method named DisplayTypes(), which will simply print the names of each class, interface, structure, enumeration, and delegate it contains. The code is refreshingly simple.

```
using System;
using System.Collections.Generic;
using System.Linq;
using System.Text;

using System.Reflection;
using System.IO;   // For FileNotFoundException definition.

namespace ExternalAssemblyReflector
{
  class Program
  {
    static void DisplayTypesInAsm(Assembly asm)
    {
      Console.WriteLine("\n***** Types in Assembly *****");
      Console.WriteLine("->{0}", asm.FullName);
      Type[] types = asm.GetTypes();
      foreach (Type t in types)
        Console.WriteLine("Type: {0}", t);
      Console.WriteLine("");
    }

    static void Main(string[] args)
    {
      Console.WriteLine("***** External Assembly Viewer *****");

      string asmName = "";
      Assembly asm = null;

      do
      {
        Console.WriteLine("\nEnter an assembly to evaluate");
        Console.Write("or enter Q to quit: ");

        // Get name of assembly.
        asmName = Console.ReadLine();

        // Does user want to quit?
        if (asmName.ToUpper() == "Q")
        {
```

```
        break;
      }

      // Try to load assembly.
      try
      {
        asm = Assembly.Load(asmName);
        DisplayTypesInAsm(asm);
      }
      catch
      {
        Console.WriteLine("Sorry, can't find assembly.");
      }
    } while (true);
  }
}
}
```

Notice that the static Assembly.Load() method has been passed only the friendly name of the assembly you are interested in loading into memory. Thus, if you wish to reflect over CarLibrary.dll, you will need to copy the CarLibrary.dll binary to the \bin\Debug directory of the ExternalAssemblyReflector application to run this program. Once you do, you will find output similar to the following:

```
***** External Assembly Viewer *****

Enter an assembly to evaluate
or enter Q to quit: CarLibrary

***** Types in Assembly *****
->CarLibrary, Version=2.0.0.0, Culture=neutral, PublicKeyToken=33a2bc294331e8b9
Type: CarLibrary.MusicMedia
Type: CarLibrary.EngineState
Type: CarLibrary.Car
Type: CarLibrary.SportsCar
Type: CarLibrary.MiniVan
```

If you wish to make ExternalAssemblyReflector more flexible, you can update your code to load the external assembly using Assembly.LoadFrom() rather than Assembly.Load(), like so:

```
try
{
  asm = Assembly.LoadFrom(asmName);
  DisplayTypesInAsm(asm);
}
```

By doing so, you can enter an absolute path to the assembly you wish to view (e.g., C:\MyApp\MyAsm.dll). Essentially, Assembly.LoadFrom() allows you to programmatically supply a <codeBase> value. With this adjustment, you can now pass in a full path to your Console Application. Thus, if CarLibrary.dll was located under C:\MyCode, you could enter the following:

```
***** External Assembly Viewer *****

Enter an assembly to evaluate
or enter Q to quit: C:\MyCode\CarLibrary.dll

***** Types in Assembly *****
->CarLibrary, Version=2.0.0.0, Culture=neutral, PublicKeyToken=33a2bc294331e8b9
Type: CarLibrary.EngineState
Type: CarLibrary.Car
Type: CarLibrary.SportsCar
Type: CarLibrary.MiniVan
```

■ **Source Code** The ExternalAssemblyReflector project is included in the Chapter 15 subdirectory.

Reflecting on Shared Assemblies

The Assembly.Load() method has been overloaded a number of times. One variation allows you to specify a culture value (for localized assemblies), as well as a version number and public key token value (for shared assemblies). Collectively speaking, the set of items identifying an assembly is termed the *display name*. The format of a display name is a comma-delimited string of name/value pairs that begins with the friendly name of the assembly, followed by optional qualifiers (that may appear in any order). Here is the template to follow (optional items appear in parentheses):

```
Name (,Version = major.minor.build.revision) (,Culture = culture token)
(,PublicKeyToken= public key token)
```

When you're crafting a display name, the convention PublicKeyToken=null indicates that binding and matching against a non–strongly named assembly is required. Additionally, Culture="" indicates matching against the default culture of the target machine, for example:

```
// Load version 1.0.0.0 of CarLibrary using the default culture.
Assembly a =
  Assembly.Load(@"CarLibrary, Version=1.0.0.0, PublicKeyToken=null, Culture=""");
```

Also be aware that the System.Reflection namespace supplies the AssemblyName type, which allows you to represent the preceding string information in a handy object variable. Typically, this class is used in conjunction with System.Version, which is an OO wrapper around an assembly's version number. Once you have established the display name, it can then be passed into the overloaded Assembly.Load() method, like so:

```
// Make use of AssemblyName to define the display name.
AssemblyName asmName;
asmName = new AssemblyName();
asmName.Name = "CarLibrary";
Version v = new Version("1.0.0.0");
asmName.Version = v;
Assembly a = Assembly.Load(asmName);
```

To load a shared assembly from the GAC, the `Assembly.Load()` parameter must specify a PublicKeyToken value. For example, assume you have a new Console Application named SharedAsmReflector, and wish to load version 4.0.0.0 of the System.Windows.Forms.dll assembly provided by the .NET base class libraries. Given that the number of types in this assembly is quite large, the following application prints out only the names of public enums, using a simple LINQ query:

```csharp
using System;
using System.Collections.Generic;
using System.Linq;
using System.Text;

using System.Reflection;
using System.IO;

namespace SharedAsmReflector
{
  public class SharedAsmReflector
  {
    private static void DisplayInfo(Assembly a)
    {
      Console.WriteLine("***** Info about Assembly *****");
      Console.WriteLine("Loaded from GAC? {0}", a.GlobalAssemblyCache);
      Console.WriteLine("Asm Name: {0}", a.GetName().Name);
      Console.WriteLine("Asm Version: {0}", a.GetName().Version);
      Console.WriteLine("Asm Culture: {0}",
        a.GetName().CultureInfo.DisplayName);
      Console.WriteLine("\nHere are the public enums:");

      // Use a LINQ query to find the public enums.
      Type[] types = a.GetTypes();
      var publicEnums = from pe in types where pe.IsEnum &&
                      pe.IsPublic select pe;

      foreach (var pe in publicEnums)
      {
        Console.WriteLine(pe);
      }
    }

    static void Main(string[] args)
    {
      Console.WriteLine("***** The Shared Asm Reflector App *****\n");

      // Load System.Windows.Forms.dll from GAC.
      string displayName = null;
      displayName = "System.Windows.Forms," +
        "Version=4.0.0.0," +
        "PublicKeyToken=b77a5c561934e089," +
        @"Culture=""";
      Assembly asm = Assembly.Load(displayName);
      DisplayInfo(asm);
      Console.WriteLine("Done!");
```

```
      Console.ReadLine();
    }
  }
}
```

■ **Source Code** The SharedAsmReflector project is included in the Chapter 15 subdirectory.

At this point, you should understand how to use some of the core members of the
System.Reflection namespace to discover metadata at runtime. Of course, I realize despite the "cool
factor," you likely will not need to build custom object browsers at your place of employment too often.
Do recall, however, that reflection services are the foundation for a number of very common
programming activities, including late binding.

Understanding Late Binding

Simply put, *late binding* is a technique in which you are able to create an instance of a given type and
invoke its members at runtime without having hard-coded compile-time knowledge of its existence.
When you are building an application that binds late to a type in an external assembly, you have no
reason to set a reference to the assembly; therefore, the caller's manifest has no direct listing of the
assembly.
    At first glance, it is not easy to see the value of late binding. It is true that if you can "bind early" to
an object (e.g., set an assembly reference and allocate the type using the C# new keyword), you should
opt to do so. For one reason, early binding allows you to determine errors at compile time, rather than at
runtime. Nevertheless, late binding does have a critical role in any extendable application you may be
building. You will have a chance to build such an "extendable" program at the end of this chapter, in the
section "Building an Extendable Application"; until then, let's examine the role of the Activator class.

The System.Activator Class

The System.Activator class (defined in mscorlib.dll) is the key to the .NET late-binding process. For the
current example, you are only interested in the Activator.CreateInstance() method, which is used to
create an instance of a type à la late binding. This method has been overloaded numerous times to
provide a good deal of flexibility. The simplest variation of the CreateInstance() member takes a valid
Type object that describes the entity you wish to allocate into memory on the fly.
    Create a new Console Application named LateBindingApp, and import the System.IO and
System.Reflection namespace via the C# using keyword. Now, update the Program class as follows:

```
// This program will load an external library,
// and create an object using late binding.
public class Program
{
  static void Main(string[] args)
  {
    Console.WriteLine("***** Fun with Late Binding *****");
    // Try to load a local copy of CarLibrary.
    Assembly a = null;
```

```
    try
    {
      a = Assembly.Load("CarLibrary");
    }
    catch(FileNotFoundException ex)
    {
      Console.WriteLine(ex.Message);
      return;
    }
    if(a != null)
      CreateUsingLateBinding(a);

    Console.ReadLine();
  }

  static void CreateUsingLateBinding(Assembly asm)
  {
    try
    {
      // Get metadata for the Minivan type.
      Type miniVan = asm.GetType("CarLibrary.MiniVan");

      // Create the Minivan on the fly.
      object obj = Activator.CreateInstance(miniVan);
      Console.WriteLine("Created a {0} using late binding!", obj);
    }
    catch(Exception ex)
    {
      Console.WriteLine(ex.Message);
    }
  }
}
```

Now, before you run this application, you will need to manually place a copy of CarLibrary.dll into the bin\Debug folder of this new application using Windows Explorer. The reason is that you are calling Assembly.Load() and, therefore, the CLR will only probe in the client folder (if you wish, you could enter a path to the assembly using Assembly.LoadFrom(); however, there is no need to do so).

■ **Note** Don't set a reference to CarLibrary.dll using Visual Studio for this example! That will record this library in the client's manifest. The whole point of late binding is that you are trying to create an object that is not known at compile time.

Notice that the Activator.CreateInstance() method returns a System.Object rather than a strongly typed MiniVan. Therefore, if you apply the dot operator on the obj variable, you will fail to see any members of the MiniVan class. At first glance, you might assume you can remedy this problem with an explicit cast, like so:

```
// Cast to get access to the members of MiniVan?
// Nope! Compiler error!
object obj = (MiniVan)Activator.CreateInstance(minivan);
```

However, because your program has not set a reference to CarLibrary.dll, you cannot make use of the C# using keyword to import the CarLibrary namespace and, therefore, you can't use a MiniVan during the casting operation! Remember that the whole point of late binding is to create instances of objects for which there is no compile-time knowledge. Given this, how can you invoke the underlying methods of the MiniVan object stored in the System.Object reference? The answer, of course, is by using reflection.

Invoking Methods with No Parameters

Assume you wish to invoke the TurboBoost() method of the MiniVan. As you recall, this method will set the state of the engine to "dead" and display an informational message box. The first step is to obtain a MethodInfo object for the TurboBoost() method using Type.GetMethod(). From the resulting MethodInfo, you are then able to call MiniVan.TurboBoost using Invoke(). MethodInfo.Invoke() requires you to send in all parameters that are to be given to the method represented by MethodInfo. These parameters are represented by an array of System.Object types (as the parameters for a given method could be any number of various entities).

Given that TurboBoost() does not require any parameters, you can simply pass null (meaning "this method has no parameters"). Update your CreateUsingLateBinding() method as follows:

```
static void CreateUsingLateBinding(Assembly asm)
{
  try
  {
    // Get metadata for the Minivan type.
    Type miniVan = asm.GetType("CarLibrary.MiniVan");

    // Create the Minivan on the fly.
    object obj = Activator.CreateInstance(miniVan);
    Console.WriteLine("Created a {0} using late binding!", obj);
    // Get info for TurboBoost.
    MethodInfo mi = miniVan.GetMethod("TurboBoost");

    // Invoke method ('null' for no parameters).
    mi.Invoke(obj, null);
  }
  catch(Exception ex)
  {
    Console.WriteLine(ex.Message);
  }
}
```

At this point, you will see the message box shown in Figure 15-2, once the TurboBoost() method is invoked.

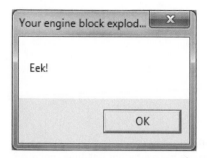

Figure 15-2. Late-bound method invocation

Invoking Methods with Parameters

When you wish to use late binding to invoke a method requiring parameters, you should package up the arguments as a loosely typed array of objects. Recall that version 2.0.0.0 of CarLibrary.dll defined the following method in the Car class:

```
public void TurnOnRadio(bool musicOn, MusicMedia mm)
{
  if (musicOn)
    MessageBox.Show(string.Format("Jamming {0}", mm));
  else
    MessageBox.Show("Quiet time...");
}
```

This method takes two parameters: a Boolean representing if the automobile's music system should be turned on or off, and an enum that represents the type of music player. Recall this enum was structured as so:

```
public enum MusicMedia
{
  musicCd,      // 0
  musicTape,    // 1
  musicRadio,   // 2
  musicMp3      // 3
}
```

Here is a new method of the Program class, which invokes TurnOnRadio(). Notice that you are using the underlying numerical values of the MusicMedia enumeration, to specify a "radio" media player.

```
static void InvokeMethodWithArgsUsingLateBinding(Assembly asm)
{
  try
  {
    // First, get a metadata description of the sports car.
    Type sport = asm.GetType("CarLibrary.SportsCar");

    // Now, create the sports car.
    object obj = Activator.CreateInstance(sport);
```

```
    // Invoke TurnOnRadio() with arguments.
    MethodInfo mi = sport.GetMethod("TurnOnRadio");
    mi.Invoke(obj, new object[] { true, 2 });
  }
  catch (Exception ex)
  {
    Console.WriteLine(ex.Message);
  }
}
```

Hopefully, at this point, you can see the relationships among reflection, dynamic loading, and late binding. To be sure, the reflection API provides many additional features beyond what has been covered here, but you should be in good shape to dig into more details if you are interested.

Again, you still might wonder exactly *when* you should make use of these techniques in your own applications. The conclusion of this chapter should shed light on this issue; however, the next topic under investigation is the role of .NET attributes.

■ **Source Code** The LateBindingApp project is included in the Chapter 15 subdirectory.

Understanding the Role of .NET Attributes

As illustrated at beginning of this chapter, one role of a .NET compiler is to generate metadata descriptions for all defined and referenced types. In addition to this standard metadata contained within any assembly, the .NET platform provides a way for programmers to embed additional metadata into an assembly using *attributes*. In a nutshell, attributes are nothing more than code annotations that can be applied to a given type (class, interface, structure, etc.), member (property, method, etc.), assembly, or module.

.NET attributes are class types that extend the abstract System.Attribute base class. As you explore the .NET namespaces, you will find many predefined attributes that you are able to make use of in your applications. Furthermore, you are free to build custom attributes to further qualify the behavior of your types by creating a new type deriving from Attribute.

The .NET base class library provides a number of attributes in various namespaces. Table 15-3 gives a snapshot of some—but by *absolutely* no means all—predefined attributes.

Table 15-3. A Tiny Sampling of Predefined Attributes

Attribute	Meaning in Life
[CLSCompliant]	Enforces the annotated item to conform to the rules of the Common Language Specification (CLS). Recall that CLS-compliant types are guaranteed to be used seamlessly across all .NET programming languages.
[DllImport]	Allows .NET code to make calls to any unmanaged C- or C++-based code library, including the API of the underlying operating system. Do note that [DllImport] is not used when communicating with COM-based software.

[Obsolete]	Marks a deprecated type or member. If other programmers attempt to use such an item, they will receive a compiler warning describing the error of their ways.
[Serializable]	Marks a class or structure as being "serializable," meaning it is able to persist its current state into a stream.
[NonSerialized]	Specifies that a given field in a class or structure should not be persisted during the serialization process.
[ServiceContract]	Marks a method as a contract implemented by a WCF service.

Understand that when you apply attributes in your code, the embedded metadata is essentially useless until another piece of software explicitly reflects over the information. If this is not the case, the blurb of metadata embedded within the assembly is ignored and completely harmless.

Attribute Consumers

As you would guess, the .NET 4.5 Framework SDK ships with numerous utilities that are indeed on the lookout for various attributes. The C# compiler (csc.exe) itself has been preprogrammed to discover the presence of various attributes during the compilation cycle. For example, if the C# compiler encounters the [CLSCompliant] attribute, it will automatically check the attributed item to ensure it is exposing only CLS-compliant constructs. By way of another example, if the C# compiler discovers an item attributed with the [Obsolete] attribute, it will display a compiler warning in the Visual Studio Error List window.

In addition to development tools, numerous methods in the .NET base class libraries are preprogrammed to reflect over specific attributes. For example, if you wish to persist the state of an object to file, all you are required to do is annotate your class or structure with the [Serializable] attribute. If the Serialize() method of the BinaryFormatter class encounters this attribute, the object is automatically persisted to file in a compact binary format.

Finally, you are free to build applications that are programmed to reflect over your own custom attributes, as well as any attribute in the .NET base class libraries. By doing so, you are essentially able to create a set of "keywords" that are understood by a specific set of assemblies.

Applying Attributes in C#

To illustrate the process of applying attributes in C#, create a new Console Application named ApplyingAttributes. Assume you wish to build a class named Motorcycle that can be persisted in a binary format. To do so, simply apply the [Serializable] attribute to the class definition. If you have a field that should not be persisted, you may apply the [NonSerialized] attribute.

```
// This class can be saved to disk.
[Serializable]
public class Motorcycle
{
  // However, this field will not be persisted.
  [NonSerialized]
  float weightOfCurrentPassengers;
```

```
// These fields are still serializable.
bool hasRadioSystem;
bool hasHeadSet;
bool hasSissyBar;
}
```

■ **Note** An attribute applies to the "very next" item. For example, the only nonserialized field of the Motorcycle class is weightOfCurrentPassengers. The remaining fields are serializable given that the entire class has been annotated with [Serializable].

At this point, don't concern yourself with the actual process of object serialization (Chapter 20 examines the details). Just notice that when you wish to apply an attribute, the name of the attribute is sandwiched between square brackets.

Once this class has been compiled, you can view the extra metadata using ildasm.exe. Notice that these attributes are recorded using the serializable token (see the red triangle immediately inside the Motorcycle class) and the notserialized token (on the weightOfCurrentPassengers field; see Figure 15-3).

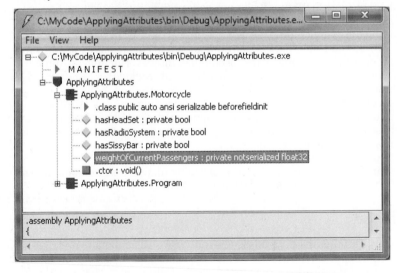

Figure 15-3. Attributes shown in ildasm.exe

As you might guess, a single item can be attributed with multiple attributes. Assume you have a legacy C# class type (HorseAndBuggy) that was marked as serializable, but is now considered obsolete for current development. Rather than deleting the class definition from your code base (and risk breaking existing software), you can mark the class with the [Obsolete] attribute. To apply multiple attributes to a single item, simply use a comma-delimited list, like so:

```
[Serializable, Obsolete("Use another vehicle!")]
public class HorseAndBuggy
```

```
{
  // ...
}
```

As an alternative, you can also apply multiple attributes on a single item by stacking each attribute as follows (the end result is identical):

```
[Serializable]
[Obsolete("Use another vehicle!")]
public class HorseAndBuggy
{
  // ...
}
```

C# Attribute Shorthand Notation

If you were consulting the .NET Framework 4.5 SDK documentation, you might have noticed that the actual class name of the [Obsolete] attribute is ObsoleteAttribute, not Obsolete. As a naming convention, all .NET attributes (including custom attributes you may create yourself) are suffixed with the Attribute token. However, to simplify the process of applying attributes, the C# language does not require you to type in the Attribute suffix. Given this, the following iteration of the HorseAndBuggy type is identical to the previous (it just involves a few more keystrokes):

```
[SerializableAttribute]
[ObsoleteAttribute("Use another vehicle!")]
public class HorseAndBuggy
{
  // ...
}
```

Be aware that this is a courtesy provided by C#. Not all .NET-enabled languages support this shorthand attribute syntax.

Specifying Constructor Parameters for Attributes

Notice that the [Obsolete] attribute is able to accept what appears to be a constructor parameter. If you view the formal definition of the [Obsolete] attribute using the Code Definition window (which can be opened using the View menu of Visual Studio), you will find that this class indeed provides a constructor receiving a System.String.

```
public sealed class ObsoleteAttribute : Attribute
{
  public ObsoleteAttribute(string message, bool error);
  public ObsoleteAttribute(string message);
  public ObsoleteAttribute();
  public bool IsError { get; }
  public string Message { get; }
}
```

Understand that when you supply constructor parameters to an attribute, the attribute is *not* allocated into memory until the parameters are reflected upon by another type or an external tool. The string data defined at the attribute level is simply stored within the assembly as a blurb of metadata.

The Obsolete Attribute in Action

Now that HorseAndBuggy has been marked as obsolete, if you were to allocate an instance of this type:

```
static void Main(string[] args)
{
  HorseAndBuggy mule = new HorseAndBuggy();
}
```

you would find that the supplied string data is extracted and displayed within the Error List window of Visual Studio, as well as on the offending line of code when you hover your mouse cursor above the obsolete type (see Figure 15-4).

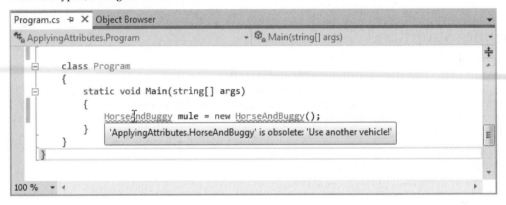

Figure 15-4. Attributes in action

In this case, the "other piece of software" that is reflecting on the [Obsolete] attribute is the C# compiler. Hopefully, at this point, you should understand the following key points regarding .NET attributes:

- Attributes are classes that derive from System.Attribute.

- Attributes result in embedded metadata.

- Attributes are basically useless until another agent reflects upon them.

- Attributes are applied in C# using square brackets.

Next up, let's examine how you can build your own custom attributes and a piece of custom software that reflects over the embedded metadata.

■ **Source Code** The ApplyingAttributes project is included in the Chapter 15 subdirectory.

Building Custom Attributes

The first step in building a custom attribute is to create a new class deriving from `System.Attribute`.
Keeping in step with the automobile theme used throughout this book, assume you have created a brand
new C# Class Library project named `AttributedCarLibrary`. This assembly will define a handful of
vehicles, each of which is described using a custom attribute named `VehicleDescriptionAttribute`, as
follows:

```
// A custom attribute.
public sealed class VehicleDescriptionAttribute : System.Attribute
{
  public string Description { get; set; }

  public VehicleDescriptionAttribute(string vehicalDescription)
  {
    Description = vehicalDescription;
  }
  public VehicleDescriptionAttribute(){ }
}
```

As you can see, `VehicleDescriptionAttribute` maintains a piece of string data manipulated using an
automatic property (`Description`). Beyond the fact that this class derived from `System.Attribute`, there
is nothing unique to this class definition.

■ **Note** For security reasons, it is considered a .NET best practice to design all custom attributes as sealed. In
fact, Visual Studio provides a code snippet named `Attribute` that will dump out a new `System.Attribute`-
derived class into your code window. See Chapter 2 for full explication of using code snippets; however, recall you
can expand any snippet by typing its name and pressing the Tab key twice.

Applying Custom Attributes

Given that `VehicleDescriptionAttribute` is derived from `System.Attribute`, you are now able to
annotate your vehicles as you see fit. For testing purposes, add the following class definitions to your
new class library:

```
// Assign description using a "named property."
[Serializable]
[VehicleDescription(Description = "My rocking Harley")]
public class Motorcycle
{
}

[SerializableAttribute]
[ObsoleteAttribute("Use another vehicle!")]
[VehicleDescription("The old gray mare, she ain't what she used to be...")]
public class HorseAndBuggy
```

```
{
}
```

```
[VehicleDescription("A very long, slow, but feature-rich auto")]
public class Winnebago
{
}
```

Named Property Syntax

Notice that the description of the Motorcycle is assigned a description using a new bit of attribute-centric syntax termed a *named property*. In the constructor of the first [VehicleDescription] attribute, you set the underlying string data by using the Description property. If this attribute is reflected upon by an external agent, the value is fed into the Description property (named property syntax is legal only if the attribute supplies a writable .NET property).

In contrast, the HorseAndBuggy and Winnebago types are not making use of named property syntax and are simply passing the string data via the custom constructor. In any case, once you compile the AttributedCarLibrary assembly, you can make use of ildasm.exe to view the injected metadata descriptions for your type. For example, Figure 15-5 shows an embedded description of the Winnebago class, specifically the data within the beforefieldinit item in ildasm.exe.

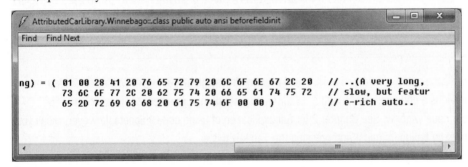

Figure 15-5. Embedded vehicle description data

Restricting Attribute Usage

By default, custom attributes can be applied to just about any aspect of your code (methods, classes, properties, and so on). Thus, if it made sense to do so, you could use VehicleDescription to qualify methods, properties, or fields (among other things).

```
[VehicleDescription("A very long, slow, but feature-rich auto")]
public class Winnebago
{
  [VehicleDescription("My rocking CD player")]
  public void PlayMusic(bool On)
  {
    ...
  }
}
```

In some cases, this is exactly the behavior you require. Other times, however, you may want to build a custom attribute that can be applied only to select code elements. If you wish to constrain the scope of a custom attribute, you will need to apply the [AttributeUsage] attribute on the definition of your custom attribute. The [AttributeUsage] attribute allows you to supply any combination of values (via an OR operation) from the AttributeTargets enumeration, like so:

```
// This enumeration defines the possible targets of an attribute.
public enum AttributeTargets
{
  All, Assembly, Class, Constructor,
  Delegate, Enum, Event, Field, GenericParameter,
  Interface, Method, Module, Parameter,
  Property, ReturnValue, Struct
}
```

Furthermore, [AttributeUsage] also allows you to optionally set a named property (AllowMultiple) that specifies whether the attribute can be applied more than once on the same item (the default is false). As well, [AttributeUsage] allows you to establish whether the attribute should be inherited by derived classes using the Inherited named property (the default is true).

To establish that the [VehicleDescription] attribute can be applied only once on a class or structure, you can update the VehicleDescriptionAttribute definition as follows:

```
// This time, we are using the AttributeUsage attribute
// to annotate our custom attribute.
[AttributeUsage(AttributeTargets.Class | AttributeTargets.Struct,
                Inherited = false)]
public sealed class VehicleDescriptionAttribute : System.Attribute
{
...
}
```

With this, if a developer attempted to apply the [VehicleDescription] attribute on anything other than a class or structure, he or she is issued a compile-time error.

Assembly-Level Attributes

It is also possible to apply attributes on all types within a given assembly using the [assembly:] tag. For example, assume you wish to ensure that every public member of every public type defined within your assembly is CLS compliant.

■ **Note** Chapter 1 mentioned the role of CLS-compliant assemblies. Recall that a CLS-compliant assembly can be used by all .NET programming languages out of the box. If you create public members of public types, which expose non–CLS compliant programming constructs (such as unsigned data or pointer parameters), other .NET languages may not be able to use your functionality. Therefore, if you are building C# code libraries that need to be used by a wide variety of .NET languages, checking for CLS compliance is a must.

To do so, simply add the following assembly-level attribute at the very top of any C# source code file. Be very aware that all assembly- or module-level attributes must be listed outside the scope of any namespace scope! If you add assembly- or module-level attributes to your project, here is a recommended file layout to follow:

```
// List "using" statements first.
using System;
using System.Collections.Generic;
using System.Linq;
using System.Text;

// Now list any assembly- or module-level attributes.
// Enforce CLS compliance for all public types in this assembly.
[assembly: CLSCompliant(true)]

// Now, your namespace(s) and types.
namespace AttributedCarLibrary
{
  // Types...
}
```

If you now add a bit of code that falls outside the CLS specification (such as an exposed point of unsigned data):

```
// Ulong types don't jibe with the CLS.
public class Winnebago
{
  public ulong notCompliant;
}
```

you are issued a compiler warning.

The Visual Studio AssemblyInfo.cs File

By default, Visual Studio projects receive a file named AssemblyInfo.cs, which can be viewed by expanding the Properties icon of the Solution Explorer (see Figure 15-6).

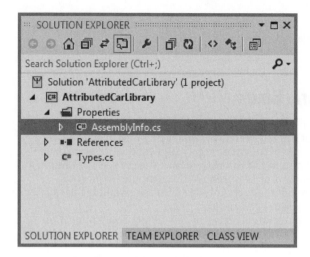

Figure 15-6. *The* `AssemblyInfo.cs` *file*

This file is a handy place to put attributes that are to be applied at the assembly level. You might recall from Chapter 14, during the examination of .NET assemblies, that the manifest contains assembly-level metadata, much of which comes from the assembly-level attributes shown in Table 15-4.

Table 15-4. *Select Assembly-Level Attributes*

Attribute	Meaning in Life
`[AssemblyCompany]`	Holds basic company information
`[AssemblyCopyright]`	Holds any copyright information for the product or assembly
`[AssemblyCulture]`	Provides information on what cultures or languages the assembly supports
`[AssemblyDescription]`	Holds a friendly description of the product or modules that make up the assembly
`[AssemblyKeyFile]`	Specifies the name of the file containing the key pair used to sign the assembly (i.e., establish a strong name)
`[AssemblyProduct]`	Provides product information
`[AssemblyTrademark]`	Provides trademark information
`[AssemblyVersion]`	Specifies the assembly's version information, in the format `<major.minor.build.revision>`

■ **Source Code** The AttributedCarLibrary project is included in the Chapter 15 subdirectory.

Reflecting on Attributes Using Early Binding

Remember that an attribute is quite useless until another piece of software reflects over its values. Once a given attribute has been discovered, that piece of software can take whatever course of action necessary. Now, like any application, this "other piece of software" could discover the presence of a custom attribute using either early binding or late binding. If you wish to make use of early binding, you'll require the client application to have a compile-time definition of the attribute in question (VehicleDescriptionAttribute, in this case). Given that the AttributedCarLibrary assembly has defined this custom attribute as a public class, early binding is the best option.

To illustrate the process of reflecting on custom attributes, create a new C# Console Application named VehicleDescriptionAttributeReader. Next, set a reference to the AttributedCarLibrary assembly. Finally, update your initial *.cs file with the following code:

```
// Reflecting on attributes using early binding.
using System;
using System.Collections.Generic;
using System.Linq;
using System.Text;

using AttributedCarLibrary;

namespace VehicleDescriptionAttributeReader
{
  class Program
  {
    static void Main(string[] args)
    {
      Console.WriteLine("***** Value of VehicleDescriptionAttribute *****\n");
      ReflectOnAttributesUsingEarlyBinding();
      Console.ReadLine();
    }

    private static void ReflectOnAttributesUsingEarlyBinding()
    {
      // Get a Type representing the Winnebago.
      Type t = typeof(Winnebago);

      // Get all attributes on the Winnebago.
      object[] customAtts = t.GetCustomAttributes(false);

      // Print the description.
      foreach (VehicleDescriptionAttribute v in customAtts)
        Console.WriteLine("-> {0}\n", v.Description);
    }
  }
}
```

The Type.GetCustomAttributes() method returns an object array that represents all the attributes applied to the member represented by the Type (the Boolean parameter controls whether the search should extend up the inheritance chain). Once you have obtained the list of attributes, iterate over each VehicleDescriptionAttribute class and print out the value obtained by the Description property.

■ **Source Code** The VehicleDescriptionAttributeReader project is included under the Chapter 15 subdirectory.

Reflecting on Attributes Using Late Binding

The previous example made use of early binding to print out the vehicle description data for the Winnebago type. This was possible due to the fact that the VehicleDescriptionAttribute class type was defined as a public member in the AttributedCarLibrary assembly. It is also possible to make use of dynamic loading and late binding to reflect over attributes.

Create a new project called VehicleDescriptionAttributeReaderLateBinding and copy AttributedCarLibrary.dll to the project's \bin\Debug directory. Now, update your Program class as follows:

```
using System;
using System.Collections.Generic;
using System.Linq;
using System.Text;

using System.Reflection;

namespace VehicleDescriptionAttributeReaderLateBinding
{
  class Program
  {
    static void Main(string[] args)
    {
      Console.WriteLine("***** Value of VehicleDescriptionAttribute *****\n");
      ReflectAttributesUsingLateBinding();
      Console.ReadLine();
    }

    private static void ReflectAttributesUsingLateBinding()
    {
      try
      {
        // Load the local copy of AttributedCarLibrary.
        Assembly asm = Assembly.Load("AttributedCarLibrary");

        // Get type info of VehicleDescriptionAttribute.
        Type vehicleDesc =
          asm.GetType("AttributedCarLibrary.VehicleDescriptionAttribute");
```

```
    // Get type info of the Description property.
    PropertyInfo propDesc = vehicleDesc.GetProperty("Description");

    // Get all types in the assembly.
    Type[] types = asm.GetTypes();

    // Iterate over each type and obtain any VehicleDescriptionAttributes.
    foreach (Type t in types)
    {
      object[] objs = t.GetCustomAttributes(vehicleDesc, false);

      // Iterate over each VehicleDescriptionAttribute and print
      // the description using late binding.
      foreach (object o in objs)
      {
        Console.WriteLine("-> {0}: {1}\n",
          t.Name, propDesc.GetValue(o, null));
      }
    }
  }
  catch (Exception ex)
  {
    Console.WriteLine(ex.Message);
  }
}
}
}
```

If you were able to follow along with the examples in this chapter, this code should be (more or less) self-explanatory. The only point of interest is the use of the PropertyInfo.GetValue() method, which is used to trigger the property's accessor. Here is the output of the current example:

```
***** Value of VehicleDescriptionAttribute *****

-> Motorcycle: My rocking Harley

-> HorseAndBuggy: The old gray mare, she ain't what she used to be...

-> Winnebago: A very long, slow, but feature-rich auto
```

■ **Source Code** The VehicleDescriptionAttributeReaderLateBinding project is included under the Chapter 15 subdirectory.

Putting Reflection, Late Binding, and Custom Attributes in Perspective

Even though you have seen numerous examples of these techniques in action, you may still be wondering when to make use of reflection, dynamic loading, late binding, and custom attributes in your programs? To be sure, these topics can seem a bit on the academic side of programming (which may or may not be a bad thing, depending on your point of view). To help map these topics to a real-world situation, you need a solid example. Assume for the moment that you are on a programming team that is building an application with the following requirement:

- The product must be extendable by the use of additional third-party tools.

What exactly is meant by *extendable*? Well, consider the Visual Studio IDE. When this application was developed, various "hooks" were inserted into the code base to allow other software vendors to "snap" (or plug in) custom modules into the IDE. Obviously, the Visual Studio development team had no way to set references to external .NET assemblies it had not developed yet (thus, no early binding), so how exactly would an application provide the required hooks? Here is one possible way to solve this problem:

- First, an extendable application must provide some input vehicle to allow the user to specify the module to plug in (such as a dialog box or command-line flag). This requires *dynamic loading*.

- Second, an extendable application must be able to determine whether the module supports the correct functionality (such as a set of required interfaces) in order to be plugged into the environment. This requires *reflection*.

- Finally, an extendable application must obtain a reference to the required infrastructure (such as a set of interface types) and invoke the members to trigger the underlying functionality. This may require *late binding*.

Simply put, if the extendable application has been preprogrammed to query for specific interfaces, it is able to determine at runtime whether the type can be activated. Once this verification test has been passed, the type in question may support additional interfaces that provide a polymorphic fabric to their functionality. This is the exact approach taken by the Visual Studio team, and despite what you might be thinking, is not at all difficult!

Building an Extendable Application

In the sections that follow, I will take you through a complete example that illustrates the process of building an extendable Windows Forms application that can be augmented by the functionality of external assemblies. If you do not have some experience building GUIs with the Windows Forms API, you might wish to load up the provided solution code and follow along.

■ **Note** Windows Forms was the initial desktop API of the .NET platform. However, since the release of .NET 3.0, the Windows Presentation Foundation (WPF) API is quickly becoming the preferred GUI framework. While this is true, I will make use of Windows Forms for a number of client GUI examples in this text, as the related code is a bit more intuitive than the corresponding WPF code.

If you are not familiar with the process of building Windows Forms applications, feel free to simply open up the supplied sample code and follow along. To serve as a road map, our extendable application entails the following assemblies:

- CommonSnappableTypes.dll: This assembly contains type definitions that will be used by each snap-in object and will be directly referenced by the Windows Forms application.

- CSharpSnapIn.dll: A snap-in written in C#, which leverages the types of CommonSnappableTypes.dll.

- VbSnapIn.dll: A snap-in written in Visual Basic, which leverages the types of CommonSnappableTypes.dll.

- MyExtendableApp.exe: This Windows Forms application will be the entity that may be extended by the functionality of each snap-in.

Again, this application will make use of dynamic loading, reflection, and late binding to dynamically gain the functionality of assemblies it has no prior knowledge of.

Building CommonSnappableTypes.dll

The first order of business is to create an assembly that contains the types that a given snap-in must leverage to be plugged into the expandable Windows Forms application. The CommonSnappableTypes Class Library project defines two types:

```
namespace CommonSnappableTypes
{
  public interface IAppFunctionality
  {
    void DoIt();
  }

  [AttributeUsage(AttributeTargets.Class)]
  public sealed class CompanyInfoAttribute : System.Attribute
  {
    public string CompanyName { get; set; }
    public string CompanyUrl { get; set; }
  }
}
```

The IAppFunctionality interface provides a polymorphic interface for all snap-ins that can be consumed by the extendable Windows Forms application. Given that this example is purely illustrative, you supply a single method named DoIt(). A more realistic interface (or a set of interfaces) might allow the object to generate scripting code, render an image onto the application's toolbox, or integrate into the main menu of the hosting application.

The CompanyInfoAttribute type is a custom attribute that can be applied on any class type that wishes to be snapped into the container. As you can tell by the definition of this class, [CompanyInfo] allows the developer of the snap-in to provide some basic details about the component's point of origin.

Building the C# Snap-In

Next up, you need to create a type that implements the IAppFunctionality interface. Again, to focus on the overall design of an extendable application, a trivial type is in order. Assume a new C# Class Library project named CSharpSnapIn defines a class type named CSharpModule. Given that this class must make use of the types defined in CommonSnappableTypes, be sure to set a reference to the CommonSnappableTypes assembly (as well as System.Windows.Forms.dll to display a noteworthy message). This being said, here is the code:

```
using System;
using System.Collections.Generic;
using System.Linq;
using System.Text;

using CommonSnappableTypes;
using System.Windows.Forms;

namespace CSharpSnapIn
{
  [CompanyInfo(CompanyName = "My Company",
      CompanyUrl = "www.MyCompany.com")]
  public class CSharpModule : IAppFunctionality
  {
    void IAppFunctionality.DoIt()
    {
      MessageBox.Show("You have just used the C# snap-in!");
    }
  }
}
```

Notice that I choose to make use of explicit interface implementation (see Chapter 9) when supporting the IAppFunctionality interface. This is not required; however, the idea is that the only part of the system that needs to directly interact with this interface type is the hosting Windows application. By explicitly implementing this interface, the DoIt() method is not directly exposed from the CSharpModule type.

Building the Visual Basic Snap-In

Now, to simulate the role of a third-party vendor who prefers Visual Basic over C#, create a new Visual Basic Class Library (VbSnapIn) that references the same external assemblies as the previous CSharpSnapIn project.

■ **Note** By default, a Visual Basic project will not display the References folder within the Solution Explorer. To add references in a VB project, use the Project ➤ Add Reference… menu option of Visual Studio.

The code is (again) intentionally simple.

```
Imports System.Windows.Forms
Imports CommonSnappableTypes

<CompanyInfo(CompanyName:="Chucky's Software", CompanyUrl:="www.ChuckySoft.com")>
Public Class VbSnapIn
  Implements IAppFunctionality

  Public Sub DoIt() Implements CommonSnappableTypes.IAppFunctionality.DoIt
    MessageBox.Show("You have just used the VB snap in!")
  End Sub
End Class
```

Notice that applying attributes in the syntax of Visual Basic requires angle brackets (< >) rather than square brackets ([ ]). Also notice that the Implements keyword is used to implement interface types on a given class or structure.

Building an Extendable Windows Forms Application

The final step is to create a new C# Windows Forms application (MyExtendableApp) that allows the user to select a snap-in using a standard Windows Open dialog box. If you have not created a Windows Forms application before, begin this final project of the chapter by selecting a Windows Forms Application project from the New Project dialog box of Visual Studio (see Figure 15-7).

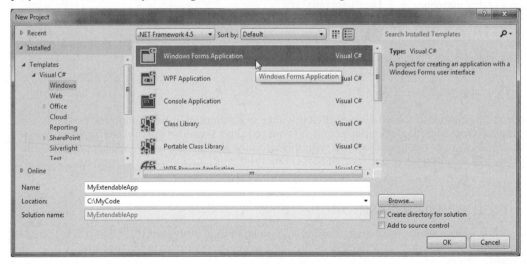

Figure 15-7. Creating a new Windows Forms project with Visual Studio

Now, set a reference to the CommonSnappableTypes.dll assembly, but *not* the CSharpSnapIn.dll or VbSnapIn.dll code libraries. As well, import the System.Reflection and CommonSnappableTypes namespaces into your form's primary code file (which you can open by right-clicking on the form designer and selecting View Code). Remember that the whole goal of this application is to make use of late binding and reflection to determine the "snapability" of independent binaries created by third-party vendors.

Again, I won't bother to examine all the details of Windows Forms development at this point in the text (see Appendix A). However, assuming you have placed a MenuStrip component onto the form designer, define a topmost menu item named File that provides a single submenu named Snap In Module. As well, the main window will contain a ListBox type (which I renamed as lstLoadedSnapIns) that will be used to display the names of each snap-in loaded by the user. Figure 15-8 shows the final GUI.

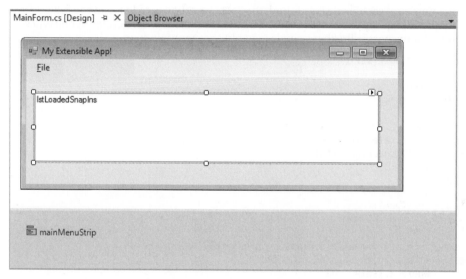

Figure 15-8. GUI for MyExtendableApp

The code that handles the Click event for the File ▸ Snap In Module menu item (which may be created simply by double-clicking the menu item from the design-time editor) displays a File Open dialog box and extracts the path to the selected file. Assuming the user did not select the CommonSnappableTypes.dll assembly (as this is purely infrastructure), the path is then sent into a helper function named LoadExternalModule() for processing (implemented next). This method will return false when it is unable to find a class implementing IAppFunctionality.

```
private void snapInModuleToolStripMenuItem_Click(object sender,
  EventArgs e)
{
  // Allow user to select an assembly to load.
  OpenFileDialog dlg = new OpenFileDialog();
  if (dlg.ShowDialog() == DialogResult.OK)
  {
    if(dlg.FileName.Contains("CommonSnappableTypes"))
      MessageBox.Show("CommonSnappableTypes has no snap-ins!");
```

```
      else if(!LoadExternalModule(dlg.FileName))
        MessageBox.Show("Nothing implements IAppFunctionality!");
    }
  }
```

The LoadExternalModule() method performs the following tasks:

- Dynamically loads the selected assembly into memory

- Determines whether the assembly contains any types implementing IAppFunctionality

- Creates the type using late binding

If a type implementing IAppFunctionality is found, the DoIt() method is called, and the fully qualified name of the type is added to the ListBox (note that the foreach loop will iterate over all types in the assembly to account for the possibility that a single assembly has multiple snap-ins).

```
private bool LoadExternalModule(string path)
{
  bool foundSnapIn = false;
  Assembly theSnapInAsm = null;
  try
  {
    // Dynamically load the selected assembly.
    theSnapInAsm = Assembly.LoadFrom(path);
  }
  catch(Exception ex)
  {
    MessageBox.Show(ex.Message);
    return foundSnapIn;
  }
  // Get all IAppFunctionality-compatible classes in assembly.
  var theClassTypes = from t in theSnapInAsm.GetTypes()
                      where t.IsClass &&
                      (t.GetInterface("IAppFunctionality") != null)
                      select t;
  // Now, create the object and call DoIt() method.
  foreach (Type t in theClassTypes)
  {
    foundSnapIn = true;
    // Use late binding to create the type.
    IAppFunctionality itfApp =
      (IAppFunctionality)theSnapInAsm.CreateInstance(t.FullName, true);
    itfApp.DoIt();
    lstLoadedSnapIns.Items.Add(t.FullName);
  }
  return foundSnapIn;
}
```

At this point, you can run your application. When you select the CSharpSnapIn.dll or VbSnapIn.dll assemblies, you should see the correct message displayed. The final task is to display the metadata provided by the [CompanyInfo] attribute. To do so, update LoadExternalModule() to call a new helper function named DisplayCompanyData() before exiting the foreach scope. Notice this method takes a single System.Type parameter.

```
private bool LoadExternalModule(string path)
{
...
  foreach (Type t in theClassTypes)
  {
...
    // Show company info.
    DisplayCompanyData(t);
  }
  return foundSnapIn;
}
```

Using the incoming type, simply reflect over the [CompanyInfo] attribute, like so:

```
private void DisplayCompanyData(Type t)
{
  // Get [CompanyInfo] data.
  var compInfo = from ci in t.GetCustomAttributes(false) where
                 (ci.GetType() == typeof(CompanyInfoAttribute))
                 select ci;
  // Show data.
  foreach (CompanyInfoAttribute c in compInfo)
  {
    MessageBox.Show(c.CompanyUrl,
      string.Format("More info about {0} can be found at", c.CompanyName));
  }
}
```

Figure 15-9 shows one possible run.

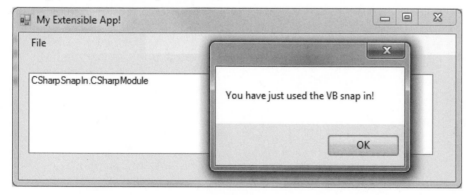

Figure 15-9. Snapping in external assemblies

Excellent! That wraps up the example application. I hope you can see that the topics presented in this chapter can be quite helpful in the real world and are not limited to the tool builders of the world.

■ **Source Code** The ExtendableApp folder under the Chapter 15 subdirectory contains the CommonSnappableTypes, CSharpSnapln, VbSnapln, and MyExtendableApp projects.

Summary

Reflection is a very interesting aspect of a robust OO environment. In the world of .NET, the keys to reflection services revolve around the System.Type class and the System.Reflection namespace. As you have seen, reflection is the process of placing a type under the magnifying glass at runtime to understand the who, what, where, when, why, and how of a given item.

Late binding is the process of creating a type and invoking its members without prior knowledge of the specific names of said members. Late binding is often a direct result of *dynamic loading*, which allows you to load a .NET assembly into memory programmatically. As shown during this chapter's extendable application example, this is a very powerful technique used by tool builders as well as tool consumers.

This chapter also examined the role of attribute-based programming. When you adorn your types with attributes, the result is the augmentation of the underlying assembly metadata.

## CHAPTER 16

Dynamic Types and the Dynamic Language Runtime

.NET 4.0 introduced a new keyword to the C# language, specifically, dynamic. This keyword allows you to incorporate scripting-like behaviors into the strongly typed world of type safety, semicolons, and curly brackets. Using this loose typing, you can greatly simplify some complex coding tasks and also gain the ability to interoperate with a number of dynamic languages (such as IronRuby or IronPython), which are .NET savvy.

In this chapter, you will learn about the C# dynamic keyword, and understand how loosely typed calls are mapped to the correct in-memory object using the *Dynamic Language Runtime* (or DLR). After you understand the services provided by the DLR, you will see examples of using dynamic types to streamline how you can perform late-bound method calls (via reflection services) and to easily communicate with legacy COM libraries.

■ **Note** Don't confuse the C# dynamic keyword with the concept of a *dynamic assembly* (see Chapter 18). While you could use the dynamic keyword when building a dynamic assembly, these are ultimately two independent concepts.

The Role of the C# dynamic Keyword

Back in Chapter 3, you learned about the var keyword, which allows you to define local variables in such a way that the underlying date type is determined at compile time, based on the initial assignment (recall that this is termed *implicit typing*). Once this initial assignment has been made, you have a strongly typed variable, and any attempt to assign an incompatible value will result in a compiler error.

To begin your investigation into the C# dynamic keyword, create a new Console Application named DynamicKeyword. Now, author the following method in your Program class, and verify that the final code statement will indeed trigger a compile time error if uncommented:

```
static void ImplicitlyTypedVariable()
{
    // a is of type List<int>.
    var a = new List<int>();
    a.Add(90);
```

```
    // This would be a compile-time error!
    // a = "Hello";
}
```

Using implicit typing simply for the sake of doing so is considered by many to be bad style (if you know you need a List<int>, just declare a List<int>). However, as you have seen in Chapter 12, implicit typing is very useful with LINQ, as many LINQ queries return back enumerations of anonymous class (via projections) which you cannot directly declare in your C# code. However, even in such cases, the implicitly typed variable is, in fact, strongly typed.

On a related note, as you learned back in Chapter 6, System.Object is the topmost parent class in the .NET framework, and can represent anything at all. Again, if you declare a variable of type object, you have a strongly typed piece of data; however, what it points to in memory can differ based on your assignment of the reference. In order to gain access to the members the object reference is pointing to in memory, you need to perform an explicit cast.

Assume you have a simple class named Person that defines two automatic properties (FirstName and LastName) both encapsulating a string. Now, observe the following code:

```
static void UseObjectVarible()
{
    // Assume we have a class named Person.
    object o = new Person() { FirstName = "Mike", LastName = "Larson" };

    // Must cast object as Person to gain access
    // to the Person properties.
    Console.WriteLine("Person's first name is {0}", ((Person)o).FirstName);
}
```

With the release of .NET 4.0, the C# language introduced a keyword named dynamic. From a high level, you can consider the dynamic keyword a specialized form of System.Object, in that any value can be assigned to a dynamic data type. At first glance, this can appear horribly confusing, as it appears you now have three ways to define data whose underlying type is not directly indicated in our code base. For example, this method:

```
static void PrintThreeStrings()
{
    var s1 = "Greetings";
    object s2 = "From";
    dynamic s3 = "Minneapolis";

    Console.WriteLine("s1 is of type: {0}", s1.GetType());
    Console.WriteLine("s2 is of type: {0}", s2.GetType());
    Console.WriteLine("s3 is of type: {0}", s3.GetType());
}
```

would print out the following if invoked from Main():

```
s1 is of type: System.String
s2 is of type: System.String
s3 is of type: System.String
```

What makes a dynamic variable much (much) different from a variable declared implicitly or via a System.Object reference is that it is *not strongly typed*. Said another way, dynamic data is not *statically typed*. As far as the C# compiler is concerned, a data point declared with the dynamic keyword can be assigned any initial value at all, and can be reassigned to any new (and possibly unrelated) value during its lifetime. Consider the following method, and the resulting output:

```
static void ChangeDynamicDataType()
{
  // Declare a single dynamic data point
  // named "t".
  dynamic t = "Hello!";
  Console.WriteLine("t is of type: {0}", t.GetType());

  t = false;
  Console.WriteLine("t is of type: {0}", t.GetType());

  t = new List<int>();
  Console.WriteLine("t is of type: {0}", t.GetType());
}
```

```
t is of type: System.String
t is of type: System.Boolean
t is of type: System.Collections.Generic.List`1[System.Int32]
```

Now, at this point in your investigation, do be aware that the previous code would compile and execute identically if you were to declare the t variable as a System.Object. However, as you will soon see, the dynamic keyword offers many additional features.

Calling Members on Dynamically Declared Data

Now, given that a dynamic data type can take on the identity of any type on the fly (just like a variable of type System.Object), the next question on your mind might be about calling members on the dynamic variable (properties, methods, indexers, register with events, etc.). Well, syntactically speaking, it will again look no different. Just apply the dot operator to the dynamic data variable, specify a public member, and supply any arguments (if required).

However (and this is a very big "however"), the validity of the members you specify will not be checked by the compiler! Remember, unlike a variable defined as a System.Object, dynamic data is not statically typed. It is not until runtime that you will know if the dynamic data you invoked supports a specified member, if you passed in the correct parameters, spelled the member correctly, and so on. Thus, as strange as it might seem, the following method compiles perfectly:

```
static void InvokeMembersOnDynamicData()
{
  dynamic textData1 = "Hello";
```

```
  Console.WriteLine(textData1.ToUpper());

  // You would expect compiler errors here!
  // But they compile just fine.
  Console.WriteLine(textData1.toupper());
  Console.WriteLine(textData1.Foo(10, "ee", DateTime.Now));
}
```

Notice the second call to WriteLine() attempts to call a method named toupper() on the dynamic data point. As you can see, textData1 is of type string and, therefore, you know it does not have a method of this name in all lowercase letters. Furthermore, string certainly does not have a method named Foo() that takes an int, string, and DateTime object!

Nevertheless, the C# compiler is satisfied. However, if you invoke this method from within Main(), you will get runtime errors similar to the following output:

```
Unhandled Exception: Microsoft.CSharp.RuntimeBinder.RuntimeBinderException:
'string' does not contain a definition for 'toupper'
```

Another very big distinction between calling members on dynamic data and strongly typed data is that when you apply the dot operator to a piece of dynamic data, you will *not* see the expected Visual Studio IntelliSense. Instead, you will find the general message shown in Figure 16-1.

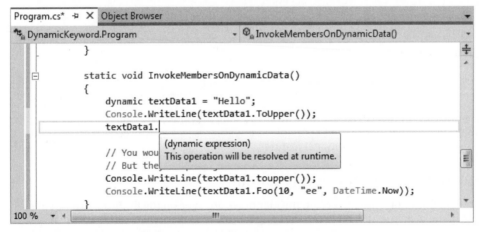

Figure 16-1. *Dynamic data will not activate IntelliSense*

It should make sense that IntelliSense is not possible with dynamic data. However, remember that this means you need to be extremely careful when you are typing C# code on such data points. Any misspelling or incorrect capitalization of a member will throw a runtime error, specifically an instance of the RuntimeBinderException class.

The Role of the Microsoft.CSharp.dll Assembly

When you create a new Visual Studio C# project, you will automatically have a reference set to an assembly named Microsoft.CSharp.dll (you can see this for yourself by looking in the References folder of the Solution Explorer). This library is very small, and defines only a single namespace (Microsoft.CSharp.RuntimeBinder) with two classes (see Figure 16-2).

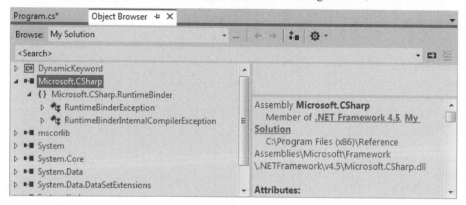

Figure 16-2. The Microsoft.CSharp.dll assembly

As you can tell by their names, both of these classes are strongly typed exceptions. The most common class, RuntimeBinderException, represents an error that will be thrown if you attempt to invoke a member on a dynamic data type, which does not actually exist (as in the case of the toupper() and Foo() methods). This same error will be raised if you specify the wrong parameter data to a member that does exist.

Because dynamic data is so volatile, whenever you are invoking members on a variable declared with the C# dynamic keyword, you could wrap the calls within a proper try/catch block, and handle the error in a graceful manner, like so:

```
static void InvokeMembersOnDynamicData()
{
  dynamic textData1 = "Hello";

  try
  {
    Console.WriteLine(textData1.ToUpper());
    Console.WriteLine(textData1.toupper());
    Console.WriteLine(textData1.Foo(10, "ee", DateTime.Now));
  }
  catch (Microsoft.CSharp.RuntimeBinder.RuntimeBinderException ex)
  {
    Console.WriteLine(ex.Message);
  }
}
```

If you call this method again, you will find the call to ToUpper() (note the capital T and U) works correctly; however, you then find the error data displayed to the console:

```
HELLO
'string' does not contain a definition for 'toupper'
```

Of course, the process of wrapping all dynamic method invocations in a try/catch block is rather tedious. As long as you watch your spelling, and parameter passing, this is not required. However, catching exceptions is handy when you might not know in advance if a member will be present on the target type.

The Scope of the dynamic Keyword

Recall that implicitly typed data (declared with the var keyword) is only possible for local variables in a member scope. The var keyword can never be used as a return value, a parameter, or a member of a class/structure. This is not the case with the dynamic keyword however. Consider the following class definition:

```
class VeryDynamicClass
{
  // A dynamic field.
  private static dynamic myDynamicField;

  // A dynamic property.
  public dynamic DynamicProperty { get; set; }

  // A dynamic return type and a dynamic paramater type.
  public dynamic DynamicMethod(dynamic dynamicParam)
  {
    // A dynamic local variable.
    dynamic dynamicLocalVar = "Local variable";

    int myInt = 10;

    if (dynamicParam is int)
    {
      return dynamicLocalVar;
    }
    else
    {
      return myInt;
    }
  }
}
```

You could now invoke the public members as expected; however, as you are operating on dynamic methods and properties, you cannot be completely sure what the data type will be! To be sure, the VeryDynamicClass definition might not be very useful in a real-world application, but it does illustrate the scope of where you can apply this C# keyword.

Limitations of the dynamic Keyword

While a great many things can be defined using the dynamic keyword, there are some limitations regarding its usage. While they are not show-stoppers, do know that a dynamic data item cannot make use of lambda expressions or C# anonymous methods when calling a method. For example, the following code will always result in errors, even if the target method does indeed take a delegate parameter that takes a string value and returns void.

```
dynamic a = GetDynamicObject();

// Error! Methods on dynamic data can't use lambdas!
a.Method(arg => Console.WriteLine(arg));
```

To circumvent this restriction, you will need to work with the underlying delegate directly, using the techniques described in Chapter 10. Another limitation is that a dynamic point of data cannot understand any extension methods (see Chapter 11). Unfortunately, this would also include any of the extension methods that come from the LINQ APIs. Therefore, a variable declared with the dynamic keyword has very limited use within LINQ to Objects and other LINQ technologies.

```
dynamic a = GetDynamicObject();

// Error! Dynamic data can't find the Select() extension method!
var data = from d in a select d;
```

Practical Uses of the dynamic Keyword

Given the fact that dynamic data is not strongly typed, not checked at compile time, has no ability to trigger IntelliSense and cannot be the target of a LINQ query, you are absolutely correct to assume that using the dynamic keyword just for the sake of doing so is very poor programming practice.

However, in a few circumstances, the dynamic keyword can radically reduce the amount of code you need to author by hand. Specifically, if you are building a .NET application that makes heavy use of late binding (via reflection), the dynamic keyword can save you typing time. As well, if you are building a .NET application that needs to communicate with legacy COM libraries (such as Microsoft Office products), you can greatly simplify your codebase via the dynamic keyword.

Like any "shortcut," you need to weigh the pros and cons. The use of the dynamic keyword is a trade-off between brevity of code, and type safety. While C# is a strongly typed language at its core, you can opt in (or opt out) of dynamic behaviors on a call-by-call basis. Always remember that you never need to use the dynamic keyword. You could always get to the same end result by authoring alternative code by hand (and typically much more of it).

■ **Source Code** The DynamicKeyword project is located under the Chapter 16 subdirectory.

The Role of the Dynamic Language Runtime (DLR)

Now that you better understand what "dynamic data" is all about, let's learn how it is processed. With the release of .NET 4.0, the Common Language Runtime (CLR) was supplemented with a complementary runtime environment named the Dynamic Language Runtime (DLR). The concept of a "dynamic runtime" is certainly not new. In fact, many programming languages such as Smalltalk, LISP, Ruby, and Python have used it for years. In a nutshell, a dynamic runtime allows a dynamic language the ability to discover types completely at runtime with no compile-time checks.

If you have a background in strongly typed languages (including C#, without dynamic types), the very notion of such a runtime might seem undesirable. After all, you typically want to receive compile-time errors, not runtime errors, wherever possible. Nevertheless, dynamic languages/runtimes do provide some interesting features, including the following:

- An extremely flexible code base. You can refactor code without making numerous changes to data types.

- A very simple way to interoperate with diverse object types built in different platforms and programming languages.

- A way to add or remove members to a type, in memory, at runtime.

One role of the DLR is to enable various dynamic languages to run with the .NET runtime and give them a way to interoperate with other .NET code. Two popular dynamic languages that make use of the DLR are IronPython and IronRuby. These languages live in a dynamic universe, where type is discovered solely at runtime. And yet, these languages have access to the richness of the .NET base class libraries. Even better, their codebases can interoperate with C# (or vice versa), thanks to the inclusion of the dynamic keyword.

■ **Note** This chapter will not address how the DLR can be used to integrate with dynamic languages. However, details can be found at the IronPython (http://ironpython.codeplex.com) and IronRuby (http://rubyforge.org/projects/ironruby) web sites.

The Role of Expression Trees

The DLR makes use of *expression trees* to capture the meaning of a dynamic call in neutral terms. For example, when the DLR encounters some C# code, such as the following:

```
dynamic d = GetSomeData();
d.SuperMethod(12);
```

it will automatically build an expression tree that says, in effect, "Call the method named SuperMethod on object d, passing in the number 12 as an argument." This information (formally termed the *payload*) is then passed to the correct runtime binder, which again could be the C# dynamic binder, the IronPython dynamic binder, or even (as explained shortly) legacy COM objects.

From here, the request is mapped into the required call structure for the target object. The nice thing about these expression trees (beyond the fact that you don't need to manually create them) is that this allows us to write a fixed C# code statement, and not worry about what the underlying target actually is (COM object, IronPython, IronRuby codebase, etc.). Figure 16-3 illustrates the concept of expression trees from a high level.

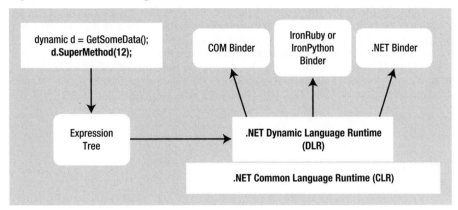

Figure 16-3. Expression trees capture dynamic calls in neutral terms and are processed by binders

The Role of the System.Dynamic Namespace

The System.Core.dll assembly includes a namespace named System.Dynamic. Truth be told, the chances are quite high that you will never need to use the types located here. However, if you were a language vendor, who wanted to enable their dynamic languages to interact with the DLR, you could make use of the System.Dynamic namespace to build a custom runtime binder.

Again, you won't need to directly dig into the types of System.Dynamic in this book; however, feel free to check it out using the .NET Framework 4.5 SDK documentation if you are interested. For practical purposes, simply know that this namespace provides the necessary infrastructure to make a dynamic language ".NET aware."

Dynamic Runtime Lookup of Expression Trees

As explained, the DLR will pass the expression trees to a target object; however, this dispatching will be influenced by a few factors. If the dynamic data type is pointing in memory to a COM object, the expression tree is sent to a low-level COM interface named IDispatch. As you might know, this interface was COM's way of incorporating its own set of dynamic services. COM objects, however, can be used in a .NET application without the use of the DLR or C# dynamic keyword. Doing so, however, (as you will see) tends to result in much more complex C# coding.

If the dynamic data is not pointing to a COM object, the expression tree may be passed to an object implementing the IDynamicObject interface. This interface is used behind the scenes to allow a language, such as IronRuby, to take a DLR expression tree and map it to Ruby specifics.

Finally, if the dynamic data is pointing to an object that is *not* a COM object and does *not* implement IDynamicObject, the object is a normal, everyday .NET object. In this case, the expression tree is dispatched to the C# runtime binder for processing. The process of mapping the expression tree to .NET specifics involves reflection services.

After the expression tree has been processed by a given binder, the dynamic data will be resolved to the real in-memory data type, after which the correct method is called with any necessary parameters. Now, let's see a few practical uses of the DLR, beginning with the simplification of late-bound .NET calls.

Simplifying Late-Bound Calls Using Dynamic Types

One instance where you might decide to use the dynamic keyword is when you are working with reflection services, specifically when making late-bound method calls. Back in Chapter 15, you saw a few examples of when this type of method call can be very useful, most commonly when you are building some type of extensible application. At that time, you learned how to use the Activator.CreateInstance() method to create an object, for which you have no compile-time knowledge of (beyond its display name). You can then make use of the types of the System.Reflection namespace to invoke members via late binding. Recall the following example from Chapter 15:

```
static void CreateUsingLateBinding(Assembly asm)
{
  try
  {
    // Get metadata for the Minivan type.
    Type miniVan = asm.GetType("CarLibrary.MiniVan");

    // Create the Minivan on the fly.
    object obj = Activator.CreateInstance(miniVan);

    // Get info for TurboBoost.
    MethodInfo mi = miniVan.GetMethod("TurboBoost");

    // Invoke method ("null" for no parameters).
    mi.Invoke(obj, null);
  }
  catch (Exception ex)
  {
    Console.WriteLine(ex.Message);
  }
}
```

While this is code works as expected, you might agree it is a bit clunky. Here, you have to manually make use of the MethodInfo class, manually query the metadata, and so forth. The following is a version of this same method, now using the C# dynamic keyword and the DLR:

```
static void InvokeMethodWithDynamicKeyword(Assembly asm)
{
  try
  {
    // Get metadata for the Minivan type.
    Type miniVan = asm.GetType("CarLibrary.MiniVan");

    // Create the Minivan on the fly and call method!
    dynamic obj = Activator.CreateInstance(miniVan);
    obj.TurboBoost();
  }
  catch (Exception ex)
  {
    Console.WriteLine(ex.Message);
  }
}
```

By declaring the obj variable using the dynamic keyword, the heavy lifting of reflection is done on your behalf, courtesy of the DRL.

Leveraging the dynamic Keyword to Pass Arguments

The usefulness of the DLR becomes even more obvious when you need to make late-bound calls on methods that take parameters. When you use "longhand" reflection calls, arguments need to be packaged up as an array of objects, which are passed to the Invoke() method of MethodInfo.

To illustrate using a fresh example, begin by creating a new C# Console Application named LateBindingWithDynamic. Next, add a Class Library project to the current solution (using the File ➤ Add New Project... menu option) named MathLibrary. Rename the initial Class1.cs of the MathLibrary project to SimpleMath.cs, and implement the class like so:

```
public class SimpleMath
{
  public int Add(int x, int y)
  {
    return x + y;
  }
}
```

After you have compiled your MathLibrary.dll assembly, place a copy of this library in the \bin\Debug folder of the LateBindingWithDynamic project (if you click the Show All Files button for each project of the Solution Explorer, you can simply drag and drop the file between projects). At this point, your Solution Explorer should look something like Figure 16-4.

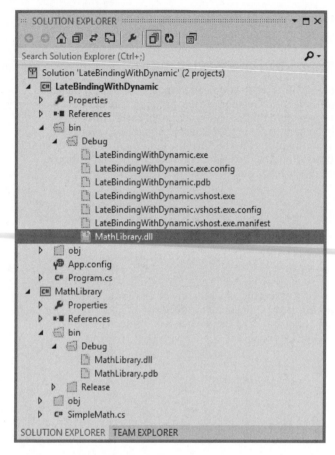

Figure 16-4. The LateBindingWithDynamic project has a private copy of MathLibrary.dll

---

■ **Note** Remember, the whole point of late binding is to allow an application to create an object for which it has no record of in the manifest. This is why you manually copied MathLibrary.dll into the output folder of the Console project, rather than reference the assembly using Visual Studio.

Now, import the System.Reflection namespace into the Program.cs file of your Console Application project. Next, add the following method to the Program class, which invokes the Add() method using typical reflection API calls:

```
private static void AddWithReflection()
{
  Assembly asm = Assembly.Load("MathLibrary");
```

```
  try
  {
    // Get metadata for the SimpleMath type.
    Type math = asm.GetType("MathLibrary.SimpleMath");

    // Create a SimpleMath on the fly.
    object obj = Activator.CreateInstance(math);

    // Get info for Add.
    MethodInfo mi = math.GetMethod("Add");

    // Invoke method (with parameters).
    object[] args = { 10, 70 };
    Console.WriteLine("Result is: {0}", mi.Invoke(obj, args));
  }
  catch (Exception ex)
  {
    Console.WriteLine(ex.Message);
  }
}
```

Now, consider the simplification of the previous logic with the dynamic keyword, via the following new method:

```
private static void AddWithDynamic()
{
  Assembly asm = Assembly.Load("MathLibrary");

  try
  {
    // Get metadata for the SimpleMath type.
    Type math = asm.GetType("MathLibrary.SimpleMath");

    // Create a SimpleMath on the fly.
    dynamic obj = Activator.CreateInstance(math);
    Console.WriteLine("Result is: {0}", obj.Add(10, 70));
  }
  catch (Microsoft.CSharp.RuntimeBinder.RuntimeBinderException ex)
  {
    Console.WriteLine(ex.Message);
  }
}
```

Not too shabby! If you call both methods from the Main() method, you'll see identical output. However, when using the dynamic keyword, you saved yourself quite a bit of work. With dynamically defined data, you no longer need to manually package up arguments as an array of objects, query the assembly metadata, or other such details. If you are building an application that makes heavy use of dynamic loading/late binding, I am sure you can see how these code savings would add up over time.

■ **Source Code** The LateBindingWithDynamic project is included under the Chapter 16 subdirectory.

Simplifying COM Interoperability Using Dynamic Data

Let's see another useful case for the dynamic keyword within the context of a COM interoperability project. Now, if you don't have much background in COM development, do be aware for this next example that a compiled COM library contains metadata, just like a .NET library; however, the format is completely different. Because of this, if a .NET program needs to communicate with a COM object, the first order of business is to generate what is known as an *interop assembly* (described in the following paragraphs). Doing so is quite straightforward. Just activate the Add Reference dialog box, select the COM tab and find the COM library you want to make use of (see Figure 16-5).

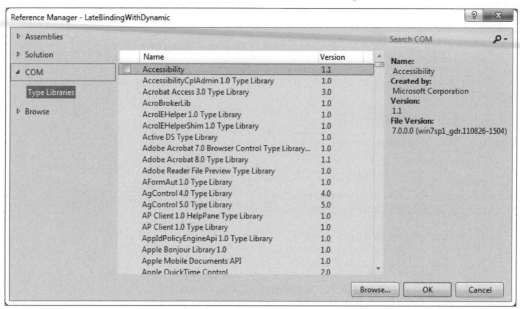

Figure 16-5. The COM tab of the Add Reference dialog box will show you all registered COM libraries on your machine

---

■ **Note** Be aware that several important Microsoft object models (including Office products) are currently accessible only through COM interoperability. Thus, even if you do not have direct experience building COM applications, you might need to consume them from a .NET program.

Once you select a COM library, the IDE will respond by generating a brand new assembly that contains .NET descriptions of COM metadata. Formally speaking, these are termed *interoperability assemblies* (or simply, *interop assemblies*). Interop assemblies do not contain any implementation code, except for a small amount that helps translate COM events to .NET events. However, these interop assemblies are very useful in that they shield your .NET codebase from the complex underbelly of COM internals.

In your C# code, you can directly program against the interop assembly, allowing the CLR (and if you use the dynamic keyword, the DLR) to automatically map .NET data types into COM types, and vice versa. Behind the scenes, data is marshaled between the .NET and COM applications using a Runtime Callable Wrapper (RCW), which is basically a dynamically generated proxy. This RCW proxy will marshal and transform .NET data types into COM types and map any COM return values into .NET equivalents. Figure 16-6 shows the big picture of .NET to COM interoperability.

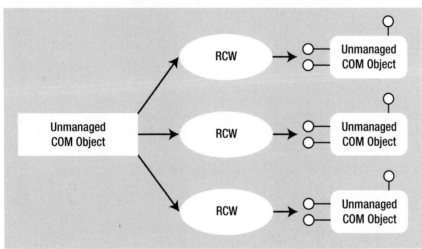

Figure 16-6. *.NET programs communicate with COM objects using a proxy termed the RCW*

The Role of Primary Interop Assemblies (PIAs)

Many COM libraries created by COM library vendors (such as the Microsoft COM libraries that allow access to the object model of Microsoft Office products) provide an "official" interoperability assembly termed a *primary interop assembly* or *PIA*. PIAs are optimized interop assemblies, which clean up (and possibly extend) the code typically generated when referencing a COM library using the Add Reference dialog box.

PIAs are typically listed in the Assemblies section of the Add Reference dialog box (under the Extensions subarea). In fact, if you reference a COM library from the COM tab of the Add Reference dialog box, Visual Studio will not generate a new interoperability library as it would normally do, but use the provided PIA instead. Figure 16-7 shows the PIA of the Microsoft Office Excel object model, which you will be using in the next example.

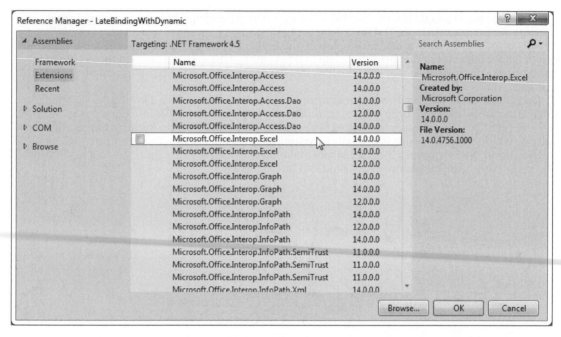

Figure 16-7. PIAs are listed in the .NET tab of the Add Reference dialog box

Embedding Interop Metadata

Before the release of .NET 4.0, when a C# application made use of a COM library (PIA or not), you needed to ensure the client machine had a copy of the interop assembly on their computer. Not only did this increase the size of your application installer package, but the install script had to check that the PIA assemblies were indeed present, and if not, install a copy to the GAC.

However, under .NET 4.0 and higher, you can now elect to embed the interoperability data directly within your compiled .NET application. When you do so, you are no longer required to ship a copy of the interoperability assembly along with your .NET application, as the necessary interoperability metadata is hardcoded in the .NET program.

By default, when you select a COM library (PIA or not) using the Add References dialog, the IDE will automatically set the Embed Interop Types property of the library to True. You can see this setting first hand by selecting a referenced interop library in the References folder of the Solution Explorer, and then investigating the Properties window (see Figure 16-8).

Figure 16-8. Interop assembly logic can be embedded directly into your .NET application

The C# compiler will only include the parts of the interop library you are actually making use of. Thus, if the real interop library has .NET descriptions of hundreds of COM objects, you will bring in only the definitions of the subset you are really making use of in your C# code. Beyond reducing the size of the application you need to ship to the client, you also have an easier installation path, as you don't need to install any missing PIAs on the target machine.

Common COM Interop Pain Points

Let's cover one more preliminary topic before the next example. Before the release of the DLR, when you authored C# code that used a COM library (via the interop assembly), you were sure to face a number of challenges. For example, many COM libraries defined methods, which took optional arguments, which were not supported in C# until .NET 3.5. This required you to specify the value Type.Missing for every occurrence of the optional argument. For example, if a COM method took five arguments, all of which were optional, you would need to write the following C# code in order to accept the default values:

```
myComObj.SomeMethod(Type.Missing, Type.Missing, Type.Missing, Type.Missing, Type.Missing);
```

Thankfully, you are now able to author the following simplified code, given that the Type.Missing values will be inserted at compile time if you don't specify a specific value.

```
myComObj.SomeMethod();
```

On a related note, many COM methods provided support for named arguments, which as you recall from Chapter 4, allows you to pass values to members in any order you require. Given that C# supports this same feature, it is very simply to "skip" over a set of optional arguments you don't care about, and only set the few you do.

Another common COM interop pain point has to do with the fact that many COM methods were designed to take and return a very particular data type, termed the Variant. Much like the C# dynamic keyword, a Variant data type could be assigned to any type of COM data on the fly (strings, interface references, numerical values, etc.). Before you had the dynamic keyword, passing or receiving Variant data points required some hoop jumping, typically by way of numerous casting operations.

When you set the Embed Interop Types property to True, all COM Variant types are automatically mapped to dynamic data. This will not only reduce the need to extraneous casting operations when working with underlying COM Variant data types, but will also further hide some COM complexities, such as working with COM indexers.

To showcase how the use of C# optional arguments, named arguments, and the dynamic keyword all work together to simplify COM interop, you will now build an application that makes use of the Microsoft Office object model. As you work through the example, you will get a chance to make use of the new features, as well as forgo them, and then compare and contrast the workload.

■ **Note** If you do not have a background in Windows Forms, you might wish to simply load the completed solution into Visual Studio and experiment with the code, rather than build this application by hand.

COM Interop Using C# Dynamic Data

Assume you have a Windows Form GUI application (named ExportDataToOfficeApp), whose main window hosts a DataGridView control named dataGridCars. This same window has two Button controls, the first of which will bring up a custom dialog box to insert a new row of data to the grid, and the other of which will export the grid's data to an Excel spreadsheet. Figure 16-9 shows the completed GUI.

Figure 16-9.The GUI of the COM interop example

The DataGridView control is filled with some initial data by handling the form's Load event as so (the Car class used as the type parameter for the generic List<T> is a simple class in the project with Color, Make, and PetName properties):

```
public partial class MainForm : Form
{
  List<Car> carsInStock = null;

  public MainForm()
  {
    InitializeComponent();
  }

  private void MainForm_Load(object sender, EventArgs e)
  {
    carsInStock = new List<Car>
    {
      new Car {Color="Green", Make="VW", PetName="Mary"},
      new Car {Color="Red", Make="Saab", PetName="Mel"},
      new Car {Color="Black", Make="Ford", PetName="Hank"},
      new Car {Color="Yellow", Make="BMW", PetName="Davie"}
    };

    UpdateGrid();
  }

  private void UpdateGrid()
  {
    // Reset the source of data.
    dataGridCars.DataSource = null;
    dataGridCars.DataSource = carsInStock;
  }
}
```

The Click event for the "Add New Entry to Inventory" button will launch a custom dialog box to allow the user to enter new data for a Car object, and if they click the OK button, the data is added to the grid (I won't bother to show the code behind the dialog box here, so please see the provided solution for details). If you are following along, however, include the NewCarDialog.cs, NewCarDialog.designer.cs, and NewCarDialog.resx files into your project (all of which are part of the code download for this text). After you have done so, implement the "Add" button click hander on the main window, as so:

```
private void btnAddNewCar_Click(object sender, EventArgs e)
{
  NewCarDialog d = new NewCarDialog();
  if (d.ShowDialog() == DialogResult.OK)
  {
    // Add new car to list.
    carsInStock.Add(d.theCar);
    UpdateGrid();
  }
}
```

The Click event handler for the "Export Current Inventory to Excel" button is the heart of this example. Using the Add Reference dialog box, add a reference to the Microsoft.Office.Interop.Excel.dll primary interop assembly (as shown previously in Figure 16-7). Add the following namespace alias to the form's primary code file. Be aware that this is not mandatory to define an alias when interacting with COM libraries. However, by doing so, you have a handy qualifier for all of the imported COM objects, which is very handy if some of these COM objects have names that would clash with your .NET types.

```
// Create an alias to the Excel object model.
using Excel = Microsoft.Office.Interop.Excel;
```

Implement this button Click event hander to call a private helper function named ExportToExcel(), like so:

```
private void btnExportToExcel_Click(object sender, EventArgs e)
{
  ExportToExcel(carsInStock);
}
```

Because you imported the COM library using Visual Studio, the PIA has been automatically configured so that the used metadata will be embedded into the .NET application (recall the role of the Embed Interop Types property). Therefore, all COM Variants are realized as dynamic data types. Furthermore, you can make use of C# optional arguments and named arguments. This being said, consider the following implementation of ExportToExcel():

```
static void ExportToExcel(List<Car> carsInStock)
{
  // Load up Excel, then make a new empty workbook.
  Excel.Application excelApp = new Excel.Application();
  excelApp.Workbooks.Add();

  // This example uses a single workSheet.
  Excel._Worksheet workSheet = excelApp.ActiveSheet;

  // Establish column headings in cells.
  workSheet.Cells[1, "A"] = "Make";
  workSheet.Cells[1, "B"] = "Color";
  workSheet.Cells[1, "C"] = "Pet Name";

  // Now, map all data in List<Car> to the cells of the spreadsheet.
  int row = 1;
  foreach (Car c in carsInStock)
  {
    row++;
    workSheet.Cells[row, "A"] = c.Make;
    workSheet.Cells[row, "B"] = c.Color;
    workSheet.Cells[row, "C"] = c.PetName;
  }

  // Give our table data a nice look and feel.
  workSheet.Range["A1"].AutoFormat(
    Excel.XlRangeAutoFormat.xlRangeAutoFormatClassic2);
```

```
  // Save the file, quit Excel, and display message to user.
  workSheet.SaveAs(string.Format(@"{0}\Inventory.xlsx", Environment.CurrentDirectory));
  excelApp.Quit();
  MessageBox.Show("The Inventory.xslx file has been saved to your app folder",
    "Export complete!");
}
```

This method begins by loading Excel into memory; however, you won't see it visible on your computer desktop. For this application, you are only interested in using the internal Excel object model. However, if you do want to actually display the UI of Excel, update your method with this additional line of code:

```
static void ExportToExcel(List<Car> carsInStock)
{
  // Load up Excel, then make a new empty workbook.
  Excel.Application excelApp = new Excel.Application();

  // Go ahead and make Excel visible on the computer.
  excelApp.Visible = true;

...
}
```

After you create an empty worksheet, you add three columns that are named similar to the properties of the Car class. Then, you fill the cells with the data of the List<Car>, and save your file under the (hardcoded) name Inventory.xlsx.

At this point, if you run your application, add a few new records, and export your data to Excel, you will then be able to open up the Inventory.xlsx file, which will be saved to the \bin\Debug folder of your Windows Forms application. Figure 16-10 shows a possible export.

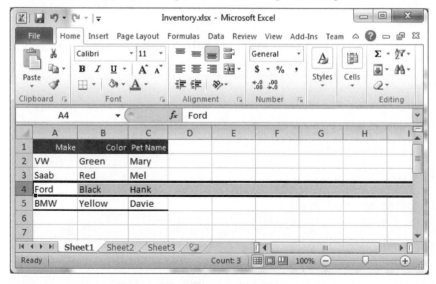

Figure 16-10. Exporting your data to an Excel file

COM interop Without C# Dynamic Data

Now, if you were to select the `Microsoft.Office.Interop.Excel.dll` assembly (in Solution Explorer), and set its Embed Interop Type property to False, you would have new compiler errors, as the COM `Variant` data is no longer realized as dynamic data, but as `System.Object` variables. This will require you to update `ExportToExcel()` with a number of explicit casting operations.

As well, if this project were compiled under .NET 3.5 or earlier, you would no longer have the benefit of optional/named parameters, and would have to explicitly mark all missing arguments. Here is a version of the `ExportToExcel()` method that would be required in earlier versions of C# (do note the increased complexity in code):

```
static void ExportToExcel2008(List<Car> carsInStock)
{
  Excel.Application excelApp = new Excel.Application();

  // Must mark missing params!
  excelApp.Workbooks.Add(Type.Missing);

  // Must cast Object as _Worksheet!
  Excel._Worksheet workSheet = (Excel._Worksheet)excelApp.ActiveSheet;

  // Must cast each Object as Range object then
  // call low-level Value2 property!
  ((Excel.Range)excelApp.Cells[1, "A"]).Value2 = "Make";
  ((Excel.Range)excelApp.Cells[1, "B"]).Value2 = "Color";
  ((Excel.Range)excelApp.Cells[1, "C"]).Value2 = "Pet Name";

  int row = 1;
  foreach (Car c in carsInStock)
  {
    row++;
    // Must cast each Object as Range and call low-level Value2 prop!
    ((Excel.Range)workSheet.Cells[row, "A"]).Value2 = c.Make;
    ((Excel.Range)workSheet.Cells[row, "B"]).Value2 = c.Color;
    ((Excel.Range)workSheet.Cells[row, "C"]).Value2 = c.PetName;
  }

  // Must call get_Range method and then specify all missing args!
  excelApp.get_Range("A1", Type.Missing).AutoFormat(
    Excel.XlRangeAutoFormat.xlRangeAutoFormatClassic2,
    Type.Missing, Type.Missing, Type.Missing,
    Type.Missing, Type.Missing, Type.Missing);

  // Must specify all missing optional args!
  workSheet.SaveAs(string.Format(@"{0}\Inventory.xlsx", Environment.CurrentDirectory),
    Type.Missing, Type.Missing, Type.Missing, Type.Missing, Type.Missing, Type.Missing,
    Type.Missing, Type.Missing, Type.Missing);

  excelApp.Quit();
  MessageBox.Show("The Inventory.xslx file has been saved to your app folder",
    "Export complete!");
}
```

Although the end result of running this program is identical, this version of the method is much more verbose, as I am sure you agree. That wraps up our look at the C# dynamic keyword and the DLR. Hopefully, you can see how these features can simplify complex programming tasks, and (perhaps more importantly) understand the trade-offs. When you opt into dynamic data, you do lose a good amount of type safety, and your code base is prone to many more runtime errors.

While there is more to say about the DLR, this chapter has tried to focus on topics that are practical and useful in your day-to-day programming. If you want to learn more about advanced features of the Dynamic Language Runtime, such as integrating with scripting languages, be sure to consult the .NET Framework 4.5 SDK documentation (look up the topic "Dynamic Language Runtime Overview" to get started).

■ **Source Code** The ExportDataToOfficeApp project is included under the Chapter 16 subdirectory.

Summary

The dynamic keyword introduced in C# 4.0 allows you to define data whose true identity is not known until runtime. When processed by the new Dynamic Language Runtime (DLR), the automatically created "expression tree" will be passed to the correct dynamic language binder, where the payload will be unpackaged and sent to the correct object member.

Using dynamic data and the DLR, a number of complex C# programming tasks can be radically simplified, especially the act of incorporating COM libraries into your .NET applications. As you have also seen in this chapter, .NET 4.0 and higher provides a number of further simplifications to COM interop (which have nothing to do with dynamic data), such as embedding COM interop data into your applications, optional arguments, and named arguments.

While these features can certainly simplify your code, always remember that dynamic data makes your C# code much less type safe, and open to runtime errors. Be sure you weigh the pros and cons of using dynamic data in your C# projects, and test accordingly!

CHAPTER 17

Processes, AppDomains, and Object Contexts

In Chapters 14 and 15, you examined the steps taken by the CLR to resolve the location of a referenced external assembly, as well as the role of .NET metadata. In this chapter, you'll drill deeper into the details of how an assembly is hosted by the CLR and come to understand the relationship between processes, application domains, and object contexts.

In a nutshell, *application domains* (or simply *AppDomains*) are logical subdivisions within a given process that host a set of related .NET assemblies. As you will see, an AppDomain is further subdivided into *contextual boundaries*, which are used to group together like-minded .NET objects. Using the notion of context, the CLR is able to ensure that objects with special runtime requirements are handled appropriately.

While it is true that many of your day-to-day programming tasks might not involve directly working with processes, AppDomains, or object contexts, understanding these topics is very important when working with numerous .NET APIs, including Windows Communication Foundation (WCF), multithreading and parallel processing, and object serialization.

The Role of a Windows Process

The concept of a "process" has existed within Windows-based operating systems well before the release of the .NET platform. In simple terms, a *process* is a running program. However, formally speaking, a process is an operating system–level concept used to describe a set of resources (such as external code libraries and the primary thread) and the necessary memory allocations used by a running application. For each *.exe loaded into memory, the OS creates a separate and isolated process for use during its lifetime.

Using this approach to application isolation, the result is a much more robust and stable runtime environment, given that the failure of one process does not affect the functioning of another. Furthermore, data in one process cannot be directly accessed by another process, unless you make use of a distributed computing programming API such as Windows Communication Foundation. Given these points, you can regard the process as a fixed, safe boundary for a running application.

Now, every Windows process is assigned a unique process identifier (PID) and may be independently loaded and unloaded by the OS as necessary (as well as programmatically). As you might be aware, the Processes tab of the Windows Task Manager utility (activated via the Ctrl+Shift+Esc keystroke combination) allows you to view various statistics regarding the processes running on a given machine, including its PID and image name (see Figure 17-1).

■ **Note** By default, the PID column of the Processes tab will not be shown. To enable this feature, activate the View ➤ Select Columns… menu option, and then check the PID (Process Identifier) checkbox.

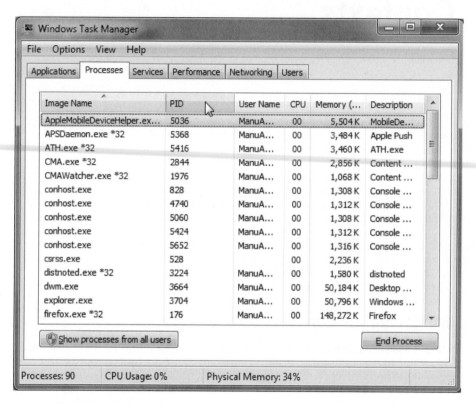

Figure 17-1. The Windows Task Manager

The Role of Threads

Every Windows process contains an initial "thread" that functions as the entry point for the application. Chapter 19 examines the details of building multithreaded applications under the .NET platform; however, to facilitate the topics presented here, you need a few working definitions. First of all, a *thread* is a path of execution within a process. Formally speaking, the first thread created by a process's entry point is termed the *primary thread*. Any .NET executable program (Console Application, Windows Forms application, WPF application, etc.) marks its entry point with the Main() method. When this method is invoked, the primary thread is created automatically.

Processes that contain a single primary thread of execution are intrinsically *thread safe*, given the fact that there is only one thread that can access the data in the application at a given time. However, a single-threaded process (especially one that is GUI-based) will often appear a bit unresponsive to the user if this single thread is performing a complex operation (such as printing out a lengthy text file, performing a mathematically intensive calculation, or attempting to connect to a remote server located thousands of miles away).

Given this potential drawback of single-threaded applications, the Windows API (as well as the .NET platform) makes it possible for the primary thread to spawn additional secondary threads (also termed *worker threads*) using a handful of Windows API functions such as CreateThread(). Each thread (primary or secondary) becomes a unique path of execution in the process and has concurrent access to all shared points of data within the process.

As you might have guessed, developers typically create additional threads to help improve the program's overall responsiveness. Multithreaded processes provide the illusion that numerous activities are happening at more or less the same time. For example, an application may spawn a worker thread to perform a labor-intensive unit of work (again, such as printing a large text file). As this secondary thread is churning away, the main thread is still responsive to user input, which gives the entire process the potential of delivering greater performance. However, this may not actually be the case: using too many threads in a single process can actually *degrade* performance, as the CPU must switch between the active threads in the process (which takes time).

On some machines, multithreading is most commonly an illusion provided by the OS. Machines that host a single (non-hyperthreaded) CPU do not have the ability to literally handle multiple threads at the same exact time. Rather, a single CPU will execute one thread for a unit of time (called a *time slice*) based in part on the thread's priority level. When a thread's time slice is up, the existing thread is suspended to allow another thread to perform its business. For a thread to remember what was happening before it was kicked out of the way, each thread is given the ability to write to Thread Local Storage (TLS) and is provided with a separate call stack, as illustrated in Figure 17-2.

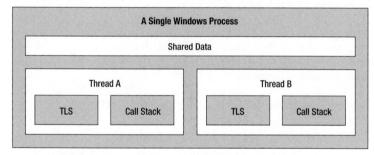

Figure 17-2. The Windows process/thread relationship

If the subject of threads is new to you, don't sweat the details. At this point, just remember that a thread is a unique path of execution within a Windows process. Every process has a primary thread (created via the executable's entry point) and may contain additional threads that have been programmatically created.

Interacting with Processes Under the .NET Platform

Although processes and threads are nothing new, the manner in which you interact with these - primitives under the .NET platform has changed quite a bit (for the better). To pave the way to understanding the world of building multithreaded assemblies (see Chapter 19), let's begin by checking out how to interact with processes using the .NET base class libraries.

The System.Diagnostics namespace defines a number of types that allow you to programmatically interact with processes and various diagnostic-related types such as the system event log and performance counters. In this chapter, you are concerned with only the process-centric types defined in Table 17-1.

Table 17-1. Select Members of the System.Diagnostics Namespace

Process-Centric Types of the System.Diagnostics Namespace	Meaning in Life
Process	The Process class provides access to local and remote processes and also allows you to programmatically start and stop processes.
ProcessModule	This type represents a module (*.dll or *.exe) that is loaded into a particular process. Understand that the ProcessModule type can represent any module—COM-based, .NET-based, or traditional C-based binaries.
ProcessModuleCollection	This provides a strongly typed collection of ProcessModule objects.
ProcessStartInfo	This specifies a set of values used when starting a process via the Process.Start() method.
ProcessThread	This type represents a thread within a given process. Be aware that ProcessThread is a type used to diagnose a process's thread set and is not used to spawn new threads of execution within a process.
ProcessThreadCollection	This provides a strongly typed collection of ProcessThread objects.

The System.Diagnostics.Process class allows you to analyze the processes running on a given machine (local or remote). The Process class also provides members that allow you to programmatically start and terminate processes, view (or modify) a process's priority level, and obtain a list of active threads and/or loaded modules within a given process. Table 17-2 lists some of the key properties of System.Diagnostics.Process.

Table 17-2. Select Properties of the Process Type

Property	Meaning in Life
ExitTime	This property gets the timestamp associated with the process that has terminated (represented with a DateTime type).
Handle	This property returns the handle (represented by an IntPtr) associated to the process by the OS. This can be useful when building .NET applications that need to communicate with unmanaged code.

Id	This property gets the PID for the associated process.
MachineName	This property gets the name of the computer the associated process is running on.
MainWindowTitle	MainWindowTitle gets the caption of the main window of the process (if the process does not have a main window, you receive an empty string).
Modules	This property provides access to the strongly typed ProcessModuleCollection type, which represents the set of modules (*.dll or *.exe) loaded within the current process.
ProcessName	This property gets the name of the process (which, as you would assume, is the name of the application itself).
Responding	This property gets a value indicating whether the user interface of the process is responding to user input (or is currently "hung").
StartTime	This property gets the time that the associated process was started (via a DateTime type).
Threads	This property gets the set of threads that are running in the associated process (represented via a collection of ProcessThread objects).

In addition to the properties just examined, System.Diagnostics.Process also defines a few useful methods (see Table 17-3).

Table 17-3. Select Methods of the Process Type

Method	Meaning in Life
CloseMainWindow()	This method closes a process that has a user interface by sending a close message to its main window.
GetCurrentProcess()	This static method returns a new Process object that represents the currently active process.
GetProcesses()	This static method returns an array of new Process objects running on a given machine.
Kill()	This method immediately stops the associated process.
Start()	This method starts a process.

Enumerating Running Processes

To illustrate the process of manipulating Process objects (pardon the redundancy), assume you have a C# Console Application named ProcessManipulator that defines the following static helper method within the Program class (be sure you import the System.Diagnostics namespace in your code file):

```
static void ListAllRunningProcesses()
{
  // Get all the processes on the local machine, ordered by
  // PID.
  var runningProcs =
    from proc in Process.GetProcesses(".") orderby proc.Id select proc;

  // Print out PID and name of each process.
  foreach(var p in runningProcs)
  {
    string info = string.Format("-> PID: {0}\tName: {1}",
      p.Id, p.ProcessName);
    Console.WriteLine(info);
  }
  Console.WriteLine("***********************************\n");
}
```

The static Process.GetProcesses() method returns an array of Process objects that represent the running processes on the target machine (the dot notation shown here represents the local computer). After you have obtained the array of Process objects, you are able to invoke any of the members seen in Tables 17-2 and 17-3. Here, you are simply displaying the PID and the name of each process, ordered by PID. Assuming the Main() method has been updated to call ListAllRunningProcesses() as follows:

```
static void Main(string[] args)
{
  Console.WriteLine("***** Fun with Processes *****\n");
  ListAllRunningProcesses();
  Console.ReadLine();
}
```

you will see the names and PIDs for all processes on your local computer. Here is some partial output from my current machine:

```
***** Fun with Processes *****

-> PID: 0        Name: Idle
-> PID: 4        Name: System
-> PID: 108      Name: iexplore
-> PID: 268      Name: smss
-> PID: 432      Name: csrss
-> PID: 448      Name: svchost
-> PID: 472      Name: wininit
-> PID: 504      Name: csrss
-> PID: 536      Name: winlogon
-> PID: 560      Name: services
-> PID: 584      Name: lsass
```

```
-> PID: 592      Name: lsm
-> PID: 660      Name: devenv
-> PID: 684      Name: svchost
-> PID: 760      Name: svchost
-> PID: 832      Name: svchost
-> PID: 844      Name: svchost
-> PID: 856      Name: svchost
-> PID: 900      Name: svchost
-> PID: 924      Name: svchost
-> PID: 956      Name: VMwareService
-> PID: 1116     Name: spoolsv
-> PID: 1136     Name: ProcessManipulator.vshost
***********************************
```

Investigating a Specific Process

In addition to obtaining a full and complete list of all running processes on a given machine, the static Process.GetProcessById() method allows you to obtain a single Process object via the associated PID. If you request access to a nonexistent PID, an ArgumentException exception is thrown. For example, if you were interested in obtaining a Process object representing a process with the PID of 987, you could write the following code:

```
// If there is no process with the PID of 987, a
// runtime exception will be thrown.
static void GetSpecificProcess()
{
  Process theProc = null;
  try
  {
    theProc = Process.GetProcessById(987);
  }
  catch(ArgumentException ex)
  {
    Console.WriteLine(ex.Message);
  }
}
```

At this point, you have learned how to get a list of all processes, or a specific process on a machine via a PID lookup. While it is somewhat useful to discover PIDs and process names, the Process class also allows you to discover the set of current threads and libraries used within a given process. Let's see how to do so.

Investigating a Process's Thread Set

The set of threads is represented by the strongly typed ProcessThreadCollection collection, which contains some number of individual ProcessThread objects. To illustrate, assume the following additional static helper function has been added to your current application:

```
static void EnumThreadsForPid(int pID)
{
  Process theProc = null;
```

```
try
{
  theProc = Process.GetProcessById(pID);
}
catch(ArgumentException ex)
{
  Console.WriteLine(ex.Message);
  return;
}

// List out stats for each thread in the specified process.
Console.WriteLine("Here are the threads used by: {0}",
  theProc.ProcessName);
ProcessThreadCollection theThreads = theProc.Threads;

foreach(ProcessThread pt in theThreads)
{
  string info =
    string.Format("-> Thread ID: {0}\tStart Time: {1}\tPriority: {2}",
      pt.Id , pt.StartTime.ToShortTimeString(), pt.PriorityLevel);
  Console.WriteLine(info);
}
Console.WriteLine("***********************************\n");
}
```

As you can see, the Threads property of the System.Diagnostics.Process type provides access to the ProcessThreadCollection class. Here, you are printing out the assigned thread ID, start time, and priority level of each thread in the process specified by the client. Now, update your program's Main() method to prompt the user for a PID to investigate, as follows:

```
static void Main(string[] args)
{
...
  // Prompt user for a PID and print out the set of active threads.
  Console.WriteLine("***** Enter PID of process to investigate *****");
  Console.Write("PID: ");
  string pID = Console.ReadLine();
  int theProcID = int.Parse(pID);

  EnumThreadsForPid(theProcID);
  Console.ReadLine();
}
```

When you run your program, you can now enter the PID of any process on your machine, and see the threads used in the process. The following output shows the threads used by PID 108 on my machine, which happens to be hosting Microsoft Internet Explorer:

```
***** Enter PID of process to investigate *****
PID: 108
Here are the threads used by: iexplore
-> Thread ID: 680      Start Time: 9:05 AM      Priority: Normal
-> Thread ID: 2040     Start Time: 9:05 AM      Priority: Normal
```

```
-> Thread ID: 880     Start Time: 9:05 AM     Priority: Normal
-> Thread ID: 3380    Start Time: 9:05 AM     Priority: Normal
-> Thread ID: 3376    Start Time: 9:05 AM     Priority: Normal
-> Thread ID: 3448    Start Time: 9:05 AM     Priority: Normal
-> Thread ID: 3476    Start Time: 9:05 AM     Priority: Normal
-> Thread ID: 2264    Start Time: 9:05 AM     Priority: Normal
-> Thread ID: 2380    Start Time: 9:05 AM     Priority: Normal
-> Thread ID: 2384    Start Time: 9:05 AM     Priority: Normal
-> Thread ID: 2308    Start Time: 9:05 AM     Priority: Normal
-> Thread ID: 3096    Start Time: 9:07 AM     Priority: Highest
-> Thread ID: 3600    Start Time: 9:45 AM     Priority: Normal
-> Thread ID: 1412    Start Time: 10:02 AM    Priority: Normal
```

The ProcessThread type has additional members of interest beyond Id, StartTime, and PriorityLevel. Table 17-4 documents some members of interest.

Table 17-4. Select Members of the ProcessThread Type

Member	Meaning in Life
CurrentPriority	Gets the current priority of the thread
Id	Gets the unique identifier of the thread
IdealProcessor	Sets the preferred processor for this thread to run on
PriorityLevel	Gets or sets the priority level of the thread
ProcessorAffinity	Sets the processors on which the associated thread can run
StartAddress	Gets the memory address of the function that the operating system called that started this thread
StartTime	Gets the time that the operating system started the thread
ThreadState	Gets the current state of this thread
TotalProcessorTime	Gets the total amount of time that this thread has spent using the processor
WaitReason	Gets the reason that the thread is waiting

Before you read any further, be very aware that the ProcessThread type is *not* the entity used to create, suspend, or kill threads under the .NET platform. Rather, ProcessThread is a vehicle used to obtain diagnostic information for the active Windows threads within a running process. Again, you will investigate how to build multithreaded applications using the System.Threading namespace in Chapter 19.

Investigating a Process's Module Set

Next up, let's check out how to iterate over the number of loaded modules that are hosted within a given process. When talking about processes, a *module* is a general term used to describe a given *.dll (or the *.exe itself) that is hosted by a specific process. When you access the ProcessModuleCollection via the Process.Modules property, you are able to enumerate over *all modules* hosted within a process: .NET-based, COM-based, or traditional C-based libraries. Ponder the following additional helper function that will enumerate the modules in a specific process based on the PID:

```
static void EnumModsForPid(int pID)
{
  Process theProc = null;
  try
  {
    theProc = Process.GetProcessById(pID);
  }
  catch(ArgumentException ex)
  {
    Console.WriteLine(ex.Message);
    return;
  }

  Console.WriteLine("Here are the loaded modules for: {0}",
    theProc.ProcessName);
  ProcessModuleCollection theMods = theProc.Modules;
  foreach(ProcessModule pm in theMods)
  {
    string info = string.Format("-> Mod Name: {0}", pm.ModuleName);
    Console.WriteLine(info);
  }
  Console.WriteLine("************************************\n");
}
```

To see some possible output, let's check out the loaded modules for the process hosting the current example program (ProcessManipulator). To do so, run the application, identify the PID assigned to ProcessManipulator.exe (via the Task Manager), and pass this value to the EnumModsForPid() method (be sure to update your Main() method accordingly). Once you do, you might be surprised to see the list of *.dlls used for a simple Console Application (GDI32.dll, USER32.dll, ole32.dll, and so forth). Consider the following output:

```
Here are the loaded modules for: ProcessManipulator
-> Mod Name: ProcessManipulator.exe
-> Mod Name: ntdll.dll
-> Mod Name: MSCOREE.DLL
-> Mod Name: KERNEL32.dll
-> Mod Name: KERNELBASE.dll
-> Mod Name: ADVAPI32.dll
-> Mod Name: msvcrt.dll
-> Mod Name: sechost.dll
-> Mod Name: RPCRT4.dll
-> Mod Name: SspiCli.dll
```

```
-> Mod Name: CRYPTBASE.dll
-> Mod Name: mscoreei.dll
-> Mod Name: SHLWAPI.dll
-> Mod Name: GDI32.dll
-> Mod Name: USER32.dll
-> Mod Name: LPK.dll
-> Mod Name: USP10.dll
-> Mod Name: IMM32.DLL
-> Mod Name: MSCTF.dll
-> Mod Name: clr.dll
-> Mod Name: MSVCR100_CLR0400.dll
-> Mod Name: mscorlib.ni.dll
-> Mod Name: nlssorting.dll
-> Mod Name: ole32.dll
-> Mod Name: clrjit.dll
-> Mod Name: System.ni.dll
-> Mod Name: System.Core.ni.dll
-> Mod Name: psapi.dll
-> Mod Name: shfolder.dll
-> Mod Name: SHELL32.dll
**********************************
```

Starting and Stopping Processes Programmatically

The final aspects of the System.Diagnostics.Process class examined here are the Start() and Kill() methods. As you can gather by their names, these members provide a way to programmatically launch and terminate a process, respectively. For example, consider the following static StartAndKillProcess() helper method:

■ **Note** You must be running Visual Studio with Administrator rights in order to start new processes. If this is not the case, you will receive a runtime error.

```
static void StartAndKillProcess()
{
  Process ieProc = null;

  // Launch Internet Explorer, and go to facebook!
  try
  {
    ieProc = Process.Start("IExplore.exe", "www.facebook.com");
  }
  catch (InvalidOperationException ex)
  {
    Console.WriteLine(ex.Message);
  }
```

```
    Console.Write("--> Hit enter to kill {0}...", ieProc.ProcessName);
    Console.ReadLine();

    // Kill the iexplore.exe process.
    try
    {
      ieProc.Kill();
    }
    catch (InvalidOperationException ex)
    {
      Console.WriteLine(ex.Message);
    }
}
```

The static `Process.Start()` method has been overloaded a few times. At minimum, you will need to specify the friendly name of the process you want to launch (such as Microsoft Internet Explorer, `iexplore.exe`). This example makes use of a variation of the `Start()` method that allows you to specify any additional arguments to pass into the program's entry point (i.e., the `Main()` method).

After you call the `Start()` method, you are returned a reference to the newly activated process. When you want to terminate the process, simply call the instance-level `Kill()` method. Here, you are wrapping the calls to `Start()` and `Kill()` within a `try/catch` block, and handling any `InvalidOperationException` errors. This is especially important when calling the `Kill()` method, as this error will be raised if the process has already been terminated prior to calling `Kill()`.

Controlling Process Startup Using the ProcessStartInfo Class

The `Start()` method also allows you to pass in a `System.Diagnostics.ProcessStartInfo` type to specify additional bits of information regarding how a given process should come to life. Here is a partial definition of `ProcessStartInfo` (see the .NET Framework 4.5 SDK documentation for full details):

```
public sealed class ProcessStartInfo : object
{
  public ProcessStartInfo();
  public ProcessStartInfo(string fileName);
  public ProcessStartInfo(string fileName, string arguments);
  public string Arguments { get; set; }
  public bool CreateNoWindow { get; set; }
  public StringDictionary EnvironmentVariables { get; }
  public bool ErrorDialog { get; set; }
  public IntPtr ErrorDialogParentHandle { get; set; }
  public string FileName { get; set; }
  public bool LoadUserProfile { get; set; }
  public SecureString Password { get; set; }
  public bool RedirectStandardError { get; set; }
  public bool RedirectStandardInput { get; set; }
  public bool RedirectStandardOutput { get; set; }
  public Encoding StandardErrorEncoding { get; set; }
  public Encoding StandardOutputEncoding { get; set; }
  public bool UseShellExecute { get; set; }
  public string Verb { get; set; }
  public string[] Verbs { get; }
  public ProcessWindowStyle WindowStyle { get; set; }
```

```
  public string WorkingDirectory { get; set; }
}
```

To illustrate how to fine-tune your process startup, here is a modified version of StartAndKillProcess(), which will load Microsoft Internet Explorer, navigate to www.facebook.com, and show the window in a maximized state:

```
static void StartAndKillProcess()
{
  Process ieProc = null;

  // Launch Internet Explorer, and go to facebook,
  // with maximized window.
  try
  {
    ProcessStartInfo startInfo = new
      ProcessStartInfo("IExplore.exe", "www.facebook.com");
    startInfo.WindowStyle = ProcessWindowStyle.Maximized;

    ieProc = Process.Start(startInfo);
  }
  catch (InvalidOperationException ex)
  {
    Console.WriteLine(ex.Message);
  }
...
}
```

Great! Now that you understand the role of Windows processes and how to interact with them from C# code, you are ready to investigate the concept of a .NET application domain.

■ **Source Code** The ProcessManipulator project is included under the Chapter 17 subdirectory.

Understanding .NET Application Domains

Under the .NET platform, executables are not hosted directly within a Windows process, as is the case in traditional unmanaged applications. Rather, a .NET executable is hosted by a logical partition within a process termed an *application domain*. As you will see, a single process may contain multiple application domains, each of which is hosting a .NET executable. This additional subdivision of a traditional Windows process offers several benefits, some of which are as follows:

- AppDomains are a key aspect of the OS-neutral nature of the .NET platform, given that this logical division abstracts away the differences in how an underlying OS represents a loaded executable.

- AppDomains are far less expensive in terms of processing power and memory than a full-blown process. Thus, the CLR is able to load and unload application domains much quicker than a formal process, and can drastically improve scalability of server applications.

- AppDomains provide a deeper level of isolation for hosting a loaded application. If one AppDomain within a process fails, the remaining AppDomains remain functional.

As mentioned, a single process can host any number of AppDomains, each of which is fully and completely isolated from other AppDomains within this process (or any other process). Given this fact, be very aware that an application running in one AppDomain is unable to obtain data of any kind (global variables or static fields) within another AppDomain, unless they make use of a distributed programming protocol (such as Windows Communication Foundation).

While a single process *may* host multiple AppDomains, this is not typically the case. At the very least, an OS process will host what is termed the *default application domain*. This specific application domain is automatically created by the CLR at the time the process launches. After this point, the CLR creates additional application domains on an as-needed basis.

The System.AppDomain Class

The .NET platform allows you to programmatically monitor AppDomains, create new AppDomains (or unload them) at runtime, load assemblies into AppDomains, and a whole slew of additional tasks, using the AppDomain class in the System namespace of mscorlib.dll. Table 17-5 documents some useful methods of the AppDomain class (consult the .NET Framework 4.5 SDK documentation for full details).

Table 17-5. Select Methods of AppDomain

Method	Meaning in Life
CreateDomain()	This static method allows you to create a new AppDomain in the current process.
CreateInstance()	This creates an instance of a type in an external assembly, after loading said assembly into the calling application domain.
ExecuteAssembly()	This method executes an *.exe assembly within an application domain, given its file name.
GetAssemblies()	This method gets the set of .NET assemblies that have been loaded into this application domain (COM-based or C-based binaries are ignored).
GetCurrentThreadId()	This static method returns the ID of the active thread in the current application domain.
Load()	This method is used to dynamically load an assembly into the current application domain.
Unload()	This is another static method that allows you to unload a specified AppDomain within a given process.

■ **Note** The .NET platform does not allow you to unload a specific assembly from memory. The only way to programmatically unload libraries is to tear down the hosting application domain via the Unload() method.

In addition, the AppDomain class also defines a set of properties that can be useful when you want to monitor activity of a given application domain. Table 17-6 documents some core properties of interest.

Table 17-6. Select Properties of AppDomain

Property	Meaning in Life
BaseDirectory	This gets the directory path that the assembly resolver uses to probe for assemblies.
CurrentDomain	This static property gets the application domain for the currently executing thread.
FriendlyName	This gets the friendly name of the current application domain.
MonitoringIsEnabled	This gets or sets a value that indicates whether CPU and memory monitoring of application domains is enabled for the current process. Once monitoring is enabled for a process, it cannot be disabled.
SetupInformation	This gets the configuration details for a given application domain, represented by an AppDomainSetup object.

Last but not least, the AppDomain class supports a set of events that correspond to various aspects of an application domain's life cycle. Table 17-7 shows some of the more useful events you can hook into.

Table 17-7. Select Events of the AppDomain Type

Event	Meaning in Life
AssemblyLoad	This occurs when an assembly is loaded into memory.
AssemblyResolve	This event will fire when the assembly resolver cannot find the location of a required assembly.
DomainUnload	This occurs when an AppDomain is about to be unloaded from the hosting process.
FirstChanceException	This event allows you to be notified that an exception has been thrown from the application domain, before the CLR will begin looking for a fitting catch statement.

ProcessExit   This occurs on the default application domain when the default application domain's parent process exits.

UnhandledException   This occurs when an exception is not caught by an exception handler.

Interacting with the Default Application Domain

Recall that when a .NET executable starts, the CLR will automatically place it into the default AppDomain of the hosting process. This is done automatically and transparently, and you never have to author any specific code to do so. However, it is possible for your application to gain access to this default application domain using the static AppDomain.CurrentDomain property. After you have this access point, you are able to hook into any events of interest, or make use of the methods and properties of AppDomain to perform some runtime diagnostics.

To learn how to interact with the default application domain, begin by creating a new Console Application named DefaultAppDomainApp. Now, update your program with the following logic, which will simply display some details about the default application domain, using a number of members of the AppDomain class:

```
class Program
{
  static void Main(string[] args)
  {
    Console.WriteLine("***** Fun with the default AppDomain *****\n");
    DisplayDADStats();
    Console.ReadLine();
  }

  private static void DisplayDADStats()
  {
    // Get access to the AppDomain for the current thread.
    AppDomain defaultAD = AppDomain.CurrentDomain;

    // Print out various stats about this domain.
    Console.WriteLine("Name of this domain: {0}", defaultAD.FriendlyName);
    Console.WriteLine("ID of domain in this process: {0}", defaultAD.Id);
    Console.WriteLine("Is this the default domain?: {0}",
      defaultAD.IsDefaultAppDomain());
    Console.WriteLine("Base directory of this domain: {0}", defaultAD.BaseDirectory);
  }
}
```

The output of this example can be seen here:

```
***** Fun with the default AppDomain *****

Name of this domain: DefaultAppDomainApp.exe
ID of domain in this process: 1
Is this the default domain?: True
Base directory of this domain: E:\MyCode\DefaultAppDomainApp\bin\Debug\
```

Notice that the name of the default application domain will be identical to the name of the executable that is contained within it (DefaultAppDomainApp.exe, in this example). Also notice that the base directory value, which will be used to probe for externally required private assemblies, maps to the current location of the deployed executable.

Enumerating Loaded Assemblies

It is also possible to discover all of the loaded .NET assemblies within a given application domain using the instance-level GetAssemblies() method. This method will return to you an array of Assembly objects, which as you recall from the Chapter 15, is a member of the System.Reflection namespace (so don't forget to import this namespace into your C# code file!).

To illustrate, define a new method named ListAllAssembliesInAppDomain() within the Program class. This helper method will obtain all loaded assemblies, and print out the friendly name and version of each.

```
static void ListAllAssembliesInAppDomain()
{
  // Get access to the AppDomain for the current thread.
  AppDomain defaultAD = AppDomain.CurrentDomain;

  // Now get all loaded assemblies in the default AppDomain.
  Assembly[] loadedAssemblies = defaultAD.GetAssemblies();
  Console.WriteLine("***** Here are the assemblies loaded in {0} *****\n",
    defaultAD.FriendlyName);
  foreach(Assembly a in loadedAssemblies)
  {
    Console.WriteLine("-> Name: {0}", a.GetName().Name);
    Console.WriteLine("-> Version: {0}\n", a.GetName().Version);
  }
}
```

Assuming you have updated your Main() method to call this new member, you will see that the application domain hosting your executable is currently making use of the following .NET libraries:

```
***** Here are the assemblies loaded in DefaultAppDomainApp.exe *****

-> Name: mscorlib
-> Version: 4.0.0.0

-> Name: DefaultAppDomainApp
```

```
-> Version: 1.0.0.0
```

Now understand that the list of loaded assemblies can change at any time as you author new C#
code. For example, assume you have updated your ListAllAssembliesInAppDomain() method to make
use of a LINQ query, which will order the loaded assemblies by name, as follows:

```
static void ListAllAssembliesInAppDomain()
{
  // Get access to the AppDomain for the current thread.
  AppDomain defaultAD = AppDomain.CurrentDomain;

  // Now get all loaded assemblies in the default AppDomain.
  var loadedAssemblies = from a in defaultAD.GetAssemblies()
    orderby a.GetName().Name select a;

  Console.WriteLine("***** Here are the assemblies loaded in {0} *****\n",
      defaultAD.FriendlyName);
  foreach (var a in loadedAssemblies)
  {
    Console.WriteLine("-> Name: {0}", a.GetName().Name);
    Console.WriteLine("-> Version: {0}\n", a.GetName().Version);
  }
}
```

If you were to run the program once again, you would see that System.Core.dll and System.dll
have also been loaded into memory, as they are required for the LINQ to Objects API:

```
***** Here are the assemblies loaded in DefaultAppDomainApp.exe *****

-> Name: DefaultAppDomainApp
-> Version: 1.0.0.0

-> Name: mscorlib
-> Version: 4.0.0.0

-> Name: System
-> Version: 4.0.0.0

-> Name: System.Core
-> Version: 4.0.0.0
```

Receiving Assembly Load Notifications

If you want to be informed by the CLR when a new assembly has been loaded into a given application
domain, you may handle the AssemblyLoad event. This event is typed against the
AssemblyLoadEventHandler delegate, which can point to any method taking a System.Object as the first
parameter, and an AssemblyLoadEventArgs as the second.

Let's add one final method to the current `Program` class called `InitDAD()`. As the name suggests, this method will initialize the default application domain, specifically by handling the `AssemblyLoad` event via a fitting lambda expression.

```
private static void InitDAD()
{
  // This logic will print out the name of any assembly
  // loaded into the applicaion domain, after it has been
  // created.
  AppDomain defaultAD = AppDomain.CurrentDomain;
  defaultAD.AssemblyLoad += (o, s) =>
    {
      Console.WriteLine("{0} has been loaded!", s.LoadedAssembly.GetName().Name);
    };
}
```

As you would expect, when you run the modified application, you will be notified when a new assembly has been loaded. Here, you are simply printing out the friendly name of the assembly, using the `LoadedAssembly` property of the incoming `AssemblyLoadedEventArgs` parameter.

■ **Source Code** The DefaultAppDomainApp project is included under the Chapter 17 subdirectory.

Creating New Application Domains

Recall that a single process is capable of hosting multiple application domains via the static `AppDomain.CreateDomain()` method. While creating new AppDomains on the fly is a rather infrequent task for most .NET applications, it is important to understand the basics of doing so. For example, as you will see later in this text, when you build *dynamic assemblies* (see Chapter 18 you will need to install them into a custom AppDomain. As well, several .NET security APIs require you to understand how to construct new AppDomains to isolate assemblies based on supplied security credentials.

To investigate how to create new application domains on the fly (and how to load new assemblies into these custom homes), create a new Console Application named CustomAppDomains. The `AppDomain.CreateDomain()` method has been overloaded a number of times. At minimum, you will specify the friendly name of the new application domain to be constructed. Update your `Program` class with the following code. Here, you are leveraging the `ListAllAssembliesInAppDomain()` method from the previous example; however, this time you are passing in the `AppDomain` object to analyze as an incoming argument.

```
class Program
{
  static void Main(string[] args)
  {
    Console.WriteLine("***** Fun with Custom AppDomains *****\n");

    // Show all loaded assemblies in default AppDomain.
    AppDomain defaultAD = AppDomain.CurrentDomain;
    ListAllAssembliesInAppDomain(defaultAD);
```

```
      // Make a new AppDomain.
      MakeNewAppDomain();
      Console.ReadLine();
    }

    private static void MakeNewAppDomain()
    {
      // Make a new AppDomain in the current process and
      // list loaded assemblies.
      AppDomain newAD = AppDomain.CreateDomain("SecondAppDomain");
      ListAllAssembliesInAppDomain(newAD);
    }

    static void ListAllAssembliesInAppDomain(AppDomain ad)
    {
      // Now get all loaded assemblies in the default AppDomain.
      var loadedAssemblies = from a in ad.GetAssemblies()
                             orderby a.GetName().Name select a;

      Console.WriteLine("***** Here are the assemblies loaded in {0} *****\n",
        ad.FriendlyName);
      foreach (var a in loadedAssemblies)
      {
        Console.WriteLine("-> Name: {0}", a.GetName().Name);
        Console.WriteLine("-> Version: {0}\n", a.GetName().Version);
      }
    }
  }
}
```

If you run the current example, you will see that the default application domain
(CustomAppDomains.exe) has loaded mscorlib.dll, System.dll, System.Core.dll, and
CustomAppDomains.exe, given the C# code base of the current project. However, the new application
domain contains only mscorlib.dll, which as you recall, is the one .NET assembly that is always loaded
by the CLR for each and every application domain:

```
***** Fun with Custom AppDomains *****

***** Here are the assemblies loaded in CustomAppDomains.exe *****

-> Name: CustomAppDomains
-> Version: 1.0.0.0

-> Name: mscorlib
-> Version: 4.0.0.0

-> Name: System
-> Version: 4.0.0.0

-> Name: System.Core
-> Version: 4.0.0.0
```

```
***** Here are the assemblies loaded in SecondAppDomain *****

-> Name: mscorlib
-> Version: 4.0.0.0
```

■ **Note** If you debug this project (via F5), you will find many additional assemblies are loaded into each AppDomain, which are used by the Visual Studio debugging process. Running this project (via Ctrl+F5) will display only the assemblies directly within each AppDomain.

This might seem counterintuitive if you have a background in traditional Windows (as you might suspect, both application domains have access to the same assembly set). Recall, however, that an assembly loads into an *application domain*, not directly into the process itself.

Loading Assemblies into Custom Application Domains

The CLR will always load assemblies into the default application domain when required. However, if you do ever manually create new AppDomains, you can load assemblies into said AppDomain using the AppDomain.Load() method. Also, be aware that the AppDomain.ExecuteAssembly() method can be called to load an *.exe assembly and execute the Main() method.

Assume that you wish to load CarLibrary.dll into your new secondary AppDomain. Provided you have copied this library to the \bin\Debug folder of the current application, you could update the MakeNewAppDomain() method as so (be sure to import the System.IO namespace, to gain access to the FileNotFoundException class):

```
private static void MakeNewAppDomain()
{
  // Make a new AppDomain in the current process.
  AppDomain newAD = AppDomain.CreateDomain("SecondAppDomain");

  try
  {
    // Now load CarLibrary.dll into this new domain.
    newAD.Load("CarLibrary");
  }
  catch (FileNotFoundException ex)
  {
    Console.WriteLine(ex.Message);
  }

  // List all assemblies.
  ListAllAssembliesInAppDomain(newAD);
}
```

This time, the output of the program would appear as so (note the presence of CarLibrary.dll):

```
***** Fun with Custom AppDomains *****

***** Here are the assemblies loaded in CustomAppDomains.exe *****

-> Name: CustomAppDomains
-> Version: 1.0.0.0

-> Name: mscorlib
-> Version: 4.0.0.0

-> Name: System
-> Version: 4.0.0.0

-> Name: System.Core
-> Version: 4.0.0.0

***** Here are the assemblies loaded in SecondAppDomain *****

-> Name: CarLibrary
-> Version: 2.0.0.0

-> Name: mscorlib
-> Version: 4.0.0.0
```

■ **Note** Remember, if you debug this application, you will see many additional libraries loaded into each application domain.

Programmatically Unloading AppDomains

It is important to point out that the CLR does not permit unloading individual .NET assemblies. However, using the AppDomain.Unload() method, you are able to selectively unload a given application domain from its hosting process. When you do so, the application domain will unload each assembly in turn.

Recall that the AppDomain type defines the DomainUnload event, which is fired when a custom application domain is unloaded from the containing process. Another event of interest is the ProcessExit event, which is fired when the default application domain is unloaded from the process (which obviously entails the termination of the process itself).

If you want to programmatically unload newAD from the hosting process, and be notified when the associated application domain is torn down, you could update MakeNewAppDomain() with the following additional logic:

```
private static void MakeNewAppDomain()
{
  // Make a new AppDomain in the current process.
  AppDomain newAD = AppDomain.CreateDomain("SecondAppDomain");
```

```
newAD.DomainUnload += (o, s) =>
{
  Console.WriteLine("The second AppDomain has been unloaded!");
};

try
{
  // Now load CarLibrary.dll into this new domain.
  newAD.Load("CarLibrary");
}
catch (FileNotFoundException ex)
{
  Console.WriteLine(ex.Message);
}

// List all assemblies.
ListAllAssembliesInAppDomain(newAD);

// Now tear down this AppDomain.
AppDomain.Unload(newAD);
}
```

If you want to be notified when the default application domain is unloaded, modify your Main() method to handle the ProcessEvent event of the default application domain, like so:

```
static void Main(string[] args)
{
  Console.WriteLine("***** Fun with Custom AppDomains *****\n");

  // Show all loaded assemblies in default AppDomain.
  AppDomain defaultAD = AppDomain.CurrentDomain;
  defaultAD.ProcessExit += (o, s) =>
  {
    Console.WriteLine("Default AD unloaded!");
  };

  ListAllAssembliesInAppDomain(defaultAD);

  MakeNewAppDomain();
  Console.ReadLine();
}
```

That wraps up our look at the .NET application domain. To conclude this chapter, let's look at one further level of partitioning, which is used to group objects into contextual boundaries.

■ **Source Code** The CustomAppDomains project is included under the Chapter 17 subdirectory.

Understanding Object Context Boundaries

As you have just seen, AppDomains are logical partitions within a process used to host .NET assemblies. On a related note, a given application domain may be further subdivided into numerous context boundaries. In a nutshell, a .NET context provides a way for a single AppDomain to establish a "specific home" for a given object.

■ **Note** Friendly FYI: While understanding processes and application domains is quite important, most .NET applications will never demand that you work with object contexts. I've included this material just to paint a more complete picture.

Using context, the CLR is able to ensure that objects that have special runtime requirements are handled in an appropriate and consistent manner by intercepting method invocations into and out of a given context. This layer of interception allows the CLR to adjust the current method invocation to conform to the contextual settings of a given object. For example, if you define a C# class type that requires automatic thread safety (using the [Synchronization] attribute), the CLR will create a "synchronized context" during allocation.

Just as a process defines a default AppDomain, every application domain has a default context. This default context (sometimes referred to as *context 0*, given that it is always the first context created within an application domain) is used to group together .NET objects that have no specific or unique contextual needs. As you might expect, a vast majority of .NET objects are loaded into context 0. If the CLR determines a newly created object has special needs, a new context boundary is created within the hosting application domain. Figure 17-3 illustrates the process/AppDomain/context relationship.

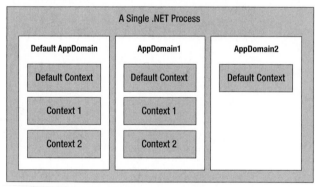

Figure 17-3. Processes, application domains, and context boundaries

Context-Agile and Context-Bound Types

.NET objects that do not demand any special contextual treatment are termed *context-agile objects*. These objects can be accessed from anywhere within the hosting AppDomain without interfering with the object's runtime requirements. Building context-agile objects is very easy, given that you simply do nothing (specifically, you do not adorn the type with any contextual attributes and do not derive from the System.ContextBoundObject base class). For example:

```
// A context-agile object is loaded into context zero.
class SportsCar{}
```

On the other hand, objects that do demand contextual allocation are termed *context-bound objects*, and they *must* derive from the System.ContextBoundObject base class. This base class solidifies the fact that the object in question can function appropriately only within the context in which it was created. Given the role of .NET context, it should stand to reason that if a context-bound object were to somehow end up in an incompatible context, bad things would be guaranteed to occur at the most inopportune times.

In addition to deriving from System.ContextBoundObject, a context-sensitive type will also be adorned by a special category of .NET attributes termed (not surprisingly) *context attributes*. All context attributes derive from the ContextAttribute base class. Let's see an example.

Defining a Context-Bound Object

Assume that you want to define a class (SportsCarTS) that is automatically thread safe in nature, even though you have not hard-coded thread synchronization logic within the member implementations. To do so, derive from ContextBoundObject and apply the [Synchronization] attribute as follows:

```
using System.Runtime.Remoting.Contexts;

// This context-bound type will only be loaded into a
// synchronized (hence thread-safe) context.
[Synchronization]
class SportsCarTS : ContextBoundObject
{}
```

Types that are attributed with the [Synchronization] attribute are loaded into a thread-safe context. Given the special contextual needs of the SportsCarTS class type, imagine the problems that would occur if an allocated object were moved from a synchronized context into a nonsynchronized context. The object is suddenly no longer thread safe and, thus, becomes a candidate for massive data corruption, as numerous threads are attempting to interact with the (now thread-volatile) reference object. To ensure the CLR does not move SportsCarTS objects outside of a synchronized context, simply derive from ContextBoundObject.

Inspecting an Object's Context

Although very few of the applications you will write will need to programmatically interact with context, here is an illustrative example. Create a new Console Application named ObjectContextApp. This application defines one context-agile class (SportsCar) and a single context-bound type (SportsCarTS) as follows:

```
using System;
using System.Runtime.Remoting.Contexts;  // For Context type.
using System.Threading;  // For Thread type.

// SportsCar has no special contextual
// needs and will be loaded into the
// default context of the AppDomain.
class SportsCar
{
  public SportsCar()
```

```
  {
    // Get context information and print out context ID.
    Context ctx = Thread.CurrentContext;
    Console.WriteLine("{0} object in context {1}",
      this.ToString(), ctx.ContextID);
    foreach(IContextProperty itfCtxProp in ctx.ContextProperties)
      Console.WriteLine("-> Ctx Prop: {0}", itfCtxProp.Name);
  }
}

// SportsCarTS demands to be loaded in
// a synchronization context.
[Synchronization]
class SportsCarTS : ContextBoundObject
{
  public SportsCarTS()
  {
    // Get context information and print out context ID.
    Context ctx = Thread.CurrentContext;
    Console.WriteLine("{0} object in context {1}",
      this.ToString(), ctx.ContextID);
    foreach(IContextProperty itfCtxProp in ctx.ContextProperties)
      Console.WriteLine("-> Ctx Prop: {0}", itfCtxProp.Name);
  }
}
```

Notice that each constructor obtains a Context object from the current thread of execution, via the static Thread.CurrentContext property. Using the Context object, you are able to print out statistics about the contextual boundary, such as its assigned ID, as well as a set of descriptors obtained via Context.ContextProperties. This property returns an array of objects implementing the IContextProperty interface, which exposes each descriptor through the Name property. Now, update Main() to allocate an instance of each class type, like so:

```
static void Main(string[] args)
{
  Console.WriteLine("***** Fun with Object Context *****\n");

  // Objects will display contextual info upon creation.
  SportsCar sport = new SportsCar();
  Console.WriteLine();

  SportsCar sport2 = new SportsCar();
  Console.WriteLine();

  SportsCarTS synchroSport = new SportsCarTS();
  Console.ReadLine();
}
```

As the objects come to life, the class constructors will dump out various bits of context-centric information (the "lease life time service property" printout is a low-level aspect of the .NET remoting layer, and can be ignored):

```
***** Fun with Object Context *****

ObjectContextApp.SportsCar object in context 0
-> Ctx Prop: LeaseLifeTimeServiceProperty

ObjectContextApp.SportsCar object in context 0
-> Ctx Prop: LeaseLifeTimeServiceProperty

ObjectContextApp.SportsCarTS object in context 1
-> Ctx Prop: LeaseLifeTimeServiceProperty
-> Ctx Prop: Synchronization
```

Given that the SportsCar class has not been qualified with a context attribute, the CLR has allocated sport and sport2 into context 0 (i.e., the default context). However, the SportsCarTS object is loaded into a unique contextual boundary (which has been assigned a context ID of 1), given the fact that this context-bound type was adorned with the [Synchronization] attribute.

■ **Source Code** The ObjectContextApp project is included under the Chapter 17 subdirectory.

Summarizing Processes, AppDomains, and Context

At this point, you hopefully have a much better idea about how a .NET assembly is hosted by the CLR. To summarize the key points:

- A .NET process hosts one to many application domains. Each AppDomain is able to host any number of related .NET assemblies. AppDomains may be independently loaded and unloaded by the CLR (or programmatically via the System.AppDomain type).

- A given AppDomain consists of one to many contexts. Using a context, the CLR is able to place a "special needs" object into a logical container, to ensure that its runtime requirements are honored.

If the previous pages have seemed to be a bit too low level for your liking, fear not. For the most part, the CLR automatically deals with the details of processes, application domains, and contexts on your behalf. The good news, however, is that this information provides a solid foundation for understanding multithreaded programming under the .NET platform.

Summary

The point of this chapter was to examine exactly how a .NET-executable image is hosted by the .NET platform. As you have seen, the long-standing notion of a Windows process has been altered under the hood to accommodate the needs of the CLR. A single process (which can be programmatically manipulated via the System.Diagnostics.Process type) is now composed of one or more application domains, which represent isolated and independent boundaries within a process.

As you have seen, a single process can host multiple application domains, each of which is capable of hosting and executing any number of related assemblies. Furthermore, a single application domain can contain any number of contextual boundaries. Using this additional level of type isolation, the CLR can ensure that special-need objects are handled correctly.

## CHAPTER 18

Understanding CIL and the Role of Dynamic Assemblies

When you are building a full-scale .NET application, you will most certainly make use of C# (or a similar managed language such as Visual Basic), given their inherent productivity and ease of use. However, as you learned in the very first chapter, the role of a managed compiler is to translate *.cs code files into terms of CIL code, type metadata, and an assembly manifest. As it turns out, CIL is a full-fledged .NET programming language, with its own syntax, semantics, and compiler (ilasm.exe).

In this chapter, you will be given a tour of .NET's mother tongue. Here you will understand the distinction between a CIL *directive*, CIL *attribute*, and CIL *opcode*. You will then learn about the role of round-trip engineering of a .NET assembly and various CIL programming tools. The remainder of the chapter will then walk you through the basics of defining namespaces, types, and members using the grammar of CIL. We'll wrap up with an examination of the role of the System.Reflection.Emit namespace and examine how it is possible to construct an assembly (with CIL instructions) dynamically at runtime.

Of course, few programmers will ever need to work with raw CIL code on a day-to-day basis. Therefore, I will start up this chapter by examining a few reasons why getting to know the syntax and semantics of this low-level .NET language might be worth your while.

Reasons for Learning the Grammar of CIL

CIL is the true mother tongue of the .NET platform. When you build a .NET assembly using your managed language of choice (C#, VB, F#, COBOL.NET, etc.), the associated compiler translates your source code into terms of CIL. Like any programming language, CIL provides numerous structural and implementation-centric tokens. Given that CIL is just another .NET programming language, it should come as no surprise that it is possible to build your .NET assemblies directly using CIL and the CIL compiler (ilasm.exe) that ships with the .NET Framework 4.5 SDK.

Now while it is true that few programmers would choose to build an entire .NET application directly with CIL, CIL is still an extremely interesting intellectual pursuit. Simply put, the more you understand the grammar of CIL, the better able you are to move into the realm of advanced .NET development. By way of some concrete examples, individuals who possess an understanding of CIL are capable of the following:

- Talking intelligently about how different .NET programming languages map their respective keywords to CIL tokens.

- Disassembling an existing .NET assembly, editing the CIL code, and recompiling the updated code base into a modified .NET binary. For example, there are some scenarios where you might need to modify CIL in order to interoperate with some advanced COM features.

- Building dynamic assemblies using the System.Reflection.Emit namespace. This API allows you to generate an in-memory .NET assembly, which can optionally be persisted to disk.

- Leveraging aspects of the CTS that are not supported by higher-level managed languages, but do exist at the level of CIL. To be sure, CIL is the only .NET language that allows you to access each and every aspect of the CTS. For example, using raw CIL, you are able to define global-level members and fields (which are not permissible in C#).

Again, to be perfectly clear, if you choose *not* to concern yourself with the details of CIL code, you are still absolutely able to gain mastery of C# and the .NET base class libraries. In many ways, knowledge of CIL is analogous to a C(++) programmer's understanding of assembly language. Those who know the ins and outs of the low-level "goo" are able to create rather advanced solutions for the task at hand and gain a deeper understanding of the underlying programming (and runtime) environment. So, if you are up for the challenge, let's begin to examine the details of CIL.

■ **Note** Understand that this chapter is not intended to be a comprehensive treatment of the syntax and semantics of CIL. If you require a full examination of the topic, I'd recommend downloading the official ECMA specification (ecma-335.pdf) from the ECMA International web site (www.ecma-international.org).

Examining CIL Directives, Attributes, and Opcodes

When you begin to investigate low-level languages such as CIL, you are guaranteed to find new (and often intimidating-sounding) names for very familiar concepts. For example, at this point in the text, if you were shown the following set of items

{new, public, this, base, get, set, explicit, unsafe, enum, operator, partial}

you would most certainly understand them to be keywords of the C# language (which is correct). However, if you look more closely at the members of this set, you might be able to see that while each item is indeed a C# keyword, it has radically different semantics. For example, the enum keyword defines a System.Enum-derived type, while the this and base keywords allow you to reference the current object or the object's parent class, respectively. The unsafe keyword is used to establish a block of code that cannot be directly monitored by the CLR, while the operator keyword allows you to build a hidden (specially named) method that will be called when you apply a specific C# operator (such as the plus sign).

In stark contrast to a higher-level language such as C#, CIL does not just simply define a general set of keywords, per se. Rather, the token set understood by the CIL compiler is subdivided into the following three broad categories based on semantics:

- CIL directives

- CIL attributes

- CIL operation codes (opcodes)

Each category of CIL token is expressed using a particular syntax, and the tokens are combined to build a valid .NET assembly.

The Role of CIL Directives

First up, there is a set of well-known CIL tokens that are used to describe the overall structure of a .NET assembly. These tokens are called *directives*. CIL directives are used to inform the CIL compiler how to define the namespaces(s), type(s), and member(s) that will populate an assembly.

Directives are represented syntactically using a single dot (.) prefix (e.g., .namespace, .class, .publickeytoken, .method, .assembly, etc.). Thus, if your *.il file (the conventional extension for a file containing CIL code) has a single .namespace directive and three .class directives, the CIL compiler will generate an assembly that defines a single .NET namespace containing three .NET class types.

The Role of CIL Attributes

In many cases, CIL directives in and of themselves are not descriptive enough to fully express the definition of a given .NET type or type member. Given this fact, many CIL directives can be further specified with various CIL *attributes* to qualify how a directive should be processed. For example, the .class directive can be adorned with the public attribute (to establish the type visibility), the extends attribute (to explicitly specify the type's base class), and the implements attribute (to list the set of interfaces supported by the type).

■ **Note** Don't confuse a ".NET attribute" (see Chapter 15) with that of a "CIL attribute," which are two very different concepts.

The Role of CIL Opcodes

Once a .NET assembly, namespace, and type set have been defined in terms of CIL using various directives and related attributes, the final remaining task is to provide the type's implementation logic. This is a job for *operation codes*, or simply *opcodes*. In the tradition of other low-level languages, many CIL opcodes tend to be cryptic and completely unpronounceable by us mere humans. For example, if you need to load a string variable into memory, you don't use a friendly opcode named LoadString, but rather ldstr.

Now, to be fair, some CIL opcodes do map quite naturally to their C# counterparts (e.g., box, unbox, throw, and sizeof). As you will see, the opcodes of CIL are always used within the scope of a member's implementation, and unlike CIL directives, they are never written with a dot prefix.

The CIL Opcode/CIL Mnemonic Distinction

As just explained, opcodes such as ldstr are used to implement the members of a given type. In reality, however, tokens such as ldstr are *CIL mnemonics* for the actual *binary CIL opcodes*. To clarify the distinction, assume you have authored the following method in C#:

```
static int Add(int x, int y)
{
  return x + y;
}
```

The act of adding two numbers is expressed in terms of the CIL opcode 0X58. In a similar vein, subtracting two numbers is expressed using the opcode 0X59, and the act of allocating a new object on the managed heap is achieved using the 0X73 opcode. Given this reality, understand that the "CIL code" processed by a JIT compiler is actually nothing more than blobs of binary data.

Thankfully, for each binary opcode of CIL, there is a corresponding mnemonic. For example, the add mnemonic can be used rather than 0X58, sub rather than 0X59, and newobj rather than 0X73. Given this opcode/mnemonic distinction, realize that CIL decompilers such as ildasm.exe translate an assembly's binary opcodes into their corresponding CIL mnemonics. For example, here would be the CIL presented by ildasm.exe for the previous C# Add() method:

```
.method private hidebysig static int32 Add(int32 x,
 int32 y) cil managed
{
// Code size     9 (0x9)
.maxstack 2
.locals init ([0] int32 CS$1$0000)
IL_0000: nop
IL_0001: ldarg.0
IL_0002: ldarg.1
IL_0003: add
IL_0004: stloc.0
IL_0005: br.s      IL_0007
IL_0007: ldloc.0
IL_0008: ret
}
```

Unless you're building some extremely low-level .NET software (such as a custom managed compiler), you'll never need to concern yourself with the literal numeric binary opcodes of CIL. For all practical purposes, when .NET programmers speak about "CIL opcodes," they're referring to the set of friendly string token mnemonics (as I've done within this text, and will do for the remainder of this chapter) rather than the underlying numerical values.

Pushing and Popping: The Stack-Based Nature of CIL

Higher-level .NET languages (such as C#) attempt to hide low-level CIL grunge from view as much as possible. One aspect of .NET development that is particularly well hidden is the fact that CIL is a stack-based programming language. Recall from the examination of the collection namespaces (see Chapter 9) that the Stack<T> class can be used to push a value onto a stack as well as pop the topmost value off of the stack for use. Of course, CIL developers do not literally use an object of type Stack<T> to load and unload the values to be evaluated; however, the same pushing and popping mind-set still applies.

Formally speaking, the entity used to hold a set of values to be evaluated is termed the *virtual execution stack*. As you will see, CIL provides a number of opcodes that are used to push a value onto the stack; this process is termed *loading*. As well, CIL defines a number of additional opcodes that transfer the topmost value on the stack into memory (such as a local variable) using a process termed *storing*.

In the world of CIL, it is impossible to access a point of data directly, including locally defined variables, incoming method arguments, or field data of a type. Rather, you are required to explicitly load the item onto the stack, only to then pop it off for later use (keep this point in mind, as it will help explain why a given block of CIL code can look a bit redundant).

■ **Note** Recall that CIL is not directly executed, but compiled on demand. During the compilation of CIL code, many of these implementation redundancies are optimized away. Furthermore, if you enable the code optimization option for your current project (using the Build tab of the Visual Studio Project Properties window), the compiler will also remove various CIL redundancies.

To understand how CIL leverages a stack-based processing model, consider a simple C# method, PrintMessage(), which takes no arguments and returns void. Within the implementation of this method, you will simply print out the value of a local string variable to the standard output stream, like so:

```
public void PrintMessage()
{
  string myMessage = "Hello.";
  Console.WriteLine(myMessage);
}
```

If you were to examine how the C# compiler translates this method in terms of CIL, you would first find that the PrintMessage() method defines a storage slot for a local variable using the .locals directive. The local string is then loaded and stored in this local variable using the ldstr (load string) and stloc.0 opcodes (which can be read as "store the current value in a local variable at storage slot zero").

The value (again, at index 0) is then loaded into memory using the ldloc.0 ("load the local argument at index 0") opcode for use by the System.Console.WriteLine() method invocation (specified using the call opcode). Finally, the function returns via the ret opcode. Here is the (annotated) CIL code for the PrintMessage() method (note that I've removed the nop opcodes from this listing, for brevity):

```
.method public hidebysig instance void PrintMessage() cil managed
{
  .maxstack  1
  // Define a local string variable (at index 0).
  .locals init ([0] string myMessage)

  // Load a string onto the stack with the value "Hello."
  ldstr  " Hello."

  // Store string value on the stack in the local variable.
  stloc.0

  // Load the value at index 0.
  ldloc.0

  // Call method with current value.
  call   void [mscorlib]System.Console::WriteLine(string)
  ret
}
```

■ **Note** As you can see, CIL supports code comments using the double-slash syntax (as well as the /*...*/ syntax, for that matter). As in C#, code comments are completely ignored by the CIL compiler.

Now that you have the basics of CIL directives, attributes, and opcodes, let's see a practical use of CIL programming, beginning with the topic of round-trip engineering.

Understanding Round-Trip Engineering

You are aware of how to use `ildasm.exe` to view the CIL code generated by the C# compiler (see Chapter 1). What you might not know, however, is that `ildasm.exe` allows you to dump the CIL contained within an assembly loaded into `ildasm.exe` to an external file. Once you have the CIL code at your disposal, you are free to edit and recompile the code base using the CIL compiler, `ilasm.exe`.

■ **Note** Also recall that `reflector.exe` can be used to view the CIL code of a given assembly, as well as to translate the CIL code into an approximate C# code base.

Formally speaking, this technique is termed *round-trip engineering*, and it can be useful under a number of circumstances, such as the following:

- You need to modify an assembly for which you no longer have the source code.

- You are working with a less-than-perfect .NET language compiler that has emitted ineffective (or flat-out incorrect) CIL code, and you wish to modify the code base.

- You are constructing a COM interoperability library and wish to account for some COM IDL attributes that have been lost during the conversion process (such as the COM [helpstring] attribute).

To illustrate the process of round-tripping, begin by creating a new C# code file (HelloProgram.cs) using a simple text editor, and define the following class type (you are free to create a new Console Application project using Visual Studio if you wish. However, be sure to delete the AssemblyInfo.cs file to decrease the amount of generated CIL code):

```
// A simple C# console app.
using System;

// Note that we are not wrapping our class in a namespace,
// to help simplify the generated CIL code.
class Program
{
  static void Main(string[] args)
  {
    Console.WriteLine("Hello CIL code!");
    Console.ReadLine();
```

```
  }
}
```

Save your file to a convenient location (for example, C:\RoundTrip) and compile your program using csc.exe, like so:

```
csc HelloProgram.cs
```

Now, open HelloProgram.exe with ildasm.exe and, using the File Dump menu option, save the raw CIL code to a new *.il file (HelloProgram.il) in the same folder containing your compiled assembly (all of the default values of the resulting dialog box are fine as is).

■ **Note** ildasm.exe will also generate a *.res file when dumping the contents of an assembly to file. These resource files can be ignored (and deleted) throughout this chapter, as you will not be making use of them.

Now you are able to view HelloProgram.il using your text editor of choice. Here is the (slightly reformatted and annotated) result:

```
// Referenced assemblies.
.assembly extern mscorlib
{
  .publickeytoken = (B7 7A 5C 56 19 34 E0 89 )
  .ver 4:0:0:0
}

// Our assembly.
.assembly HelloProgram
{
  /****  TargetFrameworkAttribute data removed for clarity! ****/

  .hash algorithm 0x00008004
  .ver 0:0:0:0
}
.module HelloProgram.exe
.imagebase 0x00400000
.file alignment 0x00000200
.stackreserve 0x00100000
.subsystem 0x0003
.corflags 0x00000003

// Definition of Program class.
.class private auto ansi beforefieldinit Program
  extends [mscorlib]System.Object
{
  .method private hidebysig static void  Main(string[] args) cil managed
  {
    // Marks this method as the entry point of the
    // executable.
```

```
    .entrypoint
    .maxstack  8
    IL_0000:  nop
    IL_0001:  ldstr  "Hello CIL code!"
    IL_0006:  call void [mscorlib]System.Console::WriteLine(string)
    IL_000b:  nop
    IL_000c:  call string [mscorlib]System.Console::ReadLine()
    IL_0011:  pop
    IL_0012:  ret
  }

  // The default constructor.
  .method public hidebysig specialname rtspecialname
    instance void  .ctor() cil managed
  {
    .maxstack  8
    IL_0000:  ldarg.0
    IL_0001:  call instance void [mscorlib]System.Object::.ctor()
    IL_0006:  ret
  }
}
```

First, notice that the *.il file opens by declaring each externally referenced assembly the current assembly is compiled against. Here, you can see a single .assembly extern token set for the always present mscorlib.dll. Of course, if your class library made use of types within other referenced assemblies, you would find additional .assembly extern directives.

Next, you find the formal definition of your HelloProgram.exe assembly, which has been assigned a default version of 0.0.0.0 (given that you did not specify a value using the [AssemblyVersion] attribute). The assembly is further described using various CIL directives (such as .module, .imagebase, and so forth).

After documenting the externally referenced assemblies and defining the current assembly, you find a definition of the Program type. Note that the .class directive has various attributes (many of which are actually optional) such as extends, shown here, which marks the base class of the type:

```
.class private auto ansi beforefieldinit Program
  extends [mscorlib]System.Object
{ ... }
```

The bulk of the CIL code represents the implementation of the class's default constructor and the Main() method, both of which are defined (in part) with the .method directive. Once the members have been defined using the correct directives and attributes, they are implemented using various opcodes.

It is critical to understand that when interacting with .NET types (such as System.Console) in CIL, you will *always* need to use the type's fully qualified name. Furthermore, the type's fully qualified name must *always* be prefixed with the friendly name of the defining assembly (in square brackets). Consider the following CIL implementation of Main():

```
.method private hidebysig static void  Main(string[] args) cil managed
{
  .entrypoint
  .maxstack  8
  IL_0000:  nop
  IL_0001:  ldstr "Hello CIL code!"
  IL_0006:  call void [mscorlib]System.Console::WriteLine(string)
```

```
 IL_000b:  nop
 IL_000c:  call string [mscorlib]System.Console::ReadLine()
 IL_0011:  pop
 IL_0012:  ret
}
```

The implementation of the default constructor in terms of CIL code makes use of yet another "load-centric" instruction (ldarg.0). In this case, the value loaded onto the stack is not a custom variable specified by you, but the current object reference (more details on this later). Also note that the default constructor explicitly makes a call to the base class constructor, as follows (which, in this case, is your good friend System.Object):

```
.method public hidebysig specialname rtspecialname
  instance void  .ctor() cil managed
{
  .maxstack  8
  IL_0000:  ldarg.0
  IL_0001:  call instance void [mscorlib]System.Object::.ctor()
  IL_0006:  ret
}
```

The Role of CIL Code Labels

One thing you certainly have noticed is that each line of implementation code is prefixed with a token of the form IL_XXX: (e.g., IL_0000:, IL_0001:, and so on). These tokens are called *code labels* and may be named in any manner you choose (provided they are not duplicated within the same member scope). When you dump an assembly to file using ildasm.exe, it will automatically generate code labels that follow an IL_XXX: naming convention. However, you may change them to reflect a more descriptive marker. For example:

```
.method private hidebysig static void  Main(string[] args) cil managed
{
  .entrypoint
  .maxstack  8
  Nothing_1:  nop
  Load_String:  ldstr  "Hello CIL code!"
  PrintToConsole: call void [mscorlib]System.Console::WriteLine(string)
  Nothing_2:  nop
  WaitFor_KeyPress: call string [mscorlib]System.Console::ReadLine()
  RemoveValueFromStack:  pop
  Leave_Function:  ret
}
```

The truth of the matter is that most code labels are completely optional. The only time code labels are truly mandatory is when you are authoring CIL code that makes use of various branching or looping constructs, as you can specify where to direct the flow of logic via these code labels. For the current example, you can remove these autogenerated labels altogether with no ill effect, like so:

```
.method private hidebysig static void Main(string[] args) cil managed
{
  .entrypoint
  .maxstack  8
  nop
```

```
    ldstr  "Hello CIL code!"
    call void [mscorlib]System.Console::WriteLine(string)
    nop
    call string [mscorlib]System.Console::ReadLine()
    pop
    ret
}
```

Interacting with CIL: Modifying an *.il File

Now that you have a better understanding of how a basic CIL file is composed, let's complete the round-tripping experiment. The goal here is to update the CIL within the existing *.il file as follows:

- Add a reference to the System.Windows.Forms.dll assembly.

- Load a local string within Main().

- Call the System.Windows.Forms.MessageBox.Show() method using the local string variable as an argument.

The first step is to add a new .assembly directive (qualified with the extern attribute) that specifies your assembly requires the System.Windows.Forms.dll assembly. To do so, update the *.il file with the following logic after the external reference to mscorlib:

```
.assembly extern System.Windows.Forms
{
  .publickeytoken = (B7 7A 5C 56 19 34 E0 89)
  .ver 4:0:0:0
}
```

Be aware that the value assigned to the .ver directive may differ depending on which version of the .NET platform you have installed on your development machine. Here, you see that System.Windows.Forms.dll version 4.0.0.0 is used and has the public key token of B77A5C561934E089. If you open the GAC (see Chapter 14) and locate your version of the System.Windows.Forms.dll assembly, you can simply copy the correct version and public key token value.

Next, you need to alter the current implementation of the Main() method. Locate this method within the *.il file and remove the current implementation code (the .maxstack and .entrypoint directives should remain intact), like so:

```
.method private hidebysig static void  Main(string[] args) cil managed
{
  .entrypoint
  .maxstack  8
  // ToDo: Write new CIL code!
}
```

Again, the goal here is to push a new string onto the stack and call the MessageBox.Show() method (rather than the Console.WriteLine() method). Recall that when you specify the name of an external type, you must make use of the type's fully qualified name (in conjunction with the friendly name of the assembly). Also notice that in terms of CIL, every method call documents the fully qualified return type. Keeping these things in mind, update the Main() method as follows:

```
.method private hidebysig static void Main(string[] args) cil managed
{
  .entrypoint
  .maxstack  8

  ldstr  "CIL is way cool"
  call valuetype [System.Windows.Forms]
    System.Windows.Forms.DialogResult
    [System.Windows.Forms]
    System.Windows.Forms.MessageBox::Show(string)
  pop
  ret
}
```

In effect, you have just updated the CIL code to correspond to the following C# class definition:

```
class Program
{
  static void Main(string[] args)
  {
    System.Windows.Forms.MessageBox.Show("CIL is way cool");
  }
}
```

Compiling CIL Code Using ilasm.exe

Assuming you have saved this modified *.il file, you can compile a new .NET assembly using the ilasm.exe (CIL compiler) utility. While the CIL compiler has numerous command-line options (all of which can be seen by specifying the -? option), Table 18-1 shows the core flags of interest.

Table 18-1. Common ilasm.exe *Command-Line Flags*

Flag	Meaning in Life
/debug	Includes debug information (such as local variable and argument names, as well as line numbers).
/dll	Produces a *.dll file as output.
/exe	Produces an *.exe file as output. This is the default setting and may be omitted.
/key	Compiles the assembly with a strong name using a given *.snk file.
/output	Specifies the output file name and extension. If you do not make use of the /output flag, the resulting file name (minus the file extension) is the same as the name of the first source file.

To compile your updated `HelloProgram.il` file into a new .NET *.exe, you can issue the following command within a Developer Command prompt:

```
ilasm /exe HelloProgram.il /output=NewAssembly.exe
```

Assuming things have worked successfully, you will see the report shown here:

```
Microsoft (R) .NET Framework IL Assembler.  Version 4.0.21006.1
Copyright (c) Microsoft Corporation.  All rights reserved.
Assembling 'HelloProgram.il'  to EXE --> 'NewAssembly.exe'
Source file is UTF-8

Assembled method Program::Main
Assembled method Program::.ctor
Creating PE file

Emitting classes:
Class 1:         Program

Emitting fields and methods:
Global
Class 1 Methods: 2;

Emitting events and properties:
Global
Class 1
Writing PE file
Operation completed successfully
```

At this point, you can run your new application. Sure enough, rather than showing a message within the console window, you will now see a message box displaying your message. While the output of this simple example is not all that spectacular, it does illustrate one practical use of programming in CIL round-tripping.

The Role of peverify.exe

When you are building or modifying assemblies using CIL code, it is always advisable to verify that the compiled binary image is a well-formed .NET image using the `peverify.exe` command-line tool, like so:

```
peverify NewAssembly.exe
```

This tool will examine all opcodes within the specified assembly for valid CIL code. For example, in terms of CIL code, the evaluation stack must always be empty before exiting a function. If you forget to pop off any remaining values, the `ilasm.exe` compiler will still generate a compiled assembly (given that compilers are concerned only with *syntax*). `peverify.exe`, on the other hand, is concerned with *semantics*. If you did forget to clear the stack before exiting a given function, `peverify.exe` will let you know before you try running your code base.

■ **Source Code** The RoundTrip example is included under the Chapter 18 subdirectory.

Understanding CIL Directives and Attributes

Now that you have seen how `ildasm.exe` and `ilasm.exe` can be used to perform a round-trip, you can get down to the business of checking out the syntax and semantics of CIL itself. The next sections will walk you through the process of authoring a custom namespace containing a set of types. However, to keep things simple, these types will not contain any implementation logic for their members (yet). After you understand how to create empty types, you can then turn your attention to the process of defining "real" members using CIL opcodes.

Specifying Externally Referenced Assemblies in CIL

Create a new file named `CILTypes.il` using your editor of choice. The first task a CIL project will require is to list the set of external assemblies used by the current assembly. For this example, you will only make use of types found within `mscorlib.dll`. To do so, the `.assembly` directive will be qualified using the external attribute. When you are referencing a strongly named assembly, such as `mscorlib.dll`, you'll want to specify the `.publickeytoken` and `.ver` directives as well, like so:

```
.assembly extern mscorlib
{
  .publickeytoken = (B7 7A 5C 56 19 34 E0 89 )
  .ver 4:0:0:0
}
```

■ **Note** Strictly speaking, you are not required to explicitly reference `mscorlib.dll` as an external reference, as `ilasm.exe` will do so automatically. However, for each external .NET library your CIL project requires, you will need to author a similar `.assembly extern` directive.

Defining the Current Assembly in CIL

The next order of business is to define the assembly you are interested in building using the `.assembly` directive. At the simplest level, an assembly can be defined by specifying the friendly name of the binary, like so:

```
// Our assembly.
.assembly CILTypes { }
```

While this indeed defines a new .NET assembly, you will typically place additional directives within the scope of the assembly declaration. For this example, update your assembly definition to include a version number of 1.0.0.0 using the `.ver` directive (note that each numerical identifier is separated by *colons*, not the C#-centric dot notation), as follows:

```
// Our assembly.
.assembly CILTypes
{
  .ver 1:0:0:0
}
```

Given that the CILTypes assembly is a single-file assembly, you will finish up the assembly definition using the following single .module directive, which marks the official name of your .NET binary, CILTypes.dll:

```
.assembly CILTypes
{
 .ver 1:0:0:0
}
// The module of our single-file assembly.
.module CILTypes.dll
```

In addition to .assembly and .module are CIL directives that further qualify the overall structure of the .NET binary you are composing. Table 18-2 lists a few of the more common assembly-level directives.

Table 18-2. Additional Assembly-Centric Directives

Directive	Meaning in Life
.mresources	If your assembly makes use of internal resources (such as bitmaps or string tables), this directive is used to identify the name of the file that contains the resources to be embedded.
.subsystem	This CIL directive is used to establish the preferred UI that the assembly wishes to execute within. For example, a value of 2 signifies that the assembly should run within a GUI application, whereas a value of 3 denotes a console executable.

Defining Namespaces in CIL

Now that you have defined the look and feel of your assembly (and the required external references), you can create a .NET namespace (MyNamespace) using the .namespace directive, like so:

```
// Our assembly has a single namespace.
.namespace MyNamespace {}
```

Like C#, CIL namespace definitions can be nested within further namespaces. There is no need to define a root namespace here; however, for the sake of argument, assume you wish to create the following root namespace named MyCompany:

```
.namespace MyCompany
{
  .namespace MyNamespace {}
}
```

Like C#, CIL allows you to define a nested namespace as follows:

```
// Defining a nested namespace.
.namespace MyCompany.MyNamespace {}
```

Defining Class Types in CIL

Empty namespaces are not very interesting, so let's now check out the process of defining a class type using CIL. Not surprisingly, the .class directive is used to define a new class. However, this simple directive can be adorned with numerous additional attributes, to further qualify the nature of the type. To illustrate, add a public class to your namespace named MyBaseClass. As in C#, if you do not specify an explicit base class, your type will automatically be derived from System.Object.

```
.namespace MyNamespace
{
  // System.Object base class assumed.
  .class public MyBaseClass {}
}
```

When you are building a class type that derives from any class other than System.Object, you make use of the extends attribute. Whenever you need to reference a type defined within the same assembly, CIL demands that you also make use of the fully qualified name (however, if the base type is within the same assembly, you can omit the assembly's friendly name prefix). Therefore, the following attempt to extend MyBaseClass results in a compiler error:

```
// This will not compile!
.namespace MyNamespace
{
  .class public MyBaseClass {}

  .class public MyDerivedClass
    extends MyBaseClass {}
}
```

To correctly define the parent class of MyDerivedClass, you must specify the full name of MyBaseClass as follows:

```
// Better!
.namespace MyNamespace
{
  .class public MyBaseClass {}

  .class public MyDerivedClass
    extends MyNamespace.MyBaseClass {}
}
```

In addition to the public and extends attributes, a CIL class definition may take numerous additional qualifiers that control the type's visibility, field layout, and so on. Table 18-3 illustrates some (but not all) of the attributes that may be used in conjunction with the .class directive.

Table 18-3. *Various Attributes Used in Conjunction with the* `.class` *Directive*

Attributes	Meaning in Life
`public`, `private`, `nested assembly`, `nested famandassem`, `nested family`, `nested famorassem`, `nested public`, `nested private`	CIL defines various attributes that are used to specify the visibility of a given type. As you can see, raw CIL offers numerous possibilities other than those offered by C#. Refer to ECMA 335 for details if you are interested.
`abstract`, `sealed`	These two attributes may be tacked onto a `.class` directive to define an abstract class or sealed class, respectively.
`auto`, `sequential`, `explicit`	These attributes are used to instruct the CLR how to lay out field data in memory. For class types, the default layout flag (`auto`) is appropriate. Changing this default can be helpful if you need to use P/Invoke to call into unmanaged C code.
`extends`, `implements`	These attributes allow you to define the base class of a type (via extends) or implement an interface on a type (via `implements`).

Defining and Implementing Interfaces in CIL

As odd as it might seem, interface types are defined in CIL using the `.class` directive. However, when the `.class` directive is adorned with the `interface` attribute, the type is realized as a CTS interface type. Once an interface has been defined, it may be bound to a class or structure type using the CIL `implements` attribute, like so:

```
.namespace MyNamespace
{
  // An interface definition.
  .class public interface IMyInterface {}

  // A simple base class.
  .class public MyBaseClass {}

  // MyDerivedClass now implements IMyInterface,
  // and extends MyBaseClass.
  .class public MyDerivedClass
    extends MyNamespace.MyBaseClass
    implements MyNamespace.IMyInterface {}
}
```

■ **Note** The extends clause must precede the implements clause. As well, the implements clause can incorporate a comma-separated list of interfaces.

As you recall from Chapter 9, interfaces can function as the base interface to other interface types in order to build interface hierarchies. However, contrary to what you might be thinking, the extends attribute cannot be used to derive interface A from interface B. The extends attribute is used only to qualify a type's base class. When you wish to extend an interface, you will make use of the implements attribute yet again. For example:

```
// Extending interfaces in terms of CIL.
.class public interface IMyInterface {}

.class public interface IMyOtherInterface
  implements MyNamespace.IMyInterface {}
```

Defining Structures in CIL

The .class directive can be used to define a CTS structure if the type extends System.ValueType. As well, the .class directive must be qualified with the sealed attribute (given that structures can never be a base structure to other value types). If you attempt to do otherwise, ilasm.exe will issue a compiler error.

```
// A structure definition is always sealed.
.class public sealed MyStruct
  extends [mscorlib]System.ValueType{}
```

Do be aware that CIL provides a shorthand notation to define a structure type. If you use the value attribute, the new type will derive the type from [mscorlib]System.ValueType automatically. Therefore, you could define MyStruct as follows:

```
// Shorthand notation for declaring a structure.
.class public sealed value MyStruct{}
```

Defining Enums in CIL

.NET enumerations (as you recall) derive from System.Enum, which is a System.ValueType (and therefore must also be sealed). When you wish to define an enum in terms of CIL, simply extend [mscorlib]System.Enum, like so:

```
// An enum.
.class public sealed MyEnum
  extends [mscorlib]System.Enum{}
```

Like a structure definition, enumerations can be defined with a shorthand notation using the enum attribute. For example:

```
// Enum shorthand.
.class public sealed enum MyEnum{}
```

You'll see how to specify the name/value pairs of an enumeration in just a moment.

■ **Note** The other fundamental .NET type, the delegate, also has a specific CIL representation. See Chapter 10 for details.

Defining Generics in CIL

Generic types also have a specific representation in the syntax of CIL. Recall from Chapter 9 that a given generic type or generic member may have one or more type parameters. For example, the List<T> type has a single type parameter, while Dictionary<TKey, TValue> has two. In terms of CIL, the number of type parameters is specified using a backward-leaning single tick, `, followed by a numerical value representing the number of type parameters. Like C#, the actual value of the type parameters is encased within angled brackets.

■ **Note** On most keyboards, the ` character can be found on the key above the Tab key (and to the left of the 1 key).

For example, assume you wish to create a List<T> variable, where T is of type System.Int32. In CIL, you would author the following (which could appear in any CIL method scope):

```
// In C#: List<int> myInts = new List<int>();
newobj instance void class [mscorlib]
   System.Collections.Generic.List`1<int32>::.ctor()
```

Notice that this generic class is defined as List`1<int32>, as List<T> has a single type parameter. However, if you needed to define a Dictionary<string, int>type, you would do so as the following:

```
// In C#: Dictionary<string, int> d = new Dictionary<string, int>();
newobj instance void class [mscorlib]
   System.Collections.Generic.Dictionary`2<string,int32>::.ctor()
```

As another example, if you have a generic type that uses another generic type as a type parameter, you would author CIL code such as the following:

```
// In C#: List<List<int>> myInts = new List<List<int>>();
newobj instance void class [mscorlib]
 System.Collections.Generic.List`1<class
 [mscorlib]System.Collections.Generic.List`1<int32>>::.ctor()
```

Compiling the CILTypes.il file

Even though you have not yet added any members or implementation code to the types you have defined, you are able to compile this *.il file into a .NET DLL assembly (which you must do, as you have not specified a Main() method). Open up a command prompt and enter the following command to ilasm.exe:

```
ilasm /dll CilTypes.il
```

After you have done so, can now open your compiled assembly into ildasm.exe to verify the creation of each type. After you have confirmed the contents of your assembly, run peverify.exe against it, like so:

```
peverify CilTypes.dll
```

Notice that you are issued errors, given that all your types are completely empty. Here is some partial output:

```
Microsoft (R) .NET Framework PE Verifier.  Version  4.0.21006.1
Copyright (c) Microsoft Corporation.  All rights reserved.

[MD]: Error: Value class has neither fields nor size parameter. [token:0x02000005]
[MD]: Error: Enum has no instance field. [token:0x02000006]
...
```

To understand how to populate a type with content, you first need to examine the fundamental data types of CIL.

.NET Base Class Library, C#, and CIL Data Type Mappings

Table 18-4 illustrates how a .NET base class type maps to the corresponding C# keyword, and how each C# keyword maps into raw CIL. As well, Table 18-4 documents the shorthand constant notations used for each CIL type. As you will see in just a moment, these constants are often referenced by numerous CIL opcodes.

Table 18-4. Mapping .NET Base Class Types to C# Keywords, and C# Keywords to CIL

.NET Base Class Type	C# Keyword	CIL Representation	CIL Constant Notation
System.SByte	sbyte	int8	I1
System.Byte	byte	unsigned int8	U1
System.Int16	short	int16	I2
System.UInt16	ushort	unsigned int16	U2
System.Int32	int	int32	I4
System.UInt32	uint	unsigned int32	U4
System.Int64	long	int64	I8
System.UInt64	ulong	unsigned int64	U8
System.Char	char	char	CHAR
System.Single	float	float32	R4
System.Double	double	float64	R8

System.Boolean	bool	bool	BOOLEAN
System.String	string	string	N/A
System.Object	object	object	N/A
System.Void	void	void	VOID

■ **Note** The System.IntPtr and System.UIntPtr types map to native int and native unsigned int (this is good to know, as many of COM interoperability and P/Invoke scenarios use these extensively).

Defining Type Members in CIL

As you are already aware, .NET types may support various members. Enumerations have some set of name/value pairs. Structures and classes may have constructors, fields, methods, properties, static members, and so on. Over the course of this book's first 17 chapters, you have already seen partial CIL definitions for the items previously mentioned, but nevertheless, here is a quick recap of how various members map to CIL primitives.

Defining Field Data in CIL

Enumerations, structures, and classes can all support field data. In each case, the .field directive will be used. For example, let's breathe some life into the skeleton MyEnum enumeration and define the following three name/value pairs (note the values are specified within parentheses):

```
.class public sealed enum MyEnum
{
 .field public static literal valuetype
  MyNamespace.MyEnum A = int32(0)
 .field public static literal valuetype
  MyNamespace.MyEnum B = int32(1)
 .field public static literal valuetype
  MyNamespace.MyEnum C = int32(2)
}
```

Fields that reside within the scope of a .NET System.Enum-derived type are qualified using the static and literal attributes. As you would guess, these attributes set up the field data to be a fixed value accessible from the type itself (e.g., MyEnum.A).

■ **Note** The values assigned to an enum value may also be in hexadecimal with a 0x prefix.

Of course, when you wish to define a point of field data within a class or structure, you are not limited to a point of public static literal data. For example, you could update MyBaseClass to support two points of private, instance-level field data, set to default values:

```
.class public MyBaseClass
{
  .field private string stringField = "hello!"
  .field private int32 intField = int32(42)
}
```

As in C#, class field data will automatically be initialized to an appropriate default value. If you wish to allow the object user to supply custom values at the time of creation for each of these points of private field data, you (of course) need to create custom constructors.

Defining Type Constructors in CIL

The CTS supports both instance-level and class-level (static) constructors. In terms of CIL, instance-level constructors are represented using the .ctor token, while a static-level constructor is expressed via .cctor (class constructor). Both of these CIL tokens must be qualified using the rtspecialname (return type special name) and specialname attributes. Simply put, these attributes are used to identify a specific CIL token that can be treated in unique ways by a given .NET language. For example, in C#, constructors do not define a return type; however, in terms of CIL, the return value of a constructor is indeed void:

```
.class public MyBaseClass
{
  .field private string stringField
  .field private int32 intField

  .method public hidebysig specialname rtspecialname
    instance void .ctor(string s, int32 i) cil managed
  {
    // TODO: Add implementation code...
  }
}
```

Note that the .ctor directive has been qualified with the instance attribute (as it is not a static constructor). The cil managed attributes denote that the scope of this method contains CIL code, rather than unmanaged code, which may be used during platform invocation requests.

Defining Properties in CIL

Properties and methods also have specific CIL representations. By way of an example, if MyBaseClass were updated to support a public property named TheString, you would author the following CIL (note again the use of the specialname attribute):

```
.class public MyBaseClass
{
...
  .method public hidebysig specialname
    instance string  get_TheString() cil managed
  {
    // TODO: Add implementation code...
```

```
  }

  .method public hidebysig specialname
    instance void  set_TheString(string 'value') cil managed
  {
    // TODO: Add implementation code...
  }

  .property instance string TheString()
  {
    .get instance string
      MyNamespace.MyBaseClass::get_TheString()
    .set instance void
      MyNamespace.MyBaseClass::set_TheString(string)
  }
}
```

In terms of CIL, a property maps to a pair of methods that take get_ and set_ prefixes. The .property directive makes use of the related .get and .set directives to map property syntax to the correct "specially named" methods.

■ **Note** Notice that the incoming parameter to the set method of a property is placed in single quotation marks, which represents the name of the token to use on the right-hand side of the assignment operator within the method scope.

Defining Member Parameters

In a nutshell, specifying arguments in CIL is (more or less) identical to doing so in C#. For example, each argument is defined by specifying its data type, followed by the parameter name. Furthermore, like C#, CIL provides a way to define input, output, and pass-by-reference parameters. As well, CIL allows you to define a parameter array argument (a.k.a. the C# params keyword), as well as optional parameters.

To illustrate the process of defining parameters in raw CIL, assume you wish to build a method that takes an int32 (by value), an int32 (by reference), a [mscorlib]System.Collection.ArrayList, and a single output parameter (of type int32). In terms of C#, this method would look something like the following:

```
public static void MyMethod(int inputInt,
  ref int refInt, ArrayList ar, out int outputInt)
{
  outputInt = 0;  // Just to satisfy the C# compiler...
}
```

If you were to map this method into CIL terms, you would find that C# reference parameters are marked with an ampersand (&) suffixed to the parameter's underlying data type (int32&).

Output parameters also make use of the & suffix, but they are further qualified using the CIL [out] token. Also notice that if the parameter is a reference type (in this case, the

672

[mscorlib]System.Collections.ArrayList type), the class token is prefixed to the data type (not to be confused with the .class directive!).

```
.method public hidebysig static void MyMethod(int32 inputInt,
  int32& refInt,
  class [mscorlib]System.Collections.ArrayList ar,
  [out] int32& outputInt) cil managed
{
  ...
}
```

Examining CIL Opcodes

The final aspect of CIL code you'll examine in this chapter has to do with the role of various operational codes (opcodes). Recall that an opcode is simply a CIL token used to build the implementation logic for a given member. The complete set of CIL opcodes (which is fairly large) can be grouped into the following broad categories:

- Opcodes that control program flow
- Opcodes that evaluate expressions
- Opcodes that access values in memory (via parameters, local variables, etc.)

To provide some insight to the world of member implementation via CIL, Table 18-5 defines some of the more useful opcodes that are directly related to member implementation logic, grouped by related functionality.

Table 18-5. Various Implementation-Specific CIL Opcodes

Opcodes	Meaning in Life
add, sub, mul, div, rem	These CIL opcodes allow you to add, subtract, multiply, and divide two values (rem returns the remainder of a division operation).
and, or, not, xor	These CIL opcodes allow you to perform bit-wise operations on two values.
ceq, cgt, clt	These CIL opcodes allow you to compare two values on the stack in various manners. For example: ceq: Compare for equality cgt: Compare for greater than clt: Compare for less than
box, unbox	These CIL opcodes are used to convert between reference types and value types.
ret	This CIL opcode is used to exit a method and return a value to the caller (if necessary).

beq, bgt, ble, blt, switch	These CIL opcodes (in addition to many other related opcodes) are used to control branching logic within a method. For example: beq: Break to code label if equal bgt: Break to code label if greater than ble: Break to code label if less than or equal to blt: Break to code label if less than All of the branch-centric opcodes require that you specify a CIL code label to jump to if the result of the test is true.
call	This CIL opcode is used to call a member on a given type.
newarr, newobj	These CIL opcodes allow you to allocate a new array or new object type into memory (respectively).

The next broad category of CIL opcodes (a subset of which is shown in Table 18-6) are used to load (push) arguments onto the virtual execution stack. Note how these load-specific opcodes take an ld (load) prefix.

Table 18-6. The Primary Stack-Centric Opcodes of CIL

Opcode	Meaning in Life
ldarg (with numerous variations)	Loads a method's argument onto the stack. In addition to the general ldarg (which works in conjunction with a given index that identifies the argument), there are numerous other variations. For example, ldarg opcodes that have a numerical suffix (ldarg_0) hard-code which argument to load. As well, variations of the ldarg opcode allow you to hard-code the data type using the CIL constant notation shown in Table 18-4 (ldarg_I4, for an int32), as well as the data type and value (ldarg_I4_5, to load an int32 with the value of 5).
ldc (with numerous variations)	Loads a constant value onto the stack.
ldfld (with numerous variations)	Loads the value of an instance-level field onto the stack.
ldloc (with numerous variations)	Loads the value of a local variable onto the stack.
ldobj	Obtains all the values gathered by a heap-based object and places them on the stack.
ldstr	Loads a string value onto the stack.

In addition to the set of load-specific opcodes, CIL provides numerous opcodes that *explicitly* pop the topmost value off the stack. As shown over the first few examples in this chapter, popping a value off the stack typically involves storing the value into temporary local storage for further use (such as a parameter for an upcoming method invocation). Given this, note how many opcodes that pop the current value off the virtual execution stack take an st (store) prefix. Table 18-7 hits the highlights.

Table 18-7. Various Pop-Centric Opcodes

Opcode	Meaning in Life
pop	Removes the value currently on top of the evaluation stack, but does not bother to store the value
starg	Stores the value on top of the stack into the method argument at a specified index
stloc (with numerous variations)	Pops the current value from the top of the evaluation stack and stores it in a local variable list at a specified index
stobj	Copies a value of a specified type from the evaluation stack into a supplied memory address
stsfld	Replaces the value of a static field with a value from the evaluation stack

Do be aware that various CIL opcodes will *implicitly* pop values off the stack to perform the task at hand. For example, if you are attempting to subtract two numbers using the sub opcode, it should be clear that sub will have to pop off the next two available values before it can perform the calculation. Once the calculation is complete, the result of the value (surprise, surprise) is pushed onto the stack once again.

The .maxstack Directive

When you write method implementations using raw CIL, you need to be mindful of a special directive named .maxstack. As its name suggests, .maxstack establishes the maximum number of variables that may be pushed onto the stack at any given time during the execution of the method. The good news is that the .maxstack directive has a default value (8), which should be safe for a vast majority of methods you might be authoring. However, if you wish to be very explicit, you are able to manually calculate the number of local variables on the stack and define this value explicitly, like so:

```
.method public hidebysig instance void
  Speak() cil managed
{
  // During the scope of this method, exactly
  // 1 value (the string literal) is on the stack.
  .maxstack  1
  ldstr "Hello there..."
  call void [mscorlib]System.Console::WriteLine(string)
  ret
}
```

Declaring Local Variables in CIL

Let's first check out how to declare a local variable. Assume you wish to build a method in CIL named `MyLocalVariables()` that takes no arguments and returns void. Within the method, you wish to define three local variables of type `System.String`, `System.Int32`, and `System.Object`. In C#, this member would appear as follows (recall that locally scoped variables do not receive a default value and should be set to an initial state before further use):

```
public static void MyLocalVariables()
{
  string myStr = "CIL code is fun!";
  int myInt = 33;
  object myObj = new object();
}
```

If you were to construct `MyLocalVariables()` directly in CIL, you could author the following:

```
.method public hidebysig static void
  MyLocalVariables() cil managed
{
  .maxstack  8
  // Define three local variables.
  .locals init ([0] string myStr, [1] int32 myInt, [2] object myObj)
  // Load a string onto the virtual execution stack.
  ldstr "CIL code is fun!"
  // Pop off current value and store in local variable [0].
  stloc.0

  // Load a constant of type "i4"
  // (shorthand for int32) set to the value 33.
  ldc.i4 33
  // Pop off current value and store in local variable [1].
  stloc.1

  // Create a new object and place on stack.
  newobj instance void [mscorlib]System.Object::.ctor()
  // Pop off current value and store in local variable [2].
  stloc.2
  ret
}
```

As you can see, the first step taken to allocate local variables in raw CIL is to make use of the `.locals` directive, which is paired with the `init` attribute. Within the scope of the related parentheses, your goal is to associate a given numerical index to each variable (seen here as [0], [1], and [2]). As you can see, each index is identified by its data type and an optional variable name. After the local variables have been defined, you load a value onto the stack (using the various load-centric opcodes) and store the value within the local variable (using the various storage-centric opcodes).

Mapping Parameters to Local Variables in CIL

You have already seen how to declare local variables in raw CIL using the `.locals init` directive; however, you have yet to see exactly how to map incoming parameters to local methods. Consider the following static C# method:

```
public static int Add(int a, int b)
{
  return a + b;
}
```

This innocent-looking method has a lot to say in terms of CIL. First, the incoming arguments (a and b) must be pushed onto the virtual execution stack using the ldarg (load argument) opcode. Next, the add opcode will be used to pop the next two values off the stack and find the summation, and store the value on the stack yet again. Finally, this sum is popped off the stack and returned to the caller via the ret opcode. If you were to disassemble this C# method using ildasm.exe, you would find numerous additional tokens injected by csc.exe, but the crux of the CIL code is quite simple.

```
.method public hidebysig static int32  Add(int32 a,
  int32 b) cil managed
{
  .maxstack  2
  ldarg.0    // Load "a" onto the stack.
  ldarg.1    // Load "b" onto the stack.
  add        // Add both values.
  ret
}
```

The Hidden this Reference

Notice that the two incoming arguments (a and b) are referenced within the CIL code using their indexed position (index 0 and index 1), given that the virtual execution stack begins indexing at position 0.

One thing to be very mindful of when you are examining or authoring CIL code is that every nonstatic method that takes incoming arguments automatically receives an implicit additional parameter, which is a reference to the current object (think the C# this keyword). Given this, if the Add() method were defined as *non*static, like so:

```
// No longer static!
public int Add(int a, int b)
{
  return a + b;
}
```

the incoming a and b arguments are loaded using ldarg.1 and ldarg.2 (rather than the expected ldarg.0 and ldarg.1 opcodes). Again, the reason is that slot 0 actually contains the implicit this reference. Consider the following pseudo-code:

```
// This is JUST pseudo-code!
.method public hidebysig static int32 AddTwoIntParams(
  MyClass_HiddenThisPointer this, int32 a, int32 b) cil managed
{
  ldarg.0    // Load MyClass_HiddenThisPointer onto the stack.
  ldarg.1    // Load "a" onto the stack.
```

```
ldarg.2    // Load "b" onto the stack.
...
}
```

Representing Iteration Constructs in CIL

Iteration constructs in the C# programming language are represented using the for, foreach, while, and do keywords, each of which has a specific representation in CIL. Consider the following classic for loop:

```
public static void CountToTen()
{
  for(int i = 0; i < 10; i++)
    ;
}
```

Now, as you may recall, the br opcodes (br, blt, and so on) are used to control a break in flow when some condition has been met. In this example, you have set up a condition in which the for loop should break out of its cycle when the local variable i is equal to or greater than the value of 10. With each pass, the value of 1 is added to i, at which point the test condition is yet again evaluated.

Also recall that when you make use of any of the CIL branching opcodes, you will need to define a specific code label (or two) that marks the location to jump to when the condition is indeed true. Given these points, ponder the following (augmented) CIL code generated via ildasm.exe (including the autogenerated code labels):

```
.method public hidebysig static void CountToTen() cil managed
{
  .maxstack  2
  .locals init ([0] int32 i)   // Init the local integer "i".
  IL_0000:  ldc.i4.0          // Load this value onto the stack.
  IL_0001:  stloc.0           // Store this value at index "0".
  IL_0002:  br.s IL_0008      // Jump to IL_0008.
  IL_0004:  ldloc.0           // Load value of variable at index 0.
  IL_0005:  ldc.i4.1          // Load the value "1" on the stack.
  IL_0006:  add               // Add current value on the stack at index 0.
  IL_0007:  stloc.0
  IL_0008:  ldloc.0           // Load value at index "0".
  IL_0009:  ldc.i4.s   10     // Load value of "10" onto the stack.
  IL_000b:  blt.s IL_0004     // Less than?  If so, jump back to IL_0004
  IL_000d:  ret
}
```

In a nutshell, this CIL code begins by defining the local int32 and loading it onto the stack. At this point, you jump back and forth between code label IL_0008 and IL_0004, each time bumping the value of i by 1 and testing to see whether i is still less than the value 10. If so, you exit the method.

■ **Source Code** The CilTypes example is included under the Chapter 18 subdirectory.

Building a .NET Assembly with CIL

Now that you've taken a tour of the syntax and semantics of raw CIL, it's time to solidify your current understanding by building a .NET application using nothing but ilasm.exe and your text editor of choice. Specifically, your application will consist of a privately deployed, single-file *.dll that contains two class type definitions, and a console-based *.exe that interacts with these types.

Building CILCars.dll

The first order of business is to build the *.dll to be consumed by the client. Open a text editor and create a new *.il file named CILCars.il. This single-file assembly will make use of two external .NET assemblies. Begin by updating your code file as follows:

```
// Reference mscorlib.dll and
// System.Windows.Forms.dll.
.assembly extern mscorlib
{
  .publickeytoken = (B7 7A 5C 56 19 34 E0 89 )
  .ver 4:0:0:0
}
.assembly extern System.Windows.Forms
{
  .publickeytoken = (B7 7A 5C 56 19 34 E0 89 )
  .ver 4:0:0:0
}

// Define the single-file assembly.
.assembly CILCars
{
  .hash algorithm 0x00008004
  .ver 1:0:0:0
}
.module CILCars.dll
```

This assembly will contain two class types. The first type, CILCar, defines two points of field data (public for simplicity in this example) and a custom constructor. The second type, CarInfoHelper, defines a single static method named DisplayCarInfo(), which takes CILCar as a parameter and returns void. Both types are in the CILCars namespace. In terms of CIL, CILCar can be implemented as follows:

```
// Implementation of CILCars.CILCar type.
.namespace CILCars
{
  .class public auto ansi beforefieldinit CILCar
    extends [mscorlib]System.Object
  {
    // The field data of the CILCar.
    .field public string petName
    .field public int32 currSpeed

    // The custom constructor simply allows the caller
    // to assign the field data.
    .method public hidebysig specialname rtspecialname
```

```
    instance void .ctor(int32 c, string p) cil managed
{
  .maxstack  8

  // Load first arg onto the stack and call base class ctor.
  ldarg.0  // "this" object, not the int32!
  call instance void [mscorlib]System.Object::.ctor()

  // Now load first and second args onto the stack.
  ldarg.0  // "this" object
  ldarg.1  // int32 arg

  // Store topmost stack (int 32) member in currSpeed field.
  stfld int32 CILCars.CILCar::currSpeed

  // Load string arg and store in petName field.
  ldarg.0  // "this" object
  ldarg.2  // string arg
  stfld string CILCars.CILCar::petName
  ret
    }
  }
}
```

Keeping in mind that the real first argument for any nonstatic member is the current object reference, the first block of CIL simply loads the object reference and calls the base class constructor. Next, you push the incoming constructor arguments onto the stack and store them into the type's field data using the stfld (store in field) opcode.

Now let's implement the second type in this namespace: CILCarInfo. The meat of the type is found within the static Display() method. In a nutshell, the role of this method is to take the incoming CILCar parameter, extract the values of its field data, and display it in a Windows Forms message box. Here is the complete implementation of CILCarInfo (which should be defined within the CILCars namespace) with analysis to follow:

```
.class public auto ansi beforefieldinit CILCarInfo
  extends [mscorlib]System.Object
{
  .method public hidebysig static void
    Display(class CILCars.CILCar c) cil managed
  {
    .maxstack  8

    // We need a local string variable.
    .locals init ([0] string caption)

    // Load string and the incoming CILCar onto the stack.
    ldstr "{0}'s speed is:"
    ldarg.0

    // Now place the value of the CILCar's petName on the
    // stack and call the static String.Format() method.
    ldfld string CILCars.CILCar::petName
    call string [mscorlib]System.String::Format(string, object)
```

```
    stloc.0

    // Now load the value of the currSpeed field and get its string
    // representation (note call to ToString()).
    ldarg.0
    ldflda int32 CILCars.CILCar::currSpeed
    call instance string [mscorlib]System.Int32::ToString()
    ldloc.0

    // Now call the MessageBox.Show() method with loaded values.
    call valuetype [System.Windows.Forms]
         System.Windows.Forms.DialogResult
         [System.Windows.Forms]
         System.Windows.Forms.MessageBox::Show(string, string)
    pop
    ret
  }
}
```

Although the amount of CIL code is a bit more than you see in the implementation of CILCar, things are still rather straightforward. First, given that you are defining a static method, you don't have to be concerned with the hidden object reference (thus, the ldarg.0 opcode really does load the incoming CILCar argument).

The method begins by loading a string ("{0}'s speed is") onto the stack, followed by the CILCar argument. After these two values are in place, you load the value of the petName field and call the static System.String.Format() method to substitute the curly bracket placeholder with the CILCar's pet name.

The same general procedure takes place when processing the currSpeed field, but note that you use the ldflda opcode, which loads the argument address onto the stack. At this point, you call System.Int32.ToString() to transform the value at said address into a string type. Finally, after both strings have been formatted as necessary, you call the MessageBox.Show() method.

At this point, you are able to compile your new *.dll using ilasm.exe with the following command:

```
ilasm /dll CILCars.il
```

and verify the contained CIL using peverify.exe, as follows:

```
peverify CILCars.dll
```

Building CILCarClient.exe

Now you can build a simple *.exe assembly with a Main() method that will

- Make a CILCar object.

- Pass the object into the static CILCarInfo.Display() method.

Create a new file named CarClient.il and define external references to mscorlib.dll and CILCars.dll (don't forget to place a copy of this .NET assembly in the client's application directory!). Next, define a single type (Program) that manipulates the CILCars.dll assembly. Here's the complete code:

```
// External assembly refs.
.assembly extern mscorlib
{
```

```
    .publickeytoken = (B7 7A 5C 56 19 34 E0 89)
    .ver 4:0:0:0
}
.assembly extern CILCars
{
    .ver 1:0:0:0
}

// Our executable assembly.
.assembly CarClient
{
    .hash algorithm 0x00008004
    .ver 1:0:0:0
}
.module CarClient.exe

// Implementation of Program type.
.namespace CarClient
{
  .class private auto ansi beforefieldinit Program
  extends [mscorlib]System.Object
  {
    .method private hidebysig static void
    Main(string[] args) cil managed
    {
      // Marks the entry point of the *.exe.
      .entrypoint
      .maxstack  8

      // Declare a local CILCar variable and push
      // values onto the stack for ctor call.
      .locals init ([0] class
      [CILCars]CILCars.CILCar myCilCar)
      ldc.i4 55
      ldstr "Junior"

      // Make new CilCar; store and load reference.
      newobj instance void
        [CILCars]CILCars.CILCar::.ctor(int32, string)
      stloc.0
      ldloc.0

      // Call Display() and pass in topmost value on stack.
      call void [CILCars]
        CILCars.CILCarInfo::Display(
            class [CILCars]CILCars.CILCar)
      ret
    }
  }
}
```

The one opcode that is important to point out is `.entrypoint`. Recall from the discussion earlier in this chapter that this opcode is used to mark which method of an *.exe functions as the entry point of the module. In fact, given that `.entrypoint` is how the CLR identifies the initial method to execute, this method can be called anything, although here you are using the standard method name of `Main()`. The remainder of the CIL code found in the `Main()` method is your basic pushing and popping of stack-based values.

Do note, however, that the creation of a `CILCar` object involves the use of the `.newobj` opcode. On a related note, recall that when you want to invoke a member of a type using raw CIL, you make use of the double-colon syntax and, as always, make use of the fully qualified name of the type. With this, you can compile your new file with `ilasm.exe`, verify your assembly with `peverify.exe`, and execute your program. Issue the following commands within your command prompt:

```
ilasm CarClient.il
peverify CarClient.exe
CarClient.exe
```

■ **Source Code** The CilCars example is included under the Chapter 18 subdirectory.

Understanding Dynamic Assemblies

To be sure, the process of building a complex .NET application in CIL would be quite the labor of love. On the one hand, CIL is an extremely expressive programming language that allows you to interact with all of the programming constructs allowed by the CTS. On the other hand, authoring raw CIL is tedious, error-prone, and painful. While it is true that knowledge is power, you might indeed wonder just how important it is to commit the laws of CIL syntax to memory. The answer is, "It depends." To be sure, most of your .NET programming endeavors will not require you to view, edit, or author CIL code. However, with the CIL primer behind you, you are now ready to investigate the world of dynamic assemblies (as opposed to static assemblies) and the role of the `System.Reflection.Emit` namespace.

The first question you may have is, "What exactly is the difference between static and dynamic assemblies?" By definition, *static assemblies* are .NET binaries loaded directly from disk storage, meaning they are located somewhere on your hard drive in a physical file (or possibly a set of files in the case of a multifile assembly) at the time the CLR requests them. As you might guess, every time you compile your C# source code, you end up with a static assembly.

A *dynamic assembly*, on the other hand, is created in memory, on the fly, using the types provided by the `System.Reflection.Emit` namespace. The `System.Reflection.Emit` namespace makes it possible to create an assembly and its modules, type definitions, and CIL implementation logic at *runtime*. After you have done so, you are then free to save your in-memory binary to disk. This, of course, results in a new static assembly. To be sure, the process of building a dynamic assembly using the `System.Reflection.Emit` namespace does require some level of understanding regarding the nature of CIL opcodes.

Although creating dynamic assemblies is a fairly advanced (and uncommon) programming task, they can be useful under various circumstances. For example:

- You are building a .NET programming tool that needs to generate assemblies on demand based on user input.

- You are building a program that needs to generate proxies to remote types on the fly, based on the obtained metadata.

- You want to load a static assembly and dynamically insert new types into the binary image.

Several aspects of the .NET runtime engine involve generating dynamic assemblies quietly in the background. For example, ASP.NET makes use of this technique to map markup and server-side script code into a runtime object model. LINQ also can generate code on the fly, based on various query expressions. This being said, let's check out the types within System.Reflection.Emit.

Exploring the System.Reflection.Emit Namespace

Creating a dynamic assembly requires you to have some familiarity with CIL opcodes, but the types of the System.Reflection.Emit namespace hide the complexity of CIL as much as possible. For example, rather than directly specifying the necessary CIL directives and attributes to define a class type, you can simply make use of the TypeBuilder class. Likewise, if you want to define a new instance-level constructor, you have no need to emit the specialname, rtspecialname, or .ctor tokens; rather, you can make use of the ConstructorBuilder. Table 18-8 documents the key members of the System.Reflection.Emit namespace.

Table 18-8. Select Members of the System.Reflection.Emit *Namespace*

Members	Meaning in Life
AssemblyBuilder	Used to create an assembly (*.dll or *.exe) at runtime. *.exes must call the ModuleBuilder.SetEntryPoint() method to set the method that is the entry point to the module. If no entry point is specified, a *.dll will be generated.
ModuleBuilder	Used to define the set of modules within the current assembly.
EnumBuilder	Used to create a .NET enumeration type.
TypeBuilder	May be used to create classes, interfaces, structures, and delegates within a module at runtime.
MethodBuilder LocalBuilder PropertyBuilder FieldBuilder ConstructorBuilder CustomAttributeBuilder ParameterBuilder EventBuilder	Used to create type members (such as methods, local variables, properties, constructors, and attributes) at runtime.
ILGenerator	Emits CIL opcodes into a given type member.
OpCodes	Provides numerous fields that map to CIL opcodes. This type is used in conjunction with the various members of System.Reflection.Emit.ILGenerator.

In general, the types of the System.Reflection.Emit namespace allow you to represent raw CIL tokens programmatically during the construction of your dynamic assembly. You will see many of these members in the example that follows; however, the ILGenerator type is worth checking out straightaway.

The Role of the System.Reflection.Emit.ILGenerator

As its name implies, the ILGenerator type's role is to inject CIL opcodes into a given type member. However, you cannot directly create ILGenerator objects, as this type has no public constructors; rather, you receive an ILGenerator type by calling specific methods of the builder-centric types (such as the MethodBuilder and ConstructorBuilder types). For example:

```
// Obtain an ILGenerator from a ConstructorBuilder
// object named "myCtorBuilder".
ConstructorBuilder myCtorBuilder =
  new ConstructorBuilder(/* ...various args... */);

ILGenerator myCILGen = myCtorBuilder.GetILGenerator();
```

Once you have an ILGenerator in your hands, you are then able to emit the raw CIL opcodes using any number of methods. Table 18-9 documents some (but not all) methods of ILGenerator.

Table 18-9. Various Methods of ILGenerator

Method	Meaning in Life
BeginCatchBlock()	Begins a catch block
BeginExceptionBlock()	Begins an exception block for a nonfiltered exception
BeginFinallyBlock()	Begins a finally block
BeginScope()	Begins a lexical scope
DeclareLocal()	Declares a local variable
DefineLabel()	Declares a new label
Emit()	Is overloaded numerous times to allow you to emit CIL opcodes
EmitCall()	Pushes a call or callvirt opcode into the CIL stream
EmitWriteLine()	Emits a call to Console.WriteLine() with different types of values
EndExceptionBlock()	Ends an exception block
EndScope()	Ends a lexical scope
ThrowException()	Emits an instruction to throw an exception

UsingNamespace()	Specifies the namespace to be used in evaluating locals and watches for the current active lexical scope

The key method of ILGenerator is Emit(), which works in conjunction with the System.Reflection.Emit.OpCodes class type. As mentioned earlier in this chapter, this type exposes a good number of read-only fields that map to raw CIL opcodes. The full set of these members are all documented within online help, and you will see various examples in the pages that follow.

Emitting a Dynamic Assembly

To illustrate the process of defining a .NET assembly at runtime, let's walk through the process of creating a single-file dynamic assembly named MyAssembly.dll. Within this module is a class named HelloWorld. The HelloWorld class supports a default constructor and a custom constructor that is used to assign the value of a private member variable (theMessage) of type string. In addition, HelloWorld supports a public instance method named SayHello(), which prints a greeting to the standard I/O stream, and another instance method named GetMsg(), which returns the internal private string. In effect, you are going to programmatically generate the following class type:

```
// This class will be created at runtime
// using System.Reflection.Emit.
public class HelloWorld
{
  private string theMessage;
  HelloWorld() {}
  HelloWorld(string s) {theMessage = s;}

  public string GetMsg() {return theMessage;}
  public void SayHello()
  {
    System.Console.WriteLine("Hello from the HelloWorld class!");
  }
}
```

Assume you have created a new Visual Studio Console Application project workspace named DynamicAsmBuilder and import the System.Reflection, System.Reflection.Emit, and System.Threading namespaces. Define a static method named CreateMyAsm(). This single method is in charge of the following:

- Defining the characteristics of the dynamic assembly (name, version, etc.)
- Implementing the HelloClass type
- Saving the in-memory assembly to a physical file

Also note that the CreateMyAsm() method takes as a single parameter a System.AppDomain type, which will be used to obtain access to the AssemblyBuilder type associated with the current application domain (see Chapter 17 for a discussion of .NET application domains). Here is the complete code, with analysis to follow:

```
// The caller sends in an AppDomain type.
public static void CreateMyAsm(AppDomain curAppDomain)
{
```

```
// Establish general assembly characteristics.
AssemblyName assemblyName = new AssemblyName();
assemblyName.Name = "MyAssembly";
assemblyName.Version = new Version("1.0.0.0");

// Create new assembly within the current AppDomain.
AssemblyBuilder assembly =
  curAppDomain.DefineDynamicAssembly(assemblyName,
  AssemblyBuilderAccess.Save);

// Given that we are building a single-file
// assembly, the name of the module is the same as the assembly.
ModuleBuilder module =
  assembly.DefineDynamicModule("MyAssembly", "MyAssembly.dll");

// Define a public class named "HelloWorld".
TypeBuilder helloWorldClass = module.DefineType("MyAssembly.HelloWorld",
  TypeAttributes.Public);

// Define a private String member variable named "theMessage".
FieldBuilder msgField =
  helloWorldClass.DefineField("theMessage", Type.GetType("System.String"),
  FieldAttributes.Private);

// Create the custom ctor.
Type[] constructorArgs = new Type[1];
constructorArgs[0] = typeof(string);
ConstructorBuilder constructor =
  helloWorldClass.DefineConstructor(MethodAttributes.Public,
  CallingConventions.Standard,
  constructorArgs);
ILGenerator constructorIL = constructor.GetILGenerator();
constructorIL.Emit(OpCodes.Ldarg_0);
Type objectClass = typeof(object);
ConstructorInfo superConstructor =
  objectClass.GetConstructor(new Type[0]);
constructorIL.Emit(OpCodes.Call, superConstructor);
constructorIL.Emit(OpCodes.Ldarg_0);
constructorIL.Emit(OpCodes.Ldarg_1);
constructorIL.Emit(OpCodes.Stfld, msgField);
constructorIL.Emit(OpCodes.Ret);

// Create the default ctor.
helloWorldClass.DefineDefaultConstructor(MethodAttributes.Public);
// Now create the GetMsg() method.
MethodBuilder getMsgMethod =
  helloWorldClass.DefineMethod("GetMsg", MethodAttributes.Public,
  typeof(string), null);
ILGenerator methodIL = getMsgMethod.GetILGenerator();
methodIL.Emit(OpCodes.Ldarg_0);
methodIL.Emit(OpCodes.Ldfld, msgField);
methodIL.Emit(OpCodes.Ret);
```

```
  // Create the SayHello method.
  MethodBuilder sayHiMethod =
    helloWorldClass.DefineMethod("SayHello",
    MethodAttributes.Public, null, null);
  methodIL = sayHiMethod.GetILGenerator();
  methodIL.EmitWriteLine("Hello from the HelloWorld class!");
  methodIL.Emit(OpCodes.Ret);

  // "Bake" the class HelloWorld.
  // (Baking is the formal term for emitting the type.)
  helloWorldClass.CreateType();

  // (Optionally) save the assembly to file.
  assembly.Save("MyAssembly.dll");
}
```

Emitting the Assembly and Module Set

The method body begins by establishing the minimal set of characteristics about your assembly, using the AssemblyName and Version types (defined in the System.Reflection namespace). Next, you obtain an AssemblyBuilder type via the instance-level AppDomain.DefineDynamicAssembly() method (recall the caller will pass in an AppDomain reference into the CreateMyAsm() method), like so:

```
// Establish general assembly characteristics
// and gain access to the AssemblyBuilder type.
public static void CreateMyAsm(AppDomain curAppDomain)
{
  AssemblyName assemblyName = new AssemblyName();
  assemblyName.Name = "MyAssembly";
  assemblyName.Version = new Version("1.0.0.0");

  // Create new assembly within the current AppDomain.
  AssemblyBuilder assembly =
    curAppDomain.DefineDynamicAssembly(assemblyName,
    AssemblyBuilderAccess.Save);
  ...
}
```

As you can see, when calling AppDomain.DefineDynamicAssembly(), you must specify the access mode of the assembly you want to define, the most common values of which are shown in Table 18-10.

Table 18-10. Common Values of the AssemblyBuilderAccess Enumeration

Value	Meaning in Life
ReflectionOnly	Represents that a dynamic assembly can only be reflected over
Run	Represents that a dynamic assembly can be executed in memory but not saved to disk

| RunAndSave | Represents that a dynamic assembly can be executed in memory and saved to disk |
| Save | Represents that a dynamic assembly can be saved to disk but not executed in memory |

The next task is to define the module set for your new assembly. Given that the assembly is a single-file unit, you need to define only a single module. If you were to build a multifile assembly using the DefineDynamicModule() method, you would specify an optional second parameter that represents the name of a given module (e.g., myMod.dotnetmodule). However, when creating a single-file assembly, the name of the module will be identical to the name of the assembly itself. In any case, once the DefineDynamicModule() method has returned, you are provided with a reference to a valid ModuleBuilder type.

```
// The single-file assembly.
ModuleBuilder module =
  assembly.DefineDynamicModule("MyAssembly", "MyAssembly.dll");
```

The Role of the ModuleBuilder Type

ModuleBuilder is the key type used during the development of dynamic assemblies. As you would expect, ModuleBuilder supports a number of members that allow you to define the set of types contained within a given module (classes, interfaces, structures, etc.) as well as the set of embedded resources (string tables, images, etc.) contained within. Table 18-11 describes a few of the creation-centric methods. (Do note that each method will return to you a related type that represents the type you want to construct.)

Table 18-11. Select Members of the ModuleBuilder Type

Method	Meaning in Life
DefineEnum()	Used to emit a .NET enum definition
DefineResource()	Defines a managed embedded resource to be stored in this module
DefineType()	Constructs a TypeBuilder, which allows you to define value types, interfaces, and class types (including delegates)

The key member of the ModuleBuilder class to be aware of is DefineType(). In addition to specifying the name of the type (via a simple string), you will also make use of the System.Reflection.TypeAttributes enum to describe the format of the type itself. Table 18-12 lists some (but not all) of the key members of the TypeAttributes enumeration.

Table 18-12. Select Members of the TypeAttributes Enumeration

Member	Meaning in Life
Abstract	Specifies that the type is abstract
Class	Specifies that the type is a class

Interface	Specifies that the type is an interface
NestedAssembly	Specifies that the class is nested with assembly visibility and is thus accessible only by methods within its assembly
NestedFamAndAssem	Specifies that the class is nested with assembly and family visibility, and is thus accessible only by methods lying in the intersection of its family and assembly
NestedFamily	Specifies that the class is nested with family visibility and is thus accessible only by methods within its own type and any subtypes
NestedFamORAssem	Specifies that the class is nested with family or assembly visibility, and is thus accessible only by methods lying in the union of its family and assembly
NestedPrivate	Specifies that the class is nested with private visibility
NestedPublic	Specifies that the class is nested with public visibility
NotPublic	Specifies that the class is not public
Public	Specifies that the class is public
Sealed	Specifies that the class is concrete and cannot be extended
Serializable	Specifies that the class can be serialized

Emitting the HelloClass Type and the String Member Variable

Now that you have a better understanding of the role of the `ModuleBuilder.CreateType()` method, let's examine how you can emit the public `HelloWorld` class type and the private string variable.

```
// Define a public class named "MyAssembly.HelloWorld".
TypeBuilder helloWorldClass = module.DefineType("MyAssembly.HelloWorld",
  TypeAttributes.Public);

// Define a private String member variable named "theMessage".
FieldBuilder msgField =
  helloWorldClass.DefineField("theMessage",
  typeof(string),
  FieldAttributes.Private);
```

Notice how the `TypeBuilder.DefineField()` method provides access to a `FieldBuilder` type. The `TypeBuilder` class also defines other methods that provide access to other "builder" types. For example, `DefineConstructor()` returns a `ConstructorBuilder`, `DefineProperty()` returns a `PropertyBuilder`, and so forth.

Emitting the Constructors

As mentioned earlier, the TypeBuilder.DefineConstructor() method can be used to define a constructor for the current type. However, when it comes to implementing the constructor of HelloClass, you need to inject raw CIL code into the constructor body, which is responsible for assigning the incoming parameter to the internal private string. To obtain an ILGenerator type, you call the GetILGenerator() method from the respective "builder" type you have reference to (in this case, the ConstructorBuilder type).

The Emit() method of the ILGenerator class is the entity in charge of placing CIL into a member implementation. Emit() itself makes frequent use of the OpCodes class type, which exposes the opcode set of CIL using read-only fields. For example, OpCodes.Ret signals the return of a method call; OpCodes.Stfld makes an assignment to a member variable; and OpCodes.Call is used to call a given method (in this case, the base class constructor). That said, ponder the following constructor logic:

```
// Create the custom constructor taking
// a single System.String argument.
Type[] constructorArgs = new Type[1];
constructorArgs[0] = typeof(string);
ConstructorBuilder constructor =
  helloWorldClass.DefineConstructor(MethodAttributes.Public,
  CallingConventions.Standard, constructorArgs);

// Now emit the necessary CIL into the ctor.
ILGenerator constructorIL = constructor.GetILGenerator();
constructorIL.Emit(OpCodes.Ldarg_0);
Type objectClass = typeof(object);
ConstructorInfo superConstructor = objectClass.GetConstructor(new Type[0]);
constructorIL.Emit(OpCodes.Call, superConstructor);  // Call base class ctor.

// Load the object's "this" pointer on the stack.
constructorIL.Emit(OpCodes.Ldarg_0);


// Load incoming argument on virtual stack and store in msgField.
constructorIL.Emit(OpCodes.Ldarg_1);
constructorIL.Emit(OpCodes.Stfld, msgField);  // Assign msgField.
constructorIL.Emit(OpCodes.Ret);              // Return.
```

Now, as you are well aware, as soon as you define a custom constructor for a type, the default constructor is silently removed. To redefine the no-argument constructor, simply call the DefineDefaultConstructor() method of the TypeBuilder type as follows:

```
// Reinsert the default ctor.
helloWorldClass.DefineDefaultConstructor(MethodAttributes.Public);
```

This single call emits the standard CIL code used to define a default constructor:

```
.method public hidebysig specialname rtspecialname
  instance void  .ctor() cil managed
{
  .maxstack  1
  ldarg.0
  call instance void [mscorlib]System.Object::.ctor()
```

```
    ret
}
```

Emitting the SayHello() Method

Last but not least, let's examine the process of emitting the SayHello() method. The first task is to obtain a MethodBuilder type from the helloWorldClass variable. After you do this, you define the method and obtain the underlying ILGenerator to inject the CIL instructions, like so:

```
// Create the SayHello method.
MethodBuilder sayHiMethod =
  helloWorldClass.DefineMethod("SayHello",
  MethodAttributes.Public, null, null);
methodIL = sayHiMethod.GetILGenerator();

// Write a line to the Console.
methodIL.EmitWriteLine("Hello there!");
methodIL.Emit(OpCodes.Ret);
```

Here you have established a public method (MethodAttributes.Public) that takes no parameters and returns nothing (marked by the null entries contained in the DefineMethod() call). Also note the EmitWriteLine() call. This helper member of the ILGenerator class automatically writes a line to the standard output with minimal fuss and bother.

Using the Dynamically Generated Assembly

Now that you have the logic in place to create and save your assembly, all that's needed is a class to trigger the logic. To come full circle, assume your current project defines a second class named AsmReader. The logic in Main() obtains the current AppDomain via the Thread.GetDomain() method that will be used to host the assembly you will dynamically create. Once you have a reference, you are able to call the CreateMyAsm() method.

To make things a bit more interesting, after the call to CreateMyAsm() returns, you will exercise some late binding (see Chapter 15) to load your newly created assembly into memory and interact with the members of the HelloWorld class. Update your Main() method as follows:

```
static void Main(string[] args)
{
  Console.WriteLine("***** The Amazing Dynamic Assembly Builder App *****");
  // Get the application domain for the current thread.
  AppDomain curAppDomain = Thread.GetDomain();

  // Create the dynamic assembly using our helper f(x).
  CreateMyAsm(curAppDomain);
  Console.WriteLine("-> Finished creating MyAssembly.dll.");

  // Now load the new assembly from file.
  Console.WriteLine("-> Loading MyAssembly.dll from file.");
  Assembly a = Assembly.Load("MyAssembly");

  // Get the HelloWorld type.
  Type hello = a.GetType("MyAssembly.HelloWorld");
```

```
  // Create HelloWorld object and call the correct ctor.
  Console.Write("-> Enter message to pass HelloWorld class: ");
  string msg = Console.ReadLine();
  object[] ctorArgs = new object[1];
  ctorArgs[0] = msg;
  object obj = Activator.CreateInstance(hello, ctorArgs);

  // Call SayHello and show returned string.
  Console.WriteLine("-> Calling SayHello() via late binding.");
  MethodInfo mi = hello.GetMethod("SayHello");
  mi.Invoke(obj, null);

  // Invoke method.
  mi = hello.GetMethod("GetMsg");
  Console.WriteLine(mi.Invoke(obj, null));
}
```

In effect, you have just created a .NET assembly that is able to create and execute .NET assemblies at runtime! That wraps up the examination of CIL and the role of dynamic assemblies. I hope this chapter has deepened your understanding of the .NET type system and the syntax and semantics of CIL.

■ **Source Code** The DynamicAsmBuilder project is included under the Chapter 18 subdirectory.

Summary

This chapter provided an overview of the syntax and semantics of CIL. Unlike higher-level managed languages such as C#, CIL does not simply define a set of keywords, but provides directives (used to define the structure of an assembly and its types), attributes (which further qualify a given directive), and opcodes (which are used to implement type members).

You were introduced to a few CIL-centric programming tools, and learned how to alter the contents of a .NET assembly with new CIL instructions using round-trip engineering. After this point, you spent time learning how to establish the current (and referenced) assembly, namespaces, types, and members. I wrapped up with a simple example of building a .NET code library and executable using little more than CIL, command-line tools, and a bit of elbow grease.

Finally, you took an introductory look at the process of creating a *dynamic assembly*. Using the System.Reflection.Emit namespace, it is possible to define a .NET assembly in memory at runtime. As you have seen firsthand, using this particular API requires you to know the semantics of CIL code in some detail. While the need to build dynamic assemblies is certainly not a common task for most .NET applications, it can be very useful for those of you who need to build support tools and other programming utilities.

## PART VI

Introducing the .NET Base Class Libraries

## CHAPTER 19

Multithreaded, Parallel, and Async Programming

Nobody enjoys working with an application that is slow and sluggish during its execution. Moreover, nobody enjoys starting a task in an application (perhaps initiated by the clicking of a toolbar item) that prevents other parts of the program from being as responsive as possible. Before the release of .NET, building applications that had the ability to perform multiple tasks required authoring very complex C++ code that made use of the Windows threading APIs. Thankfully, the .NET platform provides a number of ways for you to build software that can perform complex operations on unique paths of execution, with far fewer pain points.

This chapter begins by defining the overall nature of a "multithreaded application." Next, we will revisit the .NET delegate type to investigate its intrinsic support for *asynchronous method invocations*. As you'll see, this technique allows you to invoke a method on a secondary thread of execution without needing to manually create or configure the thread itself.

Next, you'll be introduced to the original threading namespace which has shipped since .NET 1.0, specifically System.Threading. Here you'll examine numerous types (Thread, ThreadStart, etc.) that allow you to explicitly create additional threads of execution and synchronize your shared resources, which helps ensure that multiple threads can share data in a nonvolatile manner.

The remaining parts of this chapter will examine three more recent techniques .NET developers can make use of to build multithreaded software, specifically the Task Parallel Library (TPL), Parallel LINQ (PLINQ), and the new intrinsic asynchronous keywords of C# (async and await). As you will see, these features can dramatically simplify how you can build responsive multithreaded software applications.

The Process/AppDomain/Context/Thread Relationship

In Chapter 17, a *thread* was defined as a path of execution within an executable application. While many .NET applications can live happy and productive single-threaded lives, an assembly's primary thread (spawned by the CLR when Main() executes) may create secondary threads of execution at any time to perform additional units of work. By creating additional threads, you can build more responsive (but not necessarily faster executing on single-core machines) applications.

The System.Threading namespace was released with .NET 1.0, and offers one approach to build multithreaded applications. The Thread class is perhaps the core type, as it represents a given thread. If you want to programmatically obtain a reference to the thread currently executing a given member, simply call the static Thread.CurrentThread property, like so:

```
static void ExtractExecutingThread()
{
  // Get the thread currently
  // executing this method.
```

```
    Thread currThread = Thread.CurrentThread;
}
```

Under the .NET platform, there is *not* a direct one-to-one correspondence between application domains and threads. In fact, a given AppDomain can have numerous threads executing within it at any given time. Furthermore, a particular thread is not confined to a single application domain during its lifetime. Threads are free to cross application domain boundaries as the Windows OS thread scheduler and the .NET CLR see fit.

Although active threads can be moved between AppDomain boundaries, a given thread can execute within only a single application domain at any point in time (in other words, it is impossible for a single thread to be doing work in more than one AppDomain at once). When you want to programmatically gain access to the AppDomain that is hosting the current thread, call the static Thread.GetDomain() method, like so:

```
static void ExtractAppDomainHostingThread()
{
    // Obtain the AppDomain hosting the current thread.
    AppDomain ad = Thread.GetDomain();
}
```

A single thread may also be moved into a particular context at any given time, and it may be relocated within a new context at the whim of the CLR. When you want to obtain the current context a thread happens to be executing in, make use of the static Thread.CurrentContext property (which returns a System.Runtime.Remoting.Contexts.Context object), like so:

```
static void ExtractCurrentThreadContext()
{
    // Obtain the context under which the
    // current thread is operating.
    Context ctx = Thread.CurrentContext;
}
```

Again, the CLR is the entity that is in charge of moving threads into (and out of) application domains and contexts. As a .NET developer, you can usually remain blissfully unaware where a given thread ends up (or exactly when it is placed into its new boundary). Nevertheless, you should be aware of the various ways of obtaining the underlying primitives.

The Problem of Concurrency

One of the many "joys" (read: painful aspects) of multithreaded programming is that you have little control over how the underlying operating system or the CLR makes use of its threads. For example, if you craft a block of code that creates a new thread of execution, you cannot guarantee that the thread executes immediately. Rather, such code only instructs the OS/CLR to execute the thread as soon as possible (which is typically when the thread scheduler gets around to it).

Furthermore, given that threads can be moved between application and contextual boundaries as required by the CLR, you must be mindful of which aspects of your application are *thread-volatile* (e.g., subject to multithreaded access) and which operations are *atomic* (thread-volatile operations are the dangerous ones!).

To illustrate the problem, assume a thread is invoking a method of a specific object. Now assume that this thread is instructed by the thread scheduler to suspend its activity, in order to allow another thread to access the same method of the same object.

If the original thread was not completely finished with its operation, the second incoming thread may be viewing an object in a partially modified state. At this point, the second thread is basically reading bogus data, which is sure to give way to extremely odd (and very hard to find) bugs, which are even harder to replicate and debug.

Atomic operations, on the other hand, are always safe in a multithreaded environment. Sadly, there are very few operations in the .NET base class libraries that are guaranteed to be atomic. Even the act of assigning a value to a member variable is not atomic! Unless the .NET Framework 4.5 SDK documentation specifically says an operation is atomic, you must assume it is thread-volatile and take precautions.

The Role of Thread Synchronization

At this point, it should be clear that multithreaded programs are in themselves quite volatile, as numerous threads can operate on the shared resources at (more or less) the same time. To protect an application's resources from possible corruption, .NET developers must make use of any number of threading primitives (such as locks, monitors, and the [Synchronization] attribute or language keyword support) to control access among the executing threads.

Although the .NET platform cannot make the difficulties of building robust multithreaded applications completely disappear, the process has been simplified considerably. Using types defined within the System.Threading namespace, the .NET 4.0 and higher Task Parallel Library (TPL), and the .NET 4.5 C# async and await language keywords, you are able to work with multiple threads with minimal fuss and bother.

Before diving into the System.Threading namespace, the TPL, and the C# async and await keywords, we will begin by examining how the .NET delegate type can be used to invoke a method in an asynchronous manner. While it is most certainly true that under .NET 4.5, the new C# async and await keywords offer a simpler alternative to asynchronous delegates, it is still important that you know how to interact with code using this approach (trust me; there is a ton of code in production that makes use of asynchronous delegates).

A Brief Review of the .NET Delegate

Recall that a .NET delegate is essentially a type-safe, object-oriented, function pointer. When you define a .NET delegate type, the C# compiler responds by building a sealed class that derives from System.MulticastDelegate (which in turn derives from System.Delegate). These base classes provide every delegate with the ability to maintain a list of method addresses, all of which may be invoked at a later time. Consider the following BinaryOp delegate, first defined in Chapter 10:

```
// A C# delegate type.
public delegate int BinaryOp(int x, int y);
```

Based on its definition, BinaryOp can point to any method taking two integers (by value) as arguments and returning an integer. Once compiled, the defining assembly now contains a full-blown class definition that is dynamically generated when you build your project, based on the delegate declaration. In the case of BinaryOp, this class looks more or less like the following (shown in pseudo-code):

```
public sealed class BinaryOp : System.MulticastDelegate
{
  public BinaryOp(object target, uint functionAddress);
  public int Invoke(int x, int y);
  public IAsyncResult BeginInvoke(int x, int y,
    AsyncCallback cb, object state);
  public int EndInvoke(IAsyncResult result);
}
```

Recall that the generated Invoke() method is used to invoke the methods maintained by a delegate object in a *synchronous manner*. Therefore, the calling thread (such as the primary thread of the application) is forced to wait until the delegate invocation completes. Also recall that in C#, the Invoke() method does not need to be directly called in code, but can be triggered indirectly, under the hood, when applying "normal" method invocation syntax.

Consider the following Console Application program (SyncDelegateReview), which invokes the static Add() method in a synchronous (a.k.a. blocking) manner (be sure to import the System.Threading namespace into your C# code file, as you will be calling the Thread.Sleep() method):

```
namespace SyncDelegateReview
{
  public delegate int BinaryOp(int x, int y);

  class Program
  {
    static void Main(string[] args)
    {
      Console.WriteLine("***** Synch Delegate Review *****");

      // Print out the ID of the executing thread.
      Console.WriteLine("Main() invoked on thread {0}.",
        Thread.CurrentThread.ManagedThreadId);

      // Invoke Add() in a synchronous manner.
      BinaryOp b = new BinaryOp(Add);

      // Could also write b.Invoke(10, 10);
      int answer = b(10, 10);

      // These lines will not execute until
      // the Add() method has completed.
      Console.WriteLine("Doing more work in Main()!");
      Console.WriteLine("10 + 10 is {0}.", answer);
      Console.ReadLine();
    }

    static int Add(int x, int y)
    {
      // Print out the ID of the executing thread.
      Console.WriteLine("Add() invoked on thread {0}.",
        Thread.CurrentThread.ManagedThreadId);

      // Pause to simulate a lengthy operation.
      Thread.Sleep(5000);
      return x + y;
    }
  }
}
```

Within the Add() method, you are invoking the static Thread.Sleep() method to suspend the calling thread for approximately five seconds to simulate a lengthy task. Given that you are invoking the Add()

method in a *synchronous* manner, the Main() method will not print out the result of the operation until the Add() method has completed.

Next, note that the Main() method is obtaining access to the current thread (via Thread.CurrentThread) and printing out the ID of the thread via the ManagedThreadId property. This same logic is repeated in the static Add() method. As you might suspect, given that all the work in this application is performed exclusively by the primary thread, you find the same ID value displayed to the console:

```
***** Synch Delegate Review *****
Main() invoked on thread 1.
Add() invoked on thread 1.
Doing more work in Main()!
10 + 10 is 20.

Press any key to continue . . .
```

When you run this program, you should notice that a five-second delay takes place before you see the final Console.WriteLine() logic in Main() execute. Although many (if not most) methods may be called synchronously without ill effect, .NET delegates can be instructed to call their methods asynchronously if necessary.

■ **Source Code** The SyncDelegateReview project is located under the Chapter 19 subdirectory.

The Asynchronous Nature of Delegates

If you are new to the topic of multithreading, you might wonder what exactly an *asynchronous* method invocation is all about. As you are no doubt fully aware, some programming operations take time. Although the previous Add() was purely illustrative in nature, imagine that you built a single-threaded application that is invoking a method on a remote object, calling a method performing a long-running database query, downloading a large document, or writing 500 lines of text to an external file. While performing these operations, the application could appear to hang for some amount of time. Until the task at hand has been processed, all other aspects of this program (such as menu activation, toolbar clicking, or console output) are suspended (which can aggravate users).

Therefore, the question is, how can you tell a delegate to invoke a method on a separate thread of execution to simulate numerous tasks performing "at the same time"? The good news is that every .NET delegate type is automatically equipped with this capability. The even better news is that you are *not* required to directly dive into the details of the System.Threading namespace to do so (although these entities can quite naturally work hand in hand).

The BeginInvoke() and EndInvoke() Methods

When the C# compiler processes the delegate keyword, the dynamically generated class defines two methods named BeginInvoke() and EndInvoke(). Given the definition of the BinaryOp delegate, these methods are prototyped as follows:

```
public sealed class BinaryOp : System.MulticastDelegate
{
...
  // Used to invoke a method asynchronously.
  public IAsyncResult BeginInvoke(int x, int y,
    AsyncCallback cb, object state);

  // Used to fetch the return value
  // of the invoked method.
  public int EndInvoke(IAsyncResult result);
}
```

The first set of parameters passed into BeginInvoke() will be based on the format of the C# delegate (two integers, in the case of BinaryOp). The final two arguments will always be System.AsyncCallback and System.Object. You'll examine the role of these parameters shortly; for the time being, though, I'll supply null for each. Also note that the return value of EndInvoke() is an integer, based on the return type of BinaryOp, while the single parameter of this method is always of type IAsyncResult.

The System.IAsyncResult Interface

The BeginInvoke() method always returns an object implementing the IAsyncResult interface, while EndInvoke() requires an IAsyncResult-compatible type as its sole parameter. The IAsyncResult-compatible object returned from BeginInvoke() is basically a coupling mechanism that allows the calling thread to obtain the result of the asynchronous method invocation at a later time via EndInvoke(). The IAsyncResult interface (defined in the System namespace) is defined as follows:

```
public interface IAsyncResult
{
  object AsyncState { get; }
  WaitHandle AsyncWaitHandle { get; }
  bool CompletedSynchronously { get; }
  bool IsCompleted { get; }
}
```

In the simplest case, you are able to avoid directly invoking these members. All you have to do is cache the IAsyncResult-compatible object returned by BeginInvoke() and pass it to EndInvoke() when you are ready to obtain the result of the method invocation. As you will see, you are able to invoke the members of an IAsyncResult-compatible object when you want to become "more involved" with the process of fetching the method's return value.

■ **Note** If you asynchronously invoke a method that provides a void return value, you can simply "fire and forget." In such cases, you will never need to cache the IAsyncResult-compatible object or call EndInvoke() in the first place (as there is no return value to retrieve).

Invoking a Method Asynchronously

To instruct the BinaryOp delegate to invoke Add() asynchronously, you will modify the logic in the previous project (feel free to add code to the existing project; however, in your lab downloads, you will find a new Console Application named AsyncDelegate). Update the previous Main() method as follows:

```
static void Main(string[] args)
{
  Console.WriteLine("***** Async Delegate Invocation *****");

  // Print out the ID of the executing thread.
  Console.WriteLine("Main() invoked on thread {0}.",
    Thread.CurrentThread.ManagedThreadId);

  // Invoke Add() on a secondary thread.
  BinaryOp b = new BinaryOp(Add);
  IAsyncResult iftAR = b.BeginInvoke(10, 10, null, null);

  // Do other work on primary thread...
  Console.WriteLine("Doing more work in Main()!");

  // Obtain the result of the Add()
  // method when ready.
  int answer = b.EndInvoke(iftAR);
  Console.WriteLine("10 + 10 is {0}.", answer);
  Console.ReadLine();
}
```

If you run this application, you will find that two unique thread IDs are displayed, given that there are in fact multiple threads working within the current AppDomain:

```
***** Async Delegate Invocation *****
Main() invoked on thread 1.
Doing more work in Main()!
Add() invoked on thread 3.
10 + 10 is 20.
```

In addition to the unique ID values, you will also notice upon running the application that the Doing more work in Main()! message displays immediately, while the secondary thread is occupied attending to its business.

Synchronizing the Calling Thread

If you think carefully about the current implementation of Main(), you might realize that the timespan between calling BeginInvoke() and EndInvoke() is clearly less than five seconds. Therefore, once Doing more work in Main()! prints to the console, the calling thread is now blocked and waiting for the secondary thread to complete before being able to obtain the result of the Add() method. Therefore, you are effectively making yet another *synchronous call.*

```
static void Main(string[] args)
{
...
  BinaryOp b = new BinaryOp(Add);

  // Once the next statement is processed,
  // the calling thread is now blocked until
  // BeginInvoke() completes.
  IAsyncResult iftAR = b.BeginInvoke(10, 10, null, null);

  // This call takes far less than five seconds!
  Console.WriteLine("Doing more work in Main()!");

  // Now we are waiting again for other thread to complete!
  int answer = b.EndInvoke(iftAR);
...
}
```

Obviously, asynchronous delegates would lose their appeal if the calling thread had the potential of being blocked under various circumstances. To allow the calling thread to discover whether the asynchronously invoked method has completed its work, the IAsyncResult interface provides the IsCompleted property. Using this member, the calling thread is able to determine whether the asynchronous call has indeed completed before calling EndInvoke().

If the method has not completed, IsCompleted returns false, and the calling thread is free to carry on its work. If IsCompleted returns true, the calling thread is able to obtain the result in the "least blocking manner" possible. Ponder the following update to the Main() method:

```
static void Main(string[] args)
{
...
  BinaryOp b = new BinaryOp(Add);
  IAsyncResult iftAR = b.BeginInvoke(10, 10, null, null);

  // This message will keep printing until
  // the Add() method is finished.
  while(!iftAR.IsCompleted)
  {
    Console.WriteLine("Doing more work in Main()!");
    Thread.Sleep(1000);
  }
  // Now we know the Add() method is complete.
  int answer = b.EndInvoke(iftAR);
...
}
```

Here, you enter a loop that will continue processing the Console.WriteLine() statement until the secondary thread has completed. After this has occurred, you can obtain the result of the Add() method, knowing full well the method has indeed completed. The call to Thread.Sleep(1000) is not necessary for this particular application to function correctly; however, by forcing the primary thread to wait for approximately one second during each iteration, it prevents the same message from printing hundreds of times. Here is the output (your output might differ slightly, based on the speed of your machine and when threads come to life):

```
***** Async Delegate Invocation *****
Main() invoked on thread 1.
Doing more work in Main()!
Add() invoked on thread 3.
Doing more work in Main()!
Doing more work in Main()!
Doing more work in Main()!
Doing more work in Main()!
Doing more work in Main()!
10 + 10 is 20.
```

In addition to the IsCompleted property, the IAsyncResult interface provides the AsyncWaitHandle property for more flexible waiting logic. This property returns an instance of the WaitHandle type, which exposes a method named WaitOne(). The benefit of WaitHandle.WaitOne() is that you can specify the maximum wait time. If the specified amount of time is exceeded, WaitOne() returns false. Ponder the following updated while loop, which no longer makes use of a call to Thread.Sleep():

```
while (!iftAR.AsyncWaitHandle.WaitOne(1000, true))
{
  Console.WriteLine("Doing more work in Main()!");
}
```

While these properties of IAsyncResult do provide a way to synchronize the calling thread, they are not the most efficient approach. In many ways, the IsCompleted property is much like a really annoying manager (or classmate) who is constantly asking, "Are you done yet?" Thankfully, delegates provide a number of additional (and more elegant) techniques to obtain the result of a method that has been called asynchronously.

■ **Source Code** The AsyncDelegate project is located under the Chapter 19 subdirectory.

The Role of the AsyncCallback Delegate

Rather than polling a delegate to determine whether an asynchronously invoked method has completed, it would be more efficient to have the secondary thread inform the calling thread when the task is finished. When you want to enable this behavior, you will need to supply an instance of the System.AsyncCallback delegate as a parameter to BeginInvoke(), which up until this point has been null. However, when you do supply an AsyncCallback object, the delegate will call the specified method automatically when the asynchronous call has completed.

■ **Note** The callback method will be called on the secondary thread, not the primary thread. This has important implications when using threads within a graphical user interface (WPF or Windows Forms) as controls have thread-affinity, meaning they can be manipulated only by the thread that created them. You'll see some examples of working the threads from a GUI later in this chapter, during the examination of the Task Parallel Library (TPL) and the new .NET 4.5 C# async and await keywords.

Like any delegate, AsyncCallback can invoke methods that match only a specific pattern, which in this case is a method taking IAsyncResult as the sole parameter and returning nothing:

```
// Targets of AsyncCallback must match the following pattern.
void MyAsyncCallbackMethod(IAsyncResult itfAR)
```

Assume you have another Console Application (AsyncCallbackDelegate) making use of the BinaryOp delegate. This time, however, you will not poll the delegate to determine whether the Add() method has completed. Rather, you will define a static method named AddComplete() to receive the notification that the asynchronous invocation is finished. Also, this example makes use of a class-level static bool field, which will be used to keep the primary thread in Main() running a task until the secondary thread is finished.

■ **Note** The use of this Boolean variable in this example is, strictly speaking, not thread safe, as there are two different threads which have access to its value. This will be permissible for the current example; however, as a *very* good rule of thumb, you must ensure data that can be shared among multiple threads is locked down. You'll see how to do so later in this chapter.

```
namespace AsyncCallbackDelegate
{
  public delegate int BinaryOp(int x, int y);

  class Program
  {
    private static bool isDone = false;

    static void Main(string[] args)
    {
      Console.WriteLine("***** AsyncCallbackDelegate Example *****");
      Console.WriteLine("Main() invoked on thread {0}.",
        Thread.CurrentThread.ManagedThreadId);

      BinaryOp b = new BinaryOp(Add);
      IAsyncResult iftAR = b.BeginInvoke(10, 10,
```

```
                    new AsyncCallback(AddComplete), null);

      // Assume other work is performed here...
      while (!isDone)
      {
        Thread.Sleep(1000);
        Console.WriteLine("Working....");
      }
      Console.ReadLine();
    }

    static int Add(int x, int y)
    {
      Console.WriteLine("Add() invoked on thread {0}.",
      Thread.CurrentThread.ManagedThreadId);
      Thread.Sleep(5000);
      return x + y;
    }

    static void AddComplete(IAsyncResult itfAR)
    {
      Console.WriteLine("AddComplete() invoked on thread {0}.",
        Thread.CurrentThread.ManagedThreadId);
      Console.WriteLine("Your addition is complete");
      isDone = true;
    }
  }
}
```

Again, the static `AddComplete()` method will be invoked by the `AsyncCallback` delegate when the `Add()` method has completed. If you run this program, you can confirm that the secondary thread is the thread invoking the `AddComplete()` callback:

```
***** AsyncCallbackDelegate Example *****
Main() invoked on thread 1.
Add() invoked on thread 3.
Working....
Working....
Working....
Working....
Working....
AddComplete() invoked on thread 3.
Your addition is complete
```

Like other examples in this chapter, your output might be slightly different. In fact, you might see one final "Working…" printout occur after the addition is complete. This is just a byproduct of the forced 1-second delay in `Main()`.

The Role of the AsyncResult Class

Currently, the AddComplete() method is not printing out the actual result of the operation (adding two numbers). The reason is that the target of the AsyncCallback delegate (AddComplete(), in this example) does not have access to the original BinaryOp delegate created in the scope of Main() and, therefore, you can't call EndInvoke() from within AddComplete()!

While you could simply declare the BinaryOp variable as a static member variable in the class to allow both methods to access the same object, a more elegant solution is to use the incoming IAsyncResult parameter.

The incoming IAsyncResult parameter passed into the target of the AsyncCallback delegate is actually an instance of the AsyncResult class (note the lack of an I prefix) defined in the System. Runtime.Remoting.Messaging namespace. The AsyncDelegate property returns a reference to the original asynchronous delegate that was created elsewhere.

Therefore, if you wish to obtain a reference to the BinaryOp delegate object allocated within Main(), simply cast the System.Object returned by the AsyncDelegate property into type BinaryOp. At this point, you can trigger EndInvoke() as expected.

```
// Don't forget to import
// System.Runtime.Remoting.Messaging!
static void AddComplete(IAsyncResult itfAR)
{
  Console.WriteLine("AddComplete() invoked on thread {0}.",
    Thread.CurrentThread.ManagedThreadId);
  Console.WriteLine("Your addition is complete");

  // Now get the result.
  AsyncResult ar = (AsyncResult)itfAR;
  BinaryOp b = (BinaryOp)ar.AsyncDelegate;
  Console.WriteLine("10 + 10 is {0}.", b.EndInvoke(itfAR));
  isDone = true;
}
```

Passing and Receiving Custom State Data

The final aspect of asynchronous delegates you need to address is the final argument to the BeginInvoke() method (which has been null up to this point). This parameter allows you to pass additional state information to the callback method from the primary thread. Because this argument is prototyped as a System.Object, you can pass in any type of data whatsoever, as long as the callback method knows what to expect. Assume for the sake of demonstration that the primary thread wishes to pass in a custom text message to the AddComplete() method, like so:

```
static void Main(string[] args)
{
...
  IAsyncResult iftAR = b.BeginInvoke(10, 10,
    new AsyncCallback(AddComplete),
    "Main() thanks you for adding these numbers.");
...
}
```

To obtain this data within the scope of AddComplete(), make use of the AsyncState property of the incoming IAsyncResult parameter. Notice that an explicit cast will be required; therefore, the primary and secondary threads must agree on the underlying type returned from AsyncState.

```
static void AddComplete(IAsyncResult itfAR)
{
...
  // Retrieve the informational object and cast it to string.
  string msg = (string)itfAR.AsyncState;
  Console.WriteLine(msg);
  isDone = true;
}
```

Here is the output of the final iteration:

```
*****  AsyncCallbackDelegate Example *****
Main() invoked on thread 1.
Add() invoked on thread 3.
Working....
Working....
Working....
Working....
Working....
AddComplete() invoked on thread 3.
Your addition is complete
10 + 10 is 20.
Main() thanks you for adding these numbers.
```

Now that you understand how a .NET delegate can be used to automatically spin off a secondary thread of execution to handle an asynchronous method invocation, let's turn our attention to directly interacting with threads using the System.Threading namespace. Recall that this namespace was the original .NET threading API that shipped since version 1.0.

■ **Source Code** The AsyncCallbackDelegate project is located under the Chapter 19 subdirectory.

The System.Threading Namespace

Under the .NET platform, the System.Threading namespace provides a number of types that enable the direct construction of multithreaded applications. In addition to providing types that allow you to interact with a particular CLR thread, this namespace defines types that allow access to the CLR-maintained thread pool, a simple (non–GUI-based) Timer class, and numerous types used to provide synchronized access to shared resources. Table 19-1 lists some of the important members of this namespace. (Be sure to consult the .NET Framework 4.5 SDK documentation for full details.)

Table 19-1. Core Types of the System.Threading *Namespace*

Type	Meaning in Life
Interlocked	This type provides atomic operations for variables that are shared by multiple threads.
Monitor	This type provides the synchronization of threading objects using locks and wait/signals. The C# lock keyword makes use of a Monitor object under the hood.
Mutex	This synchronization primitive can be used for synchronization between application domain boundaries.
ParameterizedThreadStart	This delegate allows a thread to call methods that take any number of arguments.
Semaphore	This type allows you to limit the number of threads that can access a resource, or a particular type of resource, concurrently.
Thread	This type represents a thread that executes within the CLR. Using this type, you are able to spawn additional threads in the originating AppDomain.
ThreadPool	This type allows you to interact with the CLR-maintained thread pool within a given process.
ThreadPriority	This enum represents a thread's priority level (Highest, Normal, etc.).
ThreadStart	This delegate is used to specify the method to call for a given thread. Unlike the ParameterizedThreadStart delegate, targets of ThreadStart must always have the same prototype.
ThreadState	This enum specifies the valid states a thread may take (Running, Aborted, etc.).
Timer	This type provides a mechanism for executing a method at specified intervals.
TimerCallback	This delegate type is used in conjunction with Timer types.

The System.Threading.Thread Class

The most primitive of all types in the System.Threading namespace is Thread. This class represents an object-oriented wrapper around a given path of execution within a particular AppDomain. This type also defines a number of methods (both static and instance level) that allow you to create new threads within the current AppDomain, as well as to suspend, stop, and destroy a particular thread. Consider the list of core static members in Table 19-2.

Table 19-2. Key Static Members of the Thread Type

Static Member	Meaning in Life
CurrentContext	This read-only property returns the context in which the thread is currently running.
CurrentThread	This read-only property returns a reference to the currently running thread.
GetDomain() GetDomainID()	These methods return a reference to the current AppDomain or the ID of the domain in which the current thread is running.
Sleep()	This method suspends the current thread for a specified time.

The Thread class also supports several instance-level members, some of which are shown in Table 19-3.

Table 19-3. Select Instance-Level Members of the Thread Type

Instance-Level Member	Meaning in Life
IsAlive	Returns a Boolean that indicates whether this thread has been started (and has not yet terminated or aborted).
IsBackground	Gets or sets a value indicating whether or not this thread is a "background thread" (more details in just a moment).
Name	Allows you to establish a friendly text name of the thread.
Priority	Gets or sets the priority of a thread, which may be assigned a value from the ThreadPriority enumeration.
ThreadState	Gets the state of this thread, which may be assigned a value from the ThreadState enumeration.
Abort()	Instructs the CLR to terminate the thread as soon as possible.
Interrupt()	Interrupts (e.g., wakes) the current thread from a suitable wait period.

Join()	Blocks the calling thread until the specified thread (the one on which Join() is called) exits.
Resume()	Resumes a thread that has been previously suspended.
Start()	Instructs the CLR to execute the thread ASAP.
Suspend()	Suspends the thread. If the thread is already suspended, a call to Suspend() has no effect.

■ **Note** Aborting or suspending an active thread is generally considered a bad idea. When you do so, there is a chance (however small) that a thread could "leak" its workload when disturbed or terminated.

Obtaining Statistics About the Current Thread of Execution

Recall that the entry point of an executable assembly (i.e., the Main() method) runs on the primary thread of execution. To illustrate the basic use of the Thread type, assume you have a new Console Application named ThreadStats. As you know, the static Thread.CurrentThread property retrieves a Thread object that represents the currently executing thread. Once you have obtained the current thread, you are able to print out various statistics, like so:

```
// Be sure to import the System.Threading namespace.
static void Main(string[] args)
{
  Console.WriteLine("***** Primary Thread stats *****\n");

  // Obtain and name the current thread.
  Thread primaryThread = Thread.CurrentThread;
  primaryThread.Name = "ThePrimaryThread";

  // Show details of hosting AppDomain/Context.
  Console.WriteLine("Name of current AppDomain: {0}",
    Thread.GetDomain().FriendlyName);
  Console.WriteLine("ID of current Context: {0}",
    Thread.CurrentContext.ContextID);

  // Print out some stats about this thread.
  Console.WriteLine("Thread Name: {0}",
    primaryThread.Name);
  Console.WriteLine("Has thread started?: {0}",
    primaryThread.IsAlive);
  Console.WriteLine("Priority Level: {0}",
    primaryThread.Priority);
  Console.WriteLine("Thread State: {0}",
    primaryThread.ThreadState);
  Console.ReadLine();
```

```
}
```

Here is the current output:

```
***** Primary Thread stats *****

Name of current AppDomain: ThreadStats.exe
ID of current Context: 0
Thread Name: ThePrimaryThread
Has thread started?: True
Priority Level: Normal
Thread State: Running
```

The Name Property

While this code is more or less self-explanatory, do notice that the Thread class supports a property called Name. If you do not set this value, Name will return an empty string. However, once you assign a friendly string moniker to a given Thread object, you can greatly simplify your debugging endeavors. If you are making use of Visual Studio, you may access the Threads window during a debugging session (select Debug ➤ Windows Threads). As you can see from Figure 19-1, you can quickly identify the thread you want to diagnose.

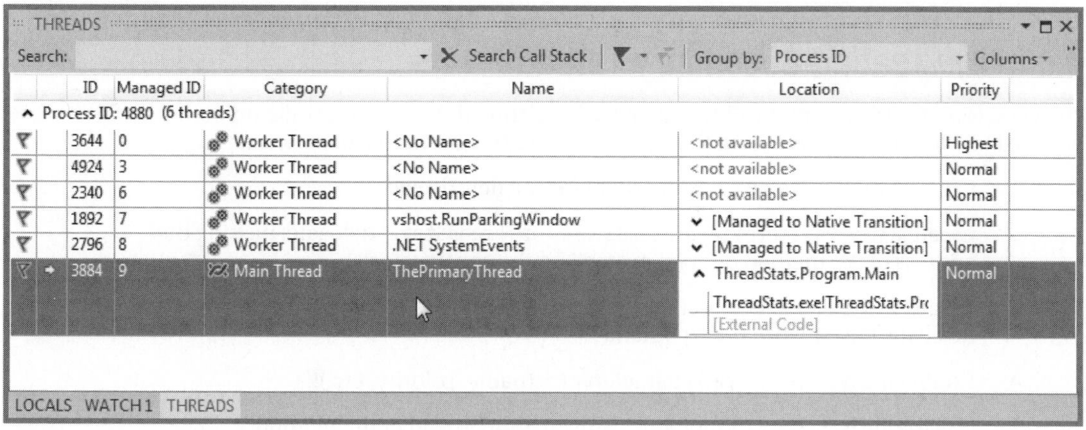

Figure 19-1. Debugging a thread with Visual Studio

The Priority Property

Next, notice that the Thread type defines a property named Priority. By default, all threads have a priority level of Normal. However, you can change this at any point in the thread's lifetime using the ThreadPriority property and the related System.Threading.ThreadPriority enumeration, like so:

```
public enum ThreadPriority
{
  Lowest,
```

```
    BelowNormal,
    Normal,  // Default value.
    AboveNormal,
    Highest
}
```

If you were to assign a thread's priority level to a value other than the default (ThreadPriority.Normal), understand that you would have no direct control over when the thread scheduler switches between threads. In reality, a thread's priority level offers a hint to the CLR regarding the importance of the thread's activity. Thus, a thread with the value ThreadPriority.Highest is not necessarily guaranteed to be given the highest precedence.

Again, if the thread scheduler is preoccupied with a given task (e.g., synchronizing an object, switching threads, or moving threads), the priority level will most likely be altered accordingly. However, all things being equal, the CLR will read these values and instruct the thread scheduler how to best allocate time slices. Threads with an identical thread priority should each receive the same amount of time to perform their work.

In most cases, you will seldom (if ever) need to directly alter a thread's priority level. In theory, it is possible to jack up the priority level on a set of threads, thereby preventing lower-priority threads from executing at their required levels (so use caution).

■ **Source Code** The ThreadStats project is included under the Chapter 19 subdirectory.

Manually Creating Secondary Threads

When you want to programmatically create additional threads to carry on some unit of work, follow this very predictable process when using the types of the System.Threading namespace:

1. Create a method to be the entry point for the new thread.

2. Create a new ParameterizedThreadStart (or ThreadStart) delegate, passing the address of the method defined in step 1 to the constructor.

3. Create a Thread object, passing the ParameterizedThreadStart/ThreadStart delegate as a constructor argument.

4. Establish any initial thread characteristics (name, priority, etc.).

5. Call the Thread.Start() method. This starts the thread at the method referenced by the delegate created in step 2 as soon as possible.

As stated in step 2, you may make use of two distinct delegate types to "point to" the method that the secondary thread will execute. The ThreadStart delegate can point to any method that takes no arguments and returns nothing. This delegate can be helpful when the method is designed to simply run in the background without further interaction.

The obvious limitation of ThreadStart is that you are unable to pass in parameters for processing. However, the ParameterizedThreadStart delegate type allows a single parameter of type System.Object. Given that anything can be represented as a System.Object, you can pass in any number of parameters via a custom class or structure. Do note, however, that the ParameterizedThreadStart delegate can only point to methods that return void.

Working with the ThreadStart Delegate

To illustrate the process of building a multithreaded application (as well as to demonstrate the usefulness of doing so), assume you have a Console Application (SimpleMultiThreadApp) that allows the end user to choose whether the application will perform its duties using the single primary thread or split its workload using two separate threads of execution.

Assuming you have imported the System.Threading namespace, your first step is to define a method to perform the work of the (possible) secondary thread. To keep focused on the mechanics of building multithreaded programs, this method will simply print out a sequence of numbers to the console window, pausing for approximately two seconds with each pass. Here is the full definition of the Printer class:

```
public class Printer
{
  public void PrintNumbers()
  {
    // Display Thread info.
    Console.WriteLine("-> {0} is executing PrintNumbers()",
      Thread.CurrentThread.Name);

    // Print out numbers.
    Console.Write("Your numbers: ");
    for(int i = 0; i < 10; i++)
    {
      Console.Write("{0}, ", i);
      Thread.Sleep(2000);
    }
    Console.WriteLine();
  }
}
```

Now, within Main(), you will first prompt the user to determine whether one or two threads will be used to perform the application's work. If the user requests a single thread, you will simply invoke the PrintNumbers() method within the primary thread. However, if the user specifies two threads, you will create a ThreadStart delegate that points to PrintNumbers(), pass this delegate object into the constructor of a new Thread object, and call Start() to inform the CLR this thread is ready for processing.

To begin, set a reference to the System.Windows.Forms.dll assembly (and import the System.Windows.Forms namespace) and display a message within Main() using MessageBox.Show() (you'll see the point of doing so after you run the program). Here is the complete implementation of Main():

```
static void Main(string[] args)
{
  Console.WriteLine("***** The Amazing Thread App *****\n");
  Console.Write("Do you want [1] or [2] threads? ");
  string threadCount = Console.ReadLine();

  // Name the current thread.
  Thread primaryThread = Thread.CurrentThread;
  primaryThread.Name = "Primary";
```

```
// Display Thread info.
Console.WriteLine("-> {0} is executing Main()",
Thread.CurrentThread.Name);

// Make worker class.
Printer p = new Printer();

switch(threadCount)
{
  case  "2":
    // Now make the thread.
    Thread backgroundThread =
      new Thread(new ThreadStart(p.PrintNumbers));
    backgroundThread.Name = "Secondary";
    backgroundThread.Start();
  break;
  case "1":
    p.PrintNumbers();
  break;
  default:
    Console.WriteLine("I don't know what you want...you get 1 thread.");
    goto case "1";
}

// Do some additional work.
MessageBox.Show("I'm busy!", "Work on main thread...");
Console.ReadLine();
}
```

Now, if you run this program with a single thread, you will find that the final message box will not display the message until the entire sequence of numbers has printed to the console. As you are explicitly pausing for approximately two seconds after each number is printed, this will result in a less-than-stellar end-user experience. However, if you select two threads, the message box displays instantly, given that a unique Thread object is responsible for printing out the numbers to the console (see Figure 19-2).

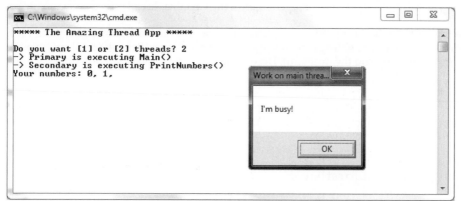

Figure 19-2. Multithreaded applications provide results in more responsive applications

---

■ **Source Code** The SimpleMultiThreadApp project is included under the Chapter 19 subdirectory.

Working with the ParameterizedThreadStart Delegate

Recall that the ThreadStart delegate can point only to methods that return void and take no arguments. While this might fit the bill in some cases, if you want to pass data to the method executing on the secondary thread, you will need to make use of the ParameterizedThreadStart delegate type. To illustrate, let's re-create the logic of the AsyncCallbackDelegate project created earlier in this chapter, this time making use of the ParameterizedThreadStart delegate type.

To begin, create a new Console Application named AddWithThreads and import the System.Threading namespace. Now, given that ParameterizedThreadStart can point to any method taking a System.Object parameter, you will create a custom type containing the numbers to be added, like so:

```
class AddParams
{
  public int a, b;

  public AddParams(int numb1, int numb2)
  {
    a = numb1;
    b = numb2;
  }
}
```

Next, create a static method in the Program class that will take an AddParams parameter and print out the sum of the two numbers involved, as follows:

```
static void Add(object data)
{
  if (data is AddParams)
  {
    Console.WriteLine("ID of thread in Add(): {0}",
      Thread.CurrentThread.ManagedThreadId);

    AddParams ap = (AddParams)data;
    Console.WriteLine("{0} + {1} is {2}",
      ap.a, ap.b, ap.a + ap.b);
  }
}
```

The code within Main() is straightforward. Simply use ParameterizedThreadStart rather than ThreadStart, like so:

```
static void Main(string[] args)
{
  Console.WriteLine("***** Adding with Thread objects *****");
  Console.WriteLine("ID of thread in Main(): {0}",
    Thread.CurrentThread.ManagedThreadId);
```

```
  // Make an AddParams object to pass to the secondary thread.
  AddParams ap = new AddParams(10, 10);
  Thread t = new Thread(new ParameterizedThreadStart(Add));
  t.Start(ap);

  // Force a wait to let other thread finish.
  Thread.Sleep(5);

  Console.ReadLine();
}
```

The AutoResetEvent Class

In these first few examples, you have made use of a few crude ways to inform the primary thread to wait until the secondary thread has completed. During your examination of asynchronous delegates you used a simple bool variable as a toggle; however, this is not a recommended solution, as both threads can access the same point of data, and this can lead to data corruption. A safer, but still undesirable alternative is to call Thread.Sleep() for a fixed amount of time. The problem here is that you don't want to wait longer than necessary.

One simple, and thread-safe way to force a thread to wait until another is completed is to use the AutoResetEvent class. In the thread that needs to wait (such as a Main() method), create an instance of this class, and pass in false to the constructor in order to signify you have not yet been notified. Then, at the point at which you are willing to wait, call the WaitOne() method. Here is the update to Program class, which will do this very thing using a static-level AutoResetEvent member variable:

```
class Program
{
  private static AutoResetEvent waitHandle = new AutoResetEvent(false);

  static void Main(string[] args)
  {
    Console.WriteLine("***** Adding with Thread objects *****");
    Console.WriteLine("ID of thread in Main(): {0}",
      Thread.CurrentThread.ManagedThreadId);
    AddParams ap = new AddParams(10, 10);
    Thread t = new Thread(new ParameterizedThreadStart(Add));
    t.Start(ap);

    // Wait here until you are notified!
    waitHandle.WaitOne();
    Console.WriteLine("Other thread is done!");

    Console.ReadLine();
  }
...
}
```

When the other thread is completed with its workload, it will call the Set() method on the same instance of the AutoResetEvent type.

```
static void Add(object data)
{
  if (data is AddParams)
  {
    Console.WriteLine("ID of thread in Add(): {0}",
      Thread.CurrentThread.ManagedThreadId);

    AddParams ap = (AddParams)data;
    Console.WriteLine("{0} + {1} is {2}",
      ap.a, ap.b, ap.a + ap.b);

    // Tell other thread we are done.
    waitHandle.Set();
  }
}
```

■ **Source Code** The AddWithThreads project is included under the Chapter 19 subdirectory.

Foreground Threads and Background Threads

Now that you have seen how to programmatically create new threads of execution using the System.Threading namespace, let's formalize the distinction between *foreground threads* and *background threads*.

- *Foreground threads* have the ability to prevent the current application from terminating. The CLR will not shut down an application (which is to say, unload the hosting AppDomain) until all foreground threads have ended.

- *Background threads* (sometimes called *daemon threads*) are viewed by the CLR as expendable paths of execution that can be ignored at any point in time (even if they are currently laboring over some unit of work). Thus, if all foreground threads have terminated, any and all background threads are automatically killed when the application domain unloads.

It is important to note that foreground and background threads are *not* synonymous with primary and worker threads. By default, every thread you create via the Thread.Start() method is automatically a foreground thread. Again, this means that the AppDomain will not unload until all threads of execution have completed their units of work. In most cases, this is exactly the behavior you require.

For the sake of argument, however, assume that you want to invoke Printer.PrintNumbers() on a secondary thread that should behave as a background thread. Again, this means that the method pointed to by the Thread type (via the ThreadStart or ParameterizedThreadStart delegate) should be able to halt safely as soon as all foreground threads are done with their work. Configuring such a thread is as simple as setting the IsBackground property to true, like so:

```
static void Main(string[] args)
{
  Console.WriteLine("***** Background Threads *****\n");
```

```
    Printer p = new Printer();
    Thread bgroundThread =
      new Thread(new ThreadStart(p.PrintNumbers));

    // This is now a background thread.
    bgroundThread.IsBackground = true;
    bgroundThread.Start();
}
```

Notice that this Main() method is *not* making a call to Console.ReadLine() to force the console to remain visible until you press the Enter key. Thus, when you run the application, it will shut down immediately because the Thread object has been configured as a background thread. Given that the Main() method triggers the creation of the primary *foreground* thread, as soon as the logic in Main() completes, the AppDomain unloads before the secondary thread is able to complete its work.

However, if you comment out the line that sets the IsBackground property, you will find that each number prints to the console, as all foreground threads must finish their work before the AppDomain is unloaded from the hosting process.

For the most part, configuring a thread to run as a background type can be helpful when the worker thread in question is performing a noncritical task that is no longer needed when the main task of the program is finished. For example, you could build an application that pings an e-mail server every few minutes for new e-mails, updates current weather conditions, or some other noncritical task.

The Issue of Concurrency

When you build multithreaded applications, your program needs to ensure that any piece of shared data is protected against the possibility of numerous threads changing its value. Given that all threads in an AppDomain have concurrent access to the shared data of the application, imagine what might happen if multiple threads were accessing the same point of data. As the thread scheduler will force threads to suspend their work at random, what if thread A is kicked out of the way before it has fully completed its work? Thread B is now reading unstable data.

To illustrate the problem of concurrency, let's build another Console Application project named MultiThreadedPrinting. This application will once again make use of the Printer class created previously, but this time the PrintNumbers() method will force the current thread to pause for a randomly generated amount of time.

```
public class Printer
{
  public void PrintNumbers()
  {
...
    for (int i = 0; i < 10; i++)
    {
      // Put thread to sleep for a random amount of time.
      Random r = new Random();
      Thread.Sleep(1000 * r.Next(5));
      Console.Write("{0}, ", i);
    }
    Console.WriteLine();
  }
}
```

The `Main()` method is responsible for creating an array of ten (uniquely named) Thread objects, each of which is making calls on the *same instance* of the Printer object as follows:

```
class Program
{
  static void Main(string[] args)
  {
    Console.WriteLine("*****Synchronizing Threads *****\n");

    Printer p = new Printer();

    // Make 10 threads that are all pointing to the same
    // method on the same object.
    Thread[] threads = new Thread[10];
    for (int i = 0; i < 10; i++)
    {
      threads[i] =
        new Thread(new ThreadStart(p.PrintNumbers));
      threads[i].Name = string.Format("Worker thread #{0}", i);
    }

    // Now start each one.
    foreach (Thread t in threads)
      t.Start();
    Console.ReadLine();
  }
}
```

Before looking at some test runs, let's recap the problem. The primary thread within this AppDomain begins life by spawning ten secondary worker threads. Each worker thread is told to make calls on the `PrintNumbers()` method on the *same* Printer instance. Given that you have taken no precautions to lock down this object's shared resources (the console), there is a good chance that the current thread will be kicked out of the way before the `PrintNumbers()` method is able to print out the complete results. Because you don't know exactly when (or if) this might happen, you are bound to get unpredictable results. For example, you might find the output shown here:

```
*****Synchronizing Threads *****

-> Worker thread #1 is executing PrintNumbers()
Your numbers: -> Worker thread #0 is executing PrintNumbers()
-> Worker thread #2 is executing PrintNumbers()
Your numbers: -> Worker thread #3 is executing PrintNumbers()
Your numbers: -> Worker thread #4 is executing PrintNumbers()
Your numbers: -> Worker thread #6 is executing PrintNumbers()
Your numbers: -> Worker thread #7 is executing PrintNumbers()
Your numbers: -> Worker thread #8 is executing PrintNumbers()
Your numbers: -> Worker thread #9 is executing PrintNumbers()
Your numbers: Your numbers: -> Worker thread #5 is executing PrintNumbers()
Your numbers: 0, 0, 0, 0, 1, 0, 0, 1, 1, 1, 2, 2, 2, 3, 3, 3, 2, 1, 0, 0, 4, 3,
4, 1, 2, 4, 5, 5, 5, 6, 6, 6, 2, 7, 7, 7, 3, 4, 0, 8, 4, 5, 1, 5, 8, 8, 9,
2, 6, 1, 0, 9, 1,
```

```
6, 2, 7, 9,
2, 1, 7, 8, 3, 2, 3, 3, 9,
8, 4, 4, 5, 9,
4, 3, 5, 5, 6, 3, 6, 7, 4, 7, 6, 8, 7, 4, 8, 5, 5, 6, 6, 8, 7, 7, 9,
8, 9,
8, 9,
9,
9,
```

Now run the application a few more times. Here is another possibility (your results will certainly differ):

```
*****Synchronizing Threads *****

-> Worker thread #0 is executing PrintNumbers()
-> Worker thread #1 is executing PrintNumbers()
-> Worker thread #2 is executing PrintNumbers()
Your numbers: -> Worker thread #4 is executing PrintNumbers()
Your numbers: -> Worker thread #5 is executing PrintNumbers()
Your numbers: Your numbers: -> Worker thread #6 is executing PrintNumbers()
Your numbers: -> Worker thread #7 is executing PrintNumbers()
Your numbers: Your numbers: -> Worker thread #8 is executing PrintNumbers()
Your numbers: -> Worker thread #9 is executing PrintNumbers()
Your numbers: -> Worker thread #3 is executing PrintNumbers()
Your numbers: 0, 0, 0, 0, 0, 0, 0, 0, 0, 0, 1, 1, 1, 1, 1, 1, 1, 1, 1, 1, 2, 2,
2, 2, 2, 2, 2, 2, 3, 3, 3, 3, 3, 3, 3, 3, 3, 3, 4, 4, 4, 4, 4, 4, 4, 4, 4,
 4, 5, 5, 5, 5, 5, 5, 5, 5, 5, 6, 6, 6, 6, 6, 6, 6, 6, 6, 7, 7, 7, 7, 7, 7
, 7, 7, 7, 7, 8, 8, 8, 8, 8, 8, 8, 8, 8, 8, 9,
9,
9,
9,
9,
9,
9,
9,
9,
9,
```

■ **Note** If you are unable to generate unpredictable outputs, increase the number of threads from 10 to 100 (for example) or introduce another call to Thread.Sleep() within your program. Eventually, you will encounter the concurrency issue.

There are clearly some problems here. As each thread is telling the Printer to print out the numerical data, the thread scheduler is happily swapping threads in the background. The result is inconsistent output. What you need is a way to programmatically enforce synchronized access to the shared resources. As you would guess, the System.Threading namespace provides a number of synchronization-centric types. The C# programming language also provides a particular keyword for the very task of synchronizing shared data in multithreaded applications.

Synchronization Using the C# lock Keyword

The first technique you can use to synchronize access to shared resources is the C# lock keyword. This keyword allows you to define a scope of statements that must be synchronized between threads. By doing so, incoming threads cannot interrupt the current thread, thus preventing it from finishing its work. The lock keyword requires you to specify a *token* (an object reference) that must be acquired by a thread to enter within the lock scope. When you are attempting to lock down a *private* instance-level method, you can simply pass in a reference to the current type, as follows:

```
private void SomePrivateMethod()
{
  // Use the current object as the thread token.
  lock(this)
  {
    // All code within this scope is thread safe.
  }
}
```

However, if you are locking down a region of code within a *public* member, it is safer (and a best practice) to declare a private object member variable to serve as the lock token, like so:

```
public class Printer
{
  // Lock token.
  private object threadLock = new object();

  public void PrintNumbers()
  {
    // Use the lock token.
    lock (threadLock)
    {
      ...
    }
  }
}
```

In any case, if you examine the PrintNumbers() method, you can see that the shared resource the threads are competing to gain access to is the console window. Therefore, if you scope all interactions with the Console type within a lock scope, as follows:

```
public void PrintNumbers()
{
  // Use the private object lock token.
  lock (threadLock)
  {
    // Display Thread info.
    Console.WriteLine("-> {0} is executing PrintNumbers()",
      Thread.CurrentThread.Name);
```

```
// Print out numbers.
Console.Write("Your numbers: ");
for (int i = 0; i < 10; i++)
{
  Random r = new Random();
  Thread.Sleep(1000 * r.Next(5));
  Console.Write("{0}, ", i);
}
Console.WriteLine();
    }
}
```

you have effectively designed a method that will allow the current thread to complete its task. Once a thread enters into a lock scope, the lock token (in this case, a reference to the current object) is inaccessible by other threads until the lock is released after the lock scope has exited. Thus, if thread A has obtained the lock token, other threads are unable to enter any scope that uses the same lock token until thread A relinquishes the lock token.

■ **Note** If you are attempting to lock down code in a static method, simply declare a private static object member variable to serve as the lock token.

If you now run the application, you can see that each thread has ample opportunity to finish its business:

```
*****Synchronizing Threads *****

-> Worker thread #0 is executing PrintNumbers()
Your numbers: 0, 1, 2, 3, 4, 5, 6, 7, 8, 9,
-> Worker thread #1 is executing PrintNumbers()
Your numbers: 0, 1, 2, 3, 4, 5, 6, 7, 8, 9,
-> Worker thread #3 is executing PrintNumbers()
Your numbers: 0, 1, 2, 3, 4, 5, 6, 7, 8, 9,
-> Worker thread #2 is executing PrintNumbers()
Your numbers: 0, 1, 2, 3, 4, 5, 6, 7, 8, 9,
-> Worker thread #4 is executing PrintNumbers()
Your numbers: 0, 1, 2, 3, 4, 5, 6, 7, 8, 9,
-> Worker thread #5 is executing PrintNumbers()
Your numbers: 0, 1, 2, 3, 4, 5, 6, 7, 8, 9,
-> Worker thread #7 is executing PrintNumbers()
Your numbers: 0, 1, 2, 3, 4, 5, 6, 7, 8, 9,
-> Worker thread #6 is executing PrintNumbers()
Your numbers: 0, 1, 2, 3, 4, 5, 6, 7, 8, 9,
-> Worker thread #8 is executing PrintNumbers()
Your numbers: 0, 1, 2, 3, 4, 5, 6, 7, 8, 9,
-> Worker thread #9 is executing PrintNumbers()
Your numbers: 0, 1, 2, 3, 4, 5, 6, 7, 8, 9,
```

■ **Source Code** The MultiThreadedPrinting project is included under the Chapter 19 subdirectory.

Synchronization Using the System.Threading.Monitor Type

The C# lock statement is really just a shorthand notation for working with the System.Threading.Monitor class. Once processed by the C# compiler, a lock scope actually resolves to the following (which you can verify using ildasm.exe):

```
public void PrintNumbers()
{
  Monitor.Enter(threadLock);
  try
  {
    // Display Thread info.
    Console.WriteLine("-> {0} is executing PrintNumbers()",
      Thread.CurrentThread.Name);

    // Print out numbers.
    Console.Write("Your numbers: ");
    for (int i = 0; i < 10; i++)
    {
      Random r = new Random();
      Thread.Sleep(1000 * r.Next(5));
      Console.Write("{0}, ", i);
    }
    Console.WriteLine();
  }
  finally
  {
    Monitor.Exit(threadLock);
  }
}
```

First, notice that the Monitor.Enter() method is the ultimate recipient of the thread token you specified as the argument to the lock keyword. Next, all code within a lock scope is wrapped within a try block. The corresponding finally clause ensures that the thread token is released (via the Monitor.Exit() method), regardless of any possible runtime exception. If you were to modify the MultiThreadPrinting program to make direct use of the Monitor type (as just shown), you would find the output is identical.

Now, given that the lock keyword seems to require less code than making explicit use of the System.Threading.Monitor type, you might wonder about the benefits of using the Monitor type directly. The short answer is control. If you make use of the Monitor type, you are able to instruct the active thread to wait for some duration of time (via the static Monitor.Wait() method), inform waiting threads when the current thread is completed (via the static Monitor.Pulse() and Monitor.PulseAll() methods), and so on.

As you would expect, in a great number of cases, the C# lock keyword will fit the bill. However, if you are interested in checking out additional members of the Monitor class, consult the .NET Framework 4.5 SDK documentation.

Synchronization Using the System.Threading.Interlocked Type

Although it always is hard to believe until you look at the underlying CIL code, assignments and simple arithmetic operations are *not atomic*. For this reason, the System.Threading namespace provides a type that allows you to operate on a single point of data atomically with less overhead than with the Monitor type. The Interlocked class defines the following key static members shown in Table 19-4.

Table 19-4. Select Static Members of the System.Threading.Interlocked Type

Member	Meaning in Life
CompareExchange()	Safely tests two values for equality and, if equal, exchanges one of the values with a third
Decrement()	Safely decrements a value by 1
Exchange()	Safely swaps two values
Increment()	Safely increments a value by 1

Although it might not seem like it from the onset, the process of atomically altering a single value is quite common in a multithreaded environment. Assume you have a method named AddOne() that increments an integer member variable named intVal. Rather than writing synchronization code such as the following:

```
public void AddOne()
{
  lock(myLockToken)
  {
    intVal++;
  }
}
```

you can simplify your code via the static Interlocked.Increment() method. Simply pass in the variable to increment by reference. Do note that the Increment() method not only adjusts the value of the incoming parameter, but also returns the new value.

```
public void AddOne()
{
  int newVal = Interlocked.Increment(ref intVal);
}
```

In addition to Increment() and Decrement(), the Interlocked type allows you to atomically assign numerical and object data. For example, if you want to assign the value of a member variable to the value 83, you can avoid the need to use an explicit lock statement (or explicit Monitor logic) and make use of the Interlocked.Exchange() method, like so:

```
public void SafeAssignment()
{
  Interlocked.Exchange(ref myInt, 83);
}
```

Finally, if you want to test two values for equality and change the point of comparison in a thread-safe manner, you are able to leverage the Interlocked.CompareExchange() method as follows:

```
public void CompareAndExchange()
{
  // If the value of i is currently 83, change i to 99.
  Interlocked.CompareExchange(ref i, 99, 83);
}
```

Synchronization Using the [Synchronization] Attribute

The final synchronization primitive examined here is the [Synchronization] attribute, which is a member of the System.Runtime.Remoting.Contexts namespace. In essence, this class-level attribute effectively locks down *all* instance member code of the object for thread safety. When the CLR allocates objects attributed with [Synchronization], it will place the object within a synchronized context. As you might recall from Chapter 17, objects that should not be removed from a contextual boundary should derive from ContextBoundObject. Therefore, if you want to make the Printer class type thread safe (without explicitly writing thread-safe code within the class members), you could update the definition as follows:

```
using System.Runtime.Remoting.Contexts;
...

// All methods of Printer are now thread safe!
[Synchronization]
public class Printer : ContextBoundObject
{
  public void PrintNumbers()
  {
    ...
  }
}
```

In some ways, this approach can be seen as the lazy way to write thread-safe code, given that you are not required to dive into the details about which aspects of the type are truly manipulating thread-sensitive data. The major downfall of this approach, however, is that even if a given method is not making use of thread-sensitive data, the CLR will *still* lock invocations to the method. Obviously, this could degrade the overall functionality of the type, so use this technique with care.

Programming with Timer Callbacks

Many applications have the need to call a specific method during regular intervals of time. For example, you might have an application that needs to display the current time on a status bar via a given helper function. As another example, you might want to have your application call a helper function every so often to perform noncritical background tasks such as checking for new e-mail messages. For situations such as these, you can use the System.Threading.Timer type in conjunction with a related delegate named TimerCallback.

To illustrate, assume you have a Console Application (TimerApp) that will print the current time every second until the user presses a key to terminate the application. The first obvious step is to write the method that will be called by the Timer type (be sure to import System.Threading into your code file).

```
class Program
{
  static void PrintTime(object state)
  {
    Console.WriteLine("Time is: {0}",
      DateTime.Now.ToLongTimeString());
  }

  static void Main(string[] args)
  {
  }
}
```

Notice the PrintTime() method has a single parameter of type System.Object and returns void. This is not optional, given that the TimerCallback delegate can only call methods that match this signature. The value passed into the target of your TimerCallback delegate can be any type of object (in the case of the e-mail example, this parameter might represent the name of the Microsoft Exchange server to interact with during the process). Also note that given that this parameter is indeed a System.Object, you are able to pass in multiple arguments using a System.Array or custom class/structure.

The next step is to configure an instance of the TimerCallback delegate and pass it into the Timer object. In addition to configuring a TimerCallback delegate, the Timer constructor allows you to specify the optional parameter information to pass into the delegate target (defined as a System.Object), the interval to poll the method, and the amount of time to wait (in milliseconds) before making the first call. For example:

```
static void Main(string[] args)
{
  Console.WriteLine("***** Working with Timer type *****\n");

  // Create the delegate for the Timer type.
  TimerCallback timeCB = new TimerCallback(PrintTime);

  // Establish timer settings.
  Timer t = new Timer(
    timeCB,      // The TimerCallback delegate object.
    null,        // Any info to pass into the called method (null for no info).
    0,           // Amount of time to wait before starting (in milliseconds).
    1000);       // Interval of time between calls (in milliseconds).

  Console.WriteLine("Hit key to terminate...");
  Console.ReadLine();
}
```

In this case, the PrintTime() method will be called roughly every second and will pass in no additional information to said method. Here is the output:

```
***** Working with Timer type *****

Hit key to terminate...
Time is: 6:51:48 PM
Time is: 6:51:49 PM
Time is: 6:51:50 PM
```

```
Time is: 6:51:51 PM
Time is: 6:51:52 PM
Press any key to continue . . .
```

If you did want to send in some information for use by the delegate target, simply substitute the null value of the second constructor parameter with the appropriate information, like so:

```
// Establish timer settings.
Timer t = new Timer(timeCB, "Hello From Main", 0, 1000);
```

You can then obtain the incoming data as follows:

```
static void PrintTime(object state)
{
  Console.WriteLine("Time is: {0}, Param is: {1}",
    DateTime.Now.ToLongTimeString(), state.ToString());
}
```

■ **Source Code** The TimerApp project is included under the Chapter 19 subdirectory.

Understanding the CLR ThreadPool

The next thread-centric topic you will examine in this chapter is the role of the CLR thread pool. When you invoke a method asynchronously using delegate types (via the BeginInvoke() method), the CLR does not literally create a brand-new thread. For purposes of efficiency, a delegate's BeginInvoke() method leverages a pool of worker threads that is maintained by the runtime. To allow you to interact with this pool of waiting threads, the System.Threading namespace provides the ThreadPool class type.

If you would like to queue a method call for processing by a worker thread in the pool, you can make use of the ThreadPool.QueueUserWorkItem() method. This method has been overloaded to allow you to specify an optional System.Object for custom state data in addition to an instance of the WaitCallback delegate.

```
public static class ThreadPool
{
  ...
  public static bool QueueUserWorkItem(WaitCallback callBack);
  public static bool QueueUserWorkItem(WaitCallback callBack,
                                    object state);
}
```

The WaitCallback delegate can point to any method that takes a System.Object as its sole parameter (which represents the optional state data) and returns nothing. Do note that if you do not provide a System.Object when calling QueueUserWorkItem(), the CLR automatically passes a null value. To illustrate queuing methods for use by the CLR thread pool, ponder the following program, which makes use of the Printer type once again. In this case, however, you are not manually creating an array of Thread objects; rather, you are assigning members of the pool to the PrintNumbers() method.

```
class Program
{
  static void Main(string[] args)
  {
    Console.WriteLine("***** Fun with the CLR Thread Pool *****\n");

    Console.WriteLine("Main thread started. ThreadID = {0}",
      Thread.CurrentThread.ManagedThreadId);

    Printer p = new Printer();

    WaitCallback workItem = new WaitCallback(PrintTheNumbers);

    // Queue the method ten times.
    for (int i = 0; i < 10; i++)
    {
      ThreadPool.QueueUserWorkItem(workItem, p);
    }
    Console.WriteLine("All tasks queued");
    Console.ReadLine();
  }

  static void PrintTheNumbers(object state)
  {
    Printer task = (Printer)state;
    task.PrintNumbers();
  }
}
```

At this point, you might be wondering if it would be advantageous to make use of the CLR-maintained thread pool rather than explicitly creating Thread objects. Consider these benefits of leveraging the thread pool:

- The thread pool manages threads efficiently by minimizing the number of threads that must be created, started, and stopped.

- By using the thread pool, you can focus on your business problem rather than the application's threading infrastructure.

However, using manual thread management is preferred in some cases. For example:

- If you require foreground threads or must set the thread priority. Pooled threads are always background threads with default priority (ThreadPriority.Normal).

- If you require a thread with a fixed identity in order to abort it, suspend it, or discover it by name.

■ **Source Code** The ThreadPoolApp project is included under the Chapter 19 subdirectory.

That wraps up your investigation of the System.Threading namespace. To be sure, understanding the topics presented thus far in the chapter (especially during our examination of concurrency issues) will be extremely valuable when creating a multithreaded application. Given this foundation, we will now turn our attention to a number of new thread-centric topics which are only available under .NET 4.0 and higher. To begin, we will examine the role of an alternative threading model, termed the TPL.

Parallel Programming Using the Task Parallel Library

At this point in the chapter, you have examined two programming techniques (using asynchronous delegates and via the members of System.Threading) that allow you to build multithreaded software. Recall that both of these approaches will work under any version of the .NET platform.

Beginning with the release of .NET 4.0, Microsoft introduced a new approach to multithreaded application development using a parallel programming library termed the *Task Parallel Library* (TPL). Using the types of System.Threading.Tasks, you can build fine-grained, scalable parallel code without having to work directly with threads or the thread pool.

This is not to say, however, that you will not use the types of System.Threading when you make use of the TPL. In reality, these two threading toolkits can work together quite naturally. This is especially true in that the System.Threading namespace still provides a majority of the synchronization primitives we examined previously (Monitor, Interlocked, and so forth). This being said, you will quite likely find that you will favor working with the TPL rather than the original System.Threading namespace, given that the same set of tasks can be performed in a more straightforward manner.

■ **Note** On a related note, be aware that the new .NET 4.5 C# async and await keywords make use of various members of the System.Threading.Tasks namespace.

The System.Threading.Tasks Namespace

Collectively speaking, the types of System.Threading.Tasks are referred to as the *Task Parallel Library*, or TPL. The TPL will automatically distribute your application's workload across available CPUs dynamically, using the CLR thread pool. The TPL handles the partitioning of the work, thread scheduling, state management, and other low-level details. The end result is that you can maximize the performance of your .NET applications, while being shielded from many of complexities of directly working with threads (see Figure 19-3).

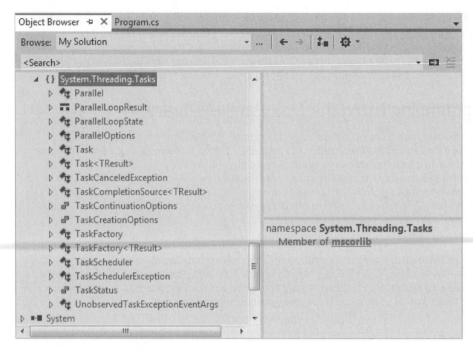

Figure 19-3. Members of the System.Threading.Tasks namespace

The Role of the Parallel Class

A key class of the TPL is System.Threading.Tasks.Parallel. This class supports a number of methods that allow you to iterate over a collection of data (specifically, an object implementing IEnumerable<T>) in a parallel fashion. If you were to look up the Parallel class in the .NET Framework 4.5 SDK documentation, you would see that this class supports two primary static methods, Parallel.For() and Parallel.ForEach(), each of which defines numerous overloaded versions.

These methods allow you to author a body of code statements that will be processed in a parallel manner. In concept, these statements are the same sort of logic you would write in a normal looping construct (via the for or foreach C# keywords). The benefit is that the Parallel class will pluck threads from the thread pool (and manage concurrency) on your behalf.

Both of these methods require you to specify an IEnumerable- or IEnumerable<T>-compatible container that holds the data you need to process in a parallel manner. The container could be a simple array, a nongeneric collection (such as ArrayList), a generic collection (such as List<T>), or the results of a LINQ query.

In addition, you will need to make use of the System.Func<T> and System.Action<T> delegates to specify the target method that will be called to process the data. You've already encountered the Func<T> delegate in Chapter 12, during your investigation of LINQ to Objects. Recall that Func<T> represents a method that can have a given return value and a varied number of arguments. The Action<T> delegate is very similar to Func<T>, in that it allows you to point to a method taking some number of parameters. However, Action<T> specifies a method that can only return void.

While you could call the Parallel.For() and Parallel.ForEach() methods and pass a strongly typed Func<T> or Action<T> delegate object, you can simplify your programming by making use of a fitting C# anonymous method or lambda expression.

Data Parallelism with the Parallel Class

The first way to use the TPL is to perform *data parallelism*. Simply put, this term refers to the task of iterating over an array or collection in a parallel manner using the Parallel.For() or Parallel.ForEach() methods. Assume you need to perform some labor-intensive file I/O operations. Specifically, you need to load a large number of *.jpg files into memory, flip them upside down, and save the modified image data to a new location.

The .NET Framework 4.5 SDK documentation provides a console-based example of this very situation; however, we will perform the same overall task using a graphical user interface, in order to examine the use of "anonymous delegates" to allow secondary threads to update the primary user interface thread (a.k.a. the UI thread).

■ **Note** When you are building a multithreaded graphical user interface (GUI) application, secondary threads can never directly access user interface controls. The reason is that controls (buttons, text boxes, labels, progress bars, etc.) have thread affinity with the thread that created them. In the following example, I'll illustrate one way to allow secondary threads to access UI items in a thread-safe manner. You'll see a more simplified approach when we examine the .NET 4.5 C# async and await keywords.

To illustrate, create a Windows Forms application named DataParallelismWithForEach, and use the Solution Explorer to rename the Form1.cs to MainForm.cs. After you do so, import the following namespaces in your primary code file:

```
// Be sure you have these namespaces!
using System.Threading.Tasks;
using System.Threading;
using System.IO;
```

The GUI of the application consists of a multiline TextBox and a single Button (named btnProcessImages). The purpose of the text area is to allow you to enter data while the work is being performed in the background, thus illustrating the nonblocking nature of the parallel task. The Click event of this Button will eventually make use of the TPL, but for now, author the following blocking code.

■ **Note** You should update the string passed into the following Directory.GetFiles() method call to point to a path on your computer that has some image files (such as a personal folder of family pictures). Here, I am just pointing to some sample pictures stored under C:\Users\Public\Pictures\Sample Pictures.

```
public partial class MainForm : Form
{
  public MainForm()
  {
    InitializeComponent();
  }

  private void btnProcessImages_Click(object sender, EventArgs e)
  {
    ProcessFiles();
  }

  private void ProcessFiles()
  {
    // Load up all *.jpg files, and make a new folder for the modified data.
    string[] files = Directory.GetFiles
      (@"C:\Users\Public\Pictures\Sample Pictures", "*.jpg",
      SearchOption.AllDirectories);
    string newDir = @"C:\ModifiedPictures";
    Directory.CreateDirectory(newDir);

    // Process the image data in a blocking manner.
    foreach (string currentFile in files)
    {
      string filename = Path.GetFileName(currentFile);

      using (Bitmap bitmap = new Bitmap(currentFile))
      {
        bitmap.RotateFlip(RotateFlipType.Rotate180FlipNone);
        bitmap.Save(Path.Combine(newDir, filename));

        // Print out the ID of the thread processing the current image.
        this.Text = string.Format("Processing {0} on thread {1}", filename,
          Thread.CurrentThread.ManagedThreadId);
      }
    }
  }
}
```

Notice that the ProcessFiles() method will rotate each *.jpg file under the specified directory, which currently contains a total of 37 files (again, be sure to update the path sent into Directory.GetFiles() as necessary). Currently, all of the work is happening on the primary thread of the executable. Therefore, if the button is clicked, the program will appear to hang. Furthermore, the caption of the window will also report that the same primary thread is processing the file, as we only have a single thread of execution.

To process the files on as many CPUs as possible, you can rewrite the current foreach loop to make use of Parallel.ForEach(). Recall that this method has been overloaded numerous times; however, in the simplest form, you must specify the IEnumerable<T>-compatible object that contains the items to process (that would be the files string array) and an Action<T> delegate that points to the method that will perform the work.

Here is the relevant update, using the C# lambda operator in place of a literal Action<T> delegate object. Notice that we are currently *commenting out* the line of code that displayed the ID of the thread executing the current image file. See the next section to find out the reason why.

```
// Process the image data in a parallel manner!
Parallel.ForEach(files, currentFile =>
  {
    string filename = Path.GetFileName(currentFile);

    using (Bitmap bitmap = new Bitmap(currentFile))
    {
      bitmap.RotateFlip(RotateFlipType.Rotate180FlipNone);
      bitmap.Save(Path.Combine(newDir, filename));

      // This code statement is now a problem! See next section.
      //  this.Text = string.Format("Processing {0} on thread {1}", filename,
      //   Thread.CurrentThread.ManagedThreadId);
    }
  }
);
```

Accessing UI Elements on Secondary Threads

You'll notice that I've commented out the previous line of code that updated the caption of the main window with the ID of the currently executing thread. As noted previously, GUI controls have "thread affinity" with the thread that created it. If secondary threads attempt to access a control it did not directly create, you are bound to run into runtime errors when debugging your software. On the flip side, if you were to *run* the application (via Ctrl+F5) you might not ever find any problems whatsoever with the original code.

■ **Note** Let me reiterate the previous point: when you debug (F5) a multithreaded application, Visual Studio is often able to catch errors that arise when a secondary thread is "touching" a control created on the primary thread. However, often times when you run (Ctrl+F5) the application, the application could appear to run correctly (or it might error straightaway). Until you take precautions (examined next), your application has the potential of raising a runtime error under such circumstances.

One approach that we can use to allow these secondary threads to access the controls in a thread-safe manner is to make use of yet another delegate centric technique, specifically an *anonymous delegate*. The Control parent class of the Windows Forms API defines a method named Invoke(), which takes a System.Delegate as input. You can call this method when you are in a coding context involving secondary threads, to provide a thread-safe manner to update the UI of the given control. Now, while we could write all of the required delegate code directly, most developers use anonymous delegates as a simple alternative. Here would be the relevant update to content with the previously commented-out code statement:

```
using (Bitmap bitmap = new Bitmap(currentFile))
{
  bitmap.RotateFlip(RotateFlipType.Rotate180FlipNone);
  bitmap.Save(Path.Combine(newDir, filename));
```

```
    // Eek! This will not work anymore!
    //this.Text = string.Format("Processing {0} on thread {1}", filename,
    //   Thread.CurrentThread.ManagedThreadId);

    // Invoke on the Form object, to allow secondary threads to access controls
    // in a thread-safe manner.
    this.Invoke((Action)delegate
      {
         this.Text = string.Format("Processing {0} on thread {1}", filename,
                    Thread.CurrentThread.ManagedThreadId);
      }
    );
}
```

■ **Note** The this.Invoke() method is unique to the Windows Forms API. When you are building a WPF application, you would write this.Dispatcher.Invoke() for the same purpose.

Now, if you run program, the TPL will indeed distribute the workload to multiple threads from the thread pool, using as many CPUs as possible. However, you will not see the window's caption display the name of each unique thread and you won't see anything if you type in the text box, until all the images have been processed! The reason is that the primary UI thread is still blocked, waiting for all of the other threads to finish up their business.

The Task Class

The Task class allows you to easily invoke a method on a secondary thread, and can be used as a simple alternative to working with asynchronous delegates. Update the Click handler of your Button control as so:

```
private void btnProcessImages_Click(object sender, EventArgs e)
{
   // Start a new "task" to process the files.
   Task.Factory.StartNew(() =>
   {
      ProcessFiles();
   });
}
```

The Factory property of Task returns a TaskFactory object. When you call its StartNew() method, you pass in an Action<T> delegate (here, hidden away with a fitting lambda expression) that points to the method to invoke in an asynchronous manner. With this small update, you will now find that the window's title will show which thread from the thread pool is processing a given file, and better yet, the text area is able to receive input, as the UI thread is no longer blocked.

Handling Cancellation Request

One improvement you can make to the current example is to provide a way for the user to stop the processing of the image data, via a second (aptly named) Cancel button. Thankfully, the Parallel.For()

and Parallel.ForEach() methods both support cancellation through the use of *cancellation tokens.* When you invoke methods on Parallel, you can pass in a ParallelOptions object, which in turn contains a CancellationTokenSource object.

First, define the following new private member variable in your Form derived class of type CancellationTokenSource named cancelToken:

```
public partial class MainForm : Form
{
  // New Form-level variable.
  private CancellationTokenSource cancelToken =
    new CancellationTokenSource();
...
}
```

Now, assuming you have added a new Button (named btnCancel) on your designer, handle the Click event, and implement the handler as so:

```
private void btnCancel_Click(object sender, EventArgs e)
{
  // This will be used to tell all the worker threads to stop!
  cancelToken.Cancel();
}
```

Now, the real modifications need to occur within the ProcessFiles() method. Consider the final implementation:

```
private void ProcessFiles()
{
  // Use ParallelOptions instance to store the CancellationToken.
  ParallelOptions parOpts = new ParallelOptions();
  parOpts.CancellationToken = cancelToken.Token;
  parOpts.MaxDegreeOfParallelism = System.Environment.ProcessorCount;

  // Load up all *.jpg files, and make a new folder for the modified data.
  string[] files = Directory.GetFiles
    (@"C:\Users\Public\Pictures\Sample Pictures", "*.jpg",
        SearchOption.AllDirectories);
  string newDir = @"C:\ModifiedPictures";
  Directory.CreateDirectory(newDir);

  try
  {
    // Process the image data in a parallel manner!
    Parallel.ForEach(files, parOpts, currentFile =>
    {
      parOpts.CancellationToken.ThrowIfCancellationRequested();

      string filename = Path.GetFileName(currentFile);
      using (Bitmap bitmap = new Bitmap(currentFile))
      {
        bitmap.RotateFlip(RotateFlipType.Rotate180FlipNone);
        bitmap.Save(Path.Combine(newDir, filename));
```

```
        this.Invoke((Action)delegate
          {
            this.Text = string.Format("Processing {0} on thread {1}", filename,
              Thread.CurrentThread.ManagedThreadId);
          }
        );
      }
    }
  );
}
catch (OperationCanceledException ex)
{
  this.Invoke((Action)delegate
  {
    this.Text = ex.Message;
  });
}
}
```

Notice that you begin the method by configuring a ParallelOptions object, setting the CancellationToken property to use the CancellationTokenSource token. Also note that when you call the Parallel.ForEach() method, you pass in the ParallelOptions object as the second parameter.

Within the scope of the looping logic, you make a call to ThrowIfCancellationRequested() on the token, which will ensure if the user clicks the Cancel button, all threads will stop and you will be notified via a runtime exception. When you catch the OperationCanceledException error, you will set the text of the main window to the error message.

■ **Source Code** The DataParallelismWithForEach project is included under the Chapter 19 subdirectory.

Task Parallelism Using the Parallel Class

In addition to data parallelism, the TPL can also be used to easily fire off any number of asynchronous tasks using the Parallel.Invoke() method. This approach is a bit more straightforward than using delegates or members from System.Threading; however, if you require more control over the way tasks are executed, you could forgo use of Parallel.Invoke() and make use of the Task class directly, as you did in the previous example.

To illustrate task parallelism, create a new Windows Forms application called MyEBookReader and be sure the System.Threading.Tasks and System.Net namespaces are imported. This example is a modification of a useful example in the .NET Framework 4.5 SDK documentation. Here, we will fetch a publically available e-book from Project Gutenberg (www.gutenberg.org), and then perform a set of lengthy tasks in parallel.

The GUI consists of a multiline TextBox control (named txtBook) and two Button controls (btnDownload and btnGetStats). Once you have designed the UI, handle the Click event for each Button, and in the form's code file, declare a class-level string variable named theEBook. Implement the Click hander for the btnDownload as so:

```
private void btnDownload_Click(object sender, EventArgs e)
{
  WebClient wc = new WebClient();
  wc.DownloadStringCompleted += (s, eArgs) =>
  {
    theEBook = eArgs.Result;
    txtBook.Text = theEBook;
  };

  // The Project Gutenberg EBook of A Tale of Two Cities, by Charles Dickens
  wc.DownloadStringAsync(new Uri("http://www.gutenberg.org/files/98/98-8.txt"));
}
```

The WebClient class is a member of System.Net. This class provides a number of methods for sending data to and receiving data from a resource identified by a URI. As it turns out, many of these methods have an asynchronous version, such as DownloadStringAsync(). This method will spin up a new thread from the CLR thread pool automatically. When the WebClient is done obtaining the data, it will fire the DownloadStringCompleted event, which you are handling here using a C# lambda expression. If you were to call the synchronous version of this method (DownloadString()) the form would appear unresponsive for quite some time.

The Click event hander for the btnGetStats Button control is implemented to extract out the individual words contained in theEBook variable, and then pass the string array to a few helper functions for processing as follows:

```
private void btnGetStats_Click(object sender, EventArgs e)
{
  // Get the words from the e-book.
  string[] words = theEBook.Split(new char[]
    { ' ', '\u000A', ',', '.', ';', ':', '-', '?', '/' },
    StringSplitOptions.RemoveEmptyEntries);

  // Now, find the ten most common words.
  string[] tenMostCommon = FindTenMostCommon(words);

  // Get the longest word.
  string longestWord = FindLongestWord(words);

  // Now that all tasks are complete, build a string to show all
  // stats in a message box.
  StringBuilder bookStats = new StringBuilder("Ten Most Common Words are:\n");
  foreach (string s in tenMostCommon)
  {
    bookStats.AppendLine(s);
  }

  bookStats.AppendFormat("Longest word is: {0}", longestWord);
  bookStats.AppendLine();
  MessageBox.Show(bookStats.ToString(), "Book info");
}
```

The FindTenMostCommon() method uses a LINQ query to obtain a list of string objects that occur most often in the string array, while FindLongestWord() locates, well, the longest word.

```csharp
private string[] FindTenMostCommon(string[] words)
{
    var frequencyOrder = from word in words
                         where word.Length > 6
                         group word by word into g
                         orderby g.Count() descending
                         select g.Key;

    string[] commonWords = (frequencyOrder.Take(10)).ToArray();
    return commonWords;
}

private string FindLongestWord(string[] words)
{
    return (from w in words orderby w.Length descending select w).FirstOrDefault();
}
```

If you were to run this project, the amount of time to perform all tasks could take a goodly amount of time, based on the CPU count of your machine and overall processor speed. Eventually, you should see the output shown in Figure 19-4.

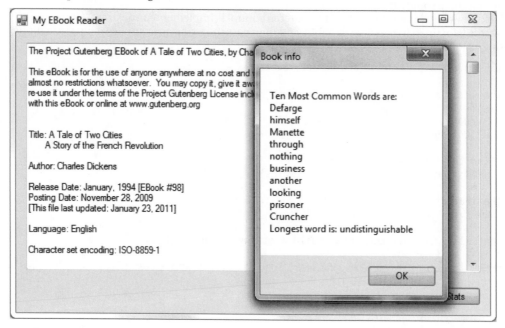

Figure 19-4. Stats about the downloaded e-book

You can help ensure that your application makes use of all available CPUs on the host machine by invoking the FindTenMostCommon() and FindLongestWord() methods in parallel. To do so, modify your btnGetStats_Click() method as so:

```
private void btnGetStats_Click(object sender, EventArgs e)
{
  // Get the words from the e-book.
  string[] words = theEBook.Split(
    new char[] { ' ', '\u000A', ',', '.', ';', ':', '-', '?', '/' },
    StringSplitOptions.RemoveEmptyEntries);
  string[] tenMostCommon = null;
  string longestWord = string.Empty;

  Parallel.Invoke(
    () =>
    {
      // Now, find the ten most common words.
      tenMostCommon = FindTenMostCommon(words);
    },
    () =>
    {
      // Get the longest word.
      longestWord = FindLongestWord(words);
    });

  // Now that all tasks are complete, build a string to show all
  // stats in a message box.
  ...
}
```

The `Parallel.Invoke()` method expects a parameter array of `Action<>` delegates, which you have supplied indirectly using lambda expressions. Again, while the output is identical, the benefit is that the TPL will now make use of all possible processors on the machine to invoke each method in parallel if possible.

■ **Source Code** The MyEBookReader project is included under the Chapter 19 subdirectory.

Parallel LINQ Queries (PLINQ)

To wrap up your look at the TPL, be aware that there is another way you can incorporate parallel tasks into your .NET applications. If you choose, you can make use of a set of extension methods, which allow you to construct a LINQ query that will perform its workload in parallel (if possible). Fittingly, LINQ queries that are designed to run in parallel are termed *PLINQ queries*.

Like parallel code authored using the `Parallel` class, PLINQ has the option of ignoring your request to process the collection in parallel if need be. The PLINQ framework has been optimized in numerous ways, which includes determining whether a query would, in fact, perform faster in a synchronous manner.

At runtime, PLINQ analyzes the overall structure of the query, and if the query is likely to benefit from parallelization, it will run concurrently. However, if parallelizing a query would hurt performance, PLINQ just runs the query sequentially. If PLINQ has a choice between a potentially expensive parallel algorithm or an inexpensive sequential algorithm, it chooses the sequential algorithm by default.

The necessary extension methods are found within the ParallelEnumerable class of the System.Linq namespace. Table 19-5 documents some useful PLINQ extensions.

Table 19-5. *Select Members of the ParallelEnumerable class*

Member	Meaning in Life
AsParallel()	Specifies that the rest of the query should be parallelized, if possible.
WithCancellation()	Specifies that PLINQ should periodically monitor the state of the provided cancellation token and cancel execution if it is requested.
WithDegreeOfParallelism()	Specifies the maximum number of processors that PLINQ should use to parallelize the query.
ForAll()	Enables results to be processed in parallel without first merging back to the consumer thread, as would be the case when enumerating a LINQ result using the foreach keyword.

To see PLINQ in action, create a final Windows Forms application named PLINQDataProcessingWithCancellation and import the System.Threading namespace. This simple form will only need two Button controls named btnExecute and btnCancel. Then the "Execute" button is clicked, and you will fire off a new Task, which executes a LINQ query that investigates a very large array of integers, looking for only the items where x % 3 == 0 is true. Here is a *nonparallel* version of the query:

```
public partial class MainForm : Form
{
...
  private void btnExecute_Click(object sender, EventArgs e)
  {
    // Start a new "task" to process the ints.
    Task.Factory.StartNew(() =>
    {
      ProcessIntData();
    });
  }

  private void ProcessIntData()
  {
    // Get a very large array of integers.
    int[] source = Enumerable.Range(1, 10000000).ToArray();

    // Find the numbers where num % 3 == 0 is true, returned
    // in descending order.
    int[] modThreeIsZero = (from num in source where num % 3 == 0
            orderby num descending select num).ToArray();

    MessageBox.Show(string.Format("Found {0} numbers that match query!",
      modThreeIsZero.Count()));
```

```
  }
}
```

Opting in to a PLINQ Query

If you want to inform the TPL to execute this query in parallel (if possible), you will want to make use of the AsParallel() extension method as so:

```
int[] modThreeIsZero = (from num in source.AsParallel() where num % 3 == 0
                        orderby num descending select num).ToArray();
```

Notice how the overall format of the LINQ query is identical to what you have seen in previous chapters. However, by including a call to AsParallel(), the TPL will attempt to pass the workload off to an available CPU.

Cancelling a PLINQ Query

It is also possible to use a CancellationTokenSource object to inform a PLINQ query to stop processing under the correct conditions (typically due to user intervention). Declare a form-level CancellationTokenSource object named cancelToken and implement the Click handler of the btnCancel to call the Cancel() method on this object. Here is the relevant code update:

```
public partial class MainForm : Form
{
  private CancellationTokenSource cancelToken = new CancellationTokenSource();

  private void btnCancel_Click(object sender, EventArgs e)
  {
    cancelToken.Cancel();
  }
...
}
```

Now, inform the PLINQ query that it should be on the lookout for an incoming cancellation request by chaining on the WithCancellation() extension method, and passing in the token. In addition, you will want to wrap this PLINQ query in a proper try/catch scope, and deal with the possible exception. Here is the final version of the ProcessIntData() method.

```
private void ProcessIntData()
{
  // Get a very large array of integers.
  int[] source = Enumerable.Range(1, 10000000).ToArray();

  // Find the numbers where num % 3 == 0 is true, returned
  // in descending order.
  int[] modThreeIsZero = null;
  try
  {
    modThreeIsZero = (from num in
      source.AsParallel().WithCancellation(cancelToken.Token)
      where num % 3 == 0 orderby num descending
      select num).ToArray();
    MessageBox.Show(string.Format("Found {0} numbers that match query!",
```

```
      modThreeIsZero.Count()));

  }
  catch (OperationCanceledException ex)
  {
    this.Invoke((Action)delegate
    {
      this.Text = ex.Message;
    });
  }
}
```

■ **Source Code** The PLINQDataProcessingWithCancellation project is included under the Chapter 19 subdirectory.

Asynchronous Calls Under .NET 4.5

We have covered a lot of terse material in this (rather lengthy) chapter. To be sure, building, debugging, and understanding complex multithreaded applications is a challenge in any framework. While the TPL, PLINQ, and the delegate type can simplify matters to some extent (especially when compared to other platforms and languages), developers are still required to be fairly savvy with the ins and outs of various advanced techniques.

With the release of .NET 4.5, the C# programming language (and for that matter, the VB programming language) has been updated with two new keywords that further simplify the process of authoring asynchronous code. In contrast to all of the examples seen in this chapter, when you make use of the new async and await keywords, the compiler will generate a good deal of threading code on your behalf, using numerous members of the System.Threading and System.Threading.Tasks namespaces.

A First Look at the C# async and await Keywords

The async keyword of C# is used to qualify that a method, lambda expression, or anonymous method should be called in an asynchronous manner *automatically*. Yes, it's true. Simply by marking a method with the async modifier, the CLR will create a new thread of execution to handle the task at hand. Furthermore, when you are calling an async method, the await keyword will *automatically* pause the current thread from any further activity until the task is complete, leaving the calling thread free to continue on its merry way.

To illustrate, create a brand new Windows Forms application named FunWithCSharpAsync and import the System.Threading namespace into the initial form's primary code file (I renamed my initial form to be MainForm). After you have done so, place a single Button control (named btnCallMethod) and a single TextBox control (named txtInput) on the designer surface, and configure any basic UI properties (colors, fonts, text) you want. Now, handle the Click event of the Button control, and within the event handler, call a private helper method named DoWork(), which forces the calling thread to wait for 10 seconds. Here is the story thus far:

```
public partial class MainForm : Form
{
  public MainForm()
  {
```

```
    InitializeComponent();
  }

  private void btnCallMethod_Click(object sender, EventArgs e)
  {
    this.Text = DoWork();
  }

  private string DoWork()
  {
    Thread.Sleep(10000);
    return "Done with work!";
  }
}
```

Now, given your work in this chapter, you know that if you were to run the program and click this button, you would need to wait 10 seconds before the text box control could receive keyword input. Furthermore, you will not see the title of the main window update with the message "Done with work!" for 10 seconds as well.

If we were to use any of the previous techniques seen in this chapter to make our program more responsive, we would have a good deal of work ahead of us. However, under .NET 4.5, we can author the following C# code base:

```
public partial class MainForm : Form
{
  public MainForm()
  {
    InitializeComponent();
  }

  private async void btnCallMethod_Click(object sender, EventArgs e)
  {
    this.Text = await DoWork();
  }

  // See below for code walkthrough...
  private Task<string> DoWork()
  {
    return Task.Run(() =>
    {
      Thread.Sleep(10000);
      return "Done with work!";
    });
  }
}
```

First, notice that our button's Click event hander has been marked with the async keyword. This marks the method as a member to be called in a nonblocking manner. Also notice that the implementation of the event handler uses the await keyword *before* naming the method that will be called. This is important: if you decorate a method with the async keyword, but do not have at least one internal await-centric method call, you have essentially built a blocking, synchronous method call (in fact, you will be given a compiler warning to this effect).

Now, notice that we are required to make use of the Task class from the System.Threading.Tasks namespace in order to refactor our DoWork() method to work as expected. Basically, rather than returning a specific return value straightaway (a string object in the current example), we return a Task<T> object, where the generic type parameter T is the underlying, actual return value (with me so far?).

The implementation of DoWork() now directly returns a Task<T> object, which is the return value of Task.Run(). The Run() method takes a Func<> or Action<> delegate, and as you know by this point in the text, we can simplify our life by using a lambda expression. Basically, our new version of DoWork() is essentially saying the following:

When you call me, I will run a new task. This task will cause the calling thread to sleep for 10 seconds, and when it is done, it gives me a string return value. I'll put this string in a new Task<string> object and return it to the caller.

Having translated this new implementation of DoWork() into more natural (poetic) language, we gain some insight into the real role of the await token. This keyword will always modify a method that returns a Task object. When the flow of logic reaches the await token, the calling thread is suspended until the call completes. If you were to run this version of the application, you would find that you could click the button and happily type within the text area immediately. Ten seconds later, your window's title would update with the completed message notification.

Naming Conventions for Async Methods

Now, let's say that the new version of DoWork() is exactly as currently shown; however, the button's Click event hander has been implemented as so:

```
private async void btnCallMethod_Click(object sender, EventArgs e)
{
  // Oops! No await keyword here!
  this.Text = DoWork();
}
```

Notice we did indeed mark the method with the async keyword, but we neglected to use the await keyword as a decorator before the DoWork() method call. At this point, we will have compiler errors, as the return value of DoWork() is a Task object, which we are attempting to assign directly to the Text property (which takes a string data type). Remember, the await token is in charge of extracting out the internal return value contained in the Task object. Since we have not used this token, we have a type mismatch. As you can see in Figure 19-5, the compiler informs us that the method we are attempting to call is "awaitable," and suggests the correct form of invoking the method.

■ **Note** An "awaitable" method is simply a method that returns a Task<T>.

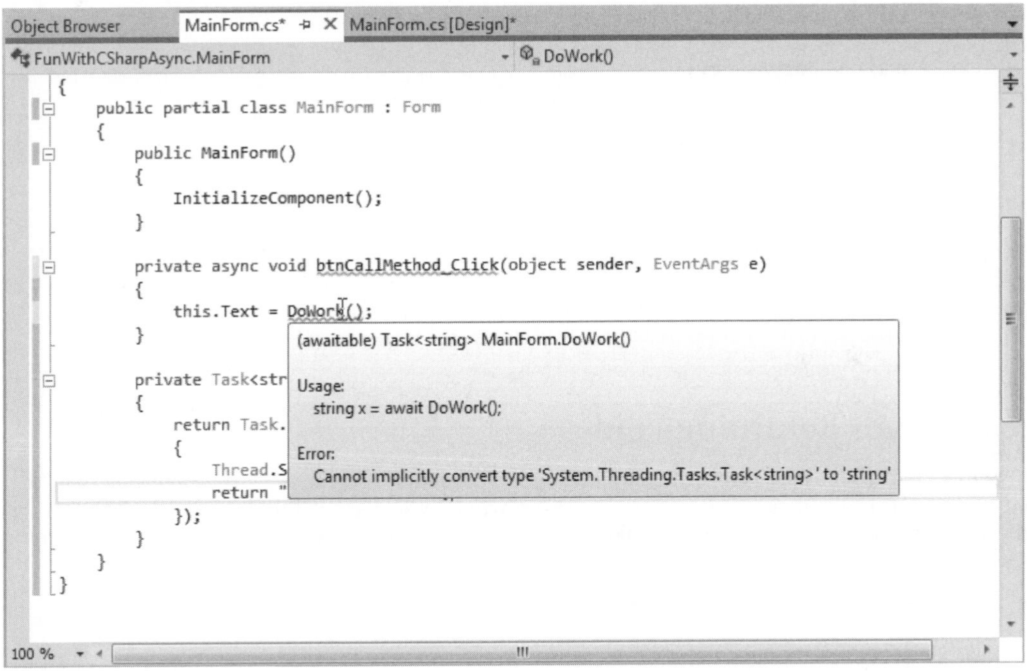

Figure 19-5. Methods that return a Task object are able to be called via await

Given the fact that methods that return Task objects can now be called in a nonblocking manner via the async and await tokens, Microsoft recommends (as a best practice) that any method returning a Task be marked with an "Async" suffix. In this way, developers who know the naming convention receive a visual reminder that the await keyword is required, if they intend to invoke the method within an asynchronous context.

___

■ **Note** Event handlers for GUI controls (such as our button Click handler) that use the async / await keywords do not follow this naming convention (by convention—pardon the redundancy!).

___

Furthermore, the DoWork() method could also be decorated with the async and await tokens (although this is not strictly required for the current example). Given these points, here is the final update to the current example, which conforms to the recommending naming conventions:

```
public partial class MainForm : Form
{
  public MainForm()
  {
    InitializeComponent();
  }
```

```
private async void btnCallMethod_Click(object sender, EventArgs e)
{
  this.Text = await DoWorkAsync();
}

private async Task<string> DoWorkAsync()
{
  return await Task.Run(() =>
  {
    Thread.Sleep(10000);
    return "Done with work!";
  });
}
}
```

Async Methods Returning Void

Currently, our DoWork() method is returning a Task, which contains "real data" for the caller that will be obtained transparently via the await keyword. However, what if you want to build an asynchronous method that returns void? In this case, we make use of the nongeneric Task class and omit any return statement, like so:

```
private async Task MethodReturningVoidAsync()
{
  await Task.Run(() => { /* Do some work here... */
                         Thread.Sleep(4000);
                       });
}
```

The caller of this method, such as a second button Click event handler, would then use the await and async keywords as so:

```
private async void btnVoidMethodCall_Click(object sender, EventArgs e)
{
  await MethodReturningVoidAsync();
  MessageBox.Show("Done!");
}
```

Async Methods with Multiple Awaits

It is completely permissible for a single async method to have multiple await contexts within its implementation. Assume our application now has a third button Click event handler that has been marked with the async keyword. In the previous parts of this example, the Click handlers purposely called some external method that runs the underlying Task; however, you could inline this logic via a set of lambda expressions as so:

```
private async void btnMutliAwaits_Click(object sender, EventArgs e)
{
  await Task.Run(() => { Thread.Sleep(2000); });
  MessageBox.Show("Done with first task!");
```

```
  await Task.Run(() => { Thread.Sleep(2000); });
  MessageBox.Show("Done with second task!");

  await Task.Run(() => { Thread.Sleep(2000); });
  MessageBox.Show("Done with third task!");
}
```

Again, here each task is not doing much more than suspending the current thread for a spell; however, any unit of work could be represented by these tasks (calling a web service, reading a database, or what have you). In any case, let's summarize the key points of this example, as follows:

- Methods (as well as lambda expressions or anonymous methods) can be marked with the async keyword to enable the method to do work in a nonblocking manner.

- Methods (as well as lambda expressions or anonymous methods) marked with the async keyword will run in a *blocking* manner until the await keyword is encountered.

- A single async method can have multiple await contexts.

- When the await expression is encountered, the calling thread is suspended until the awaited task is complete. In the meantime, control is returned to the caller of the method.

- The await keyword will hide the returned Task object from view, appearing to directly return the underlying return value. Methods with no return value simply return void.

- As a naming convention, methods that are to be called asynchronously should be marked with the "Async" suffix.

■ **Source Code** The FunWithCSharpAsync project is included under the Chapter 19 subdirectory.

Retrofitting the AddWithThreads Example Using Asycn/Await

Much earlier in this chapter, we built an example named AddWithThreads using the original threading API of the .NET platform, System.Threading. Now, let's retrofit this example to use the new C# async and await keywords, to showcase just how much cleaner our application logic can become. First, let me remind you of the basics of how the AddWithThreads project worked initially.

- We created a custom class named AddParams, which represented the data to be summed.

- We made use of the Thread class and ParameterizedThreadStart delegate to point to an Add() method receiving an AddParams object.

- We used the AutoResetEvent class to ensure the calling thread waited for the secondary thread to complete.

All in all, it was a good deal of effort to simply compute the addition of two numbers on a secondary thread of execution! Here is the same project, now refactored using the new .NET 4.5 techniques under examination (I did not reprint the AddParams class here, but recall it simply had two fields, a and b, to represent the data to sum):

```
class Program
{
  static void Main(string[] args)
  {
    AddAsync();
    Console.ReadLine();
  }

  private static async Task AddAsync()
  {
    Console.WriteLine("***** Adding with Thread objects *****");
    Console.WriteLine("ID of thread in Main(): {0}",
      Thread.CurrentThread.ManagedThreadId);

    AddParams ap = new AddParams(10, 10);
    await Sum(ap);

    Console.WriteLine("Other thread is done!");
  }

  static async Task Sum(object data)
  {
    await Task.Run(() =>
    {
      if (data is AddParams)
      {
        Console.WriteLine("ID of thread in Add(): {0}",
          Thread.CurrentThread.ManagedThreadId);

        AddParams ap = (AddParams)data;
        Console.WriteLine("{0} + {1} is {2}",
          ap.a, ap.b, ap.a + ap.b);
      }
    });
  }
}
```

The first thing I'd like to point out is that the code that was initially in Main() has been moved into a new method named AddAsync(). The reason was not only to conform to the expected naming convention, but this brings up a very important point:

■ **Note** The Main() method of an executable can not be marked with the async keyword.

Note that AddAsync() is marked with the async token, and has defined an await context. As well, the Sum() method is spinning off a new Task to perform the unit of work. In any case, lo and behold, when we run the program, we find that 10 plus 10 is still indeed 20. Note, however, that we do have two unique thread IDs (see Figure 19-6).

Figure 19-6. *Our retrofitted* System.Threading *example, now using .NET 4.5 async features*

■ **Source Code** The AddWithThreadsAsync project is included under the Chapter 19 subdirectory.

So, as you can see, the async and await keywords introduced with .NET 4.5 radically simplify the process of invoking methods on a secondary thread of execution. While we have only worked through a few examples of what can be done with this new functionality of the C# language, you are in a very good position for further exploration.

Summary

This chapter began by examining how .NET delegate types can be configured to execute a method in an asynchronous manner. As you have seen, the BeginInvoke() and EndInvoke() methods allow you to indirectly manipulate a secondary thread with minimum fuss and bother. During this discussion, you were also introduced to the IAsyncResult interface and AsyncResult class type. As you learned, these types provide various ways to synchronize the calling thread and obtain possible method return values.

The next part of this chapter examined the role of the System.Threading namespace. As you learned, when an application creates additional threads of execution, the result is that the program in question is able to carry out numerous tasks at (what appears to be) the same time. You also examined several manners in which you can protect thread-sensitive blocks of code to ensure that shared resources do not become unusable units of bogus data.

This chapter then examined some new models for working with multithreaded development introduced with .NET 4.0, specifically the Task Parallel Library and PLINQ. We wrapped things up by examining the role of the new .NET 4.5 C# async and await keywords. As you have seen, these keywords are using many types of the TPL framework in the background; however, the compiler does a majority of the work to create the complex threading and synchronization code on our behalf.

CHAPTER 20

File I/O and Object Serialization

When you create desktop applications, the ability to save information between user sessions is imperative. This chapter examines a number of I/O-related topics as seen through the eyes of the .NET Framework. The first order of business is to explore the core types defined in the System.IO namespace and learn how to modify a machine's directory and file structure programmatically. The next task is to explore various ways to read from and write to character-based, binary-based, string-based, and memory-based data stores.

After you learn how to manipulate files and directories using the core I/O types, you will examine the related topic of *object serialization*. You can use object serialization to persist and retrieve the state of an object to (or from) any System.IO.Stream-derived type. The ability to serialize objects is critical when you want to copy an object to a remote machine using various remoting technologies such as Windows Communication Foundation. However, serialization is quite useful in its own right and will likely play a role in many of your .NET applications (distributed or not).

Exploring the System.IO Namespace

In the framework of .NET, the System.IO namespace is the region of the base class libraries devoted to file-based (and memory-based) input and output (I/O) services. Like any namespace, System.IO defines a set of classes, interfaces, enumerations, structures, and delegates, most of which you can find in mscorlib.dll. In addition to the types contained within mscorlib.dll, the System.dll assembly defines additional members of the System.IO namespace. Note that all Visual Studio projects automatically set a reference to both assemblies.

Many of the types within the System.IO namespace focus on the programmatic manipulation of physical directories and files. However, additional types provide support to read data from and write data to string buffers, as well as raw memory locations. Table 20-1 outlines the core (nonabstract) classes, providing a road map of the functionality in System.IO.

Table 20-1. Key Members of the System.IO Namespace

Nonabstract I/O Class Type	Meaning in Life
BinaryReader BinaryWriter	These classes allow you to store and retrieve primitive data types (integers, Booleans, strings, and whatnot) as a binary value.
BufferedStream	This class provides temporary storage for a stream of bytes that you can commit to storage at a later time.

Directory DirectoryInfo	You use these classes to manipulate a machine's directory structure. The Directory type exposes functionality using *static members*, while the DirectoryInfo type exposes similar functionality from a valid *object reference*.
DriveInfo	This class provides detailed information regarding the drives that a given machine uses.
File FileInfo	You use these classes to manipulate a machine's set of files. The File type exposes functionality using *static members*, while the FileInfo type exposes similar functionality from a valid *object reference*.
FileStream	This class gives you random file access (e.g., seeking capabilities) with data represented as a stream of bytes.
FileSystemWatcher	This class allows you to monitor the modification of external files in a specified directory.
MemoryStream	This class provides random access to streamed data stored in memory rather than in a physical file.
Path	This class performs operations on System.String types that contain file or directory path information in a platform-neutral manner.
StreamWriter StreamReader	You use these classes to store (and retrieve) textual information to (or from) a file. These types do not support random file access.
StringWriter StringReader	Like the StreamReader/StreamWriter classes, these classes also work with textual information. However, the underlying storage is a string buffer rather than a physical file.

In addition to these concrete class types, System.IO defines a number of enumerations, as well as a set of abstract classes (e.g., Stream, TextReader, and TextWriter), that define a shared polymorphic interface to all descendants. You will read about many of these types in this chapter.

The Directory(Info) and File(Info) Types

System.IO provides four classes that allow you to manipulate individual files, as well as interact with a machine's directory structure. The first two types, Directory and File, expose creation, deletion, copying, and moving operations using various static members. The closely related FileInfo and DirectoryInfo types expose similar functionality as instance-level methods (therefore, you must allocate them with the new keyword). In Figure 20-1, the Directory and File classes directly extend System.Object, while DirectoryInfo and FileInfo derive from the abstract FileSystemInfo type.

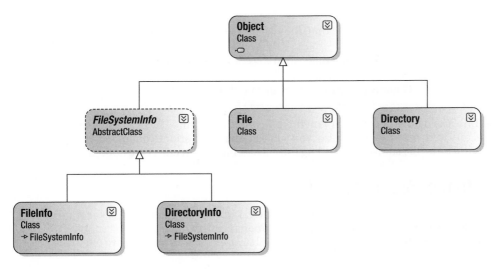

Figure 20-1. *The File- and Directory-centric types*

FileInfo and DirectoryInfo typically serve as better choices for obtaining full details of a file or directory (e.g., time created, or read/write capabilities) because their members tend to return strongly typed objects. In contrast, the Directory and File class members tend to return simple string values rather than strongly typed objects. This is only a guidline however; in many cases, you can get the same work done using File/FileInfo or Directory/DirectoryInfo.

The Abstract FileSystemInfo Base Class

The DirectoryInfo and FileInfo types receive many behaviors from the abstract FileSystemInfo base class. For the most part, you use the members of the FileSystemInfo class to discover general characteristics (such as time of creation, various attributes, and so forth) about a given file or directory. Table 20-2 lists some core properties of interest.

Table 20-2. *FileSystemInfo Properties*

Property	Meaning in Life
Attributes	Gets or sets the attributes associated with the current file that are represented by the FileAttributes enumeration (e.g., is the file or directory read-only, encrypted, hidden, or compressed?).
CreationTime	Gets or sets the time of creation for the current file or directory.
Exists	You can use this to determine whether a given file or directory exists.
Extension	Retrieves a file's extension.
FullName	Gets the full path of the directory or file.

LastAccessTime	Gets or sets the time the current file or directory was last accessed.
LastWriteTime	Gets or sets the time when the current file or directory was last written to.
Name	Obtains the name of the current file or directory.

FileSystemInfo also defines the Delete() method. This is implemented by derived types to delete a given file or directory from the hard drive. Also, you can call Refresh() prior to obtaining attribute information to ensure that the statistics regarding the current file (or directory) are not outdated.

Working with the DirectoryInfo Type

The first creatable I/O-centric type you will examine is the DirectoryInfo class. This class contains a set of members used for creating, moving, deleting, and enumerating over directories and subdirectories. In addition to the functionality provided by its base class (FileSystemInfo), DirectoryInfo offers the key members detailed in Table 20-3.

Table 20-3. Key Members of the DirectoryInfo Type

Member	Meaning in Life
Create() CreateSubdirectory()	Create a directory (or set of subdirectories) when given a path name.
Delete()	Deletes a directory and all its contents.
GetDirectories()	Returns an array of DirectoryInfo objects that represent all subdirectories in the current directory.
GetFiles()	Retrieves an array of FileInfo objects that represent a set of files in the given directory.
MoveTo()	Moves a directory and its contents to a new path.
Parent	Retrieves the parent directory of this directory.
Root	Gets the root portion of a path.

You begin working with the DirectoryInfo type by specifying a particular directory path as a constructor parameter. Use the dot (.) notation if you want to obtain access to the current working directory (the directory of the executing application). Here are some examples:

```
// Bind to the current working directory.
DirectoryInfo dir1 = new DirectoryInfo(".");
```

```
// Bind to C:\Windows,
// using a verbatim string.
DirectoryInfo dir2 = new DirectoryInfo(@"C:\Windows");
```

In the second example, you make the assumption that the path passed into the constructor (C:\Windows) already exists on the physical machine. However, if you attempt to interact with a nonexistent directory, a System.IO.DirectoryNotFoundException is thrown. Thus, if you specify a directory that is not yet created, you need to call the Create() method before proceeding, like so:

```
// Bind to a nonexistent directory, then create it.
DirectoryInfo dir3 = new DirectoryInfo(@"C:\MyCode\Testing");
dir3.Create();
```

After you create a DirectoryInfo object, you can investigate the underlying directory contents using any of the properties inherited from FileSystemInfo. To see this in action, create a new Console Application named DirectoryApp and update your C# file to import System.IO.

Update your Program class with the following new static method that creates a new DirectoryInfo object mapped to C:\Windows (adjust your path if need be), which displays a number of interesting statistics:

```
class Program
{
  static void Main(string[] args)
  {
    Console.WriteLine("***** Fun with Directory(Info) *****\n");
    ShowWindowsDirectoryInfo();
    Console.ReadLine();
  }

  static void ShowWindowsDirectoryInfo()
  {
    // Dump directory information.
    DirectoryInfo dir = new DirectoryInfo(@"C:\Windows");
    Console.WriteLine("***** Directory Info *****");
    Console.WriteLine("FullName: {0}", dir.FullName);
    Console.WriteLine("Name: {0}", dir.Name);
    Console.WriteLine("Parent: {0}", dir.Parent);
    Console.WriteLine("Creation: {0}", dir.CreationTime);
    Console.WriteLine("Attributes: {0}", dir.Attributes);
    Console.WriteLine("Root: {0}", dir.Root);
    Console.WriteLine("*************************\n");
  }
}
```

While your output might differ, you should see something similar to the following:

```
***** Fun with Directory(Info) *****

***** Directory Info *****
FullName: C:\Windows
Name: Windows
Parent:
Creation: 7/13/2012 10:22:32 PM
```

```
Attributes: Directory
Root: C:\
**************************
```

Enumerating Files with the DirectoryInfo Type

In addition to obtaining basic details of an existing directory, you can extend the current example to use some methods of the DirectoryInfo type. First, you can leverage the GetFiles() method to obtain information about all *.jpg files located under the C:\Windows\Web\Wallpaper directory.

■ **Note** If your machine does not have a C:\Windows\Web\Wallpaper directory, retrofit this code to read files of a directory on your machine (e.g., to read all *.bmp files from the C:\Windows directory).

The GetFiles() method returns an array of FileInfo objects, each of which exposes details of a particular file (you will learn the full details of the FileInfo type later in this chapter). Assume that you have the following static method of the Program class, which you call from Main():

```csharp
static void DisplayImageFiles()
{
  DirectoryInfo dir = new DirectoryInfo(@"C:\Windows\Web\Wallpaper");
  // Get all files with a *.jpg extension.
  FileInfo[] imageFiles = dir.GetFiles("*.jpg", SearchOption.AllDirectories);

  // How many were found?
  Console.WriteLine("Found {0} *.jpg files\n", imageFiles.Length);

  // Now print out info for each file.
  foreach (FileInfo f in imageFiles)
  {
    Console.WriteLine("**************************");
    Console.WriteLine("File name: {0}", f.Name);
    Console.WriteLine("File size: {0}", f.Length);
    Console.WriteLine("Creation: {0}", f.CreationTime);
    Console.WriteLine("Attributes: {0}", f.Attributes);
    Console.WriteLine("**************************\n");
  }
}
```

Notice that you specify a search option when you call GetFiles(); you do this to look within all subdirectories of the root. After you run the application, you will see a listing of all files that match the search pattern.

Creating Subdirectories with the DirectoryInfo Type

You can programmatically extend a directory structure using the DirectoryInfo.CreateSubdirectory() method. This method can create a single subdirectory, as well as multiple nested subdirectories, in a single function call. This method illustrates how to do so, extending the directory structure of the C: drive with some custom subdirectories:

```
static void ModifyAppDirectory()
{
  DirectoryInfo dir = new DirectoryInfo(@"C:\");

  // Create \MyFolder off application directory.
  dir.CreateSubdirectory("MyFolder");

  // Create \MyFolder2\Data off application directory.
  dir.CreateSubdirectory(@"MyFolder2\Data");
}
```

If you call this method from within Main() and examine your Windows directory using Windows Explorer, you will see that the new subdirectories are present and accounted for (see Figure 20-2).

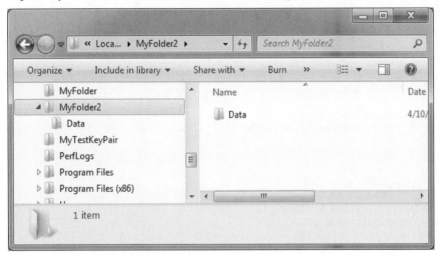

Figure 20-2. Creating subdirectories

You are not required to capture the return value of the CreateSubdirectory() method, but you should be aware that a DirectoryInfo object representing the newly created item is passed back on successful execution. Consider the following update to the previous method. Note the dot notation in the constructor of DirectoryInfo, which gives you access to the application's installation point.

```
static void ModifyAppDirectory()
{
  DirectoryInfo dir = new DirectoryInfo(".");

  // Create \MyFolder off initial directory.
  dir.CreateSubdirectory("MyFolder");

  // Capture returned DirectoryInfo object.
  DirectoryInfo myDataFolder = dir.CreateSubdirectory(@"MyFolder2\Data");
```

```
  // Prints path to ..\MyFolder2\Data.
  Console.WriteLine("New Folder is: {0}", myDataFolder);
}
```

Working with the Directory Type

You have seen the DirectoryInfo type in action; now you're ready to learn about the Directory type. For the most part, the static members of Directory mimic the functionality provided by the instance-level members defined by DirectoryInfo. Recall, however, that the members of Directory typically return string data rather than strongly typed FileInfo/DirectoryInfo objects.

Now let's look at some functionality of the Directory type; this final helper function displays the names of all drives mapped to the current computer (using the Directory.GetLogicalDrives() method) and uses the static Directory.Delete() method to remove the \MyFolder and \MyFolder2\Data subdirectories created previously.

```
static void FunWithDirectoryType()
{
  // List all drives on current computer.
  string[] drives = Directory.GetLogicalDrives();
  Console.WriteLine("Here are your drives:");
  foreach (string s in drives)
    Console.WriteLine("--> {0} ", s);

  // Delete what was created.
  Console.WriteLine("Press Enter to delete directories");
  Console.ReadLine();
  try
  {
    Directory.Delete(@"C:\MyFolder");

    // The second parameter specifies whether you
    // wish to destroy any subdirectories.
    Directory.Delete(@"C:\MyFolder2", true);
  }
  catch (IOException e)
  {
    Console.WriteLine(e.Message);
  }
}
```

■ **Source Code** You can find the DirectoryApp project under the Chapter 20 subdirectory.

Working with the DriveInfo Class Type

The System.IO namespace provides a class named DriveInfo. Like Directory.GetLogicalDrives(), the static DriveInfo.GetDrives() method allows you to discover the names of a machine's drives. Unlike Directory.GetLogicalDrives(), however, DriveInfo provides numerous other details (e.g., the drive type, available free space, and volume label). Consider the following Program class defined within a new Console Application named DriveInfoApp (don't forget to import System.IO):

```
class Program
{
  static void Main(string[] args)
  {
    Console.WriteLine("***** Fun with DriveInfo *****\n");

    // Get info regarding all drives.
    DriveInfo[] myDrives = DriveInfo.GetDrives();
    // Now print drive stats.
    foreach(DriveInfo d in myDrives)
    {
      Console.WriteLine("Name: {0}", d.Name);
      Console.WriteLine("Type: {0}", d.DriveType);

      // Check to see whether the drive is mounted.
      if(d.IsReady)
      {
        Console.WriteLine("Free space: {0}", d.TotalFreeSpace);
        Console.WriteLine("Format: {0}", d.DriveFormat);
        Console.WriteLine("Label: {0}", d.VolumeLabel);
      }
      Console.WriteLine();
    }
    Console.ReadLine();
  }
}
```

Here is some possible output:

```
***** Fun with DriveInfo *****

Name: C:\
Type: Fixed
Free space: 587376394240
Format: NTFS
Label: Mongo Drive

Name: D:\
Type: CDRom

Name: E:\
Type: CDRom

Name: F:\
Type: CDRom

Name: H:\
Type: Fixed
Free space: 477467508736
```

```
Format: FAT32
Label: My Passport
```

At this point, you have investigated some core behaviors of the Directory, DirectoryInfo, and DriveInfo classes. Next, you'll learn how to create, open, close, and destroy the files that populate a given directory.

■ **Source Code** You can find the DriveInfoApp project under the Chapter 20 subdirectory.

Working with the FileInfo Class

As shown in the previous DirectoryApp example, the FileInfo class allows you to obtain details regarding existing files on your hard drive (e.g., time created, size, and file attributes) and aids in the creation, copying, moving, and destruction of files. In addition to the set of functionality inherited by FileSystemInfo, you can find some core members unique to the FileInfo class, which you can see described in Table 20-4.

Table 20-4. FileInfo *Core Members*

Member	Meaning in Life
AppendText()	Creates a StreamWriter object (described later) that appends text to a file.
CopyTo()	Copies an existing file to a new file.
Create()	Creates a new file and returns a FileStream object (described later) to interact with the newly created file.
CreateText()	Creates a StreamWriter object that writes a new text file.
Delete()	Deletes the file to which a FileInfo instance is bound.
Directory	Gets an instance of the parent directory.
DirectoryName	Gets the full path to the parent directory.
Length	Gets the size of the current file.
MoveTo()	Moves a specified file to a new location, providing the option to specify a new file name.
Name	Gets the name of the file.

Open()	Opens a file with various read/write and sharing privileges.
OpenRead()	Creates a read-only FileStream object.
OpenText()	Creates a StreamReader object (described later) that reads from an existing text file.
OpenWrite()	Creates a write-only FileStream object.

Note that a majority of the methods of the FileInfo class return a specific I/O-centric object (e.g., FileStream and StreamWriter) that allows you to begin reading and writing data to (or reading from) the associated file in a variety of formats. You will check out these types in just a moment; however, before you see a working example, you'll find it helpful to examine various ways to obtain a file handle using the FileInfo class type.

The FileInfo.Create() Method

One way you can create a file handle is to use the FileInfo.Create() method, like so:

```
static void Main(string[] args)
{
  // Make a new file on the C drive.
  FileInfo f = new FileInfo(@"C:\Test.dat");
  FileStream fs = f.Create();

  // Use the FileStream object...

  // Close down file stream.
  fs.Close();
}
```

Notice that the FileInfo.Create() method returns a FileStream object, which exposes synchronous and asynchronous write/read operations to/from the underlying file (more details in a moment). Be aware that the FileStream object returned by FileInfo.Create() grants full read/write access to all users.

Also notice that after you finish with the current FileStream object, you must ensure you close down the handle to release the underlying unmanaged stream resources. Given that FileStream implements IDisposable, you can use the C# using scope to allow the compiler to generate the teardown logic (see Chapter 8 for details), like so:

```
static void Main(string[] args)
{
  // Defining a using scope for file I/O
  // types is ideal.
  FileInfo f = new FileInfo(@"C:\Test.dat");
  using (FileStream fs = f.Create())
  {
    // Use the FileStream object...
  }
}
```

The FileInfo.Open() Method

You can use the FileInfo.Open() method to open existing files, as well as to create new files with far more precision than you can with FileInfo.Create(). This works because Open() typically takes several parameters to qualify exactly how to iterate the file you want to manipulate. Once the call to Open() completes, you are returned a FileStream object. Consider the following logic:

```
static void Main(string[] args)
{
  // Make a new file via FileInfo.Open().
  FileInfo f2 = new FileInfo(@"C:\Test2.dat");
  using(FileStream fs2 = f2.Open(FileMode.OpenOrCreate,
    FileAccess.ReadWrite, FileShare.None))
  {
    // Use the FileStream object...
  }
}
```

This version of the overloaded Open() method requires three parameters. The first parameter of the Open() method specifies the general flavor of the I/O request (e.g., make a new file, open an existing file, and append to a file), which you specify using the FileMode enumeration (see Table 20-5 for details), like so:

```
public enum FileMode
{
  CreateNew,
  Create,
  Open,
  OpenOrCreate,
  Truncate,
  Append
}
```

Table 20-5. *Members of the* FileMode *Enumeration*

Member	Meaning in Life
CreateNew	Informs the OS to make a new file. If it already exists, an IOException is thrown.
Create	Informs the OS to make a new file. If it already exists, it will be overwritten.
Open	Opens an existing file. If the file does not exist, a FileNotFoundException is thrown.
OpenOrCreate	Opens the file if it exists; otherwise, a new file is created.
Truncate	Opens an existing file and truncates the file to 0 bytes in size.
Append	Opens a file, moves to the end of the file, and begins write operations (you can only use this flag with a write-only stream). If the file does not exist, a new file is created.

You use the second parameter of the Open() method, a value from the FileAccess enumeration, to determine the read/write behavior of the underlying stream, as follows:

```
public enum FileAccess
{
  Read,
  Write,
  ReadWrite
}
```

Finally, the third parameter of the Open() method, FileShare, specifies how to share the file among other file handlers. Here are the core names:

```
public enum FileShare
{
  Delete,
  Inheritable,
  None,
  Read,
  ReadWrite,
  Write
}
```

The FileInfo.OpenRead() and FileInfo.OpenWrite() Methods

The FileInfo.Open() method allows you to obtain a file handle in a flexible manner, but the FileInfo class also provides members named OpenRead() and OpenWrite(). As you might imagine, these methods return a properly configured read-only or write-only FileStream object, without the need to supply various enumeration values. Like FileInfo.Create() and FileInfo.Open(), OpenRead() and OpenWrite() return a FileStream object (note that the following code assumes you have files named Test3.dat and Test4.dat on your C drive):

```
static void Main(string[] args)
{
  // Get a FileStream object with read-only permissions.
  FileInfo f3 = new FileInfo(@"C:\Test3.dat");
  using(FileStream readOnlyStream = f3.OpenRead())
  {
    // Use the FileStream object...
  }

  // Now get a FileStream object with write-only permissions.
  FileInfo f4 = new FileInfo(@"C:\Test4.dat");
  using(FileStream writeOnlyStream = f4.OpenWrite())
  {
    // Use the FileStream object...
  }
}
```

The FileInfo.OpenText() Method

Another open-centric member of the FileInfo type is OpenText(). Unlike Create(), Open(), OpenRead(), or OpenWrite(), the OpenText() method returns an instance of the StreamReader type, rather than a FileStream type. Assuming you have a file named boot.ini on your C: drive, the following snippet gives you access to its contents:

```
static void Main(string[] args)
{
  // Get a StreamReader object.
  FileInfo f5 = new FileInfo(@"C:\boot.ini");
  using(StreamReader sreader = f5.OpenText())
  {
    // Use the StreamReader object...
  }
}
```

As you will see shortly, the StreamReader type provides a way to read character data from the underlying file.

The FileInfo.CreateText() and FileInfo.AppendText() Methods

The final two FileInfo methods of interest at this point are CreateText() and AppendText(). Both return a StreamWriter object, as shown here:

```
static void Main(string[] args)
{
  FileInfo f6 = new FileInfo(@"C:\Test6.txt");
  using(StreamWriter swriter = f6.CreateText())
  {
    // Use the StreamWriter object...
  }

  FileInfo f7 = new FileInfo(@"C:\FinalTest.txt");
  using(StreamWriter swriterAppend = f7.AppendText())
  {
    // Use the StreamWriter object...
  }
}
```

As you might guess, the StreamWriter type provides a way to write character data to the underlying file.

Working with the File Type

The File type uses several static members to provide functionality almost identical to that of the FileInfo type. Like FileInfo, File supplies AppendText(), Create(), CreateText(), Open(), OpenRead(), OpenWrite(), and OpenText() methods. In many cases, you can use the File and FileInfo types interchangeably. To see this in action, you can simplify each of the previous FileStream examples by using the File type instead, like so:

```
static void Main(string[] args)
```

```
{
  // Obtain FileStream object via File.Create().
  using(FileStream fs = File.Create(@"C:\Test.dat"))
  {}

  // Obtain FileStream object via File.Open().
  using(FileStream fs2 = File.Open(@"C:\Test2.dat",
    FileMode.OpenOrCreate,
    FileAccess.ReadWrite, FileShare.None))
  {}

  // Get a FileStream object with read-only permissions.
  using(FileStream readOnlyStream = File.OpenRead(@"Test3.dat"))
  {}

  // Get a FileStream object with write-only permissions.
  using(FileStream writeOnlyStream = File.OpenWrite(@"Test4.dat"))
  {}

  // Get a StreamReader object.
  using(StreamReader sreader = File.OpenText(@"C:\boot.ini"))
  {}

  // Get some StreamWriters.
  using(StreamWriter swriter = File.CreateText(@"C:\Test6.txt"))
  {}

  using(StreamWriter swriterAppend = File.AppendText(@"C:\FinalTest.txt"))
  {}
}
```

Additional File-Centric Members

The File type also supports a few members, shown in Table 20-6, which can greatly simplify the processes of reading and writing textual data.

Table 20-6. Methods of the File Type

Method	Meaning in Life
ReadAllBytes()	Opens the specified file, returns the binary data as an array of bytes, and then closes the file.
ReadAllLines()	Opens a specified file, returns the character data as an array of strings, and then closes the file.
ReadAllText()	Opens a specified file, returns the character data as a System.String, and then closes the file.

WriteAllBytes()	Opens the specified file, writes out the byte array, and then closes the file.
WriteAllLines()	Opens a specified file, writes out an array of strings, and then closes the file.
WriteAllText()	Opens a specified file, writes the character data from a specified string, and then closes the file.

You can use these methods of the File type to read and write batches of data in only a few lines of code. Even better, each of these members automatically closes down the underlying file handle. For example, the following console program (named SimpleFileIO) persists the string data into a new file on the C: drive (and reads it into memory) with minimal fuss (this example assumes you have imported System.IO):

```
class Program
{
  static void Main(string[] args)
  {
    Console.WriteLine("***** Simple I/O with the File Type *****\n");
    string[] myTasks = {
      "Fix bathroom sink", "Call Dave",
      "Call Mom and Dad", "Play Xbox 360"};

    // Write out all data to file on C drive.
    File.WriteAllLines(@"C:\tasks.txt", myTasks);

    // Read it all back and print out.
    foreach (string task in File.ReadAllLines(@"C:\tasks.txt"))
    {
      Console.WriteLine("TODO: {0}", task);
    }
    Console.ReadLine();
  }
}
```

The lesson here: when you want to obtain a file handle quickly, the File type will save you some keystrokes. However, one benefit of creating a FileInfo object first is that you can investigate the file using the members of the abstract FileSystemInfo base class.

■ **Source Code** You can find the SimpleFileIO project under the Chapter 20 subdirectory.

The Abstract Stream Class

At this point, you have seen many ways to obtain FileStream, StreamReader, and StreamWriter objects, but you have yet to read data from or write data to a file using these types. To understand how to do this, you'll need to familiarize yourself with the concept of a *stream*. In the world of I/O manipulation, a *stream* represents a chunk of data flowing between a source and a destination. Streams provide a common way to interact with *a sequence of bytes*, regardless of what kind of device (e.g., file, network connection, or printer) stores or displays the bytes in question.

The abstract System.IO.Stream class defines several members that provide support for synchronous and asynchronous interactions with the storage medium (e.g., an underlying file or memory location).

■ **Note** The concept of a stream is not limited to file I/O. To be sure, the .NET libraries provide stream access to networks, memory locations, and other stream-centric abstractions.

Again, Stream descendants represent data as a raw stream of bytes; therefore, working directly with raw streams can be quite cryptic. Some Stream-derived types support *seeking*, which refers to the process of obtaining and adjusting the current position in the stream. Table 20-7 helps you understand the functionality provided by the Stream class by describing its core members.

Table 20-7. Abstract Stream Members

Member	Meaning in Life
CanRead CanWrite CanSeek	Determines whether the current stream supports reading, seeking, and/or writing.
Close()	Closes the current stream and releases any resources (such as sockets and file handles) associated with the current stream. Internally, this method is aliased to the Dispose() method; therefore, *closing a stream* is functionally equivalent to *disposing a stream.*
Flush()	Updates the underlying data source or repository with the current state of the buffer and then clears the buffer. If a stream does not implement a buffer, this method does nothing.
Length	Returns the length of the stream in bytes.
Position	Determines the position in the current stream.
Read() ReadByte()	Reads a sequence of bytes (or a single byte) from the current stream and advances the current position in the stream by the number of bytes read.
Seek()	Sets the position in the current stream.
SetLength()	Sets the length of the current stream.
Write() WriteByte()	Writes a sequence of bytes (or a single byte) to the current stream and advances the current position in this stream by the number of bytes written.

Working with FileStreams

The FileStream class provides an implementation for the abstract Stream members in a manner appropriate for file-based streaming. It is a fairly primitive stream; it can read or write only a single byte or an array of bytes. However, you will not often need to interact directly with the members of the FileStream type. Instead, you will probably use various *stream wrappers*, which make it easier to work with textual data or .NET types. Nevertheless, you will find it helpful to experiment with the synchronous read/write capabilities of the FileStream type.

Assume you have a new Console Application named FileStreamApp (and verify that System.IO and System.Text are imported into your initial C# code file). Your goal is to write a simple text message to a new file named myMessage.dat. However, given that FileStream can operate only on raw bytes, you will be required to encode the System.String type into a corresponding byte array. Fortunately, the System.Text namespace defines a type named Encoding that provides members that encode and decode strings to (or from) an array of bytes (check out the .NET Framework 4.5 SDK documentation for more details about the Encoding type).

Once encoded, the byte array is persisted to file with the FileStream.Write() method. To read the bytes back into memory, you must reset the internal position of the stream (using the Position property) and call the ReadByte() method. Finally, you display the raw byte array and the decoded string to the console. Here is the complete Main() method:

```csharp
// Don't forget to import the System.Text and System.IO namespaces.
static void Main(string[] args)
{
  Console.WriteLine("***** Fun with FileStreams *****\n");

  // Obtain a FileStream object.
  using(FileStream fStream = File.Open(@"C:\myMessage.dat",
    FileMode.Create))
  {
    // Encode a string as an array of bytes.
    string msg = "Hello!";
    byte[] msgAsByteArray = Encoding.Default.GetBytes(msg);

    // Write byte[] to file.
    fStream.Write(msgAsByteArray, 0, msgAsByteArray.Length);

    // Reset internal position of stream.
    fStream.Position = 0;

    // Read the types from file and display to console.
    Console.Write("Your message as an array of bytes: ");
    byte[] bytesFromFile = new byte[msgAsByteArray.Length];
    for (int i = 0; i < msgAsByteArray.Length; i++)
    {
      bytesFromFile[i] = (byte)fStream.ReadByte();
      Console.Write(bytesFromFile[i]);
    }

    // Display decoded messages.
    Console.Write("\nDecoded Message: ");
    Console.WriteLine(Encoding.Default.GetString(bytesFromFile));
```

```
  }
  Console.ReadLine();
}
```

This example populates the file with data, but it also punctuates the major downfall of working directly with the FileStream type: it demands to operate on raw bytes. Other Stream-derived types operate in a similar manner. For example, if you want to write a sequence of bytes to a region of memory, you can allocate a MemoryStream. Likewise, if you want to push an array of bytes through a network connection, you can use the NetworkStream class (in the System.Net.Sockets namespace).

As mentioned previously, the System.IO namespace provides several *reader* and *writer* types that encapsulate the details of working with Stream-derived types.

■ **Source Code** You can find the FileStreamApp project is under the Chapter 20 subdirectory.

Working with StreamWriters and StreamReaders

The StreamWriter and StreamReader classes are useful whenever you need to read or write character-based data (e.g., strings). Both of these types work by default with Unicode characters; however, you can change this by supplying a properly configured System.Text.Encoding object reference. To keep things simple, assume that the default Unicode encoding fits the bill.

StreamReader derives from an abstract type named TextReader, as does the related StringReader type (discussed later in this chapter). The TextReader base class provides a limited set of functionality to each of these descendants; specifically it provides the ability to read and peek into a character stream.

The StreamWriter type (as well as StringWriter, which you will examine later in this chapter) derives from an abstract base class named TextWriter. This class defines members that allow derived types to write textual data to a given character stream.

To aid in your understanding of the core writing capabilities of the StreamWriter and StringWriter classes, Table 20-8 describes the core members of the abstract TextWriter base class.

Table 20-8. Core Members of TextWriter

Member	Meaning in Life
Close()	This method closes the writer and frees any associated resources. In the process, the buffer is automatically flushed (again, this member is functionally equivalent to calling the Dispose() method).
Flush()	This method clears all buffers for the current writer and causes any buffered data to be written to the underlying device; however, it does not close the writer.
NewLine	This property indicates the newline constant for the derived writer class. The default line terminator for the Windows OS is a carriage return, followed by a line feed (\r\n).
Write()	This overloaded method writes data to the text stream without a newline constant.
WriteLine()	This overloaded method writes data to the text stream with a newline constant.

■ **Note** The last two members of the TextWriter class probably look familiar to you. If you recall, the System.Console type has Write() and WriteLine() members that push textual data to the standard output device. In fact, the Console.In property wraps a TextWriter, and the Console.Out property wraps a TextReader.

The derived StreamWriter class provides an appropriate implementation for the Write(), Close(), and Flush() methods, and it defines the additional AutoFlush property. When set to true, this property forces StreamWriter to flush all data every time you perform a write operation. Be aware that you can gain better performance by setting AutoFlush to false, provided you always call Close() when you finish writing with a StreamWriter.

Writing to a Text File

To see the StreamWriter type in action, create a new Console Application named StreamWriterReaderApp and import System.IO. The following Main() method creates a new file named reminders.txt using the File.CreateText() method. Using the obtained StreamWriter object, you can add some textual data to the new file.

```
static void Main(string[] args)
{
  Console.WriteLine("***** Fun with StreamWriter / StreamReader *****\n");

  // Get a StreamWriter and write string data.
  using(StreamWriter writer = File.CreateText("reminders.txt"))
  {
    writer.WriteLine("Don't forget Mother's Day this year...");
    writer.WriteLine("Don't forget Father's Day this year...");
    writer.WriteLine("Don't forget these numbers:");
    for(int i = 0; i < 10; i++)
      writer.Write(i + " ");

    // Insert a new line.
    writer.Write(writer.NewLine);
  }

  Console.WriteLine("Created file and wrote some thoughts...");
  Console.ReadLine();
}
```

After you run this program, you can examine the contents of this new file (see Figure 20-3). You will find this file under the bin\Debug folder of your current application because you did not specify an absolute path at the time you called CreateText().

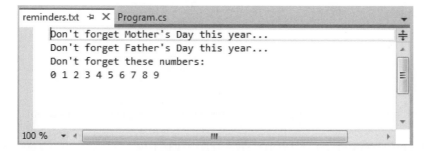

Figure 20-3. The contents of your *.txt *file*

Reading from a Text File

Next, you will learn to read data from a file programmatically by using the corresponding StreamReader type. Recall that this class derives from the abstract TextReader, which offers the functionality described in Table 20-9.

Table 20-9. TextReader Core Members

Member	Meaning in Life
Peek()	Returns the next available character without actually changing the position of the reader. A value of -1 indicates you are at the end of the stream.
Read()	Reads data from an input stream.
ReadBlock()	Reads a specified maximum number of characters from the current stream and writes the data to a buffer, beginning at a specified index.
ReadLine()	Reads a line of characters from the current stream and returns the data as a string (a null string indicates EOF).
ReadToEnd()	Reads all characters from the current position to the end of the stream and returns them as a single string.

If you now extend the current sample application to use a StreamReader, you can read in the textual data from the reminders.txt file, as shown here:

```
static void Main(string[] args)
{
  Console.WriteLine("***** Fun with StreamWriter / StreamReader *****\n");
...
  // Now read data from file.
  Console.WriteLine("Here are your thoughts:\n");
  using(StreamReader sr = File.OpenText("reminders.txt"))
  {
    string input = null;
```

```
      while ((input = sr.ReadLine()) != null)
      {
        Console.WriteLine (input);
      }
    }
    Console.ReadLine();
}
```

After you run the program, you will see the character data in reminders.txt displayed to the console.

Directly Creating StreamWriter/StreamReader Types

One of the confusing aspects of working with the types within System.IO is that you can often achieve an identical result using different approaches. For example, you have already seen that you can use the CreateText() method to obtain a StreamWriter with the File or FileInfo type. It so happens that you can work with StreamWriters and StreamReaders another way: by creating them directly. For example, you could retrofit the current application as follows:

```
static void Main(string[] args)
{
  Console.WriteLine("***** Fun with StreamWriter / StreamReader *****\n");

  // Get a StreamWriter and write string data.
  using(StreamWriter writer = new StreamWriter("reminders.txt"))
  {
    ...
  }

  // Now read data from file.
  using(StreamReader sr = new StreamReader("reminders.txt"))
  {
    ...
  }
}
```

Although it can be a bit confusing to see so many seemingly identical approaches to file I/O, keep in mind that the end result is greater flexibility. In any case, you are now ready to examine the role of the StringWriter and StringReader classes, given that you have seen how to move character data to and from a given file using the StreamWriter and StreamReader types.

■ **Source Code** You can find the StreamWriterReaderApp project under the Chapter 20 subdirectory.

Working with StringWriters and StringReaders

You can use the StringWriter and StringReader types to treat textual information as a stream of in-memory characters. This can prove helpful when you would like to append character-based information to an underlying buffer. The following Console Application (named StringReaderWriterApp) illustrates this by writing a block of string data to a StringWriter object, rather than to a file on the local hard drive:

```
static void Main(string[] args)
{
  Console.WriteLine("***** Fun with StringWriter / StringReader *****\n");

  // Create a StringWriter and emit character data to memory.
  using(StringWriter strWriter = new StringWriter())
  {
    strWriter.WriteLine("Don't forget Mother's Day this year...");
    // Get a copy of the contents (stored in a string) and dump
    // to console.
    Console.WriteLine("Contents of StringWriter:\n{0}", strWriter);
  }
  Console.ReadLine();
}
```

StringWriter and StreamWriter both derive from the same base class (TextWriter), so the writing logic is more or less identical. However, given the nature of StringWriter, you should also be aware that this class allows you to use the following GetStringBuilder() method to extract a System.Text.StringBuilder object:

```
using (StringWriter strWriter = new StringWriter())
{
  strWriter.WriteLine("Don't forget Mother's Day this year...");
  Console.WriteLine("Contents of StringWriter:\n{0}", strWriter);

  // Get the internal StringBuilder.
  StringBuilder sb = strWriter.GetStringBuilder();
  sb.Insert(0, "Hey!! ");
  Console.WriteLine("-> {0}", sb.ToString());
  sb.Remove(0, "Hey!! ".Length);
  Console.WriteLine("-> {0}", sb.ToString());
}
```

When you want to read from a stream of character data, you can use the corresponding StringReader type, which (as you would expect) functions identically to the related StreamReader class. In fact, the StringReader class does nothing more than override the inherited members to read from a block of character data, rather than from a file, as shown here:

```
using (StringWriter strWriter = new StringWriter())
{
  strWriter.WriteLine("Don't forget Mother's Day this year...");
  Console.WriteLine("Contents of StringWriter:\n{0}", strWriter);

  // Read data from the StringWriter.
  using (StringReader strReader = new StringReader(strWriter.ToString()))
  {
    string input = null;
    while ((input = strReader.ReadLine()) != null)
    {
      Console.WriteLine(input);
    }
  }
}
```

■ **Source Code** You can find the StringReaderWriterApp under the Chapter 20 subdirectory.

Working with BinaryWriters and BinaryReaders

The final writer/reader sets you will examine in this section are BinaryReader and BinaryWriter. Both derive directly from System.Object. These types allow you to read and write discrete data types to an underlying stream in a compact binary format. The BinaryWriter class defines a highly overloaded Write() method to place a data type in the underlying stream. In addition to the Write() member, BinaryWriter provides additional members that allow you to get or set the Stream-derived type; it also offers support for random access to the data (see Table 20-10).

Table 20-10. BinaryWriter Core Members

Member	Meaning in Life
BaseStream	This read-only property provides access to the underlying stream used with the BinaryWriter object.
Close()	This method closes the binary stream.
Flush()	This method flushes the binary stream.
Seek()	This method sets the position in the current stream.
Write()	This method writes a value to the current stream.

The BinaryReader class complements the functionality offered by BinaryWriter with the members described in Table 20-11.

Table 20-11. BinaryReader Core Members

Member	Meaning in Life
BaseStream	This read-only property provides access to the underlying stream used with the BinaryReader object.
Close()	This method closes the binary reader.
PeekChar()	This method returns the next available character without advancing the position in the stream.
Read()	This method reads a given set of bytes or characters and stores them in the incoming array.
ReadXXXX()	The BinaryReader class defines numerous read methods that grab the next type from the stream (e.g., ReadBoolean(), ReadByte(), and ReadInt32()).

The following example (a Console Application named BinaryWriterReader) writes a number of data types to a new *.dat file:

```
static void Main(string[] args)
{
  Console.WriteLine("***** Fun with Binary Writers / Readers *****\n");

  // Open a binary writer for a file.
  FileInfo f = new FileInfo("BinFile.dat");
  using(BinaryWriter bw = new BinaryWriter(f.OpenWrite()))
  {
    // Print out the type of BaseStream.
    // (System.IO.FileStream in this case).
    Console.WriteLine("Base stream is: {0}", bw.BaseStream);

    // Create some data to save in the file.
    double aDouble = 1234.67;
    int anInt = 34567;
    string aString = "A, B, C";

    // Write the data.
    bw.Write(aDouble);
    bw.Write(anInt);
    bw.Write(aString);
  }
  Console.WriteLine("Done!");
  Console.ReadLine();
}
```

Notice how the FileStream object returned from FileInfo.OpenWrite() is passed to the constructor of the BinaryWriter type. Using this technique makes it easy to *layer in* a stream before writing out the data. Note that the constructor of BinaryWriter takes any Stream-derived type (e.g., FileStream, MemoryStream, or BufferedStream). Thus, writing binary data to memory instead is as simple as supplying a valid MemoryStream object.

To read the data out of the BinFile.dat file, the BinaryReader type provides a number of options. Here, you call various read-centric members to pluck each chunk of data from the file stream:

```
static void Main(string[] args)
{
...
  FileInfo f = new FileInfo("BinFile.dat");
...
  // Read the binary data from the stream.
  using(BinaryReader br = new BinaryReader(f.OpenRead()))
  {
    Console.WriteLine(br.ReadDouble());
    Console.WriteLine(br.ReadInt32());
    Console.WriteLine(br.ReadString());
  }
  Console.ReadLine();
}
```

■ **Source Code** You can find the BinaryWriterReader application under the Chapter 20 subdirectory.

Watching Files Programmatically

Now that you have a better handle on the use of various readers and writers, you'll look at the role of the
FileSystemWatcher class. This type can be quite helpful when you want to monitor (or "watch") files on
your system programmatically. Specifically, you can instruct the FileSystemWatcher type to monitor files
for any of the actions specified by the System.IO.NotifyFilters enumeration (many of these members
are self-explanatory, but you should still check the .NET Framework 4.5 SDK documentation for more
details).

```
public enum NotifyFilters
{
  Attributes, CreationTime,
  DirectoryName, FileName,
  LastAccess, LastWrite,
  Security, Size
}
```

To begin working with the FileSystemWatcher type, you need to set the Path property to specify the
name (and location) of the directory that contains the files you want to monitor, as well as the Filter
property that defines the file extensions of the files you want to monitor.

At this point, you may choose to handle the Changed, Created, and Deleted events, all of which work
in conjunction with the FileSystemEventHandler delegate. This delegate can call any method matching
the following pattern:

```
// The FileSystemEventHandler delegate must point
// to methods matching the following signature.
void MyNotificationHandler(object source, FileSystemEventArgs e)
```

You can also handle the Renamed event using the RenamedEventHandler delegate type, which can call
methods that match the following signature:

```
// The RenamedEventHandler delegate must point
// to methods matching the following signature.
void MyRenamedHandler(object source, RenamedEventArgs e)
```

While you could use the traditional delegate/event syntax to handle each event, you can certainly
make use of lambda expression syntax as well (the downloadable code for this project does make use of
lambda syntax, if you are interested).

Next, let's look at the process of watching a file. Assume you have created a new directory on your C:
drive named MyFolder that contains various *.txt files (named whatever you like). The following
Console Application (named MyDirectoryWatcher) monitors the *.txt files in the MyFolder directory
and prints out messages when files are created, deleted, modified, or renamed:

```
static void Main(string[] args)
{
  Console.WriteLine("***** The Amazing File Watcher App *****\n");
```

```
// Establish the path to the directory to watch.
FileSystemWatcher watcher = new FileSystemWatcher();
try
{
  watcher.Path = @"C:\MyFolder";
}
catch(ArgumentException ex)
{
  Console.WriteLine(ex.Message);
  return;
}
// Set up the things to be on the lookout for.
watcher.NotifyFilter = NotifyFilters.LastAccess
  | NotifyFilters.LastWrite
  | NotifyFilters.FileName
  | NotifyFilters.DirectoryName;

// Only watch text files.
watcher.Filter = "*.txt";

// Add event handlers.
watcher.Changed += new FileSystemEventHandler(OnChanged);
watcher.Created += new FileSystemEventHandler(OnChanged);
watcher.Deleted += new FileSystemEventHandler(OnChanged);
watcher.Renamed += new RenamedEventHandler(OnRenamed);

// Begin watching the directory.
watcher.EnableRaisingEvents = true;

// Wait for the user to quit the program.
Console.WriteLine(@"Press 'q' to quit app.");
while(Console.Read()!='q')
  ;
}
```

The following two event handlers simply print out the current file modification:

```
static void OnChanged(object source, FileSystemEventArgs e)
{
  // Specify what is done when a file is changed, created, or deleted.
  Console.WriteLine("File: {0} {1}!", e.FullPath, e.ChangeType);
}

static void OnRenamed(object source, RenamedEventArgs e)
{
  // Specify what is done when a file is renamed.
  Console.WriteLine("File: {0} renamed to {1}", e.OldFullPath, e.FullPath);
}
```

To test this program, run the application and open Windows Explorer. Try renaming your files, creating a *.txt file, deleting a *.txt file, and so forth. You will see various bits of information generated about the state of the text files within your MyFolder, as in this example:

```
***** The Amazing File Watcher App *****

Press 'q' to quit app.
File: C:\MyFolder\New Text Document.txt Created!
File: C:\MyFolder\New Text Document.txt renamed to C:\MyFolder\Hello.txt
File: C:\MyFolder\Hello.txt Changed!
File: C:\MyFolder\Hello.txt Changed!
File: C:\MyFolder\Hello.txt Deleted!
```

■ **Source Code** You can find the MyDirectoryWatcher application under the Chapter 20 subdirectory.

That wraps up this chapter's look at fundamental I/O operations within the .NET platform. While you will certainly use these techniques in many of your applications, you might also find that *object serialization* services can greatly simplify how you persist large amounts of data.

Understanding Object Serialization

The term *serialization* describes the process of persisting (and possibly transferring) the state of an object into a stream (e.g., file stream and memory stream). The persisted data sequence contains all the necessary information you need to reconstruct (or *deserialize*) the state of the object for use later. Using this technology makes it trivial to save vast amounts of data (in various formats). In many cases, saving application data using serialization services results in less code than using the readers/writers you find in the System.IO namespace.

For example, assume you want to create a GUI-based desktop application that provides a way for end users to save their preferences (e.g., window color and font size). To do this, you might define a class named UserPrefs that encapsulates 20 or so pieces of field data. Now, if you were to use a System.IO.BinaryWriter type, you would need to save each field of the UserPrefs object *manually*. Likewise, if you were to load the data from a file back into memory, you would need to use a System.IO.BinaryReader and (once again) *manually* read in each value to reconfigure a new UserPrefs object.

This is all doable, but you can save yourself a good amount of time by marking the UserPrefs class with the [Serializable] attribute, like so:

```
[Serializable]
public class UserPrefs
{
  public string WindowColor;
  public int FontSize;
}
```

Doing this means that you can persist entire state of the object with only a few lines of code. Without getting hung up on the details for the time being, consider the following Main() method:

```
static void Main(string[] args)
{
  UserPrefs userData= new UserPrefs();
```

```
userData.WindowColor = "Yellow";
userData.FontSize = 50;

// The BinaryFormatter persists state data in a binary format.
// You would need to import System.Runtime.Serialization.Formatters.Binary
// to gain access to BinaryFormatter.
BinaryFormatter binFormat = new BinaryFormatter();

// Store object in a local file.
using(Stream fStream = new FileStream("user.dat",
  FileMode.Create, FileAccess.Write, FileShare.None))
{
  binFormat.Serialize(fStream, userData);
}
Console.ReadLine();
}
```

.NET object serialization makes it easy to persist objects; however, the processes used behind the scenes are quite sophisticated. For example, when an object is persisted to a stream, all associated data (e.g., base class data and contained objects) are automatically serialized, as well. Therefore, if you attempt to persist a derived class, all data up the chain of inheritance comes along for the ride. As you will see, you use an object graph to represent a set of interrelated objects.

.NET serialization services also allow you to persist an object graph in a variety of formats. The previous code example uses the BinaryFormatter type; therefore, the state of the UserPrefs object is persisted as a compact binary format. You can also persist an object graph into SOAP or XML format using other types. These formats can be quite helpful when you need to ensure that your persisted objects travel well across operating systems, languages, and architectures.

■ **Note** WCF prefers a slightly different mechanism for serializing objects to/from WCF service operations; it uses the [DataContract] and [DataMember] attributes. You'll learn more about this in Chapter 25.

Finally, understand that you can persist an object graph into *any* System.IO.Stream-derived type. In the previous example, you used the FileStream type to persist a UserPrefs object into a local file. However, if you would rather store an object to a specific region of memory, you could use a MemoryStream type instead. All that matters is the fact that the sequence of data correctly represents the state of objects within the graph.

The Role of Object Graphs

As mentioned previously, the CLR will account for all related objects to ensure that data is persisted correctly when an object is serialized. This set of related objects is referred to as an *object graph*. Object graphs provide a simple way to document how a set of items refer to each other. Be aware, that object graphs are *not* denoting OOP is-a or has-a relationships. Rather, you can read the arrows in an object diagram as "requires" or "depends on."

Each object in an object graph is assigned a unique numerical value. Keep in mind that the numbers assigned to the members in an object graph are arbitrary and have no real meaning to the outside world.

Once you assign all objects a numerical value, the object graph can record each object's set of dependencies.

For example, assume you have created a set of classes that model some automobiles (of course). You have a base class named Car, which *has-a* Radio. Another class named JamesBondCar extends the Car base type. Figure 20-4 shows a possible object graph that models these relationships.

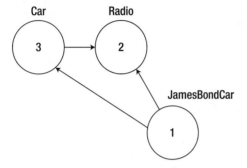

Figure 20-4. *A simple object graph*

When reading object graphs, you can use the phrase "*depends on*" or "*refers to*" when connecting the arrows. Thus, in Figure 20-4, you can see that the Car refers to the Radio class (given the *has-a* relationship). JamesBondCar refers to Car (given the *is-a* relationship), as well as to Radio (it inherits this protected member variable).

Of course, the CLR does not paint pictures in memory to represent a graph of related objects. Rather, the relationship documented in the previous diagram is represented by a mathematical formula that looks something like this:

[Car 3, ref 2], [Radio 2], [JamesBondCar 1, ref 3, ref 2]

If you parse this formula, you can see that object 3 (the Car) has a dependency on object 2 (the Radio). Object 2, the Radio, is a lone wolf and requires nobody. Finally, object 1 (the JamesBondCar) has a dependency on object 3, as well as object 2. In any case, when you serialize or deserialize an instance of JamesBondCar, the object graph ensures that the Radio and Car types also participate in the process.

The beautiful thing about the serialization process is that the graph representing the relationships among your objects is established automatically behind the scenes. As you will see later in this chapter, however, you can become more involved in the construction of a given object graph by customizing the serialization process using attributes and interfaces.

■ **Note** Strictly speaking, the XmlSerializer type (described later in this chapter) does not persist state using object graphs; however, this type still serializes and deserializes related objects in a predictable manner.

Configuring Objects for Serialization

To make an object available to .NET serialization services, all you need to do is decorate each related class (or structure) with the [Serializable] attribute. If you determine that a given type has some member data that should not (or perhaps cannot) participate in the serialization scheme, you can mark such fields with the [NonSerialized] attribute. This can be helpful if you would like to reduce the size of the persisted data, and you have member variables in a serializable class that do not need to be remembered (e.g., fixed values, random values, and transient data).

Defining Serializable Types

To get the ball rolling, create a new Console Application named SimpleSerialize. Insert a new class named Radio, which has been marked [Serializable], excluding a single member variable (radioID) that has been marked [NonSerialized] and will, therefore, not be persisted into the specified data stream.

```
[Serializable]
public class Radio
{
  public bool hasTweeters;
  public bool hasSubWoofers;
  public double[] stationPresets;

  [NonSerialized]
  public string radioID = "XF-552RR6";
}
```

Next, insert two additional class types to represent the JamesBondCar and Car classes, both of which are also marked [Serializable] and define the following pieces of field data:

```
[Serializable]
public class Car
{
  public Radio theRadio = new Radio();
  public bool isHatchBack;
}

[Serializable]
public class JamesBondCar : Car
{
  public bool canFly;
  public bool canSubmerge;
}
```

Be aware that you cannot inherit the [Serializable] attribute from a parent class. Therefore, if you derive a class from a type marked [Serializable], the child class must be marked [Serializable] as well, or it cannot be persisted. In fact, all objects in an object graph must be marked with the [Serializable] attribute. If you attempt to serialize a nonserializable object using the BinaryFormatter or SoapFormatter, you will receive a SerializationException at runtime.

Public Fields, Private Fields, and Public Properties

Notice that in each of these classes, you define the field data as public; this helps keep the example simple. Of course, private data exposed using public properties would be preferable from an OO point of view. Also, for the sake of simplicity, this example does not define any custom constructors on these types; therefore, all unassigned field data will receive the expected default values.

OO design principles aside, you might wonder how the various formatters expect a type's field data to be defined in order to be serialized into a stream. The answer is that it depends. If you persist an object's state using the BinaryFormatter or SoapFormatter, it makes absolutely no difference. These types are programmed to serialize *all* serializable fields of a type, regardless of whether they are public fields, private fields, or private fields exposed through public properties. Recall, however, that if you have points of data that you do not want to be persisted into the object graph, you can selectively mark public or private fields as [NonSerialized], as you do with the string field of the Radio type.

The situation is quite different if you use the XmlSerializer type, however. This type will *only* serialize public data fields or private data exposed by public properties. Private data not exposed from properties will be ignored. For example, consider the following serializable Person type:

```
[Serializable]
public class Person
{
  // A public field.
  public bool isAlive = true;

  // A private field.
  private int personAge = 21;

  // Public property/private data.
  private string fName = string.Empty;
  public string FirstName
  {
    get { return fName; }
    set { fName = value; }
  }
}
```

If you processed the preceding with BinaryFormatter or SoapFormatter, you would find that the isAlive, personAge, and fName fields are saved into the selected stream. However, the XmlSerializer would *not* save the value of personAge because this piece of private data is not encapsulated by a public type property. If you wished to persist the age of the person with the XmlSerializer, you would need to define the field publicly or encapsulate the private member using a public property.

Choosing a Serialization Formatter

After you configure your types to participate in the .NET serialization scheme by applying the necessary attributes, your next step is to choose which format (binary, SOAP, or XML) you should use when persisting your object's state. Each possibility is represented by the following classes:

- BinaryFormatter
- SoapFormatter
- XmlSerializer

The BinaryFormatter type serializes your object's state to a stream using a compact binary format. This type is defined within the System.Runtime.Serialization.Formatters.Binary namespace that is part of mscorlib.dll. If you want to gain access to this type, you can specify the following C# using directive:

```
// Gain access to the BinaryFormatter in mscorlib.dll.
using System.Runtime.Serialization.Formatters.Binary;
```

The SoapFormatter type persists an object's state as a SOAP message (the standard XML format for passing messages to/from a web service). This type is defined within the System.Runtime.Serialization.Formatters.Soap namespace, which is defined in a *separate assembly*. Thus, to format your object graph into a SOAP message, you must first set a reference to System.Runtime.Serialization.Formatters.Soap.dll using the Visual Studio Add Reference dialog box and then specify the following C# using directive:

```
// Must reference System.Runtime.Serialization.Formatters.Soap.dll.
using System.Runtime.Serialization.Formatters.Soap;
```

Finally, if you want to persist a tree of objects as an XML document, you can use the XmlSerializer type. To use this type, you need to specify that you are using the System.Xml.Serialization namespace and set a reference to the assembly System.Xml.dll. As luck would have it, all Visual Studio project templates automatically reference System.Xml.dll; therefore, all you need to do is use the following namespace:

```
// Defined within System.Xml.dll.
using System.Xml.Serialization;
```

The IFormatter and IRemotingFormatter Interfaces

Regardless of which formatter you choose to use, be aware that all of them derive directly from System.Object, so they do *not* share a common set of members from a serialization-centric base class. However, the BinaryFormatter and SoapFormatter types do support common members through the implementation of the IFormatter and IRemotingFormatter interfaces (strange as it might seem, the XmlSerializer implements neither).

System.Runtime.Serialization.IFormatter defines the core Serialize() and Deserialize() methods, which do the grunt work to move your object graphs into and out of a specific stream. Beyond these members, IFormatter defines the following few properties that the implementing type uses behind the scenes:

```
public interface IFormatter
{
  SerializationBinder Binder { get; set; }
  StreamingContext Context { get; set; }
  ISurrogateSelector SurrogateSelector { get; set; }
  object Deserialize(Stream serializationStream);
  void Serialize(Stream serializationStream, object graph);
}
```

The System.Runtime.Remoting.Messaging.IRemotingFormatter interface (which is leveraged internally by the .NET remoting layer) overloads the Serialize() and Deserialize() members into a manner more appropriate for distributed persistence. Note that IRemotingFormatter derives from the more general IFormatter interface.

```
public interface IRemotingFormatter  : IFormatter
{
  object Deserialize(Stream serializationStream, HeaderHandler handler);
  void Serialize(Stream serializationStream, object graph, Header[] headers);
}
```

Although you might not need to interact directly with these interfaces for most of your serialization endeavors, recall that interface-based polymorphism allows you to hold an instance of BinaryFormatter or SoapFormatter using an IFormatter reference. Therefore, if you want to build a method that can serialize an object graph using either of these classes, you could write the following:

```
static void SerializeObjectGraph(IFormatter itfFormat,
                                 Stream destStream, object graph)
{
  itfFormat.Serialize(destStream, graph);
}
```

Type Fidelity Among the Formatters

The most obvious difference among the three formatters is how the object graph is persisted to the stream (binary, SOAP, or XML). You should also be aware of a few more subtle points of distinction; specifically, how the formatters contend with *type fidelity*. When you use the BinaryFormatter type, it will persist not only the field data of the objects in the object graph, but also each type's fully qualified name and the full name of the defining assembly (name, version, public key token, and culture). These extra points of data make the BinaryFormatter an ideal choice when you want to transport objects by value (e.g., as a full copy) across machine boundaries for .NET-centric applications.

The SoapFormatter persists traces of the assembly of origin through the use of an XML namespace. For example, recall the Person type earlier in this chapter. If this type were persisted as a SOAP message, you would find that the opening element of Person is qualified by the generated xmlns. Consider this partial definition, paying special attention to the a1 XML namespace:

```
<a1:Person id="ref-1" xmlns:a1=
  "http://schemas.microsoft.com/clr/nsassem/SimpleSerialize/MyApp%2C%20
  Version%3D1.0.0.0%2C%20Culture%3Dneutral%2C%20PublicKeyToken%3Dnull">
  <isAlive>true</isAlive>
  <personAge>21</personAge>
  <fName id="ref-3">Mel</fName>
</a1:Person>
```

However, the XmlSerializer does *not* attempt to preserve full type fidelity; therefore, it does not record the type's fully qualified name or assembly of origin. This might seem like a limitation at first glance, but XML serialization is used by classic .NET web services, which can be called from clients on any platform (not just .NET). This means that there is no point serializing full .NET type metadata. Here is a possible XML representation of the Person type:

```
<?xml version="1.0"?>
<Person xmlns:xsi="http://www.w3.org/2001/XMLSchema-instance"
        xmlns:xsd="http://www.w3.org/2001/XMLSchema">
  <isAlive>true</isAlive>
  <PersonAge>21</PersonAge>
  <FirstName>Frank</FirstName>
</Person>
```

If you want to persist an object's state in a manner that can be used by any operating system (e.g., Windows, Mac OS X, and various Linux distributions), application framework (e.g., .NET, Java Enterprise Edition, and COM), or programming language, you do not want to maintain full type fidelity because you cannot assume all possible recipients can understand .NET-specific data types. Given this, SoapFormatter and XmlSerializer are ideal choices when you need to ensure as broad a reach as possible for the persisted tree of objects.

Serializing Objects Using the BinaryFormatter

You can use the BinaryFormatter type to illustrate how easy it is to persist an instance of the JamesBondCar to a physical file. Again, the two key methods of the BinaryFormatter type to be aware of are Serialize() and Deserialize().

- Serialize(): Persists an object graph to a specified stream as a sequence of bytes.

- Deserialize(): Converts a persisted sequence of bytes to an object graph.

Assume you have created an instance of JamesBondCar, modified some state data, and want to persist your spy mobile into a *.dat file. Begin by creating the *.dat file itself. You can achieve this by creating an instance of the System.IO.FileStream type. At this point, you can create an instance of the BinaryFormatter and pass in the FileStream and object graph to persist. Consider the following Main() method:

```
// Be sure to import the System.Runtime.Serialization.Formatters.Binary
// and System.IO namespaces.
static void Main(string[] args)
{
  Console.WriteLine("***** Fun with Object Serialization *****\n");

  // Make a JamesBondCar and set state.
  JamesBondCar jbc = new JamesBondCar();
  jbc.canFly = true;
  jbc.canSubmerge = false;
  jbc.theRadio.stationPresets = new double[]{89.3, 105.1, 97.1};
  jbc.theRadio.hasTweeters = true;

  // Now save the car to a specific file in a binary format.
  SaveAsBinaryFormat(jbc, "CarData.dat");
  Console.ReadLine();
}
```

You implement the SaveAsBinaryFormat() method like this:

```
static void SaveAsBinaryFormat(object objGraph, string fileName)
{
  // Save object to a file named CarData.dat in binary.
  BinaryFormatter binFormat = new BinaryFormatter();

  using(Stream fStream = new FileStream(fileName,
        FileMode.Create, FileAccess.Write, FileShare.None))
  {
    binFormat.Serialize(fStream, objGraph);
  }
}
```

```
  Console.WriteLine("=> Saved car in binary format!");
}
```

The `BinaryFormatter.Serialize()` method is the member responsible for composing the object graph and moving the byte sequence to some `Stream`-derived type. In this case, the stream happens to be a physical file. You could also serialize your object types to any `Stream`-derived type, such as a memory location or network stream.

After you run your program, you can view the contents of the `CarData.dat` file that represents this instance of the `JamesBondCar` by navigating to the `\bin\Debug` folder of the current project. Figure 20-5 shows this file opened within Visual Studio.

```
CarData.dat  ⊟ ✕  Program.cs
00000000 00 01 00 00 00 FF FF FF  FF 01 00 00 00 00 00 00  ................
00000010 00 0C 02 00 00 00 46 53  69 6D 70 6C 65 53 65 72  ......FSimpleSer
00000020 69 61 6C 69 7A 65 2C 20  56 65 72 73 69 6F 6E 3D  ialize, Version=
00000030 31 2E 30 2E 30 2E 30 2C  20 43 75 6C 74 75 72 65  1.0.0.0, Culture
00000040 3D 6E 65 75 74 72 61 6C  2C 20 50 75 62 6C 69 63  =neutral, Public
00000050 4B 65 79 54 6F 6B 65 6E  3D 6E 75 6C 6C 05 01 00  KeyToken=null...
00000060 00 00 1C 53 69 6D 70 6C  65 53 65 72 69 61 6C 69  ...SimpleSeriali
00000070 7A 65 2E 4A 61 6D 65 53  73 42 6F 6E 64 43 61 72 04  ze.JamesBondCar.
00000080 00 00 00 06 63 61 6E 46  6C 79 0B 63 61 6E 53 75  ....canFly.canSu
00000090 62 6D 65 72 67 65 08 74  68 65 52 61 64 69 6F 0B  bmerge.theRadio.
000000a0 69 73 48 61 74 68 42 42  61 63 6B 00 00 04 00 01  isHatchBack.....
000000b0 01 15 53 69 6D 70 6C 65  53 65 72 69 61 6C 69 7A  ..SimpleSerializ
000000c0 65 2E 52 61 64 69 6F 02  00 00 00 01 02 00 00 00  e.Radio.........
000000d0 01 00 09 03 00 00 00 00  05 03 00 00 00 15 53 69  ..............Si
000000e0 6D 70 6C 65 53 65 72 69  61 6C 69 7A 65 2E 52 61  mpleSerialize.Ra
000000f0 64 69 6F 03 00 00 00 0B  68 61 73 54 77 65 65 74  dio.....hasTweet
00000100 65 72 73 0D 68 61 73 53  75 62 57 6F 6F 66 65 72  ers.hasSubWoofer
00000110 73 0E 73 74 61 74 69 6F  6E 50 72 65 73 65 74 73  s.stationPresets
00000120 00 00 07 01 01 06 02 00  00 00 01 00 09 04 00 00  ................
00000130 00 0F 04 00 00 00 03 00  00 00 06 33 33 33 33 33  ...........33333
00000140 53 56 40 66 66 66 66 66  46 5A 40 66 66 66 66 66  SV@fffffFZ@fffff
00000150 46 58 40 0B                                        FX@.
```

Figure 20-5. *JamesBondCar serialized using a BinaryFormatter*

Deserializing Objects Using the BinaryFormatter

Now suppose you want to read the persisted `JamesBondCar` from the binary file back into an object variable. After you open `CarData.dat` programmatically (with the `File.OpenRead()` method), you can call the `Deserialize()` method of the `BinaryFormatter`. Be aware that `Deserialize()` returns a general `System.Object` type, so you need to impose an explicit cast, as shown here:

```
static void LoadFromBinaryFile(string fileName)
{
  BinaryFormatter binFormat = new BinaryFormatter();

  // Read the JamesBondCar from the binary file.
  using(Stream fStream = File.OpenRead(fileName))
  {
    JamesBondCar carFromDisk =
      (JamesBondCar)binFormat.Deserialize(fStream);
    Console.WriteLine("Can this car fly? : {0}", carFromDisk.canFly);
  }
}
```

Notice that when you call Deserialize(), you pass the Stream-derived type that represents the location of the persisted object graph. Once you cast the object back into the correct type, you will find the state data has been retained from the point at which you saved the object.

Serializing Objects Using the SoapFormatter

Your next choice of formatter is the SoapFormatter type, which serializes data in a proper SOAP envelope. In a nutshell, the Simple Object Access Protocol (SOAP) defines a standard process in which you can invoke methods in a platform- and OS-neutral manner.

Assuming you have set a reference to the System.Runtime.Serialization.Formatters.Soap.dll assembly (and imported the System.Runtime.Serialization.Formatters.Soap namespace), you can persist and retrieve a JamesBondCar as a SOAP message simply by replacing each occurrence of BinaryFormatter with SoapFormatter. Consider the following new method of the Program class, which serializes an object to a local file in a SOAP format:

```
// Be sure to import System.Runtime.Serialization.Formatters.Soap
// and reference System.Runtime.Serialization.Formatters.Soap.dll.
static void SaveAsSoapFormat (object objGraph, string fileName)
{
  // Save object to a file named CarData.soap in SOAP format.
  SoapFormatter soapFormat = new SoapFormatter();

  using(Stream fStream = new FileStream(fileName,
    FileMode.Create, FileAccess.Write, FileShare.None))
  {
    soapFormat.Serialize(fStream, objGraph);
  }
  Console.WriteLine("=> Saved car in SOAP format!");
}
```

As before, you use Serialize() and Deserialize() to move the object graph into and out of the stream. If you call this method from Main() and run the application, you can open the resulting *.soap file. Here you can locate the XML elements that mark the stateful values of the current JamesBondCar, as well as the relationship between the objects in the graph by using the #ref tokens (see Figure 20-6).

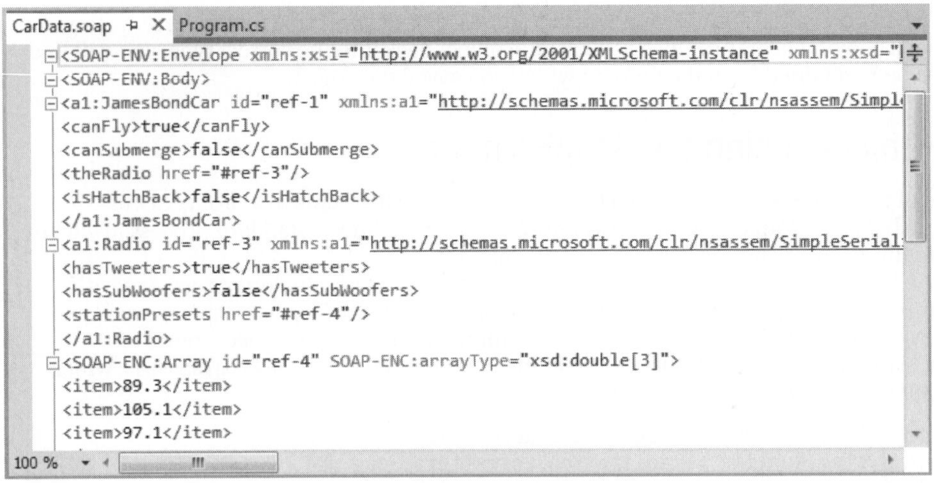

Figure 20-6. *JamesBondCar serialized using a SoapFormatter*

Serializing Objects Using the XmlSerializer

In addition to the SOAP and binary formatters, the System.Xml.dll assembly provides a third formatter, System.Xml.Serialization.XmlSerializer. You can use this formatter to persist the *public* state of a given object as pure XML, as opposed to XML data wrapped within a SOAP message. Working with this type is a bit different from working with the SoapFormatter or BinaryFormatter type. Consider the following code, which assumes you have imported the System.Xml.Serialization namespace:

```
static void SaveAsXmlFormat(object objGraph, string fileName)
{
  // Save object to a file named CarData.xml in XML format.
  XmlSerializer xmlFormat = new XmlSerializer(typeof(JamesBondCar));

  using(Stream fStream = new FileStream(fileName,
    FileMode.Create, FileAccess.Write, FileShare.None))
  {
    xmlFormat.Serialize(fStream, objGraph);
  }
  Console.WriteLine("=> Saved car in XML format!");
}
```

The key difference is that the XmlSerializer type requires you to specify type information that represents the class you want to serialize. If you were to look within the newly generated XML file (assuming you call this new method from within Main()), you would find the XML data shown here:

```
<?xml version="1.0"?>
<JamesBondCar xmlns:xsi="http://www.w3.org/2001/XMLSchema-instance"
xmlns:xsd="http://www.w3.org/2001/XMLSchema">
  <theRadio>
    <hasTweeters>true</hasTweeters>
    <hasSubWoofers>false</hasSubWoofers>
```

```
  <stationPresets>
    <double>89.3</double>
    <double>105.1</double>
    <double>97.1</double>
  </stationPresets>
  <radioID>XF-552RR6</radioID>
 </theRadio>
 <isHatchBack>false</isHatchBack>
 <canFly>true</canFly>
 <canSubmerge>false</canSubmerge>
</JamesBondCar>
```

■ **Note** The XmlSerializer demands that all serialized types in the object graph support a default constructor (so be sure to add it back if you define custom constructors). If this is not the case, you will receive an InvalidOperationException at runtime.

Controlling the Generated XML Data

If you have a background in XML technologies, you know that it is often critical to ensure the data within an XML document conforms to a set of rules that establish the *validity* of the data. Understand that a *valid* XML document does not have anything to do with the syntactic well-being of the XML elements (e.g., all opening elements must have a closing element). Rather, valid documents conform to agreed-upon formatting rules (e.g., field X must be expressed as an attribute and not a subelement), which are typically defined by an XML schema or document-type definition (DTD) file.

By default, XmlSerializer serializes all public fields/properties as XML elements, rather than as XML attributes. If you want to control how the XmlSerializer generates the resulting XML document, you can decorate types with any number of additional .NET attributes from the System.Xml.Serialization namespace. Table 20-12 documents some (but not all) of the .NET attributes that influence how XML data is encoded to a stream.

Table 20-12. Select Attributes of the System.Xml.Serialization Namespace

.NET Attribute	Meaning in Life
[XmlAttribute]	You can use this .NET attribute on a public field or property in a class to tell XmlSerializer to serialize the data as an XML attribute (rather than as a subelement).
[XmlElement]	The field or property will be serialized as an XML element named as you so choose.
[XmlEnum]	This attribute provides the element name of an enumeration member.
[XmlRoot]	This attribute controls how the root element will be constructed (namespace and element name).

| [XmlText] | The property or field will be serialized as XML text (i.e., the content between the start tag and the end tag of the root element). |
| [XmlType] | This attribute provides the name and namespace of the XML type. |

This simple example illustrates how the field data of JamesBondCar is currently persisted as XML:

```
<?xml version="1.0" encoding="utf-8"?>
<JamesBondCar xmlns:xsi="http://www.w3.org/2001/XMLSchema-instance"
              xmlns:xsd="http://www.w3.org/2001/XMLSchema">
...
  <canFly>true</canFly>
  <canSubmerge>false</canSubmerge>
</JamesBondCar>
```

If you want to specify a custom XML namespace that qualifies the JamesBondCar and encodes the canFly and canSubmerge values as XML attributes, you can do so by modifying the C# definition of JamesBondCar, like so:

```
[Serializable, XmlRoot(Namespace = "http://www.MyCompany.com")]
public class JamesBondCar : Car
{
  [XmlAttribute]
  public bool canFly;
  [XmlAttribute]
  public bool canSubmerge;
}
```

This yields the following XML document (note the opening <JamesBondCar> element):

```
<?xml version="1.0"""?>
<JamesBondCar xmlns:xsi="http://www.w3.org/2001/XMLSchema-instance"
              xmlns:xsd="http://www.w3.org/2001/XMLSchema"
  canFly="true" canSubmerge="false"
  xmlns="http://www.MyCompany.com">
...
</JamesBondCar>
```

Of course, you can use many other attributes to control how the XmlSerializer generates the resulting XML document. For full details, look up the System.Xml.Serialization namespace in the .NET Framework 4.5 SDK documentation.

Serializing Collections of Objects

Now that you have seen how to persist a single object to a stream, you're ready to examine how to save a set of objects. As you might have noticed, the Serialize() method of the IFormatter interface does not provide a way to specify an arbitrary number of objects as input (only a single System.Object). On a related note, the return value of Deserialize() is, again, a single System.Object (the same basic limitation holds true for XmlSerializer).

```
public interface IFormatter
{
...
    object Deserialize(Stream serializationStream);
    void Serialize(Stream serializationStream, object graph);
}
```

Recall that the System.Object represents a complete tree of objects. Given this, if you pass in an object that has been marked as [Serializable] and contains other [Serializable] objects, the entire set of objects is persisted in a single method call. As luck would have it, most of the types you find in the System.Collections and System.Collections.Generic namespaces have already been marked as [Serializable]. Therefore, if you would like to persist a set of objects, simply add the desired set to the container (such as a normal array, an ArrayList or a List<T>) and serialize the object to your stream of choice.

Now assume that you want to update the JamesBondCar class with a two-argument constructor, so you can set a few pieces of state data (note that you add back the default constructor as required by the XmlSerializer).

```
[Serializable,
 XmlRoot(Namespace = "http://www.MyCompany.com")]
public class JamesBondCar : Car
{
    public JamesBondCar(bool skyWorthy, bool seaWorthy)
    {
        canFly = skyWorthy;
        canSubmerge = seaWorthy;
    }
    // The XmlSerializer demands a default constructor!
    public JamesBondCar(){}
...
}
```

With this, you can now persist any number of JamesBondCars:

```
static void SaveListOfCars()
{
    // Now persist a List<T> of JamesBondCars.
    List<JamesBondCar> myCars = new List<JamesBondCar>();
    myCars.Add(new JamesBondCar(true, true));
    myCars.Add(new JamesBondCar(true, false));
    myCars.Add(new JamesBondCar(false, true));
    myCars.Add(new JamesBondCar(false, false));

    using(Stream fStream = new FileStream("CarCollection.xml",
        FileMode.Create, FileAccess.Write, FileShare.None))
    {
        XmlSerializer xmlFormat = new XmlSerializer(typeof(List<JamesBondCar>));
        xmlFormat.Serialize(fStream, myCars);
    }
    Console.WriteLine("=> Saved list of cars!");
}
```

You use XmlSerializer here, so you are required to specify type information for each of the subobjects within the root object (List<JamesBondCar>, in this case). However, the logic would be even more straightforward if you were to use the BinaryFormatter or SoapFormatter type instead, as shown here:

```
static void  SaveListOfCarsAsBinary()
{
  // Save ArrayList object (myCars) as binary.
  List<JamesBondCar> myCars = new List<JamesBondCar>();

  BinaryFormatter binFormat = new BinaryFormatter();
  using(Stream fStream = new FileStream("AllMyCars.dat",
    FileMode.Create, FileAccess.Write, FileShare.None))
  {
    binFormat.Serialize(fStream, myCars);
  }
  Console.WriteLine("=> Saved list of cars in binary!");
}
```

■ **Source Code** The SimpleSerialize application is included under the Chapter 20 subdirectory.

Customizing the Soap/Binary Serialization Process

In a majority of cases, the default serialization scheme provided by the .NET platform will be exactly what you require. Simply apply the [Serializable] attribute to your related types and pass the tree of objects to your formatter of choice for processing. In some cases, however, you might want to become more involved with how a tree is constructed and handled during the serialization process. For example, perhaps you have a business rule that says all field data must be persisted using a particular format, or perhaps you need to add additional bits of data to the stream that do not map directly to fields in the object being persisted (e.g., timestamps and unique identifiers).

When you want to become more involved with the process of object serialization, the System.Runtime.Serialization namespace provides several types that allow you to do so. Table 20-13 describes some of the core types you should be aware of.

Table 20-13. System.Runtime.Serialization Namespace Core Types

Type	Meaning in Life
ISerializable	You can implement this interface on a [Serializable] type to control its serialization and deserialization.
ObjectIDGenerator	This type generates IDs for members in an object graph.
[OnDeserialized]	This attribute allows you to specify a method that will be called immediately after the object has been deserialized.

[OnDeserializing]	This attribute allows you to specify a method that will be called before the deserialization process.
[OnSerialized]	This attribute allows you to specify a method that will be called immediately after the object has been serialized.
[OnSerializing]	This attribute allows you to specify a method that will be called before the serialization process.
[OptionalField]	This attribute allows you to define a field on a type that can be missing from the specified stream.
[SerializationInfo]	In essence, this class is a *property bag* that maintains name/value pairs representing the state of an object during the serialization process.

A Deeper Look at Object Serialization

Before you examine various ways that you can customize the serialization process, you will find it helpful to take a deeper look at what takes place behind the scenes. When the BinaryFormatter serializes an object graph, it is in charge of transmitting the following information into the specified stream:

- The fully qualified name of the objects in the graph (e.g., MyApp.JamesBondCar)

- The name of the assembly defining the object graph (e.g., MyApp.exe)

- An instance of the SerializationInfo class that contains all stateful data maintained by the members in the object graph

During the deserialization process, the BinaryFormatter uses this same information to build an identical copy of the object, using the information extracted from the underlying stream. SoapFormatter uses a quite similar process.

■ **Note** Recall that the XmlSerializer does not persist a type's fully qualified name or the name of the defining assembly; this behavior helps keep the state of the object as mobile as possible. This type is concerned only with persisting exposed public data.

Beyond moving the required data into and out of a stream, formatters also analyze the members in the object graph for the following pieces of infrastructure:

- A check is made to determine whether the object is marked with the [Serializable] attribute. If the object is not, a SerializationException is thrown.

- If the object is marked [Serializable], a check is made to determine whether the object implements the ISerializable interface. If this is the case, GetObjectData() is called on the object.

- If the object does not implement ISerializable, the default serialization process is used, serializing all fields not marked as [NonSerialized].

In addition to determining whether the type supports ISerializable, formatters are also responsible for discovering whether the types in question support members that have been adorned with the [OnSerializing], [OnSerialized], [OnDeserializing], or [OnDeserialized] attributes. You'll examine the role of these attributes in mometarily, but first you need to look at the role of ISerializable.

Customizing Serialization Using ISerializable

Objects that are marked [Serializable] have the option of implementing the ISerializable interface. Doing so lets you get "involved" with the serialization process and perform any pre- or post-data formatting.

■ **Note** Since the release of .NET 2.0, the preferred way to customize the serialization process is to use the serialization attributes (described next). However, knowledge of ISerializable is important for the purpose of maintaining existing systems.

The ISerializable interface is quite simple, given that it defines only a single method, GetObjectData().

```
// When you wish to tweak the serialization process,
// implement ISerializable.
public interface ISerializable
{
  void GetObjectData(SerializationInfo info,
    StreamingContext context);
}
```

The GetObjectData() method is called automatically by a given formatter during the serialization process. The implementation of this method populates the incoming SerializationInfo parameter with a series of name/value pairs that (typically) map to the field data of the object being persisted. SerializationInfo defines numerous variations on the overloaded AddValue() method, as well as a small set of properties that allow the type to get and set the type's name, defining assembly, and member count. Here is a partial snapshot:

```
public sealed class SerializationInfo
{
  public SerializationInfo(Type type, IFormatterConverter converter);
  public string AssemblyName { get; set; }
  public string FullTypeName { get; set; }
  public int MemberCount { get; }
  public void AddValue(string name, short value);
  public void AddValue(string name, ushort value);
  public void AddValue(string name, int value);
...
}
```

Types that implement the ISerializable interface must also define a special constructor that takes the following signature:

```
// You must supply a custom constructor with this signature
// to allow the runtime engine to set the state of your object.
[Serializable]
class SomeClass : ISerializable
{
  protected SomeClass (SerializationInfo si, StreamingContext ctx) {...}
  ...
}
```

Notice that the visibility of this constructor is set as *protected*. This is permissible because the formatter will have access to this member, regardless of its visibility. These special constructors tend to be marked as protected (or private for that matter) to ensure that the casual object user can never create an object in this manner. The first parameter of this constructor is an instance of the SerializationInfo type (which you've seen previously).

The second parameter of this special constructor is a StreamingContext type, which contains information regarding the source of the bits. The most informative member of StreamingContext is the State property, which represents a value from the StreamingContextStates enumeration. The values of this enumeration represent the basic composition of the current stream.

Unless you intend to implement some low-level custom remoting services, you will seldom need to deal with this enumeration directly. Nevertheless, here are the possible names of the StreamingContextStates enum (consult the .NET Framework 4.5 SDK documentation for full details):

```
public enum StreamingContextStates
{
  CrossProcess,
  CrossMachine,
  File,
  Persistence,
  Remoting,
  Other,
  Clone,
  CrossAppDomain,
  All
}
```

Now let's look at how to customize the serialization process using ISerializable. Assume you have a new Console Application project (named CustomSerialization) that defines a class type containing two points of string data. Also assume that you must ensure that the string objects are serialized to the stream in all uppercase, and deserialized from the stream in lowercase. To account for such rules, you could implement ISerializable like this (be sure to import the System.Runtime.Serialization namespace):

```
[Serializable]
class StringData : ISerializable
{
  private string dataItemOne = "First data block";
  private string dataItemTwo= "More data";

  public StringData(){}
  protected StringData(SerializationInfo si, StreamingContext ctx)
```

```
  {
    // Rehydrate member variables from stream.
    dataItemOne = si.GetString("First_Item").ToLower();
    dataItemTwo = si.GetString("dataItemTwo").ToLower();
  }

  void ISerializable.GetObjectData(SerializationInfo info, StreamingContext ctx)
  {
    // Fill up the SerializationInfo object with the formatted data.
    info.AddValue("First_Item", dataItemOne.ToUpper());
    info.AddValue("dataItemTwo", dataItemTwo.ToUpper());
  }
}
```

Notice that when you fill the SerializationInfo type with the GetObjectData() method, you are *not* required to name the data points identically to the type's internal member variables. This can obviously be helpful if you need to further decouple the type's data from the persisted format. Be aware, however, that you will need to obtain the values from the special, protected constructor using the same names assigned within GetObjectData().

To test your customization, assume that you want to persist an instance of MyStringData using a SoapFormatter (so update your assembly references and imports accordingly), as follows:

```
static void Main(string[] args)
{
  Console.WriteLine("***** Fun with Custom Serialization *****");

  // Recall that this type implements ISerializable.
  StringData myData = new StringData();

  // Save to a local file in SOAP format.
  SoapFormatter soapFormat = new SoapFormatter();
  using(Stream fStream = new FileStream("MyData.soap",
    FileMode.Create, FileAccess.Write, FileShare.None))
  {
    soapFormat.Serialize(fStream, myData);
  }
  Console.ReadLine();
}
```

When you view the resulting *.soap file, you will see that the string fields have been persisted in uppercase, as so:

```
<SOAP-ENV:Envelope xmlns:xsi="http://www.w3.org/2001/XMLSchema-instance"
  xmlns:xsd="http://www.w3.org/2001/XMLSchema"
  xmlns:SOAP-ENC="http://schemas.xmlsoap.org/soap/encoding/"
  xmlns:SOAP-ENV="http://schemas.xmlsoap.org/soap/envelope/"
  xmlns:clr="http://schemas.microsoft.com/soap/encoding/clr/1.0"
  SOAP-ENV:encodingStyle="http://schemas.xmlsoap.org/soap/encoding/">
<SOAP-ENV:Body>

  <a1:StringData id="ref-1" ...>
    <First_Item id="ref-3">FIRST DATA BLOCK</First_Item>
    <dataItemTwo id="ref-4">MORE DATA</dataItemTwo>
```

```
  </a1:StringData>
  </SOAP-ENV:Body>

</SOAP-ENV:Envelope>
```

Customizing Serialization Using Attributes

Although implementing the ISerializable interface is one way to customize the serialization process, the preferred way to customize the serialization process since the release of .NET 2.0 is to define methods that are attributed with any of the new serialization-centric attributes: [OnSerializing], [OnSerialized], [OnDeserializing], or [OnDeserialized]. Using these attributes is less cumbersome than implementing ISerializable because you do not need to interact manually with an incoming SerializationInfo parameter. Instead, you can modify your state data directly, while the formatter operates on the type.

■ **Note** You can find these serialization attributes defined in the System.Runtime.Serialization namespace.

When you define method decorated with these attributes, you must define the methods so they receive a StreamingContext parameter and return nothing (otherwise, you will receive a runtime exception). Note that you are not required to account for each of the serialization-centric attributes, and you can simply contend with the stages of serialization you want to intercept. The following snippet illustrates this. Here, a new [Serializable] type has the same requirements as StringData, but this time you account for using the [OnSerializing] and [OnDeserialized] attributes:

```
[Serializable]
class MoreData
{
  private string dataItemOne = "First data block";
  private string dataItemTwo= "More data";

  [OnSerializing]
  private void OnSerializing(StreamingContext context)
  {
    // Called during the serialization process.
    dataItemOne = dataItemOne.ToUpper();
    dataItemTwo = dataItemTwo.ToUpper();
  }

  [OnDeserialized]
  private void OnDeserialized(StreamingContext context)
  {
    // Called when the deserialization process is complete.
    dataItemOne = dataItemOne.ToLower();
    dataItemTwo = dataItemTwo.ToLower();
  }
}
```

If you were to serialize this new type, you would again find that the data has been persisted as uppercase and deserialized as lowercase.

■ **Source Code** You can find the CustomSerialization project under the Chapter 20 subdirectory.

With this example behind you, your exploration of the core details of object serialization services, including various ways to customize the process, is complete. As you have seen, the serialization and deserialization process makes it easy to persist large amounts of data, and it can be less labor-intensive than working with the various reader/writer classes of the System.IO namespace.

Summary

You began this chapter by examining the use of the Directory(Info) and File(Info) types. As you learned, these classes allow you to manipulate a physical file or directory on your hard drive. Next, you examined a number of classes derived from the abstract Stream class. Given that Stream-derived types operate on a raw stream of bytes, the System.IO namespace provides numerous reader/writer types (e.g., StreamWriter, StringWriter, and BinaryWriter) that simplify the process. Along the way, you also checked out the functionality provided by DriveType, learned how to monitor files using the FileSystemWatcher type, and saw how to interact with streams in an asynchronous manner.

This chapter also introduced you to the topic of object serialization services. As you have seen, the .NET platform uses an object graph to account for the full set of related objects that you want to persist to a stream. As long as each member in the object graph has been marked with the [Serializable] attribute, the data is persisted using your format of choice (binary or SOAP).

You also learned that it is possible to customize the out-of-the-box serialization process using two possible approaches. First, you learned how to implement the ISerializable interface (and support a special private constructor), which enables you to become more involved with how formatters persist the supplied data. Second, you learned about a set of .NET attributes that simplify the process of custom serialization. All you need to do is apply the [OnSerializing], [OnSerialized], [OnDeserializing], or [OnDeserialized] attribute on members that take a StreamingContext parameter, and the formatters will invoke them accordingly.

## CHAPTER 21

ADO.NET Part I: The Connected Layer

The .NET platform defines a number of namespaces that allow you to interact with relational database systems. Collectively speaking, these namespaces are known as *ADO.NET*. In this chapter, you'll learn about the overall role of ADO.NET, then move on to the topic of ADO.NET data providers. The .NET platform supports numerous data providers, each of which is optimized to communicate with a specific database management system (e.g., Microsoft SQL Server, Oracle, and MySQL).

After you understand the common functionality provided by various data providers, you will then look at the data provider factory pattern. As you will see, using types within the System.Data.Common namespace (and a related App.config file), you can build a single code base that can dynamically pick and choose the underlying data provider without the need to recompile or redeploy the application's code base.

Perhaps most importantly, this chapter will give you the chance to build a custom data access library assembly (AutoLotDAL.dll) that encapsulates various database operations performed on a custom database named AutoLot. You will expand this library in Chapters 23 and 24 and leverage it over many of this book's remaining chapters. Finally, you will wrap things up by examining the topic of database transactions.

A High-Level Definition of ADO.NET

If you have a background in Microsoft's previous COM-based data access model (Active Data Objects, or ADO), you need to understand that ADO.NET has little to do with ADO beyond the letters *A, D,* and *O.* While it is true that there is some relationship between the two systems (e.g., each has the concept of connection and command objects), some familiar ADO types (e.g., the Recordset) no longer exist. Furthermore, you can find many new ADO.NET types that have no direct equivalent under classic ADO (e.g., the data adapter).

Unlike classic ADO, which was primarily designed for tightly coupled client/server systems, ADO.NET was built with the disconnected world in mind, using DataSets. This type represents a local copy of any number of related data tables, each of which contains a collection of rows and column. Using the DataSet, the calling assembly (such as a web page or desktop executable) is able to manipulate and update a DataSet's contents while disconnected from the data source, and send any modified data back for processing using a related *data adapter*.

From a programmatic point of view, the bulk of ADO.NET is represented by a core assembly named System.Data.dll. Within this binary, you find a good number of namespaces (see Figure 21-1), many of which represent the types of a particular ADO.NET data provider (defined momentarily).

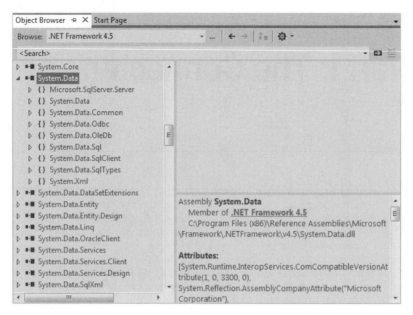

Figure 21-1. System.Data.dll is the core ADO.NET assembly

It turns out most Visual Studio project templates automatically reference this key data access assembly. You should also understand that there are other ADO.NET-centric assemblies beyond System.Data.dll, which you might need to reference manually in your current project using the Add Reference dialog box.

The Three Faces of ADO.NET

You can use the ADO.NET libraries in three conceptually unique manners: connected, disconnected, or through the Entity Framework. When you use the *connected layer* (the subject of this chapter), your code base explicitly connects to and disconnects from the underlying data store. When you use ADO.NET in this manner, you typically interact with the data store using connection objects, command objects, and data reader objects.

The *disconnected layer* (you will learn more about this in Chapter 22) allows you to manipulate a set of DataTable objects (contained within a DataSet) that functions as a client-side copy of the external data. When you obtain a DataSet using a related data adapter object, the connection is automatically opened and closed on your behalf. As you would guess, this approach helps free up connections for other callers quickly and goes a long way toward increasing the scalability of your systems.

After a caller receives a DataSet, it is able to traverse and manipulate the contents without incurring the cost of network traffic. Also, if the caller wants to submit the changes back to the data store, the data adapter (in conjunction with a set of SQL statements) is used to update the data source; at this point the connection is reopened for the database updates to occur, and then closed again immediately.

Finally in Chapter 23, you will be introduced to a data access API termed the *Entity Framework* (or simply, EF). Using EF, you are able to interact with a relational database using client-side objects that encapsulate a number of low-level database specifics from view. As well, the EF programming model allows you to interact with relational databases using strongly typed LINQ queries, using the grammar of LINQ to Entities.

Understanding ADO.NET Data Providers

ADO.NET does not provide a single set of objects that communicate with multiple database management systems (DBMSs). Rather, ADO.NET supports multiple *data providers*, each of which is optimized to interact with a specific DBMS. The first benefit of this approach is that you can program a specific data provider to access any unique features of a particular DBMS. The second benefit is that a specific data provider can connect directly to the underlying engine of the DBMS in question without an intermediate mapping layer standing between the tiers.

Simply put, a data provider is a set of types defined in a given namespace that understand how to communicate with a specific type of data source. Regardless of which data provider you use, each defines a set of class types that provide core functionality. Table 21-1 documents some of the core common types, their base class (all defined in the System.Data.Common namespace), and the key interfaces (each is defined in the System.Data namespace) they implement.

Table 21-1. *The Core Objects of an ADO.NET Data Provider*

Type of Object	Base Class	Relevant Interfaces	Meaning in Life
Connection	DbConnection	IDbConnection	Provides the ability to connect to and disconnect from the data store. Connection objects also provide access to a related transaction object.
Command	DbCommand	IDbCommand	Represents a SQL query or a stored procedure. Command objects also provide access to the provider's data reader object.
DataReader	DbDataReader	IDataReader, IDataRecord	Provides forward-only, read-only access to data using a server-side cursor.
DataAdapter	DbDataAdapter	IDataAdapter, IDbDataAdapter	Transfers DataSets between the caller and the data store. Data adapters contain a connection and a set of four internal command objects used to select, insert, update, and delete information from the data store.
Parameter	DbParameter	IDataParameter, IDbDataParameter	Represents a named parameter within a parameterized query.
Transaction	DbTransaction	IDbTransaction	Encapsulates a database transaction.

Although the specific names of these core classes will differ among data providers (e.g., SqlConnection vs. OracleConnection vs. OdbcConnection vs. MySqlConnection), each class derives from the same base class (DbConnection, in the case of connection objects) that implements identical interfaces (e.g., IDbConnection). Given this, you would be correct to assume that after you learn how to work with one data provider, the remaining providers prove quite straightforward.

■ **Note** When you refer to a connection object under ADO.NET, you're actually referring to a specific DbConnection-derived type; there is no class literally named *Connection*. The same idea holds true for a *command object*, *data adapter object*, and so forth. As a naming convention, the objects in a specific data provider are prefixed with the name of the related DBMS (e.g., SqlConnection, OracleConnection, and SqlDataReader).

Figure 21-2 shows the big picture behind ADO.NET data providers. Note how the diagram illustrates that the *Client Assembly* can literally be any type of .NET application: console program, Windows Forms application, WPF application, ASP.NET web page, WCF service, a .NET code library, and so on.

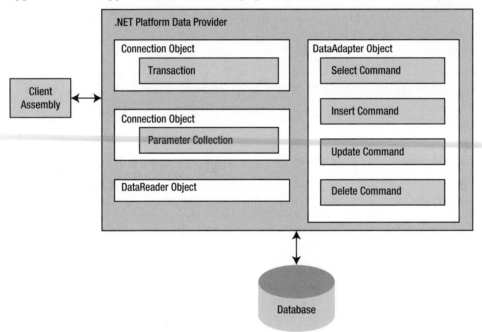

Figure 21-2. *ADO.NET data providers provide access to a given DBMS*

A data provider will supply you with other types beyond the objects shown in Figure 21-2; however, these core objects define a common baseline across all data providers.

The Microsoft-Supplied ADO.NET Data Providers

Microsoft's .NET distribution ships with numerous data providers, including a provider for Oracle, SQL Server, and OLE DB/ODBC-style connectivity. Table 21-2 documents the namespace and containing assembly for each Microsoft ADO.NET data provider.

Table 21-2. Microsoft ADO.NET Data Providers

Data Provider	Namespace	Assembly
OLE DB	System.Data.OleDb	System.Data.dll
Microsoft SQL Server	System.Data.SqlClient	System.Data.dll
Microsoft SQL Server Mobile	System.Data.SqlServerCe	System.Data.SqlServerCe.dll
ODBC	System.Data.Odbc	System.Data.dll

■ **Note** There is no specific data provider that maps directly to the Jet engine (and, therefore, Microsoft Access). If you want to interact with an Access data file, you can do so using the OLE DB or ODBC data provider.

The OLE DB data provider, which is composed of the types defined in the System.Data.OleDb namespace, allows you to access data located in any data store that supports the classic COM-based OLE DB protocol. You can use this provider to communicate with any OLE DB–compliant database simply by tweaking the Provider segment of your connection string.

However, the OLE DB provider interacts with various COM objects behind the scenes, which can affect the performance of your application. By and large, the OLE DB data provider is only useful if you interact with a DBMS that does not define a specific .NET data provider. However, given the fact that these days any DBMS worth its salt should have a custom ADO.NET data provider for download, you should consider System.Data.OleDb a legacy namespace that has little use in the .NET 4.5 world (this is even more the case with the advent of the data provider factory model introduced under .NET 2.0, which you will learn about shortly).

■ **Note** There is one case in which using the types of System.Data.OleDb is necessary: when you need to communicate with Microsoft SQL Server version 6.5 or earlier. The System.Data.SqlClient namespace can only communicate with Microsoft SQL Server version 7.0 or higher.

The Microsoft SQL Server data provider offers direct access to Microsoft SQL Server data stores— and *only* SQL Server data stores (version 7.0 and greater). The System.Data.SqlClient namespace contains the types used by the SQL Server provider and offers the same basic functionality as the OLE DB provider. The key difference is that the SQL Server provider bypasses the OLE DB layer and gives numerous performance benefits. The Microsoft SQL Server data provider also allows you to gain access to the unique features of this particular DBMS.

The remaining Microsoft-supplied providers (System.Data.Odbc and System.Data.SqlClientCe) provide access to ODBC connections, and the SQL Server Mobile edition DBMS (commonly used by handheld devices, such as Windows Mobile). The ODBC types defined within the `System.Data.Odbc` namespace are typically only useful if you need to communicate with a given DBMS for which there is no custom .NET data provider. This is true because ODBC is a widespread model that provides access to a number of data stores.

A Word Regarding System.Data.OracleClient.dll

Earlier versions of the .NET platform shipped with an assembly named `System.Data.OracleClient.dll`, which as the name suggests, offered a data provider to communicate with Oracle databases. As of .NET 4.0, however, this assembly has been marked as obsolete and will eventually be deprecated.

At first glance, this might cause you to fear that ADO.NET is slowly becoming focused squarely on Microsoft-centric data stores; however, this is not the case. Oracle provides its own custom .NET assembly, which follows the same overall design guidelines as the data providers provided by Microsoft. If you need to obtain this .NET assembly, you can visit the downloads section of Oracle's web site, found here:

`www.oracle.com/technetwork/indexes/downloads/index.html`

Obtaining Third-Party ADO.NET Data Providers

In addition to the data providers that ship from Microsoft (as well as Oracle's custom .NET library), numerous third-party data providers exist for various open source and commercial databases. While you will most likely be able to obtain an ADO.NET data provider directly from the database vendor, you should be aware of the following site:

`www.sqlsummit.com/DataProv.htm`

This web site is one of many sites that document each known ADO.NET data provider and provide links for more information and downloads. Here, you will find numerous ADO.NET providers, including SQLite, IBM DB2, MySQL, PostgreSQL, TurboDB, Sybase, and many others.

Given the large number of ADO.NET data providers, the examples in this book will use the Microsoft SQL Server data provider (`System.Data.SqlClient.dll`). Recall that this provider allows you to communicate with Microsoft SQL Server version 7.0 and higher, including SQL Server Express Edition. If you intend to use ADO.NET to interact with another DBMS, you should have no problem doing so once you understand the material presented in the pages that follow.

Additional ADO.NET Namespaces

In addition to the .NET namespaces that define the types of a specific data provider, the .NET base class libraries provide a number of additional ADO.NET-centric namespaces, some of which you can see in Table 21-3 (again, Chapter 23 will address the assemblies and namespaces specific to Entity Framework).

Table 21-3. Select Additional ADO.NET-Centric Namespaces

Namespace	Meaning in Life
Microsoft.SqlServer.Server	This namespace provides types that facilitate CLR and SQL Server 2005 and later integration services.
System.Data	This namespace defines the core ADO.NET types used by all data providers, including common interfaces and numerous types that represent the disconnected layer (e.g., DataSet and DataTable).
System.Data.Common	This namespace contains types shared between all ADO.NET data providers, including the common abstract base classes.
System.Data.Sql	This namespace contains types that allow you to discover Microsoft SQL Server instances installed on the current local network.
System.Data.SqlTypes	This namespace contains native data types used by Microsoft SQL Server. You can always use the corresponding CLR data types, but the SqlTypes are optimized to work with SQL Server (e.g., if your SQL Server database contains an integer value, you can represent it using either int or SqlTypes.SqlInt32).

Note that this chapter does not examine every type within every ADO.NET namespace (that task would require a large book all by itself); however, it is quite important that you understand the types within the System.Data namespace.

The Types of the System.Data Namespace

Of all the ADO.NET namespaces, System.Data is the lowest common denominator. You cannot build ADO.NET applications without specifying this namespace in your data access applications. This namespace contains types that are shared among all ADO.NET data providers, regardless of the underlying data store. In addition to a number of database-centric exceptions (e.g., NoNullAllowedException, RowNotInTableException, and MissingPrimaryKeyException), System.Data contains types that represent various database primitives (e.g., tables, rows, columns, and constraints), as well as the common interfaces implemented by data provider objects. Table 21-4 lists some of the core types you should be aware of.

Table 21-4. Core Members of the System.Data Namespace

Type	Meaning in Life
Constraint	Represents a constraint for a given DataColumn object.
DataColumn	Represents a single column within a DataTable object.
DataRelation	Represents a parent/child relationship between two DataTable objects.
DataRow	Represents a single row within a DataTable object.
DataSet	Represents an in-memory cache of data consisting of any number of interrelated DataTable objects.
DataTable	Represents a tabular block of in-memory data.
DataTableReader	Allows you to treat a DataTable as a fire-hose cursor (forward only, read-only data access).
DataView	Represents a customized view of a DataTable for sorting, filtering, searching, editing, and navigation.
IDataAdapter	Defines the core behavior of a data adapter object.
IDataParameter	Defines the core behavior of a parameter object.
IDataReader	Defines the core behavior of a data reader object.
IDbCommand	Defines the core behavior of a command object.
IDbDataAdapter	Extends IDataAdapter to provide additional functionality of a data adapter object.
IDbTransaction	Defines the core behavior of a transaction object.

You use the vast majority of the classes within System.Data when programming against the disconnected layer of ADO.NET. In the next chapter, you will get to know the details of the DataSet and its related cohorts (e.g., DataTable, DataRelation, and DataRow) and how to use them (and a related data adapter) to represent and manipulate client-side copies of remote data.

However, your next task is to examine the core interfaces of System.Data at a high level; this can help you understand the common functionality offered by any data provider. You will also learn specific details throughout this chapter; however, for now it's best to focus on the overall behavior of each interface type.

The Role of the IDbConnection Interface

The IDbConnection type is implemented by a data provider's *connection object*. This interface defines a set of members used to configure a connection to a specific data store. It also allows you to obtain the data provider's transaction object. Here is the formal definition of IDbConnection:

```
public interface IDbConnection : IDisposable
{
  string ConnectionString { get; set; }
  int ConnectionTimeout { get; }
  string Database { get; }
  ConnectionState State { get; }

  IDbTransaction BeginTransaction();
  IDbTransaction BeginTransaction(IsolationLevel il);
  void ChangeDatabase(string databaseName);
  void Close();
  IDbCommand CreateCommand();
  void Open();
}
```

■ **Note** Like many other types in the .NET base class libraries, the Close() method is functionally equivalent to calling the Dispose() method directly or indirectly within C# by using scope (see Chapter 13).

The Role of the IDbTransaction Interface

The overloaded BeginTransaction() method defined by IDbConnection provides access to the provider's *transaction object*. You can use the members defined by IDbTransaction to interact programmatically with a transactional session and the underlying data store.

```
public interface IDbTransaction : IDisposable
{
  IDbConnection Connection { get; }
  IsolationLevel IsolationLevel { get; }

  void Commit();
  void Rollback();
}
```

The Role of the IDbCommand Interface

Next up is the IDbCommand interface, which will be implemented by a data provider's *command object*. Like other data access object models, command objects allow programmatic manipulation of SQL statements, stored procedures, and parameterized queries. Command objects also provide access to the data provider's data reader type through the overloaded ExecuteReader() method.

```
public interface IDbCommand : IDisposable
{
  string CommandText { get; set; }
  int CommandTimeout { get; set; }
  CommandType CommandType { get; set; }
  IDbConnection Connection { get; set; }
  IDataParameterCollection Parameters { get; }
  IDbTransaction Transaction { get; set; }
  UpdateRowSource UpdatedRowSource { get; set; }

  void Cancel();
  IDbDataParameter CreateParameter();
  int ExecuteNonQuery();
  IDataReader ExecuteReader();
  IDataReader ExecuteReader(CommandBehavior behavior);
  object ExecuteScalar();
  void Prepare();
}
```

The Role of the IDbDataParameter and IDataParameter Interfaces

Notice that the Parameters property of IDbCommand returns a strongly typed collection that implements IDataParameterCollection. This interface provides access to a set of IDbDataParameter-compliant class types (e.g., parameter objects).

```
public interface IDbDataParameter : IDataParameter
{
  byte Precision { get; set; }
  byte Scale { get; set; }
  int Size { get; set; }
}
```

IDbDataParameter extends the IDataParameter interface to obtain the following additional behaviors:

```
public interface IDataParameter
{
  DbType DbType { get; set; }
  ParameterDirection Direction { get; set; }
  bool IsNullable { get; }
  string ParameterName { get; set; }
  string SourceColumn { get; set; }
  DataRowVersion SourceVersion { get; set; }
  object Value { get; set; }
}
```

As you will see, the functionality of the IDbDataParameter and IDataParameter interfaces allows you to represent parameters within a SQL command (including stored procedures) through specific ADO.NET parameter objects, rather than through hard-coded string literals.

The Role of the IDbDataAdapter and IDataAdapter Interfaces

You use *data adapters* to push and pull DataSets to and from a given data store. The IDbDataAdapter interface defines the following set of properties that you can use to maintain the SQL statements for the related select, insert, update, and delete operations:

```
public interface IDbDataAdapter : IDataAdapter
{
  IDbCommand DeleteCommand { get; set; }
  IDbCommand InsertCommand { get; set; }
  IDbCommand SelectCommand { get; set; }
  IDbCommand UpdateCommand { get; set; }
}
```

In addition to these four properties, an ADO.NET data adapter also picks up the behavior defined in the base interface, IDataAdapter. This interface defines the key function of a data adapter type: the ability to transfer DataSets between the caller and underlying data store using the Fill() and Update() methods. The IDataAdapter interface also allows you to map database column names to more user-friendly display names with the TableMappings property.

```
public interface IDataAdapter
{
  MissingMappingAction MissingMappingAction { get; set; }
  MissingSchemaAction MissingSchemaAction { get; set; }
  ITableMappingCollection TableMappings { get; }

  int Fill(DataSet dataSet);
  DataTable[] FillSchema(DataSet dataSet, SchemaType schemaType);
  IDataParameter[] GetFillParameters();
  int Update(DataSet dataSet);
}
```

The Role of the IDataReader and IDataRecord Interfaces

The next key interface to be aware of is IDataReader, which represents the common behaviors supported by a given data reader object. When you obtain an IDataReader-compatible type from an ADO.NET data provider, you can iterate over the result set in a forward-only, read-only manner.

```
public interface IDataReader : IDisposable, IDataRecord
{
  int Depth { get; }
  bool IsClosed { get; }
  int RecordsAffected { get; }

  void Close();
  DataTable GetSchemaTable();
  bool NextResult();
  bool Read();
}
```

Finally, IDataReader extends IDataRecord, which defines many members that allow you to extract a strongly typed value from the stream, rather than casting the generic System.Object retrieved from the data reader's overloaded indexer method. Here is a partial listing of the various GetXXX() methods defined by IDataRecord (see the .NET Framework 4.5 SDK documentation for a complete listing):

```
public interface IDataRecord
{
  int FieldCount { get; }
  object this[ string name ] { get; }
  object this[ int i ] { get; }
  bool GetBoolean(int i);
  byte GetByte(int i);
  char GetChar(int i);
  DateTime GetDateTime(int i);
  decimal GetDecimal(int i);
  float GetFloat(int i);
  short GetInt16(int i);
  int GetInt32(int i);
  long GetInt64(int i);
...
  bool IsDBNull(int i);
}
```

■ **Note** You can use the IDataReader.IsDBNull() method to discover programmatically whether a specified field is set to null before obtaining a value from the data reader (to avoid triggering a runtime exception). Also recall that C# supports nullable data types (see Chapter 4), which are ideal for interacting with data columns that could be null in the database table.

Abstracting Data Providers Using Interfaces

At this point, you should have a better idea of the common functionality found among all .NET data providers. Recall that even though the exact names of the implementing types will differ among data providers, you can program against these types in a similar manner—that's the beauty of interface-based polymorphism. For example, if you define a method that takes an IDbConnection parameter, you can pass in any ADO.NET connection object, like so:

```
public static void OpenConnection(IDbConnection cn)
{
  // Open the incoming connection for the caller.
  cn.Open();
}
```

■ **Note** Interfaces are not strictly required; you can achieve the same level of abstraction using abstract base classes (such as DbConnection) as parameters or return values.

The same holds true for member return values. For example, consider the following simple C# Console Application project (named MyConnectionFactory), which allows you to obtain a specific connection object based on the value of a custom enumeration. For diagnostic purposes, you simply print out the underlying connection object using reflection services, and then enter the following code:

```csharp
using System;
...

// Need these to get definitions of common interfaces,
// and various connection objects for our test.
using System.Data;
using System.Data.SqlClient;
using System.Data.Odbc;
using System.Data.OleDb;

namespace MyConnectionFactory
{
  // A list of possible providers.
  enum DataProvider
  { SqlServer, OleDb, Odbc, None }

  class Program
  {
    static void Main(string[] args)
    {
      Console.WriteLine("**** Very Simple Connection Factory *****\n");

      // Get a specific connection.
      IDbConnection myCn = GetConnection(DataProvider.SqlServer);
      Console.WriteLine("Your connection is a {0}", myCn.GetType().Name);

      // Open, use and close connection...

      Console.ReadLine();
    }

    // This method returns a specific connection object
    // based on the value of a DataProvider enum.
    static IDbConnection GetConnection(DataProvider dp)
    {
      IDbConnection conn = null;
      switch (dp)
      {
        case DataProvider.SqlServer:
          conn = new SqlConnection();
          break;
        case DataProvider.OleDb:
          conn = new OleDbConnection();
          break;
        case DataProvider.Odbc:
          conn = new OdbcConnection();
          break;
```

```
    }
    return conn;
  }
 }
}
```

The benefit of working with the general interfaces of System.Data (or for that matter, the abstract base classes of System.Data.Common) is that you have a much better chance of building a flexible code base that can evolve over time. For example, today you might be building an application that targets Microsoft SQL Server; however, it's possible your company could switch to a different database months down the road. If you build a solution that hard-codes the MS SQL Server–specific types of System.Data.SqlClient, you would obviously need to edit, recompile, and redeploy the assembly should the back-end database management system change.

Increasing Flexibility Using Application Configuration Files

To increase the flexibility of your ADO.NET applications, you could incorporate a client-side *.config file that uses custom key/value pairs within the <appSettings> element. Recall from Chapter 14 that you can obtain the custom data stored within a *.config file programmatically by using types within the System.Configuration namespace. For example, assume you have specified a data provider value within a configuration file, as in this example:

```
<configuration>
  <appSettings>
    <!-- This key value maps to one of our enum values. -->
    <add key="provider" value="SqlServer"/>
  </appSettings>
</configuration>
```

With this, you could update Main() to obtain the underlying data provider programmatically. Doing this essentially builds a *connection object factory* that allows you to change the provider, but without requiring you to recompile your code base (you simply change the *.config file). Here are the relevant updates to Main():

```
static void Main(string[] args)
{
  Console.WriteLine("**** Very Simple Connection Factory *****\n");

  // Read the provider key.
  string dataProvString = ConfigurationManager.AppSettings["provider"];

  // Transform string to enum.
  DataProvider dp = DataProvider.None;
  if(Enum.IsDefined(typeof(DataProvider), dataProvString))
    dp = (DataProvider)Enum.Parse(typeof(DataProvider), dataProvString);
  else
    Console.WriteLine("Sorry, no provider exists!");

  // Get a specific connection.
  IDbConnection myCn = GetConnection(dp);
  if(myCn != null)
    Console.WriteLine("Your connection is a {0}", myCn.GetType().Name);
```

```
  // Open, use, and close connection...

  Console.ReadLine();
}
```

■ **Note** To use the `ConfigurationManager` type, be sure to set a reference to the `System.Configuration.dll` assembly and import the `System.Configuration` namespace.

At this point, you have authored some ADO.NET code that allows you to specify the underlying connection dynamically. One obvious problem, however, is that this abstraction is only used within the `MyConnectionFactory.exe` application. If you were to rework this example within a .NET code library (e.g., `MyConnectionFactory.dll`), you would be able to build any number of clients that could obtain various connection objects using layers of abstraction.

However, obtaining a connection object is only one aspect of working with ADO.NET. To make a worthwhile data provider factory library, you would also have to account for command objects, data readers, data adapters, transaction objects, and other data-centric types. Building such a code library would not necessarily be difficult, but it would require a considerable amount of code and time.

Since the release of .NET 2.0, the kind folks in Redmond have built this exact functionality directly into the .NET base class libraries. You will examine this formal API in just a moment; however, first you need to create a custom database to use throughout this chapter (and for many chapters to come).

■ **Source Code** You can find the MyConnectionFactory project under the Chapter 21 subdirectory.

Creating the AutoLot Database

As you work through this chapter, you will execute queries against a simple SQL Server test database named `AutoLot`. In keeping with the automotive theme used throughout this book, this database will contain three interrelated tables (`Inventory`, `Orders`, and `Customers`) that contain various bits of data representing order information for a fictional automobile sales company.

The assumption in this book is that you have a copy of Microsoft SQL Server (7.0 or higher) or a copy of Microsoft SQL Server Express Edition. If you do not have either of these, please go here to download a copy:

`www.microsoft.com/sqlserver/en/us/editions/2012-editions/express.aspx`

This lightweight database server is perfect for your needs in this book: it is free, it provides a GUI front end (the SQL Server Management Tool) to create and administer your databases, and it integrates with Visual Studio/Visual C# Express Edition.

To illustrate the last point, the remainder of this section will walk you through the construction of the `AutoLot` database using Visual Studio. If you use Visual C# Express, you can perform operations similar to what is explained here by using the Database Explorer window (you can load this from the View ➤ Other Windows menu option).

■ **Note** You will use the AutoLot database throughout the rest of this book.

Creating the Inventory Table

To begin building your testing database, launch Visual Studio and open the Server Explorer using the View menu of the IDE. Next, right-click the Data Connections node and select the Create New SQL Server Database menu option (see Figure 21-3).

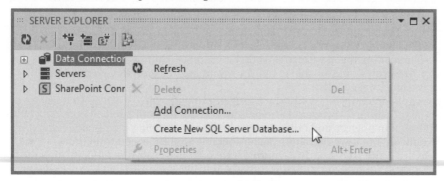

Figure 21-3. *Creating a new SQL Server database within Visual Studio*

In the resulting dialog box, you will need to enter a value into the Server name text area, which represents the machine where the database will be created. If you have installed a full version of Microsoft SQL Server on your machine, enter (local) to represent that you will create the database on your current local machine. However, if you are using Microsoft SQL Express, enter (local)\SQLEXPRESS. Name your new database AutoLot (Windows Authentication should be fine; see Figure 21-4).

Figure 21-4. Creating a new SQL Server Express database with Visual Studio

At this point, the AutoLot database is empty of any database objects (e.g., tables, stored procedures, and so on). To insert a new database table, right-click the Tables node and select Add New Table (see Figure 21-5).

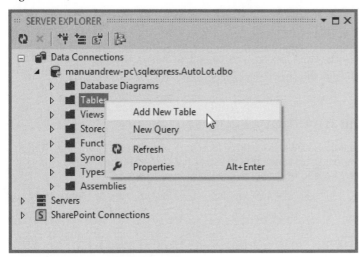

Figure 21-5. Adding the Inventory table

Use the table editor to add four columns (CarID, Make, Color, and PetName) all of type varchar(50). Ensure that the CarID column has been set to the Primary Key (do this by right-clicking the CarID row and selecting Set Primary Key). Also, notice that all columns but CarID can be assigned null values. Figure 21-6 shows the final table settings (you don't need to change anything in the Column Properties editor, but you should notice the data types for each column).

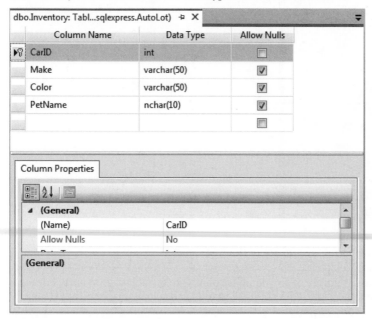

Figure 21-6. Designing the Inventory table

After you have created the table schema, save your work (via the Ctrl+S command or via File ➤ Save). When you do so, you will be asked what to name your new table. In this case, name the table Inventory. After you are done, you should see the Inventory table under the Tables node of the Server Explorer.

Adding Test Records to the Inventory Table

To add records to your first table, right-click the Inventory table icon and select Show Table Data. Enter a handful of new automobiles of your choosing (to make it interesting, be sure to include some cars that have identical colors and makes). Figure 21-7 shows one possible list of inventory.

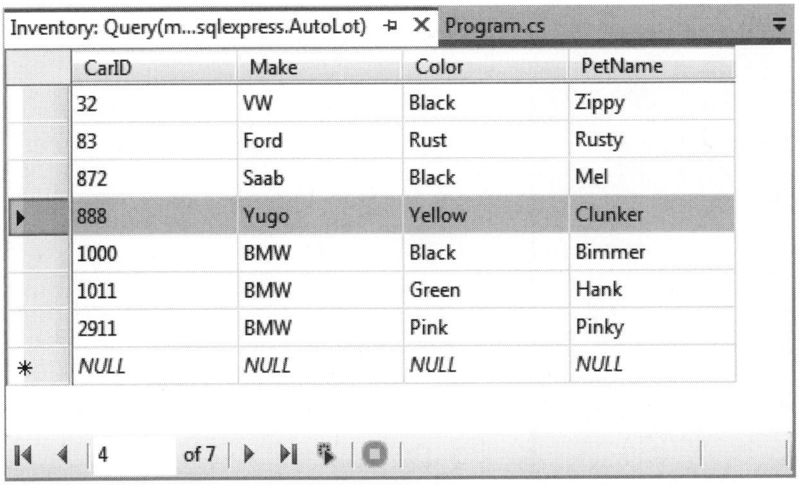

CarID	Make	Color	PetName
32	VW	Black	Zippy
83	Ford	Rust	Rusty
872	Saab	Black	Mel
888	Yugo	Yellow	Clunker
1000	BMW	Black	Bimmer
1011	BMW	Green	Hank
2911	BMW	Pink	Pinky
NULL	NULL	NULL	NULL

Figure 21-7. Populating the Inventory table

Authoring the GetPetName() Stored Procedure

Later in this chapter, you will learn how to use ADO.NET to invoke stored procedures. As you might already know, stored procedures are routines stored within a particular database that operate often on table data to yield a return value. You will add a single stored procedure that will return an automobile's pet name, based on the supplied `CarID` value. To do so, right-click the Stored Procedures node of the `AutoLot` database within the Server Explorer and select Add New Stored Procedure. Enter the following in the editor that pops up:

```
CREATE PROCEDURE GetPetName
@carID int,
@petName char(10) output
AS
SELECT @petName = PetName from Inventory where CarID = @carID
```

■ **Note** Stored procedures do not have to return data using output parameters, as shown here; however, doing things this way sets the stage for talking about the `Direction` property of the `SqlParameter`, which we will cover later in this chapter.

When you save your procedure, it will automatically be named `GetPetName`, based on your `CREATE PROCEDURE` statement (note that Visual Studio automatically changes the SQL Script to "`ALTER PROCEDURE`..." as soon as you save it for the first time). After you do this, you should see your new stored procedure within the Server Explorer (see Figure 21-8).

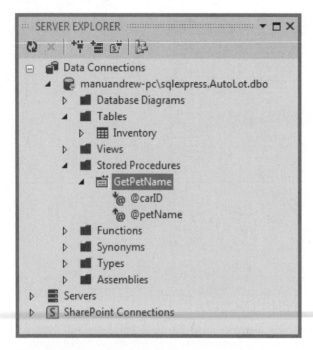

Figure 21-8. The GetPetName stored procedure

Creating the Customers and Orders Tables

The AutoLot database will have two additional tables: Customers and Orders. The Customers table (as the name suggests) will contain a list of customers and will be represented by three columns: CustID (which should be set as the primary key), FirstName, and LastName. You can create the Customers table by following the same steps you used to create the Inventory table; be sure to create the Customers table using the schema shown in Figure 21-9.

dbo.Table2: Table(...sqlexpress.AutoLot)*
dbo.GetPetName: St...qlexpress.AutoLot)
Column Name
Data Type
Allow Nulls
CustID
int
FirstName
varchar(50)
LastName
varchar(50)
Column Properties
(General)
(Name)
CustID
Allow Nulls
No
Data Type
int
Default Value or Binding
Table Designer
(General)

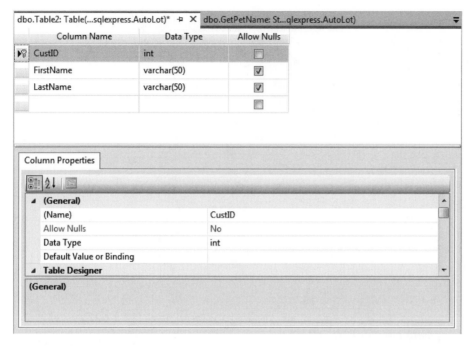

Figure 21-9. Designing the `Customers` *table*

After you save and name your table, add a handful of customer records (see Figure 21-10).

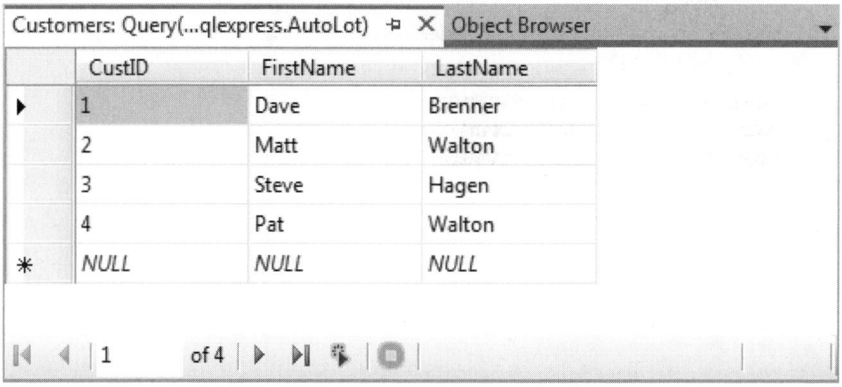

Customers: Query(...qlexpress.AutoLot)
Object Browser
CustID
FirstName
LastName
1
Dave
Brenner
2
Matt
Walton
3
Steve
Hagen
4
Pat
Walton
NULL
NULL
NULL
1
of 4

Figure 21-10. Populating the `Customers` *table*

You will use your final table, `Orders`, to represent the automobile a given customer is interested in purchasing. Do this by mapping `OrderID` values to `CarID`/`CustID` values. Figure 21-11 shows the structure of your final table (again, note that `OrderID` is the primary key).

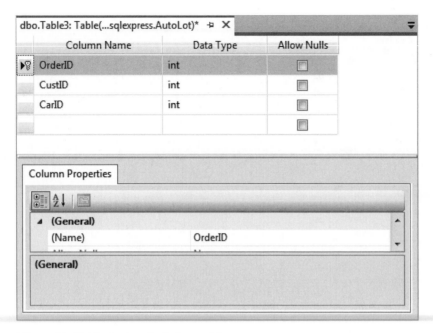

Figure 21-11. *Designing the Orders table*

Now add data to your Orders table. Assuming that the OrderID value begins at 1000, select a unique CarID for each CustID value (see Figure 21-12).

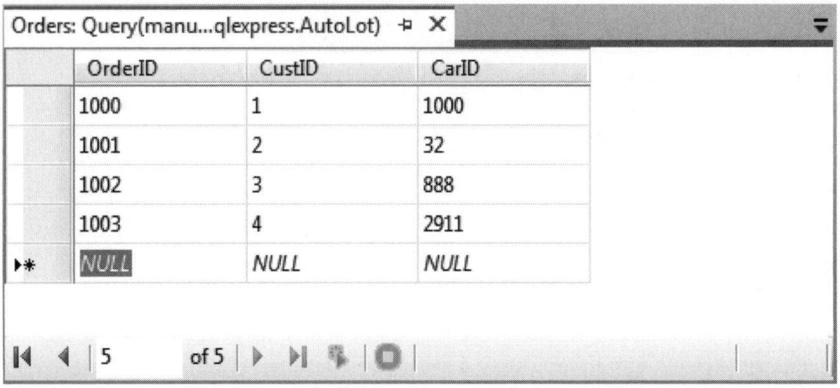

OrderID	CustID	CarID
1000	1	1000
1001	2	32
1002	3	888
1003	4	2911
NULL	NULL	NULL

Orders: Query(manu...qlexpress.AutoLot) ⊣ ✕

◄◄ ◄ | 5   of 5 | ► ►I

Figure 21-12. *Populating the Orders table*

For example, the entries used in this text indicate that Dave Brenner (CustID = 1) is interested in the black BMW (CarID = 1000), while Pat Walton (CustID = 4) has her eye on the pink BMW (CarID = 2911).

Visually Creating Table Relationships

The final task is to establish parent/child table relationships between the Customers, Orders, and Inventory tables. It is easy to do this using Visual Studio because you can elect to insert a new database diagram at design time. Using the Server Explorer, right-click the Database Diagrams node of the AutoLot database and select the Add New Diagram menu option. This brings up a dialog box that lets you pick which tables to add to the diagram. Be sure to select each of the tables from the AutoLot database (see Figure 21-13).

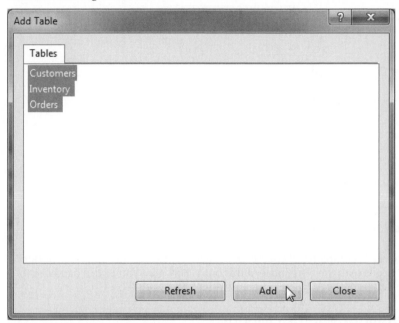

Figure 21-13. Selecting tables for your diagram

You can begin establishing the relationships between the tables by clicking the CarID key of the Inventory table and (while holding down the mouse button) drag it to the CarID field of the Orders table. Release the mouse and accept all defaults from the resulting dialog boxes. Now repeat the same process to map the CustID key of the Customers table to the CustID field of the Orders table. After you do this, you should see the class dialog box shown in Figure 21-14.

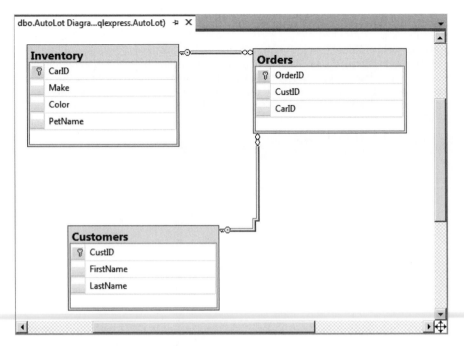

Figure 21-14. *The interconnected Orders, Inventory, and Customers tables*

With this, the AutoLot database is complete! Of course, this is a far cry from a real-world corporate database, but it will serve your needs over the remainder of this book. Now that you have a database to test with, you can dive into the details of the ADO.NET data provider factory model.

The ADO.NET Data Provider Factory Model

The .NET data provider factory pattern allows you to build a single code base using generalized data access types. Furthermore, using application configuration files (and the <connectionStrings> subelement), you can obtain providers and connection strings declaratively, without the need to recompile or redeploy the assembly that uses the ADO.NET APIs.

To understand the data provider factory implementation, recall from Table 21-1 that the classes within a data provider each derive from the same base classes defined within the System.Data.Common namespace.

- DbCommand: The abstract base class for all command classes

- DbConnection: The abstract base class for all connection classes

- DbDataAdapter: The abstract base class for all data adapter classes

- DbDataReader: The abstract base class for all data reader classes

- DbParameter: The abstract base class for all parameter classes

- DbTransaction: The abstract base class for all transaction classes

Each of the Microsoft-supplied data providers contains a class type that derives from System.Data.Common.DbProviderFactory. This base class defines several methods that retrieve provider-specific data objects. Here is a snapshot of the relevant members of DbProviderFactory:

```
public abstract class DbProviderFactory
{
...
  public virtual DbCommand CreateCommand();
  public virtual DbCommandBuilder CreateCommandBuilder();
  public virtual DbConnection CreateConnection();
  public virtual DbConnectionStringBuilder CreateConnectionStringBuilder();
  public virtual DbDataAdapter CreateDataAdapter();
  public virtual DbDataSourceEnumerator CreateDataSourceEnumerator();
  public virtual DbParameter CreateParameter();
}
```

To obtain the DbProviderFactory-derived type for your data provider, the System.Data.Common namespace provides a class type named DbProviderFactories (note the plural in this type's name). You can use the static GetFactory() method to obtain the specific DbProviderFactory object of the specified data provider; do this by specifying a string name that represents the .NET namespace containing the provider's functionality, like so:

```
static void Main(string[] args)
{
  // Get the factory for the SQL data provider.
  DbProviderFactory sqlFactory =
    DbProviderFactories.GetFactory("System.Data.SqlClient");
...
}
```

Of course, rather than obtaining a factory using a hard-coded string literal, you could instead read in this information from a client-side *.config file (much like the earlier MyConnectionFactory example). You will learn how to do this shortly; for the moment, you can obtain the associated provider-specific data objects (e.g., connections, commands, and data readers) once you have obtained the factory for your data provider.

■ **Note** For all practical purposes, you can regard the argument sent to DbProviderFactories.GetFactory() as the name of the data provider's .NET namespace. In reality, the machine.config value uses this string value to load the correct library dynamically from the Global Assembly Cache.

A Complete Data Provider Factory Example

For a complete example, you can create a new C# Console Application (named DataProviderFactory) that prints out the automobile inventory of the AutoLot database. For this initial example, you will hard-code the data access logic directly within the DataProviderFactory.exe assembly (to keep things simple for the time being). However, when you begin to dig into the details of the ADO.NET programming model, you will isolate your data logic to a specific .NET code library that you will use for the remainder of this book.

Begin by adding a reference to the System.Configuration.dll assembly and importing the System.Configuration namespace. Next, insert an App.config file to the current project and define an empty <appSettings> element. Add a new key-named provider that maps to the namespace name of the data provider you want to obtain (System.Data.SqlClient). Also, define a connection string that represents a connection to the AutoLot database (on the local instance of SQL Server Express).

```xml
<?xml version="1.0" encoding="utf-8" ?>
<configuration>
 <appSettings>
  <!-- Which provider? -->
  <add key="provider" value="System.Data.SqlClient" />

  <!-- Which connection string? -->
  <add key="cnStr" value= "Data Source=(local)\SQLEXPRESS;
          Initial Catalog=AutoLot;Integrated Security=True"/>
 </appSettings>
</configuration>
```

■ **Note** You will learn about connection strings in more detail momentarily; however, if you select your AutoLot database icon within the Server Explorer, you can copy-and-paste the correct connection string from the Connection String property of the Visual Studio Properties window.

Now that you have a proper *.config file, you can read in the provider and cnStr values using the ConfigurationManager.AppSettings indexer. The provider value will be passed to DbProviderFactories.GetFactory() to obtain the data provider–specific factory type. You will use the cnStr value to set the ConnectionString property of the DbConnection-derived type.

Assuming you have imported the System.Data and System.Data.Common namespaces, you can update your Main() method like this:

```csharp
static void Main(string[] args)
{
  Console.WriteLine("***** Fun with Data Provider Factories *****\n");

  // Get Connection string/provider from *.config.
  string dp =
    ConfigurationManager.AppSettings["provider"];
  string cnStr =
    ConfigurationManager.AppSettings["cnStr"];

  // Get the factory provider.
  DbProviderFactory df = DbProviderFactories.GetFactory(dp);

  // Now get the connection object.
  using (DbConnection cn = df.CreateConnection())
  {
    Console.WriteLine("Your connection object is a: {0}", cn.GetType().Name);
    cn.ConnectionString = cnStr;
```

```
    cn.Open();

    // Make command object.
    DbCommand cmd = df.CreateCommand();
    Console.WriteLine("Your command object is a: {0}", cmd.GetType().Name);
    cmd.Connection = cn;
    cmd.CommandText = "Select * From Inventory";

    // Print out data with data reader.
    using (DbDataReader dr = cmd.ExecuteReader())
    {
      Console.WriteLine("Your data reader object is a: {0}", dr.GetType().Name);

      Console.WriteLine("\n***** Current Inventory *****");
      while (dr.Read())
        Console.WriteLine("-> Car #{0} is a {1}.",
          dr["CarID"], dr["Make"].ToString());
    }
  }
  Console.ReadLine();
}
```

Notice that, for diagnostic purposes, you use reflection services to print the name of the underlying connection, command, and data reader. If you run this application, you will find the following current data in the Inventory table of the AutoLot database printed to the console:

```
***** Fun with Data Provider Factories *****

Your connection object is a: SqlConnection
Your command object is a: SqlCommand
Your data reader object is a: SqlDataReader

***** Current Inventory *****
-> Car #32 is a VW.
-> Car #83 is a Ford.
-> Car #872 is a Saab.
-> Car #888 is a Yugo.
-> Car #1000 is a BMW.
-> Car #1011 is a BMW.
-> Car #2911 is a BMW.
```

Now change the *.config file to specify System.Data.OleDb as the data provider (and update your connection string with a Provider segment), like so:

```
<configuration>
 <appSettings>
  <!-- Which provider? -->
  <add key="provider" value="System.Data.OleDb" />

  <!-- Which connection string? -->
  <add key="cnStr" value=
```

```
      "Provider=SQLOLEDB;Data Source=(local)\SQLEXPRESS;
        Integrated Security=SSPI;Initial Catalog=AutoLot"/>
  </appSettings>
</configuration>
```

Doing this indicates that the System.Data.OleDb types are used behind the scenes, and gives the following output:

```
***** Fun with Data Provider Factories *****

Your connection object is a: OleDbConnection
Your command object is a: OleDbCommand
Your data reader object is a: OleDbDataReader

***** Current Inventory *****
-> Car #32 is a VW.
-> Car #83 is a Ford.
-> Car #872 is a Saab.
-> Car #888 is a Yugo.
-> Car #1000 is a BMW.
-> Car #1011 is a BMW.
-> Car #2911 is a BMW.
```

Of course, based on your experience with ADO.NET, you might be a bit unsure exactly what the connection, command, and data reader objects actually *do*. Don't sweat the details for the time being (quite a few pages remain in this chapter, after all!). At this point, it's enough to know that you can use the ADO.NET data provider factory model to build a single code base that can consume various data providers in a declarative manner.

A Potential Drawback with the Data Provider Factory Model

Although this is a powerful model, you must make sure that the code base uses only types and methods common to all providers through the members of the abstract base classes. Therefore, when authoring your code base, you are limited to the members exposed by DbConnection, DbCommand, and the other types of the System.Data.Common namespace.

Given this, you might find that this generalized approach prevents you from directly accessing some of the bells and whistles of a particular DBMS. If you must be able to invoke specific members of the underlying provider (e.g., SqlConnection), you can do so using an explicit cast, as in this example:

```
using (DbConnection cn = df.CreateConnection())
{
  Console.WriteLine("Your connection object is a: {0}", cn.GetType().Name);
  cn.ConnectionString = cnStr;
  cn.Open();

  if (cn is SqlConnection)
  {
    // Print out which version of SQL Server is used.
    Console.WriteLine(((SqlConnection)cn).ServerVersion);
  }
```

```
...
}
```

When doing this, however, your code base becomes a bit harder to maintain (and less flexible) because you must add a number of runtime checks. Nevertheless, if you need to build data access libraries in the most flexible way possible, the data provider factory model provides a great mechanism for doing so.

The <connectionStrings> Element

Currently, your connection string data is in the <appSettings> element of your *.config file. Application configuration files can define an element named <connectionStrings>. Within this element, you can define any number of name/value pairs that can be programmatically read into memory using the ConfigurationManager.ConnectionStrings indexer. One advantage of this approach (as opposed to using the <appSettings> element and the ConfigurationManager.AppSettings indexer) is that you can define multiple connection strings for a single application in a consistent manner.

To see this in action, update your current App.config file as follows (note that each connection string is documented using the name and connectionString attributes rather than the key and value attributes you find in <appSettings>):

```
<configuration>
 <appSettings>
  <!-- Which provider? -->
  <add key="provider" value="System.Data.SqlClient" />
 </appSettings>

 <!-- Here are the connection strings. -->
 <connectionStrings>
  <add name ="AutoLotSqlProvider" connectionString =
       "Data Source=(local)\SQLEXPRESS;
        Integrated Security=SSPI;Initial Catalog=AutoLot"/>

  <add name ="AutoLotOleDbProvider" connectionString =
       "Provider=SQLOLEDB;Data Source=(local)\SQLEXPRESS;
        Integrated Security=SSPI;Initial Catalog=AutoLot"/>
 </connectionStrings>
</configuration>
```

You can now update your Main() method as follows:

```
static void Main(string[] args)
{
  Console.WriteLine("***** Fun with Data Provider Factories *****\n");
  string dp =
    ConfigurationManager.AppSettings["provider"];
  string cnStr =
    ConfigurationManager.ConnectionStrings["AutoLotSqlProvider"].ConnectionString;
...
}
```

At this point, you have an application that can display the results of the Inventory table of the AutoLot database using a neutral code base. Offloading the provider name and connection string to an external *.config file, means that the data provider factory model can dynamically load the correct provider in the background. With this first example behind you, you can now dive into the details of working with the connected layer of ADO.NET.

■ **Note** Now that you understand the role of ADO.NET data provider factories, the remaining examples in this book will focus on the task at hand by explicitly using the types within the System.Data.SqlClient namespace. If you use a different database management system (such as Oracle), you need to update your code base accordingly.

■ **Source Code** You can find the DataProviderFactory project under the Chapter 21 subdirectory.

Understanding the Connected Layer of ADO.NET

Recall that the *connected layer* of ADO.NET allows you to interact with a database using the connection, command, and data reader objects of your data provider. You have already used these objects in the previous DataProviderFactory application, and now you'll walk through the process again, this time using an expanded example. You need to perform the following steps when you want to connect to a database and read the records using a data reader object:

- Allocate, configure, and open your connection object.

- Allocate and configure a command object, specifying the connection object as a constructor argument or with the Connection property.

- Call ExecuteReader() on the configured command class.

- Process each record using the Read() method of the data reader.

To get the ball rolling, create a new Console Application named AutoLotDataReader and import the System.Data and System.Data.SqlClient namespaces. Here is the complete code within Main() (analysis will follow):

```
class Program
{
  static void Main(string[] args)
  {
    Console.WriteLine("***** Fun with Data Readers *****\n");

    // Create and open a connection.
    using(SqlConnection cn = new SqlConnection())
    {
      cn.ConnectionString =
        @"Data Source=(local)\SQLEXPRESS;Integrated Security=SSPI;" +
          "Initial Catalog=AutoLot";
      cn.Open();
```

```
    // Create a SQL command object.
    string strSQL = "Select * From Inventory";
    SqlCommand myCommand = new SqlCommand(strSQL, cn);

    // Obtain a data reader a la ExecuteReader().
    using(SqlDataReader myDataReader = myCommand.ExecuteReader())
    {
      // Loop over the results.
      while (myDataReader.Read())
      {
        Console.WriteLine("-> Make: {0}, PetName: {1}, Color: {2}.",
                       myDataReader["Make"].ToString(),
                       myDataReader["PetName"].ToString(),
                       myDataReader["Color"].ToString());
      }
    }
  }
  Console.ReadLine();
  }
}
```

Working with Connection Objects

The first step to take when working with a data provider is to establish a session with the data source using the connection object (which, as you recall, derives from DbConnection). .NET connection objects are provided with a formatted *connection string*; this string contains a number of name/value pairs, separated by semicolons. You use this information to identify the name of the machine you want to connect to, required security settings, the name of the database on that machine, and other data provider–specific information.

As you can infer from the preceding code, the Initial Catalog name refers to the database you want to establish a session with. The Data Source name identifies the name of the machine that maintains the database. Here, (local) allows you to define a single token to specify the current local machine (regardless of the literal name of said machine), while the \SQLEXPRESS token informs the SQL Server provider that you are connecting to the default SQL Server Express edition installation (if you created AutoLot on a full version of Microsoft SQL Server on your local computer, specify Data Source=(local)).

Beyond this, you can supply any number of tokens that represent security credentials. Here, you set the Integrated Security to SSPI (equivalent to true), which uses the current Windows account credentials for user authentication.

■ **Note** Look up the ConnectionString property of your data provider's connection object in the .NET Framework 4.5 SDK documentation to learn more about each name/value pair for your specific DBMS.

After you establish your construction string, you can use a call to Open() to establish a connection with the DBMS. In addition to the ConnectionString, Open(), and Close() members, a connection object provides a number of members that let you configure additional settings regarding your connection, such as timeout settings and transactional information. Table 21-5 lists some (but not all) members of the DbConnection base class.

Table 21-5. Members of the DbConnection Type

Member	Meaning in Life
BeginTransaction()	You use this method to begin a database transaction.
ChangeDatabase()	You use this method to change the database on an open connection.
ConnectionTimeout	This read-only property returns the amount of time to wait while establishing a connection before terminating and generating an error (the default value is 15 seconds). If you would like to change the default, specify a Connect Timeout segment in the connection string (e.g., Connect Timeout=30).
Database	This read-only property gets the name of the database maintained by the connection object.
DataSource	This read-only property gets the location of the database maintained by the connection object.
GetSchema()	This method returns a DataTable object that contains schema information from the data source.
State	This read-only property gets the current state of the connection, which is represented by the ConnectionState enumeration.

The properties of the DbConnection type are typically read-only in nature and are only useful when you want to obtain the characteristics of a connection at runtime. When you need to override default settings, you must alter the construction string itself. For example, the connection string sets the connection timeout setting from 15 seconds to 30 seconds:

```
static void Main(string[] args)
{
  Console.WriteLine("***** Fun with Data Readers *****\n");

  using(SqlConnection cn = new SqlConnection())
  {
    cn.ConnectionString =
      @"Data Source=(local)\SQLEXPRESS;" +
      "Integrated Security=SSPI;Initial Catalog=AutoLot;Connect Timeout=30";
    cn.Open();

    // New helper function (see below).
    ShowConnectionStatus(cn);
...
}
```

In the preceding code, you pass your connection object as a parameter to a new static helper method in the Program class named ShowConnectionStatus(), which you implement as follows:

```
static void ShowConnectionStatus(SqlConnection cn)
{
  // Show various stats about current connection object.
  Console.WriteLine("***** Info about your connection *****");
  Console.WriteLine("Database location: {0}", cn.DataSource);
  Console.WriteLine("Database name: {0}", cn.Database);
  Console.WriteLine("Timeout: {0}", cn.ConnectionTimeout);
  Console.WriteLine("Connection state: {0}\n", cn.State.ToString());
}
```

While most of these properties are self-explanatory, the State property is worth special mention. You can assign this property any value of the ConnectionState enumeration, as seen here:

```
public enum ConnectionState
{
  Broken, Closed,
  Connecting, Executing,
  Fetching, Open
}
```

However, the only valid ConnectionState values are ConnectionState.Open and ConnectionState.Closed (the remaining members of this enum are reserved for future use). Also, it is always safe to close a connection where connection state is currently ConnectionState.Closed.

Working with ConnectionStringBuilder Objects

Working with connection strings programmatically can be cumbersome because they are often represented as string literals, which are difficult to maintain and error-prone at best. The Microsoft-supplied ADO.NET data providers support *connection string builder objects*, which allow you to establish the name/value pairs using strongly typed properties. Consider the following update to the current Main() method:

```
static void Main(string[] args)
{
  Console.WriteLine("***** Fun with Data Readers *****\n");

  // Create a connection string via the builder object.
  SqlConnectionStringBuilder cnStrBuilder =
    new SqlConnectionStringBuilder();
  cnStrBuilder.InitialCatalog = "AutoLot";
  cnStrBuilder.DataSource = @"(local)\SQLEXPRESS";
  cnStrBuilder.ConnectTimeout = 30;
  cnStrBuilder.IntegratedSecurity = true;

  using(SqlConnection cn = new SqlConnection())
  {
    cn.ConnectionString = cnStrBuilder.ConnectionString;
    cn.Open();
```

```
      ShowConnectionStatus(cn);
...
    }
    Console.ReadLine();
}
```

In this iteration, you create an instance of SqlConnectionStringBuilder, set the properties accordingly, and obtain the internal string using the ConnectionString property. Also note that you use the default constructor of the type. If you so choose, you can also create an instance of your data provider's connection string builder object by passing in an existing connection string as a starting point (this can be helpful when you read these values dynamically from an App.config file). Once you have hydrated the object with the initial string data, you can change specific name/value pairs using the related properties, as in this example:

```
static void Main(string[] args)
{
  Console.WriteLine("***** Fun with Data Readers *****\n");

  // Assume you really obtained the cnStr value from a *.config file.
  string cnStr = @"Data Source=(local)\SQLEXPRESS;" +
                  "Integrated Security=SSPI;Initial Catalog=AutoLot";

  SqlConnectionStringBuilder cnStrBuilder =
    new SqlConnectionStringBuilder(cnStr);

  // Change timeout value.
  cnStrBuilder.ConnectTimeout = 5;
...
}
```

Working with Command Objects

Now that you understand better the role of the connection object, the next order of business is to check out how to submit SQL queries to the database in question. The SqlCommand type (which derives from DbCommand) is an OO representation of a SQL query, table name, or stored procedure. You specify the type of command using the CommandType property, which can take any value from the CommandType enum, as seen here:

```
public enum CommandType
{
  StoredProcedure,
  TableDirect,
  Text  // Default value.
}
```

When you create a command object, you can establish the SQL query as a constructor parameter or directly by using the CommandText property. Also when you create a command object, you need to specify the connection you want to use. Again, you can do so as a constructor parameter or by using the Connection property. Consider this code snippet:

```
// Create command object via ctor args.
string strSQL = "Select * From Inventory";
SqlCommand myCommand = new SqlCommand(strSQL, cn);
```

```
// Create another command object via properties.
SqlCommand testCommand = new SqlCommand();
testCommand.Connection = cn;
testCommand.CommandText = strSQL;
```

Realize that, at this point, you have not literally submitted the SQL query to the AutoLot database, but instead prepared the state of the command object for future use. Table 21-6 highlights some additional members of the DbCommand type.

Table 21-6. Members of the DbCommand Type

Member	Meaning in Life
CommandTimeout	Gets or sets the time to wait while executing the command before terminating the attempt and generating an error. The default is 30 seconds.
Connection	Gets or sets the DbConnection used by this instance of the DbCommand.
Parameters	Gets the collection of DbParameter objects used for a parameterized query.
Cancel()	Cancels the execution of a command.
ExecuteReader()	Executes a SQL query and returns the data provider's DbDataReader object, which provides forward-only, read-only access for the result of the query.
ExecuteNonQuery()	Executes a SQL non-query (e.g., an insert, update, delete, or create table).
ExecuteScalar()	A lightweight version of the ExecuteReader() method that was designed specifically for singleton queries (e.g., obtaining a record count).
Prepare()	Creates a prepared (or compiled) version of the command on the data source. As you might know, a *prepared query* executes slightly faster and is useful when you need to execute the same query multiple times (typically with different parameters each time).

Working with Data Readers

After you establish the active connection and SQL command, the next step is to submit the query to the data source. As you might guess, you have a number of ways to do this. The DbDataReader type (which implements IDataReader) is the simplest and fastest way to obtain information from a data store. Recall that data readers represent a read-only, forward-only stream of data returned one record at a time. Given this, data readers are useful only when submitting SQL selection statements to the underlying data store.

Data readers are useful when you need to iterate over large amounts of data quickly and you do not need to maintain an in-memory representation. For example, if you request 20,000 records from a table to store in a text file, it would be rather memory-intensive to hold this information in a DataSet (because a DataSet holds the entire result of the query in memory at the same time).

A better approach is to create a data reader that spins over each record as rapidly as possible. Be aware, however, that data reader objects (unlike data adapter objects, which you'll examine later) maintain an open connection to their data source until you explicitly close the connection.

You obtain data reader objects from the command object using a call to ExecuteReader().The data reader represents the current record it has read from the database. The data reader has an indexer method (e.g, [ ] syntax in C#) that allows you to access a column in the current record. You can access the column either by name or by zero-based integer.

The following use of the data reader leverages the Read() method to determine when you have reached the end of your records (using a false return value). For each incoming record that you read from the database, you use the type indexer to print out the make, pet name, and color of each automobile. Also note that you call Close() as soon as you finish processing the records, which frees up the connection object.

```
static void Main(string[] args)
{
...
  // Obtain a data reader via ExecuteReader().
  using(SqlDataReader myDataReader = myCommand.ExecuteReader())
  {
    // Loop over the results.
    while (myDataReader.Read())
    {
      Console.WriteLine("-> Make: {0}, PetName: {1}, Color: {2}.",
        myDataReader["Make"].ToString(),
        myDataReader["PetName"].ToString(),
        myDataReader["Color"].ToString());
    }
  }
  Console.ReadLine();
}
```

In the preceding snippet, you overload the indexer of a data reader object to take either a string (representing the name of the column) or an int (representing the column's ordinal position). Thus, you can clean up the current reader logic (and avoid hard-coded string names) with the following update (note the use of the FieldCount property):

```
while (myDataReader.Read())
{
  Console.WriteLine("***** Record *****");
  for (int i = 0; i < myDataReader.FieldCount; i++)
  {
    Console.WriteLine("{0} = {1} ",
      myDataReader.GetName(i),
      myDataReader.GetValue(i).ToString());
  }
  Console.WriteLine();
}
```

If you compile and run your project at this point, you should see a list of all automobiles in the Inventory table of the AutoLot database. The following output shows the initial few records from my own version of AutoLot:

```
***** Fun with Data Readers *****

***** Info about your connection *****
Database location: (local)\SQLEXPRESS
Database name: AutoLot
Timeout: 30
Connection state: Open

***** Record *****
CarID = 83
Make = Ford
Color = Rust
PetName = Rusty

***** Record *****
CarID = 107
Make = Ford
Color = Red
PetName = Snake
```

Obtaining Multiple Result Sets Using a Data Reader

Data reader objects can obtain multiple result sets using a single command object. For example, if you want to obtain all rows from the Inventory table, as well as all rows from the Customers table, you can specify both SQL select statements using a semicolon delimiter, like so:

```
string strSQL = "Select * From Inventory;Select * from Customers";
```

After you obtain the data reader, you can iterate over each result set using the NextResult() method. Note that you are always returned the first result set automatically. Thus, if you want to read over the rows of each table, you can build the following iteration construct:

```
do
{
  while (myDataReader.Read())
  {
    Console.WriteLine("***** Record *****");
    for (int i = 0; i < myDataReader.FieldCount; i++)
    {
      Console.WriteLine("{0} = {1}",
        myDataReader.GetName(i),
        myDataReader.GetValue(i).ToString());
    }
    Console.WriteLine();
  }
} while (myDataReader.NextResult());
```

At this point, you should be more aware of the functionality data reader objects bring to the table. Always remember that a data reader can only process SQL Select statements; you cannot use them to modify an existing database table using Insert, Update, or Delete requests. Modifying an existing database requires additional investigation of command objects.

■ **Source Code** You can find the AutoLotDataReader project under the Chapter 21 subdirectory.

Building a Reusable Data Access Library

The ExecuteReader() method extracts a data reader object that allows you to examine the results of a SQL Select statement using a forward-only, read-only flow of information. However, when you want to submit SQL statements that result in the modification of a given table (or any other non-query SQL statement, such as creating tables or granting permissions), you call the ExecuteNonQuery() method of your command object. This single method performs inserts, updates, and deletes based on the format of your command text.

■ **Note** Technically speaking, a *nonquery* is a SQL statement that does not return a result set. Thus, Select statements are queries, while Insert, Update, and Delete statements are not. Given this, ExecuteNonQuery() returns an int that represents the number of rows affected, not a new set of records.

Next, you will learn how to modify an existing database using nothing more than a call to ExecuteNonQuery(); your next goal is to build a custom data access library that can encapsulate the process of operating upon the AutoLot database. In a production-level environment, your ADO.NET logic will almost always be isolated to a .NET *.dll assembly for one simple reason: code reuse! The first examples of this chapter have not done so, simply so you can keep focused on the task at hand; however, it would be a waste of time to author the *same* connection logic, the *same* data reading logic, and the *same* command logic for every application that needs to interact with the AutoLot database.

Isolating data access logic to a .NET code library means that multiple applications using any sort of front end (e.g., console based, desktop based, or web based) can reference the library at hand in a language-independent manner. Thus, if you author your data library using C#, other developers can build a UI in the .NET language of their choice.

In this chapter, your data library (AutoLotDAL.dll) will contain a single namespace (AutoLotConnectedLayer) that interacts with AutoLot using the connected types of ADO.NET. In the next chapter, you will add a new namespace (AutoLotDisconnectionLayer) to this same *.dll that contains types to communicate with AutoLot using the disconnected layer. Multiple applications will take advantage of this library throughout the remainder of this book.

Begin by creating a new C# Class Library project named AutoLotDAL (short for *AutoLot Data Access Layer*) and renaming your initial C# code file to AutoLotConnDAL.cs. Next, rename your namespace scope to AutoLotConnectedLayer and change the name of your initial class to InventoryDAL; this class will define various members to interact with the Inventory table of the AutoLot database. Finally, import the following .NET namespaces:

```
using System;
...

// You will use the SQL server
// provider; however, it would also be
// permissible to use the ADO.NET
```

```
// factory pattern for greater flexibility.
using System.Data;
using System.Data.SqlClient;

namespace AutoLotConnectedLayer
{
  public class InventoryDAL
  {
  }
}
```

■ **Note** You might recall from Chapter 13 that when objects use types that manage raw resources (e.g., a database connection), it is a good practice to implement IDisposable and author a proper finalizer. In a production environment, classes such as InventoryDAL would do the same; however, you won't do that here, so you can stay focused on the particulars of ADO.NET.

Adding the Connection Logic

The first task you must attend to is to define some methods that allow the caller to connect to and disconnect from the data source using a valid connection string. You will hard-code your AutoLotDAL.dll assembly to use of the types of System.Data.SqlClient, so you need to define a private member variable of SqlConnection that is allocated at the time the InventoryDAL object is created. Also, define a method named OpenConnection() and another named CloseConnection() to interact with this member variable.

```
public class InventoryDAL
{
  // This member will be used by all methods.
  private SqlConnection sqlCn = null;

  public void OpenConnection(string connectionString)
  {
    sqlCn = new SqlConnection();
    sqlCn.ConnectionString = connectionString;
    sqlCn.Open();
  }

  public void CloseConnection()
  {
    sqlCn.Close();
  }
}
```

For the sake of brevity, your InventoryDAL type will not test for possible exceptions, nor will it throw custom exceptions under various circumstances (e.g., a malformed connection string). If you were to build an industrial-strength data access library, you would absolutely want to use structured exception handling techniques to account for any runtime anomalies.

Adding the Insertion Logic

Inserting a new record into the Inventory table is as simple as formatting the SQL Insert statement (based on user input) and calling the ExecuteNonQuery() using your command object. You can see this in action by adding a public method to your InventoryDAL type named InsertAuto() that takes four parameters that map to the four columns of the Inventory table (CarID, Color, Make, and PetName). You use these arguments to format a string type to insert the new record. Finally, use your SqlConnection object to execute the SQL statement.

```
public void InsertAuto(int id, string color, string make, string petName)
{
    // Format and execute SQL statement.
    string sql = string.Format("Insert Into Inventory" +
        "(CarID, Make, Color, PetName) Values" +
        "('{0}', '{1}', '{2}', '{3}')", id, make, color, petName);

    // Execute using our connection.
    using(SqlCommand cmd = new SqlCommand(sql, this.sqlCn))
    {
        cmd.ExecuteNonQuery();
    }
}
```

This method is syntactically fine, but you could supply an overloaded version that allows the caller to pass in a strongly typed class that represents the data for the new row. Define the following new NewCar class, which represents a new row in the Inventory table:

```
public class NewCar
{
    public int CarID { get; set; }
    public string Color { get; set; }
    public string Make { get; set; }
    public string PetName { get; set; }
}
```

Now add the following version of InsertAuto() to your InventoryDAL class:

```
public void InsertAuto(NewCar car)
{
    // Format and execute SQL statement.
    string sql = string.Format("Insert Into Inventory" +
        "(CarID, Make, Color, PetName) Values" +
        "('{0}', '{1}', '{2}', '{3}')", car.CarID, car.Make, car.Color, car.PetName);

    // Execute using our connection.
    using (SqlCommand cmd = new SqlCommand(sql, this.sqlCn))
    {
        cmd.ExecuteNonQuery();
    }
}
```

Defining classes that represent records in a relational database is a common way to build a data access library. In fact, as you will see in Chapter 23, the ADO.NET Entity Framework automatically generates strongly typed classes that allow you to interact with database data. On a related note, the *disconnected layer* of ADO.NET (see Chapter 22) generates strongly typed DataSet objects to represent data from a given table in a relational database.

■ **Note** As you might know, building a SQL statement using string concatenation can be risky from a security point of view (think: SQL injection attacks). The preferred way to build command text is to use a parameterized query, which you will learn about shortly.

Adding the Deletion Logic

Deleting an existing record is as simple as inserting a new record. Unlike when you created the code for InsertAuto(), this time you will learn about an important try/catch scope that handles the possibility of attempting to delete a car that is currently on order for an individual in the Customers table. Add the following method to the InventoryDAL class type:

```
public void DeleteCar(int id)
{
  // Get ID of car to delete, then do so.
  string sql = string.Format("Delete from Inventory where CarID = '{0}'",
    id);
  using(SqlCommand cmd = new SqlCommand(sql, this.sqlCn))
  {
    try
    {
      cmd.ExecuteNonQuery();
    }
    catch(SqlException ex)
    {
      Exception error = new Exception("Sorry! That car is on order!", ex);
      throw error;
    }
  }
}
```

Adding the Update Logic

When it comes to the act of updating an existing record in the Inventory table, the first thing you must decide is what you want to allow the caller to change, whether it's the car's color, the pet name, the make, or all of the above. One way to give the caller complete flexibility is to define a method that takes a string type to represent any sort of SQL statement, but that is risky at best.

Ideally, you want to have a set of methods that allow the caller to update a record in a variety of ways. However, for this simple data access library, you will define a single method that allows the caller to update the pet name of a given automobile, like so:

```
public void UpdateCarPetName(int id, string newPetName)
{
  // Get ID of car to modify and new pet name.
  string sql = string.Format("Update Inventory Set PetName = '{0}' Where CarID = '{1}'",
```

```
      newPetName, id);

   using(SqlCommand cmd = new SqlCommand(sql, this.sqlCn))
   {
      cmd.ExecuteNonQuery();
   }
}
```

Adding the Selection Logic

Next, you need to add a selection method. As you saw earlier in this chapter, a data provider's data reader object allows for a selection of records using a read-only, forward-only server-side cursor. As you call the Read() method, you can process each record in a fitting manner. While this is all well and good, you need to contend with the issue of how to return these records to the calling tier of your application.

One approach would be to populate and return a multidimensional array (or other such return value, such as a generic List<NewCar> object) with the data obtained by the Read() method. Here is a second way to obtain data from the Inventory table that uses the latter approach:

```
public List<NewCar> GetAllInventoryAsList()
{
   // This will hold the records.
   List<NewCar> inv = new List<NewCar>();

   // Prep command object.
   string sql = "Select * From Inventory";
   using (SqlCommand cmd = new SqlCommand(sql, this.sqlCn))
   {
      SqlDataReader dr = cmd.ExecuteReader();
      while (dr.Read())
      {
         inv.Add(new NewCar
         {
            CarID = (int)dr["CarID"],
            Color = (string)dr["Color"],
            Make = (string)dr["Make"],
            PetName = (string)dr["PetName"]
         });
      }
      dr.Close();
   }
   return inv;
}
```

Still another approach is to return a System.Data.DataTable object, which is actually part of the disconnected layer of ADO.NET. You will find complete coverage of the disconnected layer in the next chapter; however, for the time being, you should understand that a DataTable is a class type that represents a tabular block of data (e.g., a grid on a spreadsheet).

Internally, the DataTable class represents data as a collection of rows and columns. While you can fill these collections programmatically, the DataTable type provides a method named Load() that automatically populates these collections using a data reader object! Consider the following methods, which return data from Inventory as a DataTable:

```
public DataTable GetAllInventoryAsDataTable()
{
  // This will hold the records.
  DataTable inv = new DataTable();

  // Prep command object.
  string sql = "Select * From Inventory";
  using(SqlCommand cmd = new SqlCommand(sql, this.sqlCn))
  {
    SqlDataReader dr = cmd.ExecuteReader();
    // Fill the DataTable with data from the reader and clean up.
    inv.Load(dr);
    dr.Close();
  }
  return inv;
}
```

Working with Parameterized Command Objects

Currently, the insert, update, and delete logic for the InventoryDAL type uses hard-coded string literals for each SQL query. As you might know, you can use a *parameterized query* to treat SQL parameters as objects, rather than as a simple blob of text. Treating SQL queries in a more object-oriented manner helps reduce the number of typos (given strongly typed properties); plus, parameterized queries typically execute much faster than a literal SQL string because they are parsed exactly once (rather than each time the SQL string is assigned to the CommandText property). Parameterized queries also help protect against SQL injection attacks (a well-known data access security issue).

To support parameterized queries, ADO.NET command objects maintain a collection of individual parameter objects. By default, this collection is empty, but you can insert any number of parameter objects that map to a *placeholder parameter* in the SQL query. When you want to associate a parameter within a SQL query to a member in the command object's parameters collection, you can prefix the SQL text parameter with the @ symbol (at least when using Microsoft SQL Server; not all DBMSs support this notation).

Specifying Parameters Using the DbParameter Type

Before you build a parameterized query, you need to familiarize yourself with the DbParameter type (which is the base class to a provider's specific parameter object). This class maintains a number of properties that allow you to configure the name, size, and data type of the parameter, as well as other characteristics, including the parameter's direction of travel. Table 21-7 describes some key properties of the DbParameter type.

Table 21-7. Key Members of the DbParameter Type

Property	Meaning in Life
DbType	Gets or sets the native data type of the parameter, represented as a CLR data type.
Direction	Gets or sets whether the parameter is input-only, output-only, bidirectional, or a return value parameter.

IsNullable	Gets or sets whether the parameter accepts null values.
ParameterName	Gets or sets the name of the DbParameter.
Size	Gets or sets the maximum parameter size of the data in bytes; this is only useful for textual data.
Value	Gets or sets the value of the parameter.

Now let's look at how to populate a command object's collection of DBParameter-compatible objects by reworking the following version of the InsertAuto() method to leverage parameter objects (you could perform a similar reworking for your remaining methods; however, that's not necessary for this example):

```
public void InsertAuto(int id, string color, string make, string petName)
{
  // Note the "placeholders" in the SQL query.
  string sql = string.Format("Insert Into Inventory" +
      "(CarID, Make, Color, PetName) Values" +
      "(@CarID, @Make, @Color, @PetName)");

  // This command will have internal parameters.
  using(SqlCommand cmd = new SqlCommand(sql, this.sqlCn))
  {
    // Fill params collection.
    SqlParameter param = new SqlParameter();
    param.ParameterName = "@CarID";
    param.Value = id;
    param.SqlDbType = SqlDbType.Int;
    cmd.Parameters.Add(param);

    param = new SqlParameter();
    param.ParameterName = "@Make";
    param.Value = make;
    param.SqlDbType = SqlDbType.Char;
    param.Size = 10;
    cmd.Parameters.Add(param);

    param = new SqlParameter();
    param.ParameterName = "@Color";
    param.Value = color;
    param.SqlDbType = SqlDbType.Char;
    param.Size = 10;
    cmd.Parameters.Add(param);

    param = new SqlParameter();
    param.ParameterName = "@PetName";
    param.Value = petName;
    param.SqlDbType = SqlDbType.Char;
    param.Size = 10;
```

```
    cmd.Parameters.Add(param);

    cmd.ExecuteNonQuery();
  }
}
```

Again, notice that your SQL query consists of four embedded placeholder symbols, each of which is prefixed with the @ token. You can use the SqlParameter type to map each placeholder using the ParameterName property and specify various details (e.g., its value, data type, and size) in a strongly typed matter. After each parameter object is hydrated, it is added to the command object's collection through a call to Add().

■ **Note** This example uses various properties to establish a parameter object. Note, however, that parameter objects support a number of overloaded constructors that allow you to set the values of various properties (which will result in a more compact code base). Also be aware that Visual Studio provides many graphical designers that will generate a good deal of this grungy parameter-centric code on your behalf (see Chapters 22 and 23).

While building a parameterized query often requires more code, the end result is a more convenient way to tweak SQL statements programmatically, as well as to achieve better overall performance. While you are free to use this technique whenever a SQL query is involved, parameterized queries prove most helpful when you want to trigger a stored procedure.

Executing a Stored Procedure

Recall that a *stored procedure* is a named block of SQL code stored in the database. You can construct stored procedures so they return a set of rows or scalar data types or do anything else that makes sense (e.g., insert, update, or delete); you can also have them take any number of optional parameters. The end result is a unit of work that behaves like a typical function, except that it is located on a data store rather than a binary business object. Currently, your AutoLot database defines a single stored procedure named GetPetName, which you formatted as follows:

```
GetPetName
@carID int,
@petName char(10) output
AS
SELECT @petName = PetName from Inventory where CarID = @carID
```

Now consider the following final method of the InventoryDAL type, which invokes your stored procedure:

```
public string LookUpPetName(int carID)
{
  string carPetName = string.Empty;

  // Establish name of stored proc.
  using (SqlCommand cmd = new SqlCommand("GetPetName", this.sqlCn))
  {
```

```
    cmd.CommandType = CommandType.StoredProcedure;

    // Input param.
    SqlParameter param = new SqlParameter();
    param.ParameterName = "@carID";
    param.SqlDbType = SqlDbType.Int;
    param.Value = carID;

    // The default direction is in fact Input, but to be clear:
    param.Direction = ParameterDirection.Input;
    cmd.Parameters.Add(param);

    // Output param.
    param = new SqlParameter();
    param.ParameterName = "@petName";
    param.SqlDbType = SqlDbType.Char;
    param.Size = 10;
    param.Direction = ParameterDirection.Output;
    cmd.Parameters.Add(param);

    // Execute the stored proc.
    cmd.ExecuteNonQuery();

    // Return output param.
    carPetName = (string)cmd.Parameters["@petName"].Value;
  }
  return carPetName;
}
```

One important aspect of invoking a stored procedure is to keep in mind that a command object can represent a SQL statement (the default) or the name of a stored procedure. When you want to inform a command object that it will be invoking a stored procedure, you pass in the name of the procedure (as a constructor argument or by using the CommandText property) and must set the CommandType property to the value CommandType.StoredProcedure (if you fail to do this, you will receive a runtime exception because the command object is expecting a SQL statement by default).

```
SqlCommand cmd = new SqlCommand("GetPetName", this.sqlCn);
cmd.CommandType = CommandType.StoredProcedure;
```

Next, notice that the Direction property of a parameter object allows you to specify the direction of travel for each parameter passed to the stored procedure (e.g., input parameter, output parameter, in/out parameter, or return value). As before, you add each parameter object to the command object's parameters collection.

```
// Input param.
SqlParameter param = new SqlParameter();
param.ParameterName = "@carID";
param.SqlDbType = SqlDbType.Int;
param.Value = carID;
param.Direction = ParameterDirection.Input;
cmd.Parameters.Add(param);
```

After the stored procedure completes with a call to ExecuteNonQuery(), you can obtain the value of the output parameter by investigating the command object's parameter collection and casting accordingly.

```
// Return output param.
carPetName = (string)cmd.Parameters["@petName"].Value;
```

At this point, your initial iteration of the AutoLotDAL.dll data access library is complete! You can use this assembly to build any sort of front end to display and edit your data (e.g., console based, desktop GUI, or an HTML-based web application). You have not yet examined how to build graphical user interfaces, so next you will test your data library from a new console application.

■ **Source Code** You can find the AutoLotDAL project under the Chapter 21 subdirectory.

Creating a Console UI–Based Front End

Create a new Console Application named AutoLotCUIClient. After you create your new project, be sure to add a reference to your AutoLotDAL.dll assembly, as well as System.Configuration.dll. Next, add the following using statements to your C# code file:

```
using AutoLotConnectedLayer;
using System.Configuration;
using System.Data;
```

Now insert a new App.config file into your project that contains a <connectionStrings> element, which you will use to connect to your instance of the AutoLot database, as in this example:

```
<configuration>
  <connectionStrings>
    <add name ="AutoLotSqlProvider" connectionString =
    "Data Source=(local)\SQLEXPRESS;
     Integrated Security=SSPI;Initial Catalog=AutoLot"/>
  </connectionStrings>
</configuration>
```

Implementing the Main() Method

The Main() method is responsible for prompting the user for a specific course of action and executing that request using a switch statement. This program allows the user to enter the following commands:

- I: Inserts a new record into the Inventory table.
- U: Updates an existing record in the Inventory table.
- D: Deletes an existing record from the Inventory table.
- L: Displays the current inventory using a data reader.
- S: Shows these options to the user.

- P: Looks up pet name from carID.

- Q: Quits the program.

Each possible option is handled by a unique static method within the Program class. The next snippet shows the complete implementation of Main(). Notice that each method invoked from the do/while loop (with the exception of the ShowInstructions() method) takes an InventoryDAL object as its sole parameter.

```
static void Main(string[] args)
{
  Console.WriteLine("***** The AutoLot Console UI *****\n");

  // Get connection string from App.config.
  string cnStr =
    ConfigurationManager.ConnectionStrings["AutoLotSqlProvider"].ConnectionString;
  bool userDone = false;
  string userCommand = "";

  // Create our InventoryDAL object.
  InventoryDAL invDAL = new InventoryDAL();
  invDAL.OpenConnection(cnStr);

  // Keep asking for input until user presses the Q key.
  try
  {
    ShowInstructions();
    do
    {
      Console.Write("\nPlease enter your command: ");
      userCommand = Console.ReadLine();
      Console.WriteLine();
      switch (userCommand.ToUpper())
      {
      case "I":
        InsertNewCar(invDAL);
        break;
      case "U":
        UpdateCarPetName(invDAL);
        break;
      case "D":
        DeleteCar(invDAL);
        break;
      case "L":
        ListInventory(invDAL);
        break;
      case "S":
        ShowInstructions();
        break;
      case "P":
        LookUpPetName(invDAL);
        break;
      case "Q":
```

```
            userDone = true;
            break;
         default:
            Console.WriteLine("Bad data!  Try again");
            break;
      }
   } while (!userDone);
   }
   catch (Exception ex)
   {
      Console.WriteLine(ex.Message);
   }
   finally
   {
      invDAL.CloseConnection();
   }
}
```

Implementing the ShowInstructions() Method

The ShowInstructions() method does what you would expect, as seen here:

```
private static void ShowInstructions()
{
   Console.WriteLine("I: Inserts a new car.");
   Console.WriteLine("U: Updates an existing car.");
   Console.WriteLine("D: Deletes an existing car.");
   Console.WriteLine("L: Lists current inventory.");
   Console.WriteLine("S: Shows these instructions.");
   Console.WriteLine("P: Looks up pet name.");
   Console.WriteLine("Q: Quits program.");
}
```

Implementing the ListInventory() Method

You could implement the ListInventory() method in either of two ways, based on how you constructed your data access library. Recall that the GetAllInventoryAsDataTable() method of InventoryDAL returns a DataTable object. You could implement this approach like this:

```
private static void ListInventory(InventoryDAL invDAL)
{
   // Get the list of inventory.
   DataTable dt = invDAL.GetAllInventoryAsDataTable();

   // Pass DataTable to helper function to display.
   DisplayTable(dt);
}
```

The DisplayTable() helper method displays the table data using the Rows and Columns properties of the incoming DataTable (again, you will learn the full details of the DataTable object the next chapter, so don't fret over the details):

```
private static void DisplayTable(DataTable dt)
{
  // Print out the column names.
  for (int curCol = 0; curCol < dt.Columns.Count; curCol++)
  {
    Console.Write(dt.Columns[curCol].ColumnName + "\t");
  }
  Console.WriteLine("\n---------------------------------");

  // Print the DataTable.
  for (int curRow = 0; curRow < dt.Rows.Count; curRow++)
  {
    for (int curCol = 0; curCol < dt.Columns.Count; curCol++)
    {
      Console.Write(dt.Rows[curRow][curCol].ToString() + "\t");
    }
    Console.WriteLine();
  }
}
```

If you would prefer to call the GetAllInventoryAsList() method of InventoryDAL, you could implement a method named ListInventoryViaList(), like so:

```
private static void ListInventoryViaList(InventoryDAL invDAL)
{
  // Get the list of inventory.
  List<NewCar> record = invDAL.GetAllInventoryAsList();

  foreach (NewCar c in record)
  {
    Console.WriteLine("CarID: {0}, Make: {1}, Color: {2}, PetName: {3}",
      c.CarID, c.Make, c.Color, c.PetName);
  }
}
```

Implementing the DeleteCar() Method

Deleting an existing automobile is as simple as asking the user for the ID of the car and passing this to the DeleteCar() method of the InventoryDAL type, as seen here:

```
private static void DeleteCar(InventoryDAL invDAL)
{
  // Get ID of car to delete.
  Console.Write("Enter ID of Car to delete: ");
  int id = int.Parse(Console.ReadLine());

  // Just in case you have a referential integrity
  // violation!
  try
  {
    invDAL.DeleteCar(id);
  }
  catch(Exception ex)
```

```
  {
    Console.WriteLine(ex.Message);
  }
}
```

Implementing the InsertNewCar() Method

Inserting a new record into the Inventory table is a simple matter of asking the user for the new bits of data (using Console.ReadLine() calls) and passing this data into the InsertAuto() method of InventoryDAL, like so:

```
private static void InsertNewCar(InventoryDAL invDAL)
{
  // First get the user data.
  int newCarID;
  string newCarColor, newCarMake, newCarPetName;

  Console.Write("Enter Car ID: ");
  newCarID = int.Parse(Console.ReadLine());

  Console.Write("Enter Car Color: ");
  newCarColor = Console.ReadLine();

  Console.Write("Enter Car Make: ");
  newCarMake = Console.ReadLine();

  Console.Write("Enter Pet Name: ");
  newCarPetName = Console.ReadLine();

  // Now pass to data access library.
  invDAL.InsertAuto(newCarID, newCarColor, newCarMake, newCarPetName);
}
```

Recall that you overloaded InsertAuto() to take a NewCar object, rather than a set of independent arguments. Thus, you could have implemented InsertNewCar() like this:

```
private static void InsertNewCar(InventoryDAL invDAL)
{
  // First get the user data.
...

  // Now pass to data access library.
  NewCar c = new NewCar { CarID = newCarID, Color = newCarColor,
                          Make = newCarMake, PetName = newCarPetName };
  invDAL.InsertAuto(c);
}
```

Implementing the UpdateCarPetName() Method

The following implementation of UpdateCarPetName() looks similar:

```
private static void UpdateCarPetName(InventoryDAL invDAL)
{
  // First get the user data.
  int carID;
  string newCarPetName;

  Console.Write("Enter Car ID: ");
  carID = int.Parse(Console.ReadLine());
  Console.Write("Enter New Pet Name: ");
  newCarPetName = Console.ReadLine();

  // Now pass to data access library.
  invDAL.UpdateCarPetName(carID, newCarPetName);
}
```

Implementing LookUpPetName()

Obtaining the pet name of a given automobile works similarly to the previous methods; this is so because the data access library encapsulates all of the lower-level ADO.NET calls.

```
private static void LookUpPetName(InventoryDAL invDAL)
{
  // Get ID of car to look up.
  Console.Write("Enter ID of Car to look up: ");
  int id = int.Parse(Console.ReadLine());
  Console.WriteLine("Petname of {0} is {1}.",
    id, invDAL.LookUpPetName(id).TrimEnd());
}
```

With this, your console-based front end is finished! It's time to run your program and test each method. Here is some partial output that tests the L, P, and Q commands:

```
***** The AutoLot Console UI *****

I: Inserts a new car.
U: Updates an existing car.
D: Deletes an existing car.
L: Lists current inventory.
S: Shows these instructions.
P: Looks up pet name.
Q: Quits program.

Please enter your command: L

CarID   Make    Color   PetName
----------------------------------
83      Ford    Rust    Rusty
107     Ford    Red     Snake
678     Yugo    Green   Clunker
904     VW      Black   Hank
1000    BMW     Black   Bimmer
```

```
1001    BMW     Tan     Daisy
1992    Saab    Pink    Pinkey

Please enter your command: P

Enter ID of Car to look up: 904
Petname of 904 is Hank.

Please enter your command: Q

Press any key to continue . . .
```

■ **Source Code** You can find the AutoLotCUIClient application under the Chapter 21 subdirectory.

Understanding Database Transactions

Let's wrap up this examination of the connected layer of ADO.NET by taking a look at the concept of a database transaction. Simply put, a *transaction* is a set of database operations that must either *all* work or *all* fail as a collective unit. As you might imagine, transactions are quite important to ensure that table data is safe, valid, and consistent.

Transactions are important when a database operation involves interacting with multiple tables or multiple stored procedures (or a combination of database atoms). The classic transaction example involves the process of transferring monetary funds between two bank accounts. For example, if you were to transfer $500.00 from your savings account into your checking account, the following steps should occur in a transactional manner:

- The bank should remove $500.00 from your savings account.

- The bank should add $500.00 to your checking account.

It would be an extremely bad thing if the money were removed from the savings account, but not transferred to the checking account (due to some error on the bank's part) because then you would be out $500.00! However, if these steps are wrapped up into a database transaction, the DBMS ensures that all related steps occur as a single unit. If any part of the transaction fails, the entire operation is *rolled back* to the original state. On the other hand, if all steps succeed, the transaction is *committed*.

■ **Note** You might be familiar with the acronym ACID from looking at transactional literature. This represents the four key properties of a prim-and-proper transaction: *Atomic* (all or nothing); *Consistent* (data remains stable throughout the transaction); *Isolated* (transactions do not step on each other's feet); and *Durable* (transactions are saved and logged).

It turns out that the .NET platform supports transactions in a variety of ways. This chapter will look at the transaction object of your ADO.NET data provider (SqlTransaction, in the case of System.Data.SqlClient). The .NET base class libraries also provide transactional support within numerous APIs, including the following:

- System.EnterpriseServices: This namespace (located in the System.EnterpriseServices.dll assembly) provides types that allow you to integrate with the COM+ runtime layer, including its support for distributed transactions.

- System.Transactions: This namespace (located in the System.Transactions.dll assembly) contains classes that allow you to write your own transactional applications and resource managers for a variety of services (e.g., MSMQ, ADO.NET, and COM+).

- *Windows Communication Foundation*: The WCF API provides services to facilitate transactions with various distributed binding classes.

- *Windows Workflow Foundations*: The WF API provides transactional support for workflow activities.

In addition to the baked-in transactional support found within the .NET base class libraries, it is also possible to use the SQL language of your database management system. For example, you could author a stored procedure that uses the BEGIN TRANSACTION, ROLLBACK, and COMMIT statements.

Key Members of an ADO.NET Transaction Object

While transactional-aware types exist throughout the base class libraries, you will focus on transaction objects found within an ADO.NET data provider, all of which derive from DBTransaction and implement the IDbTransaction interface. Recall from the beginning of this chapter that IDbTransaction defines a handful of members as follows:

```
public interface IDbTransaction : IDisposable
{
  IDbConnection Connection { get; }
  IsolationLevel IsolationLevel { get; }

  void Commit();
  void Rollback();
}
```

Notice the Connection property, which returns a reference to the connection object that initiated the current transaction (as you'll see, you obtain a transaction object from a given connection object). You call the Commit() method when each of your database operations have succeeded. Doing this causes each of the pending changes to be persisted in the data store. Conversely, you can call the Rollback() method in the event of a runtime exception, which informs the DMBS to disregard any pending changes, leaving the original data intact.

> ■ **Note** The IsolationLevel property of a transaction object allows you to specify how aggressively a transaction should be guarded against the activities of other parallel transactions. By default, transactions are isolated completely until committed. Consult the .NET Framework 4.5 SDK documentation for full details regarding the values of the IsolationLevel enumeration.

Beyond the members defined by the IDbTransaction interface, the SqlTransaction type defines an additional member named Save(), which allows you to define *save points*. This concept allows you to roll back a failed transaction up until a named point, rather than rolling back the entire transaction. Essentially, when you call Save() using a SqlTransaction object, you can specify a friendly string moniker. When you call Rollback(), you can specify this same moniker as an argument to perform an effective *partial rollback*. Calling Rollback() with no arguments causes all of the pending changes to be rolled back.

Adding a CreditRisks Table to the AutoLot Database

Now let's look at how you use ADO.NET transactions. Begin by using the Server Explorer of Visual Studio to add a new table named CreditRisks to the AutoLot database, which has the same exact columns as the Customers table you created earlier in this chapter: CustID, which is the primary key; FirstName; and LastName. As its name suggests, CreditRisks is where you banish the undesirable customers who fail a credit check (see Figure 21-15).

Figure 21-15. The interconnected Orders, Inventory, and Customers tables

Like the earlier savings-to-checking money transfer example, this example, where you move a risky customer from the Customers table into the CreditRisks table, should occur under the watchful eye of a transactional scope (after all, you will want to remember the ID and names of those who are not creditworthy). Specifically, you need to ensure that *either* you successfully delete the current credit risks from the Customers table and add them to the CreditRisks table, or you need to ensure that neither of these database operations occurs.

> ■ **Note** In a production environment, you would not need to build a whole new database table to capture high-risk customers; instead, you could add a Boolean column named IsCreditRisk to the existing Customers table. However, this new table lets you play with a simple transaction.

Adding a Transaction Method to InventoryDAL

Now let's look at how you work with ADO.NET transactions programmatically. Begin by opening the AutoLotDAL code library project you created earlier and add a new public method named ProcessCreditRisk() to the InventoryDAL class to deal with perceived a credit risks (note that this example avoids using a parameterized query to keep the implementation simple; however, you'd want use such a query for a production-level method).

```
// A new member of the InventoryDAL class.
public void ProcessCreditRisk(bool throwEx, int custID)
{
  // First, look up current name based on customer ID.
  string fName = string.Empty;
  string lName = string.Empty;
  SqlCommand cmdSelect = new SqlCommand(
    string.Format("Select * from Customers where CustID = {0}", custID), sqlCn);
  using (SqlDataReader dr = cmdSelect.ExecuteReader())
  {
    if(dr.HasRows)
    {
      dr.Read();
      fName = (string)dr["FirstName"];
      lName = (string)dr["LastName"];
    }
    else
      return;
  }

  // Create command objects that represent each step of the operation.
  SqlCommand cmdRemove = new SqlCommand(
    string.Format("Delete from Customers where CustID = {0}", custID), sqlCn);

  SqlCommand cmdInsert = new SqlCommand(string.Format("Insert Into CreditRisks" +
                "(CustID, FirstName, LastName) Values" +
                "({0}, '{1}', '{2}')", custID, fName, lName), sqlCn);

  // You will get this from the connection object.
  SqlTransaction tx = null;
  try
  {
    tx = sqlCn.BeginTransaction();

    // Enlist the commands into this transaction.
    cmdInsert.Transaction = tx;
    cmdRemove.Transaction = tx;

    // Execute the commands.
    cmdInsert.ExecuteNonQuery();
    cmdRemove.ExecuteNonQuery();

    // Simulate error.
    if (throwEx)
```

```
  {
    throw new Exception("Sorry! Database error! Tx failed...");
  }

  // Commit it!
  tx.Commit();
  }
  catch (Exception ex)
  {
    Console.WriteLine(ex.Message);
    // Any error will roll back transaction.
    tx.Rollback();
  }
}
```

Here, you use an incoming bool parameter to represent whether you will throw an arbitrary exception when you attempt to process the offending customer. This allows you to simulate an unforeseen circumstance that will cause the database transaction to fail. Obviously, you do this here only for illustrative purposes; a true database transaction method would not want to allow the caller to force the logic to fail on a whim!

Note that you use two SqlCommand objects to represent each step in the transaction you will kick off. After you obtain the customer's first and last name based on the incoming custID parameter, you can obtain a valid SqlTransaction object from the connection object using BeginTransaction(). Next, and most importantly, you must *enlist each command object* by assigning the Transaction property to the transaction object you have just obtained. If you fail to do so, the Insert/Delete logic will not be under a transactional context.

After you call ExecuteNonQuery() on each command, you throw an exception if (and only if) the value of the bool parameter is true. In this case, all pending database operations are rolled back. If you do not throw an exception, both steps will be committed to the database tables once you call Commit(). Now compile your modified AutoLotDAL project to ensure you do not have any typos.

Testing Your Database Transaction

You could update your previous AutoLotCUIClient application with a new option to invoke the ProcessCreditRisk() method; instead, however, you will create a new Console Application named AdoNetTransaction to accomplish this. Set a reference to your AutoLotDAL.dll assembly and import the AutoLotConnectedLayer namespace.

Next, open your Customers table for data entry by right-clicking the table icon from the Server Explorer and selecting Show Table Data. Now add the following new customer who will be the victim of a low credit score:

- CustID: 333
- FirstName: Homer
- LastName: Simpson

Finally, update your Main() method as follows:

```
static void Main(string[] args)
{
  Console.WriteLine("***** Simple Transaction Example *****\n");
```

```
// A simple way to allow the transaction to succeed or not.
bool throwEx = true;
string userAnswer = string.Empty;

Console.Write("Do you want to throw an exception (Y or N): ");
userAnswer = Console.ReadLine();
if (userAnswer.ToLower() == "n")
{
  throwEx = false;
}

InventoryDAL dal = new InventoryDAL();
dal.OpenConnection(@"Data Source=(local)\SQLEXPRESS;Integrated Security=SSPI;" +
  "Initial Catalog=AutoLot");

// Process customer 333.
dal.ProcessCreditRisk(throwEx, 333);

Console.WriteLine("Check CreditRisk table for results");
Console.ReadLine();
}
```

If you were to run your program and elect to throw an exception, you would find that Homer is *not* removed from the Customers table because the entire transaction has been rolled back. However, if you did not throw an exception, you would find that Customer ID 333 is no longer in the Customers table and has been placed in the CreditRisks table instead.

■ **Source Code** You can find the AdoNetTransaction project under the Chapter 21 subdirectory.

Summary

ADO.NET is the native data access technology of the .NET platform, and you can use it in three distinct manners: connected, disconnected, or through the Entity Framework. In this chapter, you examined the connected layer and learned the role of data providers, which are essentially concrete implementations of several abstract base classes (in the System.Data.Common namespace) and interface types (in the System.Data namespace). You also saw that it is possible to build a provider-neutral code base using the ADO.NET data provider factory model.

You also learned that you can use connection objects, transaction objects, command objects, and data reader objects of the connected layer to select, update, insert, and delete records. Also, recall that command objects support an internal parameter collection, which you can use to add some type safety to your SQL queries; these also prove quite helpful when triggering stored procedures.

CHAPTER 22

ADO.NET Part II: The Disconnected Layer

The previous chapter gave you a chance to examine the *connected layer* of ADO.NET, which allows you to submit SQL statements to a database using the connection, command, and data reader objects of your data provider. In this chapter, you will learn about the *disconnected layer* of ADO.NET. Using this facet of ADO.NET lets you model database data in memory, within the calling tier, by leveraging numerous members of the System.Data namespace (most notably, DataSet, DataTable, DataRow, DataColumn, DataView, and DataRelation). By doing so, you can provide the illusion that the calling tier is continuously connected to an external data source; the reality is that the caller is operating on a local copy of relational data.

While it is possible to use this *disconnected* aspect of ADO.NET without ever making a literal connection to a relational database, you will most often obtain populated DataSet objects using the data adapter object of your data provider. As you will see, data adapter objects function as a bridge between the client tier and a relational database. Using these objects, you can obtain DataSet objects, manipulate their contents, and send modified rows back for processing. The end result is a highly scalable data-centric .NET application.

This chapter will also illustrate some data-binding techniques, using the context of a Windows Forms GUI desktop application, and examine the role of a *strongly typed* DataSet. You will also update the AutoLotDAL.dll data library you created in Chapter 21 with a new namespace that uses the disconnected layer of ADO.NET. Last but not least, you will learn about the role of LINQ to DataSet, which allows you to apply LINQ queries to your in-memory data cache.

■ **Note** You will learn about various data-binding techniques for Windows Presentation Foundation and ASP.NET applications later in this book.

Understanding the Disconnected Layer of ADO.NET

As you saw in the previous chapter, working with the connected layer allows you to interact with a database using the primary connection, command, and data reader objects. You can use this handful of classes to select, insert, update, and delete records to your heart's content (as well as invoke stored procedures or perform other data operations [e.g., DDL to create table and DCL to grant permissions]). However, you have seen only part of the ADO.NET story. Recall that you can use the ADO.NET object model in a disconnected manner.

Using the disconnected layer, it is possible to model relational data using an in-memory object model. Far beyond simply modeling a tabular block of rows and columns, the types within System.Data allow you to represent table relationships, column constraints, primary keys, views, and other database primitives. After you model the data, you can apply filters, submit in-memory queries, and persist (or load) your data in XML and binary formats. You can do all of this without ever making a literal connection to a DBMS (hence the term, *disconnected layer*) by loading data from a local XML file or manually building a DataSet in code.

───

■ **Note** In Chapter 23, you will examine the ADO.NET Entity Framework, which builds upon the concepts found in the disconnected layer examined here.

───

You could use the disconnected types without ever connecting to a database, but you will typically still use connection and command objects. In addition, you will leverage a specific object, the *data adapter* (which extends the abstract DbDataAdapter class), to fetch and update data. Unlike the connected layer, data obtained with a data adapter is not processed using data reader objects. Rather, data adapter objects use DataSet objects (or more specifically, the DataTable objects in a DataSet) to move data between the caller and data source. The DataSet type is a container for any number of DataTable objects, each of which contains a collection of DataRow and DataColumn objects.

The data adapter object of your data provider handles the database connection automatically. In an effort to increase scalability, data adapters keep the connection open for the shortest amount of time possible. After the caller receives the DataSet object, the calling tier is completely disconnected from the database and left with a local copy of the remote data. The caller is free to insert, delete, or update rows from a given DataTable, but the physical database is not updated until the caller explicitly passes a DataTable in the DataSet to the data adapter for updating. In a nutshell, DataSets allow the clients to pretend they are always connected; however, they actually operate on an in-memory database (see Figure 22-1).

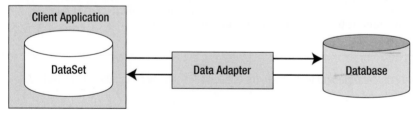

Figure 22-1. Data adapter objects move DataSets to and from the client tier

Given that the centerpiece of the disconnected layer is the DataSet class, the first task of this chapter is to learn how to manipulate a DataSet manually. Once you can do this, you will have no problem manipulating the contents of a DataSet retrieved from a data adapter object.

Understanding the Role of the DataSet

As noted previously, a DataSet is an in-memory representation of relational data. More specifically, a DataSet is a class type that internally maintains three strongly typed collections (see Figure 22-2).

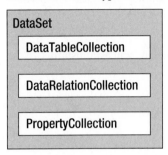

Figure 22-2. The anatomy of a DataSet

The Tables property of the DataSet allows you to access the DataTableCollection that contains the individual DataTables. Another important collection used by the DataSet is DataRelationCollection. Given that a DataSet is a disconnected version of a database schema, you can use it to represent the parent/child relationships programmatically between its tables. For example, you can create a relation between two tables to model a foreign key constraint using the DataRelation type. You can add this object to the DataRelationCollection with the Relations property. At this point, you can navigate between the related tables as you search for data. You will see how to do this later in the chapter.

The ExtendedProperties property provides access to the PropertyCollection object, which allows you to associate any extra information to the DataSet as name/value pairs. This information can be literally anything, even if it has no bearing on the database data itself. For example, you can associate your company's name to a DataSet, which can then function as in-memory metadata. Other examples of extended properties might include time stamps, an encrypted password that must be supplied to access the contents of the DataSet, a number representing a data refresh rate, and so forth.

■ **Note** The DataTable and DataColumn classes also support the ExtendedProperties property.

Key Properties of the DataSet

Before exploring too many other programmatic details, let's take a look at some core members of the DataSet. Table 22-1 describes some additional properties of interest beyond the Tables, Relations, and ExtendedProperties properties.

Table 22-1. Properties of the DataSet

Property	Meaning in Life
CaseSensitive	Indicates whether string comparisons in DataTable objects are case sensitive (or not). The default is false (string comparisons are not case sensitive by default).
DataSetName	Represents the friendly name of this DataSet. Typically, you establish this value as a constructor parameter.
EnforceConstraints	Gets or sets a value indicating whether constraint rules are followed when attempting any update operations (the default is true).
HasErrors	Gets a value indicating whether there are errors in any of the rows in any of the DataTables of the DataSet.
RemotingFormat	Allows you to define how the DataSet should serialize its content (binary or XML, which is the default).

Key Methods of the DataSet

The methods of the DataSet work in conjunction with some of the functionality provided by the aforementioned properties. In addition to interacting with XML streams, the DataSet provides methods that allow you to copy the contents of your DataSet, navigate between the internal tables, and establish the beginning and ending points of a batch of updates. Table 22-2 describes some core methods.

Table 22-2. Select Methods of the DataSet

Methods	Meaning in Life
AcceptChanges()	Commits all the changes made to this DataSet since it was loaded or the last time AcceptChanges() was called.
Clear()	Completely clears the DataSet data by removing every row in each DataTable.
Clone()	Clones the structure, but not the data, of the DataSet, including all DataTables, as well as all relations and any constraints.
Copy()	Copies both the structure and data for this DataSet.
GetChanges()	Returns a copy of the DataSet containing all changes made to it since it was last loaded or since AcceptChanges() was called. This method is overloaded, so that you can get just the new rows, just the modified rows, or just the deleted rows.

HasChanges()	Gets a value indicating whether the DataSet has changes, including new, deleted, or modified rows.
Merge()	Merges this DataSet with a specified DataSet.
ReadXml()	Allows you to define the structure of a DataSet object and populate it with data, based on XML schema and data read from a stream.
RejectChanges()	Rolls back all the changes made to this DataSet since it was created or since the last time AcceptChanges() was called.
WriteXml()	Allows you to write out the contents of a DataSet into a valid stream.

Building a DataSet

Now that you have a better understanding of the role of the DataSet (and some idea of what you can do with one), create a new Console Application named SimpleDataSet and import the System.Data namespace. Within the Main() method, define a new DataSet object that contains three extended properties that represent a time stamp, a unique identifier (represented as a System.Guid type), and your company's name, as follows:

```
static void Main(string[] args)
{
  Console.WriteLine("***** Fun with DataSets *****\n");

  // Create the DataSet object and add a few properties.
  DataSet carsInventoryDS = new DataSet("Car Inventory");

  carsInventoryDS.ExtendedProperties["TimeStamp"] = DateTime.Now;
  carsInventoryDS.ExtendedProperties["DataSetID"] = Guid.NewGuid();
  carsInventoryDS.ExtendedProperties["Company"] =
    "Mikko's Hot Tub Super Store";
  Console.ReadLine();
}
```

■ **Note** A GUID (a.k.a. a globally unique identifier) is a statically unique 128-bit number.

A DataSet object is not terribly interesting until you insert any number of DataTables. Therefore, the next task is to examine the internal composition of the DataTable, beginning with the DataColumn type.

Working with DataColumns

The DataColumn type represents a single column within a DataTable. Collectively speaking, the set of all DataColumn types bound to a given DataTable represents the foundation of a table's *schema* information. For example, if you were to model the Inventory table of the AutoLot database (see Chapter 21), you would create four DataColumns, one for each column (CarID, Make, Color, and PetName). After you create your DataColumn objects, you typically add them into the columns collection of the DataTable type (using the Columns property).

Based on your background, you might know that you can assign a given column in a database table a set of constraints (e.g., configured as a primary key, assigned a default value, or configured to contain read-only information). Also, every column in a table must map to an underlying data type. For example, the Inventory table's schema requires that the CarID column map to an integer, while Make, Color, and PetName map to an array of characters. The DataColumn class has numerous properties that allow you to configure precisely these things. Table 22-3 provides a rundown of some core properties.

Table 22-3. Properties of the DataColumn

Properties	Meaning in Life
AllowDBNull	You use this property to indicate whether a row can specify null values in this column. The default value is true.
AutoIncrement AutoIncrementSeed AutoIncrementStep	You use these properties to configure the autoincrement behavior for a given column. This can be helpful when you want to ensure unique values in a given DataColumn (such as a primary key). By default, a DataColumn does not support autoincrement behavior.
Caption	This property gets or sets the caption you want to display for this column. This allows you to define a user-friendly version of a literal database column name.
ColumnMapping	This property determines how a DataColumn is represented when a DataSet is saved as an XML document using the DataSet.WriteXml() method. You can specify that the data column should be written out as an XML element, an XML attribute, simple text content, or ignored altogether.
ColumnName	This property gets or sets the name of the column in the Columns collection (meaning how it is represented internally by the DataTable). If you do not set the ColumnName explicitly, the default values are Column with *(n+1)* numerical suffixes (e.g., Column1, Column2, and Column3).
DataType	This property defines the data type (e.g., Boolean, string, or float) stored in the column.
DefaultValue	This property gets or sets the default value assigned to this column when you insert new rows.

Expression	This property gets or sets the expression used to filter rows, calculate a column's value, or create an aggregate column.
Ordinal	This property gets the numerical position of the column in the Columns collection maintained by the DataTable.
ReadOnly	This property determines whether this column is read-only, once a row has been added to the table. The default is false.
Table	This property gets the DataTable that contains this DataColumn.
Unique	This property gets or sets a value indicating whether the values in each row of the column must be unique or if repeating values are permissible. If you assign a column a primary key constraint, then you must set the Unique property to true.

Building a DataColumn

To continue with the SimpleDataSet project (and illustrate the use of the DataColumn), assume you would like to model the columns of the Inventory table. Given that the CarID column will be the table's primary key, you will configure this DataColumn object as read-only, unique, and non-null (using the ReadOnly, Unique, and AllowDBNull properties). Next, update the Program class with a new method named FillDataSet(), which you use to build four DataColumn objects. Note this method takes a DataSet object as its only parameter.

```
static void FillDataSet(DataSet ds)
{
  // Create data columns that map to the
  // "real" columns in the Inventory table
  // of the AutoLot database.
  DataColumn carIDColumn = new DataColumn("CarID", typeof(int));
  carIDColumn.Caption = "Car ID";
  carIDColumn.ReadOnly = true;
  carIDColumn.AllowDBNull = false;
  carIDColumn.Unique = true;

  DataColumn carMakeColumn = new DataColumn("Make", typeof(string));
  DataColumn carColorColumn = new DataColumn("Color", typeof(string));
  DataColumn carPetNameColumn = new DataColumn("PetName", typeof(string));
  carPetNameColumn.Caption = "Pet Name";
}
```

Notice that when you configure the carIDColumn object, you assign a value to the Caption property. This property is helpful because it allows you to define a string value for display purposes, which can be distinct from the literal database table column name (column names in a literal database table are typically better suited for programming purposes [e.g., au_fname] than display purposes [e.g., Author First Name]). Here, you set the caption for the PetName column for the same reason, because *Pet Name* looks nicer than *PetName* to the end user.

Enabling Autoincrementing Fields

One aspect of the DataColumn you can choose to configure is its ability to *autoincrement*. You use an autoincrementing column to ensure that when a new row is added to a given table, the value of this column is assigned automatically, based on the current step of the increase. This can be helpful when you want to ensure that a column has no repeating values (e.g., a primary key).

You control this behavior using the AutoIncrement, AutoIncrementSeed, and AutoIncrementStep properties. You use the seed value to mark the starting value of the column; you use the step value to identify the number to add to the seed when incrementing. Consider the following update to the construction of the carIDColumn DataColumn:

```
static void FillDataSet(DataSet ds)
{
  DataColumn carIDColumn = new DataColumn("CarID", typeof(int));
  carIDColumn.ReadOnly = true;
  carIDColumn.Caption = "Car ID";
  carIDColumn.AllowDBNull = false;
  carIDColumn.Unique = true;
  carIDColumn.AutoIncrement = true;
  carIDColumn.AutoIncrementSeed = 0;
  carIDColumn.AutoIncrementStep = 1;
...
}
```

Here, you configure the carIDColumn object to ensure that, as rows are added to the respective table, the value for this column is incremented by 1. You set the seed at 0, so this column would be numbered 0, 1, 2, 3, and so forth.

Adding DataColumn Objects to a DataTable

The DataColumn type does not typically exist as a stand-alone entity; however, you do typically insert it into a related DataTable. For example, create a new DataTable object (fully detailed in a moment) and insert each DataColumn object in the columns collection using the Columns property, like so:

```
static void FillDataSet(DataSet ds):
{
...
  // Now add DataColumns to a DataTable.
  DataTable inventoryTable = new DataTable("Inventory");
  inventoryTable.Columns.AddRange(new DataColumn[]
    { carIDColumn, carMakeColumn, carColorColumn, carPetNameColumn });
}
```

At this point, the DataTable object contains four DataColumn objects that represent the schema of the in-memory Inventory table. However, the table is currently devoid of data, and the table is currently outside of the table collection maintained by the DataSet. You will deal with both of these shortcomings, beginning by populating the table with data using DataRow objects.

Working with DataRows

As you have seen, a collection of DataColumn objects represents the schema of a DataTable. In contrast, a collection of DataRow objects represents the actual data in the table. Thus, if you have 20 rows in the Inventory table of the AutoLot database, you can represent these records using 20 DataRow objects. Table 22-4 documents some (but not all) of the members of the DataRow type.

Table 22-4. *Key Members of the DataRow Type*

Members	Meaning in Life
HasErrors GetColumnsInError() GetColumnError() ClearErrors() RowError	The HasErrors property returns a Boolean value indicating whether there are errors in a DataRow. If so, you can use the GetColumnsInError() method to obtain the offending columns and GetColumnError()to obtain the error description. Similarly, you can use the ClearErrors() method to remove each error listing for the row. The RowError property allows you to configure a textual description of the error for a given row.
ItemArray	This property gets or sets all of the column values for this row using an array of objects.
RowState	You use this property to pinpoint the current *state* of the DataRow in the DataTable containing the DataRow, using values of the RowState enumeration (e.g., a row can be flagged as new, modified, unchanged, or deleted).
Table	You use this property to obtain a reference to the DataTable containing this DataRow.
AcceptChanges() RejectChanges()	These methods commit or reject all changes made to this row since the last time AcceptChanges() was called.
BeginEdit() EndEdit() CancelEdit()	These methods begin, end, or cancel an edit operation on a DataRow object.
Delete()	This method marks a row you want to remove when the AcceptChanges() method is called.
IsNull()	This method gets a value indicating whether the specified column contains a null value.

Working with a DataRow is a bit different from working with a DataColumn; you cannot create a direct instance of this type because there is no public constructor.

```
// Error! No public constructor!
DataRow r = new DataRow();
```

Instead, you obtain a new DataRow object from a given DataTable. For example, assume you want to insert two rows in the Inventory table. The DataTable.NewRow() method allows you to obtain the next slot in the table, at which point you can fill each column with new data using the type indexer. When doing so, you can specify either the string name assigned to the DataColumn or its (zero-based) ordinal position.

```
static void FillDataSet(DataSet ds)
{
...
  // Now add some rows to the Inventory table.
  DataRow carRow = inventoryTable.NewRow();
  carRow["Make"] = "BMW";
  carRow["Color"] = "Black";
  carRow["PetName"] = "Hamlet";
  inventoryTable.Rows.Add(carRow);

  carRow = inventoryTable.NewRow();
  // Column 0 is the autoincremented ID field,
  // so start at 1.
  carRow[1] = "Saab";
  carRow[2] = "Red";
  carRow[3] = "Sea Breeze";
  inventoryTable.Rows.Add(carRow);
}
```

■ **Note** If you pass the DataRow's indexer method an invalid column name or ordinal position, you will receive a runtime exception.

At this point, you have a single DataTable containing two rows. Of course, you can repeat this general process to create a number of DataTables to define the schema and data content. Before you insert the inventoryTable object into your DataSet object, you should check out the all-important RowState property.

Understanding the RowState Property

The RowState property is useful when you need to identify programmatically the set of all rows in a table that have changed from their original value, have been newly inserted, and so forth. You can assign this property any value from the DataRowState enumeration, as shown in Table 22-5.

Table 22-5. Values of the DataRowState Enumeration

Value	Meaning in Life
Added	The row has been added to a DataRowCollection, and AcceptChanges() has not been called.

Deleted	The row has been marked for deletion using the Delete() method of the DataRow, and AcceptChanges() has not been called.
Detached	The row has been created but is not part of any DataRowCollection. A DataRow is in this state immediately after it has been created, but before it is added to a collection. It is also in this state if it has been removed from a collection.
Modified	The row has been modified, and AcceptChanges() has not been called.
Unchanged	The row has not changed since AcceptChanges() was last called.

When you manipulate the rows of a given DataTable programmatically, the RowState property is set automatically. For example, add a new method to your Program class, which operates on a local DataRow object, printing out its row state along the way, like so:

```
private static void ManipulateDataRowState()
{
  // Create a temp DataTable for testing.
  DataTable temp = new DataTable("Temp");
  temp.Columns.Add(new DataColumn("TempColumn", typeof(int)));

  // RowState = Detached (i.e., not part of a DataTable yet).
  DataRow row = temp.NewRow();
  Console.WriteLine("After calling NewRow(): {0}", row.RowState);

  // RowState = Added.
  temp.Rows.Add(row);
  Console.WriteLine("After calling Rows.Add(): {0}", row.RowState);

  // RowState = Added.
  row["TempColumn"] = 10;
  Console.WriteLine("After first assignment: {0}", row.RowState);

  // RowState = Unchanged.
  temp.AcceptChanges();
  Console.WriteLine("After calling AcceptChanges: {0}", row.RowState);

  // RowState = Modified.
  row["TempColumn"] = 11;
  Console.WriteLine("After first assignment: {0}", row.RowState);

  // RowState = Deleted.
  temp.Rows[0].Delete();
  Console.WriteLine("After calling Delete: {0}", row.RowState);
}
```

The ADO.NET DataRow is smart enough to remember its current state of affairs. Given this, the owning DataTable is able to identify which rows have been added, updated, or deleted. This is a key feature of the DataSet because, when it comes time to send updated information to the data store, only the modified data is submitted.

Understanding the DataRowVersion Property

Beyond maintaining the current state of a row with the RowState property, a DataRow object maintains three possible versions of the data it contains using the DataRowVersion property. When a DataRow object is first constructed, it contains only a single copy of data, represented as the current version. However, as you programmatically manipulate a DataRow object (using various method calls), additional versions of the data spring to life. Specifically, you can set the DataRowVersion to any value of the related DataRowVersion enumeration (see Table 22-6).

Table 22-6. *Values of the DataRowVersion Enumeration*

Value	Meaning in Life
Current	This represents the current value of a row, even after changes have been made.
Default	This is the default version of DataRowState. For a DataRowState value of Added, Modified, or Deleted, the default version is Current. For a DataRowState value of Detached, the version is Proposed.
Original	This represents the value first inserted into a DataRow or the value the last time AcceptChanges() was called.
Proposed	This is the value of a row currently being edited due to a call to BeginEdit().

As suggested in Table 22-6, the value of the DataRowVersion property is dependent on the value of the DataRowState property in many cases. As mentioned previously, the DataRowVersion property will be changed behind the scenes when you invoke various methods on the DataRow (or, in some cases, the DataTable) object. Here is a breakdown of the methods that can affect the value of a row's DataRowVersion property:

- If you call the DataRow.BeginEdit() method and change the row's value, the Current and Proposed values become available.

- If you call the DataRow.CancelEdit() method, the Proposed value is deleted.

- After you call DataRow.EndEdit(), the Proposed value becomes the Current value.

- After you call the DataRow.AcceptChanges() method, the Original value becomes identical to the Current value. The same transformation occurs when you call DataTable.AcceptChanges().

- After you call DataRow.RejectChanges(), the Proposed value is discarded, and the version becomes Current.

Yes, this is a bit convoluted, not least because a DataRow might or might not have all versions at any given time (you'll receive runtime exceptions if you attempt to obtain a row version that is not currently tracked). Regardless of the complexity, given that the DataRow maintains three copies of data, it becomes simple to build a front end that allows an end user to alter values, change his or her mind and roll back values, or commit values permanently. You'll see various examples of manipulating these methods over the remainder of this chapter.

Working with DataTables

The DataTable type defines many members, many of which are identical in name and functionality to those of the DataSet. Table 22-7 describes some core members of the DataTable type beyond Rows and Columns.

Table 22-7. Key Members of the DataTable Type

Member	Meaning in Life
CaseSensitive	Indicates whether string comparisons within the table are case sensitive. The default value is false.
ChildRelations	Returns the collection of child relations for this DataTable (if any).
Constraints	Gets the collection of constraints maintained by the table.
Copy()	A method that copies the schema and data of a given DataTable into a new instance.
DataSet	Gets the DataSet that contains this table (if any).
DefaultView	Gets a customized view of the table that might include a filtered view or a cursor position.
ParentRelations	Gets the collection of parent relations for this DataTable.
PrimaryKey	Gets or sets an array of columns that function as primary keys for the data table.
TableName	Gets or sets the name of the table. This same property might also be specified as a constructor parameter.

To continue with the current example, you can set the PrimaryKey property of the DataTable to the carIDColumn DataColumn object. Be aware that the PrimaryKey property is assigned a collection of DataColumn objects to account for a multicolumned key. In this case, however, you need to specify only the CarID column (being the first ordinal position in the table), like so:

```
static void FillDataSet(DataSet ds)
{
...
  // Mark the primary key of this table.
  inventoryTable.PrimaryKey = new DataColumn[] { inventoryTable.Columns[0] };
}
```

Inserting DataTables into DataSets

At this point, your DataTable object is complete. The final step is to insert the DataTable into the carsInventoryDS DataSet object using the Tables collection, like this:

```
static void FillDataSet(DataSet ds)
{
...
  // Finally, add our table to the DataSet.
  ds.Tables.Add(inventoryTable);
}
```

Now update your Main() method to call FillDataSet(), passing in your local DataSet object as an argument. Next, pass the same object into a new (yet to be written) helper method named PrintDataSet(), as follows:

```
static void Main(string[] args)
{
  Console.WriteLine("***** Fun with DataSets *****\n");
...
  FillDataSet(carsInventoryDS);
  PrintDataSet(carsInventoryDS);
  Console.ReadLine();
}
```

Obtaining Data in a DataSet

The PrintDataSet() method simply iterates over the DataSet metadata (using the ExtendedProperties collection) and each DataTable in the DataSet, printing out the column names and row values using the type indexers.

```
static void PrintDataSet(DataSet ds)
{
  // Print out the DataSet name and any extended properties.
  Console.WriteLine("DataSet is named: {0}", ds.DataSetName);
  foreach (System.Collections.DictionaryEntry de in ds.ExtendedProperties)
  {
    Console.WriteLine("Key = {0}, Value = {1}", de.Key, de.Value);
  }
  Console.WriteLine();

  // Print out each table.
  foreach (DataTable dt in ds.Tables)
  {
    Console.WriteLine("=> {0} Table:", dt.TableName);

    // Print out the column names.
    for (int curCol = 0; curCol < dt.Columns.Count; curCol++)
    {
      Console.Write(dt.Columns[curCol].ColumnName + "\t");
    }
    Console.WriteLine("\n----------------------------------");
```

```
    // Print the DataTable.
    for (int curRow = 0; curRow < dt.Rows.Count; curRow++)
    {
      for (int curCol = 0; curCol < dt.Columns.Count; curCol++)
      {
        Console.Write(dt.Rows[curRow][curCol].ToString() + "\t");
      }
      Console.WriteLine();
    }
  }
}
```

If you run your program now, you'll see the following output (your time stamp and GUID value will differ, of course):

```
***** Fun with DataSets *****

DataSet is named: Car Inventory
Key = TimeStamp, Value = 1/22/2012 6:41:09 AM
Key = DataSetID, Value = 11c533ed-d1aa-4c82-96d4-b0f88893ab21
Key = Company, Value = Mikko's Hot Tub Super Store

=> Inventory Table:
CarID   Make    Color   PetName
---------------------------------
0       BMW     Black   Hamlet
1       Saab    Red     Sea Breeze
```

Processing DataTable Data Using DataTableReader Objects

Given your work in Chapter 21, you should notice that the manner in which you process data using the connected layer (e.g., data reader objects) and the disconnected layer (e.g., DataSet objects) is quite different. Working with a data reader typically involves establishing a while loop, calling the Read() method, and using an indexer to pluck out the name/value pairs. On the other hand, DataSet processing typically involves a series of iteration constructs to drill into the data within the tables, rows, and columns (remember that DataReader requires an open database connection so that it can read the data from the actual database).

DataTables support a method named CreateDataReader(). This method allows you to obtain the data within a DataTable using a data reader–like navigation scheme (the data reader will now read data from the in-memory DataTable, not from the actual database, so there's no database connection involved here). The major benefit of this approach is that you now use a single model to process data, regardless of which layer of ADO.NET you use to obtain it. Assume you have authored a new method in your Program class named PrintTable(), as follows:

```
static void PrintTable(DataTable dt)
{
  // Get the DataTableReader type.
  DataTableReader dtReader = dt.CreateDataReader();
```

```
  // The DataTableReader works just like the DataReader.
  while (dtReader.Read())
  {
    for (int i = 0; i < dtReader.FieldCount; i++)
    {
      Console.Write("{0}\t", dtReader.GetValue(i).ToString().Trim());
    }
    Console.WriteLine();
  }
  dtReader.Close();
}
```

Notice that the DataTableReader works identically to the data reader object of your data provider. A DataTableReader can be an ideal choice when you need to pump out the data within a DataTable quickly, without needing to traverse the internal row and column collections. Now assume you have updated the previous PrintDataSet() method to invoke PrintTable(), rather than drilling into the Rows and Columns collections.

```
static void PrintDataSet(DataSet ds)
{
  // Print out the DataSet name, plus any extended properties.
  Console.WriteLine("DataSet is named: {0}", ds.DataSetName);
  foreach (System.Collections.DictionaryEntry de in ds.ExtendedProperties)
  {
    Console.WriteLine("Key = {0}, Value = {1}", de.Key, de.Value);
  }
  Console.WriteLine();

  foreach (DataTable dt in ds.Tables)
  {
    Console.WriteLine("=> {0} Table:", dt.TableName);

    // Print out the column names..
    for (int curCol = 0; curCol < dt.Columns.Count; curCol++)
    {
      Console.Write(dt.Columns[curCol].ColumnName.Trim() + "\t");
    }
    Console.WriteLine("\n----------------------------------");

    // Call our new helper method.
    PrintTable(dt);
  }
}
```

When you run the application, the output is identical to that shown previously. The only difference is how you access the DataTable's contents internally.

Serializing DataTable/DataSet Objects As XML

DataSets and DataTables both support the WriteXml() and ReadXml() methods. WriteXml() allows you to persist an object's content to a local file (as well as into any System.IO.Stream-derived type) as an XML document. ReadXml() allows you to hydrate the state of a DataSet (or DataTable) from a given XML document. In addition, DataSets and DataTables both support WriteXmlSchema() and ReadXmlSchema() for saving or loading an *.xsd file.

To test this out for yourself, update your Main() method to call the following helper function (notice that you pass a DataSet as the sole parameter):

```
static void SaveAndLoadAsXml(DataSet carsInventoryDS)
{
  // Save this DataSet as XML.
  carsInventoryDS.WriteXml("carsDataSet.xml");
  carsInventoryDS.WriteXmlSchema("carsDataSet.xsd");

  // Clear out DataSet.
  carsInventoryDS.Clear();

  // Load DataSet from XML file.
  carsInventoryDS.ReadXml("carsDataSet.xml");
}
```

If you open the carsDataSet.xml file (which you will find under the \bin\Debug folder of your project), you will find that each column in the table has been encoded as an XML element.

```
<?xml version="1.0" standalone="yes"?>
<Car_x0020_Inventory>
  <Inventory>
    <CarID>0</CarID>
    <Make>BMW</Make>
    <Color>Black</Color>
    <PetName>Hamlet</PetName>
  </Inventory>
  <Inventory>
    <CarID>1</CarID>
    <Make>Saab</Make>
    <Color>Red</Color>
    <PetName>Sea Breeze</PetName>
  </Inventory>
</Car_x0020_Inventory>
```

If you were to double-click on the generated *.xsd file (also found under your \bin\Debug folder) within Visual Studio, you will open the IDE's XML schema editor (see Figure 22-3).

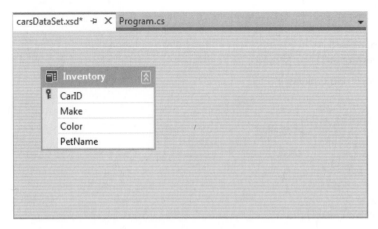

Figure 22-3. *The XSD editor of Visual Studio*

■ **Note** Chapter 24 will introduce you to the LINQ to XML API, which is the preferred manner for manipulating XML data in the .NET platform.

Serializing DataTable/DataSet Objects in a Binary Format

It is also possible to persist the contents of a DataSet (or an individual DataTable) as a compact binary format. This can be especially helpful when a DataSet object needs to be passed across a machine boundary (in the case of a distributed application). One drawback of XML data representation is that its descriptive nature can result in a good deal of overhead.

To persist DataTables or DataSets in a binary format, set the RemotingFormat property to SerializationFormat.Binary. At this point, you can use the BinaryFormatter type (see Chapter 20) as expected. Consider the following final method of the SimpleDataSet project (don't forget to import the System.IO and System.Runtime.Serialization.Formatters.Binary namespaces):

```
static void SaveAndLoadAsBinary(DataSet carsInventoryDS)
{
    // Set binary serialization flag.
    carsInventoryDS.RemotingFormat = SerializationFormat.Binary;

    // Save this DataSet as binary.
    FileStream fs = new FileStream("BinaryCars.bin", FileMode.Create);
    BinaryFormatter bFormat = new BinaryFormatter();
    bFormat.Serialize(fs, carsInventoryDS);
    fs.Close();

    // Clear out DataSet.
    carsInventoryDS.Clear();
```

```
// Load DataSet from binary file.
fs = new FileStream("BinaryCars.bin", FileMode.Open);
DataSet data = (DataSet)bFormat.Deserialize(fs);
}
```

If you call this method from Main(), you can find the *.bin file in your bin\Debug folder. Figure 22-4 shows the contents of the BinaryCars.bin file.

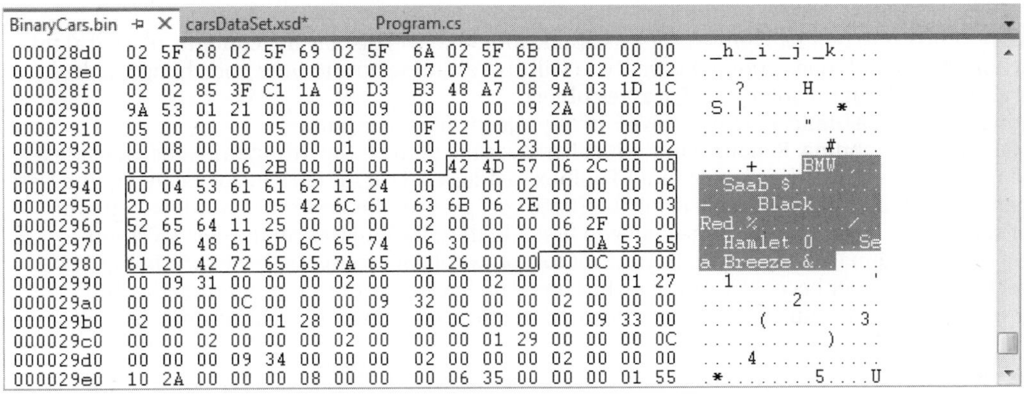

Figure 22-4. *A DataSet saved to a binary format*

■ **Source Code** You can find the SimpleDataSet application under the Chapter 22 subdirectory.

Binding DataTable Objects to Windows Forms GUIs

So far, you have examined how to create, hydrate, and iterate over the contents of a DataSet object manually using the inherit object model of ADO.NET. While understanding how to do so is quite important, the .NET platform ships with numerous APIs that have the ability to *bind* data to user interface elements automatically.

For example, the original GUI toolkit of .NET, Windows Forms, supplies a control named DataGridView that includes the built-in ability to display the contents of a DataSet or DataTable object using only a few lines of code. ASP.NET (.NET's web development API) and the Windows Presentation Foundation API (a supercharged GUI API introduced with .NET 3.0) also support the notion of data binding. You will learn to bind data to WPF and ASP.NET GUI elements later in this book; however, in this chapter, you will use Windows Forms because it is a fairly simple and straightforward programming model.

■ **Note** The next example assumes you have some experience using Windows Forms to build graphical user interfaces. If this is not the case, you might want to open the solution and follow along or return to this section after you have read Appendix A.

Your next task is to build a Windows Forms application that will display the contents of a DataTable object within its user interface. Along the way, you will also examine how to filter and change table data. You will also learn about the role of the DataView object.

Begin by creating a brand-new Windows Forms project workspace named WindowsFormsDataBinding. Rename your initial Form1.cs file to the more fitting MainForm.cs using the Solution Explorer. Next, use the Visual Studio Toolbox to drag a DataGridView control located in the Data tab (renamed to carInventoryGridView using the (Name) property of the Properties window) onto the designer surface. You might notice that when you first add the DataGridView on the designer, you activate a context menu that allows you to connect to a physical data source. For the time being, ignore this aspect of the designer because you will be binding your DataTable object programmatically. Finally, add a descriptive Label to your designer for information purposes. Figure 22-5 shows one possible look-and-feel.

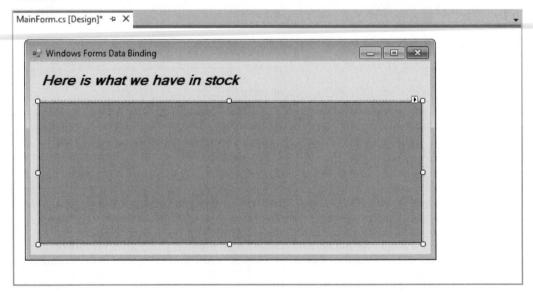

Figure 22-5. The initial GUI of your Windows Forms application

Hydrating a DataTable from a Generic List<T>

Similar to the previous SimpleDataSet example, the WindowsFormsDataBinding application will construct a DataTable that contains a set of DataColumns representing various columns and rows of data. This time, however, you will fill the rows using a generic List<T> member variable. First, insert a new C# class into your project (named Car), which you define as follows:

```
public class Car
{
  public int ID { get; set; }
  public string PetName { get; set; }
  public string Make { get; set; }
  public string Color { get; set; }
}
```

Within the default constructor of your main form, populate a List<T> member variable (named listCars) with a set of new Car objects, like so:

```
public partial class MainForm : Form
{
  // A collection of Car objects.
  List<Car> listCars = null;

  public MainForm()
  {
    InitializeComponent();

    // Fill the list with some cars.
    listCars = new List<Car>
    {
      new Car { ID = 100, PetName = "Chucky", Make = "BMW", Color = "Green" },
      new Car { ID = 101, PetName = "Tiny", Make = "Yugo", Color = "White" },
      new Car { ID = 102, PetName = "Ami", Make = "Jeep", Color = "Tan" },
      new Car { ID = 103, PetName = "Pain Inducer", Make = "Caravan",
                Color = "Pink" },
      new Car { ID = 104, PetName = "Fred", Make = "BMW", Color = "Green" },
      new Car { ID = 105, PetName = "Sidd", Make = "BMW", Color = "Black" },
      new Car { ID = 106, PetName = "Mel", Make = "Firebird", Color = "Red" },
      new Car { ID = 107, PetName = "Sarah", Make = "Colt", Color = "Black" },
    };
  }
}
```

Next, add a new member variable named inventoryTable of type DataTable to your MainForm class type, like so:

```
public partial class MainForm : Form
{
  // A collection of Car objects.
  List<Car> listCars = null;

  // Inventory information.
  DataTable inventoryTable = new DataTable();
...
}
```

Now add a new helper function to your class named CreateDataTable() and call this method within the default constructor of the MainForm class.

```
private void CreateDataTable()
{
  // Create table schema.
  DataColumn carIDColumn = new DataColumn("ID", typeof(int));
  DataColumn carMakeColumn = new DataColumn("Make", typeof(string));
  DataColumn carColorColumn = new DataColumn("Color", typeof(string));
  DataColumn carPetNameColumn = new DataColumn("PetName", typeof(string));
  carPetNameColumn.Caption = "Pet Name";
  inventoryTable.Columns.AddRange(new DataColumn[] { carIDColumn,
    carMakeColumn, carColorColumn, carPetNameColumn });

  // Iterate over the List<T> to make rows.
  foreach (Car c in listCars)
  {
    DataRow newRow = inventoryTable.NewRow();
    newRow["ID"] = c.ID;
    newRow["Make"] = c.Make;
    newRow["Color"] = c.Color;
    newRow["PetName"] = c.PetName;
    inventoryTable.Rows.Add(newRow);
  }

  // Bind the DataTable to the carInventoryGridView.
  carInventoryGridView.DataSource = inventoryTable;
}
```

The method implementation begins by creating the schema of the DataTable by creating four DataColumn objects (for the sake of simplicity, you don't need to bother autoincrementing the ID field or set it as a primary key). After you do this, you can add them to the column collection of the DataTable member variable. You map the row data from your List<Car> collection into the DataTable using a foreach iteration construct and the native ADO.NET object model.

However, notice that the final code statement within the CreateDataTable() method assigns the inventoryTable to the DataSource property of the DataGridView object. This single property is all you need to set to bind a DataTable to a Windows Forms DataGridView object. Under the hood, this GUI control reads the row and column collections internally, much like what happens with the PrintDataSet() method of the SimpleDataSet example. At this point, you should be able to run your application and see the DataTable within the DataGridView control, as shown in Figure 22-6.

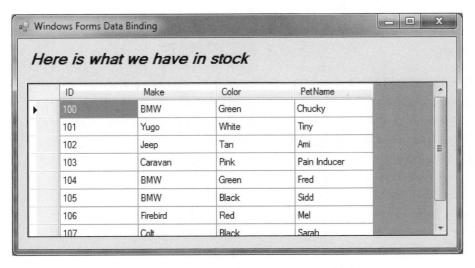

Figure 22-6. Binding a DataTable to a Windows Forms DataGridView

Deleting Rows from a DataTable

Now, assume you would like to update your graphical interface to allow the user to delete a row from the in-memory DataTable that is bound to the DataGridView. One approach is to call the Delete() method of the DataRow object that represents the row to terminate. In this case, you specify the index (or DataRow object) representing the row to remove. To allow the user to specify which row to delete, add a TextBox (named txtCarToRemove) and a Button control (named btnRemoveCar) to the current designer. Figure 22-7 shows one possible UI update (note this example wraps the two controls in a GroupBox control, illustrating how they are related).

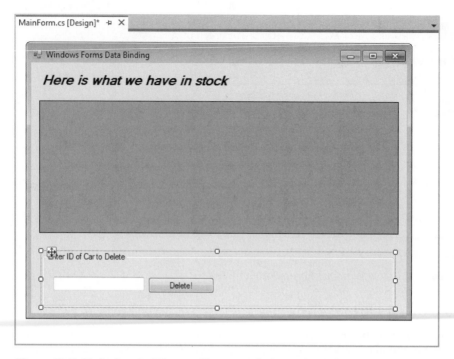

Figure 22-7. *Updating the UI to enable removal of rows from the underlying DataTable*

The following logic behind the new Button's Click event handler removes the user-specified row, based on the ID of a car, from your in-memory DataTable. The Select() method of the DataTable class allows you to specify a search criteria, which is modeled after normal SQL syntax. The return value is an array of DataRow objects that matches the search criteria.

```
// Remove this row from the DataRowCollection.
private void btnRemoveCar_Click (object sender, EventArgs e)
{
  try
  {
    // Find the correct row to delete.
    DataRow[] rowToDelete = inventoryTable.Select(
      string.Format("ID={0}", int.Parse(txtCarToRemove.Text)));

    // Delete it!
    rowToDelete[0].Delete();
    inventoryTable.AcceptChanges();
  }
  catch (Exception ex)
  {
    MessageBox.Show(ex.Message);
  }
}
```

You should now be able to run your application and specify a car ID to delete from the DataTable. As you remove DataRow objects from the DataTable, you will notice that the grid's UI is updated immediately; this occurs because it is bound to the state of the DataTable object.

Selecting Rows Based on Filter Criteria

Many data-centric applications require the need to view a small subset of a DataTable's data, as specified by some sort of filtering criteria. For example, assume you want to see only a certain make of automobile from the in-memory DataTable (e.g., only BMWs). You've already seen how the Select() method of the DataTable class allows you to find a row to delete; however, you can also use this method to grab a subset of records for display purposes.

To see this in action, update your UI again, this time allowing users to specify a string that represents the make of the automobile they want to see (see Figure 22-8) using a new TextBox (named txtMakeToView) and a new Button (named btnDisplayMakes).

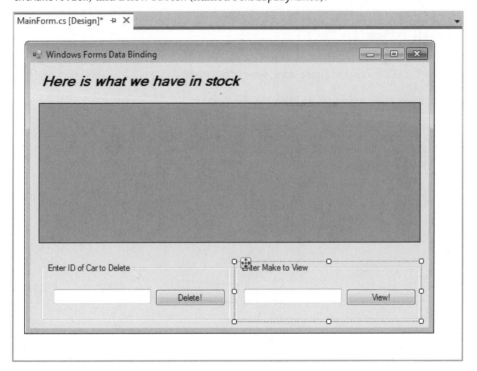

Figure 22-8. *Updating the UI to enable row filtering*

The Select() method has been overloaded a number of times to provide different selection semantics. At its most basic level, the parameter sent to Select() is a string that contains some conditional operation. To begin, observe the following logic for the Click event handler of your new button:

```
private void btnDisplayMakes_Click(object sender, EventArgs e)
{
  // Build a filter based on user input.
  string filterStr = string.Format("Make= '{0}'", txtMakeToView.Text);

  // Find all rows matching the filter.
  DataRow[] makes = inventoryTable.Select(filterStr);

  if (makes.Length == 0)
    MessageBox.Show("Sorry, no cars...", "Selection error!");
  else
  {
    string strMake = "";
    for (int i = 0; i < makes.Length; i++)
    {
      // From the current row, get the PetName value.
      strMake += makes[i]["PetName"] + "\n";
    }

    // Show the names of call cars matching the specified Make.
    MessageBox.Show(strMake,
      string.Format("We have {0}s named:", txtMakeToView.Text));
  }
}
```

Here, you begin by building a simple filter based on the value in the associated TextBox. If you specify BMW, your filter looks like this:

```
Make = 'BMW'
```

When you send this filter to the Select() method, you get back an array of DataRow types that represent each row that matches the filter (see Figure 22-9).

Figure 22-9. Displaying filtered data

Again, the filtering logic is based on standard SQL syntax. For example, assume you want to obtain the results of the previous Select() invocation alphabetically, based on the pet name. In terms of SQL, this translates into a sort based on the PetName column. Fortunately, the Select() method has been overloaded to send in a sort criterion.

```
// Sort by PetName.
makes = inventoryTable.Select(filterStr, "PetName");
```

Call Select(), as seen here, if you want the results in descending order:

```
// Return results in descending order.
makes = inventoryTable.Select(filterStr, "PetName DESC");
```

In general, the sort string contains the column name, followed by ASC (ascending, which is the default) or DESC (descending). If necessary, you can separate multiple columns by commas. Finally, understand that a filter string can be composed of any number of relational operators. For example, assume you want to find all cars with an ID greater than 5. This helper function lets you accomplish that:

```
private void ShowCarsWithIdGreaterThanFive()
{
  // Now show the pet names of all cars with ID greater than 5.
  DataRow[] properIDs;
  string newFilterStr = "ID > 5";
  properIDs = inventoryTable.Select(newFilterStr);
  string strIDs = null;
  for(int i = 0; i < properIDs.Length; i++)
```

```
  {
    DataRow temp = properIDs[i];
    strIDs += temp["PetName"]
            + " is ID " + temp["ID"] + "\n";
  }
  MessageBox.Show(strIDs, "Pet names of cars where ID > 5");
}
```

Updating Rows Within a DataTable

The final aspect of the DataTable you should be aware of is the process of updating an existing row with new values. One approach is to first obtain the row(s) that match a given filter criterion using the Select() method. Once you obtain the DataRow(s) in question, modify them accordingly. For example, assume you have a new Button on your form named btnChangeMakes that (when clicked) searches the DataTable for all rows where Make is equal to BMW. Once you identify these items, you change the Make from BMW to Yugo, as so:

```
// Find the rows you want to edit with a filter.
private void btnChangeMakes_Click(object sender, EventArgs e)
{
  // Confirm selection.
  if (DialogResult.Yes ==
    MessageBox.Show("Are you sure?? BMWs are much nicer than Yugos!",
      "Please Confirm!", MessageBoxButtons.YesNo))
  {
    // Build a filter.
    string filterStr = "Make='BMW'";
    string strMake = string.Empty;

    // Find all rows matching the filter.
    DataRow[] makes = inventoryTable.Select(filterStr);

    // Change all Beemers to Yugos!
    for (int i = 0; i < makes.Length; i++)
    {
      makes[i]["Make"] = "Yugo";
    }
  }
}
```

Working with the DataView Type

A *view object* is an alternative representation of a table (or set of tables). For example, you can use Microsoft SQL Server to create a view for your Inventory table that returns a new table containing automobiles only of a given color. In ADO.NET, the DataView type allows you to extract a subset of data programmatically from the DataTable into a stand-alone object.

One great advantage of holding multiple views of the same table is that you can bind these views to various GUI widgets (such as the DataGridView). For example, one DataGridView might be bound to a DataView showing all autos in the Inventory, while another might be configured to display only green automobiles.

To see this in action, update the current UI with an additional DataGridView type named dataGridYugosView and a descriptive Label. Next, define a member variable named yugosOnlyView of type DataView.

```
public partial class MainForm : Form
{
  // View of the DataTable.
  DataView yugosOnlyView;
...
}
```

Now create a new helper function named CreateDataView() and call this method within the form's default constructor immediately after the DataTable has been fully constructed, as shown here:

```
public MainForm()
{
...
  // Make a data table.
  CreateDataTable();

  // Make a view.
  CreateDataView();
}
```

Here is the implementation of this new helper function. Notice that the constructor of each DataView has been passed the DataTable that you will use to build the custom set of data rows.

```
private void CreateDataView()
{
  // Set the table that is used to construct this view.
  yugosOnlyView = new DataView(inventoryTable);

  // Now configure the views using a filter.
  yugosOnlyView.RowFilter = "Make = 'Yugo'";

  // Bind to the new grid.
  dataGridYugosView.DataSource = yugosOnlyView;
}
```

As you can see, the DataView class supports a property named RowFilter, which contains the string representing the filtering criteria used to extract matching rows. After you establish your view, set the grid's DataSource property accordingly. Figure 22-10 shows the completed Windows Forms data-binding application in action.

Figure 22-10. *Displaying a unique view of your data*

■ **Source Code** You can find the WindowsFormsDataBinding project under the Chapter 22 subdirectory.

Working with Data Adapters

Now that you understand the ins and outs of manipulating ADO.NET DataSets manually, it's time to turn your attention to the topic of *data adapter objects*. A data adapter is a class used to fill a DataSet with DataTable objects; this class can also send modified DataTables back to the database for processing. Table 22-8 documents the core members of the DbDataAdapter base class, the common parent to every data adapter object (e.g., SqlDataAdapter and OdbcDataAdapter).

Table 22-8. Core Members of the DbDataAdapter *Class*

Members	Meaning in Life
Fill()	Executes a SQL SELECT command (as specified by the SelectCommand property) to query the database for data and loads the data into a DataTable.
SelectCommand InsertCommand UpdateCommand DeleteCommand	Establishes the SQL commands that you will issue to the data store when the Fill() and Update() methods are called.
Update()	Executes SQL INSERT, UPDATE, and DELETE commands (as specified by the InsertCommand, UpdateCommand, and DeleteCommand properties) to persist DataTable changes to the database.

Notice that a data adapter defines four properties: SelectCommand, InsertCommand, UpdateCommand, and DeleteCommand. When you create the data adapter object for your particular data provider (e.g., SqlDataAdapter), you can pass in a string that represents the command text used by the SelectCommand's command object.

Assuming each of the four command objects has been properly configured, you can then call the Fill() method to obtain a DataSet (or a single DataTable, if you so choose). To do so, you have the data adapter execute the SQL SELECT statement specified by the SelectCommand property.

Similarly, if you want to persist a modified DataSet (or DataTable) object back to the database, you can call the Update() method, which will use any of the remaining command objects, based on the state of each row in the DataTable (you'll learn more about this in a bit).

One of the strangest aspects of working with a data adapter object is the fact that you are never required to open or close a connection to the database. Rather, the underlying connection to the database is managed on your behalf. However, you will still need to supply the data adapter with a valid connection object or a connection string (which you will use to build a connection object internally) to inform the data adapter exactly which database you want to communicate with.

■ **Note** A data adapter is agnostic by nature. You can plug in different connection objects and command objects on the fly and fetch data from a diverse variety of databases. For example, a single DataSet could contain table data obtained from SQL Server, Oracle, and MySQL database providers.

A Simple Data Adapter Example

The next step is to add new functionality to the data access library assembly (AutoLotDAL.dll) you created in Chapter 21. We will begin by creating a simple example that fills a DataSet with a single table using an ADO.NET data adapter object.

Create a new Console Application named FillDataSetUsingSqlDataAdapter and import the System.Data and System.Data.SqlClient namespaces into your initial C# code file. Now update your

`Main()` method as follows (you might need to change the connection string, based on how you created the `AutoLot` database in Chapter 21):

```
static void Main(string[] args)
{
  Console.WriteLine("***** Fun with Data Adapters *****\n");

  // Hard-coded connection string.
  string cnStr = "Integrated Security = SSPI;Initial Catalog=AutoLot;" +
    @"Data Source=(local)\SQLEXPRESS";

  // Caller creates the DataSet object.
  DataSet ds = new DataSet("AutoLot");

  // Inform adapter of the Select command text and connection string.
  SqlDataAdapter dAdapt =
    new SqlDataAdapter("Select * From Inventory", cnStr);

  // Fill our DataSet with a new table, named Inventory.
  dAdapt.Fill(ds, "Inventory");

  // Display contents of DataSet using
  // helper method created earlier in this chapter.
  PrintDataSet(ds);
  Console.ReadLine();
}
```

Notice that you construct the data adapter by specifying a string literal that will map to the SQL SELECT statement. You will use this value to build a command object internally, which you can obtain later using the `SelectCommand` property.

Next, notice that it is the job of the caller to create an instance of the `DataSet` type, which is passed into the `Fill()` method. Optionally, you can pass the `Fill()` method as a second argument a string name that you use to set the `TableName` property of the new `DataTable` (if you do not specify a table name, the data adapter will simply name the table, `Table`). In most cases, the name you assign a `DataTable` will be identical to the name of the physical table in the relational database; however, this is not required.

■ **Note** The `Fill()` method returns an integer that represents the number of rows returned by the SQL query.

Finally, notice that you do not explicitly open or close the connection to the database anywhere in the `Main()` method. You preprogram the `Fill()` method of a given data adapter to open and then close the underlying connection before returning from the `Fill()` method. Therefore, when you pass the `DataSet` to the `PrintDataSet()` method (implemented earlier in this chapter), you are operating on a local copy of disconnected data, incurring no round trips to fetch the data.

Mapping Database Names to Friendly Names

As mentioned previously, database administrators tend to create table and column names that are less than friendly to end users (e.g., au_id, au_fname, or au_lname). The good news is that data adapter objects maintain an internal strongly typed collection (named DataTableMappingCollection) of System.Data.Common.DataTableMapping objects. You can access this collection using the TableMappings property of your data adapter object.

If you so choose, you can manipulate this collection to inform a DataTable which *display names* it should use when asked to print its contents. For example, assume that you want to map the table name Inventory to Current Inventory for display purposes. For example, assume you want to display the CarID column name as Car ID (note the extra space) and the PetName column name as Name of Car. To do so, add the following code before calling the Fill() method of your data adapter object (be sure to import the System.Data.Common namespace to gain the definition of the DataTableMapping type):

```
static void Main(string[] args)
{
...
  // Now map DB column names to user-friendly names.
  DataTableMapping custMap =
    dAdapt.TableMappings.Add("Inventory", "Current Inventory");
  custMap.ColumnMappings.Add("CarID", "Car ID");
  custMap.ColumnMappings.Add("PetName", "Name of Car");
  dAdapt.Fill(ds, "Inventory");
...
}
```

If you were to run this program again, you would find that the PrintDataSet() method now displays the friendly names of the DataTable and DataRow objects, rather than the names established by the database schema:

```
***** Fun with Data Adapters *****

DataSet is named: AutoLot

=> Current Inventory Table:
Car ID  Make    Color   Name of Car
-----------------------------------
83      Ford    Rust    Rusty
107     Ford    Red     Snake
678     Yugo    Green   Clunker
904     VW      Black   Hank
1000    BMW     Black   Bimmer
1001    BMW     Tan     Daisy
1992    Saab    Pink    Pinkey
2003    Yugo    Rust    Mel
```

■ **Source Code** You can find the FillDataSetUsingSqlDataAdapter project under the Chapter 22 subdirectory.

Adding Disconnection Functionality to AutoLotDAL.dll

To illustrate the process of using a data adapter to push changes in a DataTable back to the database for processing, you will now update the AutoLotDAL.dll assembly created back in Chapter 21 to include a new namespace (named AutoLotDisconnectedLayer). This namespace contains a new class, InventoryDALDisLayer, that uses a data adapter to interact with a DataTable.

A good way to begin is by copying the entire AutoLotDAL project folder you created in Chapter 21 to a new location on your hard drive and rename this folder to AutoLotDAL (Version Two). Now use Visual Studio to activate the File ➤ Open Project/Solution... menu option, and then open the AutoLotDAL.sln file in your AutoLotDAL (Version Two) folder.

Defining the Initial Class Type

Insert a new class named InventoryDALDisLayer using the Project ➤ Add Class menu option. Next, ensure you have a public class type in your new code file. Change the name of the namespace wrapping this class to AutoLotDisconnectedLayer and import the System.Data and System.Data.SqlClient namespaces.

Unlike the connection-centric InventoryDAL type, this new class doesn't need to provide custom open/close methods because the data adapter handles the details automatically.

Begin by adding a custom constructor that sets a private string variable representing the connection string. Also, define a private SqlDataAdapter member variable, which you configure by calling a (yet to be created) helper method called ConfigureAdapter(), which takes a SqlDataAdapter output parameter.

```
namespace AutoLotDisconnectedLayer
{
  public class InventoryDALDisLayer
  {
    // Field data.
    private string cnString = string.Empty;
    private SqlDataAdapter dAdapt = null;

    public InventoryDALDisLayer(string connectionString)
    {
      cnString = connectionString;

      // Configure the SqlDataAdapter.
      ConfigureAdapter(out dAdapt);
    }
  }
}
```

Configuring the Data Adapter Using the SqlCommandBuilder

When you use a data adapter to modify tables in a DataSet, the first order of business is to assign the UpdateCommand, DeleteCommand, and InsertCommand properties with valid command objects (until you do so, these properties return null references).

Configuring the command objects manually for the InsertCommand, UpdateCommand, and DeleteCommand properties can entail a significant amount of code, especially if you use parameterized queries. Recall from Chapter 21 that a parameterized query allows you to build a SQL statement using a

set of parameter objects. Thus, if you were to take the long road, you could implement
ConfigureAdapter() to create three new SqlCommand objects manually, each of which contains a set of
SqlParameter objects. At this point, you could set each object to the UpdateCommand, DeleteCommand, and
InsertCommand properties of the adapter.

Visual Studio provides several designer tools to take care of this mundane and tedious code on your
behalf. These designers differ a bit based on which API you use (e.g., Windows Forms, WPF, or ASP.NET),
but their overall functionality is similar. You'll see examples of using these designers throughout this
book, including some Windows Forms designers later in this chapter.

You won't need to author the numerous code statements to configure a data adapter fully at this
time; instead, you can take a massive shortcut by implementing ConfigureAdapter() like this:

```
private void ConfigureAdapter(out SqlDataAdapter dAdapt)
{
  // Create the adapter and set up the SelectCommand.
  dAdapt = new SqlDataAdapter("Select * From Inventory", cnString);

  // Obtain the remaining command objects dynamically at runtime
  // using the SqlCommandBuilder.
  SqlCommandBuilder builder = new SqlCommandBuilder(dAdapt);
}
```

To simplify the construction of data adapter objects, each of the Microsoft-supplied ADO.NET data
providers provides a *command builder* type. The SqlCommandBuilder automatically generates the values
contained within the SqlDataAdapter's InsertCommand, UpdateCommand, and DeleteCommand properties,
based on the initial SelectCommand. The benefit here is that you do not need to build all the SqlCommand
and SqlParameter types by hand.

Here's an obvious question at this point: how is a command builder able to build these SQL
command objects on the fly? The short answer is metadata. When you call the Update() method of a data
adapter at runtime, the related command builder will read the database's schema data to autogenerate
the underlying insert, delete, and update command objects.

Obviously, doing so requires additional round trips to the remote database; this means it will hurt
performance if you use the SqlCommandBuilder numerous times in a single application. Here, you
minimize the negative effect by calling your ConfigureAdapter() method at the time the
InventoryDALDisLayer object is constructed, retaining the configured SqlDataAdapter for use throughout
the object's lifetime.

In the previous code snippet, you did not use the command builder object (SqlCommandBuilder, in
this case) beyond passing in the data adapter object as a constructor parameter. As odd as this might
seem, this is all you must do (at a minimum). Under the hood, this type configures the data adapter with
the remaining command objects.

While you might love the idea of getting something for nothing, you should understand that
command builders come with some critical restrictions. Specifically, a command builder is only able to
autogenerate SQL commands for use by a data adapter if all of the following conditions are true:

- The SQL SELECT command interacts with only a single table (e.g., no joins).

- The single table has been attributed with a primary key.

- The table must have a column or columns representing the primary key that you
  include in your SQL SELECT statement.

Based on the way you constructed your AutoLot database, these restrictions pose no problem.
However, in a more industrial-strength database, you will need to consider whether this type is at all

useful (if not, remember that Visual Studio will autogenerate a good deal of the required code using various database designer tools, as you will see later).

Implementing GetAllInventory()

Now that your data adapter is ready to go, the first method of your new class type will use the `Fill()` method of the `SqlDataAdapter` object to fetch a `DataTable` representing all records in the Inventory table of the `AutoLot` database, like so:

```
public DataTable GetAllInventory()
{
  DataTable inv = new DataTable("Inventory");
  dAdapt.Fill(inv);
  return inv;
}
```

Implementing UpdateInventory()

The `UpdateInventory()` method is simple, as shown here:

```
public void UpdateInventory(DataTable modifiedTable)
{
  dAdapt.Update(modifiedTable);
}
```

Here, the data adapter object examines the `RowState` value of each row of the incoming `DataTable`. Based on this value (e.g., `RowState.Added`, `RowState.Deleted`, or `RowState.Modified`), the correct command object is leveraged behind the scenes.

Setting Your Version Number

Great! At this point, the logic of the second version of your data access library is complete. You are not required to do so, but set the version number of this library to 2.0.0.0, just for good housekeeping. As described in Chapter 14, you can change the version of a .NET assembly by double-clicking the Properties node of your Solution Explorer, and then clicking the Assembly Information... button located in the Application tab. In the resulting dialog box, set the Major number of the Assembly Version to the value of 2 (see Chapter 14 for more details). After you do this, recompile your application to update the assembly manifest.

■ **Source Code** You can find the AutoLotDAL (Version Two) project under the Chapter 22 subdirectory.

Testing the Disconnected Functionality

At this point, you can build a front end to test your new `InventoryDALDisLayer` class. Once again, you will use the Windows Forms API to display your data on a graphical user interface. Create a new Windows Forms application named InventoryDALDisconnectedGUI and change your initial `Form1.cs` file to

MainForm.cs using the Solution Explorer. After you create the project, set a reference to your updated AutoLotDAL.dll assembly (be sure you pick version 2.0.0.0!) and import the following namespace:

using AutoLotDisconnectedLayer;

The design of the form consists of a single Label, DataGridView (named inventoryGrid), and Button control (named btnUpdateInventory), which you configure to handle the Click event. Here is the definition of the form:

```
public partial class MainForm : Form
{
  InventoryDALDisLayer dal = null;

  public MainForm()
  {
    InitializeComponent();

    string cnStr =
    @"Data Source=(local)\SQLEXPRESS;Initial Catalog=AutoLot;" +
      "Integrated Security=True;Pooling=False";

    // Create our data access object.
    dal = new InventoryDALDisLayer(cnStr);

    // Fill up our grid!
    inventoryGrid.DataSource = dal.GetAllInventory();
  }

  private void btnUpdateInventory_Click(object sender, EventArgs e)
  {
    // Get modified data from the grid.
    DataTable changedDT = (DataTable)inventoryGrid.DataSource;

    try
    {
      // Commit our changes.
      dal.UpdateInventory(changedDT);
    }
    catch(Exception ex)
    {
      MessageBox.Show(ex.Message);
    }
  }
}
```

After you create the InventoryDALDisLayer object, you can bind the DataTable returned from GetAllInventory() to the DataGridView object. When the user clicks the Update button, you extract the modified DataTable from the grid (with the DataSource property) and pass it into your UpdateInventory() method.

That's it! After you run this application, add a set of new rows to the grid and update/delete a few others. Assuming you click the Button control, you will see your changes have persisted into the AutoLot database.

■ **Source Code** You can find the updated InventoryDALDisconnectedGUI project under the Chapter 22 subdirectory.

Multitabled DataSet Objects and Data Relationships

So far, all of this chapter's examples have operated on a single DataTable object. However, the power of the disconnected layer shines through when a DataSet object contains numerous interrelated DataTables. In this case, you can define any number of DataRelation objects in the DataSet's DataRelation collection to account for the interdependencies of the tables. The client tier can use these objects to navigate between the table data without incurring network round trips.

■ **Note** Rather than updating AutoLotDAL.dll to account for the Customers and Orders tables, this example isolates all of the data access logic within a new Windows Forms project. However, intermixing UI and data logic in a production-level application is not recommended. The final examples of this chapter leverage various database design tools to decouple the UI logic from the data logic code.

Begin this example by creating a new Windows Forms application named MultitabledDataSetApp. The GUI is simple enough (note I changed the name of my initial Form1.cs file to MainForm.cs). In Figure 22-11, you can see three DataGridView widgets (dataGridViewInventory, dataGridViewCustomers, and dataGridViewOrders) that hold the data retrieved from the Inventory, Customers, and Orders tables of the AutoLot database. In addition, the initial Button (named btnUpdateDatabase) submits any and all changes entered within the grids back to the database for processing using data adapter objects.

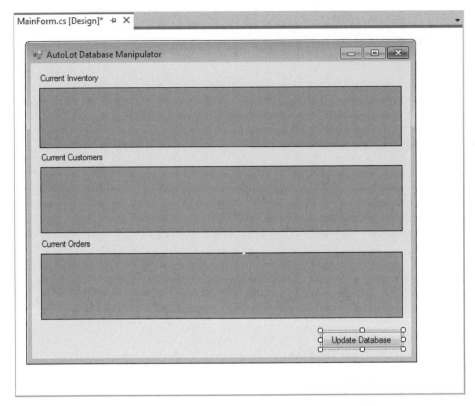

Figure 22-11. The initial UI will display data from each table of the AutoLot database

Prepping the Data Adapters

To keep the data access code as simple as possible, the MainForm will make use of command builder objects to autogenerate the SQL commands for each of the three SqlDataAdapters (one for each table). Here is the initial update to the Form-derived type (don't forget to import the System.Data.SqlClient namespace):

```
public partial class MainForm : Form
{
    // Form-wide DataSet.
    private DataSet autoLotDS = new DataSet("AutoLot");

    // Make use of command builders to simplify data adapter configuration.
    private SqlCommandBuilder sqlCBInventory;
    private SqlCommandBuilder sqlCBCustomers;
    private SqlCommandBuilder sqlCBOrders;

    // Our data adapters (for each table).
    private SqlDataAdapter invTableAdapter;
    private SqlDataAdapter custTableAdapter;
```

```
private SqlDataAdapter ordersTableAdapter;

// Form-wide connection string.
private string cnStr = string.Empty;
...
}
```

The constructor does the grunt work of creating your data-centric member variables and filling the DataSet. This example assumes you have authored an App.config file that contains the correct connection string data (and that you have referenced System.Configuration.dll and imported the System.Configuration namespace), as in this example:

```
<configuration>
  <connectionStrings>
    <add name ="AutoLotSqlProvider"  connectionString =
    "Data Source=(local)\SQLEXPRESS;
      Integrated Security=SSPI;Initial Catalog=AutoLot"
    />
  </connectionStrings>
</configuration>
```

Also note that you include a call to a private helper function, BuildTableRelationship(), as follows:

```
public MainForm()
{
  InitializeComponent();

  // Get connection string from *.config file.
  cnStr =
    ConfigurationManager.ConnectionStrings[
    "AutoLotSqlProvider"].ConnectionString;

  // Create adapters.
  invTableAdapter = new SqlDataAdapter("Select * from Inventory", cnStr);
  custTableAdapter = new SqlDataAdapter("Select * from Customers", cnStr);
  ordersTableAdapter = new SqlDataAdapter("Select * from Orders", cnStr);

  // Autogenerate commands.
  sqlCBInventory = new SqlCommandBuilder(invTableAdapter);
  sqlCBOrders = new SqlCommandBuilder(ordersTableAdapter);
  sqlCBCustomers = new SqlCommandBuilder(custTableAdapter);

  // Fill tables in DS.
  invTableAdapter.Fill(autoLotDS, "Inventory");
  custTableAdapter.Fill(autoLotDS, "Customers");
  ordersTableAdapter.Fill(autoLotDS, "Orders");

  // Build relations between tables.
  BuildTableRelationship();

  // Bind to grids.
  dataGridViewInventory.DataSource = autoLotDS.Tables["Inventory"];
  dataGridViewCustomers.DataSource = autoLotDS.Tables["Customers"];
```

```
dataGridViewOrders.DataSource = autoLotDS.Tables["Orders"];
}
```

Building the Table Relationships

The BuildTableRelationship() helper function does the grunt work to add two DataRelation objects into
the autoLotDS object. Recall from Chapter 21 that the AutoLot database expresses a number of
parent/child relationships, which you can account for with the following code:

```
private void BuildTableRelationship()
{
  // Create CustomerOrder data relation object.
  DataRelation dr = new DataRelation("CustomerOrder",
    autoLotDS.Tables["Customers"].Columns["CustID"],
    autoLotDS.Tables["Orders"].Columns["CustID"]);
  autoLotDS.Relations.Add(dr);

  // Create InventoryOrder data relation object.
  dr = new DataRelation("InventoryOrder",
    autoLotDS.Tables["Inventory"].Columns["CarID"],
    autoLotDS.Tables["Orders"].Columns["CarID"]);
  autoLotDS.Relations.Add(dr);
}
```

Note that you establish a friendly string moniker with the first parameter when you create a
DataRelation object (you'll see the usefulness of doing so in just a minute). You also establish the keys
used to build the relationship itself. Notice that the parent table (the second constructor parameter) is
specified before the child table (the third constructor parameter).

Updating the Database Tables

Now that the DataSet has been filled with data from the data source, you can manipulate each DataTable
locally. To do so, run the application and insert, update, or delete values from any of the three
DataGridViews. When you are ready to submit the data back for processing, click the Update button. You
should find it easy to follow along with the code behind the related Click event at this point.

```
private void btnUpdateDatabase_Click(object sender, EventArgs e)
{
  try
  {
    invTableAdapter.Update(autoLotDS, "Inventory");
    custTableAdapter.Update(autoLotDS, "Customers");
    ordersTableAdapter.Update(autoLotDS, "Orders");
  }
  catch (Exception ex)
  {
    MessageBox.Show(ex.Message);
  }
}
```

Now run your application and perform various updates. When you rerun the application, you
should find that your grids are populated with the recent changes.

Navigating Between Related Tables

Now let's look at how a DataRelation allows you to move between related tables programmatically. Extend your UI to include a new Button (named btnGetOrderInfo), a related TextBox (named txtCustID), and a descriptive Label (you can group these controls within a GroupBox for more visual appeal). Figure 22-12 shows one possible UI of the application.

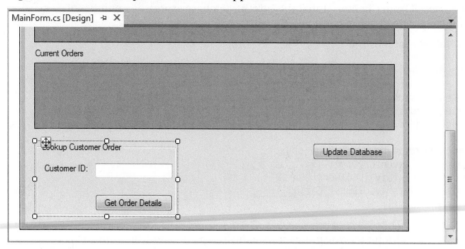

Figure 22-12. *The updated UI allows the user to look up customer order information*

This updated UI lets the user enter the ID of a customer and retrieve all the relevant information about that customer's order (e.g., name, order ID, and car order). This information will be formatted into a string type that is eventually displayed within a message box. Consider the following code behind the new Button's Click event handler:

```
private void btnGetOrderInfo_Click(object sender, System.EventArgs e)
{
  string strOrderInfo = string.Empty;
  DataRow[] drsCust = null;
  DataRow[] drsOrder = null;

  // Get the customer ID in the text box.
  int custID = int.Parse(this.txtCustID.Text);

  // Now based on custID, get the correct row in Customers table.
  drsCust = autoLotDS.Tables["Customers"].Select(
    string.Format("CustID = {0}", custID));
  strOrderInfo += string.Format("Customer {0}: {1} {2}\n",
    drsCust[0]["CustID"].ToString(),
    drsCust[0]["FirstName"].ToString(),
    drsCust[0]["LastName"].ToString());

  // Navigate from Customers table to Orders table.
  drsOrder = drsCust[0].GetChildRows(autoLotDS.Relations["CustomerOrder"]);
```

```
// Loop through all orders for this customer.
foreach (DataRow order in drsOrder)
{
  strOrderInfo += string.Format("----\nOrder Number:
    {0}\n", order["OrderID"]);

  // Get the car referenced by this order.
  DataRow[] drsInv = order.GetParentRows(autoLotDS.Relations[
    "InventoryOrder"]);

  // Get info for (SINGLE) car info for this order.
  DataRow car = drsInv[0];
  strOrderInfo += string.Format("Make: {0}\n", car["Make"]);
  strOrderInfo += string.Format("Color: {0}\n", car["Color"]);
  strOrderInfo += string.Format("Pet Name: {0}\n", car["PetName"]);
}

  MessageBox.Show(strOrderInfo, "Order Details");
}
```

Figure 22-13 shows one possible output when specifying a customer ID with the value of 3 (your output may differ based on the data within your AutoLot database tables).

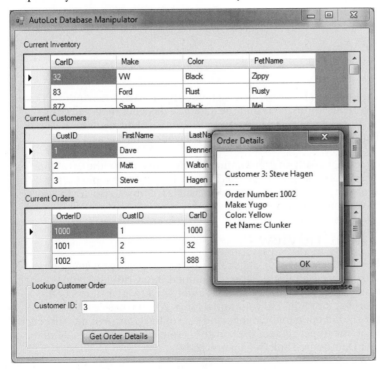

Figure 22-13. Navigating data relations

This last example should probably convince you of the usefulness of the DataSet class. Given that a DataSet is completely disconnected from the underlying data source, you can work with an in-memory copy of data and navigate around each table to make any necessary updates, deletes, or inserts without incurring any round trips to the database. After you finish this, you can submit your changes to the data store for processing. The end result is a scalable and robust application.

■ **Source Code** You can find the MultitabledDataSetApp project under the Chapter 22 subdirectory.

The Windows Forms Database Designer Tools

All of the examples thus far have involved a fair amount of elbow grease in the sense that you had to author all data access logic by hand. While you did offload a good amount of this code to a .NET code library (AutoLotDAL.dll) for reuse in later chapters of the book, you still had to create the various objects of your data provider manually before interacting with the relational database. The next task in this chapter is to look at how you use various Windows Forms database designer tools, which can produce a good deal of data access code on your behalf.

■ **Note** Windows Presentation Foundation and ASP.NET web projects have similar database designer tools; you'll look at some of these later in this chapter.

One way you can use these integrated tools is to use the designers supported by the Windows Forms DataGridView control. The problem with this approach is that the database designer tools will embed all of the data access code directly into your GUI code base! Ideally, you want to isolate all of this designer-generated code in a dedicated .NET code library, so you can easily reuse your database access logic across multiple projects.

Nevertheless, it might be helpful to begin with an examination of how you can use the DataGridView control to generate the required data access code, given that this approach does have some usefulness in small-scale projects and application prototypes. After this point, you will learn how to isolate the same designer-generated code into a third version of AutoLotDAL.dll.

Visually Designing the DataGridView

The DataGridView control has an associated wizard that can generate data access code on your behalf. Begin by creating a brand-new Windows Forms application project named DataGridViewDataDesigner. Rename the initial form to MainForm.cs using the Solution Explorer, and then add an instance of the DataGridView control (named inventoryDataGridView) to your initial form. When you select your DataGridView control, an inline editor should open to the right-hand side of the control (if not, just click on the small "triangle button" found on the upper right of the control). From the Choose Data Source drop-down box, select the Add Project Data Source link (see Figure 22-14).

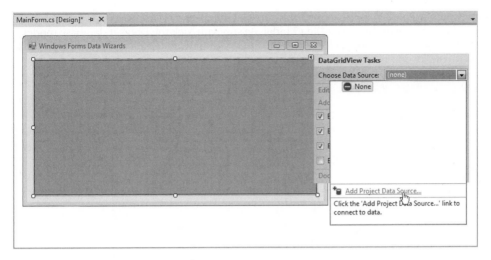

Figure 22-14. *The DataGridView editor*

This launches the Data Source Configuration Wizard. This tool guides you through a series of steps that allow you to select and configure a data source, which you can then bind to the DataGridView. The first step of the wizard asks you to identify the type of data source you want to interact with. Select Database (see Figure 22-15) and click the Next button.

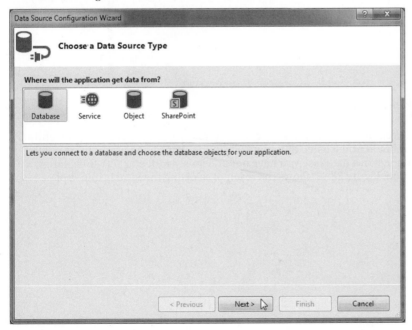

Figure 22-15. *Selecting the type of data source*

The next step (which will differ slightly based on your selection in step 1) asks whether you want to use the Dataset database model or the Entity Data Model. Be sure you pick the Dataset database model (see Figure 22-16) because you have not yet looked at the Entity Framework (you'll learn more about this in the next chapter).

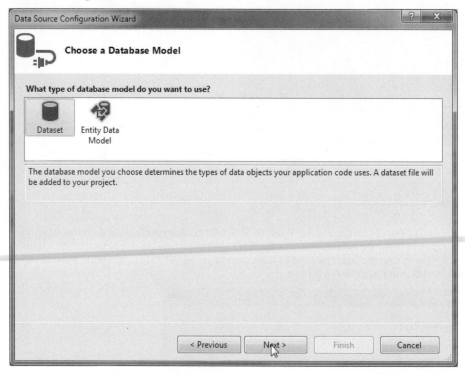

Figure 22-16. Choosing the database model

The next step allows you to configure your database connection. If you have a database currently added to Server Explorer, you should find it listed automatically in the drop-down list. If this is not the case (or if you ever need to connect to a database you have not previously added to Server Explorer), click the New Connection button. Figure 22-17 shows the result of selecting the local instance of AutoLot.

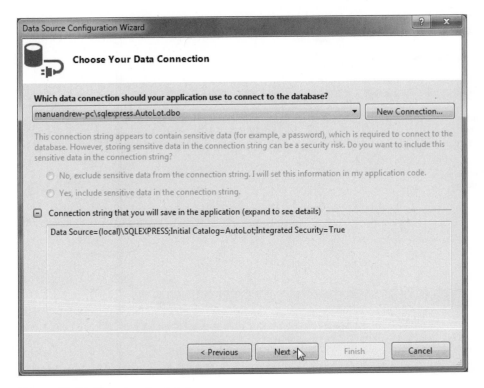

Figure 22-17. *Choosing the database*

In the wizard's next step, you will be asked if you would like to save the connection string in an application configuration file. Although I did not show the screen shot here, elect to save your connection string, and then click the Next button.

In the final step, you select the database objects that will be accounted for by the autogenerated DataSet and related data adapters. While you could select each of the data objects of the AutoLot database, here you concern yourself only with the Inventory table. Given this, change the suggested name of the DataSet to InventoryDataSet (see Figure 22-18), check the Inventory table, and click the Finish button.

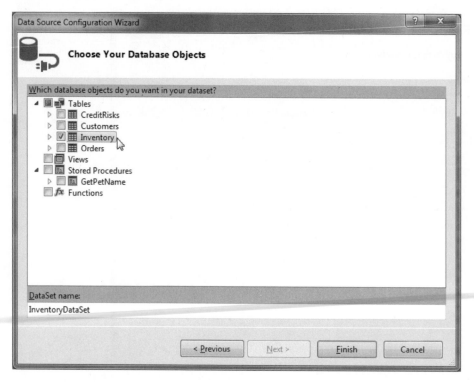

Figure 22-18. *Selecting the* Inventory *table*

After you do this, you will see that the visual designer has been updated in many ways. The most noticeable change is the fact that the DataGridView displays the schema of the Inventory table, as illustrated by the column headers. Also, you will see three components on the bottom of the form designer (in a region dubbed the *component tray*): a DataSet component, a BindingSource component, and a TableAdapter component (see Figure 22-19).

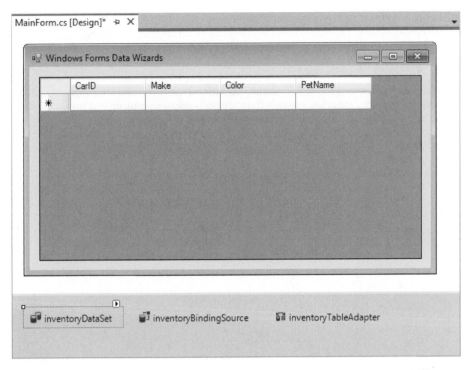

Figure 22-19. Your Windows Forms project, after running the Data Source Configuration Wizard

At this point, you can run your application, and lo and behold, the grid is filled with the records of the Inventory table! Of course, there is no magic to speak of in this case. The IDE has authored a good amount of code on your behalf and set up the grid control to use it. Let's dig into some of this autogenerated code.

The Generated App.config File

If you examine your Solution Explorer, you will find your project now contains an App.config file that contains a <connectionStrings> element that has been given a somewhat peculiar name, as shown here:

```
<?xml version="1.0" encoding="utf-8" ?>
<configuration>
  <configSections>
  </configSections>
  <connectionStrings>
    <add name="DataGridViewDataDesigner.Properties.Settings.AutoLotConnectionString"
      connectionString=
      "Data Source=(local)\SQLEXPRESS;
      Initial Catalog=AutoLot;Integrated Security=True"
      providerName="System.Data.SqlClient" />
  </connectionStrings>
</configuration>
```

The autogenerated data adapter object (which you will learn more about momentarily) uses the lengthy value, `"DataGridViewDataDesigner.Properties.Settings.AutoLotConnectionString"`.

Examining the Strongly Typed DataSet

In addition to your configuration file, the data wizard tools generated what is termed a *strongly typed DataSet*. This term describes a custom class that extends `DataSet` and exposes a number of members that allow you to interact with the database using a more intuitive object model. For example, strongly typed `DataSet` objects contain properties that map directly to the database tables names. Thus, you can use the `Inventory` property to nab the rows and columns directly, rather than having to drill into the collection of tables using the `Tables` property.

If you insert a new class diagram file into your project (by selecting the project icon in Solution Explorer and clicking the View Class Diagram button), you'll notice that the wizard has created a class named `InventoryDataSet`. This class defines a handful of members, the most important of which is a property named `Inventory` (see Figure 22-20).

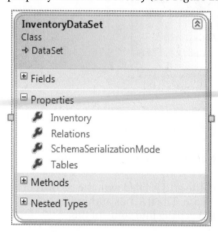

Figure 22-20. The Data Source Configuration Wizard created a strongly typed DataSet

If you double-click the `InventoryDataSet.xsd` file within Solution Explorer, you will load the Visual Studio Dataset Designer (you'll learn more details about this designer momentarily). If you right-click anywhere within this designer and select the View Code option, you will notice the following fairly empty partial class definition:

```
public partial class InventoryDataSet {
}
```

If necessary, you can add custom members to this partial class definition; however, the real action takes place within the designer-maintained file, `InventoryDataSet.Designer.cs`. If you open this file using Solution Explorer, you will see that `InventoryDataSet` extends the `DataSet` parent class. Consider the following partial code, with comments added for clarity:

```
// This is all designer-generated code!
public partial class InventoryDataSet : global::System.Data.DataSet
{
  // A member variable of type InventoryDataTable.
```

```
private InventoryDataTable tableInventory;

// Each constructor calls a helper method named InitClass().
public InventoryDataSet()
{
...
  this.InitClass();
...
}

// InitClass() preps the DataSet and adds the InventoryDataTable
// to the Tables collection.
private void InitClass()
{
  this.DataSetName = "InventoryDataSet";
  this.Prefix = "";
  this.Namespace = "http://tempuri.org/InventoryDataSet.xsd";
  this.EnforceConstraints = true;
  this.SchemaSerializationMode =
    global::System.Data.SchemaSerializationMode.IncludeSchema;
  this.tableInventory = new InventoryDataTable();
  base.Tables.Add(this.tableInventory);
}

// The read-only Inventory property returns
// the InventoryDataTable member variable.
public InventoryDataTable Inventory
{
  get { return this.tableInventory; }
}
}
```

Notice that your strongly typed DataSet has a member variable that is a *strongly typed DataTable*; in this case, the class is named InventoryDataTable. The constructor of the strongly typed DataSet class makes a call to a private initialization method named InitClass(), which adds an instance of this strongly typed DataTable to the Tables collection of the DataSet. Last but not least, notice that the implementation of the Inventory property returns the InventoryDataTable member variable.

Examining the Strongly Typed DataTable

Now return to the class diagram file and open up the Nested Types node on the InventoryDataSet icon. Here you will see the strongly typed DataTable class named InventoryDataTable and a *strongly typed* DataRow class named InventoryRow.

The InventoryDataTable class (which is the same type as the member variable of the strongly typed DataSet you examined) defines a set of properties that are based on the column names of the physical Inventory table (CarIDColumn, ColorColumn, MakeColumn, and PetNameColumn), as well as a custom indexer and a Count property to obtain the current number of records.

More interestingly, this strongly typed DataTable class defines a set of methods that allow you to insert, locate, and delete rows within the table using strongly typed members (an attractive alternative to navigating the Rows and Columns indexers manually). For example, AddInventoryRow() lets you add a new record row to the table in memory, FindByCarID() lets you do a lookup based on the primary key of the table, and RemoveInventoryRow() lets you remove a row from the strongly typed table (see Figure 22-21).

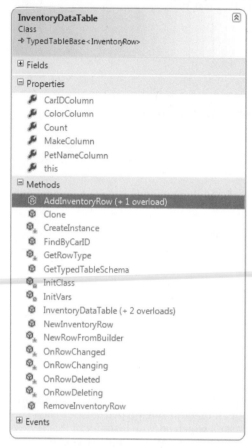

Figure 22-21. The strongly typed DataTable is nested in the strongly typed DataSet

Examining the Strongly Typed DataRow

The strongly typed DataRow class, which is also nested in the strongly typed DataSet, extends the DataRow class and exposes properties that map directly to the schema of the Inventory table. Also, the data designer tool has created a method (IsPetNameNull()) that will perform a check on whether this column has a value (see Figure 22-22).

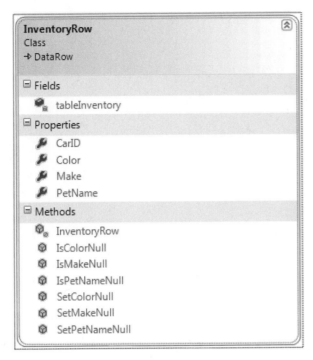

Figure 22-22. The strongly typed DataRow

Examining the Strongly Typed Data Adapter

Strong typing for your disconnected types is a solid benefit of using the Data Source Configuration
Wizard, given that creating these classes by hand would be tedious (but entirely possible). This same
wizard was kind enough to generate a custom data adapter object that can fill and update the
InventoryDataSet and InventoryDataTable objects in a strongly typed manner. Locate the
InventoryTableAdapter on the visual class designer and examine the generated members in Figure 22-23.

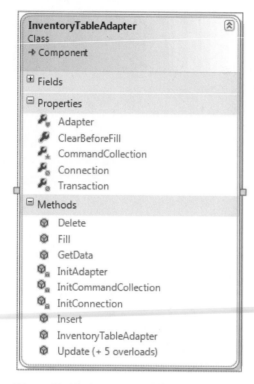

Figure 22-23. *A customized data adapter that operates on the strongly typed DataSet and DataTable*

The autogenerated InventoryTableAdapter type maintains a collection of SqlCommand objects (which you can access using the CommandCollection property), each of which has a fully populated set of SqlParameter objects. Furthermore, this custom data adapter provides a set of properties to extract the underlying connection, transaction, and data adapter objects, as well as a property to obtain an array representing each command type.

Completing the Windows Forms Application

If you examine the Load event handler of the form-derived type (in other words, if you view the code for MainForm.cs and locate the MainForm_Load() method) you will find that the Fill() method of the custom table adapter is called upon startup, passing in the custom DataTable maintained by the custom DataSet.

```
private void MainForm_Load(object sender, EventArgs e)
{
    this.inventoryTableAdapter.Fill(this.inventoryDataSet.Inventory);
}
```

You can use this same custom data adapter object to update changes to the grid. Update the UI of your form with a single Button control (named btnUpdateInventory). Next, handle the Click event and author the following code within the event handler:

```
private void btnUpdateInventory_Click(object sender, EventArgs e)
{
  try
  {
    // Save changes with the Inventory table back to the database.
    this.inventoryTableAdapter.Update(this.inventoryDataSet.Inventory);
  }
  catch(Exception ex)
  {
    MessageBox.Show(ex.Message);
  }

  // Get fresh copy for grid.
  this.inventoryTableAdapter.Fill(this.inventoryDataSet.Inventory);
}
```

Run your application again; add, delete, or update the records displayed in the grid; and click the Update button. When you run the program again, you will find your changes are present and accounted for.

Great! This example shows how helpful the DataGridView control designer can be. It lets you work with strongly typed data generates a majority of the necessary database logic on your behalf. The obvious problem is that this code is tightly connected to the window that uses it. Ideally, this sort of code belongs in your AutoLotDAL.dll assembly (or some other data access library). However, you might wonder how to harvest the code generated using the DataGridView's associated wizard in a Class Library project, given that there is no form designer by default.

■ **Source Code** You can find the DataGridViewDataDesigner project under the Chapter 22 subdirectory.

Isolating Strongly Typed Database Code into a Class Library

Fortunately, you can activate the data design tools of Visual Studio from any sort of project (UI-based or otherwise) without the need to copy-and-paste massive amounts of code between projects. You can see this in action by adding more functionality to AutoLotDAL.dll.

This time, try copying the entire AutoLotDAL (Version Two) project folder you created earlier in this chapter to a new location on your hard drive and rename this folder to AutoLotDAL (Version Three). Next, activate the Visual Studio File ➤ Open Project/Solution... menu option, and open the AutoLotDAL.sln file in your new AutoLotDAL (Version Three) folder.

Now, insert a new strongly typed DataSet class (named AutoLotDataSet.xsd) into your new project using the Project ➤ Add New Item menu option (to quickly find the DataSet project type, select the Data section of the New Item dialog; see Figure 22-24).

Figure 22-24. Inserting a new strongly typed DataSet

This opens a blank Dataset Designer surface. At this point, you can use the Server Explorer to connect to a given database (you should already have a connection to AutoLot), and drag-and-drop each table and stored procedure you want to generate onto the surface. In Figure 22-25, you can see each of the custom aspects of AutoLot are accounted for, and their relationships are realized automatically (this example does not drag over the CreditRisk table).

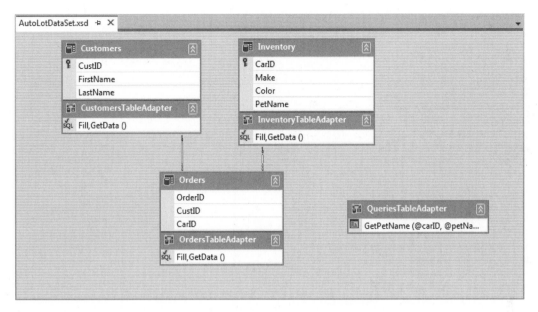

Figure 22-25. *Your custom strongly typed types, this time within a Class Library project*

Viewing the Generated Code

The DataSet designer created the exact same sort of code that the DataGridView wizard did in the previous Windows Forms example. However, this time you account for the Inventory, Customers, and Orders tables, as well as the GetPetName stored procedure, so you have many more generated classes. Basically, each database table you drag onto the designer surface gives you DataTable, DataRow, and data adapter classes contained in a strongly typed DataSet.

The strongly typed DataSet, DataTable, and DataRow classes will be placed into the root namespace of the project (AutoLotDAL). The custom table adapters will be placed within a nested namespace. You can view all of the generated types most easily by using the Class View tool, which you open from the Visual Studio View menu (see Figure 22-26).

Figure 22-26. The autogenerated strongly typed data of the AutoLot *database*

For the sake of completion, you might want use the Visual Studio Properties editor (see Chapter 14 for details) to set the version of this latest incarnation of AutoLotDAL.dll to 3.0.0.0.

■ **Source Code** You can find the AutoLotDAL (Version Three) project under the Chapter 22 subdirectory.

Selecting Data with the Generated Code

At this point, you can use your strongly typed data within any .NET application that needs to communicate with the AutoLot database. To make sure you understand the basic mechanics, create a Console Application named StronglyTypedDataSetConsoleClient. Next, add a reference to your latest-and-greatest version of AutoLotDAL.dll and import the AutoLotDAL and the AutoLotDAL.AutoLotDataSetTableAdapters namespace into your initial C# code file.

Here is a Main() method that uses the InventoryTableAdapter object to retrieve all data in the Inventory table. Notice that you do not need to specify a connection string because that information is now part of the strongly typed object model. After you fill the table, you print out the results using a helper method named PrintInventory(). Note that you can manipulate the strongly typed DataTable just as you do a "normal" DataTable using the Rows and Columns collections.

```csharp
class Program
{
  static void Main(string[] args)
  {
    Console.WriteLine("***** Fun with Strongly Typed DataSets *****\n");

    AutoLotDataSet.InventoryDataTable table =
      new AutoLotDataSet.InventoryDataTable();

    InventoryTableAdapter dAdapt = new InventoryTableAdapter();
    dAdapt.Fill(table);

    PrintInventory(table);
    Console.ReadLine();
  }

  static void PrintInventory(AutoLotDataSet.InventoryDataTable dt)
  {
    // Print out the column names.
    for (int curCol = 0; curCol < dt.Columns.Count; curCol++)
    {
      Console.Write(dt.Columns[curCol].ColumnName + "\t");
    }
    Console.WriteLine("\n--------------------------------");

    // Print the data.
    for (int curRow = 0; curRow < dt.Rows.Count; curRow++)
    {
      for (int curCol = 0; curCol < dt.Columns.Count; curCol++)
      {
        Console.Write(dt.Rows[curRow][curCol].ToString() + "\t");
      }
      Console.WriteLine();
    }
  }
}
```

Inserting Data with the Generated Code

Now assume you want to insert new records using this strongly typed object model. The following helper function adds two new rows to the current InventoryDataTable, then updates the database using the data adapter. You add the first row manually by configuring a strongly typed DataRow; you add the second row by passing in the needed column data, which allows the DataRow to be created in the background automatically.

```
public static void AddRecords(AutoLotDataSet.InventoryDataTable tb,
  InventoryTableAdapter dAdapt)
{
  try
  {
    // Get a new strongly typed row from the table.
    AutoLotDataSet.InventoryRow newRow = tb.NewInventoryRow();

    // Fill row with some sample data.
    newRow.CarID = 999;
    newRow.Color = "Purple";
    newRow.Make = "BMW";
    newRow.PetName = "Saku";

    // Insert the new row.
    tb.AddInventoryRow(newRow);

    // Add one more row, using overloaded Add method.
    tb.AddInventoryRow(888, "Yugo", "Green", "Zippy");

    // Update database.
    dAdapt.Update(tb);
  }
  catch(Exception ex)
  {
    Console.WriteLine(ex.Message);
  }
}
```

The Main() method can invoke this method; doing so updates the database table with these new records:

```
static void Main(string[] args)
{
...
  // Add rows, update, and reprint.
  AddRecords(table, dAdapt);
  table.Clear();
  dAdapt.Fill(table);
  PrintInventory(table);
  Console.ReadLine();
}
```

Deleting Data with the Generated Code

Deleting records with this strongly typed object model is also simple. The autogenerated FindBy*XXXX*() method (where *XXXX* is the name of the primary key column) of the strongly typed DataTable returns the correct (strongly typed) DataRow using the primary key. Here is another helper method that deletes the two records you just created:

```
private static void RemoveRecords(AutoLotDataSet.InventoryDataTable tb,
    InventoryTableAdapter dAdapt)
{
  try
  {
    AutoLotDataSet.InventoryRow rowToDelete = tb.FindByCarID(999);
    dAdapt.Delete(rowToDelete.CarID, rowToDelete.Make,
                  rowToDelete.Color, rowToDelete.PetName);
    rowToDelete = tb.FindByCarID(888);
    dAdapt.Delete(rowToDelete.CarID, rowToDelete.Make,
                  rowToDelete.Color, rowToDelete.PetName);
  }
  catch(Exception ex)
  {
    Console.WriteLine(ex.Message);
  }
}
```

If you call this from your Main() method and reprint the table, you should find these two test records are no longer displayed.

■ **Note** If you run this app twice and call the AddRecord() method each time, you get a VIOLATION CONSTRAINT ERROR because the AddRecord() method tries to insert the same CarID primary key value each time (which is why we wrap our data access logic in a try/catch scope). If you want to make this example more flexible, you can gather data from the user using the Console class.

Invoking a Stored Procedure Using the Generated Code

Let's look at one more example of using the strongly typed object model. In this case, you create a final method that invokes the GetPetName stored procedure. When the data adapters for the AutoLot database were created, there was a special class created named QueriesTableAdapter, which as the name implies, encapsulates the process of invoking stored procedures in the relational database. This final helper function displays the name of the specified car when called from Main():

```
public static void CallStoredProc()
{
  try
  {
    QueriesTableAdapter q = new QueriesTableAdapter();
    Console.Write("Enter ID of car to look up: ");
```

919

```
      string carID = Console.ReadLine();
      string carName = "";
      q.GetPetName(int.Parse(carID), ref carName);
      Console.WriteLine("CarID {0} has the name of {1}", carID, carName);
    }
    catch(Exception ex)
    {
      Console.WriteLine(ex.Message);
    }
  }
}
```

At this point, you know how to use strongly typed database types, and package them up into a dedicated class library. You can find more aspects of this object model to play around with, but you should be in a perfect position to dig deeper if that interests you. To wrap things up for this chapter, you will learn how to apply LINQ queries to an ADO.NET DataSet object.

■ **Source Code** You can find the StronglyTypedDataSetConsoleClient project under the Chapter 22 subdirectory.

Programming with LINQ to DataSet

You have seen in this chapter that you can manipulate the data within a DataSet in three distinct manners:

- By using the Tables, Rows, and Columns collections

- By using data table readers

- By using strongly typed data classes

When you use the various indexers of the DataSet and DataTable type, you can interact with the contained data in a straightforward but loosely typed manner. Recall that this approach requires you to treat the data as a tabular block of cells, as in this example:

```
static void PrintDataWithIndxers(DataTable dt)
{
  // Print the DataTable.
  for (int curRow = 0; curRow < dt.Rows.Count; curRow++)
  {
    for (int curCol = 0; curCol < dt.Columns.Count; curCol++)
    {
      Console.Write(dt.Rows[curRow][curCol].ToString() + "\t");
    }
    Console.WriteLine();
  }
}
```

The CreateDataReader() method of the DataTable type offers a second approach, where you can treat the data in the DataSet as a linear set of rows to be processed in a sequential manner. This allows you to apply a connected data reader programming model to a disconnected DataSet.

```
static void PrintDataWithDataTableReader(DataTable dt)
{
  // Get the DataTableReader type.
  DataTableReader dtReader = dt.CreateDataReader();
  while (dtReader.Read())
  {
    for (int i = 0; i < dtReader.FieldCount; i++)
    {
      Console.Write("{0}\t", dtReader.GetValue(i));
    }
    Console.WriteLine();
  }
  dtReader.Close();
}
```

Finally, you can use a strongly typed DataSet to yield a code base that allows you to interact with data in the object using properties that map to the column names in the relational database. Using strongly typed objects allows you to author code such as the following:

```
static void AddRowWithTypedDataSet()
{
  InventoryTableAdapter invDA = new InventoryTableAdapter();
  AutoLotDataSet.InventoryDataTable inv = invDA.GetData();
  inv.AddInventoryRow(999, "Ford", "Yellow", "Sal");
  invDA.Update(inv);
}
```

While all of these approaches have their place, the LINQ to DataSet API provides yet another option to manipulate DataSet data using LINQ query expressions.

■ **Note** You use the LINQ to DataSet API to apply LINQ queries only to DataSet objects returned by a data adapter, but this has nothing to do with applying LINQ queries directly to the database engine itself. Chapter 23 will introduce you to LINQ to Entities and the ADO.NET Entity Framework, which provide a way to represent SQL queries as LINQ queries.

Out of the box, the ADO.NET DataSet (and related types such as DataTable and DataView) do not have the necessary infrastructure to be a direct target for a LINQ query. For example, the following method (which uses types in the AutoLotDisconnectedLayer namespace) results in a compile-time error:

```
static void LinqOverDataTable()
{
  // Get a DataTable of data.
  InventoryDALDisLayer dal = new InventoryDALDisLayer(
    @"Data Source=(local)\SQLEXPRESS;" +
    "Initial Catalog=AutoLot;Integrated Security=True");
  DataTable data = dal.GetAllInventory();
```

```
    // Apply a LINQ query to the DataSet?
    var moreData = from c in data where (int)c["CarID"] > 5 select c;
}
```

If you were to compile the LinqOverDataTable() method, the compiler would inform you that the DataTable type provides a *query pattern implementation*. Similar to the process of applying LINQ queries to objects that do not implement IEnumerable<T>, ADO.NET objects must be transformed into a compatible type. To understand how to do so requires examining the types of System.Data.DataSetExtensions.dll.

The Role of the DataSet Extensions Library

The System.Data.DataSetExtensions.dll assembly, which is referenced by default in all Visual Studio projects, augments the System.Data namespace with a handful of new types (see Figure 22-27).

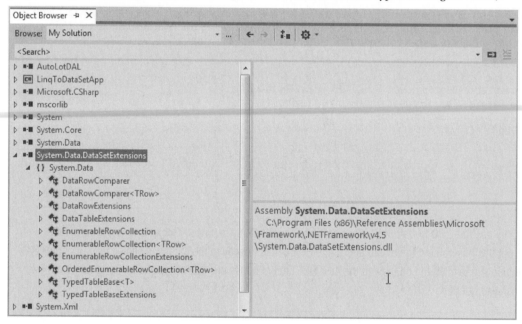

Figure 22-27. The System.Data.DataSetExtensions.dll *assembly*

The two most useful types by far are DataTableExtensions and DataRowExtensions. These classes extend the functionality of DataTable and DataRow by using a set of extension methods (see Chapter 12). The other key class is TypedTableBaseExtensions, which defines extension methods that you can apply to strongly typed DataSet objects to make the internal DataTable objects LINQ aware. All of the remaining members within the System.Data.DataSetExtensions.dll assembly are pure infrastructure, and they are not intended to be used directly in your code base.

Obtaining a LINQ-Compatible DataTable

Now let's look at how you use the DataSet extensions. Assume you have a new C# Console Application named LinqToDataSetApp. Add a reference to the latest and greatest version (3.0.0.0) of the AutoLotDAL.dll assembly and update your initial code file with the following logic:

```
using System;
...

// Location of strongly typed data containers.
using AutoLotDAL;

// Location of strongly typed data adapters.
using AutoLotDAL.AutoLotDataSetTableAdapters;

namespace LinqToDataSetApp
{
  class Program
  {
    static void Main(string[] args)
    {
      Console.WriteLine("***** LINQ over DataSet *****\n");

      // Get a strongly typed DataTable containing the current Inventory
      // of the AutoLot database.
      AutoLotDataSet dal = new AutoLotDataSet();
      InventoryTableAdapter da = new InventoryTableAdapter();
      AutoLotDataSet.InventoryDataTable data = da.GetData();

      // Invoke the methods that follow here!

      Console.ReadLine();
    }
  }
}
```

When you want to transform an ADO.NET DataTable (including a strongly typed DataTable) into a LINQ-compatible object, you must call the AsEnumerable() extension method defined by the DataTableExtensions type. This returns an EnumerableRowCollection object that contains a collection of DataRows.

You can then use the EnumerableRowCollection type to operate on each row using basic DataRow syntax (e.g., indexer syntax). Consider the following new method of your Program class, which takes a strongly typed DataTable, obtains an enumerable copy of the data, and prints out each CarID value:

```
static void PrintAllCarIDs(DataTable data)
{
  // Get enumerable version of DataTable.
  EnumerableRowCollection enumData = data.AsEnumerable();

  // Print the car ID values.
  foreach (DataRow r in enumData)
    Console.WriteLine("Car ID = {0}", r["CarID"]);
```

```
}
```

At this point, you have not applied a LINQ query; however, the point here is that the enumData object can now be the target of a LINQ query expression. Again, notice that the EnumerableRowCollection contains a collection of DataRow objects because you are applying a type indexer against each subobject to print out the value of the CarID column.

In most cases, you do not need to declare a variable of type EnumerableRowCollection to hold the return value of AsEnumerable(). Rather, you can invoke this method from within the query expression itself. Here is a more interesting method of the Program class, which obtains a projection of CarID + Makes from all entries in the DataTable where the color is red (if you don't have any red autos in your Inventory table, you update this LINQ query as necessary):

```
static void ShowRedCars(DataTable data)
{
  // Project a new result set containing
  // the ID/color for rows where Color = Red.
  var cars = from car in data.AsEnumerable()
             where
                (string)car["Color"] == "Red"
             select new
             {
                ID = (int)car["CarID"],
                Make = (string)car["Make"]
             };
  Console.WriteLine("Here are the red cars we have in stock:");
  foreach (var item in cars)
  {
    Console.WriteLine("-> CarID = {0} is {1}", item.ID, item.Make);
  }
}
```

The Role of the DataRowExtensions.Field<T>() Extension Method

One undesirable aspect of the current LINQ query expression is that you use numerous casting operations and DataRow indexers to gather the result set, which could result in runtime exceptions if you attempt to cast to an incompatible data type. To inject some strong typing into your query, you can use the Field<T>() extension method of the DataRow type. Doing so lets you increase the type safety of your query because the compatibility of data types is checked at compile time. Consider the following update:

```
var cars = from car in data.AsEnumerable()
  where
    car.Field<string>("Color") == "Red"
  select new
  {
    ID = car.Field<int>("CarID"),
    Make = car.Field<string>("Make")
  };
```

In this case, you can invoke Field<T>() and specify a type parameter to represent the underlying data type of the column. As an argument to this method, you pass in the column name itself. Given the additional compile-time checking, you should consider it a best practice to use Field<T>() (rather than the DataRow indexer) when you process the roles of a EnumerableRowCollection.

Beyond the fact that you call the AsEnumerable() method, the overall format of the LINQ query is identical to what you have already seen in Chapter 13. Given this, there is no reason to repeat the details of the various LINQ operators here. If you would like to see additional examples, you can look up the topic "LINQ to DataSet Examples" in the .NET Framework 4.5 SDK documentation.

Hydrating New DataTables from LINQ Queries

It is also possible to populate the data of a new DataTable easily, based on the results of a LINQ query and provided that you are *not* using projections. When you have a result set where the underlying type can be represented as IEnumerable<T>, you can call the CopyToDataTable<T>() extension method on the result, as in this example:

```
static void BuildDataTableFromQuery(DataTable data)
{
  var cars = from car in data.AsEnumerable()
             where
                car.Field<int>("CarID") > 5
             select car;

  // Use this result set to build a new DataTable.
  DataTable newTable = cars.CopyToDataTable();

  // Print the DataTable.
  for (int curRow = 0; curRow < newTable.Rows.Count; curRow++)
  {
    for (int curCol = 0; curCol < newTable.Columns.Count; curCol++)
    {
      Console.Write(newTable.Rows[curRow][curCol].ToString().Trim() + "\t");
    }
    Console.WriteLine();
  }
}
```

■ **Note** It is also possible to transform a LINQ query to a DataView type by using the AsDataView<T>() extension method.

You might find this technique helpful when you want to use the result of a LINQ query as the source of a data-binding operation. Recall that the DataGridView of Windows Forms (as well as an ASP.NET or WPF grid control) supports a property named DataSource. You could bind a LINQ result to the grid as follows:

```
// Assume myDataGrid is a GUI-based grid object.
myDataGrid.DataSource = (from car in data.AsEnumerable()
             where
                car.Field<int>("CarID") > 5
             select car).CopyToDataTable();
```

This wraps up the examination of the disconnected layer of ADO.NET. Using this aspect of the API, you can fetch data from a relational database, munch on the data, and return it for processing while keeping the database connection open for the shortest possible amount of time.

■ **Source Code** You can find the LinqToDataSetApp example under the Chapter 22 subdirectory.

Summary

This chapter dove into the details of the disconnected layer of ADO.NET. As you have seen, the centerpiece of the disconnected layer is the DataSet. This type is an in-memory representation of any number of tables and any number of optional interrelationships, constraints, and expressions. The beauty of establishing relations on your local tables is that you can programmatically navigate between them while disconnected from the remote data store.

You also examined the role of the data adapter type in this chapter. Using this type (and the related SelectCommand, InsertCommand, UpdateCommand, and DeleteCommand properties), the adapter can resolve changes in the DataSet with the original data store. You also learned how to navigate the object model of a DataSet using the brute-force manual approach, as well as with strongly typed objects, which the Dataset Designer tools of Visual Studio typically generate.

You wrapped up by looking at one aspect of the LINQ technology set named LINQ to DataSet. This allows you to obtain a queryable copy of the DataSet, which can receive well formatted LINQ queries.

## CHAPTER 23

ADO.NET Part III: The Entity Framework

The previous two chapters examined the fundamental ADO.NET programming models—the connected and disconnected layers, specifically. These approaches have enabled .NET programmers to work with relational data (in a relatively straightforward manner) since the initial release of the platform. However, Microsoft introduced a brand-new component of the ADO.NET API called the *Entity Framework* (or simply, *EF*) in .NET 3.5 Service Pack 1.

The overarching goal of EF is to allow you to interact with relational databases using an object model that maps directly to the business objects in your application. For example, rather than treating a batch of data as a collection of rows and columns, you can operate on a collection of strongly typed objects termed *entities*. These entities are also natively LINQ aware, and you can query against them using the same LINQ grammar you learned about in Chapter 12. The EF runtime engine translates your LINQ queries into proper SQL queries on your behalf.

This chapter will introduce you to the EF programming model. You will learn about various bits of infrastructure, including object services, entity client, LINQ to Entities, and Entity SQL. You will also learn about the format of the all-important `*.edmx` file and its role in the Entity Framework API. Next, you will learn how to generate `*.edmx` files using Visual Studio and at the command line using the EDM generator utility (`edmgen.exe`).

By the time you complete this chapter, you will have the final version of `AutoLotDAL.dll`, and you will learn how to bind entity objects to a Windows Forms desktop application.

Understanding the Role of Entity Framework

The connected and disconnected layers of ADO.NET provide you with a fabric that lets you select, insert, update, and delete data with connections, commands, data readers, data adapters, and `DataSet` objects. While this is all well and good, these aspects of ADO.NET force you to treat the fetched data in a manner that is tightly coupled to the physical database schema. Recall for example, that when you use the connected layer, you typically iterate over each record by specifying column names to a data reader. On the other hand, if you opt to use the disconnected layer, you find yourself traversing the rows and columns collections of a `DataTable` object within a `DataSet` container.

If you use the disconnected layer in conjunction with strongly typed `DataSet`s/data adapters, you end up with a programming abstraction that provides some helpful benefits. First, the strongly typed `DataSet` class exposes table data using class properties. Second, the strongly typed table adapter supports methods that encapsulate the construction of the underlying SQL statements. Recall the following `AddRecords()` method from Chapter 22:

```
public static void AddRecords(AutoLotDataSet.InventoryDataTable tb,
                              InventoryTableAdapter dAdapt)
{
    // Get a new strongly typed row from the table.
    AutoLotDataSet.InventoryRow newRow = tb.NewInventoryRow();

    // Fill row with some sample data.
    newRow.CarID = 999;
    newRow.Color = "Purple";
    newRow.Make = "BMW";
    newRow.PetName = "Saku";

    // Insert the new row.
    tb.AddInventoryRow(newRow);

    // Add one more row, using overloaded Add method.
    tb.AddInventoryRow(888, "Yugo", "Green", "Zippy");

    // Update database.
    dAdapt.Update(tb);
}
```

Things get even better if you combine the disconnected layer with LINQ to DataSet. In this case, you can apply LINQ queries to your in-memory data to obtain a new result set, which you can then optionally map to a stand-alone object such as a new DataTable, a List<T>, Dictionary<K,V>, or array of data, as follows:

```
static void BuildDataTableFromQuery(DataTable data)
{
    var cars = from car in data.AsEnumerable()
               where car.Field<int>("CarID") > 5 select car;

    // Use this result set to build a new DataTable.
    DataTable newTable = cars.CopyToDataTable();

    // Work with DataTable...
}
```

LINQ to DataSet is useful; however, you need to remember that the target of your LINQ query is the *data returned from the database*, not the database engine itself. Ideally, you could build a LINQ query that you send directly to the database engine for processing, and get back some strongly typed data in return (which is exactly what the ADO.NET Entity Framework lets you accomplish).

When you use either the connected or disconnected layer of ADO.NET, you must always be mindful of the physical structure of the back-end database. You must know the schema of each data table, author complex SQL queries to interact with said table data, and so forth. This can force you to author some fairly verbose C# code because as C# itself does not speak the language of database schema directly.

To make matters worse, the way in which a physical database is constructed (by your friendly DBA) is squarely focused on database constructs such as foreign keys, views, and stored procedures. The databases constructed by your friendly DBA can grow quite complex as the DBA endeavors to account for security and scalability. This also complicates the sort of C# code you must author in order to interact with the data store.

The ADO.NET Entity Framework (EF) is a programming model that attempts to lessen the gap between database constructs and object-oriented programming constructs. Using EF, you can interact with a relational database without ever seeing a line of SQL code (if you so choose). Rather, when you apply LINQ queries to your strongly typed classes, the EF runtime generates proper SQL statements on your behalf.

■ **Note** *LINQ to Entities* is the term that describes the act of applying LINQ queries to ADO.NET EF entity objects.

Another possible approach: rather than updating database data by finding a row, updating the row, and sending the row back for processing with a batch of SQL queries, you can simply change properties on an object and save its state. Again, the EF runtime updates the database automatically.

As far as Microsoft is concerned, the ADO.NET Entity Framework is simply another approach to the data-access APIs, and it is not intended to replace the connected or disconnected layers. However, once you spend some time working with EF, you might quickly find yourself preferring this rich object model over the more primitive world of SQL queries and row/column collections.

Nevertheless, chances are you will find uses for all three approaches in your .NET projects; in some cases, the EF model might complicate your code base. For example, if you want to build an in-house application that needs to communicate only with a single database table, you might prefer to use the connected layer to hit a batch of related stored procedures. Larger applications can particularly benefit from EF, especially if the development team is comfortable working with LINQ. As with any new technology, you will need to determine how (and when) ADO.NET EF is appropriate for the task at hand.

■ **Note** You might recall a database programming API introduced with .NET 3.5 called LINQ to SQL. This API is close in concept (and fairly close in terms of programming constructs) to ADO.NET EF. While LINQ to SQL is not formally dead, the official word from those kind folks in Redmond is that you should put your efforts into EF, not LINQ to SQL.

The Role of Entities

The strongly typed classes mentioned previously are called *entities*. Entities are a conceptual model of a physical database that maps to your business domain. Formally speaking, this model is termed an *Entity Data Model (EDM)*. The EDM is a client-side set of classes that map to a physical database, but you should understand that the entities need not map directly to the database schema in so far as naming conventions go. You are free to restructure your entity classes to fit your needs, and the EF runtime will map your unique names to the correct database schema.

For example, you might recall that you created the simple Inventory table in the AutoLot database using the database schema shown in Figure 23-1.

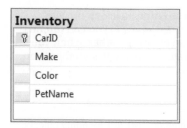

Figure 23-1. Structure of the Inventory table of the AutoLot database

If you were to generate an EDM for the Inventory table of the AutoLot database (you'll see how to do so momentarily), the entity will be called *Inventory* by default. However, you could rename this class to Car and define uniquely named properties of your choosing, which will be mapped to the columns of the Inventory table. This loose coupling means that you can shape the entities so they closely model your business domain. Figure 23-2 shows such an entity class.

Figure 23-2. The Car entity is a client-side reshaping of the Inventory schema

---

■ **Note** In many cases, the client-side entity class will be identically named to the related database table. However, remember that you can always reshape the entity to match your business situation.

We will build a full example with EF in just a bit. However, for the time being, consider the following Program class, which uses the Car entity class (and a related class named AutoLotEntities) to add a new row to the Inventory table of AutoLot. This class is termed an *object context*; the job of this class it is to communicate with the physical database on your behalf (you will learn more details soon).

```
class Program
{
  static void Main(string[] args)
  {
    // Connection string automatically read from
    // generated config file.
    using (AutoLotEntities context = new AutoLotEntities())
    {
      // Add a new record to Inventory table, using our entity.
```

```
            context.Cars.AddObject(new Car() { AutoIDNumber = 987, CarColor = "Black",
                                               MakeOfCar = "Pinto",
                                               NicknameOfCar = "Pete" });
            context.SaveChanges();
        }
    }
}
```

It is up to the EF runtime to take the client-side representation of the Inventory table (here, a class named Car) and map it back to the correct columns of the Inventory table. Notice that you see no trace of any sort of SQL INSERT statement; you simply add a new Car object to the collection maintained by the aptly named Cars property of the context object and save your changes. Sure enough, if you view the table data using the Server Explorer of Visual Studio, you will see a brand-new record (see Figure 23-3).

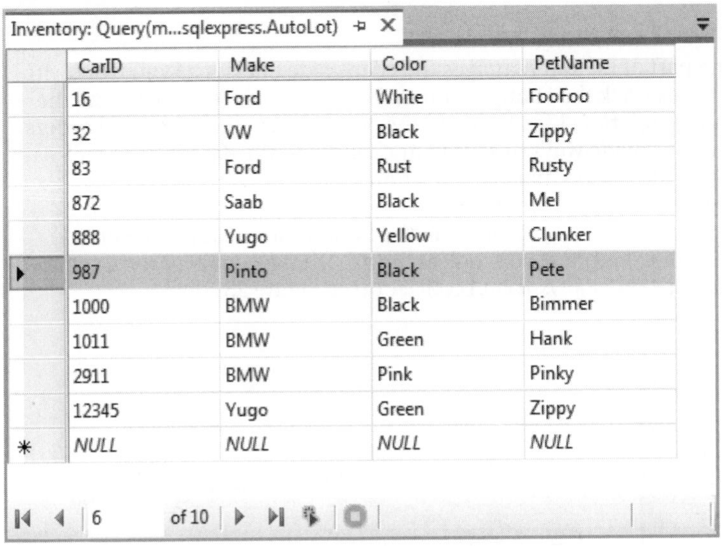

CarID	Make	Color	PetName
16	Ford	White	FooFoo
32	VW	Black	Zippy
83	Ford	Rust	Rusty
872	Saab	Black	Mel
888	Yugo	Yellow	Clunker
987	Pinto	Black	Pete
1000	BMW	Black	Bimmer
1011	BMW	Green	Hank
2911	BMW	Pink	Pinky
12345	Yugo	Green	Zippy
NULL	NULL	NULL	NULL

Figure 23-3. *The result of saving the context*

There is no magic in the preceding example. Under the covers, a connection to the database is made, a proper SQL statement is generated, and so forth. The benefit of EF is that these details are handled on your behalf. Now let's look at the core services of EF that make this possible.

The Building Blocks of the Entity Framework

The EF API sits on top of the existing ADO.NET infrastructure you have already examined in the previous two chapters. Like any ADO.NET interaction, the entity framework uses an ADO.NET data provider to communicate with the data store. However, the data provider must be updated so it supports a new set of services before it can interact with the EF API. As you might expect, the Microsoft SQL Server data provider has been updated with the necessary infrastructure, which is accounted for when using the System.Data.Entity.dll assembly.

■ **Note** Many third-party databases (e.g., Oracle and MySQL) provide EF-aware data providers. Consult your database vendor for details or log on to www.sqlsummit.com/dataprov.htm for a list of known ADO.NET data providers.

In addition to adding the necessary bits to the Microsoft SQL Server data provider, the System.Data.Entity.dll assembly contains various namespaces that account for the EF services themselves. The two key pieces of the EF API to concentrate on for the time being are *object services* and *entity client*.

The Role of Object Services

Object services is the name given to the part of EF that manages the client-side entities as you work with them in code. For example, object services track the changes you make to an entity (e.g., changing the color of a car from green to blue), manage relationships between the entities (e.g., looking up all orders for a customer named Steve Hagen), and provide ways to save your changes to the database, as well as ways to persist the state of an entity with XML and binary serialization services.

Programmatically speaking, the object services layer micromanages any class that extends the EntityObject base class. As you might suspect, EntityObject is in the inheritance chain for all entity classes in the EF programming model. For example, if you look at the inheritance chain of the Car entity class used in the previous example, you see that Car *is-a* EntityObject (see Figure 23-4).

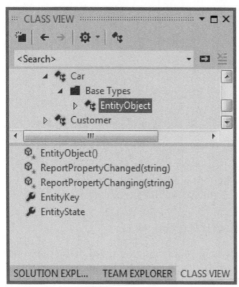

Figure 23-4. EF's object service layer can manage any class that extends EntityObject

The Role of the Entity Client

Another major aspect of the EF API is the entity client layer. This part of the EF API is in charge of working with the underlying ADO.NET data provider to make connections to the database, generate the necessary SQL statements based on the state of your entities and LINQ queries, map fetched database data into the correct shape of your entities, and manage other details you would normally perform by hand if you were not using the Entity Framework.

You can find the functionality of the entity client layer in the System.Data.EntityClient namespace. This namespace includes a set of classes that map EF concepts (such as LINQ to Entity queries) to the underlying ADO.NET data provider. These classes (e.g., EntityCommand and EntityConnection) are eerily similar to the classes you find in an ADO.NET data provider. For example, Figure 23-5 illustrates how the classes of the entity client layer extend the same abstract base classes of any other provider (e.g., DbCommand and DbConnection; you can also see Chapter 21 for more details on this subject).

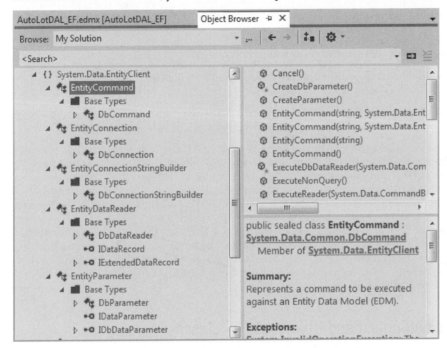

Figure 23-5. The entity client layer maps entity commands to the underlying ADO.NET data provider

The entity client layer typically works behind the scenes, but it is entirely possible to work directly with an entity client if you require full control over how it performs its duties (most notably, how it generates the SQL queries and handles the returned database data).

If you require greater control over how the entity client builds a SQL statement based on the incoming LINQ query, you can use *Entity SQL*. Entity SQL is a database-independent dialect of SQL that works directly with entities. After you build an Entity SQL query, it can be sent directly to entity client services (or if you want, to object services), where it will be formatted into a proper SQL statement for the underlying data provider. You will not work with Entity SQL to any significant extent in this chapter, but you will see a few examples of this new SQL-based grammar later in the chapter.

If you require greater control over how a fetched result set is manipulated, you can forego the automatic mapping of database results to entity objects and manually process the records using the EntityDataReader class. Unsurprisingly, the EntityDataReader allows you to process fetched data using a forward-only, read-only stream of data, just as SqlDataReader does. You will see a working example of this approach later in the chapter.

The Role of the *.edmx File (and Friends)

Recapping the story thus far, entities are client-side classes, which function as an Entity Data Model. While the client-side entities will eventually be mapped to the correct database table, there is no tight coupling between the property names of your entity classes and the column names on the data table.

For the Entity Framework API to map entity class data to database table data correctly, you need a proper definition of the mapping logic. In any data model–driven system, the entities, the real database, and the mapping layers are separated into three related parts: a *conceptual model*, a *logical model*, and a *physical model*.

- The conceptual model defines the entities and their relationships (if any).

- The logical model maps the entities and relationships into tables with any required foreign key constraints.

- The physical model represents the capabilities of a particular data engine by specifying storage details, such table schema, partitioning, and indexing.

In the world of EF, each of these three layers is captured in an XML-based file format. When you use the integrated Entity Framework designers of Visual Studio, you end up with a file that takes an *.edmx file extension (remember, EDM = entity data model). This file includes XML descriptions of the entities, the physical database, and instructions on how to map this information between the conceptual and physical models. You will examine the format of the *.edmx file in the first example of this chapter (which you will see in a moment).

When you compile your EF-based projects using Visual Studio, the *.edmx file is used to generate three stand-alone XML files: one for the conceptual model data (*.csdl), one for the physical model (*.ssdl), and one for the mapping layer (*.msl). The data of these three XML-based files is then bundled into your application in the form of binary resources. Once compiled, your .NET assembly has all the necessary data for the EF API calls you make in your code base.

The Role of the ObjectContext and ObjectSet<T> Classes

The final part of the EF puzzle is the ObjectContext class, which is a member of the System.Data.Objects namespace. When you generate your *.edmx file, you get the entity classes that map to the database tables and a class that extends ObjectContext. You typically use this class to interact with object services and entity client functionality indirectly.

ObjectContext provides a number of core services to child classes, including the ability to save all changes (which results in a database update), tweak the connection string, delete objects, call stored procedures, and handle other fundamental details. Table 23-1 describes some of the core members of the ObjectContext class (be aware that a majority of these members stay in memory until you call SaveChanges()).

Table 23-1. Common Members of ObjectContext

Member of ObjectContext	Meaning in Life
AcceptAllChanges()	Accepts all changes made to entity objects within the object context.
AddObject()	Adds an object to the object context.
DeleteObject()	Marks an object for deletion.
ExecuteFunction<T>()	Executes a stored procedure in the database.
ExecuteStoreCommand()	Allows you to send a SQL command to the data store directly.
GetObjectByKey()	Locates an object within the object context by its key.
SaveChanges()	Sends all updates to the data store.
CommandTimeout	This property gets or sets the timeout value in seconds for all object context operations.
Connection	This property returns the connection string used by the current object context.
SavingChanges	This event fires when the object context saves changes to the data store.

The ObjectContext-derived class serves as a container that manages entity objects, which are stored in a collection of type ObjectSet<T>. For example, if you generate an *.edmx file for the Inventory table of the AutoLot database, you end up with a class named (by default) AutoLotEntities. This class supports a property named Inventories (note the plural name) that encapsulates an ObjectSet<Inventory> data member. If you create an EDM for the Orders table of the AutoLot database, the AutoLotEntities class will define a second property named Orders that encapsulates an ObjectSet<Order> member variable. Table 23-2 defines some common members of System.Data.Objects.ObjectSet<T>.

Table 23-2. Common members of ObjectSet<T>

Member of ObjectSet<T>	Meaning in Life
AddObject()	Allows you to insert a new entity object into the collection.
CreateObject<T>()	Creates a new instance of the specified entity type.
DeleteObject	Marks an object for deletion.

Once you drill into the correct property of the object context, you can call any member of ObjectSet<T>. Consider again the sample code shown in the first few pages of this chapter:

```
using (AutoLotEntities context = new AutoLotEntities())
{
    // Add a new record to Inventory table, using our entity.
    context.Cars.AddObject(new Car() { AutoIDNumber = 987, CarColor = "Black",
                                       MakeOfCar = "Pinto",
                                       NicknameOfCar = "Pete" });
    context.SaveChanges();
}
```

Here, AutoLotEntities is-a ObjectContext. The Cars property gives you access to the ObjectSet<Car> variable. You use this reference to insert a new Car entity object and tell the ObjectContext to save all changes to the database.

ObjectSet<T> is typically the target of LINQ to Entity queries; as such, ObjectSet<T> supports the same extension methods you learned about in Chapter 12. Moreover, ObjectSet<T> gains a good deal of functionality from its direct parent class, ObjectQuery<T>, which is a class that represents a strongly typed LINQ (or Entity SQL) query.

All Together Now!

Before you build your first Entity Framework example, take a moment to ponder Figure 23-6, which shows you how the EF API is organized.

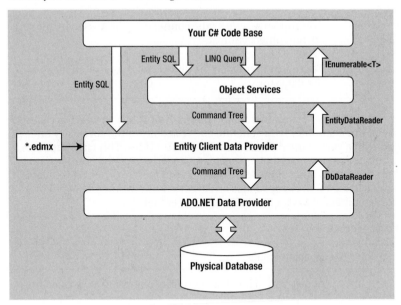

Figure 23-6. *The major components of the ADO.NET Entity Framework*

The moving parts illustrated by Figure 23-6 are not as complex as they might seem at first glance. For example, consider this common scenario. You author some C# code that applies a LINQ query to an entity you received from your context. This query is passed into object services, where it formats the LINQ command into a tree that the entity client can understand. In turn, the entity client formats this tree into a proper SQL statement for the underlying ADO.NET provider. The provider returns a data reader (e.g., a DbDataReader-derived object) that client services use to stream data to object services using an EntityDataReader. What your C# code base gets back is an enumeration of entity data (IEnumerable<T>).

Here is another scenario to consider. Your C# code base wants more control over how client services constructs the eventual SQL statement to send to the database. Thus, you author some C# code using Entity SQL that can be passed directly to entity client or object services. The end result returns as an IEnumerable<T>.

In either of these scenarios, you must make the XML data of the *.edmx file known to client services; this enables it to understand how to map database atoms to entities. Finally, remember that the client (e.g., your C# code base) can also nab the results sent from entity client by using the EntityDataReader directly.

Building and Analyzing Your First EDM

Now that you have a better understanding of what the ADO.NET Entity Framework is attempting to accomplish, as well as a high-level idea of how it all works, it's time to look at your first full example. To keep things simple for now, you will build an EDM that only allows access to the Inventory table of AutoLot. After you understand the basics, you will build a new EDM that accounts for the entire AutoLot database, and then display your data in a graphical user interface.

Generating the *.edmx File

Begin by creating a new Console Application named InventoryEDMConsoleApp. When you want to use the Entity Framework, your first step is to generate the necessary conceptual, logical, and physical model data defined by the *.edmx file. One way to do this is to use the .NET 4.5 SDK command-line tool, EdmGen.exe. Open a Developer Command Prompt and enter the following instruction:

```
EdmGen.exe -?
```

You should see a list of options that you can supply to the tool to generate the necessary files based on an existing database; you should also see options to generate a brand-new database based on existing entity files! Table 23-3 documents some common options of EdmGen.exe.

Table 23-3. Common Command-Line Flags of EdmGen.exe

EdmGen.exe Option	Meaning in Life
/mode:FullGeneration	Generate the *.ssdl, *.msl, *.csdl files and client entities from a specified database.
/project:	This is the base name to be used for the generated code and files. Typically, this is the name of the database you pull data from (it can use the short form, /p:).
/connectionstring:	This is the connection string you use to interact with the database (it can use the short form, /c:).

/language:	Allows you to specify whether you want to use C# or VB syntax for the generated code.
/pluralize	Automatically pluralize or singularize the entity set name, entity type name, and navigation property name using English language rules.

As of .NET 4.0, the EF programming model supports *domain-first* programming, which allows you to create your entities (with typical object-oriented techniques) and use them to generate a brand-new database. In this introductory look at ADO.NET EF, you will not use this model-first mentality, nor will you use EdmGen.exe to generate your client-side entity model. Instead, you will use the graphical EDM designers of Visual Studio.

Now activate the Project ➤ Add New Item... menu option and insert a new ADO.NET Entity Data Model item (be sure to highlight the Data node; see Figure 23-7) named InventoryEDM.edmx.

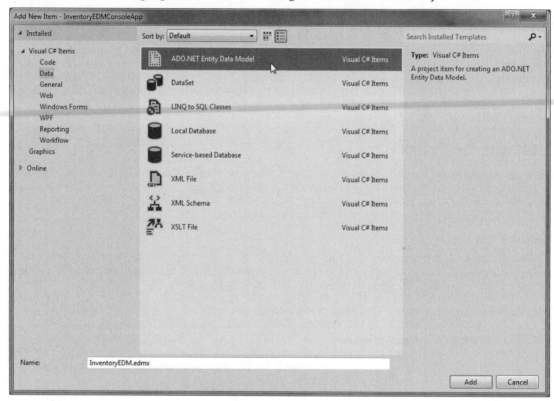

Figure 23-7. Inserting a new ADO.NET EDM project item

Clicking the Add button launches the Entity Model Data Wizard. The wizard's first step allows you to select whether you want to generate an EDM from an existing database or define an empty model (for model-first development). Select the Generate from database option and click the Next button (see Figure 23-8).

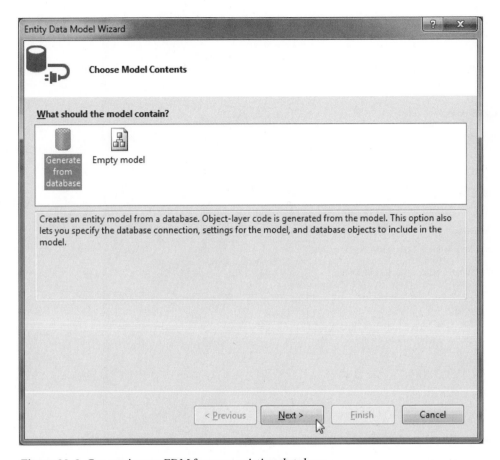

Figure 23-8. Generating an EDM from an existing database

You can select your database in the wizard's second step. If you already have a connection to a database within the Visual Studio Server Explorer, you will see it listed in the drop-down combo box. If this is not the case, you can click the New Connection button. Either way, pick your AutoLot database, and then make certain you save the connection string data in the (autogenerated) App.config file (see Figure 23-9).

Figure 23-9. *Selecting the database to generate the EDM from*

Before you click the Next button, take a moment to examine the format of your connection string.

```
metadata=res://*/InventoryEDM.csdl|res://*/InventoryEDM.ssdl|res://*/InventoryEDM.msl;
  provider=System.Data.SqlClient;provider connection string=
  "Data Source=(local)\SQLEXPRESS;
  Initial Catalog=AutoLot;Integrated Security=True;Pooling=False"
```

While your connection may differ slightly based on your machine configuration, the main point of interest here is the `metadata` flag, which you use to denote the names of the embedded XML resource data for your conceptual, physical, and mapping files (recall that the single `*.edmx` file will be broken into three separate files at compile time, and the data in these files takes the form of binary resources embedded in your assembly).

In the wizard's final step, you can select the items from the database you want to use to generate the EDM. Again, you are only concerned with the `Inventory` table in this example (see Figure 23-10).

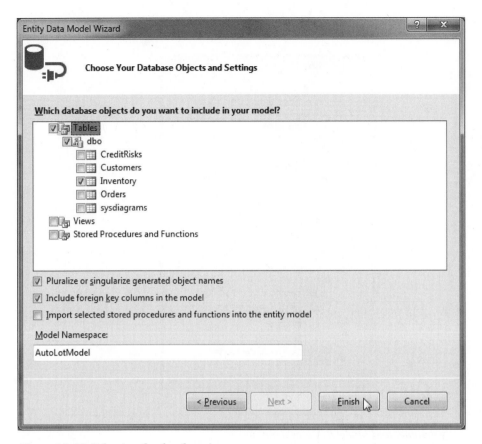

Figure 23-10. *Selecting the database items*

Now, click the Finish button to generate your EDM data.

Reshaping the Entity Data

After you complete the wizard, you will see the EDM designer open within the IDE, where you should see a single entity named *Inventory*. You can view the composition of any entity on the designer using the Entity Data Model Browser window (you open this using the View ➤ Other Windows menu option). Now look at the format of your conceptual model for the Inventory database table under the Entity Types folder (see Figure 23-11). You can see the physical model of the database under the Store node, where the name of your store will be based on the name of the database itself (AutoLotModel.Store, in this case).

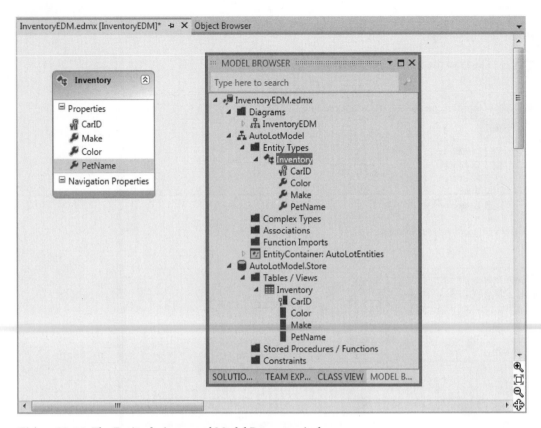

Figure 23-11. The Entity designer and Model Browser window

By default, the names of your entities will be based on the original database object names; however, recall that the names of entities in your conceptual model can be anything you choose. You can change the entity name, as well as property names of the entity, by selecting an item on the designer and renaming it using the Name property in the Visual Studio Properties window. Next, rename the Inventory entity to Car and the PetName property to CarNickname (see Figure 23-12).

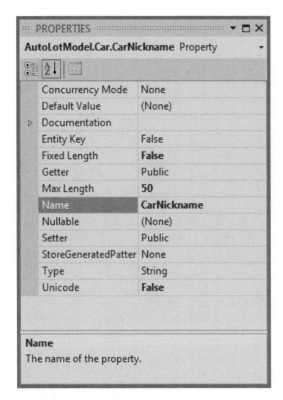

Figure 23-12. Reshaping entities using the Properties window

At this point, your conceptual model should look similar to what is shown in Figure 23-13.

Figure 23-13. The client-side model, reshaped to match your business domain

Now select the entire Car entity on the designer and look at the Properties window again. You should see that the Entity Set Name field has also been renamed from Inventories to Cars (see Figure 23-14). The Entity Set value is important because this corresponds to the name of the property on the data context class, which you will use to modify the database. Recall that this property encapsulates an ObjectSet<T> member variable in the ObjectContext derived class.

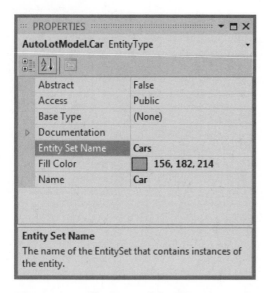

Figure 23-14. *The name of the* ObjectSet<T> *property wrapper*

Before moving on, compile your application; doing so refreshes your code base and generates the *.csdl, *.msl, and *.ssdl files based on your *.edmx file data.

Viewing the Mappings

Now that you have reshaped the data, you can view the mappings between the conceptual layer and the physical layer using the Mapping Details window (you open this using the View ➤ Other Windows... menu option). Next, look at Figure 23-15 and notice how the nodes on the left-hand side of the tree represent the data names in the physical layer, while the nodes on the right-hand side represent the names of your conceptual model.

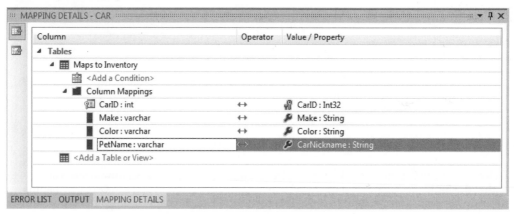

Figure 23-15. *The Mapping Details window shows the mappings of your conceptual and physical models*

Viewing the Generated *.edmx File Data

Now, let's see exactly what the EDM Wizard generated for you. Right-click the InventoryEDM.edmx file in the Solution Explorer and select the Open With... menu option. From the resulting dialog box, pick the XML (Text) Editor option. This allows you to see the underlying XML data seen in the EDM designer. The structure of this XML document is contained within the root <edmx:Edmx> element.

If you expand the root element, you have two child elements. First, <edmx:Runtime> contains metadata that's used by your application at runtime, and <Designer> contains metadata that's used by Visual Studio at development time.

Within the <edmx:Runtime> element, you find three child elements that describe the physical storage model, the logical C# object model, and the mappings between the two. Let's take a look at the storage model metadata first.

```
<!-- SSDL content. -->
<edmx:StorageModels>
  <Schema Namespace="AutoLotModel.Store" Alias="Self"
  Provider="System.Data.SqlClient"
  ProviderManifestToken="2008"
  xmlns:store=
  "http://schemas.microsoft.com/ado/2007/12/edm/EntityStoreSchemaGenerator"
  xmlns="http://schemas.microsoft.com/ado/2009/02/edm/ssdl">
    <EntityContainer Name="AutoLotModelStoreContainer">
      <EntitySet Name="Inventory" EntityType="AutoLotModel.Store.Inventory"
                 store:Type="Tables" Schema="dbo" />
    </EntityContainer>
    <EntityType Name="Inventory">
      <Key>
        <PropertyRef Name="CarID" />
      </Key>
      <Property Name="CarID" Type="int" Nullable="false" />
      <Property Name="Make" Type="varchar" Nullable="false" MaxLength="50" />
      <Property Name="Color" Type="varchar" Nullable="false" MaxLength="50" />
      <Property Name="PetName" Type="varchar" MaxLength="50" />
    </EntityType>
  </Schema>
</edmx:StorageModels>
```

Note that the <Schema> node defines the name of the ADO.NET data provider that will use this information when communicating with the database (System.Data.SqlClient). The <EntityType> node marks the name of the physical database table, as well as each column in the table.

The next major chunk of the *.edmx file is the <edmx:ConceptualModels> element, which defines the shaped client-side entities. Notice that the Cars entity defines the CarNickname property, which you change using the designer.

```
<!-- CSDL content. -->
<edmx:ConceptualModels>
  <Schema Namespace="AutoLotModel" Alias="Self"
    xmlns:annotation="http://schemas.microsoft.com/ado/2009/02/edm/annotation"
    xmlns="http://schemas.microsoft.com/ado/2008/09/edm">
    <EntityContainer
      Name="AutoLotEntities" annotation:LazyLoadingEnabled="true">
      <EntitySet Name="Cars" EntityType="AutoLotModel.Car" />
```

```
    </EntityContainer>
    <EntityType Name="Car">
      <Key>
        <PropertyRef Name="CarID" />
      </Key>
        <Property Name="CarID" Type="Int32" Nullable="false" />
        <Property Name="Make" Type="String" Nullable="false" MaxLength="50"
                Unicode="false" FixedLength="false" />
        <Property Name="Color" Type="String" Nullable="false" MaxLength="50"
                Unicode="false" FixedLength="false" />
        <Property Name="CarNickname" Type="String" MaxLength="50"
                Unicode="false" FixedLength="false" />
    </EntityType>
  </Schema>
</edmx:ConceptualModels>
```

That brings you to the mapping layer, which the Mapping Details window (and the EF runtime) uses to connect names in the conceptual model to the physical model.

```
<!-- C-S mapping content. -->
<edmx:Mappings>
  <Mapping Space="C-S"
    xmlns="http://schemas.microsoft.com/ado/2008/09/mapping/cs">
    <EntityContainerMapping StorageEntityContainer="AutoLotModelStoreContainer"
        CdmEntityContainer="AutoLotEntities">
      <EntitySetMapping Name="Cars">
        <EntityTypeMapping TypeName="AutoLotModel.Car">
          <MappingFragment StoreEntitySet="Inventory">
            <ScalarProperty Name="CarID" ColumnName="CarID" />
            <ScalarProperty Name="Make" ColumnName="Make" />
            <ScalarProperty Name="Color" ColumnName="Color" />
            <ScalarProperty Name="CarNickname" ColumnName="PetName" />
          </MappingFragment>
        </EntityTypeMapping>
      </EntitySetMapping>
    </EntityContainerMapping>
  </Mapping>
</edmx:Mappings>
```

The last part of the *.edmx file is the <Designer> element, which is not used by the EF runtime. If you view this data, you will see it contains instructions used by Visual Studio to display your entities on the visual designer surface.

Again, ensure that you have compiled your project at least once and click the Show All Files button of the Solution Explorer. Next, begin by drilling into the obj\Debug folder; and then drill into the edmxResourcesToEmbed subdirectory. Here you will find three XML files that are based on the entirety of your *.edmx file (see Figure 23-16).

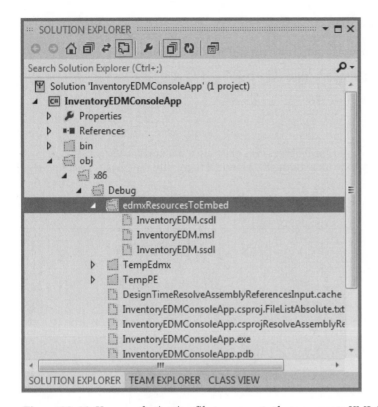

Figure 23-16. You use the *.edmx file to generate three separate XML files

The data in these files will be embedded as binary resources in your assembly. Thus, your .NET application has all the information it needs to understand the conceptual, physical, and mapping layers of the EDM.

Viewing the Generated Source Code

You are almost ready to author some code to use your EDM; before you do, however, you should check out the generated C# code base. Open the Class View window and expand your default namespace. You will see that, in addition to the Program class, the EDM Wizard generated an entity class (which you renamed to Car) and another class named AutoLotEntities.

If you go to the Solution Explorer and expand the InventoryEDM.edmx node, you will see an IDE-maintained file named InventoryEDM.Designer.cs. As with any IDE-maintained file, you should not directly edit this file because the IDE will recreate it each time you compile. However, you can open this file for viewing by double-clicking it.

The AutoLotEntities class extends the ObjectContext class, which (as you probably recall) is your entry point to the EF programming model. The constructors of AutoLotEntities provide various ways for you to feed in connection string data. The default constructor has been configured to read the connection string data automatically from the App.config file.

```
public partial class AutoLotEntities : ObjectContext
{
  public AutoLotEntities() : base("name=AutoLotEntities", "AutoLotEntities")
  {
    this.ContextOptions.LazyLoadingEnabled = true;
    OnContextCreated();
  }
  ...
}
```

Next, notice that the `Cars` property of the `AutoLotEntities` class encapsulates the `ObjectSet<Car>` data member. You can use this property to work with the EDM model to modify the physical back-end database indirectly.

```
public partial class AutoLotEntities : ObjectContext
{
  ...
  public ObjectSet<Car> Cars
  {
    get
    {
      if ((_Cars == null))
      {
        _Cars = base.CreateObjectSet<Car>("Cars");
      }
      return _Cars;
    }
  }
  private ObjectSet<Car> _Cars;
}
```

■ **Note** You will also see various methods in your `ObjectContext`-derived classes that begin with `AddTo`. While you can use them to add new entities to the `ObjectSet<T>` member variables, the preferred way to do this is with the `ObjectSet<T>` member obtained from the strongly typed properties.

The last item of interest in the designer code file is the `Car` entity class. The bulk of the code for each entity class is a collection of properties that model the shape of your conceptual model. Each of these properties implement its set logic using a call to the static `StructuralObject.SetValidValue()` method of the EF API.

Also, the set logic includes code that informs the EF runtime that the state of an entity has changed, which is important because the `ObjectContext` must know about these changes to push updates to the physical database.

In addition, the set logic makes calls on two partial methods. Recall that a C# partial method provides a simple way to deal with change notifications in your applications. If you don't implement a partial method, it is ignored by the compiler and stripped away. Here is the implementation of the `CarNickname` property of the `Car` entity class:

```
public partial class Car : EntityObject
{
...
  public global::System.String CarNickname
  {
    get
    {
      return _CarNickname;
    }
    set
    {
      OnCarNicknameChanging(value);
      ReportPropertyChanging("CarNickname");
      _CarNickname = StructuralObject.SetValidValue(value, true);
      ReportPropertyChanged("CarNickname");
      OnCarNicknameChanged();
    }
  }
  private global::System.String _CarNickname;
  partial void OnCarNicknameChanging(global::System.String value);
  partial void OnCarNicknameChanged();
}
```

Enhancing the Generated Source Code

All of the designer-generated classes have been declared with the partial keyword, which as you recall allows you to implement a class across multiple C# code files. This is especially useful when working with the EF programming model because it means you can add "real" methods to your entity classes that help you model your business domain better.

In this example, you override the ToString() method of the Car entity class to return the state of the entity with a well formatted string. You also complete the definitions of the partial OnCarNicknameChanging() and OnCarNicknameChanged() methods to serve as simple diagnostic notifications. You define the following partial class declaration in a new Car.cs file:

```
public partial class Car
{
  public override string ToString()
  {
    // Since the PetName column could be empty, supply
    // the default name of **No Name**.
    return string.Format("{0} is a {1} {2} with ID {3}.",
      this.CarNickname ?? "**No Name**",
      this.Color, this.Make, this.CarID);
  }
  partial void OnCarNicknameChanging(global::System.String value)
  {
    Console.WriteLine("\t-> Changing name to: {0}", value);
  }
  partial void OnCarNicknameChanged()
  {
```

```
      Console.WriteLine("\t-> Name of car has been changed!");
    }
  }
```

A friendly reminder: when you provide implementations to these partial methods, you can receive notifications if the properties of the *entity classes* have changed or are being changed, but not when the physical database has changed. If you need to know when the physical database has changed, you can handle the SavingChanges event on your ObjectContext-derived class.

Programming Against the Conceptual Model

Now you can author some code that interacts with your EDM. Begin by updating your Program class to call a helper method from Main(), which will print out each item in the Inventory database using your conceptual model, and another that will insert a new record to the Inventory table, as follows:

```
class Program
{
  static void Main(string[] args)
  {
    Console.WriteLine("***** Fun with ADO.NET EF *****\n");
    AddNewRecord();
    PrintAllInventory();
    Console.ReadLine();
  }

  private static void AddNewRecord()
  {
    // Add record to the Inventory table of the AutoLot
    // database.
    using (AutoLotEntities context = new AutoLotEntities())
    {
      try
      {
        // Hard-code data for a new record, for testing.
        context.Cars.AddObject(new Car() { CarID = 2222,
            Make = "Yugo", Color = "Brown" });
        context.SaveChanges();
      }
      catch(Exception ex)
      {
        Console.WriteLine(ex.InnerException.Message);
      }
    }
  }

  private static void PrintAllInventory()
  {
    // Select all items from the Inventory table of AutoLot,
    // and print out the data using our custom ToString()
    // of the Car entity class.
    using (AutoLotEntities context = new AutoLotEntities())
    {
```

```
    foreach (Car c in context.Cars)
      Console.WriteLine(c);
  }
 }
}
```

You have seen code similar to this earlier in the chapter, but now you should have a much better idea about how it works. Each helper method creates an instance of the ObjectContext-derived class (AutoLotEntities), and uses the strongly typed Cars property to interact with the ObjectSet<Car> field. Enumerating each item exposed by the Cars property enables you to submit a SQL SELECT statement indirectly to the underlying ADO.NET data provider. By inserting a new Car object with the AddObject() method of ObjectSet<Car>, and then calling SaveChanges() on the context, you have preformed a SQL INSERT.

Deleting a Record

When you want to remove a record from the database, you will first need to locate the correct item in the ObjectSet<T>, which you can find by passing an EntityKey object (which is a member of the System.Data namespace) to the GetObjectByKey() method. Assuming you have imported this namespace into your C# code file, you can now author the following helper method:

```
private static void RemoveRecord()
{
  // Find a car to delete by primary key.
  using (AutoLotEntities context = new AutoLotEntities())
  {
    // Define a key for the entity we are looking for.
    EntityKey key = new EntityKey("AutoLotEntities.Cars", "CarID", 2222);

    // See if we have it, and delete it if we do.
    Car carToDelete = (Car)context.GetObjectByKey(key);
    if (carToDelete != null)
    {
      context.DeleteObject(carToDelete);
      context.SaveChanges();
    }
  }
}
```

■ **Note** For better or for worse, calling GetObjectByKey() requires a round trip to the database before you can delete the object.

Notice that when you are creating an EntityKey object, you need use a string object to inform it which ObjectSet<T> to evaluate in a given ObjectContext-derived class. The second argument is another string; this one represents the property name on the entity class that is marked as the key, and the final constructor argument is the value of the primary key. Once you find the object in question, you can call DeleteObject() off your context and save the changes.

Updating a Record

Updating a record is also straightforward. Locate the object you want to change, set new property values on the returned entity, and save the changes, like so:

```
private static void UpdateRecord()
{
  // Find a car to delete by primary key.
  using (AutoLotEntities context = new AutoLotEntities())
  {
    // Define a key for the entity we are looking for.
    EntityKey key = new EntityKey("AutoLotEntities.Cars", "CarID", 2222);

    // Grab the car, change it, save!
    Car carToUpdate = (Car)context.GetObjectByKey(key);
    if (carToUpdate != null)
    {
      carToUpdate.Color = "Blue";
      context.SaveChanges();
    }
  }
}
```

The preceding method might seem a bit off, at least until you remember that the entity object returned from GetObjectByKey() is a reference to an existing object in the ObjectSet<T> field. Thus, when you set properties to change the state, you are changing the same object in memory.

■ **Note** Much like an ADO.NET DataRow object (see Chapter 22), any descendant of EntityObject (meaning, all of your entity classes) has a property named EntityState, which is used by the object context to determine whether the item has been modified, deleted, is detached, and so forth. This is set on your behalf as you work with the programming model; however, you can change this manually as required.

Querying with LINQ to Entities

So far, you have been working with a few simple methods on the object context and entity objects to perform selections, inserts, updates, and deletes. This is useful all by itself; however, EF becomes much more powerful when you incorporate LINQ queries. If you want to use LINQ to update or delete records, you don't need to make an EntityKey object manually. Consider the following update to the RemoveRecord() method, which will *not work* as expected at this point:

```
private static void RemoveRecord()
{
  // Find a car to delete by primary key.
  using (AutoLotEntities context = new AutoLotEntities())
  {
    // See if we have it?
    var carToDelete = from c in context.Cars where c.CarID == 2222 select c;
```

```
      if (carToDelete != null)
      {
        context.DeleteObject(carToDelete);
        context.SaveChanges();
      }
    }
  }
}
```

This code compiles, but you will receive a runtime exception when you attempt to call the DeleteObject() method. The reason: this particular LINQ query returns an ObjectQuery<T> object, not a Car object. Always remember that when you build a LINQ query that attempts to locate a single entity, you will get back an ObjectQuery<T> representing a query that is capable of bringing back the data you are looking for. To execute the query (and bring back the Car entity), you must execute a method such as FirstOrDefault() on the query object, as in the following example:

```
var carToDelete =
  (from c in context.Cars where c.CarID == 2222 select c).FirstOrDefault();
```

By calling FirstOrDefault() on the ObjectQuery<T>, you find the item you want; or, if there is no Car with the ID of 2222, a default value of null.

Given that you have already worked with many LINQ expressions in Chapter 13, a few more examples will suffice for the time being.

```
private static void FunWithLINQQueries()
{
  using (AutoLotEntities context = new AutoLotEntities())
  {
    // Get a projection of new data.
    var colorsMakes = from item in context.Cars select
        new { item.Color, item.Make };
    foreach (var item in colorsMakes)
    {
      Console.WriteLine(item);
    }

    // Get only items where CarID < 1000.
    var idsLessThan1000 = from item in context.Cars
        where item.CarID < 1000 select item;
    foreach (var item in idsLessThan1000)
    {
      Console.WriteLine(item);
    }
  }
}
```

While the syntax of these queries is simple enough, remember that you are hitting a database each time you apply a LINQ query to the object context! Recall that when you want to obtain an independent copy of data, which can be the target of new LINQ queries, you want to use immediate execution with the ToList<T>(), ToArray<T>() or ToDictionary<K,V>() extension methods (among others). Here is an update of the previous method, which performs the equivalent of a SELECT *, caches the entities as an array, and manipulates the array data using LINQ to Objects:

```
using (AutoLotEntities context = new AutoLotEntities())
{
  // Get all data from the Inventory table.
  // Could also write:
  // var allData = (from item in context.Cars select item).ToArray();
  var allData = context.Cars.ToArray();

  // Get a projection of new data.
  var colorsMakes = from item in allData select new { item.Color, item.Make };

  // Get only items where CarID < 1000.
  var idsLessThan1000 = from item in allData where
    item.CarID < 1000 select item;
}
```

Working with LINQ to Entities is much more enticing when your EDM contains multiple related tables. You'll see some example that illustrate this in a moment; however, let's wrap up this current example by looking at two other ways you can interact with your object context.

Querying with Entity SQL

To be sure, you will be querying and ObjectSet<T> with LINQ a majority of the time. The entity client will break down your LINQ query into a fitting SQL statement, passing it on to the database for processing. However, you can use Entity SQL if you want to have more control over how the query is formatted.

Entity SQL is a SQL-like query language that can be applied to entities. While the format of an Entity SQL statement is similar to a traditional SQL statement, it is not identical. Entity SQL has a unique syntax because the entities receive the query, not the physical database. Like a LINQ to Entities query, an Entity SQL query is used to pass a "real" SQL query to the database.

This chapter will not dive into the details of building Entity SQL commands, so please consult the .NET Framework 4.5 SDK documentation if you want more information. However, one example might be helpful. Consider the following method, which builds an Entity SQL statement that finds all black cars in the ObjectSet<Car> collection:

```
private static void FunWithEntitySQL()
{
  using (AutoLotEntities context = new AutoLotEntities())
  {
    // Build a string containing Entity SQL syntax.
    string query = "SELECT VALUE car FROM AutoLotEntities.Cars " +
                   "AS car WHERE car.Color='black'";

    // Now build an ObjectQuery<T> based on the string.
    var blackCars = context.CreateQuery<Car>(query);
    foreach (var item in blackCars)
    {
      Console.WriteLine(item);
    }
  }
}
```

Notice that you pass in the formatted Entity SQL statement as an argument to the CreateQuery<T> method of your object context.

Working with the Entity Client Data Reader Object

When you use LINQ to Entities or Entity SQL, the fetched data is mapped back to your entity classes automatically, thanks to the entity client service. Typically this is exactly what you require; however, you can intercept the result set before it makes its way to your entity objects and process it manually using the EntityDataReader.

Here is a final helper method for this example, which uses several members of the System.Data.EntityClient namespace to build a connection manually through a command object and data reader. This code should look familiar due to your previous work in Chapter 21; the major difference is that you use Entity SQL, rather than "normal" SQL.

```
private static void FunWithEntityDataReader()
{
  // Make a connection object, based on our *.config file.
  using (EntityConnection cn = new EntityConnection("name=AutoLotEntities"))
  {
    cn.Open();

    // Now build an Entity SQL query.
    string query = "SELECT VALUE car FROM AutoLotEntities.Cars AS car";

    // Create a command object.
    using (EntityCommand cmd = cn.CreateCommand())
    {
      cmd.CommandText = query;

      // Finally, get the data reader and process records.
      using (EntityDataReader dr =
             cmd.ExecuteReader(CommandBehavior.SequentialAccess))
      {
        while (dr.Read())
        {
          Console.WriteLine("***** RECORD *****");
          Console.WriteLine("ID: {0}", dr["CarID"]);
          Console.WriteLine("Make: {0}", dr["Make"]);
          Console.WriteLine("Color: {0}", dr["Color"]);
          Console.WriteLine("Pet Name: {0}", dr["CarNickname"]);
          Console.WriteLine();
        }
      }
    }
  }
}
```

Great! This initial example should go a long way toward helping you understand the nuts and bolts of working with the Entity Framework. As mentioned previously, things become much more interesting when your EDM contains interrelated tables, which you will learn about next.

■ **Source Code** You can find the InventoryEDMConsoleApp example under the Chapter 23 subdirectory.

AutoLotDAL Version Four, Now with Entities

Next, you will learn how to build an EDM that captures the bulk of the AutoLot database, including your GetPetName stored procedure. I strongly suggest that you make a copy of the AutoLotDAL (Version Three) project you created in Chapter 22 and rename this copy to AutoLotDAL (Version Four).

Open the latest version of the AutoLotDAL project in Visual Studio and insert a new ADO.NET Entity Data Model project item named AutoLotDAL_EF.edmx. On step three of the wizard, you should select the Inventory, Orders, and Customers tables (there's no need to nab the CreditRisks table at this time), as well as the custom stored procedure (see Figure 23-17).

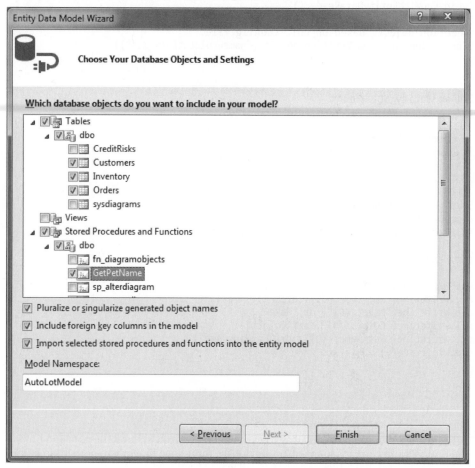

*Figure 23-17. The *.edmx file for a majority of the AutoLot database*

In contrast to the first EDM example, this time you don't bother renaming your entity class names or their properties. In any case, if you examine your Model Browser window, you will see each of your Entities is present and accounted for, in addition to your custom stored procedure (see Figure 23-18).

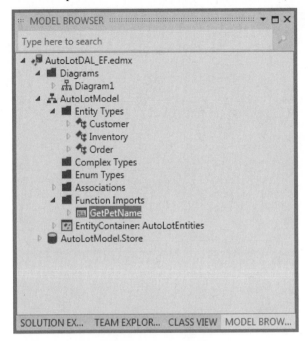

Figure 23-18. *The imported model data*

The Role of Navigation Properties

If you look at the EDM designer, you will see each table is accounted for, including new entries in the Navigation Properties section of a given entity class (see Figure 23-19).

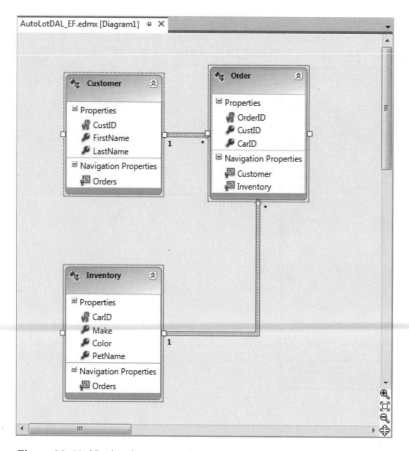

Figure 23-19. *Navigation properties*

As the name suggests, *navigation properties* allow you to capture JOIN operations in the Entity Framework programming model (without the need to author complex SQL statements). To account for these foreign key relationships, each entity in the *.edmx file now contains some new XML data that shows how entities are connected through key data. Feel free to open the *.edmx file using the XML editor if you want to see the markup directly; however, you can see this same information in the Model Browser window, under the Associations folder (see Figure 23-20).

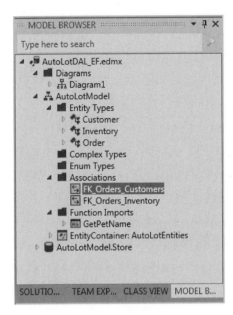

Figure 23-20. Viewing your entity relationships

If you want, change the version number of this new library to 4.0.0.0 (using the Assembly Information button within Applications tab of Properties window). Now compile your modified AutoLotDAL.dll assembly before moving to the first client application.

■ **Source Code** You can find the AutoLotDAL (Version 4) project under the Chapter 23 subdirectory.

Using Navigation Properties within LINQ to Entity Queries

Next, you will learn how to use these navigation properties within the context of LINQ to Entity queries (you could also use them with Entity SQL; however, this book doesn't delve into that aspect of this topic). Before you bind your data to a Windows Forms GUI, you make one final Console Application named AutoLotEDMClient. After you create the project, set a reference to System.Data.Entity.dll and the latest and greatest version of AutoLotDAL.dll.

Next, open the App.config file from your AutoLotDAL (Version Four) project for viewing (using the File ➤ Open… ➤ File menu option) and copy the connection string into your current configuration file (if you do not happen to have an App.config file in your project, you can simply include the entire file via Project ➤ Add Existing Item…). As well, import the AutoLotDAL namespace into your initial C# code file.

Next, you will update the physical Orders table with a few new records. Specifically, you want to ensure that a single customer has multiple orders. Using the Visual Studio Server Explorer, update the Orders table with one or two new records to ensure that a single customer has two or more orders. For example, in Figure 23-21, customer #4 has two pending orders, for cars #1992 and #83.

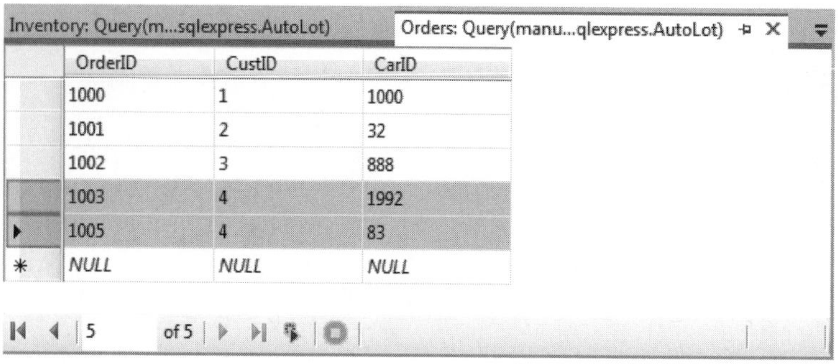

OrderID	CustID	CarID
1000	1	1000
1001	2	32
1002	3	888
1003	4	1992
1005	4	83
NULL	NULL	NULL

Inventory: Query(m...sqlexpress.AutoLot)
Orders: Query(manu...qlexpress.AutoLot)
5
of 5

***Figure 23-21.** A single customer with multiple orders*

Now update your `Program` with a new helper method (called from `Main()`). This method uses the navigation properties to select each `Inventory` object on order for a given customer.

```
private static void PrintCustomerOrders(string custID)
{
  int id = int.Parse(custID);

  using (AutoLotEntities context = new AutoLotEntities())
  {
    var carsOnOrder = from o in context.Orders
      where o.CustID == id select o.Inventory;
    Console.WriteLine("\nCustomer has {0} orders pending:", carsOnOrder.Count());
    foreach (var item in carsOnOrder)
    {
      Console.WriteLine("-> {0} {1} named {2}.",
        item.Color, item.Make, item.PetName);
    }
  }
}
```

When you run your application, you see something similar to the following output (notice that you specify a customer ID of 4 when you call `PrintCustomerOrders()` from `Main()`):

```
***** Navigation Properties *****
Please enter customer ID: 4

Customer has 2 orders pending:
-> Pink Saab named Pinky.
-> Rust Ford named Rusty.
```

Here, you find a single `Customer` entity in the context, which has the specified `CustID` value. Once you find the given customer, you can navigate to the `Inventory` table to select each car on order. The return value of your LINQ query is an enumeration of `Inventory` objects, which you print out using a standard `foreach` loop.

Invoking a Stored Procedure

In the AutoLotDAL EMD, you now have the information you need to invoke the GetPetName stored procedure. You can do this using either of two approaches. Here is the full code listing:

```
private static void CallStoredProc()
{
  using (AutoLotEntities context = new AutoLotEntities())
  {
    // Approach #1.
    ObjectParameter input = new ObjectParameter("carID", 83);
    ObjectParameter output = new ObjectParameter("petName", typeof(string));

    // Call ExecuteFunction off the context....
    context.ExecuteFunction("GetPetName", input, output);

    // Approach #2.
    // ....or use the strongly typed method on the context.
    context.GetPetName(83, output);

    Console.WriteLine("Car #83 is named {0}", output.Value);
  }
}
```

In this code listing, you can see our first approach is to call the ExecuteFunction() method of your object context. In this case, the stored procedure is identified by a string name, and each parameter is represented by an object of type ObjectParameter, which is in the System.Data.Objects namespace (don't forget to import this into your C# code file!).

However the second approach (again, seen in the previous code listing) is to use the strongly typed name in your object context. This approach proves a tad simpler because you can send input parameters (such as the carID) as typed data, rather than as an ObjectParameter object.

■ **Source Code** You can find the AutoLotEDMClient example under the Chapter 23 subdirectory.

Data Binding Entities to Windows Forms GUIs

To conclude this introductory examination of the ADO.NET Entity Framework, you will create a simple example where you bind entity objects to a Windows Forms GUI. As mentioned earlier in this chapter, you will examine data-binding operations in WPF and ASP.NET projects.

Create a new Windows Forms application named AutoLotEDM_GUI and rename your initial form to MainForm.cs. Next, set a reference to System.Data.Entity.dll and the latest and greatest version of AutoLotDAL.dll. Finally, modify the App.config file of this new project to include the connection string from your AutoLotDAL (Version Four) project and import the AutoLotDAL namespace into your Form's primary code file.

Now add a DataGridView object to the form designer and rename the control to gridInventory. After you have renamed this control, select the inline grid editor (the tiny arrow on the upper right of the widget). From the Choose Data Source drop-down box, add a project data source (see Figure 23-22).

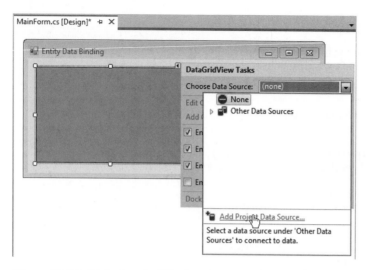

Figure 23-22. *Designing the Windows Forms* DataGridView *control*

In this case, you do not bind directly to the database; instead, you bind to an entity class, so pick the Object option (see Figure 23-23).

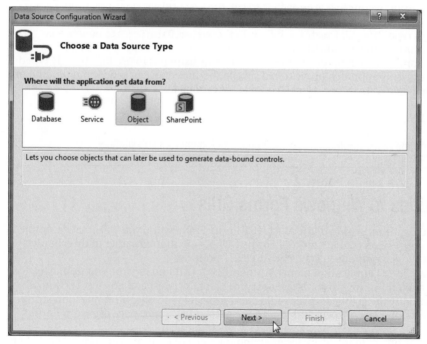

Figure 23-23. *Binding to a strongly typed object*

In the final step, check off the Inventory table of AutoLotDAL.dll as shown in Figure 23-24 (if you don't see it listed, you probably forgot to reference this library).

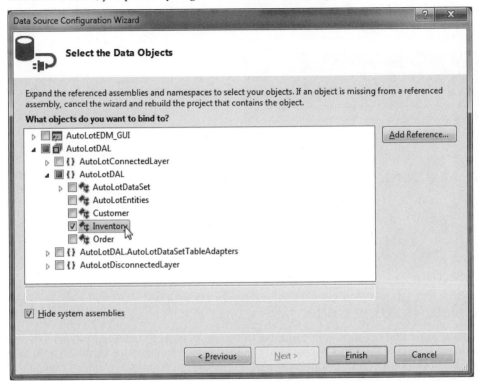

Figure 23-24. Selecting the Inventory table

When you click the Finish button, you'll see that the grid displays each property of the Inventory entity class, including the navigation properties.

To finish the UI, add a single Button control and rename it to btnUpdate. At this point, your designer should look something like what you see in Figure 23-25.

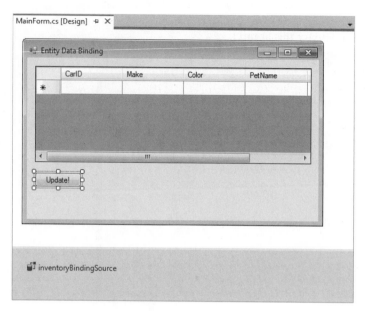

Figure 23-25. The final UI

Adding the Data-Binding Code

At this point, you have a grid that can display any number of Inventory objects; however, you need to write the code to do so. Thanks to the runtime engine of the EF, the code could not be simpler. Begin by handling the FormClosed and Load events of your MainForm class (using the Properties window) and the Click event of the Button control. After you do this, update your code file with the following snippet:

```
public partial class MainForm : Form
{
  AutoLotEntities context = new AutoLotEntities();

  public MainForm()
  {
    InitializeComponent();
  }

  private void MainForm_Load(object sender, EventArgs e)
  {
    // Bind the ObjectSet<Inventory> collection to the grid.
    gridInventory.DataSource = context.Inventories;
  }

  private void btnUpdate_Click(object sender, EventArgs e)
  {
    context.SaveChanges();
    MessageBox.Show("Data saved!");
  }
```

```
private void MainForm_FormClosed(object sender, FormClosedEventArgs e)
{
  context.Dispose();
}
}
```

This is all you need to do! If you run your application, you can now add new records to the grid, select a row and delete it, and modify existing rows. When you click your Update button, the Inventory database is updated automatically because the object context has been kind enough to generate all the necessary SQL statements for selecting, updating, deleting, and inserting automatically. Here are some key takeaways from this preceding example:

- The context remains allocated throughout the application.

- The call to context.Inventories executes SQL to fetch all rows from the Inventory table into memory.

- The context tracks *dirty* entities, so it knows what SQL to execute upon SaveChanges().

- After SaveChanges(), the entities are considered *clean* again.

Going Forward with .NET Data-Access APIs

Over the last three chapters, you have been provided with a tour of three approaches to data manipulation using ADO.NET, specifically the connection layer, the disconnected layer, and the Entity Framework. Each approach has merit, and many of your applications will likely use various aspects of each of them. Now to be sure, we have only scratched the surface of all of the topics found within the ADO.NET technology set. To dive deeper into any of the topics presented in this book (as well to examine a number of related items), I recommend consulting the .NET Framework 4.5 SDK documentation. Specifically, look up the topic "Data and Modeling." Here you will find numerous code examples (see Figure 23-26).

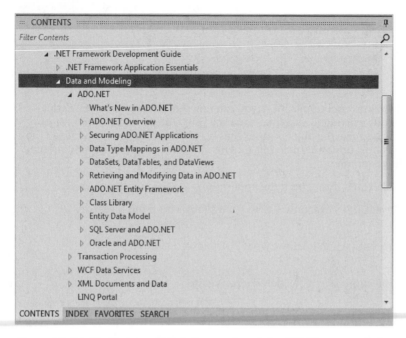

Figure 23-26. The Data and Modeling section of the .NET Framework documentation

Summary

This chapter wrapped up your formal investigation of database programming using ADO.NET by examining the role of the Entity Framework. EF allows you to program against a conceptual model that closely maps to your business domain. While you can reshape your entities in any way you choose, the EF runtime ensures that the changed data is mapped to the correct physical table data.

You learned about the role of (and composition of) *.edmx files and how to generate them using the Visual Studio IDE. Along the way, you also learned how to map stored procedures to functions in your conceptual layer, how to apply LINQ queries to the object model, the role of Entity SQL, and how to consume fetched data at the lowest level using the EntityDataReader.

You wrapped up this chapter with a simple example of binding entity classes to graphical user interfaces within the context of a Windows Forms application. You'll see other examples of binding entities to GUI applications when you examine Windows Presentation Foundation and ASP.NET.

CHAPTER 24

Introducing LINQ to XML

As a .NET developer, you are bound to encounter XML-based data in numerous places. Application and web-based configuration files store information as XML. Windows Presentation Foundation, Silverlight, and Windows Workflow Foundation all make use of an XML-based grammar (XAML) to represent desktop UIs, browser-based UIs, and workflows, respectively. ADO.NET DataSets can easily save out (or load in) data as XML. Even Windows Communication Foundation stores numerous settings as the well-formatted string called XML.

Although XML is indeed everywhere, programming with XML has historically been very tedious, very verbose, and very complex if one is not well versed in a great number of XML technologies (XPath, XQuery, XSLT, DOM, SAX, etc.). Since the inception of the .NET platform, Microsoft has provided a specific assembly, named System.Xml.dll, devoted to programming with XML documents. Within this binary are a number of namespaces and types to various XML programming techniques, as well as a few .NET-specific XML APIs such as the XmlReader/XmlWriter classes.

These days, most .NET programmers prefer to interact with XML data using the LINQ to XML API. As you will see in this chapter, the LINQ to XML programming model allows you to capture the structure of an XML data in code, and provides a much simpler way to create, manipulate, load, and save XML data. While you could use LINQ to XML as little more than a simpler way to create XML documents, you can also easily incorporate LINQ query expressions into the mix, to quickly query a document for information.

A Tale of Two XML APIs

When the .NET platform was first introduced, programmers were able to manipulate XML documents using the types within the System.Xml.dll assembly. Using the contained namespaces and types, you were able to generate XML data in memory and save it to disk storage. As well, the System.Xml.dll assembly provided types allowing you to load XML documents into memory, search an XML document for specific nodes, validate a document against a given schema, and other common programming tasks.

While this original library has been used successfully in many .NET projects, working with these types was a bit cumbersome (to put it politely), as the programming model bore no relationship to the structure of the XML document itself. For example, assume you needed to build an XML file in memory and save it to the file system. If you were to use the types of System.Xml.dll, you might author code like the following (if you want to follow along, create a new Console Application project named LinqToXmlFirstLook, and import the System.Xml namespace):

```
private static void BuildXmlDocWithDOM()
{
  // Make a new XML document in memory.
  XmlDocument doc = new XmlDocument();
```

```
// Fill this document with a root element
// named <Inventory>.
XmlElement inventory = doc.CreateElement("Inventory");

// Now, make a subelement named <Car> with
// an ID attribute.
XmlElement car = doc.CreateElement("Car");
car.SetAttribute("ID", "1000");

// Build the data within the <Car> element.
XmlElement name = doc.CreateElement("PetName");
name.InnerText = "Jimbo";
XmlElement color = doc.CreateElement("Color");
color.InnerText = "Red";
XmlElement make = doc.CreateElement("Make");
make.InnerText = "Ford";

// Add <PetName>, <Color>, and <Make> to the <Car>
// element.
car.AppendChild(name);
car.AppendChild(color);
car.AppendChild(make);

// Add the <Car> element to the <Inventory> element.
inventory.AppendChild(car);

// Insert the complete XML into the XmlDocument object,
// and save to file.
doc.AppendChild(inventory);
doc.Save("Inventory.xml");
}
```

If you were to call this method, you would be able to see that the Inventory.xml file (located in the bin\Debug folder) contains the following data:

```
<Inventory>
  <Car ID="1000">
    <PetName>Jimbo</PetName>
    <Color>Red</Color>
    <Make>Ford</Make>
  </Car>
</Inventory>
```

While this method works as expected, a few observations are in order. First, the programming model of System.Xml.dll is Microsoft's implementation of the W3C Document Object Model (DOM) specification. Under this model, an XML document is created from the bottom up. First you create a document, then you create subelements, and finally you add the elements to the document. To account for this in code, you need to author quite a bit of function calls off the XmlDocument, and XmlElement classes (among others).

For this example, it took 16 lines of code (not including code comments) to build even this very simple XML document. If you needed to build a more complex document with the System.Xml.dll assembly, you could end up with a great deal of code. While you could certainly streamline this code, by building nodes via various looping or decision constructs, the fact remains that the body of code has little visual indicators regarding the final XML tree.

LINQ to XML As a Better DOM

The LINQ to XML API is an alternative manner to create, manipulate, and query XML documents, which uses a much more functional approach than the System.Xml DOM model. Rather than building an XML document by assembling elements individually and updating the XML tree through a set of function calls, you can author top-down code such as the following:

```
private static void BuildXmlDocWithLINQToXml()
{
    // Create an XML document in a more "functional" manner.
    XElement doc =
        new XElement("Inventory",
            new XElement("Car", new XAttribute("ID", "1000"),
                new XElement("PetName", "Jimbo"),
                new XElement("Color", "Red"),
                new XElement("Make", "Ford")
            )
        );

    // Save to file.
    doc.Save("InventoryWithLINQ.xml");
}
```

Here, you are using a new set of types from the System.Xml.Linq namespace, specifically XElement and XAttribute. If you were to call this method, you would find the same XML data has been created, this time with much less fuss and bother. Notice how, through some careful indentation, your source code has the same overall structure of the resulting XML document. This is very useful in and of itself, but also notice that you have a much smaller body of code than the previous example (based on how you space your code, you saved about ten lines!)

Here, you have not made use of any LINQ query expressions, but have simply used the types of the System.Xml.Linq namespace to generate an in-memory XML document, which is then saved to file. Effectively, you have used LINQ to XML as a better DOM. As you will see later in this chapter, the classes of System.Xml.Linq are LINQ-aware, and can be the target for the same sort of LINQ queries you learned about in Chapter 12.

As you learn more about LINQ to XML, you will most likely find it much easier to work with than the initial XML libraries of .NET. This is not to say you will never use the namespaces of the original System.Xml.dll library; however, chances are that the times you will opt to use System.Xml.dll for new projects will be significantly reduced.

VB Literal Syntax As a Better LINQ to XML

Before you begin your formal examination into LINQ to XML as seen through C#, I do want to briefly mention that the Visual Basic language takes the functional approach of this API to the next level. In VB, you can define *XML literals*, which allow you to assign an XElement to a stream of inline XML markup, directly in code. Assuming you had a VB project, you could build the following method:

```vb
Public Class XmlLiteralExample
  Public Sub MakeXmlFileUsingLiterals()
    ' Notice that we can inline XML data
    ' to an XElement.
    Dim doc As XElement =
      <Inventory>
        <Car ID="1000">
          <PetName>Jimbo</PetName>
          <Color>Red</Color>
          <Make>Ford</Make>
        </Car>
      </Inventory>

    ' Save to file.
    doc.Save("InventoryVBStyle.xml")
  End Sub
End Class
```

After the VB compiler processes the XML literal, it will map the XML data into the correct underlying LINQ to XML object model. In fact, when you are working with LINQ to XML within a VB project, the IDE already understands that your XML literal syntax is just a shorthand notation for the related code. In Figure 24-1, notice how you can apply the dot operator to the </Inventory> end tag and see the same members as you would find if you apply the dot operator to a strongly typed XElement.

Figure 24-1. *VB XML literal syntax is a shorthand notation for working with the LINQ to XML object model*

Although this book is about the C# programming language, few developers can argue that VB's XML support is quite awesome. Even if you are the sort of developer who can't imagine using a language from the BASIC family for your data-to-day development, I encourage you to check out VB literal syntax using the .NET Framework 4.5 SDK documentation. You could find yourself isolating your XML data-manipulation routines to a dedicated *.dll, just so you can make use of VB to do so!

Members of the System.Xml.Linq Namespace

Somewhat surprisingly, the core LINQ to XML assembly (System.Xml.Linq.dll) defines a very small number of types in three distinct namespaces, specifically System.Xml.Linq, System.Xml.Schema, and System.Xml.XPath (see Figure 24-2).

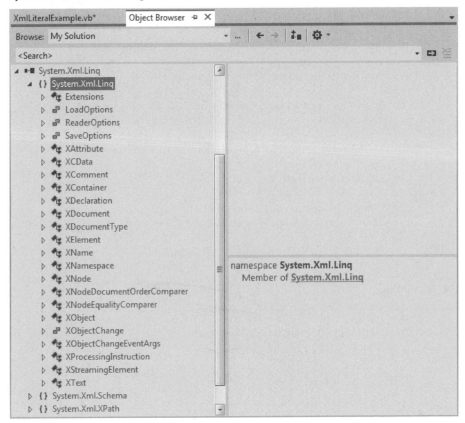

Figure 24-2. The namespaces of System.Xml.Linq.dll

The core namespace, System.Xml.Linq, contains a very manageable set of classes that represent various aspects of an XML document (its elements and their attributes, XML namespaces, XML comments, processing instructions, etc.). Table 24-1 documents the core members of System.Xml.Linq.

Table 24-1. Select Members of the System.Xml.Linq Namespace

Member of System.Xml.Linq	Meaning in Life
XAttribute	Represents an XML attribute on a given XML element.
XCData	Represents a CDATA section in the XML document. Information in a CDATA section represents data in an XML document which must be included, but does not conform to the rules of XML grammars (for example, script code).
XComment	Represents an XML comment.
XDeclaration	Represents the opening declaration of an XML document.
XDocument	Represents the entirety of an XML document.
XElement	Represents a given element within an XML document, including the root element.
XName	Represents the name of an XML element or XML attribute.
XNamespace	Represents an XML namespace.
XNode	Represents the abstract concept of a node (element, comment, document type, processing instruction, or text node) in the XML tree.
XProcessingInstruction	Represents an XML processing instruction.
XStreamingElement	Represents elements in an XML tree that supports deferred streaming output.

Figure 24-3 shows how the inheritance chain of the key class types.

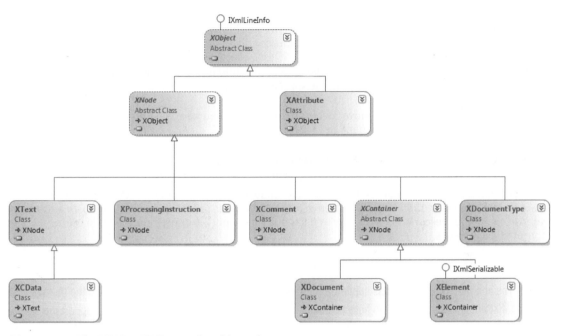

Figure 24-3. *The LINQ to XML core class hierarchy*

The LINQ to XML Axis Methods

In addition to the X* classes, System.Xml.Linq defines a class named Extensions, which (of course) defines a set of extension methods that typically extend IEnumerable<T>, where T is some descendant of XNode or XContainer. Table 24-2 documents some of the important extension methods to be aware of (as you will see, these are very useful when you want to work with LINQ queries).

Table 24-2. *Select Members of the LINQ to XML Extensions Class*

Member of Extensions	Meaning in Life
Ancestors<T>()	Returns a filtered collection of elements that contains the ancestors of every node in the source collection.
Attributes()	Returns a filtered collection of the attributes of every element in the source collection.
DescendantNodes<T>()	Returns a collection of the descendant nodes of every document and element in the source collection.
Descendants<T>	Returns a filtered collection of elements that contains the descendant elements of every element and document in the source collection.

Elements<T>	Returns a collection of the child elements of every element and document in the source collection.
Nodes<T>	Returns a collection of the child nodes of every document and element in the source collection.
Remove()	Removes every attribute in the source collection from its parent element.
Remove<T>()	Removes all occurrences of a given node from the source collection.

As you can tell from their names, these methods allow you to query a loaded XML tree to find elements, attributes, and their values. Collectively, these methods are termed *axis methods*, or simply *axes*. You can apply these methods directly to parts of a tree of nodes, or use them to build more elaborate LINQ queries.

■ **Note** The abstract XContainer class support a number of methods that are identically named to the members of Extensions. XContainer is the parent to both XElement and XDocument and, therefore, they both support the same overall functionality.

You'll see examples of using some of these axis methods over the chapter. However, here is a quick example:

```
private static void DeleteNodeFromDoc()
{
  XElement doc =
    new XElement("Inventory",
      new XElement("Car", new XAttribute("ID", "1000"),
        new XElement("PetName", "Jimbo"),
        new XElement("Color", "Red"),
        new XElement("Make", "Ford")
      )
    );

  // Delete the PetName element from the tree.
  doc.Descendants("PetName").Remove();
  Console.WriteLine(doc);
}
```

If you were to invoke this method, you'd see the following "pruned" XML tree:

```
<Inventory>
  <Car ID="1000">
    <Color>Red</Color>
    <Make>Ford</Make>
  </Car>
</Inventory>
```

The Oddness of XName (and XNamespace)

If you examine the signatures of the LINQ to XML axis methods (or the identically named members of XContainer), you'll notice that they typically require you to specify what looks to be an XName object. Consider the following signature of the Descendants() method defined by XContainer:

```
public IEnumerable<XElement> Descendants(XName name)
```

XName is "odd" in that you will never really directly make use of it in your code. In fact, since this class has no public constructor, you cannot make an XName object, as demonstrated here:

```
// Error! Can't make XName objects!
doc.Descendants(new XName("PetName")).Remove();
```

If you were to view the formal definition of XName, you would see that this class defines a custom implicit conversion operator (see Chapter 11 for information of defining custom conversion operators), which will map a simple System.String to the correct XName object.

```
// We really make an XName in the background!
doc.Descendants("PetName").Remove();
```

■ **Note** The XNamespace class also supports the same flavor of implicit string conversion.

The good news is that you can use textual values to represent the names of elements or attributes when you work with these axis methods, and allow the LINQ to XML API to map your string data to the necessary object types.

■ **Source Code** The LinqToXmlFirstLook example can be found under the Chapter 24 subdirectory.

Working with XElement and XDocument

Let's continue the investigation of LINQ to XML with a new Console Application named ConstructingXmlDocs. After you have created the project, import the System.Xml.Linq namespace into your initial code file. As you have already seen, XDocument represents the entirety of an XML document in the LINQ to XML programming model, as it can be used to define a root element, and all contained elements, processing instructions and XML declarations. Here is another example of building XML data using XDocument:

```
static void CreateFullXDocument()
{
  XDocument inventoryDoc =
    new XDocument(
      new XDeclaration("1.0", "utf-8", "yes"),
      new XComment("Current Inventory of cars!"),
      new XProcessingInstruction("xml-stylesheet",
        "href='MyStyles.css' title='Compact' type='text/css'"),
      new XElement("Inventory",
        new XElement("Car", new XAttribute("ID", "1"),
          new XElement("Color", "Green"),
          new XElement("Make", "BMW"),
          new XElement("PetName", "Stan")
        ),
        new XElement("Car", new XAttribute("ID", "2"),
          new XElement("Color", "Pink"),
          new XElement("Make", "Yugo"),
          new XElement("PetName", "Melvin")
        )
      )
    );

  // Save to disk.
  inventoryDoc.Save("SimpleInventory.xml");
}
```

Again, notice that the constructor of the XDocument object is, in fact, a tree of additional LINQ to XML objects. The constructor called here takes as the first parameter an XDeclaration, followed by a parameter array of objects (recall, C# parameter arrays allow you to pass in a comma-delimited list of arguments, which are packaged as an array on your behalf):

```
public XDocument(System.Xml.Linq.XDeclaration declaration, params object[] content)
```

If you were to invoke this method from Main(), you'd see the following data in the SimpleInventory.xml file:

```
<?xml version="1.0" encoding="utf-8" standalone="yes"?>
<!--Current Inventory of cars!-->
<?xml-stylesheet href='MyStyles.css' title='Compact' type='text/css'?>
<Inventory>
  <Car ID="1">
    <Color>Green</Color>
    <Make>BMW</Make>
    <PetName>Stan</PetName>
  </Car>
  <Car ID="2">
    <Color>Pink</Color>
    <Make>Yugo</Make>
```

```
    <PetName>Melvin</PetName>
  </Car>
</Inventory>
```

As it turns out, the default XML declaration for any XDocument is to use utf-8 encoding, XML version 1.0, as a stand-alone document. Therefore, you could completely delete the creation of the XDeclaration object and end up with the same data; given that just about every document requires this same declaration, use of XDeclaration is typically not that common.

If you do not need to define processing instructions or a custom XML declaration, you can avoid the use of XDocument all together, and simply use XElement. Remember, XElement can be used to represent the root element of the XML document and all subobjects. Thus, you could generate a commented list of inventory items as so:

```
static void CreateRootAndChildren()
{
  XElement inventoryDoc =
    new XElement("Inventory",
    new XComment("Current Inventory of cars!"),
      new XElement("Car", new XAttribute("ID", "1"),
      new XElement("Color", "Green"),
      new XElement("Make", "BMW"),
      new XElement("PetName", "Stan")
    ),
    new XElement("Car", new XAttribute("ID", "2"),
      new XElement("Color", "Pink"),
      new XElement("Make", "Yugo"),
      new XElement("PetName", "Melvin")
      )
    );

  // Save to disk.
  inventoryDoc.Save("SimpleInventory.xml");
}
```

The output is more or less identical, sans the custom processing instruction for a hypothetical style sheet:

```
<?xml version="1.0" encoding="utf-8"?>
<Inventory>
  <!--Current Inventory of cars!-->
  <Car ID="1">
    <Color>Green</Color>
    <Make>BMW</Make>
    <PetName>Stan</PetName>
  </Car>
  <Car ID="2">
    <Color>Pink</Color>
    <Make>Yugo</Make>
    <PetName>Melvin</PetName>
  </Car>
```

```
</Inventory>
```

Generating Documents from Arrays and Containers

So far, you have been building XML documents using fixed hardcoded constructor values. More commonly, you will need to generate XElements (or XDocuments) by reading data from arrays, ADO.NET objects, file data, or whatnot. One way to map in-memory data to a new XElement is by using a set of standard for loops to move data into the LINQ to XML object model. While this is certainly doable, it is more streamlined to embed a LINQ query within the construction of the XElement directly.

Assume you have an anonymous array of anonymous classes (just to avoid the amount of code for this example; any array, List<T> or other container would do here). You could map this data into an XElement as so:

```
static void MakeXElementFromArray()
{
  // Create an anonymous array of anonymous types.
  var people = new[] {
    new { FirstName = "Mandy", Age = 32},
    new { FirstName = "Andrew", Age  = 40 },
    new { FirstName = "Dave", Age  = 41 },
    new { FirstName = "Sara", Age  = 31}
  };

  XElement peopleDoc =
    new XElement("People",
      from c in people select new XElement("Person", new XAttribute("Age", c.Age),
                              new XElement("FirstName", c.FirstName))
  );
  Console.WriteLine(peopleDoc);
}
```

Here, the peopleDoc object defines the root <People> element with the results of a LINQ query. This LINQ query creates new XElements based on each item in the people array. If this embedded query is a bit hard on the eyes, you could break things down into explicit steps, like so:

```
static void MakeXElementFromArray()
{
  // Create an anonymous array of anonymous types.
  var people = new[] {
    new { FirstName = "Mandy", Age = 32},
    new { FirstName = "Andrew", Age  = 40 },
    new { FirstName = "Dave", Age  = 41 },
    new { FirstName = "Sara", Age  = 31}
  };

  var arrayDataAsXElements = from c in people
    select
      new XElement("Person",
        new XAttribute("Age", c.Age),
        new XElement("FirstName", c.FirstName));
```

```
XElement peopleDoc = new XElement("People", arrayDataAsXElements);
  Console.WriteLine(peopleDoc);
}
```

Either way, the output is the same:

```
<People>
  <Person Age="32">
    <FirstName>Mandy</FirstName>
  </Person>
  <Person Age="40">
    <FirstName>Andrew</FirstName>
  </Person>
  <Person Age="41">
    <FirstName>Dave</FirstName>
  </Person>
  <Person Age="31">
    <FirstName>Sara</FirstName>
  </Person>
</People>
```

Loading and Parsing XML Content

The XElement and XDocument types both support Load() and Parse() methods, which allow you to hydrate an XML object model from string objects containing XML data or external XML files. Consider the following method, which illustrates both approaches:

```
static void ParseAndLoadExistingXml()
{
  // Build an XElement from string.
  string myElement =
    @"<Car ID ='3'>
      <Color>Yellow</Color>
      <Make>Yugo</Make>
    </Car>";
  XElement newElement = XElement.Parse(myElement);
  Console.WriteLine(newElement);
  Console.WriteLine();

  // Load the SimpleInventory.xml file.
  XDocument myDoc = XDocument.Load("SimpleInventory.xml");
  Console.WriteLine(myDoc);
}
```

■ **Source Code** The ConstructingXmlDocs example can be found under the Chapter 24 subdirectory.

Manipulating an In-Memory XML Document

So, at this point, you have seen various ways in which LINQ to XML can be used to create, save, parse, and load XML data. The next aspect of LINQ to XML you need to examine is how to navigate a given document to locate and change specific items in the tree using LINQ queries and the LINQ to XML axis methods.

To do so, you will build a Windows Forms application that will display the data within an XML document saved on the hard drive. The GUI will allow the user to enter data for a new node, which will be added to the same XML document. Finally, you will provide a few ways for the user to perform searches on the document, via a handful of LINQ queries.

■ **Note** Given that you have already built a number of LINQ queries in Chapter 12, I won't bother to relist numerous queries. If you are interested in seeing some additional LINQ to XML specific examples, look up the topic "Querying XML Trees" in the .NET Framework 4.5 SDK documentation.

Building the UI of the LINQ to XML App

Create a Windows Forms application named LinqToXmlWinApp and change the name of your initial Form1.cs file to MainForm.cs (using the Solution Explorer). The GUI of this window is quite simple. On the left of the window, you have a TextBox control (named txtInventory), which has the Multiline property set to true, and the ScrollBars property set to Both.

Beyond that, you have one group of simple TextBox controls (txtMake, txtColor, and txtPetName) and a Button (btnAddNewItem), which will allow the user to add a new entry to the XML document. Finally, you have another group of controls (a TextBox named txtMakeToLookUp and a final Button named btnLookUpColors), which allows the user to query the XML document for a set of specified nodes. Figure 24-4 shows one possible layout.

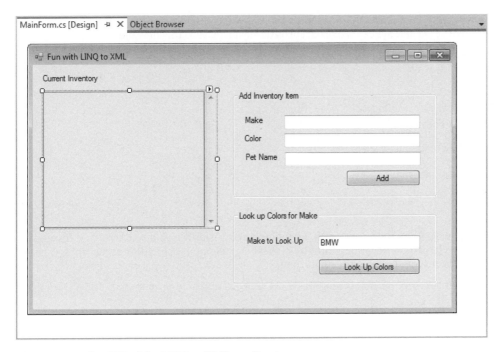

Figure 24-4. *The GUI of the LINQ to XML application*

Handle the Click event for each button to generate the event handler methods. Also handle the Load event of the form itself. You will implement these handlers in a bit.

Import the Inventory.xml File

The downloadable code for this book contains a file named Inventory.xml within the solution code for this example. It supports a set of entries within the root <Inventory> element. Import this file into your project by selecting the Project Add Existing Item menu option. As you look at the data, you will see the root element defines a set of <Car> elements, each of which is defined similar to the following:

```
<Car carID ="0">
  <Make>Ford</Make>
  <Color>Blue</Color>
  <PetName>Chuck</PetName>
</Car>
```

Before you continue on, be sure you select this file in the Solution Explorer, and then, using the Properties window, set the Copy to Output Directory property to Copy Always. This will ensure the data is deployed to your \bin\Debug folder when you compile the application.

Defining a LINQ to XML Helper Class

To isolate the LINQ to XML data, insert a new class to your project named LinqToXmlObjectModel. This class will define a set of static methods that encapsulate some LINQ to XML logic. First of all, define a method that returns a populated XDocument based on the contents of the Inventory.xml file (be sure to import the System.Xml.Linq and System.Windows.Forms namespaces into this new file):

```
public static XDocument GetXmlInventory()
{
  try
  {
    XDocument inventoryDoc = XDocument.Load("Inventory.xml");
    return inventoryDoc;
  }
  catch (System.IO.FileNotFoundException ex)
  {
    MessageBox.Show(ex.Message);
    return null;
  }
}
```

The InsertNewElement() method (shown in the following) receives the values of the "Add Inventory Item" TextBox controls to place a new node into the <Inventory> element using the Descendants() axis method. After this is done, you will save the document.

```
public static void InsertNewElement(string make, string color, string petName)
{
  // Load current document.
  XDocument inventoryDoc = XDocument.Load("Inventory.xml");

  // Generate a random number for the ID.
  Random r = new Random();

  // Make new XElement based on incoming parameters.
  XElement newElement = new XElement("Car", new XAttribute("ID", r.Next(50000)),
    new XElement("Color", color),
    new XElement("Make", make),
    new XElement("PetName", petName));

  // Add to in-memory object.
  inventoryDoc.Descendants("Inventory").First().Add(newElement);

  // Save changes to disk.
  inventoryDoc.Save("Inventory.xml");
}
```

The final method, LookUpColorsForMake() will receive the data in the final TextBox to build a string that contains the colors of a specified make, using a LINQ query. Consider the following implementation:

```
public static void LookUpColorsForMake(string make)
{
  // Load current document.
  XDocument inventoryDoc = XDocument.Load("Inventory.xml");

  // Find the colors for a given make.
  var makeInfo = from car in inventoryDoc.Descendants("Car")
        where (string)car.Element("Make") == make
```

```
      select car.Element("Color").Value;

  // Build a string representing each color.
  string data = string.Empty;
  foreach (var item in makeInfo.Distinct())
  {
    data += string.Format("- {0}\n", item);
  }

  // Show colors.
  MessageBox.Show(data, string.Format("{0} colors:", make));
}
```

Attaching the UI to Your Helper Class

All you need to do at this point is fill in the details of your event handlers. Doing so is as simple as
making calls to your static helper methods, like so:

```csharp
public partial class MainForm : Form
{
  public MainForm()
  {
    InitializeComponent();
  }

  private void MainForm_Load(object sender, EventArgs e)
  {
    // Display current XML inventory document in TextBox control.
    txtInventory.Text = LinqToXmlObjectModel.GetXmlInventory().ToString();
  }

  private void btnAddNewItem_Click(object sender, EventArgs e)
  {
    // Add new item to doc.
    LinqToXmlObjectModel.InsertNewElement(txtMake.Text, txtColor.Text, txtPetName.Text);

    // Display current XML inventory document in TextBox control.
    txtInventory.Text = LinqToXmlObjectModel.GetXmlInventory().ToString();
  }

  private void btnLookUpColors_Click(object sender, EventArgs e)
  {
    LinqToXmlObjectModel.LookUpColorsForMake(txtMakeToLookUp.Text);
  }
}
```

Figure 24-5 shows the end result.

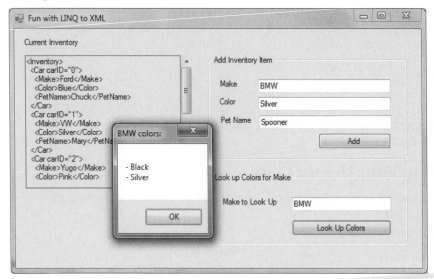

Figure 24-5. The completed LINQ to XML application

That wraps up the introductory look at LINQ to XML and your investigation of LINQ. You first encountered LINQ in Chapter 12, where you learned about LINQ to Objects. Chapter 19 showed various examples using PLINQ, while Chapter 23 showcased how you can apply LINQ queries to ADO.NET Entity objects. Using all of this information, you are in good shape to dig deeper, which you should. Microsoft has made it very clear that LINQ will continue to evolve as the .NET platform grows.

■ **Source Code** The LinqToXmlWinApp to XML example can be found under the Chapter 24 subdirectory.

Summary

This chapter examined the role of LINQ to XML. As you have seen, this API is an alternative to the initial XML manipulation library, System.Xml.dll, which shipped with the .NET platform. Using System.Xml.Linq.dll, you are able to generate new XML documents using a top-down approach, where the structure of your code has a striking resemblance to the final XML data. In this light, LINQ to XML is a better DOM. You also learned how to build XDocument and XElement objects in a variety of ways (parsing, loading from file, mapping from in-memory objects) and how to navigate and manipulate data using LINQ queries.

## CHAPTER 25

Introducing Windows Communication Foundation

.NET 3.0 introduced an API designed specifically for the process of building distributed systems: Windows Communication Foundation (WCF). Unlike other distributed APIs you might have used in the past (e.g., DCOM, .NET remoting, XML web services, message queuing), WCF provides a single, unified, and extendable programming object model that you can use to interact with a number of previously diverse distributed technologies.

This chapter begins by framing the need for WCF and examining the problems it intends to solve by way of a quick review of previous distributed computing APIs. After you look at the services provided by WCF, you'll turn your attention to examining the key .NET assemblies, namespaces, and types that represent this programming model. Over the remainder of this chapter, you'll build several WCF services, hosts, and clients using various WCF development tools.

■ **Note** In this chapter, you will author code that will require that you launch Visual Studio with administrative privileges (furthermore, you must have administrative privileges). To launch Visual Studio with the correct admin rights, right click the Visual Studio icon and select Run As Administrator.

A Potpourri of Distributed Computing APIs

The Windows operating system has historically provided many APIs for building distributed systems. While it is true that most people consider a *distributed system* to involve at least two networked computers, this term in the broader sense can refer to two executables that need to exchange data, even if they happen to be running on the same physical machine. Using this definition, selecting a distributed API for your current programming task typically involves asking the following pivotal question:

> *Will this system be used exclusively in house, or will external users require access to the application's functionality?*

If you build a distributed system for in-house use, you have a far greater chance of ensuring that each connected computer is running the same operating system and using the same programming framework (e.g., .NET, COM, or the Java platform). Running in-house systems also means that you can leverage your existing security system for purposes of authentication, authorization, and so forth. In this situation, you might be willing to select a particular distributed API that will tie you to a specific operating system/programming framework for the purposes of performance.

In contrast, if you build a system that others must reach from outside of your walls, you have a whole other set of issues to contend with. First, you will most likely *not* be able to dictate to external users which operating system(s) they can use, which programming framework(s) they can use, or how they configure their security settings.

Second, if you happen to work for a larger company or in a university setting that uses numerous operating systems and programming technologies, an in-house application suddenly faces the same challenges as an outward-facing application. In either of these cases, you need to limit yourself to a more flexible distributed API to ensure the furthest reach of your application.

Based on your answer to this key distributed computing question, the next task is to pinpoint exactly which API (or set of APIs) to use. The following sections provide a quick recap of some of the major distributed APIs historically used by Windows software developers. After you finish this brief history lesson, you will be able to see the usefulness of Windows Communication Foundation quite easily.

■ **Note** To ensure we are on the same page here, I feel compelled to point out that WCF (and the technologies it encompasses) has nothing to do with building an HTML-based web site. While it is true that web applications can be considered distributed because two machines are typically involved in the exchange, WCF is about establishing connections between machines to share the functionality of remote components—not for displaying HTML in a web browser. Chapter 32 will begin your examination of building websites with the .NET platform.

The Role of DCOM

Prior to the release of the .NET platform, the Distributed Component Object Model (DCOM) was the remoting API of choice for Microsoft-centric development endeavors. Using DCOM, it was possible to build distributed systems using COM objects, the system registry, and a good amount of elbow grease. One benefit of DCOM was that it allowed for *location transparency* of components. Simply put, this allowed you to program client software in such a way that the physical locations of the remote objects were not hard-coded in the application. Regardless of whether the remote object was on the same machine or a secondary networked machine, the code base could remain neutral because the actual location was recorded externally in the system registry.

While DCOM did enjoy some degree of success, for all practical purposes it was a Windows-centric API. DCOM alone did not provide a fabric to build comprehensive solutions involving multiple operating systems (e.g., Windows, Unix, and Mac) or promote sharing of data between diverse architectures (e.g., COM, Java, or CORBA).

■ **Note** There were some attempts to port DCOM to various flavors of Unix/Linux, but the end results were lackluster and eventually became technology footnotes.

By and large, DCOM was best suited for in-house application development because exposing COM objects outside company walls entailed a set of additional complications (firewalls and so forth). With the release of the .NET platform, DCOM quickly became a legacy programming model; and unless you maintain legacy DCOM systems, you can consider it a deprecated technology.

The Role of COM+/Enterprise Services

DCOM alone did little more than define a way to establish a communication channel between two pieces of COM-based software. To fill in the missing pieces required for building a feature-rich distributed computing solution, Microsoft eventually released Microsoft Transaction Server (MTS), which was later renamed to COM+.

Despite its name, COM+ is not used only by COM programmers—it is completely accessible to .NET professionals, as well. Since the first release of the .NET platform, the base class libraries provided a namespace named System.EnterpriseServices. Here, .NET programmers could build managed libraries that could be installed into the COM+ runtime to access the same set of services as a traditional COM+- aware COM server. In either case, once a COM+-aware library was installed into the COM+ runtime, it was termed a *serviced component.*

COM+ provides a number of features that serviced components can leverage, including transaction management, object lifetime management, pooling services, a role-based security system, a loosely coupled event model, and so on. This was a major benefit at the time, given that most distributed systems require the same set of services. Rather than forcing developers to code them by hand, COM+ provided an out-of-the-box solution.

One of the compelling aspects of COM+ was the fact that all of these settings could be configured in a declarative manner using administrative tools. Thus, if you wanted to ensure an object was monitored under a transactional context or belonged to a particular security role, you simply selected the correct check boxes.

While COM+/Enterprise Services is still in use today, this technology is a Windows-only solution that is best suited for in-house application development or as a back-end service indirectly manipulated by more agonistic front ends (e.g., a public web site that makes calls on serviced components [a.k.a. COM+ objects] in the background).

■ **Note** WCF does not provide a way to build serviced components. However, it does provide a manner for WCF services to communicate with existing COM+ objects. If you need to build serviced components using C#, you will need to make direct use of the System.EnterpriseServices namespace. Consult the .NET Framework 4.5 SDK documentation for details.

The Role of MSMQ

The Microsoft Message Queuing (MSMQ) API allows developers to build distributed systems that need to ensure reliable delivery of message data on the network. As developers know all too well, in any distributed system there is the risk that a network server is down, a database is offline, or connections are inexplicably lost. Furthermore, you must construct many applications in such a way that they hold message data for delivery at a later time (this process is known as *queuing data*).

Microsoft initially packaged MSMQ as a set of low-level C-based APIs and COM objects. With the release of the .NET platform, C# programmers could use the System.Messaging namespace to hook into MSMQ and build software that communicated with intermittently connected applications in a dependable fashion.

On a related note, the COM+ layer incorporated MSMQ functionality into the runtime (in a simplified format) using a technology termed *Queued Components* (QC). This manner of communicating with MSMQ was packaged up into the System.EnterpriseServices namespace mentioned in the previous section.

Regardless of which programming model you used to interact with the MSMQ runtime, the end result ensured that applications could deliver messages in a reliable and timely fashion. Like COM+, MSMQ is still part of the fabric of building distributed software on the Windows operating system.

The Role of .NET Remoting

As mentioned previously, DCOM quickly became a legacy distributed API after the release of the .NET platform. In its place, the .NET base class libraries shipped with the .NET remoting layer, represented by the System.Runtime.Remoting namespace. This (now legacy) API allows multiple computers to distribute objects, provided they all run the applications under the .NET platform.

The .NET remoting APIs provided a number of useful features. Most important was the use of XML-based configuration files to define declaratively the underlying plumbing used by the client and the server software. Using *.config files, it was easy to alter the functionality of your distributed system radically, simply by changing the content of the configuration files and restarting the application.

Also, given that only .NET applications can use this API, you can gain various performance benefits because data can be encoded in a compact binary format, and you can use the Common Type System (CTS) when defining parameters and return values. While it is possible to use .NET remoting to build distributed systems that span multiple operating systems (using Mono, which was briefly mentioned in Chapter 1), interoperability between other programming architectures (e.g., Java) was still not directly possible.

The Role of XML Web Services

Each of the previous distributed APIs provided little (if any) support to allow external callers to access the supplied functionality in an *agnostic manner*. When you need to expose the services of remote objects to *any* operating system and *any* programming model, XML web services provide a straightforward way of doing so.

Unlike a traditional browser-based web application, a web service provides a way to expose the functionality of remote components using standard web protocols. Since the initial release of .NET, programmers have been provided with superior support for building and consuming XML web services with the System.Web.Services namespace. In many cases, building a feature-complete web service is no more complicated than applying the [WebMethod] attribute to each public method you wish to provide access to. Furthermore, Visual Studio allows you to connect to a remote web service with the click of a button (or two).

Web services allow developers to build .NET assemblies containing types that can be accessed using simple HTTP. Furthermore, a web service encodes its data as simple XML. Given the fact that web services are based on open industry standards (e.g., HTTP, XML, and SOAP) rather than proprietary type systems and proprietary wire formats (as is the case with DCOM or .NET remoting), they allow for a high degree of interoperability and data exchange. Figure 25-1 illustrates the agnostic nature of XML web services.

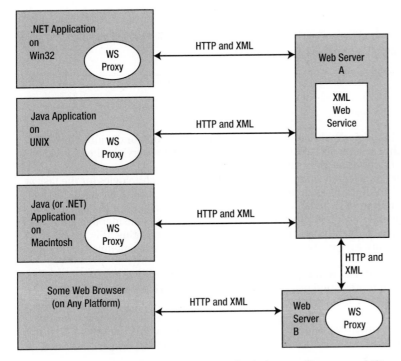

Figure 25-1. XML web services allow for a high degree of interoperability

Of course, no distributed API is perfect. One potential drawback of web services is the fact that they can suffer from some performance issues (given the use of HTTP and XML data representation). Another drawback is that they might not be an ideal solution for in-house applications where you could use a TCP-based protocol and binary formatting of data without incurring a penalty.

Web Service Standards

Another problem that web services faced early on was the fact that all of the big industry players (e.g., Microsoft, IBM, and Sun Microsystems) created web service implementations that were not 100-percent compatible with other web service implementations. Obviously, this was an issue because the whole point of web services is to achieve a high degree of interoperability across platforms and operating systems!

To ensure the interoperability of web services, groups such as the World Wide Web Consortium (W3C: www.w3.org) and the Web Services Interoperability Organization (WS-I: www.ws-i.org) began to author several specifications that laid out how a software vendor (e.g., IBM, Microsoft, or Sun Microsystems) should build web service–centric software libraries to ensure compatibility.

Collectively, all of these specifications are given the blanket name WS-*, and they cover such issues as security, attachments, the description of web services (using the *Web Service Description Language*, or *WSDL*), policies, SOAP formats, and a slew of other important details. As you will see, WCF supports many of these WS-* specifications. Typically, your WCF services will opt into various WS-* specifications based on your choice of *bindings*.

■ **Note** In addition to the distributed APIs briefly examined, developers could also make use of various interprocess communication protocols such as named pipes and sockets.

The Role of WCF

The wide array of distributed technologies makes it difficult to pick the right tool for the job. This is further complicated by the fact that several of these technologies overlap in the services they provide (most notably in the areas of transactions and security).

Even when a .NET developer has selected what appear to be the correct technologies for the task at hand, building, maintaining, and configuring such an application is complex, at best. Each API has its own programming model, its own unique set of configuration tools, and so forth. Prior to WCF, this meant that it was difficult to plug and play distributed APIs without authoring a considerable amount of custom infrastructure. For example, if you build your system using the .NET remoting APIs, and you later decide that XML web services are a more appropriate solution, you need to reengineer your code base.

WCF is a distributed computing toolkit that integrates these previously independent distributed technologies into a streamlined API represented primarily by the System.ServiceModel namespace. Using WCF, you can expose services to callers using a wide variety of techniques. For example, if you build an in-house application where all connected machines are Windows based, you can use various TCP protocols to ensure the fastest-possible performance. You can also expose this same service with HTTP and SOAP to allow external callers to leverage its functionality, regardless of the programming language or operating system.

Given the fact that WCF allows you to pick the correct protocol for the job (using a common programming model), you will find that it becomes quite easy to plug and play the underlying plumbing of your distributed application. In most cases, you can do so without having to recompile or redeploy the client/service software because the grungy details are often relegated to application configuration files.

An Overview of WCF Features

Interoperability and integration of diverse APIs are only two (important) aspects of WCF. WCF also provides a rich software fabric that complements the remoting technologies it exposes. Consider the following list of major WCF features:

- Support for strongly typed *as well as* untyped messages. This approach allows .NET applications to share custom types efficiently, while software created using other platforms (such as Java) can consume streams of loosely typed XML.

- Support for several *bindings* (e.g., raw HTTP, TCP, MSMQ, and named pipes) allows you to choose the most appropriate plumbing to transport message data.

- Support for the latest and greatest web service specifications (WS-*).

- A fully integrated security model encompassing both native Windows/.NET security protocols and numerous neutral-security techniques built on web service standards.

- Support for session-like state management techniques, as well as support for one-way or stateless messages.

As impressive as this list of features might be, it only scratches the surface of the functionality WCF provides. WCF also offers tracing and logging facilities, performance counters, a publish-and-subscribe event model, and transactional support, among other features.

An Overview of Service-Oriented Architecture

Yet another benefit of WCF is that it is based on the design principles established by *service-oriented architecture* (SOA). To be sure, SOA is a major buzzword in the industry; and like most buzzwords, SOA can be defined in numerous ways. Simply put, SOA is a way to design a distributed system where several autonomous *services* work in conjunction by passing *messages* across boundaries (either networked machines or two processes on the same machine) using well-defined *interfaces.*

In the world of WCF, you typically create these well-defined interfaces using CLR interface types (see Chapter 9). In a more general sense, however, the interface of a service simply describes the set of members that might be invoked by external callers.

The team that designed WCF observed the four tenets of SOA design principles. While these tenets are typically honored automatically simply by building a WCF application, understanding these four cardinal design rules of SOA can help you understand WCF better. The sections that follow provide a brief overview of each tenet.

Tenet 1: Boundaries Are Explicit

This tenet reiterates the fact that the functionality of a WCF service is expressed using well-defined interfaces (e.g., descriptions of each member, its parameters, and its return values). The only way that an external caller can communicate with a WCF service is through the interface, and the external caller remains blissfully unaware of the underlying implementation details.

Tenet 2: Services Are Autonomous

The term *autonomous entities* refers to the fact that a given WCF service is (as much as possible) an island unto itself. An autonomous service should be independent with regard to version, deployment, and installation issues. To help promote this tenet, you can fall back on a key aspect of interface-based programming. Once an interface is in production, it should never be changed (or you will risk breaking existing clients). When you need to extend the functionality of your WCF service, you author new interfaces that model the desired functionality.

Tenet 3: Services Communicate via Contract, Not Implementation

The third tenet is yet another byproduct of interface-based programming. The implementation details of a WCF service (e.g., the language it was written in, how it accomplishes its work, etc.) are of no concern to the external caller. WCF clients interact with services solely through their exposed public interfaces.

Tenet 4: Service Compatibility Is Based on Policy

Because CLR interfaces provide strongly typed contracts for all WCF clients (and can also be used to generate a related WSDL document based on your choice of binding), it is important to realize that interfaces and WSDL alone are not expressive enough to detail aspects of what the service is capable of doing. Given this, SOA allows you to define *policies* that further qualify the semantics of the service (e.g., the expected security requirements used to talk to the service). Using these policies, you can basically separate the low-level syntactic description of your service (the exposed interfaces) from the semantic details of how they work and how they need to be invoked.

WCF: The Bottom Line

The preceding short history lesson explains why WCF is the preferred approach for building distributed applications. WCF is the recommended API whether you want to build an in-house application using TCP protocols, move data between programs on the same machine using named pipes, or expose data to the world at large using HTTP based protocols.

This is not to say that you cannot use the original .NET distributed-centric namespaces (e.g., System.Runtime.Remoting, System.Messaging, System.EnterpriseServices, and System.Web.Services) in new development efforts. In some cases (e.g., if you need to build COM+ objects), you must do so. In any case, if you have used these APIs in previous projects, you will find learning WCF straightforward. Like the technologies that preceded it, WCF makes considerable use of XML-based configuration files, .NET attributes, and proxy generation utilities.

With this introductory foundation behind you, you can concentrate on the topic of building WCF applications. Again, you should understand that full coverage of WCF would require an entire book because each of the supported services (e.g., MSMQ, COM+, P2P, and named pipes) could be a chapter unto itself. Here, you will learn the overall process of building WCF programs using both TCP- and HTTP-based (e.g., web service) protocols. This should put you in a good position to study these topics further, as you see fit.

Investigating the Core WCF Assemblies

As you might expect, the programming fabric of WCF is represented by a set of .NET assemblies installed into the GAC. Table 25-1 describes the overall role of the core WCF assemblies you need to use in just about any WCF application.

Table 25-1. Core WCF Assemblies

Assembly	Meaning in Life
System.Runtime.Serialization.dll	This core assembly defines namespaces and types that you can use for serializing and deserializing objects in the WCF framework.
System.ServiceModel.dll	This core assembly contains the types used to build any sort of WCF application.

The two assemblies listed in Table 25-1 define many new namespaces and types. You should consult the .NET Framework 4.5 SDK documentation for complete details; however, Table 25-2 documents the roles of some of the important namespaces.

Table 25-2. *Core WCF Namespaces*

Namespace	Meaning in Life
System.Runtime.Serialization	This defines many types you use to control how data is serialized and deserialized within the WCF framework.
System.ServiceModel	This primary WCF namespace defines binding and hosting types, as well as basic security and transactional types.
System.ServiceModel.Configuration	This defines numerous types that provide programmatic access to WCF configuration files.
System.ServiceModel.Description	This defines types that provide an object model to the addresses, bindings, and contracts defined within WCF configuration files.
System.ServiceModel.MsmqIntegration	This contains types to integrate with the MSMQ service.
System.ServiceModel.Security	This defines numerous types to control aspects of the WCF security layers.

The Visual Studio WCF Project Templates

As will be explained in more detail later in this chapter, a WCF application is typically represented by three interrelated assemblies, one of which is a *.dll that contains the types that external callers can communicate with (in other words, the WCF service itself). When you want to build a WCF service, it is perfectly permissible to select a standard Class Library project template (see Chapter 14) as a starting point and manually reference the WCF assemblies.

Alternatively, you can create a new WCF service by selecting the WCF Service Library project template of Visual Studio (see Figure 25-2). This project type automatically sets references to the required WCF assemblies; however, it also generates a good deal of starter code, which you will likely often delete.

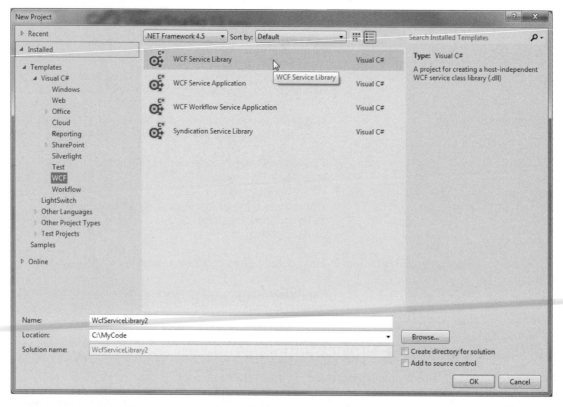

Figure 25-2. The Visual Studio WCF Service Library project template

One benefit of selecting the WCF Service Library project template is that it also supplies you with an App.config file, which might seem strange because you are building a .NET *.dll, not a .NET *.exe. However, this file is useful because, when you debug or run your WCF Service Library project, the Visual Studio IDE will automatically launch the WCF Test Client application. This program (WcfTestClient.exe) will look up the settings in the App.config file, so it can host your service for testing purposes. You'll learn more about the WCF Test Client later in this chapter.

■ **Note** The App.config file of the WCF Service Library project is also useful because it shows you the bare-bones settings used to configure a WCF host application. In fact, you can copy and paste much of this code into the configuration file of your production services.

In addition to the basic WCF Service Library template, the WCF project category of the New Project dialog box defines two WCF library projects that integrate Windows Workflow Foundation (WF) functionality into a WCF service, as well as a template to build an RSS library (see Figure 25-2). The next chapter will introduce you to the Windows Workflow Foundation, so you'll ignore these particular WCF project templates for the time being (I'll leave it to the interested reader to dig into the RSS feed project template).

The WCF Service Web Site Project Template

You can find yet another Visual Studio WCF-centric project template in the New Web Site dialog box, which you activate using the File ➤ New ➤ Web Site menu option (see Figure 25-3).

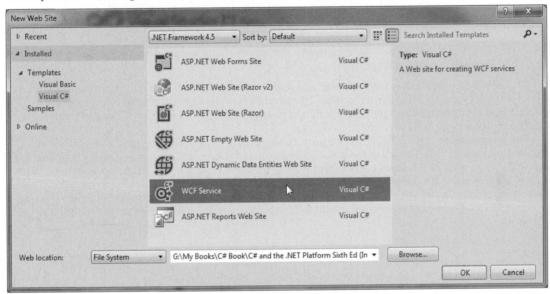

Figure 25-3. The Visual Studio web-based WCF Service project template

This WCF Service project template is useful when you know from the outset that your WCF service will use HTTP–based protocols rather than, for example, TCP or named pipes. This option can automatically create a new Internet Information Services (IIS) virtual directory to contain your WCF program files, create a proper Web.config file to expose the service through HTTP, and author the necessary *.svc file (you'll learn more about *.svc files later in this chapter). Thus, the web-based WCF Service project is a time saver because the IDE automatically sets up the required IIS infrastructure.

In contrast, if you build a new WCF service using the WCF Service Library option, you have the ability to host the service in a variety of ways (e.g., custom host, Windows service, or manually built IIS virtual directory). This option is more appropriate when you need to build a custom host for your WCF service that can work with any number of WCF bindings.

The Basic Composition of a WCF Application

When you build a WCF distributed system, you will typically do so by creating the following three interrelated assemblies:

- *The WCF Service assembly:* This *.dll contains the classes and interfaces that represent the overall functionality you want to expose to external callers.

- *The WCF Service host:* This software module is the entity that hosts your WCF service assembly.

- *The WCF client:* This is the application that accesses the service's functionality through an intervening proxy.

As mentioned previously, the WCF Service assembly is a .NET class library that contains a number of WCF contracts and their implementations. The key difference is that the interface contracts are adorned with various attributes that control data type representation, how the WCF runtime interacts with the exposed types, and so forth.

The second assembly, the WCF Service host, can be literally any .NET executable. As you will see later in this chapter, WCF was set up so that you can expose services easily from any type of application (e.g., Windows Forms, a Windows service, and WPF applications). When you build a custom host, you use the ServiceHost type and possibly a related *.config file. The latter contains details regarding the server-side plumbing you wish to use. However, if you use IISas the host for your WCF service, you don't need to build a custom host programmatically because IIS will use the ServiceHost type behind the scenes.

■ **Note** It is also possible to host a WCF service using the Windows Activation Service (WAS); you can consult the .NET Framework 4.5 SDK documentation for details.

The final assembly represents the client that makes calls into the WCF service. As you might expect, this client can be any type of .NET application. Similar to the host, client applications typically use a client-side *.config file that defines the client-side plumbing. You should also be aware that you can easily have a client application written in another framework (e.g., Java) if you build your WCF service using HTTP-based bindings.

Figure 25-4 illustrates the relationship between these three interrelated WCF assemblies (from a high level). Behind the scenes, several lower-level details are used to represent the required plumbing (e.g., factories, channels, and listeners). These low-level details are usually hidden from view; however, they can be extended or customized if required. In most cases, the default plumbing fits the bill sufficiently.

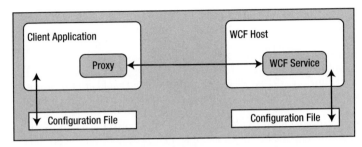

Figure 25-4. *A high-level look at a typical WCF application*

It is also worth pointing out that using a server-side or client-side *.config file is technically optional. If you want, you can hard-code the host (as well as the client) to specify the necessary plumbing (e.g., endpoints, binding, and addresses). The obvious problem with this approach is that if you need to change the plumbing details, you will need to recode, recompile, and redeploy a number of assemblies. Using a *.config file keeps your code base much more flexible because changing the plumbing is as simple as updating the file's content and restarting the application. On the other hand, programmatic configuration allows an application more dynamic flexibility—it can choose how to configure the plumbing based on *if-tests*, for example.

The ABCs of WCF

Hosts and clients communicate with each other by agreeing on the ABCs, a friendly mnemonic for remembering the core building blocks of a WCF application *address*, *binding*, and *contract*, defined as follows:

- *Address*: Describes the location of the service. In code, you represent this with a System.Uri type; however, you typically store the value in *.config files.

- *Binding*: WCF ships with a many different bindings that specify network protocols, encoding mechanisms, and the transport layer.

- *Contract*: Provides a description of each method exposed from the WCF service.

You should realize that the ABC abbreviation does not imply that a developer must define the address first, followed by binding, and ending with the contract. In many cases, a WCF developer begins by defining a contract for the service, followed by establishing an address and bindings (any order will do, as long as each aspect is accounted for). Before we move on to building our first WCF application, let's take a more detailed look at the ABCs.

Understanding WCF Contracts

Understanding the notion of a *contract* is the key to building a WCF service. While not mandatory, the vast majority of your WCF applications will begin by defining a set of .NET interface types that are used to represent the set of members a given WCF service will support. Specifically, interfaces that represent a WCF contract are called *service contracts*. The classes (or structures) that implement them are called *service types*.

WCF service contracts are adorned with various attributes, the most common of which are defined in the System.ServiceModel namespace. When the members of a service contract (the methods in the interface) contain only simple data types (e.g., numerical data, Booleans, and string data), you can build a complete WCF service using nothing more than the [ServiceContract] and [OperationContract] attributes.

However, if your members expose custom types, you will likely use various types in the System.Runtime.Serialization namespace (see Figure 25-5) of the System.Runtime.Serialization.dll assembly. Here you will find additional attributes (e.g., [DataMember] and [DataContract]) to fine-tune the process of defining how your composite types are serialized to and from XML when they are passed to and from service operations.

Strictly speaking, you are not required to use CLR interfaces to define a WCF contract. Many of these same attributes can be applied on public members of a public class (or structure). However, given the many benefits of interface-based programming (e.g., polymorphism and elegant versioning), it is safe to consider using CLR interfaces to describe a WCF contract a best practice.

Figure 25-5. System.Runtime.Serialization defines a number of attributes used when building WCF data contracts

Understanding WCF Bindings

Once you define and implement a contract (or a set of contracts) in your service library, the next logical step is to build a hosting agent for the WCF service itself. As mentioned previously, you have a variety of possible hosts to choose from, all of which must specify the *bindings* used by remote callers to gain access to the service type's functionality.

WCF ships with many of binding choices, each of which is tailored to a specific need. If none of the out-of-the-box bindings fits the bill, you can create your own by extending the CustomBinding type (something you will not do in this chapter). A WCF binding can specify the following characteristics:

- The transport layer used to move data (HTTP, MSMQ, named pipes, and TCP)

- The channels used by the transport (one-way, request-reply, and duplex)

- The encoding mechanism used to deal with the data itself (e.g., XML and binary)

- Any supported web service protocols (if permitted by the binding), such as WS-Security, WS-Transactions, WS-Reliability, and so on

Let's take a look at your basic choices.

HTTP-Based Bindings

The BasicHttpBinding, WSHttpBinding, WSDualHttpBinding, and WSFederationHttpBinding options are geared toward exposing contract types through HTTP/SOAP protocols. If you require the furthest reach possible for your service (e.g., multiple operating systems and multiple programming architectures), you want to focus on these bindings because all of these binding types encode data based on XML representation and use HTTP on the wire.

Table 25-3 shows how you can represent a WCF binding in code (using class types within the System.ServiceModel namespace) or as XML attributes defined within *.config files.

Table 25-3. The HTTP-Centric WCF Bindings

Binding Class	Binding Element	Meaning in Life
BasicHttpBinding	<basicHttpBinding>	You use this to build a WS-Basic Profile–conformant (WS-I Basic Profile 1.1) WCF service. This binding uses HTTP as the transport and Text/XML as the default message encoding.
WSHttpBinding	<wsHttpBinding>	This is similar to BasicHttpBinding, but provides more web service features. This binding adds support for transactions, reliable messaging, and WS-Addressing.
WSDualHttpBinding	<wsDualHttpBinding>	This is similar to WSHttpBinding, but intended for use with duplex contracts (e.g., the service and client can send messages back and forth). This binding supports only SOAP security and requires reliable messaging.

WSFederationHttpBinding	<wsFederationHttpBinding>	This is a secure and interoperable binding that supports the WS-Federation protocol, enabling organizations that are in a federation to authenticate and authorize users efficiently.

As its name suggests, BasicHttpBinding is the simplest of all web service–centric protocols. Specifically, this binding ensures that your WCF service conforms to a specification named WS-I Basic Profile 1.1 (defined by WS-I). The main reason to use this binding is for maintaining backward compatibility with applications that were previously built to communicate with ASP.NET web services (which have been part of the .NET libraries since version 1.0).

The WSHttpBinding protocol not only incorporates support for a subset of the WS-* specification (transactions, security, and reliable sessions), but also supports the ability to handle binary data encoding using Message Transmission Optimization Mechanism (MTOM).

The main benefit of WSDualHttpBinding is that it adds the ability to allow the caller and sender to communicate using *duplex messaging*, which is a fancy way of saying they can engage in a two-way conversation. When selecting WSDualHttpBinding, you can hook into the WCF publish/subscribe event model.

Finally, WSFederationHttpBinding is the web service–based protocol you might want to consider when security among a group of organizations is of the utmost importance. This binding supports the WS-Trust, WS-Security, and WS-SecureConversation specifications, which are represented by the WCF CardSpace APIs.

TCP-Based Bindings

If you build a distributed application involving machines that are configured with the .NET 4.5 libraries (in other words, all machines are running the Windows operating system), you can gain performance benefits by bypassing web service bindings and opting for a TCP binding, which ensures that all data is encoded in a compact binary format, rather than XML. Again, when you use the bindings shown in Table 25-4, the client and host must be .NET applications.

Table 25-4. The TCP-Centric WCF Bindings

Binding Class	Binding Element	Meaning in Life
NetNamedPipeBinding	<netNamedPipeBinding>	Serves as a secure, reliable, optimized binding for on-the-same-machine communication between .NET applications.
NetPeerTcpBinding	<netPeerTcpBinding>	Provides a secure binding for P2P network applications.
NetTcpBinding	<netTcpBinding>	Serves as a secure and optimized binding suitable for cross-machine communication between .NET applications.

The NetTcpBinding class uses TCP to move binary data between the client and WCF service. As mentioned previously, this will result in higher performance than the web service protocols, but limits you to an in-house Windows solution. On the plus side, NetTcpBinding supports transactions, reliable sessions, and secure communications.

Like NetTcpBinding, NetNamedPipeBinding supports transactions, reliable sessions, and secure communications; however, it has no ability to make cross-machine calls. If you want to find the fastest way to push data between WCF applications on the same machine (e.g., cross-application domain communications), NetNamedPipeBinding is the binding choice of champions. For more information on NetPeerTcpBinding, consult the .NET Framework 4.5 SDK documentation for details regarding P2P networking.

MSMQ-Based Bindings

Finally, the NetMsmqBinding and MsmqIntegrationBinding bindings are of immediate interest if you want to integrate with a Microsoft MSMQ server. This chapter will not examine the details of using MSMQ bindings, but Table 25-5 documents the basic role of each.

Table 25-5. The MSMQ-Centric WCF Bindings

Binding Class	Binding Element	Meaning in Life
MsmqIntegrationBinding	<msmqIntegrationBinding>	You can use this binding to enable WCF applications to send and receive messages to and from existing MSMQ applications that use COM, native C++, or the types defined in the System. Messaging namespace.
NetMsmqBinding	<netMsmqBinding>	You can use this queued binding for cross-machine communication between .NET applications. This is the preferred approach among the MSMQ-centric bindings.

Understanding WCF Addresses

Once you establish the contracts and bindings, the final piece of the puzzle is to specify an *address* for the WCF service. This is important because remote callers will be unable to communicate with the remote types if they cannot locate them! Like most aspects of WCF, an address can be hard-coded in an assembly (using the System.Uri type) or offloaded to a *.config file.

In either case, the exact format of the WCF address will differ based on your choice of binding (HTTP based, named pipes, TCP based, or MSMQ based). From a high level, WCF addresses can specify the following bits of information:

- Scheme: The transport protocol (e.g., HTTP)

- MachineName: The fully qualified domain of the machine

- Port: This is optional in many cases; for example, the default for HTTP bindings is port 80.

- Path: The path to the WCF service

This information can be represented by the following generalized template (the Port value is optional because some bindings don't use them):

```
scheme://<MachineName>[:Port]/Path
```

When you use an HTTP-based binding (e.g., basicHttpBinding, wsHttpBinding, wsDualHttpBinding, or wsFederationHttpBinding), the address breaks down like this (recall that HTTP-based protocols default to port 80 if you do not specify a port number):

```
http://localhost:8080/MyWCFService
```

If you use TCP-centric bindings (e.g., NetTcpBinding or NetPeerTcpBinding), the URI takes the following format:

```
net.tcp://localhost:8080/MyWCFService
```

The MSMQ-centric bindings (NetMsmqBinding and MsmqIntegrationBinding) are unique in their URI format because MSMQ can use public or private queues (which are available only on the local machine), and port numbers have no meaning in an MSMQ-centric URI. Consider the following URI, which describes a private queue named MyPrivateQ:

```
net.msmq://localhost/private$/MyPrivateQ
```

Last but not least, the address format used for the named-pipe binding, NetNamedPipeBinding, breaks down like this (recall that named pipes allow for interprocess communication for applications on the same physical machine):

```
net.pipe://localhost/MyWCFService
```

While a single WCF service might expose only a single address (based on a single binding), it is possible to configure a collection of unique addresses (with different bindings). You can do this in a *.config file by defining multiple <endpoint> elements. Here, you can specify any number of ABCs for the same service. This approach can be helpful when you want to allow callers to select which protocol they would like to use when communicating with the service.

Building a WCF Service

Now that you have a better understanding about the building blocks of a WCF application, it's time to create your first sample application and see how the ABCs are accounted for in code and configuration. This first example avoids using the Visual Studio WCF project templates, so you can focus on the specific steps involved in making a WCF service.

Begin by creating a new C# Class Library project named MagicEightBallServiceLib. Next, rename your initial file from Class1.cs to MagicEightBallService.cs, and then add a reference to the System.ServiceModel.dll assembly. In the initial code file, specify that you are using the System.ServiceModel namespace. At this point, your C# file should look like this (note we have a public class at this point):

```
// The key WCF namespace.
using System.ServiceModel;

namespace MagicEightBallServiceLib
{
  public class MagicEightBallService
  {
  }
}
```

```
}
```

Your class type implements a single WCF service contract represented by a strongly typed CLR interface named IEightBall. As you most likely know, the Magic 8-Ball is a toy that allows you to view one of a handful of fixed answers to a question you might ask. Your interface here will define a single method that allows the caller to pose a question to the Magic 8-Ball to obtain a random answer.

WCF service interfaces are adorned with the [ServiceContract] attribute, while each interface member is decorated with the [OperationContract] attribute (you'll learn more details regarding these two attributes in just a moment). Here is the definition of the IEightBall interface:

```
[ServiceContract]
public interface IEightBall
{
  // Ask a question, receive an answer!
  [OperationContract]
  string ObtainAnswerToQuestion(string userQuestion);
}
```

■ **Note** It is permissible to define a service contract interface that contains methods not adorned with the [OperationContract] attribute; however, such members will not be exposed through the WCF runtime.

As you know from your study of the interface type (see Chapter 8), interfaces are quite useless until they are implemented by a class or structure that fleshes out their functionality. Like a real Magic 8-Ball, the implementation of your service type (MagicEightBallService) will randomly return a canned answer from an array of strings. Also, your default constructor will display an information message that will be (eventually) displayed within the host's console window (for diagnostic purposes).

```
public class MagicEightBallService : IEightBall
{
  // Just for display purposes on the host.
  public MagicEightBallService()
  {
    Console.WriteLine("The 8-Ball awaits your question...");
  }

  public string ObtainAnswerToQuestion(string userQuestion)
  {
    string[] answers = { "Future Uncertain", "Yes", "No",
      "Hazy", "Ask again later", "Definitely" };

    // Return a random response.
    Random r = new Random();
    return answers[r.Next(answers.Length)];
  }
}
```

At this point, your WCF Service Library is complete. However, before you construct a host for this service, you need to examine some additional details of the [ServiceContract] and [OperationContract] attributes.

The [ServiceContract] Attribute

For a CLR interface to participate in the services provided by WCF, it must be adorned with the [ServiceContract] attribute. Like many other .NET attributes, the ServiceContractAttribute type supports many properties that further qualify its intended purpose. You can set two properties, Name and Namespace, to control the name of the service type and the name of the XML namespace that defines the service type. If you use an HTTP-specific binding, you use these values to define the <portType> elements of the related WSDL document.

Here, you do not bother to assign a Name value because the default name of the service type is directly based on the C# class name. However, the default name for the underlying XML namespace is simply http://tempuri.org (you should change this for all of your WCF services).

When you build a WCF service that will send and receive custom data types (which you are not currently doing), it is important that you establish a meaningful value to the underlying XML namespace because this ensures that your custom types are unique. As you might know from your experience building XML web services, XML namespaces provide a way to wrap your custom types in a unique container to ensure that your types do not clash with types in another organization.

For this reason, you can update your interface definition with a more fitting definition, which, much like the process of defining an XML namespace in a .NET Web Service project, is typically the URI of the service's point of origin, as in the following example:

```
[ServiceContract(Namespace = "http://MyCompany.com")]
public interface IEightBall
{
    ...
}
```

Beyond Namespace and Name, the [ServiceContract] attribute can be configured with the additional properties shown in Table 25-6. Be aware that some of these settings will be ignored, depending on your binding selection.

Table 25-6. *Various Named Properties of the* [ServiceContract] *Attribute*

Property	Meaning in Life
CallbackContract	Establishes whether this service contract requires callback functionality for two-way message exchange (e.g., duplex bindings).
ConfigurationName	You use this name to locate the service element in an application configuration file. The default is the name of the service implementation class.
ProtectionLevel	Allows you to specify the degree to which the contract binding requires encryption, digital signatures, or both for endpoints that expose the contract.
SessionMode	You use this to establish whether sessions are allowed, not allowed, or required by this service contract.

The [OperationContract] Attribute

Methods that you intend to use within the WCF framework must be attributed with the [OperationContract] attribute, which can also be configured with various named properties. You can use the properties shown in Table 25-7 to declare that a given method is intended to be one-way in nature, supports asynchronous invocation, requires encrypted message data, and so forth (again, many of these values might be ignored based on your binding selection).

Table 25-7. *Various Named Properties of the* [OperationContract] *Attribute*

Property	Meaning in Life
AsyncPattern	Indicates whether the operation is implemented asynchronously using a Begin/End method pair on the service. This allows the service to offload processing to another server-side thread; this has nothing to do with the client calling the method asynchronously!
IsInitiating	Specifies whether this operation can be the initial operation in a session.
IsOneWay	Indicates whether the operation consists of only a single input message (and no associated output).
IsTerminating	Specifies whether the WCF runtime should attempt to terminate the current session after the operation completes.

For the initial example, you don't need to configure the ObtainAnswerToQuestion() method with additional traits; this means you can use the [OperationContract] attribute as currently defined.

Service Types As Operational Contracts

Finally, recall that the use of interfaces is not required when building WCF service types. In fact, it is possible to apply the [ServiceContract] and [OperationContract] attributes directly to the service type itself, like so:

```
// This is only for illustrative purposes
// and not used for the current example.
[ServiceContract(Namespace = "http://MyCompany.com")]
public class ServiceTypeAsContract
{
  [OperationContract]
  void SomeMethod() { }

  [OperationContract]
  void AnotherMethod() { }
}
```

You can take this approach; however, you receive many benefits if you explicitly define an interface type to represent the service contract. The most obvious benefit is that you can apply a given interface to multiple service types (authored in a variety of languages and architectures) to achieve a high degree of polymorphism. Another benefit: You can use a service contract interface as the basis of new contracts (using interface inheritance), without having to carry any implementation baggage.

In any case, your first WCF Service Library is now complete. Compile your project to ensure you do not have any typos.

■ **Source Code** You can find the MagicEightBallServiceLib project under the `MagicEightBallServiceHTTP` subdirectory of Chapter 25.

Hosting the WCF Service

You are now ready to define a host. Although you would host a production-level service from a Windows service or an IIS virtual directory, you will make your first host a simple console named MagicEightBallServiceHost.

After you create this new Console Application project, add a reference to the `System.ServiceModel.dll` and `MagicEightBallServiceLib.dll` assemblies, and then update your initial code file by importing the `System.ServiceModel` and `MagicEightBallServiceLib` namespaces, like so:

```
using System;
...

using System.ServiceModel;
using MagicEightBallServiceLib;

namespace MagicEightBallServiceHost
{
  class Program
  {
    static void Main(string[] args)
    {
      Console.WriteLine("***** Console Based WCF Host *****");
      Console.ReadLine();
    }
  }
}
```

The first step you must take when building a host for a WCF service type is to decide whether you want to define the necessary hosting logic completely in code or to relegate several low-level details to an application configuration file. As mentioned previously, the benefit of *.config files is that the host can change the underlying plumbing without requiring you to recompile and redeploy the executable. However, always remember this is strictly optional because you can hard-code the hosting logic using the types within the System.ServiceModel.dll assembly.

This console-based host will use an application configuration file, so insert this new file (if your project does not currently have one) into your current project by using the Project ➤ Add New Item menu option, and then choosing Application Configuration File.

Establishing the ABCs Within an App.config File

When you build a host for a WCF service type, you follow a predictable set of steps—some that rely on configuration and some that rely on code. These steps are as follows:

- Define the *endpoint* for the WCF service being hosted within the host's configuration file.

- Programmatically use the ServiceHost type to expose the service types available from this endpoint.

- Ensure the host remains running to service incoming client requests. Obviously, this step is not required if you host your service types using a Windows service or IIS.

In the world of WCF, the term *endpoint* represents the address, binding, and contract rolled together in a nice, tidy package. In XML, an endpoint is expressed using the <endpoint> element and the address, binding, and contract elements. Update your *.config file to specify a single endpoint (reachable through port 8080) exposed by this host, like so:

```xml
<?xml version = "1.0" encoding = "utf-8" ?>
<configuration>
  <system.serviceModel>
    <services>
      <service name = "MagicEightBallServiceLib.MagicEightBallService">
        <endpoint address = "http://localhost:8080/MagicEightBallService"
                  binding = "basicHttpBinding"
                  contract = "MagicEightBallServiceLib.IEightBall"/>
      </service>
    </services>
  </system.serviceModel>
</configuration>
```

Notice that the <system.serviceModel> element is the root for all of a host's WCF settings. Each service exposed by the host is represented by a <service> element that is wrapped by the <services> base element. Here, your single <service> element uses the (optional) name attribute to specify the friendly name of the service type.

The nested <endpoint> element handles the task of defining the address, the binding model (basicHttpBinding, in this example), and the fully qualified name of the interface type defining the WCF service contract (IEightBall). Because you are using an HTTP-based binding, you use the http:// scheme, specifying an arbitrary port ID.

Coding Against the ServiceHost Type

With the current configuration file in place, the actual programming logic required to complete the host is simple. When your executable starts up, you will create an instance of the ServiceHost class and inform it which WCF service it is responsible for hosting. At runtime, this object will automatically read the data within the scope of the <system.serviceModel> element of the host's *.config file to determine the correct address, binding, and contract. It will then create the necessary plumbing.

```csharp
static void Main(string[] args)
{
  Console.WriteLine("***** Console Based WCF Host *****");
```

```
using (ServiceHost serviceHost = new ServiceHost(typeof(MagicEightBallService)))
{
    // Open the host and start listening for incoming messages.
    serviceHost.Open();

    // Keep the service running until the Enter key is pressed.
    Console.WriteLine("The service is ready.");
    Console.WriteLine("Press the Enter key to terminate service.");
    Console.ReadLine();
}
}
```

If you run this application now, you will find that the host is alive in memory, ready to take incoming requests from remote clients.

■ **Note** Recall that you must launch Visual Studio with administrative privileges to run many WCF project types!

Specifying Base Addresses

Currently, you create your ServiceHost using a constructor that requires only the service's type information. However, it is also possible to pass in an array of System.Uri types as a constructor argument to represent the collection of addresses this service is accessible from. Currently, you find the address using the *.config file. However, assume that you were to update the using scope like this:

```
using (ServiceHost serviceHost = new
  ServiceHost(typeof(MagicEightBallService),
  new Uri[]{new Uri("http://localhost:8080/MagicEightBallService")}))
{
  ...
}
```

If you did, you could now define your endpoint like this:

```
<endpoint address = ""
          binding = "basicHttpBinding"
          contract = "MagicEightBallServiceLib.IEightBall"/>
```

Of course, too much hard-coding within a host's code base decreases flexibility. Therefore, the current host example assumes you create the service host simply by supplying the following type information, as you did before:

```
using (ServiceHost serviceHost = new ServiceHost(typeof(MagicEightBallService)))
{
  ...
}
```

One of the (slightly frustrating) aspects of authoring host *.config files is that you have several ways to construct the XML descriptors, based on the amount of hard-coding you have in the code base (as you have just seen in the case of the optional Uri array). Here's a reworking that shows yet another way to author *.config files:

```xml
<?xml version = "1.0" encoding = "utf-8" ?>
<configuration>
  <system.serviceModel>
    <services>
      <service name = "MagicEightBallServiceLib.MagicEightBallService">

        <!-- Address obtained from <baseAddresses> -->
        <endpoint address = ""
                  binding = "basicHttpBinding"
                  contract = "MagicEightBallServiceLib.IEightBall"/>

        <!-- List all of the base addresses in a dedicated section -->
        <host>
          <baseAddresses>
            <add baseAddress = "http://localhost:8080/MagicEightBallService"/>
          </baseAddresses>
        </host>
      </service>
    </services>
  </system.serviceModel>
</configuration>
```

In this case, the address attribute of the <endpoint> element is still empty; regardless of the fact that you do not specify an array of Uri objects in code when creating the ServiceHost, the application runs as before because the value is pulled from the baseAddresses scope. The benefit of storing the base address in a <host>'s <baseAddresses> region is that other parts of a *.config file also need to know the address of the service's endpoint. Thus, rather than having to copy and paste address values within a single *.config file, you can isolate the single value, as shown in the preceding snippet.

■ **Note** In a later example, you'll be introduced to a graphical configuration tool that allows you to author configuration files in a less tedious manner.

In any case, you have a bit more work to do before you build a client application to communicate with your service. Specifically, you will dig a bit deeper into the role of the ServiceHost class type and <service.serviceModel> element, as well as the role of metadata exchange (MEX) services.

Details of the ServiceHost Type

You use the ServiceHost class type to configure and expose a WCF service from the hosting executable. However, be aware that you will only use this type directly when building a custom *.exe to host your services. If you use IIS to expose a service, the ServiceHost object is created automatically on your behalf.

As you have seen, this type requires a complete service description, which is obtained dynamically through the configuration settings of the host's *.config file. While this happens automatically when you create a ServiceHost object, it is possible to configure the state of your ServiceHost object manually using a number of members. In addition to Open() and Close() (which communicate with your service in a synchronous manner), Table 25-8 illustrates some further members of interest.

Table 25-8. Select Members of the ServiceHost Type

Members	Meaning in Life
Authorization	This property gets the authorization level for the service being hosted.
AddDefaultEndpoints()	This method is used to configure a WCF Service host programmatically so it uses any number of prebuilt endpoints supplied by the framework.
AddServiceEndpoint()	This method allows you to register an endpoint to the host programmatically.
BaseAddresses	This property obtains the list of registered base addresses for the current service.
BeginOpen() BeginClose()	These methods allow you to open and close a ServiceHost object asynchronously, using the standard asynchronous .NET delegate syntax.
CloseTimeout	This property allows you to set and get the time allowed for the service to close down.
Credentials	This property obtains the security credentials used by the current service.
EndOpen() EndClose()	These methods are the asynchronous counterparts to BeginOpen() and BeginClose().
OpenTimeout	This property allows you to set and get the time allowed for the service to start up.
State	This property gets a value that indicates the current state of the communication object, which is represented by the CommunicationState enum (e.g., opened, closed, and created).

You can see some additional aspects of ServiceHost in action by updating your Program class as follows, with a new static method that prints out the ABCs of each endpoint used by the host:

```
static void DisplayHostInfo(ServiceHost host)
{
  Console.WriteLine();
  Console.WriteLine("***** Host Info *****");

  foreach (System.ServiceModel.Description.ServiceEndpoint se
    in host.Description.Endpoints)
  {
```

```
    Console.WriteLine("Address: {0}", se.Address);
    Console.WriteLine("Binding: {0}", se.Binding.Name);
    Console.WriteLine("Contract: {0}", se.Contract.Name);
    Console.WriteLine();
  }
  Console.WriteLine("*********************");
}
```

Now, assuming that you call this new method from within Main() after opening your host:

```
using (ServiceHost serviceHost = new ServiceHost(typeof(MagicEightBallService)))
{
  // Open the host and start listening for incoming messages.
  serviceHost.Open();
  DisplayHostInfo(serviceHost);
...
}
```

the following statistics will be shown as output:

```
***** Console Based WCF Host *****

***** Host Info *****
Address: http://localhost:8080/MagicEightBallService
Binding: BasicHttpBinding
Contract: IEightBall
*********************

The service is ready.
Press the Enter key to terminate service.
```

Details of the <system.serviceModel> Element

Like any XML element, <system.serviceModel> can define a set of subelements, each of which can be qualified using various attributes. While you should consult the .NET Framework 4.5 SDK documentation for full details regarding the set of possible attributes, here is a skeleton that lists some (but not all) useful subelements:

```
<system.serviceModel>
  <behaviors>
  </behaviors>
  <client>
  </client>
  <commonBehaviors>
  </commonBehaviors>
  <diagnostics>
  </diagnostics>
  <comContracts>
  </comContracts>
  <services>
  </services>
  <bindings>
```

```
    </bindings>
</system.serviceModel>
```

You'll see more exotic configuration files as you move through the chapter; however, you can see the crux of each subelement in Table 25-9.

Table 25-9. Select Subelements of `<service.serviceModel>`

Subelement	Meaning in Life
behaviors	WCF supports various endpoint and service behaviors. In a nutshell, a *behavior* allows you to qualify further the functionality of a host, service, or client.
bindings	This element allows you to fine-tune each of the WCF-supplied bindings (e.g., basicHttpBinding and netMsmqBinding), as well as to specify any custom bindings used by the host.
client	This element contains a list of endpoints a client uses to connect to a service. Obviously, this is not particularly useful in a host's *.config file.
comContracts	This element defines COM contracts enabled for WCF and COM interoperability.
commonBehaviors	This element can only be set within a machine.config file. You can use it to define all of the behaviors used by each WCF service on a given machine.
diagnostics	This element contains settings for the diagnostic features of WCF. The user can enable/disable tracing, performance counters, and the WMI provider; the user can also add custom message filters.
services	This element contains a collection of WCF services exposed by the host.

Enabling Metadata Exchange

Recall that WCF client applications communicate with the WCF service through an intervening proxy type. While you could author the proxy code completely by hand, doing so would be tedious and error-prone. Ideally, you could use a tool to generate the necessary grunge code (including the client-side *.config file). Thankfully, the .NET Framework 4.5 SDK provides a command-line tool (svcutil.exe) for this purpose. Also, Visual Studio provides similar functionality through its Project ➤ Add Service Reference menu option.

For these tools to generate the necessary proxy code/*.config file, however, they must be able to discover the format of the WCF service interfaces and any defined data contracts (e.g., the method names and type of parameters).

Metadata exchange (MEX) is a WCF *service behavior* that you can use to fine-tune how the WCF runtime handles your service. Simply put, each <behavior> element can define a set of activities a given service can subscribe to. WCF provides numerous behaviors out of the box, and it is possible to build your own.

The MEX behavior (which is disabled by default) will intercept any metadata requests sent through HTTP GET. You must enable MEX if you want to allow svcutil.exe or Visual Studio to automate the creation of the required client-side proxy *.config file.

Enabling MEX is a matter of tweaking the host's *.config file with the proper settings (or authoring the corresponding C# code). First, you must add a new <endpoint> just for MEX. Second, you need to define a WCF behavior to allow HTTP GET access. Third, you need to associate this behavior by name to your service using the behaviorConfiguration attribute on the opening <service> element. Finally, you need to add a <host> element to define the base address of this service (MEX will look here to figure out the locations of the types to describe).

■ **Note** You can bypass this final step if you pass in a System.Uri object to represent the base address as a parameter to the ServiceHost constructor.

Consider the following updated host *.config file, which creates a custom <behavior> element (named EightBallServiceMEXBehavior) that is associated to your service through the behaviorConfiguration attribute within the <service> definition:

```xml
<?xml version = "1.0" encoding = "utf-8" ?>
<configuration>
  <system.serviceModel>
    <services>
      <service name = "MagicEightBallServiceLib.MagicEightBallService"
               behaviorConfiguration="EightBallServiceMEXBehavior">
        <endpoint address = ""
                  binding = "basicHttpBinding"
                  contract = "MagicEightBallServiceLib.IEightBall"/>

        <!-- Enable the MEX endpoint -->
        <endpoint address = "mex"
                  binding = "mexHttpBinding"
                  contract = "IMetadataExchange" />

        <!-- Need to add this so MEX knows the address of our service -->
        <host>
          <baseAddresses>
            <add baseAddress = "http://localhost:8080/MagicEightBallService"/>
          </baseAddresses>
        </host>
      </service>
    </services>

    <!-- A behavior definition for MEX -->
    <behaviors>
      <serviceBehaviors>
        <behavior name = "EightBallServiceMEXBehavior" >
          <serviceMetadata httpGetEnabled = "true" />
        </behavior>
```

```
        </serviceBehaviors>
      </behaviors>
    </system.serviceModel>
  </configuration>
```

You can now rerun your service host application and view its metadata description using the web browser of your choice. To do so, enter the address as the URL while the host is still running, like so:

```
http://localhost:8080/MagicEightBallService
```

Once you are at the homepage for your WCF service (see Figure 25-6), you are provided with basic details regarding how to interact with this service programmatically, as well as a way to view the WSDL contract by clicking the hyperlink at the top of the page. Recall that Web Service Description Language (WSDL) is a grammar that describes the structure of web services at a given endpoint.

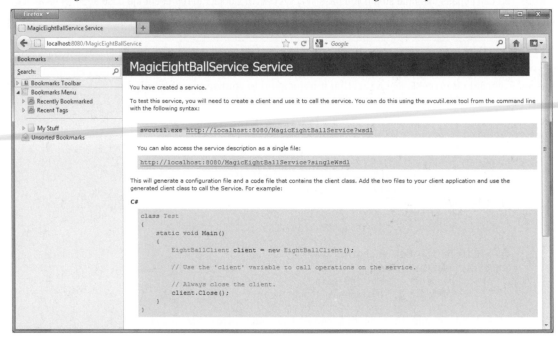

Figure 25-6. *Ready to view metadata using MEX*

Your host now exposes two different endpoints (one for the service and one for MEX), so your host's console output will appear like this:

```
***** Console Based WCF Host *****

***** Host Info *****
Address: http://localhost:8080/MagicEightBallService
Binding: BasicHttpBinding
Contract: IEightBall
```

```
Address: http://localhost:8080/MagicEightBallService/mex
Binding: MetadataExchangeHttpBinding
Contract: IMetadataExchange
**********************

The service is ready.
```

■ **Source Code** You can find the MagicEightBallServiceHost project under the `MagicEightBallServiceHTTP` subdirectory of Chapter 25.

Building the WCF Client Application

Now that your host is in place, the final task is to build a piece of software to communicate with this WCF service type. While you could take the long road and build the necessary infrastructure by hand (a feasible, but labor-intensive task), the .NET Framework 4.5 SDK provides several approaches to generate a client-side proxy quickly. Begin by creating a new Console Application project named MagicEightBallServiceClient.

Generating Proxy Code Using svcutil.exe

The first way you can build a client-side proxy is to use the `svcutil.exe` command-line tool. Using `svcutil.exe`, you can generate a new C# language file that represents the proxy code itself, as well as a client-side configuration file. You can do this by specifying the service's endpoint as the first parameter. You use the `/out:` flag to define the name of the `*.cs` file containing the proxy, and you use the `/config:` option to specify the name of the generated client-side `*.config` file.

Assuming your service is currently running, the following command set passed into `svcutil.exe` will generate two new files in the working directory (which should, of course, be entered as a single line within a Developer Command Prompt):

```
svcutil http://localhost:8080/MagicEightBallService
        /out:myProxy.cs /config:app.config
```

If you open the `myProxy.cs` file, you will find a client-side representation of the `IEightBall` interface, as well as a new class named `EightBallClient`, which is the proxy class itself. This class derives from the generic class, `System.ServiceModel.ClientBase<T>`, where T is the registered service interface.

In addition to a number of custom constructors, each method of the proxy (which is based on the original interface methods) will be implemented to use the inherited `Channel` property to invoke the correct service method. Here is a partial snapshot of the proxy type:

```
[System.Diagnostics.DebuggerStepThroughAttribute()]
[System.CodeDom.Compiler.GeneratedCodeAttribute("System.ServiceModel",
  "4.5.0.0")]
public partial class EightBallClient :
  System.ServiceModel.ClientBase<IEightBall>, IEightBall
{
...
```

```
  public string ObtainAnswerToQuestion(string userQuestion)
  {
    return base.Channel.ObtainAnswerToQuestion(userQuestion);
  }
}
```

When you create an instance of the proxy type in your client application, the base class will establish a connection to the endpoint using the settings specified in the client-side application configuration file. Much like the server-side configuration file, the generated client-side `App.config` file contains an `<endpoint>` element and details about the `basicHttpBinding` used to communicate with the service.

You will also find the following `<client>` element, which (again) establishes the ABCs from the client's perspective:

```
<client>
  <endpoint
    address = "http://localhost:8080/MagicEightBallService"
    binding = "basicHttpBinding" bindingConfiguration = "BasicHttpBinding_IEightBall"
    contract = "IEightBall" name = "BasicHttpBinding_IEightBall" />
</client>
```

At this point, you could include these two files into a client project (and reference the `System.ServiceModel.dll` assembly), and then use the proxy type to communicate with the remote WCF service. However, you'll take a different approach here, looking at how Visual Studio can help you further automate the creation of client-side proxy files.

Generating Proxy Code Using Visual Studio

Like any good command-line tool, `svcutil.exe` provides a great number of options that you can use to control how the client proxy is generated. If you do not require these advanced options, you can generate the same two files using the Visual Studio IDE. For the client project, simply select the Add Service Reference option from the Project menu.

After you activate this menu option, you will be prompted to enter the service URI. At this point, click the Go button to see the service description (see Figure 25-7).

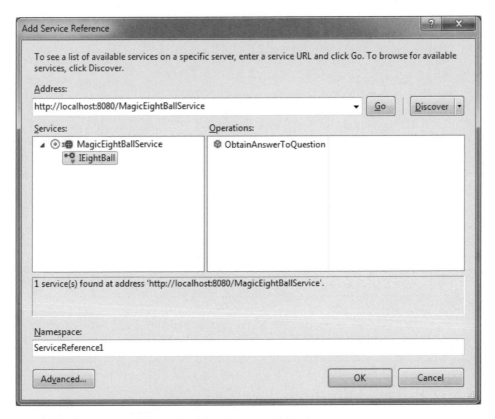

Figure 25-7. Generating the proxy files using Visual Studio

Beyond creating and inserting the proxy files into your current project, this tool is kind enough to reference the WCF assemblies automatically on your behalf. In accordance with a naming convention, the proxy class is defined within a namespace called ServiceReference1, which is nested in the client's namespace (to avoid possible name clashes). Here is the complete client code:

```
// Location of the proxy.
using MagicEightBallServiceClient.ServiceReference1;

namespace MagicEightBallServiceClient
{
  class Program
  {
    static void Main(string[] args)
    {
      Console.WriteLine("***** Ask the Magic 8 Ball *****\n");

      using (EightBallClient ball = new EightBallClient())
      {
        Console.Write("Your question: ");
        string question = Console.ReadLine();
```

```
        string answer =
           ball.ObtainAnswerToQuestion(question);
        Console.WriteLine("8-Ball says: {0}", answer);
      }
      Console.ReadLine();
    }
  }
}
```

Now assume your WCF console host is running, so you can execute the client. Here is one possible output:

```
***** Ask the Magic 8 Ball *****

Your question: Will I ever finish Skyrim?
8-Ball says: No

Press any key to continue . . .
```

■ **Source Code** You can find the MagicEightBallServiceClient project located under the MagicEightBallServiceHTTP subdirectory of Chapter 25.

Configuring a TCP-Based Binding

At this point, the host and client applications are both configured to use the simplest of the HTTP-based bindings, basicHttpBinding. Recall that the benefit of offloading settings to configuration files is that you can change the underlying plumbing in a declarative manner and expose multiple bindings for the same service.

To illustrate this, you can try a little experiment. Create a new folder on your C: drive (or wherever you happen to be saving your code) named EightBallTCP; in this new folder, create two subdirectories named Host and Client.

Next, use Windows Explorer to navigate to the \bin\Debug folder of the host project (from earlier in this chapter) and copy MagicEightBallServiceHost.exe, MagicEightBallServiceHost.exe.config, and MagicEightBallServiceLib.dll to the C:\EightBallTCP\Host folder. Now use a simple text editor to open the *.config file for editing and modify the existing contents as follows:

```
<?xml version = "1.0" encoding = "utf-8" ?>
<configuration>
  <system.serviceModel>
    <services>
      <service name = "MagicEightBallServiceLib.MagicEightBallService">
        <endpoint address = ""
                  binding = "netTcpBinding"
                  contract = "MagicEightBallServiceLib.IEightBall"/>
        <host>
          <baseAddresses>
```

```
            <add baseAddress = "net.tcp://localhost:8090/MagicEightBallService"/>
          </baseAddresses>
        </host>
      </service>
    </services>
  </system.serviceModel>
</configuration>
```

Essentially, this host's *.config file strips out all the MEX settings (because you already built the proxy) and establishes that it is using the netTcpBinding binding type through a unique port. Now run the application by double-clicking the *.exe. If all is well, you should see the host output shown here:

```
***** Console Based WCF Host *****

***** Host Info *****
Address: net.tcp://localhost:8090/MagicEightBallService
Binding: NetTcpBinding
Contract: IEightBall

*********************
The service is ready.
Press the Enter key to terminate service.
```

To complete the test, copy the MagicEightBallServiceClient.exe and MagicEightBallServiceClient.exe.config files from the \bin\Debug folder of the client application (from earlier in this chapter) into the C:\EightBallTCP\Client folder. Update the client configuration file like this:

```
<?xml version = "1.0" encoding = "utf-8" ?>
<configuration>
  <system.serviceModel>
    <client>
      <endpoint address = "net.tcp://localhost:8090/MagicEightBallService"
                binding = "netTcpBinding"
                contract = "ServiceReference1.IEightBall"
                name = "netTcpBinding_IEightBall" />
    </client>
  </system.serviceModel>
</configuration>
```

This client-side configuration file is a massive simplification compared to what the Visual Studio proxy generator authored. Notice how you have completely removed the existing <bindings> element. Originally, the *.config file contained a <bindings> element with a <basicHttpBinding> subelement that supplied numerous details of the client's binding settings (e.g., timeouts).

The truth is you never needed that detail for this example because you automatically obtain the default values of the underlying BasicHttpBinding object. If you needed to, you could of course update the existing <bindings> element to define details of the <netTcpBinding> subelement; however, doing so is not required if you are happy with the default values of the NetTcpBinding object.

In any case, you should now be able to run your client application. Assuming the host is still running in the background, you will be able to move data between your assemblies using TCP.

■ **Source Code** You can find the MagicEightBallTCP project under the Chapter 25 subdirectory.

Simplifying Configuration Settings

As you were working through the first example of the chapter, you might have noticed that the hosting configuration logic is quite verbose. For example, your host's *.config file (for the original basic HTTP binding) needed to define an <endpoint> element for the service, a second <endpoint> element for MEX, a <baseAddresses> element (technically optional) to reduce redundant URIs, and then a <behaviors> section to define the runtime nature of metadata exchange.

To be sure, learning how to author hosting *.config files can be a major hurdle when building WCF services. To make matters more frustrating, a good number of WCF services tend to require the same basic settings in a host configuration file. For example, if you were to make a brand-new WCF service and a brand-new host, and you wanted to expose this service using <basicHttpBinding> with MEX support, the required *.config file would look almost identical to the one you previously authored.

Thankfully, beginning with .NET 4.0, the Windows Communication Foundation API ships with a number of simplifications, including default settings (and other shortcuts) that make the process of building host configuration files much easier.

Leveraging Default Endpoints

Before support for default endpoints, if you called Open() on the ServiceHost object, and you had not yet specified at least one <endpoint> element in your configuration file, the runtime would throw an exception. And you would get a similar result if you called AddServiceEndpoint() in code to specify an endpoint. However, with the release of .NET 4.5, every WCF service is automatically provided with *default endpoints* that capture commonplace configuration details for each supported protocol.

If you were to open the machine.config file for .NET 4.5, you would find a new element named <protocolMapping>. This element documents which WCF bindings to use by default, if you do not specify any.

```
<system.serviceModel>
...
  <protocolMapping>
    <add scheme = "http" binding="basicHttpBinding"/>
    <add scheme = "net.tcp" binding="netTcpBinding"/>
    <add scheme = "net.pipe" binding="netNamedPipeBinding"/>
    <add scheme = "net.msmq" binding="netMsmqBinding"/>
  </protocolMapping>
  ...
</system.serviceModel>
```

To use these default bindings, all you need to do is specify base addresses in your host configuration file. To see this in action, open the HTTP-based MagicEightBallServiceHost project in Visual Studio. Now update your hosting *.config file by completely removing the <endpoint> element for your WCF service and all MEX-specific data. Your configuration file should now look like this:

```
<configuration>
  <system.serviceModel>
    <services>
```

```
      <service name = "MagicEightBallServiceLib.MagicEightBallService" >
        <host>
          <baseAddresses>
            <add baseAddress = "http://localhost:8080/MagicEightBallService"/>
          </baseAddresses>
        </host>
      </service>
    </services>
  </system.serviceModel>
</configuration>
```

Because you specified a valid HTTP `<baseAddress>`, your host will automatically use basicHttpBinding. If you run your host again, you will see the same listing of ABC data:

```
***** Console Based WCF Host *****

***** Host Info *****
Address: http://localhost:8080/MagicEightBallService
Binding: BasicHttpBinding
Contract: IEightBall
**********************
The service is ready.
Press the Enter key to terminate service.
```

You have not yet enabled MEX, but you will do so in a moment using another simplification known as *default behavior configurations*. First, however, you will learn how to expose a single WCF service using multiple bindings.

Exposing a Single WCF Service Using Multiple Bindings

Since its first release, WCF has had the ability to allow a single host to expose a WCF service using multiple endpoints. For example, you could expose the MagicEightBallService using HTTP, TCP, and named pipe bindings simply by adding new endpoints to your configuration file. Once you restart the host, all of the necessary plumbing is created automatically.

This is a huge benefit for many reasons. Before WCF, it was difficult to expose a single service using multiple bindings because each type of binding (e.g., HTTP and TCP) had its own programming model. Nevertheless, the ability to allow a caller to pick the most appropriate binding is extremely useful. In-house callers might like to use TCP bindings that an outwardly facing client (outside of your company firewall) would need to use HTTP to access, while clients on the same machine might opt to use a named pipe.

To do this before .NET 4.5, your hosting configuration file would need to define multiple `<endpoint>` elements manually. It would also have to define multiple `<baseAddress>` elements for each protocol. However, today you can simply author the following configuration file:

```
<configuration>
  <system.serviceModel>
    <services>
      <service name = "MagicEightBallServiceLib.MagicEightBallService" >
        <host>
          <baseAddresses>
            <add baseAddress = "http://localhost:8080/MagicEightBallService"/>
```

```
        <add baseAddress =
            "net.tcp://localhost:8099/MagicEightBallService"/>
        </baseAddresses>
      </host>
    </service>
  </services>
  </system.serviceModel>
</configuration>
```

If you compile your project (to refresh the deployed *.config file) and restart the host, you will now see the following endpoint data:

```
***** Console Based WCF Host *****

***** Host Info *****
Address: http://localhost:8080/MagicEightBallService
Binding: BasicHttpBinding
Contract: IEightBall

Address: net.tcp://localhost:8099/MagicEightBallService
Binding: NetTcpBinding
Contract: IEightBall

*********************
The service is ready.
Press the Enter key to terminate service.
```

Now that your WCF service can be reachable from two unique endpoints, you might wonder how the caller is able to select between them. When you generate a client-side proxy, the Add Service reference tool will give each exposed endpoint a string name in the client side *.config file. In code, you can pass in the correct string name to the proxy's constructor, and sure enough, the correct binding will be used. Before you can do this, however, you need to reestablish MEX for this modified hosting configuration file and learn how to tweak the settings of a default binding.

Changing Settings for a WCF Binding

If you specify the ABCs of a service in C# code (which you will do later in this chapter), it becomes obvious how you change the default settings of a WCF binding; you simply change the property values of the object! For example, if you want to use BasicHttpBinding, but also want to change the timeout settings, you could do so as follows:

```
void ConfigureBindingInCode()
{
  BasicHttpBinding binding = new BasicHttpBinding();
  binding.OpenTimeout = TimeSpan.FromSeconds(30);
  ...
}
```

It has always been possible to configure settings for a binding in a declarative manner. For example, .NET 3.5 let you build a host configuration file that changed the OpenTimeout property of BasicHttpBinding, like so:

```
<configuration>
  <system.serviceModel>

    <bindings>
      <basicHttpBinding>
        <binding name = "myCustomHttpBinding"
                 openTimeout = "00:00:30" />
      </basicHttpBinding>
    </bindings>

    <services>
      <service name = "WcfMathService.MyCalc">
        <endpoint address = "http://localhost:8080/MyCalc"
                  binding = "basicHttpBinding"
                  bindingConfiguration = "myCustomHttpBinding"
                  contract = "WcfMathService.IBasicMath" />
      </service>
    </services>
  </system.serviceModel>
</configuration>
```

Here, you have a configuration file for a service named WcfMathService.MyCalc, which supports a single interface named IBasicMath. Note how the <bindings> section allows you to define a named <binding> element, which tweaks settings for a given binding. Within the <endpoint> of the service, you can connect your specific settings using the bindingConfiguration attribute.

This sort of hosting configuration still works as expected; however, if you leverage a default endpoint, you can't connect the <binding> to the <endpoint>! As luck would have it, you can control the settings of a default endpoint simply by omitting the name attribute of the <binding> element. For example, this snippet changes some properties of the default BasicHttpBinding and NetTcpBinding objects used in the background:

```
<configuration>
  <system.serviceModel>
    <services>
      <service name = "MagicEightBallServiceLib.MagicEightBallService" >
        <host>
          <baseAddresses>
            <add baseAddress = "http://localhost:8080/MagicEightBallService"/>
            <add baseAddress =
              "net.tcp://localhost:8099/MagicEightBallService"/>
          </baseAddresses>
        </host>
      </service>
    </services>

    <bindings>
      <basicHttpBinding>
        <binding openTimeout = "00:00:30" />
      </basicHttpBinding>
```

```
    <netTcpBinding>
        <binding closeTimeout = "00:00:15" />
    </netTcpBinding>
  </bindings>

  </system.serviceModel>
</configuration>
```

Leveraging the Default MEX Behavior Configuration

A proxy generation tool must discover the composition of a service at runtime before it can do its work. In WCF, you allow this runtime discovery to occur by enabling MEX. Again, most host configuration files need to enable MEX (at least during development); fortunately, the way you configure MEX seldom changes, so .NET 4.5 provides a few handy shortcuts.

The most useful shortcut is out-of-the-box MEX support. You don't need to add a MEX endpoint, define a named MEX service behavior, and then connect the named binding to the service (as you did in the HTTP version of the MagicEightBallServiceHost); instead, you can now simply add the following:

```
<configuration>
  <system.serviceModel>
    <services>
      <service name = "MagicEightBallServiceLib.MagicEightBallService" >
        <host>
          <baseAddresses>
            <add baseAddress = "http://localhost:8080/MagicEightBallService"/>
            <add baseAddress =
              "net.tcp://localhost:8099/MagicEightBallService"/>
          </baseAddresses>
        </host>
      </service>
    </services>

    <bindings>
      <basicHttpBinding>
        <binding openTimeout = "00:00:30" />
      </basicHttpBinding>
      <netTcpBinding>
        <binding closeTimeout = "00:00:15" />
      </netTcpBinding>
    </bindings>

    <behaviors>
      <serviceBehaviors>
        <behavior>
          <!-- To get default MEX,
               don't name your <serviceMetadata> element -->
          <serviceMetadata httpGetEnabled = "true"/>
        </behavior>
      </serviceBehaviors>
    </behaviors>
```

```
    </system.serviceModel>
</configuration>
```

The trick is that the `<serviceMetadata>` element no longer has a `name` attribute (also notice the `<service>` element no longer needs the `behaviorConfiguration` attribute). With this adjustment, you get free MEX support at runtime. To test this, you can run your host (after you compile to refresh the configuration file) and type in the following URL in a browser:

```
http://localhost:8080/MagicEightBallService
```

After you do this, you can click the `wsdl` link at the top of the web page to see the WSDL description of the service (refer back to Figure 25-6 for a refresher). Note that you do not see the host's console window print out data for the MEX endpoint because you have not explicitly defined an endpoint for `IMetadataExchange` in your configuration file. Nevertheless, MEX is enabled, and you can start to build client proxies.

Refreshing the Client Proxy and Selecting the Binding

Assuming your updated host has been compiled and is running in the background, you will now want to open the client application and refresh the current service reference. Begin by opening the Service References folder found in the Solution Explorer. Next, right-click the current ServiceReference1 and pick the Update Service Reference menu option (see Figure 25-8).

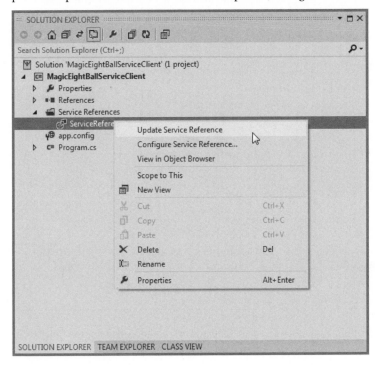

Figure 25-8. Refreshing the proxy and client-side `*.config` *file*

After you have done this, you will see that the client-side *.config file has two bindings to select from: one for HTTP and one for TCP. As you can see, you give each binding a fitting name. Here is a partial listing of the refreshed configuration file:

```
<configuration>
  <system.serviceModel>

    <bindings>
      <basicHttpBinding>
        <binding name = "BasicHttpBinding_IEightBall" ... />
      </basicHttpBinding>

      <netTcpBinding>
        <binding name = "NetTcpBinding_IEightBall" ... />
      </netTcpBinding>
    </bindings>
...
    </system.serviceModel>
</configuration>
```

The client can use these names when it creates the proxy object to select the binding it wishes to use. Thus, if your client would like to use TCP, you could update the client side C# code as follows:

```
static void Main(string[] args)
{
  Console.WriteLine("***** Ask the Magic 8 Ball *****\n");

  using (EightBallClient ball = new EightBallClient("NetTcpBinding_IEightBall"))
  {
    ...
  }
  Console.ReadLine();
}
```

If a client would rather use the HTTP binding, you could write the following:

```
using (EightBallClient ball = new
        EightBallClient("BasicHttpBinding_IEightBall"))
{
...
}
```

That wraps up the current example, which showcased a number of useful shortcuts. These features simplify how you can author hosting configuration files. Next up, you will see how to use the WCF Service Library project template.

■ **Source Code** You can find the MagicEightBallServiceHTTPDefaultBindings project located under the Chapter 25 subdirectory.

Using the WCF Service Library Project Template

You need to do one more thing before you build a more exotic WCF service that communicates with the AutoLot database you created in Chapter 21. The next example will illustrate a number of important topics, including the benefits of the WCF Service Library project template, the WCF Test Client, the WCF configuration editor, hosting WCF services within a Windows service, and asynchronous client calls. To stay focused on these new concepts, this WCF service will be kept intentionally simple.

Building a Simple Math Service

To begin, create a brand-new WCF Service Library project named MathServiceLibrary, making sure you select the correct option under the WCF node of the New Project dialog box (see Figure 25-2 if you need a nudge). Now change the name of the initial IService1.cs file to IBasicMath.cs. After you do so, *delete* all of the example code within the MathServiceLibrary namespace and replace it with the following code:

```
[ServiceContract(Namespace="http://MyCompany.com")]
public interface IBasicMath
{
  [OperationContract]
  int Add(int x, int y);
}
```

Next, change the name of the Service1.cs file to MathService.cs, delete all the example code within the MathServiceLibrary namespace (again), and implement your service contract as follows:

```
public class MathService : IBasicMath
{
  public int Add(int x, int y)
  {
    // To simulate a lengthy request.
    System.Threading.Thread.Sleep(5000);
    return x + y;
  }
}
```

Finally, open the supplied App.config file and change all occurrences of IService1 to IBasicMath, as well as all occurrences of Service1 to MathService. Also take a moment to notice that this *.config file has already been enabled to support MEX; by default, your service endpoint uses the wsHttpBinding protocol.

Testing the WCF Service with WcfTestClient.exe

One benefit of using the WCF Service Library project is that when you debug or run your library, it will read the settings in the *.config file and use them to load the WCF Test Client application (WcfTestClient.exe). This GUI-based application allows you to test each member of your service interface as you build the WCF service; this means you don't have to build a host/client manually simply for testing purposes, as you did previously.

Figure 25-9 shows the testing environment for MathService. Notice that when you double-click an interface method, you can specify input parameters and invoke the member.

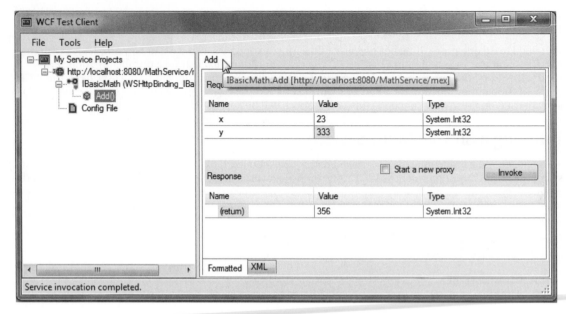

Figure 25-9. Testing the WCF service using WcfTestClient.exe

This utility works out of the box when you have created a WCF Service Library project; however, be aware that you can use this tool to test any WCF service when you start it at the command line by specifying a MEX endpoint. For example, if you were to start the MagicEightBallServiceHost.exe application, you could specify the following command at a Developer Command Prompt:

```
wcftestclient http://localhost:8080/MagicEightBallService
```

After you do this, you can invoke ObtainAnswerToQuestion() in a similar manner.

Altering Configuration Files Using SvcConfigEditor.exe

Another benefit of making use of the WCF Service Library project is that you are able to right-click the App.config file within the Solution Explorer to activate the GUI-based Service Configuration Editor, SvcConfigEditor.exe (see Figure 25-10). This same technique can be used from a client application that has referenced a WCF service.

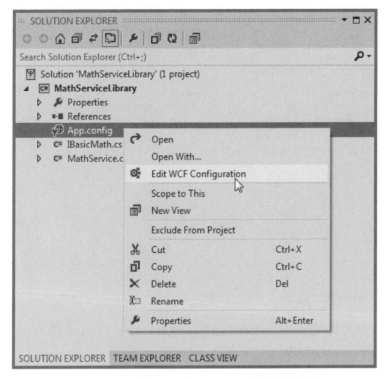

Figure 25-10. GUI-based *.config file editing starts here

After you activate this tool, you can change the XML-based data using a friendly user interface. Using a tool such as this to maintain your *.config files provides many benefits. First (and foremost), you can rest assured that the generated markup conforms to the expected format and is typo-free. Second, it is a great way to see the valid values that could be assigned to a given attribute. Finally, you no longer need to author tedious XML data manually.

Figure 25-11 shows the overall look-and-feel of the Service Configuration Editor. Truth be told, an entire chapter could be devoted to describing all of the interesting options SvcConfigEditor.exe supports (e.g., COM+ integration and creation of new *.config files). Be sure to take time to investigate this tool; also be aware that you can access a fairly detailed help system by pressing F1.

■ **Note** The SvcConfigEditor.exe utility can edit (or create) configuration files, even if you do not select an initial WCF Service Library project. Use a Developer Command window to launch the tool, and then use the File Open menu option to load an existing *.config file for editing.

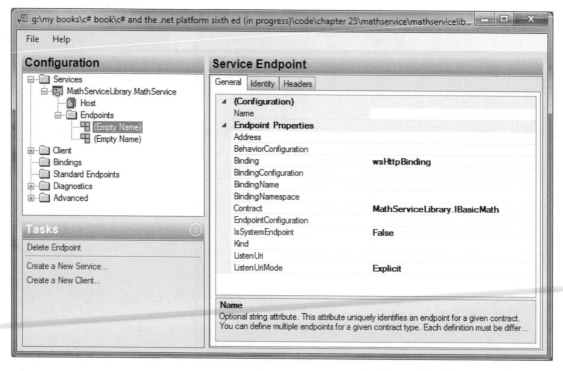

Figure 25-11. Working with the WCF Service Configuration Editor

You have no need to further configure your WCF MathService; at this point, you can move on to the task of building a custom host.

Hosting the WCF Service Within a Windows Service

Hosting a WCF service from within a console application (or within a GUI desktop application, for that matter) is not an ideal choice for a production-level server, given that the host must remain running visibly in the background to service clients. Even if you were to minimize the hosting application to the Windows taskbar, it would still be far too easy to accidentally shut down the host, thereby terminating the connection with any client applications.

■ **Note** While it is true that a desktop Windows application does not *have* to show a main window, a typical *.exe does require user interaction to load the executable. However, you can configure a Windows service (described next) to run even if no users are currently logged on to the workstation.

If you build an in-house WCF application, another alternative you have is to host your WCF Service Library from within a dedicated Windows service. One benefit of doing so is that you can configure a

Windows service to start automatically when the target machine boots up. Another benefit is that Windows services run invisibly in the background (unlike your console application) and do not require user interactivity (and you don't need IIS installed on the host computer).

Next, you will learn how to build such a host. Begin by creating a new Windows service project named MathWindowsServiceHost (see Figure 25-12). After you do this, rename your initial Service1.cs file to MathWinService.cs using Solution Explorer.

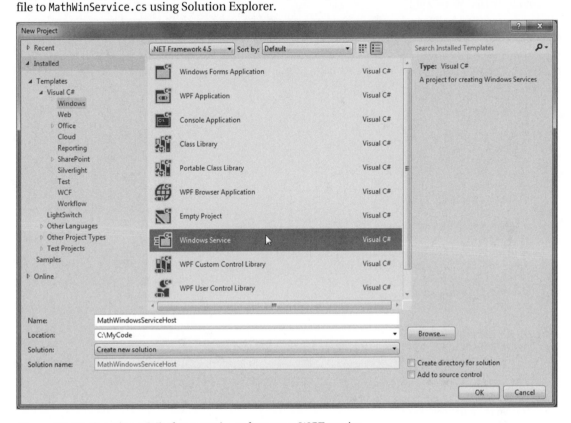

Figure 25-12. *Creating a Windows service to host your WCF service*

Specifying the ABCs in Code

Now assume you have set a reference to your MathServiceLibrary.dll and System.ServiceModel.dll assemblies. All you need to do is use the ServiceHost type in the OnStart() and OnStop() methods of your Windows service type. Open the code file for your service host class (by right-clicking the designer and selecting View Code) and add the following logic:

```
// Be sure to import these namespaces:
using MathServiceLibrary;
using System.ServiceModel;

namespace MathWindowsServiceHost
{
```

```
public partial class MathWinService: ServiceBase
{
  // A member variable of type ServiceHost.
  private ServiceHost myHost;

  public MathWinService()
  {
    InitializeComponent();
  }

  protected override void OnStart(string[] args)
  {
    // Just to be really safe.
    if (myHost != null)
    {
      myHost.Close();
      myHost = null;
    }

    // Create the host.
    myHost = new ServiceHost(typeof(MathService));

    // The ABCs in code!
    Uri address = new Uri("http://localhost:8080/MathServiceLibrary");
    WSHttpBinding binding = new WSHttpBinding();
    Type contract = typeof(IBasicMath);

    // Add this endpoint.
    myHost.AddServiceEndpoint(contract, binding, address);

    // Open the host.
    myHost.Open();
  }

  protected override void OnStop()
  {
    // Shut down the host.
    if(myHost != null)
      myHost.Close();
  }
}
}
```

While nothing prevents you from using a configuration file when building a Windows service host for a WCF service, here (for a change of pace) you establish the endpoint programmatically using the Uri, WSHttpBinding, and Type classes, rather than by using a *.config file. After you create each aspect of the ABCs, you inform the host programmatically by calling AddServiceEndpoint().

If you wish to inform the runtime that you want to gain access to each of the default endpoint bindings stored in the .NET 4.5 machine.config file, you can simplify your programming logic by specifying base addresses when you invoke the constructor of ServiceHost. In this case, you do not need to specify the ABCs manually in code or call AddServiceEndpoint(); instead, you call AddDefaultEndpoints(). Consider the following update:

```
protected override void OnStart(string[] args)
{
  if (myHost != null)
  {
    myHost.Close();
  }
  // Create the host and specify a URL for an HTTP binding.
  myHost = new ServiceHost(typeof(MathService),
          new Uri("http://localhost:8080/MathServiceLibrary"));

  // Opt in for the default endpoints!
  myHost.AddDefaultEndpoints();

  // Open the host.
  myHost.Open();
}
```

Enabling MEX

While you could enable MEX programmatically as well, here you will opt for a configuration file. Insert a new App.config file into your Windows service project that contains the following default MEX settings:

```
<?xml version = "1.0" encoding = "utf-8" ?>
<configuration>
  <system.serviceModel>
    <services>
      <service name = "MathServiceLibrary.MathService">
      </service>
    </services>

    <behaviors>
      <serviceBehaviors>
        <behavior>
          <serviceMetadata httpGetEnabled = "true"/>
        </behavior>
      </serviceBehaviors>
    </behaviors>

  </system.serviceModel>
</configuration>
```

Creating a Windows Service Installer

To register your Windows service with the operating system, you need to add an installer to your project that contains the necessary code to allow you to register the service. To do so, right-click the Windows service designer surface and select Add Installer (see Figure 25-13).

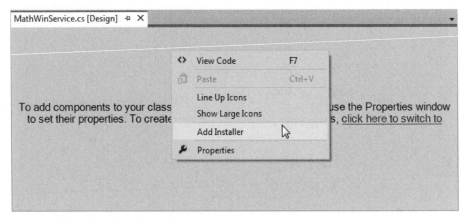

Figure 25-13. *Adding an installer for the Windows service*

Once you do this, you can see two components have been added to a new designer surface representing the installer. The first component (named serviceProcessInstaller1 by default) represents an item that can install a new Windows service on the target machine. Select this item on the designer and use the Properties window to set the Account property to LocalSystem (see Figure 25-14).

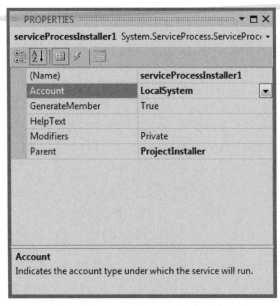

Figure 25-14. *Be sure to run the Windows service as a local system account*

The second component (named serviceInstaller1) represents a type that will install your particular Windows service. Again, use the Properties window to change the ServiceName property to MathService, set the StartType property to Automatic, and add a friendly description of your Windows service using the Description property (see Figure 25-15).

Figure 25-15. Configuring installer details

At this point, you can compile your application.

Installing the Windows Service

A Windows service can be installed on the host machine using a traditional setup program (such as an *.msi installer) or via the installutil.exe command-line tool.

■ **Note** To install a Windows service using installutil.exe, you must start the Developer Command Prompt under administrative privileges. To do so, right click the Developer Command Prompt icon and select Run As Administrator.

Using a Developer Command Prompt, change into the \bin\Debug folder of your MathWindowsServiceHost project. Now, enter the following command:

```
installutil MathWindowsServiceHost.exe
```

Assuming the installation succeeded, you can now open the Services applet located under the Administrative Tools folder of your Control Panel. You should see the friendly name of your Windows service listed alphabetically. After you locate it, make sure you start the service on your local machine using the Start link (see Figure 25-16).

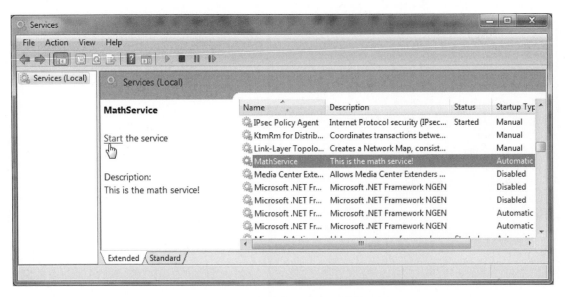

Figure 25-16. *Viewing your Windows service, which hosts your WCF service*

Now that the service is alive and kicking, the last step is to build a client application to consume its services.

■ **Source Code** You can find the MathWindowsServiceHost project located under the Chapter 25 subdirectory.

Invoking a Service Asynchronously from the Client

Create a new Console Application project named MathClient and set a Service Reference to your running WCF service (that is currently hosted by the Windows service running in the background) using the Add Service Reference option of Visual Studio (you'll need to type the URL in the Addresses box, which should be `http://localhost:8080/MathServiceLibrary`). Don't click the OK button yet, however! Notice that the Add Service Reference dialog box has an Advanced button in the lower-left corner (see Figure 25-17).

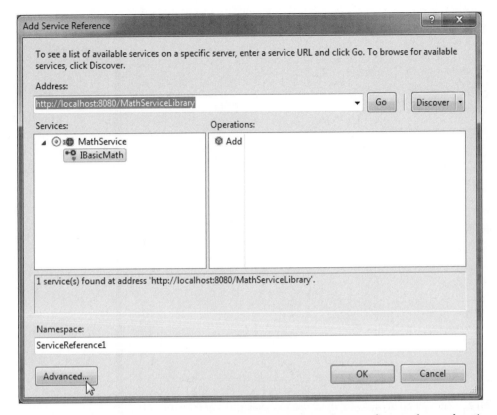

Figure 25-17. Referencing your MathService and getting ready to configure advanced settings

Click this button now to view the additional proxy configuration settings (see Figure 25-18). You can use this dialog box to generate code that allows you to call the remote methods in an asynchronous manner, provided you check the Generate asynchronous operators radio option. Go ahead and check this option for the time being.

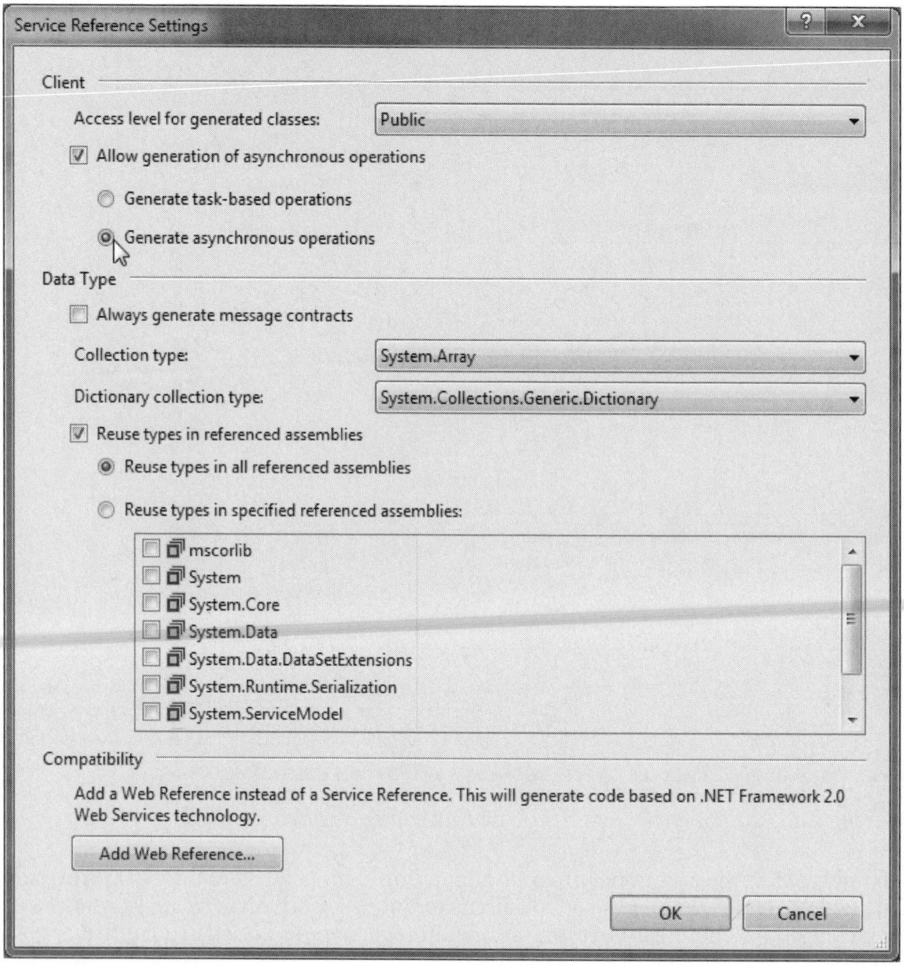

Figure 25-18. Advanced client-side proxy configuration options

At this point, the proxy code contains additional methods that allow you to invoke each member of the service contract using the expected Begin/End asynchronous invocation pattern described in Chapter 19. Here is a simple implementation that uses a lambda expression rather than a strongly typed AsyncCallback delegate:

```
using System;
using MathClient.ServiceReference1;
...

namespace MathClient
{
  class Program
  {
```

```
static void Main(string[] args)
{
  Console.WriteLine("***** The Async Math Client *****\n");

  using (BasicMathClient proxy = new BasicMathClient())
  {
    proxy.Open();

    // Add numbers in an async manner, using a lambda expression.
    IAsyncResult result = proxy.BeginAdd(2, 3,
      ar =>
      {
        Console.WriteLine("2 + 3 = {0}", proxy.EndAdd(ar));
      },
      null);

    while (!result.IsCompleted)
    {
      Thread.Sleep(200);
      Console.WriteLine("Client working...");
    }
  }
  Console.ReadLine();
}
}
}
```

■ **Source Code** You can find the MathClient project located under the Chapter 25 subdirectory.

Designing WCF Data Contracts

This chapter's final example shows you how to construct WCF *data contracts*. The previous WCF services defined simple methods that operate on primitive CLR data types. When you use of any of the HTTP binding types (e.g., basicHttpBinding and wsHttpBinding), incoming and outgoing simple data types are automatically formatted into XML elements. On a related note, if you use a TCP-based binding (such as netTcpBinding), the parameters and return values of simple data types are transmitted using a compact binary format.

■ **Note** The WCF runtime will also automatically encode any type marked with the [Serializable] attribute; however, this is not the preferred way to define WCF contracts, and it is only included for backward compatibility.

However, when you define service contracts that use custom classes as parameters or return values, it is a best practice to model such data using WCF data contracts. Simply put, a data contract is a type adorned with the [DataContract] attribute. Likewise, you must mark each field you expect to be used as part of the proposed contract with the [DataMember] attribute.

■ **Note** In earlier versions of the .NET platform, it was mandatory to use [DataContract] and [DataMember] to ensure custom data types were correctly represented. Microsoft has since relaxed this requirement; technically speaking, you are not required to use these attributes on custom data types; however, it is considered a .NET best practice.

Using the Web-Centric WCF Service Project Template

Our next WCF service will allow external callers to interact with the AutoLot database you created in Chapter 21. Moreover, this final WCF service will be created using the web-based WCF Service template and be hosted under IIS.

To begin, launch Visual Studio (with administrator rights) and access the File ➤ New ➤ Web Site menu option. Select the WCF Service project type, and ensure the Web Location drop-down is set to HTTP (which will install the service under IIS). Expose the service from the following URI:

```
http://localhost/AutoLotWCFService
```

Figure 25-19 shows the configured project.

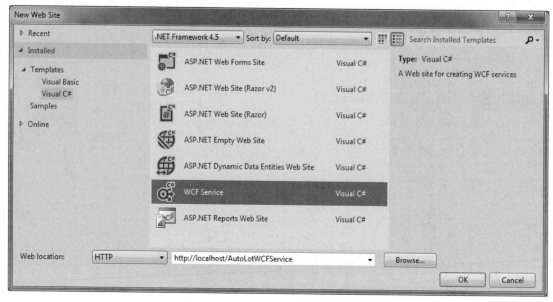

Figure 25-19. Creating a web-centric WCF service

After you have done this, set a reference to the AutoLotDAL.dll assembly you created in Chapter 21 (using the Website Add Reference menu option). You have been given some example starter code (located under the App_Code folder), which you will want to delete. Begin by renaming the initial IService.cs file to IAutoLotService.cs, and then define the initial service contract within your newly named file, like so:

```
[ServiceContract]
public interface IAutoLotService
{
  [OperationContract]
  void InsertCar(int id, string make, string color, string petname);

  [OperationContract]
  void InsertCar(InventoryRecord car);

  [OperationContract]
  InventoryRecord[] GetInventory();
}
```

This interface defines three methods, one of which returns an array of the (yet-to-be-created) InventoryRecord type. You might recall that the GetInventory() method of InventoryDAL simply returned a DataTable object, and this might make you wonder why your service's GetInventory() method does not do the same.

While it would work to return a DataTable from a WCF service method, recall that WCF was built to honor the use of SOA principles, one of which is to program against contracts, not implementations. Therefore, you won't return the .NET-specific DataTable type to an external caller; instead, you will return a custom data contract (InventoryRecord) that will be correctly expressed in the contained WSDL document in an agnostic manner.

Also note that the interface listed previously defines an overloaded method named InsertCar(). The first version takes four incoming parameters, while the second version takes an InventoryRecord type as input. You can define the InventoryRecord data contract as follows:

```
[DataContract]
public class InventoryRecord
{
  [DataMember]
  public int ID;

  [DataMember]
  public string Make;

  [DataMember]
  public string Color;

  [DataMember]
  public string PetName;
}
```

If you were to implement the IAutoLotService interface as it now stands, and then build a host and attempt to call these methods from a client, you might be surprised to see that you would get a runtime exception. The reason: one of the requirements of a WSDL description is that each method exposed from a given endpoint must be *uniquely named*. Thus, while method overloading works just fine as far as C# is concerned, the current web service specifications do not permit two identically named InsertCar() methods.

Fortunately, the [OperationContract] attribute supports a named property (Name) that allows you to specify how the C# method will be represented within a WSDL description. Given this, you can update the second version of InsertCar() as follows:

```
public interface IAutoLotService
{
...
  [OperationContract(Name = "InsertCarWithDetails")]
  void InsertCar(InventoryRecord car);
}
```

Implementing the Service Contract

Now rename Service.cs to AutoLotService.cs. The AutoLotService type implements the IAutoLotService interface as follows (be sure to import the AutoLotConnectedLayer and System.Data namespaces into this code file and update your connection string if required):

```
using AutoLotConnectedLayer;
using System.Data;

public class AutoLotService : IAutoLotService
{
  private const string ConnString =
    @"Data Source=(local)\SQLEXPRESS;Initial Catalog=AutoLot"+
      ";Integrated Security=True";

  public void InsertCar(int id, string make, string color, string petname)
  {
    InventoryDAL d = new InventoryDAL();
    d.OpenConnection(ConnString);
    d.InsertAuto(id, color, make, petname);
    d.CloseConnection();
  }

  public void InsertCar(InventoryRecord car)
  {
    InventoryDAL d = new InventoryDAL();
    d.OpenConnection(ConnString);
    d.InsertAuto(car.ID, car.Color, car.Make, car.PetName);
    d.CloseConnection();
  }

  public InventoryRecord[] GetInventory()
  {
    // First, get the DataTable from the database.
    InventoryDAL d = new InventoryDAL();
    d.OpenConnection(ConnString);
    DataTable dt = d.GetAllInventoryAsDataTable();
    d.CloseConnection();
```

```
  // Now make a List<T> to contain the records.
  List<InventoryRecord> records = new List<InventoryRecord>();

  // Copy the data table into List<> of custom contracts.
  DataTableReader reader = dt.CreateDataReader();
  while (reader.Read())
  {
    InventoryRecord r = new InventoryRecord();
    r.ID = (int)reader["CarID"];
    r.Color = ((string)reader["Color"]);
    r.Make = ((string)reader["Make"]);
    r.PetName = ((string)reader["PetName"]);
    records.Add(r);
  }

  // Transform List<T> to array of InventoryRecord types.
  return (InventoryRecord[])records.ToArray();
  }
}
```

There isn't too much to say about the preceding code. For the sake of simplicity, you hard-code the connection string value (which you might need to adjust based on your machine settings), rather than store it in your Web.config file. Given that your data access library does all the real work of communicating with the AutoLot database, all you need to do is pass the incoming parameters to the InsertAuto() method of the InventoryDAL class type. The only other point of interest is the act of mapping the DataTable object's values into a generic list of InventoryRecord types (using a DataTableReader), and then transforming the List<T> into an array of InventoryRecord types.

The Role of the *.svc File

When you create a web-centric WCF service, you will find your project contains a specific file with an *.svc file extension. This particular file is required for any WCF service hosted by IIS; it describes the name and location of the service implementation within the install point. Because you have changed the names of your starter files and WCF types, you must now update the contents of the Service.svc file as follows:

```
<%@ ServiceHost Language="C#" Debug="true"
  Service="AutoLotService" CodeBehind="~/App_Code/AutoLotService.cs" %>
```

Examining the Web.config File

The Web.config file of a WCF service created under HTTP will use a number of the WCF simplifications examined earlier in this chapter. As will be described in more detail during your examination of ASP.NET later in this book, the Web.config file serves a similar purpose to an executable's *.config file; however, it also controls a number of web-specific settings. For this example, notice that MEX is enabled, and you do not have to specify a custom <endpoint> manually:

```
<configuration>
...

  <system.serviceModel>
    <behaviors>
```

```
        <serviceBehaviors>
          <behavior>
            <!-- To avoid disclosing metadata information,
                 set the value below to false and remove the
                 metadata endpoint above before deployment -->
            <serviceMetadata httpGetEnabled="true" httpsGetEnabled="true" />
            <!-- To receive exception details in faults for debugging purposes,
                 set the value below to true.
                 Set to false before deployment to avoid
                 disclosing exception information -->
            <serviceDebug includeExceptionDetailInFaults="false"/>
          </behavior>
        </serviceBehaviors>
      </behaviors>
      <serviceHostingEnvironment aspNetCompatibilityEnabled="true"
                                 multipleSiteBindingsEnabled="true" />
  </system.serviceModel>

...
</configuration>
```

Testing the Service

Now you are free to build any sort of client to test your service, including passing in the endpoint of the `*.svc` file to the `WcfTestClient.exe` application.

```
WcfTestClient http://localhost/AutoLotWCFService/Service.svc
```

If you wish to build a custom client application, you can use the Add Service Reference dialog box, as you did for the MagicEightBallServiceClient and MathClient project examples earlier in this chapter.

■ **Source Code** You can find the AutoLotService project located under the Chapter 25 subdirectory.

That wraps up your look at the Windows Communication Foundation API. Of course, there is much more to WCF than could be covered in this introductory chapter; however, if you understand the materials presented here, you are in great shape to seek out more details as you see fit. Be sure to consult the .NET Framework 4.5 SDK documentation if you want to learn more about WCF.

Summary

This chapter introduced you to the Windows Communication Foundation (WCF) API, which has been part of the base class libraries since .NET 3.0. As explained in this chapter, the major motivation behind WCF was to provide a unified object model that exposes a number of (previously unrelated) distributed computing APIs under a single umbrella. Furthermore, a WCF service is represented by specified addresses, bindings, and contracts (which you can remember easily by the friendly abbreviation, *ABC*).

You also learned that a typical WCF application involves the use of three interrelated assemblies. The first assembly defines the service contracts and service types that represent the service's functionality. This assembly is then hosted by a custom executable, an IIS virtual directory, or a Windows service. Finally, the client assembly uses a generated code file that defines a proxy type (and settings within the application configuration file) to communicate with the remote type.

The chapter also examined how to use a number of WCF programming tools, such as SvcConfigEditor.exe (which allows you to modify *.config files), the WcfTestClient.exe application (to test a WCF service quickly), and various Visual Studio WCF project templates. You also learned about a number of configuration simplifications, including default endpoints and behaviors.

CHAPTER 26

Introducing Windows Workflow Foundation

The .NET platform supports a programming model termed *Windows Workflow Foundation* (WF). This API allows you to model, configure, monitor, and execute the *workflows* (which are used to model a business process) used internally by a given .NET program. Workflows are modeled (by default) using a declarative XML-based grammar named XAML where data used by the workflow is treated as a first class citizen.

If you are new to the topic of WF, this chapter begins by defining the role of business processes and describes how they relate to the WF API. As well, you will be exposed to the concept of a WF activity, common types of workflows and various project templates and programming tools. After we've covered the basics, we'll build several example programs that illustrate how to leverage the WF programming model to establish business processes that execute under the watchful eye of the WF runtime engine.

> ■ **Note** The entirety of the WF API cannot be covered in a single introductory chapter. If you require a deeper treatment of the topic than presented here, check out *Pro WF 4.5* by Bayer White (Apress, 2012).

Defining a Business Process

Any real-world application must be able to model various *business processes*. Simply put, a business process is a conceptual grouping of tasks that logically work as a collective whole. For example, assume you are building an application that allows a user to purchase an automobile online. When the user submits the order, a large number of activities are set in motion. You might begin by performing a credit check. If the user passes the credit verification, you might start a database transaction in order to remove the entry from an Inventory table, add a new entry to an Orders table, and update the customer account information. After the database transaction has completed, you still might need to send a confirmation e-mail to the buyer, and then invoke a remote service to place the order at the car dealership. Collectively, all of these tasks could represent a single business process.

Historically speaking, modeling a business process was yet another detail that programmers had to account for, often by authoring custom code to ensure that a business process was not only modeled correctly but also executed correctly within the application itself. For example, you might need to author code to account for points of failure, tracing, and logging support (to see what a given business process is up to); persistence support (to save the state of long-running processes); and whatnot. As you might know firsthand, building this sort of infrastructure from scratch entails a great deal of time and manual labor.

Assuming that a development team did, in fact, build a custom business process framework for their applications, their work was not yet complete. Simply put, a raw C# code base cannot be easily explained to nonprogrammers on the team who *also* need to understand the business process. The truth of the matter is that subject matter experts (SMEs), managers, salespeople, and members of a graphical design team often do not speak the language of code. Given this, as programmers, we were required to make use of other modeling tools (such as Microsoft Visio, the office whiteboard, etc.) to graphically represent our processes using skill set–neutral terms. The obvious problem here is we now have two entities to keep in sync: if we change the code, we need to update the diagrams. If we change the diagrams, we need to update the code.

Furthermore, when building a sophisticated software application using the *100% code approach*, the code base has very little trace of the internal "flow" of the application. For example, a typical .NET program might be composed of hundreds of custom types (not to mention the numerous types used within the base class libraries). While programmers might have a feel for which objects are making calls on other objects, the code itself is a far cry from a living document that explains the overall sequence of activity. While the development team might build external documentation and workflow charts, again there is the problem of multiple representations of the same process.

The Role of WF

In essence, the Windows Workflow Foundation API allows programmers to declaratively design business processes using a prefabricated set of *activities*. Thus, rather than using only a set custom of assemblies to represent a given business activity and the necessary infrastructure, we can make use of the WF designers of Visual Studio to create our business process at design time. In this respect, WF allows us to build the skeleton of a business process, which can be fleshed out through code where required.

When programming with the WF API, a single entity can then be used to represent the overall business process, as well as the code that defines it. In addition to being a friendly visual representation of the process, because a single WF document is used to represent the code driving the process, we no longer need to worry about multiple documents falling out of sync. Better yet, this WF document will clearly illustrate the process itself. With a little bit of guidance, even the most nontechnical of staff members should be able to get a grip on what your WF designer is modeling.

Building a Simple Workflow

As you build a workflow-enabled application, you will undoubtedly notice that it "feels different" from building a typical .NET application. For example, up until this point in the text, every code example began by creating a new project workspace (most often a Console Application project) and involved authoring code to represent the program at large. A WF application also consists of custom code; however, in addition, you are building *directly into the assembly* a model of the business process itself.

Another aspect of WF that is quite different from other sorts of .NET applications is that a vast majority of your workflows will be modeled in a declarative manner, using an XML-based grammar named XAML. Much of the time, you will not need to directly author this markup, as the Visual Studio IDE will do so automatically as you work with the WF designer tools. This is a big change in direction from the previous version of the WF API, which favored using C# code as the standard way to model a workflow.

■ **Note** Be aware that the XAML dialect used within WF is not identical to the XAML dialect used for WPF. You will learn about the syntax and semantics of WPF XAML in Chapter 27, as unlike WF XAML, it is quite common to directly edit designer-generated WPF XAML.

To get you into the workflow mindset, open Visual Studio. From the New Project dialog box, pick a new Workflow Console Application project named FirstWorkflowExampleApp (see Figure 26-1).

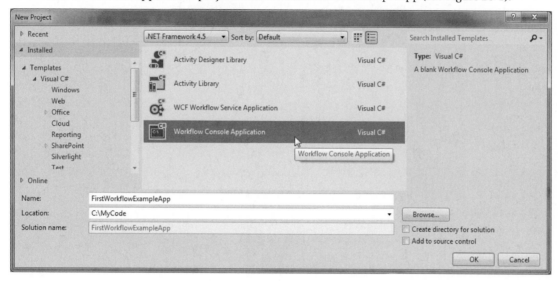

Figure 26-1. Creating a new console-based workflow application

Now, consider Figure 26-2, which illustrates the initial workflow diagram generated by Visual Studio. As you can see, there is not too much happening at this point, just a message telling you to drop activities on the designer.

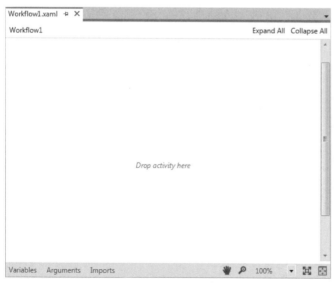

Figure 26-2. A workflow designer is a container for activities that model your business process

For this first simple test workflow, open the Visual Studio Toolbox, and locate the WriteLine activity under the Primitives section (see Figure 26-3).

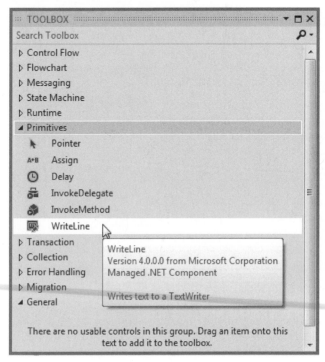

Figure 26-3. The Toolbox will show you all the default activities of WF

Once you have located this activity, drag it onto of the designer's drop target (be sure you drag it directly onto the area that says *Drop activity here*), and enter a friendly double-quoted string message into the Text edit box. Figure 26-4 shows one possible workflow.

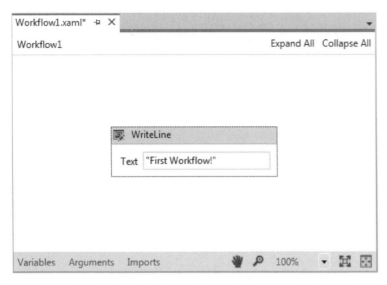

Figure 26-4. *The* WriteLine *activity will display text to a* TextWriter, *which is the console in this case*

Do understand that WF is far more than a pretty designer that allows you to model the activities of a business process. As you are building your WF diagram, your markup can always be extended using code to represent the runtime behavior of your process. In fact, if you wanted to do so, you could avoid the use of XAML all together and author the workflow using nothing but C#. If you were to this, however, you would be back to the same basic issue of having a body of code that is not readily understandable to nontechnical staff. In any case, if you were to run your application at this point, you would see your message display to the console window, like this:

```
First Workflow!
Press any key to continue . . .
```

Fair enough; however, what started this workflow? And how were you able to ensure that the console application stayed running long enough for the workflow to complete? The answers to these questions require an understanding of the workflow runtime engine.

The Workflow Runtime

The next thing to understand is that the WF API also consists of a runtime engine to load, execute, unload, and in other ways manipulate a workflow that you have defined. The WF runtime engine can be hosted within any .NET application domain; however, be aware that a single application domain can have only one running instance of the WF engine.

Recall from Chapter 17 that an AppDomain is a partition within a Windows process that plays host to a .NET application and any external code libraries. As such, the WF engine can be embedded within a simple console program, a GUI desktop application (Windows Forms or WPF), or exposed from a Windows Communication Foundation (WCF) service.

■ **Note** The WCF Workflow Service Application project template is a great starting point if you want to build a WCF service (see Chapter 25) that makes use of workflows internally.

If you are modeling a business process that needs to be used by a wide variety of systems, you also have the option of authoring your WF within a C# Class Library project of a Workflow Activity Library project. In this way, new applications can simply reference your *.dll to reuse a predefined collection of business processes. This is obviously helpful in that you would not want to have to re-create the same workflows multiple times.

Hosting a Workflow Using WorkflowInvoker

The host process of the WF runtime can interact with said runtime using a few different techniques. The simplest way to do so is to use the WorkflowInvoker class of the System.Activities namespace. This class allows you to start a workflow using a single line of code. If you were to open up the Program.cs file of your current Workflow Console Application project, you will see the following Main() method:

```
static void Main(string[] args)
{
  // Create and cache the workflow definition.
  Activity workflow1 = new Workflow1();
  WorkflowInvoker.Invoke(workflow1);
}
```

Using the WorkflowInvoker is very useful when you simply want a workflow to kick off and don't care to monitor it any further. The Invoke() method will execute the workflow in a *synchronous blocking manner*. The calling thread is blocked until the entire workflow has finished or has been terminated abruptly. Because the Invoke() method is a synchronous call, you are guaranteed that the entire workflow will indeed complete before Main() is terminated. In fact, if you were to add any code after the call to WorkflowInvoker.Invoke(), it would only execute when the workflow is completed (or in a worse-case situation, terminated abruptly).

```
static void Main(string[] args)
{
  // Create and cache the workflow definition.
  Activity workflow1 = new Workflow1();
  WorkflowInvoker.Invoke(workflow1);

  Console.WriteLine("Thanks for playing");
}
```

Passing Arguments to Your Workflow Using WorkflowInvoker

When a host process kicks off a workflow, it is very common for the host to send custom startup arguments. For example, assume that you want to let the user of your program specify which message to display in the WriteLine activity in place of the currently hard-coded text message. In normal C# code, you might create a custom constructor on a class to receive such arguments. However, a workflow is always created using the default constructor! Moreover, most workflows are defined only using XAML, not procedural code.

As it turns out, the Invoke() method has been overloaded multiple times, one version of which allows you to pass in arguments to the workflow when it starts. These arguments are represented using a Dictionary<string, object> variable that contains a set of name/value pairs that will be used to set identically named (and typed) argument variables in the workflow itself.

Defining Arguments Using the Workflow Designer

To define the arguments that will capture the incoming dictionary data, you will make use of the workflow designer. In Solution Explorer, right-click Workflow1.xaml and select View Designer. Notice on the bottom of the designer there is a button named Arguments. Click this button now, and from the resulting UI, add an input argument of type string named MessageToShow (no need to assign a default value for this new argument). As well, delete your initial message from the WriteLine activity by resetting the Text property of the WriteLine Activity via the Visual Studio Properties window. Figure 26-5 shows the end result.

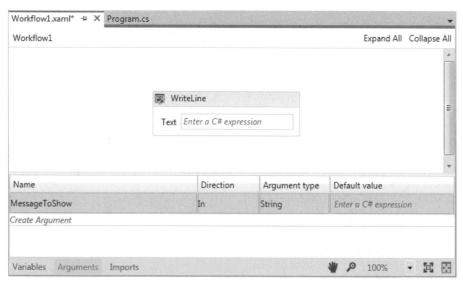

Figure 26-5. *Workflow arguments can be used to receive host-supplied arguments*

Now, in the Text property of the WriteLine activity, you can simply enter MessageToShow as the evaluation expression. As you are typing in this token, you'll notice IntelliSense will kick in (see Figure 26-6).

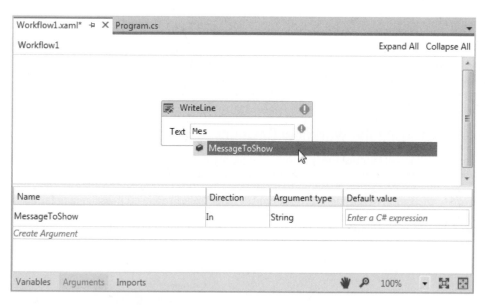

Figure 26-6. Using a custom argument as input to an activity

Now that you have the correct infrastructure in place, consider the following update to the Main() method of the Program class. Note that you will need to import the System.Collections.Generic namespace into your Program.cs file to declare the Dictionary<> variable.

```
static void Main(string[] args)
{
  Console.WriteLine("***** Welcome to this amazing WF application *****");

  // Get data from user, to pass to workflow.
  Console.Write("Please enter the data to pass the workflow: ");
  string wfData = Console.ReadLine();

  // Package up the data as a dictionary.
  Dictionary<string, object> wfArgs = new Dictionary<string,object>();
  wfArgs.Add("MessageToShow", wfData);

  // Pass to the workflow.
  Activity workflow1 = new Workflow1();
  WorkflowInvoker.Invoke(workflow1, wfArgs);

  Console.WriteLine("Thanks for playing");
}
```

Again, it is important to point out that the string values for each member of your Dictionary<> variable will need to be identically named to the related argument variable in your workflow. In any case, you will find output similar to the following when you run the modified program:

```
***** Welcome to this amazing WF application *****
Please enter the data to pass the workflow: Hello Mr. Workflow!
Hello Mr. Workflow!
Thanks for playing
Press any key to continue . . .
```

Beyond the Invoke() method, the only other really interesting members of WorkflowInvoker would be BeginInvoke() and EndInvoke(), which allow you to start up the workflow on a secondary thread using the .NET asynchronous delegate pattern (see Chapter 19). If you require more control over how the WF runtime manipulates your workflow, you can instead make use of the WorkflowApplication class.

Hosting a Workflow Using WorkflowApplication

You'll want to use WorkflowApplication (as opposed to WorkflowInvoker) if you need to save or load a long running workflow using WF persistence services, be notified of various events that fire during the lifetime of your workflow instance, work with WF "bookmarks," and other advanced features. In this case, you will want to call the Run() method of WorkflowApplication.

When you do call Run(), a new background thread will be plucked from the CLR thread pool. Therefore, if you do not add additional support to ensure the main thread waits for the secondary thread to complete, the workflow instance might not have a chance to finish its work.

One way to make sure the calling thread waits long enough for the background thread to finish its work is to use an AutoResetEvent object of the System.Threading namespace. Here is an update to the current example, which now uses WorkflowApplication rather than WorkflowInvoker:

```
static void Main(string[] args)
{
  Console.WriteLine("***** Welcome to this amazing WF application *****");

  // Get data from user, to pass to workflow.
  Console.Write("Please enter the data to pass the workflow: ");
  string wfData = Console.ReadLine();

  // Package up the data as a dictionary.
  Dictionary<string, object> wfArgs = new Dictionary<string,object>();
  wfArgs.Add("MessageToShow", wfData);

  // Used to inform primary thread to wait!
  AutoResetEvent waitHandle = new AutoResetEvent(false);

  // Pass to the workflow.
  WorkflowApplication app = new WorkflowApplication(new Workflow1(), wfArgs);

  // Hook up an event with this app.
  // When I'm done, notifiy other thread I'm done,
  // and print a message.
  app.Completed = (completedArgs) => {
    waitHandle.Set();
    Console.WriteLine("The workflow is done!");
  };
```

```
// Start the workflow!
app.Run();

// Wait until I am notified the workflow is done.
waitHandle.WaitOne();

Console.WriteLine("Thanks for playing");
}
```

The output will be similar to the previous iteration of the project:

```
***** Welcome to this amazing WF application *****
Please enter the data to pass the workflow: Hey again!
Hey again!
The workflow is done!
Thanks for playing
Press any key to continue . . .
```

The benefit of using `WorkflowApplication` is that you can hook into events (as you have done indirectly using the `Completed` property here) and can also tap into more sophisticated services (persistence, bookmarks, etc.).

■ **Note** During our introductory look at WF, we will not dive into the details of these runtime services. Be sure to check out the .NET Framework 4.5 SDK documentation for details regarding the runtime behaviors and services of the Windows Workflow Foundation runtime environment.

Recap of Your First Workflow

While this example was very trivial, you did learn a few interesting (and useful) tasks. First, you learned that you can pass in a `Dictionary` object that contains name/value pairs that will be passed to identically named arguments in your workflow. This is really useful when you need to gather user input (such as a customer ID number, SSN, name of a doctor, etc.) that will be used by the workflow to process its activities.

You also learned that a .NET workflow is defined in a declarative manner (by default) using an XML-based grammar named XAML. Using XAML, you can specify which activities your workflow contains. At runtime, this data will be used to create the correct in-memory object model. Last but not least, you looked at two different approaches to kick off a workflow using the `WorkflowInvoker` and `WorkflowApplicaion` classes.

■ **Source Code** The FirstWorkflowExampleApp project is included under the Chapter 26 subdirectory.

Examining the Workflow Activities

Recall that the purpose of WF is to allow you to model a business process in a declarative manner, which is then executed by the WF runtime engine. In the vernacular of WF, a business process is composed of any number of *activities*. Simply put, a WF activity is an atomic "step" in the overall process. When you create a new workflow application, you will find the Toolbox contains iconic representations of the built-in activities grouped by category.

These out-of-the-box activities are used to model your business process. Each activity in the Toolbox maps to a real class within the System.Activities.dll assembly (most often contained within the System.Activities.Statements namespace). You'll make use of several of these baked-in activities over the course of this chapter; however, here is a walkthrough of many of these default activities. As always, consult the .NET Framework SDK documentation for full details.

Control Flow Activities

The first category of activities in the Toolbox allow you to represent looping and decision tasks in a larger workflow. Their usefulness should be easy to understand, given that we do similar tasks in C# code quite often. In Table 26-1, notice that some of these control flow activities allow for parallel processing of activities using the Task Parallel Library behind the scenes (see Chapter 19).

Table 26-1. The Control Flow Activities of WF

Activities	Meaning in Life
DoWhile	A looping activity that executes contained activities at least once, until a condition is no longer true.
ForEach<T>	Executes an activity action once for each value provided in the ForEach<T>.Values collection.
If	Models an If-Then-Else condition.
Parallel	An activity that executes all child activities simultaneously and asynchronously.
ParallelForEach<T>	Enumerates the elements of a collection and executes each element of the collection in parallel.
Pick	Provides event-based control flow modeling.
PickBranch	A potential path of execution within a parent Pick activity.
Sequence	Executes a set of child activities sequentially.
Switch<T>	Selects one choice from a number of activities to execute, based on the value of a given expression of the type

	specified in this object's type parameter.
`While`	Executes a contained workflow element while a condition evaluates to true.

Flowchart Activities

Next are the flowchart activities, which are actually quite important given that the `Flowchart` activity will very often be the first item you place on your WF designer. This type of workflow allows you to build a workflow using the well-known flow chart model, where the execution of the workflow is based on numerous branching paths, each of which is based on the truth or falsity of some internal condition. Table 26-2 documents each member of this activity set.

Table 26-2. The Flowchart Activities of WF

Activities	Meaning in Life
`Flowchart`	Models workflows using the familiar "flow chart" paradigm. This is often the very first activity you will place on a new designer.
`FlowDecision`	A node that provides the ability to model a conditional node with two possible outcomes.
`FlowSwitch<T>`	A node that allows modeling a switch construct, with one expression and one outcome for each match.

Messaging Activities

A workflow can easily invoke members of an external XML web service or WCF service, as well as be notified by an external service using *messaging activities*. Because these activities are very closely related to WCF development, they have been packaged up in a dedicated .NET assembly, `System.ServiceModel.Activities.dll`. Within this library, you will find an identically named namespace defining the core activities seen in Table 26-3.

Table 26-3. Common Messaging Activities of WF

Activities	Meaning in Life
`CorrelationScope`	Used to manage child message activities.
`InitializeCorrelation`	Initializes correlation without sending or receiving a message.
`Receive`	Receives a message from a WCF service.
`Send`	Sends a message to a WCF service.

| SendAndReceiveReply | Sends a message to a WCF service and captures the return value. |
| TransactedReceiveScope | An activity that enables you to flow a transaction into a workflow or dispatcher-created server-side transactions. |

The most common messaging activities are Send and Receive, which allow you to communicate with external XML web services or WCF services.

The State Machine Activities

Under .NET 4.5, the WF API has been updated to include a new set of activities that allow you to model workflows that are based on *state machines*. In a nutshell, state machines allow you to define a workflow, which can be in any number of defined states at a given point of time, and the valid transitions between these states.

A well-known example of state machines is that of a soda-pop vending machine. At any given time, the "machine" can be in a single state such as (for example) "Waiting for Input," "Dispensing soda," "Refunding Payment," "Returning Change," "Displaying Selection Empty," and what have you. Among these states are a set of valid transitions. For example, if the machine is in the "Displaying Selection Empty" state, valid transitions could include "Refunding Payment" or "Dispensing Soda" (provided the user picked a different option). To build such a workflow, .NET 4.5 includes the StateMachine, State, and FinalState activities.

The Runtime and Primitives Activities

The next two categories in the Toolbox, Runtime and Primitives, allow you to build a workflow that makes calls to the workflow runtime (in the case of Persist and TerminateWorkflow) and performs common operations such as pushing text to an output stream or invoking a method on a .NET object. Consider Table 26-4, which shows some common activities of these categories.

Table 26-4. The Runtime and Primitive Activities of WF

Activities	Meaning in Life
Persist	Requests that a workflow instance persist its state into a database using the WF persistence service.
TerminateWorkflow	Terminates the running workflow instance, raises the WorkflowApplication.Completed event in the host, and reports error information. Once the workflow is terminated, it cannot be resumed.
Assign	Allows you to set properties on an activity using the assignment values you defined via the workflow designer.
Delay	Forces a workflow to stop for a fixed amount of time.

| InvokeMethod | Calls a method of a specified object or type. |
| WriteLine | Writes a specified string to a specified `TextWriter`-derived type. By default, this will be the standard output stream (a.k.a. the console); however, you can configure other streams, such as a `FileStream`. |

InvokeMethod is maybe the most interesting and useful activity of this set because it allows you to call methods of .NET classes in a declarative manner. You can also configure InvokeMethod to hold onto any return value send from the method you call. TerminateWorkflow can also be helpful when you need to account for a *point of no return*. If the workflow instance hits this activity, it will raise the Competed event, which can be caught in the host, just like you did in the first example.

The Transaction Activities

When you are building a workflow, you might need to ensure that a group of activities work in an atomic manner, meaning they must *all* succeed or *all* fail as a collective group. Even if the activities in question are not directly working with a relational database, the core activities seen in Table 26-5 allow you to add a transactional scope into a workflow.

Table 26-5. The Transaction Activities of WF

Activities	Meaning in Life
CancellationScope	Associates cancellation logic within a main path of execution.
CompensableActivity	An activity that supports compensation of its child activities.
TransactionScope	An activity that demarcates a transaction boundary.

The Collection and Error Handling Activities

The final two categories to consider in this introductory chapter allow you to declaratively manipulate generic collections and respond to runtime exceptions. The collection activities are great when you need to manipulate objects that represent business data (such as purchase orders, medical information objects, or order tracking) on the fly in XAML. Error activities, on the other hand, allow you to essentially author try/catch/throw logic within a workflow. Table 26-6 documents this final set of WF activities.

Table 26-6. *The Collection and Error Handling Activities of WF*

Activities	Meaning in Life
AddToCollection<T>	Adds an item to a specified collection.
ClearCollection<T>	Clears a specified collection of all items.
ExistsInCollection<T>	Indicates whether a given item is present in a given collection.
RemoveFromCollection<T>	Removes an item from a specified collection.
Rethrow	Throws a previously thrown exception from within a Catch activity.
Throw	Throws an exception.
TryCatch	Contains workflow elements to be executed by the workflow runtime within an exception handling block.

Now that we have seen many of the default activities at a high level, we can start to build some more interesting workflows that make use of them. Along the way, you will learn about the two key activities that typically function as the root of your workflow, Flowchart and Sequence.

Building a Flowchart Workflow

In the first example, I had you drag a simple WriteLine activity directly on the workflow designer. While it is true that any activity seen in the Visual Studio Toolbox can be the first item placed on the designer, only a few of them are able to contain subactivities (which represent a collection of related activities grouped together). When you are building a new workflow, the chances are very good that the first item you will place on your designer will be a Flowchart or Sequence activity.

Both of these built-in activities have the ability to contain any number of internal child activities (including additional Flowchart or Sequence activities) to represent the entirety of your business process. To begin, let's create a brand new Workflow Console Application named EnumerateMachineDataWF. Once you have done so, rename your initial *.xaml file to MachineInfoWF.xaml.

Now, under the Flowchart section of your Toolbox, drag a Flowchart activity onto the designer. Next, using the Properties window, change the DisplayName property to something a tad more catchy, such as Show Machine Data Flowchart (as I am sure you can guess, the DisplayName property controls how the item is named on the designer). At this point, your workflow designer should look something like Figure 26-7.

Figure 26-7. *The initial* Flowchart *activity*

Be aware that there is a grab-handle on the lower right of the Flowchart activity, which can be used to increase or decrease the size of the flowchart designer space. You'll need to increase the size as you add more and more activities.

Connecting Activities in a Flowchart

The large Start icon represents the entry point to the Flowchart activity, which in this example is the first activity in our entire workflow and will be triggered when you execute the workflow using the WorkflowInvoker or WorkflowApplication classes. This icon can be positioned anywhere on your designer, and I'd suggest you move it to the upper left, just to make some more space.

Your goal is to assemble your flowchart by connecting any number of additional activities together, making use of the FlowDecision activity during the process. To start, drag a WriteLine activity on the designer, changing the DisplayName to Greet User. Now, if you hover your mouse over the Start icon, you will see one docking tab on each side. Click and hold the docking tab closest to the WriteLine activity, and drag it to the docking tab of the WriteLine activity. After you have done so, you should see a connection between these first two items, signifying that the first activity that will be executed in your workflow will be Greet User.

Now, similar to the first example in this chapter, add a workflow argument (via the Arguments button) named UserName of type string with no default value. This will be passed in dynamically via the custom Dictionary<> object in just a bit. Finally, set the Text property of the WriteLine activity to the following code statement:

```
"Hello" + UserName
```

Add a second WriteLine activity to your designer, which is connected to the previous. This time, define a hardcoded string value of "Do you want me to list all machine drives?" for the Text property, and change the DisplayName property to Ask User. Figure 26-8 shows the connections between current workflow activities.

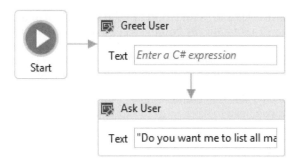

Figure 26-8. Flowchart workflows connect activities together

Working with the InvokeMethod Activity

Because the majority of a workflow is defined in a declarative manner using XAML, you are sure to make good use of the InvokeMethod activity, which allows you to invoke methods of real objects at various points in your workflow. Drag one of these items to your designer, change the DisplayName property to Get Y or N, and make a connection between it and the Ask User WriteLine activity.

The first property to configure for an InvokeMethod activity is the TargetType property, which represents the name of the class that defines a static member you want to invoke. Using the drop-down list box for the TargetType of the InvokeMethod activity, pick the Browse for Types... option (see Figure 26-9).

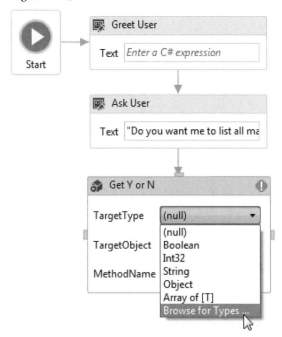

Figure 26-9. Specifying a target type for InvokeMethod

From the resulting dialog box, pick the System.Console class of mscorlib.dll (if you enter the name of the type within the Type Name edit area, the dialog will automatically find the type). When you have found the System.Console class, click the OK button.

Now, using the InvokeMethod activity on the designer, enter ReadLine as the value for the MethodName property. This will configure your InvokeMethod activity to invoke the Console.ReadLine() method when this step of the workflow is reached.

As you know, Console.ReadLine() will return a string value that contains the keystrokes entered on the keyboard before the Enter key is pressed; however, you need to have a way to capture the return value! You will do this next.

Defining Workflow-Wide Variables

Defining a workflow variable in XAML is almost identical to defining an argument, in that you can do so directly on the designer (this time with the Variables button). The difference is that *arguments* are used to capture data passed in by the host, whereas *variables* are simply points of data in the workflow that will be used to influence its runtime behavior.

Using the Variables aspect of the designer, add a new string variable named YesOrNo. Notice that if you have multiple parent containers in your workflow (for example, a Flowchart containing another Sequence), you can pick the scope of the variable. Here, your only choice is the root Flowchart (see Figure 26-10).

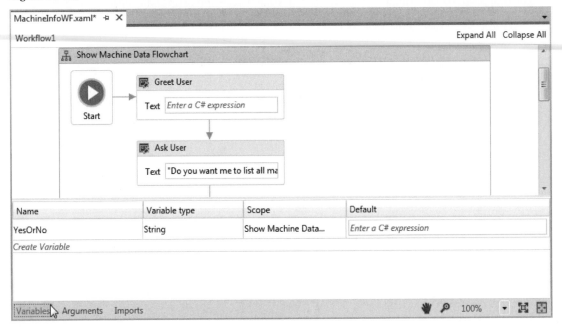

Figure 26-10. Defining a workflow variable

Next, select the InvokeMethod activity on the workflow designer, and using the Properties window of Visual Studio, set the Result property to your new variable (see Figure 26-11).

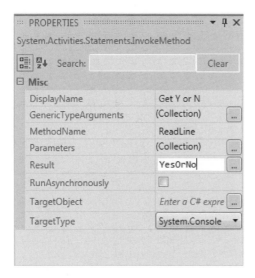

Figure 26-11. The fully configured InvokeMethod

Now that you can grab a piece of data from an external method call, you can use it to make a runtime decision in your flowchart using the FlowDecision activity.

Working with the FlowDecision Activity

A FlowDecision activity is used to take two possible courses of action, based on the truth or falsity of a Boolean variable, or a statement that resolves to a Boolean value. Drag one of these activities onto your designer, and connect it to the InvokeMethod activity (see Figure 26-12).

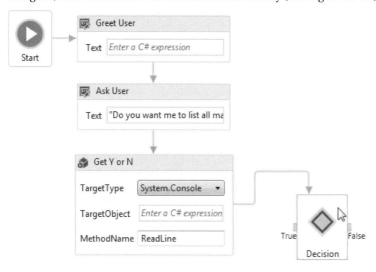

Figure 26-12. A FlowDecision can branch in two directions

■ **Note** If you need to respond to multiple branching conditions within a flowchart, make use of the
FlowSwitch<T> activity. This allows you to define any number of paths, which will be entered based on the value
of a defined workflow variable.

Set the Condition property (using the Properties window) of your FlowDecision activity to the
following code statement, which you can type directly into the editor (here, you are testing an uppercase
version of your YesOrNo variable against the value "Y"):

```
YesOrNo.ToUpper() == "Y"
```

Working with the TerminateWorkflow Activity

You now need to build the activities that will occur on each side of the FlowDecision activity. On the
"false" side, connect a final WriteLine activity that prints out a hardcoded message of your choosing,
followed by a TerminateWorkflow activity (see Figure 26-13).

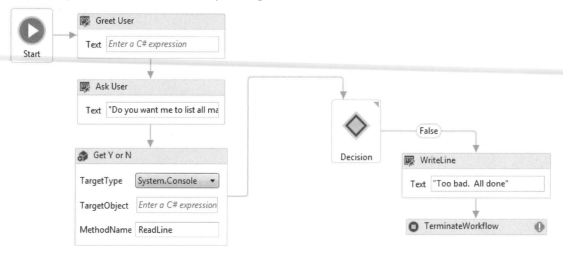

Figure 26-13. The "false" branch

Strictly speaking, you don't need to use the TerminateWorkflow activity, as this workflow would
simply end once you reach the end of the false branch. However, by using this activity type, you can
throw back an exception to the workflow host, informing them exactly why you are stopping. This
exception can be configured in the Properties window.

Assuming you have selected the TerminateWorkflow activity on the designer, use the Properties
window, and click the ellipse button for the Exception property. This will open up an editor that allows
you to throw back an exception, just like if you were doing so in code (see Figure 26-14).

Figure 26-14. *Configuring an exception to throw when the* TerminateWorkflow *activity is encountered*

Complete the configuration of this activity by setting the Reason property to "YesOrNo was false".

Building the "True" Condition

To begin building the "true" condition of the FlowDecision, connect a WriteLine activity, which simply displays a hardcoded string confirming the user has agreed to proceed. From here, connect to a new InvokeMethod activity, which will call the GetLogicalDrives() method of the System.Environment class. To do so, set the TargetType property to System.Environment and the MethodName property to GetLogicalDrives (see Figure 26-15).

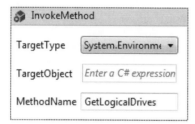

Figure 26-15. *The configured* InvokeMethod *activity*

Next, add a new workflow-level variable (using the Variables button of the workflow designer) named DriveNames of type string[]. To specify you want an array of strings, pick Array of [T] from the Variable Type drop-down list, and pick String from the resulting dialog box. Finally, set the Result property of this new InvokeMethod activity to your DriveNames variable by selecting the InvokeMethod activity on the designer and investigating the Properties window.

Working with the ForEach<T> Activity

The next part of your "true path" will be to print out the names of each drive to the console window, which is to say you need to loop over the data exposed by the DriveNames variable, which has been configured as an array of string objects. The ForEach<T> activity is the WF equivalent of the C# foreach keyword, and it is configured in a very similar manner (at least conceptually).

Drag a ForEach<T> activity on your designer and connect it to the previous InvokeMethod activity. You will configure the ForEach<T> activity in just a minute, but to complete the true condition branch, place one final `WriteLine` activity on your designer to close things off. Figure 26-16 shows the final top-level look at your workflow.

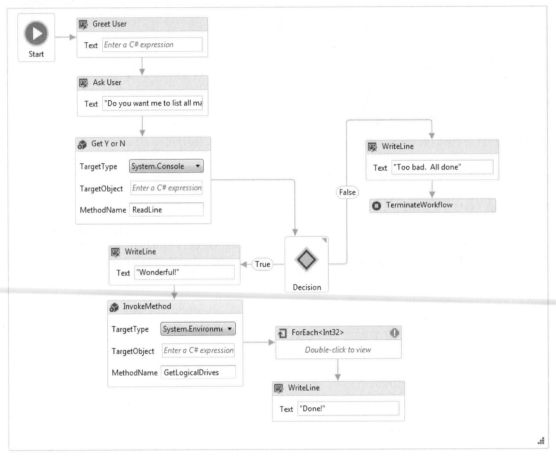

Figure 26-16. The completed top-level workflow

To get rid of the current designer error, you need to finish the configuration of the `ForEach<T>` activity. First, use the Properties window to specify the type argument to the generic, which in this example will be a `String` type. The `Values` property is where the data is coming from, which will be your `DriveNames` variable (see Figure 26-17).

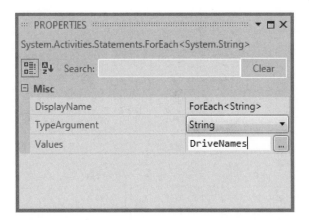

Figure 26-17. Setting the type of the ForEach enumeration

This particular activity needs to be further edited by double-clicking on the designer in order to open a mini designer just for this activity. Not all WF activities can be double-clicked on to yield a new designer, but you can easily tell if this is an option on the activity itself (it will literally say "Double-click to view"). Double click on your ForEach<String> activity, and add a single WriteLine activity, which will print out each string value in the DriveNames return value (see Figure 26-18).

Figure 26-18. The final configuration step of the ForEach<String> activity

---

■ **Note** You can add as many activities to the ForEach<T> mini designer as you require. The collective whole of these activities will execute with each iteration of the loop.

After you are done configuring the "subactivities" of ForEach<T>, you can use the links at the upper left of the workflow designer to return to the top-level workflow (you'll use these *breadcrumbs* quite a bit when drilling into a set of activities; see the mouse icon in Figure 26-19).

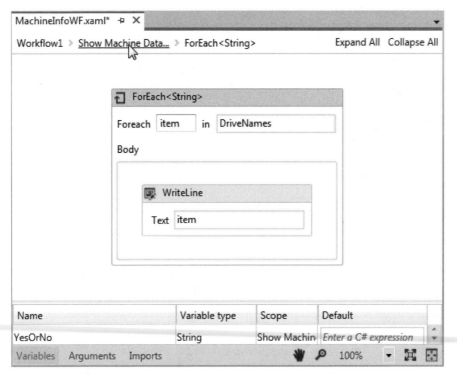

Figure 26-19. The workflow designer "breadcrumbs" allow you to return to the top-level activity

Completing the Application

You are just about done with this example! All you need to do is update the Main() method of the Program class to catch the exception that will be raised if the user says "NO" and thereby triggers the Exception object. Update your code as so (and ensure the System.Collections.Generic namespace is imported in your code file):

```
static void Main(string[] args)
{
  try
  {
    Dictionary<string, object> wfArgs = new Dictionary<string, object>();
    wfArgs.Add("UserName", "Mel");
    Activity workflow1 = new Workflow1();
    WorkflowInvoker.Invoke(workflow1, wfArgs);
  }
  catch (Exception ex)
  {
    Console.WriteLine(ex.Message);
    Console.WriteLine(ex.Data["Reason"]);
  }
}
```

Notice that the "Reason" for the exception can be obtained using the Data property of System.Exception. So, if you run the program and enter "Y" when asked to enumerate your drives, you'll see the following type of output:

```
Hello Andrew
Do you want me to list all machine drives?
y
Wonderful!
C:\
D:\
E:\
F:\
G:\
H:\
I:\
Thanks for using this workflow
```

However, if you enter "N" (or any other value other than "Y" or "y"), you will see the following:

```
Hello Andrew
Do you want me to list all machine drives?
n
Too bad. All done
YesOrNo was false
```

Reflecting on What We Have Done

Now, if you are new to working with a workflow environment, you might be wondering what you have gained by authoring this very simple business process using WF XAML rather than pure C# code. After all, you could have avoided Windows Workflow Foundation all together and authored a C# class similar to the following:

```csharp
class Program
{
  static void Main(string[] args)
  {
    try
    {
      ExecuteBusinessProcess();
    }
    catch (Exception ex)
    {
      Console.WriteLine(ex.Message);
      Console.WriteLine(ex.Data["Reason"]);
    }
  }
}
```

```
private static void ExecuteBusinessProcess()
{
  string UserName = "Andrew";
  Console.WriteLine("Hello {0}", UserName);
  Console.WriteLine("Do you want me to list all machine drives?");

  string YesOrNo = Console.ReadLine();
  if (YesOrNo.ToUpper() == "Y")
  {
    Console.WriteLine("Wonderful!");
    string[] DriveNames = Environment.GetLogicalDrives();
    foreach (string item in DriveNames)
    {
      Console.WriteLine(item);
    }
    Console.WriteLine("Thanks for using this workflow");
  }
  else
  {
    Console.WriteLine("K, Bye...");
    Exception ex = new Exception("User Said No!");
    ex.Data["Reason"] = "YesOrNo was false";
  }
}
}
```

The output of the program would be absolutely identical to the previous XAML-based workflow. So, why bother tinkering with all these activities in the first place? First of all, remember that not everyone is comfortable reading C# code. Be honest: If you had to explain this business process to a room full of salespeople and nontechnical managers, would you rather try to explain this C# code or show them the flowchart? More importantly, remember that the WF API has a whole slew of additional runtime services, including persistence of long running workflows to a database, automatic tracking of workflow events, and so on (alas, I don't have time to cover them here). When you think of the amount of work you would need to do in order to replicate this functionality in a new project, the utility of WF is even clearer.

All of this being said, the WF API is not necessarily the correct tool of choice for all .NET programs. However, for most traditional business applications, the ability to define, host, execute and monitor workflows in this manner is a very good thing indeed. Like any new technology, you will need to determine if this is useful for your current project. Let's see another example of working with the WF API, this time by packaging up a workflow in a dedicated *.dll.

■ **Source Code** The EnumerateMachineDataWF project is included under the Chapter 26 subdirectory.

Building a Sequence Workflow (in a Dedicated DLL)

While making a Workflow Console Application is great for experimenting with the WF API, a production-ready workflow will certainly need to be packaged up into a custom .NET *.dll assembly. By doing so, you can reuse your workflows at a binary level across multiple projects.

   While you could begin using a C# Class Library project as a starting point, the easiest way to build a workflow library is to start with the Activity Library project, under the Workflow node of the New Project dialog. The benefits of this project type are that it will set the required WF assembly references automatically and give you a *.xaml file to create your initial workflow.

   This workflow will model the process of querying the AutoLot database to see whether a given car of the correct make and color is in the Inventory table. If the requested car is in stock, you will build a nicely formatted response to the host via an *output parameter*. If the item in not in stock, you will generate a memo to the head of the sales division requesting that they find a car of the correct color.

Defining the Initial Project

Create a new Activity Library project named CheckInventoryWorkflowLib (see Figure 26-20). After the project is created, rename the initial Activity1.xaml file to CheckInventory.xaml.

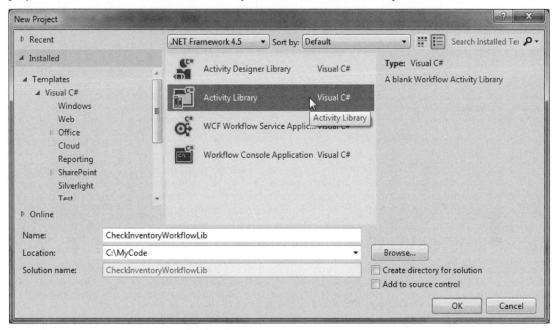

Figure 26-20. Building an Activity Library

   Now, unfortunately, when you rename a workflow XAML file, the underlying class is *not* renamed as expected. To fix the problem, right-click on your CheckInventory.xaml file in the Solution Explorer, and elect to view the code. Modify the opening <Activity> root element to reflect the correct name, as seen here:

```
<Activity mc:Ignorable="sap sap2010 sads"
  x:Class="CheckInventoryWorkflowLib.CheckInventory"
  ...
>
```

This workflow will make use of a Sequence activity as the primary activity, rather than Flowchart. Drag a new Sequence activity onto your designer (you'll find it under the Control Flow area of your Toolbox) and change the DisplayName property to Look Up Product. Figure 26-21 shows the designer thus far.

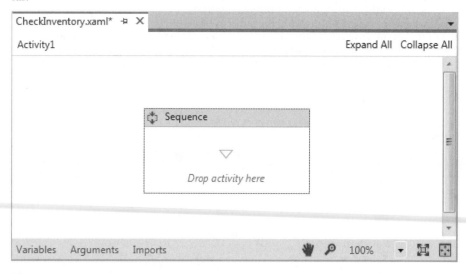

Figure 26-21. *A topmost Sequence activity*

As the name suggests, a Sequence activity allows you to easily create sequential tasks, which occur one after the other. This does not necessarily mean the children activities must follow a strict linear path, however. Your sequence could contain flowcharts, other sequences, parallel processing of data, if/else branches and whatever else might make good sense for the business process you are designing.

Importing Assemblies and Namespaces

Because your workflow will be communicating with the AutoLot database, the next step is to reference your AutoLot.dll assembly using the Add Reference dialog box of Visual Studio. This example will make use of the disconnected layer, so I'd suggest you reference the final version of this assembly created in Chapter 22 (AutoLotDAL (Version 3)).

This workflow will also be making use of the LINQ to DataSet API to query the returned DataTable in order to discover whether you have the requested item in stock. Therefore, you should also set a reference to System.Data.DataSetExtensions.dll, as this is not automatically included for new Activity Library projects.

After you have referenced these assemblies, click the Imports button located at the bottom of the workflow designer. At the top of this editor, is a text box where you can enter names of the .NET namespaces you want to make use of in your workflow scope (think of this area as a declarative version of the C# using keyword).

You can add namespaces from any referenced assembly by typing in the text box mounted on the top of the Imports editor. Import `AutoLotDisconnectedLayer` using this text area. By doing so, you can reference the contained types without needing to use fully qualified names. Figure 26-22 shows the Imports area once you are finished.

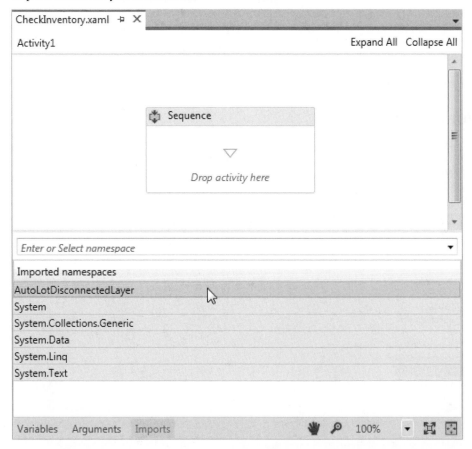

Figure 26-22. The Imports area allows you to include .NET namespaces into your workflow

Defining the Workflow Arguments

Next, we need to define two new workflow-wide input arguments, named `RequestedMake` and `RequestedColor`, both of which will be of type `String`. Like the previous examples, the host of the workflow will create a `Dictionary` object that contains data that maps to these arguments, so there is no need to assign a default value to these items using the Arguments editor. As you might have guessed, this workflow will use these incoming values to perform the database query.

As well, you can use this same Arguments editor to define an *output argument* named `FormattedResponse` of type `String`. When you need to return data from the workflow back to the host, you can create any number of output arguments that can be enumerated by the host when the workflow has completed. Figure 26-23 shows the current workflow designer.

Name	Direction	Argument type	Default value
RequestedMake	In	String	*Enter a C# expression*
RequestedColor	In	String	*Enter a C# expression*
FormattedResponse	Out	String	*Default value not supported*

Create Argument

Variables   Arguments   Imports   ✋   🔍   100%   ▼

Figure 26-23. *Input and output arguments*

Defining Workflow Variables

At this point, you need to declare a member variable in your workflow that corresponds to the InventoryDALDisLayer class of AutoLotDAL.dll. Recall from Chapter 22 that this class allows you to get all data from the Inventory returned as a DataTable. Select your Sequence activity on the designer, and using the Variables button, create a variable named AutoLotInventory. In the Variable Type drop-down list box, pick the Browse For Types... menu option, and type in InventoryDALDisLayer (see Figure 26-24).

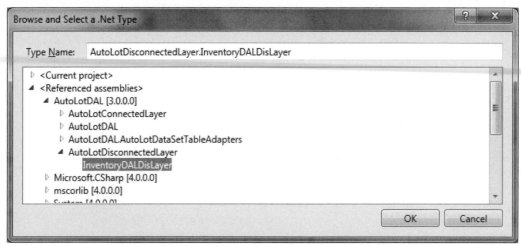

Figure 26-24. *Recall that workflow variables provide a way to declaratively define variables within a scope*

Now, making sure your new variable is selected, go to the Visual Studio Properties window and click on the ellipse button of the Default property. This will open up a code editor that you may resize as you see fit (very helpful when entering lengthy code). This editor is much easier to use when entering complex code for a variable assignment. Enter the following code (on a single line), which allocates your InventoryDALDisLayer variable:

```
new InventoryDALDisLayer(@"Data Source=(local)\SQLEXPRESS;Initial Catalog=AutoLot;Integrated
Security=True")
```

Using the WF designer, declare a second workflow variable of type System.Data.DataTable named Inventory, again using the Browse For Types... menu option (set the default value of this variable to null; see Figure 26-25).

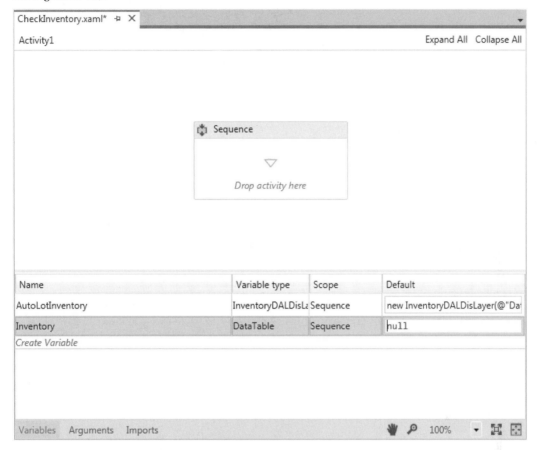

Figure 26-25. Declaring a DataTable variable in the workflow

You will be assigning the Inventory variable to the result of calling GetAllInventory() on the InventoryDALDisLayer variable in a later step.

Working with the Assign Activity

The Assign activity allows you to set a variable to a value, which can be the result of any sort of valid code statements. Drag an Assign activity (located in the Primitives area of your Toolbox) into your Sequence activity (see Figure 26-26).

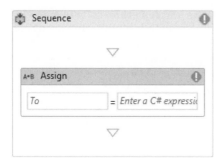

Figure 26-26. *The* Assign *activity*

In the left-side edit box, specify your Inventory variable. In the right-hand edit box, enter the following code:

```
AutoLotInventory.GetAllInventory()
```

Once the Assign activity has been encountered in your workflow, you will have a DataTable that contains all records of the Inventory table. However, you need to discover whether the correct item is in stock using the values of the RequestedMake and RequestedColor arguments sent by the host. To determine if this is the case, you will make use of the LINQ to DataSet API and a workflow If activity.

Working with the If and Switch Activities

Drag an If activity onto your Sequence node directly under the Assign activity (see Figure 26-27).

Figure 26-27. *The* If *activity*

As the If activity allows you to make runtime decisions, you first need to configure the If activity to test against a Boolean expression. In the Condition editor, enter the following check LINQ to DataSet query:

```
(from car in Inventory.AsEnumerable()
  where (string)car["Color"] == RequestedColor &&
    (string)car["Make"]  == RequestedMake select car).Any()
```

This LINQ query uses the RequestedColor and RequestedMake arguments supplied by the workflow host to fetch all records in the DataTable of correct make and color. The call to the Any() extension method will return a true or false value based on if the result of the query contains any results.

Your next task is to configure the set of activities that will execute when the specified condition is true or false. Recall that your ultimate goal here is to send a formatted message to the user if you do indeed have the car in question. However, to spice things up a tad, you will return a unique message based on which make of automobile the caller has requested (BMW, Yugo, or anything else).

Drag a Switch<T> activity (located in the Flow Control area of the Toolbox) into the Then area of the If activity. As soon as you drop this activity, Visual Studio displays a dialog box asking for the type of the generic type parameter; specify String here. After this point, use the workflow designer to set the Expression field of your Switch activity, type RequestedMake (see Figure 26-28).

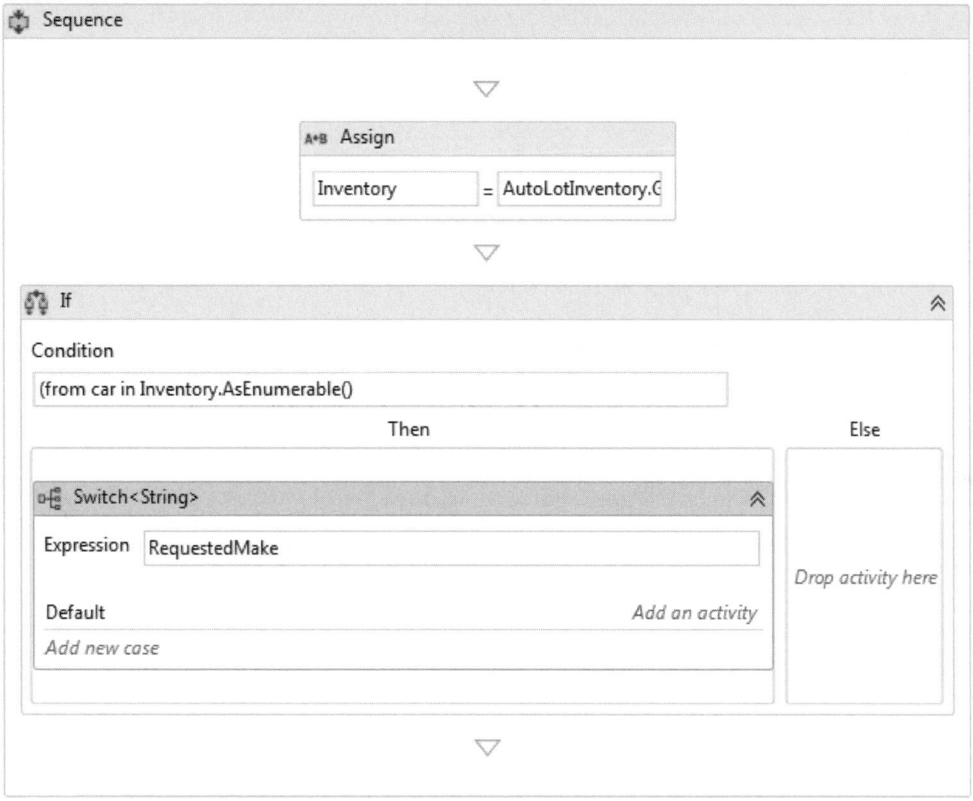

Figure 26-28. The Switch activity

You will see that a default option for the Switch activity is already in place, but you have to expand it, in order to add subactivities (by clicking "Add an Activity"). Add a single Assign activity. After you have added the Assign activity to the Default edit area, assign the FormattedResponse argument to the following code statement:

```
String.Format("Yes, we have a {0} {1} you can purchase",
          RequestedColor, RequestedMake)
```

At this point, your Switch editor will look like what is shown in Figure 26-29.

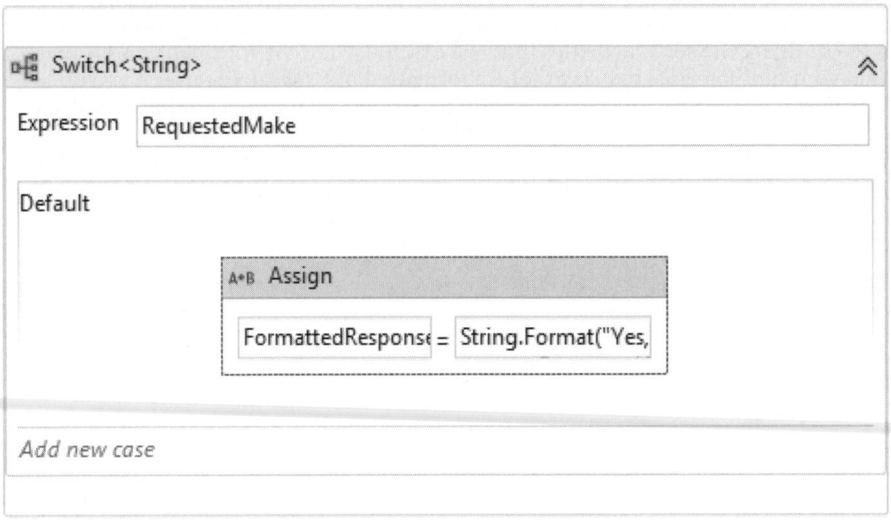

Figure 26-29. *Defining the default task for a Switch activity*

Now, click on the "Add New Case" link and enter BMW (without any double quotes) for the first case, and once again for a final case of Yugo (again, no double quotes). Within each of these case areas, drop an Assign activity, both of which assign a value to the FormattedResponse variable. For the case of BMW, assign a value such as:

```
String.Format("Yes sir! We can send you {0} {1} as soon as {2}!",
          RequestedColor, RequestedMake, DateTime.Now)
```

For the case of the Yugo, use the following expression:

```
String.Format("Please, we will pay you to get this {0} off our lot!",
          RequestedMake)
```

The Switch activity will now look something like what is shown in Figure 26-30.

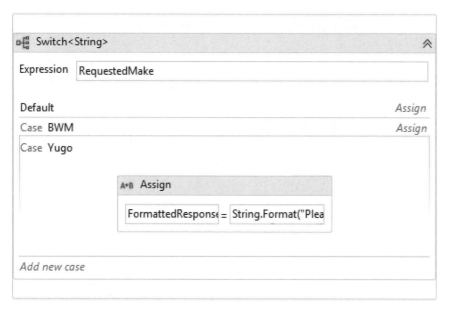

Figure 26-30. The final Switch activity

Building a Custom Code Activity

As expressive as the workflow designer experience is with its ability to embed complex code statements (and LINQ queries) in your XAML file, there will certainly be times when you just need to write code in a dedicated class. There are a number of ways to do so with the WF API, but the most straightforward way is to create a class extending CodeActivity, or if your activity needs to return a value, CodeActivity<T> (where T is the type of return value).

Here, you will make a simple custom activity that will dump out data to a text file, informing the sales staff that a request has come in for a car that is currently not in the inventory system. First, activate the Project ➤ Add New Item menu option and insert a new Code Activity named CreateSalesMemoActivity.cs (see Figure 26-31).

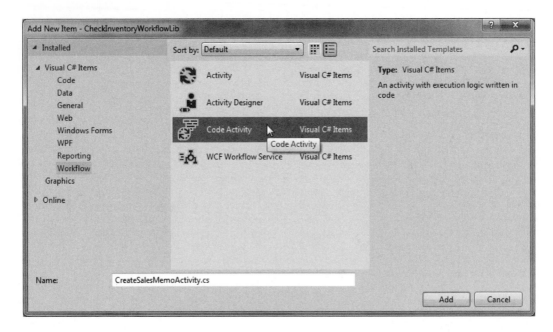

Figure 26-31. Inserting a new Code Activity

If your custom activity requires inputs to process, they will each be represented by a property encapsulating an InArgument<T> object. The InArgument<T> class type is a WF API–specific entity, which provides a way to pass through data supplied by a workflow to the custom activity class itself. Your activity will need two such properties representing the make and color of the item not in stock.

As well, a custom code activity will need to override the virtual Execute() method, which will be called by the WF runtime when this activity is encountered. Typically, this method will use the InArgument<> properties to get the workload accomplished. To get the real underlying value, you will need to do so indirectly using the GetValue() method of the incoming CodeActivityContext.

Here then is the code for your custom activity, which generates a new *.txt file describing the situation to the sales team:

```csharp
public sealed class CreateSalesMemoActivity : CodeActivity
{
  // Two properties for the custom activity.
  public InArgument<string> Make { get; set; }
  public InArgument<string> Color { get; set; }

  // If the activity returns a value, derive from CodeActivity<TResult>
  // and return the value from the Execute method.
  protected override void Execute(CodeActivityContext context)
  {
    // Dump a message to a local text file.
    StringBuilder salesMessage = new StringBuilder();
    salesMessage.AppendLine("***** Attention sales team! *****");
    salesMessage.AppendLine("Please order the following ASAP!");
    salesMessage.AppendFormat("1 {0} {1}\n",
```

```
        context.GetValue(Color), context.GetValue(Make));
      salesMessage.AppendLine("*******************************");

      System.IO.File.WriteAllText("SalesMemo.txt", salesMessage.ToString());
  }
}
```

Compile your workflow assembly. Ensuring your workflow designer is the active window within the Visual Studio IDE, examine the top area of your Toolbox. You should see your custom activity is present and accounted for (see Figure 26-32).

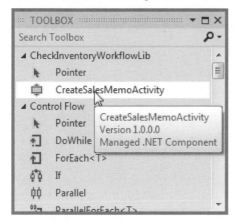

Figure 26-32. Custom code activities appear in the Visual Studio Toolbox

First, drag a new Sequence activity into the Else branch of your If activity. Next, drag your custom activity into the Sequence. At this point, you can assign values to each of the exposed properties using the Properties window. Using your RequestedMake and RequestedMake variables, set the Make and Color properties of your activity as shown in Figure 26-33.

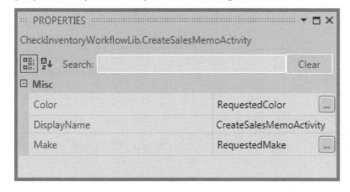

Figure 26-33. Setting the properties of your custom code activity

To complete this workflow, drag a final `Assign` activity into the Sequence activity of the `Else` branch, and set the `FormattedResponse` to the string value "Sorry, out of stock". Figure 26-34 shows the final `If` activity.

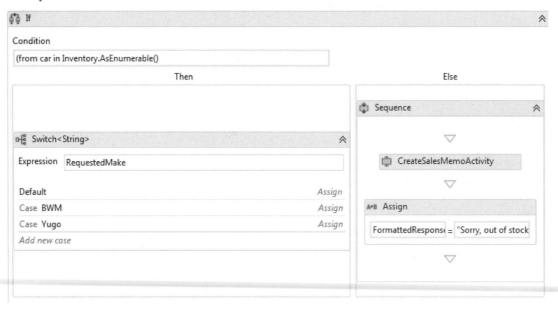

***Figure 26-34.** The completed If activity*

Compile your project and move on to the final part of this chapter, where you will build a client host to make use of the workflow.

■ **Source Code** The CheckInventoryWorkflowLib project is included under the Chapter 26 subdirectory.

Consuming the Workflow Library

Any sort of application can make use of a workflow library; however, here you will opt for simplicity and build a simple Console Application named WorkflowLibraryClient. After you make the project, you will need to set a reference not only to your `CheckInventoryWorkflowLib.dll` and `AutoLotDAL.dll` assemblies, but also the key WF library, `System.Activities.dll`. Add these library references now.

Once each assembly reference has been set, update your `Program.cs` file with the following logic:

```
using System;
...
using CheckInventoryWorkflowLib;

namespace WorkflowLibraryClient
{
```

```
class Program
{
  static void Main(string[] args)
  {
    Console.WriteLine("**** Inventory Look up ****");

    // Get user preferences.
    Console.Write("Enter Color: ");
    string color = Console.ReadLine();
    Console.Write("Enter Make: ");
    string make = Console.ReadLine();

    // Package up data for workflow.
    Dictionary<string, object> wfArgs = new Dictionary<string, object>()
    {
      {"RequestedColor", color},
      {"RequestedMake", make}
    };

    try
    {
      // Send data to workflow!
      WorkflowInvoker.Invoke(new CheckInventory(), wfArgs);
    }
    catch (Exception ex)
    {
      Console.WriteLine(ex.Message);
    }
  }
}
```

As you have done in other examples, you are using the WorkflowInvoker to spin off the workflow in a synchronous manner. While this is all well and good, how are you to get back the return value of the workflow? Remember, once the workflow terminates, you should get back a formatted response!

Retrieving the Workflow Output Argument

The WorkflowInvoker.Invoke() method will return an object implementing the IDictionary<string, object> interface. Because a workflow can return back any number of output arguments, you will need to specify the name of a given output argument as a string value to the type indexer. Update your try/catch logic as so:

```
try
{
  // Send data to workflow!
  IDictionary<string, object> outputArgs =
    WorkflowInvoker.Invoke(new CheckInventory(), wfArgs);

  // Print out the output message.
  Console.WriteLine(outputArgs["FormattedResponse"]);
}
```

```
catch (Exception ex)
{
  Console.WriteLine(ex.Message);
}
```

Now, run your program and enter a make and color that is currently in your copy of the Inventory table of the AutoLot database. You'll see output such as the following:

```
**** Inventory Look up ****
Enter Color: Black
Enter Make: BMW
Yes sir! We can send you Black BMW as soon as 2/17/2012 9:23:01 PM!
Press any key to continue . . .
```

However, if you enter information for an item not currently in stock, you will not only see output such as:

```
**** Inventory Look up ****
Enter Color: Pea Soup Green
Enter Make: Viper
Sorry, out of stock
Press any key to continue . . .
```

You will also find a new *.txt file in the \bin\Debug folder of the client application. If you open this in any text editor, you'll find the following "sales memo":

```
***** Attention sales team! *****
Please order the following ASAP!
1 Pea Soup Green Viper
*******************************
```

That wraps up your introductory look at the WF API. While this chapter has only touched on some of the key aspects of this particular aspect of the .NET platform, I hope you feel confident that you can dive into the topic further if you are interested.

■ **Source Code** The WorkflowLibraryClientproject is included under the Chapter 26 subdirectory.

Summary

In essence, WF allows you to model an application's internal business processes directly within the application itself. Beyond simply modeling the overall workflow, however, WF provides a complete runtime engine and several services that round out this API's overall functionality (persistence and tracking services, etc.). While this introductory chapter did not examine these services directly, do remember that a production-level WF application will most certainly make use of these facilities.

In this introduction to the topic, you learned about two key top-level activities, namely `Flowchart` and `Sequence`. While each of these types control the flow of logic in unique manners, they both can contain the same sort of child activities and are executed by the host in the same manner (via `WorkflowInvoker` or `WorkflowApplication`). You also learned how to pass host arguments *to* a workflow using a generic `Dictionary` object and how to retrieve output arguments *from* a workflow using a generic `IDictionary`-compatible object.

## PART VII

Windows Presentation Foundation

CHAPTER 27

Introducing Windows Presentation Foundation and XAML

When version 1.0 of the .NET platform was released, programmers who needed to build graphical desktop applications made use of two APIs named Windows Forms and GDI+, packaged up primarily in the System.Windows.Forms.dll and System.Drawing.dll assemblies. While Windows Forms/GDI+ are excellent APIs for building traditional desktop GUIs, Microsoft shipped an alternative GUI desktop API named Windows Presentation Foundation (WPF) beginning with the release of .NET 3.0.

This initial WPF chapter begins by examining the motivation behind this new GUI framework, which will help you see the differences between the Windows Forms/GDI+ and WPF programming models. Next, we will examine the different types of WPF applications supported by the API, and come to know the role of several important classes, including Application, Window, ContentControl, Control, UIElement, and FrameworkElement. During this time, you will learn to intercept keyboard and mouse activities, define application-wide data, and other common WPF tasks using nothing but C# code.

This chapter will then introduce you to an XML-based grammar named *Extensible Application Markup Language* (XAML; pronounced "zammel"). Here, you will learn the syntax and semantics of XAML (including attached property syntax, and the role of type converters and markup extensions), and come to understand how to generate, load, and parse XAML at runtime. As well, you will learn how to integrate XAML data into a C# WFP code base (and the benefits of doing so).

This chapter wraps up by investigating the integrated WPF designers of Visual Studio. Here, you will build your own custom XAML editor/parser, which will illustrate how XAML can be manipulated at runtime to build dynamic user interfaces.

The Motivation Behind WPF

Over the years, Microsoft has created numerous graphical user interface toolkits (raw C/C++/Windows API development, VB6, MFC, etc.) to build desktop executables. Each of these APIs provided a code base to represent the basic aspects of a GUI application, including main windows, dialog boxes, controls, menu systems, and other basic necessities. With the initial release of the .NET platform, the Windows Forms API quickly became the preferred model for UI development, given its simple yet very powerful object model.

While many full-featured desktop applications have been successfully created using Windows Forms, the fact of the matter is that this programming model is rather *asymmetrical*. Simply put, System.Windows.Forms.dll and System.Drawing.dll do not provide direct support for many additional technologies required to build a feature-rich desktop application. To illustrate this point, consider the ad hoc nature of GUI desktop development before the release of WPF (see Table 27-1).

Table 27-1. Pre-WPF Solutions to Desired Functionalities

Desired Functionality	Technology
Building windows with controls	Windows Forms
2D graphics support	GDI+ (System.Drawing.dll)
3D graphics support	DirectX APIs
Support for streaming video	Windows Media Player APIs
Support for flow-style documents	Programmatic manipulation of PDF files

As you can see, a Windows Forms developer must pull in types from a number of unrelated APIs and object models. While it is true that making use of these diverse APIs might look similar syntactically (it is just C# code, after all), you might also agree that each technology requires a radically different mind-set. For example, the skills required to create a 3D rendered animation using DirectX are completely different from those used to bind data to a grid. To be sure, it is very difficult for a Windows Forms programmer to master the diverse nature of each API.

Unifying Diverse APIs

WPF (introduced with .NET 3.0) was purposely created to merge these previously unrelated programming tasks into a single unified object model. Thus, if you need to author a 3D animation, you have no need to manually program against the DirectX API (although you could), as 3D functionality is baked directly into WPF. To see how well things have cleaned up, consider Table 27-2, which illustrates the desktop development model ushered in as of .NET 3.0.

Table 27-2. .NET 3.0 Solutions to Desired Functionalities

Desired Functionality	Technology
Building forms with controls	WPF
2D graphics support	WPF
3D graphics support	WPF
Support for streaming video	WPF
Support for flow-style documents	WPF

The obvious benefit here is that .NET programmers now have a single, *symmetrical* API for all common GUI desktop programming needs. After you become comfortable with the functionality of the key WPF assemblies and the grammar of XAML, you'll be amazed how quickly you can create very sophisticated UIs.

Providing a Separation of Concerns via XAML

Perhaps one of the most compelling benefits is that WPF provides a way to cleanly separate the look and feel of a GUI application from the programming logic that drives it. Using XAML, it is possible to define the UI of an application via XML *markup*. This markup (ideally generated using tools such as Microsoft Visual Studio or Microsoft Expression Blend) can then be connected to a related C# code file to provide the guts of the program's functionality.

■ **Note** XAML is not limited to WPF applications. Any application can use XAML to describe a tree of .NET objects, even if they have nothing to do with a visible user interface. For example, the Windows Workflow Foundation API uses a XAML-based grammar to define business processes and custom activities. As well, other .NET GUI frameworks such as Silverlight, Windows Phone 7, and Windows 8 applications all make use of XAML.

As you dig into WPF, you might be surprised how much flexibility this "desktop markup" provides. XAML allows you to define not only simple UI elements (buttons, grids, list boxes, etc.) in markup, but also interactive 2D and 3D graphics, animations, data binding logic, and multimedia functionality (such as video playback).

XAML also makes it very easy to customize how a control should render out its visual appearance. For example, defining a circular button control that animates your company logo requires just a few lines of markup. As shown in Chapter 31, WPF controls can be modified through styles and templates, which allow you to change the overall look and feel of an application with minimum fuss and bother. Unlike Windows Forms development, the only compelling reason to build a custom WPF control from the ground up is if you need to change the *behaviors* of a control (e.g., add custom methods, properties, or events; subclass an existing control to override virtual members). If you simply need to change the *look and feel* of a control (again, such as a circular animated button), you can do so entirely through markup.

Providing an Optimized Rendering Model

GUI toolkits such as Windows Forms, MFC, or VB6 preformed all graphical rendering requests (including the rendering of UI elements such as buttons and list boxes) using a low-level, C-based API (GDI), which has been part of the Windows OS for years. GDI provides adequate performance for typical business applications or simple graphical programs; however, if a UI application needed to tap into high-performance graphics, DirectX was required.

The WPF programming model is quite different in that GDI is *not* used when rendering graphical data. All rendering operations (e.g., 2D graphics, 3D graphics, animations, control rendering, etc.) now make use of the DirectX API. The first obvious benefit is that your WPF applications will automatically take advantage of hardware and software optimizations. As well, WPF applications can tap into very rich graphical services (blur effects, anti-aliasing, transparency, etc.) without the complexity of programming directly against the DirectX API.

■ **Note** Although WPF does push all rendering requests to the DirectX layer, I don't want to suggest that a WPF application will perform as fast as building an application using unmanaged C++ and DirectX directly. If you are intending to build a desktop application that requires the fastest possible execution speed (such as a 3D video game), unmanaged C++ and DirectX are still the best approach.

Simplifying Complex UI Programming

To recap the story thus far, Windows Presentation Foundation (WPF) is an API to build desktop applications that integrates various desktop APIs into a single object model and provides a clean separation of concerns via XAML. In addition to these major points, WPF applications also benefit from a very simple way to integrate services into your programs, which historically were quite complex to account for. The following is a quick rundown of the core WPF features:

> A number of layout managers (far more than Windows Forms) to provide extremely flexible control over placement and reposition of content.

> Use of an enhanced data-binding engine to bind content to UI elements in a variety of ways.

> A built-in style engine, which allows you to define "themes" for a WPF application.

> Use of vector graphics, which allows content to be automatically resized to fit the size and resolution of the screen hosting the application.

> Support for 2D and 3D graphics, animations, and video and audio playback.

> A rich typography API, such as support for XML Paper Specification (XPS) documents, fixed documents (WYSIWYG), flow documents, and document annotations (e.g., a Sticky Notes API).

> Support for interoperating with legacy GUI models (e.g., Windows Forms, ActiveX, and Win32 HWNDs). For example, you can incorporate custom Windows Forms controls into a WPF application, and vice versa.

Now that you have some idea of what WPF brings to the table, let's turn our attention to the various types of applications that can be created using this API. Rest assured that many of these features will be explored in detail in the chapters to come.

The Various Flavors of WPF

The WPF API can be used to build a variety of GUI-centric applications that basically differ in their navigational structure and deployment models. The sections that follow present a high-level tour through each option.

Traditional Desktop Applications

The first (and most familiar) option is to use WPF to build a traditional executable assembly that runs on a local machine. For example, you could use WPF to build a text editor, painting program, or multimedia program such as a digital music player, photo viewer, and so forth. Like any other desktop application, these *.exe files can be installed using traditional means (setup programs, Windows Installer packages, etc.) or via ClickOnce technology to allow desktop applications to be distributed and installed via a remote web server.

Programmatically speaking, this type of WPF application will make use (at a minimum) of the Window and Application class types, in addition to the expected set of dialog boxes, toolbars, status bars, menu systems, and other UI elements.

Now, you can certainly use WPF to build your basic business application that does not support any bells and whistles, but WPF really shines when you *do* incorporate such features. Consider Figure 27-1, which shows a WPF sample desktop application for viewing patient records in a medical environment.

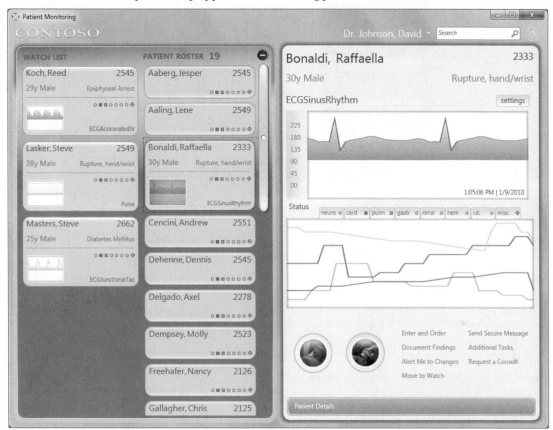

Figure 27-1. *This WPF desktop application makes use of several WPF APIs*

Sadly, the printed page does not show the full feature set of this program. For example, if you were to see this application running, you would note that the upper right of the main window is displaying a real-time graph of the patient's sinus rhythm. If you click the Patient Details button on the lower right, several animations take place to flip, rotate, and transform the UI to the look and feel shown in Figure 27-2.

Figure 27-2. Transformations and animations are very simple under WPF

Could you build this same application without WPF? Absolutely. However, the amount of code—and the complexity of the code—would be much higher.

■ **Note** This example application, and many others, can be downloaded (with source code) from the official WPF web site, `http://windowsclient.net`. Here, you will find numerous WPF (and Windows Forms) whitepapers, sample projects, technology walkthroughs, and forums.

Navigation-Based WPF Applications

WPF applications can optionally choose to make use of a navigation-based structure, which makes a traditional desktop application take on the basic behavior of a web browser application. Using this model, you can build a desktop *.exe that provides a "forward" and "back" button that allows the end user to move back and forth between various UI displays called *pages*.

This type of application maintains a list of each page and provides the necessary infrastructure to navigate between them, pass data across pages (similar to a web-based application variable), and maintain a history list. By way of a concrete example, consider Windows Explorer (see Figure 27-3), which makes use of such functionality. Notice the navigation buttons (and history list) mounted on the upper-left corner of the window.

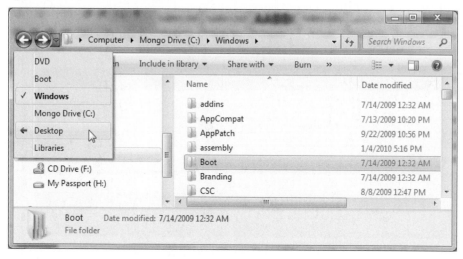

Figure 27-3. *A navigation-based desktop program*

Regardless of the fact that a WPF desktop application can take on a web-like navigational structure, understand that this is simply a UI design issue. The application itself is still little more than a local executable running on a desktop machine, and it has little to do with a web application beyond a slightly similar look and feel. Programmatically speaking, this type of WPF application is constructed using classes such as `Application`, `Page`, `NavigationWindow`, and `Frame`.

XBAP Applications

WPF also allows you to build applications that can be hosted *within* a web browser. This flavor of WPF application is termed a XAML *browser application,* or XBAP. Under this model, the end user navigates to a given URL, at which point the XBAP (which is essentially a collection of `Page` objects) is transparently downloaded and installed to the local machine. Unlike a traditional ClickOnce installation for an executable application, however, the XBAP program is hosted directly within the browser and adopts the browser's intrinsic navigational system. Figure 27-4 illustrates an XBAP program in action (specifically, the ExpenseIt WPF sample program, which can be found at `http://windowsclient.net`).

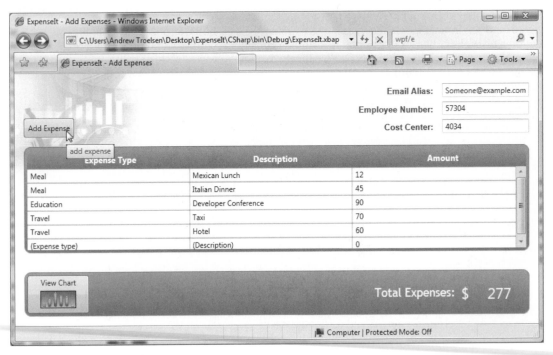

Figure 27-4. *XBAP programs are downloaded to a local machine and hosted within a web browser*

One benefit of an XBAP is that it allows you to create sophisticated UIs which are much more expressive than a typical web page built with HTML and JavaScript (however, HTML 5 certainly improves the current situation). An XBAP Page object can make use of the same WPF services as a desktop WPF application, including animations, 2D and 3D graphics, themes, and whatnot. In effect, the web browser is just a container for WPF Page objects, and is *not* displaying ASP.NET web pages.

However, given that these Page objects are deployed to a remote web server, XBAPs can be easily versioned and updated without the need to redeploy executables to the user's desktop. Like a traditional web program, you can simply update the Page objects in the web server, and the user will get the "latest and greatest" when they access the URL.

One downside to this flavor of WPF is that XBAPs must be hosted within Microsoft Internet Explorer or Firefox web browsers. If you are deploying XBAPs across a company intranet, browser compatibility should not be a problem, given that system administrators can play dictator regarding which browser should be installed on users' machines. However, if you want the outside world to make use of your XBAP, it is not possible to ensure each end user is making use of Internet Explorer/Firefox, and therefore some external users may not be able to view your WPF XBAP.

Another issue to be aware of is that the machine that is viewing an XBAP must have a local installation of the .NET framework, as the Page objects will be using the same .NET assemblies as an application running natively on the machine. Given this particular point, XBAPs are limited to Windows operating systems and, thus, cannot be viewed on a system running Mac OS X or Linux.

The WPF/Silverlight Relationship

WPF and XAML also provide the foundation for a cross-platform, cross-browser WPF-based technology termed *Silverlight*. From a high level, you can consider Silverlight as a competitor to Adobe Flash, with the benefit of using C# and XAML rather than a new set of tools and languages. Silverlight is a subset of WPF functionality, which is used to build highly interactive plug-ins for a larger HTML-based web page. In reality, however, Silverlight is a completely unique distribution of the .NET platform, which ships with a "mini" CLR and "mini" version of the .NET base class libraries.

Unlike an XBAP, the user's machine does not need a full installation of the .NET Framework. As long as the target machine has the Silverlight runtime installed, the browser will load the Silverlight runtime and display the Silverlight application automatically. Best of all, Silverlight plug-ins are not limited to the Windows operating systems. Microsoft has also created a Silverlight runtime for Mac OS X.

With Silverlight, you are able to build extremely feature-rich (and interactive) web applications. For example, like WPF, Silverlight has a vector-based graphical system, animation support, and multimedia support. Furthermore, you are able to incorporate a subset of the .NET base class library into your applications. This subset includes LINQ APIs, generic collections, support for WCF, and a healthy subset of mscorlib.dll (file I/O, XML manipulation, etc.).

■ **Note** This edition of the text does not address Silverlight; however, a majority of your WPF knowledge will map directly to the construction of Silverlight web plug-ins. If you are interested in learning more about this API, check out www.silverlight.net.

Investigating the WPF Assemblies

Regardless of which type of WPF application you want to build, WPF is ultimately little more than a collection of types bundled within .NET assemblies. Table 27-3 describes the key assemblies used to build WPF applications, each of which must be referenced when creating a new project. As you would hope, Visual Studio WPF projects reference these required assemblies automatically.

Table 27-3. Core WPF Assemblies

Assembly	Meaning in Life
PresentationCore.dll	This assembly defines numerous namespaces that constitute the foundation of the WPF GUI layer. For example, this assembly contains support for the WPF Ink API (for programming against stylus input for Pocket PCs and Tablet PCs), animation primitives, and numerous graphical rendering types.
PresentationFramework.dll	This assembly contains a majority of the WPF controls, the Application and Window classes, support for interactive 2D graphics and numerous types used in data binding.

System.Xaml.dll	This assembly provides namespaces that allow you to program against a XAML document at runtime. By and large, this library is only useful if you are authoring WPF support tools or need absolute control over XAML at runtime.
WindowsBase.dll	This assembly defines types that constitute the infrastructure of the WPF API, including those representing WPF threading types, security types, various type converters, and support for *dependency properties* and *routed events* (described in Chapter 31).

Collectively, these four assemblies define a number of new namespaces and hundreds of new .NET classes, interfaces, structures, enumerations, and delegates. While you should consult the .NET Framework 4.5 SDK documentation for complete details, Table 27-4 describes the role of some (but certainly not all) of the namespaces you should be aware of.

Table 27-4. Core WPF Namespaces

Namespace	Meaning in Life
System.Windows	This is the root namespace of WPF. Here, you will find core classes (such as Application and Window) that are required by any WPF desktop project.
System.Windows.Controls	Contains all of the expected WPF widgets, including types to build menu systems, tool tips, and numerous layout managers.
System.Windows.Data	Contains types to work with the WPF data-binding engine, as well as support for data-binding templates.
System.Windows.Documents	Contains types to work with the documents API, which allows you to integrate PDF-style functionality into your WPF applications, via the XML Paper Specification (XPS) protocol.
System.Windows.Ink	Provides support for the Ink API, which allows you to capture input from a stylus or mouse, respond to input gestures, and so forth. Very useful for Tablet PC programming; however, any WPF can make use of this API.
System.Windows.Markup	This namespace defines a number of types that allow XAML markup (and the equivalent binary format, BAML) to be parsed and processed programmatically.
System.Windows.Media	This is the root namespace to several media-centric namespaces. Within these namespaces you will find types to work with animations, 3D rendering, text rendering, and other multimedia primitives.

System.Windows.Navigation	This namespace provides types to account for the navigation logic employed by XAML browser applications (XBAPs) as well as standard desktop applications that require a navigational page model.
System.Windows.Shapes	Defines classes that allow you to render interactive 2D graphics that automatically respond to mouse input.

To begin your journey into the WPF programming model, you'll examine two members of the System.Windows namespace that are commonplace to any traditional desktop development effort: Application and Window.

■ **Note** If you have created desktop UIs using the Windows Forms API, be aware that the System.Windows.Forms.* and System.Drawing.* assemblies are not related to WPF. These libraries represent the original .NET GUI toolkit, Windows Forms/GDI+.

The Role of the Application Class

The System.Windows.Application class represents a global instance of a running WPF application. This class supplies a Run() method (to start the application), a series of events that you are able to handle in order to interact with the application's lifetime (such as Startup and Exit), and a number of events that are specific to XAML browser applications (such as events that fire as a user navigates between pages). Table 27-5 details some of the key properties to be aware of.

Table 27-5. Key Properties of the Application Type

Property	Meaning in Life
Current	This static property allows you to gain access to the running Application object from anywhere in your code. This can be very helpful when a window or dialog box needs to gain access to the Application object that created it, typically to access application-wide variables and functionality.
MainWindow	This property allows you to programmatically get or set the main window of the application.
Properties	This property allows you to establish and obtain data that is accessible throughout all aspects of a WPF application (windows, dialog boxes, etc.).
StartupUri	This property gets or sets a URI that specifies a window or page to open automatically when the application starts.

Windows	This property returns a `WindowCollection` type, which provides access to each window created from the thread that created the `Application` object. This can be very helpful when you want to iterate over each open window of an application and alter its state (such as minimizing all windows).

Constructing an Application Class

Any WPF application will need to define a class that extends `Application`. Within this class, you will define your program's entry point (the `Main()` method), which creates an instance of this subclass and typically handles the Startup and Exit events. You will build a full example project in just a moment, but here is a quick example:

```
// Define the global application object
// for this WPF program.
class MyApp : Application
{
  [STAThread]
  static void Main(string[] args)
  {
    // Create the application object.
    MyApp app = new MyApp();

    // Register the Startup/Exit events.
    app.Startup += (s, e) => { /* Start up the app */ };
    app.Exit += (s, e) => { /* Exit the app */ };
  }
}
```

Within the Startup handler, you will most often process any incoming command-line arguments and launch the main window of the program. The Exit handler, as you would expect, is where you can author any necessary shutdown logic for the program (e.g., save user preferences, write to the Windows registry).

Enumerating the Windows Collection

Another interesting property exposed by `Application` is `Windows`, which provides access to a collection representing each window loaded into memory for the current WPF application. Recall that as you create new `Window` objects, they are automatically added into the `Application.Windows` collection. Here is an example method that will minimize each window of the application (perhaps in response to a given keyboard gesture or menu option triggered by the end user):

```
static void MinimizeAllWindows()
{
  foreach (Window wnd in Application.Current.Windows)
  {
    wnd.WindowState = WindowState.Minimized;
  }
}
```

You'll build a complete Application-derived type in an upcoming example. Until then, let's check out the core functionality of the Window type and learn about a number of important WPF base classes in the process.

The Role of the Window Class

The System.Windows.Window class (located in the PresentationFramework.dll assembly) represents a single window owned by the Application-derived class, including any dialog boxes displayed by the main window. Not surprisingly, Window has a series of parent classes, each of which brings more functionality to the table. Consider Figure 27-5, which shows the inheritance chain (and implemented interfaces) for System.Windows.Window as seen through the Visual Studio object browser.

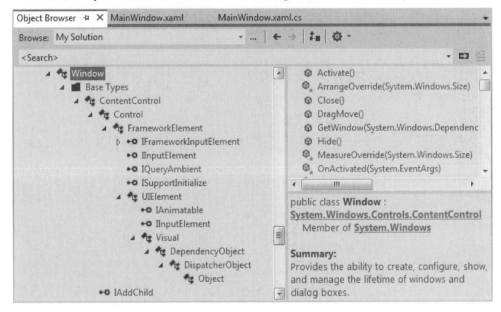

Figure 27-5. The hierarchy of the Window class

You'll come to understand the functionality provided by many of these base classes as you progress through this chapter and the chapters to come. However, to whet your appetite, the following sections present a breakdown of the functionality provided by each base class (consult the .NET Framework 4.5 SDK documentation for full details).

The Role of System.Windows.Controls.ContentControl

The direct parent of Window is ContentControl, which is quite possibly the most enticing of all WPF classes. This base class provides derived types with the ability to host a single piece of *content*, which, simply put, refers to the visual data placed within the interior of the control's surface area via the Content property. The WPF content model makes it very simple to customize the basic look and feel of a content control.

For example, when you think of a typical "button" control, you tend to assume that the content is a simple string literal (OK, Cancel, Abort, etc.). If you are using XAML to describe a WPF control, and the value you want to assign to the Content property can be captured as a simple string, you may set the Content property within the element's opening definition as so (don't fret over the exact markup at this point):

```
<!-- Setting the Content value in the opening element -->
<Button Height="80" Width="100" Content="OK"/>
```

■ **Note** The Content property can also be set in C# code, which allows you to change the interior of a control at runtime.

However, content can be almost anything. For example, let's say you want to have a "button" that has something more interesting than a simple string, perhaps a custom graphic and a blurb of text. In other UI frameworks such as Windows Forms, you would be required to build a custom control, which could entail quite a bit of code and a whole new class to maintain. With the WPF content model, there is no need to do so.

When you want to assign the Content property to a value that cannot be captured as a simple array of characters, you are unable to assign it using an attribute in the control's opening definition. Rather, you must define the content data *implicitly*, within the element's scope. For example, the following <Button> contains a <StackPanel> as content, which itself contains some unique data (an <Ellipse> and <Label>, to be exact):

```
<!-- Implicitly setting the Content property with complex data -->
<Button Height="80" Width="100">
  <StackPanel>
    <Ellipse Fill="Red" Width="25" Height="25"/>
    <Label Content ="OK!"/>
  </StackPanel>
</Button>
```

You can also make use of XAML's *property-element syntax* to set complex content. Consider the following functionally equivalent <Button> definition, which sets the Content property explicitly using property-element syntax (again, you'll find more information on XAML later in this chapter, so don't sweat the details just yet):

```
<!-- Setting the Content property using property-element syntax -->
<Button Height="80" Width="100">
  <Button.Content>
    <StackPanel>
      <Ellipse Fill="Red" Width="25" Height="25"/>
      <Label Content ="OK!"/>
    </StackPanel>
  </Button.Content>
</Button>
```

Do be aware that not every WPF control derives from ContentControl and, therefore, not all controls supports this unique content model (however, most do). As well, some WPF controls add a few refinements to the basic content model you have just examined. Chapter 28 will examine the role of WPF content in much more detail.

The Role of System.Windows.Controls.Control

Unlike `ContentControl`, all WPF controls share the `Control` base class as a common parent. This base class provides numerous core members that account for basic UI functionality. For example, `Control` defines properties to establish the control's size, opacity, tab order logic, the display cursor, background color, and so forth. Furthermore, this parent class provides support for *templating services*. As explained in Chapter 30, WPF controls can completely change the way they render their appearance using templates and styles. Table 27-6 documents some key members of the `Control` type, grouped by related functionality.

Table 27-6. Key Members of the Control Type

Members	Meaning in Life
Background, Foreground, BorderBrush, BorderThickness, Padding, HorizontalContentAlignment, VerticalContentAlignment	These properties allow you to set basic settings regarding how the control will be rendered and positioned.
FontFamily, FontSize, FontStretch, FontWeight	These properties control various font-centric settings.
IsTabStop, TabIndex	These properties are used to establish tab order among controls on a window.
MouseDoubleClick, PreviewMouseDoubleClick	These events handle the act of double-clicking a widget.
Template	This property allows you to get and set the control's template, which can be used to change the rendering output of the widget.

The Role of System.Windows.FrameworkElement

This base class provides a number of members that are used throughout the WPF framework, such as support for storyboarding (used within animations) and support for data binding, as well as the ability to name a member (via the `Name` property), obtain any resources defined by the derived type, and establish the overall dimensions of the derived type. Table 27-7 hits the highlights.

Table 27-7. Key Members of the FrameworkElement Type

Members	Meaning in Life
ActualHeight, ActualWidth, MaxHeight, MaxWidth, MinHeight, MinWidth, Height, Width	These properties control the size of the derived type.
ContextMenu	Gets or sets the pop-up menu associated with the derived type.
Cursor	Gets or sets the mouse cursor associated with the derived type.
HorizontalAlignment, VerticalAlignment	Gets or sets how the type is positioned within a container (such as a panel or list box).
Name	Allows to you assign a name to the type, in order to access its functionality in a code file.
Resources	Provides access to any resources defined by the type (see Chapter 30 for an examination of the WPF resource system).
ToolTip	Gets or sets the tool tip associated with the derived type.

The Role of System.Windows.UIElement

Of all the types within a Window's inheritance chain, the UIElement base class provides the greatest amount of functionality. The key task of UIElement is to provide the derived type with numerous events to allow the derived type to receive focus and process input requests. For example, this class provides numerous events to account for drag-and-drop operations, mouse movement, keyboard input, and stylus input (for Pocket PCs and Tablet PCs).

Chapter 29 digs into the WPF event model in detail; however, many of the core events will look quite familiar (MouseMove, KeyUp, MouseDown, MouseEnter, MouseLeave, etc.). In addition to defining dozens of events, this parent class provides a number of properties to account for control focus, enabled state, visibility, and hit testing logic, as shown in Table 27-8.

Table 27-8. Key Members of the UIElement Type

Members	Meaning in Life
Focusable, IsFocused	These properties allow you to set focus on a given derived type.
IsEnabled	This property allows you to control whether a given derived type is enabled or disabled.

IsMouseDirectlyOver, IsMouseOver	These properties provide a simple way to perform hit-testing logic.
IsVisible, Visibility	These properties allow you to work with the visibility setting of a derived type.
RenderTransform	This property allows you to establish a transformation that will be used to render the derived type.

The Role of System.Windows.Media.Visual

The Visual class type provides core rendering support in WPF, which includes hit testing of graphical data, coordinate transformation, and bounding box calculations. In fact, the Visual class interacts with the underlying DirectX subsystem to actually draw data on the screen. As will examine in Chapter 29, WPF provides three possible manners in which you can render graphical data, each of which differs in terms of functionality and performance. Use of the Visual type (and its children, such as DrawingVisual) provides the most lightweight way to render graphical data, but it also entails the greatest amount of manual code to account for all the required services. Again, more details to come in Chapter 29.

The Role of System.Windows.DependencyObject

WPF supports a particular flavor of .NET properties termed *dependency properties*. Simply put, this style of property provides extra code to allow the property to respond to several WPF technologies such as styles, data binding, animations, and so forth. In order for a type to support this new property scheme, it will need to derive from the DependencyObject base class. While dependency properties are a key aspect of WPF development, much of the time their details are hidden from view. Chapter 28 dives further into the details of dependency properties.

The Role of System.Windows.Threading.DispatcherObject

The final base class of the Window type (beyond System.Object, which I assume needs no further explanation at this point in the book) is DispatcherObject. This type provides one property of interest, Dispatcher, which returns the associated System.Windows.Threading.Dispatcher object. The Dispatcher class is the entry point to the event queue of the WPF application, and it provides the basic constructs for dealing with concurrency and threading.

Building a WPF Application Without XAML

Given all of the functionality provided by the parent classes of the Window type, it is possible to represent a window in your application by either directly creating a Window object or using this class as the parent to a strongly typed descendent. Let's examine both approaches in the following code example. Although most WPF applications will make use of XAML, doing so is technically optional. Anything that can be expressed in XAML can be expressed in code and (for the most part) vice versa. If you so desire, it is possible to build a complete WPF project using the underlying object model and procedural C# code.

To illustrate, let's create a minimal but complete application *without* the use of XAML using the Application and Window classes directly. Begin by creating a new Console Application named WpfAppAllCode (don't worry; you will use the Visual Studio WPF project template later in this chapter). Next, access the Project Add Reference dialog box and add a reference to WindowsBase.dll, PresentationCore.dll, System.Xaml.dll, and PresentationFramework.dll.

Now, update your initial C# file with the following code, which creates a window of modest functionality (here, I am only showing the namespaces that *must* be imported to compile the code; feel free to leave any auto-including using statements in place):

```
// A simple WPF application, written without XAML.
using System;
using System.Windows;
using System.Windows.Controls;

namespace WpfAppAllCode
{
  // In this first example, you are defining a single class type to
  // represent the application itself and the main window.
  class Program : Application
  {
    [STAThread]
    static void Main(string[] args)
    {
      // Handle the Startup and Exit events, and then run the application.
      Program app = new Program();
      app.Startup += AppStartUp;
      app.Exit += AppExit;
      app.Run();  // Fires the Startup event.
    }

    static void AppExit(object sender, ExitEventArgs e)
    {
      MessageBox.Show("App has exited");
    }

    static void AppStartUp(object sender, StartupEventArgs e)
    {
      // Create a Window object and set some basic properties.
      Window mainWindow = new Window();
      mainWindow.Title = "My First WPF App!";
      mainWindow.Height = 200;
      mainWindow.Width = 300;
      mainWindow.WindowStartupLocation = WindowStartupLocation.CenterScreen;
      mainWindow.Show();
    }
  }
}
```

■ **Note** The `Main()` method of a WPF application must be attributed with the `[STAThread]` attribute, which ensures any legacy COM objects used by your application are thread safe. If you do not annotate `Main()` in this way, you will encounter a runtime exception.

Note that the `Program` class extends the `System.Windows.Application` class. Within the `Main()` method, you create an instance of the application object and handle the `Startup` and `Exit` events using method group conversion syntax. Recall from Chapter 10 that this shorthand notation removes the need to manually specify the underlying delegates used by a particular event. Of course, if you want, you can specify the underlying delegates directly by name.

In the following modified `Main()` method, notice that the `Startup` event works in conjunction with the `StartupEventHandler` delegate, which can only point to methods taking an `Object` as the first parameter and a `StartupEventArgs` as the second. The `Exit` event, on the other hand, works with the `ExitEventHandler` delegate, which demands that the method pointed to take an `ExitEventArgs` type as the second parameter.

```
[STAThread]
static void Main(string[] args)
{
  // This time, specify the underlying delegates.
  Program app = new Program();
  app.Startup += new StartupEventHandler(AppStartUp);
  app.Exit += new ExitEventHandler(AppExit);
  app.Run();  // Fires the Startup event.
}
```

In any case, the `AppStartUp()` method has been configured to create a `Window` object, establish some very basic property settings, and call `Show()` to display the window on the screen in a modeless fashion (the `ShowDialog()` method can be used to launch a modal dialog). The `AppExit()` method simply makes use of the WPF `MessageBox` class to display a diagnostic message when the application is being terminated.

Once you compile and run the project, you will find a very simple main window that can be minimized, maximized, and closed. To spice things up a bit, you need to add some user interface elements. Before you do, however, you should refactor your code base to account for a strongly typed and well-encapsulated `Window`-derived class.

Creating a Strongly Typed Window

Currently, the `Application`-derived class directly creates an instance of the `Window` type upon application startup. Ideally, you would create a class deriving from `Window` in order to encapsulate its appearance and functionality. Assume that you have created the following class definition within your current `WpfAppAllCode` namespace (if you place this class in a new C# file, be sure to import the `System.Windows` namespace):

```
class MainWindow : Window
{
  public MainWindow(string windowTitle, int height, int width)
  {
    this.Title = windowTitle;
```

```
    this.WindowStartupLocation = WindowStartupLocation.CenterScreen;
    this.Height = height;
    this.Width = width;
  }
}
```

You can now update your Startup event handler to simply directly create an instance of MainWindow, like so:

```
static void AppStartUp(object sender, StartupEventArgs e)
{
  // Create a MainWindow object.
  MainWindow wnd = new MainWindow("My better WPF App!", 200, 300);
  wnd.Show();
}
```

Once the program is recompiled and executed, the output is identical. The obvious benefit is that you now have a strongly typed class representing the main window to build upon.

■ **Note** When you create a Window (or Window-derived) object, it will automatically be added to the windows collection of the Application class (via some constructor logic found in the Window class itself). You can use the Application.Windows property to iterate over the list of Window objects currently in memory.

Creating a Simple User Interface

Adding a UI element (such as a Button) to a Window in C# code will involve the following basic steps:

Define a member variable to represent the control.

Configure the control's look and feel upon Window construction.

Assign the control to the inherited Content property, or alternatively, as a parameter to the inherited AddChild() method.

Recall that the WPF control content model demands that the Content property is set to a single element. Of course, a Window that contained only a single UI control would be quite useless. Therefore, in almost every case, the "single piece of content" that is assigned to the Content property is, in reality, a layout manager, such as DockPanel, Grid, Canvas, or StackPanel. Within the layout manager, you can have any combination of internal controls, including other nested layout managers. (Read more on this aspect of WPF development in Chapter 28.)

For now, you will add a single Button control to your Window-derived class. When you click the button, you will close the current window, which will indirectly terminate the application, as you have no other windows in memory. Ponder the following update to the MainWindow class (be sure you have imported System.Windows.Controls to gain access to the Button class):

```csharp
class MainWindow : Window
{
  // Our UI element.
  private Button btnExitApp = new Button();

  public MainWindow(string windowTitle, int height, int width)
  {
    // Configure button and set the child control.
    btnExitApp.Click += new RoutedEventHandler(btnExitApp_Clicked);
    btnExitApp.Content = "Exit Application";
    btnExitApp.Height = 25;
    btnExitApp.Width = 100;

    // Set the content of this window to a single button.
    this.Content = btnExitApp;

    // Configure the window.
    this.Title = windowTitle;
    this.WindowStartupLocation = WindowStartupLocation.CenterScreen;
    this.Height = height;
    this.Width = width;
    this.Show();
  }

  private void btnExitApp_Clicked(object sender, RoutedEventArgs e)
  {
    // Close the window.
    this.Close();
  }
}
```

Notice that the Click event of the WPF Button works in conjunction with a delegate named RoutedEventHandler, which begs the question, what is a routed event? You'll examine the details of the WPF event model in the next chapter; for the time being, simply understand that targets of the RoutedEventHandler delegate must supply an object as the first parameter and a RoutedEventArgs as the second.

In any case, after you recompile and run this application, you will find the customized window shown in Figure 27-6. Notice that your button is automatically placed in the dead center of the window's client area; this is the default behavior when content is not placed within a WPF panel type.

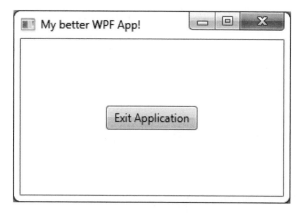

Figure 27-6. A simple WPF application writen in 100 percent C# code

Interacting with Application-Level Data

Recall that the Application class defines a property named Properties, which allows you to define a collection of name/value pairs via a type indexer. Because this indexer has been defined to operate on type System.Object, you are able to store any sort of item within this collection (including your custom classes), to be retrieved at a later time using a friendly moniker. Using this approach, it is simple to share data across all windows in a WPF application.

To illustrate, you will update the current Startup event handler to check the incoming command-line arguments for a value named /GODMODE (a common cheat code for many PC video games). If you find this token, you will establish a bool value set to true within the properties collection of the same name (otherwise, you will set the value to false).

Sounds simple enough, but how are you going to pass the incoming command-line arguments (typically obtained from the Main() method) to your Startup event handler? One approach is to call the static Environment.GetCommandLineArgs() method. However, these same arguments are automatically added to the incoming StartupEventArgs parameter and can be accessed via the Args property. That being said, here is the first update to the current code base:

```
private static void AppStartUp(object sender, StartupEventArgs e)
{
  // Check the incoming command-line arguments and see if they
  // specified a flag for /GODMODE.
  Application.Current.Properties["GodMode"] = false;
  foreach(string arg in e.Args)
  {
    if (arg.ToLower() == "/godmode")
    {
      Application.Current.Properties["GodMode"] = true;
      break;
    }
  }

  // Create a MainWindow object.
  MainWindow wnd = new MainWindow("My better WPF App!", 200, 300);
}
```

Application-wide data can be accessed from anywhere within the WPF application. All you are required to do is obtain an access point to the global application object (via Application.Current) and investigate the collection. For example, you could update the Click event handler of the Button as so:

```
private void btnExitApp_Clicked(object sender, RoutedEventArgs e)
{
  // Did user enable /godmode?
  if((bool)Application.Current.Properties["GodMode"])
    MessageBox.Show("Cheater!");

  this.Close();
}
```

With this, if the end user launches our program as follows:

```
WpfAppAllCode.exe /godmode
```

he or she will see our shameful message box displayed when terminating the application.

■ **Note** Recall that you can supply command-line arguments within Visual Studio. Simply double-click the Properties icon within Solution Explorer, click the Debug tab from the resulting editor, and enter /godmode within the "Command line arguments" editor.

Handling the Closing of a Window Object

End users can shut down a window using numerous built-in system-level techniques (e.g., clicking the "X" close button on the window's frame) or by indirectly calling the Close() method in response to some user interaction element (e.g., File ➤ Exit). In either case, WPF provides two events that you can intercept to determine whether the user is *truly* ready to shut down the window and remove it from memory. The first event to fire is Closing, which works in conjunction with the CancelEventHandler delegate.

This delegate expects target methods to take System.ComponentModel.CancelEventArgs as the second parameter. CancelEventArgs provides the Cancel property, which when set to true will prevent the window from actually closing (this is handy when you have asked the user if he really wants to close the window or if perhaps he would like to save his work first).

If the user did indeed wish to close the window, CancelEventArgs.Cancel can be set to false (which is the default setting). This will then cause the Closed event to fire (which works with the System.EventHandler delegate), making it the point at which the window is about to be closed for good.

Update the MainWindow class to handle these two events by adding these code statements to the current constructor, like so:

```
public MainWindow(string windowTitle, int height, int width)
{
  ...
  this.Closing += MainWindow_Closing;
  this.Closed += MainWindow_Closed;
}
```

Now, implement the corresponding event handlers as so:

```
private void MainWindow_Closing(object sender,
   System.ComponentModel.CancelEventArgs e)
{
   // See if the user really wants to shut down this window.
   string msg = "Do you want to close without saving?";
   MessageBoxResult result = MessageBox.Show(msg,
      "My App", MessageBoxButton.YesNo, MessageBoxImage.Warning);

   if (result == MessageBoxResult.No)
   {
      // If user doesn't want to close, cancel closure.
      e.Cancel = true;
   }
}

private void MainWindow_Closed(object sender, EventArgs e)
{
   MessageBox.Show("See ya!");
}
```

Now, run your program and attempt to close the window, either by clicking the "X" icon on the upper right of the window or by clicking the button control. You should see the confirmation dialog shown in Figure 27-7.

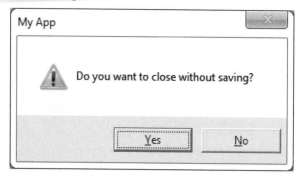

Figure 27-7. Trapping the closing event of a window

If you click the Yes button, the application will terminate; however, clicking the No button will keep the window in memory.

Intercepting Mouse Events

The WPF API provides a number of events you can capture in order to interact with the mouse. Specifically, the UIElement base class defines a number of mouse-centric events such as MouseMove, MouseUp, MouseDown, MouseEnter, MouseLeave, and so forth.

Consider, for example, the act of handling the MouseMove event. This event works in conjunction with the System.Windows.Input.MouseEventHandler delegate, which expects its target to take a System.Windows.Input.MouseEventArgs type as the second parameter. Using MouseEventArgs, you are able to extract out the (x, y) position of the mouse and other relevant details. Consider the following partial definition:

```
public class MouseEventArgs : InputEventArgs
{
...
  public Point GetPosition(IInputElement relativeTo);
  public MouseButtonState LeftButton { get; }
  public MouseButtonState MiddleButton { get; }
  public MouseDevice MouseDevice { get; }
  public MouseButtonState RightButton { get; }
  public StylusDevice StylusDevice { get; }
  public MouseButtonState XButton1 { get; }
  public MouseButtonState XButton2 { get; }
}
```

■ **Note** The XButton1 and XButton2 properties allow you to interact with "extended mouse buttons" (such as the "next" and "previous" buttons found on some mouse controls). These are often used to interact with a browser's history list to navigate between visited pages.

The GetPosition() method allows you to get the (x, y) value relative to a UI element on the window. If you are interested in capturing the position relative to the activated window, simply pass in this. Handle the MouseMove event in the constructor of your MainWindow class, like so:

```
public MainWindow(string windowTitle, int height, int width)
{
...
  this.MouseMove += MainWindow_MouseMove;
}
```

Here is an event handler for MouseMove that will display the location of the mouse in the window's title area (notice you are translating the returned Point type into a text value via ToString()):

```
private void MainWindow_MouseMove(object sender,
  System.Windows.Input.MouseEventArgs e)
{
  // Set the title of the window to the current (x,y) of the mouse.
  this.Title = e.GetPosition(this).ToString();
}
```

Intercepting Keyboard Events

Processing keyboard input for the focused window is also very straightforward. UIElement defines a number of events that you can capture to intercept keypresses from the keyboard on the active element (e.g., KeyUp, KeyDown). The KeyUp and KeyDown events both work with the System.Windows.Input.KeyEventHandler delegate, which expects the target's second event handler to be of type KeyEventArgs, which defines several public properties of interest, shown here:

```
public class KeyEventArgs : KeyboardEventArgs
{
...
  public bool IsDown { get; }
  public bool IsRepeat { get; }
  public bool IsToggled { get; }
  public bool IsUp { get; }
  public Key Key { get; }
  public KeyStates KeyStates { get; }
  public Key SystemKey { get; }
}
```

To illustrate handling the KeyDown event in the constructor of MainWindow (just like you did for the previous events), implement the following event handler that changes the content of the button with the currently pressed key:

```
private void MainWindow_KeyDown(object sender, System.Windows.Input.KeyEventArgs e)
{
  // Display key press on the button.
  btnExitApp.Content = e.Key.ToString();
}
```

As a finishing touch, double-click the Properties icon of the Solution Explorer, and under the Application tab, set the Output Type setting to Windows Application. This will prevent the console window from launching in the background of your WPF application. Figure 27-8 shows the final product of your first WPF program.

Figure 27-8. Your first WPF program, 100 percent XAML free

At this point in the chapter, WPF might look like nothing more than yet another GUI framework that is providing (more or less) the same services as Windows Forms, MFC, or VB6. If this were in fact the case, you might question the need for yet another UI toolkit. To truly see what makes WPF so unique requires an understanding of the XML-based grammar, XAML.

■ **Source Code** The WpfAppAllCode project is included under the Chapter 27 subdirectory.

Building a WPF Application Using Only XAML

A typical WPF application will *not* be composed exclusively of code, as you did in this first example. Rather, your C# code files will be paired with a related XAML source file, and together they represent the entirety of a given Window or Application, as well as other class types we have not yet examined such as UserControl and Page.

This approach is termed the *code file approach* to building a WPF application, and you will make use of this technique extensively throughout the remainder of the book's WPF coverage. However, before you do, the next example will illustrate how to build a WPF application using nothing but XAML files. While this 100-percent XAML approach is not recommended, it will help you clearly understand how blobs of markup are transformed into a corresponding C# code base, and ultimately, a .NET assembly.

■ **Note** This next example will make use of a number of XAML techniques we have not yet formally examined, so don't become concerned if you encounter some unfamiliar syntax. You might want to simply load the solution files into a text editor and follow along; however, don't use Visual Studio to do so! Some of the XAML in this sample contains markup that cannot be displayed in the Visual Studio visual designers.

In general, XAML files will contain markup that describes the look and feel of the window, while the related C# code files contain the implementation logic. For example, the XAML file for a Window might describe the overall layout system, the controls within that layout system, and specify the names of various event handlers. The related C# file would contain the implementation logic of these event handlers and any custom code required by the application.

Extensible Application Markup Language, or XAML, is an XML-based grammar that allows you to define the state (and, to some extent, the functionality) of a tree of .NET objects through markup. While XAML is frequently used when building UIs with WPF, in reality it can be used to describe any tree of *nonabstract* .NET types (including your own custom types defined in a custom .NET assembly), provided each supports a default constructor. As you will see, the markup within a *.xaml file is transformed into a full-blown object model.

Because XAML is an XML-based grammar, we gain all the benefits (and drawbacks) XML affords us. On the plus side, XAML files are very self-describing (as any XML document should be). By and large, each element in a XAML file represents a type name (such as Button, Window, or Application) within a given .NET namespace. Attributes within the scope of an opening element map to properties (Height, Width, etc.) and events (Startup, Click, etc.) of the specified type.

Given the fact that XAML is simply a declarative way to define the state of an object, it is possible to define a WPF widget via markup or procedural code. For example, the following XAML:

```
<!-- Defining a WPF Button in XAML -->
<Button Name = "btnClickMe" Height = "40" Width = "100" Content = "Click Me" />
```

can be represented programmatically as follows:

```
// Defining the same WPF Button in C# code.
Button btnClickMe = new Button();
btnClickMe.Height = 40;
btnClickMe.Width = 100;
btnClickMe.Content = "Click Me";
```

On the downside, XAML can be verbose and is (like any XML document) case sensitive. Thus, complex XAML definitions can result in a good deal of markup. Most developers will not need to manually author a complete XAML description of their WPF applications. Rather, the majority of this task will (thankfully) be relegated to development tools such as Visual Studio, Microsoft Expression Blend, or any number of third-party products. After the tools generate the basic markup, you can go in and fine-tune the XAML definitions by hand, if necessary.

Defining a Window Object in XAML

While tools can generate a good deal of XAML on your behalf, it is important for you to understand the basic workings of XAML syntax and how this markup is eventually transformed into a valid .NET assembly. To illustrate XAML in action, in the next example you'll build a WPF application using nothing more than a pair of *.xaml files.

The first Window-derived class (MainWindow) was defined in C# as a class type that extends the System.Windows.Window base class. This class contains a single Button object that calls a registered event handler when clicked. Defining this same Window type in the grammar of XAML can be achieved as follows. First, use a simple text editor (such as Notepad) to create a new file named MainWindow.xaml, and be sure to save this in a easily accessible subdirectory off your C: drive, as we will be processing this file at the command line. Now, add the following XAML:

```xml
<!-- Here is your Window definition -->
<Window x:Class="WpfAppAllXaml.MainWindow"
  xmlns="http://schemas.microsoft.com/winfx/2006/xaml/presentation"
  xmlns:x="http://schemas.microsoft.com/winfx/2006/xaml"
  Title="A Window built using 100% XAML"
  Height="200" Width="300"
  WindowStartupLocation ="CenterScreen">

  <!-- This window has a single button as content -->
  <Button x:Name="btnExitApp" Width="133" Height="24"
        Content = "Close Window" Click ="btnExitApp_Clicked"/>

  <!-- The implementation of your button's Click event handler! -->
  <x:Code>
    <![CDATA[
      private void btnExitApp_Clicked(object sender, RoutedEventArgs e)
      {
        this.Close();
      }
    ]]>
  </x:Code>
</Window>
```

First, notice that the root element <Window> makes use of the Class attribute, which is used to specify the name of the C# class that will be generated when this XAML file is processed. Also notice that the Class attribute is prefixed with the x: tag prefix. If you look within the opening <Window> element, you'll see that this XML tag prefix is assigned to the string "http://schemas.microsoft.com/winfx/2006/xaml" to build an XML namespace declaration. You will understand the details of these XML namespace definitions a bit later in the chapter, but for now, just be aware that any time you want to make reference to an item defined by the "http://schemas.microsoft.com/winfx/2006/xaml" XAML namespace, you must prefix the x: token.

Within the scope of the `<Window>` start tag, you have specified values for the `Title`, `Height`, `Width`, and `WindowStartupLocation` attributes, which are a direct mapping to properties of the same name supported by the `System.Windows.Window` class in the `PresentationFramework.dll` assembly.

Next up, notice that within the scope of the window's definition, you have authored markup to describe the look and feel of a `Button` object that will be used to implicitly set the `Content` property of the window. Beyond setting up the variable name (using the `x:Name` XAML token) and its overall dimensions, you have also handled the `Click` event of the `Button` type by assigning the method to delegate to when the `Click` event occurs.

The final aspect of this XAML file is the `<x:Code>` element, which allows you to author event handlers and other methods of this class directly within an `*.xaml` file. As a safety measure, the code itself is wrapped within a CDATA scope to prevent XML parsers from attempting to directly interpret the data (although this is not strictly required for the current example).

It is important to point out that authoring functionality within a `<Code>` element is not recommended. Although this "single-file approach" isolates all the action to one location, inline code does not provide a clear separation of concerns between UI markup and programming logic. In most WPF applications, implementation code will be found within a related C# file (which you will do eventually).

Defining the Application Object in XAML

Remember that XAML can be used to define in markup any nonabstract .NET class that supports a default constructor. Given this, you could most certainly define your application object in markup as well. Consider the following content within a new file, `MyApp.xaml`:

```
<!-- The Main() method seems to be missing!
     However, the StartupUri attribute is the
     functional equivalent -->
<Application x:Class="WpfAppAllXaml.MyApp"
  xmlns="http://schemas.microsoft.com/winfx/2006/xaml/presentation"
  xmlns:x="http://schemas.microsoft.com/winfx/2006/xaml"
  StartupUri="MainWindow.xaml">
</Application>
```

Here, you might agree, the mapping between the `Application`-derived C# class type and its XAML description is not as clear-cut as was the case for our `MainWindow`'s XAML definition. Specifically, there does not seem to be any trace of a `Main()` method. Given that any .NET executable must have a program entry point, you are correct to assume it is generated at compile time, based in part on the `StartupUri` property. The value assigned to `StartupUri` represents which XAML resource to load when the application starts up. In this example, we have set the `StartupUri` property to the name of XAML resource defining our initial `Window` object, `MainWindow.xaml`.

Although the `Main()` method is automatically created at compile time, you are free to use the `<x:Code>` element to capture other C# code blocks. For example, if you wanted to display a message when your program shuts down, you could handle the `Exit` event and implement it as so (note that the opening `<Application>` element has now set the `Exit` attribute to capture the `Exit` event of the Application class):

```
<Application x:Class="SimpleXamlApp.MyApp"
  xmlns="http://schemas.microsoft.com/winfx/2006/xaml/presentation"
  xmlns:x="http://schemas.microsoft.com/winfx/2006/xaml"
  StartupUri="MainWindow.xaml" Exit ="AppExit">
  <x:Code>
    <![CDATA[
```

```
      private void AppExit(object sender, ExitEventArgs e)
      {
        MessageBox.Show("App has exited");
      }
    ]]>
  </x:Code>
</Application>
```

Processing the XAML Files Using msbuild.exe

At this point, you are ready to transform our markup into a valid .NET assembly. However, you cannot directly use the C# compiler to do so. To date, the C# compiler does not have a native understanding of XAML markup. However, the msbuild.exe command-line utility does understand how to transform XAML into C# code and compile this code on the fly when it is informed of the correct *.targets files.

Msbuild.exe is a tool that will compile .NET code based on the instructions contained within an XML-based build script. As it turns out, these build script files contain the exact same sort of data that is found in the *.csproj file generated by Visual Studio. Therefore, it is possible to compile a .NET program at the command line using msbuild.exe or using Visual Studio itself.

■ **Note** A full examination of the msbuild.exe utility is beyond the scope of this chapter. If you'd like to learn more, perform a search for the topic "MSBuild" in the .NET Framework 4.5 SDK documentation.

Here is a very simple build script, WpfAppAllXaml.csproj, which contains just enough information to inform msbuild.exe how to transform your XAML files into a related C# code base:

```
<Project DefaultTargets="Build"
  xmlns="http://schemas.microsoft.com/developer/msbuild/2003">
  <PropertyGroup>
    <RootNamespace>WpfAppAllXaml</RootNamespace>
    <AssemblyName>WpfAppAllXaml</AssemblyName>
    <OutputType>winexe</OutputType>
  </PropertyGroup>
  <ItemGroup>
    <Reference Include="System" />
    <Reference Include="WindowsBase" />
    <Reference Include="PresentationCore" />
    <Reference Include="PresentationFramework" />
  </ItemGroup>
  <ItemGroup>
    <ApplicationDefinition Include="MyApp.xaml" />
    <Page Include="MainWindow.xaml" />
  </ItemGroup>
  <Import Project="$(MSBuildBinPath)\Microsoft.CSharp.targets" />
  <Import Project="$(MSBuildBinPath)\Microsoft.WinFX.targets" />
</Project>
```

■ **Note** This *.csproj file cannot be loaded directly into Visual Studio, as it contains only the minimal instructions necessary to build our application at the command line.

The <PropertyGroup> element is used to specify some basic aspects of the build, such as the root namespace, the name of the resulting assembly, and the output type (the equivalent of the /target:winexe option of csc.exe).

The first <ItemGroup> specifies the set of external assemblies to reference with the current build, which, as you can see, are the core WPF assemblies examined earlier in this chapter.

The second <ItemGroup> is much more interesting. Notice that the <ApplicationDefinition> element's Include attribute is assigned to the *.xaml file that defines our application object. The <Page>'s Include attribute can be used to list each of the remaining *.xaml files that define the windows (and pages, which are often used when building XAML browser applications) processed by the application object.

However, the magic of this build script is the final <Import> elements. Here, you are referencing two *.targets files, each of which contains numerous other instructions used during the build process. The Microsoft.WinFX.targets file contains the necessary build settings to transform the XAML definitions into equivalent C# code files, while Microsoft.CSharp.Targets contains data to interact with the C# compiler itself.

In any case, at this point you can use a Developer Command Prompt to process your XAML data with msbuild.exe. To do so, change to the directory containing your MainWindow.xaml, MyApp.xaml and WpfAppAllXaml.csproj files, and enter the following command:

```
msbuild WpfAppAllXaml.csproj
```

After the build process has completed, you will find that your working directory now contains a \bin and \obj subdirectory (just like a Visual Studio project). If you were to open the \bin\Debug folder, sure enough, you would find a new .NET assembly named SimpleXamlApp.exe. If you open this assembly into ildasm.exe, you can see that your XAML has been transformed into a valid executable application (see Figure 27-9).

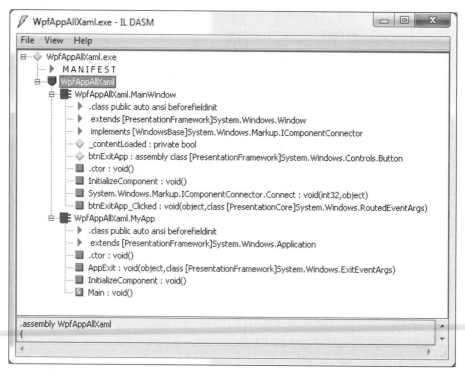

Figure 27-9. Transforming XAML into a .NET executable? Interesting...

And if you run your program by double-clicking on the executable, you will see your main window launch on the screen.

Transforming Markup into a .NET Assembly

To understand exactly *how* your markup was transformed into a .NET assembly, you need to dig a bit deeper into the msbuild.exe process and examine a number of compiler-generated files, including a particular binary resource embedded within the assembly at compile time. The first task is to learn how your *.xaml files are transformed into a corresponding C# code base.

Mapping the Window XAML Markup to C# Code

The *.targets files specified in an msbuild script contain numerous instructions to translate XAML elements into C# code. When msbuild.exe processed your *.csproj file, it produced two files with the form *.g.cs (where g denotes auto*generated*) that were saved into the \obj\Debug directory. Based on the names of your *.xaml file names, the C# files in question are MainWindow.g.cs and MyApp.g.cs.

If you open the MainWindow.g.cs file into a text editor, you will find a class named MainWindow, which extends the Window base class. The name of this class is a direct result of the x:Class attribute in the <Window> start tag. This class also contains a member variable of type System.Windows.Controls.Button, named btnExitApp. In this case, the name of the control is based on the x:Name attribute value within the opening `<Button>` declaration. This class also contains the handler for the button's `Click` event, `btnExitApp_Clicked()`. Here is a partial listing of this compiler-generated `MainWindow.g.cs` file:

```
public partial class MainWindow :
  System.Windows.Window, System.Windows.Markup.IComponentConnector
{
  internal System.Windows.Controls.Button btnExitApp;

  private void btnExitApp_Clicked(object sender, RoutedEventArgs e)
  {
    this.Close();
  }
...
}
```

This class defines a private member variable of type `bool` (named `_contentLoaded`), which was not directly accounted for in the XAML markup. This data member is used to determine (and ensure) the content of the window is assigned only once.

```
public partial class MainWindow :
  System.Windows.Window, System.Windows.Markup.IComponentConnector
{
  // This member variable will be explained soon enough.
  private bool _contentLoaded;
...
}
```

Notice that the compiler-generated class also explicitly implements the WPF `IComponentConnector` interface defined in the `System.Windows.Markup` namespace. This interface defines a single method called `Connect()`, which has been implemented to prep each control defined in the markup and rig up the event logic as specified within the original `MainWindow.xaml` file. Before the method completes, the `_contentLoaded` member variable is set to `true`. Here is the crux of the method:

```
void System.Windows.Markup.IComponentConnector.Connect(int connectionId, object target)
{
  switch (connectionId)
  {
    case 1:
      this.btnExitApp = ((System.Windows.Controls.Button)(target));
      this.btnExitApp.Click += new
        System.Windows.RoutedEventHandler(this.btnExitApp_Clicked);
    return;
  }
  this._contentLoaded = true;
}
```

Last but not least, the `MainWindow` class also defines and implements a method named `InitializeComponent()`. You might expect that this method contains code that sets up the look and feel of each control by setting various properties (`Height`, `Width`, `Content`, etc.). However, this is not the case! How then do the controls take on the correct UI? The logic with `InitializeComponent()` resolves the location of an embedded assembly resource that is named identical to the original *.xaml file, like so:

```
public void InitializeComponent()
{
  if (_contentLoaded)
  {
    return;
  }
  _contentLoaded = true;
  System.Uri resourceLocater = new
    System.Uri("/WpfAppAllXaml;component/mainwindow.xaml",
              System.UriKind.Relative);
  System.Windows.Application.LoadComponent(this, resourceLocater);
}
```

At this point, the question becomes, *what exactly is this embedded resource?*

The Role of BAML

When msbuild.exe processed our *.csproj file, it generated a file taking a *.baml file extension. The full name of this file is named based on the initial MainWindow.xaml file. Therefore, you should see a file called MainWindow.baml in the \obj\Debug folder (see Figure 27-10).

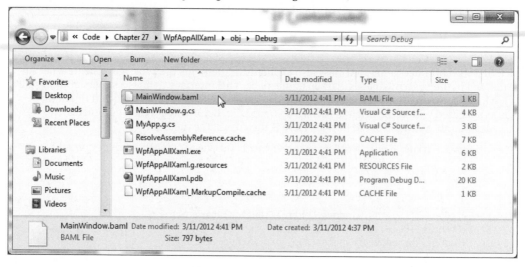

Figure 27-10. BAML is simply a compact, binary version of XAML

As you might have guessed from the name, Binary Application Markup Language (BAML) is a compact, binary representation of the original XAML data. This *.baml file is embedded as a resource (via a generated *.g.resources file) into the compiled assembly.

This BAML resource contains all of the data needed to establish the look and feel of the UI widgets (again, such as the Height and Width properties). In fact, if you open the *.baml file into Visual Studio, you can see traces of the initial XAML attributes (see Figure 27-11).

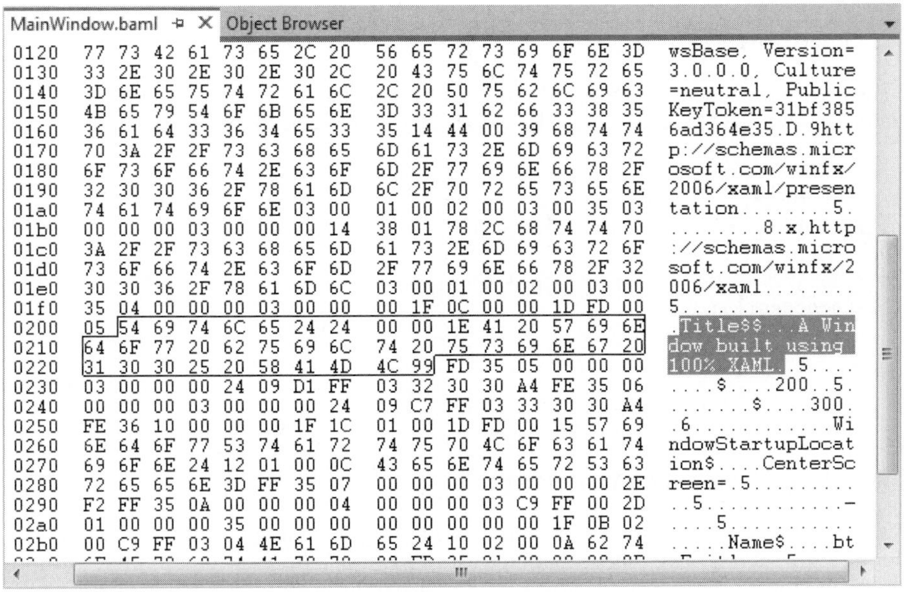

Figure 27-11. BAML contains property values used to construct objects at runtime

The important take-away here is to understand that a WPF application contains within itself a binary representation (the BAML) of the markup. At runtime, this BAML will be plucked out of the resource container and used to make sure all windows and controls are initialized to the correct look and feel.

Also, remember that the name of these binary resources are *identical* to the name of the stand-alone *.xaml files you authored. However, this does not imply in any way that you must distribute the loose *.xaml files with your compiled WPF program. Unless you build a WPF application that will dynamically load and parse *.xaml files at runtime, you will never need to ship the original markup.

Mapping the Application XAML Markup to C# Code

The final piece of the autogenerated code to examine is the MyApp.g.cs file. Here, you see your Application-derived class with a proper Main() entry point method. The implementation of this method calls InitializeComponent() on the Application-derived type, which, in turn, sets the StartupUri property, allowing each of the objects to establish its correct property settings based on the binary XAML definition.

```
namespace WpfAppAllXaml
{
  public partial class MyApp : System.Windows.Application
  {
    void AppExit(object sender, ExitEventArgs e)
    {
      MessageBox.Show("App has exited");
    }
```

```
[System.Diagnostics.DebuggerNonUserCodeAttribute()]
public void InitializeComponent()
{
  this.Exit += new System.Windows.ExitEventHandler(this.AppExit);
  this.StartupUri = new System.Uri("MainWindow.xaml", System.UriKind.Relative);
}

[System.STAThreadAttribute()]
[System.Diagnostics.DebuggerNonUserCodeAttribute()]
public static void Main() {
  SimpleXamlApp.MyApp app = new SimpleXamlApp.MyApp();
  app.InitializeComponent();
  app.Run();
}
}
}
```

XAML-to-Assembly Process Summary

So at this point in the chapter, you have created a full-blown WPF program using nothing but two XAML files and a related build script. As you have seen, msbuild.exe leverages auxiliary settings defined within the *.targets file to process the XAML files (and generate the *.baml) for the build process. Figure 27-12 illustrates the overall picture regarding the compile-time processing of *.xaml files.

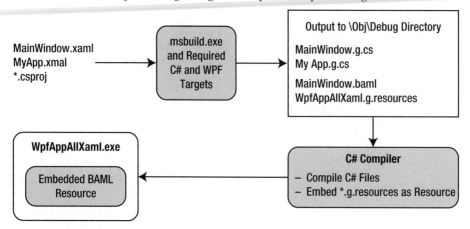

Figure 27-12. The XAML-to-assembly compile-time process

Hopefully you now have a much better idea how XAML data is used to build a .NET application. At this point, you are ready to take a look at the syntax and semantics of XAML itself.

■ **Source Code** The WpfAppAllXaml project can be found under the Chapter 27 subdirectory.

Understanding the Syntax of WPF XAML

Production-level WPF applications will typically make use of dedicated tools to generate the necessary XAML. As helpful as these tools are, it is a very good idea to have an understanding of the overall structure of XAML markup. To help in your learning process, allow me to introduce a very popular (and free) tool that allows you to easily experiment with XAML.

Introducing Kaxaml

When you are first learning the grammar of XAML, it can be very helpful to use a free tool named *Kaxaml*. You can obtain this popular XAML editor/parser from the following web site:

```
http://www.kaxaml.com
```

Kaxaml is helpful in that it has no clue about C# source code, event handlers, or implementation logic. It is a much more straightforward way to test XAML snippets than using a full-blown Visual Studio WPF project template. As well, Kaxaml has a number of integrated tools, such as a color chooser, XAML snippet manager, and even an "XAML scrubber" option that will format your XAML based on your settings. When you first open Kaxaml, you will find simple markup for a <Page> control, as follows:

```
<Page
    xmlns="http://schemas.microsoft.com/winfx/2006/xaml/presentation"
    xmlns:x="http://schemas.microsoft.com/winfx/2006/xaml">
    <Grid>

    </Grid>
</Page>
```

Like a Window, a Page contains various layout managers and controls. However, unlike a Window, Page objects cannot run as stand-alone entities. Rather, they must be placed inside of a suitable host such as a NavigationWindow, Frame, or a web browser (and in that case, you have just made an XBAP!). The good news is that you can type identical markup within a <Page> or <Window> scope.

■ **Note** If you change the <Page> and </Page> elements in the Kaxaml markup window to <Window> and </Window>, you can press the F5 key to load a new window onto the screen.

As an initial test, enter the following markup into the XAML pane at the bottom of the tool:

```
<Page
    xmlns="http://schemas.microsoft.com/winfx/2006/xaml/presentation"
    xmlns:x="http://schemas.microsoft.com/winfx/2006/xaml">
    <Grid>
        <!-- A button with custom content -->
        <Button Height="100" Width="100">
            <Ellipse Fill="Green" Height="50" Width="50"/>
        </Button>
    </Grid>
</Page>
```

You should now see your page render at the upper part of the Kaxaml editor (see Figure 27-13).

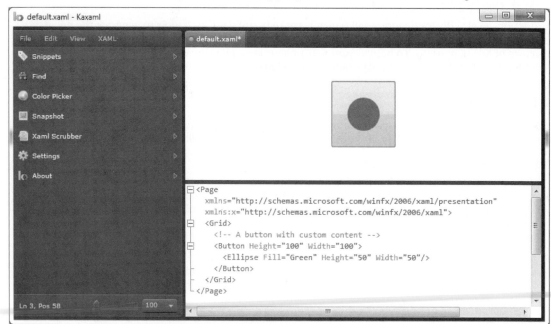

Figure 27-13. Kaxaml is a very helpful (and free) tool used to learn the grammar of XAML

As you work with Kaxaml, remember that this tool does not allow you to author any markup that entails code compilation (however, using x:Name is allowed). This includes defining a x:Class attribute (for specifying a code file), entering event handler names in markup, or using any XAML keywords that also entail code compilation (such as FieldModifier or ClassModifier). Any attempt to do so will result in a markup error.

XAML XML Namespaces and XAML "Keywords"

The root element of a WPF XAML document (such as a <Window>, <Page>, <UserControl>, or <Application> definition) will almost always make reference to the following two predefined XML namespaces:

```
<Page
  xmlns="http://schemas.microsoft.com/winfx/2006/xaml/presentation"
  xmlns:x="http://schemas.microsoft.com/winfx/2006/xaml">
  <Grid>

  </Grid>
</Page>
```

The first XML namespace, http://schemas.microsoft.com/winfx/2006/xaml/presentation, maps a slew of WPF .NET namespaces for use by the current *.xaml file (System.Windows,

System.Windows.Controls, System.Windows.Data, System.Windows.Ink, System.Windows.Media, System.Windows.Navigation, etc.).

This one-to-many mapping is actually hard-coded within the WPF assemblies (WindowsBase.dll, PresentationCore.dll, and PresentationFramework.dll) using the assembly-level [XmlnsDefinition] attribute. For example, in you were to open the Visual Studio object browser and select the PresentationCore.dll assembly, you would see listings such as the following, which essentially imports System.Windows:

```
[assembly: XmlnsDefinition("http://schemas.microsoft.com/winfx/2006/xaml/presentation",
                           "System.Windows")]
```

The second XML namespace, http://schemas.microsoft.com/winfx/2006/xaml, is used to include XAML-specific "keywords" (for lack of a better term) as well as the inclusion of the System.Windows.Markup namespace, as follows:

```
[assembly: XmlnsDefinition("http://schemas.microsoft.com/winfx/2006/xaml",
                           "System.Windows.Markup")]
```

One rule of any well-formed XML document (remember, XAML is an XML-based grammar) is that the opening root element designates one XML namespace as the *primary namespace*, which typically is the namespace that contains the most commonly used items. If a root element requires the inclusion of additional secondary namespaces (as seen here), they must be defined using a unique tag prefix (to resolve any possible name clashes). As a convention, the prefix is simply x; however, this can be any unique token you require, such as XamlSpecificStuff.

```
<Page
  xmlns="http://schemas.microsoft.com/winfx/2006/xaml/presentation"
  xmlns:XamlSpecificStuff="http://schemas.microsoft.com/winfx/2006/xaml">
  <Grid>
    <!-- A button with custom content -->
    <Button XamlSpecificStuff:Name="button1" Height="100" Width="100">
      <Ellipse Fill="Green" Height="50" Width="50"/>
    </Button>
  </Grid>
</Page>
```

The obvious downside of defining wordy XML namespace prefixes is you would be required to type XamlSpecificStuff each time your XAML file needs to refer to one of the items defined within this XAML-centric XML namespace. Given that XamlSpecificStuff requires many additional keystrokes, just stick with x.

In any case, beyond the x:Name, x:Class and x:Code keywords, the http://schemas.microsoft.com/winfx/2006/xaml XML namespace also provides access to additional XAML keywords, the most common of which are shown in Table 27-9.

Table 27-9. XAML Keywords

XAML Keyword	Meaning in Life
x:Array	Represents a .NET array type in XAML.
x:ClassModifier	Allows you to define the visibility of the C# class (internal or public) denoted by the Class keyword.
x:FieldModifier	Allows you to define the visibility of a type member (internal, public, private, or protected) for any named subelement of the root (e.g., a <Button> within a <Window> element). A *named element* is defined using the Name XAML keyword.
x:Key	Allows you to establish a key value for a XAML item that will be placed into a dictionary element.
x:Name	Allows you to specify the generated C# name of a given XAML element.
x:Null	Represents a null reference.
x:Static	Allows you to make reference to a static member of a type.
x:Type	The XAML equivalent of the C# typeof operator (it will yield a System.Type based on the supplied name).
x:TypeArguments	Allows you to establish an element as a generic type with a specific type parameter (e.g., List<int> vs. List<bool>).

In addition to these two necessary XML namespace declarations, it is possible, and sometimes necessary, to define additional tag prefixes in the opening element of a XAML document. You will typically do so whenever you need to describe in XAML a .NET class defined in an external assembly.

For example, say you have built a few custom WPF controls and packaged them in a library named MyControls.dll. Now, if you would like to create a new Window that uses these controls, you can establish a custom XML namespace that maps to your library using the clr-namespace and assembly tokens. Here is some example markup that creates a tag prefix named myCtrls, which can be used to access controls in your library:

```
<Window x:Class="WpfApplication1.MainWindow"
  xmlns="http://schemas.microsoft.com/winfx/2006/xaml/presentation"
  xmlns:x="http://schemas.microsoft.com/winfx/2006/xaml"
  xmlns:myCtrls="clr-namespace:MyControls;assembly=MyControls"
  Title="MainWindow" Height="350" Width="525">
  <Grid>
    <myCtrls:MyCustomControl />
  </Grid>
</Window>
```

The `clr-namespace` token is assigned to the name of the .NET namespace in the assembly, while the assembly token is set to the friendly name of the external `*.dll` assembly. You can use this syntax for any external .NET library you would like to manipulate in markup. While there is no need to do so at the current time, future chapters will require you to define custom XML namespace declarations to describe types in markup.

■ **Note** If you need to define a class in markup that is part of the current assembly, but in a different .NET namespace, your `xmlns` tag prefix is defined without the `assembly=` attribute. For example:

`xmlns:myCtrls="clr-namespace:SomeNamespaceInMyApp"`

Controlling Class and Member Variable Visibility

You will see many of these keywords in action where required in the chapters to come; however, by way of a simple example, consider the following XAML `<Window>` definition that makes use of the `ClassModifier` and `FieldModifier` keywords, as well as `x:Name` and `x:Class` (remember that kaxaml.exe will not allow you to make use of any XAML keyword that entails code compilation, such as `x:Code`, `x:FieldModifier`, or `x:ClassModifier`):

```
<!-- This class will now be declared internal in the *.g.cs file -->
<Window x:Class="MyWPFApp.MainWindow" x:ClassModifier ="internal"
    xmlns="http://schemas.microsoft.com/winfx/2006/xaml/presentation"
    xmlns:x="http://schemas.microsoft.com/winfx/2006/xaml">

  <!-- This button will be public in the *.g.cs file -->
  <Button x:Name ="myButton" x:FieldModifier ="public" Content = "OK"/>
</Window>
```

By default, all C#/XAML type definitions are public, while members default to internal. However, based on your XAML definition, the resulting autogenerated file contains an internal class type with a public Button variable.

```
internal partial class MainWindow : System.Windows.Window,
  System.Windows.Markup.IComponentConnector
{
  public System.Windows.Controls.Button myButton;
  ...
}
```

XAML Elements, XAML Attributes, and Type Converters

After you have established your root element and any required XML namespaces, your next task is to populate the root with a *child element*. In a real-world WPF application, the child will be a layout manager (such as a Grid or StackPanel) that contains, in turn, any number of additional UI elements that describe the user interface. The next chapter examines these layout managers in detail, so for now just assume that your `<Window>` type will contain a single Button element.

As you have already seen over the course of this chapter, XAML *elements* map to a class or structure type within a given .NET namespace, while the *attributes* within the opening element tag map to properties or events of the type. To illustrate, enter the following <Button> definition into Kaxaml:

```
<Page
  xmlns="http://schemas.microsoft.com/winfx/2006/xaml/presentation"
  xmlns:x="http://schemas.microsoft.com/winfx/2006/xaml">
  <Grid>
    <!-- Configure the look and feel of a Button -->
    <Button Height="50" Width="100" Content="OK!"
            FontSize="20" Background="Green" Foreground="Yellow"/>
  </Grid>
</Page>
```

Notice that the values assigned to each property have been captured as a simple text value. This may seem like a complete mismatch of data types because if you were to make this Button in C# code, you would *not* assign string objects to these properties but would make use of specific data types. For example, here is the same button authored in code:

```
public void MakeAButton()
{
  Button myBtn = new Button();
  myBtn.Height = 50;
  myBtn.Width = 100;
  myBtn.FontSize = 20;
  myBtn.Content = "OK!";
  myBtn.Background = new SolidColorBrush(Colors.Green);
  myBtn.Foreground = new SolidColorBrush(Colors.Yellow);
}
```

As it turns out, WPF ships with a number of *type converter* classes, which will be used to transform simple text values into the correct underlying data type. This process happens transparently (and automatically).

While this is all well and good, there will be many times when you need to assign a much more complex value to a XAML attribute, which cannot be captured as a simple string. For example, let's say you want to build a custom brush to set the Background property of the Button. If you are building the brush in code, it is quite straightforward, as seen here:

```
public void MakeAButton()
{
...
  // A fancy brush for the background.
  LinearGradientBrush fancyBruch =
    new LinearGradientBrush(Colors.DarkGreen, Colors.LightGreen, 45);
  myBtn.Background = fancyBruch;
  myBtn.Foreground = new SolidColorBrush(Colors.Yellow);
}
```

How, however, can you represent your complex brush as a string? Well, you can't! Thankfully, XAML provides a special syntax that can be used whenever you need to assign a property value to a complex object, termed *property-element syntax*.

Understanding XAML Property-Element Syntax

Property-element syntax allows you to assign complex objects to a property. Here is a XAML description for a Button that makes use of a LinearGradientBrush to set its Background property:

```
<Button Height="50" Width="100" Content="OK!"
        FontSize="20" Foreground="Yellow">
  <Button.Background>
    <LinearGradientBrush>
      <GradientStop Color="DarkGreen" Offset="0"/>
      <GradientStop Color="LightGreen" Offset="1"/>
    </LinearGradientBrush>
  </Button.Background>
</Button>
```

Notice that within the scope of the <Button> and </Button> tags, you have defined a subscope named <Button.Background>. Within this scope, you have defined a custom <LinearGradientBrush>. (Don't worry about the exact code for the brush; you'll learn about WPF graphics in Chapter 29.)

Generally speaking, any property can be set using property-element syntax, that always breaks down to the following pattern:

```
<DefiningClass>
  <DefiningClass.PropertyOnDefiningClass>
    <!-- Value for Property here! -->
  </DefiningClass.PropertyOnDefiningClass>
</DefiningClass>
```

While any property *could* be set using this syntax, if you can capture a value as a simple string, you will save yourself typing time. For example, here would be a much more verbose way to set the Width of your Button:

```
<Button Height="50" Content="OK!"
        FontSize="20" Foreground="Yellow">
...
  <Button.Width>
    100
  </Button.Width>
</Button>
```

Understanding XAML Attached Properties

In addition to property-element syntax, XAML defines a special syntax used to set a value to an *attached property*. Essentially, an attached property allows a child element to set the value for a property that is actually defined in a parent element. The general template to follow looks like this:

```
<ParentElement>
  <ChildElement ParentElement.PropertyOnParent = "Value">
</ParentElement>
```

The most common use of attached property syntax is to position UI elements within one of the WPF layout manager classes (Grid, DockPanel, etc.). The next chapter dives into these panels in some detail; for now, enter the following in Kaxaml:

```
<Page
  xmlns="http://schemas.microsoft.com/winfx/2006/xaml/presentation"
  xmlns:x="http://schemas.microsoft.com/winfx/2006/xaml">
  <Canvas Height="200" Width="200" Background="LightBlue">
    <Ellipse Canvas.Top="40" Canvas.Left="40" Height="20" Width="20" Fill="DarkBlue"/>
  </Canvas>
</Page>
```

Here, you have defined a Canvas layout manager that contains an Ellipse. Notice that the Ellipse is able to inform its parent (the Canvas) where to position its top/left position using attached property syntax.

There are a few items to be aware of regarding attached properties. First and foremost, this is not an all-purpose syntax that can be applied to *any* property of *any* parent. For example, the following XAML cannot be parsed without error:

```
<!-- Error! Set Background property on Canvas via attached property? -->
<Canvas Height="200" Width="200">
  <Ellipse Canvas.Background="LightBlue"
           Canvas.Top="40" Canvas.Left="90"
           Height="20" Width="20" Fill="DarkBlue"/>
</Canvas>
```

In reality, attached properties are a specialized form of a WPF-specific concept termed a *dependency property*. Unless a property was implemented in a very specific manner, you cannot set its value using attached property syntax. You will explore dependency properties in a detail in Chapter 31.

■ **Note** Kaxaml, Visual Studio, and Expression Blend all have IntelliSense, which will show you valid attached properties that can be set by a given element.

Understanding XAML Markup Extensions

As explained, property values are most often represented using a simple string or via property-element syntax. There is, however, another way to specify the value of a XAML attribute, using *markup extensions*. Markup extensions allow a XAML parser to obtain the value for a property from a dedicated, external class. This can be very beneficial, given that some property values require a number of code statements to execute to figure out the value.

Markup extensions provide a way to cleanly extend the grammar of XAML with new functionality. A markup extension is represented internally as a class that derives from MarkupExtension. Note that the chances of your ever needing to build a custom markup extension will be slim to none. However, a subset of XAML keywords (such as x:Array, x:Null, x:Static, and x:Type) are markup extensions in disguise!

A markup extension is sandwiched between curly brackets, like so:

```
<Element PropertyToSet = "{MarkUpExtension}"/>
```

To see some markup extensions in action, author the following into Kaxaml:

```
<Page
  xmlns="http://schemas.microsoft.com/winfx/2006/xaml/presentation"
  xmlns:x="http://schemas.microsoft.com/winfx/2006/xaml"
  xmlns:CorLib="clr-namespace:System;assembly=mscorlib">

  <StackPanel>
    <!-- The Static markup extension lets us obtain a value
         from a static member of a class -->
    <Label Content ="{x:Static CorLib:Environment.OSVersion}"/>
    <Label Content ="{x:Static CorLib:Environment.ProcessorCount}"/>

    <!-- The Type markup extension is a XAML verion of
         the C# typeof operator -->
    <Label Content ="{x:Type Button}" />
    <Label Content ="{x:Type CorLib:Boolean}" />

    <!-- Fill a ListBox with an array of strings! -->
    <ListBox Width="200" Height="50">
      <ListBox.ItemsSource>
        <x:Array Type="CorLib:String">
          <CorLib:String>Sun Kil Moon</CorLib:String>
          <CorLib:String>Red House Painters</CorLib:String>
          <CorLib:String>Besnard Lakes</CorLib:String>
        </x:Array>
      </ListBox.ItemsSource>
    </ListBox>
  </StackPanel>
</Page>
```

First, notice that the <Page> definition has a new XML namespace declaration, which allows you to gain access to the System namespace of mscorlib.dll. With this XML namespace established, you first make use of the x:Static markup extension and grab values from OSVersion and ProcessorCount of the System.Environment class.

The x:Type markup extension allows you to gain access to the metadata description of the specified item. Here, you are simply assigning the fully qualified names of the WPF Button and System.Boolean types.

The most interesting part of this markup is the ListBox. Here, you are setting the ItemsSource property to an array of strings declared entirely in markup! Notice here how the x:Array markup extension allows you to specify a set of subitems within its scope:

```
<x:Array Type="CorLib:String">
  <CorLib:String>Sun Kil Moon</CorLib:String>
  <CorLib:String>Red House Painters</CorLib:String>
  <CorLib:String>Besnard Lakes</CorLib:String>
</x:Array>
```

■ **Note** The previous XAML example is only used to illustrate a markup extension in action. As you will see in Chapter 28, there are much easier ways to populate ListBox controls!

Figure 27-14 shows the mark up of this <Page> in Kaxaml.

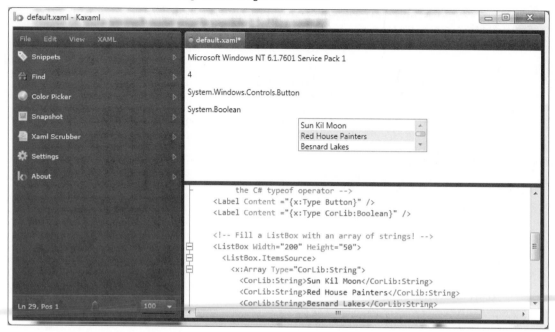

Figure 27-14. Markup extensions allow you to set values via the functionality of a dedicated class

You have now seen numerous examples that showcase each of the core aspects of XAML syntax. As you might agree, XAML is very interesting in that it allows you to describe a tree of .NET objects in a declarative manner. While this is extremely helpful when configuring graphical user interfaces, do remember that XAML can describe *any* type from *any* assembly, provided it is a nonabstract type containing a default constructor.

Building a WPF Application Using Code-Behind Files

The first two examples of this chapter illustrated the extreme ends of building a WPF application, using all code or using all XAML. The recommended way to build any WPF application, however, is to use the *code file* approach. Under this model, the XAML files of your project contain nothing but the markup that describes the general state of your classes, while the code file contains the implementation details.

Adding a Code File for the MainWindow Class

To illustrate, you will update the WpfAppAllXaml example to use code files. If you are following along, copy this entire folder and give it the name WpfAppCodeFiles. Now, create a new C# code file in this folder named MainWindow.xaml.cs (by convention, the name of a C# code-behind file takes the form *.xaml.cs). Add the following code to this new file:

```csharp
// MainWindow.xaml.cs
using System;
using System.Windows;
using System.Windows.Controls;

namespace WpfAppAllXaml
{
  public partial class MainWindow : Window
  {
    public MainWindow()
    {
      // Remember! This method is defined
      // within the generated MainWindow.g.cs file.
      InitializeComponent();
    }

    private void btnExitApp_Clicked(object sender, RoutedEventArgs e)
    {
      this.Close();
    }
  }
}
```

Here, you have defined a partial class to contain the event-handling logic that will be merged with the partial class definition of the same type in the *.g.cs file. Given that InitializeComponent() is defined within the MainWindow.g.cs file, your window's constructor makes a call in order to load and process the embedded BAML resource.

The MainWindow.xaml file will also need to be updated; this simply involves gutting all traces of the previous C# code.

```xml
<Window x:Class="WpfAppAllXaml.MainWindow"
  xmlns="http://schemas.microsoft.com/winfx/2006/xaml/presentation"
  xmlns:x="http://schemas.microsoft.com/winfx/2006/xaml"
  Title="A Window built using Code Files!"
  Height="200" Width="300"
  WindowStartupLocation ="CenterScreen">

  <!-- The event handler is now in your code file -->
  <Button x:Name="btnExitApp" Width="133" Height="24"
          Content = "Close Window" Click ="btnExitApp_Clicked"/>
</Window>
```

Adding a Code File for the MyApp Class

If desired, you could also build a code-behind file for your Application-derived type. Because most of the action takes place in the MyApp.g.cs file, the code within MyApp.xaml.cs is little more than the following:

```csharp
// MyApp.xaml.cs
using System;
using System.Windows;
using System.Windows.Controls;
```

```
namespace WpfAppAllXaml
{
  public partial class MyApp : Application
  {
    private void AppExit(object sender, ExitEventArgs e)
    {
      MessageBox.Show("App has exited");
    }
  }
}
```

The MyApp.xaml file now looks like so:

```
<Application x:Class="WpfAppAllXaml.MyApp"
  xmlns="http://schemas.microsoft.com/winfx/2006/xaml/presentation"
  xmlns:x="http://schemas.microsoft.com/winfx/2006/xaml"
  StartupUri="MainWindow.xaml"
  Exit ="AppExit">
</Application>
```

Processing the Code Files with msbuild.exe

Before you recompile your files using msbuild.exe, we need to update our *.csproj file to account for the new C# files to include in the compilation process, via the <Compile> elements (shown here in bold):

```
<Project DefaultTargets="Build" xmlns=
  "http://schemas.microsoft.com/developer/msbuild/2003">
  <PropertyGroup>
    <RootNamespace>WpfAppAllXaml</RootNamespace>
    <AssemblyName>WpfAppAllXaml</AssemblyName>
    <OutputType>winexe</OutputType>
  </PropertyGroup>
  <ItemGroup>
    <Reference Include="System" />
    <Reference Include="WindowsBase" />
    <Reference Include="PresentationCore" />
    <Reference Include="PresentationFramework" />
  </ItemGroup>
  <ItemGroup>
    <ApplicationDefinition Include="MyApp.xaml" />
    <Compile Include = "MainWindow.xaml.cs" />
    <Compile Include = "MyApp.xaml.cs" />
    <Page Include="MainWindow.xaml" />
  </ItemGroup>
  <Import Project="$(MSBuildBinPath)\Microsoft.CSharp.targets" />
  <Import Project="$(MSBuildBinPath)\Microsoft.WinFX.targets" />
</Project>
```

Once you pass the build script into msbuild.exe:

```
msbuild WpfAppAllXaml.csproj
```

you find, once again, the same executable assembly as the WpfAppAllXaml application (located in the bin\Debug folder, remember?). However, as far as development is concerned, you now have a clean partition of presentation (XAML) from programming logic (C#).

Given that this is the preferred method for WPF development, you'll be happy to know that WPF applications created using Visual Studio (or Expression Blend) always make use of the code-behind model just presented.

■ **Source Code** The WpfAppCodeFiles project can be found under the Chapter 27 subdirectory.

Building WPF Applications Using Visual Studio

Over the course of this chapter you created examples using no-frills text editors, the command-line compiler, and Kaxaml. The reason for doing so, of course, was to focus on the core syntax of WPF applications without getting distracted by the bells and whistles of a graphical designer. Now that you have seen how to build WPF applications from the ground up, let's examine how Visual Studio can simplify the construction of WPF programs.

■ **Note** Here, I will point out some key features of using Visual Studio to build WPF applications. Forthcoming chapters will illustrate additional aspects of the IDE where necessary.

The WPF Project Templates

The New Project dialog box of Visual Studio defines a set of WPF project workspaces, all of which are contained under the Window node of the Visual C# root. Here, you can choose from a WPF Application, WPF User Control Library, WPF Custom Control Library, and WPF Browser Application (i.e., XBAP). To begin, create a new WPF Application named WpfTesterApp (see Figure 27-15).

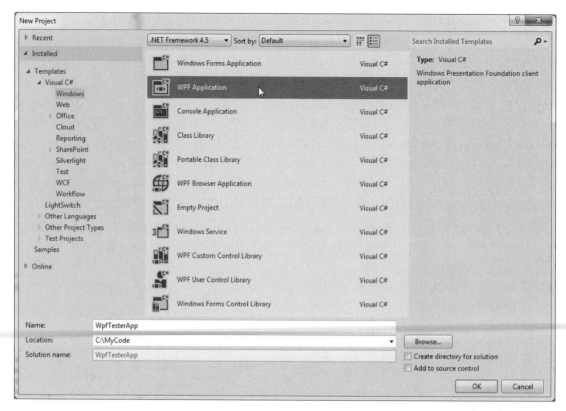

Figure 27-15. *The WPF project templates of Visual Studio can be found under the Windows node*

Beyond setting references to each of the WPF assemblies (PresentationCore.dll, PresentationFramework.dll, System.Xaml.dll, and WindowsBase.dll), you will also be provided with initial Window and Application derived classes, each represented using a XAML and C# code file. Consider Figure 27-16, which shows the Solution Explorer for this new WPF project.

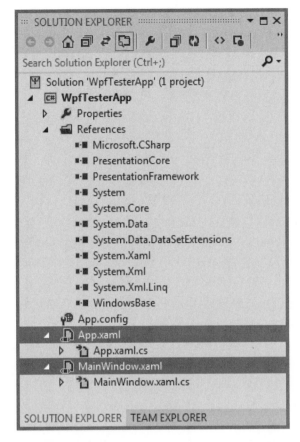

Figure 27-16. The initial files of a WPF Application project

The Toolbox and XAML Designer/Editor

Visual Studio provides a Toolbox (which you can open via the View menu) that contains numerous WPF controls (see Figure 27-17).

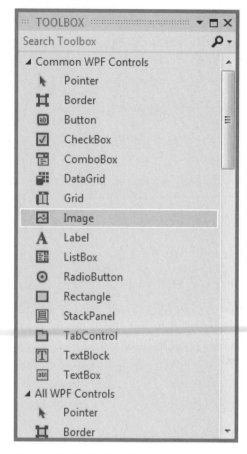

Figure 27-17. The Toolbox contains the WPF controls that can be placed on the designer surface

Using a standard mouse drag-and-drop operation, you can place any of these controls onto the Window's designer surface or drag the control into the XAML markup editor at the bottom of the designer. When you do, the initial XAML will be authored on your behalf. Use your mouse to drag a Button and Calendar control onto the designer surface. After you have done so, notice how you can relocate and resize your controls (and be sure to examine the resulting XAML generated based on your edits).

In addition to building the UI via the mouse and Toolbox, you can also manually enter your markup using the integrated XAML editor. As you can see in Figure 27-18, you do get IntelliSense support, which can help simplify the authoring of the markup. For example, try to add the Background property to the opening <Window> element.

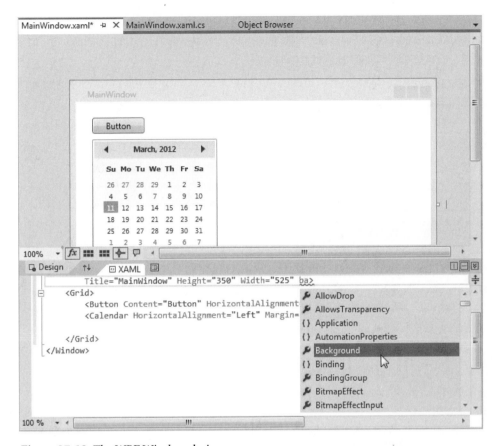

Figure 27-18. *The WPF Window designer*

Take a few moments to add some property values directly in the XAML editor. Be sure you take the time to become comfortable using this aspect of the WPF designer.

Setting Properties Using the Properties Window

After you have placed some controls onto your designer (or manually defined them in the editor), you can then make use of the Properties window to set property values for the selected control, as well as rig up event handlers for the selected control. By way of a simple test, select your Button control on the designer. Now, use the Properties window to change the Background color of the Button using the integrated brush editor (see Figure 27-19; you will learn more about the Brushes editor in Chapter 29, during our examination of WPF graphics).

■ **Note** The Properties window provides a Search text area mounted on the very top. Type in the name of a property you would like to set to quickly find the item in question.

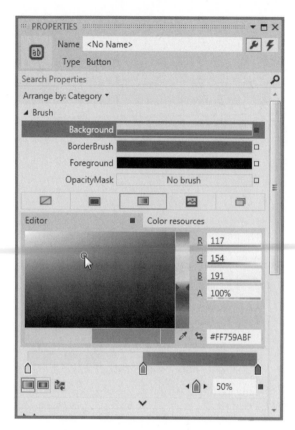

Figure 27-19. The Properties window can be used to configure the UI of a WPF control

After you have finished tinkering with the brush editor, check out the generated markup. It might look something like this:

```
<Button Content="Button" Height="23" HorizontalAlignment="Left" Margin="12,12,0,0"
        Name="button1" VerticalAlignment="Top" Width="75">
  <Button.Background>
    <LinearGradientBrush EndPoint="1,0.5" StartPoint="0,0.5">
      <GradientStop Color="#FF7488CE" Offset="0" />
      <GradientStop Color="#FFC11E1E" Offset="0.837" />
    </LinearGradientBrush>
  </Button.Background>
</Button>
```

Handling Events Using the Properties Window

If you want to handle events for a given control, you can also make use of the Properties window, but this time you need to click on the Events button on the upper right of the Properties window (look for the lightning bolt icon). Ensure that the button is selected on your designer, click on the Events tab, and locate the Click event. Once you do, double-click directly on the Click event entry. This will cause Visual Studio to automatically build an event handler that takes the following general form:

NameOfControl_NameOfEvent

Since you did not rename your button, the Properties window shows it generated an event handler named Button_Click_1 (see Figure 27-20).

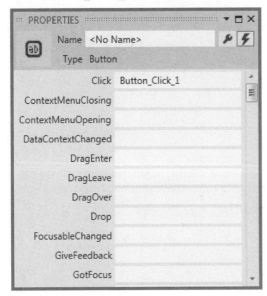

Figure 27-20. *Handling events using the Properties window*

As well, Visual Studio generated the corresponding C# event handler in your window's code file. Here, you can add any sort of code that must execute when the button is clicked. For a quick test, just enter the following code statement:

```
public partial class MainWindow : Window
{
  public MainWindow()
  {
    InitializeComponent();
  }

  private void Button_Click_1(object sender, RoutedEventArgs e)
  {
    MessageBox.Show("You clicked the button!");
  }
}
```

Handling Events in the XAML Editor

You can also handle events directly in the XAML editor. By way of an example, place your mouse within the <Window> element and type in the MouseMove event, followed by the equals sign. Once you do, you will see that Visual Studio displays any compatible handlers in your code file (if they exist), as well as the <New Event Handler> option (see Figure 27-21).

Figure 27-21. *Handling events using the XAML editor*

If you double-click <New Event Handler>, the IDE will generate a fitting handler in your C# code file. Enter the following code in your MouseMove event handler, then run the application to see the end result:

```
private void Window_MouseMove (object sender, MouseEventArgs e)
{
    this.Title = e.GetPosition(this).ToString();
}
```

The Document Outline Window

When you are working with any XAML-based project (WPF, Silverlight, Windows Phone 7, or a Windows 8 Application), you will certainly make use of a healthy amount of markup to represent your UIs. When you begin to work with more complex XAML, it can be useful to visualize the markup in order to quickly select an item to edit on the Visual Studio designer.

Currently, our markup is quite tame, as we have only defined a few controls within the initial <Grid>. Nevertheless, locate the Documents Outline window in your IDE, mounted by default on the lower left of the IDE (if you cannot locate it, simply activate it using the View ▸ Other Windows menu option). Now, make sure your XAML designer is the active window in the IDE (rather than a C# code file), and you will notice the Document Outline displays the nested elements (see Figure 27-22).

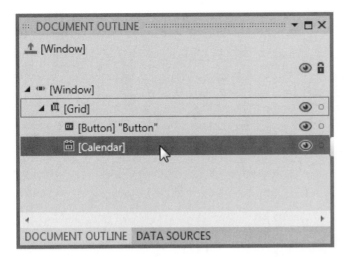

Figure 27-22. *Visualizing your XAML via the Document Outline window*

This tool also provides a way to temporarily hide a given item (or set of items) on the designer as well as lock items to prevent additional edits from taking place. In the next chapter, you will see how the Document Outline window also provides many other features to group selected items into new layout managers (among other features).

Viewing the AutoGenerated Code Files

Before building the last example of this chapter, locate the Solution Explorer window, and click on the Show All Files button (seen in Figure 27-23). Notice that the BAML and *.g.cs files are present and accounted for (in the obj\Debug folder). While it is never advised that you would add your own code to these autogenerated files, the previous examples of the chapter should have helped clarify exactly how your XAML is processed.

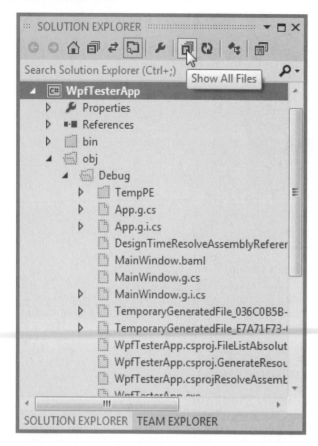

Figure 27-23. Viewing the output files of a WPF project using Solution Explorer

Building a Custom XAML Editor with Visual Studio

Now that you have seen the basic tools used within Visual Studio to design a WPF window, our final example of this chapter will walk you through how to build an application that will allow you to manipulate XAML at runtime. Close down your current project, and create a fresh WPF Application named MyXamlPad. This project (when finished) will function similar to Kaxaml without the bells and whistles. Specifically, this application will allow you to type in any well-formed markup, and click a button to dynamically render the XAML into a new Window object.

Designing the GUI of Our Window

The WPF API supports the ability to load, parse, and save XAML descriptions programmatically. Doing so can be quite useful in a variety of situations. For example, assume you have five different XAML files that describe the look and feel of a Window type. As long as the names of each control (and any necessary event handlers) are identical within each file, it would be possible to dynamically apply "skins" to the window (perhaps based on a startup argument passed into the application).

Interacting with XAML at runtime revolves around the XamlReader and XamlWriter types, both of which are defined within the System.Windows.Markup namespace. To illustrate how to programmatically hydrate a Window object from an external *.xaml file, you will build an application that mimics the basic functionality of the Kaxaml.

■ **Note** The XamlReader and XamlWriter classes provide basic functionality to manipulate XAML at runtime. If you ever have a need to gain full control over the XAML object model, you will want to explore the System.Xaml.dll assembly.

While your application will certainly not be as feature-rich as Kaxaml, it will provide the ability to enter valid XAML markup, view the results, and save the XAML to an external file. To begin, update the initial XAML definition of your <Window> as shown next (I'd suggest perhaps just manually typing the XAML at this point; however, use the IDE to generate event handlers as shown previously).

■ **Note** The next chapter will dive into the details of working with controls and panels, so don't fret over the details of the control declarations.

```
<Window x:Class="MyXamlPad.MainWindow"
  xmlns="http://schemas.microsoft.com/winfx/2006/xaml/presentation"
  xmlns:x="http://schemas.microsoft.com/winfx/2006/xaml"
  Title="My Custom XAML Editor"
  Height="338" Width="1041"
  Loaded="Window_Loaded" Closed="Window_Closed"
  WindowStartupLocation="CenterScreen">

  <!-- You will use a DockPanel, not a Grid -->
  <DockPanel LastChildFill="True" >

    <!-- This button will launch a window with defined XAML -->
    <Button DockPanel.Dock="Top" Name = "btnViewXaml" Width="100" Height="40"
            Content ="View Xaml" Click="btnViewXaml_Click" />

    <!-- This will be the area to type within -->
    <TextBox AcceptsReturn ="True" Name ="txtXamlData"
            FontSize ="14" Background="Black" Foreground="Yellow"
            BorderBrush ="Blue" VerticalScrollBarVisibility="Auto"
            AcceptsTab="True"/>
  </DockPanel>
</Window>
```

First, notice that you have replaced the initial <Grid> with a <DockPanel> layout manager that contains a Button (named btnViewXaml) and a TextBox (named txtXamlData), and that the Click event of the Button type has been handled.

Also notice that the Loaded and Closed events of the Window itself have been handled within the opening <Window> element (again, use the IDE to generate the event handlers as described earlier in this section of the chapter). If you have used the designer to handle your events, you should find the following code in your MainWindow.xaml.cs file:

```
public partial class MainWindow : Window
{
  public MainWindow()
  {
    InitializeComponent();
  }

  private void btnViewXaml_Click(object sender, RoutedEventArgs e)
  {
  }

  private void Window_Closed(object sender, EventArgs e)
  {
  }

  private void Window_Loaded(object sender, RoutedEventArgs e)
  {
  }
}
```

Before continuing, be sure to import the following namespaces into your MainWindow.xaml.cs file:

```
using System.IO;
using System.Windows.Markup;
```

Implementing the Loaded Event

The Loaded event of your main window is in charge of determining whether there is currently a file named YourXaml.xaml in the folder containing the application. If this file does exist, you will read in the data and place it into the TextBox on the main window. If not, you will fill the TextBox with an initial default XAML description of an empty window (this description is the exact same markup as an initial window definition, except that you are using a <StackPanel> rather than a <Grid>).

■ **Note** The string you are building to represent the initial markup to display in your editor is a bit cumbersome to type, given the escape characters required for the embedded quotations, so type carefully.

```
private void Window_Loaded(object sender, RoutedEventArgs e)
{
  // When the main window of the app loads,
  // place some basic XAML text into the text block.
```

```
  if (File.Exists("YourXaml.xaml"))
  {
    txtXamlData.Text = File.ReadAllText("YourXaml.xaml");
  }
  else
  {
    txtXamlData.Text =
    "<Window xmlns=\"http://schemas.microsoft.com/winfx/2006/xaml/presentation\"\n"
    +"xmlns:x=\"http://schemas.microsoft.com/winfx/2006/xaml\"\n"
    +"Height =\"400\" Width =\"500\" WindowStartupLocation=\"CenterScreen\">\n"
    +"<StackPanel>\n"
    +"</StackPanel>\n"
    +"</Window>";
  }
}
```

Using this approach, your application will be able to load the XAML entered in a previous session or supply a default block of markup if necessary. At this point, you should be able to run your program and find the display shown in Figure 27-24 within the TextBox type.

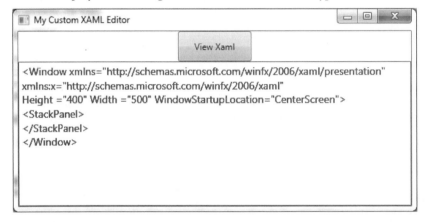

Figure 27-24. The first run of MyXamlPad.exe

Implementing the Button's Click Event

When you click the Button, you will first save the current data in the TextBox into the YourXaml.xaml file. At this point, you will read in the persisted data via File.Open() to obtain a FileStream. This is necessary, as the XamlReader.Load() method requires a Stream-derived type (rather than a simple System.String) to represent the XAML to be parsed.

After you have loaded the XAML description of the <Window> you would like to construct, create an instance of System.Windows.Window based on the in-memory XAML and display the Window as a modal dialog, like so:

```
private void btnViewXaml_Click(object sender, RoutedEventArgs e)
{
  // Write out the data in the text block to a local *.xaml file.
  File.WriteAllText("YourXaml.xaml", txtXamlData.Text);
```

```
// This is the window that will be dynamically XAML-ed.
Window myWindow = null;
// Open local *.xaml file.
try
{
  using (Stream sr = File.Open("YourXaml.xaml", FileMode.Open))
  {
    // Connect the XAML to the Window object.
    myWindow = (Window)XamlReader.Load(sr);

    // Show window as a dialog and clean up.
    myWindow.ShowDialog();
    myWindow.Close();
    myWindow = null;

  }
}
catch (Exception ex)
{
  MessageBox.Show(ex.Message);
}
}
```

Note that you are wrapping much of our logic within a try/catch block. In this way, if the
YourXaml.xaml file contains ill-formed markup, you can see the error of your ways within the resulting
message box. For example, run your program, and purposely misspell <StackPanel> by adding an extra
letter P in the opening element or whatnot. If you click the button, you will see an error similar to
Figure 27-25.

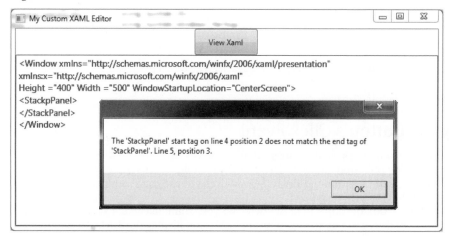

Figure 27-25. Catching markup errors

Implementing the Closed Event

Finally, the Closed event of your Window type will ensure that the latest and greatest data in the TextBox is persisted to the YourXaml.xaml file.

```
private void Window_Closed(object sender, EventArgs e)
{
  // Write out the data in the text block to a local *.xaml file.
  File.WriteAllText("YourXaml.xaml", txtXamlData.Text);
  Application.Current.Shutdown();
}
```

Testing Your Application

Now fire up your program and enter some XAML into your text area. Do be aware that (like Kaxaml) this program does not allow you to specify any code generation–centric XAML attributes (such as Class or any event handlers). As a first test, enter the following XAML within your <StackPanel> scope:

```
<Button Height = "100" Width = "100" Content = "Click Me!">
  <Button.Background>
    <LinearGradientBrush StartPoint = "0,0" EndPoint = "1,1">
      <GradientStop Color = "Blue" Offset = "0" />
      <GradientStop Color = "Yellow" Offset = "0.25" />
      <GradientStop Color = "Green" Offset = "0.75" />
      <GradientStop Color = "Pink" Offset = "0.50" />
    </LinearGradientBrush>
  </Button.Background>
</Button>
```

When you click the button, you will see a window appear that renders your XAML definitions (or possibly you'll see a parsing error in the message box—watch your typing!). Figure 27-26 shows possible output.

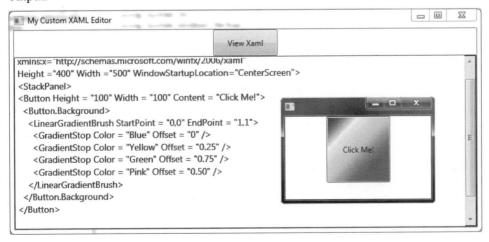

Figure 27-26. MyXamlPad.exe in action

Now, enter the following XAML markup directly after the current `<Button>` definition:

```
<Label Content = "Interesting...">
  <Label.Triggers>
    <EventTrigger RoutedEvent = "Label.Loaded">
      <EventTrigger.Actions>
        <BeginStoryboard>
          <Storyboard TargetProperty = "FontSize">
            <DoubleAnimation From = "12" To = "100" Duration = "0:0:4"
              RepeatBehavior = "Forever"/>
          </Storyboard>
        </BeginStoryboard>
      </EventTrigger.Actions>
    </EventTrigger>
  </Label.Triggers>
</Label>
```

This markup is a great example of how powerful XAML really is. When you test this markup, you'll notice you have created a simple animation sequence. Animation services (as well as graphical renderings) will be examined in detail in upcoming chapters; however, feel free to tweak the XAML and see the end result.

Exploring the WPF Documentation

To close this chapter, I want to point out that the .NET 4.5 Framework SDK documentation provides an entire section devoted to the topic of WPF. As you explore this API and read over the remaining WPF-centric chapters, you will do yourself a great service if you consult the help system early and often. Here, you will find a huge amount of sample XAML, detailed tutorials on a wide variety of topics ranging from 3D graphics programing to complex data binding operations.

The WPF documentation is located under the .NET Framework 4.5 ➤ .NET Framework Development Guide ➤ Developing Client Applications path (see Figure 27-27).

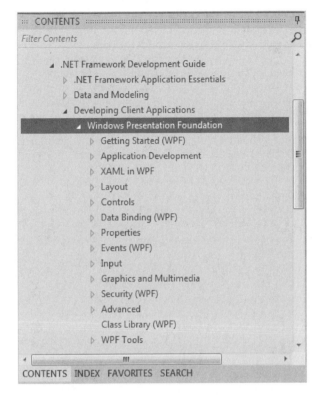

Figure 27-27. The .NET 4.5 Framework SDK documentation provides an extensive WPF help area

As you dig around this part of the help system, you will run into numerous XAML examples you can copy directly to your clipboard and paste into your custom XAML editor. However, you will need to make sure the root element is changed from <Page> to <Window> before testing (our application was not programmed to display Page objects, only full Window objects). Before moving on to the next chapter, take time to dig into topics that interest you and test additional markup in your custom tool.

■ **Source Code** The MyXamlPad project can be found under the Chapter 27 subdirectory.

Summary

Windows Presentation Foundation (WPF) is a user interface toolkit introduced since the release of .NET 3.0. The major goal of WPF is to integrate and unify a number of previously unrelated desktop technologies (2D graphics, 3D graphics, window and control development, etc.) into a single, unified programming model. Beyond this point, WPF programs typically make use of Extendable Application Markup Language (XAML), which allows you to declare the look and feel of your WPF elements via markup.

Recall that XAML allows you to describe trees of .NET objects using a declarative syntax. During this chapter's investigation of XAML, you were exposed to several new bits of syntax, including property-element syntax and attached properties, as well as the role of type converters and XAML markup extensions.

While XAML is a key aspect for any production-level WPF application, your first example of this chapter illustrated how you can build a WPF program using nothing but C# code. Next, you discovered how you could build a WPF program using nothing but XAML (this is not recommended; however, it was a useful learning exercise!). Finally, you learned about the use of "code-behind files," which allow you to partition look-and-feel from functionality.

The final example of this chapter gave you a chance to build a WPF application that allowed you to programmatically interact with XAML definitions using the XamlReader and XamlWriter classes. Along the way, you took a tour of the core WPF designers of Visual Studio. You will learn much more about the WPF designers in upcoming chapters.

CHAPTER 28

Programming with WPF Controls

Chapter 27 provided a foundation for the WPF programming model, including an examination of the Window and Application classes, the grammar of XAML, and the use of code files. Chapter 27 also introduced you to the process of building WPF applications using the designers of Visual Studio. In this chapter, you will dig into the construction of more sophisticated graphical user interfaces using several new controls and layout managers, learning about additional features of the WPF designers of Visual Studio along the way.

This chapter will also examine some important related WPF control topics such as the data-binding programming model and the use of control commands. You will also learn how to use the Ink and Documents APIs, which allow you to capture stylus (or mouse) input and build rich text documents using the XML Paper Specification, respectively.

■ **Note** Previous editions of this text made use of a product named Microsoft Expression Blend to facilitate building GUIs using the WPF API. However, the latest version of Visual Studio provides sufficient functionality to build WPF UIs for the topics examined in this text. If you would like to learn the details of working with Expression Blend, check out my book *Pro Expression Blend 4* (2011, Apress).

A Survey of the Core WPF Controls

Unless you are new to the concept of building graphical user interfaces (which is fine), the general purpose of the major WPF controls should not raise too many issues. Regardless of which GUI toolkit you might have used in the past (e.g., VB 6.0, MFC, Java AWT/Swing, Windows Forms, Mac OS X [Cocoa], or GTK+/GTK# [among others]), the core WPF controls listed in Table 28-1 are likely to look familiar.

Table 28-1. *The Core WPF Controls*

WPF Control Category	Example Members	Meaning in Life
Core user input controls	Button, RadioButton, ComboBox, CheckBox, Calendar, DatePicker, Expander, DataGrid, ListBox, ListView, ToggleButton, TreeView, ContextMenu, ScrollBar, Slider, TabControl, TextBlock, TextBox, RepeatButton, RichTextBox, Label	WPF provides an entire family of controls you can use to build the crux of a user interface.
Window and control adornments	Menu, ToolBar, StatusBar, ToolTip, ProgressBar	You use these UI elements to decorate the frame of a Window object with input devices (such as the Menu) and user informational elements (e.g., StatusBar and ToolTip).
Media controls	Image, MediaElement, SoundPlayerAction	These controls provide support for audio/video playback and image display.
Layout controls	Border, Canvas, DockPanel, Grid, GridView, GridSplitter, GroupBox, Panel, TabControl, StackPanel, Viewbox, WrapPanel	WPF provides numerous controls that allow you to group and organize other controls for the purpose of layout management.

The WPF Ink Controls

In addition to the common WPF controls listed in Table 28-1, WPF defines additional controls for working with the digital Ink API. This aspect of WPF development is useful during Tablet PC development because it lets you capture input from the stylus. However, this is not to say a standard desktop application cannot leverage the Ink API because the same controls can capture input using the mouse.

The System.Windows.Ink namespace of PresentationCore.dll contains various Ink API support types (e.g., Stroke and StrokeCollection); however, a majority of the Ink API controls (e.g., InkCanvas and InkPresenter) are packaged up with the common WPF controls under the System.Windows.Controls namespace in the PresentationFramework.dll assembly. You'll work with the Ink API later in this chapter.

The WPF Document Controls

WPF also provides controls for advanced document processing, allowing you to build applications that incorporate Adobe PDF-style functionality. Using the types within the System.Windows.Documents namespace (also in the PresentationFramework.dll assembly), you can create print-ready documents that support zooming, searching, user annotations (sticky notes), and other rich text services.

Under the covers, however, the document controls do not use Adobe PDF APIs; rather, they use the XML Paper Specification (XPS) API. To the end user, there will really appear to be no difference because PDF documents and XPS documents have an almost identical look-and-feel. In fact, you can find many free utilities that allow you to convert between the two file formats on the fly. You'll work with some aspects of the document controls in an upcoming example.

WPF Common Dialog Boxes

WPF also provides you with a few common dialog boxes such as OpenFileDialog and SaveFileDialog. These dialog boxes are defined within the Microsoft.Win32 namespace of the PresentationFramework.dll assembly. Working with either of these dialog boxes is a matter of creating an object and invoking the ShowDialog() method, like so:

```
using Microsoft.Win32;

namespace WpfControls
{
  public partial class MainWindow : Window
  {
    public MainWindow()
    {
      InitializeComponent();
    }

    private void btnShowDlg_Click(object sender, RoutedEventArgs e)
    {
      // Show a file save dialog.
      SaveFileDialog saveDlg = new SaveFileDialog();
      saveDlg.ShowDialog();
    }
  }
}
```

As you would hope, these classes support various members that allow you to establish file filters and directory paths, and gain access to user-selected files. You will put these file dialogs to use in later examples; you will also learn how to build custom dialog boxes to gather user input.

The Details Are in the Documentation

Despite what you might be thinking, the intent of this chapter is *not* to walk through each and every member of each and every WPF control. Rather, you will receive an overview of the various controls with an emphasis on the underlying programming model and key services common to most WPF controls.

To round out your understanding of the particular functionality of a given control, be sure to consult the .NET Framework 4.5 SDK documentation—specifically, the Control Library section of the help system, which you can find under Windows Presentation Foundation Controls (see Figure 28-1).

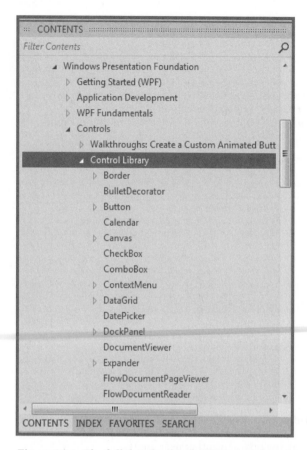

Figure 28-1. The full details of each WPF control are just a keypress away (F1)

Here you will find full details of each control, various code samples (in XAML, as well as C#), and information regarding a control's inheritance chain, implemented interfaces, and applied attributes. Make sure you take time to look up the controls examined in this chapter for complete details.

A Brief Review of the Visual Studio WPF Designer

A majority of these standard WPF controls have been packaged up in the System.Windows.Controls namespace of the PresentationFramework.dll assembly. When you build a WPF application using Visual Studio, you will find most of these common controls contained in the Toolbox, provided you have a WPF designer open as the active window (see Figure 28-2).

Figure 28-2. The Visual Studio Toolbox exposes the many commonly used WPF controls

Similar to other UI frameworks created with Visual Studio, you can drag these controls onto the WPF window designer and configure them using the Properties window (which you learned about in Chapter 27). While Visual Studio will generate a good amount of the XAML on your behalf, it is not uncommon to edit the markup yourself manually. Let's review the basics.

Working with WPF Controls Using Visual Studio

You might recall from Chapter 27 that when you place a WPF control onto the Visual Studio designer, you want to set the x:Name property through the Properties window because this allows you to access the object in your related C# code file. You might also recall that you can use the Events tab of the Properties window to generate event handlers for a selected control. Thus, you could use Visual Studio to generate the following markup for a simple Button control:

```
<Button x:Name="btnMyButton" Content="Click Me!" Height="23" Width="140"
        Click="btnMyButton_Click" />
```

Here, you set the Content property of the Button to a simple string with the value "Click Me!". However, thanks to the WPF control content model, you could fashion a Button that contains the following complex content:

```
<Button x:Name="btnMyButton" Height="121" Width="156" Click="btnMyButton_Click">
  <Button.Content>
    <StackPanel Height="95" Width="128" Orientation="Vertical">
      <Ellipse Fill="Red" Width="52" Height="45" Margin="5"/>
      <Label Width="59" FontSize="20" Content="Click!" Height="36" />
    </StackPanel>
  </Button.Content>
</Button>
```

You might also recall that the immediate child element of a ContentControl-derived class is the implied content; therefore, you do not need to define a <Button.Content> scope explicitly when specifying complex content. You could simply author the following:

```
<Button x:Name="btnMyButton" Height="121" Width="156" Click="btnMyButton_Click">
  <StackPanel Height="95" Width="128" Orientation="Vertical">
    <Ellipse Fill="Red" Width="52" Height="45" Margin="5"/>
    <Label Width="59" FontSize="20" Content="Click!" Height="36" />
  </StackPanel>
</Button>
```

In either case, you set the button's Content property to a <StackPanel> of related items. You can author this sort of complex content using the Visual Studio designer, as well. After you define the layout manager for a content control, you can select it on the designer to serve as a drop target for the internal controls. At this point, you can edit each using the Properties window. If you were to use the Properties window to handle the Click event for the Button control (as seen in the previous XAML declarations), the IDE would generate an empty event handler, to which you could add your own custom code. For example:

```
private void btnMyButton_Click(object sender, RoutedEventArgs e)
{
  MessageBox.Show("You clicked the button!");
}
```

Working with the Document Outline Editor

You should also be aware that the Document Outline window of Visual Studio (which you can open using the View ➤ Other Windows menu) is useful when designing a WPF control that has complex content. Notice in Figure 28-3 how the logical tree of XAML is displayed for the Window you are building. If you click any of these nodes it is automatically selected in the designer for editing.

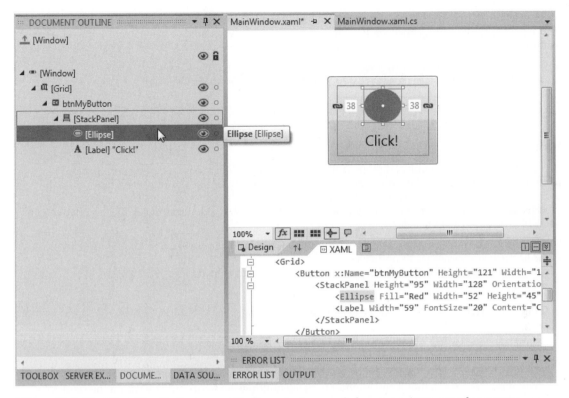

Figure 28-3. *The Visual Studio Document Outline window can help you navigate complex content*

With the current edition of Visual Studio, the Document Outline editor has a few additional features that you might find useful. Notice that to the right of any node you will find an icon that looks similar to an eyeball. When you click toggle this button, you can opt to hide or show an item on the designer, which can be helpful when you want to focus in on a particular segment to edit (note that this will *not* hide the item at runtime; this is only hiding items on the designer surface).

Right next to the "eyeball icon" is a second toggle that allows you to "lock" an item on the designer. As you might guess, this can be very helpful when you want to make sure you (or your coworkers) do not accidently change the XAML for a given item. In effect, locking an item makes it read-only at design time (however, you can obviously change the object's state at runtime).

Controlling Content Layout Using Panels

A WPF application invariably contains a good number of UI elements (e.g., user input controls, graphical content, menu systems, and status bars) that need to be well organized within various windows. After you place the UI elements, you need to make sure they behave as intended when the end user resizes the window or possibly a portion of the window (as in the case of a splitter window). To ensure your WPF controls retain their position within the hosting window, you can take advantage of a good number of *panel types* (also known as *layout managers*).

By default, a new WPF `Window` created with Visual Studio will use a layout manager of type `<Grid>` (more details in just a bit). However, for now, assume a `Window` with no declared layout manager. For example:

```
<Window x:Class="MyWPFApp.MainWindow"
   xmlns="http://schemas.microsoft.com/winfx/2006/xaml/presentation"
   xmlns:x="http://schemas.microsoft.com/winfx/2006/xaml"
...
   Title="Fun with Panels!" Height="285" Width="325">

</Window>
```

When you declare a control directly inside a window that doesn't use panels, the control is positioned dead-center in the container. Consider the following simple window declaration, which contains a single `Button` control. Regardless of how you resize the window, the UI widget is always equidistant from all four sides of the client area. The `Button`'s size is determined by the assigned `Height` and `Width` properties of the `Button`.

```
<!-- This button is in the center of the window at all times -->
<Window x:Class="MyWPFApp.MainWindow"
   xmlns="http://schemas.microsoft.com/winfx/2006/xaml/presentation"
   xmlns:x="http://schemas.microsoft.com/winfx/2006/xaml"
...
   Title="Fun with Panels!" Height="285" Width="325">

   <Button x:Name="btnOK" Height = "100"
           Width="80" Content="OK"/>
</Window>
```

You might also recall that if you attempt to place multiple elements directly within the scope of a `<Window>`, you will receive markup and compile-time errors. The reason for these errors is that a window (or any descendant of `ContentControl` for that matter) can assign only a single object to its `Content` property. Therefore, the following XAML yields markup and compile time errors:

```
<!-- Error! Content property is implicitly set more than once! -->
<Window x:Class="MyWPFApp.MainWindow"
   xmlns="http://schemas.microsoft.com/winfx/2006/xaml/presentation"
   xmlns:x="http://schemas.microsoft.com/winfx/2006/xaml"
...
   Title="Fun with Panels!" Height="285" Width="325">

   <!-- Error! Two direct child elements of the <Window>! -->
   <Label x:Name="lblInstructions" Width="328" Height="27"
          FontSize="15" Content="Enter Information"/>
   <Button x:Name="btnOK" Height = "100" Width="80" Content="OK"/>
</Window>
```

Obviously, a window that can only contain a single control is of little use. When a window needs to contain multiple elements, those elements must be arranged within any number of panels. The panel will contain all of the UI elements that represent the window, after which the panel itself is used as the single object assigned to the `Content` property.

The `System.Windows.Controls` namespace provides numerous panels, each of which controls how subelements are maintained. You can use panels to establish how the controls behave if the end user resizes the window, if the controls remain exactly where they were placed at design time, if the controls reflow horizontally from left-to-right or vertically from top-to-bottom, and so forth.

You can also intermix panel controls within other panels (e.g., a DockPanel that contains a StackPanel of other items) to provide a great deal of flexibility and control. Table 28-2 documents the role of some commonly used WPF panel controls.

Table 28-2. *Core WPF Panel Controls*

Panel Control	Meaning in Life
Canvas	Provides a classic mode of content placement. Items stay exactly where you put them at design time.
DockPanel	Locks content to a specified side of the panel (Top, Bottom, Left, or Right).
Grid	Arranges content within a series of cells, maintained within a tabular grid.
StackPanel	Stacks content in a vertical or horizontal manner, as dictated by the Orientation property.
WrapPanel	Positions content from left-to-right, breaking the content to the next line at the edge of the containing box. Subsequent ordering happens sequentially from top-to-bottom or from right-to-left, depending on the value of the Orientation property.

In the next few sections, you will learn how to use these commonly used panel types by copying some predefined XAML data into the MyXamlPad.exe application you created in Chapter 27 (you could also load this data into kaxaml.exe, if you so choose). You can find all these loose XAML files contained inside the PanelMarkup subfolder of your Chapter 28 code download folder (see Figure 28-4).

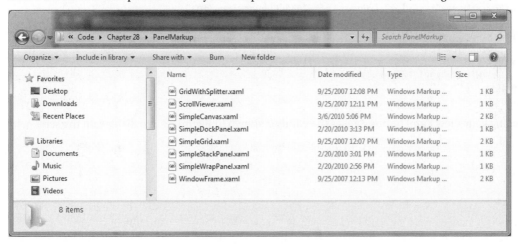

Figure 28-4. *You will be loading the supplied XAML data into your MyXamlPad.exe appliction to test various layouts*

Positioning Content Within Canvas Panels

You will probably feel most at home with the Canvas panel because it allows for absolute positioning of UI content. If the end user resizes the window to an area that is smaller than the layout maintained by the Canvas panel, the internal content will not be visible until the container is stretched to a size equal to or larger than the Canvas area.

To add content to a Canvas, you begin by defining the required controls within the scope of the opening <Canvas> and closing </Canvas> tags. Next, specify the upper-left corner for each control; this is where the rendering should begin using the Canvas.Top and Canvas.Left properties. You can specify the bottom-right area indirectly in each control by setting its Height and Width properties, or directly by using the Canvas.Right and Canvas.Bottom properties.

To see Canvas in action, open the provided SimpleCanvas.xaml file using a text editor and copy the content into MyXamlPad.exe (or kaxaml.exe). You should see the following Canvas definition:

```
<Window
  xmlns="http://schemas.microsoft.com/winfx/2006/xaml/presentation"
  xmlns:x="http://schemas.microsoft.com/winfx/2006/xaml"
...
  Title="Fun with Panels!" Height="285" Width="325">
  <Canvas Background="LightSteelBlue">
    <Button x:Name="btnOK" Canvas.Left="212" Canvas.Top="203"
            Width="80" Content="OK"/>
    <Label x:Name="lblInstructions" Canvas.Left="17" Canvas.Top="14"
            Width="328" Height="27" FontSize="15"
            Content="Enter Car Information"/>
    <Label x:Name="lblMake" Canvas.Left="17" Canvas.Top="60"
            Content="Make"/>
    <TextBox x:Name="txtMake" Canvas.Left="94" Canvas.Top="60"
            Width="193" Height="25"/>
    <Label x:Name="lblColor" Canvas.Left="17" Canvas.Top="109"
            Content="Color"/>
    <TextBox x:Name="txtColor" Canvas.Left="94" Canvas.Top="107"
            Width="193" Height="25"/>
    <Label x:Name="lblPetName" Canvas.Left="17" Canvas.Top="155"
            Content="Pet Name"/>
    <TextBox x:Name="txtPetName" Canvas.Left="94" Canvas.Top="153"
            Width="193" Height="25"/>
  </Canvas>
</Window>
```

Clicking your View Xaml button causes the window shown in Figure 28-5 to display on the screen.

Figure 28-5. The Canvas layout manager allows for absolute positioning of content

Note that the order you declare content within a Canvas is not used to calculate placement; instead, placement is based on the control's size and the Canvas.Top, Canvas.Bottom, Canvas.Left, and Canvas.Right properties.

■ **Note** If subelements within a Canvas do not define a specific location using attached property syntax (e.g., Canvas.Left and Canvas.Top), they automatically attach to the extreme upper-left corner of Canvas.

Using the Canvas type might seem like the preferred way to arrange content (because it feels so familiar), but this approach does suffer from some limitations. First, items within a Canvas do not dynamically resize themselves when applying styles or templates (e.g., their font sizes are unaffected). Second, the Canvas will not attempt to keep elements visible when the end user resizes the window to a smaller surface.

Perhaps the best use of the Canvas type is for positioning *graphical content*. For example, if you were building a custom image using XAML, you certainly would want the lines, shapes, and text to remain in the same location, rather than see them dynamically repositioned as the user resizes the window! You'll revisit Canvas in Chapter 29 when you examine WPF's graphical rendering services.

Positioning Content Within WrapPanel Panels

A WrapPanel allows you to define content that will flow across the panel as the window is resized. When positioning elements in a WrapPanel, you do not specify top, bottom, left, and right docking values as you typically do with Canvas. However, each subelement is free to define a Height and Width value (among other property values) to control its overall size in the container.

Because content within a WrapPanel does not dock to a given side of the panel, the order in which you declare the elements is important (content is rendered from the first element to the last). If you were to load the XAML data found within the SimpleWrapPanel.xaml file, you would find it contains the following markup (enclosed within a <Window> definition):

```
<WrapPanel Background="LightSteelBlue">
  <Label x:Name="lblInstruction" Width="328"
         Height="27" FontSize="15" Content="Enter Car Information"/>
  <Label x:Name="lblMake" Content="Make"/>
  <TextBox x:Name="txtMake" Width="193" Height="25"/>
  <Label x:Name="lblColor" Content="Color"/>
  <TextBox x:Name="txtColor" Width="193" Height="25"/>
  <Label x:Name="lblPetName" Content="Pet Name"/>
  <TextBox x:Name="txtPetName" Width="193" Height="25"/>
  <Button x:Name="btnOK" Width="80" Content="OK"/>
</WrapPanel>
```

When you load this markup, the content looks out of sorts as you resize the width because it flows from left-to-right across the window (see Figure 28-6).

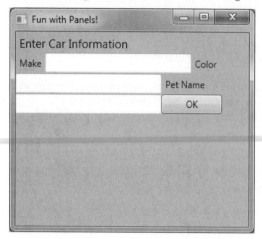

Figure 28-6. Content in a WrapPanel behaves much like a traditional HTML page

By default, content within a WrapPanel flows from left-to-right. However, if you change the value of the Orientation property to Vertical, you can have content wrap in a top-to-bottom manner.

```
<WrapPanel Background="LightSteelBlue" Orientation ="Vertical">
```

You can declare a WrapPanel (as well as some other panel types) by specifying ItemWidth and ItemHeight values, which control the default size of each item. If a subelement does provide its own Height and/or Width value, it will be positioned relative to the size established by the panel. Consider the following markup:

```
<WrapPanel Background="LightSteelBlue" ItemWidth ="200" ItemHeight ="30">
  <Label x:Name="lblInstruction"
         FontSize="15" Content="Enter Car Information"/>
  <Label x:Name="lblMake" Content="Make"/>
  <TextBox x:Name="txtMake"/>
  <Label x:Name="lblColor" Content="Color"/>
  <TextBox x:Name="txtColor"/>
  <Label x:Name="lblPetName" Content="Pet Name"/>
```

```
  <TextBox x:Name="txtPetName"/>
  <Button x:Name="btnOK" Width ="80" Content="OK"/>
</WrapPanel>
```

When you see this code rendered, you find the output shown in Figure 28-7 (notice the size and position of the Button control, which has specified a unique Width value).

Figure 28-7. *A WrapPanel can establish the width and height of a given item*

As you might agree after looking at Figure 28-7, a WrapPanel is not typically the best choice for arranging content directly in a window because its elements can become scrambled as the user resizes the window. In most cases, a WrapPanel will be a subelement to another panel type, allowing a small area of the window to wrap its content when resized (e.g., a ToolBar control).

Positioning Content Within StackPanel Panels

Like a WrapPanel, a StackPanel control arranges content into a single line that can be oriented horizontally or vertically (the default), based on the value assigned to the Orientation property. The difference, however, is that the StackPanel will *not* attempt to wrap the content as the user resizes the window. Rather, the items in the StackPanel will simply stretch (based on their orientation) to accommodate the size of the StackPanel itself. For example, the SimpleStackPanel.xaml file contains the following markup, which results in the output shown in Figure 28-8:

```
<StackPanel Background="LightSteelBlue">
  <Label x:Name="lblInstruction"
         FontSize="15" Content="Enter Car Information"/>
  <Label x:Name="lblMake" Content="Make"/>
  <TextBox Name="txtMake"/>
  <Label x:Name="lblColor" Content="Color"/>
  <TextBox x:Name="txtColor"/>
  <Label x:Name="lblPetName" Content="Pet Name"/>
  <TextBox x:Name="txtPetName"/>
  <Button x:Name="btnOK" Width ="80" Content="OK"/>
</StackPanel>
```

Figure 28-8. Vertical stacking of content

If you assign the Orientation property to Horizontal as follows, the rendered output will match that shown in Figure 28-9:

```
<StackPanel Background="LightSteelBlue" Orientation="Horizontal">
```

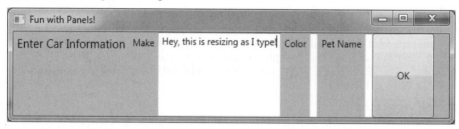

Figure 28-9. Horizontal stacking of content

Again, as is the case with the WrapPanel, you will seldom want to use a StackPanel to arrange content directly within a window. Instead, you'll be better off using StackPanel as a subpanel to a master panel.

Positioning Content Within Grid Panels

Of all the panels provided with the WPF APIs, Grid is far and away the most flexible. Like an HTML table, the Grid can be carved up into a set of cells, each one of which provides content. When defining a Grid, you perform three steps:

1. Define and configure each column.

2. Define and configure each row.

3. Assign content to each cell of the grid using attached property syntax.

■ **Note** If you do not define any rows or columns, the <Grid> defaults to a single cell that fills the entire surface of the window. Furthermore, if you do not assign a cell value for a subelement within a <Grid>, it automatically attaches to column 0, row 0.

You achieve the first two steps (defining the columns and rows) by using the <Grid.ColumnDefinitions> and <Grid.RowDefinitions> elements, which contain a collection of <ColumnDefinition> and <RowDefinition> elements, respectively. Each cell within a grid is indeed a true .NET object, so you can configure the look-and-feel and behavior of each cell as you see fit.

Here is a <Grid> definition (that you can find in the SimpleGrid.xaml file) that arranges your UI content as shown in Figure 28-10:

```
<Grid ShowGridLines ="True" Background ="LightSteelBlue">
  <!-- Define the rows/columns -->
  <Grid.ColumnDefinitions>
    <ColumnDefinition/>
    <ColumnDefinition/>
  </Grid.ColumnDefinitions>
  <Grid.RowDefinitions>
    <RowDefinition/>
    <RowDefinition/>
  </Grid.RowDefinitions>

  <!-- Now add the elements to the grid's cells -->
  <Label x:Name="lblInstruction" Grid.Column ="0" Grid.Row ="0"
         FontSize="15" Content="Enter Car Information"/>
  <Button x:Name="btnOK"  Height ="30" Grid.Column ="0"
         Grid.Row ="0" Content="OK"/>
  <Label x:Name="lblMake" Grid.Column ="1"
         Grid.Row ="0" Content="Make"/>
  <TextBox x:Name="txtMake" Grid.Column ="1"
          Grid.Row ="0" Width="193" Height="25"/>
  <Label x:Name="lblColor" Grid.Column ="0"
         Grid.Row ="1" Content="Color"/>
  <TextBox x:Name="txtColor" Width="193" Height="25"
          Grid.Column ="0" Grid.Row ="1" />

  <!-- Just to keep things interesting, add some color to the pet name cell -->
  <Rectangle Fill ="LightGreen" Grid.Column ="1" Grid.Row ="1" />
  <Label x:Name="lblPetName" Grid.Column ="1" Grid.Row ="1" Content="Pet Name"/>
  <TextBox x:Name="txtPetName" Grid.Column ="1" Grid.Row ="1"
          Width="193" Height="25"/>
</Grid>
```

Notice that each element (including a light green Rectangle element thrown in for good measure) connects itself to a cell in the grid using the Grid.Row and Grid.Column attached properties. By default, the ordering of cells in a grid begins at the upper left, which you specify using Grid.Column="0" Grid.Row="0". Given that your grid defines a total of four cells, you can identify the bottom-right cell using Grid.Column="1" Grid.Row="1".

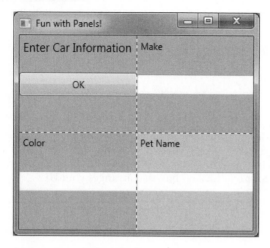

Figure 28-10. *The Grid panel in action*

Grids with GridSplitter Types

Grid objects can also support *splitters*. As you might know, splitters allow the end user to resize rows or columns of a grid type. As this is done, the content within each resizable cell will reshape itself based on how the items have been contained. Adding splitters to a Grid is easy to do; you simply define the <GridSplitter> control, using attached property syntax to establish which row or column it affects.

Be aware that you must assign a Width or Height value (depending on vertical or horizontal splitting) for the splitter to be visible on the screen. Consider the following simple Grid type with a splitter on the first column (Grid.Column = "0"). The contents of the provided GridWithSplitter.xaml file look like this:

```
<Grid Background ="LightSteelBlue">
  <!-- Define columns -->
  <Grid.ColumnDefinitions>
    <ColumnDefinition Width ="Auto"/>
    <ColumnDefinition/>
  </Grid.ColumnDefinitions>

  <!-- Add this label to cell 0 -->
  <Label x:Name="lblLeft" Background ="GreenYellow"
        Grid.Column="0" Content ="Left!"/>

  <!-- Define the splitter -->
  <GridSplitter Grid.Column ="0" Width ="5"/>

  <!-- Add this label to cell 1 -->
  <Label x:Name="lblRight" Grid.Column ="1" Content ="Right!"/>
</Grid>
```

First and foremost, notice that the column that will support the splitter has a Width property of Auto. Next, notice that the <GridSplitter> uses attached property syntax to establish which column it is working with. If you were to view this output, you would find a five-pixel splitter that allows you to resize

1172

each Label. Note that the content fills up the entire cell because you have not specified Height or Width properties for either Label (see Figure 28-11).

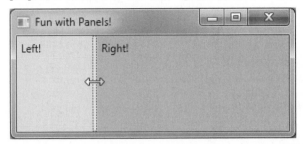

Figure 28-11. Grid types containing splitters

Positioning Content Within DockPanel Panels

DockPanel is typically used as a container that holds any number of additional panels for grouping related content. DockPanels use attached property syntax (as seen with the Canvas or Grid types) to control where each item docks itself within the DockPanel.

The SimpleDockPanel.xaml file defines the following simple DockPanel definition that results in the output shown in Figure 28-12:

```
<DockPanel LastChildFill ="True">
  <!-- Dock items to the panel -->
  <Label x:Name="lblInstruction" DockPanel.Dock ="Top"
         FontSize="15" Content="Enter Car Information"/>
  <Label x:Name="lblMake" DockPanel.Dock ="Left" Content="Make"/>
  <Label x:Name="lblColor" DockPanel.Dock ="Right" Content="Color"/>
  <Label x:Name="lblPetName" DockPanel.Dock ="Bottom" Content="Pet Name"/>
  <Button x:Name="btnOK" Content="OK"/>
</DockPanel>
```

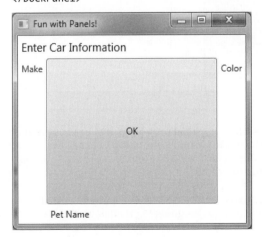

Figure 28-12. A simple DockPanel

■ **Note** If you add multiple elements to the same side of a DockPanel, they will stack along the specified edge in the order that they are declared.

The benefit of using DockPanel types is that, as the user resizes the window, each element remains connected to the specified side of the panel (through DockPanel.Dock). Also notice that the opening <DockPanel> tag in our example sets the LastChildFill attribute to true. Given that the Button control is indeed the "last child" in the container, it will therefore be stretched within the remaining space.

Enabling Scrolling for Panel Types

It is worth pointing out the WPF supplies a ScrollViewer class, which provides automatic scrolling behaviors for data within panel objects. The ScrollViewer.xaml file defines the following:

```
<ScrollViewer>
  <StackPanel>
    <Button Content ="First" Background = "Green" Height ="40"/>
    <Button Content ="Second" Background = "Red" Height ="40"/>
    <Button Content ="Third" Background = "Pink" Height ="40"/>
    <Button Content ="Fourth" Background = "Yellow" Height ="40"/>
    <Button Content ="Fifth" Background = "Blue" Height ="40"/>
  </StackPanel>
</ScrollViewer>
```

You can see the result of the previous XAML definition in Figure 28-13.

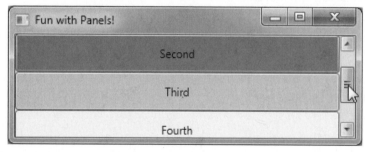

Figure 28-13. Working with the ScrollViewer type

As you would expect, each panel provides numerous members that allow you to fine-tune content placement. On a related note, many WPF controls support two properties of interest (Padding and Margin) that allow the control itself to inform the panel how it wishes to be treated. Specifically, the Padding property controls how much extra space should surround the interior control, while Margin controls the extra space around the exterior of a control.

This wraps up this chapter's look at the major panel types of WPF, as well as the various ways they position their content. Next, let's learn how to use the Visual Studio designers to create layouts.

Configuring Panels Using the Visual Studio Designers

Now that you have been given a walkthrough of the XAML used to define some common layout managers, you will be happy to know that Visual Studio has some very good design-time support for constructing your layouts. The key to doing so lies with the Document Outline window described earlier in this chapter. To illustrate some of the basics, create a new WPF Application project named VisualLayoutTesterApp (this example is just here to illustrate working with the layout editors, so I have not included it in the book's provided source code).

Now, notice how your initial Window is making use of a Grid layout by default, as follows:

```
<Window x:Class="VisualLayoutTesterApp.MainWindow"
        xmlns="http://schemas.microsoft.com/winfx/2006/xaml/presentation"
        xmlns:x="http://schemas.microsoft.com/winfx/2006/xaml"
        Title="MainWindow" Height="350" Width="525">
    <Grid>

    </Grid>
</Window>
```

If you are happy using the Grid layout system, notice in Figure 28-14, you can easily carve out and resize the grid's cells using the visual layout. To do so, first select the Grid component in your Document Outline window, and then click on the grid's border to create new rows and columns.

Figure 28-14. The Grid control can be visually cut into cells using the IDE's designer

Now, let's say you have defined a grid with some number of cells. You can then drag and drop controls into a given cell of the layout system, and the IDE will automatically set the Grid.Row and

`Grid.Column` properties of the control in question. Here is some possible markup generated by the IDE after dragging a `Button` into a predefined cell:

```
<Button Content="Button" HorizontalAlignment="Left" Margin="10,10,0,0"
        Grid.Row="1" VerticalAlignment="Top" Width="75"
        Grid.Column="1"/>
```

Now, let's say you would rather not use a `Grid` at all. If you right-click on any layout node in the Document Outline window, you will find a menu option that allows you to change the current container into another (see Figure 28-15). Be very aware that when you do so, you will (most likely) radically change the positioning of the controls, as the controls will conform to the rules of the new panel type.

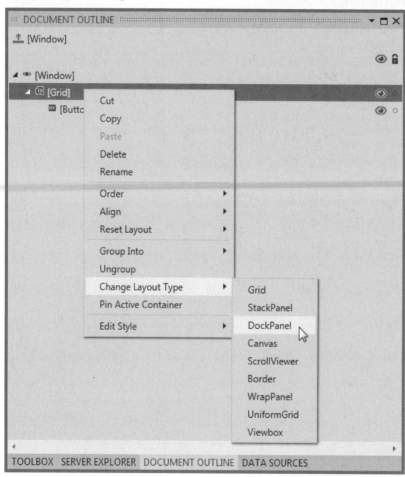

Figure 28-15. The Document Outline window allows you to convert to new panel types

Another handy trick is the ability to select a set of controls on the visual designer and group them into a new, nested layout manager. Assume you have a `Canvas` that defines a set of random objects (if you want to try, convert the initial Grid to a Canvas using the technique shown in the Figure 28-15). Now, select a set of items on the designer by holding down the CTRL key and clicking on each item with the left mouse button. If you then right-click on the selection, you can group the selected items into a new subpanel (see Figure 28-16).

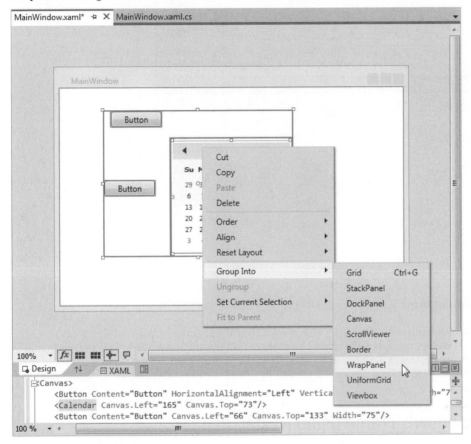

Figure 28-16. Grouping items into a new subpanel.

After you have done so, examine the Document Outline window once again to verify the nested layout system. As you build full-featured WPF windows, you will most likely always need to make use of a nested layout system, rather than simply picking a single panel for all the UI display (in fact, the remaining WPF examples in the text will typically do so). On a final note, do know that the nodes in the Document Outline window are all drag and droppable. For example, if you wanted to move a control currently in the Canvas into the parent panel, you could do so as suggested in Figure 28-17.

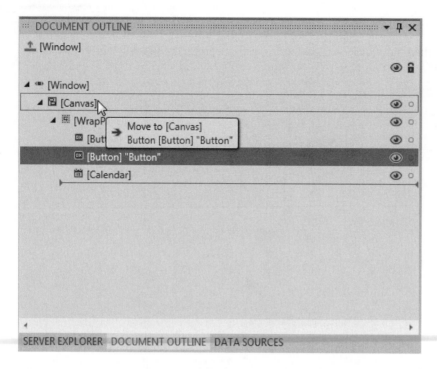

Figure 28-17. Relocating items via the Document Outline window

As you work through the remaining WPF chapters, I'll point out additional layout shortcuts where possible. However, I will let you know that it will be most definitely worth your time to experiment and test out various features yourself. To keep us moving in the right direction, the next example in the chapter will illustrate how to build a nested layout manager for a custom text processing application (with spell checking!).

Building a Window's Frame Using Nested Panels

As mentioned previously, a typical WPF window will not use a single panel control, but instead will nest panels within other panels to gain the desired layout system. Begin by creating a new WPF Application named MyWordPad.

Your goal is to construct a layout where the main window has a topmost menu system, a toolbar under the menu system, and a status bar mounted on the bottom of the window. The status bar will contain a pane to hold text prompts that are displayed when the user selects a menu item (or toolbar button), while the menu system and toolbar will offer UI triggers to close the application and display spelling suggestions in an Expander widget. Figure 28-18 shows the initial layout you are shooting for; it also displays spelling suggestions for "XAML."

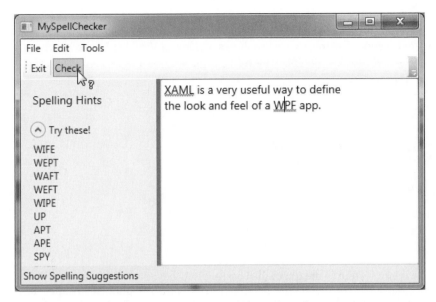

Figure 28-18. *Using nested panels to establish a window's UI*

Notice that the two toolbar buttons are not supporting an expected image, but a simple text value. This would not be sufficient for a production-level application, but assigning images to toolbar buttons typically involves using embedded resources, a topic that you will examine in Chapter 29 (so text data will do for now). Also note that, as the mouse button is placed over the Check button, the mouse cursor changes and the single pane of the status bar displays a useful UI message.

To begin building this UI, update the initial XAML definition for your Window type so it uses a <DockPanel> child element, rather than the default <Grid>, as follows:

```
<Window x:Class="MyWordPad.MainWindow"
  xmlns="http://schemas.microsoft.com/winfx/2006/xaml/presentation"
  xmlns:x="http://schemas.microsoft.com/winfx/2006/xaml"
  Title="MySpellChecker" Height="331" Width="508"
  WindowStartupLocation ="CenterScreen" >

  <!-- This panel establishes the content for the window -->
  <DockPanel>
  </DockPanel>

</Window>
```

Building the Menu System

Menu systems in WPF are represented by the Menu class, which maintains a collection of MenuItem objects. When building a menu system in XAML, you can have each MenuItem handle various events. The most notable of these events is Click, which occurs when the end user selects a subitem. In this example, you begin by building the two topmost menu items (File and Tools; you will build the Edit menu later in this example), which expose Exit and Spelling Hints subitems, respectively.

In addition to handling the Click event for each subitem, you also need to handle the MouseEnter and MouseExit events, which you will use to set the status bar text in a later step. Add the following markup within your <DockPanel> scope (feel free to use Properties window of Visual Studio to handle each event; see Chapter 27 for a walkthrough on how to do so):

```
<!-- Dock menu system on the top -->
<Menu DockPanel.Dock ="Top"
      HorizontalAlignment="Left" Background="White" BorderBrush ="Black">
  <MenuItem Header="_File">
    <Separator/>
    <MenuItem Header ="_Exit" MouseEnter ="MouseEnterExitArea"
              MouseLeave ="MouseLeaveArea" Click ="FileExit_Click"/>
  </MenuItem>
  <MenuItem Header="_Tools">
    <MenuItem Header ="_Spelling Hints"
        MouseEnter ="MouseEnterToolsHintsArea"
        MouseLeave ="MouseLeaveArea" Click ="ToolsSpellingHints_Click"/>
  </MenuItem>
</Menu>
```

Notice that you dock the menu system to the top of the DockPanel. Also, you use the <Separator> element to insert a thin horizontal line in the menu system, directly before the Exit option. Also notice that the Header values for each MenuItem contain an embedded underscore token (e.g., _Exit). You use this token to establish which letter will be underlined when the end user presses the Alt key (for keyboard shortcuts).

So far you've implemented the complete the menu system definition; next, you need to implement the various event handlers. First, you have the File Exit handler, FileExit_Click(), which simply closes the window, which in turn terminates the application because this is your topmost window. The MouseEnter and MouseExit event handlers for each subitem will eventually update your status bar; however, for now, you will simply provide shells. Finally, the ToolsSpellingHints_Click() handler for the Tools Spelling Hints menu item will also remain a shell for the time being. Here are the current updates to your code-behind file:

```
public partial class MainWindow : System.Windows.Window
{
  public MainWindow()
  {
    InitializeComponent();
  }

  protected void FileExit_Click(object sender, RoutedEventArgs args)
  {
    // Close this window.
    this.Close();
  }

  protected void ToolsSpellingHints_Click(object sender, RoutedEventArgs args)
  {
  }
  protected void MouseEnterExitArea(object sender, RoutedEventArgs args)
  {
  }
```

```
    protected void MouseEnterToolsHintsArea(object sender, RoutedEventArgs args)
    {
    }
    protected void MouseLeaveArea(object sender, RoutedEventArgs args)
    {
    }
}
```

Building Menus Visually

While it is always good to know how to manually define items in XAML, it can be a tad on the tedious side. Visual Studio supports visual design support for menu systems, toolbars, status bars and many other UI controls. By way of a quick example, assume you had a fresh Menu control on a new Window (you might want to insert a test Window via the Project ➤ Add Window menu option and follow along). Now, if you right-click on the Menu control, you will notice an Add MenuItem option (see Figure 28-19).

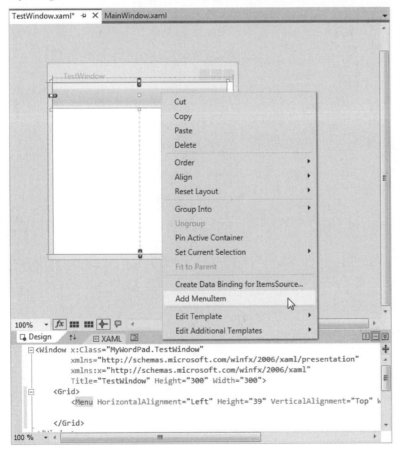

Figure 28-19. Visually adding items to a Menu object

After you have added a set of topmost items, you can then add submenu items, separators, expand or collapse the menu itself, and perform other menu-centric operations via a second right-click. Figure 28-20 shows one possible way to visually design a simple menu system (be sure you examine the generated XAML).

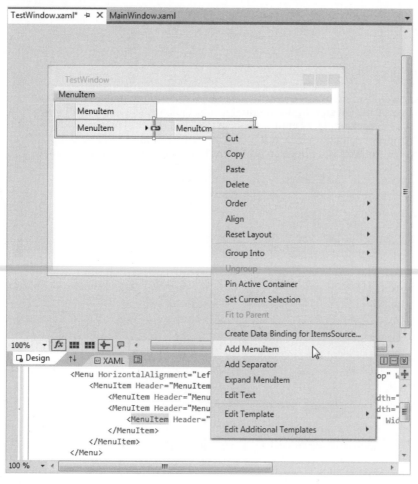

Figure 28-20. *Visually adding items to a MenuItem object*

As you read over the reminder of the current MyWordPad example, I'll typically show you the final generated XAML; however, do take the time to experiment with the visual designers to simplify the task at hand.

Building the ToolBar

Toolbars (represented by the ToolBar class in WPF) typically provide an alternative manner for activating a menu option. Add the following markup directly after the closing scope of your <Menu> definition:

```
<!-- Put Toolbar under the Menu -->
<ToolBar DockPanel.Dock ="Top" >
  <Button Content ="Exit" MouseEnter ="MouseEnterExitArea"
        MouseLeave ="MouseLeaveArea" Click ="FileExit_Click"/>
  <Separator/>
  <Button Content ="Check" MouseEnter ="MouseEnterToolsHintsArea"
        MouseLeave ="MouseLeaveArea" Click ="ToolsSpellingHints_Click"
        Cursor="Help" />
</ToolBar>
```

Your ToolBar control consists of two Button controls, which just so happen to handle the same events and are handled by the same methods in your code file. Using this technique, you can double-up your handlers to serve both menu items and toolbar buttons. Although this toolbar uses the typical push buttons, you should appreciate that the ToolBar type "is-a" ContentControl; therefore, you are free to embed any types into its surface (e.g., drop-down lists, images, and graphics). The only other point of interest here is that the Check button supports a custom mouse cursor through the Cursor property.

■ **Note** You can optionally wrap the ToolBar element within a <ToolBarTray> element, which controls layout, docking, and drag-and-drop operations for a set of ToolBar objects. Consult the .NET Framework 4.5 SDK documentation for details.

Building the StatusBar

A StatusBar control will be docked to the lower portion of the <DockPanel> and contain a single <TextBlock> control, which you have not used prior to this point in the chapter. You can use a TextBlock to hold text that supports numerous textual annotations, such as bold text, underlined text, line breaks, and so forth. Add the following markup directly after the previous ToolBar definition:

```
<!-- Put a StatusBar at the bottom -->
<StatusBar DockPanel.Dock ="Bottom" Background="Beige" >
  <StatusBarItem>
    <TextBlock Name="statBarText" Text="Ready"/>
  </StatusBarItem>
</StatusBar>
```

Finalizing the UI Design

The final aspect of your UI design is to define a splittable Grid that defines two columns. On the left you place an Expander control that will display a list of spelling suggestions, wrapped within a <StackPanel>. On the right, you place a TextBox control that supports multiple lines and scrollbars, and includes enabled spell checking. You mount the entire <Grid> to the left of the parent <DockPanel>. Add the following XAML markup directly under the markup describing the StatusBar to complete the definition of our Window's UI:

```xml
<Grid DockPanel.Dock ="Left" Background ="AliceBlue">
  <!-- Define the rows and columns -->
  <Grid.ColumnDefinitions>
    <ColumnDefinition />
    <ColumnDefinition />
  </Grid.ColumnDefinitions>

  <GridSplitter Grid.Column ="0" Width ="5" Background ="Gray" />
  <StackPanel Grid.Column="0" VerticalAlignment ="Stretch" >
    <Label Name="lblSpellingInstructions" FontSize="14" Margin="10,10,0,0">
      Spelling Hints
    </Label>

    <Expander Name="expanderSpelling" Header ="Try these!"
            Margin="10,10,10,10">
      <!-- This will be filled programmatically -->
      <Label Name ="lblSpellingHints" FontSize ="12"/>
    </Expander>
  </StackPanel>

  <!-- This will be the area to type within -->
  <TextBox  Grid.Column ="1"
            SpellCheck.IsEnabled ="True"
            AcceptsReturn ="True"
            Name ="txtData"  FontSize ="14"
            BorderBrush ="Blue"
            VerticalScrollBarVisibility="Auto"
            HorizontalScrollBarVisibility="Auto">
  </TextBox>
</Grid>
```

Implementing the MouseEnter/MouseLeave Event Handlers

At this point, the UI of your window is complete. The only remaining tasks are to provide an implementation for the remaining event handlers. Begin by updating your C# code file so that each of the MouseEnter and MouseLeave handlers set the text pane of the status bar with a fitting message to help the end user, like so:

```csharp
public partial class MainWindow : System.Windows.Window
{
...
  protected void MouseEnterExitArea(object sender, RoutedEventArgs args)
  {
    statBarText.Text = "Exit the Application";
  }
  protected void MouseEnterToolsHintsArea(object sender, RoutedEventArgs args)
  {
    statBarText.Text = "Show Spelling Suggestions";
  }
```

```
protected void MouseLeaveArea(object sender, RoutedEventArgs args)
{
    statBarText.Text = "Ready";
}
}
```

At this point, you can run your application. You should see your status bar change its text, based on which menu item/toolbar button you hover your mouse over.

Implementing the Spell Checking Logic

The WPF API ships with built-in spell checker support, which is independent of Microsoft Office products. This means you don't need to use the COM interop layer to use the spell checker of Microsoft Word; instead, you can easily add the same type of support with only a few lines of code.

You might recall that when you defined the <TextBox> control, you set the SpellCheck.IsEnabled property to true. When you do this, misspelled words are underlined with a red squiggle, just as they are in Microsoft Office. Even better, the underlying programming model gives you access to the spell-checker engine, which allows you to get a list of suggestions for misspelled words. Add the following code to your ToolsSpellingHints_Click() method:

```
protected void ToolsSpellingHints_Click(object sender, RoutedEventArgs args)
{
    string spellingHints = string.Empty;

    // Try to get a spelling error at the current caret location.
    SpellingError error = txtData.GetSpellingError(txtData.CaretIndex);
    if (error != null)
    {
        // Build a string of spelling suggestions.
        foreach (string s in error.Suggestions)
        {
            spellingHints += string.Format("{0}\n", s);
        }

        // Show suggestions and expand the expander.
        lblSpellingHints.Content = spellingHints;
        expanderSpelling.IsExpanded = true;
    }
}
```

The preceding code is quite simple. You simply figure out the current location of the caret in the text box by using the CaretIndex property to extract a SpellingError object. If there is an error at said location (meaning the value is not null), you loop over the list of suggestions using the aptly named Suggestions property. After you have all of the suggestions for the misspelled word, you connect the data to the Label in the Expander.

So there you have it! With only a few lines of procedural code (and a healthy dose of XAML), you have the beginnings of a functioning word processor. An understanding of *control commands* can help you add a bit more pizzazz.

Understanding WPF Commands

Windows Presentation Foundation provides support for what might be considered *control-agnostic events* via the *command architecture*. A typical .NET event is defined within a specific base class and can be used only by that class or a derivative thereof. Therefore, normal .NET events are tightly coupled to the class in which they are defined.

In contrast, WPF commands are event-like entities that are independent from a specific control and, in many cases, can be successfully applied to numerous (and seemingly unrelated) control types. By way of a few examples, WPF supports copy, paste, and cut commands, which you can apply to a wide variety of UI elements (e.g., menu items, toolbar buttons, and custom buttons), as well as keyboard shortcuts (e.g., Ctrl+C, and Ctrl+V).

While other UI toolkits (such as Windows Forms) provided standard events for such purposes, using them typically left you with redundant and hard-to-maintain code. Under the WPF model, you can use commands as an alternative. The end result typically yields a smaller and more flexible code base.

The Intrinsic Command Objects

WPF ships with numerous built-in control commands, all of which you can configure with associated keyboard shortcuts (or other input gestures). Programmatically speaking, a WPF command is any object that supports a property (often called Command) that returns an object implementing the ICommand interface, as shown here:

```
public interface ICommand
{
  // Occurs when changes occur that affect whether
  // or not the command should execute.
  event EventHandler CanExecuteChanged;

  // Defines the method that determines whether the command
  // can execute in its current state.
  bool CanExecute(object parameter);

  // Defines the method to be called when the command is invoked.
  void Execute(object parameter);
}
```

WPF provides various command classes, which expose close to 100 command objects, out of the box. These classes define numerous properties that expose specific command objects, each of which implements ICommand. Table 28-3 documents some of the standard command objects available (be sure to consult the .NET Framework 4.5 SDK documentation for complete details).

Table 28-3. *The Intrinsic WPF Control Command Objects*

WPF Class	Command Objects	Meaning in Life
ApplicationCommands	Close, Copy, Cut, Delete, Find, Open, Paste, Save, SaveAs, Redo, Undo	Various application-level commands
ComponentCommands	MoveDown, MoveFocusBack, MoveLeft, MoveRight, ScrollToEnd, ScrollToHome	Various commands common to UI components
MediaCommands	BoostBase, ChannelUp, ChannelDown, FastForward, NextTrack, Play, Rewind, Select, Stop	Various media-centric commands
NavigationCommands	BrowseBack, BrowseForward, Favorites, LastPage, NextPage, Zoom	Various commands relating to the WPF navigation model
EditingCommands	AlignCenter, CorrectSpellingError, DecreaseFontSize, EnterLineBreak, EnterParagraphBreak, MoveDownByLine, MoveRightByWord	Various commands relating to the WPF Documents API

Connecting Commands to the Command Property

If you want to connect any of the WPF command properties to a UI element that supports the Command property (such as a Button or MenuItem), you have little work to do. You can see how to do this by updating the current menu system so it supports a new topmost menu item named Edit and three subitems to account for copying, pasting, and cutting of textual data, like so:

```
<Menu DockPanel.Dock ="Top"
      HorizontalAlignment="Left"
      Background="White" BorderBrush ="Black">
  <MenuItem Header="_File" Click ="FileExit_Click" >
    <MenuItem Header ="_Exit" MouseEnter ="MouseEnterExitArea"
              MouseLeave ="MouseLeaveArea" Click ="FileExit_Click"/>
  </MenuItem>

  <!-- New menu item with commands! -->
  <MenuItem Header="_Edit">
    <MenuItem Command ="ApplicationCommands.Copy"/>
    <MenuItem Command ="ApplicationCommands.Cut"/>
    <MenuItem Command ="ApplicationCommands.Paste"/>
  </MenuItem>
```

```
<MenuItem Header="_Tools">
  <MenuItem Header ="_Spelling Hints"
            MouseEnter ="MouseEnterToolsHintsArea"
            MouseLeave ="MouseLeaveArea"
            Click ="ToolsSpellingHints_Click"/>
</MenuItem>
</Menu>
```

Notice that each of the subitems on the Edit menu has a value assigned to the Command property. Doing this means that the menu items automatically receive the correct name and shortcut key (e.g., Ctrl+C for a cut operation) in the menu item UI; it also means that the application is now *copy, cut, and paste* aware with no procedural code!

If you were to run the application and select some of your text, you would be able to use your new menu items, out of the box. As a bonus, your application is also equipped to respond to a standard right-click operation to present the user with the same options (see Figure 28-21).

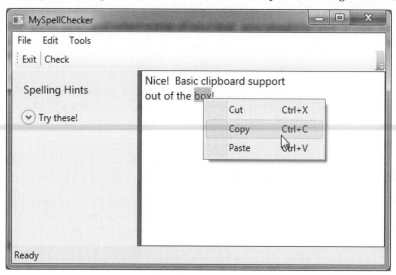

Figure 28-21. *Command objects provide a good deal of built-in functionality for free*

Connecting Commands to Arbitrary Actions

If you want to connect a command object to an arbitrary (application-specific) event, you will need to drop down to procedural code. Doing so is not complex, but it does involve a bit more logic than you see in XAML. For example, assume that want to have the entire window respond to the F1 key, so that when the end user presses this key, he will activate an associated help system. Also, assume your code file for the main window defines a new method named SetF1CommandBinding(), which you call within the constructor after the call to InitializeComponent().

```
public MainWindow()
{
  InitializeComponent();
  SetF1CommandBinding();
}
```

This new method will programmatically create a new CommandBinding object, which you can use whenever you need to bind a command object to a given event handler in your application. Here, you configure your CommandBinding object to operate with the ApplicationCommands.Help command, which is automatically F1-aware:

```
private void SetF1CommandBinding()
{
  CommandBinding helpBinding = new CommandBinding(ApplicationCommands.Help);
  helpBinding.CanExecute += CanHelpExecute;
  helpBinding.Executed += HelpExecuted;
  CommandBindings.Add(helpBinding);
}
```

Most CommandBinding objects will want to handle the CanExecute event (which allows you to specify whether the command occurs based on the operation of your program) and the Executed event (which is where you can author the content that should occur once the command occurs). Add the following event handlers to your Window-derived type (note the format of each method, as required by the associated delegates):

```
private void CanHelpExecute(object sender, CanExecuteRoutedEventArgs e)
{
  // Here, you can set CanExecute to false if you want to prevent the
  // command from executing.
  e.CanExecute = true;
}

private void HelpExecuted(object sender, ExecutedRoutedEventArgs e)
{
  MessageBox.Show("Look, it is not that difficult. Just type something!",
                  "Help!");
}
```

In the preceding snippet, you implemented CanHelpExecute() so it always allows F1 help to launch; you do this by simply returning true. However, if you have certain situations where the help system should not display, you can account for this and return false when necessary. Your "help system" displayed within HelpExecuted() is little more than a message box. At this point, you can run your application. When you press the F1 key on your keyboard, you will see your (less than helpful, if not a bit insulting) user-guidance system (see Figure 28-22).

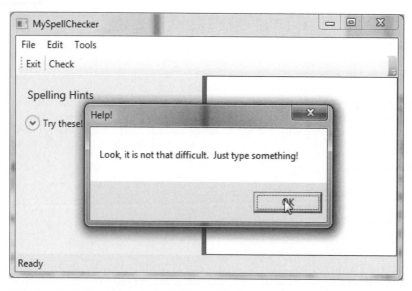

Figure 28-22. Your custom help system (which might not be as helpful as the user would hope)

Working with the Open and Save Commands

To complete the current example, you will add functionality to save your text data to an external file and open up *.txt files for editing. If you want to take the long road, you can manually add programming logic that enables or disables new menu items based on whether your TextBox has data inside it. Once again, however, you can use commands to decrease your burden.

Begin by updating the <MenuItem> element that represents your topmost File menu by adding the following two new submenus that use the Save and Open ApplicationCommands objects:

```
<MenuItem Header="_File">
  <MenuItem Command ="ApplicationCommands.Open"/>
  <MenuItem Command ="ApplicationCommands.Save"/>
  <Separator/>
  <MenuItem Header ="_Exit"
          MouseEnter ="MouseEnterExitArea"
          MouseLeave ="MouseLeaveArea" Click ="FileExit_Click"/>

</MenuItem>
```

Again, remember that all command objects implement the ICommand interface, which defines two events (CanExecute and Executed). Now you need to enable the entire window, so it can check whether it is currently okay to fire these commands; if so, you can define an event handler to execute the custom code.

You do this by populating the CommandBindings collection maintained by the window. To do so in XAML requires that you use property element syntax to define a <Window.CommandBindings> scope in which you place two <CommandBinding> definitions. Update your <Window> like this:

```
<Window x:Class="MyWordPad.MainWindow"
  xmlns="http://schemas.microsoft.com/winfx/2006/xaml/presentation"
  xmlns:x="http://schemas.microsoft.com/winfx/2006/xaml"
  Title="MySpellChecker" Height="331" Width="508"
  WindowStartupLocation ="CenterScreen" >

  <!-- This will inform the Window which handlers to call,
       when testing for the Open and Save commands. -->
  <Window.CommandBindings>
    <CommandBinding Command="ApplicationCommands.Open"
                    Executed="OpenCmdExecuted"
                    CanExecute="OpenCmdCanExecute"/>
    <CommandBinding Command="ApplicationCommands.Save"
                    Executed="SaveCmdExecuted"
                    CanExecute="SaveCmdCanExecute"/>
  </Window.CommandBindings>

  <!-- This panel establishes the content for the window -->
  <DockPanel>
  ...
  </DockPanel>
</Window>
```

Now right-click each of the Executed and CanExecute attributes in your XAML editor and pick the Navigate to Event Handler menu option. As you might recall from Chapter 27, this will automatically generate stub code for the event itself. At this point, you should have four empty handlers in the C# code file for the window.

The implementation of CanExecute event handlers will tell the window that it is okay to fire the corresponding Executed events at any time by setting the CanExecute property of the incoming CanExecuteRoutedEventArgs object.

```
private void OpenCmdCanExecute(object sender, CanExecuteRoutedEventArgs e)
{
  e.CanExecute = true;
}

private void SaveCmdCanExecute(object sender, CanExecuteRoutedEventArgs e)
{
  e.CanExecute = true;
}
```

The corresponding Executed handlers perform the actual work of displaying the open and save dialog boxes; they also send the data in your TextBox to a file. Begin by making sure that you import the System.IO and Microsoft.Win32 namespaces into your code file. The following completed code is straightforward:

```
private void OpenCmdExecuted(object sender, ExecutedRoutedEventArgs e)
{
  // Create an open file dialog box and only show XAML files.
  OpenFileDialog openDlg = new OpenFileDialog();
  openDlg.Filter = "Text Files |*.txt";
```

```
  // Did they click on the OK button?
  if (true == openDlg.ShowDialog())
  {
    // Load all text of selected file.
    string dataFromFile = File.ReadAllText(openDlg.FileName);

    // Show string in TextBox.
    txtData.Text = dataFromFile;
  }
}

private void SaveCmdExecuted(object sender, ExecutedRoutedEventArgs e)
{
  SaveFileDialog saveDlg = new SaveFileDialog();
  saveDlg.Filter = "Text Files |*.txt";

  // Did they click on the OK button?
  if (true == saveDlg.ShowDialog())
  {
    // Save data in the TextBox to the named file.
    File.WriteAllText(saveDlg.FileName, txtData.Text);
  }
}
```

That wraps up this example and your initial look at working with WPF controls. Here, you learned how to work with basic commands, menu systems, status bars, toolbars, nested panels, and a few basic UI controls, such as TextBox and Expander. The next example will work with some more exotic controls, while examining several important WPF services at the same time.

■ **Source Code** You can find the MyWordPad project under the Chapter 28 subdirectory.

A Deeper Look at WPF APIs and Controls

The remainder of this chapter will give you a chance to build a brand-new WPF application using Visual Studio. The goal is to create a UI that consists of a TabControl widget containing a set of tabs. Each tab will illustrate some new WPF controls and interesting APIs you might want to make use of in your software projects. Along the way, you will also learn additional features of the Visual Studio WPF designers.

Working with the TabControl

To get started, create a new WPF Application named WpfControlsAndAPIs. As mentioned, your initial window will contain a TabControl with four different tabs, each of which shows off a set of related controls and/or WPF APIs. Locate the TabControl control in the Visual Studio Toolbox, drop one onto your designer and resize the component to take up a majority of the display area and rename this UI element to myTabSystem.

You will notice that you are given two tab items automatically. In order to add additional tabs, you simply need to right-click the TabControl node in the Document Outline window and select the Add TabItem menu option (you can also right-click the TabControl on the designer to activate the same menu option). Add two additional tabs using either approach (Figure 28-23 shows the Document Outline approach).

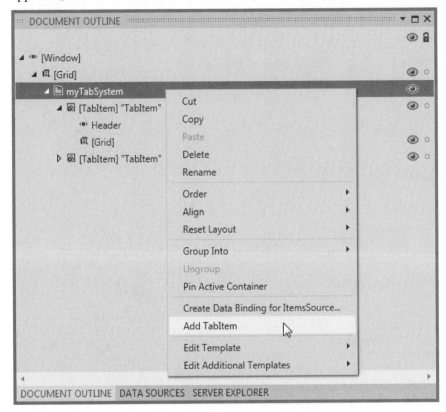

Figure 28-23. Visually adding TabItems

Now, select each TabItem control (on the designer or via the Document Outline window) and change the Header property for each tab, naming them Ink API, Documents, Data Binding, and DataGrid. At this point, your window designer should look like what you see in Figure 28-24.

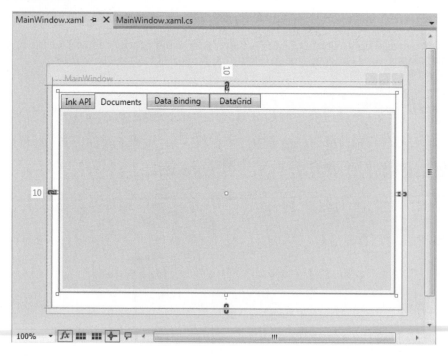

Figure 28-24. *The initial layout of the tab system*

Now click each tab again and use the Properties window to give each tab a unique, proper name. Be aware that when you select a tab for editing, that tab becomes the active tab, and you can design that tab by dragging controls from the Toolbox window. Before you begin to design each tab, take a peek at the XAML that the IDE generates on your behalf. You should see markup similar to the following (your markup might differ based on the properties you set):

```
<TabControl x:Name="myTabSystem" HorizontalAlignment="Left" Height="280"
        Margin="10,10,0,0" VerticalAlignment="Top" Width="489">
    <TabItem Header="Ink API">
        <Grid Background="#FFE5E5E5"/>
    </TabItem>
    <TabItem Header="Documents">
        <Grid Background="#FFE5E5E5"/>
    </TabItem>
    <TabItem Header="Data Binding" HorizontalAlignment="Left" Height="20"
            VerticalAlignment="Top" Width="95" Margin="-2,-2,-36,0">
        <Grid Background="#FFE5E5E5"/>
    </TabItem>
    <TabItem Header="DataGrid" HorizontalAlignment="Left" Height="20"
            VerticalAlignment="Top" Width="74" Margin="-2,-2,-15,0">
        <Grid Background="#FFE5E5E5"/>
    </TabItem>
</TabControl>
```

Now that we have the core TabControl defined, we can work out the details tab by tab, and learn more features of the WPF API along the way.

Building the Ink API Tab

The first tab shows the overall role of WPF's digital Ink API, which allows you to incorporate painting functionality into a program easily. Of course, the application does not literally need to be a painting application; you can use this API for a wide variety of purposes, including capturing handwriting input with a stylus for a Tablet PC.

Begin by locating the node that represents the Ink API tab in your Document Outline area and expand it. You should see that the default layout manager for this TabItem is a <Grid>. Right-click this and change it to a StackPanel (see Figure 28-25).

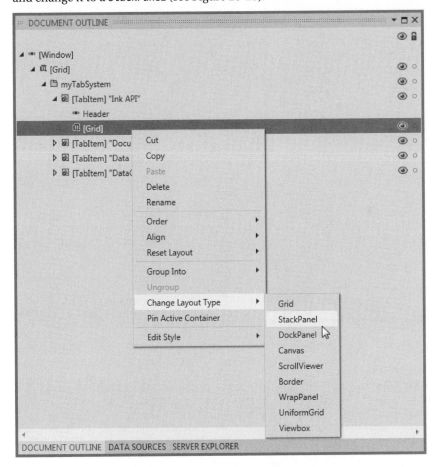

Figure 28-25. *Changing the layout manager of the first tab item*

Designing the ToolBar

Ensure that the StackPanel is the currently selected node in the Document Outline editor and insert a new ToolBar control named inkToolbar. Next, select the inkToolbar for editing and set the Height of the Toolbar control to 60 (the current Width value should be fine). Now find the Common section of the Properties window and click the ellipse button for the Items (Collection) property (see Figure 28-26).

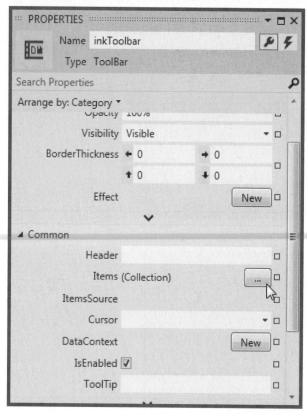

Figure 28-26. Populating the ToolBar with items begins here

After you click this button, you are presented with a dialog box that allows you to select the controls you want to add to the ToolBar. Click the drop-down list box on the bottom center of the dialog, and add three RadioButton controls. You can use the embedded Properties editor of this dialog to give each RadioButton a Height of 50 and a Width of 100 (again, you can find these properties in the Layout area). Also, set the Content property (located in the Common area) of each RadioButton to the values Ink Mode!, Erase Mode!, and Select Mode! (see Figure 28-27).

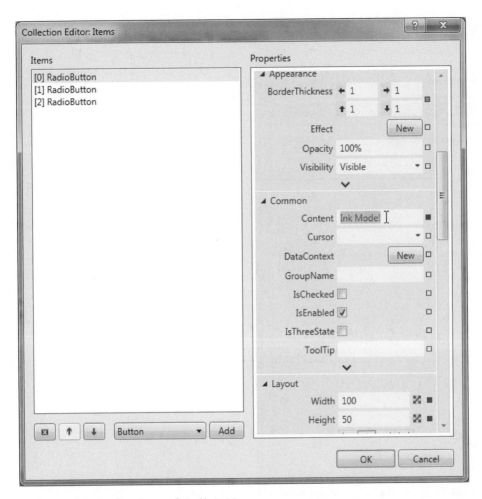

Figure 28-27. Configuring each RadioButton

After you add your three RadioButton controls, add a Separator control using the drop-down list of the Items editor. Now you need to add the final ComboBox (not ComboBoxItem) control listed in the drop-down. When you need to insert nonstandard controls using the Items dialog, just select the <Other Type…> option from the drop-down. This opens the Select Object editor, where you can type in the name of the control you want. Make sure the Show all assemblies option is checked, and then do a search for your control of interest (see Figure 28-28).

Figure 28-28. Using the Select Object editor to add unique items to the toolbar

Set the Width property of the ComboBox to 100 and add three ComboBoxItem objects to the ComboBox using the Items (Collection) property (again) in the Common section of the Properties editor. Set the Content property of each ComboBoxItem to the strings Red, Green, and Blue.

After you do this, close the editor to return to the window designer. The last task for this section is to use the Name property to assign variable names to your new items. Name your three RadioButton controls inkRadio, selectRadio, and eraseRadio. Also, name your ComboBox control comboColors. When all is said and done, the XAML for your first TabItem control should look similar to the following:

```
<TabItem Header="Ink API">
  <StackPanel Background="#FFE5E5E5">
    <ToolBar x:Name="inkToolbar" HorizontalAlignment="Left" Width="479" Height="60">
      <RadioButton x:Name="inkRadio" Content="Ink Mode!" Height="50" Width="100"/>
      <RadioButton x:Name="selectRadio" Content="Erase Mode!" Height="50" Width="100"/>
```

```
        <RadioButton x:Name="eraseRadio" Content="Select Mode!" Height="50" Width="100"/>
        <Separator/>
        <ComboBox x:Name="comboColors" Width="100">
          <ComboBoxItem Content="Red"/>
          <ComboBoxItem Content="Green"/>
          <ComboBoxItem Content="Blue"/>
        </ComboBox>
      </ToolBar>
    </StackPanel>
</TabItem>
```

■ **Note** As you built your toolbar using the IDE, you might have thought to yourself how much quicker your task would be if you could simply edit the XAML by hand. If you feel comfortable typing in the markup directly, you are certainly free to do so. However, I do encourage you to spend time becoming comfortable with the Visual Studio WPF Properties editor. As you will see, a number of advanced features are exposed via this editor.

The RadioButton Control

In this example, you want these three RadioButton controls to be mutually exclusive. In other GUI frameworks, ensuring that a group of related controls (such as radio buttons) were mutually exclusive required that you place them in the same group box. You don't need to do this under WPF. Instead, you can simply assign them all to the same *group name*. This is helpful because the related items do not need to be physically collected in the same area, but can be anywhere in the window.

Do this by selecting each RadioButton on the designer (you can select all three using a Shift-Click operation), and then setting the GroupName property (located in the Common Properties area of the Properties window) to InkMode.

When a RadioButton control is not placed inside of a parent panel control, it will take on a UI identical to a Button control! However, unlike a Button, the RadioButton class includes an IsChecked property, which toggles between true and false when the end user clicks the UI element. Furthermore, RadioButton provides two events (Checked and Unchecked) that you can use to intercept this state change.

To configure your RadioButton controls to look like typical radio buttons, select each control on the designer using a Shift+Click operation, then right-click the selection and pick the Group Into ▶ Border menu option (see Figure 28-29).

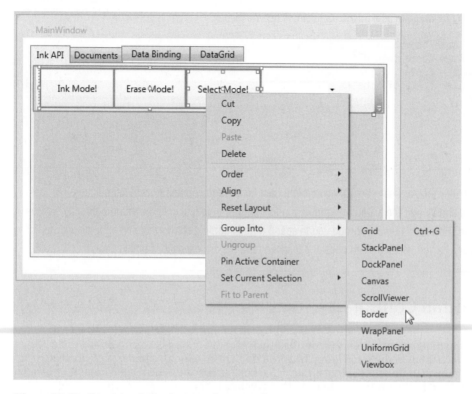

Figure 28-29. *Grouping items in a Border control*

At this point, you're ready to test the program, which you can do by pressing the F5 key. You should now see three mutually exclusive radio buttons and a combo box with three selections (see Figure 28-30).

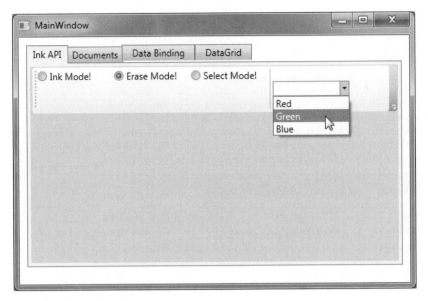

Figure 28-30. *The completed toolbar system*

Handling Events for the Ink API Tab

The next step for the Ink API tab is to handle the Click event for each RadioButton control. Like you have done in other WPF projects in this book, simply select the Lightning Bolt button of the Visual Studio Properties editor to enter the names of event handlers. Using this approach, route the Click event for each button to the same handler, named RadioButtonClicked. After you handle all three Click events, handle the SelectionChanged event of the ComboBox using a handler named ColorChanged. When you finish, you should have the following C# code:

```
public partial class MainWindow : Window
{
  public MainWindow()
  {
    this.InitializeComponent();

    // Insert code required on object creation below this point.
  }
  private void RadioButtonClicked(object sender, System.Windows.RoutedEventArgs e)
  {
    // TODO: Add event handler implementation here.
  }

  private void ColorChanged(object sender,
    System.Windows.Controls.SelectionChangedEventArgs e)
  {
    // TODO: Add event handler implementation here.
  }
}
```

You will implement these handlers in a later step, so leave them empty for the time being.

The InkCanvas Control

To finish the UI of this tab, you need to place an InkCanvas control into the StackPanel, so it appears below the Toolbar you have just created. Unfortunately, the Visual Studio Toolbox will *not* show you every possible WPF component by default. While you could simply type in the necessary XAML, you should know that you can indeed update the items to be displayed in the Toolbox.

To do so, right-click anywhere in the Toolbox area and select the Choose Items... menu option. After a moment or two, you will see a list of possible components to add to the Toolbox. For our purposes, we are interested in adding the InkCanvas control (see Figure 28-31).

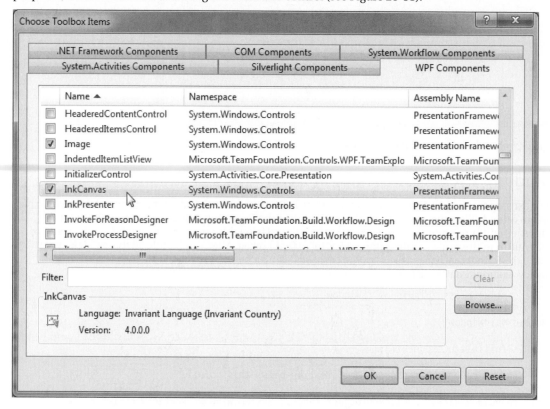

Figure 28-31. Adding new components to the Visual Studio Toolbox

Select the StackPanel for the tabInk object in the Document Outline editor, then add an InkCanvas named myInkCanvas. Resize this new control so that it takes up a majority of the tab area. Also, you might opt to use the Brushes editor to give your InkCanvas a unique background color (you'll learn much more about the Brushes editor in the next chapter). After you do this, run your program by pressing the F5 key. You will see the canvas is already able to draw data when you click-and-drag the left-mouse button (see Figure 28-32).

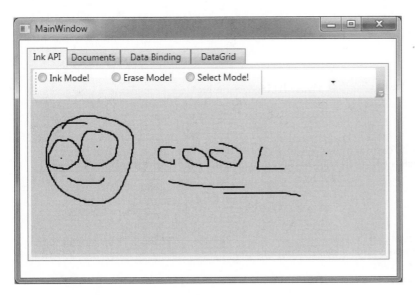

Figure 28-32. The InkCanvas in action

The InkCanvas does more than draw mouse (or stylus) strokes; it also supports a number of unique editing modes, controlled by the EditingMode property. You can assign this property any value from the related InkCanvasEditingMode enumeration. For this example, you are interested in Ink mode, which is the default option you just witnessed; Select mode, which allows the user to select a region with the mouse to move or resize; and EraseByStoke, which will delete the previous mouse stroke.

■ **Note** A *stroke* is the rendering that takes place during a single mouse down/mouse up operation. The InkCanvas stores all strokes in a StrokeCollection object, which you can access using the Strokes property.

Update your RadioButtonClicked() hander with the following logic, which places the InkCanvas in the correct mode, based on the selected RadioButton:

```
private void RadioButtonClicked(object sender,
  System.Windows.RoutedEventArgs e)
{
  // Based on which button sent the event, place the InkCanvas in a unique
  // mode of operation.
  switch((sender as RadioButton).Content.ToString())
  {
    // These strings must be the same as the Content values for each
    // RadioButton.
    case "Ink Mode!":
      this.myInkCanvas.EditingMode = InkCanvasEditingMode.Ink;
    break;
```

```
    case "Erase Mode!":
      this.myInkCanvas.EditingMode = InkCanvasEditingMode.EraseByStroke;
    break;

    case "Select Mode!":
      this.myInkCanvas.EditingMode = InkCanvasEditingMode.Select;
    break;
  }
}
```

Also, set the mode to Ink by default in the window's constructor. And while you are at it, set a default selection for the ComboBox (more details on this control in the next section), as follows:

```
public MainWindow()
{
  this.InitializeComponent();

  // Be in Ink mode by default.
  this.myInkCanvas.EditingMode = InkCanvasEditingMode.Ink;
  this.inkRadio.IsChecked = true;
  this.comboColors.SelectedIndex = 0;
}
```

Now run your program again by pressing F5. Enter Ink mode and draw some data. Next, enter Erase mode and remove the previous mouse stroke you entered (you'll notice the mouse icon automatically looks like an eraser). Finally, enter Select mode and select some strokes by using the mouse as a lasso. After you circle the item, you can move it around the canvas and resize its dimensions. Figure 28-33 shows your edit modes at work.

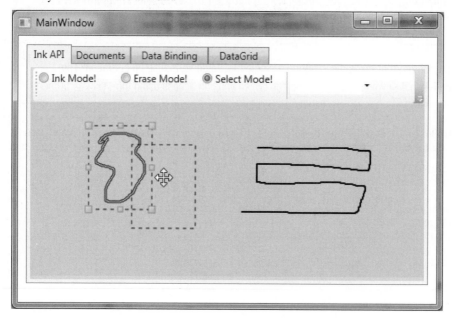

Figure 28-33. The InkCanvas in action, with edit modes!

The ComboBox Control

After you populate a ComboBox control (or a ListBox), you have three ways to determine the selected item. First, if you want to find the numerical index of the item selected, you can use the SelectedIndex property (which is zero-based; a value of -1 represents no selection). Second, if you want to obtain the object within the list that has been selected, the SelectedItem property fits the bill. Third, the SelectedValue allows you to obtain the value of the selected object (typically obtained using a call to ToString()).

You need to add the last bit of code for this tab to change the color of the strokes entered on the InkCanvas. The DefaultDrawingAttributes property of InkCanvas returns a DrawingAttributes object that allows you to configure numerous aspect of the pen nib, including its size and color (among other settings). Update your C# code with this implementation of the ColorChanged() method:

```
private void ColorChanged(object sender,
  System.Windows.Controls.SelectionChangedEventArgs e)
{
  // Get the selected value in the combo box.
  string colorToUse =
    (this.comboColors.SelectedItem as ComboBoxItem).Content.ToString();

  // Change the color used to render the strokes.
  this.myInkCanvas.DefaultDrawingAttributes.Color =
    (Color)ColorConverter.ConvertFromString(colorToUse);
}
```

Now recall that the ComboBox has a collection of ComboBoxItems. If you were to view the generated XAML, you'd see the following definition:

```
<ComboBox x:Name="comboColors" Width="100" SelectionChanged="ColorChanged">
  <ComboBoxItem Content="Red"/>
  <ComboBoxItem Content="Green"/>
  <ComboBoxItem Content="Blue"/>
</ComboBox>
```

When you call SelectedItem, you grab the selected ComboBoxItem, which is stored as a general Object. After you cast the Object as a ComboBoxItem, you pluck out the value of the Content, which will be the string Red, Green, or Blue. This string is then converted to a Color object using the handy ColorConverter utility class. Now run your program again. You should be able to change between colors as you render your image.

Note that the ComboBox and ListBox controls can contain complex content as well, rather than a list of text data. You can get a sense of some of the things that are possible by opening the XAML editor for your window and changing the definition of your ComboBox so it contains a set of <StackPanel> elements, each of which contains an <Ellipse> and a <Label> (notice that the Width of the ComboBox is 200).

```
<ComboBox x:Name="comboColors" Width="200" SelectionChanged="ColorChanged">
  <StackPanel Orientation ="Horizontal" Tag="Red">
    <Ellipse Fill ="Red" Height ="50" Width ="50"/>
    <Label FontSize ="20" HorizontalAlignment="Center"
           VerticalAlignment="Center" Content="Red"/>
  </StackPanel>

  <StackPanel Orientation ="Horizontal" Tag="Green">
    <Ellipse Fill ="Green" Height ="50" Width ="50"/>
    <Label FontSize ="20" HorizontalAlignment="Center"
```

```
            VerticalAlignment="Center" Content="Green"/>
  </StackPanel>

  <StackPanel Orientation ="Horizontal" Tag="Blue">
    <Ellipse Fill ="Blue" Height ="50" Width ="50"/>
    <Label FontSize ="20" HorizontalAlignment="Center"
           VerticalAlignment="Center" Content="Blue"/>
  </StackPanel>
</ComboBox>
```

Notice that each StackPanel assigns a value to its Tag property, which is a simple, fast, and convenient way to discover which stack of items has been selected by the user (there are better ways to do this, but this will do for now). With this adjustment, you need to change the implementation of your ColorChanged() method, like this:

```
private void ColorChanged(object sender,
  System.Windows.Controls.SelectionChangedEventArgs e)
{
  // Get the Tag of the selected StackPanel.
  string colorToUse = (this.comboColors.SelectedItem
      as StackPanel).Tag.ToString();
  ...
}
```

Now run your program again and take note of your unique ComboBox (see Figure 28-34).

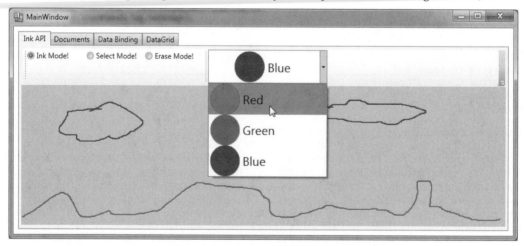

Figure 28-34. A custom ComboBox, thanks to the WPF content model

Saving, Loading, and Clearing InkCanvas Data

The last part of this tab will enable you to save and load your canvas data, as well as clear it of all content. At this point in the chapter, you might feel a bit more comfortable designing a UI, so the instructions will be short and sweet.

Begin by importing the System.IO and System.Windows.Ink namespaces to your code file. Now add three more Button controls to your ToolBar named btnSave, btnLoad, and btnClear. Next, handle the Click event for each control, then implement the handlers, like this:

```
private void SaveData(object sender, System.Windows.RoutedEventArgs e)
{
  // Save all data on the InkCanvas to a local file.
  using (FileStream fs = new FileStream("StrokeData.bin", FileMode.Create))
  {
    this.myInkCanvas.Strokes.Save(fs);
    fs.Close();
  }
}

private void LoadData(object sender, System.Windows.RoutedEventArgs e)
{
  // Fill StrokeCollection from file.
  using(FileStream fs = new FileStream("StrokeData.bin",
    FileMode.Open, FileAccess.Read))
  {
    StrokeCollection strokes = new StrokeCollection(fs);
    this.myInkCanvas.Strokes = strokes;
  }
}

private void Clear(object sender, System.Windows.RoutedEventArgs e)
{
  // Clear all strokes.
  this.myInkCanvas.Strokes.Clear();
}
```

You should now be able to save your data to a file, load it from the file, and clear the InkCanvas of all data. That wraps up the first tab of the TabControl, as well as your examination of the WPF digital Ink API. To be sure, there is more to say about this technology; however, you should be in a good position to dig into the topic further if that interests you. Next, you will learn how to use the WPF Documents API.

Introducing the Documents API

WPF ships with many controls that allow you to capture or display simple blurbs of textual data, including Label, TextBox, TextBlock, and PasswordBox. These controls are useful, but some WPF applications require the use of sophisticated, highly formatted text data, similar to what you might find in an Adobe PDF file. The Documents API of WPF provides such functionality; however, it uses the XML Paper Specification (XPS) format rather than the PDF file format.

You can use the Documents API to construct a print-ready document by leveraging several classes from the System.Windows.Documents namespace. Here you will find a number of types that represent pieces of a rich XPS document, such as List, Paragraph, Section, Table, LineBreak, Figure, Floater, and Span.

Block Elements and Inline Elements

Formally speaking, the items you add to an XPS document belong to one of two broad categories: *block elements* and *inline elements*. This first category, block elements, consists of classes that extend the System.Windows.Documents.Block base class. Examples of block elements include List, Paragraph, BlockUIContainer, Section, and Table. You use classes from this category to group together other content (e.g., a list containing paragraph data, and a paragraph containing subparagraphs for different text formatting).

The second category, inline elements, consists of classes that extend the System.Windows.Documents.Inline base class. You nest inline elements within another block item (or possibly within another inline element inside a block element). Some common inline elements include Run, Span, LineBreak, Figure, and Floater.

These classes possess names that you might encounter when building a rich document with a professional editor. As with any other WPF control, you can configure these classes in XAML or through code. Therefore, you can either declare an empty <Paragraph> element that is populated at runtime (you'll see how to do such tasks in this example) or define a populated <Paragraph> element with static text.

Document Layout Managers

You might think you can simply place inline and block elements directly into a panel container such as a Grid; however, you need to wrap them in a <FlowDocument> element or a <FixedDocument> element.

It is ideal to place items in a FlowDocument when you would like to let your end user change the way the data is presented on the computer screen. The user can do this by zooming text or changing how the data is presented (e.g., a single long page or a pair of columns). You're better off using FixedDocument for true print-ready (WYSIWYG), unchangeable document data.

For this example, you will only concern yourself with the FlowDocument container. After you insert inline and block items to your FlowDocument, the FlowDocument object is placed in one of four specialized XPS-aware layout managers, listed in Table 28-4.

Table 28-4. XPS Control Layout Managers

Panel Control	Meaning in Life
FlowDocumentReader	Displays data in a FlowDocument and adds support for zooming, searching, and content layout in various forms.
FlowDocumentScrollViewer	Displays data in a FlowDocument; however, the data is presented as a single document viewed with scrollbars. This container does not support zooming, searching, or alternative layout modes.
RichTextBox	Displays data in a FlowDocument and adds support for user editing.
FlowDocumentPageViewer	Displays the document page-by-page, one page at a time. Data can also be zoomed, but not searched.

The most feature-rich way to display a FlowDocument is to wrap it within a FlowDocumentReader manager. When you do this, the user can alter the layout, search for words in the document, and zoom

in on the data using the provided UI. The one limitation of this container (as well as of
FlowDocumentScrollViewer and FlowDocumentPageViewer) is that the content you display with it is read
only. However, if you do want to allow the end user to enter new information to the FlowDocument, you
can wrap it in a RichTextBox control.

Building the Documents Tab

Click on the Documents tab of your TabItem and use the designer to open this control for editing. You
should already have a default <Grid> control as the direct child of the TabItem control; however, change it
to a StackPanel here using the Document Outline window. This tab will be used to display a
FlowDocument that allows the user to highlight selected text, as well as add annotations using the Sticky
Notes API.

Begin by defining the following ToolBar control, which has three simple (and unnamed!) Button
controls. You will be rigging up a few new commands to these controls later on, so you do not need to
refer to them in code (feel free to enter the XAML directly, or use the IDE if you prefer).

```
<TabItem x:Name="tabDocuments" Header="Documents" VerticalAlignment="Bottom"
        Height="20">
  <StackPanel>
    <ToolBar>
      <Button BorderBrush="Green" Content="Add Sticky Note"/>
      <Button BorderBrush="Green" Content="Delete Sticky Notes"/>
      <Button BorderBrush="Green" Content="Highlight Text"/>
    </ToolBar>
  </StackPanel>
</TabItem>
```

If you want, you can update the Toolbox of Visual Studio to include a FlowDocumentReader control
(using the same technique as you did when adding the InkCanvas), or update the current TabItem
manually using the XAML editor.

In either case, add a FlowDocumentReader into your StackPanel, rename it to myDocumentReader, and
stretch it out over the surface of your StackPanel. To this new component, add an empty
<FlowDocument>.

```
<FlowDocumentReader x:Name="myDocumentReader" Height="269.4">
  <FlowDocument/>
</FlowDocumentReader>
```

At this point, you can add document classes (e.g., List, Paragraph, Section, Table, LineBreak, Figure,
Floater, and Span) to the <FlowDocument> element. Here is one possible way to configure the
FlowDocument:

```
<FlowDocumentReader x:Name="myDocumentReader" Height="269.4">
  <FlowDocument>
    <Section Foreground = "Yellow" Background = "Black">
      <Paragraph FontSize = "20">
        Here are some fun facts about the WPF Documents API!
      </Paragraph>
    </Section>
    <List/>
    <Paragraph/>
  </FlowDocument>
</FlowDocumentReader>
```

```
</FlowDocumentReader>
```

If you run your program now (hit the F5 key), you should already be able to zoom your document (using the lower-right slider bar), search for a keyword (using the lower-left search editor), and display the data in one of three manners (using the layout buttons).

Before moving to the next step, you might want to edit your XAML to use a different FlowDocument container, such as the FlowDocumentScrollViewer or a RichTextBox, rather than the FlowDocumentReader. After you have done this, run the application again and notice the different ways the document data is handled. Be sure to roll back to the FlowDocumentReader type when you finish this task.

Populating a FlowDocument Using Code

Now, let's build the List block and the remaining Paragraph block in code. This is important because you might need to populate a FlowDocument based on user input, external files, database information, or what have you. Before you do so, use the XAML editor to give the List and Paragraph elements proper names, so you can access them in code.

```
<List x:Name="listOfFunFacts"/>
<Paragraph x:Name="paraBodyText"/>
```

In your code file, define a new private method named PopulateDocument(). This method first adds a set of new ListItems to the List, each of which has a Paragraph with a single Run. Also, your helper method dynamically builds a formatted paragraph using three separate Run objects, as in the following example:

```
private void PopulateDocument()
{
  // Add some data to the List item.
  this.listOfFunFacts.FontSize = 14;
  this.listOfFunFacts.MarkerStyle = TextMarkerStyle.Circle;
  this.listOfFunFacts.ListItems.Add(new ListItem( new
    Paragraph(new Run("Fixed documents are for WYSIWYG print ready docs!"))));
  this.listOfFunFacts.ListItems.Add(new ListItem(
    new Paragraph(new Run("The API supports tables and embedded figures!"))));
  this.listOfFunFacts.ListItems.Add(new ListItem(
    new Paragraph(new Run("Flow documents are read only!"))));
  this.listOfFunFacts.ListItems.Add(new ListItem(new Paragraph(new Run
    ("BlockUIContainer allows you to embed WPF controls in the document!")
    )));

  // Now add some data to the Paragraph.
  // First part of sentence.
  Run prefix = new Run("This paragraph was generated ");

  // Middle of paragraph.
  Bold b = new Bold();
  Run infix = new Run("dynamically");
  infix.Foreground = Brushes.Red;
  infix.FontSize = 30;
  b.Inlines.Add(infix);

  // Last part of paragraph.
  Run suffix = new Run(" at runtime!");
```

```
    // Now add each piece to the collection of inline elements
    // of the Paragraph.
    this.paraBodyText.Inlines.Add(prefix);
    this.paraBodyText.Inlines.Add(infix);
    this.paraBodyText.Inlines.Add(suffix);
}
```

Make sure you call this method from your window's constructor. After you do this, you can run the application and see your new, dynamically generated document content.

Enabling Annotations and Sticky Notes

So far, so good. You can now build a document with interesting data using XAML and C# code; however, you still need to address the three buttons on your toolbar for the Documents tab. WPF ships with a set of commands that are used specifically with the Documents API. You can use these commands to allow the user to select a part of a document for highlighting or to add sticky note annotations. Best of all, you can add all of this with a few lines of code (and a tad of markup).

You can find the command objects for the Documents API bundled in the System.Windows.Annotations namespace of PresentationFramework.dll. Thus, you need to define a custom XML namespace in the opening element of the <Window> to use such objects in XAML (notice that the tag prefix is a), like so:

```
<Window
...
  xmlns:a=
  "clr-namespace:System.Windows.Annotations;assembly=PresentationFramework"
  x:Class="WpfControlsAndAPIs.MainWindow"
  x:Name="Window"
  Title="MainWindow"
  Width="856" Height="383" mc:Ignorable="d"
    WindowStartupLocation="CenterScreen" >
...
</Window>
```

Now update your three <Button> definitions to set the Command property to three of the supplied annotation commands, as follows:

```
<ToolBar>
    <Button BorderBrush="Green" Content="Add Sticky Note"
          Command="a:AnnotationService.CreateTextStickyNoteCommand"/>
    <Button BorderBrush="Green" Content="Delete Sticky Notes"
          Command="a:AnnotationService.DeleteStickyNotesCommand"/>
    <Button BorderBrush="Green" Content="Highlight Text"
          Command="a:AnnotationService.CreateHighlightCommand"/>
</ToolBar>
```

The last thing you need to do is to enable annotation services for the FlowDocumentReader object, which you named myDocumentReader. Add another private method in your class named EnableAnnotations(), which is called from the constructor of the window. Now import the following namespaces:

```
using System.Windows.Annotations;
using System.Windows.Annotations.Storage;
```

Next, implement this method:

```
private void EnableAnnotations()
{
  // Create the AnnotationService object that works
  // with our FlowDocumentReader.
  AnnotationService anoService = new AnnotationService(myDocumentReader);

  // Create a MemoryStream that will hold the annotations.
  MemoryStream anoStream = new MemoryStream();

  // Now, create an XML-based store based on the MemoryStream.
  // You could use this object to programmatically add, delete,
  // or find annotations.
  AnnotationStore store = new XmlStreamStore(anoStream);

  // Enable the annotation services.
  anoService.Enable(store);
}
```

The AnnotationService class allows a given document layout manger to opt in to annotation support. Before you call the Enable() method of this object, you need to provide a location for the object to store annotation data, which in this example is a chunk of memory represented by a MemoryStream object. Notice that you connect the AnnotationService object with the Stream using the AnnotationStore.

Now, run your application. When you select some text, you can click the Add Sticky Note button and type in some information. Also, when you select some text, you can highlight data (the color is yellow by default). Finally, you can delete created notes by selecting them and clicking the Delete Sticky Note button. Figure 28-35 shows a test run.

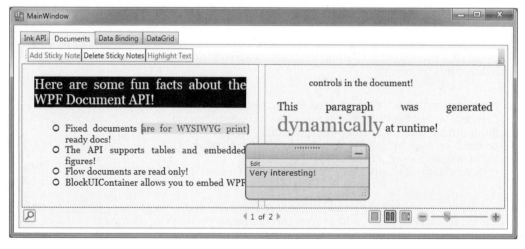

Figure 28-35. Sticky notes!

Saving and Loading a Flow Document

Let's wrap up this look at the Documents API by looking at how simple it is to save a document out to a file, as well as read a document in from a file. Recall that, unless you wrap your FlowDocument object in a RichTextBox, the end user cannot edit the document; however, part of the document was created dynamically at runtime, so you might like to save it for later use. The ability to load an XPS-style document could also be useful in many WPF applications because you might want to define a blank document and load it all on the fly.

This next snippet assumes you will add two new Buttons to the Toolbar of the Documents tab, which you declare like this (note that you did not handle any events in your markup):

```
<Button x:Name="btnSaveDoc" HorizontalAlignment="Stretch"
        VerticalAlignment="Stretch" Width="75" Content="Save Doc"/>
<Button x:Name="btnLoadDoc" HorizontalAlignment="Stretch"
        VerticalAlignment="Stretch" Width="75" Content="Load Doc"/>
```

Now, in the constructor of your window, author the following lambda expressions to save and load the FlowDocument data (you'll need to import the System.Windows.Markup namespace to gain access to the XamlReader and XamlWriter classes):

```
public MainWindow()
{
...
  // Rig up some Click handlers for the save/load of the flow doc.
  btnSaveDoc.Click += (o, s) =>
  {
    using(FileStream fStream = File.Open(
      "documentData.xaml", FileMode.Create))
    {
      XamlWriter.Save(this.myDocumentReader.Document, fStream);
    }
  };

  btnLoadDoc.Click += (o, s) =>
  {
    using(FileStream fStream = File.Open("documentData.xaml", FileMode.Open))
    {
      try
      {
        FlowDocument doc = XamlReader.Load(fStream) as FlowDocument;
        this.myDocumentReader.Document = doc;
      }
      catch(Exception ex) {MessageBox.Show(ex.Message, "Error Loading Doc!");}
    }
  };
}
```

That is all you need to do to save the document (note that you did not save any annotations; however, you can also accomplish that using annotation services). If you click your Save button, you will see a new *.xaml file in your \bin\Debug folder. This file contains the current document data.

That wraps up your look at the WPF Documents API. To be sure, there is more to this API than you have seen here; but at this point, you know a good deal about the basics. To wrap up this chapter, you will look at a handful of data-binding topics and complete the current application.

Introducing the WPF Data-Binding Model

Controls are often the target of various data-binding operations. Simply put, *data binding* is the act of connecting control properties to data values that might change over the course of your application's lifetime. Doing so lets a user interface element display the state of a variable in your code. For example, you might use data binding to accomplish the following:

- Check a CheckBox control based on a Boolean property of a given object.

- Display data in DataGrid objects from a relational database table.

- Connect a Label to an integer that represents the number of files in a folder.

When you use the intrinsic WPF data-binding engine, you must be aware of the distinction between the *source* and the *destination* of the binding operation. As you might expect, the source of a data-binding operation is the data itself (e.g., a Boolean property or relational data), while the destination (target) is the UI control property that uses the data content (e.g., a property on a CheckBox or TextBox control).

Truth be told, using the WPF data-binding infrastructure is always optional. If you were to roll your own data-binding logic, the connection between a source and destination typically would involve handling various events and authoring procedural code to connect the source and destination. For example, if you had a ScrollBar on a window that needed to display its value on a Label type, you might handle the ScrollBar's ValueChanged event and update the Label's content accordingly.

However, you can use WPF data binding to connect the source and destination directly in XAML (or use C# code in your code file) without the need to handle various events or hard-code the connections between the source and destination. Also, based on how you set up your data-binding logic, you can ensure that the source and destination stay in sync if either of their values changes.

Building the Data Binding Tab

Using the Document Outline editor, change the Grid of your third tab to a StackPanel. Now, use the Toolbox and Properties editor of Visual Studio to build the following initial layout:

```
<TabItem x:Name="tabDataBinding" Header="Data Binding">
  <StackPanel Width="250">
    <Label Content="Move the scroll bar to see the current value"/>

    <!-- The scrollbar's value is the source of this data bind. -->
    <ScrollBar x:Name="mySB" Orientation="Horizontal" Height="30"
          Minimum = "1" Maximum = "100" LargeChange="1" SmallChange="1"/>

    <!-- The label's content will be bound to the scroll bar! -->
    <Label x:Name="labelSBThumb" Height="30" BorderBrush="Blue"
          BorderThickness="2" Content = "0"/>
  </StackPanel>
</TabItem>
```

Notice that the <ScrollBar> object (named mySB here) has been configured with a range between 1 and 100. The goal is to ensure that, as you reposition the thumb of the scrollbar (or click the left or right arrow), the Label will automatically update with the current value. Currently, the Content property of the Label control is set to the value "0"; however, we will change this via a data-binding operation.

Establishing Data Bindings Using Visual Studio

The glue that makes it possible to define a binding in XAML is the {Binding} markup extension. If you would like to establish a binding between controls using Visual Studio, you can do so easily. For this example, locate the Content property of the Label object (in the Common area of the Properties window) and click the small square next to the property to open a context menu. From here, select Data Binding (see Figure 28-36).

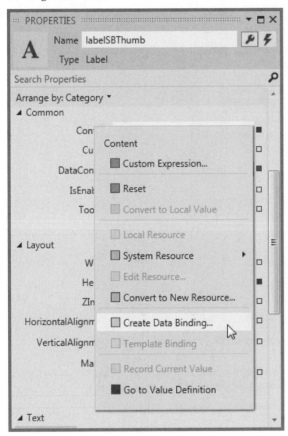

Figure 28-36. *Configuring a data-binding operation*

Next, select the ElementName option from the Binding Type drop-down list, which will give you a list of all items in your XAML file that can be selected as the source of the data-binding operation. In the Element Name tree control, find your ScrollBar object (named mySB). In the Path tree, find the Value property (see Figure 28-37). Click the OK button once you do this.

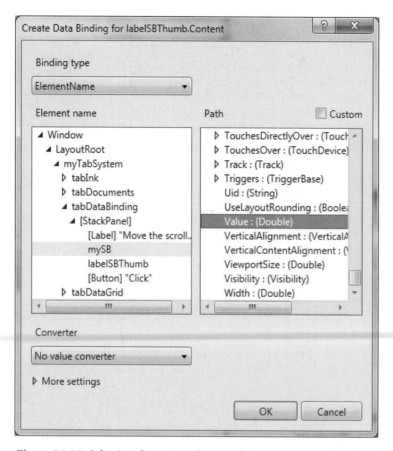

Figure 28-37. *Selecting the source object and the property on the object*

If you run your program again, you will find that the content of the label updates as you move the thumb! Now look at the following XAML the data-binding tool generated on your behalf:

```
<Label x:Name="labelSBThumb" Height="30" BorderBrush="Blue" BorderThickness="2"
    Content = "{Binding Value, ElementName=mySB}"/>
```

Note the value assigned to the Label's Content property. Here, the ElementName value represents the source of the data-binding operation (the ScrollBar object), while the first item after the Binding keyword (Value) represents (in this case) the property of the element to obtain.

If you have worked with WPF data binding previously, you might expect to see the use of the Path token to set the property to observe on the object. For example, the following markup would also update the Label correctly:

```
<Label x:Name="labelSBThumb" Height="30" BorderBrush="Blue"
    BorderThickness="2" Content = "{Binding Path=Value, ElementName=mySB }"/>
```

By default, the Path= aspect of the data-binding operation is omitted unless the property is a subproperty of another object (e.g., myObject.MyProperty.Object2.Property2).

The DataContext Property

You can define a data-binding operation in XAML using an alternative format, where it is possible to break out the values specified by the {Binding} markup extension by explicitly setting the DataContext property to the source of the binding operation, as follows:

```
<!-- Breaking object/value apart via DataContext -->
<Label x:Name="labelSBThumb" Height="30" BorderBrush="Blue"
       BorderThickness="2"
       DataContext = "{Binding ElementName=mySB}"
       Content = "{Binding Path=Value}" />
```

In the current example, the output would be identical if you were to modify the markup in this way. Given this, you might wonder when you would want to set the DataContext property explicitly. Doing so can be helpful because subelements can inherit its value in a tree of markup.

In this way, you can easily set the same data source to a family of controls, rather than having to repeat a bunch of redundant "{Binding ElementName=X, Path=Y}" XAML values to multiple controls. For example, assume you have added the following new Button to the <StackPanel> of this tab (you'll see why it is so large in just a moment):

```
<Button Content="Click" Height="140"/>
```

You could use Visual Studio to generate data bindings for multiple controls, but instead try entering the modified markup manually using the XAML editor, like so:

```
<!-- Note the StackPanel sets the DataContext property. -->
<StackPanel Width="250" DataContext = "{Binding ElementName=mySB}">
  <Label Content="Move the scroll bar to see the current value"/>

  <ScrollBar Orientation="Horizontal" Height="30" Name="mySB"
             Maximum = "100" LargeChange="1" SmallChange="1"/>

  <!-- Now both UI elements use the scrollbar's value in unique ways. -->
  <Label x:Name="labelSBThumb" Height="30" BorderBrush="Blue" BorderThickness="2"
         Content = "{Binding Path=Value}"/>

  <Button Content="Click" Height="200"
          FontSize = "{Binding Path=Value}"/>
</StackPanel>
```

Here, you set the DataContext property on the <StackPanel> directly. Therefore, as you move the thumb, you see not only the current value on the Label, but also see the font size of the Button grow and shrink accordingly, based on the same value (see Figure 28-38 shows one possible output).

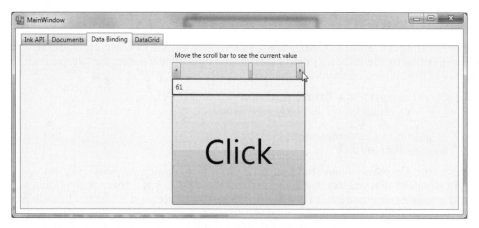

Figure 28-38. Binding the ScrollBar value to a Label and a Button

Data Conversion Using IValueConverter

The ScrollBar type uses a double to represent the value of the thumb, rather than an expected whole number (e.g., an integer). Therefore, as you drag the thumb, you will find various floating-point numbers displayed within the Label (e.g., 61.0576923076923). The end user would find this rather unintuitive because he is most likely expecting to see whole numbers (e.g., 61, 62, and 63).

If you want to convert the value of a data-binding operation into an alternative format, you could create a custom class that implements the IValueConverter interface of the System.Windows.Data namespace. This interface defines two members that allow you to perform the conversion to and from the target and destination (in the case of a two-way data binding). After you define this class, you can use it to qualify further the processing of your data-binding operation.

Assuming that you want to display whole numbers within the Label control, you can build the following custom conversion class. Activate the Project Add Class menu and insert a class named MyDoubleConverter. Next, add the following:

```csharp
class MyDoubleConverter : IValueConverter
{
  public object Convert(object value, Type targetType, object parameter,
                    System.Globalization.CultureInfo culture)
  {
    // Convert the double to an int.
    double v = (double)value;
    return (int)v;
  }

  public object ConvertBack(object value, Type targetType, object parameter,
                      System.Globalization.CultureInfo culture)
  {
    // You won't worry about "two-way" bindings
    // here, so just return the value.
    return value;
  }
}
```

The Convert() method is called when the value is transferred from the source (the ScrollBar) to the destination (the Text property of the TextBox). You receive many incoming arguments, but you only need to manipulate the incoming object for this conversion, which is the value of the current double. You can use this type to cast the type into an integer and return the new number.

The ConvertBack() method will be called when the value is passed from the destination to the source (if you have enabled a two-way binding mode). Here, you simply return the value straightaway. Doing so lets you type a floating-point value into the TextBox (e.g., 99.9) and have it automatically convert to a whole number value (e.g., 99) when the user tabs off the control. This "free" conversion happens due to the fact that the Convert() method is called again, after a call to ConvertBack(). If you were simply to return null from ConvertBack(), your binding would appear to be out of sync because the text box would still be displaying a floating-point number.

Establishing Data Bindings in Code

With this class in place, you are ready to register your custom converter with any control that wishes to use it. You could accomplish this exclusively in XAML; however, to do so, you would need to define some custom object resources, which you will not learn how to do until the next chapter. For now, you can register your data conversion class in code. Begin by cleaning up the current definition of the <Label> control in your data binding tab, so that it no longer uses the {Binding} markup extension.

```
<Label x:Name="labelSBThumb" Height="30" BorderBrush="Blue"
       BorderThickness="2" Content = "0"/>
```

In your window's constructor, call a new private helper function called SetBindings(). In this method, add the following code:

```
private void SetBindings()
{
  // Create a Binding object.
  Binding b = new Binding();

  // Register the converter, source, and path.
  b.Converter = new MyDoubleConverter();
  b.Source = this.mySB;
  b.Path = new PropertyPath("Value");

  // Call the SetBinding method on the Label.
  this.labelSBThumb.SetBinding(Label.ContentProperty, b);
}
```

The only part of this function that probably looks a bit off is the call to SetBinding(). Notice that the first parameter calls a static, read-only field of the Label class named ContentProperty. As you will learn about in Chapter 31, you are specifying what is known as a *dependency property*. For the time being, just know that when you set bindings in code, the first argument will nearly always require you to specify the name of the class that wants the binding (the Label, in this case), followed by a call to the underlying property with the Property suffix (again, you'll learn more about this in Chapter 31). In any case, running the application illustrates that the Label only prints out whole numbers.

Building the DataGrid Tab

The previous data-binding example illustrated how to configure two (or more) controls to participate in a data-binding operation. While this is helpful, it is also possible to bind data from XML files, database data, and in-memory objects. To complete this example, you will design the final tab of your tab control, so it displays data obtained from the Inventory table of the AutoLot database.

As with the other tabs, you begin by changing the current Grid to a StackPanel. Do this by directly updating the XAML using Visual Studio. Now define a DataGrid control in your new StackPanel named gridInventory, like so:

```
<TabItem x:Name="tabDataGrid" Header="DataGrid">
  <StackPanel>
    <DataGrid x:Name="gridInventory" Height="288"/>
  </StackPanel>
</TabItem>
```

Next, reference the AutoLotDAL.dll assembly you created in Chapter 23 (where you used the Entity Framework). When you do so, Visual Studio will automatically reference the required System.Data.Entity.dll assembly, as well as the related App.config file which contains the required connection string data (check your Solution Explorer to verify this is the case; if not, manually add the required items).

Open the code file for your window and add a final helper function called ConfigureGrid();make sure you call this from your constructor. Assuming that you did import the AutoLotDAL namespace, all you need to do is add a few lines of code, like so:

```
private void ConfigureGrid()
{
  using (AutoLotEntities context = new AutoLotEntities())
  {
    // Build a LINQ query that gets back some data from the Inventory table.
    var dataToShow = from c in context.Inventories
      select new { c.CarID, c.Make, c.Color, c.PetName };
    this.gridInventory.ItemsSource = dataToShow;
  }
}
```

Notice that you do not directly bind context.Inventories to the grid's ItemsSource collection; instead, you build a LINQ query that appears to ask for the same data in the entities. The reason for this approach: the Inventory object set *also* contains additional EF (Entity Framework) properties that would appear on the grid, but which don't map to the physical database.

If we were to run the project as is, you would see an extremely plain grid. To make the grid a bit less of an eyesore, use the Visual Studio Properties window to edit the Rows category of the DataGrid. At a minimum, set the AlternationCount property to 2 and pick a custom brush using the integrated editor for the AlternatingRowBackground and RowBackground properties. You can see the final tab for this example in Figure 28-39.

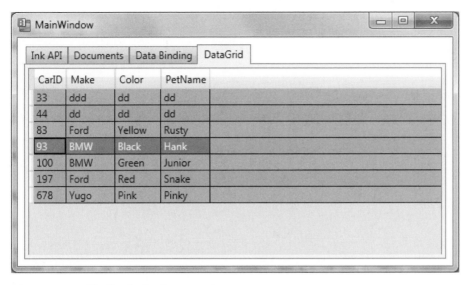

Figure 28-39. The final tab of your project

That wraps up the current example. You'll use some other controls in action during later chapters; at this point, however, you should feel comfortable with the process of building UIs in Visual Studio and manually using XAML and C# code.

■ **Source Code** You can find the WpfControlsAndAPIs project under the Chapter 28 subdirectory.

Summary

This chapter examined several aspects of WPF controls, beginning with an overview of the control toolkit and the role of layout managers (panels). The first example gave you a chance to build a simple word processor application that illustrated the integrated spell-checking functionality of WPF, as well as how to build a main window with menu systems, status bars, and toolbars.

More importantly, you examined how to use WPF commands. Recall that you can attach these control-agnostic events to a UI element or an input gesture to inherit out-of-the-box services automatically (e.g., clipboard operations).

You also learned quite a bit about using Visual Studio to build out UIs via the integrated visual designers. Specifically, you built a complex user interface using numerous aspects of the tool, and you learned about the WPF Ink and Document APIs at the same time. You also received an introduction to WPF data-binding operations, including how to use the WPF DataGrid class to display data from your custom AutoLot database.

CHAPTER 29

WPF Graphics Rendering Services

In this chapter, we'll examine the graphical rendering capabilities of WPF. As you'll see, WPF provides three separate ways to render graphical data—shapes, drawings, and visuals. After you understand the pros and cons of each approach, you will start learning about the world of interactive 2D graphics using the classes within System.Windows.Shapes. After this, you'll see how drawings and geometries allow you to render 2D data in a more lightweight manner. And last but not least, you'll learn how the visual layer gives you the greatest level of power and performance.

Along the way, you will explore a number of related topics, such as the creation of custom brushes and pens, how to apply graphical transformations to your renderings, and how to perform hit-test operations. In particular, you'll see how the integrated tools of Visual Studio, and an additional tool named Expression Design, can help simplify your graphical coding endeavors.

■ **Note** Graphics are a key aspect of WPF development. Even if you are not building a graphics-heavy application (such as a video game or multimedia application), the topics in this chapter are critical when you work with services such as control templates, animations, and data-binding customization.

Understanding WPF's Graphical Rendering Services

WPF uses a particular flavor of graphical rendering that goes by the term *retained-mode graphics*. Simply put, this means that as you are using XAML or procedural code to generate graphical renderings, it is the responsibility of WPF to persist these visual items and ensure they are correctly redrawn and refreshed in an optimal manner. Thus, when you render graphical data, it is always present, even when the end user hides the image by resizing or minimizing the window, by covering the window with another, and so forth.

In stark contrast, previous Microsoft graphical rendering APIs (including Windows Form's GDI+) were *immediate-mode* graphical systems. In this model, it was up to the programmer to ensure that rendered visuals were correctly "remembered" and updated during the life of the application. For example, in a Windows Forms application, rendering a shape such as a rectangle involved handling the Paint event (or overriding the virtual OnPaint() method), obtaining a Graphics object to draw the rectangle and, most important, adding the infrastructure to ensure that the image was persisted when the user resized the window (for example, creating member variables to represent the position of the rectangle and calling Invalidate() throughout your program).

The shift from immediate-mode to retained-mode graphics is indeed a good thing, as programmers have far less grungy graphics code to author and maintain. However, I'm not suggesting that the WPF graphics API is *completely* different from earlier rendering toolkits. For example, like GDI+, WPF supports various brush types and pen objects, techniques for hit-testing, clipping regions, graphical transformations, and so on. So, if you currently have a background in GDI+ (or C/C++-based GDI), you already know a good deal about how to perform basic renderings under WPF.

WPF Graphical Rendering Options

As with other aspects of WPF development, you have a number of choices regarding how to perform your graphical rendering, beyond the decision to do so via XAML or procedural C# code (or perhaps a combination of both). Specifically, WPF provides the following three distinct ways to render graphical data:

- **Shapes**: WPF provides the System.Windows.Shapes namespace, which defines a small number of classes for rendering 2D geometric objects (rectangles, ellipses, polygons, etc.). While these types are very simple to use, and very powerful, they do come with a fair amount of memory overhead if used with reckless abandon.

- **Drawings and Geometries**: The WPF API provides a second way to render graphical data, using descendants from the System.Windows.Media.Drawing abstract class. Using classes such as GeometryDrawing or ImageDrawing (in addition to various *geometry objects*) you can render graphical data in a more lightweight (but less feature-rich) manner.

- **Visuals**: The fastest and most lightweight way to render graphical data under WPF is using the visual layer, which is accessible only through C# code. Using descendants of System.Windows.Media.Visual, you can speak directly to the WPF graphical subsystem.

The reason for offering different ways to do the exact same thing (i.e., render graphical data) has to do with memory use and, ultimately, application performance. Because WPF is such a graphically intensive system, it is not unreasonable for an application to render hundreds or even thousands of different images on a window's surface, and the choice of implementation (shapes, drawings, or visuals) could have a huge impact.

Do understand that when you build a WPF application, chances are good you'll use all three options. As a rule of thumb, if you need a modest amount of *interactive* graphical data that can be manipulated by the user (receive mouse input, display tooltips, etc.), you'll want to use members in the System.Windows.Shapes namespace.

In contrast, drawings and geometries are more appropriate when you need to model complex, generally noninteractive, vector-based graphical data using XAML or C#. While drawings and geometries can still respond to mouse events, hit-testing, and drag-and-drop operations, you will typically need to author more code to do so.

Last but not least, if you require the fastest possible way to render massive amounts of graphical data, the visual layer is the way to go. For example, let's say you are using WPF to build a scientific application that can plot out thousands of points of data. Using the visual layer, you can render the plot points in the most optimal way possible. As you will see later in this chapter, the visual layer is only accessible via C# code, and is not XAML-friendly.

No matter which approach you take (shapes, drawings and geometries, or visuals) you will make use of common graphical primitives such as brushes (which fill interiors), pens (which draw exteriors), and transformation objects (which, well, transform the data). To begin the journey, we will begin working with the classes of System.Windows.Shapes.

■ **Note** WPF also ships with a full-blown API that can be used to render and manipulate 3D graphics, which is not addressed in this edition of the text. Please consult the .NET Framework 4.5 SDK documentation if you are interested in incorporating 3D graphics in your applications.

Rendering Graphical Data Using Shapes

Members of the System.Windows.Shapes namespace provide the most straightforward, most interactive, yet most memory-intensive way to render a two-dimensional image. This namespace (defined in the PresentationFramework.dll assembly) is quite small and consists of only six sealed classes that extend the abstract Shape base class: Ellipse, Rectangle, Line, Polygon, Polyline, and Path.

Create a new WPF Application named RenderingWithShapes. Now, if you locate the abstract Shape class in the Visual Studio object browser (see Figure 29-1) and expand each of the parent nodes, you can see that each descendant of Shape receives a great deal of functionality up the inheritance chain.

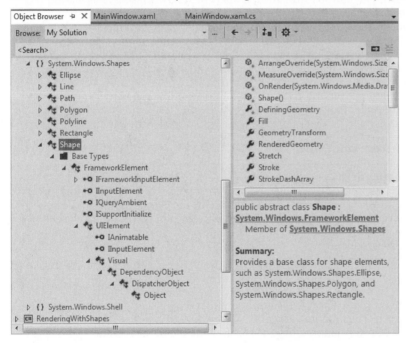

Figure 29-1. The Shape base class receives a good deal of functionality from its parent classes

Now, given your work in the previous two chapters, some of these parent classes might ring a bell. Recall, for example, that UIElement defines numerous methods to receive mouse input and deal with drag-and-drop events, while FrameworkElement defines members to deal with sizing, tooltips, mouse cursors, and whatnot. Given this inheritance chain, be aware that when you render graphical data using Shape-derived classes, the objects are just about as functional (as far as user interactivity is concerned) as a WPF control!

For example, determining whether the user has clicked on your rendered image is no more complicated than handling the MouseDown event. By way of a simple example, if you authored the following XAML of a Rectangle object in the Grid of your initial Window:

```
<Rectangle x:Name="myRect" Height="30" Width="30"
           Fill="Green" MouseDown="myRect_MouseDown"/>
```

you could implement a C# event handler for the MouseDown event that changes the rectangle's background color when clicked, like so:

```
private void myRect_MouseDown(object sender, MouseButtonEventArgs e)
{
  // Change color of Rectangle when clicked.
  myRect.Fill = Brushes.Pink;
}
```

Unlike with other graphical toolkits you may have used, you do *not* need to author a ton of infrastructure code that manually maps mouse coordinates to the geometry, manually calculates hit-testing, renders to an off-screen buffer, and so forth. The members of System.Windows.Shapes simply respond to the events you register with, just like a typical WPF control (e.g., Button, etc.).

The downside of all this out-of-the-box functionality is that the shapes do take up a fair amount of memory. Again, if you're building a scientific application that plots thousands of points on the screen, using shapes would be a poor choice (essentially, it would be about as memory-intensive as rendering thousands of Button objects!). However, when you need to generate an interactive 2D vector image, shapes are a wonderful choice.

Beyond the functionality inherited from the UIElement and FrameworkElement parent classes, Shape defines a number of members for each of the children; some of the more useful ones are shown in Table 29-1.

Table 29-1. Key Properties of the Shape Base Class

Properties	Meaning in Life
DefiningGeometry	Returns a Geometry object that represents the overall dimensions of the current shape. This object contains *only* the plot points that are used to render the data, and has no trace of the functionality from UIElement or FrameworkElement.
Fill	Allows you to specify a "brush object" to render the interior portion of a shape.
GeometryTransform	Allows you to apply transformations to a shape, *before* it is rendered on the screen. The inherited RenderTransform property (from UIElement) applies the transformation *after* it has been rendered on the screen.
Stretch	Describes how to fill a shape within its allocated space, such as its position within a layout manager. This is controlled using the corresponding System.Windows.Media.Stretch enumeration.
Stroke	Defines a brush object, or in some cases, a pen object (which is really a brush in disguise) that is used to paint the border of a shape.

StrokeDashArray, StrokeEndLineCap, StrokeStartLineCap, StrokeThickness	These (and other) stroke-related properties control how lines are configured when drawing the border of a shape. In a majority of cases, these properties will configure the brush used to draw a border or line.

■ **Note** If you forget to set the Fill and Stroke properties, WPF will give you "invisible" brushes and, therefore, the shape will not be visible on the screen!

Adding Rectangles, Ellipses, and Lines to a Canvas

Later in this chapter, you will learn to use Expression Design to generate XAML descriptions of graphical data. For now, we will build a WPF application that can render shapes using XAML and C#, and while doing so, learn a bit about the process of hit-testing. First of all, go ahead and remove the current Rectangle description and the C# event handler logic. Now, update the initial XAML of the <Window> to define a <DockPanel>, containing a (now empty) <ToolBar> and a <Canvas>. Note that we have given each contained item a fitting name via the Name property.

```
<DockPanel LastChildFill="True">
  <ToolBar DockPanel.Dock="Top" Name="mainToolBar" Height="50">
  </ToolBar>
  <Canvas Background="LightBlue" Name="canvasDrawingArea"/>
</DockPanel>
```

Now, populate the <ToolBar> with a set of <RadioButton> objects, each of which contains a specific Shape-derived class as content. Notice that each <RadioButton> is assigned to the same GroupName (to ensure mutual exclusivity) and is also given a fitting name.

```
<ToolBar DockPanel.Dock="Top" Name="mainToolBar" Height="50">
  <RadioButton Name="circleOption" GroupName="shapeSelection">
    <Ellipse Fill="Green" Height="35" Width="35" />
  </RadioButton>

  <RadioButton Name="rectOption" GroupName="shapeSelection">
    <Rectangle Fill="Red" Height="35"
               Width="35" RadiusY="10" RadiusX="10" />
  </RadioButton>

  <RadioButton Name="lineOption" GroupName="shapeSelection">
    <Line  Height="35" Width="35"
           StrokeThickness="10" Stroke="Blue"
           X1="10" Y1="10" Y2="25" X2="25"
           StrokeStartLineCap="Triangle" StrokeEndLineCap="Round" />
  </RadioButton>
</ToolBar>
```

As you can see, declaring Rectangle, Ellipse, and Line objects in XAML is quite straightforward and requires little comment. Recall that the Fill property is used to specify a *brush* to paint the interior of a shape. When you require a solid-colored brush, you can simply specify a hard-coded string of known values and the underlying type converter will generate the correct object. One interesting feature of the Rectangle type is that it defines RadiusX and RadiusY properties to allow you to render curved corners if you require.

Line represents its starting and end points using the X1, X2, Y1, and Y2 properties (given that *height* and *width* make little sense when describing a line). Here we are setting up a few additional properties that control how to render the starting and ending points of the Line, as well as how to configure the stroke settings. Figure 29-2 shows the rendered toolbar, as seen through the Visual Studio WPF designer.

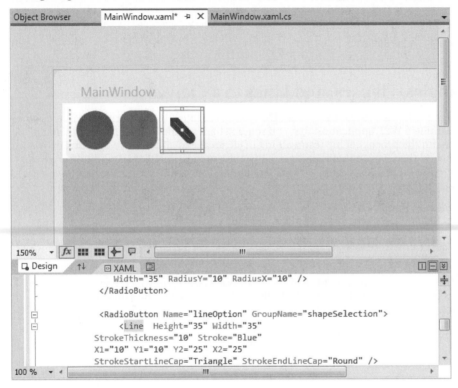

Figure 29-2. Using Shapes as content for a set of RadioButtons

Now, using the Properties window of Visual Studio, handle the MouseLeftButtonDown event for the Canvas, and the Click event for each RadioButton. In your C# file, your goal is to render the selected shape (a circle, square, or line) when the user clicks within the Canvas. First, define the following nested enum (and corresponding member variable) within your Window derived class:

```
public partial class MainWindow : Window
{
  private enum SelectedShape
  { Circle, Rectangle, Line }

  private SelectedShape currentShape;
...
}
```

Within each Click event handler, set the currentShape member variable to the correct SelectedShape value. For example, here is the implementation code for the Click event of the circleOption RadioButton. Implement the remaining two Click handlers in a similar manner.

```
private void circleOption_Click(object sender, RoutedEventArgs e)
{
  currentShape = SelectedShape.Circle;
}
```

With the MouseLeftButtonDown event handler of the Canvas, you will render out the correct shape (of a predefined size), using the X,Y position of the mouse cursor as a starting point. Here is the complete implementation, with analysis to follow:

```
private void canvasDrawingArea_MouseLeftButtonDown(object sender, MouseButtonEventArgs e)
{
  Shape shapeToRender = null;

  // Configure the correct shape to draw.
  switch (currentShape)
  {
    case SelectedShape.Circle:
      shapeToRender = new Ellipse() { Fill = Brushes.Green, Height = 35, Width = 35 };
      break;
    case SelectedShape.Rectangle:
      shapeToRender = new Rectangle()
        { Fill = Brushes.Red, Height = 35, Width = 35, RadiusX = 10, RadiusY = 10 };
      break;
    case SelectedShape.Line:
      shapeToRender = new Line()
      {
        Stroke = Brushes.Blue,
        StrokeThickness = 10,
        X1 = 0, X2 = 50, Y1 = 0, Y2 = 50,
        StrokeStartLineCap= PenLineCap.Triangle,
        StrokeEndLineCap = PenLineCap.Round
      };
      break;
    default:
      return;
  }

  // Set top/left position to draw in the canvas.
  Canvas.SetLeft(shapeToRender, e.GetPosition(canvasDrawingArea).X);
  Canvas.SetTop(shapeToRender, e.GetPosition(canvasDrawingArea).Y);

  // Draw shape!
  canvasDrawingArea.Children.Add(shapeToRender);
}
```

■ **Note** You might notice that the Ellipse, Rectangle, and Line objects being created in this method have the same property settings as the corresponding XAML definitions! As you might hope, we can streamline this code—but that requires an understanding of the WPF object resources, which we will examine in Chapter 30.

As you can see, we are testing the currentShape member variable to create the correct Shape-derived object. After this point, we set the top-left value within the Canvas using the incoming MouseButtonEventArgs. Last but not least, we add the new Shape-derived type to the collection of UIElement objects maintained by the Canvas. If you run your program now, you should be able to click anywhere in the canvas and see the selected shape rendered at the location of the left mouse-click.

Removing Rectangles, Ellipses, and Lines from a Canvas

With the Canvas maintaining a collection of objects, you might wonder how you can dynamically remove an item, perhaps in response to the user right-clicking on a shape. You can certainly do this, using a class in the System.Windows.Media namespace called the VisualTreeHelper. In Chapter 31, you will come to know the role of "visual trees" and "logical trees" in some detail. Until then, handle the MouseRightButtonDown event on your Canvas object, and implement the corresponding event handler, like so:

```
private void canvasDrawingArea_MouseRightButtonDown(object sender, MouseButtonEventArgs e)
{
  // First, get the X,Y location of where the user clicked.
  Point pt = e.GetPosition((Canvas)sender);

  // Use the HitTest() method of VisualTreeHelper to see if the user clicked
  // on an item in the canvas.
  HitTestResult result = VisualTreeHelper.HitTest(canvasDrawingArea, pt);

  // If the result is not null, they DID click on a shape!
  if (result != null)
  {
    // Get the underlying shape clicked on, and remove it from
    // the canvas.
    canvasDrawingArea.Children.Remove(result.VisualHit as Shape);
  }
}
```

This method begins by obtaining the exact X,Y location the user clicked in the Canvas, and performs a hit-test operation via the static VisualTreeHelper.HitTest() method. The return value, a HitTestResult object, will be set to null if the user does not click on a UIElement within the Canvas. If HitTestResult is *not* null, we can obtain the underlying UIElement that was clicked via the VisualHit property, which we are casting into a Shape-derived object (remember, a Canvas can hold any UIElement, not just shapes!). Again, you'll get more details on exactly what a "visual tree" is in the next chapter.

▪ **Note** By default, VisualTreeHelper.HitTest() returns the topmost UIElement clicked on, and does not provide information on other objects below that item (e.g., objects overlapping by Z-order).

With this modification, you should be able to add a shape to the canvas with a left mouse-click, and delete an item from the canvas with a right mouse-click! Figure 29-3 shows the functionality of the current example.

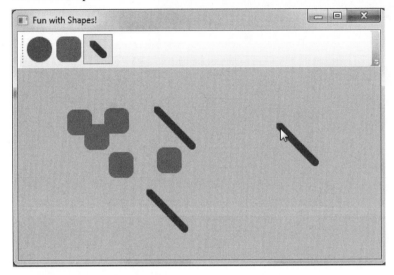

Figure 29-3. Fun with shapes

So far, so good. At this point, you have used Shape-derived objects to render content on RadioButtons using XAML, and populated a Canvas using C#. We will add a bit more functionality to this example when we examine the role of brushes and graphical transformations. On a related note, a different example in this chapter will illustrate drag-and-drop techniques on UIElement objects. Until then, we will examine the remaining members of System.Windows.Shapes.

Working with Polylines and Polygons

The current example used only three of the Shape-derived classes. The remaining child classes (Polyline, Polygon, and Path) are extremely tedious to render correctly without tool support (such as Expression Blend or Expression Design), simply because they require a large number of plot points to represent their output. You'll learn about the role of Expression Design in just a moment, but until then, here is an overview of the remaining Shapes types.

The Polyline type lets you define a collection of (x, y) coordinates (via the Points property) to draw a series of line segments that do not require connecting ends. The Polygon type is similar; however, it is programmed so that it will always close the starting and ending points and fill the interior with the specified brush. Assume you have authored the following <StackPanel> in the kaxaml editor, or better yet, in the custom XAML editor you created in Chapter 27:

```
<!-- Polylines do not automatically connect the ends. -->
<Polyline Stroke ="Red" StrokeThickness ="20" StrokeLineJoin ="Round"
          Points ="10,10  40,40  10,90  300,50"/>

<!-- A Polygon always closes the end points. -->
<Polygon Fill ="AliceBlue" StrokeThickness ="5" Stroke ="Green"
         Points ="40,10 70,80 10,50" />
```

Figure 29-4 shows the rendered output.

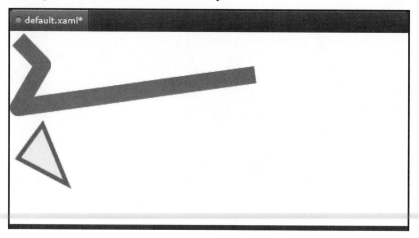

Figure 29-4. Polygons and polylines

Working with Paths

Using the Rectangle, Ellipse, Polygon, Polyline, and Line types alone to draw a detailed 2D vector image would be extremely complex, as these primitives do not allow you to easily capture graphical data such as curves, unions of overlapping data, and so forth. The final Shape-derived class, Path, provides the ability to define complex 2D graphical data represented as a collection of independent *geometries*. After you have defined a collection of such geometries, you can assign them to the Data property of the Path class, where this information will be used to render your complex 2D image.

The Data property takes a System.Windows.Media.Geometry-derived class, which contains the key members described in Table 29-2.

Table 29-2. Select Members of the System.Windows.Media.Geometry Type

Member	Meaning in Life
Bounds	Establishes the current bounding rectangle containing the geometry.
FillContains()	Determines whether a given Point (or other Geometry object) is within the bounds of a particular Geometry-derived class. This is useful for hit-testing calculations.

GetArea()	Returns the entire area a Geometry-derived type occupies.
GetRenderBounds()	Returns a Rect that contains the smallest possible rectangle that could be used to render the Geometry-derived class.
Transform	Assigns a Transform object to the geometry to alter the rendering.

The classes that extend Geometry (see Table 29-3) look very much like their Shape-derived counterparts. For example, EllipseGeometry has similar members to Ellipse. The big distinction is that Geometry-derived classes *do not know* how to render themselves directly, as they are not UIElements. Rather, Geometry-derived classes represent little more than a collection of plot-point data, which say in effect "If a Path uses my data, this is how I would render myself."

■ **Note** Path is not the only class in WPF that can use a collection of geometries. For example, DoubleAnimationUsingPath, DrawingGroup, GeometryDrawing, and even UIElement can all use geometries for rendering, using the PathGeometry, ClipGeometry, Geometry, and Clip properties, respectively.

Table 29-3. Geometry-Derived Classes

Geometry Class	Meaning in Life
LineGeometry	Represents a straight line.
RectangleGeometry	Represents a rectangle.
EllipseGeometry	Represents an ellipse.
GeometryGroup	Allows you to group together several Geometry objects.
CombinedGeometry	Allows you to merge two different Geometry objects into a single shape.
PathGeometry	Represents a figure composed of lines and curves.

Here is a Path defined in kaxaml that makes use of a few Geometry-derived types. Notice that we are setting the Data property of Path to a GeometryGroup object that contains other Geometry-derived objects such as EllipseGeometry, RectangleGeometry, and LineGeometry. Figure 29-5 shows the output.

```
<!-- A Path contains a set of geometry objects,
     set with the Data property. -->
<Path Fill = "Orange" Stroke = "Blue" StrokeThickness = "3">
  <Path.Data>
    <GeometryGroup>
      <EllipseGeometry Center = "75,70"
```

```
        RadiusX = "30" RadiusY = "30" />
      <RectangleGeometry Rect = "25,55 100 30" />
      <LineGeometry StartPoint="0,0" EndPoint="70,30" />
      <LineGeometry StartPoint="70,30" EndPoint="0,30" />
    </GeometryGroup>
  </Path.Data>
</Path>
```

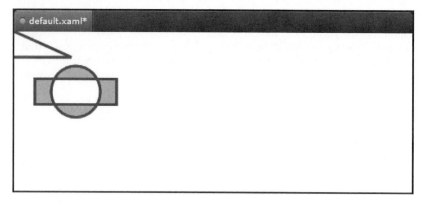

Figure 29-5. *A Path containing various Geometry objects*

The image in Figure 29-5 could have been rendered using the Line, Ellipse, and Rectangle classes shown earlier. However, this would have put various UIElement objects in memory. When you use geometries to model the plot points of what to draw, and then place the geometry collection into a container that can render the data (Path, in this case), you reduce the memory overhead.

Now recall that Path has the same inheritance chain as any other member of System.Windows.Shapes, and therefore has the ability to send the same event notifications as other UIElements. Thus, if you were to define this same <Path> element in a Visual Studio project, you could determine whether the user clicked anywhere in the sweeping line simply by handling a mouse event (remember, kaxaml does not allow you to handle events for the markup you have authored).

The Path "Modeling Mini-Language"

Of all the classes listed in Table 29-3, PathGeometry is the most complex to configure in terms of XAML or code. This has to do with the fact that each *segment* of the PathGeometry is composed of objects that contain various segments and figures (for example, ArcSegment, BezierSegment, LineSegment, PolyBezierSegment, PolyLineSegment, PolyQuadraticBezierSegment, etc.). Here is an example of a Path object whose Data property has been set to a <PathGeometry> composed of various figures and segments:

```
<Path Stroke="Black" StrokeThickness="1" >
  <Path.Data>
    <PathGeometry>
      <PathGeometry.Figures>
        <PathFigure StartPoint="10,50">
          <PathFigure.Segments>
            <BezierSegment
              Point1="100,0"
```

```
                Point2="200,200"
                Point3="300,100"/>
            <LineSegment Point="400,100" />
            <ArcSegment
              Size="50,50" RotationAngle="45"
              IsLargeArc="True" SweepDirection="Clockwise"
              Point="200,100"/>
          </PathFigure.Segments>
        </PathFigure>
      </PathGeometry.Figures>
    </PathGeometry>
  </Path.Data>
</Path>
```

Now, to be perfectly honest, very few programmers will ever need to manually build complex 2D images by directly describing Geometry- or PathSegment-derived classes. In reality, complex paths will be composed on your behalf when you are working with Expression Design.

Even with the assistance of these tools, the amount of XAML required to define a complex Path object would be ghastly, as the data consists of full descriptions of various Geometry- or PathSegment-derived classes. In order to produce more concise and compact markup, the Path class has been designed to understand a specialized "mini-language."

For example, rather than setting the Data property of Path to a collection of Geometry- and PathSegment-derived types, you can set the Data property to a single string literal containing a number of known symbols and various values that define the shape to be rendered. In fact, when you use the Expression tools to build a Path object, the mini-language is used automatically. Here is a simple example, and the resulting output (see Figure 29-6).

```
<Path Stroke="Black" StrokeThickness="3"
      Data="M 10,75 C 70,15 250,270 300,175 H 240" />
```

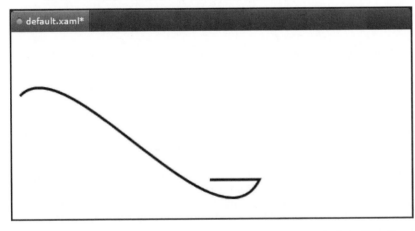

Figure 29-6. The path mini-language allows you to compactly describe a Geometry/PathSegment object model

The M command (short for *move*) takes an X,Y position that represents the starting point of the drawing. The C command takes a series of plot points to render a *curve* (a cubic Bézier curve to be exact), while H draws a *horizontal* line.

Now, to be perfectly honest, the chances that you will ever need to manually build or parse a string literal containing path mini-language instructions are slim to none. However, at the very least, you will no longer be surprised when you view XAML-generated dedicated tools. If you are interested in examining the details of this particular grammar, look up "Path Markup Syntax" in the .NET Framework 4.5 SDK documentation.

WPF Brushes and Pens

Each of the WPF graphical rendering options (shape, drawing and geometries, and visuals) makes extensive use of *brushes*, which allow you to control how the interior of a 2D surface is filled. WPF provides six different brush types, all of which extend System.Windows.Media.Brush. While Brush is abstract, the descendants described in Table 29-4 can be used to fill a region with just about any conceivable option.

Table 29-4. WPF Brush-Derived Types

Brush Type	Meaning in Life
DrawingBrush	Paints an area with a Drawing-derived object (GeometryDrawing, ImageDrawing, or VideoDrawing)
ImageBrush	Paints an area with an image (represented by an ImageSource object)
LinearGradientBrush	Paints an area with a linear gradient
RadialGradientBrush	Paints an area with a radial gradient
SolidColorBrush	Paints a single color, set with the Color property
VisualBrush	Paints an area with a Visual-derived object (DrawingVisual, Viewport3DVisual, and ContainerVisual)

The DrawingBrush and VisualBrush classes allow you to build a brush based on an existing Drawing- or Visual-derived class. These brush classes are used when you are working with the other two graphical options of WPF (drawings or visuals) and will be examined later in this chapter.

ImageBrush, as the name suggests, lets you build a brush that displays image data from an external file or embedded application resource, by setting the ImageSource property. The remaining brush types (LinearGradientBrush and RadialGradientBrush) are quite straightforward to use, though typing in the required XAML can be a tad verbose. Thankfully, Visual Studio supports integrated brush editors that make it simple to generate stylized brushes.

Configuring Brushes Using Visual Studio

Let's update our WPF drawing program, RenderingWithShapes, to use some more interesting brushes. The three shapes we've employed so far to render data on our toolbar use simple, solid colors, so we can capture their values using simple string literals. To spice things up a tad, we will now use the integrated brush editor. Ensure that the XAML editor of your initial window is the open window within the IDE, and select the Ellipse element. Now, in the Properties window, locate the Brush category and then click Fill property listed on the top (see Figure 29-7).

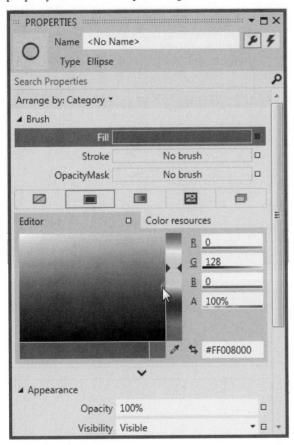

Figure 29-7. *Any property that requires a brush can be configured with the integrated brush editor*

At the top of the Brushes editor, you will see a set of properties that are all "brush compatible" for the selected item (i.e., Fill, Stroke, and OpacityMask). Below this, you will see a series of tabs that allow you to configure different types of brushes, including the current solid color brush. You can use the color selector tool, as well as the ARGB (alpha, red, green, and blue, where "alpha" controls transparency) editors to control the color of the current brush. Using these sliders and the related color selection area, you can create any sort of solid color. Go ahead and use these tools to change the Fill color of your Ellipse, and view the resulting XAML. You'll notice the color is stored as a hexadecimal value. For example:

```
<Ellipse Fill="#FF47CE47" Height="35" Width="35" />
```

More interestingly, this same editor allows you to configure gradient brushes, which are used to define a series of colors and transition points. Recall this Brushes editor provides you a set of tabs, the first of which lets you set a *null brush* for no rendered output. The other four allow you to set up a solid color brush (what we just examined), gradient brush, tile brush, or image brush.

Click the gradient brush button and the editor will display a few new options (see Figure 29-8). The three buttons on the lower left allow you to pick a linear gradient, a radial gradient, or to reverse the gradient stops. The bottommost strip will show you the current color of each gradient stop, each of which is marked by a "thumb" on the strip. As you drag these thumbs around the gradient strip, you can control the gradient offset. Furthermore, when you click on a given thumb, you can change the color for that particular gradient stop via the color selector. Finally, if you click directly on the gradient strip, you can add additional gradient stops.

Take a few minutes to play around with this editor to build a radial gradient brush containing three gradient stops, set to your colors of choice. Figure 29-8 shows the brush I just constructed, using three different shades of green.

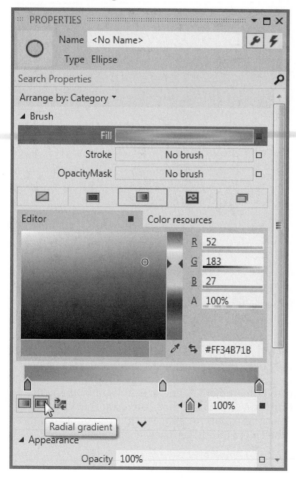

Figure 29-8. *The Visual Studio brush editor allows you to build basic gradient brushes*

When you are done, the IDE will update your XAML with a custom brush, set to a brush-compatible property (the Fill property of the Ellipse in our example) using property-element syntax. For example:

```
<Ellipse Height="35" Width="35">
  <Ellipse.Fill>
    <RadialGradientBrush>
      <GradientStop Color="#FF87E71B" Offset="0.589" />
      <GradientStop Color="#FF2BA92B" Offset="0.013" />
      <GradientStop Color="#FF34B71B" Offset="1" />
    </RadialGradientBrush>
  </Ellipse.Fill>
</Ellipse>
```

Configuring Brushes in Code

Now that we have built a custom brush for the XAML definition of our Ellipse, the corresponding C# code is out of date, in that it will still render a solid green circle. To sync things back up, update the correct case statement to use the same brush you just created. Here is the necessary update, which looks more complex than you might expect, just because we are converting the hexadecimal value to a proper Color object via the System.Windows.Media.ColorConverter class (see Figure 29-9 for the modified output):

```
case SelectedShape.Circle:
  shapeToRender = new Ellipse() { Height = 35, Width = 35 };

  // Make a RadialGradientBrush in code!
  RadialGradientBrush brush = new RadialGradientBrush();
  brush.GradientStops.Add(new GradientStop(
    (Color)ColorConverter.ConvertFromString("#FF87E71B"), 0.589));
  brush.GradientStops.Add(new GradientStop(
    (Color)ColorConverter.ConvertFromString("#FF2BA92B"), 0.013));
  brush.GradientStops.Add(new GradientStop(
    (Color)ColorConverter.ConvertFromString("#FF34B71B"), 1));

  shapeToRender.Fill = brush;
  break;
```

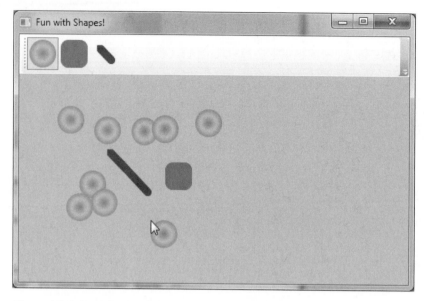

Figure 29-9. *Drawing circles with a bit more pizzazz!*

By the way, you can build GradientStop objects by specifying a simple color as the first constructor parameter using the Colors enumeration, which returns a configured Color object.

```
GradientStop g = new GradientStop(Colors.Aquamarine, 1);
```

Or, if you require even finer control, you can pass in a configured Color object. For example:

```
Color myColor = new Color() { R = 200, G = 100, B = 20, A = 40 };
GradientStop g = new GradientStop(myColor, 34);
```

Of course, the Colors enum and Color class are not limited to gradient brushes. You can use them anytime you need to represent a color value in code.

Configuring Pens

In comparison with brushes, a *pen* is an object for drawing borders of geometries, or in the case of the Line or PolyLine class, the line geometry itself. Specifically, the Pen class allows you to draw a specified thickness, represented by a double value. In addition, a Pen can be configured with the same sort of properties seen in the Shape class, such as starting and stopping pen caps, dot-dash patterns, and so forth. For example:

```
<Pen Thickness="10" LineJoin="Round" EndLineCap="Triangle" StartLineCap="Round" />
```

In many cases, you won't need to directly create a Pen object, as this will be done indirectly when you assign a value to properties, such as StrokeThickness to a Shape-derived type (as well as other UIElements). However, building a custom Pen object is very handy when working with Drawing-derived types (described later in the chapter). Visual Studio does not have a pen editor, *per se*, but it does allow you to configure all of the stroke-centric properties of a selected item using the Properties window.

Applying Graphical Transformations

To wrap up our discussion of using shapes, let's address the topic of *transformations*. WPF ships with numerous classes that extend the System.Windows.Media.Transform abstract base class. Table 29-5 documents many of the key out-of-the-box Transform-derived classes.

Table 29-5. Key Descendants of the System.Windows.Media.Transform Type

Type	Meaning in Life
MatrixTransform	Creates an arbitrary matrix transformation that is used to manipulate objects or coordinate systems in a 2D plane
RotateTransform	Rotates an object clockwise about a specified point in a 2D (x, y) coordinate system
ScaleTransform	Scales an object in the 2D (x, y) coordinate system
SkewTransform	Skews an object in the 2D (x, y) coordinate system
TranslateTransform	Translates (moves) an object in the 2-D (x-y) coordinate system
TransformGroup	Represents a composite Transform composed of other Transform objects

Transformations can be applied to any UIElement (e.g., descendants of Shape as well as controls such as Buttons, TextBoxes, and the like). Using these transformation classes, you can render graphical data at a given angle, skew the image across a surface, and expand, shrink, or flip the target item in a variety of ways.

■ **Note** While transformation objects can be used anywhere, you will find them most useful when working with WPF animations and custom control templates. As you will see later in the text, you can use WPF animations to incorporate visual cues to the end user for a custom control.

Transformation objects (or a whole set of them) can be assigned to a target object (e.g., Button, Path, etc.) using two common properties. The LayoutTransform property is helpful in that the transformation occurs *before* elements are rendered into a layout manager, and therefore the transformation will not affect z-ordering operations (in other words, the transformed image data will not overlap).

The RenderTransform property, on the other hand, occurs after the items are in their container, and therefore it is quite possible that elements can be transformed in such a way that they could overlap each other, based on how they were arranged in the container.

A First Look at Transformations

We will add some transformational logic to our RenderingWithShapes project in just a moment. However, to see transformation objects in action, open kaxaml (or your custom XAML editor) and define a simple <StackPanel> in the root <Page> or <Window>, and set the Orientation property to Horizontal. Now, add the following <Rectangle>, which will be drawn at a 45-degree angle using a RotateTransform object:

```
<!-- A Rectangle with a rotate transformation. -->
<Rectangle Height ="100" Width ="40" Fill ="Red">
  <Rectangle.LayoutTransform>
    <RotateTransform Angle ="45"/>
  </Rectangle.LayoutTransform>
</Rectangle>
```

Here is a <Button> that is skewed across the surface by 20 percent, using a <SkewTransform>:

```
<!-- A Button with a skew transformation. -->
<Button Content ="Click Me!" Width="95" Height="40">
  <Button.LayoutTransform>
    <SkewTransform AngleX ="20" AngleY ="20"/>
  </Button.LayoutTransform>
</Button>
```

And for good measure, here is an <Ellipse> that is scaled by 20 percent with a ScaleTransform (note the values set to the initial Height and Width), as well as a <TextBox> that has a group of transformation objects applied to it:

```
<!-- An Ellipse that has been scaled by 20%. -->
<Ellipse Fill ="Blue" Width="5" Height="5">
  <Ellipse.LayoutTransform>
    <ScaleTransform ScaleX ="20" ScaleY ="20"/>
  </Ellipse.LayoutTransform>
</Ellipse>
```

```
<!-- A TextBox that has been rotated and skewed. -->
<TextBox Text ="Me Too!" Width="50" Height="40">
  <TextBox.LayoutTransform>
    <TransformGroup>
      <RotateTransform Angle ="45"/>
      <SkewTransform AngleX ="5" AngleY ="20"/>
    </TransformGroup>
  </TextBox.LayoutTransform>
</TextBox>
```

Note that when a transformation is applied, you are not required to perform any manual calculations to correctly respond to hit-testing, input focus, or whatnot. The WPF graphics engine handles such tasks on your behalf. For example, in Figure 29-10, you can see that the TextBox is still responsive to keyboard input.

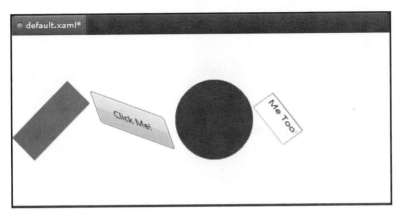

Figure 29-10. The results of graphical transformation objects

Transforming Our Canvas Data

Now, let's see how we can incorporate some transformational logic into our RenderingWithShapes example. In addition to applying a transformation object to a single item (e.g., Rectangle, TextBox, etc.), you can also apply transformation objects to a layout manager, to transform all of the internal data. You could, for example, render the entire <DockPanel> of the main window at an angle, like so:

```
<DockPanel LastChildFill="True">
  <DockPanel.LayoutTransform>
    <RotateTransform Angle="45"/>
  </DockPanel.LayoutTransform>
...
</DockPanel>
```

This is a bit extreme for this example, so let's add a final (less aggressive) feature that allows the user to flip the entire Canvas and all contained graphics. Begin by adding a final <ToggleButton> to your <ToolBar>, defined as follows:

```
<ToggleButton Name="flipCanvas" Click="flipCanvas_Click" Content="Flip Canvas!"/>
```

Within the Click event handler, you create a RotateTransform object and connect it to the Canvas object via the LayoutTransform property if this new ToggleButton is clicked. If the ToggleButton is not clicked, you remove the transformation by setting the same property to null.

```
private void flipCanvas_Click(object sender, RoutedEventArgs e)
{
  if (flipCanvas.IsChecked == true)
  {
    RotateTransform rotate = new RotateTransform(-180);
    canvasDrawingArea.LayoutTransform = rotate;
  }
  else
  {
    canvasDrawingArea.LayoutTransform = null;
  }
}
```

Run your application and add a bunch of graphics throughout the canvas area. If you click your new button, you will find that the shape data flows outside of the boundaries of the canvas! This is because we have not defined a clipping region (see Figure 29-11).

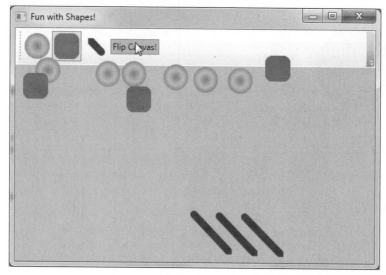

Figure 29-11. Oops! Our data is flowing outside of the canvas after the transformation!

Fixing this is trivial. Rather than manually authoring complex clipping-logic code, simply set the ClipToBounds property of the <Canvas> to true, which prevents child elements from being rendered outside the parent's boundaries. If you run your program again, you'll find the data will not bleed off the canvas boundary.

```
<Canvas ClipToBounds = "True" ... >
```

The last tiny modification to make has to do with the fact that when you flip the canvas by pressing your toggle button, and then click on the canvas to draw a new shape, the point at which you click is *not* the point where the graphical data is applied. Rather the data is rendered above the mouse cursor.

To resolve this issue, check out the solution code for this example where I have added one final Boolean member variable (isFlipped), which will apply the same transformation object to the shape being drawn before the rendering occurs (via RenderTransform). Here is the crux of the code:

```
private void canvasDrawingArea_MouseLeftButtonDown(object sender, MouseButtonEventArgs e)
{
  Shape shapeToRender = null;
...

  // isFlipped is a private boolean field. This is toggled when the
  // toggle button is clicked.
  if (isFlipped)
  {
    RotateTransform rotate = new RotateTransform(-180);
    shapeToRender.RenderTransform = rotate;
  }
```

```
// Set top/left to draw in the canvas.
Canvas.SetLeft(shapeToRender, e.GetPosition(canvasDrawingArea).X);
Canvas.SetTop(shapeToRender, e.GetPosition(canvasDrawingArea).Y);

// Draw shape!
canvasDrawingArea.Children.Add(shapeToRender);
}
```

This wraps up our examination of System.Windows.Shapes, brushes, and transformations. Before turning our attention to the role of rendering graphics using drawings and geometries, let's see how Expression Blend can be used to simplify how we work with primitive graphics.

■ **Source Code** The RenderingWithShapes project can be found under the Chapter 29 subdirectory.

Working with the Visual Studio Transform Editor

In the previous example, you applied various transformations by manually entering markup and authoring some C# code. While this is certainly useful, you will be happy to know that the latest version of Visual Studio ships with an integrated transformation editor, which allows you to easily generate the necessary transformational markup using integrated tools. Now recall, any UI element can be the recipient of transformational services, including a layout system contain various UI elements. To illustrate the use of Visual Studio's transform editor, create a new WPF Application named FunWithTransforms.

Building the Initial Layout

First, split your initial Grid into two columns using the integrated grid editor (the exact size does not matter). Now, locate the StackPanel control within your Toolbox and add this item to take up the entire space of the first column of the Grid. For example:

```
<Grid>
  <Grid.ColumnDefinitions>
    <ColumnDefinition Width="221*"/>
    <ColumnDefinition Width="288*"/>
  </Grid.ColumnDefinitions>
  <StackPanel HorizontalAlignment="Left" Height="292" Margin="10,10,0,0"
              VerticalAlignment="Top" Width="201"/>
</Grid>
```

Next, select your new StackPanel in the Document Outline panel and add three Button controls to the StackPanel container (see Figure 29-12).

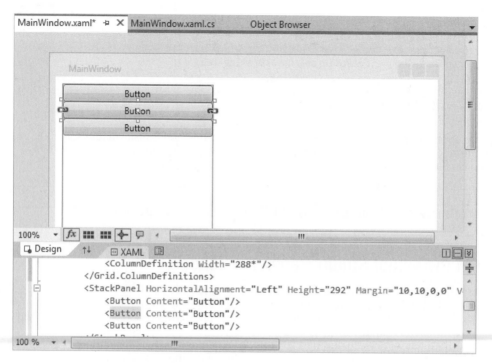

Figure 29-12. A StackPanel of Button controls

Now, select each Button one at a time and change the Content property (located in the Common Properties section of the Properties window) to the values Skew, Rotate, and Flip. As well, use the Name area of the Properties panel to given each button a proper name, such as btnSkew, btnRotate, and btnFile; and using the Events tab of the Properties panel, handle the Click event for each Button. We will implement these handlers in just a bit.

To finalize the UI, create a graphic of your choosing (using any of the techniques seen in this chapter) defined in the second column of the Grid. Figure 29-13 shows the final layout. Here, I have two Ellipse controls grouped into a Canvas control, which has been named myCanvas.

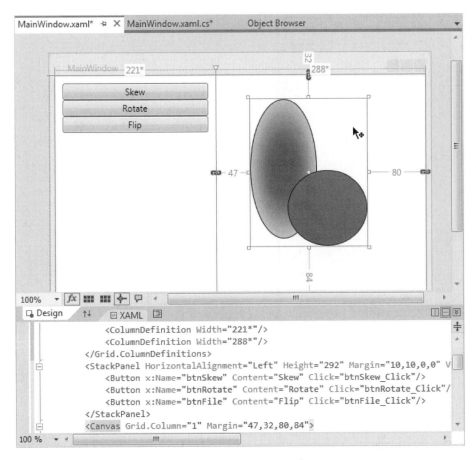

Figure 29-13. The layout of our transformation example

Applying Transformations at Design Time

As mentioned, Visual Studio provides an integrated Transform editor which can be found in the Properties panel. Locate this area, and make sure you expand the Transform section to view the RenderTransform and LayoutTransform sections of the editor (see Figure 29-14).

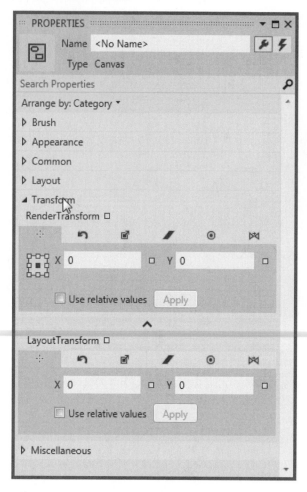

Figure 29-14. *The Transform editor*

Similar to the Brushes section, the Transform section provides a number of tabs to configure various types of graphical transformation to the currently selected item. Table 29-6 describes each transformation option, listed in the order of evaluating each tab left to right.

Table 29-6. *Blend Transformation Options*

Transformation Option	Meaning in Life
Translate	Allows you to offset the location of an item on an X, Y position.
Rotate	Allows you to rotate an item on a 360-degree angle.

Scale	Allows you to grow or shrink an item by a factor in the X and Y directions.
Skew	Allows you to skew the bounding box containing the selected item by a factor in the X and Y directions.
Center Point	When you rotate or flip an object, the item moves relative to a fixed point, called the object's center point. By default, an object's center point is located at the object's center; however, this transformation allows you to change an object's center point in order to rotate or flip the object around a different point.
Flip	Flips a selected item based on an X or Y center point.

I'd suggest you test each of these transformations using your custom shape as a target (just press Ctrl+Z to undo the previous operation). Like many other aspects of the Transform Properties panel, each transformation section has a unique set of configuration options, which should become fairly understandable as you tinker. For example, the Skew transform editor allows you to set the X and Y skew values, the Flip transform editor allows you to flip on the X or Y axis, and so forth.

Transforming the Canvas in Code

The implementation of each Click event handler will be more or less the same. We will configure a transformation object, and assign it to the myCanvas object. Thus, when you run the application, you can click on a button to see the result of the applied transformation. Here is the complete code for each event handler (notice I am setting the LayoutTransform property, so the shape data remains positioned relative to the parent container):

```
private void btnFlip_Click(object sender, System.Windows.RoutedEventArgs e)
{
  myCanvas.LayoutTransform  = new ScaleTransform(-1, 1);
}

private void btnRotate_Click(object sender, System.Windows.RoutedEventArgs e)
{
  myCanvas.LayoutTransform = new RotateTransform(180);
}

private void btnSkew_Click(object sender, System.Windows.RoutedEventArgs e)
{
  myCanvas.LayoutTransform = new SkewTransform(40, -20);
}
```

■ **Source Code** The FunWithTransformations project can be found under the Chapter 29 subdirectory.

Rendering Graphical Data Using Drawings and Geometries

While the Shape types allow you to generate any sort of interactive two-dimensional surface, they entail quite a bit of memory overhead due to their rich inheritance chain. And though the Path class can help remove some of this overhead using contained geometries (rather than a large collection of other shapes), WPF provides a sophisticated drawing and geometry programming interface that renders even more lightweight 2D vector images.

The entry point into this API is the abstract System.Windows.Media.Drawing class (in PresentationCore.dll), which on its own does little more than define a bounding rectangle to hold the rendering. Notice in Figure 29-15, the inheritance chain of the Drawing class is significantly more lightweight than Shape, given that neither UIElement nor FrameworkElement is in the inheritance chain.

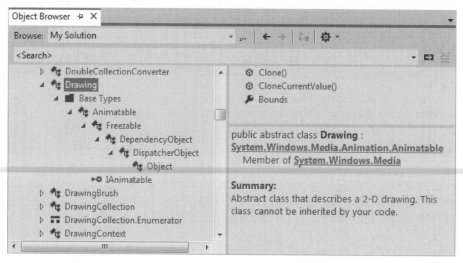

Figure 29-15. The Drawing class is more lightwight than Shape

WPF provides various classes that extend Drawing, each of which represents a particular way of drawing the content, as described in Table 29-7.

Table 29-7. WPF Drawing-Derived Types

Type	Meaning in Life
DrawingGroup	Used to combine a collection of separate Drawing-derived objects into a single composite rendering.
GeometryDrawing	Used to render 2D shapes in a very lightweight manner.
GlyphRunDrawing	Used to render textual data using WPF graphical rendering services.
ImageDrawing	Used to render an image file, or geometry set, into a bounding rectangle.

VideoDrawing	Used to play an audio file or video file. This type can only be fully exploited using procedural code. If you would like to play videos via XAML, the MediaPlayer type is a better choice.

Because they are more lightweight, Drawing-derived types do not have intrinsic support for handling input events, as they are not UIElements or FrameworkElements (although it is possible to programmatically perform hit-testing logic).

Another key difference between Drawing-derived types and Shape-derived types is that Drawing-derived types have no ability to render themselves, as they do not derive from UIElement! Rather, derived types must be placed within a hosting object (specifically, DrawingImage, DrawingBrush, or DrawingVisual) to display their content.

DrawingImage allows you to place drawing and geometries inside of a WPF Image control, which typically is used to display data from an external file. DrawingBrush allows you to build a brush based on a drawing and its geometries, in order to set a property that requires a brush. Finally, DrawingVisual is used only in the "visual" layer of graphical rendering, which is driven completely via C# code.

Although using drawings is a bit more complex than using simple shapes, this decoupling of graphical composition from graphical rendering makes the Drawing-derived types much more lightweight than the Shape-derived types, while still retaining key services.

Building a DrawingBrush Using Geometries

Earlier in this chapter, we filled a Path with a group of geometries, like so:

```
<Path Fill = "Orange" Stroke = "Blue" StrokeThickness = "3">
  <Path.Data>
    <GeometryGroup>
      <EllipseGeometry Center = "75,70"
        RadiusX = "30" RadiusY = "30" />
      <RectangleGeometry Rect = "25,55 100 30" />
      <LineGeometry StartPoint="0,0" EndPoint="70,30" />
      <LineGeometry StartPoint="70,30" EndPoint="0,30" />
    </GeometryGroup>
  </Path.Data>
</Path>
```

By doing this, we gain interactivity from Path but are still fairly lightweight given our geometries. However, if you want to render the same output and have no need for any (out-of-the-box) interactivity, you can place the same <GeometryGroup> inside a DrawingBrush, like this:

```
<DrawingBrush>
  <DrawingBrush.Drawing>
    <GeometryDrawing>
      <GeometryDrawing.Geometry>
        <GeometryGroup>
          <EllipseGeometry Center = "75,70"
                           RadiusX = "30" RadiusY = "30" />
          <RectangleGeometry Rect = "25,55 100 30" />
          <LineGeometry StartPoint="0,0" EndPoint="70,30" />
          <LineGeometry StartPoint="70,30" EndPoint="0,30" />
        </GeometryGroup>
      </GeometryDrawing.Geometry>
```

```
        <!-- A custom pen to draw the borders. -->
        <GeometryDrawing.Pen>
          <Pen Brush="Blue" Thickness="3"/>
        </GeometryDrawing.Pen>
        <!-- A custom brush to fill the interior. -->
        <GeometryDrawing.Brush>
          <SolidColorBrush Color="Orange"/>
        </GeometryDrawing.Brush>
      </GeometryDrawing>
    </DrawingBrush.Drawing>
  </DrawingBrush>
</DrawingBrush>
```

When you place a group of geometries into a DrawingBrush, you also need to establish the Pen object used to draw the boundaries, as we no longer inherit a Stroke property from the Shape base class. Here, I created a <Pen> with the same settings used in the Stroke and StrokeThickness values of the previous Path example.

Furthermore, since we no longer inherit a Fill property from Shape, we also need to use property-element syntax to define a brush object to use for the <DrawingGeometry>, which here is a solid colored orange brush, just like the previous Path settings.

Painting with the DrawingBrush

Now that you have a DrawingBrush, you can use it to set the value of any property requiring a brush object. For example, if you are authoring this markup in kaxaml, you could use property-element syntax to paint your drawing over the entire surface of a Page:

```
<Page
  xmlns="http://schemas.microsoft.com/winfx/2006/xaml/presentation"
  xmlns:x="http://schemas.microsoft.com/winfx/2006/xaml">

  <Page.Background>
    <!-- Same DrawingBrush as seen above. -->
    <DrawingBrush>
      ...
    </DrawingBrush>
  </Page.Background>
</Page>
```

Or, you can use this <DrawingBrush> to set a different brush-compatible property, such as the Background property of a Button:

```
<Page
  xmlns="http://schemas.microsoft.com/winfx/2006/xaml/presentation"
  xmlns:x="http://schemas.microsoft.com/winfx/2006/xaml">

  <Button Height="100" Width="100">
    <Button.Background>
      <!-- Same DrawingBrush as seen above. -->
      <DrawingBrush>
        ...
      </DrawingBrush>
    </Button.Background>
```

```
    </Button>

</Page>
```

No matter which brush-compatible property you set with your custom <DrawingBrush>, the bottom line is you are rendering a 2D vector image with much less overhead than the same 2D image rendered with shapes.

Containing Drawing Types in a DrawingImage

The DrawingImage type allows you to plug your drawing geometry into a WPF <Image> control. Consider the following:

```
<Page
  xmlns="http://schemas.microsoft.com/winfx/2006/xaml/presentation"
  xmlns:x="http://schemas.microsoft.com/winfx/2006/xaml">
  <Image Height="100" Width="100">
    <Image.Source>
      <DrawingImage>
        <DrawingImage.Drawing>
          <GeometryDrawing>
            <GeometryDrawing.Geometry>
              <GeometryGroup>
                <EllipseGeometry Center = "75,70"
                                 RadiusX = "30" RadiusY = "30" />
                <RectangleGeometry Rect = "25,55 100 30" />
                <LineGeometry StartPoint="0,0" EndPoint="70,30" />
                <LineGeometry StartPoint="70,30" EndPoint="0,30" />
              </GeometryGroup>
            </GeometryDrawing.Geometry>

            <!-- A custom pen to draw the borders. -->
            <GeometryDrawing.Pen>
              <Pen Brush="Blue" Thickness="3"/>
            </GeometryDrawing.Pen>

            <!-- A custom brush to fill the interior. -->
            <GeometryDrawing.Brush>
              <SolidColorBrush Color="Orange"/>
            </GeometryDrawing.Brush>
          </GeometryDrawing>
        </DrawingImage.Drawing>
      </DrawingImage>
    </Image.Source>
  </Image>
</Page>
```

In this case, our <GeometryDrawing> has been placed into a <DrawingImage>, rather than a <DrawingBrush>. Using this <DrawingImage>, we can set the Source property of the Image control.

The Role of Expression Design

As you might agree, it would be quite challenging for a graphic artist to create a complex vector-based image using the tools and techniques provided by Visual Studio. As luck would have it, Microsoft Expression Design can be used to create much more sophisticated graphical data, which can then be exported into a variety of file formats, including XAML. If the data has been exported as XAML, it can easily be imported into a WPF. At this point, you can program against the generated object model using Visual Studio.

■ **Note** The next example application will illustrate how it is possible to export graphical data as XAML, and import this markup into a new Visual Studio WPF application. However, if you do not have a copy of Expression Design, fear not. The necessary bear_paper.xaml file is included in the Chapter 29 folder of your code download file.

Exporting a Sample Design File As XAML

Before we can import complex graphical data into a new WPF application, our first task is to generate said graphical data. Launch Expression Design. Now, if you happen to have some graphical skills, you could draw a custom graphic for this example. However, if you are like myself and are a bit artistically challenged, simply activate the Help ➤ Samples menu option. Here, you will find a number of different *.design files you can load, such as bear_paper.design (see Figure 29-16).

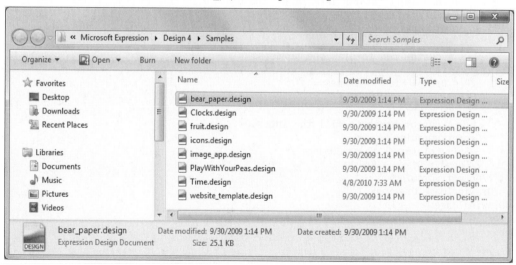

Figure 29-16. The teddy bear sample graphic

■ **Note** Coverage of Expression Design is beyond the scope of this book (and to be honest, outside of my current skill set). If you are interested in learning more about using Design to create your own custom graphics, launch the Expression Design User Guide using the Help menu.

At this point, you should see a portion of the teddy bear image appear in the Expression Design art board. Press the Ctrl+A keyboard combination to select the entire image, and resize the image data so it is contained within the viewport, similar to Figure 29-17.

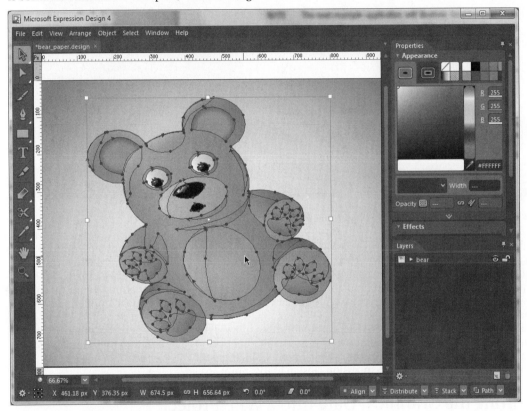

Figure 29-17. Resizing the teddy bear graphic

After the graphical data has been finalized, you can export the data (or parts of the data) using the File ➤ Export… menu option. Using the Format list box, you will see a number of popular file formats, but for this example we are interested in XAML Silverlight 4/WPF Canvas option (see Figure 29-18).

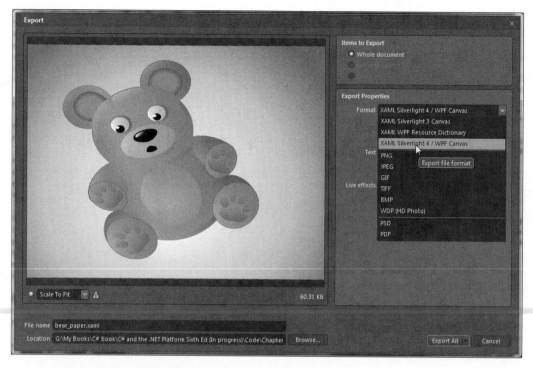

Figure 29-18. Exporting the teddy bear sample graphic as XAML

After you have selected the correct XAML file format, uncheck the Always name objects option. Recall that when an element has an x:Name attribute, you can interact with the item in code. However, this teddy bear will be described using a great number of XAML elements. If we told the tool to name every possible object, we could end up with a large number of member variables added to our C# code base, which we are not really going to use (and this can increase the size of the final compiled application).

Also, make sure you have selected a location for this exported data (bear_paper.xaml) that will be easy to find later (such as on your Windows desktop). All other options can be left to their defaults. When you are ready, click the Export All button, and lo and behold, the teddy bear image data has been captured as XAML. You can close Expression Design at this point.

Importing the Graphical Data into a WPF Project

At this point, we can build a new WPF Application (named InteractiveTeddyBear) using Visual Studio. After you have done so, resize the dimensions of the initial Window to the following Height and Width, and delete the initial Grid control:

```
<Window x:Class="InteractiveTeddyBear.MainWindow"
        xmlns="http://schemas.microsoft.com/winfx/2006/xaml/presentation"
        xmlns:x="http://schemas.microsoft.com/winfx/2006/xaml"
        Title="MainWindow" Height="824" Width="1056">
</Window>
```

1256

Now, activate the Project ➤ Add Existing Item menu option, and using the resulting dialog box, navigate to the location of your exported bear_paper.xaml file. Click the Add button, and you'll find that this XAML file has been added to your project (which you can verify by examining the Solution Explorer panel). Double-click on this file to load the teddy bear graphical data into Visual Studio designer.

If you view the Document Outline editor of the bear_paper.xaml file, you will see that each XAML element is present and accounted for. The goal here is to locate the *left eyeball*, and *right inner ear* of the bear, and give each item a name. While you could manually hunt for the correct objects (which would be very tedious), simply click these items using the visual designer. This will automatically highlight the correct node in the Document Outline editor. Select the left eyeball, and use the Properties editor to name this object leftEye. Select a portion of the right ear (whichever part you want to select) and name it rightEar. Figure 29-19 shows the basic process.

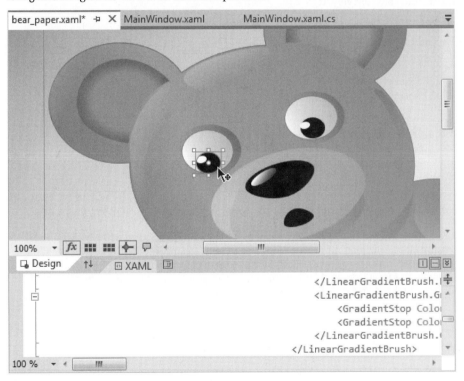

Figure 29-19. Locating and naming objects

Now, copy the entire XAML Canvas to your clipboard. At this point, you can close the bear_paper.xaml file. Switch back to the designer for the initial Window and paste in the Canvas data between the opening and closing <Window> elements. You should now see the teddy bear data displayed within the main window of your application. Feel free to adjust the exact location of the bear image in your layout manager if you like. However as long as the left eye and right ear are visible, you are ready to interact with these objects from code.

Interacting with the Bear

At this point, you can handle events for the leftEye and rightEar objects. To do so, select each object on the designer, activate the Events area of the Properties window, and enter event handler names as required. For the current example, handle the MouseLeftButtonDown event for each object, specifying a unique method name each time.

Here is some simple C# code that will change the look and feel of each object when clicked (if you don't feel like typing all the code seen here, you could simply add a MessageBox.Show() statement for each handler, and display a fitting message).

```
private void leftEye_MouseLeftButtonDown(object sender,
  System.Windows.Input.MouseButtonEventArgs e)
{
  // Change the color of the eye when clicked.
  leftEye.Fill = new SolidColorBrush(Colors.Red);
}

private void rightEar_MouseLeftButtonDown(object sender,
  System.Windows.Input.MouseButtonEventArgs e)
{
  // Blur the ear when clicked.
  System.Windows.Media.Effects.BlurEffect blur =
    new System.Windows.Media.Effects.BlurEffect();
  blur.Radius = 10;
  rightEar.Effect = blur;
}
```

Now, run your application. Go ahead and click on the bear's left eyeball and right ear to see the effects.

You now understand the process of importing complex graphical data created with Expression Design into an Expression Blend project, and more importantly, how to interact with the graphical data in code. As you might agree, the ability for professional graphic artists to generate complex graphical data and export the data as XAML is extremely powerful. Once the graphical data has been generated, developers can import the markup and program against the object model.

■ **Source Code** The InteractiveTeddyBear project can be found under the Chapter 29 subdirectory.

Rendering Graphical Data Using the Visual Layer

The final option for rendering graphical data with WPF is termed the *visual layer*. As mentioned, you can only gain access to this layer through code (it is not XAML-friendly). While a vast majority of your WPF applications will work just fine using shapes, drawings, and geometries, the visual layer does provide the fastest possible way to render huge amounts of graphical data. Oddly, this very low-level graphical layer can also be useful when you need render to single image over a very large area. For example, if you need to fill the background of a window with a plain static image, the visual layer will be the fastest way to do so, and it can be useful if you need to change between window backgrounds very quickly, based on user input or whatnot.

While we won't spend too much time delving into the details of this aspect of WPF programming, let's build a small sample program that illustrates the basics.

The Visual Base Class and Derived Child Classes

The abstract System.Windows.Media.Visual class type supplies a minimal set of services (rendering, hit-testing, transformations) to render graphics, but it does not provide support for additional nonvisual services, which can lead to code bloat (input events, layout services, styles, and data binding). Notice the simple inheritance chain of the Visual type, as shown in Figure 29-20.

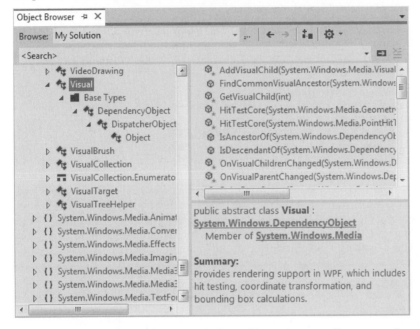

Figure 29-20. *The Visual type provides basic hit-testing, coordinate transformation, and bounding box calculations*

Given that Visual is an abstract base class, we need to use one of the derived types to perform actual rendering operations. WPF provides a handful of subclasses, including DrawingVisual, Viewport3DVisual, and ContainerVisual.

In this example, we will focus only on DrawingVisual, a lightweight drawing class that is used to render shapes, images, or text.

A First Look at Using the DrawingVisual Class

To render data onto a surface using a DrawingVisual, you need to take the following basic steps:

- Obtain a DrawingContext object from the DrawingVisual.

- Use the DrawingContext to render the graphical data.

These two steps represent the bare minimum necessary for rendering some data to a surface. However, if you want the graphical data you've rendered to be responsive to hit-testing calculations (which would be important for adding user interactivity), you will also need to perform these additional steps:

- Update the logical and visual trees maintained by the container you are rendering on top of.

- Override two virtual methods from the FrameworkElement class, allowing the container to obtain the visual data you have created.

We will examine these final two steps in a bit. First, to illustrate how you can use the DrawingVisual class to render 2D data, create a new WPF application with Visual Studio named RenderingWithVisuals. Our first goal is to use a DrawingVisual to dynamically assign data to a WPF Image control. Begin by updating the XAML of your window, like so:

```
<Window x:Class="RenderingWithVisuals.MainWindow"
        xmlns="http://schemas.microsoft.com/winfx/2006/xaml/presentation"
        xmlns:x="http://schemas.microsoft.com/winfx/2006/xaml"
        Title=" Fun with the Visual Layer" Height="350" Width="525"
        Loaded="Window_Loaded" WindowStartupLocation="CenterScreen">
    <StackPanel Background="AliceBlue" Name="myStackPanel">
        <Image Name="myImage" Height="80"/>
    </StackPanel>
</Window>
```

Notice that our <Image> control does not yet have a Source value, as that will happen at runtime. Also notice that we are handling the Loaded event of the window, which will do the work of building the in-memory graphical data, using a DrawingBrush object. Here is the implementation of the Loaded event handler:

```
private void Window_Loaded(object sender, RoutedEventArgs e)
{
  const int TextFontSize = 30;

  // Make a System.Windows.Media.FormattedText object.
  FormattedText text = new FormattedText("Hello Visual Layer!",
    new System.Globalization.CultureInfo("en-us"),
    FlowDirection.LeftToRight,
    new Typeface(this.FontFamily, FontStyles.Italic,
              FontWeights.DemiBold, FontStretches.UltraExpanded),
    TextFontSize,
    Brushes.Green);

  // Create a DrawingVisual, and obtain the DrawingContext.
  DrawingVisual drawingVisual = new DrawingVisual();
  using(DrawingContext drawingContext = drawingVisual.RenderOpen())
  {
    // Now, call any of the methods of DrawingContext to render data.
    drawingContext.DrawRoundedRectangle(Brushes.Yellow, new Pen(Brushes.Black, 5),
      new Rect(5, 5, 450, 100), 20, 20);
    drawingContext.DrawText(text, new Point(20, 20));
```

```
}

// Dynamically make a bitmap, using the data in the DrawingVisual.
RenderTargetBitmap bmp = new RenderTargetBitmap(500, 100, 100, 90,
  PixelFormats.Pbgra32);
bmp.Render(drawingVisual);

// Set the source of the Image control!
myImage.Source = bmp;
}
```

This code introduces a number of new WPF classes, which I will briefly comment on here (be sure to check the .NET Framework 4.5 SDK documentation for full details if you are interested). The method begins by creating a new FormattedText object that represents the textual portion of the in-memory image we are constructing. As you can see, the constructor allows us to specify numerous attributes such as font size, font family, foreground color, and the text itself.

Next, we obtain the necessary DrawingContext object via a call to RenderOpen() on the DrawingVisual instance. Here, we are rendering a colored, rounded rectangle into the DrawingVisual, followed by our formatted text. In both cases, we are placing the graphical data into the DrawingVisual using hard-coded values, which is not necessarily a great idea for production, but fine for our simple test.

■ **Note** Be sure to look up the DrawingContext class within the .NET Framework 4.5 SDK documentation to view all rendering members. If you have worked with the Windows Forms Graphics object in the past, DrawingContext should look very similar.

The last few statements map the DrawingVisual into a RenderTargetBitmap object, which is a member of the System.Windows.Media.Imaging namespace. This class will take a visual object, and transform it into an in-memory bitmap image. After this point, we set the Source property of the Image control, and sure enough, we see the output in Figure 29-21.

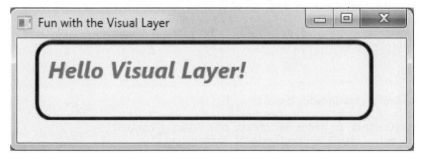

Figure 29-21. Using the visual layer to render an in-memory bitmap

---

■ **Note** The `System.Windows.Media.Imaging` namespace contains a number of additional encoding classes that let you save the in-memory `RenderTargetBitmap` object to a physical file in a variety of formats. Check out the `JpegBitmapEncoder` class (and friends) for more information.

Rendering Visual Data to a Custom Layout Manager

While it is interesting to use `DrawingVisual` to paint onto the background of a WPF control, it is perhaps more common to build a custom layout manager (Grid, StackPanel, Canvas, etc.) that uses the visual layer internally to render its content. After you have created such a custom layout manager, you can plug it into a normal Window (or Page, or UserControl) and have a part of the UI using a highly optimized rendering agent, while the noncritical aspects of the hosting Window use shapes and drawings for the remainder of the graphical data.

If you don't require the extra functionality provided by a dedicated layout manager, you could opt to simply extend FrameworkElement, which does have the necessary infrastructure to also contain visual items. To illustrate how this could be done, insert a new class to your project named CustomVisualFrameworkElement. Extend this class from FrameworkElement and import the System.Windows, System.Windows.Input, and System.Windows.Media namespaces.

This class will maintain a member variable of type VisualCollection, which contains two fixed DrawingVisual objects (of course, you could add new members to this collection via a mouse operation, but this example will keep it simple). Update your class with the following new functionality:

```
class CustomVisualFrameworkElement : FrameworkElement
{
    // A collection of all the visuals we are building.
    VisualCollection theVisuals;

    public CustomVisualFrameworkElement()
    {
        // Fill the VisualCollection with a few DrawingVisual objects.
        // The ctor arg represents the owner of the visuals.
        theVisuals = new VisualCollection(this);
        theVisuals.Add(AddRect());
        theVisuals.Add(AddCircle());
    }
    private Visual AddCircle()
    {
        DrawingVisual drawingVisual = new DrawingVisual();

        // Retrieve the DrawingContext in order to create new drawing content.
        using (DrawingContext drawingContext = drawingVisual.RenderOpen())
        {
            // Create a circle and draw it in the DrawingContext.
            Rect rect = new Rect(new Point(160, 100), new Size(320, 80));
            drawingContext.DrawEllipse(Brushes.DarkBlue, null, new Point(70, 90), 40, 50);
        }
        return drawingVisual;
    }
```

```
private Visual AddRect()
{
  DrawingVisual drawingVisual = new DrawingVisual();
  using (DrawingContext drawingContext = drawingVisual.RenderOpen())
  {
    Rect rect = new Rect(new Point(160, 100), new Size(320, 80));
    drawingContext.DrawRectangle(Brushes.Tomato, null, rect);
  }
  return drawingVisual;
}
}
```

Now, before we can use this custom FrameworkElement in our Window, we must override two key virtual methods mentioned previously, both of which are called internally by WPF during the rendering process. The GetVisualChild() method returns a child at the specified index from the collection of child elements. The read-only VisualChildrenCount property returns the number of visual child elements within this visual collection. Both methods are easy to implement, as we can delegate the real work to the VisualCollection member variable.

```
protected override int VisualChildrenCount
{
  get { return theVisuals.Count; }
}

protected override Visual GetVisualChild(int index)
{
  // Value must be greater than zero, so do a sainity check.
  if (index < 0 || index >= theVisuals.Count)
  {
    throw new ArgumentOutOfRangeException();
  }

  return theVisuals[index];
}
```

We now have just enough functionality to test our custom class. Update the XAML description of the Window to add one of your CustomVisualFrameworkElement objects to the existing StackPanel. Doing so will require you to build a custom XML namespace that maps to your .NET namespace (see Chapter 28).

```
<Window x:Class="RenderingWithVisuals.MainWindow"
  xmlns="http://schemas.microsoft.com/winfx/2006/xaml/presentation"
  xmlns:x="http://schemas.microsoft.com/winfx/2006/xaml"
  xmlns:custom="clr-namespace:RenderingWithVisuals"
  Title="Fun with the Visual Layer" Height="350" Width="525"
  Loaded="Window_Loaded" WindowStartupLocation="CenterScreen">
    <StackPanel Background="AliceBlue" Name="myStackPanel">
        <Image Name="myImage" Height="80"/>
        <custom:CustomVisualFrameworkElement/>
    </StackPanel>
</Window>
```

If all is well, you should see something similar to Figure 29-22 when you run your program.

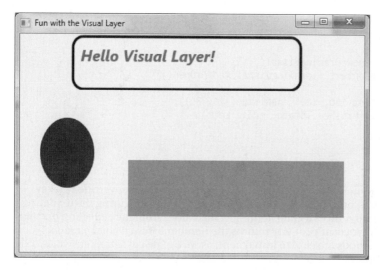

Figure 29-22. *Using the visual layer to render data to a custom* `FrameworkElement`

Responding to Hit-Test Operations

Because `DrawingVisual` does not have any of the infrastructure of `UIElement` or `FrameworkElement`, you will need to programmatically add in the ability to calculate hit-test operations. Thankfully, this is fairly easy to do in the visual layer because of the concept of *logical* and *visual* trees. As it turns out, when you author a blob of XAML, you are essentially building a logical tree of elements. However, behind every logical tree is a much richer description known as the visual tree, which contains lower-level rendering instructions.

Chapter 31 will delve into these trees in more detail but for now, just understand that until you register your custom visuals with these data structures, you will not be able to perform hit-testing operations. Luckily, the `VisualCollection` container does this on your behalf (which explains why we needed to pass in a reference to the custom `FrameworkElement` as a constructor argument).

First, update the `CustomVisualFrameworkElement` class to handle the `MouseDown` event in the class constructor using standard C# syntax, like so:

```
this.MouseDown += MyVisualHost_MouseDown;
```

The implementation of this handler will call the `VisualTreeHelper.HitTest()` method to see whether the mouse is within the boundaries of one of the rendered visuals. To do this, we specify as a parameter to `HitTest()`, a `HitTestResultCallback` delegate that will perform the calculations. If we did click on a visual, we will toggle between a skewed rendering of the visual and the original rendering. Add the following methods to your `CustomVisualFrameworkElement` class:

```
void MyVisualHost_MouseDown(object sender, MouseButtonEventArgs e)
{
  // Figure out where the user clicked.
  Point pt = e.GetPosition((UIElement)sender);

  // Call helper function via delegate to see if we clicked on a visual.
  VisualTreeHelper.HitTest(this, null,
```

```
    new HitTestResultCallback(myCallback), new PointHitTestParameters(pt));
}

public HitTestResultBehavior myCallback(HitTestResult result)
{
  // Toggle between a skewed rendering and normal rendering,
  // if a visual was clicked.
  if (result.VisualHit.GetType() == typeof(DrawingVisual))
  {
    if (((DrawingVisual)result.VisualHit).Transform == null)
    {
      ((DrawingVisual)result.VisualHit).Transform = new SkewTransform(7, 7);
    }
    else
    {
      ((DrawingVisual)result.VisualHit).Transform = null;
    }
  }

  // Tell HitTest() to stop drilling into the visual tree.
  return HitTestResultBehavior.Stop;
}
```

Now, run your program once again. You should now be able to click on either rendered visual and see the transformation in action! While this is just a very simple example of working with the visual layer of WPF, remember that you make use of the same brushes, transformations, pens, and layout managers as you would when working with XAML. As a result, you already know quite a bit about working this Visual-derived classes.

■ **Source Code** The RenderingWithVisuals project can be found under the Chapter 29 subdirectory.

That wraps up our investigation of the graphical rendering services of Windows Presentation Foundation. While we covered a number of interesting topics, the reality is that we have only scratched the surface of WPF's graphical capabilities. I will leave it in your hands to dig deeper into the topics of shapes, drawings, brushes, transformations, and visuals (and, to be sure, you will see some additional details of these topics in the remaining WPF chapters).

Summary

Because Windows Presentation Foundation is such a graphically intensive GUI API, it comes as no surprise that we are given a number of ways to render graphical output. This chapter began by examining each of three ways a WPF application can do so (shapes, drawings, and visuals), and along the way discussed various rendering primitives such as brushes, pens, and transformations.

Remember that when you need to build interactive 2D renderings, shapes make the process very simple. However, static, noninteractive renderings can be rendered in a more optimal manner by using drawings and geometries, while the visual layer (accessible only in code) gives you maximum control and performance.

C H A P T E R 30

WPF Resources, Animations, and Styles

This chapter introduces you to three important (and interrelated) topics that will deepen your understanding of the Windows Presentation Foundation (WPF) API. The first order of business is to learn the role of *logical resources*. As you will see, the logical resource (also known as an *object resource*) system is a way to name and refer to commonly used objects within a WPF application. While logical resources are often authored in XAML, they can also be defined in procedural code.

Next, you will learn how to define, execute, and control an animation sequence. Despite what you might think, WPF animations are not limited to video game or multimedia applications. Under the WPF API, animations can be as subtle as making a button appear to glow when it receives focus, or expanding the size of a selected row in a DataGrid. Understanding animations is a key aspect of building custom control templates (as you'll see in Chapter 31).

We'll wrap up by exploring the role of WPF styles. Much like a web page that uses CSS or the ASP.NET theme engine, a WPF application can define a common look and feel for a set of controls. You can define these styles in markup and store them as object resources for later use, and you can also apply them dynamically at runtime.

Understanding the WPF Resource System

Our first task is to examine the topic of embedding and accessing application resources. WPF supports two flavors of resources. The first is a *binary resource*, and this category typically includes items most programmers consider a resource in the traditional sense (embedded image files or sound clips, icons used by the application, and so on).

The second flavor, termed *object resources* or *logical resources*, represents a named .NET object that can be packaged and reused throughout the application. While any .NET object can be packaged as an object resource, logical resources are particularly helpful when working with graphical data of any sort, given that you can define commonly used graphic primitives (brushes, pens, animations, etc.) and refer to them when required.

Working with Binary Resources

Before we get to the topic of object resources, let's quickly examine how to package up *binary resources* such as icons or image files (e.g., company logos or images for an animation) into your applications. If you'd like to follow along, create a new WPF application named BinaryResourcesApp using Visual Studio. Update the markup for your initial window to use a DockPanel as the layout root, like so:

```
<Window x:Class="BinaryResourcesApp.MainWindow"
  xmlns="http://schemas.microsoft.com/winfx/2006/xaml/presentation"
  xmlns:x="http://schemas.microsoft.com/winfx/2006/xaml"
  Title="Fun with Binary Resources" Height="500" Width="649">

  <DockPanel LastChildFill="True">
  </DockPanel>

</Window>
```

Now, let's say your application needs to display one of three image files inside part of the window, based on user input. The WPF Image control can be used to not only display a typical image file (*.bmp, *.gif, *.ico, *.jpg, *.png, *.wdp, or *.tiff) but also data in a DrawingImage (as you saw in Chapter 29). You might build a UI for your window that supports a DockPanel containing a simple toolbar with Next and Previous buttons. Below this toolbar you can place an Image control, which currently does not have a value set to the Source property, as we will do this in code:

```
<Window x:Class="BinaryResourcesApp.MainWindow"
  xmlns="http://schemas.microsoft.com/winfx/2006/xaml/presentation"
  xmlns:x="http://schemas.microsoft.com/winfx/2006/xaml"
  Title="Fun with Binary Resources" Height="500" Width="649">

  <DockPanel LastChildFill="True">
    <ToolBar Height="60" Name="picturePickerToolbar" DockPanel.Dock="Top">
      <Button x:Name="btnPreviousImage" Height="40" Width="100" BorderBrush="Black"
              Margin="5" Content="Previous" Click="btnPreviousImage_Click"/>
      <Button x:Name="btnNextImage" Height="40" Width="100" BorderBrush="Black"
              Margin="5" Content="Next" Click="btnNextImage_Click"/>
    </ToolBar>

    <!-- We will fill this Image in code. -->
    <Border BorderThickness="2" BorderBrush="Green">
      <Image x:Name="imageHolder" Stretch="Fill" />
    </Border>
  </DockPanel>

</Window>
```

Please note that the Click event has been handled for each Button object. Assuming you have used the IDE to handle these events, you will have two empty methods in your C# code file. So, how can we code the Click event handlers to cycle through the image data? More importantly, do we want to have the image data located on the user's hard drive or embedded in our compiled assembly? Let's examine our options.

Including Loose Resource Files in a Project

Let's assume you want to ship your image files as a set of loose files in a subdirectory of the application install path. Using the Solution Explorer window of Visual Studio, you can right-click on your project node and select the Add ➤ New Folder menu option to create such a subdirectory, which I have called Images.

Now, when you right-click on this folder, you can select the Add ➤ Existing Item menu option, to copy the image files into the new subdirectory. In the downloadable source code for this project, you will find three image files named Welcome.jpg, Dogs.jpg, and Deer.jpg that you can include in this project, or simply add three image files of your choice. Figure 30-1 shows the current setup.

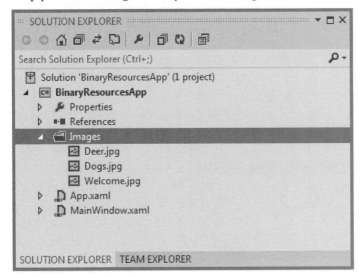

Figure 30-1. A new subdirectory that contains image data in our WPF project

Configuring the Loose Resources

When you want Visual Studio to copy project content to your output directory, you need to adjust a few settings using the Properties window. To ensure that the content of your \Images folder is copied to the \bin\Debug folder, begin by selecting each image in the Solution Explorer. Now, with these images still selected, use the Properties window to set the Build Action property to Resource, and the Copy to Output Directory property to Copy always (see Figure 30-2).

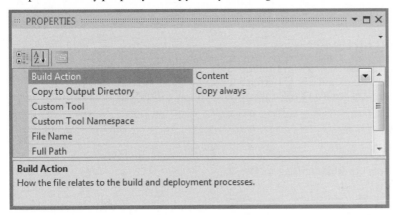

Figure 30-2. Configuring the image data to be copied to our output directory

If you recompile your program, you can now click on the Show all Files button of the Solution Explorer and view the copied Image folder under your \bin\Debug directory (you might need to click the refresh button). See Figure 30-3.

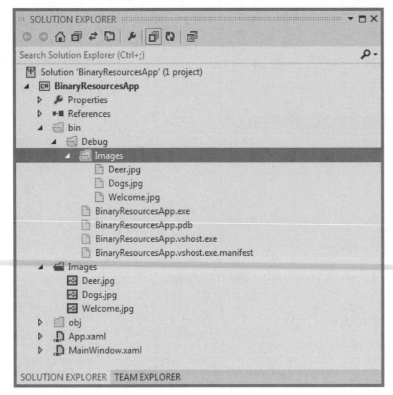

Figure 30-3. *The copied data*

Programmatically Loading an Image

WPF provides a class named BitmapImage, which is part of the System.Windows.Media.Imaging namespace. This class allows you to load data from an image file whose location is represented by a System.Uri object. If you handle the Loaded event of your window, you might fill a List<T> of BitmapImages like so:

```
public partial class MainWindow : Window
{
  // A List of BitmapImage files.
  List<BitmapImage> images = new List<BitmapImage>();

  // Current position in the list.
  private int currImage = 0;
  private const int MAX_IMAGES = 2;
```

```
private void Window_Loaded(object sender, RoutedEventArgs e)
{
  try
  {
    string path = Environment.CurrentDirectory;

    // Load these images when the window loads.
    images.Add(new BitmapImage(new Uri(string.Format(@"{0}\Images\Deer.jpg", path))));
    images.Add(new BitmapImage(new Uri(string.Format(@"{0}\Images\Dogs.jpg", path))));
    images.Add(new BitmapImage(new Uri(string.Format(@"{0}\Images\Welcome.jpg", path))));

    // Show first image in the List<>.
    imageHolder.Source = images[currImage];
  }
  catch (Exception ex)
  {
    MessageBox.Show(ex.Message);
  }
}
...
}
```

Notice that this class also defines an int member variable (currImage) that will allow the Click event handlers to loop through each item in the List<T> and display it in the Image control by setting the Source property. (Here, our Loaded event handler sets the Source property to the first image in the List<T>.) In addition, our MAX_IMAGES constant will let us test for upper and lower limits as we iterate over the list. Here are the Click handlers that do exactly this:

```
private void btnPreviousImage_Click(object sender, RoutedEventArgs e)
{
  if (--currImage < 0)
    currImage = MAX_IMAGES;
  imageHolder.Source = images[currImage];
}

private void btnNextImage_Click(object sender, RoutedEventArgs e)
{
  if (++currImage > MAX_IMAGES)
    currImage = 0;
  imageHolder.Source = images[currImage];
}
```

At this point, you can run your program and flip through each picture.

Embedding Application Resources

If you'd rather configure your image files to be compiled directly into your .NET assembly as binary resources, select the image files in Solution Explorer (in the \Images folder, not in the \bin\Debug\Images folder). Then change the Build Action property to Resource, and the Copy to Output Directory property to Do not copy (see Figure 30-4).

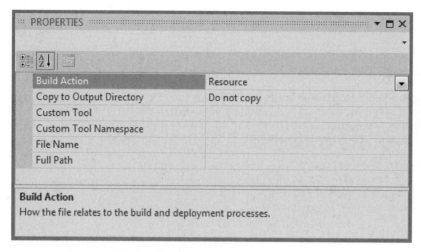

Figure 30-4. *Configuring the images to be embedded resources*

Now, using Visual Studio's Build menu, select the Clean Solution option to wipe out the current contents of \bin\Debug\Images, then rebuild your project. Refresh the Solution Explorer, and observe the absence of data in your \bin\Debug\Images directory. With the current build options, your graphical data is no longer copied to the output folder and is now embedded within the assembly itself.

With this adjustment, we will now need to modify our code to load these images by extracting them from the compiled assembly:

```
private void Window_Loaded(object sender, RoutedEventArgs e)
{
  try
  {
    images.Add(new BitmapImage(new Uri(@"/Images/Deer.jpg", UriKind.Relative)));
    images.Add(new BitmapImage(new Uri(@"/Images/Dogs.jpg", UriKind.Relative)));
    images.Add(new BitmapImage(new Uri(@"/Images/Welcome.jpg", UriKind.Relative)));
    imageHolder.Source = images[currImage];
  }
  catch (Exception ex)
  {
    MessageBox.Show(ex.Message);
  }
}
```

Notice in this case, we no longer need to determine the installation path and can simply list the resources by name, which takes into account the name of the original subdirectory. Also notice, when we create our Uri objects, we specify a UriKind value of Relative. In any case, at this point our executable is a stand-alone entity that can be run from any location on the machine, as all compiled data is within the binary. Figure 30-5 shows the completed application.

Figure 30-5. Our simple picture viewer

■ **Source Code** The BinaryResourcesApp can be found under the Chapter 30 subdirectory.

Working with Object (Logical) Resources

When you are building a WPF application, it is very common to define a blurb of XAML to use in multiple locations within a window, or perhaps across multiple windows or projects. For example, say you have created the *perfect* linear gradient brush, which consists of ten lines of markup. Now, you want to use that brush as the background color for every Button control in the project (which consists of eight windows) for a total of 16 Buttons.

The worst thing you could do is to copy and paste the XAML to each and every control. Clearly, this would be a nightmare to maintain, as you would need to make numerous changes anytime you wanted to tweak the look and feel of the brush.

Thankfully, *object resources* allow us to define a blob of XAML, give it a name, and store it in a fitting dictionary for later use. Like a binary resource, object resources are often compiled into the assembly that requires them. However, you don't need to tinker with the Build Action property to do so. As long as you place your XAML into the correct location, the compiler will take care of the rest.

Working with object resources is a big part of WPF development. As you will see, object resources can be far more complex than a custom brush. You could define a XAML-based animation, a 3D rendering, a custom control style, data template, control template, and more, and package each one as a reusable resource.

The Role of the Resources Property

As mentioned, object resources must be placed in a fitting dictionary object in order to be used across an application. As it stands, every descendant of FrameworkElement supports a Resources property. This property encapsulates a ResourceDictionary object that contains the defined object resources. The ResourceDictionary can hold any type of item as it operates on System.Object types and may be manipulated via XAML or procedural code.

In WPF, all controls, Windows, Pages (used when building navigation applications or XBAP programs), and UserControls extend FrameworkElement, so just about all widgets provide access to a ResourceDictionary. Furthermore, the Application class, while not extending FrameworkElement, supports an identically named Resources property for the same purpose.

Defining Window-Wide Resources

To begin exploring the role of object resources, create a new WPF application named ObjectResourcesApp using Visual Studio and change the initial Grid to a horizontally aligned StackPanel layout manager. Into this StackPanel, define two Button controls (we really don't need much to illustrate the role of object resources, so this will do):

```
<Window x:Class="ObjectResourcesApp.MainWindow"
  xmlns="http://schemas.microsoft.com/winfx/2006/xaml/presentation"
  xmlns:x="http://schemas.microsoft.com/winfx/2006/xaml"
  Title="Fun with Object Resources" Height="350" Width="525">

  <StackPanel Orientation="Horizontal">
    <Button Margin="25" Height="200" Width="200" Content="OK" FontSize="20"/>
    <Button Margin="25" Height="200" Width="200" Content="Cancel" FontSize="20"/>
  </StackPanel>

</Window>
```

Now, select the OK button and set the Background color property to a custom brush type using the integrated brush editor (discussed in Chapter 29). After you've done so, notice how the brush is embedded within the scope of the <Button> and </Button> tags, as shown here:

```
<Button Margin="25" Height="200" Width="200" Content="OK" FontSize="20">
  <Button.Background>
    <RadialGradientBrush>
      <GradientStop Color="#FFC44EC4" Offset="0" />
      <GradientStop Color="#FF829CEB" Offset="1" />
      <GradientStop Color="#FF793879" Offset="0.669" />
    </RadialGradientBrush>
  </Button.Background>
</Button>
```

To allow the Cancel button to use this brush as well, we should promote the scope of our <RadialGradientBrush> to a parent element's resource dictionary. For example, if we move it to the

<StackPanel>, both buttons can use the same brush, as they are child elements of the layout manager. Even better, we could package the brush into the resource dictionary of the window itself, so all aspects of the window's content (nested panels, etc.) can freely make use of it.

When you need to define a resource, you use property element syntax to set the Resources property of the owner. You also give the resource item an x:Key value, which will be used by other parts of the window when they want to refer to the object resource. Be aware that x:Key and x:Name are not the same! The x:Name attribute allows you to gain access to the object as a member variable in your code file, while the x:Key attribute allows you to refer to an item in a resource dictionary.

Visual Studio allows you to promote a resource to a higher scope using their respective Properties windows. To do so, first identify the property that has the complex object you want to package as a resource (the Background property, in our example). Next to the property, you'll see a small white square that, when clicked, will open a pop-up menu. From here, select the Convert to New Resource... option (see Figure 30-6).

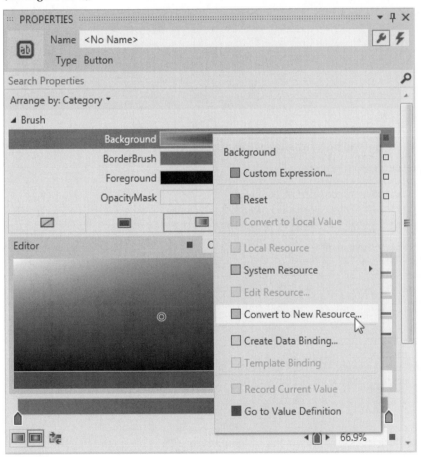

Figure 30-6. Moving a complex object into a resource container

You are now asked to name your resource (myBrush), and specify where to place it. For this example, leave the default selection of the current document (see Figure 30-7).

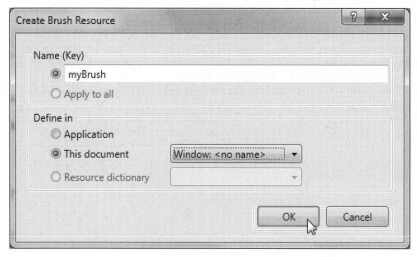

Figure 30-7. Naming the object resource

When you're done, the markup will be restructured like this:

```
<Window x:Class="ObjectResourcesApp.MainWindow"
    xmlns="http://schemas.microsoft.com/winfx/2006/xaml/presentation"
    xmlns:x="http://schemas.microsoft.com/winfx/2006/xaml"
    Title="Fun with Object Resources" Height="350" Width="525">

    <Window.Resources>
        <RadialGradientBrush x:Key="myBrush">
            <GradientStop Color="#FFC44EC4" Offset="0" />
            <GradientStop Color="#FF829CEB" Offset="1" />
            <GradientStop Color="#FF793879" Offset="0.669" />
        </RadialGradientBrush>
    </Window.Resources>

    <StackPanel Orientation="Horizontal">
        <Button Margin="25" Height="200" Width="200" Content="OK"
                FontSize="20" Background="{StaticResource myBrush}"></Button>
        <Button Margin="25" Height="200" Width="200" Content="Cancel" FontSize="20"/>
    </StackPanel>

</Window>
```

Notice the new `<Window.Resources>` scope, which now contains the `RadialGradientBrush` object, which has a key value of `myBrush`.

The {StaticResource} Markup Extension

The other change that took place when we extracted our object resource was that the property that was the target of the extraction (again, Background) now makes use of the {StaticResource} markup extension. As you can see, the key name is specified as an argument. Now, if the Cancel button opts to use the same brush to paint its background, it is free to do so. Or, if the Cancel button had some complex content, any subelement of that Button could also use the window-level resource—for example, the Fill property of an Ellipse:

```
<StackPanel Orientation="Horizontal">
  <Button Margin="25" Height="200" Width="200" Content="OK" FontSize="20"
          Background="{StaticResource myBrush}">
  </Button>

  <Button Margin="25" Height="200" Width="200" FontSize="20">
    <StackPanel>
      <Label HorizontalAlignment="Center" Content= "No Way!"/>
      <Ellipse Height="100" Width="100" Fill="{StaticResource myBrush}"/>
    </StackPanel>
  </Button>
</StackPanel>
```

The {DynamicResource} Markup Extension

It is also possible for a property to use the {DynamicResource} markup extension when connecting to a keyed resource. To understand the difference, name your OK button btnOK and handle the Click event. In this event handler, use the Resources property to obtain the custom brush, and then change some aspect of it, like so:

```
private void btnOK_Click(object sender, RoutedEventArgs e)
{
  // Get the brush and make a change.
  RadialGradientBrush b = (RadialGradientBrush)Resources["myBrush"];
  b.GradientStops[1] = new GradientStop(Colors.Black, 0.0);
}
```

■ **Note** We are using the Resources indexer to locate a resource by name here. Be aware, however, that this will throw a runtime exception if the resource can't be found. You could also use the TryFindResource() method, which will not throw a runtime error but simply return null if the specified resource can't be located.

If you run this application and click the OK button, you will see the brush's change is accounted for and each button updates to render the modified brush. However, what if you completely changed the type of brush specified by the myBrush key? For example:

```
private void btnOK_Click(object sender, RoutedEventArgs e)
{
  // Put a totally new brush into the myBrush slot.
  Resources["myBrush"] = new SolidColorBrush(Colors.Red);
```

```
}
```

This time, when you click the button, neither updates as expected. This is because the {StaticResource} markup extension applies the resource only once and stays "connected" to the original object during the life of the application. However, if we change each occurrence of {StaticResource} to {DynamicResource} in our markup, we find our custom brush has been replaced with the expected solid red brush.

Essentially, the {DynamicResource} markup extension is able to detect whether the underlying keyed object has been replaced with a new object. As you might guess, this requires some extra runtime infrastructure, so you should typically stick to using {StaticResource} unless you know you have an object resource that will be swapped with a different object at runtime, and you want all items using that resource to be informed.

Application-Level Resources

When you have object resources in a window's resource dictionary, all items in the window are free to make use of it, but other windows in the application cannot. Give your Cancel button a name of btnCancel and handle the Click event. Insert a new window into your current project (named TestWindow.xaml) that contains a single Button, which, when clicked, will close the window.

```
public partial class TestWindow : Window
{
  public TestWindow()
  {
    InitializeComponent();
  }

  private void btnClose_Click(object sender, RoutedEventArgs e)
  {
    this.Close();
  }
}
```

Now, in the Click handler of the Cancel button on your first window, just load and display this new window, like so:

```
private void btnCancel_Click(object sender, RoutedEventArgs e)
{
  TestWindow w = new TestWindow();
  w.Owner = this;
  w.WindowStartupLocation = WindowStartupLocation.CenterOwner;
  w.ShowDialog();
}
```

So, if the new window wants to use myBrush, it currently won't be able to as it is not within the correct "scope." The solution is to define the object resource at the application level, rather than at the level of a specific window. There is no way to automate this within Visual Studio, so simply cut the current brush object out of the <Windows.Resources> scope, and place it in the <Application.Resources> scope in your App.xaml file.

```
<Application x:Class="ObjectResourcesApp.App"
  xmlns="http://schemas.microsoft.com/winfx/2006/xaml/presentation"
  xmlns:x="http://schemas.microsoft.com/winfx/2006/xaml"
```

```
    StartupUri="MainWindow.xaml">

    <Application.Resources>
      <RadialGradientBrush x:Key="myBrush">
        <GradientStop Color="#FFC44EC4" Offset="0" />
        <GradientStop Color="#FF829CEB" Offset="1" />
        <GradientStop Color="#FF793879" Offset="0.669" />
      </RadialGradientBrush>
    </Application.Resources>

</Application>
```

Now your TestWindow is free to use this same brush to paint its background. If you find the
Background property for this new Window, click the "Brush resources" tab to view your your application-
level resources (see Figure 30-8)

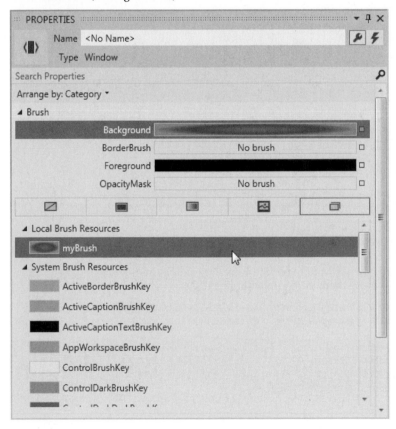

Figure 30-8. Applying application-level resources

Defining Merged Resource Dictionaries

Application-level resources are a good starting point, but what if you need to define a set of complex (or not so complex) resources that need to be reused across multiple WPF projects? In this case, you want to define what is known as a *merged resource dictionary*. This is nothing more than a `.xaml` file that contains a collection of object resources. A single project can have as many of these files as required (one for brushes, one for animations, and so forth), each of which can be inserted using the Add New Item dialog box activated via the Project menu (see Figure 30-9).

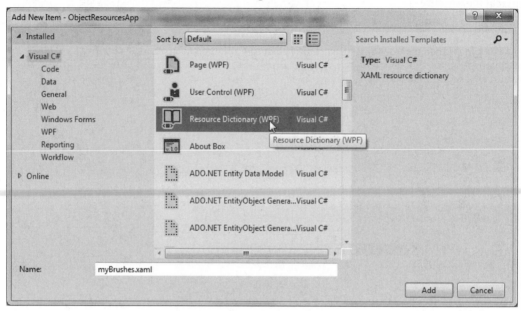

Figure 30-9. *Inserting a new merged resource dictionary*

In the new `MyBrushes.xaml` file, we will want to cut the current resources in the `Application.Resources` scope and move them into our dictionary, like so:

```
<ResourceDictionary xmlns="http://schemas.microsoft.com/winfx/2006/xaml/presentation"
                    xmlns:x="http://schemas.microsoft.com/winfx/2006/xaml">

  <RadialGradientBrush x:Key="myBrush">
    <GradientStop Color="#FFC44EC4" Offset="0" />
    <GradientStop Color="#FF829CEB" Offset="1" />
    <GradientStop Color="#FF793879" Offset="0.669" />
  </RadialGradientBrush>

</ResourceDictionary>
```

Now, even though this resource dictionary is part of our project, we will get runtime errors. The reason is that all resource dictionaries must be merged (typically at the application level) into an existing resource dictionary. To do this, use the following format (note that multiple resource dictionaries can be

merged by adding multiple <ResourceDictionary> elements within the
<ResourceDictionary.MergedDictionaries> scope):

```xml
<Application x:Class="ObjectResourcesApp.App"
  xmlns="http://schemas.microsoft.com/winfx/2006/xaml/presentation"
  xmlns:x="http://schemas.microsoft.com/winfx/2006/xaml"
  StartupUri="MainWindow.xaml">

  <!-- Bring in the logical resources
       from the MyBrushes.xaml file. -->
  <Application.Resources>
    <ResourceDictionary>
      <ResourceDictionary.MergedDictionaries>
        <ResourceDictionary Source = "MyBrushes.xaml"/>
      </ResourceDictionary.MergedDictionaries>
    </ResourceDictionary>
  </Application.Resources>

</Application>
```

Defining a Resource-Only Assembly

Last but not least, it is possible to create .NET class libraries that contain nothing but dictionaries of
object resources. This can be useful if you have defined a set of themes that need to be used on a
machine-wide level. You could package up the object resource into a dedicated assembly, and then
applications that need to make use of them could load them into memory.

The easiest way to build a resource-only assembly is to actually begin with a WPF User Control
Library project. Add such a project (named MyBrushesLibrary) to your current solution, using the Add ➤
New Project menu option of Visual Studio (see Figure 30-10).

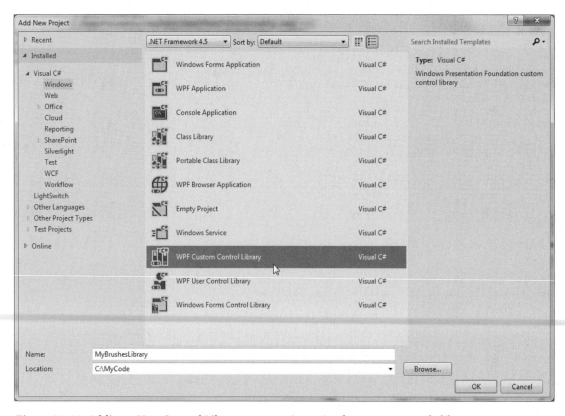

Figure 30-10. Adding a User Control Library as a starting point for a resource-only library

Now, completely delete the UserControl1.xaml file from the project (the only items we really want are the referenced WPF assemblies). Next, drag and drop the MyBrushes.xaml file into your MyBrushesLibrary project and delete it from the ObjectResourcesApp project. Your Solution Explorer should now look like Figure 30-11.

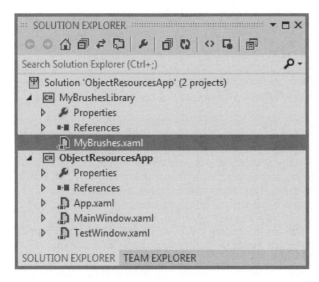

Figure 30-11. Moving the MyBrushes.xaml file into our new library project

Compile your User Control Library project. Next, reference this library from the ObjectResourcesApp project using the Add Reference dialog box. Now, you will want to merge these binary resources into the application-level resource dictionary of the ObjectResourcesApp project. Doing so, however, requires some rather funky syntax, shown here:

```
<Application.Resources>
  <ResourceDictionary>
    <ResourceDictionary.MergedDictionaries>
      <!--The syntax is /NameOfAssembly;Component/NameOfXamlFileInAssembly.xaml -->
      <ResourceDictionary Source = "/MyBrushesLibrary;Component/MyBrushes.xaml"/>
    </ResourceDictionary.MergedDictionaries>
  </ResourceDictionary>
</Application.Resources>
```

First, be aware that this string is space-sensitive. If you have extra white space around your semicolon or forward slashes, you will generate runtime errors. The first part of the string is the friendly name of the external library (no file extension). After the semicolon, you type in the word Component followed by the name of the compiled binary resource, which will be identical to the original XAML resource dictionary.

That wraps up our examination of WPF's resource management system. You will make good use of these techniques for most of your applications, as well as during the remainder of the WPF chapters of this text. Next up, let's investigate the integrated animation API of Windows Presentation Foundation.

■ **Source Code** The ObjectResourcesApp project can be found under the Chapter 30 subdirectory.

Understanding WPF's Animation Services

In addition to the graphical rendering services you examined in Chapter 29, WPF supplies a programming interface to support animation services. The term *animation* may bring to mind visions of spinning company logos, a sequence of rotating image resources (to provide the illusion of movement), text bouncing across the screen, or specific types of programs such as video games or multimedia applications.

While WPF's animation APIs could certainly be used for such purposes, animation can be used any time you want to give an application additional flair. For example, you could build an animation for a button on a screen that magnifies slightly when the mouse cursor hovers within its boundaries (and shrinks back once the mouse cursor moves beyond the boundaries). Or you could animate a window so that it closes using a particular visual appearance, such as slowly fading into transparency. In fact, WPF's animation support can be used within any sort of application (a business application, multimedia programs, video games, etc.) whenever you want to provide a more engaging user experience.

As with many other aspects of WPF, the notion of building animations is nothing new. What is new is that, unlike other APIs you might have used in the past (including Windows Forms), developers are not required to author the necessary infrastructure by hand. Under WPF, there's no need to create the background threads or timers used to advance the animation sequence, define custom types to represent the animation, erase and redraw images, or bother with tedious mathematical calculations. Like other aspects of WPF, we can build an animation entirely using XAML, entirely using C# code, or using a combination of the two.

■ **Note** Visual Studio has no support for authoring animations using GUI animation tools. If you author an animation with Visual Studio, you will do so by typing in the XAML directly. However, Expression Blend does indeed have a built-in animation editor that can simplify your life a good deal.

The Role of the Animation Class Types

To understand WPF's animation support, we must begin by examining the animation classes within the `System.Windows.Media.Animation` namespace of `PresentationCore.dll`. Here you will find over 100 different class types that are named using the `Animation` token.

All of these classes can be placed into one of three broad categories. First, any class that follows the name convention *DataType*`Animation` (`ByteAnimation`, `ColorAnimation`, `DoubleAnimation`, `In32Animation`, etc.) allows you to work with linear interpolation animations. This enables you to change a value smoothly over time from a start value to a final value.

Next, the classes that follow the naming convention *DataType*`AnimationUsingKeyFrames` (`StringAnimationUsingKeyFrames`, `DoubleAnimationUsingKeyFrames`, `PointAnimationUsingKeyFrames`, etc.) represent "key frame animations," which allow you to cycle through a set of defined values over a period of time. For example, you could use key frames to change the caption of a button by cycling through a series of individual characters.

Finally, classes that follow the *DataType*`AnimationUsingPath` naming convention (`DoubleAnimationUsingPath`, `PointAnimationUsingPath`, among others) are path-based animations that allow you to animate objects to move along a path you define. By way of an example, if you were building a GPS application, you could use a path-based animation to move an item along the quickest travel route to the user's destination.

Now, obviously, these classes are *not* used to somehow provide an animation sequence directly to a variable of a particular data type (after all, how exactly could we animate the value "9" using an Int32Animation?).

For example, consider the Label type's Height and Width properties, both of which are dependency properties wrapping a double. If you wanted to define an animation that would increase the height of a label over a time span, you could connect a DoubleAnimation object to the Height property and allow WPF to take care of the details of performing the actual animation itself. By way of another example, if you wanted to transition the color of a brush type from green to yellow over a period of five seconds, you could do so using the ColorAnimation type.

To be very clear, these Animation classes can be connected to any *dependency property* of a given object that matches the underlying types. As explained in Chapter 31, dependency properties are a specialized form of property required by many WPF services including animation, data binding, and styles.

By convention, a dependency property is defined as a static, read-only field of the class, and is named by suffixing the word Property to the normal property name. For example, the dependency property for the Height property of a Button would be accessed in code using Button.HeightProperty.

The To, From, and By Properties

All Animation classes define the following handful of key properties that control the starting and ending values used to perform the animation:

- To: This property represents the animation's ending value.

- From: This property represents the animation's starting value.

- By: This property represents the total amount by which the animation changes its starting value.

Despite the fact that all Animation classes support the To, From, and By properties, they do not receive them via virtual members of a base class. The reason for this is that the underlying types wrapped by these properties vary greatly (integers, colors, Thickness objects, etc.), and representing all possibilities using a single base class would result in very complex coding constructs.

On a related note, you might also wonder why .NET generics were not used to define a single generic animation class with a single type parameter (e.g., Animate<T>). Again, given that there are so many underlying data types (colors, vectors, ints, strings, etc.) used to animated dependency properties, it would not be as clean a solution as you might expect (not to mention XAML has only limited support for generic types).

The Role of the Timeline Base Class

Although a single base class was not used to define virtual To, From, and By properties, the Animation classes do share a common base class: System.Windows.Media.Animation.Timeline. This type provides a number of additional properties that control the pacing of the animation, as described in Table 30-1.

Table 30-1. Key Members of the Timeline *Base Class*

Properties	Meaning in Life
AccelerationRatio, DecelerationRatio, SpeedRatio	These properties can be used to control the overall pacing of the animation sequence.
AutoReverse	This property gets or sets a value that indicates whether the timeline plays in reverse after it completes a forward iteration (the default value is false).
BeginTime	This property gets or sets the time at which this timeline should begin. The default value is 0, which begins the animation immediately.
Duration	This property allows you to set a duration of time to play the timeline.
FillBehavior, RepeatBehavior	These properties are used to control what should happen once the timeline has completed (repeat the animation, do nothing, etc.).

Authoring an Animation in C# Code

Specifically, we will build a Window that contains a Button, which has the odd behavior of spinning in a circle (based on the upper-left corner) whenever the mouse enters its surface area. Begin by creating a new WPF application named SpinningButtonAnimationApp, using Visual Studio. Update the initial markup like the following (note we are handling the button's MouseEnter event):

```
<Window x:Class="SpinningButtonAnimationApp.MainWindow"
    xmlns="http://schemas.microsoft.com/winfx/2006/xaml/presentation"
    xmlns:x="http://schemas.microsoft.com/winfx/2006/xaml"
    Title="Animations in C# code" Height="350"
    Width="525" WindowStartupLocation="CenterScreen">
    <Grid>
        <Button x:Name="btnSpinner" Height="50" Width="100" Content="I Spin!"
                MouseEnter="btnSpinner_MouseEnter"/>
    </Grid>
</Window>
```

Now, import the System.Windows.Media.Animation namespace and add the following code in the window's C# code file:

```
public partial class MainWindow : Window
{
    private bool isSpinning = false;

    private void btnSpinner_MouseEnter(object sender, MouseEventArgs e)
    {
        if (!isSpinning)
        {
            isSpinning = true;
```

```
    // Make a double animation object, and register
    // with the Completed event.
    DoubleAnimation dblAnim = new DoubleAnimation();
    dblAnim.Completed += (o, s) => { isSpinning = false; };

    // Set the start value and end value.
    dblAnim.From = 0;
    dblAnim.To = 360;

    // Now, create a RotateTransform object, and set
    // it to the RenderTransform property of our
    // button.
    RotateTransform rt = new RotateTransform();
    btnSpinner.RenderTransform = rt;

    // Now, animation the RotateTransform object.
    rt.BeginAnimation(RotateTransform.AngleProperty, dblAnim);
  }
 }
}
```

The first major task of this method is to configure a DoubleAnimation object, which will start at the value 0 and end at the value 360. Notice that we are handling the Completed event on this object as well, to toggle a class-level bool variable that is used to ensure that if an animation is currently being performed, we don't "reset" it to start again.

Next, we create a RotateTransform object that is connected to the RenderTransform property of our Button control (btnSpinner). Last but not least, we inform the RenderTransform object to begin animating its Angle property using our DoubleAnimation object. When you are authoring animations in code, you typically do so by calling BeginAnimation(), and pass in the underlying *dependency property* you would like to animate (remember, by convention, this is a static field on the class), followed by a related animation object.

Let's add another animation to the program, which will cause the button to fade into invisibility when clicked. First, handle the Click event of the btnSpinner object, then add the following code in the resulting event handler:

```
private void btnSpinner_Click(object sender, RoutedEventArgs e)
{
  DoubleAnimation dblAnim = new DoubleAnimation();
  dblAnim.From = 1.0;
  dblAnim.To = 0.0;
  btnSpinner.BeginAnimation(Button.OpacityProperty, dblAnim);
}
```

Here, we are changing the Opacity property value to fade the button out of view. Currently, however, this is hard to do, as the button is spinning very fast! How, then, can we control the pace of an animation? Glad you asked.

Controlling the Pace of an Animation

By default, an animation will take approximately one second to transition between the values assigned to the From and To properties. Therefore, our button has one second to spin around a full 360-degree angle, while the button will fade away to invisibility (when clicked) over the course of one second.

If you want to define a custom amount of time for an animation's transition, you may do so via the animation object's Duration property, which can be set to an instance of a Duration object. Typically, the time span is established by passing a TimeSpan object to the Duration's constructor. Consider the following update that will give the button a full four seconds to rotate:

```
private void btnSpinner_MouseEnter(object sender, MouseEventArgs e)
{
  if (!isSpinning)
  {
    isSpinning = true;

    // Make a double animation object, and register
    // with the Completed event.
    DoubleAnimation dblAnim = new DoubleAnimation();
    dblAnim.Completed += (o, s) => { isSpinning = false; };

    // Button has four seconds to finish the spin!
    dblAnim.Duration = new Duration(TimeSpan.FromSeconds(4));
...
  }
}
```

With this adjustment, you should have a fighting chance to click the button while it is spinning, at which point it will fade away.

■ **Note** The BeginTime property of an Animation class also takes a TimeSpan object. Recall that this property can be set to establish a wait time before starting an animation sequence.

Reversing and Looping an Animation

You can also tell Animation objects to play an animation in reverse at the completion of the animation sequence by setting the AutoReverse property to true. For example, if you want to have the button come back into view after it has faded away, you could author the following:

```
private void btnSpinner_Click(object sender, RoutedEventArgs e)
{
  DoubleAnimation dblAnim = new DoubleAnimation();
  dblAnim.From = 1.0;
  dblAnim.To = 0.0;

  // Reverse when done.
  dblAnim.AutoReverse = true;
  btnSpinner.BeginAnimation(Button.OpacityProperty, dblAnim);
```

```
}
```

If you'd like to have an animation repeat some number of times (or to never stop once activated), you can do so using the RepeatBehavior property, which is common to all Animation classes. If you pass in a simple numerical value to the constructor, you can specify a hard-coded number of times to repeat. On the other hand, if you pass in a TimeSpan object to the constructor, you can establish an amount of time the animation should repeat. Finally, if you want an animation to loop ad infinitum, you can simply specify RepeatBehavior.Forever. Consider the following ways we could change the repeat behaviors of either of the DoubleAnimation objects used in this example:

```
// Loop forever.
dblAnim.RepeatBehavior = RepeatBehavior.Forever;

// Loop three times.
dblAnim.RepeatBehavior = new RepeatBehavior(3);

// Loop for 30 seconds.
dblAnim.RepeatBehavior = new RepeatBehavior(TimeSpan.FromSeconds(30));
```

That wraps up our investigation about how to animate aspects of an object using C# code and the WPF animation API. Next, we will learn how to do the same using XAML.

───

■ **Source Code** The SpinningButtonAnimationApp project can be found under the Chapter 30 subdirectory.

───

Authoring Animations in XAML

Authoring animations in markup is similar to authoring them in code, at least for simple, straightforward animation sequences. When you need to capture more complex animations, which may involve changing the values of numerous properties at once, the amount of markup can grow considerably. Even if you use a tool to generate XAML-based animations, it is important to know the basics of how an animation is represented in XAML, as this will make it easier for you to modify and tweak tool-generated content.

───

■ **Note** You will find a number of XAML files in the XamlAnimations folder of the downloadable source code. As you go through the next several pages, copy these markup files into your custom XAML editor, or into the Kaxaml editor, to see the results.

───

For the most part, creating an animation is similar to what you have already seen. You still configure an Animation object and associate it to an object's property. One big difference, however, is that WPF is not function call–friendly. As a result, instead of calling BeginAnimation(), you use a *storyboard* as a layer of indirection.

Let's walk through a complete example of an animation defined in terms of XAML, followed by a detailed breakdown. The following XAML definition will display a window that contains a single label. As soon as the Label object loads into memory, it begins an animation sequence in which the font size increases from 12 points to 100 over a period of four seconds. The animation will repeat for as long as the Window object is loaded in memory. You can find this markup in the GrowLabelFont.xaml file, so copy it into your MyXamlPad.exe application (or Kaxaml) and observe the behavior.

```
<Window
  xmlns="http://schemas.microsoft.com/winfx/2006/xaml/presentation"
  xmlns:x="http://schemas.microsoft.com/winfx/2006/xaml"
  Height="200" Width="600" WindowStartupLocation="CenterScreen" Title="Growing Label Font!">
  <StackPanel>
    <Label Content = "Interesting...">
      <Label.Triggers>
        <EventTrigger RoutedEvent = "Label.Loaded">
          <EventTrigger.Actions>
            <BeginStoryboard>
              <Storyboard TargetProperty = "FontSize">
                <DoubleAnimation From = "12" To = "100" Duration = "0:0:4"
                                 RepeatBehavior = "Forever"/>
              </Storyboard>
            </BeginStoryboard>
          </EventTrigger.Actions>
        </EventTrigger>
      </Label.Triggers>
    </Label>
  </StackPanel>
</Window>
```

Now, lets break this example down, bit by bit.

The Role of Storyboards

Working from the innermost element outward, we first encounter the <DoubleAnimation> element, which makes use of the same properties we set in procedural code (From, To, Duration, and RepeatBehavior).

```
<DoubleAnimation From = "12" To = "100" Duration = "0:0:4"
                 RepeatBehavior = "Forever"/>
```

As mentioned, Animation elements are placed within a <Storyboard> element, which is used to map the animation object to a given property on the parent type via the TargetProperty property—which in this case is FontSize. A <Storyboard> is always wrapped in a parent element named <BeginStoryboard>.

```
<BeginStoryboard>
  <Storyboard TargetProperty = "FontSize">
    <DoubleAnimation From = "12" To = "100" Duration = "0:0:4"
                     RepeatBehavior = "Forever"/>
  </Storyboard>
</BeginStoryboard>
```

The Role of Event Triggers

After the <BeginStoryboard> element has been defined, we need to specify some sort of action that will cause the animation to begin executing. WPF has a few different ways to respond to runtime conditions in markup, one of which is termed a *trigger*. From a high level, you can consider a trigger a way of responding to an event condition in XAML, without the need for procedural code.

Typically, when you respond to an event in C#, you author custom code that will execute when the event occurs. A trigger, however, is just a way to be notified that some event condition has happened ("I'm loaded into memory", "The mouse is over me!", "I have focus!").

Once you've been notified that an event condition has occurred, you can start the storyboard. In this example, we are responding to the Label being loaded into memory. Because it is the Label's Loaded event we are interested in, the <EventTrigger> is placed in the Label's trigger collection.

```
<Label Content = "Interesting...">
  <Label.Triggers>
    <EventTrigger RoutedEvent = "Label.Loaded">
      <EventTrigger.Actions>
        <BeginStoryboard>
          <Storyboard TargetProperty = "FontSize">
            <DoubleAnimation From = "12" To = "100" Duration = "0:0:4"
                             RepeatBehavior = "Forever"/>
          </Storyboard>
        </BeginStoryboard>
      </EventTrigger.Actions>
    </EventTrigger>
  </Label.Triggers>
</Label>
```

Let's see another example of defining an animation in XAML, this time using a *key frame* animation.

Animation Using Discrete Key Frames

Unlike the linear interpolation animation objects, which can only move between a starting point and an ending point, the *key frame* counterparts allow us to create a collection of specific values for an animation that should take place at specific times.

To illustrate the use of a discrete key frame type, assume you want to build a Button control that animates its content so that over the course of three seconds, the value "OK!" appears, one character at a time. You'll find the following markup in the StringAnimation.xaml file. Copy this markup into your MyXamlPad.exe program (or Kaxaml) and view the results.

```
<Window xmlns="http://schemas.microsoft.com/winfx/2006/xaml/presentation"
  xmlns:x="http://schemas.microsoft.com/winfx/2006/xaml"
  Height="100" Width="300"
  WindowStartupLocation="CenterScreen" Title="Animate String Data!">
  <StackPanel>
    <Button Name="myButton" Height="40"
            FontSize="16pt" FontFamily="Verdana" Width = "100">
      <Button.Triggers>
        <EventTrigger RoutedEvent="Button.Loaded">
          <BeginStoryboard>
            <Storyboard>
              <StringAnimationUsingKeyFrames RepeatBehavior = "Forever"
                  Storyboard.TargetName="myButton"
                  Storyboard.TargetProperty="Content"
                  Duration="0:0:3">
                <DiscreteStringKeyFrame Value="" KeyTime="0:0:0" />
                <DiscreteStringKeyFrame Value="O" KeyTime="0:0:1" />
                <DiscreteStringKeyFrame Value="OK" KeyTime="0:0:1.5" />
```

```
                    <DiscreteStringKeyFrame Value="OK!" KeyTime="0:0:2" />
                </StringAnimationUsingKeyFrames>
            </Storyboard>
        </BeginStoryboard>
      </EventTrigger>
    </Button.Triggers>
  </Button>
 </StackPanel>
</Window>
```

First, notice that we have defined an event trigger for our button to ensure that our storyboard executes when the button has loaded into memory. The StringAnimationUsingKeyFrames class is in charge of changing the content of the button, via the Storyboard.TargetName and Storyboard.TargetProperty values.

Within the scope of the <StringAnimationUsingKeyFrames> element, we defined four DiscreteStringKeyFrame elements, which change the button's Content property over the course of two seconds (note that the duration established by StringAnimationUsingKeyFrames is a total of three seconds, so we will see a slight pause between the final "!" and looping "O").

Now that you have a better feel for how to build animations in C# code and XAML, let's turn our attention of the role of WPF styles, which make heavy use of graphics, object resources, and animations.

■ **Source Code** These loose XAML files can be found under the XamlAnimations subdirectory of Chapter 30.

Understanding the Role of WPF Styles

When you are building the UI of a WPF application, it is not uncommon for a family of controls to require a shared look and feel. For example, you might want all button types have the same height, width, background color, and font size for their string content. Though you could handle this by setting each button's individual properties to identical values, such an approach makes it difficult to implement changes down the road, as you'd need to reset the same set of properties on multiple objects for every change.

Thankfully, WPF offers a simple way to constrain the look and feel of related controls using *styles*. Simply put, a WPF style is an object that maintains a collection of property/value pairs. Programmatically speaking, an individual style is represented using the System.Windows.Style class. This class has a property named Setters, which exposes a strongly typed collection of Setter objects. It is the Setter object that allows you to define the property/value pairs.

In addition to the Setters collection, the Style class also defines a few other important members that allow you to incorporate triggers, restrict where a style can be applied, and even create a new style based on an existing style (think of it as "style inheritance"). In particular, be aware of the following members of the Style class:

- Triggers: Exposes a collection of trigger objects, which allow you to capture various event conditions within a style.

- BasedOn: Allows you to build a new style based on an existing style.

- TargetType: Allows you to constrain where a style can be applied.

Defining and Applying a Style

In almost every case, a Style object will be packaged as an object resource. Like any object resource, you can package it at the window or application level, as well as within a dedicated resource dictionary (this is great, because it makes the Style object easily accessible throughout your application). Now recall that the goal is to define a Style object that fills (at minimum) the Setters collection with a set of property/value pairs.

Create a new WPF application named WpfStyles using Visual Studio. Let's build a style that captures the basic font characteristics of a control in our application. Open your App.xaml file and define the following named style:

```
<Application x:Class="WpfStyles.App"
  xmlns="http://schemas.microsoft.com/winfx/2006/xaml/presentation"
  xmlns:x="http://schemas.microsoft.com/winfx/2006/xaml"
  StartupUri="MainWindow.xaml">

  <Application.Resources>
    <Style x:Key ="BasicControlStyle">
      <Setter Property = "Control.FontSize" Value ="14"/>
      <Setter Property = "Control.Height" Value = "40"/>
      <Setter Property = "Control.Cursor" Value = "Hand"/>
    </Style>
  </Application.Resources>

</Application>
```

Notice that our BasicControlStyle adds three Setter objects to the internal collection. Now, let's apply this style to a few controls in our main window. Because this style is an object resource, the controls that want to use it still need to use the {StaticResource} or {DynamicResource} markup extension to locate the style. When they find the style, they will set the resource item to the identically named Style property. Consider the following <Window> definition:

```
<Window x:Class="WpfStyles.MainWindow"
  xmlns="http://schemas.microsoft.com/winfx/2006/xaml/presentation"
  xmlns:x="http://schemas.microsoft.com/winfx/2006/xaml"
  Title="A Window with Style!" Height="229"
  Width="525" WindowStartupLocation="CenterScreen">

  <StackPanel>
    <Label x:Name="lblInfo" Content="This style is boring..."
           Style="{StaticResource BasicControlStyle}" Width="150"/>
    <Button x:Name="btnTestButton" Content="Yes, but we are reusing settings!"
           Style="{StaticResource BasicControlStyle}" Width="250"/>
  </StackPanel>

</Window>
```

If you run this application, you'll find that both controls support the same cursor, height, and font size.

Overriding Style Settings

Here we have a `Button` and `Label` that have both opted in to the constraints enforced by our style. Of course, if a control wants to apply a style and then change some of the defined settings, that's fine. For example, the `Button` will now use the `Help` cursor (rather than the `Hand` cursor defined in the style):

```
<Button x:Name="btnTestButton" Content="Yes, but we are reusing settings!"
        Cursor="Help" Style="{StaticResource BasicControlStyle}" Width="250" />
```

Styles are processed before the individual property settings of the control using the style; therefore, controls can "override" settings on a case-by-case basis.

Automatically Applying a Style with TargetType

Currently, our style is defined in such a way that any control can adopt it (and has to do so explicitly by setting the control's `Style` property), given that each property is qualified by the `Control` class. For a program that defines dozens of settings, this would entail a good amount of repeated code. One way to clean this style up a bit is to use the `TargetType` attribute. When you add this attribute to a `Style`'s opening element, you can mark exactly once where it can be applied.

```
<Style x:Key ="BasicControlStyle" TargetType="Control">
  <Setter Property = "FontSize" Value ="14"/>
  <Setter Property = "Height" Value = "40"/>
  <Setter Property = "Cursor" Value = "Hand"/>
</Style>
```

■ **Note** When you are building a style that is using a base class type, you needn't be concerned if you assign a value to a dependency property not supported by derived types. If the derived type does not support a given dependency property, it is ignored.

This is somewhat helpful, but we still have a style that can apply to any control. The `TargetType` attribute is more useful when you want to define a style that can be applied to only a particular type of control. Add the following new style to the application's resource dictionary:

```
<Style x:Key ="BigGreenButton" TargetType="Button">
  <Setter Property = "FontSize" Value ="20"/>
  <Setter Property = "Height" Value = "100"/>
  <Setter Property = "Width" Value = "100"/>
  <Setter Property = "Background" Value = "DarkGreen"/>
  <Setter Property = "Foreground" Value = "Yellow"/>
</Style>
```

This style will work only on `Button` controls (or a subclass of `Button`) and if you apply it on an incompatible element, you will get markup and compiler errors. If the `Button` uses this new style, like so:

```
<Button x:Name="btnTestButton" Content="OK!"
        Cursor="Help" Style="{StaticResource BigGreenButton}" Width="250"  />
```

you'd see the output like that shown in Figure 30-12.

Figure 30-12. *Controls with different styles*

Subclassing Existing Styles

You can also build new styles using an existing style, via the BasedOn property. The style you are extending must have been given a proper x:Key in the dictionary, as the derived style will reference it by name using the {StaticResource} markup extension. Here is a new style based on BigGreenButton, which rotates the button element by 20 degrees:

```
<!-- This style is based on BigGreenButton. -->
<Style x:Key ="TiltButton" TargetType="Button" BasedOn = "{StaticResource BigGreenButton}">
  <Setter Property = "Foreground" Value = "White"/>
  <Setter Property = "RenderTransform">
    <Setter.Value>
      <RotateTransform Angle = "20"/>
    </Setter.Value>
  </Setter>
</Style>
```

This time, the output appears as in Figure 30-13.

Figure 30-13. *Using a derived style*

The Role of Unnamed Styles

Assume you need to ensure that all TextBox controls have the same look and feel. Now assume you have defined a style as an application-level resource, so all windows in the program have access to it. While this is a step in the right direction, if you have numerous windows with numerous TextBox controls, you'll need to set the Style property numerous times!

WPF styles can be implicitly applied to all controls within a given XAML scope. To create such a style, you use the TargetType property but you don't assign the Style resource an x:Key value. This "unnamed style" now applies to all controls of the correct type. Here is another application-level style that will apply automatically to all TextBox controls in the current application:

```
<!-- The default style for all text boxes. -->
<Style TargetType="TextBox">
  <Setter Property = "FontSize" Value ="14"/>
  <Setter Property = "Width" Value = "100"/>
  <Setter Property = "Height" Value = "30"/>
  <Setter Property = "BorderThickness" Value = "5"/>
  <Setter Property = "BorderBrush" Value = "Red"/>
  <Setter Property = "FontStyle" Value = "Italic"/>
</Style>
```

We can now define any number of TextBox controls and they will automatically get the defined look. If a given TextBox does not want this default look and feel, it can opt out by setting the Style property to {x:Null}. For example, txtTest will get the default unnamed style, while txtTest2 is doing things its own way:

```
<TextBox x:Name="txtTest"/>
<TextBox x:Name="txtTest2" Style="{x:Null}" BorderBrush="Black"
         BorderThickness="5" Height="60" Width="100" Text="Ha!"/>
```

Defining Styles with Triggers

WPF styles can also contain triggers, by packaging up Trigger objects within the Triggers collection of the Style object. Using triggers in a style allows you to define certain <Setter> elements in such a way that they will be applied only if a given trigger condition is true. For example, perhaps you want to increase the size of a font when the mouse is over a button. Or maybe you want to make sure that the text box with the current focus is highlighted with a given color. Triggers are very useful for these sorts of situations, in that they allow you to take specific actions when a property changes, without the need to author explicit C# code in a code-behind file.

Here is an update to the TextBox style that ensures that when a TextBox has the input focus, it will receive a yellow background:

```
<!-- The default style for all text boxes. -->
<Style TargetType="TextBox">
  <Setter Property = "FontSize" Value ="14"/>
  <Setter Property = "Width" Value = "100"/>
  <Setter Property = "Height" Value = "30"/>
  <Setter Property = "BorderThickness" Value = "5"/>
  <Setter Property = "BorderBrush" Value = "Red"/>
  <Setter Property = "FontStyle" Value = "Italic"/>
  <!-- The following setter will be applied only when the text box is
       in focus. -->
  <Style.Triggers>
    <Trigger Property = "IsFocused" Value = "True">
      <Setter Property = "Background" Value = "Yellow"/>
    </Trigger>
  </Style.Triggers>
</Style>
```

If you test this style, you'll find that as you tab between various TextBox objects, the currently selected TextBox has a bright yellow background (provided it has not opted out by assigning {x:Null} to the Style property).

Property triggers are also very smart, in that when the trigger's condition is *not true*, the property automatically receives the default assigned value. Therefore, as soon as a TextBox loses focus, it also automatically becomes the default color without any work on your part. In contrast, event triggers (examined when we looked at WPF animations) do not automatically revert to a previous condition.

Defining Styles with Multiple Triggers

Triggers can also be designed in such a way that the defined <Setter> elements will be applied when *multiple conditions* are true (similar to building an if statement for multiple conditions). Let's say we want to set the background of a TextBox to Yellow only if it has the active focus and the mouse is hovering within its boundaries. To do so, we can make use of the <MultiTrigger> element to define each condition, like so:

```
<!-- The default style for all text boxes. -->
<Style TargetType="TextBox">
  <Setter Property = "FontSize" Value ="14"/>
  <Setter Property = "Width" Value = "100"/>
  <Setter Property = "Height" Value = "30"/>
  <Setter Property = "BorderThickness" Value = "5"/>
  <Setter Property = "BorderBrush" Value = "Red"/>
  <Setter Property = "FontStyle" Value = "Italic"/>
  <!-- The following setter will be applied only when the text box is
  in focus AND the mouse is over the text box. -->
  <Style.Triggers>
    <MultiTrigger>
      <MultiTrigger.Conditions>
          <Condition Property = "IsFocused" Value = "True"/>
          <Condition Property = "IsMouseOver" Value = "True"/>
      </MultiTrigger.Conditions>
      <Setter Property = "Background" Value = "Yellow"/>
    </MultiTrigger>
  </Style.Triggers>
</Style>
```

Animated Styles

Styles can also incorporate triggers that kick off an animation sequence. Here is one final style that, when applied to Button controls, will cause the controls to grow and shrink in size when the mouse is inside the button's surface area:

```
<!-- The growing button style! -->
<Style x:Key = "GrowingButtonStyle" TargetType="Button">
  <Setter Property = "Height" Value = "40"/>
  <Setter Property = "Width" Value = "100"/>
  <Style.Triggers>
    <Trigger Property = "IsMouseOver" Value = "True">
      <Trigger.EnterActions>
        <BeginStoryboard>
          <Storyboard TargetProperty = "Height">
            <DoubleAnimation From = "40" To = "200"
                             Duration = "0:0:2" AutoReverse="True"/>
```

```
        </Storyboard>
      </BeginStoryboard>
    </Trigger.EnterActions>
  </Trigger>
</Style.Triggers>
</Style>
```

Here, our triggers collection is on the lookout for the IsMouseOver property to return true. When this occurs, we define a <Trigger.EnterActions> element to execute a simple storyboard that forces the button to grow to a Height value of 200 (and then return to a Height of 40) over two seconds. If you want to perform other property changes, you could also define a <Trigger.ExitActions> scope to define any custom actions to take when IsMouseOver is false.

Assigning Styles Programmatically

Recall that a style can be applied at runtime as well. This can be helpful if you want to let end users choose how their UI looks and feels, or if you need to enforce a look and feel based on security settings (e.g., the DisableAllButton style) or what have you.

During this project, you have defined a number of styles, many of which can apply to Button controls. So, let's retool the UI of our main window to allow the user to pick from some of these styles by selecting names in a ListBox. Based on the user's selection, we will apply the appropriate style. Here is the new (and final) markup for the <Window> element:

```
<Window x:Class="WpfStyles.MainWindow"
  xmlns="http://schemas.microsoft.com/winfx/2006/xaml/presentation"
  xmlns:x="http://schemas.microsoft.com/winfx/2006/xaml"
  Height="350" Title="A Window with Style!"
  Width="525" WindowStartupLocation="CenterScreen">

  <DockPanel >
    <StackPanel Orientation="Horizontal" DockPanel.Dock="Top">
      <Label Content="Please Pick a Style for this Button" Height="50"/>
      <ListBox x:Name ="lstStyles" Height ="80" Width ="150" Background="LightBlue"
               SelectionChanged ="comboStyles_Changed" />
    </StackPanel>
    <Button x:Name="btnStyle" Height="40" Width="100" Content="OK!"/>
  </DockPanel>

</Window>
```

The ListBox control (named lstStyles) will be filled dynamically within the window's constructor, like so:

```
public MainWindow()
{
  InitializeComponent();

  // Fill the list box with all the Button
  // styles.
  lstStyles.Items.Add("GrowingButtonStyle");
  lstStyles.Items.Add("TiltButton");
  lstStyles.Items.Add("BigGreenButton");
  lstStyles.Items.Add("BasicControlStyle");
```

```
}
```

The final task is to handle the SelectionChanged event in the related code file. Notice in the following code how we are able to extract the current resource by name, using the inherited TryFindResource() method:

```
private void comboStyles_Changed(object sender, SelectionChangedEventArgs e)
{
  // Get the selected style name from the list box.
  Style currStyle = (Style)
    TryFindResource(lstStyles.SelectedValue);
  if (currStyle != null)
  {
    // Set the style of the button type.
    this.btnStyle.Style = currStyle;
  }
}
```

When you run this application, you can pick from one of these four button styles on the fly. Figure 30-14 shows our completed application.

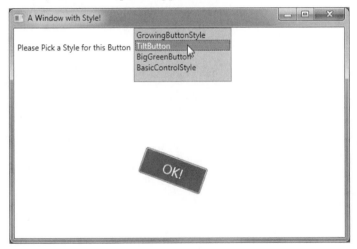

Figure 30-14. Controls with different styles

■ **Source Code** The WpfStyles project can be found under the Chapter 30 subdirectory.

Summary

The first part of this chapter examined the resource management system of WPF. We began by looking at how to work with binary resources, then quickly turned our attention of the role of object resources. As you learned, object resources are named blobs of XAML that can be stored at various locations, in order to reuse content.

Next, you learned about WPF's animation framework. Here you had a chance to create some animations using C# code, as well as with XAML. You learned that if you define an animation in markup, you use <Storyboard> elements and triggers to control execution. We wrapped up by looking at the WPF style mechanism, which makes heavy use of graphics, object resources, and animations.

CHAPTER 31

Dependency Properties, Routed Events, and Templates

This chapter concludes your investigation of the WPF programming model by introducing you to the process of building customized control templates. While it is true that the content model and style mechanism do allow you to add unique bits to a standard WPF control, the process of building custom templates allows you to fully define how a control should render its output, respond to state transitions, and integrate into the WPF APIs.

This chapter begins by examining two topics that are important when creating a custom control, specifically *dependency properties* and *routed events*. Once you understand these topics, you will then learn about the role of a *default template* and how to view them programmatically at runtime. After this foundation has been laid, the remainder of this chapter will examine how to build custom control templates, and how to incorporate visual cues using the WPF trigger framework.

■ **Note** Building production level templates will most certainly require the use of Expression Blend, due to the numerous built-in template tools. Here, you will build some **simple** templates which can be easily created in Visual Studio proper. Again, consult my book *Pro Expression Blend* (Apress, 2011) for details of the Blend IDE.

Understanding the Role of Dependency Properties

Like any .NET API, WPF makes use of each member of the .NET type system (classes, structures, interfaces, delegates, enumerations) and each type member (properties, methods, events, constant data, read-only fields, etc.) within its implementation. However, WPF also supports a unique programming concept termed a *dependency property*.

Like a "normal" .NET property (often termed a *CLR property* in the WPF literature), dependency properties can be set declaratively using XAML or programmatically within a code file. Furthermore, dependency properties (like CLR properties) ultimately exist to encapsulate data fields of a class and can be configured as read-only, write-only, or read-write.

To make matters more interesting, in almost every case you will be blissfully unaware that you have actually set (or accessed) a dependency property as opposed to a CLR property! For example, the Height and Width properties that WPF controls inherit from FrameworkElement, as well as the Content member inherited from ControlContent, are all, in fact, dependency properties.

```
<!-- Set three dependency properties! -->
<Button x:Name = "btnMyButton" Height = "50" Width = "100" Content = "OK"/>
```

Given all of these similarities, why does WPF define a new term for such a familiar concept? The answer lies in how a dependency property is implemented within the class. You'll see a coding example in just a little bit; however, from a high level, all dependency properties are created in the following manner:

- First, the class that defined a dependency property must have DependencyObject in its inheritance chain.

- A single dependency property is represented as a public, static, read-only field in the class of type DependencyProperty. By convention, this field is named by suffixing the word Property to the name of the CLR wrapper (see final bullet point).

- The DependencyProperty variable is registered via a static call to DependencyProperty.Register(), which typically occurs in a static constructor or inline when the variable is declared.

- Finally, the class will define a XAML-friendly CLR property, which makes calls to methods provided by DependencyObject to get and set the value.

Once implemented, dependency properties provide a number of powerful features that are used by various WPF technologies including data binding, animation services, styles, templates and so forth. In a nutshell, the motivation of dependency properties is to provide a way to compute the value of a property based on the value of other inputs. Here is a list of some of these key benefits, which go well beyond those of the simple data encapsulation found with a CLR property:

- Dependency properties can inherit their values from a parent element's XAML definition. For example, if you defined a value for the FontSize attribute in the opening tag of a <Window>, all controls in that Window would have the same font size by default.

- Dependency properties support the ability to have values set by elements contained within their XAML scope, such as a Button setting the Dock property of a DockPanel parent. (Recall from Chapter 28 that *attached properties* do this very thing, as attached properties are a form of dependency properties.)

- Dependency properties allow WPF to compute a value based on multiple external values, which can be very important for animation and data-binding services.

- Dependency properties provide infrastructure support for WPF triggers (also used quite often when working with animation and data binding).

Now remember, in many cases you will interact with an existing dependency property in a manner identical to a normal CLR property (thanks to the XAML wrapper). However, when I covered data binding in Chapter 28, you learned that if you need to establish a data binding in code, you must call the SetBinding() method on the object that is the destination of the operation and specify the *dependency property* it will operate on, like so:

```
private void SetBindings()
{
  Binding b = new Binding();
  b.Converter = new MyDoubleConverter();
```

```
b.Source = this.mySB;
b.Path = new PropertyPath("Value");

// Specify the dependency property!
this.labelSBThumb.SetBinding(Label.ContentProperty, b);
}
```

You also saw similar code when you examined how to start an animation in code, back in the previous chapter.

```
// Specify the dependency property!
rt.BeginAnimation(RotateTransform.AngleProperty, dblAnim);
```

The only time when you would need to build your own custom dependency property is when you are authoring a custom WPF control. For example, if you are building a UserControl that defines four custom properties and you want these properties to integrate well within the WPF API, you should author them using dependency property logic.

Specifically, if your properties need to be the target of a data-binding or animation operation, if the property must broadcast when it has changed, if it must be able to work as a Setter in a WPF style, or if it must be able to receive their values from a parent element, a normal CLR property will *not* be enough. If you were to use a normal CLR property, other programmers may indeed be able to get and set a value; however, if they attempt to use your properties within the context of a WPF service, things will not work as expected. Because you can never know how others might want to interact with the properties of your custom UserControl classes, you should get in the habit of *always* defining dependency properties when building custom controls.

Examining an Existing Dependency Property

Before you learn how to build a custom dependency property, let's take a look at how the Height property of the FrameworkElement class has been implemented internally. The relevant code is shown here (with my included comments:

```
// FrameworkElement is-a DependencyObject.
public class FrameworkElement : UIElement, IFrameworkInputElement,
  IInputElement, ISupportInitialize, IHaveResources, IQueryAmbient
{
...
  // A static read-only field of type DependencyProperty.
  public static readonly DependencyProperty HeightProperty;

  // The DependencyProperty field is often registered
  // in the static constructor of the class.
  static FrameworkElement()
  {
    ...
    HeightProperty = DependencyProperty.Register(
      "Height",
      typeof(double),
      typeof(FrameworkElement),
      new FrameworkPropertyMetadata((double) 1.0 / (double) 0.0,
        FrameworkPropertyMetadataOptions.AffectsMeasure,
        new PropertyChangedCallback(FrameworkElement.OnTransformDirty)),
      new ValidateValueCallback(FrameworkElement.IsWidthHeightValid));
```

```
    }

    // The CLR wrapper, which is implemented using
    // the inherited GetValue()/SetValue() methods.
    public double Height
    {
      get { return (double) base.GetValue(HeightProperty); }
      set { base.SetValue(HeightProperty, value); }
    }
  }
```

As you can see, dependency properties require quite a bit of additional code from a normal CLR property! And in reality, a dependency can be even more complex than what you see here (thankfully, many implementations are simpler than Height).

First and foremost, remember that if a class wants to define a dependency property, it must have DependencyObject in the inheritance chain, as this is the class that defines the GetValue() and SetValue() methods used in the CLR wrapper. Because FrameworkElement is-a DependencyObject, this requirement is satisfied.

Next, recall that the entity that will hold the actual value of the property (a double in the case of Height) is represented as a public, static, read-only field of type DependencyProperty. The name of this field should, by convention, always be named by suffixing the word Property to the name of the related CLR wrapper, like so:

```
public static readonly DependencyProperty HeightProperty;
```

Given that dependency properties are declared as static fields, they are typically created (and registered) within the static constructor of the class. The DependencyProperty object is created via a call to the static DependencyProperty.Register() method. This method has been overloaded many times; however, in the case of Height, DependencyProperty.Register() is invoked as follows:

```
HeightProperty = DependencyProperty.Register(
  "Height",
  typeof(double),
  typeof(FrameworkElement),
  new FrameworkPropertyMetadata((double)0.0,
    FrameworkPropertyMetadataOptions.AffectsMeasure,
    new PropertyChangedCallback(FrameworkElement.OnTransformDirty)),
  new ValidateValueCallback(FrameworkElement.IsWidthHeightValid));
```

The first argument to DependencyProperty.Register() is the name of the normal CLR property on the class (Height, in this case), while the second argument is the type information of the underlying data type it is encapsulating (a double). The third argument specifies the type information of the class that this property belongs to (FrameworkElement, in this case). While this might seem redundant (after all, the HeightProperty field is already defined within the FrameworkElement class), this is a very clever aspect of WPF in that it allows one class to register properties on another (even if the class definition has been sealed!).

The fourth argument passed to DependencyProperty.Register() in this example is what really gives dependency properties their own unique flavor. Here, a FrameworkPropertyMetadata object is passed that describes various details regarding how WPF should handle this property with respect to callback notifications (if the property needs to notify others when the value changes) and various options (represented by the FrameworkPropertyMetadataOptions enum) that control what is effected by the property in question (Does it work with data binding?, Can it be inherited?, etc.). In this case, the constructor arguments of FrameworkPropertyMetadata break down as so:

```
new FrameworkPropertyMetadata(
  // Default value of property.
  (double)0.0,

  // Metadata options.
  FrameworkPropertyMetadataOptions.AffectsMeasure,

  // Delegate pointing to method called when property changes.
  new PropertyChangedCallback(FrameworkElement.OnTransformDirty)
)
```

Because the final argument to the FrameworkPropertyMetadata constructor is a delegate, note that its constructor parameter is pointing to a static method on the FrameworkElement class named OnTransformDirty(). I won't bother to show the code behind this method, but be aware that any time you are building a custom dependency property, you can specify a PropertyChangedCallback delegate to point to a method that will be called when your property value has been changed.

This brings me to the final parameter passed to the DependencyProperty.Register() method, a second delegate of type ValidateValueCallback, which points to a method on the FrameworkElement class that is called to ensure the value assigned to the property is valid.

```
new ValidateValueCallback(FrameworkElement.IsWidthHeightValid)
```

This method contains logic you might normally expect to find in the set block of a property (more information on this point in the next section).

```
private static bool IsWidthHeightValid(object value)
{
  double num = (double) value;
  return ((!DoubleUtil.IsNaN(num) && (num >= 0.0))
    && !double.IsPositiveInfinity(num));
}
```

After the DependencyProperty object has been registered, the final task is to wrap the field within a normal CLR property (Height, in this case). Notice, however, that the get and set scopes do not simply return or set a class-level double-member variable, but do so indirectly using the GetValue() and SetValue() methods from the System.Windows.DependencyObject base class, as follows:

```
public double Height
{
  get { return (double) base.GetValue(HeightProperty); }
  set { base.SetValue(HeightProperty, value); }
}
```

Important Notes Regarding CLR Property Wrappers

So, just to recap the story thus far, dependency properties look like a normal everyday property when you get or set their values in XAML or code, but behind the scenes they are implemented with much more elaborate coding techniques. Remember, the whole reason to go through this process is to build a custom control that has custom properties that need to integrate with WPF services that demand communication with a dependency property (e.g., animation, data binding, and styles).

Even though part of the implementation of a dependency property includes defining a CLR wrapper, *you should never put validation logic in the set block*. For that matter, the CLR wrapper of a dependency property *should never do anything other than call GetValue() or SetValue()*.

The reason is that the WPF runtime has been constructed in such a way that when you write XAML that seems to set a property, such as

```
<Button x:Name="myButton" Height="100" .../>
```

the runtime will completely bypass the set block of the Height property and *directly* call SetValue()! The reason for this odd behavior has to do with a simple optimization technique. If the WPF runtime were to call the set block of the Height property, it would have to perform runtime reflection to figure out where the DependencyProperty field (specified by the first argument to SetValue()) is located, reference it in memory, and so forth. The same story holds true if you were to write XAML that retrieves the value of the Height property—GetValue() would be called directly.

Since this is the case, why do you need to build this CLR wrapper at all? Well, WPF XAML does not allow you to call functions in markup, so the following markup would be an error:

```
<!-- Nope! Can't call methods in WPF XAML! -->
<Button x:Name="myButton" this.SetValue("100") .../>
```

In effect, when you set or get a value in markup using the CLR wrapper, think of it as a way to tell the WPF runtime, "Hey! Go call GetValue()/SetValue() for me, since I can't directly do it in markup!" Now, what if you call the CLR wrapper in code like so:

```
Button b = new Button();
b.Height = 10;
```

In this case, if the set block of the Height property contained code other than a call to SetValue(), it *would* execute, as the WPF XAML parser optimization is not involved.

The basic rule to remember is that when registering a dependency property, use a ValidateValueCallback delegate to point to a method that performs the data validation. This ensures that the correct behavior will occur, regardless of whether you use XAML or code to get/set a dependency property.

Building a Custom Dependency Property

If you have a slight headache at this point in the chapter, this is a perfectly normal response. Building dependency properties can take some time to get used to. However, for better or worse, it is part of the process of building many custom WPF controls, so let's take a look at how to build a dependency property.

Begin by creating a new WPF Application named CustomDepPropApp. Now, using the Project menu, activate the Add User Control menu option, and create a control named ShowNumberControl.xaml (see Figure 31-1).

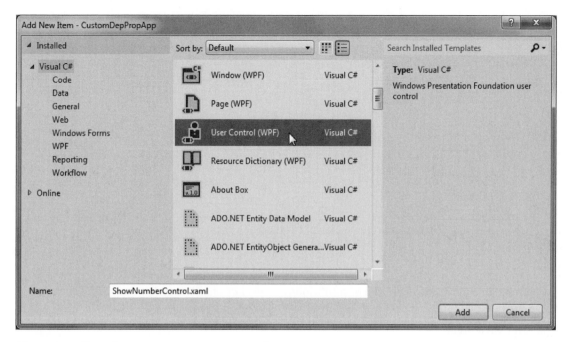

Figure 31-1. *Inserting a new custom* UserControl

■ **Note** You will learn more details about the WPF UserControl later in this chapter, so just follow along as shown for now.

Just like a window, WPF UserControl types have a XAML file and a related code file. Update the XAML of your user control to define a single Label control in the Grid, like so:

```
<UserControl x:Class="CustomDepPropApp.ShowNumberControl"
  xmlns="http://schemas.microsoft.com/winfx/2006/xaml/presentation"
  xmlns:x="http://schemas.microsoft.com/winfx/2006/xaml"
  xmlns:mc="http://schemas.openxmlformats.org/markup-compatibility/2006"
  xmlns:d="http://schemas.microsoft.com/expression/blend/2008"
  mc:Ignorable="d"
  d:DesignHeight="300" d:DesignWidth="300">
  <Grid>
    <Label x:Name="numberDisplay" Height="50" Width="200" Background="LightBlue"/>
  </Grid>
</UserControl>
```

In the code file of this custom control, create a normal, everyday .NET property that wraps an int and sets the Content property of the Label with the new value, as follows:

```
public partial class ShowNumberControl : UserControl
{
  public ShowNumberControl()
  {
    InitializeComponent();
  }

  // A normal, everyday .NET property.
  private int currNumber = 0;
  public int CurrentNumber
  {
    get { return currNumber; }
    set
    {
      currNumber = value;
      numberDisplay.Content = CurrentNumber.ToString();
    }
  }
}
```

Now, update the XAML definition of your window to declare an instance of your custom control within a StackPanel layout manger. Because your custom control is not part of the core WPF assembly stack, you will need to define a custom XML namespace that maps to your control (see Chapter 27). Here is the required markup:

```
<Window x:Class="CustomDepPropApp.MainWindow"
  xmlns="http://schemas.microsoft.com/winfx/2006/xaml/presentation"
  xmlns:x="http://schemas.microsoft.com/winfx/2006/xaml"
  xmlns:myCtrls="clr-namespace:CustomDepPropApp"
  Title="Simple Dependency Property App" Height="150" Width="250"
  WindowStartupLocation="CenterScreen">

  <StackPanel>
    <myCtrls:ShowNumberControl x:Name="myShowNumberCtrl" CurrentNumber="100"/>
  </StackPanel>
</Window>
```

As you can see, the Visual Studio designer appears to correctly display the value that you set in the CurrentNumber property (see Figure 31-2).

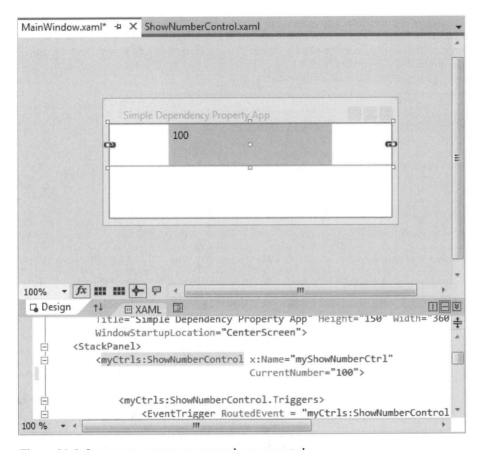

Figure 31-2. It appears your property works as expected

However, what if you want to apply an animation object to the CurrentNumber property so that the value changes from 100 to 200 over a period of 10 seconds? If you wanted to do so in markup, you might update your <myCtrls:ShowNumberControl> scope as so:

```
<myCtrls:ShowNumberControl x:Name="myShowNumberCtrl" CurrentNumber="100">
  <myCtrls:ShowNumberControl.Triggers>
    <EventTrigger RoutedEvent = "myCtrls:ShowNumberControl.Loaded">
      <EventTrigger.Actions>
        <BeginStoryboard>
          <Storyboard TargetProperty = "CurrentNumber">
            <Int32Animation From = "100" To = "200" Duration = "0:0:10"/>
          </Storyboard>
        </BeginStoryboard>
      </EventTrigger.Actions>
    </EventTrigger>
  </myCtrls:ShowNumberControl.Triggers>
</myCtrls:ShowNumberControl>
```

If you attempt to run your application, the animation object cannot find a proper target, so it is ignored. The reason is that the CurrentNumber property has not been registered as a dependency property! To fix matters, return to the code file of your custom control, and completely comment out the current property logic (including the private backing field). Now, position your mouse cursor within the scope of the class and type in the propdp code snippet (see Figure 31-3).

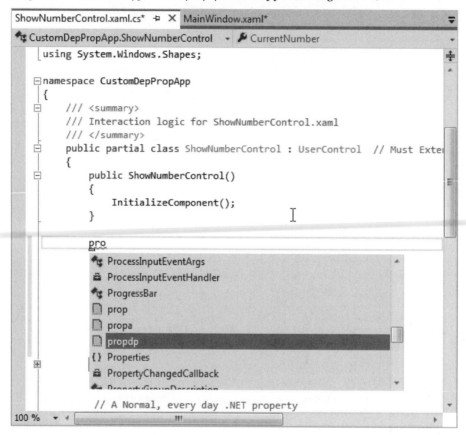

Figure 31-3. The propdp code snippet provides a starting point for building a dependency property

After you have typed propdp, press the Tab key twice. You will find the snippet expands to give you the basic skeleton of a dependency property (see Figure 31-4).

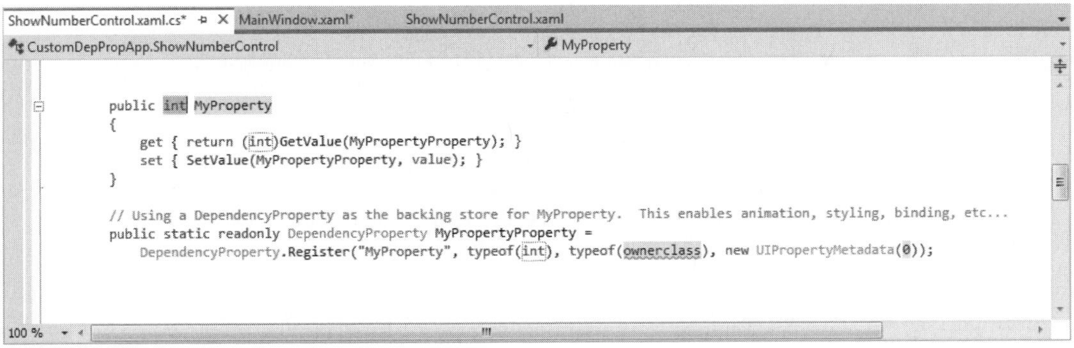

Figure 31-4. The expanded snippet

The simplest version of the CurrentNumber property will look like so:

```
public partial class ShowNumberControl : UserControl
{
  public int CurrentNumber
  {
    get { return (int)GetValue(CurrentNumberProperty); }
    set { SetValue(CurrentNumberProperty, value); }
  }

  public static readonly DependencyProperty CurrentNumberProperty =
     DependencyProperty.Register("CurrentNumber",
     typeof(int),
     typeof(ShowNumberControl),
     new UIPropertyMetadata(0));
  ...
}
```

This is similar to what you saw in the implementation of the Height property; however, the code snippet registers the property inline rather than within a static constructor (which is fine). Also notice that a UIPropertyMetadata object is used to define the default value of the integer (0) rather than the more complex FrameworkPropertyMetadata object.

Adding a Data Validation Routine

Although you now have a dependency property named CurrentNumber, you still won't see your animation take hold. The next adjustment you might want to make is to specify a function to call to perform some data validation logic. For this example, assume that you need to ensure that the value of CurrentNumber is between 0 and 500.

To do so, add a final argument to the DependencyProperty.Register() method of type ValidateValueCallback, which points to a method named ValidateCurrentNumber.

ValidateValueCallback is a delegate that can only point to methods returning bool and take an object as the only argument. This object represents the new value that is being assigned. Implement ValidateCurrentNumber to return true or false, if the incoming value is within the expected range.

1311

```
public static readonly DependencyProperty CurrentNumberProperty =
  DependencyProperty.Register("CurrentNumber", typeof(int), typeof(ShowNumberControl),
  new UIPropertyMetadata(100),
  new ValidateValueCallback(ValidateCurrentNumber));

public static bool ValidateCurrentNumber(object value)
{
  // Just a simple business rule. Value must be between 0 and 500.
  if (Convert.ToInt32(value) >= 0 && Convert.ToInt32(value) <= 500)
    return true;
  else
    return false;
}
```

Responding to the Property Change

Okay, so now you have a valid number, but still no animation. The final change you need to make is to specify a second argument to the constructor of UIPropertyMetadata, which is a PropertyChangedCallback object. This delegate can point to any method that takes a DependencyObject as the first parameter and a DependencyPropertyChangedEventArgs as the second. First, update your code as so:

```
// Note the second param of UIPropertyMetadata construtor.
public static readonly DependencyProperty CurrentNumberProperty =
  DependencyProperty.Register("CurrentNumber", typeof(int), typeof(ShowNumberControl),
  new UIPropertyMetadata(100,
                      new PropertyChangedCallback(CurrentNumberChanged)),
  new ValidateValueCallback(ValidateCurrentNumber));
```

Within the CurrentNumberChanged() method, your ultimate goal is to change the Content of the Label to the new value assigned by the CurrentNumber property. You have one big problem, however: the CurrentNumberChanged() method is static, as it must be to work with the static DependencyProperty object. So how are you supposed to gain access to the Label for the current instance of ShowNumberControl? That reference is contained in the first DependencyObject parameter. You can find the new value using the incoming event arguments. Here is the necessary code that will change the Content property of the Label:

```
private static void CurrentNumberChanged(DependencyObject depObj,
    DependencyPropertyChangedEventArgs args)
{
  // Cast the DependencyObject into ShowNumberControl.
  ShowNumberControl c = (ShowNumberControl)depObj;

  // Get the Label control in the ShowNumberControl.
  Label theLabel = c.numberDisplay;

  // Set the Label with the new value.
  theLabel.Content = args.NewValue.ToString();
}
```

Whew! That was a long way to go just to change the output of a label. The benefit is that your CurrentNumber dependency property can now be the target of a WPF style, an animation object, the target of a data-binding operation, and so forth. If you run your application once again, you should now see the value change during execution.

That wraps up your look at WPF dependency properties. While I hope you have a much better idea about what these constructs allow you to do and have a better idea of how to make your own, please be aware that there are many details I have not covered here.

If you find yourself in a position where you are building a number of custom controls that support custom properties, please look up the topic "Properties" under the "WPF Fundamentals" node of the .NET Framework 4.5 SDK documentation. Here, you will find many more examples of building dependency properties, attached properties, various ways to configure property metadata, and a slew of other details.

■ **Source Code** The CustomDepPropApp project is included under the Chapter 31 subdirectory.

Understanding Routed Events

Properties are not the only .NET programming construct to be given a facelift in order to work well within the WPF API. The standard CLR event model has also been refined just a bit to ensure that events can be processed in a manner that is fitting for XAML's description of a tree of objects. Assume you have a new WPF Application project named WPFRoutedEvents. Now, update the XAML description of the initial window by adding the following <Button> control, which defines some complex content:

```
<Button Name="btnClickMe" Height="75" Width = "250"
        Click ="btnClickMe_Clicked">
  <StackPanel Orientation ="Horizontal">
    <Label Height="50" FontSize ="20">Fancy Button!</Label>
    <Canvas Height ="50" Width ="100" >
    <Ellipse Name = "outerEllipse" Fill ="Green" Height ="25"
            Width ="50" Cursor="Hand" Canvas.Left="25" Canvas.Top="12"/>
    <Ellipse Name = "innerEllipse" Fill ="Yellow" Height = "15" Width ="36"
            Canvas.Top="17" Canvas.Left="32"/>
    </Canvas>
  </StackPanel>
</Button>
```

Notice in the <Button>'s opening definition you have handled the Click event by specifying the name of a method to be called when the event is raised. The Click event works with the RoutedEventHandler delegate, which expects an event handler that takes an object as the first parameter and a System.Windows.RoutedEventArgs as the second. Implement this handler as so:

```
public void btnClickMe_Clicked(object sender, RoutedEventArgs e)
{
  // Do something when button is clicked.
  MessageBox.Show("Clicked the button");
}
```

If you run your application, you will see this message box display, regardless of which part of the button's content you click on (the green Ellipse, the yellow Ellipse, the Label, or the Button's surface). This is a good thing. Imagine how tedious WPF event handling would be if you were forced to handle a

Click event for each and every one of these subelements. Not only would the creation of separate event handlers for each aspect of the Button be labor intensive, you would end up with some mighty nasty code to maintain down the road.

Thankfully, WPF *routed events* take care of ensuring that your single Click event handler will be called regardless of which part of the button is clicked automatically. Simply put, the routed events model automatically propagates an event up (or down) a tree of objects, looking for an appropriate handler.

Specifically speaking, a routed event can make use of three *routing strategies*. If an event is moving from the point of origin up to other defining scopes within the object tree, the event is said to be a *bubbling event*. Conversely, if an event is moving from the outermost element (e.g., a Window) down to the point of origin, the event is said to be a *tunneling event*. Finally, if an event is raised and handled only by the originating element (which is what could be described as a normal CLR event), it is said to be a *direct event*.

The Role of Routed Bubbling Events

In the current example, if the user clicks the inner yellow oval, the Click event bubbles out to the next level of scope (the Canvas), then to the StackPanel, and finally to the Button where the Click event handler is handled. In a similar way, if the user clicks the Label, the event is bubbled to the StackPanel and then finally to the Button element.

Given this bubbling routed event pattern, you have no need to worry about registering specific Click event handlers for all members of a composite control. However, if you wanted to perform custom clicking logic for multiple elements within the same object tree, you can do so.

By way of illustration, assume you need to handle the clicking of the outerEllipse control in a unique manner. First, handle the MouseDown event for this subelement (graphically rendered types such as the Ellipse do not support a Click event; however, they can monitor mouse button activity via -MouseDown, MouseUp, etc.).

```
<Button Name="btnClickMe" Height="75" Width = "250"
        Click ="btnClickMe_Clicked">
  <StackPanel Orientation ="Horizontal">
    <Label Height="50" FontSize ="20">Fancy Button!</Label>
    <Canvas Height ="50" Width ="100" >
      <Ellipse Name = "outerEllipse" Fill ="Green"
               Height ="25" MouseDown ="outerEllipse_MouseDown"
               Width ="50" Cursor="Hand" Canvas.Left="25" Canvas.Top="12"/>
      <Ellipse Name = "innerEllipse" Fill ="Yellow" Height = "15" Width ="36"
               Canvas.Top="17" Canvas.Left="32"/>
    </Canvas>
  </StackPanel>
</Button>
```

Then implement an appropriate event handler, which for illustrative purposes will simply change the Title property of the main window, like so:

```
public void outerEllipse_MouseDown(object sender, MouseButtonEventArgs e)
{
  // Change title of window.
  this.Title = "You clicked the outer ellipse!";
}
```

With this, you can now take different courses of action depending on where the end user has clicked (which boils down to the outer ellipse and everywhere else within the button's scope).

■ **Note** Routed bubbling events always move from the point of origin to the *next defining scope*. Thus, in this example, if you were to click the innerEllipse object, the event would be bubbled to the Canvas, *not* to the outerEllipse, as they are both Ellipse types within the scope of Canvas.

Continuing or Halting Bubbling

Currently, if the user clicks the outerEllipse object, it will trigger the registered MouseDown event handler for this Ellipse object, at which point the event bubbles to the button's Click event. If you want to inform WPF to stop bubbling up the tree of objects, you can set the Handled property of the EventArgs parameter to true, as follows:

```
public void outerEllipse_MouseDown(object sender, MouseButtonEventArgs e)
{
  // Change title of window.
  this.Title = "You clicked the outer ellipse!";

  // Stop bubbling!
  e.Handled = true;
}
```

In this case, you would find that the title of the window is changed, but you will not see the MessageBox displayed by the Click event handler of the Button. In a nutshell, routed bubbling events make it possible to allow a complex group of content to act either as a single logical element (e.g., a Button) or as discrete items (e.g., an Ellipse within the Button).

The Role of Routed Tunneling Events

Strictly speaking, routed events can be *bubbling* (as just described) or *tunneling* in nature. Tunneling events (which all begin with the Preview suffix—e.g., PreviewMouseDown) drill down from the topmost element into the inner scopes of the object tree. By and large, each bubbling event in the WPF base class libraries is paired with a related tunneling event that fires *before* the bubbling counterpart. For example, before the bubbling MouseDown event fires, the tunneling PreviewMouseDown event fires first.

Handling a tunneling event looks just like the processing of handling any other events; simply assign the event handler name in XAML (or, if needed, use the corresponding C# event-handling syntax in your code file) and implement the handler in the code file. Just to illustrate the interplay of tunneling and bubbling events, begin by handling the PreviewMouseDown event for the outerEllipse object, like so:

```
<Ellipse Name = "outerEllipse" Fill ="Green" Height ="25"
         MouseDown ="outerEllipse_MouseDown"
         PreviewMouseDown ="outerEllipse_PreviewMouseDown"
         Width ="50" Cursor="Hand" Canvas.Left="25" Canvas.Top="12"/>
```

Next, retrofit the current C# class definition by updating each event handler (for all objects) to append data about the current event into a string member variable named mouseActivity, using the incoming event args object. This will allow you to observe the flow of events firing in the background.

```
public partial class MainWindow : Window
{
  string mouseActivity = string.Empty;
  public MainWindow()
  {
    InitializeComponent();
  }

  public void btnClickMe_Clicked(object sender, RoutedEventArgs e)
  {
    AddEventInfo(sender, e);
    MessageBox.Show(mouseActivity, "Your Event Info");

    // Clear string for next round.
    mouseActivity = "";
  }

  private void AddEventInfo(object sender, RoutedEventArgs e)
  {
    mouseActivity += string.Format(
      "{0} sent a {1} event named {2}.\n", sender,
      e.RoutedEvent.RoutingStrategy,
      e.RoutedEvent.Name);
  }

  private void outerEllipse_MouseDown(object sender, MouseButtonEventArgs e)
  {
    AddEventInfo(sender, e);
  }

  private void outerEllipse_PreviewMouseDown(object sender, MouseButtonEventArgs e)
  {
    AddEventInfo(sender, e);
  }
}
```

Notice that you are not halting the bubbling of an event for any event handler. If you run this application, you will see a unique message box display based on where you click the button. Figure 31-5 shows the result of clicking on the outer Ellipse object.

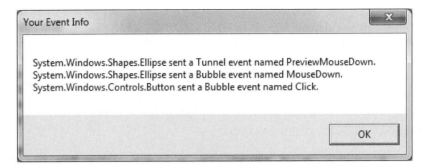

Figure 31-5. Tunneling first, bubbling second

So, why do WPF events typically tend to come in pairs (one tunneling and one bubbling)? The answer is that by previewing events, you have the power to perform any special logic (data validation, disable bubbling action, etc.) before the bubbling counterpart fires. By way of an example, assume you have a TextBox that should contain only numerical data. You could handle the PreviewKeyDown event, and if you see the user has entered nonnumerical data, you could cancel the bubbling event by setting the Handled property to true.

As you would guess, when you are building a custom control that contains custom events, you could author the event in such a way that it can bubble (or tunnel) through a tree of XAML. For the purpose of this chapter, I will not be examining how to build custom routed events (however, the process is not that different from building a custom dependency property). If you are interested, check out the topic "Routed Events Overview" within the .NET Framework 4.5 SDK documentation. Here, you will find a number of tutorials that will help you on your way.

■ **Source Code** The WPFRoutedEvents project is included under the Chapter 31 subdirectory.

Logical Trees, Visual Trees, and Default Templates

There are a few more preparatory topics to investigate before you begin learning how to build custom controls. Specifically, you need to learn the distinction between a *logical tree*, a *visual tree* and a *default template*. When you are typing XAML into Visual Studio, or a tool such as kaxaml.exe, your markup is the *logical view* of the XAML document. As well, if you author C# code that adds new items to a StackPanel control, you are inserting new items into the logical tree. Essentially, a logical view represents how your content will be positioned within the various layout managers for a main Window (or another root element, such as Page or NavigationWindow).

However, behind every logical tree, there is a much more verbose representation termed a *visual tree*, which is used internally by WPF to correctly render out elements onto the screen. Within any visual tree, there will be full details of the templates and styles used to render out each object, including any necessary drawings, shapes, visuals, and animations.

It is useful to understand the distinction between logical and visual trees because when you are building a custom control template, you are essentially replacing all or part of the default visual tree of a control and inserting your own. Therefore, if you want a Button control to be rendered as a star shape, you could define a new star template and plug it into the Button's visual tree. Logically, the Button is still of type Button, and it supports all of the properties, methods, and events as expected. But visually, it has taken on a whole new appearance. This fact alone makes WPF an extremely useful API, given that other toolkits would require you to build a brand-new class to make a star-shaped button. With WPF, you simply need to define new markup.

■ **Note** WPF controls are often described as *lookless*. This refers to the fact that the look and feel of a WPF control is completely independent (and customizable) from its behavior.

Programmatically Inspecting a Logical Tree

While analyzing a window's logical tree at runtime is not a tremendously common WPF programming activity, it is worth mentioning that the System.Windows namespace defines a class named LogicalTreeHelper, which allows you to inspect the structure of a logical tree at runtime. To illustrate the connection between logical trees, visual trees, and control templates, create a new WPF Application named TreesAndTemplatesApp.

Update the markup for your window so that it contains two Button controls and a large read-only TextBox with scrollbars enabled. Make sure you use the IDE to handle the Click event of each button. The following XAML will do nicely:

```
<Window x:Class="TreesAndTemplatesApp.MainWindow"
    xmlns="http://schemas.microsoft.com/winfx/2006/xaml/presentation"
    xmlns:x="http://schemas.microsoft.com/winfx/2006/xaml"
    Title="Fun with Trees and Templates" Height="518"
    Width="836" WindowStartupLocation="CenterScreen">

    <DockPanel LastChildFill="True">
        <Border Height="50"  DockPanel.Dock="Top" BorderBrush="Blue">
            <StackPanel Orientation="Horizontal">
                <Button x:Name="btnShowLogicalTree" Content="Logical Tree of Window"
                        Margin="4" BorderBrush="Blue" Height="40" Click="btnShowLogicalTree_Click"/>
                <Button x:Name="btnShowVisualTree" Content="Visual Tree of Window"
                        BorderBrush="Blue" Height="40" Click="btnShowVisualTree_Click"/>
            </StackPanel>
        </Border>
        <TextBox x:Name="txtDisplayArea" Margin="10" Background="AliceBlue" IsReadOnly="True"
                BorderBrush="Red" VerticalScrollBarVisibility="Auto"
                HorizontalScrollBarVisibility="Auto" />
    </DockPanel>

</Window>
```

Within your C# code file, define a string member variable named dataToShow. Now, within the Click handler for the btnShowLogicalTree object, call a helper function that calls itself recursively in order to populate the string variable with the logical tree of the Window. To do so, you will call the static GetChildren() method of LogicalTreeHelper. Here is the code:

```
private void btnShowLogicalTree_Click(object sender, RoutedEventArgs e)
{
  dataToShow = "";
  BuildLogicalTree(0, this);
  this.txtDisplayArea.Text = dataToShow;
}

void BuildLogicalTree(int depth, object obj)
{
  // Add the type name to the dataToShow member variable.
  dataToShow += new string(' ', depth) + obj.GetType().Name + "\n";

  // If an item is not a DependencyObject, skip it.
  if (!(obj is DependencyObject))
    return;

  // Make a recursive call for each logical child.
  foreach (object child in LogicalTreeHelper.GetChildren(
    obj as DependencyObject))
      BuildLogicalTree(depth + 5, child);
}
```

If you run your application and click this first button, you will see a tree print out in the text area, which is just about an exact replica of the original XAML (see Figure 31-6).

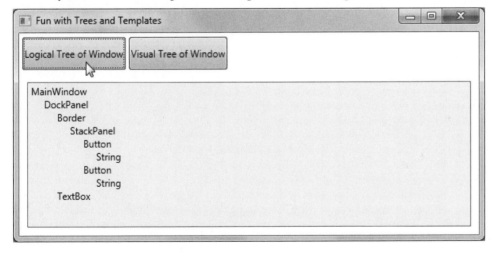

Figure 31-6. *Viewing a logical tree at runtime*

Programmatically Inspecting a Visual Tree

A Window's visual tree can also be inspected at runtime using the VisualTreeHelper class of System.Windows.Media. Here is a Click implementation of the second Button control (btnShowVisualTree), which performs similar recursive logic to build a textual representation of the visual tree:

```
private void btnShowVisualTree_Click(object sender, RoutedEventArgs e)
{
  dataToShow = "";
  BuildVisualTree(0, this);
  this.txtDisplayArea.Text = dataToShow;
}

void BuildVisualTree(int depth, DependencyObject obj)
{
  // Add the type name to the dataToShow member variable.
  dataToShow += new string(' ', depth) + obj.GetType().Name + "\n";
  // Make a recursive call for each visual child.
  for (int i = 0; i < VisualTreeHelper.GetChildrenCount(obj); i++)
    BuildVisualTree(depth + 1, VisualTreeHelper.GetChild(obj, i));
}
```

As you can see in Figure 31-7, the visual tree exposes a number of lower-level rendering agents such as ContentPresenter, AdornerDecorator, TextBoxLineDrawingVisual, and so forth.

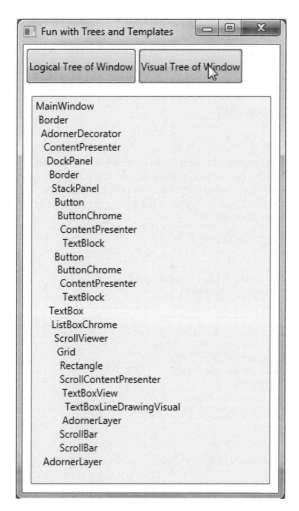

Figure 31-7. Viewing a visual tree at runtime

Programmatically Inspecting a Control's Default Template

Recall that a visual tree is used by WPF to understand how to render a Window and all contained elements. Every WPF control stores its own set of rendering commands within its default template. Programmatically speaking, any template can be represented as an instance of the ControlTemplate class. As well, you can obtain a control's default template by using the aptly named Template property, like so:

```
// Get the default template of the Button.
Button myBtn = new Button();
ControlTemplate template = myBtn.Template;
```

Likewise, you could create a new `ControlTemplate` object in code and plug it into a control's `Template` property as follows:

```
// Plug in a new template for the button to use.
Button myBtn = new Button();
ControlTemplate customTemplate = new ControlTemplate();

// Assume this method adds all the code for a star template.
MakeStarTemplate(customTemplate);
myBtn.Template = customTemplate;
```

While you could build a new template in code, it is far more common to do so in XAML. However, before you start building your own templates, let's finish the current example and add the ability to view the default template of a WPF control at runtime. This can be a really useful way to take a look at the overall composition of a template. First, update the markup of your window with a new `StackPanel` of controls docked to the left side of the master `DockPanel`, defined as so:

```
<Border DockPanel.Dock="Left" Margin="10" BorderBrush="DarkGreen"
        BorderThickness="4" Width="358">
  <StackPanel>
    <Label Content="Enter Full Name of WPF Control" Width="340" FontWeight="DemiBold" />
    <TextBox x:Name="txtFullName" Width="340" BorderBrush="Green"
             Background="BlanchedAlmond" Height="22"
             Text="System.Windows.Controls.Button" />
    <Button x:Name="btnTemplate" Content="See Template" BorderBrush="Green"
            Height="40" Width="100" Margin="5"
            Click="btnTemplate_Click" HorizontalAlignment="Left" />
    <Border BorderBrush="DarkGreen" BorderThickness="2" Height="260"
            Width="301" Margin="10" Background="LightGreen" >
      <StackPanel x:Name="stackTemplatePanel" />
    </Border>
  </StackPanel>
</Border>
```

Do take note of the empty `StackPanel`, `stackTemplatePanel`, as you will refer to it in code. Anyway, your window should now look something like Figure 31-8.

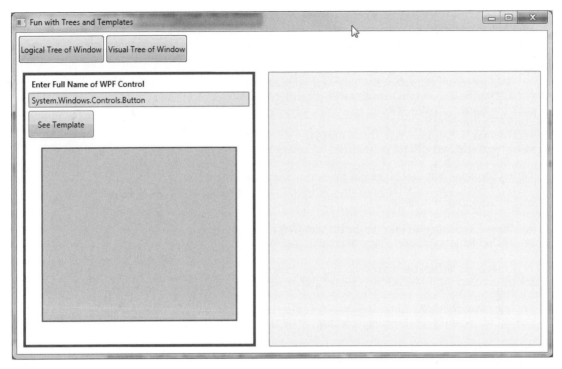

Figure 31-8. The updated UI of your window

The upper-left text area allows you to enter in the fully qualified name of a WPF control located in the `PresentationFramework.dll` assembly. Once the library is loaded, you will dynamically create an instance of the object and display it in the large square in the bottom left. Last but not least, the control's default template will be displayed in the right-hand text area. First, add a new member variable to your C# class of type `Control`, like so:

```
private Control ctrlToExamine = null;
```

Here is the remaining code, which will require you to import the `System.Reflection`, `System.Xml`, and `System.Windows.Markup` namespaces:

```
private void btnTemplate_Click(object sender, RoutedEventArgs e)
{
  dataToShow = "";
  ShowTemplate();
  this.txtDisplayArea.Text = dataToShow;
}

private void ShowTemplate()
{
  // Remove the control that is currently in the preview area.
  if (ctrlToExamine != null)
    stackTemplatePanel.Children.Remove(ctrlToExamine);
  try
```

```
    {
      // Load PresentationFramework, and create an instance of the
      // specified control. Give it a size for display purposes, then add to the
      // empty StackPanel.
      Assembly asm = Assembly.Load("PresentationFramework, Version=4.0.0.0," +
        "Culture=neutral, PublicKeyToken=31bf3856ad364e35");
      ctrlToExamine = (Control)asm.CreateInstance(txtFullName.Text);
      ctrlToExamine.Height = 200;
      ctrlToExamine.Width = 200;
      ctrlToExamine.Margin = new Thickness(5);
      stackTemplatePanel.Children.Add(ctrlToExamine);

      // Define some XML settings to preserve indentation.
      XmlWriterSettings xmlSettings = new XmlWriterSettings();
      xmlSettings.Indent = true;

      // Create a StringBuilder to hold the XAML.
      StringBuilder strBuilder = new StringBuilder();

      // Create an XmlWriter based on our settings.
      XmlWriter xWriter = XmlWriter.Create(strBuilder, xmlSettings);

      // Now save the XAML into the XmlWriter object based on the ControlTemplate.
      XamlWriter.Save(ctrlToExamine.Template, xWriter);

      // Display XAML in the text box.
      dataToShow = strBuilder.ToString();
    }
    catch (Exception ex)
    {
      dataToShow = ex.Message;
    }
  }
```

The bulk of the work is just tinkering with the compiled BAML resource to map it into a XAML string. Figure 31-9 shows your final application in action, displaying the default template of the System.Windows.Controls.DatePicker control.

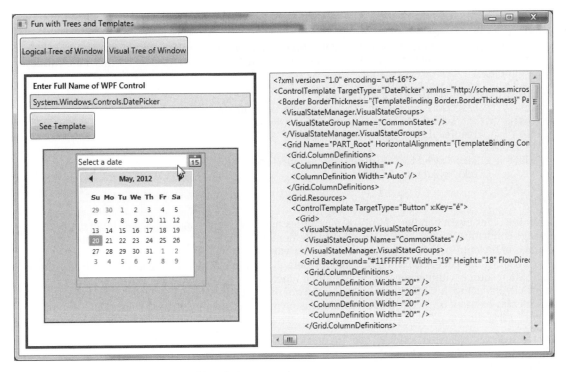

Figure 31-9. Investigating a ControlTemplate *at runtime*

Great! Hopefully you have a better idea about how logical trees, visual trees, and control default templates work together. Now you can spend the remainder of this chapter learning how to build custom templates and user controls.

■ **Source Code** The TreesAndTemplatesApp project is included under the Chapter 31 subdirectory.

Building a Control Template with the Trigger Framework

When you are building a custom template for a control, you could do so with nothing but C# code. Using this approach, you would be adding data to a ControlTemplate object and then assigning it to a control's Template property. Most of the time, however, you will define the look and feel of a ControlTemplate using XAML and add bits of code (or possible quite a bit of code) to drive the runtime behavior.

For the remainder of this chapter you will examine how to build custom templates using Visual Studio. Along the way, you will come to learn about the WPF trigger framework, the Visual State Manager (VSM), and see how to use animations to incorporate visual cues for the end user. As you will see, using Visual Studio alone to build complex templates can entail a fair amount of typing and a bit of heavy lifting. To be sure, production-level templates will benefit from the use of Expression Blend. However, given that this edition of the text does not include coverage of Blend, it's time to roll up our sleeves and pound out some markup.

To begin, create a brand-new WPF Application named ButtonTemplate. For this project, you are more interested in the mechanics of creating and using templates, so the markup for this main window is very simple.

```
<Window x:Class="ButtonTemplate.MainWindow"
  xmlns="http://schemas.microsoft.com/winfx/2006/xaml/presentation"
  xmlns:x="http://schemas.microsoft.com/winfx/2006/xaml"
  Title="Fun with Templates" Height="350" Width="525">
  <StackPanel>
    <Button x:Name="myButton" Width="100" Height="100"
            Click="myButton_Click"/>
  </StackPanel>
</Window>
```

In the Click event handler, simply display a message box (via MessageBox.Show()) that displays a message confirming the clicking of the control. Remember, when you build custom templates, the *behavior* of the control is constant but the *look* may vary.

Currently, this Button is rendered using the default template, which, as the last example illustrated, is a BAML resource within a given WPF assembly. When you want to define your own template, you are essentially replacing this default visual tree with your own creation. To begin, update the definition of the <Button> element to specify a new template using property element syntax. This template will give the control a round appearance.

```
<Button x:Name="myButton" Width="100" Height="100"
        Click="myButton_Click">
  <Button.Template>
    <ControlTemplate>
      <Grid x:Name="controlLayout">
        <Ellipse  x:Name="buttonSurface" Fill = "LightBlue"/>
        <Label x:Name="buttonCaption" VerticalAlignment = "Center"
               HorizontalAlignment = "Center"
               FontWeight = "Bold" FontSize = "20" Content = "OK!"/>
      </Grid>
    </ControlTemplate>
  </Button.Template>
</Button>
```

Here, you have defined a template that consists of a named Grid control containing a named Ellipse and a Label. Because your Grid has no defined rows or columns, each child stacks on top of the previous control, allowing you to have centering of content. Now, if you run your application, you will notice that the Click event will fire *only* when the mouse cursor is within the bounds of the Ellipse (i.e., not in the corners around the edges of the ellipse)! This is a great feature of the WPF template architecture: you do not need to recalculate hit-testing, bounds checking, or any other low-level detail. So, if your template used a Polygon object to render some oddball geometry, you can rest assured that the mouse hit-testing details are relative to the shape of the control, not the larger bounding rectangle.

Templates As Resources

Currently, your template is embedded to a specific Button control, which limits your reuse options. Ideally, you would place your template into a resource dictionary, so you can reuse your round button template between projects, or at minimum, move it into the application resource container for reuse within this project. Let's move the local Button resource to the application level. First, locate the Template property for your Button in the Properties editor (you'll find it under the Miscellaneous section). Now, click on the small white square icon and select "Convert to New Resource…" (see Figure 31-10).

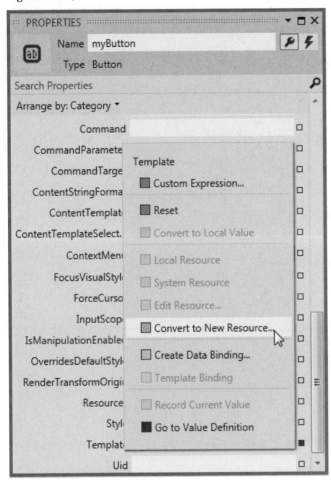

Figure 31-10. *Extracting a local resource*

From the resulting dialog box, define a new template named RoundButtonTemplate, which is stored at Application level (i.e., in App.xaml; see Figure 31-11).

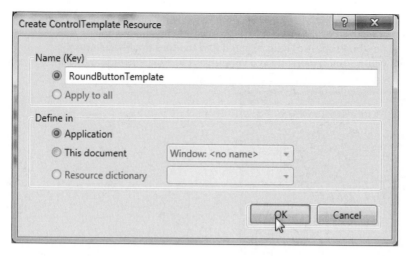

Figure 31-11. *Placing your resource into* App.xaml

At this point, you will find the following data in your Application object's markup:

```
<Application x:Class="ButtonTemplate.App"
  xmlns="http://schemas.microsoft.com/winfx/2006/xaml/presentation"
  xmlns:x="http://schemas.microsoft.com/winfx/2006/xaml"
  StartupUri="MainWindow.xaml">
  <Application.Resources>
    <ControlTemplate x:Key="RoundButtonTemplate" TargetType="{x:Type Button}">
      <Grid x:Name="controlLayout">
        <Ellipse  x:Name="buttonSurface" Fill = "LightBlue"/>
        <Label x:Name="buttonCaption" VerticalAlignment = "Center"
               HorizontalAlignment = "Center"
               FontWeight = "Bold" FontSize = "20" Content = "OK!"/>
      </Grid>
    </ControlTemplate>
  </Application.Resources>
</Application>
```

Now, because this resource is available for the entire application, you can define any number of round buttons. Go ahead and create two additional Button controls that use this template for testing purposes (no need to handle the Click event for these new items).

```
<StackPanel>
  <Button x:Name="myButton" Width="100" Height="100"
          Click="myButton_Click"
          Template="{StaticResource RoundButtonTemplate}"></Button>
  <Button x:Name="myButton2" Width="100" Height="100"
          Template="{StaticResource RoundButtonTemplate}"></Button>
  <Button x:Name="myButton3" Width="100" Height="100"
          Template="{StaticResource RoundButtonTemplate}"></Button>
</StackPanel>
```

Incorporating Visual Cues Using Triggers

When you define a custom template, all of the visual cues of the default template are removed as well. For example, the default button template contains markup that informs the control how to look when certain UI events occur, such as when it receives focus, when it is clicked with the mouse, when it is enabled (or disabled), and so on. Users are quite accustomed to these sort of visual cues, as it gives the control somewhat of a tactile response. However, your RoundButtonTemplate does not define any such markup, so the look of the control is identical regardless of the mouse activity. Ideally, your control should look slightly different when clicked (maybe via a color change or drop shadow) to let the user know the visual state has changed.

When WPF was first released, the way to add in such visual cues was to add to the template any number of triggers that would typically change values of object properties or start a storyboard animation (or both) when the trigger condition was true. By way of example, update your RoundButtonTemplate with the following markup, which will change the color of the control to blue and the foreground color to yellow when the mouse is over the surface:

```
<ControlTemplate x:Key="RoundButtonTemplate" TargetType="Button" >
  <Grid x:Name="controlLayout">
    <Ellipse x:Name="buttonSurface" Fill="LightBlue" />
    <Label x:Name="buttonCaption" Content="OK!" FontSize="20" FontWeight="Bold"
           HorizontalAlignment="Center" VerticalAlignment="Center" />
  </Grid>
    <ControlTemplate.Triggers>
      <Trigger Property = "IsMouseOver" Value = "True">
        <Setter TargetName = "buttonSurface" Property = "Fill" Value = "Blue"/>
        <Setter TargetName = "buttonCaption" Property = "Foreground"
                Value = "Yellow"/>
      </Trigger>
    </ControlTemplate.Triggers>
</ControlTemplate>
```

If you run the program yet again, you should find the color does toggle based on whether or not the mouse is within the Ellipse area. Here is another trigger, which will shrink the size of the Grid (and, therefore, all child elements) when the control is pressed via the mouse. Add this to your <ControlTemplate.Triggers> collection:

```
<Trigger Property = "IsPressed" Value="True">
  <Setter TargetName="controlLayout"
          Property="RenderTransformOrigin" Value="0.5,0.5"/>
  <Setter TargetName="controlLayout" Property="RenderTransform">
    <Setter.Value>
      <ScaleTransform ScaleX="0.8" ScaleY="0.8"/>
    </Setter.Value>
  </Setter>
</Trigger>
```

The Role of the {TemplateBinding} Markup Extension

Your template can only be applied to Button controls and, therefore, it would stand to reason that you could set properties on the <Button> elementthat will cause the template to render itself in a unique manner. For example, right now, the Fill property of the Ellipse is hard-coded to be blue and the

Content of the Label is always set to the string value "OK". Of course, you might want buttons of different colors and text values, so you might try to define the following buttons in your main window:

```
<StackPanel>
    <Button x:Name="myButton" Width="100" Height="100"
            Background="Red" Content="Howdy!"
            Click="myButton_Click"
            Template="{StaticResource RoundButtonTemplate}" />
    <Button x:Name="myButton2" Width="100" Height="100"
            Background="LightGreen" Content="Cancel!"
            Template="{StaticResource RoundButtonTemplate}" />
    <Button x:Name="myButton3" Width="100" Height="100"
             Background="Yellow" Content="Format"
            Template="{StaticResource RoundButtonTemplate}" />
</StackPanel>
```

However, regardless of the fact that each Button is setting a unique Background and Content value, you still end up with three blue buttons that contain the text "OK". The problem is that the properties of the control using the template (Button) have properties that do not match identically with the items on the template (such as the Fill property of the Ellipse). As well, although the Label does have a Content property, the value defined in the <Button> scope is not automatically routed to the internal child of the template.

You can solve these issues by using the {TemplateBinding} markup extension when you build your template. This allows you to capture property settings defined by the control using your template and use them to set values in the template itself. Here is a reworked version of RoundButtonTemplate, which now uses this markup extension to map the Background property of the Button to the Fill property of the Ellipse; it also makes sure the Content of the Button is indeed passed to the Content property of the Label.

```
<ControlTemplate x:Key="RoundButtonTemplate" TargetType="Button">
    <Grid x:Name="controlLayout">
        <Ellipse x:Name="buttonSurface" Fill="{TemplateBinding Background}"/>
        <Label x:Name="buttonCaption" Content="{TemplateBinding Content}"
               FontSize="20" FontWeight="Bold"
               HorizontalAlignment="Center" VerticalAlignment="Center" />
    </Grid>
    <ControlTemplate.Triggers>
      ...
    </ControlTemplate.Triggers>
</ControlTemplate>
```

With this update, you can now create buttons of various colors and textual values (see Figure 31-12).

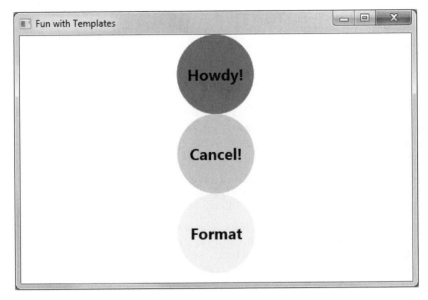

Figure 31-12. Template bindings allow values to pass through to the internal controls

The Role of ContentPresenter

When you designed your template, you used a Label to display the textual value of the control. Like the Button, the Label supports a Content property. Therefore, given your use of {TemplateBinding}, you could define a Button which contained complex content beyond that of a simple string. For example:

```
<Button x:Name="myButton4" Width="100" Height="100" Background="Yellow"
        Template="{StaticResource RoundButtonTemplate}">
  <Button.Content>
    <ListBox Height="50" Width="75">
      <ListBoxItem>Hello</ListBoxItem>
      <ListBoxItem>Hello</ListBoxItem>
      <ListBoxItem>Hello</ListBoxItem>
    </ListBox>
  </Button.Content>
</Button>
```

For this particular control, things work just as hoped. However, what if you need to pass in complex content to a template member that does *not* have a Content property? When you want to define a generalized *content display area* in a template, you can use the ContentPresenter class as opposed to a specific type of control (Label or TextBlock). You have no need to do so for this example; however, here is some simple markup that illustrates how you could build a custom template that uses ContentPresenter to show the value of the Content property of the control using the template:

```
<!-- This button template will display whatever is set
     to the Content of the hosting button. -->
<ControlTemplate x:Key="NewRoundButtonTemplate" TargetType="Button">
  <Grid>
```

```
      <Ellipse Fill="{TemplateBinding Background}"/>
      <ContentPresenter HorizontalAlignment="Center"
                        VerticalAlignment="Center"/>
   </Grid>
</ControlTemplate>
```

Incorporating Templates into Styles

Currently, your template simply defines a basic look and feel of the Button control. However, the process of establishing the basic properties of the control (content, font size, font weight, etc.) is the responsibility of the Button itself.

```
<!-- Currently the Button must set basic property values, not the template. -->
<Button x:Name ="myButton" Foreground ="Black" FontSize ="20" FontWeight ="Bold"
        Template ="{StaticResource RoundButtonTemplate}" Click ="myButton_Click"/>
```

If you want, you could establish these values *in the template*. By doing so, you can effectively create a default look and feel. As you might have already realized, this is a job for WPF styles. When you build a style (to account for basic property settings), you can define a template *within the style!* Here is your updated application resource in the application resources in App.xaml, which has been rekeyed as RoundButtonStyle:

```
<!-- A style containing a template. -->
<Style x:Key ="RoundButtonStyle" TargetType ="Button">
  <Setter Property ="Foreground" Value ="Black"/>
  <Setter Property ="FontSize" Value ="14"/>
  <Setter Property ="FontWeight" Value ="Bold"/>
  <Setter Property="Width" Value="100"/>
  <Setter Property="Height" Value="100"/>
  <!-- Here is the template! -->
  <Setter Property ="Template">
    <Setter.Value>
      <ControlTemplate TargetType ="Button">
        <Grid x:Name="controlLayout">
          <Ellipse x:Name="buttonSurface" Fill="{TemplateBinding Background}"/>
          <Label x:Name="buttonCaption" Content ="{TemplateBinding Content}"
                 HorizontalAlignment="Center" VerticalAlignment="Center" />
        </Grid>
        <ControlTemplate.Triggers>
          <Trigger Property = "IsMouseOver" Value = "True">
            <Setter TargetName = "buttonSurface" Property = "Fill" Value = "Blue"/>
            <Setter TargetName = "buttonCaption" Property = "Foreground" Value = "Yellow"/>
          </Trigger>
          <Trigger Property = "IsPressed" Value="True">
            <Setter TargetName="controlLayout"
                    Property="RenderTransformOrigin" Value="0.5,0.5"/>
            <Setter TargetName="controlLayout" Property="RenderTransform">
              <Setter.Value>
                <ScaleTransform ScaleX="0.8" ScaleY="0.8"/>
              </Setter.Value>
            </Setter>
          </Trigger>
```

```
        </ControlTemplate.Triggers>
      </ControlTemplate>
    </Setter.Value>
  </Setter>
</Style>
```

With this update, you can now create button controls by setting the Style property as so:

```
<Button x:Name="myButton" Background="Red" Content="Howdy!"
        Click="myButton_Click" Style="{StaticResource RoundButtonStyle}"/>
```

While the rendering and behavior of the button is identical, the benefit of nesting templates within styles is that you are able to provide a canned set of values for common properties. That wraps up your look at how to use Visual Studio and the trigger framework to build custom templates for a control. While there is still much more about the Windows Presentation Foundation API than has been examined here, you should be in a solid position for further study.

■ **Source Code** The ButtonTemplate project can be found under the Chapter 31 subdirectory.

Summary

This chapter examined a number of related WPF topics, all of which are focused on the construction of custom user controls. You started by investigating how WPF places a unique spin on traditional .NET programming primitives, specifically properties and events. As you have seen, a *dependency property* allows you to build a property that can integrate within the WPF set of services (animations, data bindings, styles, and so on). On a related note, *routed events* provide a way for an event to flow up or down a tree of markup.

You then examined the relationship between a *logical tree* and a *visual tree*. The logical tree is basically a one-to-one correspondence of the markup you would author to describe a WPF root element. Behind this logic tree is a much deeper visual tree that contains detailed rendering instructions.

The role of a *default template* was then examined. Remember, when you are building custom templates, you are essentially ripping out all (or part) of a control's visual tree and replacing it with your own custom implementation.

## PART VIII

ASP.NET Web Forms

Introducing ASP.NET Web Forms

Until now, all of the examples in this book have focused on console-based and desktop graphical user interfaces created using the WPF API. The remainder of the text will explore how the .NET platform facilitates the construction of browser-based presentation layers using a technology named ASP.NET. To begin, you'll quickly overview a number of key web development concepts (HTTP, HTML, client-side scripting, postbacks) and examine the role of Microsoft's commercial web server (IIS) as well as that of the ASP.NET Development Web Server.

With this brief web primer out of the way, the remainder of this chapter concentrates on the structure of the ASP.NET web form programming model (including the single-page and code-behind model) and examines the functionality of the Page base class. Along the way, you'll be introduced to the role of ASP.NET web controls, the directory structure of an ASP.NET web site, and how to use a web.config file to control the runtime operation of your web sites.

■ **Note** If you would like to load any of the ASP.NET web site projects found within this book's downloadable source code, launch Visual Studio and select the File ➤ Open ➤ Web Site... menu option. From the resulting dialog box, click on the File System button (mounted on the left-hand side), and select the folder containing the web project files. This will load all content for the current web application into the Visual Studio IDE.

The Role of HTTP

Web applications are very different animals from graphical desktop applications. The first obvious difference is that a production-level web application involves at least two networked machines: one hosting the web site and the other viewing data within a web browser. Of course, during development it is entirely possible to have a single machine play the role of both the browser-based client and the hosting web server that serves up content. Given the nature of web applications, the networked machines in question must agree upon a particular wire protocol to determine how to send and receive data. The wire protocol that connects the computers in question is the Hypertext Transfer Protocol (HTTP).

The HTTP Request/Response Cycle

When a client machine launches a web browser (such as Google Chrome, Opera, Mozilla Firefox, Apple Safari, or Microsoft Internet Explorer), an HTTP *request* is made to access a particular resource (typically a web page) on the remote server machine. HTTP is a text-based protocol that is built upon a standard request/ response paradigm. For example, if you navigate to http://www.facebook.com, the browser software leverages a web technology termed *Domain Name Service* (DNS) that converts the registered URL into a numerical value termed an *IP address*. At this point, the browser opens a socket connection (typically via port 80 for a nonsecure connection) and sends the HTTP request for processing to the target site.

The web server receives the incoming HTTP request and may choose to parse out any client-supplied input values (such as values within a text box, check box, or list box) in order to format a proper HTTP *response*. Web programmers may leverage any number of server-side technologies (PHP, ASP.NET, JSP, etc.) to dynamically generate the content to be emitted into the HTTP response. At this point, the client-side browser renders the returned HTML sent from the web server. Figure 32-1 illustrates the basic HTTP request/response cycle.

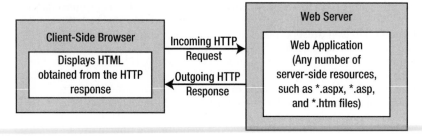

Figure 32-1. The HTTP request/response cycle

HTTP Is a Stateless Protocol

Another aspect of web development that is markedly different from traditional desktop programming is the fact that HTTP is essentially a *stateless* wire protocol. As soon as the web server sends a response to the client browser, everything about the previous interaction is forgotten. This is certainly not the case in a traditional desktop application, where the state of the executable is most often alive and kicking until the user shuts down the main window of the application.

Given this point, as a web developer, it is up to you take specific steps to "remember" information (such as items in a shopping cart, credit card numbers, and home addresses) about the users who are currently logged on to your site. As you will see in Chapter 34, ASP.NET provides numerous ways to handle state, using techniques such as session variables, cookies, and the application cache as well as the ASP.NET profile management API.

Understanding Web Applications and Web Servers

A *web application* can be understood as a collection of files (e.g., *.htm, *.aspx, image files, XML-based file data) and related components (such as a .NET code library) stored within a particular set of directories on a web server. As shown in Chapter 34, ASP.NET web applications have a specific life cycle and provide numerous events (such as initial startup or final shutdown) that you can hook into to perform specialized processing during your web site's operation.

A *web server* is a software product in charge of hosting your web applications; it typically provides a number of related services such as integrated security, File Transfer Protocol (FTP) support, mail exchange services, and so forth. Internet Information Services (IIS) is the Microsoft enterprise-level web server product, and it offers intrinsic support for ASP.NET web applications.

Assuming you have IIS properly installed on your workstation, you can interact with IIS from the Administrative Tools folder (located in the Control Panel folder) by double-clicking the Internet Information Services applet. Figure 32-2 shows the Default Web Site node of IIS where a majority of the configuration details occur (if you are running earlier versions of IIS, your UI will look different).

Figure 32-2. The IIS applet can be used to configure the runtime behavior of Microsoft IIS

The Role of IIS Virtual Directories

A single IIS installation is able to host numerous web applications, each of which resides in a *virtual directory*. Each virtual directory is mapped to a physical directory on the machine's hard drive. For example, if you create a new virtual directory named CarsAreUs, the outside world can navigate to this site using a URL such as http://www.MyDomain.com/CarsAreUs (assuming your site's IP address has been registered with a DNS of www.MyDomain.com). Under the hood, this virtual directory maps to a physical root directory on the web server that contains the content of the CarsAreUs web application.

As you will see later in this chapter, when you create ASP.NET web applications using Visual Studio, you have the option of having the IDE generate a new virtual directory for the current web site automatically. However, if required, you are certainly able to manually create a virtual directory by hand by right-clicking the Default Web Site node of IIS and selecting Add Virtual Directory from the context menu.

The ASP.NET Development Web Server

In earlier versions of the .NET platform, ASP.NET developers were required to make use of IIS virtual directories during the development and testing of their web applications. In many cases, this tight dependency on IIS made team development more complex than necessary, not to mention that many network administrators frowned upon installing IIS on every developer's machine.

Happily, there is the option of a lightweight web server named the ASP.NET Development Web Server. This utility allows developers to host an ASP.NET web application outside the bounds of IIS. Using this tool, you can build and test your web pages from any folder on your machine. This is quite helpful for team development scenarios and for building ASP.NET web applications on versions of Windows that do not support IIS installations.

Most of the examples in this book will make use of the ASP.NET Development Web Server (via the correct Visual Studio project option) rather than hosting web content under an IIS virtual directory. While this approach can simplify the development of your web application, be aware that this web server is *not* intended to host production-level web applications. It is intended purely for development and testing purposes. When your web application is ready for prime time, your site will need to be copied to an IIS virtual directory.

■ **Note** Visual Studio provides a built-in tool to copy a local web application to a production-level web server. Doing so is literally as simple as the click (or two) of a button. To start the process, you need to select your web project in the Visual Studio Solution Explorer, and then click on the Copy Web Site button. At this point you can select the intended destination of the deployment.

The Role of HTML

After you have configured a directory to host your web application and you have chosen a web server to serve as the host, you need to create the content itself. Recall that a web application is simply a set of files that constitute the functionality of the site. To be sure, many of these files will contain Hypertext Markup Language (HTML) statements. HTML is a standard markup language used to describe how literal text, images, external links, and various HTML controls are to be rendered within the client-side browser.

While it is true that modern IDEs (including Visual Studio) and web development platforms (such as ASP.NET) generate much of the HTML automatically, you will do well to have a working knowledge of HTML as you work with ASP.NET.

■ **Note** Recall from Chapter 2 that Microsoft has released a number of free IDEs under the Express family of products (such as Visual C# Express). If you are interested in web development, you might want to also download Visual Web Developer Express. This free IDE is geared exclusively toward the construction of ASP.NET web applications using C# or VB.

While this section will most certainly not cover all aspects of HTML, it will touch on some basics. This will help you better understand the markup generated on your behalf by the ASP.NET web forms programming model.

HTML Document Structure

A typical HTML file consists of a set of tags that describe the look and feel of a given web page. The basic structure of an HTML document tends to remain the same. For example, *.htm files (or, equivalently, *.html files) open and close with <html> and </html> tags, typically define a <body> section, and so forth.

To illustrate some HTML basics, open Visual Studio and create an empty HTML Page file via the File ➤ New ➤ File menu selection (notice that you are not making a web project at this point, you are just creating a blank HTML file for editing). After you have done so, save it as default.htm to a convenient location on your hard drive. You should see some initial markup such as the following (the exact HTML may differ based on how you have configured Visual Studio):

```
<!DOCTYPE html>

<html lang="en" xmlns="http://www.w3.org/1999/xhtml">
<head>
    <meta charset="utf-8" />
    <title>Untitled Page</title>
</head>
<body>

</body>
</html>
```

First, notice that this HTML file opens with a DOCTYPE processing instruction. This, in conjunction with the opening <html> tag establishes that the contained HTML tags should be validated against the HTML 5.0 standard. As mentioned, traditional HTML was *very loose* in its syntax. Beyond the case insensitivity issue, it was permissible to define an opening element (such as <br> for a line break) that did not have a corresponding closing break (</br>, in this case). The HTML 5.0 standard is a W3C specification that adds many new features to vanilla-flavored markup.

■ **Note** By default, Visual Studio validates all HTML documents against the HTML 5.0 validation scheme to ensure the markup is in sync with the HTML 5 standard. If you need to specify an alternative validation scheme, activate the Tools ➤ Options dialog box, expand the Text Editor node, expand the HTML node, and then select the Validation node. On a related note, if you would rather not see validation warnings, simply uncheck the Show Errors check box found in the same location.

The <body> scope is where the vast majority of the actual content is defined. To spruce things up just a bit, update the title of your page as so:

```
<head>
  <title>This is my simple web page</title>
</head>
```

Not surprisingly, the <title> tags are used to specify the text string that should be placed in the title bar of the hosting web browser.

The Role of an HTML Form

An *HTML form* is simply a named group of related UI elements, typically used to gather user input. Do not confuse an HTML form with the entire display area shown by a given browser. In reality, an HTML form is more of a *logical grouping* of widgets placed in the <form> and </form> tag set. For example:

```
<!DOCTYPE html>

<html xmlns="http://www.w3.org/1999/xhtml">
```

```
<head>
    <title>This is my simple web page</title>
</head>
<body>
  <form id="defaultPage">
    <!-- Insert web UI content here -->
  </form>
</body>
</html>
```

This form has been assigned the id of "defaultPage". Typically, the opening <form> tag supplies an action attribute that specifies the URL to which to submit the form data, as well as the method of transmitting that data itself (POST or GET). For the time being, let's look at the sorts of items that can be placed in an HTML form (beyond simple literal text).

The Visual Studio HTML Designer Tools

Visual Studio provides an HTML tab on the Toolbox that allows you to select an HTML control that you may place on your HTML designer (see Figure 32-3).

Figure 32-3. The HTML tab of the Toolbox

■ **Note** When you are building ASP.NET web pages using the web form programming model, you will typically not be using these HTML controls to create the user interface. Rather, you will use the ASP.NET web controls, which will render back the correct HTML on your behalf. You'll learn about the role of web controls a bit later in this chapter.

Similar to the process of building a WPF application, these HTML controls can be dragged onto the HTML designer surface or directly into the HTML markup. If you click the Split button on the bottom of the HTML editor, the bottom pane of the HTML editor will display the HTML visual layout and the upper pane will show the related markup. Another benefit of this editor is that as you select markup or an HTML UI element, the corresponding representation is highlighted (see Figure 32-4).

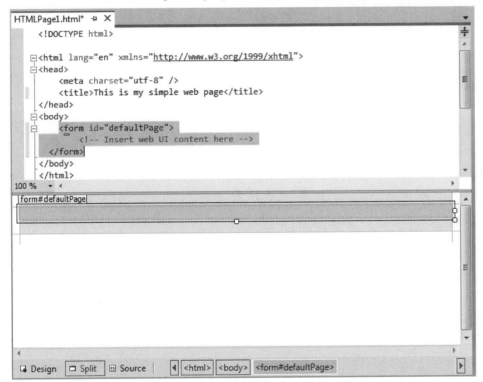

Figure 32-4. The Visual Studio HTML designer

Visual Studio also allows you to edit the overall look and feel of the *.htm file or a given HTML control in the <form> using the Properties window. For example, if you select DOCUMENT from the drop-down list of the Properties window, you are able to configure various aspects of the HTML page (see Figure 32-5).

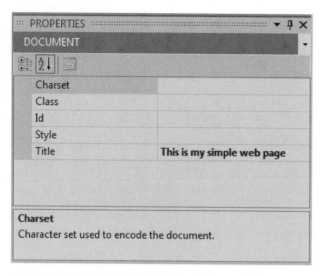

Figure 32-5. *The Visual Studio Properties window can be used to configure the HTML markup*

As you use the Properties window to configure an aspect of your web page, the IDE will update the HTML accordingly. Feel free to use the IDE to help edit your HTML pages as you read over the remaining chapters of the book.

Building an HTML Form

For now, update the `<body>` of the initial file to display some literal text that prompts the user to enter a message. Be aware that you can enter and format literal textual content by typing directly in the HTML designer. Here, you are using the `<h1>` tag to set a header weight, `<p>` for a paragraph block, and `<i>` for italic text:

```
<html xmlns="http://www.w3.org/1999/xhtml">
<head>
  <title>This is my simple web page</title>
</head>
<body>
  <!-- Prompt for user input. -->
  <h1>Simple HTML Page</h1>
  <p>
    <br/>
    <i>Please enter a message</i>.
  </p>

  <form id="defaultPage">
  </form>

</body>
</html>
```

Now let's build the form's input area. In general, each HTML control is described using an id attribute (used to identify the item programmatically) and a type attribute (used to specify which input control you are interested in placing in the <form> declaration). Depending on which UI widget you have declared, you will find additional attributes specific to the control that can be modified using the Properties window.

The UI you will build here will contain one text field and two button types. The first button will be used to run a client-side script and the other to reset the form input fields to the default values. Update your HTML form as so:

```
<!-- Build a form to get user info. -->
<form id="defaultPage">
  <p>
    Your Message:
    <input id="txtUserMessage" type="text"/></p>
  <p>
    <input id="btnShow" type="button" value="Show!"/>
    <input id="btnReset" type="reset" value="Reset"/>
  </p>
</form>
```

Notice that you have assigned relevant ids to each control (txtUserMessage, btnShow, and btnReset). Also notice that each input item has an extra attribute named type that marks these input controls as UI items that automatically clear all fields to their initial values (type="reset"), receive text input (type="text"), or function as a simple client-side button that does not post back to the web server (type="button").

Save your file, then right-click on the designer and select the View in Browser menu option. Figure 32-6 shows the current page with the Firefox web browser.

Figure 32-6. Your simple HTML page

■ **Note** When you select the View in Browser option for an HTML file, Visual Studio will automatically launch the ASP.NET Development Web Server to host your content.

The Role of Client-Side Scripting

In addition to GUI elements, a given `*.htm` file may contain blocks of script code that will be processed by the requesting browser. The following are two major reasons why client-side scripting is used:

- To validate user input in the browser before posting back to the web server

- To interact with the Document Object Model (DOM) of the browser

Regarding the first point, understand that the inherent evil of a web application is the need to make frequent round-trips (termed *postbacks*) to the server machine to update the HTML to be rendered into the browser. While postbacks are unavoidable, you should always be mindful of ways to minimize travel across the wire. One technique that saves postbacks is to use client-side scripting to validate user input before submitting the form data to the web server. If an error is found, such as not supplying data within a required field, you can alert the user to the error without incurring the cost of posting back to the web server. (After all, nothing is more annoying to users than posting back on a slow connection, only to receive instructions to address input errors!)

■ **Note** Be aware that even when performing client-side validation (for improved response time), validation should *also* occur on the web server itself. This will ensure that the data has not been tampered with as it was sent across the wire. The ASP.NET validation controls will automatically perform client- and server-side validation (more on this in Chapter 33).

Client-side scripts can also be used to interact with the underlying object model (the Document Object Model or DOM) of the web browser itself. Most commercial browsers expose a set of objects that can be leveraged to control how the browser should behave.

When a browser parses an HTML page, it builds an object tree in memory, representing all the contents of the Web page (forms, input controls, etc.). Browsers provide an API called DOM that exposes the object tree and allows you to modify its contents programmatically. For example, you can write JavaScript that executes in the browser to get the values from specific controls, change the color of a control, add new controls to the page dynamically, and so forth.

One major annoyance is the fact that different browsers tend to expose similar, *but not identical*, object models. Thus, if you emit a block of client-side script code that interacts with the DOM, it might not work identically on all browsers (thus, testing is always a must!).

ASP.NET provides the `HttpRequest.Browser` property, which allows you to determine at runtime the capacities of the browser and device that sent the current request. You can use this information to stylize how to emit back the HTTP response in the most optimal manner. But you rarely need to worry about this, unless you are implementing custom controls, because all the standard Web controls in ASP.NET automatically know how to render themselves appropriately based on the browser type. This remarkable capability is known as *adaptive rendering*, and it's implemented out-of-the-box for all standard ASP.NET controls.

There are various scripting languages that can be used to author client-side script code, but the most popular by far is JavaScript. It's important to note that JavaScript is in no way, shape, or form the same as the Java language. While JavaScript and Java have a somewhat similar syntax, JavaScript is less powerful than Java. The good news is that all modern-day web browsers support JavaScript, which makes it a natural candidate for client-side scripting logic.

A Client-Side Scripting Example

To illustrate the role of client-side scripting, let's first examine how to intercept events sent from client-side GUI widgets. To capture the click event for the Show button, update the definition of the btnShow widget to support an onclick attribute, which is assigned to a JavaScript method named btnShow_onclick().

```
<input id="btnShow" type="button" value="Show!"
    onclick="return btnShow_onclick()" />
```

Now, add the following JavaScript function directly after the opening <head> element, that will be called when the user clicks the button. Use the alert() method to display a client-side message box containing the value in the text box via the value property.

```
<script lang="javascript" type="text/javascript">
// <![CDATA[
  function btnShow_onclick() {
    alert(txtUserMessage.value);
  }
// ]]>
</script>
```

Note that the scripting block has been wrapped within a CDATA section. The reason for this is simple: if your page ends up on a browser that does not support JavaScript, the code will be treated as a comment block and ignored. Of course, your page may be less functional, but the upside is that your page will not blow up when rendered by the browser. In any case, if you view your page in a browser once again, you should be able to type a message and see it pop up in a client-side message box (see Figure 32-7).

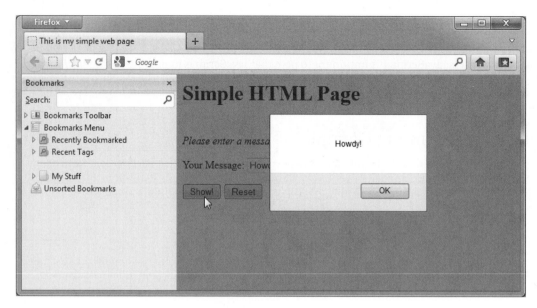

Figure 32-7. Invoking a client-side JavaScript function

As well, when you click on the Reset button, you should find that the text area is cleared of data, as this particular button has been created by specifying `type="reset"`.

Posting Back to the Web Server

This simple HTML page is executing all functionality within the hosting browser. A *real* web page needs to post back to a resource on the web server, passing all of the input data at the same time. Once the server-side resource receives this data, it can use it to build a proper, dynamically generated, HTTP response.

The `action` attribute on the opening `<form>` tag specifies the recipient of the incoming form data. Possible receivers include mail servers, other HTML files on the web server, a classic Active Server Pages (ASP) file, an ASP.NET web page, and so forth.

Beyond the `action` attribute, you will also likely have a `submit` button, which when clicked, will transmit the form data to the web application via an HTTP request. You have no need to do so for this example; however, here is an update to the file, specifying the following attribute in the opening `<form>` tag:

```
<form id="defaultPage"
    action="http://localhost/Cars/ClassicAspPage.asp" method="GET">
  <input id="btnPostBack" type="submit" value="Post to Server!"/>
...
</form>
```

When the `submit` button for this form is clicked, the form data is sent to the `ClassicAspPage.asp` at the specified URL. When you specify `method="GET"` as the mode of transmission, the form data is appended to the query string as a set of name/value pairs separated by ampersands. You might have seen this sort of data in your browser before. For example:

```
http://www.google.com/search?hl=en&source=hp&q=vikings&cts=1264370773666&aq=
f&aql=&aqi=g1g-z1g1g-z1g1g-z1g4&oq=
```

The other method of transmitting form data to the web server is to specify method="POST", like so:

```
<form id="defaultPage"
    action="http://localhost/Cars/ClassicAspPage.asp" method = "POST">
...
</form>
```

In this case, the form data is not appended to the query string. Using POST, the form data is not directly visible to the outside world. More important, POST data does not have a character-length limitation; many browsers have a limit for GET queries.

Postbacks Under ASP.NET

When you are building ASP.NET-based web sites using web forms, the framework will take care of the posting mechanics on your behalf. One of the many benefits of building a web site using ASP.NET is that the programming model layers on top of the standard HTTP request/response protocol of an event-driven system. Thus, rather than manually setting an action attribute and defining an HTML submit button, you can simply handle events on the ASP.NET web controls using standard C# syntax.

Using this event-driven model, you can very easily post back to the web server using a large number of controls. If you require, you can post back to the web server if the user clicks on a radio button, an item in a list box, a day on a calendar control, and so on. In each case, you simply handle the correct event, and the ASP.NET runtime will automatically emit back the correct HTML posting data.

■ **Source Code** The SimpleWebPage web site is included under the Chapter 32 subdirectory.

An Overview of the ASP.NET API

At this point, your whirlwind review of classic web application development is complete, and you are ready to dive into ASP.NET itself. As you would expect, each edition of the .NET platform adds more functionality to the web programming APIs, and this is certainly true under .NET 4.5. Regardless of which version of .NET you happen to be targeting, the following features are commonplace for ASP.NET web applications:

- ASP.NET provides a model termed *code-behind*, which allows you to separate presentation logic (HTML) from business logic (C# code).

- ASP.NET pages are coded using .NET programming languages, rather than server-side scripting languages. The code files are compiled into valid .NET *.dll assemblies (which translates into much faster execution).

- ASP.NET web controls can be used to build a web UI in a model similar to that of building a desktop windows application.

- ASP.NET web applications can make use of any of the assemblies within the .NET base class libraries and are constructed using the object-oriented techniques examined in this book (classes, interfaces, structures, enums, and delegates).

- ASP.NET web applications can be easily configured via a web application configuration file (web.config).

The first point I want to elaborate on here is the fact that the UI of an ASP.NET web page can be constructed using various *web controls*. Unlike a typical HTML control, web controls are executed on the web server and will emit back to the HTTP response their correct HTML tags. This alone is a huge benefit of ASP.NET in that the amount of HTML you must manually author by hand diminishes greatly. By way of a quick example, assume you have defined the following ASP.NET web control in an ASP.NET web page:

```
<asp:Button ID="btnMyButton" runat="server" Text="Button" BorderColor="Blue"
        BorderStyle="Solid" BorderWidth="5px" />
```

You'll learn the details of declaring ASP.NET web controls soon enough, but for right now, notice that many attributes of the <asp:Button> control look very similar to the properties you have encountered in the WPF examples. The same is true for all ASP.NET web controls because when Microsoft built the web control toolkit, these widgets were purposely designed to look and feel like their desktop counterparts.

Now, if a browser makes a call to the *.aspx file containing this control, the control responds by emitting into the output stream the following HTML declaration:

```
<input type="submit" name="btnMyButton" value="Button" id="btnMyButton"
        style="border-color:Blue;border-width:5px;border-style:Solid;" />
```

Notice how the web control emits back standard HTML that can be rendered in any browser. Given this, understand that using ASP.NET web controls in no way ties you to the Microsoft family of operating systems or to Microsoft Internet Explorer. Any operating system or browser (including those on handheld devices such as the Apple iPhone or BlackBerry devices) can view an ASP.NET web page.

Next, note from the previous list of features that an ASP.NET web application will be compiled into a .NET assembly. Thus, your web projects are no different than any .NET *.dll built during this book. The compiled web application will be composed of CIL code, an assembly manifest, and type metadata. This has a number of huge benefits, most notably performance gains, strong typing, and the ability to be micromanaged by the CLR (e.g., garbage collection, etc.).

Finally, ASP.NET web applications provide a programming model whereby you can partition your page's markup from its related C# code base using *code files*. Using code files, the markup you type will map to a full-blown object model that is merged with your C# code file via partial class declarations.

Major Features of ASP.NET 2.0 and Higher

ASP.NET 1.0 was a major step in the right direction, and ASP.NET 2.0 provided many additional bells and whistles that helped ASP.NET move from a way to build dynamic *web pages* to a way to build feature-rich *web sites*. Consider this partial list of key features:

- Introduction of the ASP.NET Development Web Server (which means developers no longer need IIS installed on their development computers).

- A large number of new web controls that handle many complex situations (navigation controls, security controls, new data-binding controls, etc.).

- The introduction of *master pages*, which allow developers to attach a common UI frame to a set of related pages.

- Support for *themes*, which offer a declarative manner to change the look and feel of the entire web application on the web server.

- Support for *Web Parts*, which allow end users to customize the look and feel of a web page and store their settings for later use (à la portals).

- Introduction of a web-based configuration and management utility that maintains the various `web.config` files.

Beyond the ASP.NET Development Web Server, one of the biggest additions brought forth with ASP.NET 2.0 was the introduction of *master pages*. As you are aware, most web sites have a look and feel that is common to all pages on the site. Consider a commercial web site such as `www.amazon.com`. Every page has the same elements, such as a common header, common footer, common navigation menus, and so on.

Using a master page, you can model this common functionality and define *placeholders* that other `*.aspx` files can plug into. This makes it very easy to quickly reshape the overall look and feel of your site (reposition the navigation bar, change the header logo, and so on) by simply changing the master page, leaving the other `*.aspx` files unmodified.

■ **Note** Master pages are so useful that as of Visual Studio 2010, all new ASP.NET web projects include a master page by default.

ASP.NET 2.0 also added many new web controls into the mix, including controls that automatically incorporate common security features (log in controls, password recovery controls, etc.), controls that allow you to layer a navigational structure on top of a set of related `*.aspx` files, and even more controls for performing complex data-binding operations, where the necessary SQL queries could be generated using a set of ASP.NET web controls.

Major Features of ASP.NET 3.5 (and .NET 3.5 SP1) and Higher

.NET 3.5 added the ability for ASP.NET web applications to make use of the LINQ programming model (also introduced in .NET 3.5) and the following web-centric features:

- Support for data binding against ADO.NET entity classes (see Chapter 23).

- Support for ASP.NET Dynamic Data. This is a Ruby on Rails–inspired web framework that can be used to build data-driven web applications. It exposes tables in a database by encoding it in the URI of the ASP.NET web service, and the data in the table is automatically rendered to HTML.

- Integrated support for Ajax-style development, which essentially allows for micro-postbacks to refresh part of a web page as quickly as possible.

The ASP.NET Dynamic Data project templates, introduced with .NET 3.5 Service Pack 1, provide a new model to build sites that are driven heavily by a relational database. Of course, most web sites will need to communicate with databases to some extent, but the ASP.NET Dynamic Data projects are tightly connected to the ADO.NET Entity Framework and are squarely focused on the rapid development of data-driven sites (similar to what one might build when using Ruby).

Major Features of ASP.NET 4.0 and 4.5

.NET 4.0 and 4.5 add even more features to the Microsoft web development platform; here is a hit list of some of the key web-centric features:

- The ability to compress "view state" data using the GZIP standard.

- Updated browser definitions to ensure that ASP.NET pages render correctly on new browsers and devices (Google Chrome, Apple iPhone, BlackBerry devices, etc.).

- Ability to customize the output of validation controls using a cascading style sheet (CSS).

- Inclusion of the ASP.NET Chart control, which allows for building ASP.NET pages that include intuitive charts for complex statistical or financial analysis.

- Support for ASP.NET Model View Controller project templates, which decrease the dependency among application layers by using the Model-View-Controller (MVC) pattern. This is a completely different approach to web site development and has little resemblance to the web form programming model examined in this edition of the text.

- Numerous updates to support HTML 5.0.

- Integration with the new asynchronous language features of C# and VB.

As you might agree, the feature set of ASP.NET is quite deep (and this API has many more features than I have briefly enumerated here). Truth be told, if I were to cover every possible feature of ASP.NET, this book would easily double in size (triple, perhaps). Since this is not realistic, the goal for the remainder of the text is to examine the core features of ASP.NET that you will likely use on a day-to-day basis. Be sure to make use of the .NET Framework 4.5 SDK documentation to check out the features not covered here.

■ **Note** If you require a comprehensive treatment of building web applications using ASP.NET, I suggest picking up a copy of *Pro ASP.NET 4.5 in C#, Fifth Edition* by Adam Freeman and Matthew MacDonald (Apress).

Building a Single-File ASP.NET Web Page

An ASP.NET web page can be constructed using one of two primary approaches, the first of which is to build a single *.aspx file that contains a blend of server-side code and HTML. Using this *single-file page model* approach, the server-side code is placed within a <script> scope, but the code itself is *not* script code proper (e.g., VBScript/JavaScript). Rather, the code within a <script> block is written in your .NET language of choice (C#, Visual Basic, etc.).

If you are building a web page that contains very little code (but a good deal of static HTML), a single-file page model may be easier to work with, as you can see the code and the markup in one unified *.aspx file. In addition, placing your procedural code and HTML markup into a single *.aspx file provides a few other advantages:

- Pages written using the single-file model are slightly easier to deploy or to send to another developer.

- Because there is no dependency between multiple files, a single-file page is easier to rename.

- Managing files in a source code control system is slightly easier, as all the action is taking place in a single file.

On the downside, the single-file page model can lead to some complex files, as the UI markup and programming logic is isolated to one location. Nevertheless, you'll begin your journey of ASP.NET by examining the single-file page model.

Your goal is to build an *.aspx file that displays the Inventory table of the AutoLot database (created in Chapter 21) using the connected layer (but, as you would guess, you could also use the disconnected layer or the Entity Framework). To begin, launch Visual Studio and create a new Web Form using the File ➤ New ➤ File menu option (see Figure 32-8; note you will need to pick the Web ➤ C# node from the left-side tree view).

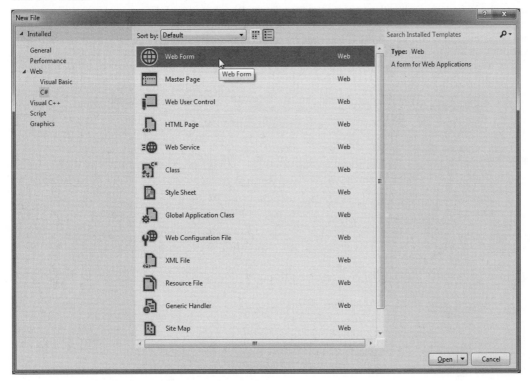

Figure 32-8. *Creating a new single-file ASP.NET page*

After you have done so, save this file as Default.aspx under a new directory on your hard drive so that you can easily find it later (for example, C:\MyCode\SinglePageModel).

Referencing AutoLotDAL.dll

Next, use Windows Explorer to create a subdirectory under the SinglePageModel folder named bin. The specially named bin subdirectory is a registered name with the ASP.NET runtime engine. Into the \bin folder of a web site's root, you are able to deploy any private assemblies used by the web application. For this example, place a copy of AutoLotDAL.dll (see Chapter 21) into the C:\MyCode\SinglePageModel\bin folder.

■ **Note** As shown later in this chapter, when you use Visual Studio to create a ASP.NET web project, the IDE will maintain the \bin folder on your behalf and copy any references to private assemblies here by default.

Designing the UI

Now, using the Visual Studio Toolbox, select the Standard tab and drag and drop a Button, Label, and GridView control (the GridView widget can be found under the Data tab of the Toolbox) onto the page designer between the opening and closing form elements. Feel free to make use of the Properties window to set various visual property settings as you choose. Also, be sure to give each web widget a proper name via the ID attribute. Figure 32-9 shows one possible design. (I kept the example's look and feel intentionally bland to minimize the amount of control markup, but feel free to spruce things up to your liking.)

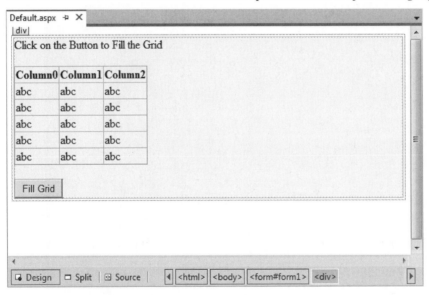

Figure 32-9. The Default.aspx GUI

Now, locate the <form> section of your page. Notice how each web control has been defined using an <asp:> tag. After this tag prefix, you will find the name of an ASP.NET web control (Label, GridView, and Button). Before the closing tag of a given element, you will find a series of name/value pairs that correspond to the settings you made in the Properties window. For example:

```
<form id="form1" runat="server">
<div>
  <asp:Label ID="lblInfo" runat="server"
    Text="Click on the Button to Fill the Grid">
  </asp:Label>
  <br />
  <br />
  <asp:GridView ID="carsGridView" runat="server">
  </asp:GridView>
  <br />
  <asp:Button ID="btnFillData" runat="server" Text="Fill Grid" />
</div>
</form>
```

You will dig into the full details of ASP.NET web controls later in Chapter 33. Until then, recall that web controls are objects processed on the web server that emit back their HTML representation into the outgoing HTTP response automatically. Beyond this major benefit, ASP.NET web controls mimic a desktop-like programming model in that the names of the properties, methods, and events typically mimic an equivalent Windows Forms/WPF counterpart.

Adding the Data Access Logic

Now, switch to the definer, and handle the Click event for the Button type using either the Visual Studio Properties window (via the lightning bolt icon). After you do so, you will find your Button's definition has been updated with an OnClick attribute that is assigned to the name of the Click event handler you entered. For example:

```
<asp:Button ID="btnFillData" runat="server"
    Text="Fill Grid" OnClick="btnFillData_Click"/>
```

Now, within the *.aspx server-side <script> block author the Click event handler. Notice that the incoming parameters are a dead-on match for the target of the System.EventHandler delegate, which you have seen in many examples in this book.

```
<script runat="server">
  protected void btnFillData_Click(object sender, EventArgs args)
  {
  }
</script>
```

The next step is to populate the GridView using the functionality of your AutoLotDAL.dll assembly. To do so, you must use the <%@ Import %> directive to specify that you are using the AutoLotConnectedLayer namespace.

■ **Note** You will only need to use the <%@ Import %> directive if you are building a page with the single-file code model. If you are using the default code file approach, you will simply use the using keyword of C# to include namespaces in your code file. The same is true for the <%@ Assembly %> directive, described next.

In addition, you need to inform the ASP.NET runtime that this single-file page is referencing the AutoLotDAL.dll assembly via the <%@ Assembly %> directive (more details on directives in just a moment). Here is the remaining relevant page logic of the Default.aspx file (be sure to modify your connection string as required):

```
<%@ Page Language="C#" %>
<%@ Import Namespace = "AutoLotConnectedLayer" %>
<%@ Assembly Name ="AutoLotDAL" %>

<!DOCTYPE html>

<script runat="server">
  protected void btnFillData_Click(object sender, EventArgs args)
  {
    InventoryDAL dal = new InventoryDAL();
    dal.OpenConnection(@"Data Source=(local)\SQLEXPRESS;" +
      "Initial Catalog=AutoLot;Integrated Security=True");

    carsGridView.DataSource = dal.GetAllInventoryAsList();
    carsGridView.DataBind();
    dal.CloseConnection();
  }

</script>
```

Before you dive into the details behind the format of this *.aspx file, let's try a test run. First, save your *.aspx file. Now, right-click anywhere on the *.aspx designer and select the View in Browser menu option, which will launch the ASP.NET Development Web Server, which, in turn, hosts your page.

When the page is served, you will initially see your Label and Button controls. However, when you click your button control, a postback occurs to the web server, at which point the web controls render back their corresponding HTML tags. Figure 32-10 shows the output once you click the Fill Grid button.

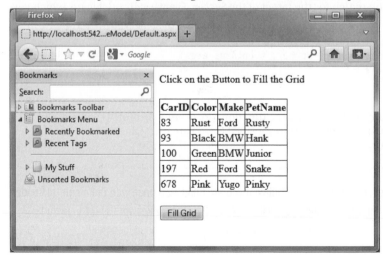

Figure 32-10. ASP.NET provides a declarative data-binding model

Given, the current UI is quite bland. To spice up the current example, select the GridView control on the Visual Studio designer, and using the context menu (that tiny arrow on the upper right of the control), select the Auto Format option (see Figure 32-11).

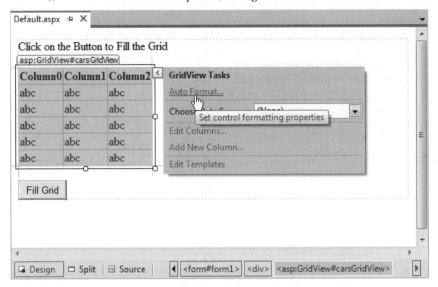

Figure 32-11. *Configuring the ASP.NET GridView control*

From the resulting dialog box, pick a template that suits your fancy (I picked "Slate"). After you click OK, view the generated control declaration, which is quite a bit richer than before.

```
<asp:GridView ID="carsGridView" runat="server" BackColor="White"
        BorderColor="#E7E7FF" BorderStyle="None" BorderWidth="1px" CellPadding="3"
        GridLines="Horizontal">
    <AlternatingRowStyle BackColor="#F7F7F7" />
    <FooterStyle BackColor="#B5C7DE" ForeColor="#4A3C8C" />
    <HeaderStyle BackColor="#4A3C8C" Font-Bold="True" ForeColor="#F7F7F7" />
    <PagerStyle BackColor="#E7E7FF" ForeColor="#4A3C8C" HorizontalAlign="Right" />
    <RowStyle BackColor="#E7E7FF" ForeColor="#4A3C8C" />
    <SelectedRowStyle BackColor="#738A9C" Font-Bold="True" ForeColor="#F7F7F7" />
    <SortedAscendingCellStyle BackColor="#F4F4FD" />
    <SortedAscendingHeaderStyle BackColor="#5A4C9D" />
    <SortedDescendingCellStyle BackColor="#D8D8F0" />
    <SortedDescendingHeaderStyle BackColor="#3E3277" />
</asp:GridView>
```

If you view your application again and click on your button, you will now see a more interesting UI (see Figure 32-12).

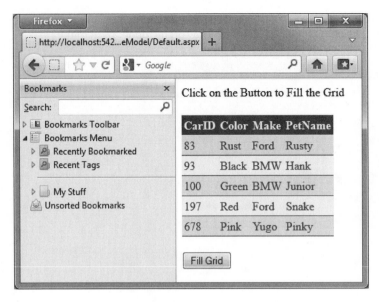

Figure 32-12. A richer display for our test page

That was simple, yes? Of course, as they say, the devil is in the details, so let's dig a bit deeper into the composition of this *.aspx file, beginning with examining the role of the <%@Page… %> directive. Do be aware that the topics you examine will apply directly to the more preferred *code file* model examined next.

The Role of ASP.NET Directives

A given *.aspx file will typically open with a set of *directives*. ASP.NET directives are always denoted with <%@ ... %> markers and may be qualified with various attributes to inform the ASP.NET runtime how to process the attribute in question.

Every *.aspx file will have at minimum a <%@Page%> directive that is used to define the managed language used within the page (via the language attribute). Also, the <%@Page%> directive may define the name of the related code-behind file (examined soon), and so on. Table 32-1 documents some of the more interesting <%@Page%>-centric attributes.

Table 32-1. Select Attributes of the <%@Page%> Directive

Attribute	Meaning in Life
CodePage	Specifies the name of the related code-behind file
EnableTheming	Establishes whether the controls on the *.aspx page support ASP.NET themes
EnableViewState	Indicates whether view state is maintained across page requests (more details on this property in Chapter 33)

Inherits	Defines a class in the code-behind page the *.aspx file derives from, which can be any class derived from System.Web.UI.Page
MasterPageFile	Sets the master page used in conjunction with the current *.aspx page
Trace	Indicates whether tracing is enabled

In addition to the <%@Page%> directive, a given *.aspx file may specify various <%@Import%> directives to explicitly state the namespaces required by the current page and <%@Assembly%> directives to specify the external code libraries used by the site (typically placed under the \bin folder of the web site).

In this example, you specified you were making use of the types within the AutoLotConnectedLayer namespace within the AutoLotDAL.dll assembly. As you would guess, if you need to make use of additional .NET namespaces, you simply specify multiple <%@Import%>/<%@Assembly%> directives.

To be sure, ASP.NET does define a number of other directives that may appear in an *.aspx file above and beyond <%@Page%>, <%@Import%>, and <%@Assembly%>; however, I'll reserve commenting on those for the time being. You'll see examples of other directives as you progress through the remaining chapters.

Analyzing the "Script" Block

Under the single-file page model, an *.aspx file may contain server-side scripting logic that executes on the web server. In this case, it is *critical* that all of your server-side code blocks are defined to execute at the server, using the runat="server" attribute. If the runat="server" attribute is not supplied, the runtime assumes you have authored a block of *client-side* script to be emitted into the outgoing HTTP response, and it will throw an exception. That being said, here is a proper server-side <script> block:

■ **Note** All ASP.NET web controls will need to have the runat="server" attribute in their opening declaration. If not, they will not render their HTML into the outbound HTTP response.

```
<script runat="server">
  protected void btnFillData_Click(object sender, EventArgs args)
  {
    InventoryDAL dal = new InventoryDAL();
    dal.OpenConnection(@"Data Source=(local)\SQLEXPRESS;" +
        "Initial Catalog=AutoLot;Integrated Security=True");
    carsGridView.DataSource = dal.GetAllInventory();
    carsGridView.DataBind();
    dal.CloseConnection();
  }
</script>
```

The signature of this helper method should look strangely familiar. Recall that a given control event handler must match the pattern defined by a related .NET delegate. The delegate in question is System.EventHandler that can only call methods that take System.Object as the first parameter and System.EventArgs as the second.

Analyzing the ASP.NET Control Declarations

The final point of interest in this first example is the declaration of the Button, Label, and GridView web controls. Like classic ASP and raw HTML, ASP.NET web widgets are scoped within <form> elements. This time, however, the opening <form> element is marked with the runat="server" attribute. As well, the controls are qualified with the asp: tag prefix. Any control that takes this prefix is a member of the ASP.NET control library and has a corresponding C# class representation in a given .NET namespace of the .NET base class libraries. Here you find:

```
<form id="form1" runat="server">
<div>
  <asp:Label ID="lblInfo" runat="server"
    Text="Click on the Button to Fill the Grid">
  </asp:Label>
  <br />
  <br />
  <asp:GridView ID="carsGridView" runat="server">
    ...
  </asp:GridView>
  <br />
  <asp:Button ID="btnFillData" runat="server" Text="Fill Grid" OnClick="btnFillData_Click"/>
</div>
</form>
```

The System.Web.UI.WebControls namespace of the System.Web.dll assembly contains a majority of the ASP.NET web controls. If you were to open the Visual Studio Object Browser, you could, for example, locate the DataGrid control (see Figure 32-13).

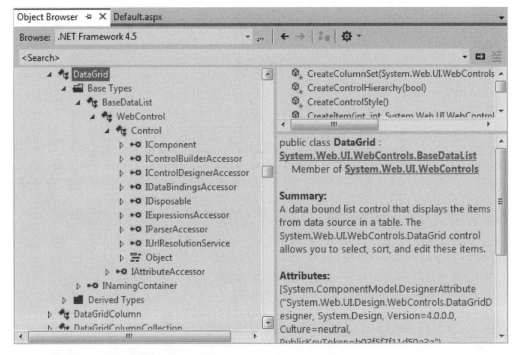

Figure 32-13. All ASP.NET control declarations map to a .NET class type

As you can see, an ASP.NET web control has an inheritance chain with System.Object at the very top. The WebControl parent class is a common base to all ASP.NET controls and defines all the common UI properties you would expect (BackColor, Height, etc.). The Control class is also very common within the framework; however, it defines more infrastructure-centric members (data binding, view state, etc.) rather than a child's graphical look and feel. You'll learn more about these classes in Chapter 33.

■ **Source Code** The SinglePageModel web site is included under the Chapter 32 subdirectory.

Building an ASP.NET Web Page Using Code Files

While the single-file code model can be helpful at times, the default approach taken by Visual Studio (when creating a new web project) is to make use of a technique known as *code-behind*, which allows you to separate your server-side programming code from your HTML presentation logic using two distinct files. This model works quite well when your pages contain a significant amount of code or when multiple developers are working on the same web site. The code-behind model offers other benefits as well, such as the following:

- Because code-behind pages offer a clean separation of HTML markup and code, it is possible to have designers working on the markup while programmers author the C# code.

- Code is not exposed to page designers or others who are working only with the page markup (as you might guess, HTML folks are not always interested in viewing reams of C# code).

- Code files can be used across multiple *.aspx files.

Regardless of which approach you take, there is *no* difference in terms of performance. In fact, many ASP.NET web applications will benefit from building sites that make use of both approaches. To illustrate the code-behind page model, let's recreate the previous example using a blank Visual Studio Web Site template. Activate the File ➤ New ➤ Web Site menu option and select the ASP.NET Empty Web Site template, as shown in Figure 32-14.

Figure 32-14. The Empty Web Site template

Notice in Figure 32-14 that you are able to select the location of your new site. If you select File System, your content files will be placed within a local directory and pages will be served via the ASP.NET Development Web Server. If you select FTP or HTTP, your site will be hosted within a new virtual directory maintained by IIS. For this example, it makes no difference which option you select, but for simplicity I suggest selecting the File System option and specifying a new folder named C:\CodeBehindPageModel.

■ **Note** The Empty Web Site project template will automatically include a web.config file, which is similar to an App.config file for a desktop executable. You'll learn about the format of this file later in the chapter.

Now, using the Website ➤ Add New Item... menu option, insert a new Web Form item named Default.aspx. You'll notice that, by default, the Place code in separate file check box is checked automatically, which is exactly what you want (see Figure 32-15).

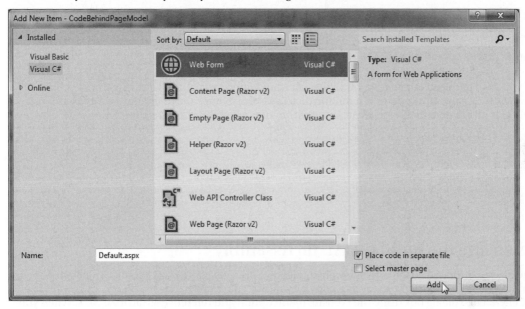

Figure 32-15. Inserting a new Web Form with code separation

Once again, make use of the designer to build a UI consisting of a Label, Button, and GridView, and make use of the Properties window to build a UI of your liking. If you like you can copy the previous ASP.NET control declarations from the SingleFilePageModel example directly into your new *.aspx file. Given that this is the exact same markup, I won't bother to relist it here (just be sure to paste the control declarations between the <form> and </form> tags).

Now, notice that the <%@Page%> directive used within the code file model has been updated with a few new attributes, as so:

```
<%@ Page Language="C#" AutoEventWireup="true"
        CodeFile="Default.aspx.cs" Inherits="_Default" %>
```

The CodeFile attribute is used to specify the related external file that contains this page's coding logic. By default, these code-behind files are named by adding the suffix .cs to the name of the *.aspx file (Default.aspx.cs, in this example). If you examine Solution Explorer, you will see this code-behind file is visible via a subnode on the Web Form icon (see Figure 32-16).

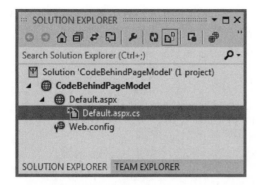

*Figure 32-16. The associated code-behind file for a given *.aspx file*

If you were to open your code-behind file, you would find a partial class deriving from System.Web.UI.Page with support for handling the Load event. Notice that the name of this class (_Default) is identical to the Inherits attribute within the <%@Page%> directive.

```
public partial class _Default : System.Web.UI.Page
{
  protected void Page_Load(object sender, EventArgs e)
  {

  }
}
```

Referencing the AutoLotDAL.dll Assembly

As previously mentioned, when creating web application projects using Visual Studio, you do not need to manually build a \bin subdirectory and copy private assemblies by hand. For this example, activate the Add Reference dialog box using the Website menu option and reference AutoLotDAL.dll. When you do so, you will see the new \bin folder within Solution Explorer, as shown in Figure 32-17.

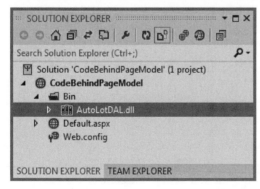

Figure 32-17. Visual Studio web projects make use of special ASP.NET folders

Updating the Code File

Handle the Click event for the Button type by double-clicking the Button placed on the designer. As before, the Button definition has been updated with an OnClick attribute. However, the server-side event handler is no longer placed within a <script> scope of the *.aspx file but as a method of the _Default class type.

To complete this example, add a using statement for AutoLotConnectedLayer inside your code-behind file and implement the handler using the previous logic (again, update your connection string if necessary).

```
using AutoLotConnectedLayer;

public partial class _Default : System.Web.UI.Page
{
  protected void Page_Load(object sender, EventArgs e)
  {
  }
  protected void btnFillData_Click(object sender, EventArgs e)
  {
    InventoryDAL dal = new InventoryDAL();
    dal.OpenConnection(@"Data Source=(local)\SQLEXPRESS;" +
      "Initial Catalog=AutoLot;Integrated Security=True");
    carsGridView.DataSource = dal.GetAllInventoryAsList();
    carsGridView.DataBind();
    dal.CloseConnection();
  }
}
```

At this point, you can run your web site by pressing the Ctrl+F5 key combination. Once again, the ASP.NET Development Web Server will fire up, serving your page into your hosting browser.

Debugging and Tracing ASP.NET Pages

When you are building ASP.NET web projects, you can use the same debugging techniques as you would with any other sort of Visual Studio project type. Thus, you can set breakpoints in your code-behind file (as well as embedded "script" blocks in an *.aspx file), start a debug session (via the F5 key, by default), and step through your code.

However, to debug your ASP.NET web applications, your site must contain a properly configured web.config file. By default, all Visual Studio web projects will automatically have a web.config file. However, debugging support is initially disabled. When you start a debugging session, the IDE will prompt you whether you would like to modify web.config to enable debugging. Once you have opted to do so, the <compilation> element of the web.config file is updated like so:

```
<compilation debug="true" targetFramework="4.5"/>
```

On a related note, you are also able to enable *tracing support* for an *.aspx file by setting the Trace attribute to true within the <%@Page%> directive (it is also possible to enable tracing for your entire site by modifying the web.config file).

```
<%@ Page Language="C#" AutoEventWireup="true"
        CodeFile="Default.aspx.cs" Inherits="_Default" Trace="true" %>
```

Once you do so, the emitted HTML contains numerous details regarding the previous HTTP request/response (server variables, session and application variables, request/response, etc.).

To insert your own trace messages into the mix, you can use the Trace property inherited from System.Web.UI.Page. Anytime you would like to log a custom message (from a script block or C# source code file), simply call the static Trace.Write() method. The first argument represents the name of your custom category; the second argument specifies the trace message. To illustrate, update the Click handler of your Button with the following code statement:

```
protected void btnFillData_Click(object sender, EventArgs e)
{
  Trace.Write("CodeFileTraceInfo!", "Filling the grid!");

  ...
}
```

Run your project once again and click the button. You will find your custom category and custom message are present and accounted for. In Figure 32-18, take note of the highlighted message that displays the trace information.

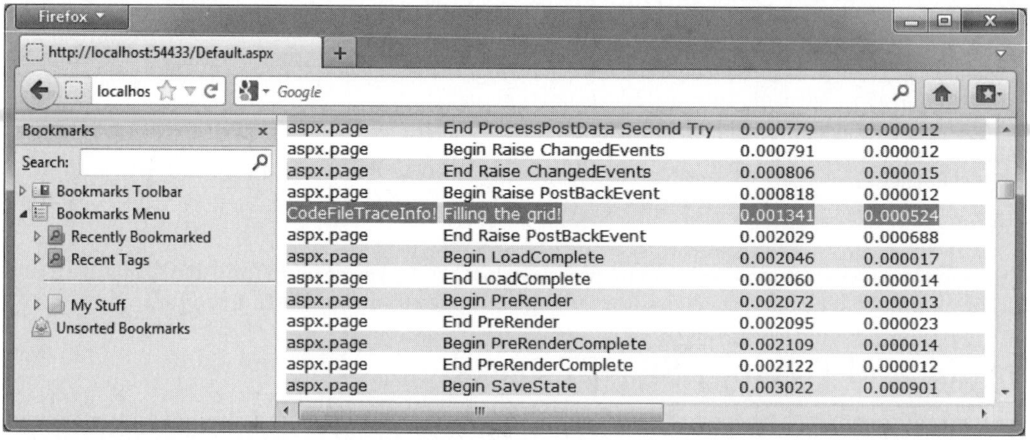

Figure 32-18. Logging custom trace messages

At this point, you have seen how to build a single ASP.NET web page using the single-file and code-file approach. The remaining topics of this chapter will take a deeper look into the composition of an ASP.NET web project, as well as ways to interact with the HTTP request/response and the life cycle of a Page-derived class. Before you dive in, I need to clarify the distinction between an ASP.NET Web Site and an ASPNET Web Application.

■ **Source Code** The CodeBehindPageModel web site is included under the Chapter 32 subdirectory.

ASP.NET Web Sites vs. ASP.NET Web Applications

When you are about to build a new ASP.NET web project, you will need to make a choice regarding which of two project formats you will make use of, specifically an *ASPNET Web Site* or an *ASP.NET Web Application*. Your choice of web project will control the way in which Visual Studio organizes and processes your web application starter files, the type of initial project files that are created, and how much control you have over the resulting composition of the compiled .NET assembly.

When ASP.NET was first released with .NET 1.0, the only option was to build what is now termed *a web application*. Under this model, you have direct control over the name and location of the compiled output assembly.

Web applications are useful when you are migrating older .NET 1.1 web sites into .NET 2.0 and higher projects. Web applications are also helpful when you want to build a single Visual Studio Solution that can contain multiple projects (for example, the web application and any related .NET code libraries). To build an ASP.NET Web Application, you activate the File ➤ New Project... menu item and pick a template from the Web category (see Figure 32-19).

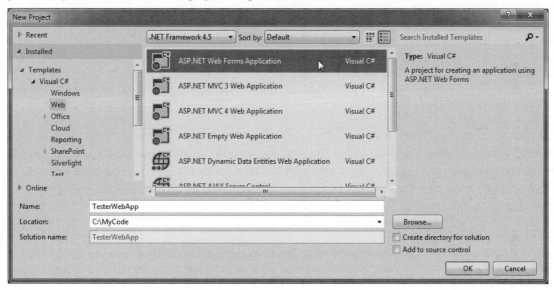

Figure 32-19. *The Visual Studio Web Application templates*

You have no need to do so now; however, assume you did create a new ASP.NET Web Application project. You will find a large number of starter files (which will make sense as you work through the chapters to come), but most importantly note that each ASP.NET web page is composed of three files: the `*.aspx` file (for markup), the `*.designer.cs` file (for designer-generated C# code), and the primary C# code file (for your event handlers, custom methods, and whatnot). See Figure 32-20.

Figure 32-20. Under the Web Application model, each web page is composed of three files

---

■ **Note** Because the Visual Studio ASP.NET project templates can generate a great deal of starter code (master pages, content pages, script libraries, a log in page, etc.), this book will opt to use the Blank web site template. However, after you have completed reading the ASP.NET chapters of this text, make sure you create a new ASPNET Web Site project and examine this starter code first hand.

In stark contrast, the Visual Studio ASP.NET Web Site project templates (found under the File ➤ New Web Site... menu option) hides the *.designer.cs file in favor of an in-memory partial class. Moreover, ASP.NET Web Site projects support a number of specially named folders, such as App_Code. Within this folder, you can place any C# (or VB) code files that are not directly mapped to your web pages, and the runtime compiler will dynamically compile them as required. This is a great simplification to the normal act of building a dedicated .NET code library and referencing it in new projects.

On a related note, a Web Site project can be pushed as-is to a production web server without the need to precompile the site as you would need to do with an ASP.NET Web Application.

In this book, I'll make use of ASP.NET Web Site project types, as they do offer some simplifications to the process of building web applications under the .NET platform. However, regardless of which approach you take, you will have access to the same overall programming model.

The ASP.NET Web Site Directory Structure

When you create a new ASP.NET Web Site project, your project may contain any number of specifically named subdirectories, each of which has a special meaning to the ASP.NET runtime. Table 32-2 documents these special subdirectories.

Table 32-2. *Special ASP.NET Subdirectories*

Subfolder	Meaning in Life
App_Browsers	Folder for browser definition files that are used to identify individual browsers and determine their capabilities.
App_Code	Folder for source code for components or classes that you want to compile as part of your application. ASPNET compiles the code in this folder when pages are requested. Code in the App_Code folder is automatically accessible by your application.
App_Data	Folder for storing Access *.mdb files, SQL Express *.mdf files, XML files, or other data stores.
App_GlobalResources	Folder for *.resx files that are accessed programmatically from application code.
App_LocalResources	Folder for *.resx files that are bound to a specific page.
App_Themes	Folder that contains a collection of files that define the appearance of ASP.NET web pages and controls.
App_WebReferences	Folder for proxy classes, schemas, and other files associated with using a web service in your application.
Bin	Folder for compiled private assemblies (*.dll files). Assemblies in the Bin folder are automatically referenced by your application.

If you are interested in adding any of these known subfolders to your current web application, you may do so explicitly using the Website ➤ Add ASP.NET Folder menu option. However, in many cases, the IDE will automatically do so as you naturally insert related files into your site. For example, inserting a new class file into your project will automatically add an App_Code folder to your directory structure if one does not currently exist.

Referencing Assemblies

Although the Web Site templates do generate an *.sln file to load your *.aspx files into the IDE, there is no longer a related *.csproj file. However, an ASP.NET Web Application project records all external assemblies within *.csproj. So where are the external assemblies recorded under ASP.NET?

As you have seen, when you reference a private assembly, Visual Studio will automatically create a \bin directory within your directory structure to store a local copy of the binary. When your code base makes use of types within these code libraries, they are automatically loaded on demand.

If you reference a shared assembly located in the Global Assembly Cache, Visual Studio will automatically insert a web.config file into your current web solution (if one is not currently in place) and record the external reference within the <assemblies> element. For example, if you again activate the Website ▸ Add Reference menu option and this time select a shared assembly (such as System.Security.dllyou will find that your web.config file has been updated as follows:

```
<assemblies>
  <add assembly="System.Security, Version=4.0.0.0,
      Culture=neutral, PublicKeyToken=B03F5F7F11D50A3A"/>
</assemblies>
```

As you can see, each assembly is described using the same information required for a dynamic load via the Assembly.Load() method (see Chapter 15).

The Role of the App_Code Folder

The App_Code folderis used to store source code files that are not directly tied to a specific web page (such as a code-behind file) but are to be compiled for use by your web site. Code within the App_Code folder will be automatically compiled on the fly on an as-needed basis. After this point, the assembly is accessible to any other code in the web site. To this end, the App_Code folder is much like the Bin folder, except that you can store source code in it instead of compiled code. The major benefit of this approach is that it is possible to define custom types for your web application without having to compile them independently.

A single App_Code foldercan contain code files from multiple languages. At runtime, the appropriate compiler kicks in to generate the assembly in question. If you would rather partition your code, however, you can define multiple subdirectories that are used to hold any number of managed code files (*.vb, *.cs, etc.).

For example, assume you have added an App_Code folder to the root directory of a web site application that has two subfolders, MyCSharpCode and MyVbNetCode that contain language-specific files. After you have done so, you are able to update your web.config file to specify these subdirectories using a <codeSubDirectories> element nested within the <configuration> element, like so:

```
<compilation debug="true" strict="false" explicit="true">
  <codeSubDirectories>
    <add directoryName="MyCSharpCode" />
    <add directoryName="MyVbNetCode" />
  </codeSubDirectories>
</compilation>
```

■ **Note** The App_Code directory will also be used to contain files that are not language files but are useful nonetheless (*.xsd files, *.wsdl files, etc.).

Beyond Bin and App_Code, the App_Data and App_Themes folders are two additional special subdirectories that you should be familiar with, both of which will be detailed in the next several chapters. As always, consult the .NET Framework 4.5 SDK documentation for full details of the remaining ASP.NET subdirectories if you require further information.

The Inheritance Chain of the Page Type

All .NET web pages eventually derive from System.Web.UI.Page. Like any base class, this type provides a polymorphic interface to all derived types. However, the Page type is not the only member in your inheritance hierarchy. If you were to locate the System.Web.UI.Page class (within the System.Web.dll assembly) using the Visual Studio object browser, you would find that Page is-a TemplateControl which is-a Control, which is-an Object (see Figure 32-21).

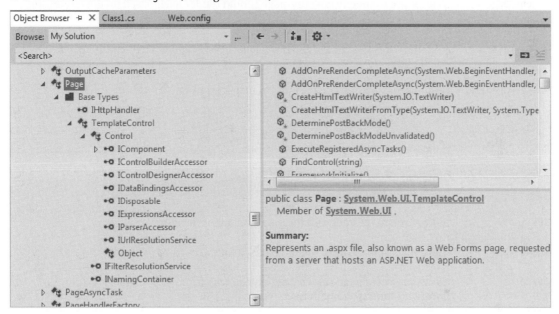

Figure 32-21. The inheritance chain of Page

Each of these base classes brings a good deal of functionality to each and every *.aspx file. For the majority of your projects, you will make use of the members defined within the Page and Control parent classes. The functionality gained from the System. Web.UI.TemplateControl class is only of interest if you are building custom Web Form controls or interacting with the rendering process.

The first parent class of interest is Page itself. Here you will find numerous properties that enable you to interact with various web primitives such as application and session variables, the HTTP request/response theme support, and so forth. Table 32-3 describes some (but by no means all) of the core properties.

Table 32-3. Select Properties of the Page Type

Property	Meaning in Life
Application	Allows you to interact with data that can be accessed across the entire web site for all users
Cache	Allows you to interact with the cache object for the current web site
ClientTarget	Allows you to specify how this page should render itself based on the requesting browser
IsPostBack	Gets a value indicating whether the page is being loaded in response to a client postback or whether it is being loaded and accessed for the first time
MasterPageFile	Establishes the master page for the current page
Request	Provides access to the current HTTP request
Response	Allows you to interact with the outgoing HTTP response
Server	Provides access to the HttpServerUtility object, which contains various server-side helper functions
Session	Allows you to interact with the session data for the current caller
Theme	Gets or sets the name of the theme used for the current page
Trace	Provides access to a TraceContext object, which allows you to log custom messages during debugging sessions

Interacting with the Incoming HTTP Request

As you saw earlier in this chapter, the basic flow of a web application begins with a client requesting a web page, possibly filling in user information, and clicking a "Submit button" to post back the HTML form data to a given web page for processing. In most cases, the opening tag of the form statement specifies an action attribute and a method attribute that indicates the file on the web server that will be sent the data in the various HTML widgets, as well as the method of sending this data (GET or POST).

```
<form name="defaultPage" id="defaultPage"
    action="http://localhost/Cars/ClassicAspPage.asp" method = "GET">
...
</form>
```

All ASPNET pages support the System.Web.UI.Page.Request property, which provides access to an instance of the HttpRequest class type (see Table 32-4 for some common members of this class).

Table 32-4. Members of the HttpRequest Class

Member	Meaning in Life
ApplicationPath	Gets the ASP.NET application's virtual application root path on the server
Browser	Provides information about the capabilities of the client browser
Cookies	Gets a collection of cookies sent by the client browser
FilePath	Indicates the virtual path of the current request
Form	Gets a collection of HTTP form variables
Headers	Gets a collection of HTTP headers
HttpMethod	Indicates the HTTP data transfer method used by the client (GET, POST)
IsSecureConnection	Indicates whether the HTTP connection is secure (i.e., HTTPS)
QueryString	Gets the collection of HTTP query string variables
RawUrl	Gets the current request's raw URL
RequestType	Indicates the HTTP data transfer method used by the client (GET, POST)
ServerVariables	Gets a collection of web server variables
UserHostAddress	Gets the IP host address of the remote client
UserHostName	Gets the DNS name of the remote client

In addition to these properties, the HttpRequest type has a number of useful methods, including the following:

- MapPath(): Maps the virtual path in the requested URL to a physical path on the server for the current request.

- SaveAs: Saves details of the current HTTP request to a file on the web server, which can prove helpful for debugging purposes.

- ValidateInput(): If the validation feature is enabled via the Validate attribute of the Page directive, this method can be called to check all user input data (including cookie data) against a predefined list of potentially dangerous input data.

Obtaining Browser Statistics

The first interesting aspect of the `HttpRequest` type is the `Browser` property, which provides access to an underlying `HttpBrowserCapabilities` object. `HttpBrowserCapabilities`, in turn, exposes numerous members that allow you to programmatically investigate statistics regarding the browser that sent the incoming HTTP request.

Create a new ASP.NET Empty Web Site project (named FunWithPageMembers) using the File ➤ New Website menu option, again electing to use the File System option. Next, insert a new Web Form file into your project using the Website ➤ Add New Item menu option).

Your first task is to build a UI that allows users to click a `Button` web control (named btnGetBrowserStats) to view various statistics about the calling browser. These statistics will be generated dynamically and attached to a `Label` type (named lblOutput). Add these two controls to the web page designer anywhere to your liking. Next, handle the `Click` event, and implement the handler as shown here:

```
protected void btnGetBrowserStats_Click(object sender, EventArgs e)
{
  string theInfo = "";
  theInfo += string.Format("<li>Is the client AOL? {0}</li>",
    Request.Browser.AOL);
  theInfo += string.Format("<li>Does the client support ActiveX? {0}</li>",
    Request.Browser.ActiveXControls);
  theInfo += string.Format("<li>Is the client a Beta? {0}</li>",
    Request.Browser.Beta);
  theInfo += string.Format("<li>Does the client support Java Applets? {0}</li>",
    Request.Browser.JavaApplets);
  theInfo += string.Format("<li>Does the client support Cookies? {0}</li>",
    Request.Browser.Cookies);
  theInfo += string.Format("<li>Does the client support VBScript? {0}</li>",
    Request.Browser.VBScript);
  lblOutput.Text = theInfo;
}
```

Here you are testing for a number of browser capabilities. As you would guess, it is (very) helpful to discover a browser's support for ActiveX controls, Java applets, and client-side VBScript code. If the calling browser does not support a given web technology, your *.aspx page will be able to take an alternative course of action.

Access to Incoming Form Data

Other aspects of the `HttpRequest` type are the `Form` and `QueryString` properties. These two properties allow you to examine the incoming form data using name/value pairs. While you could make use of the `HttpRequest.Form` and `HttpRequest.QueryString` properties to access client-supplied form data on the web server, ASP.NET provides a more elegant, object-oriented approach. Given that ASP.NET supplies you with server-side web controls, you are able to treat HTML UI elements as true objects. Therefore, rather than obtaining the value within a text box as follows:

```
protected void btnGetFormData_Click(object sender, System.EventArgs e)
{
  // Get value for a widget with ID txtFirstName.
  string firstName = Request.Form("txtFirstName");
```

```
  // Use this value in your page...
}
```

you can simply ask the server-side widget directly via the Text property for use in your program, like so:

```
protected void btnGetFormData_Click(object sender, System.EventArgs e)
{
  // Get value for a widget with ID txtFirstName.
  string firstName = txtFirstName.Text;

  // Use this value in your page...
}
```

Not only does this approach lend itself to solid OO principles, but also you do not need to concern yourself with how the form data was submitted (GET or POST) before obtaining the values. Furthermore, working with the widget directly is much more type safe, given that typing errors are discovered at compile time rather than runtime. Of course, this is not to say that you will *never* need to make use of the Form or QueryString property in ASP.NET; rather, the need to do so has greatly diminished and is usually optional.

The IsPostBack Property

Another very important member of Page is the IsPostBack property. Recall that "postback" refers to a web page posting back to the same URL at the web server. Given this definition, understand that the IsPostBack property will return true if the current HTTP request has been sent by a user currently in session, and false if this is the user's first interaction with the page.

Typically, the need to determine whether the current HTTP request is indeed a postback is most helpful when you need to execute a block of code only when the user first accesses a given page. For example, you might want to populate an ADO.NET DataSet when the user first accesses an *.aspx file and cache the object for later use. When the caller returns to the page, you can avoid the need to hit the database unnecessarily (of course, some pages might require that the DataSet always be updated upon each request, but that is another issue). Assuming your *.aspx file has handled the page's Load event (described in detail later in this chapter), you could programmatically test for postback conditions as follows:

```
protected void Page_Load(object sender, EventArgs e)
{
  // Fill DataSet only the very first time
  // the user comes to this page.
  if (!IsPostBack)
  {
    // Populate DataSet and cache it!
  }
  // Use cached DataSet.
}
```

Interacting with the Outgoing HTTP Response

Now that you have a better understanding of how the Page type allows you to interact with the incoming HTTPrequest, the next step is to see how to interact with the outgoing HTTP response. In ASP.NET, the Response property of the Page class provides access to an instance of the HttpResponse type. This type defines a number of properties that allow you to format the HTTP response sent back to the client browser. Table 32-5 lists some core properties.

Table 32-5. Properties of the HttpResponse Type

Property	Meaning in Life
Cache	Returns the caching semantics of the web page (see Chapter 34)
ContentEncoding	Gets or sets the HTTP character set of the output stream
ContentType	Gets or sets the HTTP MIME type of the output stream
Cookies	Gets the HttpCookie collection that will be returned to the browser
Output	Enables text output to the outgoing HTTP content body
OutputStream	Enables binary output to the outgoing HTTP content body
StatusCode	Gets or sets the HTTP status code of output returned to the client
StatusDescription	Gets or sets the HTTP status string of output returned to the client
SuppressContent	Gets or sets a value indicating that HTTP content will not be sent to the client

Also, consider the partial list of methods supported by the HttpResponse type, described in Table 32-6.

Table 32-6. Methods of the HttpResponse Type

Method	Meaning in Life
Clear()	Clears all headers and content output from the buffer stream
End()	Sends all currently buffered output to the client and then closes the socket connection
Flush()	Sends all currently buffered output to the client
Redirect()	Redirects a client to a new URL
Write()	Writes values to an HTTP output content stream
WriteFile()	Writes a file directly to an HTTP content output stream

Emitting HTML Content

Perhaps the most well-known aspect of the HttpResponse type is the ability to write content directly to the HTTP output stream. The HttpResponse.Write() method allows you to pass in any HTMLtags and/or text literals. The HttpResponse.WriteFile() method takes this functionality one step further, in that you can specify the name of a physical file on the web server whose contents should be rendered to the output stream (this is quite helpful to quickly emit the contents of an existing *.htm file).

To illustrate, assume you have added another Button to your current *.aspx file that implements the server-side Click event handler, like so:

```
protected void btnHttpResponse_Click(object sender, EventArgs e)
{
  Response.Write("<b>My name is:</b><br>");
  Response.Write(this.ToString());
  Response.Write("<br><br><b>Here was your last request:</b><br>");
  Response.WriteFile("MyHTMLPage.htm");
}
```

The role of this helper function (which you can assume is called by some server-side event handler) is quite simple. The only point of interest is the fact that the HttpResponse.WriteFile() method is now emitting the contents of a server-side *.htm file within the root directory of the web site.

Again, while you can always take this old-school approach and render HTML tags and content using the Write() method, this approach is far less common under ASP.NET than with classic ASP. The reason is (once again) due to the advent of server-side web controls. Thus, if you want to render a block of textual data to the browser, your task is as simple as assigning a string to the Text property of a Label widget.

Redirecting Users

Another aspect of the HttpResponse type is the ability to redirect the user to a new URL. For example:

```
protected void btnWasteTime_Click(object sender, EventArgs e)
{
  Response.Redirect("http://www.facebook.com");
}
```

If this event handler is invoked via a client-side postback, the user will automatically be redirected to the specified URL.

■ **Note** The HttpResponse.Redirect() method will always entail a trip back to the client browser. If you simply want to transfer control to an *.aspx file in the same virtual directory, the HttpServerUtility.Transfer() method, accessed via the inherited Server property, is more efficient.

So much for investigating the functionality of System.Web.UI.Page. I will examine the role of the System.Web.UI.Control base class in the next chapter. Next up, let's examine the life and times of a Page-derived object.

■ **Source Code** The FunWithPageMembers web site is included under the Chapter 32 subdirectory.

The Life Cycle of an ASP.NET Web Page

Every ASP.NET web page has a fixed life cycle. When the ASP.NET runtime receives an incoming request for a given *.aspx file, the associated System.Web.UI.Page-derived type is allocated into memory using the type's default constructor. After this point, the framework will automatically fire a series of events. By default, the Load event is automatically accounted for, where you can add your custom code.

```
public partial class _Default : System.Web.UI.Page
{
  protected void Page_Load(object sender, EventArgs e)
  {
    Response.Write("Load event fired!");
  }
}
```

Beyond the Load event, a given Page is able to intercept any of the core events in Table 32-7, which are listed in the order in which they are encountered (consult the .NET Framework 4.5 SDK documentation for details on all possible events that may fire during a page's lifetime).

Table 32-7. Select Events of the Page Type

Event	Meaning in Life
PreInit	The framework uses this event to allocate any web controls, apply themes, establish the master page, and set user profiles. You may intercept this event to customize the process.
Init	The framework uses this event to set the properties of web controls to their previous values via postback or view state data.
Load	When this event fires, the page and its controls are fully initialized, and their previous values are restored. At this point, it is safe to interact with each web widget.
"Event that triggered the postback"	There is, of course, no event of this name. This "event" simply refers to whichever event caused the browser to perform the postback to the web server (such as a Button click).
PreRender	All control data binding and UI configuration has occurred and the controls are ready to render their data into the outbound HTTP response.
Unload	The page and its controls have finished the rendering process, and the page object is about to be destroyed. At this point, it is a runtime error to interact with the outgoing HTTP response. You may, however, capture this event to perform any page-level cleanup (close file or database connections, perform any form of logging activity, dispose of objects, etc.).

When a C# programmer needs to handle events beyond Load, you might be surprised to find that there is no IDE support to do so! Rather, you must manually author a method in your code file taking the name Page_*NameOfEvent*. For example, here is how you can handle the Unload event:

```
public partial class _Default : System.Web.UI.Page
{
  protected void Page_Load(object sender, EventArgs e)
  {
    Response.Write("Load event fired!");
  }

  protected void Page_Unload(object sender, EventArgs e)
  {
    // No longer possible to emit data to the HTTP
    // response, so we will write to a local file.
    System.IO.File.WriteAllText(@"C:\MyLog.txt", "Page unloading!");
  }
}
```

■ **Note** Each event of the Page type works in conjunction with the System.EventHandler delegate; therefore, the subroutines that handle these events always take an Object as the first parameter and an EventArgs as the second parameter.

The Role of the AutoEventWireup Attribute

When you want to handle events for your page, you will need to update your <script> block or code-behind file with an appropriate event handler. However, if you examine the <%@Page%> directive, you will notice a specific attribute named AutoEventWireUp, which, by default, is set to true.

```
<%@ Page Language="C#" AutoEventWireup="true"
    CodeFile="Default.aspx.cs" Inherits="_Default" %>
```

With this default behavior, each page-level event handler will automatically be handled if you enter the appropriately named method. However, if you disable AutoPageWireUp by setting this attribute to false, like so:

```
<%@ Page Language="C#" AutoEventWireup="false"
    CodeFile="Default.aspx.cs" Inherits="_Default" %>
```

the page-level events will no longer be captured. As its name suggests, this attribute (when enabled) will generate the necessary event riggings within the autogenerated partial class described earlier in this chapter. Even if you disable AutoEventWireup, you can still process page-level events by making use of C# event-handling logic. For example:

```
public _Default()
{
  // Explicitly hook into the Load and Unload events.
  this.Load += Page_Load;
  this.Unload += Page_Unload;
```

```
}
```

As you might suspect, you will usually leave AutoEventWireup enabled.

The Error Event

Another event that may occur during your page's life cycle is Error. This event will be fired if a method on the Page-derived type triggered an exception that was not explicitly handled. Assume that you have handled the Click event for a given Button on your page, and within the event handler (which I named btnGetFile_Click), you attempt to write out the contents of a local file to the HTTP response.

Also assume you have *failed* to test for the presence of this file via standard structured exception handling. If you have rigged up the page's Error event in the default constructor, you have one final chance to deal with the problem on this page before the end user finds an ugly error. Consider the following code:

```
public partial class _Default : System.Web.UI.Page
{
  void Page_Error(object sender, EventArgs e)
  {
    Response.Clear();
    Response.Write("I am sorry...I can't find a required file.<br>");
    Response.Write(string.Format("The error was: <b>{0}</b>",
        Server.GetLastError().Message));
    Server.ClearError();
  }

  protected void Page_Load(object sender, EventArgs e)
  {
    Response.Write("Load event fired!");
  }

  protected void Page_Unload(object sender, EventArgs e)
  {
    // No longer possible to emit data to the HTTP
    // response at this point, so we will write to a local file.
    System.IO.File.WriteAllText(@"C:\MyLog.txt", "Page unloading!");
  }

  protected void btnPostback_Click(object sender, EventArgs e)
  {
    // Nothing happens here. This is just to ensure a
    // postback to the page.
  }
  protected void btnTriggerError_Click(object sender, EventArgs e)
  {
    System.IO.File.ReadAllText(@"C:\IDontExist.txt");
  }
}
```

Notice that your Error event handler begins by clearing out any content currently within the HTTP response and emits a generic error message. If you want to gain access to the specific System.Exception object, you may do so using the `HttpServerUtility.GetLastError()` method exposed by the inherited Server property.

```
Exception e = Server.GetLastError();
```

Finally, note that before exiting this generic error handler, you are explicitly calling the `HttpServerUtility.ClearError()` method via the Server property. This is required, as it informs the runtime that you have dealt with the issue at hand and require no further processing. If you forget to do so, the end user will be presented with the runtime's error page.

At this point, you should feel confident with the composition of an ASP.NET Page type. Now that you have such a foundation, you can turn your attention to the role of ASP.NET web controls, themes, and master pages, all of which are the subject of remaining chapters. To wrap up this chapter, however, let's examine the role of the `web.config` file.

■ **Source Code** The PageLifeCycle web site is included under the Chapter 32 subdirectory.

The Role of the web.config File

By default, all C# ASP.NET web applications created with Visual Studio are automatically provided with a `web.config` file. However, if you ever need to manually insert a `web.config` file into your site (e.g., when you are working with the single-page model and have not created a web solution), you may do so using the Website ➤ Add New Item menu option. In either case, within this scope of a `web.config` file you are able to add settings that control how your web application will function at runtime.

Recall during your examination of .NET assemblies (in Chapter 14) that you learned client applications can leverage an XML-based configuration file to instruct the CLR how it should handle binding requests, assembly probing, and other runtime details. The same holds true for ASP.NET web applications, with the notable exception that web-centric configuration files are always named `web.config` (unlike *.exe configuration files, which are named based on the related client executable).

The full structure of a `web.config` file is rather verbose. However, Table 32-8 outlines some of the more interesting subelements that can be found within a `web.config` file.

Table 32-8. Select Elements of a `web.config` File

Element	Meaning in Life
`<appSettings>`	This element is used to establish custom name/value pairs that can be programmatically read in memory for use by your pages using the `ConfigurationManager` type.
`<authentication>`	This security-related element is used to define the authentication mode for this web application.
`<authorization>`	This is another security-centric element used to define which users can access which resources on the web server.

`<connectionStrings>`	This element is used to hold external connection strings used within this web site.
`<customErrors>`	This element is used to tell the runtime exactly how to display errors that occur during the functioning of the web application.
`<globalization>`	This element is used to configure the globalization settings for this web application.
`<namespaces>`	This element documents all of the namespaces to include if your web application has been precompiled using the new `aspnet_compiler.exe` command-line tool.
`<sessionState>`	This element is used to control how and where session state data will be stored by the .NET runtime.
`<trace>`	This element is used to enable (or disable) tracing support for this web application.

A `web.config` file may contain additional subelements above and beyond the set presented in Table 32-8. The vast majority of these items are security related, while the remaining items are useful only during advanced ASP.NET scenarios, such as creating custom HTTP headers or custom HTTP modules (topics that are not covered here).

The ASP.NET Web Site Administration Utility

Although you are always free to modify the content of a `web.config` file directly using Visual Studio, ASP.NET web projects can make use of a handy web-based editor that will allow you to graphically edit numerous elements and attributes of your project's `web.config` file. To launch this tool, activate the Website ➤ ASP.NET Configuration menu option.

If you were to click the tabs located on the top of the page, you would quickly notice that most of this tool's functionality is used to establish security settings for your web site. However, this tool also makes it possible to add settings to your `<appSettings>` element, define debugging and tracing settings, and establish a default error page.

You'll see more of this tool in action where necessary; however, do be aware that this utility will *not* allow you to add all possible settings to a `web.config` file. There will most certainly be times when you will need to manually update this file using your text editor of choice.

Summary

Building web applications requires a different frame of mind than is used to assemble traditional desktop applications. In this chapter, you began with a quick and painless review of some core web topics, including HTML, HTTP, the role of client-side scripting, and server-side scripts using classic ASP. The bulk of this chapter was spent examining the architecture of an ASP.NET page. As you have seen, each `*.aspx` file in your project has an associated `System.Web.UI.Page`-derived class. Using this OO approach, ASP.NET allows you to build more reusable and OO-aware systems.

After examining some of the core functionality of a page's inheritance chain, this chapter then discussed how your pages are ultimately compiled into a valid .NET assembly. We wrapped up by exploring the role of the `web.config` file and overviewed the ASP.NET Web Site Administration tool.

## CHAPTER 33

ASP.NET Web Controls, Master Pages, and Themes

The previous chapter concentrated on the general composition of an ASP.NET web page and the role of the Page class. This chapter will dive into the details of the *web controls* that make up a page's user interface. After examining the overall nature of an ASP.NET web control, you will come to understand how to make use of several UI elements, including the validation controls and various data-binding techniques.

The good portion of this chapter will examine the role of *master pages* and show how they provide a simplified manner to establish a common UI skeleton that will be replicated across the pages in your web site. Closely related to the topic of master pages is the use of site navigation controls (and a related *.sitemap file) that allow you to define the navigational structure of a multipaged site via a server-side XML file.

To wrap things up, you will learn about the role of ASP.NET themes. Conceptually, themes serve the same purpose as a cascading style sheet (CSS); however, ASP.NET themes are applied on the web server (as opposed to within the client-side browser) and, therefore, have access to server-side resources.

Understanding the Nature of Web Controls

A major benefit of ASP.NET is the ability to assemble the UI of your pages using the types defined in the System.Web.UI.WebControls namespace. As you have seen, these controls (which go by the names *server controls*, *web controls*, or *Web Form controls*) are extremely helpful in that they automatically generate the necessary HTML for the requesting browser and expose a set of events that may be processed on the web server. Furthermore, because each ASP.NET control has a corresponding class in the System.Web.UI.WebControls namespace, it can be manipulated in an object-oriented manner.

When you configure the properties of a web control using the Visual Studio Properties window, your edits are recorded in the opening control tag of a given element in the *.aspx file as a series of name/value pairs. Thus, if you add a new TextBox to the designer of a given *.aspx file and change the ID, BorderStyle, BorderWidth, BackColor, and Text properties, the opening <asp:TextBox> tag is modified accordingly (however, note that the Text value becomes the inner text of the TextBox scope).

```
<asp:TextBox ID="txtNameTextBox" runat="server" BackColor="#C0FFC0"
    BorderStyle="Dotted" BorderWidth="3px">Enter Your Name</asp:TextBox>
```

Given that the declaration of a web control eventually becomes a member variable from the System.Web.UI.WebControls namespace (via the dynamic compilation cycle mentioned in Chapter 32), you are able to interact with the members of this type within a server-side <script> block or more commonly via the page's code-behind file. Thus, if you were to add a new Button control to an *.aspx file, you could handle the Click event and write a server-side handler that changes the background color of the TextBox, like so:

```
partial class _Default : System.Web.UI.Page
{
  protected void btnChangeTextBoxColor_Click(object sender, EventArgs e)
  {
    // Change color of text box object in code.
    this.txtNameTextBox.BackColor = System.Drawing.Color.DarkBlue;
  }
}
```

All ASP.NET web controls ultimately derive from a common base class named `System.Web.UI.WebControls.WebControl`. In turn, `WebControl` derives from `System.Web.UI.Control` (which derives from `System.Object`). `Control` and `WebControl` each define a number of properties common to all server-side controls. Before I examine the inherited functionality, let's formalize what it means to handle a server-side event.

Understanding Server-Side Event Handling

Given the current state of the World Wide Web, it is impossible to avoid the fundamental nature of browser/web server interaction. Whenever these two entities communicate, there is always an underlying, stateless HTTP request-and-response cycle. While ASP.NET server controls do a great deal to shield you from the details of the raw HTTP protocol, always remember that treating the Web as an event-driven entity is just a magnificent smoke-and-mirrors show provided by the .NET platform, and it is not identical to the event-driven model of a Windows-based desktop GUI framework such as WPF.

For example, although the WPF-centric `System.Windows.Controls` namespace and the ASP.NET `System.Web.UI.WebControls` namespace both define classes with the same simple names (`Button`, `TextBox`, `Label`, and so on) they do not expose an identical set of properties, methods, or events. For example, there is no way to handle a server-side `MouseMove` event when the user moves the cursor over a Web Form `Button` control.

The bottom line is that a given ASP.NET web control will expose a limited set of events, all of which ultimately result in a postback to the web server. Any necessary client-side event processing will require you to author blurbs of *client-side* JavaScript/VBScript script code to be processed by the requesting browser's scripting engine. Given that ASP.NET is primarily a server-side technology, I will not be addressing the topic of authoring client-side scripts.

■ **Note** Handling an event for a given web control using Visual Studio can be done in an identical manner as doing so for a Windows GUI control. Simply select the widget from the designer and click the lightning bolt icon on the Properties window.

The AutoPostBack Property

It is also worth pointing out that many of the ASP.NET web controls support a property named `AutoPostBack` (most notably, the `CheckBox`, `RadioButton`, and `TextBox` controls, as well as any widget that derives from the abstract `ListControl` type). By default, this property is set to `false`, which disables an immediate postback to the server (even if you have indeed rigged up the event in the code-behind file). In most cases, this is the exact behavior you require, given that UI elements, such as check boxes, typically don't require postback functionality. In other words, you don't want to post back to the server immediately after the user checks or unchecks a check box, as the page object can obtain the state of the widget within a more natural Button Click event handler.

However, if you want to cause any of these widgets to post back to a server-side event handler immediately, simply set the value of AutoPostBack to true. This technique can be helpful if you would like to have the state of one widget automatically populate another value within another widget on the same page. To illustrate, assume you have a web page that contains a single TextBox (named txtAutoPostback) and a single ListBox control (named lstTextBoxData). Here is the relevant markup:

```
<form id="form1" runat="server">
  <asp:TextBox ID="txtAutoPostback" runat="server"></asp:TextBox>
  <br/>
  <asp:ListBox ID="lstTextBoxData" runat="server"></asp:ListBox>
</form>
```

Now, if you were to handle the TextChanged event of the TextBox, the server-side event handler could attempt to populate the ListBox with the current value in the TextBox, like so:

```
partial class _Default : System.Web.UI.Page
{
  protected void txtAutoPostback_TextChanged(object sender, EventArgs e)
  {
    lstTextBoxData.Items.Add(txtAutoPostback.Text);
  }
}
```

If you run the application as is, you will find that as you type in the TextBox, nothing happens. Furthermore, if you type in the TextBox and tab to the next control, nothing happens. The reason is that the AutoPostBack property of the TextBox is set to false by default. However, if you set this property to true, like so:

```
<asp:TextBox ID="txtAutoPostback" runat="server"
             AutoPostBack="true" ... >
</asp:TextBox>
```

you will find that when you tab away from the TextBox (or press the Enter key), the ListBox is automatically populated with the current value in the TextBox. To be sure, beyond the need to populate the items of one widget based on the value of another widget, you will typically not need to alter the state of a widget's AutoPostBack property (and even then, sometimes this can be accomplished purely in client script, removing the need for server interaction at all).

The Control and WebControl Base Classes

The System.Web.UI.Control base class defines various properties, methods, and events that allow the ability to interact with core (typically non-GUI) aspects of a web control. Table 33-1 documents some, but not all, members of interest.

Table 33-1. Select Members of System.Web.UI.Control

Member	Meaning in Life
Controls	This property gets a ControlCollection object that represents the child controls within the current control.

DataBind()	This method binds a data source to the invoked server control and all its child controls.
EnableTheming	This property establishes whether the control supports theme functionality (the default is true).
HasControls()	This method determines whether the server control contains any child controls.
ID	This property gets or sets the programmatic identifier assigned to the server control.
Page	This property gets a reference to the Page instance that contains the server control.
Parent	This property gets a reference to the server control's parent control in the page control hierarchy.
SkinID	This property gets or sets the skin to apply to the control, which allows you to set the look and feel using server-side resources.
Visible	This property gets or sets a value that indicates whether a server control is rendered as a UI element on the page.

Enumerating Contained Controls

The first aspect of System.Web.UI.Control we will examine is the fact that all web controls (including Page itself) inherit a custom controls collection (accessed via the Controls property). Much like in a Windows Forms application, the Controls property provides access to a strongly typed collection of WebControl derived types. Like any .NET collection, you have the ability to add, insert, and remove items dynamically at runtime.

While it is technically possible to add web controls directly to a Page-derived type, it is easier (and more robust) to make use of a Panel control. The Panel class represents a container of widgets that may or may not be visible to the end user (based on the value of its Visible and BorderStyle properties).

To illustrate, create a new Empty Web Site named DynamicCtrls and add a new Web Form to your project. Using the Visual Studio page designer, add a Panel control (named myPanel) that contains a TextBox, Button, and HyperLink widget named whatever you choose (be aware that the designer requires that you drag internal items within the UI of the Panel type). Next, place a Label widget outside the scope of the Panel (named lblControlInfo) to hold the rendered output. Here is one possible HTML description:

```
<html xmlns="http://www.w3.org/1999/xhtml">
<head runat="server">
  <title>Dynamic Control Test</title>
</head>
<body>
  <form id="form1" runat="server">
    <div>
```

```
      <hr />
      <h1>Dynamic Controls</h1>
      <asp:Label ID="lblTextBoxText" runat="server"></asp:Label>
      <hr />
      </div>

      <!-- The Panel has three contained controls -->
      <asp:Panel ID="myPanel" runat="server" Width="200px"
          BorderColor="Black" BorderStyle="Solid" >
        <asp:TextBox ID="TextBox1" runat="server"></asp:TextBox><br/>
        <asp:Button ID="Button1" runat="server" Text="Button"/><br/>
        <asp:HyperLink ID="HyperLink1" runat="server">HyperLink
        </asp:HyperLink>
      </asp:Panel>
   <br />
   <br />
   <asp:Label ID="lblControlInfo" runat="server"></asp:Label>
</form>
</body>
</html>
```

With this markup, your page designer will look something like that of Figure 33-1.

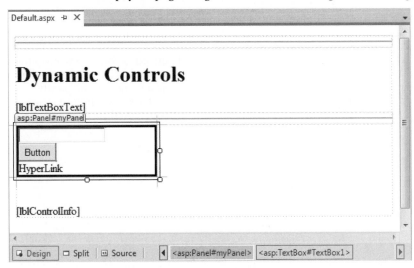

Figure 33-1. *The UI of the Dynamic Controls web page*

Assume in the Page_Load() event, you want to obtain details regarding the controls contained within the Panel and assign this information to the Label control (named lblControlInfo). Consider the following C# code:

```
public partial class _Default : System.Web.UI.Page
{
  private void ListControlsInPanel()
  {
```

```
    string theInfo = "";
    theInfo = string.Format("<b>Does the panel have controls? {0} </b><br/>",
      myPanel.HasControls());

    // Get all controls in the panel.
    foreach (Control c in myPanel.Controls)
    {
      if (!object.ReferenceEquals(c.GetType(),
        typeof(System.Web.UI.LiteralControl)))
      {
        theInfo += "***************************<br/>";
        theInfo += string.Format("Control Name? {0} <br/>", c.ToString());
        theInfo += string.Format("ID? {0} <br>", c.ID);
        theInfo += string.Format("Control Visible? {0} <br/>", c.Visible);
        theInfo += string.Format("ViewState? {0} <br/>", c.EnableViewState);
      }
    }
    lblControlInfo.Text = theInfo;
  }

  protected void Page_Load(object sender, System.EventArgs e)
  {
    ListControlsInPanel();
  }
}
```

Here, you iterate over each WebControl maintained on the Panel and perform a check to see whether the current type is of type System.Web.UI.LiteralControl, and if so, we skip over it. This class is used to represent literal HTML tags and content (such as <br>, text literals, etc.). If you do not do this sanity check, you might be surprised to find many more controls in the scope of the Panel (given the *.aspx declaration seen previously). Assuming the control is not literal HTML content, you then print out some various statistics about the widget. Figure 33-2 shows the output.

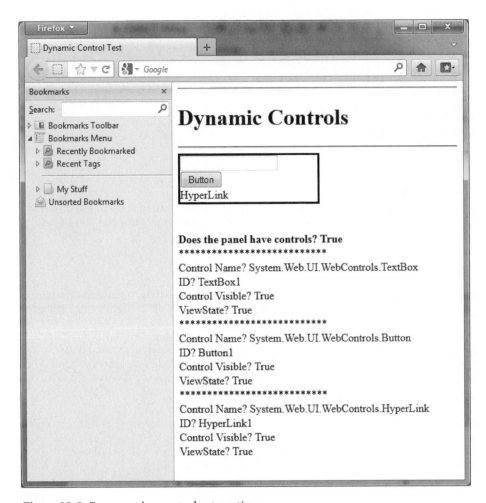

Figure 33-2. Enumerating controls at runtime

Dynamically Adding and Removing Controls

Now, what if you want to modify the contents of a Panel at runtime? Let's update the current page to support an additional Button (named btnAddWidgets) that dynamically adds three new TextBox controls to the Panel and another Button (named btnClearPanel) that clears the Panel widget of all controls. The Click event handlers for each are shown here:

```
protected void btnClearPanel_Click(object sender, System.EventArgs e)
{
  // Clear all content from the panel, then relist items.
  myPanel.Controls.Clear();
  ListControlsInPanel();
}
```

```
protected void btnAddWidgets_Click(object sender, System.EventArgs e)
{
  for (int i = 0; i < 3; i++)
  {
    // Assign an ID so we can get
    // the text value out later
    // using the incoming form data.
    TextBox t = new TextBox();
    t.ID = string.Format("newTextBox{0}", i);
    myPanel.Controls.Add(t);
    ListControlsInPanel();
  }
}
```

Notice that you assign a unique ID to each TextBox (e.g., newTextBox0, newTextBox1, and so on). If you run your page, you should be able to add new items to the Panel control and clear the Panel of all content.

Interacting with Dynamically Created Controls

Now, if you want to obtain the values within these dynamically generated TextBoxes, you can do so in a variety of ways. First, update your UI with one additional Button (named btnGetTextData), a final Label control named lblTextBoxData, and handle the Click event for the Button.

To get access to the data within the dynamically created text boxes, you have a few options. One approach is to loop over each item contained within the incoming HTML form data (accessed via HttpRequest.Form) and concatenate the textual information to a locally scoped System.String. Once you have exhausted the collection, assign this string to the Text property of the new Label control, like so:

```
protected void btnGetTextData_Click(object sender, System.EventArgs e)
{
  string textBoxValues = "";
  for (int i = 0; i < Request.Form.Count; i++)
  {
    textBoxValues += string.Format("<li>{0}</li><br/>", Request.Form[i]);
  }
  lblTextBoxData.Text = textBoxValues;
}
```

When you run the application, you will find that you are able to view the content of each text box, including some rather long (unreadable) string data. This string contains the *view state* for each control on the page. You'll learn about the role of view state in Chapter 34.

To clean up the output, you could instead pluck out the textual data for your uniquely named items (newTextBox0, newTextBox1, and newTextBox2). Consider the following update:

```
protected void btnGetTextData_Click(object sender, System.EventArgs e)
{
  // Get each text box by name.
  string lableData = string.Format("<li>{0}</li><br/>",
    Request.Form.Get("newTextBox0"));
  lableData += string.Format("<li>{0}</li><br/>",
    Request.Form.Get("newTextBox1"));
  lableData += string.Format("<li>{0}</li><br/>",
    Request.Form.Get("newTextBox2"));
```

```
lblTextBoxData.Text = lableData;
}
```

Using either approach, you will notice that once the request has been processed, the text boxes disappear. Again, the reason has to do with the stateless nature of HTTP. If you want to maintain these dynamically created TextBoxes between postbacks, you need to persist these objects using ASP.NET state programming techniques (again, see Chapter 34).

■ **Source Code** The DynamicCtrls web site is included under the Chapter 33 subdirectory.

Functionality of the WebControl Base Class

As you can tell, the Control type provides a number of non–GUI-related behaviors (the controls collection, autopostback support, etc.). On the other hand, the WebControl base class provides a graphical polymorphic interface to all web widgets, as suggested in Table 33-2.

Table 33-2. Select Properties of the WebControl *Base Class*

Property	Meaning in Life
BackColor	Gets or sets the background color of the web control.
BorderColor	Gets or sets the border color of the web control.
BorderStyle	Gets or sets the border style of the web control.
BorderWidth	Gets or sets the border width of the web control.
Enabled	Gets or sets a value indicating whether the web control is enabled.
CssClass	Allows you to assign a class defined within a Cascading Style Sheet to a web widget.
Font	Gets font information for the web control.
ForeColor	Gets or sets the foreground color (typically the color of the text) of the web control.
Height, Width	Get or set the height and width of the web control.
TabIndex	Gets or sets the tab index of the web control.
ToolTip	Gets or sets the tool tip for the web control to be displayed when the cursor is over the control.

Almost all of these properties are self-explanatory, so rather than drill through the use of them one by one, let's instead check out a number of ASP.NET Web Form controls in action.

Major Categories of ASP.NET Web Controls

The ASP.NET web control library can be broken down into several broad categories, all of which can be viewed within the Visual Studio Toolbox (provided you have an *.aspx page open for design) (see Figure 33-3).

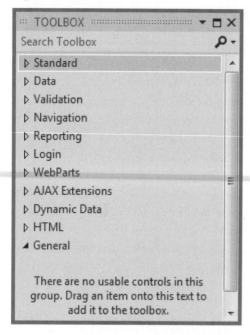

Figure 33-3. The categories of ASP.NET web controls

Under the Standard area of the Toolbox, you will find the most frequently used controls, including Button, Label, TextBox, and ListBox. In addition to these vanilla-flavored UI elements, the Standard area also lists more exotic web controls, such as Calendar, Wizard, and AdRotator (see Figure 33-4).

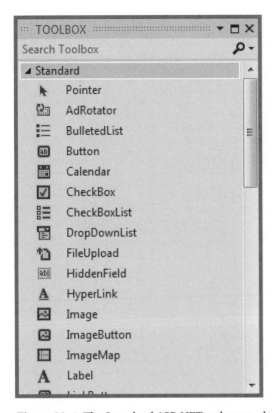

Figure 33-4. The Standard ASP.NET web controls

The Data section is where you can find a set of controls used for data-binding operations, including the ASP.NET Chart control, which allows you to render out graphical chart data (pie charts, line charts) typically as the result of a data-binding operation (see Figure 33-5).

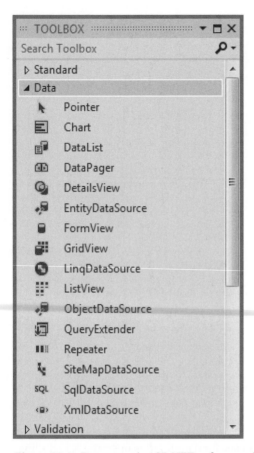

Figure 33-5. Data-centric ASP.NET web controls

The ASP.NET validation controls (found in the Validation area of the Toolbox) are very interesting in that they can be configured to emit back blocks of client-side JavaScript that will test input fields for valid data. If a validation error occurs, the user will see an error message and will not be allowed to post back to the web server until the error is corrected.

The Navigation node of the Toolbox is where you will find a small set of controls (Menu, SiteMapPath, and TreeView), which typically work in conjunction with a *.sitemap file. As briefly mentioned earlier in this chapter, these navigation controls allow you to describe the structure of a multipaged site using XML descriptions.

The most exotic set of ASP.NET web controls would have to be the Login controls (see Figure 33-6).

Figure 33-6. Security ASP.NET web controls

These controls can radically simplify how to incorporate basic security features (password recovery, login screens, etc.) into your web applications. In fact, these controls are so powerful, they will even dynamically create a dedicated database to store credentials (saved under the App_Data folder of your web site) if you do not already have a specific security database.

■ **Note** The remaining categories of web controls shown in the Visual Studio Toolbox (such as WebParts, AJAX Extensions, and Dynamic Data) are for more specialized programming needs and will not be examined here.

A Brief Word Regarding System.Web.UI.HtmlControls

Truth be told, there are two distinct web control toolkits that ship with ASP.NET. In addition to the ASP.NET web controls (within the System.Web.UI.WebControls namespace), the base class libraries also provides the System.Web.UI.HtmlControls control library.

The HTML controls are a collection of types that allow you to make use of traditional HTML controls on a Web Forms page. However, unlike simple HTML tags, HTML controls are object-oriented entities that can be configured to run on the server and, thus, support server-side event handling. Unlike ASP.NET web controls, HTML controls are quite simplistic in nature and offer little functionality beyond standard HTML tags (HtmlButton, HtmlInputControl, HtmlTable, etc.).

The HTML controls can be useful if your team has a clear division between those who build HTML UIs and .NET developers. HTML folks can make use of their web editor of choice using familiar markup tags and pass the HTML files to the development team. At this point, developers can configure these HTML controls to run as server controls (by right-clicking an HTML widget within Visual Studio). This will allow developers to handle server-side events and work with the HTML widget programmatically.

The HTML controls provide a public interface that mimics standard HTML attributes. For example, to obtain the information within an input area, you make use of the Value property rather than the web control–centric Text property. Given that the HTML controls are not as feature-rich as the ASP.NET web controls, I won't make further mention of them in this text.

Web Control Documentation

You will get a chance to work with a number of ASP.NET web controls during the remainder of this book; however, you should certainly take a moment to search the .NET Framework 4.5 SDK documentation for the System.Web.UI.WebControls namespace. Here, you will find explanations and code examples for each member of the namespace (see Figure 33-7).

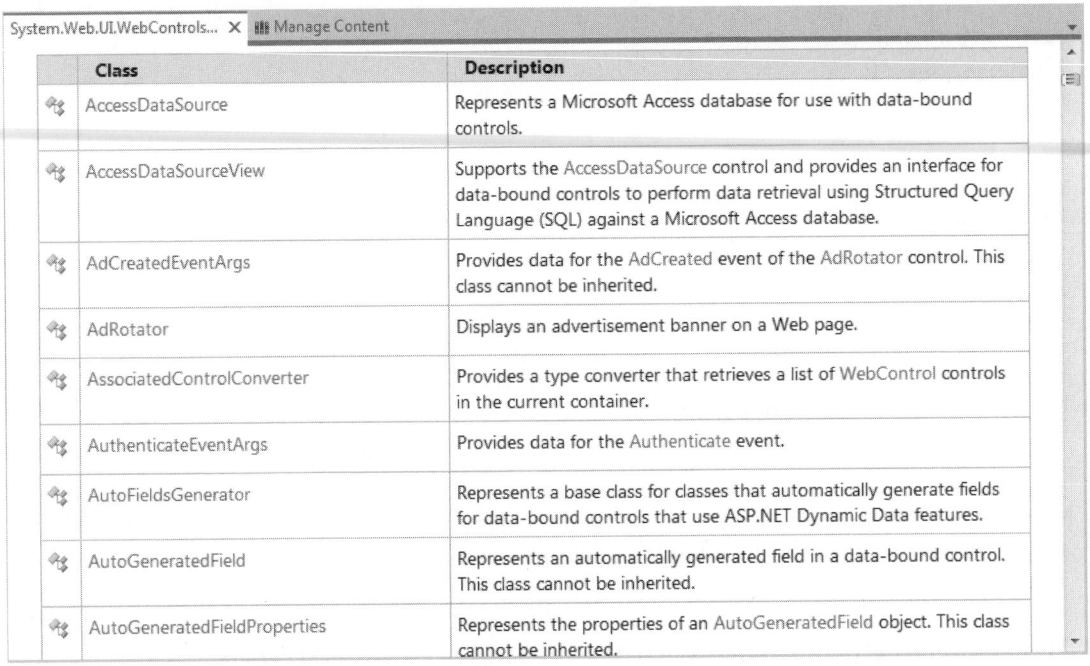

Class	Description
AccessDataSource	Represents a Microsoft Access database for use with data-bound controls.
AccessDataSourceView	Supports the AccessDataSource control and provides an interface for data-bound controls to perform data retrieval using Structured Query Language (SQL) against a Microsoft Access database.
AdCreatedEventArgs	Provides data for the AdCreated event of the AdRotator control. This class cannot be inherited.
AdRotator	Displays an advertisement banner on a Web page.
AssociatedControlConverter	Provides a type converter that retrieves a list of WebControl controls in the current container.
AuthenticateEventArgs	Provides data for the Authenticate event.
AutoFieldsGenerator	Represents a base class for classes that automatically generate fields for data-bound controls that use ASP.NET Dynamic Data features.
AutoGeneratedField	Represents an automatically generated field in a data-bound control. This class cannot be inherited.
AutoGeneratedFieldProperties	Represents the properties of an AutoGeneratedField object. This class cannot be inherited.

Figure 33-7. All ASP.NET web controls are documented in the .NET Framework 4.5 SDK documentation

Building the ASP.NET Cars Web Site

Given that many of the "simple" controls look and feel so close to their Windows GUI counterparts, I won't bother to enumerate the details of the basic widgets (Buttons, Labels, TextBoxes, etc.). Rather, let's build a new web site that illustrates working with several of the more exotic controls, as well as the

ASP.NET master page model and aspects of the data-binding engine. Specifically, this next example will illustrate the following techniques:

- Working with master pages

- Working with site map navigation

- Working with the GridView control

- Working with the Wizard control

To begin, create an Empty Web Site project named AspNetCarsSite. Note that we are not yet creating a new full ASP.NET Web Site project, as this will add a number of starter files to the mix that we have not yet examined. For this project, we will add what we need manually.

Working with ASP.NET Master Pages

Many web sites provide a consistent look and feel across multiple pages (a common menu navigation system, common header and footer content, company logo, etc.). A master page is little more than an ASP.NET page that takes a *.master file extension. On their own, master pages are not viewable from a client-side browser (in fact, the ASP.NET runtime will not serve this flavor of web content). Rather, master pages define a common UI layout shared by all pages (or a subset of pages) in your site.

As well, a *.master page will define various content placeholder areas that establish a region of UI real estate that other *.aspx files may plug into. As you will see, *.aspx files that plug their content into a master file look and feel a bit different from the *.aspx files we have been examining. Specifically, this flavor of an *.aspx file is termed a *content page*. Content pages are *.aspx files that do not define an HTML <form> element (that is the job of the master page).

However, as far as the end user is concerned, a request is made to a given *.aspx file. On the web server, the related *.master file and any related *.aspx content pages are blended into a single unified HTML page declaration.

To illustrate the use of master pages and content pages, begin by inserting a new master page into your web site via the Website   Add New Item menu selection (Figure 33-8 shows the resulting dialog box).

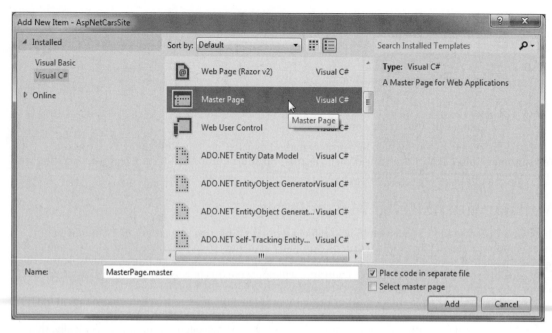

Figure 33-8. *Inserting a new* *.master file*

The initial markup of the MasterPage.master file looks like the following:

```
<%@ Master Language="C#" AutoEventWireup="true"
    CodeFile="MasterPage.master.cs" Inherits="MasterPage" %>

<!DOCTYPE html>

<html xmlns="http://www.w3.org/1999/xhtml">
<head runat="server">
  <title> </title>
  <asp:ContentPlaceHolder id="head" runat="server">
  </asp:ContentPlaceHolder>
</head>
<body>
  <form id="form1" runat="server">
  <div>
    <asp:ContentPlaceHolder id="ContentPlaceHolder1" runat="server">
    </asp:ContentPlaceHolder>
  </div>
  </form>
</body>
</html>
```

The first point of interest is the new <%@Master%> directive. For the most part, this directive supports the same attributes as the <%@Page%> directive described in Chapter 32. Like Page types, a master page derives from a specific base class, which in this case is MasterPage. If you were to open up your related code file, you would find the following class definition:

```
public partial class MasterPage : System.Web.UI.MasterPage
{
  protected void Page_Load(object sender, EventArgs e)
  {
  }
}
```

The other point of interest within the markup of the master is the <asp:ContentPlaceHolder> definition. This region of a master page represents the area of the master that the UI widgets of the related *.aspx content file may plug into, not the content defined by the master page itself.

If you do intend to plug in an *.aspx file within this region, the scope within the <asp:ContentPlaceHolder> and </asp:ContentPlaceHolder> tags will typically remain empty. However, if you so choose, you are able to populate this area with various web controls that function as a default UI to use in the event that a given *.aspx file in the site does not supply specific content. For this example, assume that each *.aspx page in your site will indeed supply custom content and, therefore, your <asp:ContentPlaceHolder> elements will be empty.

■ **Note** A *.master page may define as many content placeholders as necessary. As well, a single *.master page may nest additional *.master pages.

You are able to build a common UI of a *.master file using the same Visual Studio designers used to build *.aspx files. For this site, you will add a descriptive Label (to serve as a common welcome message), an AdRotator control (which will randomly display one of two image files), and a TreeView control (to allow the user to navigate to other areas of the site). Here is the markup I ended up with after designing my master page via the IDE:

```
<html xmlns="http://www.w3.org/1999/xhtml">
<head runat="server">
    <title> </title>
    <asp:ContentPlaceHolder id="head" runat="server">
    </asp:ContentPlaceHolder>
</head>
<body>
    <form id="form1" runat="server">
    <div>
      <hr />
      <asp:Label ID="Label1" runat="server" Font-Size="XX-Large"
        Text="Welcome to the ASP.NET Cars Super Site!"></asp:Label>
      <asp:AdRotator ID="myAdRotator" runat="server"/>
       <br />
      <br />
      <asp:TreeView ID="navigationTree" runat="server">
      </asp:TreeView>
      <hr />
    </div>
```

```
    <div>
        <asp:ContentPlaceHolder id="ContentPlaceHolder1" runat="server">
        </asp:ContentPlaceHolder>
    </div>
    </form>
</body>
</html>
```

Figure 33-9 shows the design time view of the current master page (note the display area of your AdRotator control will be empty for the time being).

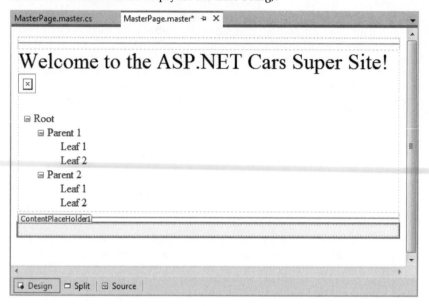

Figure 33-9. The *.master file's shared UI

Feel free to enhance the look of your TreeView control by using the inline editor of the control and selecting the Auto Format... link. As well, feel free to spice up the display of the remaining controls using the Properties editor. When you are happy with your results, move to the next section.

Configuring the TreeView Control Site Navigation Logic

ASP.NET ships with several web controls that allow you to handle site navigation: SiteMapPath, TreeView, and Menu. As you would expect, these web widgets can be configured in multiple ways. For example, each of these controls can dynamically generate its nodes via an external XML file (or an XML-based *.sitemap file), programmatically generate nodes in code, or through markup using the designers of Visual Studio.

Your navigation system will be dynamically populated using a *.sitemap file. The benefit of this approach is that we can define the overall structure of our web site in an external file and then bind it to a TreeView (or Menu) control on the fly. This way, if the navigational structure of your web site changes, you simply need to modify the *.sitemap file and reload the page. To begin, insert a new Web.sitemap file into your project using the Website ➤ Add New Item menu option to bring up the dialog box shown in Figure 33-10.

Figure 33-10. *Inserting a new* Web.sitemap *file*

As you can see, the initial Web.sitemap file defines a topmost item with two subnodes, as follows:

```xml
<?xml version="1.0" encoding="utf-8" ?>
<siteMap xmlns="http://schemas.microsoft.com/AspNet/SiteMap-File-1.0" >
  <siteMapNode url="" title="" description="">
    <siteMapNode url="" title="" description="" />
    <siteMapNode url="" title="" description="" />
  </siteMapNode>
</siteMap>
```

If we were to bind this structure to a Menu control, we would find a topmost item with two subitems. Therefore, when you want to define subitems, simply define new <siteMapNode> elements within the scope of an existing <siteMapNode>. In any case, the goal is to define the overall structure of your web site within a Web.sitemap file using various <siteMapNode> elements. Each one of these elements can define a title and URL attribute. The URL attribute represents which *.aspx file to navigate to when the user clicks a given menu item (or node of a TreeView). Your site map will contain three site map nodes (underneath the top-level site map node), as follows:

- *Home*: Default.aspx

- *Build a Car*: BuildCar.aspx

- *View Inventory*: Inventory.aspx

We will add these three new ASP.NET web pages to our project in the pages to come. For the time being, we will simply configure the site map file.

Your navigation system has a single topmost Welcome item with three subelements. Therefore, you can update the Web.sitemap file as follows, but be aware that each url value must be unique (if not, you will receive a runtime error):

```
<?xml version="1.0" encoding="utf-8" ?>
<siteMap xmlns="http://schemas.microsoft.com/AspNet/SiteMap-File-1.0" >
  <siteMapNode url="" title="Welcome!" description="">
    <siteMapNode url="~/Default.aspx" title="Home"
      description="The Home Page" />
    <siteMapNode url="~/BuildCar.aspx" title="Build a car"
      description="Create your dream car" />
    <siteMapNode url="~/Inventory.aspx" title="View Inventory"
      description="See what is in stock" />
  </siteMapNode>
</siteMap>
```

■ **Note** The ~/ prefix before each page in the url attribute is a notation that represents the root of the web site.

Now, despite what you might be thinking, you do not associate a Web.sitemap file directly to a Menu or TreeView control using a given property. Rather, the *.master or *.aspx file that contains the UI widget that will display the Web.sitemap file must contain a SiteMapDataSource component. This component will automatically load the Web.sitemap file into its object model when the page is requested. The Menu and TreeView types then set their DataSourceID property to point to the SiteMapDataSource instance.

To add a new SiteMapDataSource to your *.master file and automatically set the DataSourceID property, you can make use of the Visual Studio designer. Activate the inline editor of the TreeView control (i.e., click the tiny arrow in the top-right corner of the TreeView) , expand the Choose Data Source drop-down list, and select New Data Source, as shown in Figure 33-11.

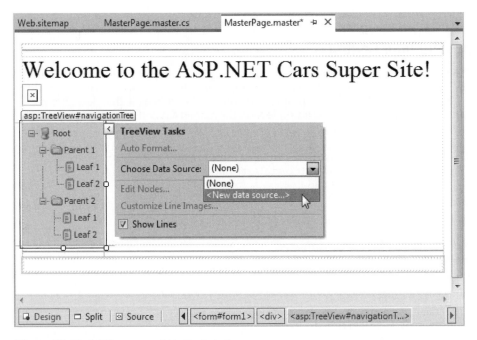

Figure 33-11. *Adding a new* SiteMapDataSource

From the resulting dialog box, select the SiteMap icon. This will set the DataSourceID property of the Menu or TreeView control, as well as add a new SiteMapDataSource component to your page. This is all you need to do to configure your TreeView control to navigate to the additional pages on your site. If you would like to perform additional processing when the user selects a given menu item, you may do so by handling the SelectedNodeChanged event on the TreeView control. There is no need to do so for this example, but be aware that you are able to determine which menu item was selected using the incoming event arguments.

Establishing Breadcrumbs with the SiteMapPath Type

Before moving on to the AdRotator control, add a SiteMapPath type (located in the Navigation tab in the Toolbox) onto your *.master file, beneath the content placeholder elements. This widget will automatically adjust its content based on the current selection of the menu system. As you might know, this can provide a helpful visual cue for the end user (formally, this UI technique is termed *breadcrumbs*). Once you complete this example, you will notice that when you select the Welcome Build a Car menu item, the SiteMapPath widget updates accordingly automatically.

Configuring the AdRotator Control

The role of the ASP.NET AdRotator widget is to randomly display a given image at some position in the browser. Recall at this point, the AdRotator is displaying an empty placeholder. This control cannot do its magic until you assign the AdvertisementFile property to point to the source file that describes each image. For this example, the data source will be a simple XML file named Ads.xml.

To add the XML file to the web site, go to the Website Add New Item menu option and select XML file. Name the file Ads.xml and specify a unique <Ad> element for each image you want to display. At minimum, each <Ad> element specifies the image to display (ImageUrl), the URL to navigate to if the image is selected (TargetUrl), mouseover text (AlternateText), and the weight of the ad (Impressions).

```
<Advertisements>
  <Ad>
    <ImageUrl>SlugBug.jpg</ImageUrl>
    <TargetUrl>http://www.Cars.com</TargetUrl>
    <AlternateText>Your new Car?</AlternateText>
    <Impressions>80</Impressions>
  </Ad>
  <Ad>
    <ImageUrl>car.gif</ImageUrl>
    <TargetUrl>http://www.CarSuperSite.com</TargetUrl>
    <AlternateText>Like this Car?</AlternateText>
    <Impressions>80</Impressions>
  </Ad>
</Advertisements>
```

Here, you have specified two image files (slugbug.jpg and car.gif). As a result, you will need to ensure that these files are in the root of your web site (these files have been included with this book's code download). To add them to your current project, select the Website Add Existing Item menu option. At this point, you can associate your XML file to the AdRotator control via the AdvertisementFile property (in the Properties window), like so:

```
<asp:AdRotator ID="myAdRotator" runat="server"
               AdvertisementFile="~/Ads.xml"/>
```

Later, when you run this application and post back to the page, you will be randomly presented with one of two image files.

Defining the Default Content Page

Now that you have a master page established, you can begin designing the individual *.aspx pages that will define the UI content to merge within the <asp:ContentPlaceHolder> tag of the master page. The *.aspx files that are merged within a master page are called *content pages* and have a few key differences from a normal, stand-alone ASP.NET web page.

In a nutshell, the *.master file defines the <form> section of the final HTML page. Therefore, the existing <form> area within the *.aspx file will need to be replaced with an <asp:Content> scope. While you could update the markup of your initial *.aspx file by hand, you can insert a new content page to your project; simply right-click anywhere on the designer surface of the *.master file and select the Add Content Page menu option (see Figure 33-12).

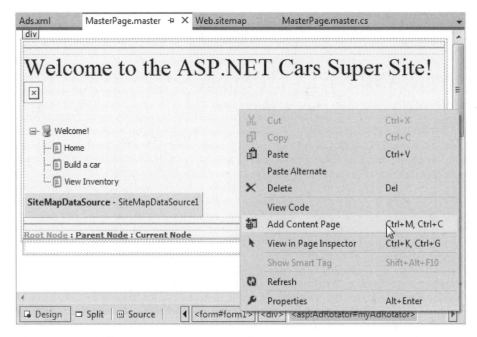

Figure 33-12. Adding a new content page to the master page

This will generate a new *.aspx file with the following initial markup:

```
<%@ Page Language="C#" MasterPageFile="~/MasterPage.master"
        AutoEventWireup="true" CodeFile="Default.aspx.cs"
        Inherits="_Default" Title="" %>

<asp:Content ID="Content1"
  ContentPlaceHolderID="head" Runat="Server">
</asp:Content>
<asp:Content ID="Content2"
  ContentPlaceHolderID="ContentPlaceHolder1" Runat="Server">
</asp:Content>
```

First, notice that the <%@Page%> directive has been updated with a new MasterPageFile attribute that is assigned to your *.master file. Also note that rather than having a <form> element, we have an <asp:Content> scope (currently empty) that has set the ContentPlaceHolderID value identical to the <asp:ContentPlaceHolder> component in the master file.

Given these associations, the content page understands where to plug in its content, while the master's content is displayed in a read-only nature on the content page. There is no need to build a complex UI for your Default.aspx content area. For this example, simply add some literal text that provides some basic site instructions, as you see in Figure 33-13 (also notice on the upper right of the content page in the designer that there is a link to switch to the related master file).

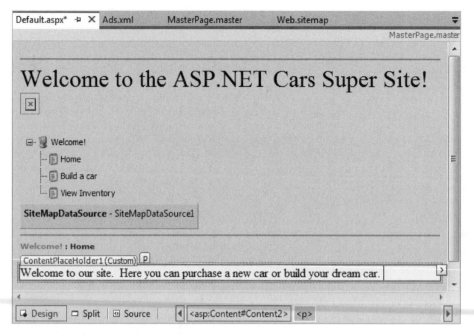

Figure 33-13. *Authoring the first content page*

Now, if you run your project, you will find that the UI content of the *.master and Default.aspx files has been merged into a single stream of HTML. As you can see from Figure 33-14, the browser (or end user) is unaware that the master page even exists (note the browser is simply showing the HTML from Default.aspx). Also, as you refresh the page (via the F5 key), you should see the AdRotator randomly displaying one of two images.

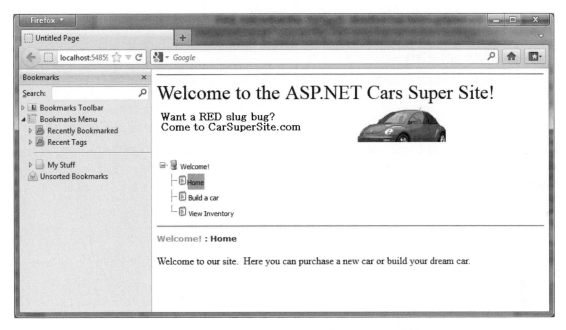

Figure 33-14. At runtime, master files and content pages render back a single form

Designing the Inventory Content Page

To insert the Inventory.aspx content page into your current project, open the *.master page in the IDE, select Website Add Content Page, and use the Solution Explorer to rename this file to Inventory.aspx. The role of the Inventory content page is to display the contents of the Inventory table of the AutoLot database within a GridView control. However, unlike the previous chapter, this GridView will be configured to interact with the AutoLot database using some built-in data-binding support.

The ASP.NET GridView control has the ability to represent connection string data and SQL Select, Insert, Update, and Delete statements (or alternatively stored procedures) *in markup*. Therefore, rather than authoring all of the necessary ADO.NET code by hand, you can allow the SqlDataSource class to generate the markup for you. Using the visual designers, you are able to assign the DataSourceID property of the GridView to the SqlDataSource component.

With a few simple mouse clicks, you can configure the GridView to automatically select, update, and delete records of the underlying data store. While this "zero-code mindset" greatly simplifies the amount of boilerplate code, understand that this simplicity comes with a loss of control and might not be the best approach for an enterprise-level application. This model can be wonderful for low-trafficked pages, prototyping a web site, or smaller in-house applications.

To illustrate how to work with the GridView (and the data access logic) in a declarative manner, begin by updating the Inventory.aspx content page with a descriptive Label control. Next, open the Server Explorer tool (via the View menu) and make sure you have added a data connection to the AutoLot database created during your examination of ADO.NET (see Chapter 21 for a walkthrough of the process of adding a data connection). Now, select the Inventory table in Server Explorer and drag it onto the content area of the Inventory.aspx file. After you have done so, the IDE responds by performing the following steps:

1. Your web.config file is updated with a new <connectionStrings> element.

2. A SqlDataSource component is configured with the necessary Select, Insert, Update, and Delete logic.

3. The DataSourceID property of the GridView is now set to the new SqlDataSource component.

■ **Note** As an alternative to dragging tables from the Server Explorer, you can configure a GridView widget using the inline editor (via the editor on the right corner). Select New Data Source from the Choose Data Source drop-down box. This will activate a wizard that walks you through a series of steps to connect this component to the required data source.

If you examine the opening declaration of the GridView control, you will see that the DataSourceID property has been set to the SqlDataSource you just defined, as follows:

```
<asp:GridView ID="GridView1" runat="server" AutoGenerateColumns="False"
    DataKeyNames="CarID" DataSourceID="SqlDataSource1"
    EmptyDataText="There are no data records to display.">
  <Columns>
    <asp:BoundField DataField="CarID" HeaderText="CarID" ReadOnly="True"
        SortExpression="CarID" />
    <asp:BoundField DataField="Make" HeaderText="Make" SortExpression="Make" />
    <asp:BoundField DataField="Color" HeaderText="Color" SortExpression="Color" />
    <asp:BoundField DataField="PetName" HeaderText="PetName"
                    SortExpression="PetName" />
  </Columns>
</asp:GridView>
```

The SqlDataSource element is where a majority of the action is taking place. In the markup that follows, notice that this element has recorded the necessary SQL statements (with parameterized queries, no less) to interact with the Inventory table of the AutoLot database. As well, using the $ syntax of the ConnectionString property, this component will automatically read the <connectionStrings> value from web.config.

```
<asp:SqlDataSource ID="SqlDataSource1" runat="server"
 ConnectionString="<%$ ConnectionStrings:AutoLotConnectionString1 %>"
  DeleteCommand="DELETE FROM [Inventory] WHERE [CarID] = @CarID"
  InsertCommand="INSERT INTO [Inventory] ([CarID], [Make], [Color], [PetName])
    VALUES (@CarID, @Make, @Color, @PetName)"
  ProviderName="<%$ ConnectionStrings:AutoLotConnectionString1.ProviderName %>"
  SelectCommand="SELECT [CarID], [Make], [Color], [PetName] FROM [Inventory]"
  UpdateCommand="UPDATE [Inventory] SET [Make] = @Make,
    [Color] = @Color, [PetName] = @PetName WHERE [CarID] = @CarID">
  <DeleteParameters>
    <asp:Parameter Name="CarID" Type="Int32" />
  </DeleteParameters>
  <UpdateParameters>
```

```
      <asp:Parameter Name="Make" Type="String" />
      <asp:Parameter Name="Color" Type="String" />
      <asp:Parameter Name="PetName" Type="String" />
      <asp:Parameter Name="CarID" Type="Int32" />
   </UpdateParameters>
   <InsertParameters>
      <asp:Parameter Name="CarID" Type="Int32" />
      <asp:Parameter Name="Make" Type="String" />
      <asp:Parameter Name="Color" Type="String" />
      <asp:Parameter Name="PetName" Type="String" />
   </InsertParameters>
</asp:SqlDataSource>
```

At this point, you are able to run your web program, click the View Inventory menu item, and view your data, as shown in Figure 33-15. (Note that I updated my GridView with a unique look and feel using the inline designer.)

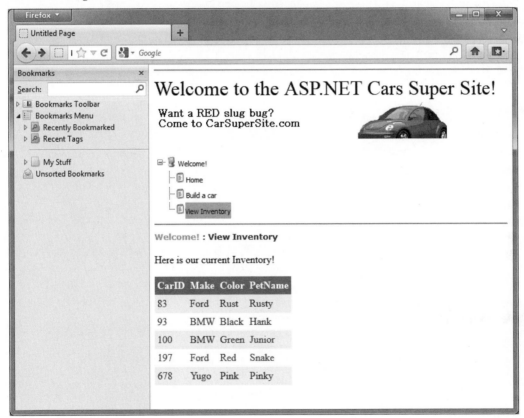

Figure 33-15. The zero-code model of the SqlDataSource component

Enabling Sorting and Paging

The GridView control can easily be configured for sorting (via column name hyperlinks) and paging (via numeric or next/previous hyperlinks). To do so, activate the inline editor and check the appropriate options, as shown in Figure 33-16.

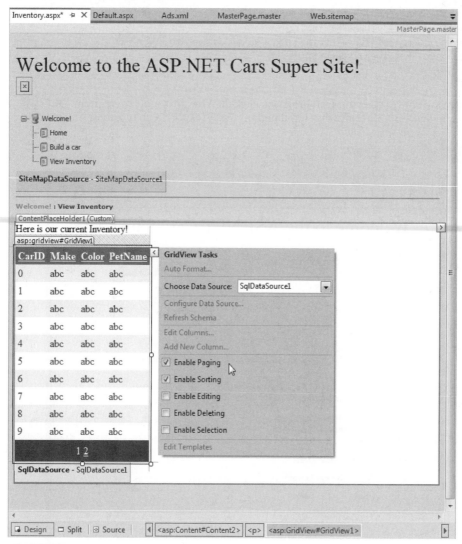

Figure 33-16. Enabling sorting and paging

When you run your page again, you will be able to sort your data by clicking the column names and scrolling through your data via the paging links (provided you have enough records in the Inventory table!).

Enabling In-Place Editing

The final detail of this page is to enable the GridView control's support for in-place activation. Given that your SqlDataSource already has the necessary Delete and Update logic, all you need to do is check the Enable Deleting and Enable Editing check boxes of the GridView (see Figure 33-16 for a reference point). Sure enough, when you navigate back to the Inventory.aspx page, you are able to edit and delete records (as shown in Figure 33-17) and update the underlying Inventory table of the AutoLot database.

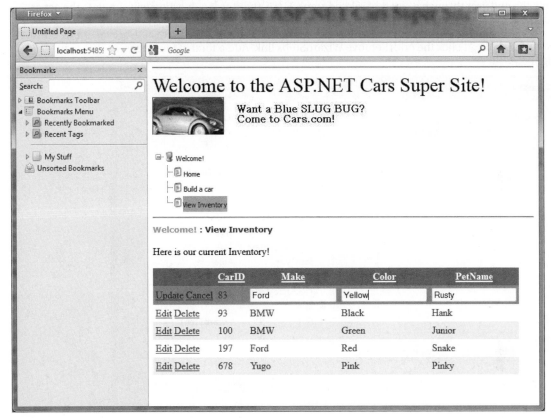

Figure 33-17. Editing and deleting functionality

■ **Note** Enabling in-place editing for a GridView requires that the database table be assigned a primary key. If you do not see these options enabled, chances are you forgot to set CarID as the primary key of the Inventory table within the AutoLot database.

Designing the Build-a-Car Content Page

The final task for this example is to design the BuildCar.aspx content page. To do so, make sure you have your *.master file open for editing, then insert this file into the current project (via the Website Add Content Page menu option; this is an alternative to right-clicking on the project's master page). Rename this new file to BuildCar.aspx using the Solution Explorer.

This new page will make use of the ASP.NET Wizard web control, which provides a simple way to walk the end user through a series of related steps. Here, the steps in question will simulate the act of building an automobile for purchase.

Place a descriptive Label and Wizard control onto the content area. Next, activate the inline editor for the Wizard and click the Add/Remove WizardSteps link. Add a total of four steps, as shown in Figure 33-18.

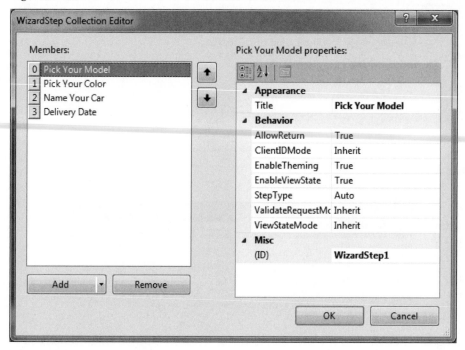

Figure 33-18. Configuring our wizard

After you have defined these steps, you will notice that the Wizard defines an empty content area where you can now drag and drop controls for the currently selected step. For this example, update each step with the following UI elements (be sure to provide a fitting ID value for each item using the Properties window):

- *Pick Your Model*: A TextBox control

- *Pick Your Color*: A ListBox control

- *Name Your Car*: A TextBox control

- *Delivery Date*: A Calendar control

The ListBox control is the only UI element of the Wizard that requires additional steps. Select this item on the designer (making sure you first select the Pick Your Color link) and fill this widget with a set of colors using the Items property of the Properties window. After you do so, you will find markup much like the following within the scope of the Wizard definition:

```
<asp:ListBox ID="ListBoxColors" runat="server" Width="237px">
  <asp:ListItem>Purple</asp:ListItem>
  <asp:ListItem>Green</asp:ListItem>
  <asp:ListItem>Red</asp:ListItem>
  <asp:ListItem>Yellow</asp:ListItem>
  <asp:ListItem>Pea Soup Green</asp:ListItem>
  <asp:ListItem>Black</asp:ListItem>
  <asp:ListItem>Lime Green</asp:ListItem>
</asp:ListBox>
```

Now that you have defined each of the steps, you can handle the FinishButtonClick event for the autogenerated Finish button. Be aware, however, that you won't see this Finish button until you select the final step of the wizard on the designer. Once you have selected the final step, simply double-click on the Finish button to generate the event handler. Within the server-side event handler, obtain the selections from each UI element and build a description string that is assigned to the Text property of an additional Label type named lblOrder, like so:

```
public partial class BuildCarPage : System.Web.UI.Page
{
  protected void Page_Load(object sender, EventArgs e)
  {
  }

  protected void carWizard_FinishButtonClick(object sender,
    WizardNavigationEventArgs e)
  {
    // Get each value.
    string order = string.Format("{0}, your {1} {2} will arrive on {3}.",
    txtCarPetName.Text, ListBoxColors.SelectedValue,
    txtCarModel.Text,
    carCalendar.SelectedDate.ToShortDateString());

    // Assign to label.
    lblOrder.Text = order;
  }
}
```

At this point, your AspNetCarsSite web application is complete! Figure 33-19 shows the Wizard in action.

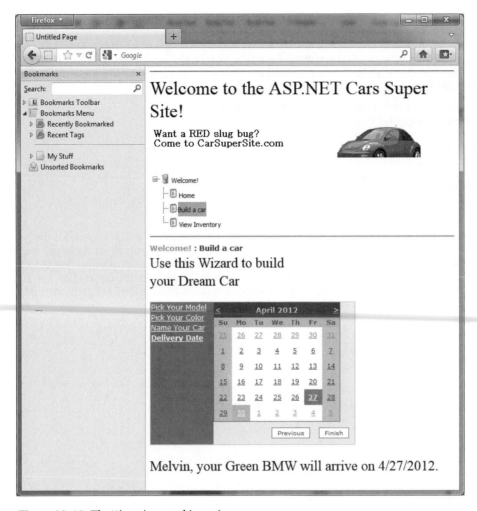

Figure 33-19. *The Wizard control in action*

That wraps up your first look of various ASP.NET web controls, master pages, content pages, and site map navigation. Next up, let's look at the functionality of the ASP.NET validation controls. To keep the topics in this chapter somewhat isolated and atomic, we will build a new web site to illustrate validation techniques; however, you could most certainly add validation controls to your current project.

■ **Source Code** The AspNetCarsSite web site is included under the Chapter 33 subdirectory.

The Role of the Validation Controls

The next set of Web Form controls we will examine are known collectively as *validation controls*. Unlike the other Web Form controls we've examined, validation controls are not used to emit HTML for rendering purposes, but are used to emit client-side JavaScript for the purpose of form validation. As illustrated at the beginning of this chapter, client-side form validation is quite useful because you can ensure that various constraints are in place before posting back to the web server, thereby avoiding expensive round-trips. Table 33-3 gives a rundown of the ASP.NET validation controls.

Table 33-3. ASP.NET Validation Controls

Control	Meaning in Life
CompareValidator	Validates that the value of an input control is equal to a given value of another input control or a fixed constant.
CustomValidator	Allows you to build a custom validation function that validates a given control.
RangeValidator	Determines that a given value is in a predetermined range.
RegularExpressionValidator	Checks whether the value of the associated input control matches the pattern of a regular expression.
RequiredFieldValidator	Ensures that a given input control contains a value (i.e., is not empty).
ValidationSummary	Displays a summary of all validation errors of a page in a list, bulleted list, or single-paragraph format. The errors can be displayed inline and/or in a pop-up message box.

All of the validation controls (minus ValidationSummary) ultimately derive from a common base class named System.Web.UI.WebControls.BaseValidator and, therefore, they have a set of common features. Table 33-4 documents the key members.

Table 33-4. Common Properties of the ASP.NET Validators

Member	Meaning in Life
ControlToValidate	Gets or sets the input control to validate.
Display	Gets or sets the display behavior of the error message in a validation control.
EnableClientScript	Gets or sets a value indicating whether client-side validation is enabled.
ErrorMessage	Gets or sets the text for the error message.

ForeColor	Gets or sets the color of the message displayed when validation fails.

To illustrate working with these validation controls, create a new Empty Web Site project named ValidatorCtrls and insert a new Web Form named Default.aspx. To begin, place four (well-named) TextBox controls (with four corresponding and descriptive Labels) onto your page. Next, place a RequiredFieldValidator, RangeValidator, RegularExpressionValidator, and CompareValidator control adjacent to each respective input field. Finally, add a single Button and final Label. Figure 33-20 shows one possible layout.

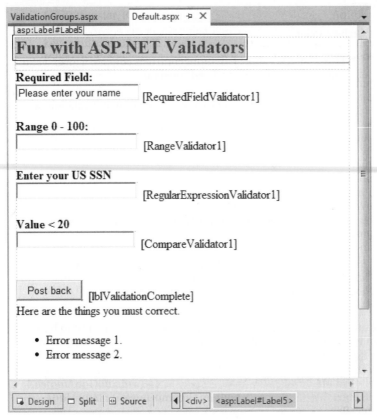

Figure 33-20. *ASP.NET validation controls will ensure your form data is correct before allowing postback*

Now that you have an initial UI to experiment with, let's walk through the process of configuring each validator control and see the end result of doing so. However, before doing so, we need to modify the current web.config file to allow client-side processing of our validation controls.

Enabling Client-Side JavaScript Validation Support

Beginning with ASP.NET 4.5, Microsoft has introduced a new setting that can be used to control how validation controls respond at runtime. If you were to open your current web.config file, you should find the following setting:

```
<appSettings>
...
  <add key="ValidationSettings:UnobtrusiveValidationMode" value="WebForms" />
</appSettings>
```

When this setting is in your web configuration file, the web site will process validation using various HTML 5 data attributes, rather than sending back blurbs of client-side JavaScript code to be processed by the web browser. Given that this edition of the text does not dive into the details of HTML 5, we need to comment out (or remove) this line in order for the current validation example to work correctly. Thus, simply comment out this section of the <appSettings> section as so:

```
<appSettings>
...
  <!--
  <add key="ValidationSettings:UnobtrusiveValidationMode" value="WebForms" />
  -->
</appSettings>
```

The RequiredFieldValidator

Configuring the RequiredFieldValidator is straightforward. Simply set the ErrorMessage and ControlToValidate properties accordingly using the Visual Studio Properties window. Here is the resulting markup that ensures the txtRequiredField text box is not empty:

```
<asp:RequiredFieldValidator ID="RequiredFieldValidator1"
  runat="server" ControlToValidate="txtRequiredField"
  ErrorMessage="Oops!  Need to enter data.">
</asp:RequiredFieldValidator>
```

The RequiredFieldValidator supports an InitialValue property. You can use this property to ensure that the user enters any value other than the initial value in the related TextBox. For example, when the user first posts to a page, you might want to configure a TextBox to contain the value "Please enter your name". Now, if you did not set the InitialValue property of the RequiredFieldValidator, the runtime would assume that the string "Please enter your name" is valid. Thus, to ensure a required TextBox is valid only when the user enters anything other than "Please enter your name", configure your widgets as follows:

```
<asp:RequiredFieldValidator ID="RequiredFieldValidator1"
  runat="server" ControlToValidate="txtRequiredField"
  ErrorMessage="Oops!  Need to enter data."
  InitialValue="Please enter your name">
</asp:RequiredFieldValidator>
```

The RegularExpressionValidator

The RegularExpressionValidator can be used when you want to apply a pattern against the characters entered within a given input field. To ensure that a given TextBox contains a valid U.S. Social Security number, you could define the widget as follows:

```
<asp:RegularExpressionValidator ID="RegularExpressionValidator1"
  runat="server" ControlToValidate="txtRegExp"
  ErrorMessage="Please enter a valid US SSN."
  ValidationExpression="\d{3}-\d{2}-\d{4}">
</asp:RegularExpressionValidator>
```

Notice how the RegularExpressionValidator defines a ValidationExpression property. If you have never worked with regular expressions before, all you need to be aware of for this example is that they are used to match a given string pattern. Here, the expression "\d{3}-\d{2}-\d{4}" is capturing a standard U.S. Social Security number of the form xxx-xx-xxxx (where x is any digit).

This particular regular expression is fairly self-explanatory; however, assume you wanted to test for a valid Japanese phone number. The correct expression now becomes much more complex: "(0\d{1,4}-|\(0\d{1,4}\)?)?\d{1,4}-\d{4}". The good news is that when you select the ValidationExpression property using the Properties window, you can pick from a predefined set of common regular expressions by clicking the ellipse button.

■ **Note** If you are interested in regular expressions, you will be happy to know that the .NET platform supplies two namespaces (System.Text.RegularExpressions and System.Web.RegularExpressions) devoted to the programmatic manipulation of such patterns.

The RangeValidator

In addition to a MinimumValue and MaximumValue property, RangeValidators have a property named Type. Because you are interested in testing the user-supplied input against a range of whole numbers, you need to specify Integer (which is *not* the default!), as so:

```
<asp:RangeValidator ID="RangeValidator1"
  runat="server" ControlToValidate="txtRange"
  ErrorMessage="Please enter value between 0 and 100."

  MaximumValue="100" MinimumValue="0" Type="Integer">
</asp:RangeValidator>
```

The RangeValidator can also be used to test whether a given value is between a currency value, date, floating-point number, or string data (the default setting).

The CompareValidator

Finally, notice that the CompareValidator supports the following Operator property:

```
<asp:CompareValidator ID="CompareValidator1" runat="server"
  ControlToValidate="txtComparison"
  ErrorMessage="Enter a value less than 20." Operator="LessThan"
  ValueToCompare="20" Type="Integer">
</asp:CompareValidator>
```

Given that the role of this validator is to compare the value in the text box against another value using a binary operator, it should be no surprise that the Operator property may be set to values such as LessThan, GreaterThan, Equal, and NotEqual. Also note that the ValueToCompare is used to establish a value to compare against. Do notice here that we have set the Type attribute to Integer. By default, the CompareValidator will be testing against string values!

■ **Note** The CompareValidator can also be configured to compare a value within another Web Form control (rather than a hard-coded value) using the ControlToCompare property.

To finish up the code for this page, handle the Click event for the Button control and inform the user that he or she has succeeded in the validation logic, like so:

```
public partial class _Default : System.Web.UI.Page
{
  protected void Page_Load(object sender, EventArgs e)
  {

  }
  protected void btnPostback_Click(object sender, EventArgs e)
  {
    lblValidationComplete.Text = "You passed validation!";
  }
}
```

Now, navigate to this page using your browser of choice. At this point, you should not see any noticeable changes. However, when you attempt to click the Submit button after entering bogus data, your error message is suddenly visible. When you enter valid data, the error messages are removed and postback occurs. If you look at the HTML rendered by the browser, you see that the validation controls generate a client-side JavaScript function that makes use of a specific library of JavaScript functions that is automatically downloaded to the user's machine. After the validation has occurred, the form data is posted back to the server, where the ASP.NET runtime will perform the same validation tests on the web server (just to ensure that no along-the-wire tampering has taken place).

On a related note, if the HTTP request was sent by a browser that does not support client-side JavaScript, all validation will occur on the server. In this way, you can program against the validation controls without being concerned with the target browser; the returned HTML page redirects the error processing back to the web server.

Creating Validation Summaries

The next validation-centric topic we will examine here is the use of the ValidationSummary widget. Currently, each of your validators displays its error message at the exact place in which it was positioned at design time. In many cases, this might be exactly what you are looking for. However, on a complex form with numerous input widgets, you might not want to have random blobs of red text pop up. Using the ValidationSummary type, you can instruct all of your validation types to display their error messages at a specific location on the page.

The first step is to simply place a ValidationSummary on your *.aspx file. You may optionally set the HeaderText property of this type as well as the DisplayMode, which by default will list all error messages as a bulleted list.

```
<asp:ValidationSummary id="ValidationSummary1"
  runat="server" Width="353px"
  HeaderText="Here are the things you must correct.">
</asp:ValidationSummary>
```

Next, you need to set the Display property to None for each of the individual validators (e.g., RequiredFieldValidator, RangeValidator) on the page. This will ensure that you do not see duplicate error messages for a given validation failure (one in the summary pane and another at the validator's location). Figure 33-21 shows the summary pane in action.

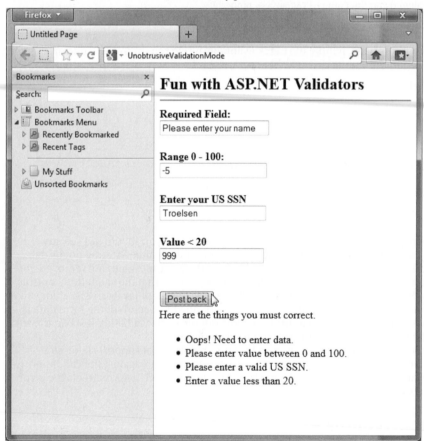

Figure 33-21. *Using a validation summary*

Last but not least, if you would rather have the error messages displayed using a client-side MessageBox, set the ValidationSummary control's ShowMessageBox property to true and the ShowSummary property to false.

Defining Validation Groups

It is also possible to define *groups* for validators to belong to. This can be very helpful when you have regions of a page that work as a collective whole. For example, you could have one group of controls in a Panel object to allow the user to enter his or her mailing address and another Panel containing UI elements to gather credit card information. Using groups, you can configure each group of controls to be validated independently.

Insert a new page into your current project named ValidationGroups.aspx that defines two Panels. The first Panel object expects a TextBox to contain some form of user input (via a RequiredFieldValidator) and the second Panel expects a U.S. SSN value (via a RegularExpressionValidator). Figure 33-22 shows one possible UI.

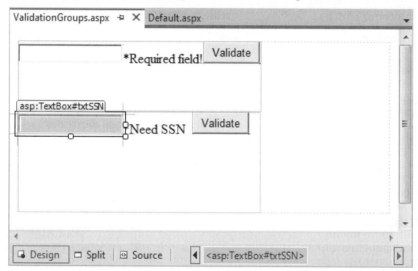

Figure 33-22. *These Panel objects will independently configure their input areas*

To ensure that the validators function independently, simply assign each validator and the control being validated to a uniquely named group using the ValidationGroup property. In the following possible markup, note that the Click event handlers used here are essentially empty stubs in the code file:

```
<form id="form1" runat="server">

  <asp:Panel ID="Panel1" runat="server" Height="83px" Width="296px">
    <asp:TextBox ID="txtRequiredData" runat="server"
              ValidationGroup="FirstGroup">
    </asp:TextBox>
    <asp:RequiredFieldValidator ID="RequiredFieldValidator1" runat="server"
        ErrorMessage="*Required field!" ControlToValidate="txtRequiredData"
```

```
            ValidationGroup="FirstGroup">
    </asp:RequiredFieldValidator>
    <asp:Button ID="bntValidateRequired" runat="server"
        OnClick="bntValidateRequired_Click"
        Text="Validate" ValidationGroup="FirstGroup" />
</asp:Panel>

<asp:Panel ID="Panel2" runat="server" Height="119px" Width="295px">
    <asp:TextBox ID="txtSSN" runat="server"
        ValidationGroup="SecondGroup">
    </asp:TextBox>
    <asp:RegularExpressionValidator ID="RegularExpressionValidator1"
        runat="server" ControlToValidate="txtSSN"
        ErrorMessage="*Need SSN" ValidationExpression="\d{3}-\d{2}-\d{4}"
        ValidationGroup="SecondGroup">
    </asp:RegularExpressionValidator> 
    <asp:Button ID="btnValidateSSN" runat="server"
        OnClick="btnValidateSSN_Click" Text="Validate"
      ValidationGroup="SecondGroup" />
</asp:Panel>

</form>
```

Now, right-click this page's designer and select the View In Browser menu option to verify each panel's widgets operate in a mutually exclusive manner.

■ **Source Code** The ValidatorCtrls web site is included under the Chapter 33 subdirectory.

Working with Themes

At this point, you have had the chance to work with numerous ASP.NET web controls. As you have seen, each control exposes a set of properties (many of which are inherited by System.Web.UI.WebControls.WebControl) that allow you to establish a given UI look and feel (background color, font size, border style, and whatnot). Of course, on a multipaged web site, it is quite common for the site as a whole to define a common look and feel for various types of widgets. For example, all TextBoxes might be configured to support a given font, all Buttons have a custom image, and all Calendars have a light blue border.

Obviously, it would be very labor intensive (and error prone) to establish the *same* property settings for *every* widget on *every* page within your web site. Even if you were able to manually update the properties of each UI widget on each page, imagine how painful it would be when you now need to change the background color for each TextBox yet again. Clearly, there must be a better way to apply site-wide UI settings.

One approach to simplifying the application of a common UI look and feel is to define *style sheets*. If you have a background in web development, you are aware that style sheets define a common set of UI-centric settings that are applied on the browser. As you would hope, ASP.NET web controls can be assigned a given style by assigning the CssStyle property.

However, ASP.NET ships with a complementary technology to define a common UI termed *themes*. Unlike a style sheet, themes are applied on the web server (rather than the browser) and can be done so programmatically or declaratively. Given that a theme is applied on the web server, it has access to all the server-side resources on the web site. Furthermore, themes are defined by authoring the same markup you would find within any *.aspx file (as you might agree, the syntax of a style sheet is a bit on the terse side).

Recall from Chapter 32 that ASP.NET web applications may define any number of special subdirectories, one of which is App_Themes. This single subdirectory may be further partitioned with additional subdirectories, each of which represents a possible theme on your site. For example, consider Figure 33-23, which illustrates a single App_Themes folder containing three subdirectories, each of which has a set of files that make up the theme itself.

Figure 33-23. A single App_Theme folder may define numerous themes

Understanding *.skin Files

The one file that every theme subdirectory is sure to have is a *.skin file. These files define the look and feel for various web controls. To illustrate, create a new Empty Web Site named FunWithThemes, and insert a new Default.aspx Web Form. On this new page, add a Calendar, TextBox, and Button control. We don't need to configure these controls in any special way, and the names of these controls are irrelevant for the current example. As you will see, these controls will be the targets for our custom skins.

Next, insert a new *.skin file (using the Website Add New Item menu option) named BasicGreen.skin, as shown in Figure 33-24.

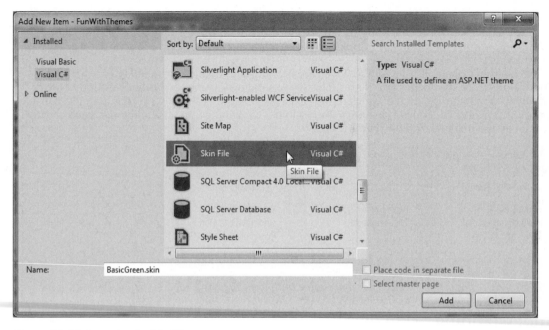

Figure 33-24. *Inserting* *.skin *files*

Visual Studio will prompt you to confirm this file can be added into an App_Themes folder (which is exactly what we want). If you were now to look in your Solution Explorer, you would indeed find your App_Themes folder has a subfolder named BasicGreen containing your new BasicGreen.skin file.

A *.skin file is where you are able to define the look and feel for various widgets using ASP.NET control declaration syntax. Sadly, the IDE does not provide designer support for *.skin files. One way to reduce the amount of typing time is to insert a temporary *.aspx file into your program (temp.aspx, for example) that can be used to build up the UI of the widgets using the Visual Studio page designer.

The resulting markup can then be copied and pasted into your *.skin file. When you do so, however, you *must* delete the ID attribute for each web control! This should make sense, given that we are not trying to define a UI look and feel for a *particular* Button (for example), rather *all* Buttons.

This being said, here is the markup for BasicGreen.skin that defines a default look and feel for the Button, TextBox, and Calendar types:

```
<asp:Button runat="server" BackColor="#80FF80"/>
<asp:TextBox runat="server" BackColor="#80FF80"/>
<asp:Calendar runat="server" BackColor="#80FF80"/>
```

Notice that each widget still has the runat="server" attribute (which is mandatory), and none of the widgets have been assigned an ID attribute.

Now, let's define a second theme named CrazyOrange. Using the Solution Explorer, right-click your App_Themes folder and add a new theme named CrazyOrange. This will create a new subdirectory under your site's App_Themes folder.

Next, right-click the new CrazyOrange folder within the Solution Explorer and select Add New Item. From the resulting dialog box, add a new *.skin file. Update the CrazyOrange.skin file to define a unique UI look and feel for the same web controls. For example:

```
<asp:Button runat="server" BackColor="#FF8000"/>
<asp:TextBox runat="server" BackColor="#FF8000"/>
<asp:Calendar BackColor="White" BorderColor="Black"
  BorderStyle="Solid" CellSpacing="1"
  Font-Names="Verdana" Font-Size="9pt" ForeColor="Black" Height="250px"
  NextPrevFormat="ShortMonth" Width="330px" runat="server">
  <SelectedDayStyle BackColor="#333399" ForeColor="White" />
  <OtherMonthDayStyle ForeColor="#999999" />
  <TodayDayStyle BackColor="#999999" ForeColor="White" />
  <DayStyle BackColor="#CCCCCC" />
  <NextPrevStyle Font-Bold="True" Font-Size="8pt" ForeColor="White" />
  <DayHeaderStyle Font-Bold="True" Font-Size="8pt"
    ForeColor="#333333" Height="8pt" />
  <TitleStyle BackColor="#333399" BorderStyle="Solid"
    Font-Bold="True" Font-Size="12pt"
    ForeColor="White" Height="12pt" />
</asp:Calendar>
```

At this point, your Solution Explorer should like Figure 33-25.

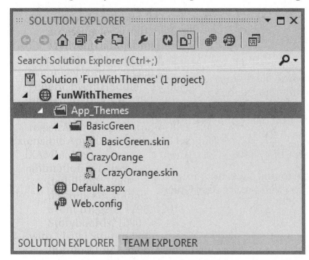

Figure 33-25. A single web site with multiple themes

Now that your site has a few themes defined, the next logical step is to apply them to your pages. As you might guess, there are many ways to do so.

■ **Note** To be sure, these example themes are quite bland by design (in order to reduce the amount of markup on the printed page). Feel free to spruce things up to your liking.

Applying Site-Wide Themes

If you would like to make sure that every page in your site adheres to the same theme, the simplest way to do so is to update your web.config file. Open your current web.config file and define a <pages> element within the scope of your <system.web> root element. If you add a theme attribute to the <pages> element, this will ensure that every page in your web site is assigned the selected theme (which is, of course, the name of one of the subdirectories under App_Theme). Here is the critical update:

```
<configuration>
  <system.web>
    ...
    <pages controlRenderingCompatibilityVersion="4.5"
        theme="BasicGreen">
    </pages>
  </system.web>
</configuration>
```

If you were to run this page, you would find each widget has the UI of BasicGreen. If you were to update the theme attribute to CrazyOrange and run the page again, you would find the UI defined by this theme is used instead.

Applying Themes at the Page Level

It is also possible to assign themes on a page-by-page level. This can be helpful in a variety of circumstances. For example, perhaps your web.config file defines a site-wide theme (as described in the previous section); however, you want to assign a different theme to a specific page. To do so, you can simply update the <%@Page%> directive. If you are using Visual Studio to do so, you will be happy to find that IntelliSense will display each defined theme within your App_Theme folder.

```
<%@ Page Language="C#" AutoEventWireup="true"
    CodeFile="Default.aspx.cs" Inherits="_Default" Theme ="CrazyOrange" %>
```

Because you assigned the CrazyOrange theme to this page, but the web.config file specified the BasicGreen theme, all pages *but this page* will be rendered using BasicGreen.

The SkinID Property

Sometimes you might need to define a set of possible UI look and feel scenarios for a single widget. For example, assume you want to define two possible UIs for the Button type within the CrazyOrange theme. When you want do so, you may differentiate each look and feel using the SkinID property of a control within the *.skin file:

```
<asp:Button runat="server" BackColor="#FF8000"/>
<asp:Button runat="server" SkinID = "BigFontButton"
        Font-Size="30pt" BackColor="#FF8000"/>
```

Now, if you have a page that makes use of the CrazyOrange theme, each Button will, by default, be assigned the unnamed Button skin. If you want to have various buttons within the *.aspx file make use of the BigFontButton skin, simply specify the SkinID property within the markup, like so:

```
<asp:Button ID="Button2" runat="server"
        SkinID="BigFontButton" Text="Button" /><br />
```

Assigning Themes Programmatically

Last but not least, it is possible to assign a theme in code. This can be helpful when you want to provide a way for end users to select a theme for their current session. Of course, I have not yet shown you how to build stateful web applications, so the current theme selection will be forgotten between postbacks. In a production-level site, you might want to store the user's current theme selection within a session variable, or persist the theme selection to a database.

To illustrate how to assign a theme programmatically, update the UI of your Default.aspx file with three new Button controls, as shown in Figure 33-26. After you have done so, handle the Click event for each Button.

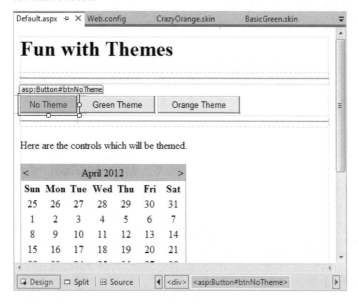

Figure 33-26. *The updated UI of the themes example*

Now, be aware that you can only assign a theme programmatically during specific phases of your page's life cycle. Typically, this will be done within the Page_PreInit event. This being said, update your code file as follows:

```
partial class _Default : System.Web.UI.Page
{
  protected void btnNoTheme_Click(object sender, System.EventArgs e)
  {
    // Empty strings result in no theme being applied.
    Session["UserTheme"] = "";

    // Triggers the PreInit event again.
    Server.Transfer(Request.FilePath);
  }

  protected void btnGreenTheme_Click(object sender, System.EventArgs e)
  {
```

```
    Session["UserTheme"] = "BasicGreen";

    // Triggers the PreInit event again.
    Server.Transfer(Request.FilePath);
}

protected void btnOrangeTheme_Click(object sender, System.EventArgs e)
{
    Session["UserTheme"] = "CrazyOrange";

    // Triggers the PreInit event again.
    Server.Transfer(Request.FilePath);
}

protected void Page_PreInit(object sender, System.EventArgs e)
{
    try
    {
        Theme = Session["UserTheme"].ToString();
    }
    catch
    {
        Theme = "";
    }
}
}
```

Notice that we are storing the selected theme within a session variable (see Chapter 34 for details) named UserTheme, which is formally assigned within the Page_PreInit() event handler. Also note that when the user clicks a given Button, we programmatically force the PreInit event to fire by calling Server.Transfer() and requesting the current page once again. If you were to run this page, you would now find that you can establish your theme via various Button clicks.

■ **Source Code** The FunWithThemes web site is included under the Chapter 33 subdirectory.

Summary

This chapter examined how to make use of various ASP.NET web controls. We began by examining the role of the Control and WebControl base classes, and you learned how to dynamically interact with a panel's internal controls collection. Along the way, you were exposed to the new site navigation model (*.sitemap files and the SiteMapDataSource component), the new data-binding engine (via the SqlDataSource component and the GridView control), and various validation controls.

The latter half of this chapter examined the role of master pages and themes. Recall that master pages can be used to define a common layout for a set of pages on your site. Also recall that the *.master file defines any number of content placeholders to which content pages plug in their custom UI content. Finally, as you were shown, the ASP.NET theme engine allows you to declaratively or programmatically apply a common UI look and feel to your widgets on the web server.

CHAPTER 34

ASP.NET State Management Techniques

The previous two chapters concentrated on the composition and behavior of ASP.NET pages and the web controls they contain. This chapter builds on that information by examining the role of the `Global.asax` file and the underlying `HttpApplication` type. As you will see, the functionality of `HttpApplication` allows you to intercept numerous events that enable you to treat your web application as a cohesive unit, rather than a set of stand-alone *.aspx files driven by a master page.

In addition to investigating the `HttpApplication` type, this chapter also addresses the all-important topic of state management. Here you will learn the role of view state, session and application variables (including the application cache), cookie data, and the ASP.NET Profile API.

The Issue of State

At the beginning of the Chapter 32, I pointed out that HTTP on the Web results in a *stateless* wire protocol. This very fact makes web development extremely different from the process of building an executable assembly. For example, when you are building a Windows desktop UI application, you can rest assured that any member variables defined in the `Form`-derived class will typically exist in memory until the user explicitly shuts down the executable.

```
public partial class MainWindow : Window
{
  // State data!
  private string userFavoriteCar = "Yugo";
}
```

In the World Wide Web environment, however, you are not afforded the same luxurious assumption. To prove the point, create a new Empty Web Site project named SimpleStateExample and insert a new Web Form. In the code-behind file of your *.aspx file, define a page-level string variable named userFavoriteCar, as follows:

```
public partial class _Default : System.Web.UI.Page
{
  // State data?
  private string userFavoriteCar = "Yugo";

  protected void Page_Load(object sender, EventArgs e)
  {
```

1429

```
    }
}
```

Next, construct a very simple web UI as shown in Figure 34-1.

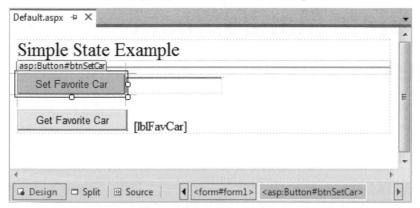

Figure 34-1. *The UI for the simple state page*

The server-side Click event handler for the Set button (named btnSetCar) allows the user to assign the string member variable to the value within the TextBox (named txtFavCar), like so:

```
protected void btnSetCar_Click(object sender, EventArgs e)
{
  // Store favorite car in member variable.
  userFavoriteCar = txtFavCar.Text;
}
```

The Click event handler for the Get button (btnGetCar) displays the current value of the member variable within the page's Label widget (lblFavCar), as follows:

```
protected void btnGetCar_Click(object sender, EventArgs e)
{
  // Show value of member variable.
  lblFavCar.Text = userFavoriteCar;
}
```

Now, if you were building a Windows GUI application, you would be right to assume that once the user sets the initial value, it would be remembered throughout the life of the desktop application. Sadly, when you run this web application, you find that each time you post back to the web server (by clicking either button), the value of the userFavoriteCar string variable is set back to the initial value of "Yugo"; therefore, the Label's text is continuously fixed.

Again, given that HTTP has no clue how to automatically remember data once the HTTP response has been sent, it stands to reason that the Page object is destroyed almost instantly. As a result, when the client posts back to the *.aspx file, a new Page object is constructed that will reset any page-level member variables. This is clearly a major issue. Imagine how useless online shopping would be if every time you posted back to the web server, any and all information you previously entered (such as the items you wished to purchase) were discarded. When you want to remember information regarding the users who are logged on to your site, you need to make use of various state management techniques.

■ **Note** This issue is in no way limited to ASP.NET. Java web applications, CGI applications, classic ASP applications, and PHP applications all must contend with the thorny issue of state management.

To remember the value of the userFavoriteCar string type between postbacks, one approach is to store the value of this string type in a *session variable*. We will examine the details of session state in the pages that follow. For the sake of completion, however, here are the necessary updates for the current page (note that you are no longer using the private string member variable, so feel free to comment out or remove the definition altogether).

```
public partial class _Default : System.Web.UI.Page
{
  // State data?
  // private string userFavoriteCar = "Yugo";

  protected void Page_Load(object sender, EventArgs e)
  {
  }

  protected void btnSetCar_Click(object sender, EventArgs e)
  {
    // Store value to be remembered in session variable.
    Session["UserFavCar"] = txtFavCar.Text;
  }

  protected void btnGetCar_Click(object sender, EventArgs e)
  {
    // Get session variable value.
    lblFavCar.Text = (string)Session["UserFavCar"];
  }
}
```

If you now run the application, the value of your favorite automobile will be preserved across postbacks, thanks to the HttpSessionState object manipulated indirectly by the inherited Session property. Session data (which will be examined in greater detail later in this chapter) is just one way to "remember" information in your web sites. Over the next several pages, you will examine each of the major options supported by ASP.NET.

■ **Source Code** The SimpleStateExample web site is included under the Chapter 34 subdirectory.

ASP.NET State Management Techniques

ASP.NET provides several mechanisms you can use to maintain stateful information in your web applications. Here are some common options:

- Use ASP.NET view state.

- Use ASP.NET control state.

- Define application-level data.

- Use the cache object.

- Define session-level data.

- Define cookie data.

In addition to these techniques, if you want to persist user data in a permanent manner, ASP.NET provides an out-of-the-box Profile API. We'll examine the details of each approach in turn, beginning with the topic of ASP.NET view state.

Understanding the Role of ASP.NET View State

The term *view state* has been thrown out a few times here and in the previous chapters without a formal definition, so let's demystify this term. Without framework support, web developers are required to manually repopulate the values of the incoming form widgets during the process of constructing the outgoing HTTP response.

Using ASP.NET, we no longer have to manually scrape out and repopulate the values in the HTML widgets because the ASP.NET runtime automatically embeds a hidden form field (named __VIEWSTATE), which will flow between the browser and a specific page. The data assigned to this field is a Base64-encoded string that contains a set of name/value pairs representing the values of each GUI widget on the page at hand.

The System.Web.UI.Page base class's Init event handler is the entity in charge of reading the incoming values in the __VIEWSTATE field to populate the appropriate member variables in the derived class. (This is why it is risky at best to access the state of a web widget within the scope of a page's Init event handler.)

Also, just before the outgoing response is emitted back to the requesting browser, the __VIEWSTATE data is used to repopulate the form's widgets. Clearly, the best thing about this aspect of ASP.NET is that it just happens without any work on your part. Of course, you are always able to interact with, alter, or disable this default functionality if you so choose. To understand how to do this, let's see a concrete view state example.

Demonstrating View State

First, create a new Empty Web Site called ViewStateApp and insert a new Web Form. On your *.aspx page, add a single ASP.NET ListBox web control named myListBox and a single Button control named btnPostback.

Now, using the Visual Studio Properties window, access the Items property and add four ListItems to the ListBox using the associated dialog box. The resulting markup should look something like so:

```
<asp:ListBox ID="myListBox" runat="server">
  <asp:ListItem>Item One</asp:ListItem>
  <asp:ListItem>Item Two</asp:ListItem>
  <asp:ListItem>Item Three</asp:ListItem>
  <asp:ListItem>Item Four</asp:ListItem>
</asp:ListBox>
```

Note that you are hard-coding the items in the ListBox directly within the *.aspx file. As you already know, all <asp:> definitions in an ASP.NET Web Form will automatically render back their HTML representation before the final HTTP response (provided they have the runat="server" attribute).

The <%@Page%> directive has an optional attribute called EnableViewState that by default is set to true. To disable this behavior, simply update the <%@Page%> directive as follows:

```
<%@ Page Language="C#" AutoEventWireup="true"
        CodeFile="Default.aspx.cs" Inherits="_Default"
        EnableViewState ="false" %>
```

So, what exactly does it mean to disable view state? The answer is, it depends. Given the previous definition of the term, you would think that if you disable view state for an *.aspx file, the values in your ListBox would not be remembered between postbacks to the web server. However, if you were to run this application as is, you might be surprised to find that the information in the ListBox is retained regardless of how many times you post back to the page.

In fact, if you examine the source HTML returned to the browser (by right-clicking the page within the browser and selecting View Source), you might be further surprised to see that the hidden __VIEWSTATE field is *still present*.

```
<input type="hidden" name="__VIEWSTATE" id="__VIEWSTATE"
        value="/wEPDwUKLTM4MTM2MDM4NGRkqGC6gjEV25JnddkJiRmoIc1OSIA=" />
```

However, assume that your ListBox is dynamically populated within the code-behind file rather than within the HTML <form> definition. First, remove the <asp:ListItem> declarations from the current *.aspx file.

```
<asp:ListBox ID="myListBox" runat="server">
</asp:ListBox>
```

Next, fill the list items within the Load event handler in your code-behind file, like so:

```
protected void Page_Load(object sender, EventArgs e)
{
  if (!IsPostBack)
  {
    // Fill ListBox dynamically!
    myListBox.Items.Add("Item One");
    myListBox.Items.Add("Item Two");
    myListBox.Items.Add("Item Three");
    myListBox.Items.Add("Item Four");
  }
}
```

If you post to this updated page, you'll find that the first time the browser requests the page, the values in the ListBox are present and accounted for. However, on postback, the ListBox is suddenly empty. The first rule of ASP.NET view state is that its effect is only realized when you have widgets whose values are dynamically generated through code. If you hard-code values within the *.aspx file's <form> tags, the state of these items is always remembered across postbacks (even when you set EnableViewState to false for a given page).

If the idea of disabling view state for the entire *.aspx file seems a bit too aggressive, know that every descendant of the System.Web.UI.Control base class inherits the EnableViewState property, which makes it very simple to disable view state on a control-by-control basis.

```
<asp:GridView id="myHugeDynamicallyFilledGridOfData" runat="server"
 EnableViewState="false">
</asp:GridView>
```

■ **Note** Beginning with .NET 4.0, large view state data values are automatically compressed, to help reduce the size of this hidden form field.

Adding Custom View State Data

In addition to the EnableViewState property, the System.Web.UI.Control base class provides a protected property named ViewState. Under the hood, this property provides access to a System.Web.UI.StateBag type, which represents all the data contained within the __VIEWSTATE field. Using the indexer of the StateBag type, you can embed custom information within the hidden __VIEWSTATE form field using a set of name/value pairs. Here's a simple example:

```
protected void btnAddToVS_Click(object sender, EventArgs e)
{
  ViewState["CustomViewStateItem"] = "Some user data";
  lblVSValue.Text = (string)ViewState["CustomViewStateItem"];
}
```

Because the System.Web.UI.StateBag type has been designed to operate on System.Object types, when you want to access the value of a given key, you should explicitly cast it into the correct underlying data type (in this case, a System.String). Be aware, however, that values placed within the __VIEWSTATE field cannot literally be any object. Specifically, the only valid types are Strings, Integers, Booleans, ArrayLists, Hashtables, or an array of these types.

So, given that *.aspx pages can insert custom bits of information into the __VIEWSTATE string, the next logical step is to figure out when you would want to do so. Most of the time, custom view-state data is best suited for user-specific preferences. For example, you could establish view-state data that specifies how a user wants to view the UI of a GridView (such as a sort order). However, view-state data is not well-suited for full-blown user data, such as items in a shopping cart or cached DataSets. When you need to store this sort of complex information, you must work with session or application data. Before we get to that point, though, you need to understand the role of the Global.asax file.

■ **Source Code** The ViewStateApp web site is included under the Chapter 34 subdirectory.

The Role of the Global.asax File

At this point, an ASP.NET application might seem little more than a set of .aspx files and their respective web controls. While you could build a web application by simply linking a set of related web pages, you will most likely need a way to interact with the web application as a whole. To this end, an ASP.NET application may choose to include an optional Global.asax file via the Web Site ➤ Add New Item menu option, as shown in Figure 34-2 (notice you are selecting the Global Application Class icon).

Figure 34-2. The Global.asax *file*

Simply put, Global.asax is just about as close to a traditional double-clickable *.exe as you can get in the world of ASP.NET, meaning this type represents the runtime behavior of the web site itself. When you insert a Global.asax file into a web project, you'll see it's little more than a <script> block containing a set of event handlers, like this:

```
<%@ Application Language="C#" %>

<script runat="server">
  void Application_Start(object sender, EventArgs e)
  {
    // Code that runs on application startup.
  }

  void Application_End(object sender, EventArgs e)
  {
    // Code that runs on application shutdown.
  }

  void Application_Error(object sender, EventArgs e)
  {
    // Code that runs when an unhandled error occurs.
  }
```

```
    void Session_Start(object sender, EventArgs e)
    {
        // Code that runs when a new session is started.
    }
    void Session_End(object sender, EventArgs e)
    {
        // Code that runs when a session ends.
        // Note: The Session_End event is raised only when the sessionstate mode
        // is set to InProc in the web.config file. If session mode is set to
        // StateServer or SQLServer, the event is not raised.
    }
</script>
```

Looks can be deceiving, however. At runtime, the code within this <script> block is assembled into a class type deriving from System.Web.HttpApplication. Therefore, within any of the provided event handlers, you can access parent class members via the this or base keywords.

As mentioned, the members defined inside Global.asax are event handlers that allow you to interact with application-level (and session-level) events. Table 34-1 documents the role of each member.

Table 34-1. Core Types of the System.Web *Namespace*

Event Handler	Meaning in Life
Application_Start()	This event handler is called the very first time the web application is launched. Thus, this event will fire exactly once over the lifetime of a web application. It is an ideal place to define application-level data used throughout your web application.
Application_End()	This event handler is called when the application is shutting down. This will occur when the last user times out or if you manually shut down the application via IIS.
Session_Start()	This event handler is fired when a new user reaches your application. Here you can establish any user-specific data points you want to preserve across postbacks.
Session_End()	This event handler is fired when a user's session has terminated (typically through a predefined timeout).
Application_Error()	This is a global error handler that will be called when an unhandled exception is thrown by the web application.

The Global Last-Chance Exception Event Handler

First, let me point out the role of the Application_Error() event handler. Recall that a specific page may handle the Error event to process any unhandled exception that occurred within the scope of the page itself. In a similar light, the Application_Error() event handler is the final place to handle an exception that was not handled by a given page. As with the page-level Error event, you are able to access the specific System.Exception using the inherited Server property, like so:

```
void Application_Error(object sender, EventArgs e)
{
  // Obtain the unhandled error.
  Exception ex = Server.GetLastError();

  // Process error here...

  // Clear error when finished.
  Server.ClearError();
}
```

Given that the Application_Error() event handler is the last-chance exception handler for your web application, it is quite common to implement this method in such a way that the user is transferred to a predefined error page on the server. Other common duties could include sending an e-mail to the web administrator or writing to an external error log.

The HttpApplication Base Class

As mentioned, the Global.asax script is dynamically generated as a class deriving from the System.Web.HttpApplication base class, which supplies some of the same sort of functionality as the System.Web.UI.Page type (without a visible user interface). Table 34-2 documents the key members of interest.

Table 34-2. Key Members Defined by the System.Web.HttpApplication *Type*

Property	Meaning in Life
Application	This property allows you to interact with application-level data, using the exposed HttpApplicationState type.
Request	This property allows you to interact with the incoming HTTP request, using the underlying HttpRequest object.
Response	This property allows you to interact with the incoming HTTP response, using the underlying HttpResponse object.
Server	This property gets the intrinsic server object for the current request, using the underlying HttpServerUtility object.
Session	This property allows you to interact with session-level data, using the underlying HttpSessionState object.

Again, given that the Global.asax file does not explicitly document that HttpApplication is the underlying base class, it is important to remember that all of the rules of the "is-a" relationship do indeed apply.

Understanding the Application/Session Distinction

Under ASP.NET, application state is maintained by an instance of the HttpApplicationState type. This class enables you to share global information across all users (and all pages) using your ASP.NET application. Not only can application data be shared by all users on your site, but also if the value of an application-level data point changes, the new value is seen by all users on their next postback.

On the other hand, session state is used to remember information for a specific user (again, such as items in a shopping cart). Physically, a user's session state is represented by the HttpSessionState class type. When a new user reaches an ASP.NET web application, the runtime will automatically assign that user a new session ID, which by default will expire after 20 minutes of inactivity. Thus, if 20,000 users are logged on to your site, you have 20,000 distinct HttpSessionState objects, each of which is automatically assigned a unique session ID. The relationship between a web application and web sessions is shown in Figure 34-3.

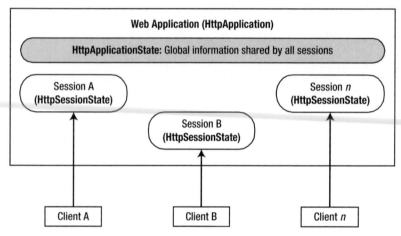

Figure 34-3. The application/session state distinction

Maintaining Application-Level State Data

The HttpApplicationState type enables developers to share global information across multiple users in an ASP.NET application. Table 34-3 describes some core members of this type.

Table 34-3. Members of the HttpApplicationState Type

Members	Meaning in Life
Add()	This method allows you to add a new name/value pair to the HttpApplicationState object. Do note that this method is typically *not* used in favor of the indexer of the HttpApplicationState class.
AllKeys	This property returns an array of string objects that represent all the names in the HttpApplicationState type.

Clear()	This method deletes all items in the HttpApplicationState object. This is functionally equivalent to the RemoveAll() method.
Count	This property gets the number of item objects in the HttpApplicationState type.
Lock(), UnLock()	These two methods are used when you want to alter a set of application variables in a thread-safe manner.
RemoveAll(), Remove(), RemoveAt()	These methods remove a specific item (by string name) within the HttpApplicationState object. RemoveAt() removes the item via a numerical indexer.

To illustrate working with application state, create a new Empty Web Site project named AppState (and insert a new Web Form). Next, insert a new Global.asax file. When you create data members that can be shared among all users, you need to establish a set of name/value pairs. In most cases, the most natural place to do so is within the Application_Start() event handler in Global.asax.cs. For example:

```
void Application_Start(Object sender, EventArgs e)
{
    // Set up some application variables.
    Application["SalesPersonOfTheMonth"] = "Chucky";
    Application["CurrentCarOnSale"] = "Colt";
    Application["MostPopularColorOnLot"] = "Black";
}
```

During the lifetime of your web application (which is to say, until the web application is manually shut down or until the final user times out), any user on any page may access these values as necessary. Assume you have a page that will display the current discount car within a Label via a button Click event handler, like so:

```
protected void btnShowCarOnSale_Click(object sender, EventArgs arg)
{
    lblCurrCarOnSale.Text = string.Format("Sale on {0}'s today!",
        (string)Application["CurrentCarOnSale"]);
}
```

As with the ViewState property, notice how you should cast the value returned from the HttpApplicationState object into the correct underlying type because the Application property operates on general System.Object types.

Now, given that the Application property can hold any type, it should stand to reason that you can place custom types (or any .NET object) within your site's application state. Assume you'd rather maintain the three current application variables within a strongly typed class named CarLotInfo, as follows:

```
public class CarLotInfo
{
    public CarLotInfo(string s, string c, string m)
    {
        SalesPersonOfTheMonth = s;
        CurrentCarOnSale = c;
```

```
        MostPopularColorOnLot = m;
    }
    public string SalesPersonOfTheMonth { get; set; }
    public string CurrentCarOnSale { get; set; }
    public string MostPopularColorOnLot { get; set; }
}
```

With this helper class in place, you could modify the Application_Start() event handler as follows:

```
void Application_Start(Object sender, EventArgs e)
{
    // Place a custom object in the application data sector.
    Application["CarSiteInfo"] =
        new CarLotInfo("Chucky", "Colt", "Black");
}
```

You could then access the information using the public field data within a server-side Click event handler for a Button control named btnShowAppVariables, as follows:

```
protected void btnShowAppVariables_Click(object sender, EventArgs e)
{
    CarLotInfo appVars =
        ((CarLotInfo)Application["CarSiteInfo"]);
    string appState =
        string.Format("<li>Car on sale: {0}</li>",
        appVars.CurrentCarOnSale);
    appState +=
        string.Format("<li>Most popular color: {0}</li>",
        appVars.MostPopularColorOnLot);
    appState +=
        string.Format("<li>Big shot SalesPerson: {0}</li>",
        appVars.SalesPersonOfTheMonth);
    lblAppVariables.Text = appState;
}
```

Given that the current car-on-sale data is now exposed from a custom class type, your btnShowCarOnSale Click event handler would also need to be updated, like so:

```
protected void btnShowCarOnSale_Click(object sender, EventArgs e)
{
    lblCurrCarOnSale.Text = String.Format("Sale on {0}'s today!",
        ((CarLotInfo)Application["CarSiteInfo"]).CurrentCarOnSale);
}
```

Modifying Application Data

You may programmatically update or delete any or all application-wide data items using members of the HttpApplicationState type during the execution of your web application. For example, to delete a specific item, simply call the Remove() method. If you want to destroy all application-level data, call RemoveAll().

```
private void CleanAppData()
{
    // Remove a single item via string name.
```

```
    Application.Remove("SomeItemIDontNeed");

    // Destroy all application data!
    Application.RemoveAll();
}
```

If you want to change the value of an existing application-level data item, you need only make a new assignment to the data item in question. Assume your page now has a Button that allows your user to change the current hotshot salesperson by reading in a value from a TextBox named txtNewSP. The Click event handler here is as you'd expect:

```
protected void btnSetNewSP_Click(object sender, EventArgs e)
{
    // Set the new Salesperson.
    ((CarLotInfo)Application["CarSiteInfo"]).SalesPersonOfTheMonth
        = txtNewSP.Text;
}
```

If you run the web application, you'll find that the application-level data item has been updated. Furthermore, given that application variables are accessible by any user on any page in the Web application, if you launched three or four instances of your web browser, you'd find that if one instance changes the current salesperson, each of the other browsers displays the new value on postback. Figure 34-4 shows some possible output.

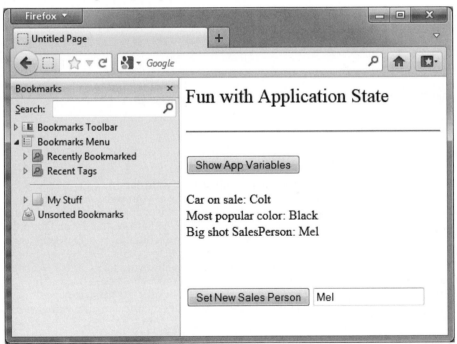

Figure 34-4. Displaying application data

Understand that if you have a situation where a set of application-level variables must be updated as a unit, you risk the possibility of data corruption (since it is technically possible that an application-level data point may be changed while another user is attempting to access it!). You could take the long road and manually lock down the logic using threading primitives of the System.Threading namespace, but the HttpApplicationState type has the following two methods, Lock() and Unlock(), that automatically ensure thread safety:

```
// Safely access related application data.
Application.Lock();
Application["SalesPersonOfTheMonth"] = "Maxine";
Application["CurrentBonusedEmployee"] = Application["SalesPersonOfTheMonth"];
Application.UnLock();
```

Handling Web Application Shutdown

The HttpApplicationState type is designed to maintain the values of the items it contains until one of two situations occurs: the last user on your site times out (or manually logs out) or someone manually shuts down the web site via IIS. In either case, the Application_End() method of the HttpApplication-derived type will automatically be called. Within this event handler, you are able to perform whatever sort of cleanup is necessary.

```
void Application_End(Object sender, EventArgs e)
{
  // Write current application variables
  // to a database or whatever else you need to do.
}
```

■ **Source Code** The AppState web site is included under the Chapter 34 subdirectory.

Working with the Application Cache

ASP.NET provides a second and more flexible way to handle application-wide data. As you recall, the values within the HttpApplicationState object remain in memory as long as your web application is alive and kicking. Sometimes, however, you might want to maintain a piece of application data only for a specific period of time. For example, you might want to obtain an ADO.NET DataSet that is valid for only five minutes. After that time, you might want to obtain a fresh DataSet to account for possible database updates. While it's technically possible to build this infrastructure using HttpApplicationState and some sort of handcrafted monitor, the ASP.NET application cache greatly simplifies your task.

As its name suggests, the ASP.NET System.Web.Caching.Cache object (which is accessible via the Context.Cache property) allows you to define objects that are accessible by all users from all pages for a fixed amount of time. In its simplest form, interacting with the cache looks identical to interacting with the HttpApplicationState type.

```
// Add an item to the cache.
// This item will *not* expire.
Context.Cache["SomeStringItem"] = "This is the string item";
// Get item from the cache.
```

```
string s = (string)Context.Cache["SomeStringItem"];
```

■ **Note** If you want to access the cache from within Global.asax, you need to use the Context property. However, if you are within the scope of a System.Web.UI.Page-derived type, you can access the Cache object directly via the page's Cache property.

The System.Web.Caching.Cache class defines only a small number of members beyond the type's indexer. You can use the Add() method to insert a new item into the cache that is not currently defined (if the specified item is already present, Add() effectively does nothing). The Insert() method will also place a member into the cache. If the item is currently defined, however, Insert() will replace the current item with the new object. Since this is generally the behavior you'll desire, I'll focus on the Insert() method exclusively.

Fun with Data Caching

Let's see an example. To begin, create a new Empty Web Site named CacheState and insert a Web Form and a Global.asax file. Like an application-level data item maintained by the HttpApplicationState type, the cache may hold any System.Object-derived type and is often populated within the Application_Start() event handler. For this example, the goal is to automatically update the contents of a DataSet every 15 seconds. The DataSet in question will contain the current set of records from the Inventory table of the AutoLot database created during our discussion of ADO.NET.

Given these design notes, set a reference to AutoLotDAL.dll (see Chapter 21) and update your Global.asax like so (code analysis to follow):

```
<%@ Application Language="C#" %>
<%@ Import Namespace = "AutoLotConnectedLayer" %>
<%@ Import Namespace = "System.Data" %>

<script runat="server">
  // Define a static-level Cache member variable.
  static Cache theCache;

  void Application_Start(Object sender, EventArgs e)
  {
    // First assign the static "theCache" variable.
    theCache = Context.Cache;

    // When the application starts up,
    // read the current records in the
    // Inventory table of the AutoLot DB.
    InventoryDAL  dal = new InventoryDAL();
    dal.OpenConnection(@"Data Source=(local)\SQLEXPRESS;" +
      "Initial Catalog=AutoLot;Integrated Security=True");
    DataTable theCars = dal.GetAllInventoryAsDataTable();
    dal.CloseConnection();
```

```
    // Now store DataTable in the cache.
    theCache.Insert("AppDataTable",
        theCars,
        null,
        DateTime.Now.AddSeconds(15),
        Cache.NoSlidingExpiration,
        CacheItemPriority.Default,
        new CacheItemRemovedCallback(UpdateCarInventory));
    }

    // The target for the CacheItemRemovedCallback delegate.
    static void UpdateCarInventory(string key, object item,
        CacheItemRemovedReason reason)
    {
        InventoryDAL  dal = new InventoryDAL();
        dal.OpenConnection(@"Data Source=(local)\SQLEXPRESS;" +
            "Initial Catalog=AutoLot;Integrated Security=True");
        DataTable theCars = dal. GetAllInventoryAsDataTable();
        dal.CloseConnection();

        // Now store in the cache.
        theCache.Insert("AppDataTable",
            theCars,
            null,
            DateTime.Now.AddSeconds(15),
            Cache.NoSlidingExpiration,
            CacheItemPriority.Default,
            new CacheItemRemovedCallback(UpdateCarInventory));
    }
    ...
</script>
```

First, notice we've defined a static Cache member variable. The reason is that we've defined two static members that need to access the Cache object. Recall that static methods do not have access to inherited members, so you can't use the Context property!

Inside the Application_Start() event handler, you fill a DataTable and insert it into the application cache. As you would guess, the Context.Cache.Insert() method has been overloaded a number of times. Here, you supply a value for each possible parameter. Consider the following commented call to Insert():

```
theCache.Insert("AppDataTable",       // Name used to identify item in the cache.
    theCars,                          // Object to put in the cache.
    null,                             // Any dependencies for this object?
    DateTime.Now.AddSeconds(15),      // Absolute timeout value.
    Cache.NoSlidingExpiration,        // Don't use sliding expiration (see below).
    CacheItemPriority.Default,        // Priority level of cache item.
    // Delegate for CacheItemRemove event.
    new CacheItemRemovedCallback(UpdateCarInventory));
```

The first two parameters simply make up the name/value pair of the item. The third parameter allows you to define a CacheDependency object (which is null in this case, as the DataTable does not depend on anything).

The DateTime.Now.AddSeconds(15) parameter specifies an absolute expiration time. It means the cache item will definitely be evicted from the cache after 15 seconds. Absolute expiration is useful for data items that need to be constantly refreshed (such as a stock ticker).

The Cache.NoSlidingExpiration parameter specifies that the cache item doesn't use sliding expiration. Sliding expiration is a way of keeping an item in the cache for at least a certain amount of time. For example, if you set a sliding expiration of 60 seconds for a cache item, it will live in the cache for at least 60 seconds. If any web page accesses the cache item within that time, the clock is reset and the cache item has a fresh 60 seconds to live. If no web page accesses the cache item in 60 seconds, the item is removed from the cache. Sliding expiration is useful for data that might be expensive (time-wise) to generate, but which might not be used very frequently by web pages.

Note that you can't specify both an absolute expiration and a sliding expiration for a given cache item. You set either an absolute expiration (and use Cache.NoSlidingExpiration) or a sliding expiration (and use Cache.NoAbsoluteExpiration).

Finally, as you can see from the signature of the UpdateCarInventory() method, the CacheItemRemovedCallback delegate can only call methods that match the following signature:

```
void UpdateCarInventory(string key, object item, CacheItemRemovedReason reason)
{
}
```

So, at this point, when the application starts up, the DataTable is populated and cached. Every 15 seconds, the DataTable is purged, updated, and reinserted into the cache. To see the effects of doing this, you need to create a page that allows for some degree of user interaction.

Modifying the *.aspx File

In Figure 34-5, you can see I constructed a UI that allows the user to enter the necessary data to insert a new record into the database (via four different TextBox controls). The Click event for the single Button control will be coded (in just a bit) to handle the database manipulation. Finally, minus a number of descriptive Label controls, the GridView on the bottom of the page will be used to display the set of current records in the Inventory table.

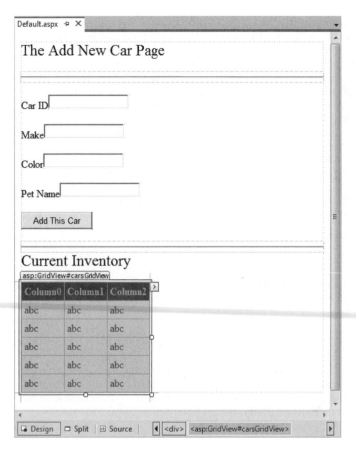

Figure 34-5. The cache application GUI

In the page's Load event handler, configure your GridView to display the current contents of the cached DataTable the first time the user posts to the page (be sure to import the System.Data and AutoLotConnectedLayer namespaces within your code file).

```
protected void Page_Load(object sender, EventArgs e)
{
  if (!IsPostBack)
  {
    carsGridView.DataSource = (DataTable)Cache["AppDataTable"];
    carsGridView.DataBind();
  }
}
```

In the Click event handler of the Add This Car button, insert the new record into the AutoLot database using the InventoryDAL type. After the record has been inserted, call a helper function named RefreshGrid(), which will update the UI.

```
protected void btnAddCar_Click(object sender, EventArgs e)
{
  // Update the Inventory table
  // and call RefreshGrid().
  InventoryDAL dal = new InventoryDAL();
  dal.OpenConnection(@"Data Source=(local)\SQLEXPRESS;" +
    "Initial Catalog=AutoLot;Integrated Security=True");
  dal.InsertAuto(int.Parse(txtCarID.Text), txtCarColor.Text,
    txtCarMake.Text, txtCarPetName.Text);
  dal.CloseConnection();
  RefreshGrid();
}

private void RefreshGrid()
{
  InventoryDAL dal = new InventoryDAL();
  dal.OpenConnection(@"Data Source=(local)\SQLEXPRESS;" +
    "Initial Catalog=AutoLot;Integrated Security=True");
  DataTable theCars = dal.GetAllInventoryAsDataTable();
  dal.CloseConnection();

  carsGridView.DataSource = theCars;
  carsGridView.DataBind();
}
```

Now, to test the use of the cache, begin by running the current program (Ctrl+F5) and copy the URL appearing in the browser to your clipboard. Next, launch a second instance of your browser (using the Start button) and paste the URL into this instance. At this point, you should have two instances of your web browser, both viewing Default.aspx and showing identical data.

In one instance of the browser, add a new automobile entry. Obviously, this results in an updated GridView viewable from the browser that initiated the postback.

In the second browser instance, click the Refresh button (F5). You should not see the new item, since the Page_Load event handler is reading directly from the cache. (If you did see the value, the 15 seconds had already expired. Either type faster or increase the amount of time the DataTable will remain in the cache.) Wait a few seconds and click the Refresh button from the second browser instance one more time. Now you should see the new item, given that the DataTable in the cache has expired and the CacheItemRemovedCallback delegate target method has automatically updated the cached DataTable.

As you can see, the major benefit of the Cache type is that you can ensure that when an item is removed, you have a chance to respond. In this example, you certainly could avoid using the Cache and simply have the Page_Load() event handler always read directly from the AutoLot database (but this would potentially be much slower than the caching approach). Nevertheless, the point should be clear: the cache allows you to automatically refresh data using the cache mechanism.

■ **Source Code** The CacheState web site is included under the Chapter 34 subdirectory.

Maintaining Session Data

So much for our examination of application-level and cached data. Next, let's check out the role of per-user data. As mentioned earlier in the chapter, a *session* is little more than a given user's ongoing interaction with a web application, which is represented via a unique HttpSessionState object. To maintain stateful information for a particular user, you can use the Session property in your web page class or in Global.asax. The classic example of the need to maintain per-user data is an online shopping cart. Again, if 10 people all log on to an online store, each individual will have a unique set of items that she (might) intend to purchase, and that data needs to be maintained.

When a new user joins to your web application, the .NET runtime automatically assigns the user a unique session ID, which is used to identify that user. Each session ID identifies a custom instance of the HttpSessionState type to hold on to user-specific data. Inserting or retrieving session data is syntactically identical to manipulating application data. For example:

```
// Add/retrieve session data for current user.
Session["DesiredCarColor"] = "Green";
string color = (string) Session["DesiredCarColor"];
```

In Global.asax, you can intercept the beginning and end of a session via the Session_Start() and Session_End() event handlers. Within Session_Start(), you can freely create any per-user data items, while Session_End() allows you to perform any work you might need to do when the user's session has terminated.

```
<%@ Application Language="C#" %>
...
void Session_Start(Object sender, EventArgs e)
{
  // New session! Prep if required.
}

void Session_End(Object sender, EventArgs e)
{
  // User logged off/timed out. Tear down if needed.
}
```

Like application state, session state may hold any System.Object-derived type, including your custom classes. For example, assume you have a new Empty Web Site project (named SessionState) that defines a class named UserShoppingCart, as follows:

```
public class UserShoppingCart
{
  public string DesiredCar {get; set;}
  public string DesiredCarColor {get; set;}
  public float DownPayment {get; set;}
  public bool IsLeasing {get; set;}
  public DateTime DateOfPickUp {get; set;}

  public override string ToString()
  {
    return string.Format
      ("Car: {0}<br>Color: {1}<br>$ Down: {2}<br>Lease: {3}<br>Pick-up Date: {4}",
        DesiredCar, DesiredCarColor, DownPayment, IsLeasing,
        DateOfPickUp.ToShortDateString());
```

```
    }
}
```

Now, insert a Global.asax file. Within the Session_Start() event handler, you can now assign each user a new instance of the UserShoppingCart class, like so:

```
void Session_Start(Object sender, EventArgs e)
{
  Session["UserShoppingCartInfo"] = new UserShoppingCart();
}
```

As the user traverses your web pages, you are able to pluck out the UserShoppingCart instance and fill the fields with user-specific data. For example, assume you have a simple *.aspx page that defines a set of input controls that correspond to each field of the UserShoppingCart type, a Button for setting the values, and two Labels that will be used to display the user's session ID and session information (see Figure 34-6).

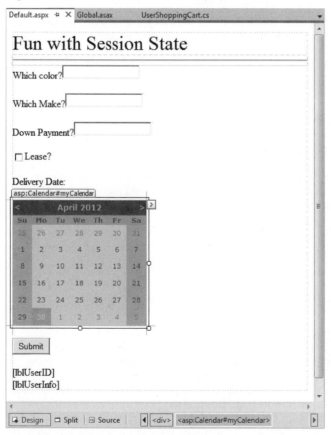

Figure 34-6. The session application GUI

The server-side Click event handler for the Button control is straightforward (scrape out values from TextBoxes and display the shopping cart data on a Label control).

```
protected void btnSubmit_Click(object sender, EventArgs e)
{
  // Set current user prefs.
  UserShoppingCart cart =
    (UserShoppingCart)Session["UserShoppingCartInfo"];
  cart.DateOfPickUp = myCalendar.SelectedDate;
  cart.DesiredCar = txtCarMake.Text;
  cart.DesiredCarColor = txtCarColor.Text;
  cart.DownPayment = float.Parse(txtDownPayment.Text);
  cart.IsLeasing = chkIsLeasing.Checked;
  lblUserInfo.Text = cart.ToString();
  Session["UserShoppingCartInfo"] = cart;
}
```

Within Session_End(), you might elect to persist the fields of the UserShoppingCart to a database or whatnot (however, as you will see at the conclusion of this chapter, the ASP.NET Profile API will do so automatically). As well, you might want to implement Session_Error() to trap any faulty input (or perhaps make use of various validation controls on the Default.aspx page to account for such user errors).

In any case, if you were to launch two or three instances of your browser of choice all posting to the same URL (via a copy/paste operation as you did for the data cache example), you would find that each user is able to build a custom shopping cart that maps to his unique instance of HttpSessionState.

Additional Members of HttpSessionState

The HttpSessionState class defines a number of other members of interest beyond the type indexer. First, the SessionID property will return the current user's unique ID. If you would like to view the automatically assigned session ID for this example, handle the Load event of your page as follows:

```
protected void Page_Load(object sender, EventArgs e)
{
  lblUserID.Text = string.Format("Here is your ID: {0}",
    Session.SessionID);
}
```

The Remove() and RemoveAll() methods may be used to clear items out of the user's instance of HttpSessionState. For example:

```
Session.Remove("SomeItemWeDontNeedAnymore");
```

The HttpSessionState type also defines a set of members that control the expiration policy of the current session. Again, by default each user has 20 minutes of inactivity before the HttpSessionState object is destroyed. Thus, if a user enters your web application (and, therefore, obtains a unique session ID), but then does not return to the site within 20 minutes, the runtime assumes the user is no longer interested and destroys all session data for that user. You are free to change this default 20-minute expiration value on a user-by-user basis using the Timeout property. The most common place to do so is within the scope of your Session_Start() method, like so:

```
void Session_Start(Object sender, EventArgs e)
{
  // Each user has 5 minutes of inactivity.
  Session.Timeout = 5;
  Session["UserShoppingCartInfo"]
    = new UserShoppingCart();
}
```

■ **Note** If you do not need to tweak each user's Timeout value, you can alter the 20-minute default for all users via the timeout attribute of the <sessionState> element within the web.config file (examined at the end of this chapter).

The benefit of the Timeout property is that you have the ability to assign specific timeout values separately for each user. For example, imagine you have created a web application that allows users to pay cash for a given membership level. You could specify that Gold members should time out within one hour, while Wood members should get only 30 seconds. This possibility begs the question, how can you remember user-specific information (such as the current membership level) if users close the browser and come back at a later time? One possible answer is through the use of the HttpCookie type. (And speaking of cookies . . .)

■ **Source Code** The SessionState web site is included under the Chapter 34 subdirectory.

Understanding Cookies

The next state management technique we'll examine is the persisting of data within a *cookie*, which is often realized as a text file (or set of files) on the user's machine. When a user joins a given site, the browser checks to see whether the user's machine has a cookie file for the URL in question and, if so, appends this data to the HTTP request.

The receiving server-side web page can then read the cookie data to create a GUI based on the current user preferences. I'm sure you've noticed that when you visit certain of your favorite web sites, they somehow "just know" the sort of content you would like to see. The reason (in part) may have to do with a cookie stored on your computer that contains information relevant to a given web site.

■ **Note** The exact location of your cookie files will depend on which browser and operating system you happen to be using.

The contents of a given cookie file will obviously vary among web sites, but keep in mind that they are ultimately text files. Thus, cookies are a horrible choice for maintaining sensitive information about the current user (such as a credit card number, password, and the like). Even if you take the time to encrypt the data, a crafty hacker could decrypt the value and use it for evil purposes. In any case, cookies do play a role in the development of web applications, so let's check out how ASP.NET handles this particular state management technique.

Creating Cookies

First of all, understand that ASP.NET cookies can be configured to be either persistent or temporary. A *persistent* cookie is typically regarded as the classic definition of cookie data, in that the set of name/value pairs is physically saved to the user's hard drive. A *temporary* cookie (also termed a *session cookie*) contains the same data as a persistent cookie, but the name/value pairs are never saved to the user's hard drive; rather, they exist *only* while the browser is open. When the user shuts down the browser, all data contained in the session cookie is destroyed.

The System.Web.HttpCookie type is the class that represents the server side of the cookie data (persistent or temporary). When you want to create a new cookie in your web page code, you access the Response.Cookies property. Once the new HttpCookie is inserted into the internal collection, the name/value pairs flow back to the browser within the HTTP header.

To check out cookie behavior firsthand, create a new Empty Web Site (named CookieStateApp) and create the UI of the first Web Form (which you will need to insert) displayed in Figure 34-7.

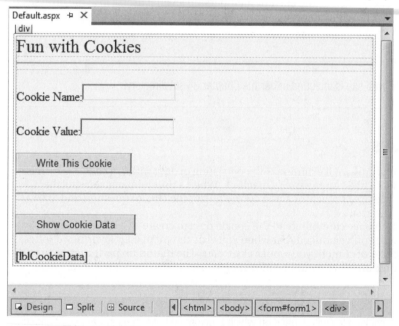

Figure 34-7. *The UI of* CookieStateApp

Within the first button's Click event handler, build a new HttpCookie and insert it into the Cookie collection exposed from the HttpRequest.Cookies property. Be very aware that the data will not persist itself to the user's hard drive unless you explicitly set an expiration date using the HttpCookie.Expires property. Thus, the following implementation will create a temporary cookie that is destroyed when the user shuts down the browser:

```
protected void btnCookie_Click(object sender, EventArgs e)
{
  // Make a temp cookie.
  HttpCookie theCookie =
    new HttpCookie(txtCookieName.Text,
    txtCookieValue.Text);
  Response.Cookies.Add(theCookie);
}
```

However, the following generates a persistent cookie that will expire three months from today:

```
protected void btnCookie_Click(object sender, EventArgs e)
{
  HttpCookie theCookie =
    new HttpCookie(txtCookieName.Text,
    txtCookieValue.Text);
  theCookie.Expires = DateTime.Now.AddMonths(3);
  Response.Cookies.Add(theCookie);
}
```

Reading Incoming Cookie Data

Recall that the browser is the entity in charge of accessing persisted cookies when navigating to a previously visited page. If a browser decides to send a cookie to the server, you can access the incoming data in your *.aspx page via the HttpRequest.Cookies property. To illustrate, implement the Click event handler for the second button like so:

```
protected void btnShowCookie_Click(object sender, EventArgs e)
{
  string cookieData = "";
  foreach (string s in Request.Cookies)
  {
    cookieData +=
      string.Format("<li><b>Name</b>: {0}, <b>Value</b>: {1}</li>",
      s, Request.Cookies[s].Value);
  }
  lblCookieData.Text = cookieData;
}
```

If you now run the application and click your new button, you will find that the cookie data has indeed been sent by your browser and accessed successfully in your *.aspx code at the server.

▪ **Source Code** The CookieStateApp web site is included under the Chapter 34 subdirectory.

The Role of the <sessionState> Element

At this point in the chapter, you have examined numerous ways to remember information about your users. As you have seen, view state and application, cache, session, and cookie data are manipulated programmatically in more or less the same way (via a class indexer). As you have also seen, Global.asax has methods that allow you to intercept and respond to events that occur during your web application's lifetime.

By default, ASP.NET will store session state in-process. The plus side is that access to the information is as fast as possible. However, the downside is that if this AppDomain crashes (for whatever reason), all of the user's state data is destroyed. Furthermore, when you store state data as an in-process *.dll, you cannot interact with a networked web farm. This default mode of storage works just fine if your web application is hosted by a single web server. As you might guess, however, this model is not ideal for a farm of web servers, given that session state is "trapped" within a given AppDomain.

Storing Session Data in the ASP.NET Session State Server

Under ASP.NET, you can instruct the runtime to host the session state *.dll in a surrogate process named the ASP.NET session state server (aspnet_state.exe). When you do so, you are able to offload the *.dll from aspnet_wp.exe into a unique *.exe, which can be located on any machine within the web farm. Even if you intend to run the aspnet_state.exe process on the same machine as the web server, you gain the benefit of partitioning the state data in a unique process (as it is more durable).

To make use of the session state server, the first step is to start the aspnet_state.exe Windows service on the target machine by typing the following in a Developer Command Prompt window (note that you will need admin privileges to do so):

```
net start aspnet_state
```

Alternatively, you can start aspnet_state.exe using the Services applet accessed from the Administrative Tools folder of the Control Panel, as shown in Figure 34-8.

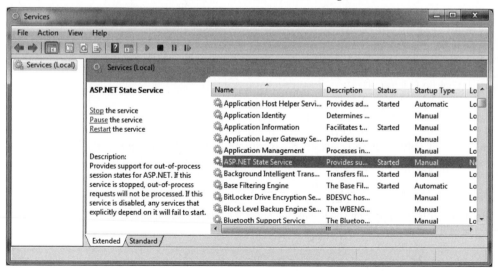

Figure 34-8. Starting aspnet_state.exe using the Services applet

The key benefit of this approach is that you can use the Properties window to configure aspnet_state.exe to start automatically when the machine boots up. In any case, once the session state server is running, add the following <sessionState> element of your web.config file as follows:

```
<system.web>
  <sessionState
    mode="StateServer"
    stateConnectionString="tcpip=127.0.0.1:42626"
    sqlConnectionString="data source=127.0.0.1;Trusted_Connection=yes"
    cookieless="false"
    timeout="20"
  />
...
</system.web>
```

That's it! At this point, the CLR will host session-centric data within aspnet_state.exe. In this way, if the AppDomain hosting the web application crashes, the session data is preserved. Moreover, note that the <sessionState> element can also support a stateConnectionString attribute. The default TCP/IP address value (127.0.0.1) points to the local machine. If you would rather have the .NET runtime use the aspnet_state.exe service located on another networked machine (again, think web farms), you are free to update this value.

Storing Session Data in a Dedicated Database

Finally, if you require the highest degree of isolation and durability for your web application, you may choose to have the runtime store all your session state data within Microsoft SQL Server. The following appropriate update to the web.config file is simple:

```
<sessionState
  mode="SQLServer"
  stateConnectionString="tcpip=127.0.0.1:42626"
  sqlConnectionString="data source=127.0.0.1;Trusted_Connection=yes"
  cookieless="false"
  timeout="20"
/>
```

However, before you attempt to run the associated web application, you need to ensure that the target machine (specified by the sqlConnectionString attribute) has been properly configured. When you install the .NET Framework 4.5 SDK (or Visual Studio proper), you will be provided with two files named InstallSqlState.sql and UninstallSqlState.sql, located by default under C:\Windows\Microsoft.NET\Framework\<version>. On the target machine, you must run the InstallSqlState.sql file using a tool such as the Microsoft SQL Server Management Studio (which ships with Microsoft SQL Server).

After you have run InstallSqlState.sql, you will find a new SQL Server database has been created (ASPState), which contains a number of stored procedures called by the ASP.NET runtime, as well as a set of tables used to store the session data itself. (Also, the tempdb database has been updated with a set of tables for swapping purposes.) As you'd guess, configuring your web application to store session data within SQL Server is the slowest of all possible options. The benefit is that user data is as durable as possible (even if the web server is rebooted).

■ **Note** If you make use of the ASP.NET session state server or SQL Server to store your session data, you must make sure that any custom types placed in the HttpSessionState object have been marked with the [Serializable] attribute.

Introducing the ASP.NET Profile API

So far you have examined numerous techniques that allow you to remember user-level and application-level bits of data. However, many web sites require the ability to persist user information across sessions. For example, perhaps you need to give users the ability to build an account on your site. Maybe you need to persist instances of a ShoppingCart class across sessions (for an online shopping site). Or perhaps you need to persist basic user preferences (themes, etc.).

While you most certainly could build a custom database (with several stored procedures) to hold such information, you would then need to build a custom code library to interact with these database objects. This is not necessarily a complex task, but the bottom line is that *you* are the individual in charge of building this sort of infrastructure.

To help simplify matters, ASP.NET ships with an out-of-the-box user profile management API and database system for this very purpose. In addition to providing the necessary infrastructure, the Profile API allows you to define the data to be persisted directly within your web.config file (for purposes of simplification); however, you are also able to persist any [Serializable] type. Before we get too far ahead of ourselves, let's check out where the Profile API will be storing the specified data.

The ASPNETDB.mdf Database

Every ASP.NET web site built with Visual Studio can support an App_Data subdirectory. By default, the Profile API (as well as other services, such as the ASP.NET role membership API, which is not examined in this text) is configured to make use of a local SQL Server database named ASPNETDB.mdf, located within the App_Data folder. This default behavior is due to settings within the machine.config file for the current .NET installation on your machine. In fact, when your code base makes use of any ASP.NET service requiring the App_Data folder, the ASPNETDB.mdf data file will be automatically created on the fly if a copy does not currently exist.

If you'd rather have the ASP.NET runtime communicate with an ASPNETDB.mdf file located on another networked machine, or you'd prefer to install this database on an instance of SQL Server 7.0 (or higher), you will need to manually build ASPNETDB.mdf using the aspnet_regsql.exe command-line utility. Like any good command-line tool, aspnet_regsql.exe provides numerous options; however, if you run the tool with no arguments (from a Developer Command Prompt window), like so:

```
aspnet_regsql
```

you will launch a GUI-based wizard that will walk you through the process of creating and installing ASPNETDB.mdf on your machine (and version of SQL Server) of choice.

Now, assuming your site is not using a local copy of the database under the App_Data folder, the final step is to update your web.config file to point to the unique location of your ASPNETDB.mdf. Assume you have installed ASPNETDB.mdf on a machine named ProductionServer. The following (partial) machine.config file would instruct the Profile API where to find the necessary database items in their default location (you could add a custom web.config to change these defaults):

```
<configuration>
  <connectionStrings>
    <add name="LocalSqlServer"
         connectionString ="Data Source=ProductionServer;Integrated
         Security=SSPI;Initial Catalog=aspnetdb;"
         providerName="System.Data.SqlClient"/>
  </connectionStrings>
  <system.web>
    <profile>
      <providers>
        <clear/>
        <add name="AspNetSqlProfileProvider"
             connectionStringName="LocalSqlServer"
             applicationName="/"
             type="System.Web.Profile.SqlProfileProvider, System.Web,
             Version=4.0.0.0,
             Culture=neutral, PublicKeyToken=b03f5f7f11d50a3a" />
      </providers>
    </profile>
  </system.web>
</configuration>
```

Like most *.config files, this looks much worse than it is. Basically we are defining a
<connectionString> element with the necessary data, followed by a named instance of the
SqlProfileProvider (this is the default provider used regardless of physical location of the
ASPNETDB.mdf).

■ **Note** For simplicity, I will assume that you'll use the autogenerated ASPNETDB.mdf database located under your
web application's App_Data subdirectory.

Defining a User Profile Within web.config

As mentioned, a user profile is defined within a web.config file. The really nifty aspect of this approach is
that you can interact with this profile in a strongly typed manner using the inherited Profile property in
your code files. To illustrate this, create a new Empty Web Site named FunWithProfiles, add a new
*.aspx file, and open your web.config file for editing.

Our goal is to make a profile that models the home address of the users who are in session, as well as
the total number of times they have posted to this site. Not surprisingly, profile data is defined within a
<profile> element using a set of name/data type pairs. Consider the following profile, which is created
within the scope of the <system.web> element:

```
<profile>
  <properties>
    <add name="StreetAddress" type="System.String" />
    <add name="City" type="System.String" />
    <add name="State" type="System.String" />
    <add name="TotalPost" type="System.Int32" />
  </properties>
```

1457

```
</profile>
```

Here, we have specified a name and CLR data type for each item in the profile (of course, we could add additional items for zip code, name, and so forth, but I am sure you get the idea). Strictly speaking, the type attribute is optional; however, the default is a System.String. As you would guess, there are many other attributes that can be specified in a profile entry to further qualify how this information should be persisted in ASPNETDB.mdf. Table 34-4 illustrates some of the core attributes.

Table 34-4. *Select Attributes of Profile Data*

Attribute	Example Values	Meaning in Life
allowAnonymous	True I False	Restricts or allows anonymous access to this value. If it is set to false, anonymous users won't have access to this profile value.
defaultValue	String	The value to return if the property has not been explicitly set.
Name	String	A unique identifier for this property.
Provider	String	The provider used to manage this value. It overrides the defaultProvider setting in web.config or machine.config.
readOnly	True I False	Restricts or allows write access (the default is false; i.e., it's not read-only).
serializeAs	String I XML I Binary	The format of a value when persisting in the data store.
type	Primitive I User-defined type	A .NET primitive type or class. Class names must be fully qualified (e.g., MyApp.UserData.ColorPrefs).

We will see some of these attributes in action as we modify the current profile. For now, let's see how to access this data programmatically from within our pages.

Accessing Profile Data Programmatically

Recall that the whole purpose of the ASP.NET Profile API is to automate the process of writing data to (and reading data from) a dedicated database. To test this out for yourself, update the UI of your Default.aspx file with a set of TextBoxes (and descriptive Labels) to gather the street address, city, and state of the user. As well, add a Button (named btnSubmit) and a final Label (named lblUserData) that will be used to display the persisted data, as shown in Figure 34-9.

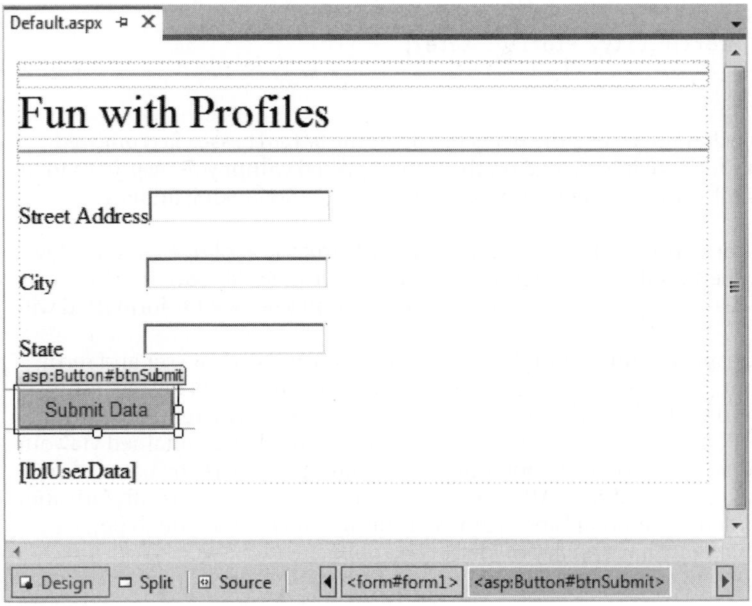

Figure 34-9. The UI of the FunWithProfiles Default.aspx *page*

Now, within the Click event handler of the button, make use of the inherited Profile property to persist each point of profile data based on what the user has entered in the related TextBox. After you have persisted each piece of data within ASPNETDB.mdf, read each piece of data out of the database and format it into a string that is displayed on the lblUserData Label type. Finally, handle the page's Load event, and display the same information on the Label type. In this way, when users come to the page, they can see their current settings. Here is the complete code file:

```
public partial class _Default : System.Web.UI.Page
{
  protected void Page_Load(object sender, EventArgs e)
  {
    GetUserAddress();
  }
  protected void btnSubmit_Click(object sender, EventArgs e)
  {
    // Database writes happening here!
    Profile.StreetAddress = txtStreetAddress.Text;
    Profile.City = txtCity.Text;
    Profile.State = txtState.Text;

    // Get settings from database.
    GetUserAddress();
  }

  private void GetUserAddress()
  {
    // Database reads happening here!
```

```
        lblUserData.Text = String.Format("You live here: {0}, {1}, {2}",
            Profile.StreetAddress, Profile.City, Profile.State);
    }
}
```

Now if you run this page, you will notice a lengthy delay the first time Default.aspx is requested. The reason is that the ASPNETDB.mdf file is being created on the fly and placed within your App_Data folder (you can verify this for yourself by refreshing the Solution Explorer window and looking under the App_Data folder).

You will also find that the first time you come to this page, the lblUserData Label does not display any profile data, as you have not yet entered your data into the correct table of ASPNETDB.mdf. After you enter values in the TextBox controls and post back to the server, you will find this Label is formatted with the persisted data.

Now, for the really interesting aspect of this technology. If you shut down your browser and rerun your web site, you will find that your previously entered profile data has indeed been persisted, as the Label displays the correct information. This begs the obvious question, how were you remembered?

For this example, the Profile API used your Windows network identity, which was obtained via your current machine credentials. However, when you are building public web sites (where the users are not part of a given domain), rest assured that the Profile API integrates with the Forms-based authentication model of ASP.NET and also supports the notion of "anonymous profiles," which allow you to persist profile data for users who do not currently have an active identity on your site.

■ **Note** This edition of the text does not address ASP.NET security topics (such as Forms-based authentication or anonymous profiles). Consult the .NET Framework 4.4 SDK documentation for details.

Grouping Profile Data and Persisting Custom Objects

To wrap up this chapter, allow me to make a few additional comments on how profile data may be defined within a web.config file. The current profile simply defined four pieces of data that were exposed directly from the profile type. When you build more complex profiles, it can be helpful to group related pieces of data under a unique name. Consider the following update:

```
<profile>
  <properties>
    <group name ="Address">
      <add name="StreetAddress" type="String" />
      <add name="City" type="String" />
      <add name="State" type="String" />
    </group>
    <add name="TotalPost" type="Integer" />
  </properties>
</profile>
```

This time, we have defined a custom group named Address to expose the street address, city, and state of our user. To access this data in our pages would now require us to update our code base by specifying Profile.Address to get each subitem. For example, here is the updated GetUserAddress() method (the Click event handler for the Button would need to be updated in a similar manner):

```
private void GetUserAddress()
{
  // Database reads happening here!
  lblUserData.Text = String.Format("You live here: {0}, {1}, {2}",
    Profile.Address.StreetAddress,
    Profile.Address.City, Profile.Address.State);
}
```

Before you run this example, you need to delete ASPNETDB.mdf from your App_Data folder, to ensure the database schema is refreshed. After you have done so, you should be able to run your web site example without error.

■ **Note** A profile can contain as many groups as you feel are necessary. Simply define multiple <group> elements within your <properties> scope.

Finally, it is worth pointing out that a profile may also persist (and obtain) custom objects to and from ASPNETDB.mdf. To illustrate, assume you wanted to build a custom class (or structure) that will represent the user's address data. The only requirement expected by the Profile API is that the type be marked with the [Serializable] attribute. For example:

```
[Serializable]
public class UserAddress
{
  public string Street = string.Empty;
  public string City = string.Empty;
  public string State = string.Empty;
}
```

With this class in place, our profile definition can now be updated as follows (notice I removed the custom group, although this is not mandatory):

```
<profile>
  <properties>
    <add name="AddressInfo" type="UserAddress" serializeAs ="Binary"/>
    <add name="TotalPost" type="Integer" />
  </properties>
</profile>
```

Note that when you are adding [Serializable] types to a profile, the type attribute is the fully qualified name of the type being persisted. As you will see from the Visual Studio IntelliSense, your core choices are binary, XML, or string data. Now that we are capturing street address information as a custom class type, we (once again) need to update our code base as follows:

```
private void GetUserAddress()
{
  // Database reads happening here!
  lblUserData.Text = String.Format("You live here: {0}, {1}, {2}",
    Profile.AddressInfo.Street, Profile.AddressInfo.City,
    Profile.AddressInfo.State);
```

}

To be sure, there is much more to the Profile API than I've had space to cover here. For example, the `Profile` property actually encapsulates a type named `ProfileCommon`. Using this type, you are able to programmatically obtain all information for a given user, delete (or add) profiles to `ASPNETDB.mdf`, update aspects of a profile, and so forth.

Moreover, the Profile API has numerous points of extensibility that can allow you to optimize how the profile manager accesses the tables of the `ASPNETDB.mdf` database. As you would expect, there are many ways to decrease the number of "hits" this database takes. Interested readers are encouraged to consult the .NET Framework 4.5 SDK documentation for further details.

■ **Source Code** The FunWithProfiles web site is included under the Chapter 34 subdirectory.

Summary

In this chapter, you rounded out your knowledge of ASP.NET by examining how to leverage the `HttpApplication` type. As you have seen, this type provides a number of default event handlers that allow you to intercept various application- and session-level events. The bulk of this chapter was spent exploring a number of state management techniques. Recall that view state is used to automatically repopulate the values of HTML widgets between postbacks to a specific page. Next, you checked out the distinction of application- and session-level data, cookie management, and the ASP.NET application cache.

Finally, this chapter exposed you to the ASP.NET Profile API. As you have seen, this technology provides an out-of-the-box solution to the issue of persisting user data across sessions. Using your web site's `web.config` file, you can define any number of profile items (including groups of items and `[Serializable]` types) that will automatically be persisted into `ASPNETDB.mdf`.

Index

■ B

■ F

■ G

■ J

■ K

■ L

■ M

■ X, Y, Z